Caravan
& Camping
Europe 2007

GW00587581

To contact us:
Advertisement Sales: advertisingsales@theAA.com
Editorial: lifestyleguides@theAA.com

Picture credit: Front cover AA World Travel Library/S L Day
Typeset by Keenes, Andover, Hampshire UK
Printed and bound by Graficas Estella
Published by AA Publishing, a trading name of
Automobile Association Developments Limited,
whose registered office is:
Fanum House, Basing View, Basingstoke,
Hampshire, RG21 4EA
Registered number 1878835
A CIP catalogue record for this book is available from
the British Library
ISBN 10: 0-7495-5105-4
ISBN 13: 978-0-7495-5105-6
A02829

Mapping produced by the Cartography Department of The Automobile Association from the Automaps database using electronic and computer technology

Maps© Automobile Association Developments Limited 2007

Contents

Using the guide

Each country in this guide is divided into regions, within which the site locations are listed in alphabetical order. Regions and locations are shown on the country maps at the back of the guide, and are listed in the index. For route planning you should use a road atlas, such as the *AA Road Atlas Europe*. AA road atlases are also available for France, Germany, Italy and Spain. The AA Route Planner Europe on www.theAA.com covers most of the countries in the guide.

Campsite entries

In order to update our information we send a questionnaire each year to every campsite. Inevitably a number of the questionnaires are not returned in time for publication, in which case the campsite name is printed in italics. Most of the sites accept both tents and caravans unless otherwise stated.

Websites

Campsite web addresses are included where available. The AA cannot be held responsible for the content of any of these websites.

Opening times

Dates shown are inclusive. All information was correct at the time of going to press, but we recommend you check with the site before arriving. Sometimes only restricted facilities are available between October and April.

Prices

Prices are given per night, per adult, car, caravan and tent. Prices are in euros except for Switzerland (Swiss francs). We do not give charges for children as these vary. To determine the cost of one night, simply add up the prices that apply to your party. Exceptions are:

pp Campsite charges per person per night. The charge includes the vehicle and caravan/tent. For a party of four people, multiply the pp price by four.

pitch The price per pitch, regardless of whether it is a caravan or a tent. Where the word pitch follows the L for adult price, you should multiply the L price by the number of adults in the party, then add the pitch price to that total to obtain the cost per night for your party.

Booking

It is best to book well in advance for peak holiday seasons, or for your first and last stop close to a ferry crossing port. However, we do find that some sites do not accept reservations. Specimen booking letters in English, French, German, Italian and Spanish are on page 8. Please note that, although it is not common practice, some campsites may regard your deposit as a booking fee which is not deductible from the final account.

Complaints

If you have any complaint about a site, discuss the problem with the site proprietor immediately so that the matter can be dealt with promptly. We regret that the AA cannot act as intermediary in any dispute, or attempt to gain refunds or compensation. Your comments, however, help us to update new editions. Please use the Reader's Report Form at the back of the guide.

Symbols

Abbreviations and symbols are explained at the foot of the gazetteer pages. Please note also:

CM camping municipal, parque municipal de campismo, or parque de la camara municipal (local authority site)

Online information

This selection of websites contains useful travel information, though the AA is not responsible for their content.

Camping

www.calorgas.co.uk
Official site of Calor Gas

www.lpga.co.uk
Offical site of LP Gas, suppliers of liquid petroleum gas

www.campingandcaravanningclub.co.uk
www.caravanclub.co.uk
Britain's major caravan clubs

www.gear-zone.co.uk
Major suppliers of camping gear

www.campingeurope.com
The European Federation of Campingsite Organisations (EFCO)

UK Government

www.fco.gov.uk/travel
The Foreign and Commonwealth Office travel information

www.hmce.gov.uk
HM Revenue & Customs

www.passport.gov.uk
UK Passport Service

www.defra.gov.uk/animalh/quarantine/index.htm
Pet travel information and quarantine regulations

EU, euro

europa.eu.int
The European Union

Tourism

www.austria.info
Austrian National Tourist Office

www.belgium-tourism.net
OPT (Office for the Promotion of Tourism in Walloon & Brussels)

www.visitflanders.com
Toerisme Vlaanderen (Tourism Flanders)

www.franceguide.com
Maison de la France (French government tourist office)

www.germany-tourism.de
German National Tourist Board

www.enit.it
Italian State Tourism Board (ENIT)

www.luxembourg.co.uk
Luxembourg Tourist Office (London)

www.holland.com
Netherlands Board of Tourism

www.portugal.org
Government of Portugal

www.okspain.org
Tourism in Spain

www.turisme.ad
Andorra Ministry of Tourism

www.myswitzerland.com
Switzerland Tourism

Booking letters

Please use capitals and enclose an International Reply Coupon, obtainable from a Post Office. Be sure to include your name, address, post code and country.

English

Dear Sir

I intend to stay at your site for ... days, arriving on ... (date and month) and departing on ... (date and month). -

We are a party of ... people, including ... adults and ... children (aged ...) and would like a pitch for... tent(s) and/or parking space for our car/caravan/caravan trailer.

We would like to hire a tent/caravan/bungalow.

Please quote full charges when replying and advise on the deposit required, which will be forwarded without delay.

French

Monsieur

Je me propose de séjourner à votre terrain de camping pour ... jours, depuis le ... jusqu'au ...

Nous sommes ... personnes en tout, y compris ... adultes et ... enfants (âgés de ...) et nous aurons besoin d'un emplacement pour ... tente(s), et/ou un parking pour notre voiture/caravane/remorque.

Nous voudrions louer une tente/caravane/bungalow.

Veuillez me donner dans votre réponse une idée de vos prix, m'indiquant en même temps le montant qu'il faut payer en avance, ce qui vous sera envoyé sans délai.

German

Sehr geehrter Herr!

Ich beabsichtige, mich auf Ihrem Campingplatz ... Tage aufzuhalten, und zwar vom ... bis zum ...

Wir sind im ganzen ... Personen, ...

Erwachsene und ... Kinder (in Alter von ...), und benötigen Platz für Zelt(e) und/oder unseren Wagen/Wohnwagen/Wohnwagenanhänger.

Wir möchten ein Zelt/Wohnwagen/Bungalow mieten.

Bitte, geben Sie mir in Ihrem Antwortschreiben die vollen Preise bekannt, und ebenso die Höhe der von mir zu leistenden Anzahlung, die Ihnen alsdann unverzüglich überwiesen wird.

Italian

Egregio Signore

Ho intenzione di remanere presso di voi per ... giorni. Arriverò il ... e partirò il ...

Siamo un gruppo di ... persone in totale, compreso ... adulti e ... bambini (de età ...) e vorremo un posto per ... tenda(tende) e/o spazio per parcheggiare la nostra vetture/carovana/roulette.

Desideriamo affittare una tenda/carovana/bungalow.

Vi preghiamo di quotare i prezzi completi quando ci risponderete, e darci informazioni sul deposito richiesto, che vi sarà rimesso senza ritardo.

Spanish

Muy señor mio

Desearia me reservara espacio por ... dias, a partir del ... hasta el ...

Nuestro grupo comprende .....personas todo comprendido, ... adultos y ... niños (... de años de edad). Necesitarimos un espacio por ... tienda(s) y/o espacio para apacar nuestro choche/caravana/remolque.

Deseariamos alquilar una tienda de campana/caravan/bungalow.

Le ruego nos comunique los precios y nos informe sobre el depósito que debemos remitirle.

Motoring regulations, documents & equipment

Planning your journey

Before leaving

General advice for driving in Europe is available at www.theaa.com/motoring_advice/overseas/index.html. You can also buy AA European Breakdown Cover online at the website or call 0800 085 2840.

Before departure, AA members can arrange a thorough check of their car by DEKRA, a pan-European company, whose inspection service is approved by the AA. For more information and charges visit www.dekra-assured.com or call 0800 043 0999.

AA UK travel news

When heading for your UK port of departure, check the traffic and weather on the AA's information line 09003 401 100 or 401 100 from your mobile (calls cost up to 60p per minute). Or click on to Travel & Check Traffic at www.theAA.com.

BBC World Service

The international radio arm of the BBC broadcasts in English and 42 other languages. World news is on the hour every hour and there are regular bulletins of British news. If you want to listen to World Service when you are abroad, go to www.bbc.co.uk/worldservice or write for information to:

BBC World Service, Bush House, Strand
London WC2B 4PH
Tel 020 7240 3456
Email worldservice@bbc.co.uk

Camping Card International

A CCI is recognised at most campsites in Europe. At some campsites a reduction to the advertised charge may be allowed on presentation of the card. The CCI, which is valid for 12 months, provides third-party insurance cover for up to 11 people camping away from home or staying in

rented accommodation or at a hotel.

AA personal members may purchase a CCI from the Caravan Club. If you require further information please call the Caravan Club on 01342 327410 (Mon-Fri 9.15-5.15) and be prepared to quote your AA membership number.

Caravans & trailers

Take a list of contents, especially if any valuable or unusual equipment is being carried, as this may be required at a frontier.

A towed vehicle - boat trailer, caravan or trailer - must have a unique chassis number. The identification plate should be in an accessible position and show the name of the maker of the vehicle and the production or serial number.

Direction indicators

Most standard car-flasher units will be overloaded by the extra lamps of a caravan or trailer, and a special heavy duty unit or relay device should be fitted.

Disabled travellers

The AA Disability Helpline provides information on a range of disability related subjects, such as motoring in the UK and overseas. AA members can call this service free on 0800 26 20 50. The comprehensive *AA Disabled Traveller's Guide* is also free to all members of the public and contains information on motoring. Call free on 0800 26 20 50 to claim a copy. A pdf version of the guide is available for download at www.theAA.com/services/breakdowncover/breakdown_disabilities_info.html.

A standard blue parking badge for disabled people has been introduced throughout the EU. All EU member states with reciprocal arrangements in place, operate the Blue Badge parking scheme. Badge holders across the participating EU states can enjoy the same parking concessions provided in the host country by displaying the badge issued under their own national scheme. (Badge holders should check local notices to ensure that they are parking within the law.) These arrangements apply only to badge holders themselves and are not for the benefit of non-disabled companions. Wrongful display of the badge may incur a fine.

For details of the Blue Badge parking scheme or for planning a trip abroad contact: Department for Transport, Great Minster House, 76 Marsham Street, London SW1P 4DR Tel 020 7944 9643 www.direct.gov.uk/DisabledPeople.

Documents & insurance

Always carry your national driving licence (and International Driving Permit if necessary), the original vehicle registration document and your passport. Remember, if the registration document is not in your name, ask the registered keeper to provide you with a letter of authority. If the vehicle is hired or leased ask the company concerned to supply you with a Vehicle on Hire Certificate.

The IDP, for which a statutory charge is made, is issued by the AA to applicants who holds a valid full British driving licence and who are over 18. Go to www.theAA.com/getaway/idp/index.html and Advice & Information, or call 0870 240 1456.

When driving abroad you must carry your certificate of motor insurance with you at all times. Third-party is the minimum legal requirement in most countries. Before taking a vehicle, caravan or trailer abroad, contact your insurer or broker to notify them of your intentions and ask their advice. Check that you are covered against damage in transit (e.g. on the ferry) when the vehicle is not being driven. Motorists can obtain all types of insurance at www.theAA.com or call 0800 316 2456.

Of the countries covered by this guide, a Green Card is compulsory in Andorra. This document is issued by your motor insurer and provides proof of insurance. The Green Card must be signed on receipt.

Electrical

The electricity supply in Europe is usually 220 volts (50 cycles) AC (alternating current), but can be as low as 110 volts. In some isolated areas, low voltage DC (direct current) is provided. Continental circular two-pin plugs and screw-type bulbs are usually the rule. Check for correct polarity when using a mains hook-up on a touring caravan.

Electrical adapters (not voltage transformers), which can be used in Continental power sockets, shaver points and light bulb sockets, are available in the UK from electrical retailers or from on-board ferry shops.

Euro

Apart from Switzerland (Swiss franc), the currency of all the the countries in this guide is the euro. For further information visit the European Central Bank at www.ecb.int.

Notes have denominations of 5, 10, 20, 50, 100, 200 and 500 euros; the coins 1 and 2 euros, and 1, 2, 5, 10, 20 and 50 cents.

There is no limit to the amount of sterling notes you may take abroad. Some countries have curency import or export restrictions and you should check this with your bank or currency supplier.

Credit and debit cards are as easy to use abroad as they are at home. Their use is subject to the conditions set out by the issuing bank.

Establishments display the symbols of cards that they accept. However, it is recommended that you don't rely exclusively on any one payment method. A combination of traveller's cheques, a payment card and a small amount of local currency is suggested.

Traveller's cheques can often be used like cash. Your bank will be able to recommend currency traveller's cheques for the countries you are visiting.

Fire extinguisher/first aid kit
In some countries it is compulsory to equip your vehicle with these items (see country introductions). A fire extinguisher is not required for two-wheeled vehicles.

Foodstuffs
Countries have regulations governing the types and quantities of foodstuffs that may be imported. Although they are usually not strictly applied, visitors should know that they exist and only take reasonable quantities of food with them.

Lights
For driving abroad you should alter your headlamps so that the dipped beam does not dazzle oncoming drivers. You can do this by using headlamp beam converters or contact your vehicle dealer if in doubt. It is a wise precaution to carry replacement bulbs even when it is not a compulsory requirement (compulsory in Andorra and Spain; see country introductions).

AA Headlamp Beam Converters and/or AA Bulb Kits, or an AA Motoring Abroad Kit, which includes bulb kit, first-aid kit, GB sticker, headlamp beam converters and warning triangle, can be purchased from the AA's Dover shop (Eastern Docks Terminal) or the AA's Folkestone shop (Eurotunnel Passenger Terminal).

Medical treatment
EU/EEA nationals temporarily visiting another country in the European Economic Area (EEA) or Switzerland are entitled to receive state-provided medical care in the case of illness or an accident. A European Health Insurance Card (which replaced the E111 form in 2004) entitles you to reduced-cost or free public medical treatment for an illness or accident while you're in a European Economic Area (EEA) country or Switzerland. The EHIC can be obtained online via ww.dh.gov.uk, or call 0845 606 2030, or pick up a EHIC form from the Post Office.

Nationality plate
Vehicles must display a nationality sticker of the approved design on a vertical surface at the rear (and caravan or trailer). Fines are imposed for failing to display the correct distinguishing sign.

UK registration plates displaying the GB Euro-symbol (Euro-Plates) must comply with British Standard AU 145d. These plates make display of a conventional sticker unnecessary when circulating within the EU. The Euro-Plate is only legally recognised in the EU; it is still a requirement to display a GB sticker when travelling outside the EU.

A GB sign can be purchased from the AA's Dover shop (Eastern Docks Terminal) or the AA's Folkestone shop (Eurotunnel Passenger Terminal). GB signs are also available on-board ferries.

Passports
Each person must hold, or be named on, a valid passport. Always carry your passport and a separate note of the number, date and place of issue. The only type of passport now is the standard UK passport.

All passports issued to children under the age of 16 years are for 5 years only. After 5 years a new application must be made. To obtain a passport application call 0870 521 0410 or visit the UK Passport Service at www.passport.gov.uk.

Pet Travel Scheme
For information on how to bring pet cats and dogs back into the UK from certain countries without quarantine contact the Pets Helpline on 0870 241 1710 or visit the Department for Environment, Food & Rural Affairs (DEFRA) website www.defra.gov.uk/animalh/quarantine/index.html.

Vehicle licence
When taking a vehicle out of the UK for a temporary visit, the vehicle licence (tax disc) must to be valid throughout your journey and on your return.

Agreement within the EU provides for the temporary use of foreign-registered vehicles within the member states. A vehicle which is properly registered and taxed in its home country should not be subject to the domestic taxation and registration laws of the host country during a temporary stay.

Visas

EU citizens travelling within the EU do not require visas. A visa is not normally required by United Kingdom and Republic of Ireland passport holders when visiting non-EU countries within western Europe for periods of three months or less. However, if you hold a passport of any other nationality, a UK passport not issued in this country, or if you are in any doubt at all, check with the embassies or consulates of the countries you intend to visit.

Warning triangle & reflective jacket

The use of a warning triangle is compulsory in most European countries in the event of accident or breakdown (not required for two-wheeled vehicles). In certain circumstances two triangles are required. Additionally, reflective jackets/waistcoats are compulsory in Austria, Italy, Portugal and Spain.

The triangle should should be clearly visible from up to 100m by day and night, about 0.6m from the edge of the road, but not in such a position as to be a danger to oncoming traffic. It should be set up about 30m behind the obstruction, but this distance should be increased to 100m on motorways.

Warning triangles and reflective jackets or waistcoats can be purchased from the AA's Dover shop (Eastern Docks Terminal) or the AA's Folkestone shop (Eurotunnel Passenger Terminal).

Weather

For weather information on the Continent visit **www.metoffice.com** or call the Met Office on 0870 9000 100, or from outside the UK on +44 (0)1392 885680.

During your journey

Accidents

If you are in an accident you must stop. A warning triangle should be placed on the road at the appropriate distance; the use of hazard warning lights does not affect the regulations governing the use of warning triangles. The accident must be reported to the police if the accident has caused death or bodily injury; or if an unoccupied vehicle or property has been damaged (see country openers for emergency telephone numbers). If the accident necessitates calling the police, leave the vehicle in position. If it obstructs other traffic, mark the position of the vehicle on the road and get the details confirmed by independent witnesses before moving it. Notify your insurance company (by letter) within 24 hours, making sure all the essential particulars are noted (see the conditions of your policy).

If a third party is injured, contact your insurers for advice or, if you have a Green Card, notify the company or bureau given on the back of your Green Card; this company or bureau will deal with any compensation claim from the injured party.

It is useful to take photographs of the scene. Include the other vehicles involved, their registration plates and any background that could help later enquiries or when completing the insurance company's accident form.

Breakdown

Try to move the car to the side of the road so that it does not obstruct traffic flow. Place a warning triangle to the rear of the vehicle at the appropriate distance. Find the nearest telephone to call for assistance. On motorways emergency telephones are generally located every 2km and automatically connect you to the official motorway breakdown service.

Motorists are advised to take out **AA European Breakdown Cover** and travel insurance from the AA. They are available at **www.theAA.com** or call 0800 085 2840.

Beaches

Pollution of seawater at certain Continental coastal resorts can represent a health hazard. Countries of the European Union publish detailed information on the quality of their bathing beaches, including maps, which are available from national authorities and the European Union.

In many (though not all) popular resorts where the water quality may present risk, signs (generally small) forbid bathing:

France
No bathing
Défense de se baigner
Bathing prohibited
Il est défendu de se baigner
Italy
No bathing
Vietato bagnarsi
Bathing prohibited
Evietato bagnarsi
Spain
No bathing
Prohibido bañarse
Bathing prohibited
Se prohibe bañarse
Germany
Baden verboten

British Embassies/Consulates

Many Continental countries have at least one British consulate in addition to the British embassy. British consulates (and consular sections in embassies) can help British travellers in distress overseas but there are limitations to what they can do. For example, they cannot pay your hotel, medical or any other bills, nor will they do the work of a travel agent, information bureau or the police.

Report any loss or theft of property to the local police in the first instance, not to the consular offices. If you need to obtain an emergency passport or guidance on how to transfer funds from the UK, contact the nearest British embassy or consulate. Note that the hours and functions of honorary consuls are more restricted than full consular posts.

For up-to-date advice on travelling abroad, visit **www.fco.gov.uk/knowbeforeyougo** or call 0845 850 2829.

Cycle carriers

If you are taking bicycles on a rear-mounted cycle rack, make sure that they do not obstruct rear lights and/or number plate, or you risk an on-the-spot fine.
N.B. Rear-mounted cycle racks are illegal in Portugal, see page 310.

Crash helmets

The wearing of crash or safety helmets by motorcyclists and their passengers is compulsory in all countries.

Customs regulations

People travelling within the EU are free to take not only personal belongings but a motor vehicle, boat, caravan or trailer across the internal frontiers without being subject to customs formalities. The EU countries are Austria, Belgium, Cyprus, Czech Republic, Denmark, Estonia, Finland, France, Germany, Greece, Hungary, Republic of Ireland, Italy, Latvia, Lithuania, Luxembourg, Malta, the Netherlands, Poland, Portugal, Slovakia, Slovenia, Spain (but not the Canaries), Sweden and the UK (but not the Channel Islands). Gibraltar is part of the EU, but customs allowances for outside the EU apply.

When you return to the UK, use the blue exit reserved for EU travellers. You do not have to pay any tax or duty in the UK on goods you have bought in other EU countries for your own use. The law sets out guidelines for the amount of alcohol and tobacco you can bring into the UK. If you bring in more, you must be able to satisfy the customs officer that the goods are for your own use. If you cannot, the goods may be taken from you, and your vehicle may also be seized.

The guidelines are:
3,200 cigarettes, 400 cigarillos, 200 cigars, 3kg smoking tobacco, 10 litres spirits, 20 litres fortified wine, 90 litres wine, 110 litres beer.

People under 17 are not allowed to bring in alcohol or tobacco.

When you enter the UK from a non-EU country, or from an EU country having travelled through a non-EU country, you must pass through customs. If you have any goods over the allowance, or if you are not sure what to declare you must use the red exit. If you do not declare items on which you should pay duty you are breaking the law.

Customs allowances for travellers from outside the EU are:
200 cigarettes or 100 cigarillos or 50 cigars or 250gms tobacco; 60cc/ml of perfume; 250cc/ml of toilet water; 2 litres still table wine; 1 litre of spirits or strong liqueurs over 22% volume or 2 litres fortified wine, sparkling wine or other liqueurs; £145 worth of all other goods including gifts and souvenirs.

For more information, see the HM Revenue & Customs & website www.hmce.gov.uk or call 0845 010 9000.

Fines

Some countries impose on-the-spot fines for minor traffic offences. Fines are paid in the currency of the country concerned to the police or local post office against a ticket issued. A receipt should be obtained as proof of payment. If you drink, don't drive - the laws are strict and the penalties severe.

Horn

In built-up areas, the general rule is that you should not use it unless safety demands it. In many large towns and resorts, and in areas indicated by the international sign (a horn inside a red circle, crossed through) use of the horn is banned.

Hot weather

In hot weather and at high altitude, excessive heat cause engine problems. If towing a caravan, consult the manufacturers of your vehicle about the limitations of the cooling system, and the operating temperature of the gearbox fluid for automatics.

Journey times

As there are many factors to consider when travelling abroad it is extremely difficult to estimate how long a journey will take. Volume of traffic, road and weather conditions will all affect calculations. On motorways the average speed will be about 60mph, on all-purpose roads out of town the average can be about 45mph, and in urban areas it may be as low as 15-20mph. Remember to allow for refreshments, petrol and toilet stops, and if making for a port or airport to add extra time for checking in and unforeseen delays.

At peak travel periods delays may occur on some main routes and at frontier crossing points. Mountain passes and alpine roads may be closed during the winter months.

Mobile phones

The use of hand-held mobile phones while driving is prohibited in many countries.

Off-site camping

Off-site camping may contravene local regulations. You are strongly advised never to camp by the roadside and in isolated areas.

Parking

Heavy fines are imposed for parking offences and unaccompanied offending cars can be towed away. Make sure you understand all parking related signs. Always park on the right-hand side of the road or at an authorised place. If possible, park off the main carriageway.

Petrol & diesel

You will find familiar brands and comparable grades of petrol along the main routes in most countries. However, leaded petrol is no longer generally available in northern European countries. Diesel fuel is generally known as diesel or gas-oil.

While you may wish to carry a reserve can of fuel, remember that all ferry and rail operators will either forbid the carriage of fuel in spare cans or insist that spare cans must be empty. In Luxembourg motorists are forbidden to carry petrol in cans in the vehicle.

Road signs

Most road signs throughout Europe conform to international standards and most will be familiar. Watch for road markings - do not cross a solid white or yellow line marked on the road centre. In Belgium there are three official languages, and signs will be in Dutch, French or German. In the Basque and Catalonian areas of Spain local and national place names appear on signposts.

Road signs also indicate priority or loss of priority, and tourists must be sure that they understand such signs. Particular care should be exercised when circulating anti-clockwise on a roundabout. It is advisable to keep to the outside lane if possible, to make your exit easier.

Rule of the road

In all countries in this guide, drive on the right and overtake on the left.

When overtaking on roads with two lanes or more in each direction, signal in good time, and also signal your return to the inside lane. Do not remain in any other lane. Failure to comply with this regulation, particularly in France, will incur an on-the-spot fine (immediate deposit in France).

Do not overtake at level crossings, intersections, the crest of a hill or pedestrian crossings. When being overtaken, keep to the right and reduce speed if necessary.

Seat belts

All countries in this guide require seat belts to be worn.

Signposting

Signposting between major towns and along main roads is generally efficient, but on some secondary roads and in open country advance direction signs may be less frequent. Signs are often of the pointer type and placed on walls or railings on the far side of the turn; they tend to point across the road they indicate which can be confusing at first. Difficulties may arise with spellings when crossing frontiers, and place names may not be so easily recognised when written in a different language. Extra difficulties may arise in countries with two or more official languages or dialects, although some towns may have both spellings, eg San Sebastian - Donostia in Spain, Antwerpen - Anvers in Belgium, Basel - Bâle in Switzerland.

Speed limits

Speed limits for individual countries are listed in the country openers. Lower limits may apply to motorcycles in some countries and also generally when towing a trailer unless indicated otherwise. It can be an offence to travel so slowly as to obstruct traffic flow without good reason.

Tolls

Tolls are payable on most motorways in France, Italy, Portugal, Spain and on sections in Austria. Over long distances, charges can be considerable.

Always have some local currency ready to pay the tolls, as traveller's cheques are not accepted at toll booths. Credit cards are accepted at toll booths in France and Spain. In Austria and Switzerland authorities levy a tax for using motorway netways. See country openers.

Trams

Trams take priority over other vehicles. Always give way to passengers boarding and alighting. Never position a vehicle so that it impedes the free passage of a tram. Trams must be overtaken on the right, except in one-way streets.

Channel crossings

Brittany Ferries
Tel 08709 076 103
www.brittanyferries.com

Cork to Roscoff
Plymouth to Roscoff
Plymouth to Santander
Portsmouth to Caen
Poole to Cherbourg
Portsmouth to Cherbourg
Portsmouth to St Malo
Plymouth to St Malo

Condor Ferries
Tel 0870 243 5140
www.condorferries.com

Poole to St Malo (via Channel Islands)
Portsmouth to Cherbourg (seasonal)
Weymouth to St Malo (via Channel Islands)

Eurotunnel
Tel 08705 35 35 35
www.eurotunnel.com

Folkstone to Calais

Irish Ferries
Tel 0818 300 400 (from Northern Ireland &
Republic of Ireland)
Tel 08705 17 17 17 (from Great Britain)
www.irishferries.com

Rosslare to Cherbourg
Rosslare to Roscoff

LD Lines
Tel 0870 420 1267
www.ldline.co.uk

Portsmouth to Le Havre

Norfolk Line
Tel 0870 870 10 20
www.norfolkline-ferries.com

Dover to Dunkerque

P&O Ferries
Tel 08705 980 333
www.poferries.com

Dover to Calais
Portsmouth to Bilbao
Hull to Rotterdam
Hull to Zeebrugge

Seafrance
Tel 0870 443 1653
www.seafrance.com

Dover to Calais

Speed Ferries
Tel 0870 22 00 570
www.speedferries.com

Dover to Boulogne

Transmanche Ferries
Tel 0800 917 1201
www.transmancheferries.com

Newhaven to Dieppe

You always forget something when you go on holiday.
Don't let it be European Breakdown Cover.

10% DISCOUNT FOR AA MEMBERS

AA European Breakdown Cover from just £10.80*

Breaking down abroad without the right cover can be expensive; recovery back to the UK alone could cost you up to £1,000.† But with AA European Breakdown Cover from just £10.80* for AA Members, you know you'll always have help if you need it. So you can relax. After all, that's what holidays are for.

Benefits of cover include:

- Roadside assistance and emergency repair
- 24 hr English speaking telephone assistance
- Emergency car hire and accommodation
- Vehicle recovery for you and your passengers
- Vehicle transported back to UK

0800 085 7254
www.theAA.com

You've got **AA** *friend*

Principle mountain passes

It is best not to attempt to cross mountain passes at night, and daily schedules should make allowances for the comparatively slow speeds inevitable in mountainous areas.

Gravel surfaces (such as dirt and stone chips) vary considerably; they are dusty when dry, slippery when wet. Where known to exist, this type of surface has been noted. Road repairs can be carried out only during the summer, and may interrupt traffic. Precipitous road sides are rarely, if ever, totally unguarded; on the older roads, stone pillars are placed at close intervals.

Gradient figures take the mean figure on hairpin bends, and may be steeper on the inside of the curves, particularly on the older roads.

Gradients

All steep hill signs show the grade in percentage terms. The following conversion table may be used as a guide:

30%	= 1 in 3	14%	= 1 in 7
25%	= 1 in 4	12%	= 1 in 8
20%	= 1 in 5	11%	= 1 in 9
16%	= 1 in 6	10%	= 1 in 10

Before attempting late evening or early morning journeys across frontier passes, check the times of opening of the frontier controls. A number close at night and throughout the winter.

Always engage a low gear before either ascending or descending steep gradients, and keep well to the right-hand side of the road and avoid cutting corners. Avoid excessive use of brakes. If the engine overheats, pull off the road, making sure that you do not cause an obstruction, leave the engine idling, and put the heater controls (including the fan) into the maximum heat position.

Under no circumstances should you remove the radiator cap until the engine has cooled down. Do not fill the coolant system of a hot engine with cold water.

Always engage a lower gear before taking a hairpin bend, give priority to vehicles ascending

and remember that as your altitude increases, so your engine power decreases. Always give priority to postal coaches travelling in either direction. Their route is usually signposted.

Caravans

Passes suitable for caravans are indicated in the table on the following pages. Those shown to be negotiable by caravans are best used only by experienced drivers in cars with ample power; the rest are probably best avoided. A correct power-to-load ratio is always essential.

Winter

Winter conditions are given in italics in the last column. UO means usually open, although a severe fall of snow may temporarily obstruct the road for 24 to 48 hours, and wheel chains are often necessary; OC means occasionally closed, UC, usually closed, between the dates stated. Dates for opening and closing the passes are approximate only. Warning notices are usually posted at the foot of a pass if it is closed, or if chains or snow tyres should or must be used.

Wheel chains may be needed early and late in the season, and between short spells (a few hours) of obstruction. At these times, conditions are usually more difficult for caravans.

In fair weather, wheel chains or snow tyres are only necessary on the higher passes, but in severe weather you will probably need to use them (as a rough guide) at altitudes exceeding 610 metres.

Pass Height	From To	Distances from summit & max gradient	Min width of road	Conditions (see page 18 for abbreviations)
*Albula 2312m Switzerland	Tiefencastel 851m La Punt 1687m	30km 1 in 10 9km 1 in 10	3.5m	UC Nov-early Jun. An inferior alternative to the Julier; tar and gravel, fine scenery. Alternative rail tunnel.
Allosa 2250m France 1235m	Barcelonnette 1132m Colmars	20km 1 in 10 24km 1 in 12	4m	UC Early Nov-early Jun. Very winding, narrow mostly unguarded but not difficult otherwise; passing bays on southern slope, poor surface (maximum width vehicles 1.8m)
Aprica 1176m Italy	Tresenda 375m Edolo 699m	14km 1 in 11 15km 1 in 16	4m	UO Fine scenery, good surface, well graded; suitable for caravans
Aravis 1498m France	LaClusaz 1040m Flumet 917m	8km 1 in 11 12km 1 in 11	4m	OC Dec-Mar. Outstanding scenery, and a fairly easy road.
Arlberg 1802m Austria	Bludenz 581m Landeck 816m	35km 1 in 8 32km 1 in 7.5	6m	OC Dec-Apr. Modern road; short, steep stretch from west easing towards the summit; heavy traffic; parallel toll road tunnel. Suitable for caravans; using tunnel (see chapter on Major Road and Rail Tunnels). Pass road closed to vehicles towing trailers.
Aubisque 1710m France	Eaux Bonnes 750m Argelés-Gazost 463m	12km 1 in 10 30km 1 in 10	3.5m	UC Mid Oct-Jun. A very winding road; continuous but easy ascent; the descent incorporates the Col de Soulor (1450m, 4757ft); 8km (5 miles) of very narrow, rough unguarded road, with a steep drop.
Ballon d'Alsace 1178m France	Giromagny 476m St-Maurice-sur-Moselle 549m	17km 1 in 9 9km 1 in 9	4m	OC Dec-Mar. A fairly straightforward ascent and descent, but numerous bends; negotiable by caravans.
Bayard 1248m France	Chauffayer 911m (2989ft) Gap 733m (2405ft)	18km 1 in 12 8km 1 in 7	6m	UO Part of the Route Napoléon. Fairly easy, steepest on the southern side with several hairpin bends; negotiable by caravans from north to south.
*Bernina 2330m Switzerland	Pontresina 1805m (5922ft) Poschiavo 1019m (3343ft)	15.5km 1 in 10 18.5km 1 in 8	5m	OC Dec-Mar. A good road on both sides; negotiable by caravans.
Bonaigua 2072m Spain	Viella 974m Esterri d`Aneu 957m	23km 1 in 12 23km 1 in 12	4.3m	UC Nov-Apr. A sinuous and narrow road with many hairpin bends and some precipitous drops; the alternative route to Lleida (Lérida) through the Viella tunnel is open in winter.
Bracco 613m Italy	Riva Trigoso 43m Borghetto di Vara 104m	15km 1 in 7 18km 1 in 7	5m	UO A two-lane road with continuous bends; passing usually difficult; negotiable by caravans; alternative toll motorway available.
Brenner 1374m Austria-Italy	Innsbruck 574m Vipiteno 948m	36km 1 in 12 15km 1 in 7	6m	UO Parallel toll motorway open; heavy traffic; suitable for caravans using toll motorway. Pass road closed to vehicles towing trailers.

* Maximum vehicle width 2.28m + Maximum vehicle width 2.49m ++ Maximum vehicle length 9.14m

Pass Height	From To	Distances from summit & max gradient	Min width of road	Conditions (see page 18 for abbreviations)
Brünig 1007m Switzerland	Brienzwiler Station 575m Giswil 485m	6km 1 in 12 13km 1 in 12	6m	UO An easy but winding road, heavy traffic at weekends; suitable for caravans.
Bussang 721m France	Thann 340m St Maurice-sur-Moselle 549m	24km 1 in 14 8km 1 in 14	4m	UO A very easy road over the Vosges; beautiful scenery; suitable for caravans.
Cabre 1180m France	Luc-en-Diois 580m Aspres sur Buëch 764m	24km 1 in 11 17km 1 in 14	5.5m	UO An easy pleasant road; suitable for caravans.
Campolongo 1875m Italy	Corvara in Badia 1568m Arabba 1602m	6km 1 in 8 4km 1 in 8	5m	OC Dec–Mar. A winding but easy ascent; long level stretch on summit followed by easy descent; good surface; suitable for caravans.
Cayolle 2326m France	Barcelonnette 1132m Guillaumes 819m	30km 1 in 10 33km 1 in 10	4m	UC early Nov–early Jun. Narrow and winding road with hairpin bends; poor surface and broken edges; steep drops. Long stretches of single-track road with passing places.
Costalunga (Karer) 1753m Italy	Cardano 282m Pozza 1290m	24km 1 in 6 11km 1 in 8	5m	OC Dec–Apr. A good well-engineered road but mostly winding; caravans prohibited.
Croix 1778m Switzerland	Villars-sur-Ollon 1253m Les Diablerets 1155m	8km 1 in 7.5 9km 1 in 11	3.5m	UC Nov–May. A narrow and winding route but extremely picturesque.
Croix-Haute 1179m France	Monestier-de-Clermont 832m Aspres-sur-Buëch 764m	34km 1 in 14 29km 1 in 14	5.5m	UO Well engineered; several hairpin bends on the north side; suitable for caravans.
Envalira 2407m Andorra	Pas de la Casa 2091m Andorra 1029m	5km 1 in 10 25km 1 in 8	6m	OC Nov–Apr. A good road with wide bends on ascent and descent; fine views; negotiable by caravans (maximum height vehicles 3.5m, on northern approach near l'Hospitalet).
Falzárego 2117m Italy	Cortina d'Ampezzo 1224m Andraz 1428m	17km 1 in 12 9km 1 in 12	5m	OC Dec–Apr. Well engineered bitumen surface; many hairpin bends on both sides; negotiable by caravans.
Faucille 1323m France	Gex 628m Morez 702m	11km 1 in 10 27km 1 in 12	5m	UO Fairly wide, winding road across the Jura mountains; negotiable by caravans, but it is probably better to follow La Cure-St-Cergue-Nyon.
Fern 1209m Austria	Nassereith 843m Lermoos 995m	10km 1 in 10 10km 1 in 10	6m	UO An easy pass, but slippery when wet; heavy traffic at summer weekends; suitable for caravans.

* Maximum vehicle width 2.28m + Maximum vehicle width 2.49m ++ Maximum vehicle length 9.14m

Pass Height	From To	Distances from summit & max gradient	Min width of road	Conditions (see page 18 for abbreviations)
Flexen 1784m Austria	Lech 1447m Rauzalpe (near Arlberg Pass) 1628m	6.5km 1 in 10 3.5km 1 in 10	5.5m	UO The magnificent 'Flexenstrasse', a well engineered mountain road with tunnels and galleries. The road from Lech to Warth, north of the pass, is usually closed between November and April due to danger of avalanches.
*Flüela 2383m Switzerland	Davos-Dorf 1563m Susch 1438m	14km 1 in 10 14km 1 in 8	5m	OC Nov-May. Easy ascent from Davos; some acute hairpin bends on the eastern side; bitumen surface; negotiable by caravans.
+Forclaz 1527m Switzerland France	Martigny 476m Argentière 1253m	13km 1 in 12 19km 1 in 12	5m	UO Forclaz; OC Montets Dec-early Apr. A good road over the pass and to the frontier; in France, narrow and rough over Col des Montets (1461m); negotiable by caravans.
Foscagno 2291m Italy	Bormio 1225m Livigno 1816m	24km 1 in 8 14km 1 in 8	3.3m	OC Nov-May. Narrow and winding through lonely mountains, generally poor surface. Long winding ascent with many blind bends; not always well guarded. The descent includes winding rise and fall over the Passo d'Eira (2200m).
Fugazze 1159m Italy	Rovereto 201m Valli del Pasubio 350m	27km 1 in 7 12km 1 in 7	3.5m	UO Very winding with some narrow sections, particularly on northern side. The many blind bends and several hairpin bends call for extra care.
*Furka 2431m Switzerland	Gletsch 1757m Realp 1538m	10km 1 in 9 13km 1 in 10	4m	UC Oct-Jun. A well graded road, with narrow sections and several sharp hairpin bends on both ascent and descent. Fine views of the Rhône glacier. Alternative rail tunnel available.
Galibier 2645m France	Lautaret Pass 2058m St-Michel-de-Maurienne 712m	7km 1 in 9 34km 1 in 8	3m	UC Oct-Jun. Mainly wide, well surfaced but unguarded. Ten hairpin bends on descent then 5km (3.1 miles) narrow and rough. Rise over the Col du Télégraphe (1600m), then 11 more hairpin bends. (The tunnel under the Galibier summit is closed.)
Gardena (Grödner-Joch) 2121m Italy	Val Gardena 1862m Corvara in Badia 1568m	6km 1 in 8 10km 1 in 8	5m	OC Dec-Jun. A well engineered road, very winding on descent.
Gavia 2621m Italy	Bormio 1225m Ponte di Legno 1258m	25km 1 in 5.5 18km 1 in 5.5	3m	UC Oct-Jul. Steep and narrow, but with frequent passing bays; many hairpin bends and a gravel surface; not for the faint-hearted; extra care necessary. (Maximum width for vehicles 1.8m.)
Gerlos 1628m Austria	Zell am Ziller 575m Wald 885m	29km 1 in 12 15km 1 in 11	4m	UO Hairpin ascent out of Zell to modern toll road; the old, steep, narrow, and winding route with passing bays and 1-in-7 gradient is not recommended, but is negotiable with care; caravans prohibited.

* Maximum vehicle width 2.28m + Maximum vehicle width 2.49m ++ Maximum vehicle length 9.14m

Pass Height	From To	Distances from summit & max gradient	Min width of road	Conditions (see page 18 for abbreviations)
+Grand St Bernard 2473m Switzerland-Italy	Martigny 476m Aosta 583m	46km 1 in 9 34km 1 in 9	4m	UC Oct-Jun. Modern road to entrance of road tunnel (usually open) then narrow over summit to frontier; also good surface in Italy; suitable for caravans using tunnel. Pass road closed to vehicles towing trailers.
*Grimsel 2164m Switzerland	Innerkirchen 630m Gletsch 1757m	26km 1 in 10 6km 1 in 10	5m	UC mid Oct-late Jun. A fairly easy road, but heavy traffic weekends. A long winding ascent, finally hairpin bends; then a terraced descent (six hairpins) into the Rhône valley. Negotiable by caravans.
Grossglockner 2503m Austria	Bruck an der Glocknerstrasse 755m Heiligenblut 1301m	34km 1 in 8 15m 1 in 8	5.5m	UC late Oct-early May. Numerous well engineered hairpin bends; moderate but very long ascent, toll road; very fine scenery; heavy tourist traffic; negotiable preferably from south to north, by caravans. Road closed 22.00-05.00.
Hochtannberg 1679m Austria	Schröcken 1269m Warth (near Lech) 1500m	5.5km 1 in 7 4.5km 1 in 11	4m	OC Jan-Mar. A reconstructed modern road.
Ibañeta (Roncesvalles) 1057m France-Spain	St-Jean-Pied-de-Port 163m Pamplona 415m	27km 1 in 10 49km 1 in 10	4m	UO A slow and winding, scenic route; negotiable by caravans.
Iseran 2770m France	Bourg-St-Maurice 840m Lanslebourg 1399m	47km 1 in 12 33km 1 in 9	4m	UC mid Oct-late Jun. The second highest pass in the Alps. Well graded with reasonable bends, average surface; several unlit tunnels on northern approach.
Izoard 2360m France	Guillestre 1000m Briançon 1321m	32km 1 in 8 22km 1 in 8	5m	UC late Oct-mid Jun. A winding and sometimes narrow road with many hairpin bends. Care is required at several unlit tunnels near Guillestre.
*Jaun 1509m Switzerland	Broc 718m Reidenbach 845m	25km 1 in 10 8km 1 in 10	4m	UO A modernised but generally narrow road; some poor sections on ascent, and several hairpin bends on descent; negotiable by caravans.
+Julier 2284m Switzerland	Tiefencastel 851m Silvaplana 1815m	35km 1 in 10 7km 1 in 7.5	4m	UO Well engineered road, approached from Chur by Lenzerheide Pass (1549m); negotiable by caravans, preferably from north to south.
Katschberg 1641m Austria	Spittal 554m St Michael 1068m 662m	37km 1 in 5 6km 1 in 6	6m	UO Steep though not particularly difficult, parallel toll motorway, including tunnel available; negotiable by light caravans, using tunnel.
*Klausen 1948m Switzerland	Altdorf 458m Linthal	25km 1 in 10 23km 1 in 11	5m	UC late Oct-early Jun. Narrow and winding in places, but generally easy, in spite of a number of sharp bends; no through route for caravans as they are prohibited from using the road between Unterschächen and Linthal.

* Maximum vehicle width 2.28m + Maximum vehicle width 2.49m ++ Maximum vehicle length 9.14m

Pass Height	From To	Distances from summit & max gradient	Min width of road	Conditions (see page 18 for abbreviations)
Larche (della Maddalena) 1994m France-Italy	La Condamine-Châtelard 1308m Vinadio 910m	19km 1 in 12 32km 1 in 12	3.5m	OC Dec-Mar. An easy, well graded road; narrow ascent, wider on descent; suitable for caravans.
Lautaret 2058m France	Le Bourg-d'Oisans 719m Briançon 1321m	38km 1 in 8 28km 1 in 10	4m	OC Dec-Mar. Modern, evenly graded, but winding, and unguarded in places; very fine scenery; suitable for caravans.
Loibl (Ljubelj) 1067m Austria-Slovenia	Unterloibl 518m Kranj 385m	10km 1 in 5.5 26km 1 in 8	6m	UO Steep rise and fall over Little Loibl pass to tunnel (1.6km, 1 mile long) under summit. The old road over the summit is closed to through traffic.
*Lukmanier (Lucomagno) 1916m Switzerland	Olivone 893m Disentis 1133m	20km 1 in 11 20km 1 in 11	5m	UC early Nov-late May. Rebuilt, modern road; suitable for caravans.
+Maloja 1815m Switzerland	Silvaplana 1815m Chiavenna 333m	11km level 32km 1 in 11	4m	UO Escarpment facing south; fairly easy, but many hairpin bends on descent; negotiable by caravans, possibly difficult on ascent.
Mauria 1298m Italy	Lozzo Cadore 753m Ampezzo 560m	13km 1 in 14 31km 1 in 14	5m	UO A well designed road with easy, winding ascent and descent; suitable for caravans.
Mendola 1363m Italy	Appiano (Eppan) 411m Sarnonico 978m	15km 1 in 8 9km 1 in 10	5m	UO A fairly straightforward but winding road, well guarded; suitable for caravans.
Mont Cenis 2083m France-Italy	Lanslebourg 1399m Susa 503m	11km 1 in 10 28km 1 in 8	5m	UC Nov-May. Approach by industrial valley. An easy highway, with mostly very good surface; spectacular scenery; suitable for caravans. Alternative Fréjus road tunnel.
Monte Croce di Comélico (Kreuzberg) 1636m Italy	San Candido 1174m Santo Stefano di Cadore 908m	15km 1 in 12 21km 1 in 12	5m	UO A winding road with moderate gradients, beautiful scenery; suitable for caravans.
Montgenèvre 1850m France-Italy	Briançon 1321m Cesana Torinese 1344m	12km 1 in 14 8km 1 in 11	5m	UO An easy, modern road; suitable for caravans.
Monte Giovo (Jaufen) 2094m Italy	Merano 324m Vipiteno 948m	40km 1 in 8 19km 1 in 11	4m	UC Nov-May. Many well engineered hairpin bends; caravans prohibited.
Montets (see Forclaz)				
Morgins 1369m France-Switzerland	Abondance 930m Monthey 424m	14km 1 in 11 15km 1 in 7	4m	UO A lesser used route through pleasant, forested countryside crossing the French-Swiss border.

* Maximum vehicle width 2.28m + Maximum vehicle width 2.49m ++ Maximum vehicle length 9.14m

Pass Height	From To	Distances from summit & max gradient	Min width of road	Conditions (see page 18 for abbreviations)
*Mosses 1445m Switzerland	Aigle 417m Château d`Oex 958m	16km 1 in 12 15km 1 in 12	4m	UO A modern road; suitable for caravans.
Nassfeld (Pramollo) 1530m Austria-Italy	Tröpolach 601m Pontebba 568m	10km 1 in 5 10km 1 in 10	4m	OC late Nov-Mar. The winding descent in Italy has been improved.
*Nufenen (Novena) 2478m Switzerland	Ulrichen 1346m Airolo 1142m	13km 1 in 10 24km 1 in 10	4.0m	UC mid Oct-mid Jun. The approach roads are narrow, with tight bends, but the road over the pass is good; negotiable by caravans.
*Oberalp 2044m Switzerland	Andermatt 1447m Disentis 1133m	10km 1 in 10 21km 1 in 10	5m	UC Nov-late May. A widened road with a modern surface; many hairpin bends, but long level stretch on summit; negotiable by caravans. Alternative rail tunnel for winter.
*Ofen (Fuorn) 2149m Switzerland	Zernez 1474m Santa Maria im Münstertal 1375m	22km 1 in 10 14km 1 in 8	4m	UO Good, fairly easy road through the Swiss National Park; negotiable by caravans.
Petit St Bernard 2188m France-Italy	Bourg-St-Maurice 840m Pré St-Didier 1000m	30km 1 in 16 23km 1 in 12	5m	UC mid Oct-Jun. Outstanding scenery; a fairly easy approach, but poor surface and unguarded broken edges near the summit; good on the descent in Italy; negotiable by light caravans.
Peyresourde 1563m France	Arreau 704m Luchon 630m	18km 1 in 10 14km 1 in 10	4m	UO Somewhat narrow with several hairpin bends, though not difficult.
*Pillon 1546m Switzerland	Le Sépey 974m Gsteig 1184m	15km 1 in 11 7km 1 in 11	4m	OC Jan-Feb. A comparatively easy modern road; suitable for caravans.
Plöcken (Monte Croce-Carnico) 1362m Austria-Italy	Kötschach 706m Paluzza 600m	16km 1 in 7 16km 1 in 14	5m	OC Dec-Apr. A modern road with long, reconstructed sections; heavy traffic at summer weekends; delay likely at the frontier; negotiable by caravans, best used only by experienced drivers in cars with ample power.
Pordoi 2239m Italy	Arabba 1602m Canazei 1465m	9km 1 in 10 12km 1 in 10	5m	OC Dec-Apr. An excellent modern road with numerous hairpin bends; negotiable by caravans.
Port 1249m France	Tarascon 474m Massat 650m	18km 1 in 10 12km 1 in 10	4m	OC Nov-Mar. A fairly easy road, but narrow on some bends; negotiable by caravans.
Portet-d'Aspet 1069m France	Audressein 508m Fronsac 472m	18km 1 in 7 29km 1 in 7	3.5m	UO Approached from the west by the easy Col des Ares (797m) and Col de Buret (599m); well engineered road, but calls for particular care on hairpin bends; rather narrow.

* Maximum vehicle width 2.28m + Maximum vehicle width 2.49m ++ Maximum vehicle length 9.14m

Pass Height	From To	Distances from summit & max gradient	Min width of road	Conditions (see page 18 for abbreviations)
Pötschen 982m Austria	Bad Ischl 469m Bad Aussee 659m	19km 1 in 11 9 km 1 in 11	7m	UO A modern road; suitable for caravans.
Pourtalet 1792m France-Spain	Eaux-Chaudes 656m Biescas 860m	23km 1 in 10 32km 1 in 10	3.5m	UC late Oct-early Jun. A fairly easy, unguarded road, but narrow in places.
Puymorens 1915m France	Ax-les-Thermes 720m Bourg-Madame 1130m	28km 1 in 10 27km 1 in 10	5.5m	OC Nov-Apr. A generally easy, modern tarmac road, but narrow, winding and with a poor surface in places; not suitable for night driving; suitable for caravans (max height vehicles 3.5m). Parallel toll road tunnel available.
Quillane 1714m France	Quillan 291m Mont-Louis 1600m	63km 1 in 12 6 km 1 in 12	5m	OC Nov-Mar. An easy, straight forward ascent and descent; suitable for caravans.
Radstädter-Tauern Austria	Radstadt 1738m Mauterndorf 1122m	21km 1 in 6 862m 17km 1 in 7	5m	OC Jan-Mar. Northern ascent steep, but not difficult otherwise; parallel toll motorway including tunnel; negotiable by light caravans, using tunnel.
Résia (Reschen) 1504m Italy-Austria	Spondigna 885m Pfunds 970m	29km 1 in 10 21km 1 in 10	6m	UO A good, straightforward alternative to the Brenner Pass; suitable for caravans.
Restefond (La Bonette) 2802m France	Jausiers (near Barcelonnette) 1220m St-Etienne-de-Tinée 1144m	23km 1 in 8 27km 1 in 6	3m	UC Oct-Jun. The highest pass in the Alps, completed in 1962. Narrow, rough, unguarded ascent with many blind bends, and nine hairpins. Descent easier, winding with 12 hairpin bends. Not for the faint-hearted; extra care required.
Rolle 1970m Italy	Predazzo 1018m Mezzano 637m	21km 1 in 11 27km 1 in 14	5m	OC Dec-Mar. A well engineered road with many hairpin bends on both sides; very beautiful scenery; good surface; negotiable by caravans.
Rombo (see Timmelsjoch)				
Routes des Crêtes 1283m France	St-Dié 343m Cernay 296m	1 in 8 1 in 8	4m	UC Nov-Apr. A renowned scenic route crossing seven ridges, with the highest point at 'Hôtel du Grand Ballon'.
+St Gotthard (San Gottardo) 2108m Switzerland	Göschenen 1106m Airolo 1142m	18km 1 in 10 15km 1 in 10	6m	UC mid Oct-early Jun. Modern, fairly easy two to three-lane road. Heavy traffic; negotiable by caravans. Alternative road tunnel.
*San Bernardino 2066m Switzerland	Mesocco 790m Hinterrhein 1620m	21km 1 in 10 9.5km 1 in 10	4m	UC Oct-late Jun. Easy, modern roads on northern and southern approaches to tunnel. Narrow and winding over summit, via tunnel suitable for caravans.
Schlucht 1139m France	Gérardmer 665m Munster 381m	15km 1 in 14 18km 1 in 14	5m	UO An extremely picturesque route crossing the Vosges mountains, with easy, wide bends on the descent; suitable for caravans.

* Maximum vehicle width 2.28m + Maximum vehicle width 2.49m ++ Maximum vehicle length 9.14m

Pass Height	From To	Distances from summit & max gradient	Min width of road	Conditions (see page 18 for abbreviations)
Seeberg (Jezersko) 1218m Austria-Slovenia	Eisenkappel 555m Kranj 385m	14km 1 in 8 33km 1 in 10	5m	UO An alternative to the steeper Loibl and Wurzen passes; moderate climb with winding, hairpin ascent and descent.
Sella 2240m Italy	Plan 1606m Canazei 1465m	9km 1 in 9 12km 1 in 9	5m	OC Dec-Jun. A finely engineered, winding road; exceptional views of the Dolomites.
Semmering 985m Austria	Mürzzuschlag im Mürztal 672m Gloggnitz 457m	14km 1 in 16 17km 1 in 16	6m	UO A fine, well engineered highway; suitable for caravans.
Sestriere 2033m Italy	Cesana Torinese 1344m Pinerolo 376m	12km 1 in 10 55km 1 in 10	6m	UO Mostly bitumen surface; negotiable by caravans.
Silvretta (Bielerhöhe) 2032m Austria	Partenen 1051m Galtür 1584m	16km 1 in 9 10km 1 in 9	5m	UC late Oct-early Jun. For the most part reconstructed; 32 easy hairpin bends on western ascent; eastern side more straightforward. Toll road; caravans prohibited.
+Simplon 2005m Switzerland-Italy	Brig 681m Domodóssola 280m	22km 1 in 9 41km 1 in 11	7m	OC Nov-Apr. An easy, reconstructed modern road, but 13 miles long, continuous ascent to summit; suitable for caravans.
Somport 1632m France-Spain	Bedous 416m Jaca 820m	31km 1 in 10 32km 1 in 10	3.5m	UO A favoured, old-established route; generally easy, but in parts narrow and unguarded; fairly well surfaced road; suitable for caravans.
*Splügen 2113m Switzerland-Italy	Splügen 1457m Chiavenna 330m	9km 1 in 9 30km 1 in 7.5	3.5m	UC Nov-Jun. Mostly narrow and winding, with many hairpin bends, and not well guarded; care is also required at many tunnels and galleries (max height vehicles 2.79m).
++Stelvio 2757m Italy	Bormio 1225m Spondigna 885m	22km 1 in 8 28km 1 in 8	4m	UC Oct-late Jun. the third highest pass in the Alps; the number of acute hairpin bends, all well engineered, is exceptional - from 40 to 50 on either side; the surface is good, the traffic heavy. Hairpin bends are too acute for long vehicles.
+Susten 2224m Switzerland	Innertkirchen 630m Wassen 916m	28km 1 in 11 19km 1 in 11	6m	UC Nov-Jun. A very scenic and well guarded mountain road; easy gradients and turns; heavy traffic at weekends; negotiable by caravans - extra care required. Not for the faint-hearted.
Tenda (Tende) 1321m Italy-France	Borgo S Dalmazzo 641m La Giandola 308m	24km 1 in 11 29km 1 in 11	6m	UO Well guarded, modern road with several hairpin bends; road tunnel at summit; suitable for caravans; but prohibited during the winter.
+Thurn 1274m Austria	Kitzbühel 762m Mittersill 789m	19km 1 in 12 10km 1 in 16	5m	UO A good road with narrow stretches; northern approach rebuilt; suitable for caravans.

* Maximum vehicle width 2.28m + Maximum vehicle width 2.49m ++ Maximum vehicle length 9.14m

Pass Height	From To	Distances from summit & max gradient	Min width of road	Conditions (see page 18 for abbreviations)
Timmelsjoch (Rombo) 2509m Austria-Italy	Obergurg 1910m Moso 1007m	14km 1 in 7 23km 1 in 8	3.5m	UC mid Oct-late Jun. Pass open to private cars (without trailers) only as some tunnels on the Italian side are too narrow for larger vehicles; toll road. Border closed 20.00-07.00.
Tonale 1883m Italy	Edolo 699m Dimaro 766m	30km 1 in 12 27km 1 in 10	5m	UO A relatively easy road; suitable for caravans.
Toses (Tosas) 1800m Spain	Puigcerdá 1152m Ribes de Freser 920m	26km 1 in 10 25km 1 in 10	5m	UO Now a fairly straightforward, but continuously winding, two-lane road with many sharp bends; negotiable by caravans.
Tourmalet 2114m France	Luz 711m Ste-Marie-de-Campan 857m	18km 1 in 8 17km 1 in 8	4m	UC Oct-mid Jun. The highest of the French Pyrenean routes; the approaches are good, though winding and exacting over summit; sufficiently guarded.
Tre Croci 1809m Italy	Cortina d'Ampezzo 1224m Auronzo di Cadore 864m	7km 1 in 9 26 km 1 in 9	6m	OC Dec-Mar. An easy pass; very fine scenery; suitable for caravans.
Turracher Höhe 1763m Austria	Predlitz 922m Ebene-Reichenau 1062m	20km 1 in 5.5 8km 1 in 4.5	4m	UO Formerly one of the steepest mountain roads in Austria; now much improved. A steep, fairly straightforward ascent is followed by a very steep descent; good surface and mainly two-lane width; fine scenery.
*Umbrail 2501m Switzerland-Italy	Santa Maria im Münstertal 1375m Bormio 1225m	14km 1 in 11 19km 1 in 11	4.3m	UC early Nov-early Jun. Highest of the Swiss passes; narrow; mostly gravel surfaced with 34 hairpin bends, but not too difficult.
Vars 2109m France	St-Paul-sur-Ubaye 1470m Guillestre 1000m	8km 1 in 10 20km 1 in 10	5m	OC Dec-Mar. Easy winding ascent with seven hairpin bends; gradual winding descent with another seven hairpin bends; good surface; negotiable by caravans.
Wurzen (Koren) 1073m Austria-Slovenia	Riegersdorf 541m Kranjska Gora 810m	7km 1 in 5.5 6km 1 in 5.5	4m	UO A steep two-lane road, which otherwise is not particularly difficult; heavy traffic at summer weekends; delay likely at the frontier; caravans prohibited.
Zirler Berg 1009m Austria	Seefeld 1180m Zir 622m	6km 1 in 7 5km 1 in 6	7m	UO An escarpment facing south, part of the route from Garmisch to Innsbruck; a good, modern road, but heavy tourist traffic and a long steep descent, with one hairpin bend, into the Inn Valley. Steepest section from the hairpinbend down to Zirl; caravans prohibited northbound.

* Maximum vehicle width 2.28m + Maximum vehicle width 2.49m ++ Maximum vehicle length 9.14m

Country regions

The country directories, except Andorra and Luxembourg, are divided into regions. See the country maps at the end of the guide. The lists below of country regions show the corresponding national departments, districts or administrative areas.

Austria

TIROL – Tirol
CARINTHIA – Kärnten
STYRIA – Steiermark
LOWER AUSTRIA – Niederösterreich, Burgenland
UPPER AUSTRIA – Oberösterreich, Salzburg
VORARLBERG VIENNA – Wien

Belgium

SOUTH WEST/COAST – Hainaut, West-Vlaanderen
NORTH/CENTRAL – Brabant, Oost-Vlaanderen
NORTH EAST – Antwerpen, Limburg
SOUTH EAST – Liège, Luxembourg, Namur

France

ALPS/EAST – Ain, Doubs, Hautes-Alpes, Haute Saône, Haute Savoie, Jura, Isère, Savoie, Territoire-de-Belfort
ALSACE/LORRAINE – Bas-Rhin, Haut-Rhin, Meurthe-et-Moselle, Meuse, Moselle, Vosges
BURGUNDY/CHAMPAGNE – Aube, Ardennes, Côte-d'Or, Haute-Marne, Marne, Nièvre, Saône-et-Loire, Yonne
SOUTH WEST/ PYRENEES – Ariège, Dordogne, Gers, Gironde, Haute-Garonne, Hautes-Pyrénées, Landes, Lot, Lot-et-Garonne, Pyrénées-Atlantiques, Tarn, Tarn-et-Garonne
LOIRE/CENTRAL – Charente, Charente-Maritime, Cher, Corrèze, Creuse, Deux-Sèvres, Eure-et-Loir, Haute-Vienne, Indre, Indre-et-Loire, Loire-Atlantique, Loiret, Loir-et-Cher, Maine-et-Loire, Mayenne, Sarthe, Vendée, Vienne
BRITTANY/NORMANDY – Calvados, Côtes-d'Armor, Eure, Finistère, Ille-et-Vilaine, Manche, Morbihan, Orne, Seine-Maritime
PARIS/NORTH – Aisne, Essonne, Hauts-de-Seine, Nord, Oise, Paris, Pas-de-Calais, Seine-et-Marne, Seine-St-Denis, Somme, Val-de-Marne, Val d'Oise, Yvelines
AUVERGNE – Allier, Aveyron, Cantal, Haute-Loire, Loire, Lozère, Puy-de-Dôme, Rhône
SOUTH COAST/RIVIERA – Alpes-Maritimes, Alpes-de-Haute-Provence, Ardèche, Aude, Bouches-du-Rhône, Drôme, Gard, Hérault, Monaco, Pyrénées-Orientales, Var, Vaucluse
CORSICA – Corse-du-Sud, Haute-Corse

Germany

SOUTH EAST – Bayern
SOUTH WEST – Baden-Württemberg
BERLIN AND EASTERN PROVINCES – Brandenburg, Sachsen, Thüringen
CENTRAL – Hessen, Nordrhein-Westfalen, Rheinland-Pfalz, Saarland
NORTH – Bremen, Hamburg, Niedersachsen, Schleswig-Holstein

Italy

NORTH WEST/ALPS/LAKES – Aosta, Alessandria, Asti, Beramo, Bolzano, Brescia, Como, Cremona, Cuneo, Mantova, Milano, Novara, Pavia, Sondrio, Trento, Torino, Varese, Vercelli
VENICE/NORTH – Belluno, Gorizia, Padova, Pordenone, Rovigo, Treviso, Trieste, Udine, Venezia, Verona, Vicenza,
NORTH WEST/MED COAST – Arezzo, Firenze, Genova, Grosseto, Imperia, Livorno, Lucca, Massa Carrara, Pisa, Pistoia, Savona, Siena, La Spezia
NORTH EAST/ADRIATIC – Ancona, L'Aquila, Ascoli Piceno, Bologna, Campobasso, Chieti, Ferrara, Forli, Iserina, Macerata, Modena, Parma, Perugia, Pescara, Pesaro & Urbino, Piacenza, Ravenna, Reggio nell'Emilia, Teramo, Terni
ROME – Frosinone, Latina, Roma, Rieti, Viterbo
SOUTH – Avellino, Bari, Benevento, Brindisi,

Caserta, Catanzaro, Cosenza, Foggia, Lecce, Matera, Napoli, Potenza, Reggio di Calabria, Salerno, Taranto
SARDINIA – Cagliari, Nuoro, Oristano, Sassari
SICILY – Agrigento, Caltanissetta, Catania, Enna, Messina, Palermo, Ragusa, Siracusa, Trapani

Netherlands

NORTH – Ameland, Drenthe, Friesland, Groningen
CENTRAL – Flevoland, Gelderland, Noord-Holland, Overijssel, Utrecht
SOUTH – Limburg, Noord-Brabant, Zeeland, Zuid-Holland

Portugal

SOUTH – Algarve, Baixo-Alentejo
NORTH – Costa Verde, Douro Litoral, Minho, Tras os Montes, Alto Douro
CENTRAL – Alto Alentejo, Beira Alta, Beira Baixo, Beira Litoral, Costa de Prata, Estremadura, Ribatejo

Spain

NORTH EAST COAST – Barcelona, Girona
CENTRAL – Albacete, Avila, Badajoz, Cáceres, Ciudad Real, Cuenca, Guadalajara, Madrid, Salamanca, Segovia, Soria, Teruel, Toledo
SOUTH EAST COAST – Alicante, Castellón, Tarragona, Valencia
NORTH COAST – Asturias, Cantabria, Guipúzcoa, La Coruña, Lugo, Vizcaya
NORTH EAST – Alava, Burgos, Huesca, Lleida, La Rioja, Navarra, Zaragoza
NORTH WEST – Léon, Logrono Orense, Palencia, Pontevedra, Valladolid, Zamora
SOUTH – Almeria, Cádiz, Cordoba, Granada, Huelva, Jaén, Málaga, Murcia, Sevilla
ISLANDS – Ibiza, Mallorca Menorca

Switzerland

NORTH – Aargau, Basel, Solothurn
NORTH EAST – Appenzell, Liechtenstein, St Gallen, Schaffhausen, Thurgau, Zürich
NORTH WEST/CENTRAL – Bern, Jura, Luzern, Neuchâtel, Nidwalden, Obwalden, Schwyz, Uri, Zug
EAST – Glarus, Graubünden
SOUTH – Ticino
SOUTH WEST – Fribourg, Genève, Valais, Vaud

Austria

Accidents & emergencies
fire 122　**police** 133　**ambulance** 144

The European emergency call number is also in use – dial 112 and ask for the service required.

Driving requirements
Minimum age 18 for UK licence holders driving temporarily imported motorcycle (over 50cc) or car. UK driving licences that do not incorporate a photograph will not be recognised unless accompanied by photographic proof of identity, e.g. a passport.

Lights
Daytime use of dipped headlights is mandatory for both cars and motorcycles. Parking lights are required in areas where there are no all-night street lamps (lamps with red-banded posts will go off at midnight).

Motorways
All vehicles using Austrian motorways and expressways must display a tax sticker *(vignette)*. The stickers may be purchased at many petrol stations close to the border in neighbouring countries and in Austria, at the frontier or in OAMTC offices within Austria. Fines are imposed for non-display. Charges may change and are a guide only.

Passengers & children
Children under 14 and 1.5m high must not travel in the front or rear seat unless using a suitable restraint system. Never fit a rear-facing child restraint in a seat with a frontal airbag.

Size restrictions
Motor vehicle or trailer
height 4m, width 2.55m, length 12m

Vehicle + trailer
length 18.75m

Speed limits
Unless signed otherwise:

Car without trailer, motorcycle

Built-up areas	50kph
Outside built-up areas	100kph
Motorways	130kph

Car towing caravan not exceeding 750kg

Built-up areas	50kph
Outside built-up areas	100kph
Motorways	100kph

Car towing caravan over 750kg

Built-up areas	50kph
Outside built-up areas	80kph
Motorways	100kph

Car towing caravan exceeding 3500kg in total weight

Built-up areas	50kph
Outside built-up areas	60kph
Motorways	70kph

The weight of any caravan equipped with over-run brakes must not exceed maximum weight of towing vehicle.

Tourist office
Austrian National Tourist Office
9-11 Richmond Buildings, London W1D 3HF
Tel 0845 1011 818
www.austria.info

Additional information
First-aid kit and warning triangle compulsory. Restrictions in some areas to prevent the circulation of tourist vehicles when levels of pollution reach certain limits. Reflective jacket/waiscoat compulsory for use by driver and/or passengers when exiting vehicle in case of breakdown/accident.

Tolls

Tolls Vignette	car	car & caravan
10 day vignette	€7.60	€7.60
2 month vignette	€21.80	€21.80
Annual vignette	€72.60	€72.60
A10 Tauern Autobahn	€13.00	€19.00
A13 Innsbruck - Brenner pass	€23.50	€32.90
A16 St Anton - Arlberg	€13.30	€18.60
Bridges & tunnels		
A9 Bosruck Tunnel/ Gleinalm Tunnel	€6.60	€9.20
A9 Gleinalm Tunnel	€9.50	€13.30
A9 Bosruck Tunnel/ Gleinalm Tunnel	€16.00	€22.00
A11 Karawanken Tunnel	€9.00	€12.60

TIROL

ASCHAU TIROL

Aufenfeld
Distelberg 1, 6274 ☎ 05282 2916 🖹 05282 291611
e-mail camping.fiegl@tirol.com
website www.camping-zillertal.at
A well-equipped family site on level meadowland backed by thickly
wooded slopes.
➲ *Signed from Aschau road.*
Open 9 Dec-2 Nov **Site** 12HEC ⚊ ⚊ 🏠 **Prices** ♦ 5-9 pitch 7-10.50
Facilities 🝙 🛁 ⊙ 🔌 ∅ ⚐ ℗ **Services** 🛒 🍽 🗐 **Leisure** ≋ LP
Off-site ≋R ➕

EHRWALD TIROL

International Dr-Ing E Lauth
Zugspitzstr 34, 6632 ☎ 05673 2666 🖹 05673 26664
e-mail info@campingehrwald.at
website www.campingehrwald.at
On undulating grassland, surrounded by high conifers, below the
Wetterstein mountain range. Cars may park by tents in winter.
➲ *To right of access road to Zugspitz funicular.*
Open All year **Site** 1HEC ⚊ ⚊ ⚊ 🏠 🔌 Ă **Prices** ♦ 8.60-8.75 Ă 4.70
pitch 5.90-6.20 **Facilities** 🝙 ⊙ 🔌 ∅ ⚐ ℗ **Services** 🛒 🍽 ➕ 🗐
Off-site 🛁 ≋P

Tiroler Zugspitzcamp
Obermoos 1, 6632 ☎ 05673 2309 🖹 05673 230951
e-mail camping@zugspitze.at
website www.ferienanlage-zugspitze.at
A well-equipped site on several grassy terraces surrounded by
woodland. Modern sanitary installations with bathrooms.
➲ *Near the Zugspitz funicular station.*
Open All year **Site** 5HEC ⚊ **Prices** ♦ 11.25-13.25 pitch 6-8 **Facilities** 🝙 🛁
⊙ 🔌 ∅ ℗ **Services** 🛒 🍽 **Leisure** ≋ P

FIEBERBRUNN TIROL

Tirol-Camp
6391 ☎ 05354 56666 🖹 05354 52516
e-mail office@tirol-camp.at
website www.tirol-camp.at
A summer and winter site in pleasant Alpine surroundings.
Open All year **Site** 7HEC ⚊ ⚊ **Facilities** 🝙 🛁 ⊙ 🔌 ∅ ⚐ ℗ **Services** 🛒
🍽 ➕ 🗐 **Leisure** ≋ LP **Off-site** ≋L

FÜGEN TIROL

Hell
Gagering 212b, 6263 ☎ 05288 62203 🖹 05288 622034
e-mail info@zillertal-camping.at
website www.zillertal-camping.at
Meadow setting around a farm with fine views of the surrounding
mountains.
➲ *1km N of Fügen on B169.*
Open All year **Site** 4HEC ⚊ ⚊ 🔌 **Prices** ♦ 4.20-6.50 pitch 6-14.50
Facilities 🝙 🛁 ⊙ 🔌 ∅ ⚐ ℗ **Services** 🛒 🍽 ➕ 🗐 **Leisure** ≋ P
Off-site ≋L

HAIMING TIROL

Center Oberland
Bundestr 9, 6425 ☎ 05266 88294 🖹 05266 882949
e-mail oberland@tirol.com
website www.camping_oberland.at
On a sloping meadow in a picturesque mountain setting. A variety of
sports facilities are available.
➲ *Off B171 at Km485.*
Open May-Oct **Site** 4HEC ⚊ ⚊ 🏠 🔌 Ă **Prices** ♦ 4.50-5 ♠ 3.50 🔌 3.50
Ă 3.50 **Facilities** 🝙 🛁 ⊙ 🔌 ∅ ⚐ ℗ **Services** 🛒 🍽 ➕ 🗐 **Leisure** ≋ P
Off-site ≋R

HEITERWANG TIROL

Heiterwangersee
Hotel Fisher am See, 6611 ☎ 05674 5116 🖹 05674 5260
e-mail fischer.am.see@tirol.com
A quiet meadow location beside a lake behind the hotel.
➲ *By Hotel Fischer am See.*
Open All year **Site** 1HEC ⚊ ⚊ ⚊ **Facilities** 🝙 ⊙ 🔌 ∅ ⚐ ℗
Services 🛒 🍽 ➕ 🗐 **Leisure** ≋ L

HOPFGARTEN TIROL

Schlossberg
Brixentalerstr. 11, Itter, 6361 ☎ 05335 2181 🖹 05335 2182
e-mail info@camping-itter.at
website www.camping-itter.at
A family site on terraced meadowland below Schloss Itter on the
Brixental Ache. Good leisure facilities.
➲ *2km W on B170.*
Open Dec-15 Nov **Site** 4HEC ⚊ ⚊ ⚊ **Prices** ♦ 4-6 pitch 4-9 **Facilities** 🝙
🛁 ⊙ 🔌 ∅ ⚐ ℗ **Services** 🛒 🍽 🗐 **Leisure** ≋ PR **Off-site** ≋L ➕

HUBEN TIROL

Ötztaler Naturcamping
6444 ☎ 05253 5855 🖹 05253 5538
e-mail info@oetztalernaturcamping.com
website www.oetztalernaturcamping.com
A well-kept site in a beautiful wooded location beside a mountain
stream.
➲ *S of town, signed from Km27 on B186.*
Open All year **Site** 0.5HEC ⚊ ⚊ **Prices** ♦ 5-5.20 ♠ 2.50-2.70
🔌 4.50-6.20 Ă 3.40-4.50 **Facilities** 🝙 ⊙ 🔌 ∅ ⚐ ℗ **Services** 🍽 ➕ 🗐
Off-site 🍽 ∅

IMST TIROL

Imst-West
Langgasse 62, 6460 ☎ 05412 66293 🖹 05412 6629319
e-mail fink.franz@aon.at
website www.imst-west.com
On open meadowland in the Langgasse area.
➲ *Off bypass near turning for the Pitztal.*
Open All year **Site** 1HEC ⚊ ⚊ **Prices** ♦ 4-5 pitch 6-7.50 **Facilities** 🝙 🛁 ⊙
🔌 ∅ ⚐ ℗ **Services** 🛒 🗐 **Off-site** 🍽 ≋LPR ➕

Facilities 🛁 shop 🝙 shower ⊙ electric points for razors 🔌 electric points for caravans ℗ parking by tents permitted 🅿 compulsory separate car park
Services 🍽 café/restaurant 🛒 bar ∅ Camping Gaz International ⚐ gas other than Camping Gaz ➕ first aid facilities 🗐 laundry
Leisure ≋ swimming L-Lake P-Pool R-River S-Sea **Off-site** All facilities within 2km

Austria

Ideally located near the forest yet so close to a town! Open year-round, great bus connection to the old part of the town of Innsbruck, "Inntal" bike way only 150m away, motor caravan services, restaurant, Internet access point Bus tickets, excursion and rambling tips as well as the All-inclusive Innsbruck Card are available at reception point. Receive many discounts with guest cards. Free guided mountain hikes from June to September. Free ski bus service in winter in the Olympic ski world surrounding Innsbruck.

www.campinginnsbruck.com, Tel. + Fax +43 512 28 41 80

INNSBRUCK TIROL

Innsbruck-Kranebitten

Kranebitter Allee 214, 6020 ☎ 0512 284180 🖹 0512 284180
e-mail campinnsbruck@hotmail.com
website www.campinginnsbruck.com
A pleasant location close to the city. An Innsbruck Card giving reductions to many places of interest and some forms of public transport is available at the site.
➲ Signed off A12.
Open All year **Site** 3HEC ❤️ ❤️ 🚐 ⚠️ **Prices** ⚡5.40 🚗 3.40 🚐 3.40-3 ⚠️ 3.40 🚐 (static)280 **Facilities** 🍴 🛁 ⊙ 🚻 🤝 ♨️ ⑦ **Services** 🕽 🍽️ 🛒 🛒 **Leisure** ♨️ R **Off-site** ♨️P

See advertisement on this page

KITZBÜHEL TIROL

Schwarzsee

6370 ☎ 05356 62806 🖹 05356 6447930
e-mail office@bruggerhof-camping.at
website www.bruggerhof-camping.at
Meadowland site on the edge of a wood behind a large restaurant.
➲ B170 from town towards Wörgl, 2km turn right, 400m after Schwarzsee railway station.
Open All year **Site** 6HEC ❤️ ❤️ 🚐 **Prices** ⚡8.70-9.70 pitch 8.50-9.90 **Facilities** 🍴 🛁 ⊙ 🚻 ⚠️ ♨️ ⑦ **Services** 🕽 🍽️ 🛒 🛒 **Leisure** ♨️ L

KÖSSEN TIROL

Wilder Kaiser

Kranebittau 18, 6345 ☎ 05375 6444 🖹 05375 2113
e-mail info@eurocamp-koessen.com
website www.eurocamp-koessen.com
Situated in a lovely position below Unterberg. The level site is adjoined on three sides by woodland.
➲ Road to Unterberg lift & turn right for 200m.
Open 5 Nov-3 Dec **Site** 5HEC ❤️ ❤️ 🚐 **Prices** ⚡6.20-7.20 pitch 6.30-9.30 **Facilities** 🍴 🛁 ⊙ 🚻 ⚠️ ♨️ ⑦ **Services** 🕽 🍽️ 🛒 🛒 **Leisure** ♨️ P **Off-site** ♨️L

KRAMSACH TIROL

Stadlerhof

6233 ☎ 05337 63371 🖹 05337 65311
e-mail camping.stadlerhof@chello.at
website www.camping-stadlerhof.at
A pleasant, year-round site on the Reintaler See with well-defined pitches and good leisure facilities.
➲ Via A12.
Open All year **Site** 3HEC ❤️ ❤️ 🚐 🚐 **Prices** pitch 16-24.50 (incl 2 persons) **Facilities** 🍴 🛁 ⊙ 🚻 ⚠️ ♨️ ⑦ **Services** 🕽 🍽️ 🛒 🛒 **Leisure** ♨️ LPR

KUFSTEIN TIROL

Kufstein

Salurner Str 36, 6330 ☎ 05372 62229 🖹 05372 636894
e-mail kufstein@hotelbaeren.at
website www.hotelbaeren.at
A pleasant location with a variety of sports facilities.
➲ 1km W of Kufstein between River Inn & B171.
Open May-Oct **Site** 1HEC ❤️ ❤️ **Facilities** 🍴 🛁 ⊙ 🚻 ⚠️ ♨️ ⑦ **Services** 🕽 🍽️ 🛒 🛒 **Off-site** ♨️LPR

LANDECK TIROL

Riffler

6500 ☎ 05442 64898 🖹 05442 648984
e-mail lorenz.schimpfoessi@aon.at
website www.camping-riffler.at
Site on meadowland between residential housing and the banks of the Sanna.
Open Jun-Apr **Site** 0.3HEC ❤️ ❤️ 🚐 **Prices** ⚡4.60 🚗 2.40 🚐 7.50-8.70 ⚠️ 4.50-7.50 **Facilities** 🍴 ⊙ 🚻 ⑦ **Services** 🛒 🛒 **Leisure** ♨️ R **Off-site** 🛁 🕽 🍽️ ⚠️ ♨️P

Sport Camp Tirol

Mühlkanal 1, 6500 ☎ 05442 64636 🖹 05442 64037
e-mail info@sportcamptirol.at
website www.sportcamptirol.at
Meadowland site with many fruit trees.
➲ On B316.
Open All year **Site** 1.5HEC ❤️ ❤️ 🚐 **Facilities** 🍴 🛁 ⊙ 🚻 ⚠️ ♨️ ⑦ **Services** 🕽 🍽️ 🛒 🛒 **Leisure** ♨️ R **Off-site** ♨️LP

LÄNGENFELD TIROL

Ötztal

6444 ☎ 05253 5348 🖹 05253 5909
e-mail info@camping-oetztal.com
website www.camping-oetztal.com
Meadowland with some tall trees on the edge of woodland.
➲ Turn right off E186 at fire station.
Open All year **Site** 2.6HEC ❤️ ❤️ 🚐 🚐 **Prices** ⚡5.40-5.90 pitch 6.50-10.70 **Facilities** 🍴 🛁 ⊙ 🚻 ⚠️ ♨️ ⑦ **Services** 🕽 🍽️ 🛒 🛒 **Off-site** 🍽️ ♨️P

LANGKAMPFEN TIROL

Hager

Kufsteinerstrasse 38, 6336 ☎ 05372 64170 🖹 05332 7296635
e-mail office@hager-stb.at
Site situated on level meadowland.
Open All year **Site** 0.5HEC ❤️ ❤️ **Prices** pitch 17 (incl 2 persons) **Facilities** 🍴 🛁 ⊙ 🚻 ⚠️ ♨️ ⑦ **Services** 🕽 🍽️ 🛒 🛒 **Off-site** ♨️LR

Site 6HEC (site size) ❤️ grass 🔵 sand ❤️ stone 🌿 little shade 🌿 partly shaded 🌳 mainly shaded 🏠 bungalows for hire 🚐 caravans for hire ⚠️ tents for hire ⊗ no dogs **Prices** ⚡ adult per night 🚗 car per night pp per person per night 🚐 caravan per night ⚠️ tent per night 🚐 (static)-caravan hire per week

Austria

LERMOOS TIROL

Happy Camp Hofherr

Garmischer Str 21, 6631 ☎ 05673 2980 ▤ 05673 29805
e-mail info@camping-lermoos.com
website www.camping-lermoos.com
Well-equipped site in a wooded location with fine views of the surrounding mountains.
➲ *0.5km from town, off B187 towards Ehrwald.*
Open 15 Dec-Apr & Jun-Oct **Site** 0.8HEC ☸ ☸ **Prices** ♠ 7.10-8.10
☲ 6.50-8.20 **Facilities** ⋒ ⊙ ☲ ⚞ ☝ ⑳ **Services** ☎ ᐅ ⊠ **Off-site** ☖ ⌀
☀PR ➕

LEUTASCH TIROL

Holiday-Camping

6105 ☎ 05214 65700 ▤ 05214 657030
e-mail info@holiday-camping.at
website www.holiday-camping.at
A modern site on level grassland screened by trees on the Leutascher Ache.
➲ *Off B313 Mittenwald-Scharnitz towards Leutasch.*
Open 7 Dec-5 Nov **Site** 2.6HEC ☸ ☸ ☲ ☲ **Prices** ♠ 9 pitch 9-10
Facilities ⋒ ☖ ⊙ ☲ ⌀ ⚞ ⑳ **Services** ☎ ᐅ ➕ ⊠ **Leisure** ☀ PR

LIENZ TIROL

Falken

Falkenweg 7, 9900 ☎ 04852 64022 ▤ 04852 640226
e-mail camping.falken@tirol.com
website www.camping-falken.com
On open ground on the outskirts of the town with modern sanitary facilities.
➲ *S of Lienz, signed from B100.*
Open 21 Dec-19 Oct **Site** 2.5HEC ☸ ☸ **Prices** ♠ 5-6 pitch 6.50-8.50
Facilities ⋒ ☖ ⊙ ☲ ⌀ ⚞ ⑳ **Services** ☎ ᐅ ⊠ **Off-site** ☀LPR ➕

MAURACH TIROL

Karwendel

6212 ☎ 05243 6116 ▤ 05243 20036
e-mail info@karwendel-camping.at
website www.karwendel-camping.at
On a level meadow with fine views of the surrounding mountains.
➲ *Off B181 in town onto Pertisau road.*
Open All year **Site** 1.8HEC ☸ ☸ ☲ **Prices** ♠ 4.50 ☲ 3 ☲ 4.50 ☖ 4
Facilities ⋒ ⊙ ☲ ⌀ ⚞ ⑳ **Services** ☎ ᐅ ⊠ **Off-site** ☖ ☀LP ➕

MAYRHOFEN TIROL

Mayrhofen

Laubichl 125, 6290 ☎ 05285 6258051 ▤ 05285 6258060
e-mail camping@alpenparadies.com
website www.alpenparadies.com
A modern site with good facilities, a short walk from the village.
➲ *Near farm at N entrance to village.*
Open 21 Dec-Oct **Site** 2HEC ☸ ☸ **Prices** ♠ 4.90-7 ☲ 2.50 ☲ 2.90-5
☖ 2.90-5 **Facilities** ⋒ ☖ ⊙ ☲ ⌀ ⚞ ⑳ **Services** ☎ ᐅ ➕ **Leisure** ☀ P
Off-site ☀R

NATTERS TIROL

Natterer See

Natterer See 1, 6161 ☎ 0512 546732 ▤ 0512 54673216
e-mail info@natterersee.com
website www.natterersee.com
A terraced site beautifully situated among woodland and mountains on the shore of Natterersee. A variety of leisure facilities are available.
➲ *Brenner motorway exit Innsbruck Süd, via Natters, onto B182 & signed.*
Open 15 Dec-Oct **Site** 9HEC ☸ ☸ ☲ ☲ ☖ **Prices** ♠ 5.70-7.80 pitch 7.80-
10 ☲ (static)258.30-489.30 **Facilities** ⋒ ☖ ⊙ ☲ ⌀ ⚞ ⑳ **Services** ☎ ᐅ
➕ ⊠ **Leisure** ☀ L

NAUDERS TIROL

Alpencamping Nauders

6543 ☎ 05473 87217 ▤ 05473 8721750
e-mail alpencamping@tirol.com
website www.camping-nauders.at
A year-round family site in a delightful Alpine location with good recreational facilities.
➲ *Via B315.*
Open 17 Dec-Oct **Site** 3HEC ☸ ☸ **Facilities** ⋒ ☖ ⊙ ☲ ⌀ ⑳ **Services** ⊠
Off-site ☎ ᐅ ☀L

PETTNEU AM ARLBERG TIROL

Arlberg

☎ 05448 22266 ▤ 05448 2226630
e-mail info@camping-arlberg.at
website www.camping-arlberg.at
Site in the Tyrolean mountains suitable for hiking and mountaineering in summer and close to winter sports resorts.
➲ *S16 exit for Pettneu.*
Open All year **Site** 4.8HEC ☸ ☸ ☲ ☲ **Prices** ♠ 9-10 pitch 8-22
☲ (static)420 **Facilities** ⋒ ☖ ⊙ ☲ ⌀ ⑳ ⑳ **Services** ☎ ᐅ ➕ ⊠
Leisure ☀ PR

PILL TIROL

Plankenhof

6130 ☎ 05242 641950 ▤ 05242 72344
e-mail m.khuen-belasi@tirol.com
Site in meadow.
➲ *On B171 near Gasthof Plankenhof.*
Open May-1 Oct **Site** 0.6HEC ☸ ☸ **Prices** ♠ 4.05 pitch 6-10 **Facilities** ⋒
⊙ ☲ ⑳ **Services** ☎ ᐅ ➕ ⊠ **Leisure** ☀ P **Off-site** ☖ ☀LR

PRUTZ TIROL

Aktiv-Camping Prutz

Beim Sauerbrunn, 6522 ☎ 05472 2648 ▤ 05472 26484
e-mail info@aktiv-camping.at
website www.aktiv-camping.at
A pleasant site in a beautiful mountain setting with modern facilities.
Open All year **Site** 1.5HEC ☸ ☸ ☲ ☲ **Prices** ♠ 3.50-5.50 ☲ 5.10-10.50
☲ (static)210-380 **Facilities** ⋒ ☖ ⊙ ☲ ⌀ ⚞ ⑳ **Services** ᐅ ➕ ⊠
Leisure ☀ R **Off-site** ᐅ ☀LP

Facilities ☖ shop ⋒ shower ⊙ electric points for razors ☲ electric points for caravans ⑳ parking by tents permitted ⑳ compulsory separate car park
Services ᐅ café/restaurant ☎ bar ⌀ Camping Gaz International ⚞ gas other than Camping Gaz ➕ first aid facilities ⊠ laundry
Leisure ☀ swimming L-Lake P-Pool R-River S-Sea **Off-site** All facilities within 2km

Austria

REUTTE TIROL

Seespitze

6600 ☎ 05672 78121 🖹 05672 63372
e-mail agrar.breitenwang@aon.at
website www.camping-plansee.at
Open May-15 Oct **Site** 2HEC 🏕 🏕 **Prices** ↟4.50 ♠2 ♣5 Å 4-5
Facilities ↑ ⌂ ☉ ⊖ ⬤ ⌀ ⌸ ⑫ **Services** ⦿ ⊞ ⓢ **Leisure** ♨ L **Off-site** ⦿

Sennalpe

6600 ☎ 05672 78115 🖹 05672 63372
e-mail agrar.breitenwang@aon.at
website www.camping-plansee.at
A quiet location next to the lake.
➲ On Reutte-Oberammergau road 200m from Hotel Forelle.
Open 15 Dec-15 Oct **Site** 4HEC 🏕 🏕 **Facilities** ↑ ⌂ ☉ ⊖ ⬤ ⌀ ⌸ ⑫
Services ⦿ ⊞ ⓢ **Leisure** ♨ L **Off-site** ⦿

RIED BEI LANDECK TIROL

Dreiländereck

6531 ☎ 05472 6025 🖹 05472 60254
e-mail camping-drellandereck@tirol.com
website www.tirolcamping.at
Level site in centre of village beside a lake with spectacular views.
Open All year **Site** 1HEC 🏕 🏕 🏠 ♣ **Prices** ↟4-5.50 pitch 8-10.50
♣ (static)280-420 **Facilities** ↑ ⌂ ☉ ⊖ ⬤ ⌀ ⑫ **Services** ⦿ ⊞ ⓢ
Off-site ⦿ ⌸ ♨LPR

RINN TIROL

Judenstein

Judenstein 40, 6074 ☎ 05223 78620 🖹 05223 7887715
e-mail kommunalgmbh@rinn.tirol.gv.at
website www.tiscover.at/camping.judenstein
A wooded location with fine views.
➲ Motorway exit Hall.
Open May-Sep **Site** 0.6HEC 🏕 🏕 **Facilities** ↑ ☉ ⊖ ⬤ ⑫ **Services** ⊞ ⓢ
Off-site ⌂ ⦿ ⦿

ST JOHANN TIROL

Michelnhof

Weiberndorf 6, 6380 ☎ 05352 62584 🖹 05352 625844
e-mail camping@michelnhof.at
website www.camping-michelnhof.at
➲ 1.5km S via B161 St-Johann-Kitzbühel.
Open All year **Site** 3HEC 🏕 🏕 **Prices** ↟5 ♠3.50 ♣4 Å 4 **Facilities** ↑
⌂ ☉ ⊖ ⬤ ⌀ ⑫ **Services** ⦿ ⊞ ⓢ **Off-site** ⌂ ⦿ ♨PR

SCHWAZ TIROL

AT WEER (6KM W)

Alpencamping Mark

Maholmhof, 6114 ☎ 05224 68146 🖹 05244 681466
e-mail alpcamp.mark@aou.at
website www.alpencampingmark.com
Situated on meadowland by a farm on the edge of a forest.
➲ Off B171.
Open Apr-Oct **Site** 2HEC 🏕 🏕 **Prices** ↟4.30-5.50 ♣6 pitch 4.50-6
Facilities ↑ ⌂ ☉ ⊖ ⑫ **Services** ⦿ ⦿ ⊞ ⓢ **Leisure** ♨ P
Off-site ⌀ ♨L

SEEFELD TIROL

Alpin

Leutascher Str 810 ☎ 05212 4848 🖹 05212 4868
e-mail info@camp-alpin.at
website www.camp-alpin.at
Terraced site on an alpine plateau with fine mountain views, open for
summer vacations and winter sports.
Open All year **Site** 1.1HEC 🏕 🏕 **Facilities** ↑ ⌂ ☉ ⊖ ⬤ ⌀ ⌸ ⑫
Services ⦿ ⦿ ⊞ ⓢ **Off-site** ♨LP

SÖLDEN TIROL

Sölden

Wohlfahrtstr 22, 6450 ☎ 05254 26270 🖹 05254 26275
e-mail info@camping-soelden.com
website www.camping-soelden.com
Situated on meadowland on the Ötztaler tributary. Beautiful views of
the surrounding mountains.
➲ By Grauer Bär Inn at Km36 on the B186.
Open Jan-Apr, Jul-Dec **Site** 1.3HEC 🏕 🏕 **Prices** ↟6-7.10 pitch 6.70-8.20
Facilities ↑ ☉ ⊖ ⬤ ⌀ ⌸ ⑫ **Services** ⊞ ⓢ **Off-site** ⌂ ⦿ ⦿ ♨P

STAMS TIROL

Eichenwald

Schiessstand weg 10, 6422 ☎ 05263 6159
Well-managed terraced site in oak wood.
➲ Off B171 at Esso fuel station towards abbey, onto steep
narrow access road.
Site 2HEC 🏕 🏕 🏠 ♣ **Facilities** ↑ ⌂ ☉ ⊖ ⬤ ⌀ ⑫ **Services** ⦿ ⦿ ⊞ ⓢ
Leisure ♨ P **Off-site** ♨R

THIERSEE TIROL

Rueppenhof

Seebauern 8, 6335 ☎ 05376 5694 🖹 05376 5142
e-mail atzl.barbara@tirol.com
website www.rueppenhof-motinfo.com
Site made up of several meadows surrounding a farm that lies on the
banks of the lake.
➲ A12 exit Kufstein-Nord, signed Thiersee.
Open Apr-Oct **Site** 1.5HEC 🏕 🏕 **Facilities** ↑ ☉ ⊖ ⬤ ⌀ ⑫ **Services** ⊞
Leisure ♨ L **Off-site** ⌂ ⦿ ⦿

UMHAUSEN TIROL

Ötztal Arena Camp Krismer

6441 ☎ 05255 5390 🖹 05255 5390
e-mail info@oetztal-camping.at
website www.oetztal-camping.at
➲ Signed from B186.
Open All year **Site** 1HEC 🏕 🏕 **Prices** ↟5.60-5.80 pitch 3-8 **Facilities** ↑
⌂ ☉ ⊖ ⬤ ⌀ ⌸ ⑫ **Services** ⦿ ⦿ ⊞ ⓢ **Leisure** ♨ LR

UNTERPERFUSS TIROL

Farm

6175 ☎ 05232 2209 🖹 05232 22094
e-mail brangerbrau@aon.at
website www.brangeralm.at
Modern site on gently sloping meadow in a beautiful mountain
setting.
➲ W end of village near Amberg railway & main road.
Open All year **Site** 1.5HEC 🏕 🏕 **Facilities** ↑ ☉ ⊖ ⬤ ⌀ ⑫ **Services** ⦿ ⦿
⊞ **Off-site** ⌂ ⦿

Site 6HEC (site size) 🏕 grass ♠ sand 🏕 stone ♣ little shade 🏕 partly shaded 🏕 mainly shaded 🏠 bungalows for hire
♣ caravans for hire Å tents for hire ⊗ no dogs **Prices** ↟ adult per night ♠ car per night pp per person per night ♣ caravan per night
Å tent per night ♣ (static)-caravan hire per week

VÖLS TIROL

Völs

Bahnhofstr 10, 6176 ☎ 0512 303533
➲ *Motorway exit Innsbruck-Kranebitten.*
Open Apr-Nov **Site** 0.4HEC ⚕ ♣ **Facilities** 🏠 ⊙ 🖳 ⑫ **Services** 🚽 🍴
➕ 🔄 **Off-site** 🏢 ∅ ⚫LPR

WAIDRING TIROL

Steinplatte

Unterwasser 43, 6384 ☎ 05353 5345 📠 05353 5406
e-mail camping-steinplatte@aon.at
website www.camping-steinplatte.at
On a level meadow with fine panoramic views of the surrounding mountains.
Open All year **Site** 4HEC ⚕ ♣ ♣ **Prices** 🅰 5.80 🅰 5-5.80 pitch 5-7.80
Facilities 🏠 🏢 ⊙ 🖳 ∅ ⚒ ⑫ **Services** 🚽 🍴 ➕ **Leisure** ⚫ L
Off-site ⚫PR

WALCHSEE TIROL

Seespitz

Wassersportzentrum, 6344 ☎ 05374 5359 📠 05374 5845
e-mail camping.seespitz@netway.at
website www.camping-seespitz.at
Pleasant surroundings beside the Walchsee with good recreational facilities.
➲ *Between B172 & lake.*
Open All year **Site** 3HEC ⚕ ♣ ♣ **Prices** 🅰 5.50-6 🚗 2.50-3 🚐 5-5.50
🅰 5-5.50 **Facilities** 🏠 🏢 ⊙ 🖳 ⑫ **Services** 🍴 ➕ 🔄 **Leisure** ⚫ L

Terrassencamping Süd-See

Seestr 76, 6344 ☎ 05374 5339 📠 05374 5529
e-mail campingwalchsee@aon.at
website www.camp-sud-see.com
A lakeside site in wooded surroundings with extensive terracing and fine mountain views.
➲ *0.5km W on B172 onto no through road, continue 1.5km.*
Open All year **Site** 11HEC ⚕ ♣ ⚕ ♣ **Facilities** 🏠 🏢 ⊙ 🖳 ∅ ⚒ ⑫
Services 🚽 🍴 ➕ 🔄 **Leisure** ⚫ L

WESTENDORF TIROL

Panorama

Mühltal 70, A-6363 ☎ 05334 6166 📠 05334 6843
e-mail info@panoramacamping.at
website www.panoramacamping.at
A beautiful Alpine setting with modern facilities, including well-furnished studio apartments.
➲ *B170 W towards Wörgl.*
Open 3 Dec-13 Nov **Site** 2.2HEC ⚕ ♣ **Prices** 🅰 5.50 🚗 3.50 🚐 3.50
🅰 3.50 **Facilities** 🏠 🏢 ⊙ 🖳 ∅ ⚒ ⑫ **Services** 🚽 🍴 ➕ 🔄 **Off-site** ⚫P

ZELL AM ZILLER TIROL

Hofer

Gerlossasstr 33, 6280 ☎ 05282 2248 📠 05282 22488
e-mail info@campingdorf.at
website www.campingdorf.at
On meadowland with some fruit trees.
➲ *Site at end of Zillertal off road to Gerlos Pass.*
Open All year **Site** 1.5HEC ⚕ ♣ **Prices** 🅰 5.60-6.60 pitch 6-6.80
Facilities 🏠 🏢 ⊙ 🖳 ∅ ⚒ ⑫ **Services** 🚽 🍴 ➕ 🔄 **Leisure** ⚫ P

ZIRL TIROL

Alpenfrieden

Eigenhofen 11, 6170 ☎ 05238 53520
Terraced site in orchard surroundings.
➲ *Near B171.*
Open May-Sep **Site** 1HEC ⚕ ♣ ♣ **Facilities** 🏠 ⊙ 🖳 ⑫ **Services** 🚽
🍴 ➕ **Leisure** ⚫ P **Off-site** ⚫R

CARINTHIA

DELLACH KÄRNTEN

Neubauer

9872 ☎ 04766 2532 📠 04766 25324
e-mail info@camping-neubauer.at
website www.camping-neubauer.at
A terraced site with direct access to the Millstättersee.
➲ *Off B100 Leinz-Spittal, signed in village.*
Open May-15 Oct **Site** 1.5HEC ⚕ ♣ **Facilities** 🏠 ⊙ 🖳 ⑫ **Services** 🚽
🍴 🔄 **Leisure** ⚫ L **Off-site** 🏢 🍴 ∅

DELLACH IM DRAUTAL KÄRNTEN

Waldbad

9772 ☎ 04714 288 & 234 📠 04714 2343
e-mail info@camping-waldbad.at
website www.camping-waldbad.at
A small site in a delightful wooded setting with two large swimming pools.
➲ *Off A10 at Spittal onto B100.*
Open May-Sep **Site** 2HEC ⚕ ♣ 🚐 **Prices** pitch 14-23 (incl 2 persons)
pp4.50-7 **Facilities** 🏠 🏢 ⊙ 🖳 ∅ ⑫ **Services** 🍴 ➕ 🔄 **Leisure** ⚫ P
Off-site 🚽 ⚫R

DÖBRIACH KÄRNTEN

Brunner am See

Glanzerstr 108, 9873 ☎ 04246 7189 📠 04246 718914
e-mail office@camping-brunner.at
website www.camping-brunner.at
Tidily arranged with poplar trees. Private bathing area.
➲ *Off A10, at E end of Lake Millstatt.*
Open All year **Site** 3.5HEC ⚕ ♣ ♣ ♣ **Prices** 🅰 5-7.50 pitch 7-10.90
Facilities 🏠 🏢 ⊙ 🖳 ∅ ⚒ ⑫ **Services** 🚽 🍴 ➕ 🔄 **Leisure** ⚫ L

Burgstaller

Seefeldstr 16, 9873 ☎ 04246 7774 📠 04246 77744
e-mail info@burgstaller.co.at
website www.burgstaller.co.at
A quiet site 100m from the lake, with modern facilities.
➲ *From B98 towards SE end of Lake Millstatt for 1km.*
Open All year **Site** 12HEC ⚕ ♣ ♣ 🚐 **Prices** 🅰 5-8 pitch 4.70-11.50
Facilities 🏠 🏢 ⊙ 🖳 ∅ ⚒ ⑫ **Services** 🚽 🍴 ➕ 🔄 **Leisure** ⚫ LP

Facilities 🏢 shop 🏠 shower ⊙ electric points for razors 🖳 electric points for caravans ⑫ parking by tents permitted 🅿 compulsory separate car park
Services 🍴 café/restaurant 🚽 bar ∅ Camping Gaz International ⚒ gas other than Camping Gaz ➕ first aid facilities 🔄 laundry
Leisure ⚫ swimming L-Lake P-Pool R-River S-Sea **Off-site** All facilities within 2km

Austria

DÖLLACH KÄRNTEN

Zirknitzer

9843 ☎ 04825 451 ▤ 04825 45117
e-mail camping.zirknitzer@utanet.at
Beside the River Möu.
➥ *Between Km8 & Km9 on B107 Glocknerstr.*
Open 21 Dec-4 Nov **Site** 0.6HEC ⚌ ⚌ ⛺ ⚎ **Prices** ♠ 3.20-4 ♠ 2-2.20
⚎ 2-2.50 ⚠ 1.20-2 **Facilities** ♠ ⚏ ⊙ ⚎ ⚎ ⚎ **Services** ⚐ ⚎ ⚎ ⚎
Leisure ⚎ R **Off-site** ⚎ ⚎P

FELDKIRCHEN KÄRNTEN

Seewirt-Spiess

Maltschach am See 2, 9560 ☎ 04277 2637 ▤ 04277 26374
e-mail office@seewirl-spiess.com
website www.seewirl-spiess.com
A pleasant wooded location on the shore of the Maltschacher See.
➥ *Off B95 towards Klagenfurt.*
Open May-Sep **Site** 1.2HEC ⚌ ⚌ ⛺ ⚎ **Facilities** ♠ ⊙ ⚎ ⚎ ⚎ **Services** ⚐
⚎ ⚎ **Leisure** ⚎ L **Off-site** ⚏ ⚎P ⚎

HEILIGENBLUT KÄRNTEN

Grossglockner

9844 ☎ 04824 2048 ▤ 04824 24622
e-mail nationalpark-camping@heiligenblut.at
website www.heiligenblut.at/nationalpark-camping
Meadowland site surrounded by woodland within a national park.
➥ *Signed.*
Open May-Oct & Dec-Apr **Site** 2.5HEC ⚌ ⚌ **Prices** ♠ 6.90-7.60 ♠ 2.50
⚎ 2.50 **Facilities** ♠ ⚏ ⊙ ⚎ ⚎ ⚎ **Services** ⚐ ⚎ ⚎ ⚎ **Leisure** ⚎ R
Off-site ⚎P

HERMAGOR KÄRNTEN

Schluga

9620 ☎ 04282 2051 ▤ 04282 288120
e-mail camping@schluga.com
website www.schluga.com
Well-equipped family site in a rural setting 4km from Presseger See.
Open All year **Site** 5.5HEC ⚌ ⚌ ⚎ ⚠ **Facilities** ♠ ⚏ ⊙ ⚎ ⚎ ⚎ ⚎
Services ⚐ ⚎ ⚎ ⚎ **Leisure** ⚎ LP **Off-site** ⚎R

Schluga Seecamping

9620 ☎ 04282 2051 ▤ 04282 288120
e-mail camping@schluga.com
website www.schluga.com
A well-equipped family site 300m north of a lake in meadowland with
some terraces and fine views.
➥ *6km E of Hermagor.*
Open 20 May-20 Sep **Site** 8.8HEC ⚌ ⚌ ⚎ ⚠ **Facilities** ♠ ⚏ ⊙ ⚎ ⚎ ⚎
⚎ **Services** ⚐ ⚎ ⚎ ⚎ **Leisure** ⚎ L **Off-site** ⚎R

KEUTSCHACH KÄRNTEN

Strandcamping Süd

9074 ☎ 04273 2773 ▤ 04273 27734
e-mail info@strandcampingbruecklersued.at
website www.strandcampingsued.at
A pleasant setting among shrubs and trees on south side of the
Keutschachersee.
➥ *Motorway exit Valden, towards Keutschacher-Seental.*
Open May-Sep **Site** 2HEC ⚌ ⚌ **Prices** ♠ 5.50-7 pitch 7-8 **Facilities** ♠ ⚏
⊙ ⚎ ⚎ **Services** ⚎ ⚎ ⚎ **Leisure** ⚎ L

KLAGENFURT KÄRNTEN

Strandbad

9020 ☎ 0463 21169 ▤ 0463 21193
e-mail camping@stw.at
website www.tiscover.at/camping-klagenfurt
Large site divided into sections by trees and bushes.
➥ *B83 from town centre towards Velden, left just outside town
towards bathing area.*
Open 15 Apr-5 Oct **Site** 4HEC ⚌ ⚌ ⚎ **Prices** ♠ 6-8.80 pitch 9
Facilities ♠ ⚏ ⊙ ⚎ ⚎ **Services** ⚐ ⚎ ⚎ ⚎ **Leisure** ⚎ L

KÖTSCHACH-MAUTHEN KÄRNTEN

Alpencamp Kötschach-Mauthen

9640 ☎ 04715 429 ▤ 04715 429
e-mail info@alpencamp.at
website www.alpencamp.at
On level meadowland beside River Gail with good facilities for water
sports.
➥ *In S of village, off B110, 0.8km towards Lesachtal.*
Open 15 Dec-Oct **Site** 1.8HEC ⚌ ⚌ ⛺ ⚎ **Prices** ♠ 4.10-6.40 pitch 4.40-
6.90 **Facilities** ♠ ⚏ ⊙ ⚎ ⚎ ⚎ ⚎ ⚎ **Services** ⚐ ⚎ ⚎ ⚎ **Off-site** ⚎ ⚎PR

MALTA KÄRNTEN

Maltatal

9854 ☎ 4733 2340 ▤ 4733 23416
e-mail info@maltacamp.at
website www.maltacamp.at
On a gently rising alpine meadow with breathtaking views of the
surrounding mountains.
➥ *Off B99 in Gmünd for 5.5km through Malta valley.*
Open 31 Mar-Oct **Site** 3.5HEC ⚌ ⚌ ⛺ ⚎ **Prices** ♠ 4.70-6.90 pitch 4.80-
10.90 ⚎ (static)259-511 **Facilities** ♠ ⚏ ⊙ ⚎ ⚎ ⚎ ⚎ ⚎ **Services** ⚐ ⚎ ⚎
⚎ **Leisure** ⚎ PR

MÖLLBRÜCKE KÄRNTEN

Rheingold

Mölltalstr 65, 9813 ☎ 04769 2338
➥ *Site on main road from Spittal to Mallnitz, next to swimming
pool.*
Open All year **Site** 2HEC ⚌ ⚌ **Facilities** ♠ ⊙ ⚎ ⚎ **Services** ⚐ ⚎
Leisure ⚎ P **Off-site** ⚏

OBERVELLACH KÄRNTEN

Sport Erlebnis

9821 ☎ 04782 2727 ▤ 04782 3183
e-mail info@sporterlebnis.at
website www.sporterlebnis.at
Open May-Sep **Site** 10HEC ⚌ ⚌ ⛺ **Facilities** ♠ ⚎ ⚎ ⚎ **Services** ⚐ ⚎
⚎ ⚎ **Leisure** ⚎ R **Off-site** ⚏ ⚎ ⚎ ⚎P

OSSIACH KÄRNTEN

Ossiach

9570 ☎ 04243 436 ▤ 04243 8171
e-mail martinz@camping.at
website www.terrassen.camping.at
Divided into pitches with generally well-placed terraces.
➥ *Off B94 on E bank of Kale Ossiacher.*
Open May-Sep **Site** 10HEC ⚌ ⚌ ⛺ ⚎ **Prices** ♠ 5.20-7.70 pitch 7.20-11.50
⚎ (static)245-483 **Facilities** ♠ ⚏ ⊙ ⚎ ⚎ ⚎ ⚎ ⚎ **Services** ⚐ ⚎ ⚎ ⚎
Leisure ⚎ L

Site 6HEC (site size) ⚌ grass ⚌ sand ⚌ stone ⚌ little shade ⚌ partly shaded ⚌ mainly shaded ⛺ bungalows for hire
⚎ caravans for hire ⚠ tents for hire ⊗ no dogs **Prices** ♠ adult per night ♠ car per night pp per person per night ⚎ caravan per night
⚠ tent per night ⚎ (static)-caravan hire per week

Austria

Parth
9570 ☎ 04243 27440 🗎 04243 274415
e-mail camping@parth.at
website www.parth.at
On hilly ground on S shore of the lake. Steep, but there are some terraces.
➲ Off B94 on S bank of Lake Ossiach.
Open 26 Dec-11 Nov **Site** 1.8HEC ⚌ ♣ ⚌ 🚐 **Prices** ♦ 4.80-7.90 ▲ 4.10-6.50 pitch 6.90-10.50 🚐 (static)79 **Facilities** 🌲 🖾 ⊙ 🚭 ⌀ 🚠 ⚉ **Services** 🍴 ➕ 🗟 **Leisure** ⚬ L

Seecamping Berghof
Ossiachersee-Süduferstr 241, 9523
☎ 04242 41133 🗎 04242 4113330
e-mail office@seecamping-berghof.at
website www.seecamping-berghof.at
Attractive terraced meadowland with a 0.8km-long promenade with bathing areas. Dogs not allowed in July and August.
➲ E shore of Lake Ossiacher.
Open Apr-20 Oct **Site** 10HEC ⚌ ♣ ⚌ 🚐 **Prices** ♦ 5-8 pitch 7.50-12.50 **Facilities** 🌲 🖾 ⊙ 🚭 ⌀ 🚠 ⚉ **Services** 🍴 🍴 ➕ 🗟 **Leisure** ⚬ L

SACHSENBURG KÄRNTEN

Markt Sachsenburg
Ringmauergasse 8, 9751 ☎ 04769 3131 🗎 04769 292520
e-mail info@draucamping.at
website www.draucamping.at
A modern family site with good facilities in a delightful mountain setting.
➲ A10 between Spittal & Lienz.
Open May-Sep **Site** 1.3HEC ⚌ ♣ **Prices** pitch 16.50-24 (incl 2 persons) pp8-9 **Facilities** 🌲 🖾 ⊙ 🚭 ⚉ **Off-site** 🖾 🍴 🍴 ⚬P ➕

ST PRIMUS KÄRNTEN

Strandcamping Turnersee Breznik
9123 ☎ 04239 2350 🗎 04239 235032
e-mail info@breznik.at
website www.breznik.at
A quiet site in a picturesque mountain setting with a variety of recreational facilities.
➲ B70 Klagenfurt-Graz towards Kopenersee.
Open 6 Apr-11 Nov **Site** 7.5HEC ⚌ ♣ ⚌ 🚐 **Prices** ♦ 4.60-7.70 pitch 6.10-9.40 🚐 (static)161-455 **Facilities** 🌲 🖾 ⊙ 🚭 ⚉ **Services** 🍴 🍴 **Leisure** ⚬ L **Off-site** ➕

SEEBODEN KÄRNTEN

Ferienpark Lieseregg
Kras 27, 9871 ☎ 04762 2723 🗎 04762 33857
e-mail info@ferienpark-lieseregg.at
website www.ferienpark-lieseregg.at
A family site on a large level meadow with terraces and asphalt drives surrounded by woodland.
➲ B99 from Spittal N to B98, then left for 1.5km.
Open May-1 Oct **Site** 3HEC ⚌ ♣ ⚌ **Facilities** 🌲 🖾 ⊙ 🚭 ⌀ 🚠 ⚉ **Services** 🍴 ➕ 🗟 **Leisure** ⚬ P

SPITTAL AN DER DRAU KÄRNTEN

Draufluss
9800 ☎ 04762 2466 🗎 04762 2466
e-mail drauwirt@aon.at
website www.drauwirt.com
A long, narrow riverside site, partly surrounded by a hedge.
➲ From town centre to river towards Goldeckbahn.
Open 15 Apr-15 Oct **Site** 0.7HEC ⚌ ♣ **Prices** ♦ 4-4.50 🚐 3-3.50 🚐 3-3.50 ▲ 3-3.50 **Facilities** 🌲 ⊙ 🚭 ⚉ **Services** 🍴 🍴 ➕ 🗟 **Leisure** ⚬ PR **Off-site** 🖾 ⌀ 🚠

STOCKENBOI KÄRNTEN

Ronacher
Möse 6, 9714 ☎ 04761 256 🗎 04761 2564
e-mail terrassencamping.ronacher@net4you.at
website www.campingronacher.at
Situated on meadow between forest slopes, gently sloping to the shore of Weissensee. Shop only open in summer.
➲ Approach for caravans via Weissensee.
Open May-10 Oct **Site** 1.7HEC ⚌ ♣ **Facilities** 🌲 🖾 ⊙ 🚭 ⌀ 🚠 ⚉ **Services** 🍴 ➕ **Leisure** ⚬ L

VILLACH KÄRNTEN

Gerli
Badstr 23, 9500 ☎ 04242 57402 🗎 04242 582909
e-mail gerli.meidl@utanet.at
Level, isolated site with a heated swimming pool (open to the public).
➲ Off B100, turn right just before Villach & continue 2km.
Open All year **Site** 2.3HEC ⚌ ♣ ⚌ 🚐 **Prices** ♦ 3.90-4.50 pitch 3.90-4.50 **Facilities** 🌲 🖾 ⊙ 🚭 ⌀ ⚉ **Services** 🍴 ➕ 🗟 **Off-site** 🍴 ⚬P

AT FAAK AM SEE (10KM SE)

Strandcamping Arneitz
Seeuferlandesstrasse 53, A-9583 ☎ 04254 2137 🗎 04254 3044
e-mail camping@arneitz.at
website www.arneitz.at
On a wooded peninsula jutting into the Faakersee with good sports facilities.
Open 21 Apr-Sep **Site** 6HEC ⚌ ⚌ ♣ ⚌ 🚐 **Prices** ♦ 6.80-7.50 pitch 10-13 **Facilities** 🌲 🖾 ⊙ 🚭 ⌀ 🚠 ⚉ **Services** 🍴 🍴 ➕ 🗟 **Leisure** ⚬ L

Strandcamping Gruber
9583 ☎ 04254 2298 🗎 04254 22987
e-mail gruber@strandcamping.at
website www.strandcamping.at
On level ground beside the lake with fine views of the surrounding mountains.
Open May-Sep **Site** 2.5HEC ⚌ ⚌ ♣ **Prices** ♦ 4.60-6.70 pitch 8.40-17.50 **Facilities** 🌲 🖾 ⊙ 🚭 ⚉ **Services** 🍴 🍴 ➕ 🗟 **Leisure** ⚬ L **Off-site** ⌀ 🚠 ⚬P

Strandcamping Sandbank
Badeweg 3, 9583 ☎ 04254 2261 🗎 04254 3943
e-mail info@camping-sandbank.at
website www.camping-sandbank.at
A partially shaded site between the lakeside and the road.
➲ From road by Hotel Fürst.
Open May-25 Sep **Site** 3.5HEC ⚌ ♣ ⚌ 🚐 **Facilities** 🌲 🖾 ⊙ 🚭 ⌀ ⚉ **Services** 🍴 ➕ 🗟 **Leisure** ⚬ L **Off-site** 🍴 🚠

Facilities 🖾 shop 🌲 shower ⊙ electric points for razors 🚭 electric points for caravans ⚉ parking by tents permitted 🅿 compulsory separate car park
Services 🍴 café/restaurant 🍴 bar ⌀ Camping Gaz International 🚠 gas other than Camping Gaz ➕ first aid facilities 🗟 laundry
Leisure ⚬ swimming L-Lake P-Pool R-River S-Sea **Off-site** All facilities within 2km

Austria

WERTSCHACH KÄRNTEN

Alpenfreude
9612 ☎ 04256 2708 🖷 04256 27084
e-mail camping.alpenfreude@aon.at
website www.alpenfreude.at
Open May-Sep **Site** 5HEC ❀ ♣ ✿ 🜨 **Facilities** ↿ 🖾 ☺ 🖳 🖉 🜂 ⓟ **Services** 🍴 🛨 🖻 **Leisure** ➛ P **Off-site** 🏪

STYRIA

AUSSEE, BAD STEIERMARK

Traun
Grundlseer Str 21, 8990 ☎ 03622 54565 🖷 03622 52427
e-mail gh.staudnwirt@aussee.at
website www.aussee.at/staudnwirt
Pleasant wooded surroundings.
➪ 2.5km from Bad Aussee towards Grundlsee.
Open All year **Site** 0.4HEC ❀ ♣ 🜨 **Prices** ♣ 6.60 pitch 3 🜨 (static)168-294 **Facilities** ↿ ☺ 🖳 ⓟ **Services** 🏪 🍴 🖻 **Leisure** ➛ R **Off-site** 🖾 🖉 🜂 ➛L 🛨

GRAZ STEIERMARK

S C Central
Martinhofstr 3, 8054 ☎ 0676 3785102 🖷 0316 697824
e-mail freizeit@netway.at
A site with many lawns separated by asphalt paths and partly divided into pitches.
➪ Off B70 in Strassgang S of Graz & continue 300m.
Open Apr-Oct **Site** 4HEC ❀ ✿ 🜨 **Facilities** ↿ 🖾 ☺ 🖳 🜂 ⓟ **Services** 🏪 🍴 🛨 🖻 **Leisure** ➛ P

HIRSCHEGG STEIERMARK

Hirschegg
8584 ☎ 03141 2201
e-mail info@camping-hirschegg.at
website www.camping-hirschegg.at
Delightful Alpine setting.
➪ A2 towards Klagenfurt, exit Modriach.
Open All year **Site** 2HEC ❀ ✿ 🜨 Å **Prices** ♠ 3.50 ➛ 2.20 🜨 2.20 Å 2.20 **Facilities** ↿ ☺ 🖳 🖉 ⓟ **Services** 🖻 **Off-site** 🖾 🏪 🍴 ➛LR 🛨

LANGENWANG-MÜRTZAL STEIERMARK

Europa
Siglstr 5, 8665 ☎ 03854 2950
e-mail europa.camping.stmk@aon.at
website www.campsite.at/europa.camping.langenwang
On level meadow with some trees, surrounded by hedges. The site occupies an attractive alpine setting.
➪ B306 (E7) bypasses town, so exit 6km S of Mürzzuschlag.
Open All year **Site** 0.6HEC ❀ ✿ **Prices** ♠ 4.60 ➛ 3.20 🜨 3.20 Å 3.20 **Facilities** ↿ ☺ 🖳 🜂 ⓟ **Services** 🖻 **Off-site** 🖾 🏪 🍴 ➛R 🛨

LEIBNITZ STEIERMARK

Leibnitz
R-H-Bartsch-Gasse 33, 8430 ☎ 03452 82463 🖷 03452 71491
e-mail stadtgemeinde@leibnitz.at
website www.camping-steiermark.at
A well-equipped site in pleasant wooded surroundings with plenty of leisure facilities.
➪ Signed W of town.
Open May-15 Oct **Site** 0.7HEC ❀ ✿ **Facilities** ↿ ☺ 🖳 ⓟ **Services** 🏪 🛨 🖻 **Leisure** ➛ PR **Off-site** 🖾 🏪 🖉 🜂 ➛L

MARIA LANKOWITZ STEIERMARK

Piberstein
Am See 1, 8591 ☎ 03144 7095950 🖷 03144 7095974
e-mail office@piberstein.at
website www.piberstein.at
Large well-equipped site surrounding a series of lakes. Plenty of sports facilities.
➪ S of Maria Lankowitz towards Pack.
Open May-15 Oct **Site** 5.6HEC ❀ ♣ 🜨 **Facilities** ↿ 🖾 ☺ 🖳 ⓟ **Services** 🏪 🛨 🖻 **Leisure** ➛ L **Off-site** 🏪 🖉 🜂

MITTERNDORF, BAD STEIERMARK

Grimmingsicht
8983 ☎ 03623 2985
e-mail camping@grimmingsicht.at
website www.grimmingsicht.at
A modern site in a picturesque mountain setting with a variety of sports facilities.
Open All year **Site** 0.6HEC ❀ ♣ ✿ 🜨 **Facilities** ↿ ☺ 🖳 ⓟ **Services** 🏪 🍴 🛨 🖻 **Leisure** ➛ R **Off-site** 🖾 🍴 🜂 ➛P

MÜHLEN STEIERMARK

Badsee
Hitzmannsdorf 2, 8822 ☎ 03586 2418 🖷 03586 2204
e-mail office@camping-am-badsee.at
website www.camping-am-badsee.at
Family site with direct access to the lake.
➪ N via B92, signed.
Open May-Sep **Site** 1.5HEC ❀ ♣ ✿ **Facilities** ↿ 🖾 ☺ 🖳 ⓟ **Services** 🏪 🛨 🖻 **Leisure** ➛ L **Off-site** 🖉 🜂 ➛P

OBERWÖLZ STEIERMARK

Burg Rothenfels
8832 ☎ 03581 76980
e-mail camping@rothenfels.at
website www.rothenfels.at
Set in the grounds of a castle with picturesque Alpine surroundings. Good recreational facilities.
➪ On SE outskirts.
Open All year **Site** 8HEC ❀ ♣ ✿ 🜨 **Prices** ♠ 4.50 ➛ 3.50 🜨 4 Å 2.50 🜨 (static)245 **Facilities** ↿ 🖾 ☺ 🖳 ⓟ **Services** 🍴 🖻 **Leisure** ➛ L **Off-site** 🖾 🏪 🍴 🖉 ➛PR 🛨

Site 6HEC (site size) ❀ grass ● sand ✿ stone ♣ little shade ♣ partly shaded ✿ mainly shaded 🜨 bungalows for hire 🜨 caravans for hire Å tents for hire ⊗ no dogs **Prices** ♠ adult per night ➛ car per night pp per person per night 🜨 caravan per night Å tent per night 🜨 (static)-caravan hire per week

Austria

ST GEORGEN STEIERMARK

Olachgut
8861 ☎ 03532 2162 📠 03532 2162
e-mail olachgut@murau.at
website www.murau.at/olachgut
On a level meadow, surrounded by beautiful mountain scenery.
➲ *Signed.*
Open All year **Site** 10HEC ♨ ♣ ♠ ♥ 🏃 **Prices** ♠ 6.50-7.50 pitch 20-21
(incl 2 persons) ♥ (static)287-329 **Facilities** ♠ 🛱 ⊙ ♥ ∅ ⚲ ⑦
Services 🍽 🖪 **Leisure** ♨ L **Off-site** ♨PR

ST SEBASTIAN STEIERMARK

Erlaufsee
Erholungszentrum Erlaufseestr 3, 8630
☎ 03882 4937 📠 03882 214822
e-mail gemeinde@st-sebastian.at
website www.st-sebastian.at
A picturesque Alpine setting in woodland, 100m from the lake.
➲ *Signed.*
Open May-15 Sep **Site** 1HEC ♨ ♣ **Prices** ♠ 4 ♥ 2.70 ♥ 3 🏃 3
Facilities ♠ ⊙ ♥ ⑨ **Off-site** 🏃 🍽 ♨LR ✚

SCHLADMING STEIERMARK

Zirngast
Linke Ennsau 633, 8970 ☎ 03687 23195 📠 03687 23495
e-mail camping@zirngast.at
website www.zirngast.at
Meadowland site on the River Enns next to the railway.
➲ *Off B308 towards town, site by fuel station.*
Open All year **Site** 1.5HEC ♨ ♣ **Facilities** ♠ 🛱 ⊙ ♥ ⚲ ⑦ **Services**
🏃 🍽 ✚ 🖪 **Leisure** ♨ R **Off-site** ♨P ✚

UNGERSDORF BEI FROHNLEITEN STEIERMARK

Lanzmaierhof
Ungersdorf 16, 8130 ☎ 03126 2360 📠 03126 4174
e-mail lanzmaierhof@tele2.at
website www.camping-steiermark.at
➲ *Signed 2km S of Frohnleiten on Graz road.*
Open All year **Site** 0.5HEC ♨ ♣ ♠ ♥ 🏃 **Prices** ♠ 5 ♥ 2.50-3.70 ♥ 2.50
🏃 1.50-3 **Facilities** ♠ ⊙ ♥ ∅ ⚲ ⑦ **Services** 🍽 ✚ 🖪 **Off-site** 🛱 ♨P

WEISSKIRCHEN STEIERMARK

50Plus Campingpark Fisching
Fisching 9, 8741 ☎ 03577 82284 📠 03577 822846
e-mail campingpark@fisching.at
website www.camping50plus.at
A modern site with fine sanitary and sports facilities, catering for over
50s. 6km from the Formula 1 circuit (A1-Ring) in Zeltweg.
➲ *S36 exit Zeltweg-Ost for Obdach & signs for B78, signed
from centre of Fisching.*
Open Apr-15 Oct **Site** 1.5HEC ♨ ♣ ♠ **Prices** ♠ 4.60 pitch 8.80-11
Facilities ♠ ⊙ ♥ ∅ ⚲ ⑦ **Services** 🏃 🍽 ✚ 🖪 **Leisure** ♨ P **Off-site** 🛱

WILDALPEN STEIERMARK

Wildalpen
8924 ☎ 03636 342 & 341 📠 03636 313
e-mail camping@wildalpen.at
website www.wildalpen.at
Located in a nature reserve beside the River Salza with good canoeing
facilities.
Open Apr-Oct **Site** 0.8HEC ♨ ♣ ♠ **Prices** ♠ 3.65-4.15 ♥ 2.70 ♥ 3
🏃 1.70-4 **Facilities** ♠ ⊙ ♥ ⑦ **Services** 🖪 **Leisure** ♨ R **Off-site** 🛱 🏃
🍽 ∅ ♨P ✚

LOWER AUSTRIA

BREITENBRUNN BURGENLAND

Seebad
7091 ☎ 02683 5252 📠 02683 5252
Open May-Sep **Site** 1HEC ♨ ♣ ⊗ **Facilities** ♠ ⊙ ♥ ⑨ **Services** ✚ 🖪
Leisure ♨ L **Off-site** 🛱 🍽 ♨P

GMÜND NIEDERÖSTERREICH

Assangteich
Albrechtser Str 10, 3950 ☎ 02852 51552 📠 02852 52506500
e-mail info@sole-felsen-bad.at
website www.tiscover.at/camping.gmuend
A pleasant location with a variety of recreational facilities.
➲ *Signed off B41.*
Open 5 Apr-8 Oct **Site** 0.5HEC ♨ ♣ **Prices** ♠ 4.06 pitch 6.20 **Facilities** ♠
⊙ ♥ ⑦ **Services** 🖪 **Off-site** 🏃 🍽 ∅ ⚲ ♨LP ✚

HIRTENBERG NIEDERÖSTERREICH

Hirtenberg
Leobersdorfefstr, 2552 ☎ 02256 81111 📠 02256 8111117
➲ *A2 exit Leobersdorf, B18 W for 0.8km.*
Open 15 May-15 Sep **Site** 1.5HEC ♨ ♣ ⊗ **Facilities** ♠ ⊙ ♥ ⑦
Services 🖪 **Off-site** 🛱 🍽 ∅ ♨P ✚

JENNERSDORF BURGENLAND

Jennersdorf
Freizeitzentrum 3, 8380 ☎ 03329 46133 📠 03329 4626121
e-mail post@jennersdorf.bgld.gv.at
website www.jennersdorf.net
A pleasant site in wooded surroundings.
➲ *A2 exit Fürstenfeld.*
Open 16 Mar-Oct **Site** 1HEC ♨ ♣ **Prices** ♠ 5 pitch 5 **Facilities** ♠ ⊙ ♥
⑦ **Services** ✚ 🖪 **Leisure** ♨ P **Off-site** 🛱 🏃 🍽 ∅ ♨R

LAXENBURG NIEDERÖSTERREICH

Schlosspark Laxenburg
Münchendorfer Str, 2361 ☎ 02236 71333 📠 02236 73966
e-mail camping.laxenburg@verkehrsbuero.at
On level meadowland with surfaced roads. The site lies in a recreation
centre within the grounds of the historic Laxenburg castle.
➲ *0.6km S on road to B16.*
Open Apr-Oct **Site** 2.4HEC ♨ ♣ **Facilities** ♠ 🛱 ⊙ ♥ ∅ ⑦ **Services** 🍽
✚ 🖪 **Leisure** ♨ P **Off-site** 🍽

Facilities 🛱 shop ♠ shower ⊙ electric points for razors ♥ electric points for caravans ⑦ parking by tents permitted ⑨ compulsory separate car park
Services 🍽 café/restaurant 🏃 bar ∅ Camping Gaz International ⚲ gas other than Camping Gaz ✚ first aid facilities 🖪 laundry
Leisure ♨ swimming L-Lake P-Pool R-River S-Sea **Off-site** All facilities within 2km

MARBACH NIEDERÖSTERREICH

Marbacher

3671 ☎ 0664 5581815 📧 07413 703533
e-mail info@marbach-freizeit.at
website www.marbach-freizeit.at
A pleasant location beside the River Danube.
➲ A1 exit Ybbs.
Open Apr-Oct **Site** 0.4HEC 👑 👙 🏠 **Prices** ♠ 5.30 🚗 3.50 🚐 4.50 Å 4
Facilities 🌣 ⊙ 🖾 ⌀ 🏵 **Services** 🛒 🍴 ➕ 🖾 **Leisure** ◈ R
Off-site 🏠 ◈P

MARKT ST MARTIN BURGENLAND

Markt St Martin

Mühlweg 2, 7341 ☎ 02618 2239 📧 02618 22394
e-mail post@markt-st-martin.bgld.gv.at
On a level meadow with plenty of trees and bushes.
➲ A2 exit Krumbach/Schäffern.
Open May-Sep **Site** 0.5HEC 👑 👙 🏠 🏵 **Prices** ♠ 4.90 🚐 4 Å 1.50
Facilities 🌣 ⊙ 🖾 🏵 **Services** 🛒 🍴 ➕ 🖾 **Leisure** ◈ PR **Off-site** 🏠 🍴

RECHNITZ BURGENLAND

GC

Hauptpl 10, 7471 ☎ 03363 79202 📧 03363 7920222
e-mail post@rechnitz.bgld.gv.at
website www.rechnitz.com
On an artificial lake in the heart of the beautiful Faludi valley.
Open Jun-Aug **Site** 1HEC 👑 👙 **Prices** ♠ 4.30 🚐 5.10 Å 2.90 **Facilities** 🌣
⊙ 🖾 🏵 **Services** 🍴 **Leisure** ◈ L **Off-site** 🏠 🛒 🍴 ⌀ ⌗ ➕

RUST BURGENLAND

Rust

7071 ☎ 02685 595 📧 02685 595
e-mail office@gmeiner.co.at
website www.gmeiner.co.at
Situated on level meadowland with young trees.
➲ From Rust onto road to lake.
Open Apr-Oct **Site** 56HEC 👑 👙 **Facilities** 🌣 🏠 ⊙ 🖾 ⌀ 🏵 **Services** 🛒
🍴 ➕ 🖾 **Leisure** ◈ L **Off-site** ⌗ ◈P

SCHÖNBÜHEL NIEDERÖSTERREICH

Stumpfer

3392 ☎ 02752 8510 📧 02752 851017
e-mail office@stumpfer.com
website www.stumpfer.com
A small site in a wooded location attached to a guesthouse close to
the River Donau.
➲ SW of town.
Open Apr-Oct **Site** 1.5HEC 👑 👙 🏠 **Prices** ♠ 4.80 🚐 6 Å 2.50-6
Facilities 🌣 🏠 ⊙ 🖾 ⌀ 🏵 **Services** 🛒 🍴 ➕ 🖾 **Leisure** ◈ R

TRAISEN NIEDERÖSTERREICH

Terrassen-Camping Traisen

Kulmhof 1, 3160 ☎ 02762 62900 📧 02762 629004
e-mail info@camping-traisen.at
website www.camping-traisen.at
Set out in a circular formation around the main buildings with plenty
of trees around the pitches.
➲ 0.6km W via B20.
Open All year **Site** 2.1HEC 👑 👙 🏠 **Prices** ♠ 5.50-6 pitch 5.50-6
Facilities 🌣 🏠 ⊙ 🖾 ⌀ ⌗ 🏵 **Services** ➕ 🖾 **Leisure** ◈ P **Off-site** 🛒 🍴

TULLN NIEDERÖSTERREICH

Donaupark-Camping Tulln

Hafenstr, 3430 ☎ 02272 65200 📧 02272 65201
e-mail camptulln@oeamtc.at
website www.campingtulln.at
A modern site in a peaceful location with good facilities close to the
River Danube. Summer bus service to Vienna.
Open Apr-Oct **Site** 10HEC 👑 👙 🏠 🏠 **Prices** ♠ 6.50 🚗 4.50 🚐 7.50-11
Å 2.50 **Facilities** 🌣 🏠 ⊙ 🖾 ⌀ 🏵 **Services** 🛒 🍴 ➕ 🖾 **Leisure** ◈ L
Off-site ◈PR

WAIDHOFEN AN DER THAYA NIEDERÖSTERREICH

Thayapark

Badgasse, 3830 ☎ 02842 50350 📧 02842 50399
e-mail info@waidhofen-thaya-stadt.at
website www.waidhofen-thaya.at
A family site in wooded surroundings close to the River Thaya.
➲ Signed from village.
Open May-Sep **Site** 10HEC 👑 👙 **Facilities** 🌣 ⊙ 🖾 🏵 **Services** ➕ 🖾
Leisure ◈ R **Off-site** 🏠 🛒 🍴 ◈P

UPPER AUSTRIA/SALZBURG

ABERSEE SALZBURG

Wolfgangblick

Seestrasse 115, 5342 ☎ 06227 3475 📧 06227 3218
e-mail camping@wolfgangblick.at
website www.wolfgangblick.at
A pleasant position on the Wolfgangsee.
➲ Signed from village. 6km from St Gilgen via B1598.
Open May-1 Oct **Site** 2HEC 👑 👙 **Prices** ♠ 4.50 pitch 5.80-7.60
Facilities 🌣 🏠 ⊙ 🖾 ⌀ 🏵 **Services** 🛒 🍴 ➕ 🖾 **Leisure** ◈ LR
Off-site ⌗ ➕

ABTENAU SALZBURG

Oberwötzhof

Erlfeld 37, 5441 ☎ 06243 2698 📧 06243 269855
e-mail oberwoetzlhof@sbg.at
A summer and winter site on a level meadow with panoramic views of
the surrounding mountains.
➲ NW of Abtenau.
Open All year **Site** 2HEC 👑 👙 👙 **Facilities** 🌣 🏠 ⊙ 🖾 ⌗ 🏵 **Services** 🍴
➕ **Leisure** ◈ P **Off-site** ◈R

ALTMÜNSTER OBERÖSTERREICH

Schweizerhof

Hauptstr 14, 4813 ☎ 07612 89313 📧 07612 872764
e-mail office@schweizerhof.cc
website www.schweizerhof.cc
A modern site on the shore of Lake Traunsee with plenty of sports
facilities.
➲ Signed from motorway.
Open May-Sep **Site** 0.6HEC 👑 👙 👙 **Facilities** 🌣 🏠 ⊙ 🖾 🏵 **Services** 🍴
🍴 ➕ 🖾 **Leisure** ◈ L **Off-site** ⌀ ⌗

Site 6HEC (site size) 👑 grass 👙 sand 👙 stone 👙 little shade 👙 partly shaded 👙 mainly shaded 🏠 bungalows for hire
🚐 caravans for hire Å tents for hire ⊗ no dogs **Prices** ♠ adult per night 🚗 car per night pp per person per night 🚐 caravan per night
Å tent per night 🚐 (static)-caravan hire per week

BRUCK AN DER GROSSGLOCKNERSTRASSE SALZBURG

Woferlgut
Kroessenbach 40, 5671 ☎ 06545 73030 🗎 06545 73033
e-mail info@sportcamp.at
website www.sportcamp.at
Set in a beautiful valley beside a lake with good recreational facilities.
Some noise from the main road that bisects the site.
➲ *Via Bruck-Süd or Grossglockner on B311.*
Open All year **Site** 17HEC ⚙ ⚙ ⛺ ⛽ Å **Prices** ⚡ 4.90-7.50 pitch 9.40-12
⛽ (static)392-546 **Facilities** � 🏕 ⊙ ⚡ ⌀ ⚒ ⚑ **Services** 🍴 🍽 ➕
Leisure ⚓ LP **Off-site** ⚓R ➕

ESTERNBERG OBERÖSTERREICH

Pyrawang
4092 ☎ 07714 6504 🗎 07714 6504
➲ *On B130 Passau-Linz at Km45.5.*
Open Apr-Oct **Site** 3HEC ⚙ ⚙ **Prices** ⚡ 3 ⊷ 3 ⛽ 2.50 Å 1.50
Facilities � ⊙ ⚡ ⚒ **Services** 🍴 🍽 ➕ **Off-site** ⚓R

GLEINKERAU OBERÖSTERREICH

Pyhrn Priel
4582 ☎ 07562 7066 🗎 07562 7192
e-mail pousek@pyhrn-priel.at
website www.pyhrn-priel.at
A year-round site with a variety of facilities.
➲ *2.5km from town, signed from Windischgarsten towards
Gleinkersee.*
Open May-Oct **Site** 1HEC ⚙ ⚙ **Facilities** � ⊙ ⚡ ⚑ ⚒ **Services** 🍴 🍽
➕ 🗄 **Off-site** ⚓R

KAPRUN SALZBURG

Mühle
N-Gassner Str 38, 5710 ☎ 06547 8254 🗎 06547 825489
e-mail muehle@kaprun.at
website www.kaprun.at/muehle
A pleasant family site on long stretch of meadow by the Kapruner
Ache.
➲ *S end of village towards cable lift.*
Open All year **Site** 1.5HEC ⚙ ⚙ **Facilities** � 🏕 ⊙ ⚡ ⌀ ⚑ ⚒
Services 🍴 🍽 ➕ 🗄 **Leisure** ⚓ P

MAISHOFEN SALZBURG

Kammerlander
Oberreit 18, 5751 ☎ 06542 68755 🗎 06542 687555
e-mail landhaus-christa@sbg.at
website www.sbg.at/landhaus-christa
➲ *On B168.*
Open May-15 Sep **Site** ⚙ ⚙ **Prices** ⚡ 3 ⊷ 1.50 ⛽ 1.50 Å 1.50
Facilities � ⊙ ⚡ ⚒ **Off-site** 🏕 ⚓L

MONDSEE OBERÖSTERREICH

Mond-See-Land
Punzau 21, 5310 ☎ 06232 2600 🗎 06232 27218
e-mail austria@campmondsee.at
website www.campmondsee.at
A picturesque and peaceful site between the lakes Mondsee and Irrsee
with good facilities.
➲ *A1 exit Mondsee, B154 towards Strasswalden for 1.5km, onto
Haider-Mühle road for 2km.*
Open Apr-Oct **Site** 3HEC ⚙ ⚙ ⛺ ⛽ **Prices** ⚡ 4.90-5.50 pitch 6.50-7.50
⛽ (static)210-252 **Facilities** � 🏕 ⊙ ⚡ ⌀ ⚑ ⚒ **Services** 🍴 🍽 ➕ 🗄
Leisure ⚓ P

NUSSDORF OBERÖSTERREICH

Gruber
Dortstr 63, 4865 ☎ 07666 80450 🗎 07666 80456
On fairly long meadow parallel to the promenade.
➲ *S of village. Off B151 at Km19.7 towards lake (Attersee).*
Open 15 Apr-15 Oct **Site** 2.6HEC ⚙ ⚙ **Facilities** � 🏕 ⊙ ⚡ ⚒
Services 🍴 🍽 ➕ 🗄 **Leisure** ⚓ LP **Off-site** ⌀

PERWANG AM GRABENSEE OBERÖSTERREICH

Perwang
5163 ☎ 06217 8288 🗎 06217 824715
e-mail gemeinde@perwang.ooe.gv.at
website www.tiscover.com/perwang
Site beside lake.
Open May-Oct **Site** 1.5HEC ⚙ ⚙ ⚙ **Prices** ⚡ 3.80 Å 4 **Facilities** � ⊙
⚡ ⚐ **Services** 🍴 🍽 ➕ 🗄 **Leisure** ⚓ L **Off-site** 🏕

RADSTADT SALZBURG

Forellencamp
Gaismairallee 51, 5550 ☎ 06452 7861 🗎 06452 5092
e-mail info@forellencamp.com
website www.forellencamp.com
Flat meadowland near town
➲ *SW via B99.*
Open All year **Site** 1HEC ⚙ ⚙ ⚙ **Prices** ⚡ 4.50 ⊷ 2.40 ⛽ 4.50 Å 2.40
Facilities � 🏕 ⊙ ⚡ ⚑ ⚒ **Services** 🍴 🍽 ➕ **Off-site** ⌀ ⚓PR

ST JOHANN IM PONGAU SALZBURG

Hirschenwirt
Bundesstr 1, 5600 ☎ 06412 6012 🗎 06412 60128
e-mail hirschenwirt@aon.at
website www.hirschenwirt.com
A small, pleasant site well placed for the Salzburg-Badgastein road or
as a base for exploring this region of mountains and lakes. The flat
open site has grass pitches on either side of gravel roads. A small pool
is open in summer. Being on a major route there is traffic noise.
➲ *Site behind Gasthof Hirschenwirt at St Johann im Pongau on
B311.*
Open All year **Site** 0.8HEC ⚙ ⚙ **Prices** ⚡ 4.50-5.50 pitch 6-9 **Facilities** �
⊙ ⚡ ⚑ ⚒ **Services** 🍴 🍽 **Leisure** ⚓ P **Off-site** ⌀ ⚓R

Facilities 🏕 shop � shower ⊙ electric points for razors ⚡ electric points for caravans ⚒ parking by tents permitted ⚐ compulsory separate car park
Services 🍽 café/restaurant 🍴 bar ⌀ Camping Gaz International ⚑ gas other than Camping Gaz ➕ first aid facilities 🗄 laundry
Leisure ⚓ swimming L-Lake P-Pool R-River S-Sea **Off-site** All facilities within 2km

Austria *(side tab)*

Wieshof
Wieshofgasse 8, 5600 ☎ 06412 8519 📠 06412 82929
e-mail info@camping-wieshof.at
website www.camping-wieshof.at
On gently sloping meadow behind pension and farmhouse. Modern facilities. Big spa house with sauna, massage facilities and health bars, adjacent to site.
➲ *Off B311 towards Zell am Zee.*
Open All year **Site** 1.6HEC ❄ ❄ **Prices** ♠ 5.50 pitch 5.50 **Facilities** ℟ 🔋 ⊙ ⊟ ⊘ ® **Services** ▣ **Off-site** ฿ ♨LP ⊞

ST MARTIN BEI LOFER SALZBURG

Park Grubhof
5092 ☎ 06588 8237 📠 06588 82377
e-mail camping@lofer.net
website www.grubhof.com
Situated in meadowland on the banks of the River Saalach. Separate sections for dog owners, families, teenagers and groups.
➲ *B311 S of Lofer, 1.5km turn left.*
Open 21 Apr-3 Oct **Site** 10HEC ❄ ❄ 🏠 **Facilities** ℟ 🔋 ⊙ ⊟ ⊘ ♨ ®
Services ฿ ▣ ⊞ ▣ **Leisure** ♨ R **Off-site** ♨P

ST WOLFGANG OBERÖSTERREICH

Appesbach
Au 99, 5360 ☎ 06138 2206 📠 06138 220633
e-mail camping@appesbach.at
website www.appesbach.at
On sloping meadow facing lake with no shade at upper end.
➲ *0.8km E of St Wolfgang between lake & Strobl road.*
Open Mar-Oct **Site** 2.2HEC ❄ ❄ 🏠 **Prices** ♠ 5-6.50 🏠 6-11 ▲ 4-6 pitch 4-8 🏠 (static)315-420 **Facilities** ℟ 🔋 ⊙ ⊟ ⊘ ♨ ® **Services** ฿ ▣ ▣
Leisure ♨ L **Off-site** ⊞

Berau
Schwarzenbach 16, 5360 ☎ 06138 2543 📠 06138 254355
e-mail camping@berau.at
website www.berau.com
A family-run site in a picturesque setting on the edge of the Wolfgangsee. Spacious, level pitches and modern facilities.
➲ *A1 exit Talgau, N158 signed Hof/Bad Ischl, through Strobl towards St Wolfgang & signed.*
Open All year **Site** 2HEC ❄ ❄ 🏠 **Prices** ♠ 4.40-6.10 🏠 2.10-3.80 🏠 7.50-10.80 ▲ 4.30-5.60 **Facilities** ℟ 🔋 ⊙ ⊟ ⊘ ♨ ® **Services** ฿ ▣ ⊞ ▣
Leisure ♨ L

SALZBURG SALZBURG

Kasern
C-Zuckmayerstr 26, 5101 ☎ 0662 450576 📠 0662 450576
e-mail schwarzkopf@aon.at
➲ *A1 exit Salzburg-Nord.*
Open Apr-Oct **Site** 0.9HEC ❄ ❄ ▲ **Facilities** ℟ 🔋 ⊙ ⊟ ® **Services** ▣
▣ **Off-site** ฿ ▣ ⊘

Nord Sam
Samstr 22A, 5023 ☎ 0662 660494 📠 0662 660494
e-mail office@camping-nord-sam.com
website www.camping-nord-sam.com
Site divided into pitches.
➲ *Salzburg Nord autobahn exit, site 400m.*
Open 14 Apr-Sep **Site** 2HEC ❄ ❄ ❄ **Prices** ♠ 5-7 pitch 7.50-9
Facilities ℟ 🔋 ⊙ ⊟ ® **Services** ▣ ⊞ ▣ **Leisure** ♨ P
Off-site ฿ ▣ ⊘ ♨

Panorama Camping Stadtblick
Rauchenbichlerstr 21, 5020 ☎ 0662 450652 📠 0662 458018
e-mail info@ panorama-camping.at
website www.panorama-camping.at
A terraced site affording spectacular views of the surrounding mountains.
➲ *Motorway exit Salzburg-Nord & signed.*
Open 20 Mar-5 Nov **Site** 0.8HEC ❄ ❄ ❄ 🏠 **Prices** ♠ 6.20-6.50 ▲ 2-4 pitch 6.50-7 🏠 (static)200 **Facilities** ℟ 🔋 ⊙ ⊟ ⊘ ♨ ® **Services** ฿ ▣
⊞ ▣ **Off-site** ♨L

Schloss Aigen
A5026 ☎ 0662 622079 📠 0662 622079
e-mail camping.aigen@elsnet.at
website www.campingaigen.com
Site divided into pitches in partial clearing on mountain slope.
➲ *Motorway exit Salzburg-Süd, Anif & Glasenbach.*
Open May-Sep **Site** 25HEC ❄ ❄ **Prices** ♠ 4.80 pitch 4.60-5.50
Facilities ℟ 🔋 ⊙ ⊟ ⊘ ♨ ® **Services** ฿ ▣ ⊞ ▣

SCHLÖGEN OBERÖSTERREICH

Terrassencamping Pension Schlögen
A-4083 ☎ 07279 8241 📠 07279 824122
e-mail schloegen.freizeit@netway.at
website www.schloegen.at
On level ground beside the River Donau, backed by woods and mountains.
Open Apr-20 Oct **Site** 2.8HEC ❄ ❄ **Facilities** ℟ 🔋 ⊙ ⊟ ® **Services** ฿
▣ ⊞ ▣ **Leisure** ♨ PR

SEEKIRCHEN SALZBURG

Strand
Seestr 2, 5201 ☎ 06212 4088 📠 06212 4088
Beside the Wallersee in beautiful meadow.
Open 15 Apr-15 Oct **Site** 2HEC ❄ ❄ **Facilities** ℟ 🔋 ⊙ ⊟ ⊘ ®
Services ฿ ▣ ⊞ ▣ **Leisure** ♨ LP **Off-site** 🔋

Zell am Wallersee
5201 ☎ 06212 4080 📠 06212 4080
e-mail franz.klampfer@aon.at
Level meadowland separated from the lake by the lido.
➲ *A1 exit Wallersee, via Seekirchen to Zell.*
Open 11 May-19 Oct **Site** 3HEC ❄ ❄ **Facilities** ℟ ⊙ ⊟ ® **Services** ▣
⊞ ▣ **Leisure** ♨ LP

Site 6HEC (site size) ❄ grass ❄ sand ❄ stone ❄ little shade ❄ partly shaded ❄ mainly shaded 🏠 bungalows for hire 🏠 caravans for hire ▲ tents for hire ⊗ no dogs **Prices** ♠ adult per night 🏠 car per night pp per person per night 🏠 caravan per night ▲ tent per night 🏠 (static)-caravan hire per week

UNTERACH OBERÖSTERREICH

Insel

4866 ☎ 07665 8311 🖷 07665 7255
e-mail camping@inselcamp.at
website www.inselcamp.at
Quiet family site on the shore of Lake Attersee, divided into two by
the River Seeache.

➲ *Entrance below B152 towards Steinbach at Km24.5, 300m
from B151 junct.*

Open 15 May-15 Sep **Site** 1.8HEC ❈ ♣ **Prices** ♠ 4-4.73 ♠ 2.50 ♠ 3.50
▲ 2.70 **Facilities** ↿ 🖻 ⊙ ♠ ⑰ **Services** 🖫 **Leisure** ♠ LR **Off-site** 🕱 🍴
⌀ ➕

WALD SALZBURG

S.N.P

Lahn 65, 5742 ☎ 06565 84460 🖷 06565 84464
e-mail info@snp-camping.at
website www.snp-camping.at
A small family site in a beautiful Alpine setting.

➲ *W of town.*

Open All year **Site** 0.7HEC ❈ ♣ **Facilities** ↿ 🖻 ⊙ ♠ ⌀ ⑰ **Services** 🕱
🍴 ➕ 🖫 **Off-site** 🍴 ♠LP

WESENUFER OBERÖSTERREICH

Nibelungen

4085 ☎ 07718 7589 🖷 07718 7589
e-mail nibelungen.camping@utanet.at
Pleasant rural setting beside the River Donau.

➲ *0.5km from B130.*

Open Apr-Sep **Site** 1.2HEC ❈ ♣ **Prices** ♠ 3 ▲ 2.30 pitch 4 **Facilities** ↿
⊙ ♠ ⑰ **Services** ➕ 🖫 **Leisure** ♠ R **Off-site** 🖻 🍴 ♠P

ZELL AM SEE SALZBURG

Seecamp Zell am See

Thumersbacherstr 34, 5700 ☎ 06542 72115 🖷 06542 7211515
e-mail zell@seecamp.at
website www.seecamp.at
Pleasant wooded location beside the lake with excellent site and
recreational facilities.

➲ *B311 N of lake towards Thumersbach, signed.*

Open All year **Site** 3.2HEC ❈ ♣ ♣ **Prices** ♠ 6.30-7.90 ♠ 2-2.50 ♠ 7.40-
9.20 ▲ 3.70-4.60 **Facilities** ↿ 🖻 ⊙ ♠ ⌀ ♨ ⑰ **Services** 🕱 🍴 ➕ 🖫
Leisure ♠ L **Off-site** ♠P

Süedufer

Thumersbach, Seeuferstr 196, 5700
☎ 06542 56228 🖷 06542 562284
e-mail zell@camping-suedufer.at
website www.camping-suedufer.at
A family site on level ground in a picturesque spot on the southern
bank of the Zeller See.

➲ *S via B311 towards Thumersbach.*

Open All year **Site** 0.6HEC ❈ ♣ **Prices** ♠ 4.90-6.40 ♠ 2.50-3 ♠ 4.90-
5.90 ▲ 3.90-5.70 **Facilities** ↿ 🖻 ⊙ ♠ ⌀ ♨ ⑰ **Services** 🍴 ➕ 🖫
Off-site 🕱 🍴 ♠LPR

BEZAU VORARLBERG

Bezau

Ach 206, 6870 ☎ 05514 2964
e-mail campingplatz.bezau@aon.at
website www.campingfuehrer.at
Small family-owned site with modern sanitary facilities.

➲ *S via B200 Dornbirn-Warth.*

Open All year **Site** 0.5HEC ❈ ♣ **Facilities** ↿ ⊙ ♠ ⑰ **Off-site** 🖻 🕱 🍴
♠PR ➕

BLUDENZ VORARLBERG

AT BRAZ (7KM SE)

Traube

Klostertalerstr 12, 6751 ☎ 05552 28103 🖷 05552 2810340
e-mail traube.braz@aon.at
website www.traubebraz.at
On sloping grassland in the picturesque Klostertal valley with modern
facilities.

➲ *7km SE of Bludenz. Off S16 near railway, signed.*

Open All year **Site** 2HEC ❈ ♣ ⑳ **Prices** pitch 19.80-28.20 (incl 2
persons) **Facilities** ↿ 🖻 ⊙ ♠ ⌀ ♨ ⑰ **Services** 🍴 ➕ 🖫 **Leisure** ♠ P
Off-site ♠R

DALAAS VORARLBERG

Erne

6752 ☎ 05585 7223 🖷 05585 20049
e-mail info@etpc.at
website www.etpc.at
Site in the town, attached to a guesthouse and next to the swimming
pool.

➲ *S16 exit Dalass.*

Open All year **Site** 0.6HEC ❈ ♣ **Prices** pitch 21.50 (incl 2 persons)
Facilities ↿ ⊙ ♠ ⌀ ♨ ⑰ **Leisure** ♠ R **Off-site** ♠ 🖻 🍴 ♠P ➕

DORNBIRN VORARLBERG

In der Enz

6850 ☎ 05572 29119
e-mail camping@camping-enz.at
website www.camping-enz.at
A municipal site beside a public park, in a wooded area some 100m
beyond the Karren cable lift.

➲ *Autobahn exit Dornbirn-Süd.*

Open Apr-Sep **Site** 10HEC ❈ ♣ **Prices** ♠ 4.40 ♠ 2.10 ♠ 4.50 ▲ 4.50
Facilities ↿ ⊙ ♠ ⌀ ⑳ ⑰ **Services** 🕱 🍴 ➕ 🖫 **Off-site** ♠PR ➕

LINGENAU VORARLBERG

Feurstein

Haidach 185, 6951 ☎ 05513 6114 🖷 05513 61144
A small site located in a meadow adjacent to some farm buildings
with sufficient facilities for a pleasant stay.

Open All year **Site** 1HEC ❈ ♣ **Prices** ♠ 6.50 ♠ 1.10 ♠ 3.50 ▲ 2-3.50
Facilities ↿ ⊙ ♠ ♨ ⑰ **Services** ➕ 🖫 **Off-site** 🖻 🕱 🍴

Facilities 🖻 shop ↿ shower ⊙ electric points for razors ♠ electric points for caravans ⑳ parking by tents permitted ⑰ compulsory separate car park
Services 🍴 café/restaurant 🕱 bar ⌀ Camping Gaz International ♨ gas other than Camping Gaz ➕ first aid facilities 🖫 laundry
Leisure ♠ swimming L-Lake P-Pool R-River S-Sea **Off-site** All facilities within 2km

Austria

NENZING VORARLBERG
Alpencamping Nenzing
6710 ☎ 05525 62491 🖷 05525 635676
e-mail office@alpencamping.at
website www.alpencamping.at
A well-appointed site in magnificent Alpine scenery. There are fine sports facilities and modern sanitary blocks.
➲ Signed from B190 from Nenzing, 2km towards Gurtis.
Open Jan-11 Apr & 30 Apr-Dec **Site** 3HEC ⛺ ⛱ ⛺ ⛺ **Facilities** ⚕ 🖭 ⊙ 🖭 ⌀ ⚑ **Services** ⛽ 🍴 ⊞ 🖫 **Leisure** ⚓ P

AT NÜZIDERS (2.5KM NW)
Sonnenberg
Hinteroferst 12, 6714 ☎ 05552 64035 🖷 05552 33900
e-mail sonnencamp@aon.at
website www.camping-sonnenberg.com
Clean site with modern facilities in gently sloping meadowland and splendid mountain scenery.
➲ Via Bludenz-Nüziders road, at 1st fork go up hill.
Open 3 May-3 Oct **Site** 1.9HEC ⛺ ⛱ ⛺ **Prices** ⚑ 5-5.70 pitch 5-10 **Facilities** ⚕ 🖭 ⊙ 🖭 ⌀ ⚑ **Services** ⊞ 🖫 **Off-site** ⛽ 🍴 ⚑ ⚓ R

RAGGAL-PLAZERA VORARLBERG
Grosswalsertal
6741 ☎ 05553 209 🖷 05553 2094
e-mail info@camping-grosswalsertal.at
website www.camping-grosswalsertal.at
A family site in a quiet location on gently sloping terrain, with pleasant views.
➲ On NE outskirts.
Open 8 Apr-15 Nov **Site** 0.8HEC ⛺ ⛱ **Facilities** ⚕ 🖭 ⊙ 🖭 ⌀ ⚑ **Services** 🖫 **Leisure** ⚓ P **Off-site** ⛽ 🍴 ⊞

TSCHAGGUNS VORARLBERG
Zelfen
6774 ☎ 0664 2002326
e-mail kunsttischlerei.tschofen@utanet.at
website www.camping-zelfen.at
Partly uneven, grassy site in a wooded location beside River Ill. Good recreational facilities.
➲ A14 to Bludenz, then B188 to Tschagguns.
Open All year **Site** 2HEC ⛺ ⛱ **Prices** ⚑ 5.60-6.30 pitch 19-22 **Facilities** ⚕ 🖭 ⊙ 🖭 ⌀ ⚑ **Services** ⛽ 🍴 ⊞ 🖫 **Leisure** ⚓ R **Off-site** ⚓ P

VIENNA (WIEN)

WIEN (VIENNA) WIEN
Donaupark Klosterneuburg
In der Au, 3400 ☎ 02243 25877 🖷 02243 25878
e-mail campklosterneuburg@oeamtc.at
website www.campingklosterneuburg.at
A modern site in delightful wooded surroundings with fine recreational facilities and within easy reach of the city centre.
➲ Signed from A1.
Open 15 Mar-07 Nov **Site** 2.2HEC ⛺ ⛱ ⛺ **Prices** ⚑ 6.50 ⚑ 4.50 pitch 7.50-11 **Facilities** ⚕ 🖭 ⊙ 🖭 ⌀ ⚑ **Services** 🍴 ⊞ 🖫 **Off-site** ⚓PR

Neue Donau
Am Kleehäufel, 1220 ☎ 01 2024010 🖷 01 2024020
e-mail neuedonau@campingwien.at
website www.campingwien.at
Situated in a meadow surrounded by trees beside the Danube within a leisure park.
➲ On E bank of river via A4 & A22.
Open Etr-Sep **Site** 3.3HEC ⛺ ⛱ ⛺ Å **Prices** ⚑ 5.90-6.90 Å 5.50-6.50 pitch 8.50-9.50 **Facilities** ⚕ 🖭 ⊙ 🖭 ⚑ **Services** ⛽ 🍴 ⊞ 🖫 **Off-site** ⌀ ⚑ ⚓LPR

Wien-West
Hüttelbergstr 80, 1140 ☎ 01 9142314 🖷 01 9113594
e-mail west@campingwien.at
website www.campingwien.at
On slightly rising meadow with asphalt paths.
➲ End of A1 Linz-Wien to Bräuhausbrücke, turn left & across road to Linz for 1.8km.
Open Jan & Mar-Dec **Site** 3.5HEC ⛺ ⛱ ⛺ **Prices** ⚑ 5.90-6.90 Å 5.50-6.50 pitch 8.50-9.50 **Facilities** ⚕ 🖭 ⊙ 🖭 ⚑ **Services** ⛽ 🍴 ⊞ 🖫 **Off-site** ⌀ ⚑

AT RODAUN (4KM SW)
Rodaun
An der Au 2, 1230 ☎ 01 8884154 🖷 01 8884154
➲ Between An der Austr & Leising River dam, via Breitenfürter Str N492.
Open 20 Jun-20 Oct **Site** 0.8HEC ⛺ ⛱ ⛺ **Prices** ⚑ 6 ⚑ 1.20 ⚑ 6 Å 6 **Facilities** ⚕ 🖭 ⊙ 🖭 ⌀ ⚑ **Services** ⊞ 🖫 **Off-site** 🖭 ⛽ 🍴

Belgium

Accidents & emergencies

fire 100   **police** 101   **ambulance** 100

The European emergency call number is also in use - dial 112 and ask for the service required. 112 must be used from a mobile.

Driving requirements

Minimum age 18 for UK licence holders driving temporarily imported car or motorcycle.

Lights

Dipped headlights required during poor daytime visibility: front and rear lights (or parking lights) required for parked vehicles when visibility reduced to less than 200m or at night when public lighting does not make vehicle visible from 100m. Motorcyclists must use dipped headlights during the day.

Passengers & children

Children under 3 must not travel in the front unless using a suitable restraint system; children under 3 in rear must use restraint if suitable restraint system available in vehicle. Children over 3 and under 12 must not travel in front or rear seats unless using seat belts or restraint system appropriate to the size and weight of the child. Never fit a rear-facing child restraint in a seat with a frontal airbag.

Size restrictions

Motor vehicle or trailer
height 4m, width 2.55m, length 12m

Vehicle + trailer
length 18m

Speed Limits

Unless signed otherwise:

Car with/without trailer, motorcycle	
Built-up areas	50kph
Outside built-up areas	90kph
Motorways/dual carriageways	120kph

Tourist office

Belgian National Tourist Office
(Brussels & Wallonia)
217 Marsh Wall
London E14 9FJ
Tel 0800 9545 245
www.belgium-tourism.net
www.belgiumtheplaceto.be

Tourism Flanders-Brussels
Flanders House
1a Cavendish Square
London W1G 0LD
Tel 020 7307 7738
www.visitflanders.com

Additonal information

Traffic on roundabouts must give way to traffic from the right, unless indicated otherwise by road signs. Warning Triangle compulsory. Recently introduced road sign bans use of cruise control on congested motorways. Any vehicle standing must have its engine switched off, unless absolutely necessary.

Tolls

Tolls Bridges & tunnels	car	car & caravan
R2 Llefkenshoek Tunnel	€5.00	€16.00

45

SOUTH WEST/COAST

BLANKENBERGE WEST-VLAANDEREN

Bonanza I
Zeebruggelaan 137, 8370 ☎ 050 416658 ▤ 050 427349
e-mail bonanza1@kmonet.be
website www.bonanza1.be
A family site in wooded surroundings 1km from both the village and the sea.
Open 15 Mar-15 Sep **Site** 4.5HEC ❧ ♣ **Facilities** ♠ ⓑ ☺ ☻ ∅ ⚏ **④**
Services ☲ ✐ ➕ ⓢ **Leisure** ☜ P **Off-site** ☜LS

Dallas
Ruzettelaan 191, 8370 ☎ 050 418157 ▤ 050 429479
Well-equipped family site near a large department store 50m from the beach.
Open 15 Mar-1 Oct **Site** 2.6HEC ❧ ♣ **Facilities** ♠ ⓑ ☺ ☻ ∅ ⓔ **④**
Services ➕ ⓢ **Off-site** ☲ ✐ ☜LPS

JABBEKE WEST-VLAANDEREN

Recreatiepark Klein Strand
Varsenareweg 29, 8490 ☎ 050 811440 ▤ 050 814289
e-mail info@kleinstrand.be
website www.kleinstrand.be
A lakeside site with modern facilities and a variety of leisure activities.
➲ Off Oostende-Brugge road.
Open All year **Site** 28HEC ❧ ♣ ☎ ⚏ **Prices** pitch 15-28 ⚏ (static)195-665 **Facilities** ♠ ⓑ ☺ ☻ ∅ ⓔ ☻ **④ Services** ☲ ✐ ➕ ⓢ **Leisure** ☜ LP
Off-site ☜R

KNOKKE-HEIST WEST-VLAANDEREN

De Vuurtoren
Heistlaan 168, 8301 ☎ 050 511782
e-mail kampvuurtoren@attglobal.net
website www.knokke-heist.be
On level meadow with tarred roads.
➲ From Knokke to Oostende for 4km, turn S & signed.
Open 15 Mar-15 Oct **Site** 6.6HEC ❧ ♣ **Facilities** ♠ ⓑ ☺ ☻ ⓔ
Services ☲ ✐ ➕ ⓢ **Off-site** ∅ ⓔ ☜PS

Zilvermeeuw
Heistlaan 166, 8301 ☎ 050 512726 ▤ 050 512703
e-mail info.campingzilvermeeuw@skynet.be
website www.camping-zilvermeeuw.be
Level site in wooded surroundings.
➲ SW via N300.
Open Mar-15-Oct **Site** 7HEC ❧ ♣ **Prices** ♦ 3-4 ⚘ 1 ⚏ 9-11 ⚑ 6-8
Facilities ♠ ⓑ ☺ ☻ ∅ ⓔ **Services** ✐ ➕ ⓢ **Off-site** ✐ ✐ ☜LPS

KOKSIJDE WEST-VLAANDEREN

Blekker & Blekkerdal
Jachtwakerstr 12, 8670 ☎ 058 511633 ▤ 058 511307
e-mail camping.deblekker@belgacom.net
website www.deblekker.be
A peaceful location surrounded by trees. Good modern facilities.
➲ Between Dunkerque & Oostende, 5km from Belgian frontier. Motorway exit towards Veurne.
Open Apr-30 Oct **Site** 3HEC ❧ ♣ ⊗ **Prices** pitch 20-30 (incl 4 persons)
Facilities ♠ ☺ ☻ ⓔ **Services** ➕ ⓢ **Off-site** ⓑ ✐ ✐ ∅ ☜ ☜PS

LOMBARDSIJDE WEST-VLAANDEREN

Lombarde
Elisabethlaan 4, 8434 ☎ 058 236839 ▤ 058 239908
e-mail info@delombarde.be
website www.delombarde.be
A well-equipped family site 400m from the sea and close to the centre of the village. Some facilities only available March to early November.
➲ E40 exit Nieuwpoort. At Nieuwpoort take N34 direction Ostende, site signed on right.
Open All year **Site** 8.5HEC ❧ ♣ ☎ **Prices** ⚏ 15-27.50 **Facilities** ♠ ⓑ ☺
☻ ∅ ⚏ **④ Services** ☲ ✐ ➕ ⓢ **Leisure** ☜ L **Off-site** ✐ ☜RS

Zomerzon
Elisabethlaan 1, 8434 ☎ 058 237396 ▤ 058 232817
A quiet location with good facilities, 0.8km from the dunes and beach.
Open 24 Mar-11 Nov **Site** 10HEC ❧ ♣ ☎ ⊗ **Facilities** ♠ ☺ ☻
Services ☲ ➕ ⓢ **Off-site** ⓑ ✐ ∅ ☜PS

LOPPEM WEST-VLAANDEREN

Lac Loppem
8210 ☎ 050 824262
Surrounded by fir trees on the edge of a lake.
➲ A10 exit Torhout, right by Esso fuel station.
Open All year **Site** 14HEC ❧ ♣ **Facilities** ♠ ☺ ☻ ∅ ⓔ **④ Services** ☲
✐ ➕ **Leisure** ☜ L

MIDDELKERKE WEST-VLAANDEREN

Myn Plezier
Duinenweg 489, 8430 ☎ 059 300279 ▤ 059 314503
Wooded surroundings close to the castle. The camp shop only open in summer.
Open Apr-10 Sep **Site** 3HEC ❧ ♣ **Facilities** ♠ ☺ ☻ ∅ ✐ ⓔ
Services ☲ ✐ ➕ ⓢ **Off-site** ⓑ ☜S

MONS HAINAUT

Waux-Hall
av St-Pierre 17, 7000 ☎ 065 337923 ▤ 065 363848
A secluded position 1km from the town centre, with direct access to the Parc du Waux-Hall.
➲ From town ring road exit for Beaumont/Binche, Charleroi, right at lights & sharp right.
Open All year **Site** 1.4HEC ❧ ♣ ☎ **Prices** ♦ 3.35 ⚘ 0.90 ⚏ 1.90-6.10
⚑ 1.90 **Facilities** ♠ ☺ ☻ ⓔ **Services** ➕ ⓢ **Off-site** ⓑ ☲ ✐ ∅ ✐ ☜L

NIEUWPOORT WEST-VLAANDEREN

Info
Brugsesteenweg 49, 8620 ☎ 058 236037 ▤ 058 232682
e-mail nieuwpoort@kompascamping.be
website www.kompascamping.be
A family site in pleasant wooded surroundings. Plenty of recreational facilities including water sports.
➲ E40 exit 4 for Diksmuide & Nieuwpoort, signed from St Joris.
Open 30 Mar-12 Nov **Site** 24HEC ❧ ♣ ☎ ☎ **Prices** pitch 20.25-31.50
⚏ (static)280-630 **Facilities** ♠ ⓑ ☺ ☻ ∅ ⓔ **Services** ☲ ✐ ➕ ⓢ
Leisure ☜ P **Off-site** ✐ ☜LRS

Site 6HEC (site size) ❧ grass ⬤ sand ❧ stone ♣ little shade ♣ partly shaded ❧ mainly shaded ☎ bungalows for hire
⚏ caravans for hire ⚑ tents for hire ⊗ no dogs **Prices** ♦ adult per night ⚘ car per night pp per person per night ⚏ caravan per night
⚑ tent per night ⚏ (static)-caravan hire per week

OOSTENDE (OSTENDE) WEST-VLAANDEREN

Asterix
Duinenstr 200, 8450 ☎ 059 331000 🗏 059 324202
A family site in wooded surroundings, 0.5km from the sea.
➲ N34 from Oostende towards Knokke-Heist, 7km right for Bredene-Dorp.
Open All year Site 3HEC ⛺ ♣ ♠ ➾ Prices pitch 12 ➾ (static)280
Facilities ♠ ⊙ ➡ ∅ ♨ ⊕ ❷ Services ⬱ ⍥ ➊ ⑤ Off-site ⓐ ✦LPS

TOURNAI HAINAUT

Orient
Vieux Chemin de Mons 8, 7500 ☎ 069 222635 🗏 069 890229
e-mail tourisme@tournai.be
website www.tournai.be
A pleasant site in an area of woodland with good recreational facilities.
➲ Motorway exit Tournai Est for town centre, left at 1st x-rds & signed.
Open All year Site 20HEC ⛺ ♣ Facilities ♠ ⊙ ➡ ⊕ Services ⬱ ➊
⑤ Leisure ✦ LP Off-site ⓐ ⍥

WAREGEM WEST-VLAANDEREN

Gemeentelijk
Sportstadion Zuiderlaan 13, 8790 ☎ 056 609532 🗏 056 621290
e-mail toerisme@waregem.be
website www.waregem.be
Set in a sports and leisure centre south-east of the town centre.
➲ Via E17 Kortrijk-Gent.
Open Apr-Sep Site 1HEC ⛺ ♣ Facilities ♠ ⊙ ➡ ⊕ Services ➊
Off-site ⓐ ⬱ ⍥ ∅ ♨ ✦P

WESTENDE WEST-VLAANDEREN

KACB
Bassevillestr 81, 8434 ☎ 058 237343 🗏 058 233505
e-mail campingkacbwestende@pi.be
website www.kacb.be
A well-appointed site close to the beach.
➲ Between Westende & Lombardsijde towards sea.
Open All year Site 6.5HEC ⛺ ♣ ♠ Facilities ♠ ⓐ ⊙ ➡ ∅ ⊕
Services ⬱ ⍥ ➊ ⑤ Off-site ♨ ✦LPS

NORTH/CENTRAL

BACHTE-MARIA-LEERNE OOST-VLAANDEREN

Groeneveld
Groenevelddreef, 9800 ☎ 09 3801014 🗏 09 3801760
e-mail info@campinggroeneveld.be
website www.campinggroeneveld.be
Well-equipped site beside a fishing lake.
➲ Approach via E17 or E40.
Open 24 Mar-12 Nov Site 1.7HEC ⛺ ♣ ♠ Prices pitch 17-20 (incl 2 persons) Facilities ♠ ⊙ ➡ ⊕ Services ⬱ ⍥ ➊ Off-site ✦R

BEGYNENDYK BRABANT

Roygaerden
Betekomsesteenweg 75, 3130 ☎ 016 531087 🗏 016531087
e-mail info@immovdb.be
website www.camping-deroygaerden.be
Pitches are in wooded surroundings beside a lake.
Open All year Site 5HEC ⛺ ♣ ♠ Prices ♠ 3.75 ➾ 8.70 ♣ 3
Facilities ♠ ⊙ ➡ ∅ ♨ ⊕ ❷ Services ⬱ ⍥ ➊ Off-site ⓐ ✦LP

BEVERE OOST-VLAANDEREN

Kompas Camping Oudenaarde
Kortrijkstr 342, 9700 ☎ 055 315473 🗏 055 300865
e-mail oudenaarde@kompascamping.be
website www.kompascamping.be
A family site with good recreational facilities.
➲ Signed from N453.
Open Apr-mid Nov Site 24HEC ⛺ ♣ ♠ ➾ ♣ Prices pitch 18.75-28.50
Facilities ♠ ⓐ ⊙ ➡ ∅ ⊕ Services ⍥ ➊ ⑤ Leisure ✦ LP

GENT (GAND) OOST-VLAANDEREN

Blaarmeersen
Zuiderlaan 12, 9000 ☎ 09 2668160 🗏 09 2668166
e-mail camping.blaarmeersen@gent.be
website www.gent.be/blaarmeersen
Pleasant wooded surroundings SW of Gent towards the railway station.
Open Mar-15 Oct Site 6HEC ⛺ ♣ ♠ Prices ♠ 3.50-4.50 ➾ 2-2.50 pitch 3.50-4.50 Facilities ♠ ⓐ ⊙ ➡ ⊕ ❷ Services ⬱ ⍥ ➊ ⑤ Leisure ✦ L

GRIMBERGEN BRABANT

Grimbergen
Veldkanstr 64, 1850 ☎ 0479 760378 🗏 02 2701215
e-mail camping.grimbergen@telenet.be
➲ Bruxelles ring road exit 7.
Open Apr-Oct Site 1.5HEC ⛺ ♣ Prices ♠ 4.50 ➾ 2 ➾ 3 ♣ 3
Facilities ♠ ⊙ ➡ ⊕ Services ➊ ⑤ Off-site ⓐ ⬱ ⍥ ✦P

HEVERLEE BRABANT

Ter Munck
Sint Jansbergsesteenweg 152, 3001 ☎ 016 228515
➲ Via E40 or E413.
Open 18 Jun-9 Sep Site 1.5HEC ⛺ ♣ Facilities ♠ ⊙ ➡ ⊕ Services ⬱
⍥ ➊ ⑤ Off-site ⓐ ⍥ ∅ ♨ ✦P

ONKERZELE OOST-VLAANDEREN

Gavers
Onkerzelestr 280, 9500 ☎ 054 416324 🗏 054 410388
e-mail gavers@oost-vlaanderen.be
A quiet, well-equipped site beside a lake between the Dendre valley and the foothills of the Ardennes. There are good sports and sanitary facilities.
➲ NE of town towards river.
Open All year Site 15HEC ⛺ ♣ ♠ Facilities ♠ ⓐ ⊙ ➡ ⊕ ❷
Services ⬱ ⍥ ➊ ⑤ Leisure ✦ LPR

Facilities ⓐ shop ♠ shower ⊙ electric points for razors ➡ electric points for caravans ⊕ parking by tents permitted ❷ compulsory separate car park
Services ⍥ café/restaurant ⬱ bar ∅ Camping Gaz International ♨ gas other than Camping Gaz ➊ first aid facilities ⑤ laundry
Leisure ✦ swimming L-Lake P-Pool R-River S-Sea **Off-site** All facilities within 2km

Belgium *(vertical side tab)*

STEKENE OOST-VLAANDEREN

Eurocamping Baudeloo
Heirweg 183, 9190 ☎ 03 7890663 🖥 03 7890663
Open All year **Site** 4.5HEC ❤ ♣ **Facilities** 🏪 ⊙ ❿ ⑳ **Services** ☎ 🍴 🔝
🗄 **Leisure** ⚓ P **Off-site** 🛉 🍴 ⌀

Reinaert
Lunterbergstr 4, 9190 ☎ 03 7798525
e-mail peter.vandenbranden@skynet.be
Open Apr-Oct **Site** 5HEC ❤ ♣ **Facilities** 🏪 ⊙ ❿ ⚍ ⑳ **Services** ☎ 🍴
🔝 🗄 **Off-site** 🛉 🍴

WACHTEBEKE OOST-VLAANDEREN

Puyenbroeck
Puyenbrug 1A, 9185 ☎ 09 3424231 🖥 09 3424258
website www.puyenbroeck.be
Open Apr-Sep **Site** 500HEC ❤ ♣ ❿ **Facilities** 🏪 ⊙ ❿ ⑳ **Services** 🔝 🗄
Off-site 🛉 ☎ 🍴 ⚓LP

NORTH EAST

BRECHT ANTWERPEN

Floreal Het Veen
Eekhoornlaan 1, St-Job In't Goor, 2960 ☎ 03 6361327
A comfortable site in a pleasant wooded setting with residential and touring pitches.
➲ E19 exit St Job In't Goor.
Open Mar-Oct **Site** 7.5HEC ❤ ♣ ♣ ❿ **Facilities** 🏪 🛉 ⊙ ❿ ⑳ **Services** ☎
🍴 🔝 🗄 **Leisure** ⚓ R **Off-site** ⌀ ⚍

EKSEL LIMBURG

Lage Kempen
Kiefhoek str 19, B-3941 ☎ 011 402243 🖥 011 348812
e-mail info@lagekempen.be
website www.lagekempen.be
Situated in the middle of a forest with a variety of recreational facilities.
➲ Route 67 from Hasselt & signed left Lage Kampen.
Open Etr-2 Nov **Site** 3.8HEC ❤ ♣ ♣ ❿ **Prices** ⚹ 4 ⇜ 2.75 ⇜ 3.75-6.50
⚠ 2-3.75 **Facilities** 🏪 🛉 ⊙ ❿ ⌀ ⚍ ⑳ **Services** ☎ 🍴 🔝 🗄
Leisure ⚓ P

GIERLE ANTWERPEN

Lilse Bergen
Strandweg 6, 2275 ☎ 014 557901 🖥 014 554454
e-mail info@lilsebergen.be
website www.lilsebergen.be
A very well-equipped family site surrounding a private lake.
➲ E39 exit 22.
Open All year **Site** 60HEC ⊜ ♣ ❿ ❿ **Prices** pitch 18-24 **Facilities** 🏪 🛉
⊙ ❿ ⌀ ⚍ ⑳ **Services** ☎ 🍴 🔝 🗄 **Leisure** ⚓ L

HOUTHALEN LIMBURG

Hengelhoef
Hengelhoefdreef 1, 3530 ☎ 089 844583 🖥 089 386940
e-mail camp.hengelhoef@belgacom.net
A family site in pleasant wooded surroundings with modern facilities.
➲ E314 exit 30.
Open All year **Site** 15HEC ❤ ♣ ❿ **Facilities** 🏪 ⊙ ❿ ⑳ **Services** 🍴 🔝
🗄 **Off-site** 🛉 🍴

MOL ANTWERPEN

Zilvermeer
Zilvermeerlaan 2, 2400 ☎ 014 829500 🖥 014 829501
e-mail info@zilvermeer.provant.be
A pleasant lakeside site with good recreational facilities.
Site 45HEC ❤ ⊜ ♣ ❿ **Facilities** 🏪 🛉 ⊙ ❿ ⌀ ⚍ ⑳ ❿ **Services** ☎ 🍴
🔝 🗄 **Leisure** ⚓ L

OPGLABBEEK LIMBURG

Boseind
Speeltuinstr 8, 3660 ☎ 089 854347 🖥 089 854319
e-mail info@hetlaer.be
website www.hetlaer.be
A family site adjoining a wood. A variety of recreational facilities is available.
➲ N730 from town centre towards Bree & signed.
Open Apr-Sep **Site** 8HEC ❤ ♣ **Facilities** 🏪 🛉 ⊙ ❿ ⑳ **Services** ☎ 🍴
🔝 **Leisure** ⚓ P **Off-site** ⌀

Wilhelm Tell
Hoeverweg 87, 3660 ☎ 089 854444 🖥 089 810010
e-mail receptie@wilhelmtell.com
website www.wilhelmtell.com
A family site set in a vast nature reserve with heathland, woodland and marshlands. The large variety of water attractions on site includes a water chute and a swimming pool with a wave machine. Also an indoor family pool and bubble bath.
➲ E313 exit 32 for Opglabbeek.
Open All year **Site** 4HEC ❤ ♣ ❿ ❿ **Prices** pitch 10.50-15 (incl 2 persons)
pp4.20-6 ❿ (static)250-650 **Facilities** 🏪 🛉 ⊙ ❿ ⌀ ⑳ **Services** ☎ 🍴 🔝
🗄 **Leisure** ⚓ P

RETIE ANTWERPEN

Berkenstrand
Brand 78, 2470 ☎ 014 377590 🖥 014 375139
e-mail info@berkenstrand.be
website www.berkenstrand.be
Wooded surroundings beside a lake.
➲ 3km NE on road to Postel.
Open Apr-15 Oct **Site** 10HEC ❤ ♣ ❿ ❿ **Facilities** 🏪 🛉 ⊙ ❿ ⑳
Services ☎ 🍴 🔝 🗄 **Leisure** ⚓ L

TURNHOUT ANTWERPEN

Baalse Hei
Roodhuisstr 10, B-2300 ☎ 014 448470 🖥 014 448474
e-mail info@baalsehei.be
website www.baalsehei.be
A family site in pleasant wooded surroundings with plenty of recreational facilities.
Open 16 Jan-15 Dec **Site** 30HEC ❤ ♣ ❿ ❿ **Prices** pitch 15-22
❿ (static)275-475 **Facilities** 🏪 🛉 ⊙ ❿ ⌀ ⚍ ⑳ **Services** ☎ 🍴 🔝 🗄
Leisure ⚓ L

Site 6HEC (site size) ❤ grass ⊜ sand ♣ stone ♣ little shade ❿ partly shaded ❿ mainly shaded ❿ bungalows for hire
❿ caravans for hire ⚠ tents for hire ⑳ no dogs **Prices** ⚹ adult per night ⇜ car per night pp per person per night ❿ caravan per night
⚠ tent per night ❿ (static)-caravan hire per week

Belgium

VORST-LAAKDAL ANTWERPEN

Kasteel Meerlaer
Verboekt 115, 2430 ☎ 013 661420 🖹 013 667512
e-mail camp.meerlaer@skynet.be
website www.camping.be
➲ *E313 exit 24 for Hosselt. Or exit 24 for Antwerp.*
Open All year **Site** 6HEC ❦ ♣ **Prices** ✦ 3 ♠ 3 ♣ 3 **Å** 3 **Facilities** ⋔ ⊙
🔃 ∅ ♨ 🅟 **Services** 🚩 ⦿ ➕ 🖺 **Off-site** 🛆 ⦿

ZONHOVEN LIMBURG

Holsteenbron
Hengelhoelseweg 9, 3520 ☎ 011 817140 🖹 011 817140
e-mail camping.holsteenbron@skynet.be
website www.holsteenbron.be
A rural family site in a wooded location.
➲ *E314 exit 29 for Zondhoven.*
Open Apr-11Nov **Site** 4HEC ❦ ♣ ♣ **Prices** pitch 16-18 **Facilities** ⋔ ⊙
🔃 ℗ **Services** 🚩 ⦿ ➕ 🖺

SOUTH EAST

AISCHE-EN-REFAIL NAMUR

Manoir de lá Bas
rte de Gembloux 180, 5310 ☎ 081 655353
e-mail europa-camping.sa@skynet.be
website www.camping-manoirdelabas.be
A beautiful location within the wooded grounds of a former manor house.
➲ *5km W of Eghezée.*
Open Apr-Oct **Site** 21HEC ❦ ♣ **Prices** ✦ 4 ♣ 5 **Å** 5 **Facilities** ⋔ ⊙ 🔃
♨ ℗ **Services** 🚩 ⦿ ➕ 🖺 **Leisure** ♨ P **Off-site** 🛆

AMBERLOUP LUXEMBOURG

Tonny
r Tonny 35-36, 6680 ☎ 061 688285 🖹 061 688285
e-mail camping.tonny@belgacom.net
website www.campingtonny.be
Set in a pleasant valley beside the River Ourthe with fine sports facilities.
➲ *E25 or A4 to Bastogne, then N826.*
Open 15 Feb-15 Nov **Site** 3.5HEC ❦ ♣ ♣ **Prices** ✦ 3.50 pitch 8
♣ (static)230-410 **Facilities** ⋔ 🛆 ⊙ 🔃 ∅ ♨ 🅟 **Services** 🚩 ⦿ ➕ 🖺
Leisure ♨ R

AMONINES LUXEMBOURG

Val de l'Aisne
Rue de TTA, 6997 ☎ 086 470067 🖹 086 470043
e-mail info@levaldelaisne.be
website www.levaldelaisne.be
Open All year **Site** 25HEC ❦ ♣ ♣ ♣ **Å Facilities** ⋔ 🛆 ⊙ 🔃 ∅ ♨ ℗
Services 🚩 ⦿ ➕ 🖺 **Leisure** ♨ LR

BARVAUX-SUR-OURTHE LUXEMBOURG

Hazalles
Chainrue 77a, 6940 ☎ 086 211642 🖹 086 211642
Situated in an orchard beside a stream with well-maintained facilities, 0.6km from the village.
Open Apr-Sep **Site** 0.4HEC ❦ ♣ ♣ **Prices** ✦ 1.75 **Å** 2.50 pitch 3.75
Facilities ⋔ ⊙ 🔃 ℗ **Services** ➕ 🖺 **Off-site** 🛆 🚩 ⦿ ∅ ♨ PR

Rives de l'Ourthe
r Inzespres 70, 6940 ☎ 086 211730
A large site with plenty of touring pitches beside the River Ourthe.
➲ *200m from village towards river.*
Open Apr-Sep **Site** 2HEC ❦ ♣ 🔃 ⊙ 🔃 ℗ **Services** 🚩 ⦿ ➕
Leisure ♨ R **Off-site** 🛆 ⦿ ∅ ♨ LP

BERTRIX LUXEMBOURG

Kompas
rte de Mortehan, 6880 ☎ 061 412281 🖹 061 412588
e-mail bertrix@kompascamping.be
website www.kompascamping.be
Well-equipped family site in a pleasant wooded setting.
➲ *Via E411 exit 25 onto N89.*
Open 30 Mar-11 Nov **Site** 14HEC ❦ ♣ ♣ ♣ **Prices Å** 9.50 pitch 19.50-
30.50 ♣ (static)280-630 **Facilities** ⋔ 🛆 ⊙ 🔃 ∅ ℗ **Services** 🚩 ⦿ ➕
🖺 **Leisure** ♨ P

BÜLLINGEN (BULLANGE) LIÈGE

Hêtraie
Rotheck 14, 4760 ☎ 080 642413 🖹 080 642413
This site is on a sloping meadow near a fish pond, surrounded by groups of beautiful beech trees and conifers.
➲ *From village towards Amel, left for 2km & signed.*
Open Apr-15 Nov **Site** 3HEC ❦ ♣ ♣ **Prices** ✦ 2 ♣ 1 ♣ 3.50 **Å** 2.50
Facilities ⋔ ⊙ 🔃 ℗ **Services** ➕ 🖺 **Leisure** ♨ P **Off-site** ♨ R

BURE LUXEMBOURG

Parc la Clusure
30 Chemin de la Clusure, 6927 ☎ 084 360050 🖹 084 366777
e-mail info@parclaclusure.be
website www.parclaclusure.be
Pleasant site with good facilities in the centre of the Ardennes.
➲ *E411 & N846 from Tellin.*
Open All year **Site** 12HEC ❦ ♣ ♣ ♣ **Å Prices** ✦ 4-5 **Å** 3 pitch 19-26
(incl 2 persons) ♣ (static)252-770 **Facilities** ⋔ 🛆 ⊙ 🔃 ∅ ℗ **Services** 🚩
⦿ ➕ 🖺 **Leisure** ♨ PR

BÜTGENBACH LIÈGE

Worriken
Worriken Center 1, 4750 ☎ 080 446358 🖹 080 447089
e-mail camping.worriken@swing.be
Situated on the shores of a lake.
Open All year **Site** 8HEC ❦ ♣ **Facilities** ⋔ ⊙ 🔃 ℗ **Services** 🚩 ⦿ ➕
🖺 **Leisure** ♨ L **Off-site** 🛆 ∅ ♨ PR

CHEVETOGNE NAMUR

Domaine Provincial
5590 ☎ 083 687211 🖹 083 688677
Located in the grounds of a castle and surrounded by fine ornamental gardens. There is a variety of leisure activities.
Open All year **Site** 0.5HEC ❦ ♣ ♣ **Facilities** ⋔ ⊙ 🔃 ℗ 🅟 **Services** 🚩
⦿ ➕ 🖺 **Leisure** ♨ L **Off-site** ♨ P

Facilities 🛆 shop ⋔ shower ⊙ electric points for razors 🔃 electric points for caravans ℗ parking by tents permitted 🅟 compulsory separate car park
Services ⦿ café/restaurant 🚩 bar ∅ Camping Gaz International ♨ gas other than Camping Gaz ➕ first aid facilities 🖺 laundry
Leisure ♨ swimming L-Lake P-Pool R-River S-Sea **Off-site** All facilities within 2km

Belgium

COO-STAVELOT LIÈGE

Cascade
Chemin des Faravennes 5, 4970 ☎ 080 684312
e-mail info@campingcoo.be
website www.campingcoo.be
A small touring and holiday site beside the River Amblève.
⮕ *Motorway exit 10 or 11, site 3km from Trois-Ponts.*
Open Mar-Sep **Site** 0.8HEC 😈 🛇 **Prices** ⋔ 2.75-2.85 🚗 3.75 🚐 3 🛆 3-3.10 **Facilities** 🖍 ⊙ 🗟 ⑦ **Services** ⚑ 🍴 🛨 🗟 **Leisure** 🛇 R **Off-site** 🍴 ⌀

EUPEN LIÈGE

`An der Hill'
Hutte 46, 4700 ☎ 087 744617 🖺 087 557232
Set in wooded surroundings with well-defined pitches.
⮕ *SW of town via N67 towards Monschau.*
Open All year **Site** 0.6HEC 😈 🛇 **Facilities** 🖍 ⊙ 🗟 ⌀ ⚒ ⑦ **Services** ⚑ 🍴 🛨 🗟 **Off-site** 🗟 🛇P

FLORENVILLE LUXEMBOURG

Rosière
Rive Gauche de la Semois, 6820 ☎ 061 311937 🖺 061 314873
e-mail larosiere@pi.be
website www.larosiere.be
Wooded surroundings close to the town centre.
⮕ *E411 exit 26 for Verlaine/Nuefchâteau.*
Open Apr-10 Nov **Site** 10HEC 😈 🛇 **Facilities** 🖍 🗟 ⊙ 🗟 ⌀ ⚒ ⑦ **Services** ⚑ 🍴 🛨 🗟 **Leisure** 🛇 PR

FORRIÈRES LUXEMBOURG

Pré du Blason
r de la Ramée 30, 6953 ☎ 084 212867 🖺 084 223650
e-mail info@camping-predublason.be
website www.camping-predublason.be
This well-kept site lies on a meadow surrounded by wooded hills and is completely divided into pitches and crossed by rough gravel drives.
⮕ *Off N49 Masbourg road.*
Open Apr-Oct **Site** 3HEC 😈 🛇 🚐 **Prices** ⋔ 2 🚐 7.20 🛆 5.50 🚐 (static)200 **Facilities** 🖍 🗟 ⊙ 🗟 ⌀ ⚒ ⑦ **Services** ⚑ 🍴 🛨 🗟 **Leisure** 🛇 R

GEMMENICH LIÈGE

Kon Tiki
Terstraeten 141, 4851 ☎ 087 785973 🖺 087 785973
e-mail campingkontiki@skynet.be
Open All year **Site** 12HEC 😈 🛇 **Prices** pitch 12-16 (incl 5 persons)
Facilities 🖍 🗟 ⊙ 🗟 ⑦ **Services** ⚑ 🍴 🛨 🗟 **Leisure** 🛇 PR

GOUVY LUXEMBOURG

Lac de Cherapont
Cherapont 2, 6670 ☎ 080 517082 🖺 080 517093
e-mail cherapont@skynet.be
website www.cherapont.be
On an extensive lakeside tourist complex with a variety of recreational facilities.
⮕ *E25 exit 51. Or E42 exit 15.*
Open Apr-Oct **Site** 10HEC 😈 🛇 🛎 🚐 **Facilities** 🖍 🗟 ⊙ 🗟 ⚒ ⑦ **Services** ⚑ 🍴 🛨 🗟 **Leisure** 🛇 LR **Off-site** ⌀

GRAND-HALLEUX LUXEMBOURG

Neuf Prés
av de la Résistance, 6698 ☎ 080 216882
A family site in pleasant wooded surroundings beside a river.
⮕ *Via E42.*
Open Apr-Sep **Site** 4HEC 😈 🛇 **Facilities** 🖍 ⊙ 🗟 ⑦ **Services** ⚑ 🍴 🗟 **Leisure** 🛇 PR **Off-site** 🗟 🍴 ⌀ ⚒ 🛨

HABAY-LA-NEUVE LUXEMBOURG

Portail de la Forêt
r du Bon-Bois 3, 6720 ☎ 063 422312 🖺 063 423410
e-mail athiry@belgacom.net
Park-like, terraced site on a hill surrounded by woodland.
⮕ *E25/E411 exit 29.*
Open 15 Mar-15 Oct **Site** 2.5HEC 😈 🛇 **Facilities** 🖍 ⊙ 🗟 ⑦ **Off-site** 🗟 ⚑ 🍴 ⌀ ⚒ 🛇PR 🛨

HOGNE NAMUR

Relais
16 r de Serinchamps, 5377 ☎ 084 311580 🖺 084 312400
e-mail info@campinglerelais.com
website www.campinglerelais.com
A pleasant site in a wooded park beside a lake.
⮕ *N4 from Courrière to Hogne via Marche.*
Open Mar-4 Jan **Site** 12HEC 😈 🛇 🛎 🚐 **Prices** ⋔ 3 🛆 5.20-8 pitch 10-16 🚐 (static)180-400 **Facilities** 🖍 🗟 ⊙ 🗟 ⌀ ⚒ ⑦ **Services** ⚑ 🍴 🛨 🗟 **Leisure** 🛇 LR

HOUFFALIZE LUXEMBOURG

Chasse et Pêche
r de la Roche 63, 6660 ☎ 061 288314 🖺 061 289660
e-mail info@cpbuitensport.com
website www.cpbuitensport.com
A pleasant site attached to a café-restaurant with good recreational facilities.
⮕ *3km NW off E25.*
Open All year **Site** 2HEC 😈 🛇 🛎 🚐 **Prices** ⋔ 5 🚗 3.50 🚐 5 🛆 3.50 **Facilities** 🖍 ⊙ 🗟 ⌀ ⑦ ⑨ **Services** ⚑ 🍴 🛨 🗟 **Leisure** 🛇 R

Moulin de Rensiwez
Moulin de Rensiwez 1, 6663 ☎ 061 289027 🖺 061 289027
A good stopover site on a series of terraces beside the River Ourthe close to an old water-mill.
Open All year **Site** 5HEC 😈 🛇 🛎 🚐 **Facilities** 🖍 🗟 ⊙ 🗟 ⌀ ⑦ ⑨ **Services** ⚑ 🍴 🛨 🗟 **Leisure** 🛇 R

LOUVEIGNÉ LIÈGE

Moulin du Rouge-Thier
Rouge-Thier 8, 4141 ☎ 04 3608341 🖺 04 3608341
A well-equipped site in a pleasant wooded location.
⮕ *S of town towards Deigné.*
Open Apr-30 Oct **Site** 8HEC 😈 🛇 🛎 🚐 **Facilities** 🖍 ⊙ 🗟 ⌀ ⚒ ⑦ **Services** ⚑ 🍴 🛨 🗟

Site 6HEC (site size) 😈 grass 🛇 sand 🛇 stone 🛇 little shade 🛇 partly shaded 😈 mainly shaded 🛎 bungalows for hire 🚐 caravans for hire 🛆 tents for hire ⊗ no dogs **Prices** ⋔ adult per night 🚗 car per night pp per person per night 🚐 caravan per night 🛆 tent per night 🚐 (static)-caravan hire per week

Belgium

MALONNE NAMUR

Trieux
Les Tris 99, 5020 ☎ 081 445583 🗏 081 44 5583
e-mail camping.les.trieux@skynet.be
website www.campinglestrieux.be
Open Apr-30 Oct **Site** 2.2HEC ⛺ ♣ 🚐 **Prices** ▲ 4-5 pitch 20-40 pp3.50
🚐 (static)175-280 **Facilities** 🚿 🖻 ⊙ 🔌 ⊘ ♨ ℗ **Services** 🖃 🖺
Off-site 🍴 🍽 🏊PR

MARCHE-EN-FAMENNE LUXEMBOURG

Euro Camping Paola
r du Panorama 10, 6900 ☎ 084 311704 🗏 084 314722
e-mail camping.paola@skynet.be
A long site on a hill with beautiful views. The only noise comes from a
railway line that passes the site.
➲ *Towards Hotton, right after cemetery for 1km.*
Open All year **Site** 13HEC ⛺ 🍴 ♣ 🚐 **Prices** ⚡ 2.20 🚗 2.50 🚐 5 ▲ 4-5
🚐 (static)200 **Facilities** 🚿 ⊙ 🔌 ♨ ℗ **Services** 🍽 🖃 **Off-site** 🖻 🍴
🍽 🏊P

NEUFCHÂTEAU LUXEMBOURG

International Spineuse
r de Malome 7, rte de Florenville, 6840
☎ 061 277320 🗏 061 277104
e-mail info@camping-spineuse.be
website www.camping-spineuse.be
Camp shop only open July and August.
➲ *2km from Florenville towards Neufchâteau.*
Open All year **Site** 2.5HEC ⛺ ♣ 🚐 **Prices** ⚡ 3.10 pitch 9-11.25
🚐 (static)245-370 **Facilities** 🚿 🖻 ⊙ 🔌 ⊘ ♨ ℗ **Services** 🍴 🍽 🖃 🖺
Leisure 🏊 LPR

OLLOY-SUR-VIROIN NAMUR

Try des Baudets
r de la Champagne, 5670 ☎ 060 390108 🗏 060 390108
e-mail masson_p@yahoo.fr
A peaceful location on the edge of a forest.
Open All year **Site** 11HEC ⛺ ♣ 🚐 **Facilities** 🚿 ⊙ 🔌 ♨ ℗ **Services** 🍴
🍽 🖃 🖺 **Off-site** 🖻 🍴

OTEPPE LIÈGE

Hirondelle
r du Château 1, 4210 ☎ 085 711131 🗏 085 711021
e-mail info@lhirondelle.be
website www.lhirondelle.be
Ideal family site with modern facilities in the picturesque Burdinale
valley.
➲ *Signed N of town between E40 & E42.*
Open Apr-Sep **Site** 65HEC ⛺ ♣ 🍴 🚐 **Prices** ⚡ 2.75-4 🚗 1.50 🚐 6.75-9.75
▲ 6.75-9.75 **Facilities** 🚿 🖻 ⊙ 🔌 ⊘ ♨ ℗ **Services** 🍴 🍽 🖃 🖺
Leisure 🏊 P

POLLEUR LIÈGE

Polleur
r de Congrès 90, 4910 ☎ 087 541033 🗏 087 542530
e-mail info@campingpolleur.be
website www.campingpolleur.be
A family site in a pleasant wooded location.
➲ *Signed off A27.*
Open Apr-Oct **Site** 3.7HEC ⛺ ♣ 🚐 **Facilities** 🚿 🖻 ⊙ 🔌 ⊘ ℗
Services 🍴 🍽 🖃 🖺 **Leisure** 🏊 PR

PURNODE NAMUR

Camping du Bocq
av de la Vallée 2, 5530 ☎ 082 612269 🗏 082 646814
e-mail campingdubocq@scarlet.be
website www.camping-dubocq.be
A beautiful wooded location beside the river.
➲ *E411 exit 19 Spontin for Yvoir, exit Purnode.*
Open Apr-Oct **Site** 3.5HEC ⛺ ♣ 🚐 **Prices** ⚡ 3.25 🚗 2.50 pitch 3.25
🚐 (static)120-210 **Facilities** 🚿 ⊙ 🔌 ♨ ℗ **Services** 🍴 🍽 🖃 🖺
Leisure 🏊 R **Off-site** 🖻

REMOUCHAMPS LIÈGE

Eden
r de Trois Ponts 92, 4920 ☎ 04 3844165 🗏 04 3840055
e-mail edencamping@swing.be
Open Apr-Oct **Site** 3.2HEC ⛺ ♣ 🍴 🚐 **Facilities** 🚿 🖻 ⊙ 🔌 ⊘ ♨ ℗
Services 🍴 🍽 🖃 **Leisure** 🏊 R **Off-site** 🍴

RENDEUX LUXEMBOURG

Festival
rte de la Roche 89, 6987 ☎ 084 477371 🗏 084 477364
website www.lefestival.be
Unspoiled surroundings beside the River Ourthe.
Open Etr-Sep **Site** 11HEC ⛺ ♣ 🍴 🚐 **Facilities** 🚿 🖻 ⊙ 🔌 ⊘ ℗ 🅿
Services 🍴 🍽 🖃 **Leisure** 🏊 R

ROBERTVILLE LIÈGE

Plage
33 rte des Bains, B-4950 ☎ 080 446658 🗏 080 446178
Open All year **Site** 1.8HEC ⛺ ♣ 🚐 **Facilities** 🚿 🖻 ⊙ 🔌 ⊘ ♨ ℗
Services 🍴 🍽 🖃 **Leisure** 🏊 LPR

ROCHE-EN-ARDENNE, LA LUXEMBOURG

Grillon
r des Echarées, 6980 ☎ 084 412062 🗏 084 412128
Well-equipped family site in a pleasant wooded setting.
Open Etr-Oct **Site** 3.5HEC ⛺ ♣ **Facilities** 🚿 🖻 ⊙ 🔌 ⊘ ♨ ℗
Services 🍴 🖃 🖺 **Leisure** 🏊 R **Off-site** 🍽 🏊P

Lohan
20a rte de Houffalize, 6980 ☎ 084 411545
Set in a park surrounded by woodland, on the N bank of the River
Ourthe.
➲ *3km E of La Roche towards Maboge & Houffalize.*
Open Apr-1 Nov **Site** 4HEC ⛺ ♣ ⊗ **Prices** ⚡ 2.50 pitch 7-8 **Facilities** 🚿
🖻 ⊙ 🔌 ⊘ ℗ **Services** 🍴 🍽 🖃 🖺 **Leisure** 🏊 R

Facilities 🖻 shop 🚿 shower ⊙ electric points for razors 🔌 electric points for caravans ℗ parking by tents permitted 🅿 compulsory separate car park
Services 🍽 café/restaurant 🍴 bar ⊘ Camping Gaz International ♨ gas other than Camping Gaz 🖃 first aid facilities 🖺 laundry
Leisure 🏊 swimming L-Lake P-Pool R-River S-Sea **Off-site** All facilities within 2km

Ourthe

6980 ☎ 084 411459
e-mail info@campingdelourthe.be
website www.campingdelourthe.be
Well-kept site beside the River Ourthe.
➔ *On SW bank of Ourthe below N34.*
Open 15 Mar-15 Oct **Site** 2HEC ❤ ♣ ⚓ ☎ **Prices** ⚹ 2 pitch 6
☎ (static)200 **Facilities** ⚐ 🗟 ⊙ ❤ ⬰ ℗ ℗ **Services** ⊞ 🗟 **Leisure** ⚓ R
Off-site ⚐ ⛱ ⚓P ⊞

SART-LEZ-SPA LIÈGE

Touring Club

Stockay 17, 4845 ☎ 087 474400 🖹 087 475277
e-mail info@campingspador.be
website www.campingspador.be
➔ *Signed E of Spa.*
Open All year **Site** 6HEC ❤ ♣ ⚓ Å **Prices** pitch 16-24 (incl 2 persons)
pp4.90-5.90 ☎ (static)700 **Facilities** ⚐ 🗟 ⊙ ❤ ⬰ ℗ **Services** ⚐ ⛱
⊞ 🗟 **Leisure** ⚓ PR **Off-site** ⚓L

SIPPENAEKEN LIÈGE

Vieux Moulin

114 Tebruggen, 4851 ☎ 087 784255
website www.camping-vieuxmoulin.be
A family site with good recreational facilities, set in a pleasant wooded
location close to a nature reserve.
➔ *E40 exit Battile for Aubel-Hombourg-Sippenaeken.*
Open Apr-Sep **Site** 6HEC ❤ ♣ ⚓ **Prices** ⚹ 4 pitch 3.50 **Facilities** ⚐ 🗟 ⊙
❤ ℗ **Services** ⚐ ⛱ ⊞ 🗟 **Leisure** ⚓ PR

SPA LIÈGE

Parc des Sources

r de la Sauvenière 141, 4900 ☎ 087 772311 🖹 087 475965
e-mail info@campingparcdessources.be
website www.campingparcdessources.be
On the outskirts of the town close to a forest.
➔ *S of town centre on N32 towards Malmédy.*
Open All year **Site** 2.5HEC ❤ ♣ **Prices** pitch 16.50 (incl 2 persons)
Facilities ⚐ 🗟 ⊙ ❤ ⬰ 🚿 ℗ **Services** ⚐ ⛱ 🗟 **Leisure** ⚓ P **Off-site** ⚐
⛱ 🚿 ⊞

SPRIMONT LIÈGE

Tultay

r de Tultay 22, 4140 ☎ 04 3821162 🖹 04 3821162
e-mail r3cb.tultay@teledismet.net
website www.rcccb.com
A pleasant site in wooded surroundings on the edge of a nature
reserve.
➔ *E25 exit 45*
Open All year **Site** 1.5HEC ❤ ♣ **Prices** ⚹ 2.50 pitch 5 **Facilities** ⚐ ⊙ ❤
℗ **Services** ⚐ ⛱ ⊞ 🗟 **Off-site** 🗟 ⛱ 🚿

STAVELOT LIÈGE

Domaine de l'Eau Rouge

Cheneux 25, 4970 ☎ 080 863075
website www.campingleaurouge.be
A pleasant riverside site with good sports facilities.
➔ *Via E42 to Francorchamps or Malmédy.*
Open All year **Site** 4HEC ❤ ♣ ⚓ **Facilities** ⚐ ⊙ ❤ 🚿 ℗ ℗ **Services** ⚐
⛱ ⊞ 🗟 **Leisure** ⚓ R **Off-site** ⚓P

TENNEVILLE LUXEMBOURG

Pont de Berguème

r Berguème 9, 6970 ☎ 084 455443 🖹 084 456231
e-mail info@pontbergueme.be
website www.pontbergueme.be
A peaceful wooded setting in the beautiful Ardennes area with
modern facilities.
➔ *Off N4 towards Berguème, then turn right.*
Open All year **Site** 3HEC ❤ ♣ ⚓ **Prices** ⚹ 3.50 pitch 5.75 **Facilities** ⚐ 🗟
⊙ ❤ ⬰ ℗ **Services** ⚐ ⛱ ⊞ 🗟 **Leisure** ⚓ R **Off-site** ⛱

THOMMEN-REULAND LIÈGE

Hohenbusch

Grüfflingen 44, 4791 ☎ 080 227523
e-mail info@hohenbusch.be
website www.hohenbusch.be
A well-appointed family site on a wooded meadow with plenty of
recreational facilities.
➔ *Off N26 SW of St-Vith.*
Open Apr-Oct **Site** 5HEC ❤ ♣ ⚓ **Facilities** ⚐ 🗟 ⊙ ❤ ⬰ ℗
Services ⛱ 🗟 **Leisure** ⚓ P

VIELSALM LUXEMBOURG

Salm

chemin de la Vallée, B-6690 ☎ 080 216241 🖹 080 217266
website www.vielsham.be
Open All year **Site** 2.5HEC ❤ ♣ **Facilities** ⚐ ⊙ ❤ ⬰ ℗ **Services** ⚐ ⛱
⊞ 🗟 **Leisure** ⚓ R **Off-site** 🗟 ⛱ ⬰ ⚓LP

VIRTON LUXEMBOURG

Colline de Rabais

r du Bonlieu, 6760 ☎ 063 571195 🖹 063 583342
e-mail info@collinederabais.be
website www.collinederabais.be
A secluded family site in the heart of the Gaume region close to a lake
with good recreational facilities.
➔ *NE of Virton between N87 & N82.*
Open All year **Site** 8HEC ❤ ♣ ⚓ ☎ Å **Prices** ⚹ 3.20-4.50 pitch 5.90-8
(incl 2 persons) **Facilities** ⚐ 🗟 ⊙ ❤ ⬰ 🚿 ℗ **Services** ⚐ ⛱ ⊞ 🗟
Leisure ⚓ P **Off-site** ⚓L

WAIMES LIÈGE

Anderegg

Bruyères 4, 4950 ☎ 080 679393 🖹 080 679396
e-mail campinganderegg@skynet.be
website www.campinganderegg.be
A peaceful location beside the Lac de Robertville.
Open All year **Site** 1.5HEC ❤ ♣ **Prices** ⚹ 3.75 ☎ 6 Å 6 **Facilities** ⚐ 🗟
⊙ ❤ ⬰ 🚿 ℗ **Services** ⚐ ⛱ ⊞ 🗟

Site 6HEC (site size) ❤ grass ⬟ sand ❤ stone ♣ little shade ♣ partly shaded ❤ mainly shaded ⚓ bungalows for hire
☎ caravans for hire Å tents for hire ⊗ no dogs **Prices** ⚹ adult per night ⬰ car per night pp per person per night ☎ caravan per night
Å tent per night ☎ (static)-caravan hire per week

France

Accidents & emergencies
fire 18   **police** 17   **ambulance** 15

The European emergency call number is also in use - dial 112 and ask for the service required.

Driving requirements
Minimum age 18 for UK licence holders driving temporarily imported cars (or motorcycles over 80cc). Visiting motorists who have held a driving licence for less than two years must adhere to the wet weather speed limit.

Lights
Dipped headlights must be used in poor daytime visibility and on motorcycles at all times. Replacement set of vehicle bulbs strongly recommended. Hazard warning lights compulsory; warning triangle compulsory when vehicle over 3500kg or if towing caravan/trailer with total authorised laden weight exceeding 500kg (otherwise recommended that warning triangle always be carried).

Passengers & children
Children under 10 must not travel in the front with the exception of babies up to 9 months and less than 9kg in rear facing restraint system appropriate to age and weight. Children under 10 in rear must use restraint system appropriate to weight (between 9-15kg child seat, over 15kg booster seat in conjunction with normal seat belts). Never fit a rear-facing child restraint in a seat with a frontal airbag.

Size restrictions
Motor vehicle or trailer
height 4m, width 2.55m, length 12m

Vehicle + trailer
length 18.75m

Speed limits
Unless signed otherwise:

Car with or without caravan/trailer (total weight less than 3.5 tonnes**), motorcycle (over 125cc)
Built-up areas	50kph
Outside built-up areas	90kph
Dual carriageways	110kph
Motorways	130kph*

* minimum speed in overtaking lane during good daytime visibility 80kph; maximum speed on urban motorway 80kpm on the Paris ring road and 110kpm elsewhere.

** if the caravan weight exceeds that of the car by less than 30% a limit of 65kph applies, by more than 30% 45kph.

In conditions of rain, snow or sleet, limits are reduced as follows: outside built-up areas 80kph; 100kph on dual carriageways; motorways 110kph. In fog when visibility is reduced to 50m, 50kph on all roads. Holders of EU driving licences exceeding speed limit by more than 40kph will have their licences confiscated on the spot by the police.

Tourist office
French Government Tourist Office
178 Piccadilly, London W1J 9AL
Tel 09068 244123 (premium rate information line Mon-Fri 09.00-19.30 hrs)
www.franceguide.com

Additional information
The holder of a UK passport who is not a British citizen may require a visa. Check with:
French Consulate General, 6A Cromwell Place, London SW7 2EN
Tel 020 7073 1250 (recorded information)

Motorways
www.autoroutes.fr
To join a motorway follow signs with the international motorway symbol or signs with the word *par Autoroute* added. Signs with the words *péage* or *par péage* lead to toll roads. Motorcycles under 50cc are prohibited. Use green alternative routes to avoid traffic jams on major highways.

Services
It is usually possible to obtain 24-hour service for a car and/or occupants every 40km. Rest stops, most of which have toilet facilities, can be found every 15km. Free emergency telephones are sited every 2km on most motorways.

Breakdown
Use of hazard warning lights or warning triangle compulsory.

Tolls
Most motorways charge tolls except certain sections near large towns such as Paris, Bordeaux, Lille, Lyon, Marseille and Metz.

Toll payments, *péage*

On the majority of toll motorways a travel ticket is issued on entry and toll is paid on leaving the motorway and also at occasional intermediate points. On some motorways the toll collection is automatic – have the correct change ready to throw in the collecting basket. If change is required use marked separate lane. Toll booths will not exchange traveller's cheques – ensure you have sufficient currency to meet the high toll charges (credit cards are accepted at the toll booths).
The charges in the following tables are a guide only and may change.

Tolls

		car	car & caravan
A1	Lille - Paris	€13.10	€19.20
A2/A1	Valenciennes - Paris	€12.00	€17.60
A2/A26	Valenciennes - Reims	€10.60	€15.90
A4	Paris - Reims	€9.00	€13.50
A4	Paris - Metz	€21.00	€31.50
A4	Metz - Strasbourg	€10.90	€16.70
A4	Paris - Strasbourg	€31.90	€48.20
A5/A31/			
A6	Paris - Lyon (via Troyes)	€28.20	€36.90
A6	Paris - Beaune	€17.90	€23.40
A6	Paris - Macon	€23.40	€30.60
A6	Paris - Lyon	€28.20	€36.90
A7/A8	Lyon - Aix-en-Provence	€20.60	€31.80
A7/A9	Lyon - Montpellier	€20.90	€32.50
A8	Aix-en-Provence - Cannes	€12.00	€18.20
A8	Cannes - Nice	€3.80	€5.70
A8	Nice - Menton (Italian frontier)	€1.90	€2.90
A9	Orange - Montpellier	€6.50	€10.00
A9	Montpellier - Le Perthus (Spanish frontier)	€16.50	€17.90
A9/A54	Montpellier - Arles	€4.60	€7.10
A10	Paris - Tours	€19.60	€31.30
A10	Tours - Bordeaux	€27.80	€43.30
A10	Tours - Poitiers	€8.70	€14.50
A10	Poitiers - Saintes	€9.30	€14.30
A10/A71	Paris - Clermont-Ferrand	€31.50	€46.80
A10/A837	Bordeaux - Rochefort	€11.30	€17.30
A11	Paris - Angers	€23.10	€35.30
A11	Angers - Nantes	€7.50	€11.40
A11/A81	Paris - Rennes	€25.20	€39.10
A13	Le Havre-St Saens	€6.30	€9.50
A13	Caen - Paris	€18.80	€31.60
A13	Le Havre - Paris	€16.10	€27.40
A13	Rouen - Paris	€11.50	€20.80
A14	Orgeval-Paris (La defense)	€8.80	€13.00
A16	Calais - Paris	€18.50	€28.20
A26	Calais - Reims	€18.70	€27.00
A26	Reims - Troyes	€9.20	€13.40
A26/A1	Calais - Paris	€18.50	€28.20
A26/A5	Reims - Lyon	€33.80	€45.60
A26/A5/ A39/A40	Reims - Chamonix	€47.00	€66.80
A29	Le Havre - St Saens(A28)	€6.50	€9.80
A29/A26	Amiens - Reims	€10.90	€16.40
A31	Toul - Langres	€7.40	€9.70

Tolls

		car	car & caravan
A31	Langres - Dijon	€3.20	€4.20
A31	Dijon - Beaune	€2.20	€2.60
A36	Beaune - Besancon	€6.20	€8.10
A36	Besancon - Belfort	€6.30	€8.30
A36	Belfort - Mulhouse	€2.40	€3.00
A39	Dijon - Dole	€2.50	€3.30
A39	Dole - Bourg-en-Bresse	€7.40	€9.70
A40	Macon - Geneve	€13.50	€20.00
A40	Geneve - Chamonix	€5.00	€8.80
A41	Grenoble - Chambery	€5.10	€7.40
A41	Chambery - Geneve	€4.80	€7.50
A41/A40	Chambery - Chamonix	€11.00	€17.40
A42/A40	Lyon - Geneve	€13.30	€19.70
A43	Lyon - Chambery	€9.40	€15.10
A43/A48	Lyon - Grenoble	€8.90	€14.30
A43/A430	Chambery - Albertville	€4.60	€7.10
A49	Valence - Grenoble	€7.60	€12.00
A52/A50	Aix-en-Provence - Toulon	€6.50	€9.80
A51	Aix-en-Provence - La Saulce	€9.90	€16.10
A54/A7	Montpellier - Aix-en-Provence	€8.30	€12.70
A57	Toulon - Le Cannet de Maures	€2.00	€3.00
A61/A9	Toulouse - Montpellier	€17.40	€26.40
A61/A9	Toulouse - Le Perthus	€16.20	€25.10
A62	Bordeaux - Toulouse	€15.40	€24.00
A63	Bordeaux - Hendaye (Spanish frontier)	€6.40	€9.90
A64	Bayonne - Toulouse	€16.20	€24.80
A72	Clermont-Ferrand - St Etienne	€9.30	€14.40
A83/A10	Nantes - Bordeaux	€24.30	€37.10
A85	Angers - Bourgueil	€5.40	€7.60
A87	Angers - Cholet	€4.40	€4.90
A89	Bordeaux - Mussidan	€5.40	€8.40
A89	Tulle- St Julien	€8.40	€13.10

Bridges & tunnels

	car	car & caravan
Pont de Normandie	€5.00	€5.80
Pont de Tancarville	€2.30	€2.90
Tunnel du Puymorens	€5.40	€10.90
Tunnel Maurice Lemaire (Closed until Late 2007)		
Tunnel du Frejus	€31.20	€41.30
Tunnel du Mont Blanc	€31.90	€42.10
Tunnel Prado Carenage (cars only)	€2.40	
A75 le Viaduc de Millau (summer)	€6.50	€9.70
A75 le Viaduc de Millau (rest of the year)	€4.90	€7.30

ALPS/EAST

ABRETS, LES ISÈRE

Coin Tranquille
6 chemin des Vignes, 38490 ☎ 476321348 ▨ 476374067
e-mail contact@coin-tranquille.com
website www.coin-tranquille.com
Completely divided into pitches with attractive flower beds in rural surroundings.
⮕ *2km E of village, 0.5km off N6.*
Open Apr-Oct **Site** 8HEC ⛺ ♨ 🚐 **Prices** ⚐ 4-6.50 pitch 15-27 (incl 2 persons) **Facilities** 🚿 🏠 ⊙ 🔌 🖉 ⑫ **Services** 🍴 🍽 ➕ 🗑 **Leisure** ⚊ P

ALBENS SAVOIE

Beauséjour
rte de la Rippe, 73410 ☎ 479541520
website www.campingbeausejour-albens.com
A peaceful wooded setting between Aix-les-Bains and Annecy.
⮕ *SW via rte de la Chambotte, signed.*
Open Jun-20 Sep **Site** 2HEC ⛺ ♨ 🚐 🔌 **Prices** ⚐ 2 pitch 4 🔌 (static)170
Facilities 🚿 ⊙ 🔌 🖉 ⑫ **Services** 🗑 **Off-site** 🏠 🍴 🍽 ⚊R ➕

ALLEVARD ISÈRE

Clair Matin
20 rte de Pommiers, 38580 ☎ 476975519 ▨ 476458715
e-mail jdavallet1@aol.com
website www.achatgrenoble.com/campingclairmatin
Gently sloping terraced area divided into pitches.
⮕ *S of village, 300m off D525.*
Open 10 May-15 Oct **Site** 5.5HEC ⛺ ♨ 🚐 🔌 **Prices** ⚐ 2.95 pitch 5.60-11.20 🔌 (static)113-445 **Facilities** 🚿 ⊙ 🔌 🖉 🏔 ⑫ **Services** 🍴 ➕ 🗑
Leisure ⚊ P **Off-site** 🏠 🍴 🍽 ⚊LR

ARBOIS JURA

CM Vignes
av Gl-Leclerc, 39600 ☎ 384661412 ▨ 384661412
Terraced site. Shop only open July and August.
⮕ *E on D107 Mesnay road at stadium.*
Open Apr-Sep **Site** 5HEC ⛺ ♨ 🚐 **Prices** pitch 12-13 (incl 2 persons)
Facilities 🚿 🏠 ⊙ 🔌 🖉 ⑫ **Services** 🍴 🍽 ➕ 🗑 **Off-site** 🏔 ⚊PR

ARGENTIÈRE HAUTE-SAVOIE

Glacier d'Argentière
161 chemin des Chosalets, 74400 ☎ 450541736 ▨ 450540373
website www.camping-chamonix.com
Set on sloping meadowland in a beautiful location at the foot of the Mont Blanc Massif.
⮕ *1km S of Argentière. Off N506 towards Cableway Lognan et de Grandes Montets & 200m to site.*
Open 15 May-Sep **Site** 1.5HEC ⛺ ♨ 🚐 **Prices** ⚐ 4.60 ♨ 1.70 🚐 3.30
⛺ 2.30 🔌 (static)182 **Facilities** 🚿 ⊙ 🔌 🖉 ⑫ **Services** ➕ 🗑 **Off-site** 🏠 🍴 🍽 🏔

In the Isère, you will find countryside, mountains, lakes and rivers: extraordinary advantages for all the family in every season!

One sole address:
www.campingisere.com

ARS-SUR-FORMANS AIN

Bois de la Dame
Chemin du Bois de la Dame, 1480 ☎ 474007723
Compulsory separate car park for arrivals after 22.00 hrs.
⮕ *A6 exit Villefranche for Jassans-Riottier.*
Open Apr-Sep **Site** 1.5HEC ⛺ ♨ **Prices** pitch 9.90 **Facilities** 🚿 ⊙ 🔌 ⑫ ⓟ **Services** ➕ 🗑 **Off-site** 🏠 🍴 🍽 ⚊P

AUTRANS ISÈRE

Caravaneige du Vercors
Les Gaillards, 38880 ☎ 476953188 ▨ 476953682
e-mail camping.le.vercors@wanadoo.fr
website www.camping-du-vercors.fr
Ideal for summer or winter holidays, situated in the heart of the Vercors with easy access to skiing.
⮕ *0.6km S via D106 towards Méaudre.*
Open 20 May-20 Sep, Dec-Mar **Site** 1HEC ⛺ ♨ 🚐 **Prices** pitch 12.80-15.30 (incl 2 persons) pp4.20 **Facilities** 🚿 ⊙ 🔌 🖉 🏔 ⑫ **Services** ➕ 🗑
Leisure ⚊ P **Off-site** 🏠 🍴 🍽

Joyeux Réveil
38880 ☎ 476953344 ▨ 476957298
e-mail camping-au-joyeux-reveil@wanadoo.fr
website camping-au-joyeux-reveil.fr
A beautiful location surrounded by woodland, with fine mountain views.
⮕ *NE of town via rte de Montaud.*
Open Dec-Mar & May-Sep **Site** 1.5HEC ⛺ ♨ 🚐 **Prices** pitch 16.50-26 (incl 2 persons) 🚐 (static)300-650 **Facilities** 🚿 ⊙ 🔌 🏔 ⑫ **Services** 🍴 🍽 ➕ 🗑 **Leisure** ⚊ P **Off-site** 🏠 🍴 🍽 🖉

BARATIER HAUTES-ALPES

Verger
5200 ☎ 492431587 ▨ 4924981
e-mail campingleverger@wanadoo.fr
website www.campingleverger.fr
Terraced site in plantation of fruit trees with fine views of Alps. Divided into pitches.
⮕ *From N94 drive 2.5km S of Embrun, 1.5km E on D40.*
Open Apr-Sep **Site** 4HEC ⛺ ♨ 🚐 🔌 **Facilities** 🚿 ⊙ 🔌 🏔 ⑫
Services ➕ 🗑 **Leisure** ⚊ P **Off-site** 🏠 🍴 🍽 🖉 ⚊LR

Facilities 🏠 shop 🚿 shower ⊙ electric points for razors 🔌 electric points for caravans ⑫ parking by tents permitted ⓟ compulsory separate car park
Services 🍽 café/restaurant 🍴 bar 🖉 Camping Gaz International 🏔 gas other than Camping Gaz ➕ first aid facilities 🗑 laundry
Leisure ⚊ swimming L-Lake P-Pool R-River S-Sea **Off-site** All facilities within 2km

France

BELFORT TERRITOIRE-DE-BELFORT

Étang des Forges
r du Général Béthouart, 90000 ☎ 384225492 📄 384227655
e-mail contact@campings-belfort.com
website www.campings-belfort.com
Situated by Malsaucy lake in the regional nature reserve of Ballons des Vosges. Ideal terrain for hiking and water activities.
➲ *A36 exit 2, off D13 Richtung-Offemont.*
Open 7 Apr-Sep **Site** 3.5HEC 🌊 🏖 🛖 **Prices** ⚡ 3.50-3.80 pitch 7.50-8.50 (incl 2 persons) 🚐 (static)220-400 **Facilities** 🏠 🏚 ⊙ 🏪 🅿 🅰 ⓔ **Services** 🍴 🍽 ➕ 🍴 **Leisure** ⚓ P **Off-site** 🛒 ⚓L

BOURG-D'OISANS, LE ISÈRE

Caravaneige le Vernis
38520 ☎ 476800268
e-mail levernis.camping@wanadoo.fr
website www.oisans.com/levernis
Well-kept site at foot of mountain in summer skiing area.
➲ *2.5km of N91, rte de Briançon.*
Open Jun-10 Sept **Site** 1.2HEC 🌊 🏖 🛖 ⊗ **Prices** ⚡ 4 pitch 17 (incl 2 persons) 🚐 (static)250 **Facilities** 🏠 ⊙ 🅰 ⓔ **Services** ➕ 🍽 **Leisure** ⚓ P **Off-site** 🛒 🍴 🍽 ⚓ 🅰

Cascade
rte de l'Alpe-d'Huez, 38520 ☎ 476800242 📄 476802263
e-mail lacascade@wanadoo.fr
website www.lacascadesarenne.com
Set at the foot of a mountain with a waterfall and modern, very well-kept sanitary arrangements. TV lounge with library, open fireplace. Booking essential.
➲ *From Grenoble signs Stations de l'Oisans & from Bourg-d'Oisans towards Alpe-d'Huez.*
Open 15 Dec-Sep **Site** 2.5HEC 🌊 🏖 🛖 **Prices** pitch 8.20 **Facilities** 🏠 ⊙ 🅰 🅰 ⓔ **Services** 🍴 🍽 **Leisure** ⚓ PR **Off-site** 🛒 🍽 ➕

Colporteur
le Mas du Plan, 38520 ☎ 476791144 📄 476791149
e-mail info@camping-colporteur.com
website www.camping-colporteur.com
Situated 200m from the centre of Bourg d'Oisans, in the centre of a plain surrounded by mountains.
Open mid May-mid Sep **Site** 4HEC 🌊 🏖 🛖 **Prices** pitch 22 (incl 2 persons) **Facilities** 🏠 ⊙ 🅰 ⓔ **Services** 🍴 🍽 🍽 **Leisure** ⚓ R **Off-site** 🛒 🅰 ⚓P ➕

Rencontre du Soleil
rte de l'Alpe-d'Huez, 38520 ☎ 476791222 📄 476802637
e-mail rencontre.soleil@wanadoo.fr
website www.alarencontredusoleil.com
Charming site in a lovely setting in the Dauphiny Alps at the foot of a mountain. Fine rustic common room with open fireplace. TV, playroom for children.
➲ *At foot of hairpin road to L'Alp-d'Huez, off N91 in Le Bourg d'Osians.*
Open 5 May-16 Sep **Site** 1.6HEC 🌊 🏖 🛖 **Prices** pitch 15-24.80 (incl 2 persons) pp5.10-6.20 **Facilities** 🏠 ⊙ 🅰 ⓔ **Services** 🍴 🍽 🍽 **Leisure** ⚓ P **Off-site** 🛒 🍽 🅰 ⚓R

AT VENOSC (10KM SE ON N91 AND D530)

Champ de Moulin
38520 ☎ 476800738 📄 476802444
website www.champ-du-moulin.com
Picturesque location with fine views of the surrounding mountains and a direct cablecar to local ski slopes. Separate car park for late arrivals.
Open Jan-15 Sep, 15-31 Dec **Site** 1HEC 🌊 🏖 🛖 🚐 **Facilities** 🏠 🏚 ⊙ 🅰 🅰 ⓔ **Services** 🍴 🍽 **Leisure** ⚓ R **Off-site** ⚓P ➕

BOURG-EN-BRESSE AIN

CM de Challes
5 allée du Centre Nautique, 01000 ☎ 474453721 📄 474224032
e-mail camping_municipal_bourgenbresse@wanadoo.fr
Set in a football ground near the swimming pool.
➲ *Signed from outskirts of town.*
Open Apr-14 Oct **Site** 2.7HEC 🌊 🏖 🛖 **Prices** ⚡ 3.32 🅰 5.28 pitch 6.25 **Facilities** 🏠 🏚 ⊙ 🅰 ⓔ ⓔ **Services** 🍴 🍽 ➕ 🍽 **Leisure** ⚓ P **Off-site** 🅰 🅰 ⚓L

BOURGET-DU-LAC, LE SAVOIE

CM Ile aux Cygnes
73370 ☎ 479250176 📄 479253294
e-mail camping@bourgetdulac.com
website www.bourgetdulac.com
A family site on the shore of the Lac Bourdeau with plenty of recreational facilities.
➲ *Via N514.*
Open 13 Apr-13 Oct, May-Sept **Site** 4.5HEC 🌊 🏖 🛖 **Facilities** 🏠 🏚 ⊙ 🅰 🅰 ⓔ **Services** ➕ 🍽 **Leisure** ⚓ LR **Off-site** 🍴 🍽

BOURG-ST-MAURICE SAVOIE

Versoyen
rte des Arcs, 73700 ☎ 479070345 📄 479072541
e-mail leversoyen@wanadoo.fr
website www.leversoyen.com
Many secluded pitches in a wood with two communal sanitary blocks (one heated). Skiing facilities.
➲ *Via RN90*
Open May-2 Nov & 15 Dec-2 May **Site** 4HEC 🌊 🏖 🛖 🚐 **Prices** ⚡ 4.61-5.18 pitch 3.60-4.50 🚐 (static)202.81-452.81 **Facilities** 🏠 ⊙ 🅰 🅰 ⓔ **Services** ➕ 🍽 **Off-site** 🛒 🍴 🍽 🅰 🅰 ⚓PR

BOUT-DU-LAC HAUTE-SAVOIE

International du Lac Bleu
rte de la Plage, 74210 ☎ 450443018 📄 450448435
e-mail lac-bleu@nwc.fr
website www.camping-lac-bleu.com
Modern, well-kept site. Overflow area with own sanitary blocks.
➲ *On S shore of Lake Annecy via N508, opp ANTAR garage.*
Open 15 Apr-25 Sep **Site** 3.3HEC 🌊 🏖 🛖 🚐 **Facilities** 🏠 ⊙ 🅰 ⓔ **Services** 🍴 🍽 ➕ 🍽 **Leisure** ⚓ LP **Off-site** 🛒 🅰 🅰

Nublière
74210 ☎ 450443344 📄 450443178
e-mail nubliere@wanadoo.fr
website www.campeoles.fr
Extensive site divided into pitches in attractive surroundings.
➲ *150m off N508 at S end of Lac d'Annecy.*
Open May-Sep **Site** 9HEC 🌊 🏖 🛖 🅰 **Facilities** 🏠 🏚 ⊙ 🅰 🅰 ⓔ **Services** ➕ 🍽 **Leisure** ⚓ L **Off-site** 🍴 🍽 🅰 ⚓R

Site 6HEC (site size) 🌊 grass 🏖 sand 🌊 stone 🏖 little shade 🏖 partly shaded 🌊 mainly shaded 🛖 bungalows for hire 🚐 caravans for hire 🅰 tents for hire ⊗ no dogs **Prices** ⚡ adult per night 🚗 car per night pp per person per night 🚐 caravan per night 🅰 tent per night 🚐 (static)-caravan hire per week

France *(side tab)*

CHALEZEULE DOUBS

Plage
12 rte de Belfort, 25220 ☎ 381880426 🖹 381505462
e-mail laplage.besancon@ffcc.asso.fr
website www.ffcc.asso.fr
A modern site with good facilities near the main roads and close to the River Doubs.
➲ *N83 towards Belfort.*
Open Apr-Sep **Site** 1.8HEC ❦ ♣ **Facilities** ⚑ ⊙ ⬚ ∅ ⬜ ⑫ **Services** ⬚
⦿ ⊞ ⬚ **Leisure** ❧ PR **Off-site** ⬚ ∅ ⬜

CHAMONIX-MONT-BLANC HAUTE-SAVOIE

Mer de Glace
200 Chemin de la Bagna, 74400 ☎ 450534403 🖹 450536083
e-mail info@chamonix-camping.com
website www.chamonix-camping.com
A forested setting with pitches divided by hedges. Enjoys fine mountain views.
➲ *2km NE to Les Praz. On approach to village (from Chamonix) turn right under railway bridge.*
Open 27 Apr-1 Oct **Site** 2.2HEC ❦ ♣ ♣ **Prices** ⚑ 5.50-6.30 pitch 5.20-7
Facilities ⚑ ⊙ ⬚ ⑫ **Services** ⦿ ⊞ ⬚ **Off-site** ⬚ ⬚ ⦿ ∅ ❧P

Rosières
121 Clos des Rosières, 74400 ☎ 450531042 🖹 450532955
e-mail info@campinglesrosieres.com
website www.campinglesrosieres.com
Picturesque site at the foot of the Mont Blanc range.
➲ *1.2km NE via N506.*
Open 8 Jun-10 Sep **Site** 1.5HEC ❦ ♣ ♣ ⭑ **Prices** ⚑ 5.70-6.40 ▲ 3.20
pitch 5-6.60 **Facilities** ⚑ ⊙ ⬚ ∅ ⬜ ⑫ **Services** ⬚ ⦿ ⊞ ⬚
Off-site ⬚ ⬚ ⦿ ❧P

AT BOSSONS, LES (3KM W)

Cimes
28 rte des Tissieres, 74400 ☎ 450535893
e-mail info@campinglescimesmontblanc.com
website www.campinglescimesmontblanc.com
A wooded meadow at the foot of Mont Blanc Massif. Ideal for hiking and mountain tours.
Open 15 Jun-20 Sep **Site** 1HEC ❦ ♣ ⭑ **Prices** ⚑ 5.80 pitch 3.80
⭑ (static)230 **Facilities** ⚑ ⊙ ⬚ ⑫ **Services** ⬚ **Leisure** ❧ R **Off-site** ⬚
⬚ ⦿ ❧L ⊞

Deux Glaciers
80 rte des Tissieres, 74400 ☎ 450531584 🖹 450559081
e-mail glaciers@clubinternet.fr
A glacial stream runs through the site. Pitches shaded by trees, very modern, well-kept sanitary installations. Rustic common room with open fires.
➲ *Off N506 towards road underpass, 250m to site.*
Open All year **Site** 16HEC ❦ ♣ **Facilities** ⚑ ⊙ ⬚ ⬜ ⑫ **Services** ⬚ ⦿
⊞ ⬚ **Off-site** ⬚

CHAMPAGNOLE JURA

CM Boyse
r G-Vallery, 39300 ☎ 384520032 🖹 384520116
e-mail boyse@frce.fr
website www.tourisme.champagnole.com
Clean and tidy site in the grounds of a municipal swimming pool with asphalt drives and divided into pitches.
➲ *Onto D5 before town & 1.3km to site.*
Open Jun-15 Sep **Site** 8HEC ❦ ♣ ♣ ⭑ **Facilities** ⚑ ⬚ ⊙ ⬚ ∅ ⬜ ⑫
Services ⬚ ⦿ ⊞ ⬚ **Leisure** ❧ PR

CHÂTEAUROUX-LES-ALPES HAUTES-ALPES

Cariamas
Fontmolines, 05380 ☎ 492432263
e-mail p.tim@free.fr
website les.cariamas.free.fr
On a meadow in an attractive mountain setting beside the River Durance.
➲ *1.5km SE.*
Open Apr-Oct **Site** 6HEC ❦ ♣ ⭑ ⭑ ▲ **Prices** ⚑ 4.50 pitch 5.50
⭑ (static)200-370 **Facilities** ⚑ ⬚ ⊙ ⬚ ∅ ⬜ ⑫ **Services** ⬚ **Leisure** ❧ P
Off-site ⬚ ⦿

CHÂTILLON JURA

Domaine de l'Epinette
15 r de l'Epinette ☎ 384257144 🖹 384257596
e-mail contact@domaine-epinette.com
website www.domaine-epinette.com
A small campsite situated beside the Ain river in an area of lakes and mountains.
Open 15 Jun-15 Sep **Site** 7HEC ❦ ♣ ⭑ ▲ **Facilities** ⚑ ⬚ ⊙ ⬚ ∅ ⑫ ⭑
Services ⦿ ⊞ **Leisure** ❧ PR

CHOISY HAUTE-SAVOIE

Chez Langin
74330 ☎ 450774165 🖹 450774101
e-mail 352@wanadoo.fr
Pleasant wooded surroundings.
➲ *1.3km NE via D3.*
Open 14 Apr-Sep **Site** 3HEC ❦ ♣ ⭑ **Prices** pitch 19 (incl 2 persons)
Facilities ⚑ ⊙ ⬚ ∅ ⬜ ⑫ **Services** ⬚ ⦿ ⊞ ⬚ **Leisure** ❧ P

CHORANCHE ISÈRE

Gouffre de la Croix
38680 ☎ 476360713 🖹 476360713
e-mail camping.gouffre.croix@wanadoo.fr
website camping-choranche.com
A quiet location beside the River Bourne with fine views of the surrounding mountains and modern facilities.
➲ *A49 exit St-Marcellin or Hostun.*
Open 30 Apr-15 Sep **Site** 2.5HEC ❦ ♣ ⭑ ⭑ **Prices** ⚑ 3-4 ⭑ 1.50-2 pitch
3-4 **Facilities** ⚑ ⊙ ⬚ ∅ ⑫ **Services** ⬚ ⦿ ⊞ ⬚ **Leisure** ❧ R

Facilities ⬚ shop ⚑ shower ⊙ electric points for razors ⬚ electric points for caravans ⑫ parking by tents permitted ⦿ compulsory separate car park
Services ⦿ café/restaurant ⬚ bar ∅ Camping Gaz International ⬜ gas other than Camping Gaz ⊞ first aid facilities ⬚ laundry
Leisure ❧ swimming L-Lake P-Pool R-River S-Sea **Off-site** All facilities within 2km

CLAIRVAUX-LES-LACS JURA

Fayolan

39130 ☎ 384252619 📠 384252620
e-mail reservation@rs139.com
website www.vacances-nature.com
Wooded location beside the lake.

➲ *1.2km SE via D118.*

Open 16 May-9 Sep **Site** 17HEC ⛺ ♣ ⛺ ⛺ Å **Prices** pitch 17-32 (incl 2 persons) pp5-6.50 **Facilities** 🌲 🛁 ⊙ 🚰 ⊘ 🚿 ⊕ **Services** 🍴 🍽 🛒 **Leisure** ⚓ LP **Off-site** ➕

Grisière et Europe Vacances

39130 ☎ 384258048 📠 384252234
e-mail la-grisiere.com
website www.la-grisiere.com
Fenced in meadowland with some trees, sloping down to the Grand Lac. The site is guarded during July and August.

➲ *From village centre off N78 onto D118 towards Châtel-de-Joux for 0.8km.*

Open May-Sep **Site** 11HEC ⛺ ♣ ⛺ **Facilities** 🌲 🛁 ⊙ 🚰 ⊘ ⊕ **Services** 🍴 🍽 ➕ 🛒 **Leisure** ⚓ L

CLUSAZ, LA HAUTE-SAVOIE

Plan du Fernuy

1800, rte des Confins, 74220 ☎ 450024475 📠 450326702
e-mail info@plandufernuy.com
website www.plandufernuy.com
Well placed for skiing or walking. Airing rooms. 30 ski-lifts nearby and several cable cars.

➲ *Off N50 E of La Clusaz towards Les Confins, 2km to site.*

Open 17 Jun-2 Sep & 20 Dec-Apr **Site** 1.3HEC ⛺ ♣ ♣ ⛺ **Prices** pitch 20-23 (incl 2 persons) pp4.50-5 **Facilities** 🌲 🛁 ⊙ 🚰 🚿 ⊕ **Services** 🍴 🍽 🛒 **Leisure** ⚓ P **Off-site** 🍽 ⊘ ➕

DIVONNE-LES-BAINS AIN

Fleutron

Quartier Villard, 01220 ☎ 450200195 📠 450200035
e-mail info@homair-vacances.fr
website www.homair-vacances.fr
Set in wooded surroundings with large individual pitches.

➲ *A40 exit Bellegarde, then D984 to Divonne. A33 exit Poligny, then RN5 to Gex, then D984 to Divonne.*

Open 30 Mar-21 Oct **Site** 8HEC ⛺ ♣ ⛺ ⛺ Å **Prices** ⋔ 4.50-7.50 🚗 2.50-3.50 pitch 5-9.50 ⛺ (static)168-399 **Facilities** 🌲 🛁 ⊙ 🚰 ⊕ 🅿 **Services** 🍴 🍽 🛒 **Leisure** ⚓ P **Off-site** ⚓LR ➕

DOLE JURA

Pasquier

18 Chelin Theremot, 39100 ☎ 384720261 📠 384792344
e-mail lola@camping-le-pasquier.com
website www.camping-le-pasquier.com
Meadow site near River Doubs.

➲ *0.9km SE of town centre.*

Open 15 Mar-15 Oct **Site** 2HEC ⛺ ♣ ♣ ⛺ ⛺ **Facilities** 🌲 🛁 ⊙ 🚰 ⊘ ⊕ **Services** 🍴 🍽 ➕ 🛒 **Leisure** ⚓ PR **Off-site** 🍽 🚿 ⚓L

DOUCIER JURA

Domaine de Chalain

39130 ☎ 384257878 📠 384257006
e-mail chalain@chalain.com
website www.chalain.com
A large site beside Lake Chalain with a variety of recreational facilities.

➲ *3km NE.*

Open May-21 Sep **Site** 20HEC ⛺ ♣ ⛺ ⛺ **Prices** pitch 17.30-28 (incl 3 persons) pp6.53-9 ⛺ (static)317-580 **Facilities** 🌲 🛁 ⊙ 🚰 ⊘ 🚿 ⊕ **Services** 🍴 🍽 ➕ 🛒 **Leisure** ⚓ LP

DOUSSARD HAUTE-SAVOIE

Ravoire

rte de la Ravoire, 74210 ☎ 450443780 📠 45032960
e-mail info@camping-la-ravoire.fr
website www.camping-la-ravoire.fr
A well-appointed, modern site on level ground 0.8km from Lake Annecy. Spectacular mountain views.

➲ *Autoroute exit Annecy Sud for Albertville, N508 to Duingt & signed.*

Open 15 May-15 Sep **Site** 2HEC ⛺ ♣ ⛺ **Prices** pitch 29.30-33.40 (incl 2 persons) pp6 **Facilities** 🌲 🛁 ⊙ 🚰 ⊘ ⊕ **Services** 🍴 🍽 🛒 **Leisure** ⚓ P **Off-site** 🍽 ⚓L

Serraz

r de la Poste, 74210 ☎ 450443068 📠 450448107
e-mail info@campinglaserraz.com
website www.campinglaserraz.com
Modern site divided into pitches. Cosy bar in rustic style.

➲ *At E end of village, N508 onto D181 for 0.5km.*

Open 15 May - 15 Sep **Site** 4HEC ⛺ ♣ ⛺ **Prices** ⋔ 3-5.80 pitch 14.50-31.50 **Facilities** 🌲 ⊙ 🚰 ⊕ **Services** 🍴 🍽 ➕ 🛒 **Leisure** ⚓ P **Off-site** ⊘ ⚓L

EMBRUN HAUTES-ALPES

CM Clapière

av du Lac, 05200 ☎ 492430183
Well-managed site with shaded pitches on stony ground, on N shore of lake. Site shop only open in summer.

➲ *2.5km SW on N94.*

Open May-Sep **Site** 5.3HEC ⛺ ♣ ♣ **Prices** pitch 11.70-14.20 (incl 2 persons) pp4.80 **Facilities** 🌲 ⊙ 🚰 ⊕ **Services** 🛒 **Off-site** 🛁 🍴 🍽 ⊘ 🚿 ⚓LPR ➕

ENTRE-DEUX-GUIERS ISÈRE

Arc en Ciel

r des Berges, 38380 ☎ 476660697 📠 476668805
e-mail info@camping-arc-en-ciel.com
website www.camping-arc-en-ciel.com
A wooded location by the river with well-shaded pitches.

➲ *On D520 300m from N6.*

Open Mar-15 Oct **Site** 1.2HEC ⛺ ♣ ⛺ **Facilities** 🌲 ⊙ 🚰 ⊘ 🚿 ⊕ **Services** ➕ 🛒 **Leisure** ⚓ PR **Off-site** 🛁 🍴 🍽

Site 6HEC (site size) ⛺ grass ⛺ sand ♣ stone ♣ little shade ⛺ partly shaded ⛺ mainly shaded ⛺ bungalows for hire ⛺ caravans for hire Å tents for hire ⊗ no dogs **Prices** ⋔ adult per night 🚗 car per night pp per person per night ⛺ caravan per night Å tent per night ⛺ (static)-caravan hire per week

France

ÉVIAN-LES-BAINS HAUTE-SAVOIE

Clos Savoyard
Maxilly sur Ciman, 74500 ☎ 450752584 📠 450753019
Attractive site with fine views of the lake and the mountains.
➲ Onto D21 in town 1.2km after Hôtel le Maximillien & continue uphill.
Open Jul-Aug **Site** 2HEC 👪 ♣ ♠ ♠ **Facilities** 🗈 ⊙ 🖳 ⑫ **Services** 🛨 🗟
Off-site 🗈 🛨 🍴 ⌀ ♨L

AT AMPHION-LES-BAINS (3.5KM W ON N5)

Plage
304 rue de la Garenne, Amphion les Bains, 74500
☎ 450700046 📠 450708445
e-mail info@camping-dela-plage.com
website www.camping-dela-plage.com
A pleasant site with direct access to the lake. There are good recreational facilities and modern, well-equipped bungalows and chalets are available for hire.
➲ NW of town on N5, 150m from lake.
Open All year **Site** 1HEC 👪 ♣ ♠ **Prices** ♠ 6.10-6.50 pitch 16-22 (incl 2 persons) **Facilities** 🗈 ⊙ 🖳 ♨ ⑫ **Services** 🛨 🍴 🛨 🗟 **Leisure** ♨ P
Off-site 🗈 🍴 ⌀ ♨ ♨LR

FERRIÈRE-D'ALLEVARD ISÈRE

CM Neige et Nature
chemin de Montarmand, 38580 ☎ 476451984
e-mail contact@neige-nature.fr
website www.neige-nature.fr
A beautiful location with spectacular mountain views and modern facilities.
➲ From Allevard D525A towards Le Pleynet.
Open 15 May-15 Sep **Site** 1.2HEC 👪 ♣ ♠ **Prices** ♠ 4.70 pitch 4.70
Facilities 🗈 ⊙ 🖳 ⑫ **Services** 🛨 🍴 🛨 🗟 **Leisure** ♨ PR
Off-site 🗈 ⌀ ♨

GRESSE-EN-VERCORS ISÈRE

4 Saisons
38650 ☎ 0476343027 📠 0476343952
e-mail pieter.aalmoes@wanadoo.fr
website www.camping-les4saisons.com
A picturesque mountain setting with good facilities.
➲ A51 Grenoble-Sisteron exit at Monestier de Clermont and follow signs Gresse-en-Vercors.
Open May-Sept, 20 Dec-15 Mar **Site** 2.2HEC 👪 ♣ ♠ **Prices** ♠ 5.10
♠ 3.50 pitch 14.30 (incl 2 persons) ♠ (static)276-436 **Facilities** 🗈 ⊙ 🖳
⌀ ♨ ⑫ **Services** 🛨 🍴 🗟 **Leisure** ♨ P **Off-site** 🗈 🛨 🍴 ♨R 🛨

GUILLESTRE HAUTES-ALPES

Villard
Le Villard, 5600 ☎ 492450654 📠 492450052
website www.camping-levillard.com
A magnificent location between the Ecrins and Queyras regional parks with good facilities. Bar and café only open July and August.
➲ 2km W via D902A & N4 rte de Gap.
Open All year **Site** 3HEC 👪 ♣ ♠ ♠ Å **Facilities** 🗈 🗈 ⊙ 🖳 ⌀ ♨ ⑫
Services 🛨 🍴 🗟 **Leisure** ♨ PR **Off-site** ⌀ ♨L 🛨

HAUTECOURT-ROMANÈCHE AIN

Ile Chambod
01250 ☎ 474372541 📠 474372828
e-mail camping.chambod@free.fr
website www.campingilechambod.com
A well-equipped site close to the River Ain where swimming is supervised by lifeguards. Good sanitary and recreational facilities.
➲ From Bourg-en-Bresse D979 towards Geneva.
Open May-Sep **Site** 2.5HEC 👪 ♣ ♠ Å **Facilities** 🗈 🗈 ⊙ 🖳 ⌀ ♨ ⑫
Services 🛨 🍴 🛨 🗟 **Leisure** ♨ P **Off-site** ♨LR

HUANNE-MONTMARTIN DOUBS

Bois de Reveuge
25680 ☎ 381843860 📠 381844404
website www.campingduboisdereveuge.com
A terraced site in a 20-hectare park surrounded by the Vosges and Jura mountains with good recreational facilities.
➲ A36 exit Baumes-les-Dames.
Open 23 Apr-17 Sep **Site** 24HEC 👪 ♣ ♠ ♠ **Facilities** 🗈 🗈 ⊙ 🖳 ⌀
♨ ⑫ **Services** 🛨 🍴 🛨 🗟 **Leisure** ♨ LP

ISLE-SUR-LE-DOUBS, L' DOUBS

CM Lumes
10 r des Lumes, 25250 ☎ 381927305 📠 381927305
e-mail jp-paillard@tiscali.fr
The site lies close to the town. Common room with TV.
➲ Off N83. Entrance near bridge over the Doubs.
Open 15 Apr-Sep **Site** 1.5HEC 👪 ♣ ♠ ♠ **Facilities** 🗈 🗈 ⊙ 🖳 ⑫
Services 🗟 **Leisure** ♨ R **Off-site** 🗈 🛨 🍴 ⌀ ♨

LANDRY SAVOIE

Eden
73210 ☎ 479076181 📠 479076217
e-mail info@camping-eden.net
website www.camping-eden.net
A modern site with excellent sports and sanitary facilities, situated in the heart of the Savoie Olympic area.
Open 18 Dec-8 May & Jun-15 Sep **Site** 2.7HEC 👪 ♣ ♠ **Prices** ♠ 3.42-5.70
pitch 3.60-10 ♠ (static)210-315 **Facilities** 🗈 ⊙ 🖳 ♨ ⑫ **Services** 🛨 🍴
🛨 🗟 **Leisure** ♨ PR **Off-site** 🗈 🍴 ⌀ ♨

LONS-LE-SAUNIER JURA

Majorie
640 bd de l'Europe, 39000 ☎ 384242694 📠 384240840
e-mail info@camping-marjorie.com
website www.camping-marjorie.com
Clean, tidy site with tent and caravan sections separated by a stream. Caravan pitches (80 sq m) are gravelled and surrounded by hedges. Heated common room with TV, reading area, kitchen.
➲ Near swimming stadium on outskirts of town.
Open Apr-15 Oct **Site** 9HEC 👪 ♣ ♠ ♠ **Prices** ♠ 1.50-3.80 pitch 10-17.40 (incl 2 persons) **Facilities** 🗈 🗈 ⊙ 🖳 ⌀ ♨ ⑫ **Services** 🛨 🍴 🛨 🗟
Off-site 🍴 ♨P

Facilities 🗈 shop 🗈 shower ⊙ electric points for razors 🖳 electric points for caravans ⑫ parking by tents permitted 🅿 compulsory separate car park
Services 🍴 café/restaurant 🛨 bar ⌀ Camping Gaz International ♨ gas other than Camping Gaz 🛨 first aid facilities 🗟 laundry
Leisure ♨ swimming L-Lake P-Pool R-River S-Sea **Off-site** All facilities within 2km

France

LUGRIN HAUTE-SAVOIE

Myosotis

28 chemin du Grand Tronc, 74500 ☎ 450760759

A terraced site with fine views over the lake and of the surrounding mountains.

➲ *Via D321*

Open 10 May-20 Sep **Site** 0.9HEC 👑 ♣ 🌑 **Prices** ♠ 2.40-2.70 pitch 6.20-6.60 **Facilities** ⋔ ⊙ 🖪 ℗ **Services** ➕ 🗑 **Off-site** 🏠 ⛽ 🍴 🅐 🏖L

Rys

Route le Rys, 74500 ☎ 450760575 🖹 450760575

e-mail jeanmichel.blanc@wanadoo.fr

Calm shady site with panoramic views of the lake and mountains. 10min walk from the beach

➲ *Signed W of town.*

Open 30 Apr-1 Oct **Site** 1.5HEC 👑 ♣ 🌑 🚐 **Prices** ♠ 3 pitch 6 (incl 2 persons) 🚐 (static)245 **Facilities** ⋔ ⊙ 🖪 🅐 🏔 ℗ **Services** ➕ 🗑 **Off-site** 🏠 ⛽ 🍴 🏖L

Vieille Église

74500 ☎ 450760195 🖹 450761312

e-mail campingvieilleeglise@wanadoo.fr

website www.camping-vieille-eglise.com

On rising meadow between lake and mountains with good views. Close to lake Léman and its beaches.

➲ *D24 to Neuvecelle, onto D21, 1km on right after Maxilly.*

Open 10 Apr-20 Oct **Site** 1.5HEC 👑 ♣ 🌑 🚐 **Prices** pitch 17.50 (incl 2 persons) 🚐 (static)198-395 **Facilities** ⋔ 🏠 ⊙ 🖪 🅐 🏔 ℗ **Services** ➕ 🍴 ➕ 🗑 **Leisure** 🏊 P **Off-site** 🏠 🏔 🏖L

MALBUISSON DOUBS

Fuvettes

25160 ☎ 381693150 🖹 381697046

e-mail les-fuvettes@wanadoo.fr

website camping-fuvettes.com

Mainly level site with some terraces at an altitude of 900m in the Jura mountains, gently sloping towards a lake.

➲ *0.5km S on D437.*

Open Apr-Sep **Site** 6HEC 👑 ♣ 🌑 🚐 **Facilities** ⋔ 🏠 ⊙ 🖪 🅐 🏔 ℗ **Services** ➕ 🍴 ➕ 🗑 **Leisure** 🏊 LP

MARIGNY JURA

Sunelia la Pergola

39130 ☎ 384257003 🖹 384257596

e-mail contact@lapergola.com

website www.lapergola.com

A well-equipped, terraced site with direct access to the lake.

➲ *S of Marigny off D27.*

Open 15 May-19 Sep **Site** 12HEC 👑 🌑 ♣ 🚐 **Facilities** ⋔ 🏠 ⊙ 🖪 🅐 ℗ **Services** ➕ 🍴 ➕ 🗑 **Leisure** 🏊 LP **Off-site** 🏖R

MATAFELON-GRANGES AIN

Gorges de l'Oignin

r du Lac, 1580 ☎ 474768097 🖹 474768097

e-mail camping.lesgorgesdeloignin@wanadoo.fr

Rural site on the banks of a lake surrounded by low mountains.

➲ *A404 exit 11, site signed after 1.6km.*

Open Apr-Sep **Site** 2.6HEC 👑 ♣ 🚐 **Prices** pitch 12.60-15.20 (incl 2 persons) **Facilities** ⋔ 🏠 ⊙ 🖪 🏔 ℗ **Services** ➕ 🍴 ➕ 🗑 **Leisure** 🏊 LP

MÉAUDRE ISÈRE

Buissonnets

38112 ☎ 476952104 🖹 476952614

e-mail camping-les-buissonnets@wanadoo.fr

website www.camping-les-buissonets.com

A quiet, friendly site in the heart of the Vercors regional park, with modern sanitary blocks and a range of summer and winter recreational facilities.

➲ *200m from village centre.*

Open 15 Dec-1 Nov **Site** 2.7HEC 👑 ♣ 🚐 **Prices** ⛺ 10 pitch 14 (incl 2 persons) pp4 **Facilities** ⋔ 🏠 ⊙ 🖪 🏔 🅖 **Services** 🗑 **Off-site** ➕ 🍴 🅐 🏖PR ➕

MESNOIS JURA

Beauregard

2 Grande Rue ☎ 384483251 🖹 384483251

e-mail reception@juracampingbeuregard.com

website www.juracampingbeauregard.com

Open Apr-Sep **Site** 6HEC 👑 ♣ 🚐 ⛺ **Prices** ⛺ 3.20-4 pitch 16-21 **Facilities** ⋔ 🏠 ⊙ 🖪 🅐 🏔 ℗ **Services** ➕ 🍴 ➕ 🗑 **Leisure** 🏊 PR **Off-site** 🏖L

See advertisement on this page

MESSERY HAUTE-SAVOIE

Relais du Léman
74140 ☎ 450947111 🖹 450947766
e-mail info@relaisduleman.com
website www.relaisduleman.com
Well-equipped site in a wooded location on the shore of Lac Léman.
➜ *1.5km SW via D25.*
Open Apr-Sep **Site** 3.5HEC ⛺ ♣ ⌂ ⚏ **Prices** ♠ 6 ♠ 5 ⚏ 5.50 ⚑ 5.50
⚏ (static)420 **Facilities** 🌃 ⊙ 🖳 ⊘ 🅿 **Services** ⛽ 🍴 🖻 **Leisure** ⚓ P
Off-site 🖻 ⚓LP ⛨

MEYRIEU-LES-ÉTANGS ISÈRE

Moulin
38440 ☎ 474593034 🖹 474583612
e-mail basedeloisirs.du.moulin@wanadoo.fr
website www.camping-meyrieu.com
A quiet rural setting with good recreational facilities.
➜ *On D552 between Vienne & Bourgoin-Jallieu.*
Open 15 Apr-Sep **Site** 1.5HEC ⛺ ⌂ 🌃 🖻 ⊙ 🖳 🅿
Services ⛽ 🍴 ⛨ 🖻 **Leisure** ⚓ L **Off-site** 🍴

MIRIBEL-LES-ÉCHELLES ISÈRE

Balcon de Chartreuse
950 chemin de la Foiet, 38380 ☎ 476552853 🖹 476552582
e-mail balcondechartreuse@wanadoo.fr
website www.camping-balcondechartreuse.com
A peaceful site in the heart of the Parc Régional de Chartreuse, with
fine views of the surrounding mountains.
➜ *400m from village centre.*
Open Apr-Oct **Site** 2.5HEC ⛺ ♣ ⌂ 🌃 **Facilities** 🌃 ⊙ 🖳 ⚒ 🅿
Services ⛽ 🍴 ⛨ 🖻 **Leisure** ⚓ P **Off-site** 🖻 ⛨

MONTMAUR HAUTES-ALPES

Mon Repos
5400 ☎ 592580314
Generally well-kept site on wooded terrain with shaded pitches.
➜ *1km E on D937 & D994.*
Open May-Oct **Site** 7HEC ⛺ ♣ ⌂ 🌃 **Facilities** 🌃 ⊙ 🖳 ⊘ 🅿
Services ⛽ 🍴 ⛨ 🖻 **Leisure** ⚓ LR **Off-site** 🍴

MONTREVEL-EN-BRESSE AIN

Plaine Tonique
Base de Plein Air, 01340 ☎ 474308052 🖹 474308077
e-mail plaine.tonique@wanadoo.fr
website www.laplainetonique.com
A well-equipped site divided into a series of self contained sections
beside the lake. Entrance closed between 22.00 & 07.00 hrs. Booking
advised for July and August.
➜ *0.5km E on D28.*
Open 19 Apr-26 Sep **Site** 17HEC ⛺ ♣ 🌃 **Prices** ♠ 3.10-5.10 pitch 7-11.50
Facilities 🌃 ⊙ 🖳 ⊘ ⚒ 🅿 **Services** ⛽ 🍴 ⛨ 🖻 **Leisure** ⚓ LP
Off-site ⚓R

MURS-ET-GELIGNIEUX AIN

Ile de la Comtesse
rte des Abrets, 1300 ☎ 479872333 🖹 479872333
e-mail camping.comtesse@wanadoo.fr
website www.ile-de-la-comtesse.com
A stunning natural setting beneath the Alps next to Lake Cuchet (part
of the Rhone), with direct access to the water.
➜ *A43 exit 10, D592 to La Bruyere, site off route to Belley.*
Open 17 May-1 Sep **Site** 3HEC ⛺ ♣ 🌃 **Prices** ♠ 5.60-6.90 pitch 18-23
(incl 2 persons) 🌃 (static)250-580 **Facilities** 🌃 🖻 ⊙ 🖳 ⚒ 🅿
Services ⛽ 🍴 🖻 **Leisure** ⚓ PR **Off-site** ⚓L

NEYDENS HAUTE-SAVOIE

Colombière
74160 ☎ 450351314 🖹 450351340
e-mail la.colombiere@wanadoo.fr
website www.camping-la-colombiere.com
A pleasant, friendly site with good recreational facilities.
➜ *Via A40.*
Open Apr-Sep **Site** 2.2HEC ⛺ ♣ ♣ ⌂ **Facilities** 🌃 🖻 ⊙ 🖳 ⊘ 🅿
Services ⛽ 🍴 ⛨ 🖻 **Leisure** ⚓ P **Off-site** 🖻 ⚓R

NOVALAISE SAVOIE

Charmilles
Lac d'Aiguebelette, 73470 ☎ 479360467 🖹 479360467
e-mail camping.les.charmilles@wanadoo.fr
website www.marmotte.com/charmilles
A terraced site in a beautiful mountain setting, 150m from the lake.
➜ *On W shore of lake on D941 towards St-Alban-de-Montbel.*
Open Jul-Aug **Site** 2.3HEC ⛺ ♣ ♣ **Facilities** 🌃 🖻 ⊙ 🖳 ⊘ 🅿
Services ⛨ 🖻 **Off-site** ⛽ 🍴 ⚓L

ORNANS DOUBS

Chanet
9 chemin de Chanet, 25290 ☎ 381622344 🖹 381621397
e-mail contact@lechanet.com
website www.lechanet.com
Comfortable site with good facilities in the peaceful Loue valley.
➜ *1.5km SW on D241, green signs.*
Open Mar-Oct **Site** 2.2HEC ⛺ ♣ ⌂ 🌃 ⚑ **Facilities** 🌃 🖻 ⊙ 🖳 ⊘ 🅿
Services ⛽ 🍴 ⛨ 🖻 **Leisure** ⚓ P **Off-site** ⚒ ⚓R

ORPIERRE HAUTES-ALPES

Princes d'Orange
05700 ☎ 492662253 🖹 492663108
e-mail campingorpierre@wanadoo.fr
website www.campingorpierre.com
The site lies on a meadow with terraces.
➜ *N75 exit Eyguians onto D30.*
Open Apr-28 Oct **Site** 20HEC ⛺ ♣ ♣ 🌃 ⚑ **Prices** pitch 15-20 (incl 2
persons) 🌃 (static)285-525 **Facilities** 🌃 ⊙ 🖳 🅿 **Services** ⛽ 🍴 ⛨ 🖻
Leisure ⚓ P **Off-site** 🖻 ⊘ ⚓R

France

Facilities 🖻 shop 🌃 shower ⊙ electric points for razors 🖳 electric points for caravans 🅿 parking by tents permitted 🅿 compulsory separate car park
Services 🍴 café/restaurant ⛽ bar ⊘ Camping Gaz International ⚒ gas other than Camping Gaz ⛨ first aid facilities 🖻 laundry
Leisure ⚓ swimming L-Lake P-Pool R-River S-Sea **Off-site** All facilities within 2km

France

OUNANS JURA

Plage Blanche

3 r de la Plage, 39380 ☎ 384376963 📠 384376021
e-mail reservation@la-plage-blanche.com
website www.la-plage-blanche.com
Pleasant location beside the River Loue with good recreational facilities.
➲ *1.5km S via D71 rte de Montbarcy.*
Open Apr-Sep **Site** 7HEC ❤️ ❤️ 🏠 ⛺ **Prices** ⚹ 4.70 pitch 5.90
Facilities 🍴 🏠 ⊙ ⚑ ⑦ **Services** 🗲 ⍟ 🖸 **Leisure** ⚓ PR **Off-site** ⌀

PARCEY JURA

Bords de Loue

Chemin du Val d'Amour, 39100 ☎ 384710382 📠 384710342
e-mail contact@jura-camping.com
website www.jura-camping.com
A quiet site on the River Loue.
➲ *1.5km from village centre via N5, signed.*
Open 20 Apr-10 Sep **Site** 18HEC ❤️ ❤️ 🏠 ⛺ ⛺ **Prices** ⚹ 4.30 pitch 4.90
⛺ (static)130-310 **Facilities** 🍴 ⊙ ⚑ ⌀ ⑦ **Services** 🗲 ⍟ 🖸 🖸
Leisure ⚓ PR **Off-site** 🏠 ⍟

PATORNAY JURA

Moulin

39130 ☎ 384483121 📠 384447121
e-mail contact@camping-moulin.com
website www.camping-moulin.com
A modern site on a level meadow in a peaceful, wooded location on the banks of the River Ain.
➲ *NE via N78 rte de Clairvaux-les-Lacs.*
Open 20 May-17 Sep **Site** 5HEC ❤️ ❤️ 🏠 ⛺ **Prices** ⚹ 5 **Facilities** 🍴 🏠 ⊙
⚑ ⌀ 🛒 ⑦ **Services** 🗲 ⍟ 🖸 **Leisure** ⚓ PR **Off-site** ⍟ ⚓L 🖸

PLAGNE-MONTCHAVIN SAVOIE

Montchavin les Coches

73210 ☎ 479078323 📠 479078018
e-mail info@montchavin-lescoches.com
website www.montchavin-lescoches.com
A summer and winter site overlooking the Tarentaise valley with modern facilities.
Open Nov-Sep **Site** 1.3HEC ❤️ ❤️ **Prices** pitch 12.50 (incl 2 persons)
Facilities 🍴 ⊙ ⚑ 🛒 ⑦ **Services** 🖸 🖸 **Off-site** 🏠 🗲 ⍟ ⌀ ⚓P

PONT-DE-VAUX AIN

Rives du Soleil

Port de Fleurville, 01190 ☎ 385303365 📠 385303365
e-mail info@rivesdusoleil.com
website www.rivesdusoleil.com
A family site beside the River Saône with good facilities.
➲ *3km from Pont-de-Vaux via N6.*
Open Apr-Sep **Site** 7HEC ❤️ ❤️ 🏠 ⛺ **Facilities** 🍴 🏠 ⊙ ⚑ ⌀ 🛒 ⑦
Services 🗲 ⍟ 🖸 🖸 **Leisure** ⚓ PR

PORT-SUR-SAÔNE HAUTE-SAÔNE

CM Maladière

70170 ☎ 384915132 📠 384781809
A quiet, comfortable site with modern facilities, close to the River Saône.
➲ *S on the D6, between River Saône & canal.*
Open 15 May-15 Sep **Site** 2HEC ❤️ ❤️ **Facilities** 🍴 ⊙ ⚑ ⑦ **Services** 🖸
🖸 **Off-site** 🏠 🗲 ⍟ ⌀ ⚓PR

PRESLE SAVOIE

Combe Léat

73110 ☎ 479255402
A quiet mountain site.
➲ *Via A43 & D207.*
Open 15 Jun-5 Sep **Site** 4HEC ❤️ ❤️ ⛺ **Facilities** 🍴 ⊙ ⚑ ⑦
Services 🖸 🖸

RENAGE ISÈRE

Verdon

185 av de la Piscine, 38140 ☎ 476914802
➲ *5km N of Tullins on D45.*
Open Apr-15 Oct **Site** 1.5HEC ❤️ ❤️ **Facilities** 🍴 ⊙ ⚑ ⌀ ⑦
Services 🖸 🖸 **Off-site** 🏠 🗲 ⍟ 🛒 ⚓PR

ROCHETTE, LA SAVOIE

Lac St-Clair

73110 ☎ 479257355 📠 479257825
website www.la-rochette.com
At the foot of the Belledonne mountains, 1km from a lake with good fishing.
➲ *Via D925B Grenoble-Albertville.*
Open Jul-Sep **Site** 3HEC ❤️ ❤️ 🏠 ⛺ **Prices** ⚹ 15 ⛟ 7 ⛺ 11 **Facilities** 🍴
⊙ ⚑ ⑦ **Services** 🗲 ⍟ 🖸 🖸 **Leisure** ⚓ L **Off-site** 🏠 ⍟ ⌀ 🛒 ⚓P

ROSIÈRE-DE-MONTVALEZAN, LA SAVOIE

Forêt

73700 ☎ 79068621 📠 79401625
e-mail campinglaforet@free.fr
website www.campinglaforet.free.fr
A peaceful site in pleasant wooded surroundings, with modern facilities.
➲ *2km S via N90 towards Bourg-St-Maurice.*
Open 10 Jun-15 Sep & 15 Dec-1 May **Site** 2.7HEC ❤️ ❤️ 🏠 ⛺ ⛺
Prices ⚹ 4.03 ⛟ 4.10 🚗 2.60 ⛺ (static)425 **Facilities** 🍴 ⊙ ⚑ 🛒 ⑦
Services 🗲 ⍟ 🖸 🖸 **Leisure** ⚓ P **Off-site** 🏠 ⍟ ⌀ ⚓R

ROUGEMONT DOUBS

🏠 Val de Bonnal

Bonnal, 25680 ☎ 381869087 📠 381860392
e-mail val-de-bonnal@wanadoo.fr
Quiet woodland site beside the River Ognon. Supervised swimming in lake with beach.
Open 8 May-5 Sep **Site** 15HEC ❤️ ❤️ 🏠 ⛺ **Facilities** 🍴 🏠 ⊙ ⚑ ⌀ ⑦
Services 🗲 ⍟ 🖸 🖸 **Leisure** ⚓ LPR

Site 6HEC (site size) ❤️ grass ❤️ sand ❤️ stone ❤️ little shade ❤️ partly shaded ❤️ mainly shaded 🏠 bungalows for hire
⛺ caravans for hire ⛺ tents for hire ⊗ no dogs **Prices** ⚹ adult per night ⛟ car per night pp per person per night ⛺ caravan per night
⛺ tent per night ⛺ (static)-caravan hire per week

France

ST-CLAIR-DU-RHÔNE ISÈRE

Daxia
rte du Péage, 38370 ☎ 474563920 ▤ 474569346
A riverside site with good sanitary and recreational facilities.
➾ *Via N7/A7.*
Open Apr-Sep **Site** 7.5HEC ♨ ♣ ♠ ⇎ **Facilities** ☏ ⊙ ⊟ ℗ **Services** �'○' ▣ **Leisure** ⚓ PR

ST-CLAUDE JURA

Martinet
39200 ☎ 384450040
A wooded location close to the Centre Nautique.
➾ *2km SE beside river.*
Open May-Sep **Site** 3HEC ♨ ♣ **Facilities** ☏ ☖ ⊙ ⊟ ℗ **Services** ▤' '○' ▣ **Leisure** ⚓ R **Off-site** ⚒ ⚓P

ST-GERVAIS-LES-BAINS HAUTE-SAVOIE

Dômes de Miage
197 rte des Contamines, 74170 ☎ 450934596 ▤ 450781075
e-mail info@camping-mont-blanc.com
website www.camping-mont-blanc.com
On a beautiful wooded plateau with fine views of the surrounding mountains.
➾ *2km S on D902.*
Open 12 May-23 Sep **Site** 2.5HEC ♨ ♣ **Prices** pitch 16.50-20.50 (incl 2 persons) **Facilities** ☏ ☖ ⊙ ⊟ ⊘ ℗ **Services** ▤' '○' ➕ ▣ **Off-site** ⚒ ⚓P

ST-JEAN-DE-COUZ SAVOIE

International la Bruyère
73160 ☎ 479657911 ▤ 479657427
e-mail bearob@libertysurf.fr
website www.camping-labruyere.com
Wooded surroundings close to the Grande Chartreuse range with a variety of sports facilities.
➾ *2km S via N6 towards Côte-Barrier.*
Open 25 Apr-10 Oct **Site** 1HEC ♨ ♣ ♠ **Prices** ♠ 3.10 pitch 3 ⇎ (static)260 **Facilities** ☏ ☖ ⊙ ⊟ ℗ **Services** ▤' '○'➕▣ **Off-site** ⚓R

ST JEAN-DE-MAURIENNE SAVOIE

CM des Grands Cols
408-436 Av du Mont-Cenis ☎ 479642802 ▤ 479642802
e-mail camping@saintjeandemaurienne.fr
website www.saintjeandemaurienne.fr/tourisme/campfr.html
A tranquil site at the mouth of the Arvan valley with panoramic views of the Alps on the outskirts of the city.
➾ *In town signs for camping municipal, site opp high school.*
Open May-15 Sep **Site** 3HEC ♨ ♣ ♠ ⚠ **Facilities** ☏ ⊙ ⊟ ℗ **Services** ▤' '○' ▣ **Off-site** ☖ ⊘ ⚓P ➕

ST-JEAN-ST-NICOLAS HAUTES-ALPES

CM le Châtelard
Pont-du-Fossé, 5260 ☎ 492559431
e-mail comstjeanstnicolas@wanadoo.fr
Open 15 Jun-15 Sep **Site** 4HEC ♨ ♣ **Prices** ♠ 3.40 ⇎ 4.60 ⚠ 3.80 **Facilities** ☏ ⊙ ⊟ ℗ **Services** ➕ ▣ **Leisure** ⚓ R **Off-site** ☖ ⊘ '○' ⊘ ⚒ ⚓LP

ST-JORIOZ HAUTE-SAVOIE

Europa
1444 rte d'Albertville, 74410 ☎ 450685101 ▤ 450685520
e-mail info@camping-europa.com
website www.camping-europa.com
Well-equipped site in picturesque surroundings close to Lake Annecy.
➾ *1.4km SE.*
Open 7 May-15 Sep **Site** 3.7HEC ♨ ♣ ♠ ⇎ **Prices** pitch 18.50-30.50 (incl 2 persons) **Facilities** ☏ ⊙ ⊟ ℗ **Services** ▤' '○' ▣ **Leisure** ⚓ P **Off-site** ☖ ⊘ ⚒ ⚓L ➕

International du Lac d'Annecy
74410 ☎ 450686793 ▤ 450090122
e-mail campannecy@wanadoo.fr
website www.campannecy.com
➾ *N508 towards Albertville.*
Open 20 May-15 Sep **Site** 2.5HEC ♨ ♣ ♠ **Prices** pitch 14.50-18 (incl 2 persons) ⇎ (static)260-560 **Facilities** ☏ ⊙ ⊟ ℗ **Services** ▤' '○' ➕ ▣ **Leisure** ⚓ P **Off-site** ☖ ⊘ ⚒ ⚓L

ST-LAURENT-EN-BEAUMONT ISÈRE

Belvédère de l'Obiou
rte Napoléon, Lieu-dit les Egats, 38350
☎ 476304080 ▤ 476304486
e-mail info@camping-obiou.com
website www.camping-obiou.com
Terraced meadow site at the foot of mountains with hedge surrounds.
➾ *1.6km from Ortsteil Les Egats on N85, signed.*
Open Apr-15 Oct **Site** 1HEC ♨ ♣ ♠ ⇎ **Facilities** ☏ ⊙ ⊟ ⊘ ⚒ ℗ **Services** '○' ➕ ▣ **Leisure** ⚓ P **Off-site** ▤' ➕

ST-MARTIN-SUR-LA-CHAMBRE SAVOIE

Bois Joli
St Martin-sur-la-Chambre, 73130 ☎ 479562128
e-mail camping-le-bois-joli@wanadoo.fr
website www.campingleboisjoli.com
Well-kept site with pitches and individual washing cabins.
➾ *1km N of St-Avre, off N6-E70 via La Chambre.*
Open 15 Apr-15 Oct **Site** 4HEC ♨ ♣ ♠ **Prices** pitch 10-13 (incl 2 persons) **Facilities** ☏ ⊙ ⊟ ℗ **Services** ▤' '○' ➕ ▣ **Leisure** ⚓ P **Off-site** ☖

ST-PIERRE-DE-CHARTREUSE ISÈRE

Martinière
rte du Col de Porte, 38380 ☎ 476886036 ▤ 476886910
e-mail brice.gaude@wanadoo.fr
website www.campingdemartiniere.com
Pleasant position among the Chartreuse mountains and close to the famous monastery.
➾ *2km SW off D512.*
Open 28 Apr-16 Sep **Site** 2.5HEC ♨ ♣ ♠ **Prices** pitch 13.50-17 (incl 2 persons) **Facilities** ☏ ☖ ⊙ ⊟ ⊘ ⚒ ℗ **Services** ▤' '○' ➕ ▣ **Leisure** ⚓ P **Off-site** '○'

Facilities ☖ shop ☏ shower ⊙ electric points for razors ⊟ electric points for caravans ℗ parking by tents permitted ⦿ compulsory separate car park
Services '○' café/restaurant ▤' bar ⊘ Camping Gaz International ⚒ gas other than Camping Gaz ➕ first aid facilities ▣ laundry
Leisure ⚓ swimming L-Lake P-Pool R-River S-Sea **Off-site** All facilities within 2km

SALLE-EN-BEAUMONT, LA ISÈRE

Champ-Long

38350 ☎ 476304181 ▤ 476304721
e-mail champ.long@tiscali.fr
website www.camping-champlong.com
A beautiful Alpine setting at the entrance to the Ecrins park at an altitude of 700m.
➲ *1.5km NW off N85*

Open 15 Nov-15 Oct **Site** 5HEC 😃 ♨ ♣ 🏠 🚐 Å **Prices** ⋔ 3.80-3.80 pitch 13-15 🚐 (static)200-280 **Facilities** 🌣 🏠 ⊙ 🚰 ♨ ⊕ ❷ **Services** ⋮ 🍴 ⊞ 🖺 **Leisure** ⇌ P **Off-site** ⊘ ⇌LR

SÉEZ SAVOIE

Reclus

rte de Tignes, 73700 ☎ 479410105 ▤ 479410479
e-mail campinglereclus@wanadoo.fr
website www.campingsavoie.com
Pleasant wooded location within easy reach of the ski slopes.
➲ *NW on N90.*

Open Dec-Oct **Site** 1.8HEC 😃 ♨ 🚐 **Facilities** 🌣 ⊙ 🚰 ℗ **Services** ⊞ 🖺 **Leisure** ⇌ R **Off-site** 🏠 ⋮ 🍴 ⊘ ♨ ⇌P

SERRES HAUTES-ALPES

Barillons

05700 ☎ 492671735
e-mail camping.les.barillons@wanadoo.fr
Well-laid out with terraces.
➲ *1km SE on N75.*

Open Mid May-Mid Sep **Site** 3HEC 😃 ♨ 🚐 Å **Prices** ⋔ 3.60 pitch 13.30 (incl 2 persons) 🚐 (static)150-230 **Facilities** 🌣 ⊙ 🚰 ⊘ ℗ **Services** ⋮ 🍴 ⊞ 🖺 **Leisure** ⇌ P **Off-site** 🏠 🍴 ⇌LR

Domaine des 2 Soleils

05700 ☎ 492670133 ▤ 492670802
e-mail dom.2.soleils@wanadoo.fr
website perso.orange.fr/2soleils
Well-kept terraced site in Buéch valley.
➲ *S of town off N75, signed.*

Open May-Sep **Site** 12HEC 😃 ♨ ♣ 🏠 🚐 **Prices** ⋔ 11.65-17.90 🚐 (static)290 **Facilities** 🌣 🏠 ⊙ 🚰 ⊘ ♨ ℗ **Services** ⋮ 🍴 ⊞ 🖺 **Leisure** ⇌ P **Off-site** ⇌LR

SEVRIER HAUTE-SAVOIE

Coeur du Lac

☎ 450524645 ▤ 450190145
e-mail info@aucoeurdulac.com
website www.campingaucoeurdulac.com
Site adjacent to Lake Annecy with direct access to the lake and beach and fine views of the Alps.
➲ *RN508 exit Albertville, through Annecy to Sevrier, 100m after McDonald's.*

Open Apr-Sep **Site** 2.7HEC 😃 ♨ ♣ 🚐 **Prices** pitch 14.70-18 pp3-3.40 **Facilities** 🌣 🏠 ⊙ 🚰 ⊘ ℗ **Services** 🍴 ⊞ 🖺 **Leisure** ⇌ L **Off-site** ⋮ ♨

SEYSSEL AIN

International de Seyssel

chemin de la Barotte, 01420 ☎ 450592847 ▤ 450592847
e-mail camp.inter@wanadoo.fr
A quiet site on steep, terraced meadowland, with individual washbasins and clean sanitary installations.
➲ *1km SW off Culoz road.*

Open 15 Jun-15 Sep **Site** 1.5HEC 😃 ♨ 🏠 🚐 **Facilities** 🌣 ⊙ 🚰 ⊘ ♨ ℗ **Services** ⋮ 🍴 ⊞ 🖺 **Leisure** ⇌ P **Off-site** 🏠 ⇌LR

TALLOIRES HAUTE-SAVOIE

Lanfonnet

Angon, 74290 ☎ 450607212 ▤ 45060712 & 450233882
e-mail camping.le.lanfonnet@wanadoo.fr
website www.camping-lanfonnet.com
A well-equipped site 100m from the lake.
➲ *1.5km SE.*

Open May-Sep **Site** 2.5HEC 😃 ♨ 🏠 🚐 **Facilities** 🌣 🏠 ⊙ 🚰 ⊘ ℗ **Services** ⋮ 🍴 ⊞ 🖺 **Leisure** ⇌ L

THOISSEY AIN

CM

01140 ☎ 474040425
e-mail mairie.thoissey@wanadoo.fr
Situated between the rivers Saône and Chalaronne.
➲ *1km SW on D7.*

Open 20 Apr-20 Sep **Site** 15HEC 😃 ♨ 🚐 **Facilities** 🌣 ⊙ 🚰 ℗ **Services** ⋮ 🍴 ⊞ 🖺 **Leisure** ⇌ PR **Off-site** 🏠 ⊘ ♨

THONON-LES-BAINS HAUTE-SAVOIE

Morcy

74200 ☎ 450704487 ▤ 450704487
A quiet location close to Lac Léman and the thermal spa.
➲ *2.5km W of town.*

Open 15 Apr-15 Sep **Site** 1.2HEC 😃 ♨ 🏠 🚐 **Facilities** 🌣 ⊙ 🚰 ⊘ ℗ **Services** ⋮ 🍴 ⊞ **Off-site** 🏠 🍴 ⇌LR

TIGNES-LES-BRÉVIÈRES SAVOIE

Europeen dea Brevieres

rte des Boisses, 73320 ☎ 479064586 ▤ 479040745
e-mail contact@camping-de-tignes.com
website www.camping-de-tignes-les-brevieres.com
A well-equipped site 1km from the centre of the village.
➲ *Signed from D902*

Open 15 May-15 Oct **Site** 4.5HEC 😃 ♣ 🏠 **Facilities** 🌣 🏠 ⊙ 🚰 ⊘ ℗ **Services** ⋮ 🍴 ⊞ 🖺 **Leisure** ⇌ P **Off-site** ⇌LPR

TREPT ISÈRE

3 Lac

La Plaine, 38460 ☎ 474929206 ▤ 474834381
e-mail info@les3lacsdusoleil.com
website www.les3lacsdusoleil.com
Situated at the gateway to the Alps, an undulating wooded area with small lakes.
➲ *2.5km W on D517*

Open May-10 Sep **Site** 26HEC 😃 ♣ 🏠 **Prices** pitch 15.50-31 (incl 2 persons) pp3-7 **Facilities** 🌣 🏠 ⊙ 🚰 ⊘ ℗ **Services** ⋮ 🍴 ⊞ 🖺 **Leisure** ⇌ LP

Site 6HEC (site size) 😃 grass ⊜ sand ♨ stone ♣ little shade ♧ partly shaded ⊜ mainly shaded 🏠 bungalows for hire 🚐 caravans for hire Å tents for hire ⊗ no dogs **Prices** ⋔ adult per night 🚗 car per night pp per person per night 🚐 caravan per night Å tent per night 🚐 (static)-caravan hire per week

VERNIOZ ISÈRE

Bontemps
38150 ☎ 474578352 🖷 474578370
e-mail info@campinglebontemps.com
website www.campinglebontemps.com
A pleasantly landscaped site beside the River Varèze.
➲ N7 onto D131
Open Apr-Sept **Site** 8HEC 😃 🏕 **Prices** ♠ 5 ♠ 2 ♠ 6.50 ▲ 6.50
Facilities ⚡ 🖻 ⊙ 🖸 ⊘ 🚿 ⑳ **Services** 🍴 🍽 ➕ 🖫 **Leisure** ♨ PR

VILLARD-DE-LANS ISERE

L'Oursière
38250 ☎ 476951477 🖷 476955811
e-mail info@camping-oursiere.fr
website www.camping-oursiere.fr
Peaceful site in the Vercors regional park. Summer and winter facilities.
➲ N off D531 towards Grenoble.
Open 4 Dec-Sep **Site** 4.2HEC 😃 🏕 **Prices** pitch 13.50-15.75 (incl 2
persons) pp3.80-4.50 ♠ (static)229-599 **Facilities** ⚡ ⊙ 🖸 ⊘ 🚿 ⑳
Services 🍴 🍽 ➕ 🖫 **Leisure** ♨ R **Off-site** ♨P

VILLARS-LES-DOMBES AIN

Intercommunal des Autières
164 av des Nations, 01330 ☎ 474980021 🖷 474980582
e-mail autieres@campingendombes.fr
website www.campingendombes.fr
Clean and tidy park-like site divided into plots and pitches. Part
reserved for overnight campers. Clean, modern sanitary installations.
➲ SW off N83.
Open 8 Apr-24 Sep **Site** 4.5HEC 😃 🏕 **Prices** ♠ 4 ♠ 2.50 pitch 8
Facilities ⚡ ⊙ 🖸 ⑳ **Services** 🍴 🍽 🖫 **Leisure** ♨ PR
Off-site 🖻 ⊘ 🚿 ➕

ALSACE/LORRAINE

ANOULD VOSGES

Acacias
88650 ☎ 329571106 🖷 329571106
e-mail contact@acaciascamp.com
website www.acaciascamp.com
Pleasant surroundings with well-defined pitches in the heart of the
Hautes-Vosges region.
➲ NE of town centre towards ski slopes.
Open Dec-10 Oct **Site** 2.5HEC 😃 🏕 **Prices** ♠ 3.50 pitch 3.60
♠ (static)120-320 **Facilities** ⚡ 🖻 ⊙ 🖸 ⊘ 🚿 ⑳ **Services** 🍴 🍽 ➕ 🖫
Leisure ♨ P **Off-site** 🖻 ♨R

AUBURE HAUT-RHIN

CM La Ménère
68150 ☎ 389739299 🖷 389739345
e-mail aubure@cc-ribeauville.fr
A peaceful site at an altitude of 800m.
➲ N415 or D416 onto D11.
Open 15 May-Sep **Site** 1.8HEC 😃 🏕 **Prices** ♠ 3.70 pitch 3.15
Facilities ⚡ ⊙ 🖸 ⑳ **Services** ➕ 🖫 **Off-site** 🖻 🍴 🍽

BAERENTHAL MOSELLE

Ramstein Plage
Base de Baerenthal, Ramstein Plage, 57230
☎ 387065073 🖷 387065073
e-mail camping.ramstein@wanadoo.fr
website www.baerenthal.eu
The River Zinsel runs through this rural wooded site close to the
border with Germany.
➲ W via r du Ramstein.
Open Apr-Sep **Site** 14HEC 😃 🏕 **Prices** ♠ 3.80 pitch 5.30-9.50
Facilities ⚡ ⊙ 🖸 ⑳ **Services** 🍴 🍽 ➕ 🖫 **Leisure** ♨ LP
Off-site 🖻 ⊘ ♨R

BIESHEIM HAUT-RHIN

Ile du Rhin
Zone Touristique, 68600 ☎ 389725795 🖷 389721421
e-mail camping@paysdebrisach.fr
website www.campingiledurhin.com
On the Ile du Rhin, between the Canal d'Alsace and the River Rhine in
pleasant wooded surroundings.
➲ From Colmar N415 to Rhine bridge.
Open early Apr-early Oct **Site** 3HEC 😃 🏕 **Prices** ♠ 4.10 pitch 13.96 (incl
2 persons) **Facilities** ⚡ 🖻 ⊙ 🖸 ⑳ **Services** 🍴 🍽 ➕ 🖫 **Off-site** ♨PR
See advertisement on this page

BRESSE, LA VOSGES

Belle Hutte
Belle Hutte, 88250 ☎ 329254975 🖷 329255263
e-mail camping-belle-hutte@wanadoo.fr
website www.camping-belle-hutte.com
Terraced site beside the River Moselotte.
➲ D34 towards Col de la Schlucht.
Open All year **Site** 3.2HEC 😃 🏕 **Prices** ♠ 3.70-6.20 ♠ 2.30-2.75
♠ 2.30-3.70 ▲ 2.30-3.70 **Facilities** ⚡ 🖻 ⊙ 🖸 ⊘ 🚿 ⑳ **Services** 🍴 🖫
Leisure ♨ PR **Off-site** 🍽 ♨L ➕

BURNHAUPT-LE-HAUT HAUT-RHIN

Le Castors
4 rte de Guewenheim, 68520 ☎ 389487858 🖷 389627466
e-mail camping.les.castors@wanadoo.fr
A modern site in a rural setting close to a river and surrounded by
woodland.
➲ E of Burnhaupt on D466 towards Guewenheim.
Open 15 Feb-Dec **Site** 2.5HEC 😃 🏕 **Prices** ♠ 3.60 pitch 3.80
♠ (static)245 **Facilities** ⚡ 🖻 ⊙ 🖸 ⑳ **Services** 🍴 🍽 ➕ 🖫 **Leisure** ♨ R
Off-site 🖻 ⊘

France

BUSSANG VOSGES

Domaine de Champé
14 Les Champs Navés, 88540 ☎ 329858645 🖷 329615690
e-mail info@domaine-de-champe.com
website www.domaine-de-champe.com
Pleasant surroundings beside the River Moselle.
➲ On N57.
Open All year **Site** 3.5HEC 😃 ♣ 🏠 **Facilities** 🍴 🚿 ☺ 🗲 ⑦ **Services** ⛽
🍽 🚻 🖾 **Leisure** ⌖ PR **Off-site** ⌀ ♒ ⌖L

CELLES-SUR-PLAINE VOSGES

Lac
Base de Loisirs, Les Lacs de Pierre-Percée, 88110
☎ 329412800 🖷 329411869
e-mail camping@sma-lacs-pierre-percee.fr
website www.sma-lacs-pierre-percee.fr
Set among wooded hills in an extensive natural leisure area around
the Lakes of Pierre-Percée.
➲ Via D392A.
Open Apr-Sep **Site** 3HEC 😃 ♣ 🏠 **Facilities** 🍴 🚿 ☺ 🗲 ⑦
Services ⛽ 🍽 🚻 🖾 **Leisure** ⌖ PR **Off-site** 🍽 ♒ ⌖L

CERNAY HAUT-RHIN

CM Acacias
16 rue Réne Guibert, 68700 ☎ 389755697 🖷 389397229
e-mail lesacacias.cernay@ffcc.fr
Clean, quiet site on the River Thur.
➲ Off N83 between Colmar & Belfort.
Open Apr-10 Oct **Site** 4HEC 😃 ♣ **Facilities** 🍴 🚿 ☺ 🗲 ⑦ **Services** 🖾
Off-site ⌖P 🚻

COLMAR HAUT-RHIN

Intercommunal de l'Ill
68180 ☎ 389411594 🖷 389411594
e-mail camping.ill@calixo.net
website www.campingdelill.com
On a meadow beside the river with modern facilities. Separate
sections for campers in transit.
➲ 2km E on N415.
Open 21 Mar-21 Dec **Site** 2.2HEC 😃 ♣ **Prices** ⚥ 3.45 🚗 1.65 pitch 3.60
Facilities 🍴 🚿 ☺ 🗲 ⑦ **Services** ⛽ 🍽 🚻 🖾 **Leisure** ⌖ R **Off-site** ⌖P

CORCIEUX VOSGES

Domaine des Bains
r J-Wiese, 88430 ☎ 329516467 🖷 329516465
e-mail les_bans@domaines_des_bans.com
On meadowland divided into pitches with a variety of recreational
facilities.
➲ E of village off D8.
Open All year **Site** 30HEC 😃 ♣ 🏠 🚐 **Facilities** 🍴 🚿 ☺ 🗲 ⌀ ♒ ⑦
Services ⛽ 🍽 🚻 🖾 **Leisure** ⌖ LP **Off-site** 🍽

DABO MOSELLE

Rocher
CD 45, 57850 ☎ 387074751 🖷 387074773
e-mail info@ot-dabo.fr
website www.ot-dabo.fr
Beautiful position close to the historic town of Dabo in the Vosges
mountains.
➲ 1.5km SW via D45.
Open 5 Apr-1 Nov **Site** 0.5HEC 😃 ♣ 🚐 **Prices** ⚥ 2.70 🚗 1 🚐 3.40
⚊ 1.50 **Facilities** 🍴 🚿 ☺ 🗲 ⑦ **Off-site** 🚿 ⛽ 🍽 ⌀ ♒ 🚻

DAMBACH-LA-VILLE BAS-RHIN

CM
rte d'Ebersheim, 67650 ☎ 388924860
e-mail info.tourisme@darnbach-la-ville.fr
website www.pays-de-barr.com/dambach-la-ville
A wooded location close to the town centre. Booking advised for July
and August.
➲ 1km E via D120.
Open Jun-end Sep **Site** 1.8HEC 😃 ♣ **Prices** ⚥ 2.60 🚗 1.65 🚐 2.10
⚊ 1.65 **Facilities** 🍴 🚿 ☺ 🗲 ⑦ **Services** 🖾 **Off-site** 🚿 ⛽ 🍽 ⌀ ♒ 🚻

EGUISHEIM HAUT-RHIN

CM Aux Trois Châteaux
10 r du Bassin, 68420 ☎ 389231939 🖷 389241019
e-mail camping.eguisheim@wanadoo.fr
Peaceful location surrounded by vineyards at an altitude of 210m.
➲ 6km S of Colmar on N83.
Open Apr-Sep **Site** 1.8HEC 😃 ♣ ♣ ⊗ **Prices** ⚥ 3.60-3.80 pitch 3.90-4.10
Facilities 🍴 🚿 ☺ 🗲 ⌀ ⑦ **Services** 🖾 **Off-site** 🚿 ⛽ 🍽 🚻

FONTENOY-LE-CHÂTEAU VOSGES

Fontenoy
rte de la Vierge, 88240 ☎ 329363474
e-mail marliesfontenoy@hotmail.com
website www.campingfontenoy.com
Set on a hill in peaceful, wooded surroundings.
➲ 2.2km S via D40.
Open 15 Apr-Sep **Site** 1.2HEC 😃 ♣ 🚐 **Prices** ⚥ 2.80 🚗 2.25 🚐 3 ⚊ 3
🚐 (static)250 **Facilities** 🍴 🚿 ☺ 🗲 ⌀ ⑦ **Services** ⛽ 🍽 🚻 🖾 **Leisure** ⌖ P
Off-site ♒ ⌖R 🚻

GEMAINGOUTTE VOSGES

CM 'Le Violu'
88520 ☎ 329577070 🖷 329517260
e-mail communedegemaingoutte@wanadoo.fr
➲ W beside river via N59.
Open May-Sep **Site** 0.9HEC 😃 ♣ **Facilities** 🍴 ☺ 🗲 ⑦ **Services** 🚻 🖾
Leisure ⌖ R **Off-site** 🍽 ⛽ 🍽

GÉRARDMER VOSGES

Ramberchamp
21 chemin du Tour du Lac, 88400 ☎ 329630382 🖷 329632609
e-mail boespflug.helene@wanadoo.fr
website www.camping-de-ramberchamp.com/fra.html
On a level meadow on S side of Lac de Gérardmer.
➲ 2km from village centre via N417 or 486.
Open 20 Apr-20 Sep **Site** 3.5HEC 😃 ⚊ ♣ 🏠 **Prices** pitch 16 (incl 2
persons) 🚐 (static)480 **Facilities** 🍴 🚿 ☺ 🗲 ⌀ ⑦ **Services** ⛽ 🍽 🖾
Leisure ⌖ L

Site 6HEC (site size) 😃 grass ⚊ sand ♣ stone ♣ little shade ♣ partly shaded ♣ mainly shaded 🏠 bungalows for hire
🚐 caravans for hire ⚊ tents for hire ⊗ no dogs **Prices** ⚥ adult per night 🚗 car per night pp per person per night 🚐 caravan per night
⚊ tent per night 🚐 (static)-caravan hire per week

GRANGES-SUR-VOLOGNE VOSGES

Château
2 Les Chappes, 88640 ☎ 329575083
e-mail camping-du-chateau@wanadoo.fr
A terraced site with good sports facilities 1km from the village,
Open 15 Jun-15 Sep **Site** 2HEC ⚏ ⚏ ⚏ ⚏ **Prices** ♠ 3.50 pitch 3.40-3.20
⚏ (static)200 **Facilities** ⚏ ⚏ ⚏ ⚏ ⚏ **Services** ⚏ **Leisure** ⚏ P
Off-site ⚏ ⚏ ⚏R ⚏

Gina-Park
88460 ☎ 329514195
website www.ginapark.com
A pleasant park at the foot of a wooded mountain. Streams cross the
site and there is a lake and facilities for a variety of sports.
➲ 1km SE of town centre.
Open All year **Site** 4.5HEC ⚏ ⚏ ⚏ ⚏ **Prices** ♠ 2.90 pitch 3.05
⚏ (static)150-330 **Facilities** ⚏ ⚏ ⚏ ⚏ ⚏ ⚏ **Services** ⚏ ⚏ ⚏
Leisure ⚏ PR **Off-site** ⚏ ⚏

HEIMSBRUNN HAUT-RHIN

Chaumière
62 r de la Galfingue, 68990 ☎ 389819343 ▤ 389819343
e-mail infos@camping-lachaumiere.com
website www.camping-lachaumiere.com
A pleasant wooded location with modern facilities.
➲ Signed from village centre.
Open All year **Site** 1HEC ⚏ ⚏ ⚏ ⚏ ⚏ **Facilities** ⚏ ⚏ ⚏ ⚏ ⚏ ⚏
Services ⚏ **Leisure** ⚏ P **Off-site** ⚏ ⚏ ⚏ ⚏R

HOHWALD, LE BAS-RHIN

CM
67140 ☎ 388083090 ▤ 388083090
e-mail lecamping.herreenhaus@orange.fr
A well-equipped terraced site in beautiful wooded surroundings.
➲ W via D425.
Open All year **Site** 2HEC ⚏ ⚏ **Prices** ♠ 3.45 ⚏ 1.70 ⚏ 2 ⚏ 2
Facilities ⚏ ⚏ ⚏ ⚏ **Services** ⚏ **Off-site** ⚏ ⚏ ⚏ ⚏ ⚏ ⚏

ISSENHEIM HAUT-RHIN

Florival
rte de Soultz, 68500 ☎ 389742047 ▤ 389742047
e-mail contact@camping-leflorival.com
website www.camping-leflorival.com
Level meadowland site, situated in a regional park and surrounded by
a forest.
➲ N83 Colmar-Mulhouse exit for Issenheim, site signed.
Open Apr-Oct **Site** 3.5HEC ⚏ ⚏ ⚏ **Prices** ♠ 3.20 pitch 6 (incl 2 persons)
Facilities ⚏ ⚏ ⚏ ⚏ **Services** ⚏ **Off-site** ⚏ ⚏ ⚏ ⚏ ⚏ ⚏ ⚏P ⚏

KAYSERSBERG HAUT-RHIN

CM
r des Acacias, 68240 ☎ 389471447
e-mail camping@ville-kaysersberg.fr
Between a sports ground and the River Weiss. Subdivided by low
hedges.
➲ 200m from N415, signed.
Open Apr-Sep **Site** 1.5HEC ⚏ ⚏ **Facilities** ⚏ ⚏ ⚏ ⚏ **Services** ⚏ ⚏
Leisure ⚏ R **Off-site** ⚏ ⚏ ⚏ ⚏ ⚏ ⚏P

KRUTH HAUT-RHIN

Schlossberg
r du Bourbach, 68820 ☎ 389822676 ▤ 389822017
e-mail contact@schlossberg.fr
website www.schlossberg.fr
A quiet location in the heart of the Parc des Ballons with modern
facilities.
➲ 2.3km NW via D13b.
Open Etr-1 Oct **Site** 5.2HEC ⚏ ⚏ ⚏ ⚏ **Prices** ♠ 4 pitch 3.70
⚏ (static)210-290 **Facilities** ⚏ ⚏ ⚏ ⚏ ⚏ ⚏ **Services** ⚏ ⚏ ⚏ ⚏
Leisure ⚏ R **Off-site** ⚏ ⚏ ⚏L

LAUTERBOURG BAS-RHIN

CM des Mouettes
chemin des Mouettes, 67630 ☎ 388546860 ▤ 388546860
e-mail camping-lauterbourg@wanadoo.fr
A level site on the shores of a lake.
➲ D63 from Haguenau.
Open 19 Apr-Nov **Site** 3HEC ⚏ ⚏ ⚏ ⚏ ⚏ ⚏ **Facilities** ⚏ ⚏ ⚏ ⚏ ⚏ ⚏
Services ⚏ ⚏ ⚏ ⚏ **Leisure** ⚏ L **Off-site** ⚏R

LUTTENBACH HAUT-RHIN

Amis de la Nature
4 r du Château, 68140 ☎ 389773860 ▤ 389772572
e-mail camping.an@wanadoo.fr
Situated on a long strip of land, in the heart of Luttenbach
countryside. Divided into pitches.
➲ D10 from Munster for 1km.
Open All year **Site** 7HEC ⚏ ⚏ **Facilities** ⚏ ⚏ ⚏ ⚏ ⚏ **Services** ⚏ ⚏
⚏ ⚏ **Leisure** ⚏ R **Off-site** ⚏ ⚏ ⚏P

MASEVAUX HAUT-RHIN

Masevaux
3 r du Stade, 68290 ☎ 389824229 ▤ 389824229
e-mail info@camping-masevaux.com
Wooded surroundings beside the River Doller.
➲ Off main road to Ballon-d'Alsace.
Open 15 Feb-Dec **Site** 3.5HEC ⚏ ⚏ ⚏ ⚏ **Prices** ♠ 3 pitch 3
⚏ (static)252.90 **Facilities** ⚏ ⚏ ⚏ ⚏ **Services** ⚏ ⚏ ⚏ ⚏
Off-site ⚏ ⚏PR

METZERAL HAUT-RHIN
AT MITTLACH (3KM SW)

CM
68380 ☎ 389776377 ▤ 0389777436
e-mail mairiemittlach@wanadoo.fr
website commune-de-mittlach.ifrance.com
Very quiet forested area by a small village.
➲ From Munster signs for Metzeral then Mittlach D10.
Open May-Oct **Site** 3HEC ⚏ ⚏ **Prices** ♠ 3.25 ⚏ 1.15 ⚏ 2.45 ⚏ 1.50
Facilities ⚏ ⚏ ⚏ ⚏ ⚏ ⚏ **Services** ⚏ **Leisure** ⚏ R

France

France

MOOSCH HAUT-RHIN

Mine d'Argent

r de la Mine d'Argent, 68690 ☎ 389823066

e-mail serge.sorribas@free.fr

A well-established site in a peaceful wooded setting.

➲ *1.5km SW off N66.*

Open 15 Apr-15 Oct **Site** 2.5HEC ⚑ ♣ ⬛ ⬛ **Prices** ⚹ 3.60 pitch 3.60 ⬛ (static)125-215 **Facilities** ⬛ ⊙ ⬛ ⬛ ⬛ ⬛ **Services** ⬛ ⬛ **Leisure** ⬛ R
Off-site ⬛ ⬛ ⬛ ⬛LPR

MULHOUSE HAUT-RHIN

CM III

av P-de-Coubertin, 68100 ☎ 389062066 ▤ 389611834

e-mail campingdelill@aol.com

website www.camping-de-lill.com

Set in the park between the canal and the River Ill, a short walk from the city centre.

➲ *From town centre signs for Fribourg & Allemagne, signed at Ile Napoléon.*

Open Apr-Oct **Site** 6HEC ⚑ ♣ ⬛ ⬛ ⚊ **Prices** ⚹ 3.50-4.70 pitch 3.50-4.70 ⬛ (static)100-150 **Facilities** ⬛ ⬛ ⊙ ⬛ ⬛ **Services** ⬛ ⬛ ⬛ ⬛ **Leisure** ⬛ P **Off-site** ⬛R

MUNSTER HAUT-RHIN

CM Parc de la Fecht

rte de Gunsbach, 68140 ☎ 389773108 ▤ 389770455

e-mail ville.munster@worldonline.fr

Well-maintained site close to the town centre, in a park-like area surrounded by high walls and trees.

➲ *On D417, 200m after entering Munster town centre, near swimming pool.*

Open Apr-Sep **Site** 4HEC ⚑ ♣ **Facilities** ⬛ ⬛ ⊙ ⬛ ⬛ ⬛ **Services** ⬛ ⬛ **Leisure** ⬛ R **Off-site** ⬛ ⬛ ⬛ ⬛P

OBERBRONN BAS-RHIN

CM Eichelgarten

3 r du Frohret, 67110 ☎ 388097196 ▤ 388099787

e-mail oasis.oberbronn@laregie.fr

➲ *Signed W from D28 Oberbronn-Zinswiller.*

Open 11 Mar-11 Nov **Site** 4HEC ⚑ ♣ ⬛ **Prices** ⚹ 3.61-3.80 ⬛ 1.80-1.90 pitch 2.37-2.50 **Facilities** ⬛ ⬛ ⊙ ⬛ ⬛ **Services** ⬛ ⬛ **Leisure** ⬛ P
Off-site ⬛ ⬛ ⬛ ⬛

OBERNAI BAS-RHIN

CM

rue de Berlin, 67210 ☎ 388953848 ▤ 388483147

e-mail camping@obernai.fr

website www.obernai.fr

Partly terraced site in a park.

➲ *W on D426 towards Ottrott.*

Open All year **Site** 3HEC ⚑ ♣ **Prices** ⚹ 3.60 pitch 4.40 **Facilities** ⬛ ⬛ ⊙ ⬛ ⬛ **Services** ⬛ ⬛ **Off-site** ⬛ ⬛ ⬛ ⬛P

RIBEAUVILLE HAUT-RHIN

Pierre de Coubertin

23 r de Landau, 68150 ☎ 389736671 ▤ 389736671

e-mail camping.ribeauville@wanadoo.fr

website www.camping-alsace.com

Peaceful location. Shop only open in summer.

➲ *Via D106.*

Open 15 Mar-14 Nov **Site** 3.5HEC ⚑ ♣ **Prices** ⚹ 3.80 pitch 4 **Facilities** ⬛ ⬛ ⊙ ⬛ ⬛ ⬛ **Services** ⬛ ⬛ **Off-site** ⬛ ⬛ ⬛P

RIQUEWIHR HAUT-RHIN

Inter Communal

rte des Vins, 68340 ☎ 389479008 ▤ 389490563

e-mail campingriquewihr@wanadoo.fr

Extensive site overlooking vineyards.

➲ *2km E on D16. Turn W off N83 at Ostheim.*

Open Apr-Dec **Site** 4HEC ⚑ ♣ **Facilities** ⬛ ⬛ ⊙ ⬛ ⬛ ⬛ **Services** ⬛ **Off-site** ⬛ ⬛ ⬛ ⬛

ST-MAURICE-SUR-MOSELLE VOSGES

Deux Ballons

17 r du Stade, 88560 ☎ 329251714

e-mail vero@camping-deux-ballons.fr

website www.camping-deux-ballons.fr

Well-maintained site beside a stream and surrounded by woodland and mountains.

➲ *1km W on N66 near Avia fuel station.*

Open 28 Apr-16 Sep **Site** 4HEC ⚑ ♣ ⬛ **Prices** pitch 14.90-24.30 (incl 2 persons) **Facilities** ⬛ ⊙ ⬛ ⬛ ⬛ **Services** ⬛ ⬛ ⬛ ⬛ **Leisure** ⬛ P
Off-site ⬛ ⬛ ⬛ ⬛R

ST-PIERRE BAS-RHIN

Beau Séjour

r de l'Église, F.67140 ☎ 388085224 ▤ 388085224

e-mail commune.saintpierre@wanadoo.fr

website www.pays-de-barr.com/beau-sejour/

Situated midway between Strasbourg and Colmar with modern facilities.

Open 15 May-1 Oct **Site** 0.6HEC ⚑ ♣ **Prices** pitch 10.50 (incl 2 persons) pp3 **Facilities** ⬛ ⊙ ⬛ ⬛ **Services** ⬛ ⬛ **Leisure** ⬛ R **Off-site** ⬛ ⬛ ⬛

STE-CROIX-EN-PLAINE HAUT-RHIN

Clair Vacances

rte de Herrlisheim, 68127 ☎ 389492728 ▤ 389493137

e-mail clairvacances@wanadoo.fr

website www.clairvacances.com

A pleasant woodland setting with good facilities for a family holiday.

➲ *On D1 towards Herrlisheim.*

Open Etr-17 Oct **Site** 3.5HEC ⚑ ♣ ⬛ ⊗ **Facilities** ⬛ ⊙ ⬛ ⬛ ⬛ **Services** ⬛ ⬛ **Leisure** ⬛ P **Off-site** ⬛ ⬛ ⬛

SAVERNE BAS-RHIN

CM

67700 ☎ 388913565 ▤ 388913565

A pleasant site at the foot of the Rocher du Haut Barr.

➲ *1.3km SW via D171*

Open Apr-Sep **Site** 2.5HEC ⚑ ♣ **Facilities** ⬛ ⊙ ⬛ ⬛ **Services** ⬛ ⬛ **Off-site** ⬛ ⬛ ⬛ ⬛

Site 6HEC (site size) ⚑ grass ⬤ sand ⬤ stone ♣ little shade ♣ partly shaded ⬤ mainly shaded ⬛ bungalows for hire
⬛ caravans for hire ⬛ tents for hire ⊗ no dogs **Prices** ⚹ adult per night ⬛ car per night pp per person per night ⬛ caravan per night
⬛ tent per night ⬛ (static)-caravan hire per week

SÉLESTAT BAS-RHIN

CM Cigognes
r de la 1-er DFL, 67600 ☎ 388920398
Rural setting at an altitude of 175m.
➲ 0.9km from town centre.
Open May-Sep **Site** 0.7HEC ♨ ♣ Å **Facilities** ⋒ ☉ ⌷ ⅌ **Services** ⑤
Off-site ⓐ ⌷ P ✚

SEPPOIS-LE-BAS HAUT-RHIN

CM les Lupins
r de l'Ancienne Gare, 68580 ☎ 389256537 ▤ 389256537
e-mail leslupins@wanadoo.fr
website www.campingalsace.com
Picturesque site close to the German and Swiss borders.
➲ A36 exit Burnhaupt for Dannemarie.
Open Apr-Oct **Site** 4HEC ♨ ♣ ☎ **Facilities** ⋒ ☉ ⌷ ∅ ⅌ ⑫
Services ✚ ⑤ **Leisure** ⌷ P **Off-site** ⓐ ⅰ⑭ ♨ ⌷R

SIVRY-SUR-MEUSE MEUSE

Brouzel
26 r du Moulin, 55110 ☎ 329858645
Open Apr-1 Oct **Site** 1.5HEC ♨ ♣ **Facilities** ⋒ ☉ ⌷ ⅌ **Services** ✚ ⑤
Off-site ⓐ ⑭ ⅰ⑭ ∅ ♨ ⌷R

THOLY, LE VOSGES

Noir Rupt
chemin de l'Étang de Noirrupt, 88530 ☎ 329618127 ▤ 329618305
e-mail info@jpvacances.com
website www.jpvacances.com
A peaceful site in a beautiful wooded location. Plenty of facilities.
➲ 2km SE on D417.
Open 15 Apr-14 Oct **Site** 3HEC ♨ ♣ **Prices** ⚬ 3.71-5.30 pitch 6.16-8.80
Facilities ⋒ ☉ ⌷ ∅ ⅌ ⑫ **Services** ⑤ **Leisure** ⌷ P **Off-site** ⅰ⑭ ♨
♨R ✚

TONNOY MEURTHE-ET-MOSELLE

Grande Vanné
54210 ☎ 383266236 ▤ 383266395
➲ W via D74, beside the River Moselle.
Open 15 Jun-15 Sep **Site** 7HEC ♨ ♣ **Facilities** ⋒ ☉ ⌷ ⅌ **Services** ⑭
ⅰ⑭ ⑤ **Leisure** ⌷ R **Off-site** ⓐ ⅰ⑭

TURCKHEIM HAUT-RHIN

Cigognes
68230 ☎ 389270200
website www.turckheim-alsace.com
➲ N417 from Colmar to Wintzenheim then Turckheim, left
before bridge, pass railway station & stadium.
Open 15 March -30 Oct **Site** 2.5HEC ♨ ♣ **Prices** ⚬ 3.50 pitch 3.80
Facilities ⋒ ☉ ⌷ ∅ ⅌ **Services** ✚ ⑤ **Leisure** ⌷ R **Off-site** ⅰ⑭

URBÈS HAUT-RHIN

CM Benelux Bâle
68121 ☎ 389827876
A well-maintained site with good facilities.
➲ W of rte de Bussang.
Open Apr-Oct **Site** 2.4HEC ♨ ♣ ⌷ Å **Facilities** ⋒ ☉ ⌷ ⅌ **Services** ✚
⑤ **Off-site** ⓐ ∅ ♨ ♨R

VAGNEY VOSGES

CM du Mettey
88120 ☎ 329248135
e-mail ocvbr@wanadoo.fr
➲ 1.3km E on road to Gérardmer.
Open 15 Jun-15 Sep **Site** 2HEC ♨ ♣ **Prices** pitch 8.40 (incl 2 persons)
Facilities ⋒ ☉ ⌷ ⅌ **Services** ✚ ⑤ **Off-site** ∅ ♨

VERDUN MEUSE

Breuils
allée des Breuils, 55100 ☎ 329861531 ▤ 329867576
e-mail contact@camping-lesbreuils.com
website www.camping-lesbreuils.com
A family site in peaceful surroundings. Pitches are divided by trees and
bushes and the sanitary facilities are well-maintained.
➲ SW via D34, signed.
Open Apr-Sep **Site** 5.5HEC ♨ ♣ ☎ **Prices** ⚬ 5 pitch 4.40 **Facilities** ⋒ ⓐ
☉ ⌷ ∅ ♨ ⅌ **Services** ⑭ ⅰ⑭ ✚ ⑤ **Leisure** ⌷ P **Off-site** ♨LR

VILLERS-LÈS-NANCY MEURTHE-ET-MOSELLE

Campeole le Brabois
av Paul Muller, 54600 ☎ 383271828 ▤ 383400643
e-mail campeoles.brabois@wanadoo.fr
website www.camping-brabois.com
Beautiful wooded surroundings with well-defined pitches and good
recreational facilities.
➲ SW in Brabois park.
Open Apr-15 Oct **Site** 6HEC ♨ ♣ ☎ **Facilities** ⋒ ⓐ ☉ ⌷ ∅ ⅌
Services ⑭ ⅰ⑭ ✚ ⑤ **Off-site** ⓐ ⑭ ⅰ⑭ ∅ ✚

WASSELONNE BAS-RHIN

CM
rte de Romanswiller, 67310 ☎ 388870008
e-mail camping-wasselonne@wanadoo.fr
On a level meadow adjoining the local sports complex.
➲ 1km W on D224.
Open Apr-15 Oct **Site** 2.5HEC ♨ ♣ ☎ **Prices** ⚬ 3-3.30 pitch 7.30
Facilities ⋒ ⓐ ☉ ⌷ ∅ ⅌ **Services** ⑭ ⅰ⑭ ✚ ⑤ **Leisure** ⌷ P
Off-site ⅰ⑭ ♨

WATTWILLER HAUT-RHIN

Sources
rte des Crêtes, 68700 ☎ 389754494 ▤ 389757198
e-mail camping.les.sources@wanadoo.fr
website www.camping-les-sources.com
A family site on the edge of the Vosges forest close to the Route du
Vin.
➲ N83 exit Cernay Nord.
Open 5 Apr-Sep **Site** 14HEC ♨ ♣ ☎ ⌷ **Prices** pitch 13-27 (incl 2
persons) pp5-7 ⌷ (static)192-686 **Facilities** ⋒ ⓐ ☉ ⌷ ∅ ⅌ ⑫
Services ⑭ ⅰ⑭ ✚ ⑤ **Leisure** ⌷ P

France

Facilities ⓐ shop ⋒ shower ☉ electric points for razors ⌷ electric points for caravans ⅌ parking by tents permitted ⑫ compulsory separate car park
Services ⅰ⑭ café/restaurant ⑭ bar ∅ Camping Gaz International ♨ gas other than Camping Gaz ✚ first aid facilities ⑤ laundry
Leisure ♨ swimming L-Lake P-Pool R-River S-Sea **Off-site** All facilities within 2km

France

WIHR-AU-VAL HAUT-RHIN

Route Verte
13 r de la Gare, 68230 ☎ 389711010
e-mail info@camping-routeverte.com
website camping-routeverte.com
Near the centre of the village at an altitude of 320m.
➲ *Approach via D10.*
Open May-Sep **Site** 1HEC ❤ ● ❤ **Prices** ☀ 2.65 pitch 3.65 **Facilities** ⚲ ☺
🏪 ⌀ ☂ **Services** 🗓 **Off-site** 🏠 ⅋🗍 🍴 ⇷R ➕

XONRUPT/LONGEMER VOSGES

L'Eau-Vive
rte de Colmar, 88400 ☎ 329630737 🖷 329630737
e-mail campingeauvive@wanadoo.fr
website www.monsite.wanadoo.fr/camping_eau_vive
On a meadow surrounded by trees, close to the ski slopes.
➲ *2km SE on D67A next to Lac de Longemer.*
Open All year **Site** 1HEC ❤ ● ❤ 🏪 **Facilities** ⚲ ☺ 🏪 ⌀ 🗸 ☂
Services 🗍 🍴 ➕ 🗓 **Leisure** ⇷ R **Off-site** 🏠 ⇷L

Jonquilles
rte du Lac, 88400 ☎ 329633401 🖷 329600928
A delightful wooded lakeside setting. Booking advised for July and
August.
➲ *2km SE on D67A beside Lac de Longemer.*
Open 14 Apr-1 Oct **Site** 4HEC ❤ ● **Prices** pitch 8-12 (incl 2 persons)
Facilities ⚲ 🏠 ☺ 🏪 ⌀ ☂ **Services** 🗍 🍴 ➕ 🗓 **Leisure** ⇷ L
Off-site 🍴 🗸

BURGUNDY/CHAMPAGNE

ACCOLAY YONNE

Moulin Jacquot
route de Bazarnes, 89460 ☎ 386815687 🖷 386815687
A well-equipped site in a pleasant rural setting, close to the village.
➲ *W to Canal du Nivernais.*
Open Apr-Sep **Site** 0.8HEC ❤ ● **Facilities** ⚲ ☺ 🏪 ☂ **Services** 🗓
Off-site 🏠 🗍 🍴 ⌀ 🗸 ⇷R ➕

ANCY-LE-FRANC YONNE

CM
rte de Cusy, 89160 ☎ 386751321
A sheltered position just beyond the village.
➲ *Via Montbard road.*
Open Jun-15 Sep **Site** 0.8HEC ❤ ● **Prices** ☀ 2 🚗 1 ♺ 2 🛆 1
Facilities ⚲ ☺ 🏪 ☂ **Services** 🗓 **Off-site** 🏠 🗍 🍴 ⌀ 🗸 ⇷R ➕

ANDRYES YONNE

Bois Joli
89480 ☎ 386817048 🖷 386817048
e-mail info@campingauboisjoli.com
website www.campingauboisjoli.com
A small site in pleasant Burgundian countryside.
➲ *0.6km SW via N151.*
Open Apr-Oct **Site** 5HEC ❤ ●● ● 🛆 **Prices** ☀ 2.75-3.75 🚗 2.15 ♺ 2.10-
3.10 🛆 2.10-3.10 **Facilities** ⚲ 🏠 ☺ 🏪 ⌀ 🗸 ☂ **Services** ➕ 🗓 **Leisure** ⇷ P
Off-site 🍴 ⇷L

ARNAY-LE-DUC CÔTE-D'OR

Fouché
r du 8 mai 1945, 21230 ☎ 380900223 🖷 380901191
e-mail info@campingfouche.com
website www.campingfouche.com
A quiet location beside a lake with good recreational facilities, close to
the medieval town of Arnay-le-Duc.
➲ *0.7km E on CD17.*
Open 15 Apr-15 Oct **Site** 8HEC ❤ ● ❤ **Prices** ☀ 3.10-4.30 pitch 3.90-6.10
Facilities ⚲ 🏠 ☺ 🏪 ⌀ ☂ 🗸 **Services** 🗍 🍴 ➕ 🗓 **Leisure** ⇷ LP
Off-site 🏠 🗍 🍴 🗸

AUXERRE YONNE

CM
8 rte de Vaux, 89000 ☎ 386521115 🖷 386511754
e-mail camping.mairie@auxerre.com
➲ *SE towards Vaux.*
Open 15 Apr-Sep **Site** 3HEC ❤ ● **Prices** ☀ 2.40-3 pitch 2.65 **Facilities** ⚲
🏠 ☺ 🏪 ⌀ ☂ **Services** ➕ 🗓 **Off-site** 🗍 🍴 🗸 ⇷PR

AUXONNE CÔTE-D'OR

Arquebuse
rte d'Athée, 21130 ☎ 380310689 🖷 380311302
e-mail camping.arquebuse@wanadoo.fr
website www.campingarquebuse.com
Clean, well-equipped site on the River Saône, near a bathing area.
➲ *N5 W from Auxonne for 3km, N onto D24 towards Athée &*
Pontailler-sur-Saône.
Open All year **Site** 4HEC ❤ ● 🏪 ♺ **Prices** ☀ 3.60 🚗 1.80 ♺ 3.50
🛆 3.50 ♺ (static)300 **Facilities** ⚲ 🏠 ☺ 🏪 ⌀ 🗸 ☂ **Services** 🗍 🍴 🗓
Off-site ⇷PR ➕

AVALLON YONNE

CM Sous Roche
1 r Sous-Roche, 89200 ☎ 386341039 🖷 386341039
e-mail campingsousroches@ville-avallon.fr
➲ *2km SE by D944 & D427.*
Open 15 Mar-15 Oct **Site** 2HEC ❤ ● **Facilities** ⚲ 🏠 ☺ 🏪 ☂
Services 🍴 ➕ 🗓 **Leisure** ⇷ R **Off-site** ⇷P

BANNES HAUTE-MARNE

Hautoreille
52360 ☎ 325848340 🖷 325848340
e-mail campinghautoreille@free.fr
website www.campinghautoreille.com
Small grassy site with modern facilities, offering large pitches, many in
shaded positions. Separate car park for late arrivals.
➲ *D74 direction S towards Langres.*
Open All year **Site** 3.5HEC ❤ ● ❤ **Prices** ☀ 4-4.50 pitch 5 ♺ (static)190-
225 **Facilities** ⚲ 🏠 ☺ 🏪 ☂ **Services** 🗍 🍴 ➕ 🗓 **Off-site** ⇷LR

BAR-SUR-AUBE AUBE

Gravière
av du Parc, 10200 ☎ 325271294 🖷 325271294
➲ *0.5km E of D13.*
Open 15 Mar-15 Oct **Site** 2.8HEC ❤ ● **Facilities** ⚲ ☺ 🏪 ☂ **Services** 🗓
Leisure ⇷ PR **Off-site** 🏠 🗍 🍴 ⌀ 🗸 ⇷P

Site 6HEC (site size) ❤ grass ● sand ❤ stone 🗸 little shade ● partly shaded ❤ mainly shaded 🏠 bungalows for hire
♺ caravans for hire 🛆 tents for hire ⊗ no dogs **Prices** ☀ adult per night 🚗 car per night pp per person per night ♺ caravan per night
🛆 tent per night ♺ (static)-caravan hire per week

France (side tab)

BAZOLLES NIÈVRE

Baye
58110 ☎ 386389033
Open Apr-Oct **Site** 1.5HEC ♨ ♣ ♣ ♠ **Facilities** ↑ ⊙ ⊕ ℗
Services 🔁 🖲 **Leisure** ⚓ L **Off-site** 🗎 📶 🍴 ⌀ ♨

BEAUNE CÔTE-D'OR

CM Cent Vignes
10 rue August Dubois, 21200 ☎ 380220391 🖨 380220391
On outskirts of town. Site divided into pitches, clean, well-looked after
sanitary installations. From 20 June to August it is advisable to arrive
before 1600 hrs.
➲ *On N74 on Savigny-les-Beaune road.*
Open 15 Mar-Oct **Site** 2HEC ♨ ♣ ♣ **Facilities** ↑ 🗎 ⊙ ⊕ ⌀ ℗
Services 📶 🍴 🔁 🖲 **Off-site** ♨ ⚓LP

BOURBON-LANCY SAÔNE-ET-LOIRE

St-Prix
r du St-Prix, 71140 ☎ 385892098 🖨 385892098
e-mail aquadis1@wanadoo.fr
website www.camping-chalets-bourbon-lancy.com
A well-equipped family site close to an extensive water-sports centre.
➲ *By swimming pool off D979a.*
Open Apr-Oct **Site** 2.5HEC ♨ ♣ ♠ ♣ **Prices** pitch 15-17 (static)289
Facilities ↑ 🗎 ⊙ ⊕ ⌀ ♨ ℗ **Services** 📶 🍴 🖲 **Leisure** ⚓ P **Off-site** 🍴
⚓L 🔁

BOURBONNE-LES-BAINS HAUTE-MARNE

Montmorency
r du Stade, BP N7, 52400 ☎ 325900864 🖨 325842374
e-mail c.montmorency@wanadoo.fr
website www.camping-montmorency.com
A well-equipped site in a pleasant natural setting.
Open Mar-Nov **Site** 2HEC ♨ ♣ ♣ ♣ **Prices** ⚲ 3.50 pitch 3.40 **Facilities** ↑
⊙ ⊕ ⌀ ℗ **Services** 🔁 🖲 **Off-site** ⚓P

BOURG HAUTE-MARNE

Croix d'Arles
RN 74, 52200 ☎ 325882402 🖨 325882402
e-mail croix.arles@wanadoo.fr
website www.croixdarles.com
A peaceful site in flat wooded surroundings close to Langres.
➲ *A31 exit 6, D428 towards Langres, onto RN74 for Dijon, site
2km on right.*
Open 15 Mar-1 Nov **Site** 7HEC ♨ ♣ ♠ ♣ ♠ **Prices** ⚲ 2.50-4 pitch 6-6.50
♣ (static)175-490 **Facilities** ↑ 🗎 ⊙ ⊕ ℗ **Services** 📶 🍴 🔁 🖲
Leisure ⚓ P

BOURG-FIDÈLE ARDENNES

Murée
35 r Catherine de Clè, 08230 ☎ 324542445
e-mail campingdelamuree@wanadoo.fr
website www.campingdelamuree.com
A lakeside site in wooded surroundings.
➲ *1km N via D22.*
Open All year **Site** 1.3HEC ♨ ♣ ♠ ♣ **Prices** ⚲ 3 ♣ 1.60 pitch 4.60
♣ (static)195 **Facilities** ↑ ⊙ ⊕ ℗ **Services** 📶 🍴 🖲 **Off-site** 🗎 ⌀ ♨
⚓P 🔁

BUZANCY ARDENNES

Samaritaine
☎ 324300888 🖨 324302939
e-mail info@campinglasamaritaine.com
website www.campinglasamaritaine.com
Site set in a peaceful location in a small village in the heart of the
Ardennes. The forests in the area are well-suited for walking, horse-
riding or cycling.
➲ *D12 onto D947 towards Buzancy for 17km.*
Open 4 May-Sep **Site** 2.5HEC ♨ ♣ ♠ ♣ **Prices** ⚲ 3.95-4.95 pitch 7-12
♣ (static)294-497 **Facilities** ↑ ⊙ ⊕ ℗ **Services** 🍴 🔁 🖲 **Off-site** 🗎 📶
🍴 ⌀ ♨ ⚓L

CHAGNY SAÔNE-ET-LOIRE

Pâquier Fané
20 Rue de Paquier, 71150 ☎ 385872142
e-mail campingchagny@aol.com
A clean site 0.6km W of the church.
➲ *D974 from town centre.*
Open 15 Apr-Oct **Site** 1.8HEC ♨ ♣ ♣ **Prices** ⚲ 3.10 pitch 4.90 **Facilities** ↑
🗎 ⊙ ⊕ ⌀ ♨ ℗ **Services** 📶 🍴 🔁 🖲 **Leisure** ⚓ R **Off-site** ⚓P

CHÂLONS-EN-CHAMPAGNE MARNE

CM
r de Plaisance, 51000 ☎ 326683800 🖨 326683800
e-mail camping.mairie.chalons@wanadoo.fr
website www.chalons-en-champagne.net
Pleasant wooded location with good recreational facilities.
➲ *N44 NE/N77 S*
Open Apr-Oct **Site** 7.5HEC ♨ ♣ ♣ **Prices** ⚲ 4.70 ♣ 3.10 pitch 4.70
Facilities ↑ ⊙ ⊕ ⌀ ℗ **Services** 📶 🍴 🔁 🖲 **Off-site** 🗎 ⚓P

CHAROLLES SAÔNE-ET-LOIRE

CM
rte de Viny, 71120 ☎ 385240490 🖨 385240490
e-mail mairie.charolles@wanadoo.fr
Pleasant wooded surroundings with modern sanitary facilities.
➲ *NE of town on D33 towards Viry, signed.*
Open Apr-5 Oct **Site** 0.6HEC ♨ ♣ ♠ **Prices** ⚲ 2 ♣ 1.50 ♣ 2.50
🄰 2.50 ♣ (static)200-330 **Facilities** ↑ ⊙ ⊕ ℗ **Services** 📶 🔁 🖲
Leisure ⚓ PR **Off-site** 🗎 🍴 ⌀ ♨

CHÂTILLON-SUR-SEINE CÔTE-D'OR

CM
espl St-Vorles, 21400 ☎ 380910305 🖨 380912146
e-mail tourism-chatillon-sur-seine@wanadoo.fr
Hilly shaded site near the historic Renaissance church of St Vorles.
➲ *SE of town off D928 rte de Langres.*
Open Apr-Sep **Site** 0.8HEC ♨ ♣ ♣ **Prices** ⚲ 3.25 ♣ 1.35 ♣ 3.15 🄰 3.15
Facilities ↑ ⊙ ⊕ ⌀ ℗ **Services** 📶 🔁 🖲 **Off-site** 🗎 🍴 ♨ ⚓P

CHATONRUPT HAUTE-MARNE

Jardinot
52300 ☎ 325948007 🖨 325948007
Open May-Sep **Site** 1.1HEC ♨ ♣ **Prices** ⚲ 1.10 ♣ 1 ♣ 1 🄰 1
Facilities ↑ ⊙ ⊕ ℗ **Services** 🖲 **Leisure** ⚓ R **Off-site** 🗎 🍴 ♨

Facilities 🗎 shop ↑ shower ⊙ electric points for razors ⊕ electric points for caravans ℗ parking by tents permitted ◐ compulsory separate car park
Services 🍴 café/restaurant 📶 bar ⌀ Camping Gaz International ♨ gas other than Camping Gaz 🔁 first aid facilities 🖲 laundry
Leisure ⚓ swimming L-Lake P-Pool R-River S-Sea **Off-site** All facilities within 2km

CHEVIGNY NIÈVRE

Hermitage de Chevigny

58230 ☎ 386845097

A pleasant site with good facilities in wooded surroundings within the Morvan nature reserve. There is direct access to the lake and water sports are available.

Open Apr-Sep **Site** 2.5HEC 🌱 🏖 🐾 **Prices** ⚥ 4.50 🚗 3 pitch 2.50 🚐 (static)175 **Facilities** ⌂ 🛁 ⊙ 🚰 ∅ ♨ ☺ **Services** ⚑ ⫯⊙⫯ ➕ ⊠ **Leisure** ⚓ LR

CLAMECY NIÈVRE

Pont Picot

rte de Chenoches, 58500 ☎ 386270597

A pleasant location between the River Yonne and the Canal du Nivernais.

Open May-Sep **Site** 1.2HEC 🌱 🏖 **Facilities** ⌂ ⊙ 🚰 ☺ **Services** ⊠ **Leisure** ⚓ R **Off-site** 🛁 ⚑ ⫯⊙⫯ ∅ ♨ ⚓P ➕

COSNE-SUR-LOIRE NIÈVRE

Loire & Nohain

Ile de Cosne, 18300 ☎ 386282792 🖷 386281810

e-mail campingile18@aol.com

Site borders River Loire.

➲ D955 W towards Sancerre.

Open All year **Site** 4HEC 🌱 🏖 🏖 🌱 🏖 🐾 🐾 Ⓐ **Facilities** ⌂ 🛁 ⊙ 🚰 ∅ ♨ ☺ **Services** ⚑ ⫯⊙⫯ ➕ ⊠ **Leisure** ⚓ PR **Off-site** ♨ ⚓P

CRÊCHES-SUR-SAÔNE SAÔNE-ET-LOIRE

CM Le Port d'Arciat

71680 ☎ 385371183 🖷 385365791

e-mail camping-creches.sur.saone@wanadoo.fr

Wooded location beside the River Saône.

➲ 1.5km E via D31.

Open 15 May-15 Sep **Site** 6HEC 🌱 🏖 **Facilities** ⌂ ⊙ 🚰 ∅ ☺ **Services** ⚑ ⫯⊙⫯ ➕ ⊠ **Leisure** ⚓ LR **Off-site** 🛁 ∅ ♨

DIGOIN SAÔNE-ET-LOIRE

CM Chevrette

r de la Chevrette, 71160 ☎ 385531149 🖷 385885970

e-mail lachevrette@wanadoo.fr

website www.lachevrette.com

On the banks of the river Loire set in peaceful countryside.

➲ W of village on N79 exit 23/24.

Open Mar-Oct **Site** 1.5HEC 🌱 🏖 🏖 🐾 🐾 Ⓐ **Prices** ⚥ 2.80-3.15 pitch 5.40-6 🚐 (static)105 **Facilities** ⌂ 🛁 ⊙ 🚰 ☺ **Services** ⚑ ⫯⊙⫯ ➕ ⊠ **Leisure** ⚓ PR **Off-site** ∅ ♨

DIJON CÔTE-D'OR

Lac

3 bd Chanoine Kir, 21000 ☎ 380435472 🖷 380435472

website www.ville-dijon.fr

A well-maintained site in natural surroundings, an ideal base for exploring the historic town of Dijon.

➲ 1.5km W on N5.

Open Apr-15 Oct **Site** 2.5HEC 🌱 🏖 🏖 **Facilities** ⌂ ⊙ 🚰 ☺ **Services** ⚑ ⫯⊙⫯ ➕ ⊠ **Off-site** 🛁 ∅ ♨ ⚓LP

DOMPIERRE-LES-ORMES SAÔNE-ET-LOIRE

Village des Meuniers

71520 ☎ 385503660 🖷 385503661

e-mail levillagedesmeuniers@wanadoo.fr

website www.villagedesmeuniers.com

A well-equipped site in the heart of the southern Burgundy countryside. Booking advised for July and August.

➲ Via N79, signed.

Open 28 Apr-Sep **Site** 4HEC 🌱 🏖 🐾 **Prices** ⚥ 5.85-8 pitch 6.95-9.60 **Facilities** ⌂ 🛁 ⊙ 🚰 ∅ ♨ ☺ **Services** ⚑ ⫯⊙⫯ ➕ ⊠ **Leisure** ⚓ P

ÉCLARON-BRAUCOURT HAUTE-MARNE

Presqu'île de Champaubert

52290 ☎ 325041320 🖷 325943351

e-mail info@lacduder.com

website www.lacduder.com

Situated on a lake peninsula.

Open Apr-Sep **Site** 3.5HEC 🌱 🏖 **Facilities** ⌂ 🛁 ⊙ 🚰 ∅ ☺ **Services** ⚑ ⫯⊙⫯ ➕ ⊠ **Off-site** ⚓L

EPINAC SAÔNE-ET-LOIRE

Pont Vert

Rue de la Piscine, 71360 ☎ 385820026 🖷 385821367

e-mail info@campingdupontvert.com

website www.campingdupontvert.com

Wooded location on the banks of the river. Modern facilities and motel within the site.

➲ S via D43 beside River Drée.

Open Apr-Sep **Site** 4HEC 🌱 🏖 🐾 Ⓐ **Facilities** ⌂ 🛁 ⊙ 🚰 ∅ ☺ **Services** ⚑ ⫯⊙⫯ ➕ ⊠ **Leisure** ⚓ R **Off-site** ⫯⊙⫯ ∅ ♨

FRONCLES HAUTE-MARNE

Deux Ponts

r des Ponts, 52320 ☎ 325023121 🖷 325020980

A peaceful location beside the River Marne.

Open 15 Mar-15 Oct **Site** 3HEC 🏖 **Prices** ⚥ 1.90 pitch 2.40 **Facilities** ⌂ 🚰 ☺ **Off-site** 🛁 ⚑ ⫯⊙⫯ ⚓R ➕

GIBLES SAÔNE-ET-LOIRE

Château de Montrouant

Montrouant, 71800 ☎ 385845113 🖷 385845430

A small site in the Charollais hill region with access to extensive parkland.

➲ 1.6km NE beside lake.

Open Jun-9 Sep **Site** 1HEC 🌱 🏖 🏖 🐾 Ⓐ **Facilities** ⌂ ⊙ 🚰 ☺ **Services** ⚑ ⫯⊙⫯ ➕ ⊠ **Leisure** ⚓ LPR **Off-site** 🛁 ∅ ♨

GIFFAUMONT MARNE

Plage

Chemin de la Cachotte, Station Nautique, 51290 ☎ 326726184

A well-maintained site at the Station Nautique.

➲ 2km from village.

Open May-10 Sep **Site** 1.5HEC 🌱 🏖 **Prices** ⚥ 4.70 pitch 4.10 **Facilities** ⌂ ⊙ 🚰 ∅ ☺ **Services** ⚑ ➕ ⊠ **Off-site** 🛁 ⫯⊙⫯ ♨ ⚓L

Site 6HEC (site size) 🌱 grass 🏖 sand 🐾 stone 🌱 little shade 🏖 partly shaded 🐾 mainly shaded 🏠 bungalows for hire 🚐 caravans for hire Ⓐ tents for hire ⊗ no dogs **Prices** ⚥ adult per night 🚗 car per night pp per person per night 🚐 caravan per night Ⓐ tent per night 🚐 (static)-caravan hire per week

GIGNY-SUR-SAÔNE SAÔNE-ET-LOIRE

Château de l'Epervière
71240 ☎ 385441690 📠 385941697
e-mail domaine-de-leperviere@wanadoo.fr
website www.domaine-eperviere.com
Quiet site in the park surrounding a 16th-century château. Close to the River Saône for fishing and sailing.
➲ N6 to Sennecey-le-Grand & signed.
Open Apr-Sep **Site** 10HEC 😃 ♨ ♠ **Prices** 🏕 5.40-7.30 pitch 7.90-10.50 **Facilities** 🚿 🛁 ⊙ 🔌 ⊘ ⓟ **Services** 🍴 🍽 ⨹ 🔲 **Leisure** ♦ P **Off-site** ♦R

GRANDPRÉ ARDENNES

CM
8250 ☎ 324305071
A peaceful riverside site.
➲ 150m from village centre on D6.
Open Apr-Sep **Site** 2HEC 😃 ♨ ♠ **Prices** 🏕 1.80 ♠ 0.90 ♠ 1-1.10 ⛺ 1-1.10 **Facilities** 🚿 ⊙ 🔌 ⓟ **Services** ⨹ **Leisure** ♦ R **Off-site** 🛁 🍽 🍴 ⊘ ⨺

ISSY-L'ÉVÊQUE SAÔNE-ET-LOIRE

CM de l'Étang Neuf
71760 ☎ 385249605
e-mail info@camping-etang-neuf.com
website www.camping-etang-neuf.com
A fine position beside the lake, with views of the château.
Open May-15 Sep **Site** 4HEC 😃 ♨ ♠ ⛺ **Prices** pitch 17-20 (incl 2 persons) ♠ (static)499 **Facilities** 🚿 🛁 ⊙ 🔌 ⊘ ⓟ **Services** 🍴 🍽 ⨹ 🔲 **Leisure** ♦ LP **Off-site** ⨺

LAIVES SAÔNE-ET-LOIRE

Lacs 'La Heronnière'
Les Bois de Laives, 71240 ☎ 385449885 📠 385449885
e-mail camping.laives@wanadoo.fr
website perso.orange.fr/camping.laives
Compulsory separate car park for arrivals after 22.00 hrs.
➲ Autoroute exit Chalon Sud towards Mâcon.
Open May-15 Sep **Site** 2HEC 😃 ♨ ♠ ♠ **Facilities** 🚿 🛁 ⊙ 🔌 ⊘ ⓟ **Services** 🍴 🍽 ⨹ 🔲 **Leisure** ♦ P **Off-site** 🍴 🍽 ♦LR

MÂCON SAÔNE-ET-LOIRE

CM
71000 ☎ 385381622 📠 385393918
e-mail camping@ville-macon.fr
Site divided into pitches with a water-sports centre and pool nearby.
➲ 2km N on N6.
Open 15 Mar-Oct **Site** 5HEC 😃 ♨ **Prices** pitch 9.90-14.10 (incl 2 persons) **Facilities** 🚿 🛁 ⊙ 🔌 ⊘ ⓟ **Services** 🍴 🍽 ⨹ 🔲 **Leisure** ♦ P **Off-site** ⨺ ♦R⨹

MARCENAY CÔTE-D'OR

Grebes
Laignes, 21330 ☎ 380816172 📠 380816199
e-mail marcenay@club-internet.fr
A peaceful site in unspoiled contryside with separate hedged pitches. Direct access to lake.
Open 30 Mar-15 Sep **Site** 2.4HEC 😃 ♨ ♠ **Facilities** 🚿 🛁 ⊙ 🔌 ⊘ ⓟ **Services** ⨹ 🔲 **Leisure** ♦ L **Off-site** 🍴 🍽

MATOUR SAÔNE-ET-LOIRE

CM Le Paluet
Le Paluet, 71520 ☎ 385597058 📠 385597454
e-mail mairie.matour@wanadoo.fr
website www.matour.com
Pleasant countryside beside the river.
Open May-Sep **Site** 2HEC 😃 ♨ ♠ ♠ ⛺ **Prices** 🏕 3.10-4.10 pitch 4.20-5.30 **Facilities** 🚿 ⊙ 🔌 ⓟ **Services** 🍴 🍽 🔲 **Leisure** ♦ P **Off-site** ⊘ ⨺ ⨹

MESNIL-ST PÈRE AUBE

Voie Colette
10140 ☎ 325412715 📠 325412715
e-mail voiecolette@yahoo.fr
Grassland, with trees, ornamental shrubs and flower beds. Slightly sloping, with a man-made lake nearby.
➲ 2km from Mesnil-St-Père, signed from centre.
Open Apr-10 Oct **Site** 4HEC 😃 ♨ ♠ **Facilities** 🚿 ⊙ 🔌 ⊘ ⓟ **Services** 🍴 ⨹ 🔲 **Off-site** 🛁 🍴 🍽 ♦L

MEURSAULT CÔTE-D'OR

Grappe d'Or
2 rte de Volnay, 21190 ☎ 380212248 📠 380216574
e-mail camping.lagrappedor@wanadoo.fr
website www.camping-meursault.com
Clean terraced site on an open meadow. Mountain bikes are available for hire.
➲ 0.7km NE on D11b.
Open Apr-15 Sep **Site** 5.5HEC 😃 ♨ ♠ ♠ **Prices** pitch 13.50-16.50 (incl 2 persons) pp3-3.70 ♠ (static)275-490 **Facilities** 🚿 🛁 ⊙ 🔌 ⊘ ⓟ **Services** 🍽 ⨹ 🔲 **Leisure** ♦ P **Off-site** 🍴

MONTAPAS NIÈVRE

CM La Chênaie
La Chênaie, 58110 ☎ 386583432 📠 386582905
Wooded location beside a lake with plenty of recreational facilities.
➲ 0.5km from town centre via D259, beside lake.
Open Apr-Oct **Site** 1HEC 😃 ♨ **Facilities** 🚿 ⊙ 🔌 ⓟ **Services** 🍴 🍽 🔲 **Leisure** ♦ L **Off-site** 🛁 ⊘ ⨺ ⨹

MONTBARD CÔTE-D'OR

CM
r M-Servet, 21500 ☎ 380922160 📠 380922160
e-mail camping.montbard@wanadoo.fr
website www.montbard.com
➲ NW via rte de Laignes.
Open Mar-27 Oct **Site** 2.5HEC 😃 ♨ ♠ **Prices** 🏕 3.50 pitch 6.50 ♠ (static)175-500 **Facilities** 🚿 🛁 ⊙ 🔌 ⊘ ⓟ **Services** 🍴 🍽 🔲 **Leisure** ♦ P **Off-site** 🍽 ⊘ ⨺ ♦R⨹

MONTHERMÉ ARDENNES

Base de Loisirs Départementale
8800 ☎ 324328161 📠 324323766
A pleasant wooded location.
➲ 0.8km NE beside the River Semoy.
Open All year **Site** 16HEC 😃 ♨ ♠ **Prices** 🏕 2.60 ♠ 1.40 ♠ 1.40 ⛺ 1.40 **Facilities** 🚿 ⊙ 🔌 ⓟ **Services** 🔲 **Leisure** ♦ R

Facilities 🛁 shop 🚿 shower ⊙ electric points for razors 🔌 electric points for caravans ⓟ parking by tents permitted ⓟ compulsory separate car park
Services 🍴 café/restaurant ⨹ bar ⊘ Camping Gaz International ⨺ gas other than Camping Gaz ⨹ first aid facilities 🔲 laundry
Leisure ♦ swimming L-Lake P-Pool R-River S-Sea **Off-site** All facilities within 2km

France

MONTSAUCHE NIÈVRE

Mesanges
Lac des Settons, Rive Gauche, 58230
☎ 386845577 ▤ 386845577
On Lac des Settons.
Open May-15 Sep **Site** 5HEC ♨ ♣ **Prices** ♠ 3.90 ♠ 2.60 pitch 3.30 **Facilities** ↑ ☎ ⊙ ❷ ⌀ **Services** ➕ ▨ **Off-site** ✴ ᵀⓄᴵ ⌀ ♨ ♠LPR

Plage du Midi
58230 ☎ 386845197 ▤ 386845731
e-mail plagedumidi@aol.com
website www.settons-camping.com
Wooded setting on Lac des Settons with good facilities.
➲ D193 from town centre to Les Sultons & site.
Open Etr-15 Oct **Site** 4HEC ♨ ♣ ☎ **Facilities** ↑ ☎ ⊙ ❷ ⌀ ❷ **Services** ✴ ᵀⓄᴵ ➕ ▨ **Leisure** ♠ L **Off-site** ᵀⓄᴵ ♨

PARAY-LE-MONIAL SAÔNE-ET-LOIRE

Mambré
rte du Gué-Léger, 71600 ☎ 385888920 ▤ 385888781
On a level meadow with modern facilities.
➲ Signed from outskirts of town.
Open Apr-Oct **Site** 4HEC ♨ ♣ ☎ ❷ **Facilities** ↑ ☎ ⊙ ❷ ♨ ❷ **Services** ✴ ᵀⓄᴵ ▨ **Leisure** ♠ P **Off-site** ☎ ✴ ᵀⓄᴵ ⌀ ♠R ➕

PONT-SAINTE-MARIE AUBE

CM de Troyes
7 r Roger Salengro, 10150 ☎ 325810264 ▤ 325810264
e-mail info@troyescamping.net
website www.troyescamping.net
Wooded site a short walk from the town of Troyes.
Open Apr-15 Oct **Site** 3.8HEC ♨ ♣ **Prices** ♠ 4.20 pitch 5.80 **Facilities** ↑ ☎ ⊙ ❷ ⌀ ❷ **Services** ᵀⓄᴵ ➕ ▨ **Off-site** ✴ ᵀⓄᴵ ♨

POUGUES-LES-EAUX NIÈVRE

CM Chanternes
Av de Paris, 58320 ☎ 386688618
➲ 7km N of Nevers on N7.
Open Jun-Sep **Site** 1.4HEC ♨ ♣ **Facilities** ↑ ⊙ ❷ ❷ **Services** ➕ ▨ **Off-site** ☎ ✴ ᵀⓄᴵ ♨ ♠PR

PREMEAUX CÔTE-D'OR

Saule Guillaume
21700 ☎ 380612799 ▤ 380613519
Pleasant site beside a lake.
➲ 1.5km E via D109C.
Open 15 Jun-5 Sep **Site** 2.1HEC ♨ ♣ **Facilities** ↑ ☎ ⊙ ❷ ❷ **Services** ➕ ▨ **Off-site** ✴ ᵀⓄᴵ ⌀ ♠P

RADONVILLIERS AUBE

Garillon
Rue des Anciens Combattants, 10500 ☎ 325922146 ▤ 325922134
Beside the river, 250m from the lake.
Open May-15 Sep **Site** 1HEC ♨ ♣ ❷ **Facilities** ↑ ⊙ ❷ ❷ **Services** ▨ **Off-site** ✴ ᵀⓄᴵ ♠LR ➕

RIEL-LES-EAUX CÔTE-D'OR

Riel-les-Eaux
21570 ☎ 380937276 ▤ 380937276
A lakeside site with fishing and boating facilities.
➲ 2.2km W via D13.
Open Apr-Oct **Site** 0.2HEC ♨ ♣ ☎ **Prices** ♠ 2 ♠ 1 pitch 2.50 **Facilities** ↑ ☎ ⊙ ❷ ⌀ ❷ **Services** ✴ ᵀⓄᴵ ▨ **Leisure** ♠ L **Off-site** ♨

ST-HILAIRE-SOUS-ROMILLY AUBE

Domaine de La Noue des Rois
chemin des Brayes, 10100 ☎ 325244160 ▤ 325243418
e-mail michele.desmont@wanadoo.fr
website www.lanouedesrois.com
A quiet site in a pine forest on the Basin d'Arcachon. Booking advised for July and August.
➲ 2km NE.
Open All year **Site** 30HEC ♨ ♣ ☎ ⊗ **Facilities** ↑ ☎ ⊙ ❷ ♨ ❷ ❷ **Services** ✴ ᵀⓄᴵ ➕ ▨ **Leisure** ♠ LP

ST-HONORÉ NIÈVRE

Bains
15 av J-Mermoz, 58360 ☎ 386307344 ▤ 386306188
e-mail camping-les-bains@wanadoo.fr
website www.campinglesbains.com
A family site with good facilities close to the Morvan national park.
➲ Via A6 & D985.
Open May-5 Sep **Site** 4.5HEC ♨ ♣ ☎ **Facilities** ↑ ⊙ ❷ ⌀ ❷ **Services** ✴ ᵀⓄᴵ ➕ ▨ **Leisure** ♠ P **Off-site** ☎ ᵀⓄᴵ ♨

ST-PÉREUSE NIÈVRE

Manoir de Bezolle
58110 ☎ 386844255 ▤ 386844377
e-mail info@bezolle.com
website www.bezolle.com
A well-kept site divided by hedges in the grounds of a manor house, at the edge of a national park.
➲ At x-rds of D11 & D978.
Open May-15 Sept **Site** 8HEC ♨ ♣ ☎ ❷ A **Facilities** ↑ ☎ ⊙ ❷ ⌀ ❷ **Services** ✴ ᵀⓄᴵ ➕ ▨ **Leisure** ♠ P

STE-MENEHOULD MARNE

CM de la Grelette
51800 ☎ 326607389
A well-equipped municipal site.
➲ E of town towards Metz, beside River Aisne.
Open May-Sep **Site** 1HEC ♨ ♣ **Facilities** ↑ ⊙ ❷ ❷ **Services** ▨ **Off-site** ☎ ✴ ᵀⓄᴵ ⌀ ♨ ♠PR ➕

SAULIEU CÔTE-D'OR

CM Perron
21210 ☎ 380641619 ▤ 380641619
e-mail camping.saulieu@wanadoo.fr
website www.saulieu.fr
On level, open ground with good recreational facilities.
➲ 1km NW on N6.
Open Apr-Sep **Site** 4.5HEC ♨ ♣ ☎ **Prices** ♠ 3-3 A 3 pitch 12-13 (incl 2 persons) **Facilities** ↑ ☎ ⊙ ❷ ❷ **Services** ✴ ➕ ▨ **Leisure** ♠ P **Off-site** ☎ ✴ ᵀⓄᴵ ⌀ ♨ ♠LP

Site 6HEC (site size) ♨ grass ⬤ sand ♨ stone ♣ little shade ♣ partly shaded ● mainly shaded ☎ bungalows for hire ❷ caravans for hire A tents for hire ⊗ no dogs **Prices** ♠ adult per night ♠ car per night pp per person per night ❷ caravan per night A tent per night ❷ (static)-caravan hire per week

SEDAN ARDENNES

CM de la Prairie

bd Fabert, 08200 ☎ 324271305 ▤ 324271305

A well-equipped municipal site on the banks of the River Meuse, close to the centre of the village.

Open Apr-Sept **Site** 1.5HEC ❤ ♣ **Prices** ♠ 1.20-2.55 ⊕ 2.15-2.35 **Facilities** ↑ ⊙ ⊕ ⊛ **Services** ➕ ⬚ **Off-site** ⬤LP

SEURRE CÔTE-D'OR

Piscine

21250 ☎ 380204922 ▤ 380203401

A well-equipped municipal site with direct access to the river.

➲ N73 W from town centre for 0.6km towards Beaune.

Open 15 May-15 Sep **Site** ❤ ♣ **Facilities** ↑ ⊙ ⊕ ⊘ ⊛ **Services** ➕ ⎚ ➕ ⬚ **Leisure** ⬤ PR **Off-site** ⬚ ➕ ⎚

SÉZANNE MARNE

CM

rte de Launat, 51120 ☎ 326805700

e-mail campingdesezanne@wanadoo.fr

➲ 1.5km W on D239, rte de Launat.

Open Apr-1 Oct **Site** 1HEC ❤ ♣ **Facilities** ↑ ⊙ ⊕ ⊛ **Services** ⬚ **Leisure** ⬤ P **Off-site** ⬚ ➕ ⎚

SIGNY-LE-PETIT ARDENNES

Pré Hugon

Base de Loisirs, 08380 ☎ 324535473 ▤ 324535473

e-mail campingprehugon@wanadoo.fr

website www.signy-le-petit.com

A pleasant site in wooded surroundings.

➲ Via N43.

Open 12 Apr-Sep **Site** 0.8HEC ❤ ♣ ⚑ **Prices** ♠ 3 ⊕ 2 ⊕ 2 Å 2 **Facilities** ↑ ⊙ ⊕ ⊛ **Services** ➕ ⎚ ⬚ **Leisure** ⬤ P **Off-site** ⬚ ➕ ⎚ ⊘ ⬟ ⬤LR ➕

SOULAINES-DHUYS AUBE

La Croix Badeau

10200 ☎ 325270543

e-mail steveheusghem@hotmail.com

website www.croix-badeau.com

Open Apr-15 Oct **Site** 1.5HEC ❤ ♣ **Prices** ♠ 2.70 ⊕ 3.20 Å 3.20 **Facilities** ↑ ⊙ ⊕ ⊛ **Services** ⬚ **Off-site** ⬚ ➕ ⎚ ⊘ ⬟ ⬤R ➕

TAZILLY NIÈVRE

Château de Chigy

58170 ☎ 386301080 ▤ 386300922

A beautiful location within the extensive grounds of a magnificent château. Good sports facilities and entertainment programme.

➲ 4km from Luzy on D973 Luzy-Moulins.

Open May-Sep **Site** 7HEC ❤ ♣ ⚑ **Facilities** ↑ ⬚ ⊙ ⊕ ⊘ ⊛ **Services** ➕ ⎚ ➕ ⬚ **Leisure** ⬤ LP

THONNANCE-LES-MOULINS HAUTE-MARNE

Forge de Ste-Marie

52230 ☎ 325944200 ▤ 325944143

e-mail la.forge.de.sainte.marie@wanadoo.fr

website www.laforgedesaintemarie.com

Partially terraced, on the site of an 18th-century forge containing a lake.

➲ Via N67 & D427.

Open May-Sep **Site** 11HEC ❤ ♣ ⚑ ⚑ **Prices** ♠ 3.50-7 pitch 11-15 **Facilities** ↑ ⬚ ⊙ ⊕ ⊘ ⊛ **Services** ➕ ⎚ ➕ ⬚ **Leisure** ⬤ PR

TOULON-SUR-ARROUX SAÔNE-ET-LOIRE

CM du Val d'Arroux

rte d'Uxeau, 73120 ☎ 385795122 ▤ 385796217

e-mail mairie.toulon@wanadoo.fr

On W outskirts beside the River Arroux.

➲ D985 onto Uxeau road.

Open late Apr-late Oct **Site** 0.6HEC ❤ ♣ **Prices** ♠ 1.80 ⊕ 1.35 ⊕ 2.80 **Facilities** ↑ ⊙ ⊕ ⊛ **Services** ➕ ⬚ **Leisure** ⬤ R **Off-site** ⬚ ➕ ⎚ ⊘ ⬟

UCHIZY SAÔNE-ET-LOIRE

National 6

71700 ☎ 385405390 ▤ 385405390

e-mail camping.uchizylen6@wanadoo.fr

website camping.uchizy.free.fr

Site surrounded by poplar trees on banks of river.

➲ Off N6 towards Saône 6km S of Tournus & continue 0.8km.

Open Apr-1 Oct **Site** 6HEC ❤ ♣ ⚑ ⚑ **Prices** ♠ 3.30-4.30 pitch 3.90-4.90 ⚑ (static)260-340 **Facilities** ↑ ⬚ ⊙ ⊕ ⊘ ⬟ ⊛ **Services** ➕ ⎚ ➕ ⬚ **Leisure** ⬤ PR

VAL-DES-PRÉS MARNE

Gentianes

La Vachette, 5100 ☎ 492212141 ▤ 492212412

A delightful wooded location bordered by a river and backed by imposing mountains.

➲ On edge of village, 3km SE of Briançon.

Open All year **Site** 2HEC ❤ ♣ ♣ ⚑ ⚑ **Prices** ♠ 4.70 pitch 4.70 pp2.10 ⚑ (static)302-407 **Facilities** ↑ ⬚ ⊙ ⊕ ⬟ ⊛ **Services** ➕ ⎚ ➕ ⬚ **Leisure** ⬤ PR **Off-site** ⊘

VANDENESSE-EN-AUXOIS CÔTE-D'OR

Lac de Panthier

21320 ☎ 380492194 ▤ 380492580

e-mail info@lac-de-panthier.com

website www.lac-de-panthier.com

Wooded location beside Lake Panthier with a variety of sports facilities.

➲ 5km SE from Pouilly-en-Auxois on A6.

Open 18 Apr-27 Sep **Site** 6HEC ❤ ♣ ⚑ **Facilities** ↑ ⬚ ⊙ ⊕ ⊘ ⊛ **Services** ➕ ⎚ ➕ ⬚ **Leisure** ⬤ LP

France

VENAREY-LES-LAUMES CÔTE-D'OR

Alésia
r Dr-Roux, 21150 ☎ 380960776 🖹 380960776
e-mail camping.venary@wanadoo.fr
website www.alesia-tourisme.net
A peaceful site close to the lake and river.
Open All year **Site** 2HEC 👑 👑 🏚 **Prices** ♠ 2.50 🚗 4 Å 1.60
Facilities ♠ ⊙ 🗭 ⑳ **Services** 🍴 🖸 🗟 **Off-site** 🛉 ⚖️ ⊘ ⚖LR 🖸

VERMENTON YONNE

Coulemières
89270 ☎ 386815302 🖹 386815302
website www.vermenton.fr
A peaceful meadowland site with good facilities.
➲ On N6 S of Auxerre.
Open Apr-Sep **Site** 1.5HEC 👑 👑 **Facilities** ♠ ⊙ 🗭 ⑳ **Services** 🖸 🗟
Leisure ⚖ R **Off-site** 🛉 ⊘

VILLENEUVE-LES-GENÊTS YONNE

Bois Guillaume
89350 ☎ 386454541 🖹 386454920
e-mail camping@bois-guillaume.com
website www.bois-guillaume.com
Wooded surroundings with modern facilities.
➲ 2.7km NE.
Open All year **Site** 8HEC 👑 👑 🏚 **Prices** ♠ 3.70-3.90 🚗 2.60 pitch 2.70
Facilities ♠ ⊙ 🗭 ⊘ ⚖ ⑳ **Services** 🍴 🍴 🖸 🗟 **Leisure** ⚖ P
Off-site ⚖R

VINCELLES YONNE

Ceriselles
rte de Vincelottes, 89290 ☎ 386425047 🖹 386423939
e-mail lesceriselles@wanadoo.fr
website www.campingceriselles.com
Rural location beside the river Yonne, close to the local village.
➲ RN6 exit between Avallon & Auxerre, signed.
Open Apr-Oct **Site** 1.5HEC 👑 👑 🏚 **Facilities** ♠ ⊙ 🗭 ⊘ ⑳
Services 🍴 🍴 🖸 🗟 **Off-site** 🛉 ⚖R 🖸

SOUTH WEST/PYRÉNÉES

ABZAC GIRONDE

Paradis
rte de Périgueux, 33230 ☎ 557490510 🖹 557491888
e-mail campingleparadis@free.fr
website www.campingleparadis.free.fr
Meadowland Site near an artificial lake. Pedal boats and fishing nearby. A region of gastronomic importance.
➲ N89 W from Périgueux, after St-Médard-de-Guizières onto D17E & signed.
Open Feb-15 Nov **Site** 5HEC 👑 👑 🏚 🏚 **Facilities** ♠ 🛉 ⊙ 🗭 ⊘ ⚖ ⑳
Services 🍴 🍴 🖸 🗟 **Leisure** ⚖ LR

AIGNAN GERS

Castex
32290 ☎ 562092513 🖹 562092479
e-mail info@gers-vacances.com
website www.gers-vacances.com
Wooded site in peaceful surroundings.
➲ 0.8km from D48.
Open 15 Mar-15 Oct **Site** 3HEC 👑 👑 🏚 🏚 **Prices** pitch 12-14 (incl 2 persons) 🚐 (static)375-600 **Facilities** ♠ ⊙ 🗭 ⑳ **Services** 🍴 🍴 🖸 🗟
Leisure ⚖ P **Off-site** 🛉 🍴 ⊘ ⚖ ⚖LR

AIRE-SUR-L'ADOUR LANDES

Ombrages de l'Adour
r des Graviers, 40800 ☎ 558717510 🖹 558713259
e-mail hetapsarl@yahoo.fr
website www.camping-adour-landes.com
A clean, tidy site next to a sports stadium beside the river. Clean sanitary installations.
Open Apr-Oct **Site** 2HEC 👑 👑 🏚 🏚 Å **Prices** ♠ 2.50-3.50 🚗 1.50-2 pitch 3-4 🚐 (static)130-240 **Facilities** ♠ ⊙ 🗭 ⚖ ⑳ **Services** 🖸 🗟
Leisure ⚖ R **Off-site** ⚖P

ALBI TARN

Languedoc
allée du Camping Caussels, 81000 ☎ 563603706 🖹 563603706
The site is owned by the local automobile club. It lies on terraced land in a forest next to municipal swimming pools.
➲ N99 from village towards Millau, left onto D100, left to site.
Open Apr-Oct **Site** 1.5HEC 👑 👑 🏚 **Prices** ♠ 11.50 pitch 11.50 (incl 2 persons) **Facilities** ♠ ⊙ 🗭 ⑳ **Services** 🖸 🗟 **Off-site** 🛉 🍴 🍴 ⊘ ⚖P

ALLAS-LES-MINES DORDOGNE

Domaine Le Cro Magnon
☎ 553291370 🖹 553291579
e-mail contact@domaine-cro-magnon.com
website www.domaine-cro-magnon.com
Spacious pitches in a generously wooded 25 hectare estate.
➲ D25 southwards exit Marnac Berbiguières.
Open May-15 Sep **Site** 22HEC 👑 👑 🏚 **Prices** ♠ 3.40-7 pitch 5-17.10 🚐 (static)320-886 **Facilities** ♠ 🛉 ⊙ 🗭 ⊘ ⑳ **Services** 🍴 🍴 🖸
Leisure ⚖ P **Off-site** ⚖R

ALLES-SUR-DORDOGNE DORDOGNE

Port de Limeuil
24480 ☎ 553632976 🖹 553630419
e-mail didierbonvallet@aol.com
website www.leportdelimeuil.com
Situated in a conservation area at the confluence of the Dordogne and Vézère rivers, with a 400m-long beach.
➲ Signed off D51.
Open May-Sep **Site** 7HEC 👑 👑 👑 **Prices** pitch 14-24.90 (incl 2 persons) pp4.50-5.50 **Facilities** ♠ 🛉 ⊙ 🗭 ⑳ **Services** 🍴 🍴 🖸 🗟
Leisure ⚖ PR

Site 6HEC (site size) 👑 grass 👑 sand 👑 stone ♣ little shade ♣ partly shaded 👑 mainly shaded 🏚 bungalows for hire
🚐 caravans for hire Å tents for hire ⊗ no dogs **Prices** ♠ adult per night 🚗 car per night pp per person per night 🚐 caravan per night
Å tent per night 🚐 (static)-caravan hire per week

ANDERNOS-LES-BAINS GIRONDE

Fontaine-Vieille
4 bd du Colonel Wurtz, 33510 ☎ 556820167 🖹 556820981
e-mail fontaine-vieille-sa@wanadoo.fr
website www.fontaine-vieille.com
On level ground in sparse forest.
➲ S of village centre.
Open Apr-Sep **Site** 12.6HEC 🛖 🛋 🚐 🚗 **Prices** ⚑ 3-5 🚐 2-3 pitch 16-24 (incl 2 persons) **Facilities** ⋔ 🛒 ⊙ 🖽 🐝 🚿 ⚲ **Services** ⌿ 🍴 ⊞ 🗒 **Leisure** ⚓ PS

See advertisement on this page

Pleine Forêt
33510 ☎ 556821718
A quiet location among pines.
➲ Off D106E or D106 Andernos-les-Bains-Bordeaux road.
Open All year **Site** 6HEC 🛖 🛋 🚐 🚗 🚐 **Facilities** ⋔ ⊙ 🖽 🐝 🚿 **Services** ⌿ 🍴 ⊞ 🗒 **Leisure** ⚓ P **Off-site** 🍴 ⚲ ⚓S

ANGLARS-JUILLAC LOT

Floiras
46140 ☎ 565362739 🖹 565214100
e-mail campingfloiras@aol.com
website www.campingfloiras.com
A quiet level site beside the River Lot, surrounded by vineyards in a hilly landscape dotted with villages, castles and caves. Facilities for boating.
➲ SW via D8.
Open Apr-15 Oct **Site** 1HEC 🛖 🛋 ⚐ **Prices** ⚑ 3.50-3.85 pitch 5.25-7 **Facilities** ⋔ ⊙ 🖽 ⚲ 🚿 **Services** ⌿ 🍴 ⊞ 🗒 **Leisure** ⚓ R **Off-site** 🛒 🍴

ANGLES TARN

Manoir de Boutaric
rte de Lacabarede, 81260 ☎ 563709606 🖹 563709605
e-mail manoir@boutaric.com
website www.boutaric.com
The site lies in the grounds of an old manor house in the heart of the Haute Languedoc region.
➲ S of village on D52 towards Lacabarède.
Open Etr-Sep **Site** 3.3HEC 🛖 🛋 🚐 **Prices** ⚑ 3.10-5.50 pitch 13-26 (incl 2 persons) **Facilities** ⋔ ⊙ 🖽 ⚲ 🚿 **Services** ⌿ 🍴 ⊞ 🗒 **Leisure** ⚓ P **Off-site** 🛒 ⚓LR

ANGLET PYRÉNÉES-ATLANTIQUES

Parme
Quartier Brindos, 64600 ☎ 559230300 🖹 559412955
e-mail campingdeparme@wanadoo.fr
website campingdeparme.com
Wooded area with good facilities on the outskirts of Biarritz.
➲ 3km SW off N10.
Open Apr-30 Oct **Site** 3.5HEC 🛖 🛋 🚐 **Prices** 🚐 (static)210-680 **Facilities** ⋔ 🛒 ⊙ 🖽 ⚲ 🚿 **Services** ⌿ 🍴 ⊞ 🗒 **Leisure** ⚓ P **Off-site** ⚓LRS

CAMPING CARAVANING FONTAINE VIEILLE
★ ★ ★
Bassin d'Arcachon

WATER COMPLEX

4, Boulevard du Colonel Wurtz
33510 Andernos-Les-Bains
Tél.: 05 56 82 01 67
Fax: 05 56 82 09 81
www.fontainevieille.com
GPS 44° 43.550-N 001° 04797-0

ARCACHON GIRONDE

Camping Club d'Arcachon
av de la Galaxie, Les Abatilles, 33120 ☎ 556832415 🖹 557522851
e-mail camparcachon@hotmail.com
A delightful wooded position 0.8km from the town and 1km from the beaches.
➲ 1.5km S.
Open All year **Site** 6HEC 🛖 🛋 🚐 🚗 **Prices** pitch 10-26 (incl 3 persons) **Facilities** ⋔ 🛒 ⊙ 🖽 ⚲ 🚿 🐝 ❂ **Services** ⌿ 🍴 ⊞ 🗒 **Leisure** ⚓ P **Off-site** ⚓S

ARCIZANS-AVANT HAUTES-PYRÉNÉES

Lac
29 chemin d'Azun, 65400 ☎ 562970188 🖹 562970188
e-mail campinglac@campinglac65.fr
website www.campinglac65.fr
Set in delightful Pyrenean surroundings on outskirts of village. Lakeside site close to a château.
➲ S on N21, onto D13 through St-Savin.
Open 15 May-Sep **Site** 4HEC 🛖 🛋 🚐 **Prices** ⚑ 6.50 pitch 6.50 **Facilities** ⋔ 🛒 ⊙ 🖽 ⚲ 🚿 ❂ **Services** ⊞ 🗒 **Leisure** ⚓ P **Off-site** ⌿ 🍴 🐝 ⚓LR

Facilities 🛒 shop ⋔ shower ⊙ electric points for razors 🖽 electric points for caravans ❂ parking by tents permitted ❂ compulsory separate car park
Services 🍴 café/restaurant ⌿ bar ⚲ Camping Gaz International 🐝 gas other than Camping Gaz ⊞ first aid facilities 🗒 laundry
Leisure ⚓ swimming L-Lake P-Pool R-River S-Sea **Off-site** All facilities within 2km

France

ARÈS GIRONDE

Canadienne
rte de Lège, 82 r du Gl-de-Gaulle, 33740
☎ 556602491 ▤ 557704085
e-mail camping-la-canadienne@wanadoo.fr
website www.lacanadienne.com
A family site surrounded by pine and oak trees with good facilities.
➲ *1km N off D106.*
Open Jan-Nov **Site** 2HEC ❤ ❤ ❀ **Facilities** ↑ ⊙ ◘ ⌂ ⚿ **Services** ⚐
⏰ ➕ ⊠ **Leisure** ⚭ P **Off-site** ⌀ ⚭L

Cigale
rte de Lège, 33740 ☎ 556602259 ▤ 557704166
e-mail campinglacigaleares@wanadoo.fr
website www.camping-lacigale-ares.com
Clean tidy site among pine trees. Grassy pitches and good recreational facilities.
➲ *0.5km N on D106, between sea & Arcachon Basin.*
Open 5 May-Sep **Site** 2.8HEC ❤ ❤ ❀ **Prices** pitch 18-29 (incl 2 persons) ➡ (static)260-620 **Facilities** ↑ ⊞ ⊙ ◘ ⚿ **Services** ⚐ ⏰ ➕ ⊠
Leisure ⚭ P **Off-site** ⌀ ⚌ ⚭S

Goëlands
av de la Libération, 33740 ☎ 556825564 ▤ 556820751
e-mail camping-les-goelands@wanadoo.fr
Situated among oak trees 200m from the beach with good facilities.
➲ *1.7km SE.*
Open Mar-Oct **Site** 10HEC ❤ ❤ ❀ **Prices** pitch 15-21.22 (incl 2 persons) **Facilities** ↑ ⊞ ⊙ ◘ ⌀ ⚿ **Services** ⚐ ⏰ ➕ ⊠ **Off-site** ⚭L

Pasteur
1 r du Pilote, 33704 ☎ 556603333
website www.atlantic-vacances.com
➲ *S of D3, 300m from the sea.*
Open Apr-Sep **Site** 1HEC ❤ ❤ ❀ ➡ **Prices** pitch 12.50-23 (incl 2 persons) pp3-5 ➡ (static)220-600 **Facilities** ↑ ⊙ ◘ ⚿ **Services** ⚐
⏰ ➕ ⊠ **Leisure** ⚭ P **Off-site** ⊞ ⚭S

ARGELÈS-GAZOST HAUTES-PYRÉNÉES
AT AGOS-VIDALOS (5KM NE)

Soleil du Pibeste
65400 ☎ 562975323´
e-mail info@campingpibeste.com
A beautiful wooded setting in the heart of the Pyrénées.
➲ *S on N21.*
Open All year **Site** 1.5HEC ❤ ❤ ❀ **Facilities** ↑ ⊞ ⊙ ◘ ⌀ ⚌ ⚿
Services ⚐ ⏰ ➕ ⊠ **Leisure** ⚭ P **Off-site** ⚭R

ARREAU HAUTES-PYRÉNÉES

Refuge International
RD 929, 65240 ☎ 562986334 ▤ 562986334
e-mail camping.international.arreau@wanadoo.fr
Enclosed terrace site.
➲ *2km N on D929.*
Open All year **Site** 15HEC ❤ ❤ ❀ ➡ **Facilities** ↑ ⊙ ◘ ⚌ ⚿
Services ⚐ ⏰ ➕ ⊠ **Leisure** ⚭ PR **Off-site** ⊞ ⏰ ⌀ ⚌ ⚭L

ASCAIN PYRÉNÉES-ATLANTIQUES

Nivelle
64310 ☎ 559540194 ▤ 559540194
e-mail campinglanivelle@wanadoo.fr
website www.camping-lanivelle.com
Picturesque location beside the River Nivelle.
➲ *2km N of town on D918 to St-Jean-de-Luz.*
Open Apr-Oct **Site** 2.8HEC ❤ ❤ ❀ ➡ **Facilities** ↑ ⊞ ⊙ ◘ ⚿ ⚐
Services ⏰ ➕ ⊠ **Leisure** ⚭ R **Off-site** ⊞ ⚐ ⏰ ⌀ ➕

ASCARAT PYRÉNÉES-ATLANTIQUES

Europ' Camping
64220 ☎ 559371278 ▤ 559372982
Rural surroundings of mountains and vineyards, 300m from the River Nive.
➲ *1km W of St-Jean-Pied-de-Port on D918.*
Open Etr-Sep **Site** 2HEC ❤ ❤ ❀ **Facilities** ↑ ⊞ ⊙ ◘ ⚿ **Services** ⚐ ⏰
➕ ⊠ **Leisure** ⚭ P **Off-site** ⌀ ⚌ ⚭R

ATUR DORDOGNE

Grand Dague
24750 ☎ 553042101 ▤ 553042201
e-mail info@legranddague.fr
website www.legranddague.fr
Well-equipped family site in the heart of the Dordogne region, with pitches divided by bushes and hedges.
➲ *NE of Atur via D2.*
Open Etr-15 Sep **Site** 22HEC ❤ ❤ ❀ ➡ **Prices** ⚲ 4.25-5.75 pitch 4.95-7.95 ➡ (static)185-635 **Facilities** ↑ ⊞ ⊙ ◘ ⌀ ⚌ ⚿ **Services** ⚐ ⏰ ➕ ⊠
Leisure ⚭ P

AUREILHAN LANDES

Aurilandes Camping
1001 promenade de l'Étang, 40200 ☎ 558091088 ▤ 558090189
e-mail info@campingterreoceane.com
website www.campingterreoceane.com
Quiet site separated by a small road on the banks of Lake Aureilhan.
➲ *D626, 2km before Mimizan, on right.*
Open Jun-Sep **Site** 8HEC ❤ ❤ ❀ ⚑ **Facilities** ↑ ⊞ ⊙ ◘ ⌀ ⚌ ⚿
Services ⚐ ⏰ ➕ ⊠ **Leisure** ⚭ LP **Off-site** ⚭PS

Parc St-James Eurolac
Promenade de l'Étang, 40200 ☎ 558090287 ▤ 558094189
e-mail info@camping-parcstjames.com
website www.camping-parcstjames.com
Well-tended site with deciduous trees providing shade, and partly open meadow.
➲ *Off N10 at Labouheyre onto D626 to Aureilhan & signed.*
Open Apr-Sep **Site** 13HEC ❤ ❤ ❀ ⚑ **Prices** ⚑ 5 pitch 8.50-26.50 (incl 2 persons) ➡ (static)258-744 **Facilities** ↑ ⊞ ⊙ ◘ ⌀ ⚿ **Services** ⚐
⏰ ➕ ⊠ **Leisure** ⚭ LP

Site 6HEC (site size) ❤ grass ❤ sand ❤ stone ❀ little shade ❀ partly shaded ❀ mainly shaded ❀ bungalows for hire
➡ caravans for hire ⚑ tents for hire ⊗ no dogs **Prices** ⚲ adult per night ⚏ car per night pp per person per night ➡ caravan per night
⚑ tent per night ➡ (static)-caravan hire per week

AZUR LANDES

Camping Azu' Rivage

720 Route des Campings, Au bord du lac, 40140
☎ 558483072 ▤ 558483072
e-mail info@campingazurivage.com
website www.campingazurivage.com
A family site in wooded surroundings close to Lac de Soustons and
8km from the coast.
➲ *2km S of Azur.*
Open 15 June-15 Sep **Site** 7HEC 👜 ♣ ♣ 🏠 **Prices** ⚑ 2.60-3.60 pitch
10.10-16.70 (incl 2 persons) **Facilities** 🌰 🖆 ⊙ ♀ ⌀ 🚯 ⑳ **Services** ⚑ 🍴
➕ 🖾 **Leisure** ⚓ LPR

BAGNÈRES-DE-BIGORRE HAUTES-PYRÉNÉES

Bigourdan

rte de Tarbes, 65200 ☎ 562951357
website www.camping-bigourdan.com
A level site recommended for caravans in a beautiful Pyrenean setting.
➲ *2.5km NW at Pouzac.*
Open 31 Mar-21 Oct **Site** 1HEC 👜 ♣ 🏠 ♀ **Prices** ⚑ 3.80 pitch 3.90
♀ (static)150-390 **Facilities** 🌰 ⊙ ♀ ⑳ **Services** 🖾 **Leisure** ⚓ P
Off-site 🖆 ⚑🍴 🍴 ⌀ 🚯 ⚓R ➕

Tilleuls

12 av Maréchal Alan Brooke, 65200 ☎ 562952604
A well-equipped site at an altitude of 500m. There are good
recreational facilities and a bakery operates during July and August.
Open May-Sep **Site** 2.6HEC 👜 ♣ **Facilities** 🌰 ⊙ ♀ ⑳ **Services** 🖾
Off-site 🖆 ⚑🍴 🍴 ⌀ 🚯 ⚓P ➕

AT TRÉBONS (4KM N ON D935)

Parc des Oiseaux

RD26, 65200 ☎ 562953026
Clean, well-kept site with large pitches.
Open All year **Site** 2.8HEC 👜 ♣ 🏠 ♀ **Facilities** 🌰 ⊙ ♀ 🚯 ⑳
Services ⚑🍴 ➕ 🖾 **Leisure** ⚓ R **Off-site** 🍴 ⚓P

BASTIDE-DE-SEROU, LA ARIÈGE

Arize

rte de Nescus, 9240 ☎ 561658151 ▤ 561658334
e-mail camparize@aol.com
website www.camping-arize.com
A well-run site with a range of facilities in a peaceful wooded location
at the foot of the Pyrénées.
Open Apr-Oct **Site** 1.8HEC 👜 ♣ 🏠 ♀ ⚐ **Facilities** 🌰 🖆 ⊙ ♀ ⌀ ⑳
Services ⚑🍴 ➕ 🖾 **Leisure** ⚓ PR **Off-site** 🍴 ➕

BEAUCENS-LES-BAINS HAUTES-PYRÉNÉES

Viscos

65400 ☎ 562970545
A secluded location at the foot of the Pyrénées.
➲ *1km N on D13 rte de Lourdes.*
Open 10 May-Sep **Site** 2HEC 👜 ♣ **Prices** ⚑ 3.50 pitch 3.50 **Facilities** 🌰
⊙ ♀ ⌀ ⑳ **Services** ➕ 🖾 **Off-site** ⚓R

BELVÈS DORDOGNE

Hauts de Ratebout

24170 ☎ 553290210 ▤ 553290828
e-mail camping@hauts-ratebout.fr
website www.hauts-ratebout.fr
A well-equipped site on an old Périgord farm, set in extensive grounds
on top of a hill.
➲ *D710 to Fumel, after Vaurez-de-Belvès onto D54 to Casals.*
Open 12 May-9 Sep **Site** 12HEC 👜 ♣ 🏠 ♀ ⑳ **Prices** ⚑ 5.50-7.50 pitch
20.60-33 ♀ (static)365-766 **Facilities** 🌰 🖆 ⊙ ♀ ⌀ ⑳ **Services** ⚑🍴 🍴 ➕
🖾 **Leisure** ⚓ P

Nauves

Bos Rouge, 24170 ☎ 553291264 ▤ 553291264
e-mail campinglesnauves@hotmail.com
Located on a site of 40 hectares surrounded by forest.
➲ *4.5km SW via D53.*
Open Apr- Sep **Site** 7HEC 👜 ♣ 🏠 ♀ **Facilities** 🌰 🖆 ⊙ ♀ ♀ ⑳ ♀
Services ⚑🍴 🍴 ➕ 🖾 **Leisure** ⚓ P

RCN Le Moulin de la Pique

24170 ☎ 553290115 ▤ 553282909
e-mail info@rcn-lemoulindelapique,fr
website www.rcn-campings.fr
A quiet well-equipped site set out around an imposing villa and a
small lake. There are fine entertainment facilities and modern sanitary
installations.
➲ *0.5km S on D710.*
Open 14 Apr-6 Oct **Site** 12HEC 👜 ♣ 🏠 ♀ **Prices** pitch 13.75 (incl 2
persons) ♀ (static)260-805 **Facilities** 🌰 🖆 ⊙ ♀ ⌀ 🚯 ⑳ **Services** ⚑🍴 🍴
➕ 🖾 **Leisure** ⚓ LPR

BEYNAC-ET-CAZENAC DORDOGNE

Capeyrou

24220 ☎ 553295495 ▤ 553283627
e-mail lecapeyrou@wanadoo.fr
website www.camping-dordogne.com/lecapeyrou
Situated beside the River Dordogne close to the gates of the
picturesque medieval town of Beynac.
➲ *Via D703.*
Open Etr-Sep **Site** 5HEC 👜 ♣ **Facilities** 🌰 ⊙ ♀ ⑳ **Services** ⚑🍴 🍴 ➕ 🖾
Leisure ⚓ P **Off-site** 🖆 🍴 ⌀ 🚯 ⚓R

BEZ, LE TARN

Plô

81260 ☎ 563740082
e-mail info@leplo.com
website www.leplo.com
A pleasant site in wooded surroundings.
➲ *0.9km W via D30.*
Open May-Sep **Site** 4.2HEC 👜 ♣ ♀ 🛆 **Facilities** 🌰 🖆 ⊙ ♀ ⑳
Services ⚑🍴 🍴 ➕ 🖾 **Off-site** 🍴 ⌀ ⚓R

France

BIARRITZ PYRÉNÉES-ATLANTIQUES

Biarritz

28 r d'Harcet, 64200 ☎ 559230012 📄 559437467
e-mail biarritz.camping@wanadoo.fr
website www.biarritz-camping.fr
A pleasant site with spacious pitches, 200m from the beach.

➲ *2km from town centre on N10, signed Espagne.*

Open 6 May-16 Sep **Site** 2.6HEC 😃 😃 😨 🐟 **Prices** ⚹ 3-4.15 pitch 15-21.50 (incl 2 persons) 🐟 (static)230-600 **Facilities** 🏱 🏠 ⊙ 🐟 ⌀ ☜ **Services** 🍴 🍴 🚻 🗄 **Leisure** ⌂ P **Off-site** 🏠 🍴 🍴 🚲 ⌂S 🚻

AT BIDART (4KM SW)

Jean Paris

Quartier M-Pierre, 64210 ☎ 559265558 📄 559265558
Site lies 0.6km from beaches.

➲ *S of town, cross railway, site on S side of N10.*

Open Jun-Sep **Site** 1.1HEC 😃 😃 **Facilities** 🏱 🏠 ⊙ 🐟 ☜ **Services** 🍴 🍴 🚻 🗄 **Off-site** 🍴 ⌂S

Oyam

Ferme Oyamburua, 64210 ☎ 559549161 📄 559549161
e-mail accueil@camping-oyam.com
website www.camping-oyam.com/
Level meadow site near farm. Views of the Pyrénées. Simple but pleasant site.

➲ *Turn off beyond church onto N10 towards Arbonne for 1km.*

Open Jun-Sep **Site** 6HEC 😃 😃 😨 🅰 **Prices** ⚹ 1.70-4.80 pitch 12-23 (incl 2 persons) **Facilities** 🏱 ⊙ 🐟 🚲 ☜ **Services** 🍴 🍴 🗄 **Leisure** ⌂ P **Off-site** 🏠 ⌀ ⌂S 🚻

Pavillon Royal

av Prince de Galles, 64210 ☎ 559230054 📄 559234447
e-mail info@pavillon-royal.com
website www.pavillon-royal.com
A beautiful, well-kept site beside a rocky beach, divided into pitches, most of which have a sea view.

➲ *2km N.*

Open 15 May-25 Sep **Site** 5HEC 😃 😃 😨 ⊗ **Prices** pitch 18-41 (incl 2 persons) pp2.50 **Facilities** 🏱 🏠 ⊙ 🐟 🚲 ☜ **Services** 🍴 🍴 🚻 🗄 **Leisure** ⌂ P **Off-site** ⌂S

Résidence des Pins

rte de Biarritz, 64210 ☎ 559230029 📄 559412459
e-mail contact@campingdespins.com
website www.campingdespins.com
Terraced site with numbered pitches, 0.8km from the sea.

➲ *2km N on N106 Biarritz road.*

Open 15 May-Sep **Site** 7HEC 😃 😃 😨 **Prices** pitch 15.60-24 (incl 2 persons) **Facilities** 🏱 🏠 ⊙ 🐟 ⌀ 🚲 ☜ **Services** 🍴 🍴 🚻 🗄 **Leisure** ⌂ P **Off-site** ⌂LS

Ruisseau

rte d'Arbonne, 64210 ☎ 559419450 📄 559419573
e-mail francoise.dumont3@wanadoo.fr
website www.camping-le-ruisseau.fr
A well-equipped site in wooded surroundings set out around two lakes.

➲ *2km E on D255.*

Open 19 May-16 Sep **Site** 15HEC 😃 😃 😨 **Prices** ⚹ 5-6.50 pitch 15-30 (incl 2 persons) **Facilities** 🏱 🏠 ⊙ 🐟 ⌀ 🚲 ☜ **Services** 🍴 🍴 🚻 🗄 **Leisure** ⌂ LP

Sunelia Berrua

rte Berrua, 64210 ☎ 559549666 📄 559547830
e-mail contact@berrua.com
website www.berrua.com
A well-equipped family site 1km from the beach and 0.5km from the village.

Open 30 Mar-15 Oct **Site** 5HEC 😃 😃 😨 🐟 **Prices** ⚹ 3.20-6.15 pitch 16.10-30.20 🐟 (static)264-945 **Facilities** 🏱 🏠 ⊙ 🐟 ⌀ ☜ **Services** 🍴 🍴 🚻 🗄 **Leisure** ⌂ P **Off-site** ⌂RS

Ur-Onéa

r de la Chapelle, 64210 ☎ 559265361 📄 559265394
e-mail uronea@wanadoo.fr
website www.uronea.com
A well-equipped site lying at the foot of the Pyrénées with good recreational facilities.

➲ *Off RN10.*

Open 7 Apr-15 Sep **Site** 5HEC 😃 😃 😨 🐟 **Prices** pitch 13-23.50 (incl 2 persons) 🐟 (static)225-440 **Facilities** 🏱 🏠 ⊙ 🐟 ⌀ ☜ ⓟ **Services** 🍴 🍴 🚻 🗄 **Leisure** ⌂ P **Off-site** 🍴 🚲 ⌂RS

BIAS LANDES

CM Le Tatiou

40710 ☎ 558090476 📄 558824430
e-mail campingletatiou@wanadoo.fr
website www.campingletatiou.com
Well-equipped family site in a forested setting 4km from the sea.

➲ *2km W towards Lespecier.*

Open 4 Apr-14 Oct **Site** 10HEC 😃 😃 😃 😨 🐟 **Prices** pitch 13.30 (incl 2 persons) 🐟 (static)300 **Facilities** 🏱 🏠 ⊙ 🐟 ⌀ ☜ **Services** 🍴 🍴 🚻 🗄 **Leisure** ⌂ P **Off-site** 🚲 ⌂S

BIRON DORDOGNE

Sunêlia le Moulinal

24540 ☎ 553408460 📄 553408149
e-mail lemoulinal@perigord.com
website www.lemoulinal.com
A pleasant location beside a lake close to the former mill of Château de Biron. The modern holiday village has a variety of recreational facilities.

➲ *2km S on the Lacapelle-Biron road.*

Open 7Apr-23 Sep **Site** 18HEC 😃 😃 😨 🅰 **Prices** pitch 17-36 (incl 2 persons) pp4-10 **Facilities** 🏱 🏠 ⊙ 🐟 ⌀ 🚲 ☜ **Services** 🍴 🍴 🚻 🗄 **Leisure** ⌂ LP

BISCARROSSE LANDES

Bimbo

176 chemin de Bimbo, 40600 ☎ 558098233 📄 558098014
e-mail camping.bimbo@free.fr
website campingbimbo.com
Delightful wooded surroundings 0.5km from the lake and 10 minutes from the sea. Booking advised.

➲ *3.5km N towards Sanguinet.*

Open All year **Site** 6HEC 😃 😃 😨 **Facilities** 🏱 🏠 ⊙ 🐟 ⌀ 🚲 ☜ **Services** 🍴 🍴 🚻 🗄 **Leisure** ⌂ P **Off-site** ⌂L

Site 6HEC (site size) 😃 grass 😃 sand 😨 stone ♣ little shade 😃 partly shaded 😃 mainly shaded 😨 bungalows for hire 🐟 caravans for hire 🅰 tents for hire ⊗ no dogs **Prices** ⚹ adult per night 🚗 car per night pp per person per night 🐟 caravan per night 🅰 tent per night 🐟 (static)-caravan hire per week

France

Ecureuils

Port Navarrosse, 40600 ☎ 558098000
e-mail camping.les.ecureuils@wanadoo.fr
website www.ecureuils.fr
A pleasant wooded location 200m from the lake. Plenty of recreational facilities.
⮑ *Via D652.*
Open Apr-Sep **Site** 7HEC ♨ ♨ **Facilities** ⋔ ⊙ ⊕ ℗ **Services** ☎ ⦙⦙
⊠ **Leisure** ⚓ P **Off-site** ▣ ⊘ ⚓L

Rive

rte de Bordeaux, 40600 ☎ 558781233 ▤ 558781292
e-mail info@camping-de-la-rive.fr
website www.larive.fr
Level site in tall pine forest on E side of lake. Private port and beach.
⮑ *N of town off D652 Sanguinet road.*
Open Apr-25 Sep **Site** 15HEC ♨ ♨ ♨ ♨ **Prices** pitch 20-36 (incl 2 persons) ⊞ (static)266-973 **Facilities** ⋔ ▣ ⊙ ⊕ ⊘ ⚒ ℗ **Services** ☎ ⦙⦙
⊞ ⊠ **Leisure** ⚓ LP

BLAYE GIRONDE

AT MAZION (5.5KM NE ON N937)

Tilleuls

33390 ☎ 557421813 ▤ 557421301
⮑ *5.5km NE on N937.*
Open May-Oct **Site** 0.5HEC ♨ ♨ **Prices** ⚘ 4 pitch 2.50 **Facilities** ⋔ ⊙ ⚘
℗ **Services** ⊞ ⊠ **Off-site** ▣ ☎ ⦙⦙

BOURNEL LOT-ET-GARONNE

Ferme de Bourgade

47210 ☎ 553366715
e-mail bourgade47@libertysurf.fr
website www.bourgade-holidays.co.uk
A small, tranquil site with good, clean facilities.
⮑ *Signed from N21 between Castillonnès & Villeréal.*
Open 15 June- 15 Sep **Site** 1HEC ♨ ♨ **Facilities** ⋔ ⊕ ℗ **Services** ⊞ ⊠
Leisure ⚓ L **Off-site** ☎ ⦙⦙

BRETENOUX LOT

Bourgnatelle

46130 ☎ 565108904 ▤ 565108918
e-mail contact@dordogne-vacances.fr
website ww.dordogne-vacances.fr
A pleasant location beside the River Cére. Separate car park for arrivals after 22.30hrs.
⮑ *D940 towards Rocamadour.*
Open May-Sep **Site** 2HEC ♨ ♨ ⚘ **Prices** pitch 12-15 (incl 2 persons) pp3.50-4 ⊞ (static)150-580 **Facilities** ⋔ ⊙ ⊕ ⊘ ℗ **Services** ⊠
Leisure ⚓ PR **Off-site** ▣ ☎ ⦙⦙ ⚒ ⊞

BUGUE, LE DORDOGNE

Brin d'Amour

Saint Cirq, 24260 ☎ 553072373 ▤ 553072373
e-mail brindamour2@wanadoo.fr
website www.campings-dordogne.com/brindamour
A fine location overlooking the Vézère valley with good facilities.
Open Apr-10 Oct **Site** 3.8HEC ♨ ♨ ⚘ **Prices** ⚘ 3.40-4.20 pitch 4.20-5
⊞ (static)240-450 **Facilities** ⋔ ▣ ⊙ ⊕ ⚒ ℗ **Services** ☎ ⦙⦙ ⊞ ⊠
Leisure ⚓ P **Off-site** ⚓LR

Rocher de la Granelle

rte du Buisson, 24260 ☎ 53072432
e-mail info@lagranelle.com
website www.lagranelle.com
Surrounded by woodland with pitches set out among trees and bushes on the banks of the Vézère with a variety of leisure facilities.
⮑ *From Le Bugue centre over bridge & signed.*
Open Apr-Sep **Site** 8HEC ♨ ♨ ⚘ **Prices** pitch 12.50-17.50
(incl 2 persons) **Facilities** ⋔ ▣ ⊙ ⊕ ⊘ ⚒ ℗ **Services** ☎ ⦙⦙ ⊞ ⊠
Leisure ⚓ PR

St-Avit Loisirs

St-Avit-de-Vialard, 24260 ☎ 553026400 ▤ 553026439
e-mail contact@saint-avit.loisirs.com
website www.saint-avit-loisirs.com
A pleasant site in natural wooded surroundings.
⮑ *W of town via C201.*
Open Apr-Sep **Site** 7HEC ♨ ♨ ⚘ **Prices** ⚘ 3.90-9.50 pitch 6.10-13.70
Facilities ⋔ ▣ ⊙ ⊕ ⊘ ℗ **Services** ☎ ⦙⦙ ⊞ ⊠ **Leisure** ⚓ P
Off-site ⚓R

CAHORS LOT

Rivière de Cabessut

r de la Rivière, 46000 ☎ 565300630 ▤ 565239946
e-mail contact@cabessut.com
website www.cabessut.com
⮑ *N of town via Cabessut Bridge over River Lot.*
Open Apr-Sep **Site** 3HEC ♨ ♨ ⚘ **Prices** ⚘ 3 pitch 8 **Facilities** ⋔ ▣ ⊙ ⊕
⊘ ℗ **Services** ☎ ⦙⦙ ⊞ ⊠ **Leisure** ⚓ PR **Off-site** ⦙⦙ ⚒

AT ESCLAUZELS (18KM SE)

Pompit

46090 ☎ 565315340 ▤ 565317800
Situated in the heart of a large forest close to the magnificent Lot valley.
⮑ *5km NW of Esclauzels village.*
Open All year **Site** 3.5HEC ♨ ♨ ♨ ⚘ ⚘ **Facilities** ⋔ ▣ ⊙ ⊕ ⊘ ℗
Services ☎ ⦙⦙ ⊞ ⊠ **Leisure** ⚓ P

CALVIAC LOT

Chênes Verts

rte de Sarlat, Souillac, 24370 ☎ 553592107
A beautiful wooded setting in the Périgord countryside. A variety of recreational facilities is available.
⮑ *On D704A between Sarlat & Calviac.*
Open May-Sep **Site** 6HEC ♨ ♨ ⚘ **Facilities** ⋔ ▣ ⊙ ⊕ ⊘ ℗
Services ☎ ⦙⦙ ⊞ ⊠ **Leisure** ⚓ P **Off-site** ⚓LR

Trois Sources

Le Peyratel, 46190 ☎ 565330301 ▤ 565330301
e-mail info@les-trois-sources.com
website www.les-trois-sources.com
Wooded location, family site with plenty of leisure facilities.
⮑ *D653 onto D25 to Calviac.*
Open 28 Apr-Sep **Site** 7.5HEC ♨ ♨ ♨ ⚘ **Prices** ⚘ 2.75-4.25 pitch 3.50-7.25 ⊞ (static)131-640.50 **Facilities** ⋔ ▣ ⊙ ⊕ ⊘ ℗ **Services** ☎ ⦙⦙ ⊞ ⊠
Leisure ⚓ LPR

Facilities ▣ shop ⋔ shower ⊙ electric points for razors ⊕ electric points for caravans ℗ parking by tents permitted ℗ compulsory separate car park
Services ⦙⦙ café/restaurant ☎ bar ⊘ Camping Gaz International ⚒ gas other than Camping Gaz ⊞ first aid facilities ⊠ laundry
Leisure ⚓ swimming L-Lake P-Pool R-River S-Sea **Off-site** All facilities within 2km

CAMBO-LES-BAINS PYRÉNÉES-ATLANTIQUES

Bixta Eder
rte de St-Jean-de-Luz, 64250 ☎ 5559299423 📠 559292370
e-mail camping.bixtaeden@wanadoo.fr
website www.camping-bixtaeder.com
Modern site with good sports facilities.
➾ *Near junct D932 & D10.*
Open 15 Apr **Site** 1HEC 🌱 🌱 🌱 **Facilities** 🅵 ⊙ 🅔 ⊕ **Services** 🔢
Off-site ⚫LP 🕀

CAPBRETON LANDES

Pointe
Quartier la Pointe, 40130 ☎ 558721498 📠 558723197
Family site in a wooded location on the banks of a river, 0.8km from
the sea. Good recreational facilities.
➾ *2km S on N652 towards Labenne.*
Open Apr-Oct **Site** 13HEC 🌱 🌱 🍄 **Facilities** 🅵 🛆 ⊙ 🅔 🖉 🔺 ⊕ 🅟
Services 🔢 🍴 🕀 🔢 **Leisure** ⚫ PRS

CAP FERRET GIRONDE

Truc Vert
rte Forestière, 33970 ☎ 556608955 📠 556609947
e-mail camping.truc-vert@worldonline.fr
website www.trucvert.com
A very pleasant location on a slope in a pine wood close to the beach.
➾ *On D106 towards Cap Ferret to Petit Piquey, turn right &
signed.*
Open May-Sep **Site** 11HEC 🌱 🌱 **Prices** 🔺 3-4.20 🅰 9.45 pitch 12-17.90
(incl 2 persons) **Facilities** 🅵 🛆 ⊙ 🅔 🖉 ⊕ **Services** 🔢 🍴 🕀 🔢
Off-site ⚫S

CARLUCET LOT

Château de Lacomté
46500 ☎ 565387546 📠 565331768
e-mail chateaulacomte@wanadoo.fr
website www.campingchateaulacomte.com
Set in wooded surroundings with good size pitches and a variety of
recreational facilities.
➾ *Signed from D677/D32.*
Open 15 May-Sep **Site** 12HEC 🌱 🌱 🌱 🍄 🍄 🅰 **Prices** 🔺 3.77-8 🅰 3.70
pitch 4.80-10 🍄 (static)175-470 **Facilities** 🅵 🛆 ⊙ 🅔 ⊕ **Services** 🔢 🍴 🕀
🔢 **Leisure** ⚫ P

CASTELJALOUX LOT-ET-GARONNE

Club de Clarens
rte de Mont-de-Marsan, 47700 ☎ 553930745 📠 553939309
A large site with direct access to the 17-hectare Lac de Clarens and
good recreational facilities.
Open Jun-Sep **Site** 2HEC 🌱 🌱 🍄 🍄 **Facilities** 🅵 ⊙ 🅔 ⊕ **Services** 🔢
🍴 🕀 🔢 **Leisure** ⚫ LR **Off-site** 🍴 ⚫P

CM de la Piscine
rte de Marmande, 47700 ☎ 553935468 📠 553934807
➾ *NW on D933 Marmande road.*
Open Apr-Nov **Site** 1HEC 🌱 🌱 **Prices** 🔺 2 pitch 2-3.35 **Facilities** 🅵 ⊙ 🅔
⊕ **Services** 🔢 **Off-site** 🛆 🔢 🍴 🖉 🔺 ⚫PR 🕀

CASTELNAUD-LA-CHAPELLE DORDOGNE

Maisonneuve
24250 ☎ 553295129 📠 553302706
e-mail contact@campingmaisonneuve.com
website www.campingmaisonneuve.com
Picturesque surroundings 0.8km from the village, close to the River
Céou in the Périgord Noir region.
➾ *10km S of Sarlat on D57.*
Open 29 Mar-15 Oct **Site** 6HEC 🌱 🌱 🍄 **Prices** 🔺 3.50-5 pitch 4.90-7
Facilities 🅵 🛆 ⊙ 🅔 ⊕ **Services** 🔢 🍴 🕀 🔢 **Leisure** ⚫ PR
Off-site 🖉 🔺

CLAOUEY GIRONDE

Airotel les Viviers
rte du Cap Ferret, 33950 ☎ 556607004 📠 557703777
e-mail lesviviers@wanadoo.fr
website www.airotel.les.viviers.com
Extensive site in a beautiful forest divided by seawater channels.
➾ *On D106 1km S of the town.*
Open 8 Apr-1 Oct **Site** 33HEC 🌱 🌱 🍄 **Facilities** 🅵 🛆 ⊙ 🅔 ⊕
Services 🔢 🍴 🕀 🔢 **Leisure** ⚫ LPS

CONTIS-PLAGE LANDES

Lous Seurrots
40170 ☎ 558428582 📠 558424911
e-mail info@lous-seurrots.com
website www.lous-seurrots.com
Well-equipped site in a pine forest on outskirts of village between a
road and a stream.
➾ *Via D41.*
Open Apr-Sep **Site** 15HEC 🌱 🌱 🍄 **Prices** pitch 17-36 (incl 2 persons)
pp4-6 **Facilities** 🅵 🛆 ⊙ 🅔 🖉 🔺 ⊕ **Services** 🔢 🍴 🕀 🔢 **Leisure** ⚫ PRS

CORDES TARN

Moulin de Julien
81170 ☎ 563561110 📠 563561110
website www.cordes_sur_ciel.org
A beautiful valley with good pitches for caravans and tents and plenty
of modern facilities.
➾ *0.9km E on D600 & D922.*
Open 15 May-Sep **Site** 6HEC 🌱 🌱 🍄 🍄 **Facilities** 🅵 ⊙ 🅔 🖉 ⊕
Services 🔢 🍴 🕀 🔢 **Leisure** ⚫ LP **Off-site** 🛆 🍴 🔺 ⚫R

COUX-ET-BIGAROQUE DORDOGNE

Clou
Meynard, 24220 ☎ 553316332 📠 553316933
e-mail info@camping-le-clou.com
website www.camping-le-clou.com
Separate section for dog owners.
➾ *Via D703 Le Bugue-Delve road.*
Open 25 Apr-Sep **Site** 3.5HEC 🌱 🌱 🍄 🍄 🅰 **Prices** 🔺 3.50-4.90 pitch 4-7.50
Facilities 🅵 🛆 ⊙ 🅔 🖉 🔺 ⊕ **Services** 🔢 🍴 🕀 🔢 **Leisure** ⚫ P

Site 6HEC (site size) 🌱 grass 🌱 sand 🌱 stone 🌱 little shade 🌱 partly shaded 🌱 mainly shaded 🍄 bungalows for hire
🍄 caravans for hire 🅰 tents for hire ⊗ no dogs **Prices** 🔺 adult per night 🔺 car per night pp per person per night 🍄 caravan per night
🅰 tent per night 🍄 (static)-caravan hire per week

Faval

24220 ☎ 553316044 🖷 553283971
e-mail camping.la.faval@libertysurf.fr
website www.lafaval.com
Wooded location 200m from the River Dordogne. A family site with good recreational facilities.
➲ 1km E of village on D703, near D710 junct.
Open Apr-Sep **Site** 3HEC 👪 �# 🚐 **Facilities** 🦌 🛆 ⊙ 🚐 ⌀ ⅋ **Services** 🕎 🍴 ➕ 🗵 **Leisure** 🏊 P **Off-site** 🏖 🏊R

Valades

Les Valades, 24220 ☎ 553291427 🖷 553281928
e-mail camping.valades@wanadoo.fr
website www.lesvalades.com
Wooded surroundings within a pleasant valley. Well-equipped pitches available.
➲ 5km N of town off N703.
Open Apr-Sept **Site** 12HEC 👪 �# 🚐 **Prices** 🧍 4.60 pitch 6.20 **Facilities** 🦌 🛆 ⊙ 🚐 ⅋ **Services** 🕎 🍴 ➕ 🗵 **Leisure** 🏊 LP

CRÉON GIRONDE

Bel Air

33670 ☎ 556230190 🖷 556230838
e-mail info@camping-bel-air.com
website www.camping-bel-air.com
A well-equipped, roomy site on a level meadow shaded by tall trees.
➲ 1.6km W of Créon on D671.
Open All year **Site** 2HEC 👪 �# 🚐 **Facilities** 🦌 🛆 ⊙ 🚐 ⌀ 🏔 ⅋ **Services** 🍴 ➕

DAGLAN DORDOGNE

Moulin de Paulhiac

24250 ☎ 553282088 🖷 553293345
e-mail francis.armagnac@wanadoo.fr
website www.moulin-de-paulhiac.com
Picturesque wooded surroundings with wide, well-marked pitches and modern facilities.
➲ 4km N via D57 beside the Céou.
Open 15 May-15 Sep **Site** 5HEC 👪 �# 🚐 **Facilities** 🦌 🛆 ⊙ 🚐 ⌀ ⅋ **Services** 🕎 🍴 ➕ 🗵 **Leisure** 🏊 PR

DAX LANDES

Chênes

Au Bois-de-Boulogne, 40100 ☎ 558900553 🖷 558904243
e-mail camping-chenes@wanadoo.fr
website www.camping-les-chenes.fr
A wooded park on the edge of the Bois-de-Boulogne with good facilities.
➲ 1.5km W of town beside River Adour.
Open 24 Mar-3 Nov **Site** 5HEC 👪 �# 🚐 **Prices** pitch 10.70-18.40 (incl 2 persons) **Facilities** 🦌 🛆 ⊙ 🚐 ⌀ ⅋ **Services** 🗵 **Leisure** 🏊 P **Off-site** 🕎 🍴 🏊R ➕

DOMME DORDOGNE

Perpetuum

Au Bord de la Dordogne ☎ 553283518 🖷 553296364
e-mail luc.parsy@wanadoo.fr
website www.campingleperpetuum.com
Open All year **Site** 4HEC 👪 �# 🚐 **Prices** 🧍 4-5 pitch 4-6 🚐 (static)200-650 **Facilities** 🦌 🛆 ⊙ 🚐 ⌀ 🏔 ⅋ **Services** 🕎 🍴 🗵 **Leisure** 🏊 PR

See advertisement on this page

DURAVEL LOT

Club de Vacances

Port de Vire, 46700 ☎ 565246506 🖷 565246496
e-mail clubduravel@wanadoo.fr
website www.clubdevacances.fr
A pleasant site with good facilities beside the River Lot.
➲ 2.3km S via D58.
Open 25 Apr-Sep **Site** 7HEC 👪 �# 🚐 🏕 ⅄ **Prices** 🧍 4.30-6.15 pitch 6.85-9.75 🚐 (static)215-600 **Facilities** 🦌 🛆 ⊙ 🚐 ⌀ ⅋ **Services** 🕎 🍴 ➕ 🗵 **Leisure** 🏊 PR

DURFORT ARIÈGE

Bourdieu

09130 ☎ 561673017 🖷 561672900
e-mail lebourdieu@wanadoo.fr
website www.lebourdieu.com
Well-equipped site in a picturesque setting with fine views of the Pyrénées.
➲ Off D14 Le Fossat-Saverdun.
Open All year **Site** 20HEC 👪 �# 🚐 **Facilities** 🦌 🛆 ⊙ 🚐 🏔 ⅋ **Services** 🕎 🍴 ➕ 🗵 **Leisure** 🏊 PR

ESTAING HAUTES-PYRÉNÉES

Pyrénées Natura

rte du Lac, 65400 ☎ 562974544 🖷 562974581
e-mail sarl.ruysschaert@wanadoo.fr
website www.camping-pyrenees-natura.com
A well-run site at an altitude of 1000m, situated on the edge of the national park with views of the surrounding mountains.
➲ From Argèles-Gazost towards Arrens & D13 for Lac d'Estaing.
Open May-Sep **Site** 2.5HEC 👪 �# 🚐 **Prices** pitch 15.50-24 (incl 2 persons) 🚐 (static)240-590 **Facilities** 🦌 🛆 ⊙ 🚐 ⌀ ⅋ **Services** 🕎 🍴 ➕ 🗵 **Leisure** 🏊 R **Off-site** 🍴

Facilities 🛆 shop 🦌 shower ⊙ electric points for razors 🚐 electric points for caravans ⅋ parking by tents permitted 🅟 compulsory separate car park
Services 🍴 café/restaurant 🕎 bar ⌀ Camping Gaz International 🏔 gas other than Camping Gaz ➕ first aid facilities 🗵 laundry
Leisure 🏊 swimming L-Lake P-Pool R-River S-Sea **Off-site** All facilities within 2km

France (side tab)

ÉYZIES-DE-TAYAC, LES DORDOGNE

Pech Charmant
24620 ☎ 553359708
e-mail info@lepech.com
website www.lepech.com
Located on the side of a wooded hill and contains a small farm with donkeys, goats, horses and chickens.

Open 15 Apr-1 Oct **Site** 17HEC 👪 🏖 🐾 🐾 Å **Prices** 🕯 3-5.05 pitch 5-8.25 🚐 (static)200-435 **Facilities** 🍴 ⊙ 🐾 🖉 🚿 🏵 **Services** 🕯 🏵
➕ 🖻 **Leisure** 🏊 P **Off-site** 🛈 🏊R

FIGEAC LOT

Rives du Célé
Domaine du Surgie, 46100 ☎ 565345900 🗎 565348383
e-mail surgie.camp.lois@wanadoo.fr
website www.domainedesurgie.com
A pleasant wooded location on the banks of the River Célé with plenty of leisure facilities. The site lies within a large recreation area. Separate car park for late arrivals.

Open Apr-Sep **Site** 2HEC 👪 🏖 🐾 **Prices** pitch 25.20 (incl 4 persons) **Facilities** 🍴 🛈 ⊙ 🐾 🚿 🏵 **Services** 🕯 🍽 ➕ 🖻 **Leisure** 🏊 LPR
Off-site 🖉

FOIX ARIÈGE

Lac
RN 20, 09000 ☎ 561651158 🗎 561651998
e-mail camping-du-lac@wanadoo.fr
website www.campingdulac.com
On well-kept meadow beside the Lac de Labarre.

➲ *3km N on N20.*

Open All year **Site** 5HEC 👪 🏖 🐾 **Prices** pitch 13.50-19.50 **Facilities** 🍴 ⊙ 🐾 🏵 **Services** 🕯 🍽 🖻 **Leisure** 🏊 LP **Off-site** 🛈 🕯 🍽 🖉 ➕

FONTRAILLES HAUTES-PYRÉNÉES

Fontrailles
☎ 562356252
e-mail detm.paddon@free.fr
website www.fontraillescamping.com
Set in a peaceful location, next to a shady oak wood and small fishing lake.

➲ *2km N of Trie-sur-Baise, left off D939 Tarbes-Mirande, signed.*

Open Jul-Sep **Site** 1.5HEC 👪 🏖 **Prices** 🕯 4 pitch 6 **Facilities** 🍴 ⊙ 🐾 🏵 **Services** ➕ **Leisure** 🏊 P **Off-site** 🛈 🕯 🍽 🖉 🚿

GASTES LANDES

Réserve
40160 ☎ 0870 242 7777 🗎 0870 242 9999
website www.haveneurope.com
A large, popular site situated in one of the largest forests in Europe. Plenty of sports and entertainment facilities.

➲ *3km SW via D652*

Open 28 Apr-14 Sep **Site** 32HEC 👪 🏖 🐾 Å 🛇 **Facilities** 🍴 🛈 🐾 🖉 🚿 🏵 **Services** 🕯 🍽 ➕ 🖻 **Leisure** 🏊 LP

GAUGEAC DORDOGNE

Moulin de David
24540 ☎ 553226525 🗎 553239976
e-mail info@moulin-de-david.com
website www.moulin-de-david.com
Situated in a wooded valley alongside a small stream, with well-defined pitches and good recreational facilities.

➲ *3km from town towards Villeréal.*

Open 19 May-15 Sep **Site** 14HEC 👪 🏖 🐾 🐾 Å **Prices** 🕯 3.90-6.95 pitch 5.30-10 🚐 (static)213.50-539 **Facilities** 🍴 🛈 ⊙ 🐾 🖉 🚿 🏵 **Services** 🕯 🍽 ➕ 🖻 **Leisure** 🏊 LP

GOURDON LOT

Paradis
La Peyrugue, 46300 ☎ 565416501 🗎 565416501
e-mail contact@campingleparadis.com
website www.campingleparadis.com
On a pleasant wooded meadow surrounded by hills.

➲ *1.6km SW off N673.*

Open 15 May-15 Sep **Site** 2HEC 👪 🏖 🐾 🐾 **Prices** 🕯 4.75 pitch 2.50 🚐 (static)250 **Facilities** 🍴 ⊙ 🐾 🖉 🚿 🏵 **Services** ➕ 🖻 **Leisure** 🏊 LP **Off-site** 🛈 🕯 🍽 🏊LR

AT ST-MARTIAL-DE-NABIRAT (6KM W)

Carbonnier
24250 ☎ 553284253 🗎 553285131
Family site in a small, wooded valley with a variety of recreational facilities.

➲ *Off D46.*

Open Etr-15 Sep **Site** 8HEC 👪 🏖 🐾 **Facilities** 🍴 🛈 ⊙ 🐾 🖉 🚿 🏵 **Services** 🕯 🍽 ➕ 🖻 **Leisure** 🏊 LP

GOURETTE PYRÉNÉES-ATLANTIQUES

Ley
64440 ☎ 559051147 🗎 559051147
Terraced site with gravel and asphalt caravan pitches. TV, common room.

➲ *E from Laruns to Eaux-Bonnes & uphill to Gourette.*

Open Dec-Apr & Jul-Aug **Site** 2HEC 👪 🏖 🐾 🐾 **Prices** 🕯 7 pitch 10.70 **Facilities** 🍴 ⊙ 🐾 🚿 🏵 **Services** 🕯 🍽 ➕ 🖻 **Leisure** 🏊 R **Off-site** 🛈 🖉 🏊L

GRAULGES, LES DORDOGNE

Crozes les Graulges
24340 ☎ 553607473 🗎 553607473
e-mail info@lesgraulges.com
website www.lesgraulges.com
A picturesque setting in woodland beside a lake.

➲ *Off D939 between Angoulême & Périgueux.*

Open Apr-Sep **Site** 8HEC 👪 🏖 🐾 🐾 **Prices** 🕯 3.75-4.50 🚐 4.50-5.50 🚐 (static)495 **Facilities** 🍴 🛈 ⊙ 🐾 🏵 **Services** 🕯 🍽 ➕ **Leisure** 🏊 LPR

GRISOLLES TARN-ET-GARONNE

Aquitaine
rte Nationalle 20, 82170 ☎ 563673322
e-mail campingaquitaine@aol.com
➲ *1.5km N off 'X' roads N20/N113.*

Open All year **Site** 3HEC 👪 🏖 🐾 🐾 **Facilities** 🍴 ⊙ 🐾 🏵 **Services** ➕ 🖻 **Leisure** 🏊 P **Off-site** 🛈 🕯 🍽 🖉 🚿 🏊R

Site 6HEC (site size) 👪 grass 🏖 sand 🐾 stone 🌿 little shade 🌳 partly shaded 🌲 mainly shaded 🏠 bungalows for hire
🚐 caravans for hire Å tents for hire 🛇 no dogs **Prices** 🕯 adult per night 🚗 car per night pp per person per night 🚐 caravan per night
Å tent per night 🚐 (static)-caravan hire per week

GROLÉJAC

Granges

24250 ☎ 553281115 🖹 553285713

e-mail lesueur.francine@wanadoo.fr

website lesgranges-fr.com

Beautifully situated terraces on a hill with big pitches. The site has been constructed around a disused railway station, incorporating the old ticket office and the bridge into the modern design. Facilities for sports and entertainment.

➲ Off D704 in village towards Domme.

Open 2 May-14 Sep **Site** 6.5HEC 👪 🏕 🚁 **Prices** pitch 15-23.60 (incl 2 persons) pp6.20 **Facilities** ⋔ ⊙ 🕿 ⊛ **Services** ⊉ ⓘ⌁ 🏢 🗐 **Leisure** 🏊 PR **Off-site** 🗐 ⊘ 🏊L

HASPARREN PYRÉNÉES-ATLANTIQUES

Chapital

rte de Cambo, 64240 ☎ 559296294 🖹 559296971

On level ground, surrounded by woodland. Good facilities for families.

➲ 0.5km W via D22. Or via A64 towards Hasparren.

Open Etr-Oct **Site** 2.6HEC 👪 🏕 🚁 🚁 **Facilities** ⋔ ⊙ 🕿 ⊛ ⊛ **Services** 🏢 🗐 **Off-site** 🗐 ⊉ ⓘ 🏊 🏊P

HAUTEFORT DORDOGNE

Moulin des Loisirs

L'étang du Coucou, 24390 ☎ 553504655

e-mail moulin.des.loisirs@wanadoo.fr

website www.moulin-des-loisirs.fr

➲ 2km SW via D72 & D71, 100m from Coucou lake.

Open Etr-Sep **Site** 4HEC 👪 🏕 🚁 **Facilities** ⋔ ⊙ 🕿 ⊛ **Services** ⊉ ⓘ 🗐 **Leisure** 🏊 LP **Off-site** ⊘ 🏊 🏊L 🏢

HENDAYE PYRÉNÉES-ATLANTIQUES

Acacias

64700 ☎ 559207876 🖹 559207876

e-mail info@les-acacias.com

website www.les-campings.com/acacias

A pleasant family site in parkland, 5 minutes from the beach.

➲ 1.8km E (rte de la Glacière).

Open Apr-Sep **Site** 5HEC 👪 🏕 🚁 **Prices** pitch 17-21 **Facilities** ⋔ ⊙ 🕿 ⊛ ⊕ **Services** ⊉ ⓘ 🏢 🗐 **Leisure** 🏊 L **Off-site** 🗐 ⊉ ⓘ 🏊S

Airotel Eskualduna

rte de la Corniche (D-912), 64700 ☎ 559200464 🖹 559200464

website www.camping-eskualduna.fr

On gently sloping meadow.

➲ 2km from village on N10c.

Open 15 Jun-Sep **Site** 10HEC 👪 🏕 🚁 🚁 **Facilities** ⋔ 🗐 ⊙ 🕿 ⊘ 🏊 ⊛ **Services** ⊉ ⓘ 🏢 🗐 **Leisure** 🏊 PR **Off-site** 🏊S

HOURTIN GIRONDE

Acacia

Ste-Hélène, 33990 ☎ 556738080

e-mail camping.lacacia@wanadoo.fr

website www.camping-lacacia.com

Pleasant, quiet site on the edge of a forest with good sanitary facilities. Compulsory car park for arrivals after 23.30hrs.

➲ Off D3 towards lake.

Open 15 May-15 Oct **Site** 5HEC 👪 🏕 🚁 **Facilities** ⋔ ⊙ 🕿 ⊛ **Services** ⊉ 🏢 🗐 **Off-site** 🏊L

Mariflaude

33990 ☎ 556091197 🖹 556092401

Level meadowland, shaded by pines, in rural setting 2km from one of the biggest lakes in the country.

➲ Onto D4 at pharmacy & E towards Pauillac.

Open May-15 Sep **Site** 7HEC 👪 🏕 🚁 **Facilities** ⋔ 🗐 ⊙ 🕿 ⊘ 🏊 ⊛ **Services** ⊉ ⓘ 🏢 🗐 **Leisure** 🏊 P **Off-site** 🏊L

Ourmes

90 av du Lac, 33990 ☎ 556091276 🖹 556092390

e-mail lesourmes@free.fr

website www.lesourmes.com

Wooded surroundings close to the beach and 0.5km from the largest freshwater lake in France.

➲ D4 towards lake.

Open Apr-Sep **Site** 7HEC 👪 🏕 🚁 **Prices** pitch 20-23 (incl 2 persons) 🚁 (static)250-640 **Facilities** ⋔ 🗐 ⊙ 🕿 ⊛ **Services** ⊉ ⓘ 🗐 **Leisure** 🏊 P **Off-site** 🏊 🏊LS 🏢

HOURTIN-PLAGE GIRONDE

Côte d'Argent

33990 ☎ 556091025 🖹 556092496

e-mail info@camping-cote-dargent.com

website www.camping-cote-dargent.com

Set in a pine and oak forest with good facilities, 0.5km from the beach.

➲ D101 from Hourtin.

Open mid May-mid Sep **Site** 20HEC 🌊 👪 🏕 🚁 **Prices** pitch 19-41 (incl 2 persons) 🚁 (static)343-998 **Facilities** ⋔ 🗐 ⊙ 🕿 ⊘ 🏊 ⊛ **Services** ⊉ ⓘ 🏢 🗐 **Leisure** 🏊 LPS

LABENNE LANDES

Pins Bleus

av de l'Océan, 40530 ☎ 559454113 🖹 559454470

e-mail lespinsbleus@wanadoo.fr

website www.lespinsbleus.com

➲ On RN10.

Open Apr-4 Nov **Site** 6.5HEC 🌊 👪 🏕 🚁 🏕 Å **Prices** pitch 11.65-16 (incl 2 persons) **Facilities** ⋔ ⊙ 🕿 ⊛ **Services** ⊉ ⓘ 🏢 🗐 **Leisure** 🏊 P **Off-site** 🗐 ⊘ 🏊 🏊LRS 🏢

LABENNE-OCÉAN LANDES

Boudigau

40530 ☎ 559454207 🖹 559457776

e-mail info@boudigau.com

website www.boudigau.com

Situated in a pine forest.

➲ Turn right after bridge into site.

Open 15 May-15 Sep **Site** 6HEC 🌊 👪 🏕 🚁 🚁 **Prices** pitch 12-26 (incl 2 persons) 🚁 (static)400-590 **Facilities** ⋔ 🗐 ⊙ 🕿 ⊘ 🕿 **Services** ⊉ ⓘ 🏢 🗐 **Leisure** 🏊 P **Off-site** 🏊S

Côte d'Argent

60 av de l'Océan, 40530 ☎ 559454202 🖹 559457331

e-mail info@camping-cotedargent.com

website www.camping-cotedargent.com

Very well-managed modern site attached to holiday village.

➲ 3km W on D126.

Open Apr-Oct **Site** 4HEC 🌊 👪 🏕 🚁 🏕 Å **Prices** pitch 9.70-22.50 (incl 2 persons) pp2.90-4.45 **Facilities** ⋔ ⊙ 🕿 🏊 ⊛ **Services** ⊉ ⓘ 🏢 🗐 **Leisure** 🏊 P **Off-site** 🗐 ⊘ 🏊RS

France

Facilities 🗐 shop ⋔ shower ⊙ electric points for razors 🕿 electric points for caravans ⊛ parking by tents permitted ⊕ compulsory separate car park
Services ⓘ café/restaurant ⊉ bar ⊘ Camping Gaz International 🏊 gas other than Camping Gaz 🏢 first aid facilities 🗐 laundry
Leisure 🏊 swimming L-Lake P-Pool R-River S-Sea **Off-site** All facilities within 2km

Mer

rte de la Plage, 40530 ☎ 559454209 🖷 559454307
e-mail campinglamer@wanadoo.fr
website www.campinglamer.com
Set in a pine forest 0.7km from the beach.

➲ *On D126 rte de la Plage.*

Open Etr-Sep **Site** 6.5HEC 🌿 🏖 🏕 ♨ Å **Prices** ♠ 2.70-6 pitch 9.50-21 (incl 2 persons) ♨ (static)200-860 **Facilities** 🅟 ⊙ 🚻 ⌀ ⓔ **Services** 🍴 🍽 🛒 🔌 **Leisure** ⚓ PR **Off-site** 🛒 ⚓S

Yelloh Village Le Sylvamar

av de l'Océan ☎ 559457516 🖷 559454639
website www.sylvamar.fr
Situated in a tranquil location in a pine forest.

➲ *Access via D126.*

Open Apr-Sep **Site** 15HEC 🌿 🏖 🏖 🏕 ♨ Å **Facilities** 🅟 🚻 ⊙ 🚻 ⓔ **Services** 🍴 🍽 🛒 🔌 **Leisure** ⚓ P **Off-site** ⚓S

See advertisement on this page

LACANAU-OCÉAN GIRONDE

Airotel de l'Océan

24 Rue du Répos, 33680 ☎ 556032445 🖷 557700187
e-mail airotel.lacanau@wanadoo.fr
website www.airotel-ocean.com
On rising ground in a pine forest, 0.8km from the beach.

Open 8 Apr-24 Sep **Site** 9.5HEC 🏖 🌿 🏕 ♨ **Facilities** 🅟 🚻 ⊙ 🚻 ⌀ ⓔ ⓟ **Services** 🍴 🍽 🛒 🔌 **Leisure** ⚓ P **Off-site** ⚓S

Yelloh Village Grands Pins

Plages Nord, 33680 ☎ 556032077 🖷 557700389
e-mail reception@lesgrandspins.com
website www.lesgrandspins.com
On very hilly terrain in woodland, 350m from the beach through dunes.

➲ *A10 exit 7, D6 to Lacanau.*

Open 7 Apr-22 Sep **Site** 12HEC 🌿 🏖 🏕 **Prices** pitch 16-38 **Facilities** 🅟 🚻 ⊙ 🚻 ♨ ⚒ ⓟ **Services** 🍴 🍽 🛒 🔌 **Leisure** ⚓ P **Off-site** ⚓S

AT MEDOC (8KM E)

Talaris

rte de l'Océan, 33680 ☎ 556030415 🖷 556262156
e-mail talarisvacances@free.fr
website www.talaris-vacances.fr
A family site in delightful wooded surroundings 1.2km from the lake. Separate car park for arrivals after 22.30hrs.

➲ *2km E on rte de Lacanau.*

Open 7 Apr-15 Sep **Site** 8.2HEC 🌿 🏖 🏕 Å **Prices** Å 3.90 pitch 16.50-28.50 (incl 2 persons) ♨ (static)250-635 **Facilities** 🅟 🚻 ⊙ 🚻 ⌀ ⚒ ⓔ **Services** 🍴 🍽 🛒 🔌 **Leisure** ⚓ P **Off-site** ⚓L 🔌

AT MOUTCHIC (5KM E)

Lac

33680 ☎ 556030026

➲ *On D6 rte de Lacanau, 60m from lake.*

Open Apr-15 Oct **Site** 1HEC 🌿 🏖 **Facilities** 🅟 🚻 ⊙ 🚻 ⌀ ⓔ **Services** 🍴 🍽 🛒 🔌 **Off-site** ⚓L

Site 6HEC (site size) 🌿 grass 🏖 sand 🏕 stone ♣ little shade 🌲 partly shaded 🌳 mainly shaded 🏠 bungalows for hire
♨ caravans for hire Å tents for hire ⊗ no dogs **Prices** ♠ adult per night ⚓ car per night pp per person per night ♨ caravan per night
Å tent per night ♨ (static)-caravan hire per week

Tedey
rte de Longarisse, 33680 ☎ 55603015 📠 556030190
e-mail camping@le-tedey.com
website www.le-tedey.com
Quiet site in pine forest, on edge of Lake Lacanau. Private bathing area.
➲ *Off D6 onto narrow track through forest for 0.5km.*
Open 28 Apr-19 Sep **Site** 14HEC 👪 🏕 🚐 ⊗ **Prices** pitch 19.80-24 (incl 2 persons) 🚐 (static)280-650 **Facilities** 🏪 🖻 ⊙ 🔌 🗑 ⑫ **Services** 📶 🍽 🔁 🔟 **Leisure** 🏊 L

LACAPELLE-MARIVAL LOT

CM Bois de Sophie
Route d'Aymac, 46120 ☎ 565408259 📠 565408259
e-mail lacapelle.mairie@wanadoo.fr
A pleasant wooded location with a variety of sports facilities.
➲ *1km NW via D940.*
Open 15 May-Sep **Site** 1HEC 👪 🏕 🚐 🏕 **Prices** 👤 2.20-3.25 🔺 3.20-4.25 🔺 2 🚐 (static)97-175 **Facilities** 🏪 ⊙ 🔌 ⑫ **Services** 🔟 **Leisure** 🏊 P
Off-site 🖻 📶 🍽 🗑 ⚱ 🏊 R 🔁

LANTON GIRONDE

Roumingue
33138 ☎ 556829748 📠 556829609
website www.roumingue.fr
Level terrain under a few deciduous trees partially in open meadow on the Bassin d'Arcachon.
➲ *1km NW of village towards sea.*
Open 15 Mar-15 Nov **Site** 10HEC 👪 🏕 🏕 🚐 🏕 **Prices** pitch 11.50-27.80 (incl 2 persons) 🚐 (static)288-680 **Facilities** 🏪 🖻 ⊙ 🔌 🏕 ⑫ **Services** 📶 🍽 🔁 🔟 **Leisure** 🏊 PS **Off-site** 🗑 ⚱

LARNAGOL LOT

Ruisseau de Treil
Le Ruisseau, 46160 ☎ 565312339 📠 565312327
e-mail lotcamping@wanadoo
website www.lotcamping.com
A quiet site within a small valley, with well-defined pitches and good leisure facilities.
➲ *0.6km E of Larnagol off D662 towards Cajarc.*
Open May-Sep **Site** 3.2HEC 👪 🏕 🏕 🏕 🚐 🏕 **Prices** 👤 4.10-5.90 pitch 5.30-7.50 🚐 (static)160-395 **Facilities** 🏪 🖻 ⊙ 🔌 ⑫ **Services** 📶 🍽 🔁 🔟 **Leisure** 🏊 P **Off-site** 🏊 R

LARUNS PYRÉNÉES-ATLANTIQUES

Gaves
64440 ☎ 559053237 📠 559054714
e-mail campingdesgaves@wanadoo.fr
website www.campingdesgaves.com
On the bank of the Gave d'Ossan amid beautiful Pyrenean scenery. Some pitches reserved for caravans.
➲ *1km S.*
Open All year **Site** 2.5HEC 👪 🏕 🏕 **Prices** 👤 2.90-3.70 🔺 5.70-8.80 pitch 7.40-9.60 **Facilities** 🏪 ⊙ 🔌 🗑 🏕 ⑫ **Services** 📶 🍽 🔟 **Leisure** 🏊 R **Off-site** 🖻 🍽 🏊 P 🔁

LARUSCADE GIRONDE

Relais du Chavan
33620 ☎ 557686305
On well-kept meadow edged by a strip of forest. Some traffic noise.
➲ *6.5km NW on N10 near Km20.3.*
Open 15 May-Sep **Site** 3.6HEC 👪 🏕 🚐 🏕 **Facilities** 🏪 🖻 ⊙ 🔌 🗑 ⚱ ⑫ **Services** 🔁 🔟 **Leisure** 🏊 P

LECTOURE GERS

Lac des Trois Vallées
32700 ☎ 562688233 📠 562688882
e-mail lac.des.trois.vallees@wanadoo.fr
website lac-des-3-vallees.com
This rural site is part of a large park and lies next to a lake. It has spacious marked pitches.
➲ *3km SE on N21.*
Open 20 May-10 Sep **Site** 40HEC 👪 🏕 🏕 🚐 🔺 **Facilities** 🏪 🖻 ⊙ 🔌 🗑 ⚱ ⑫ **Services** 📶 🍽 🔁 🔟 **Leisure** 🏊 LP

LÉON LANDES

Airotel Lou Puntaou
Av du Lac, 40550 ☎ 558487430 📠 558487042
e-mail reception@loupuntaou.com
website www.loupuntaou.com
Set in an oak wood with separate sections for caravans.
➲ *Off N652 in village onto D142 towards lake for 1.5km.*
Open Apr-1 Oct **Site** 8HEC 👪 🏕 🏕 🚐 🏕 **Prices** 👤 3-6 pitch 9-27 (incl 2 persons) 🚐 (static)320-892 **Facilities** 🏪 🖻 ⊙ 🔌 🗑 ⑫ **Services** 📶 🍽 🔁 🔟 **Leisure** 🏊 P **Off-site** 🗑 ⚱ 🏊 LRS

St-Antoine
St-Michel-Escalus, 40550 ☎ 558487850 📠 558487190
e-mail campingstantoine@wanadoo.fr
A pleasant, well-equipped site beside a river in peaceful wooded surroundings.
Open Mar-Sep **Site** 6HEC 👪 🏕 🏕 🏕 **Prices** 👤 3.50 pitch 5 **Facilities** 🏪 🖻 ⊙ 🔌 🗑 ⑫ **Services** 📶 🍽 🔁 🔟 **Leisure** 🏊 R

LESCAR PYRÉNÉES-ATLANTIQUES

Terrier
av du Vert Galant, 64230 ☎ 559810182 📠 559812683
e-mail camping.terrier@wanadoo.fr
website www.camping-terrier.com
Meadowland site divided in two with pitches surrounded by hedges in foreground.
➲ *From Pau N117 towards Bayonne for 6.5km, left onto D501 towards Monein to site towards bridge.*
Open All year **Site** 4HEC 👪 🏕 🏕 🏕 **Prices** 👤 3.80 🚐 1.60 pitch 5 **Facilities** 🏪 🖻 ⊙ 🔌 🗑 ⚱ ⑫ **Services** 📶 🍽 🔁 🔟 **Leisure** 🏊 PR **Off-site** 🖻 🍽 🏊 L 🔁

LINXE LANDES

CM Le Grandjean
rte de Mixe, 40260 ☎ 558429000 📠 558429467
A modern family site on the edge of a forest.
➲ *Off Castets road onto D42 towards Linxe.*
Open 25 Jun-27 Aug **Site** 2.7HEC 👪 🏕 🏕 🏕 **Prices** 👤 2.90 🚐 0.70 🚐 5.80 🔺 3.40 **Facilities** 🏪 ⊙ 🔌 ⑫ **Services** 🔁 **Off-site** 📶 🍽 🔁

Facilities 🖻 shop 🏪 shower ⊙ electric points for razors 🔌 electric points for caravans ⑫ parking by tents permitted 🅿 compulsory separate car park
Services 🍽 café/restaurant 📶 bar 🗑 Camping Gaz International ⚱ gas other than Camping Gaz 🔁 first aid facilities 🔟 laundry
Leisure 🏊 swimming L-Lake P-Pool R-River S-Sea **Off-site** All facilities within 2km

France

LIT-ET-MIXE LANDES

Vignes

rte du Cap de l'Homy, 40170 ☎ 558428560 ▤ 558427436

e-mail contact@les-vignes.com

website www.les-vignes.com

Set in a pine forest with good sanitary and sports facilities.

➲ 3km S via D652 & D89.

Open Jun-15 Sep **Site** 15HEC 🌿 🏖 🌿 🏘 🚐 🅰 ⊗ **Facilities** 🏧 🛎 ☺ 🚽 🅰 🚿 🅿 🅶 **Services** 🍴 🍽 🛒 **Leisure** 🏊 P

LIVERS-CAZELLES TARN

Rédon

81170 ☎ 563561464 ▤ 563561464

e-mail info@campredon.com

website www.campredon.com

A quiet site with fine views over the surrounding area and modern facilities.

➲ 4km SE of Cordes on D600.

Open 28 Mar-30 Oct **Site** 4HEC 🌿 🏖 🌿 🏘 **Prices** pitch 13.50 **Facilities** 🏧 🛎 ☺ 🚽 🅰 🚿 **Services** 🍴 🍽 🛒 **Leisure** 🏊 P

LOUPIAC LOT

Hirondelles

☎ 565376625 ▤ 565376665

e-mail camp.les-hirondelles@wanadoo.fr

website www.les-hirondelles.com

A natural setting in the heart of the Quercy region with a variety of recreational facilities.

➲ 3km N via N20.

Open Apr-15 Sep **Site** 2.5HEC 🌿 🏖 🏘 🚐 🅰 **Facilities** 🏧 🛎 ☺ 🚽 🅰 🚿 🅿 🅶 **Services** 🍴 🍽 🛒 **Leisure** 🏊 P

See advertisement on this page

LOURDES HAUTES-PYRÉNÉES

Arrouach

9 r des Trois Archanges, Quartier Biscaye, 65100

☎ 562421143 ▤ 562420527

e-mail camping.arrouach@wanadoo.fr

website www.camping-arrouach.com

Pleasant wooded surroundings on N outskirts.

➲ On D947 Soumoulou road.

Open 15 Mar-Dec **Site** 13HEC 🌿 🏖 **Prices** 🧍 3.70 pitch 4.40 **Facilities** 🏧 ☺ 🚽 🅰 🚿 **Services** 🍴 🛒 **Off-site** 🛎 🍽 🚿 🏊LPR

Domec

rte de Julos, 65100 ☎ 562940879 ▤ 562940879

➲ Off N21 Tarbes road N of town centre.

Open Etr-Oct **Site** 2HEC 🌿 🏖 🏘 🚐 **Facilities** 🏧 🛎 ☺ 🚽 🅰 🚿 🅿 **Services** 🛒 🛒 **Off-site** 🍴 🍽 🏊 🚿PR

LUZ-ST-SAUVEUR HAUTES-PYRÉNÉES

Bergons

rte de Barèges, 65120 ☎ 562929077

e-mail abordenave@club-internet.fr

website www.camping-bergons.com

A beautiful setting on a level meadow surrounded by woodland close to the main Pyrenean ski resorts.

➲ 0.6km E on D618 Barèges road.

Open Dec-20 Oct **Site** 1HEC 🌿 🏖 🏘 **Prices** pitch 5.17-9.34 (incl 2 persons) **Facilities** 🏧 ☺ 🚽 🅰 🚿 🅶 **Services** 🛒 **Off-site** 🛎 🍴 🍽 🚿PR 🛒

Pyrénées International

rte de Lourdes, 65120 ☎ 562928202 ▤ 562929687

e-mail camping.international.luz@wanadoo.fr

Set in a wooded valley at an altitude of 700m with panoramic views of the surrounding mountains.

➲ 1.3km NW on N21.

Open 15 Dec-20 Apr & Jun-Sep **Site** 4HEC 🌿 🏖 🏘 **Facilities** 🏧 🛎 ☺ 🚽 🅰 🚿 🅶 **Services** 🍴 🍽 🛒 🛒 **Leisure** 🏊 P **Off-site** 🚿R

Pyrénévasion

rte de Luz-Ardiden, Sazos, 65120 ☎ 562929154 ▤ 562929834

e-mail camping-pyrenevasion@wanadoo.fr

website www.campingpyrenevasion.com

A quiet site in an idyllic mountain setting close to the ski-runs. The pitches are well-defined and all facilities are clean and modern.

➲ 2km from town on Luz-Ardiden road.

Open All year **Site** 3HEC 🌿 🏖 🏘 **Prices** 🧍 5 pitch 14 **Facilities** 🏧 ☺ 🚽 🅰 🚿 🅶 **Services** 🍴 🍽 🛒 🛒 **Leisure** 🏊 P **Off-site** 🍽 🚿R 🛒

MARCILLAC-ST-QUENTIN DORDOGNE

Tailladis

24200 ☎ 553591095 ▤ 553294756

e-mail tailladis@aol.com

website www.tailladis.com

Well-maintained family site with good recreational facilities.

➲ 2km N near D48.

Open All year **Site** 4HEC 🌿 🏖 🏘 🚐 🅰 **Facilities** 🏧 🛎 ☺ 🚽 🅰 🚿 🅶 **Services** 🍴 🍽 🛒 🛒 **Leisure** 🏊 LP

MARTRES-TOLOSANE HAUTE-GARONNE

Moulin

31220 ☎ 561988640 ▤ 561986690

e-mail info@campinglemoulin.com

website www.campinglemoulin.com

A beautiful wooded location beside the River Garonne at the foot of the Pyrénées. Well maintained with a variety of recreational facilities.

➲ 1.5km SE off N117.

Open 15 Apr-Sep **Site** 12HEC 🌿 🏖 🏘 🚐 **Prices** 🧍 4.20-6 pitch 5.95-8.50 🚐 (static)195-350 **Facilities** 🏧 🛎 ☺ 🚽 🅰 🚿 🅶 **Services** 🍴 🍽 🛒 **Leisure** 🏊 PR **Off-site** 🛎 🍽 🚿L 🛒

Site 6HEC (site size) 🌿 grass 🏖 sand 🌿 stone 🌿 little shade 🏖 partly shaded 🏖 mainly shaded 🏘 bungalows for hire
🚐 caravans for hire 🅰 tents for hire ⊗ no dogs **Prices** 🧍 adult per night 🚗 car per night pp per person per night 🚐 caravan per night
🅰 tent per night 🚐 (static)-caravan hire per week

MAULÉON-LICHARRE PYRÉNÉES-ATLANTIQUES

Saison

rte de Libarrenx, 64130 ☎ 559281879 📄 559280623

e-mail camping.uhaitza@wanadoo.fr

website www.camping-uhaitza.com

A peaceful site beside the river, near the town centre.

➔ *1.5km S on D918.*

Open Mar-Nov **Site** 1.1HEC 🌣 ♣ ⚏ 🚃 **Prices** ♦ 3.40-4.10 🚐 2-2.50 pitch 3.90-4.55 🚐 (static)185-480 **Facilities** 🏪 🛁 ☺ ⚏ 🅟 ⚏ ⛁ 🅟 **Services** ⛽ 🍴 ➕ 🔲 **Leisure** ⚱ R **Off-site** 🍴 ⚱P

MESSANGES LANDES

Acacias

rte d'Azur, Quartier Delest ☎ 558480178 📄 558482312

e-mail lesacacias@lesacacias.com

website www.lesacacias.com

Open 25 Mar-25 Oct **Site** 3.4HEC 🌣 ♣ ⚏ 🚃 **Prices** pitch 8.90-13.50 (incl 2 persons) pp2.60-3.40 🚐 (static)170-550 **Facilities** 🏪 🛁 ☺ ⚏ ⚱ ⛁ 🅟 **Services** ➕ 🔲 **Off-site** ⛽ 🍴 ⚱

Albret Plage

40660 ☎ 558480367 📄 558482191

e-mail albretplage@wanadoo.fr

website www.albretplage.fr

Site with direct access to beach (300m). 1km from town of Vieux Boucau.

Open Apr-Oct **Site** 6HEC 🌣 ♣ ⚏ 🚃 **Prices** pitch 11-15.20 🚐 (static)211-585 **Facilities** 🏪 🛁 ☺ ⚏ ⚱ ⛁ 🅟 **Services** ⛽ 🍴 🔲 **Leisure** ⚱ S

Off-site ⚱LR   *See advertisement on this page*

Côte

rte de Vieux Boucau, 40660 ☎ 558489494 📄 558489444

e-mail info@campinglacote.com

website www.campinglacote.com

A picturesque wooded area 1km from the beach.

➔ *2.3km S via D652.*

Open Apr-Sep **Site** 4HEC 🌣 ♣ ⚏ **Prices** ♦ 3-4.50 pitch 9.50-16.20 (incl 2 persons) **Facilities** 🏪 🛁 ☺ ⚏ ⚱ ⛁ 🅟 **Services** ➕ 🔲 **Off-site** ⛽ 🍴 ⚱ ⚱LS

Moïsan

rte de la Plage, 40660 ☎ 558489206 📄 558489206

e-mail sarl@bsclub-internet.fr

website www.camping-moisan.com

Set in a pine forest 0.8km from the sea with modern facilities.

Open 15 May-Sep **Site** 7HEC 🌣 ♣ 🌣 ♣ ⚏ 🚃 **Prices** pitch 8-16.20 (incl 2 persons) pp2.50-4.50 🚐 (static)100-320 **Facilities** 🏪 🛁 ☺ ⚏ ⚱ ⛁ 🅟 **Services** ⛽ 🍴 ➕ 🔲 **Off-site** ⚱PS

Vieux Port

Plage Sud, 40660 ☎ 172039160 📄 558480169

e-mail contact@levieuxport.com

website www.levieuxport.com

A family site in the heart of the Landes forest with direct access to the beach. Good recreational facilities.

➔ *2.5km SW via D652.*

Open Apr-Sep **Site** 30HEC 🌣 ♣ 🌣 ♣ ⚏ 🚃 **Prices** ♦ 3.50-6 pitch 12-37 (incl 2 persons) 🚐 (static)250-580 **Facilities** 🏪 🛁 ☺ ⚏ ⚱ ⚏ 🅟 **Services** ⛽ 🍴 ➕ 🔲 **Leisure** ⚱ PS **Off-site** ⚱ ⚱LR ➕

MÉZOS LANDES

Sen Yan

40170 ☎ 558426005 📄 558426456

e-mail reception@sen-yan.com

website www.sen-yan.com

A pleasant site in exotic tropical gardens, surrounded by a pine wood.

➔ *1km E.*

Open 26 May-16 Sep **Site** 8HEC 🌣 ♣ ⚏ 🚃 **Prices** pitch 24-34 (incl 2 persons) pp5-6 **Facilities** 🏪 🛁 ☺ ⚏ ⚱ ⛁ 🅟 **Services** ⛽ 🍴 ➕ 🔲 **Leisure** ⚱ P **Off-site** ⚱ ⚱R

France

Facilities 🛁 shop 🏪 shower ☺ electric points for razors ⚏ electric points for caravans 🅟 parking by tents permitted 🅟 compulsory separate car park
Services 🍴 café/restaurant 🔲 bar ⚏ Camping Gaz International ⚱ gas other than Camping Gaz ➕ first aid facilities 🔲 laundry
Leisure ⚱ swimming L-Lake P-Pool R-River S-Sea **Off-site** All facilities within 2km

France

MIERS LOT

Pigeonnier
46500 ☎ 565337195 ▤ 565337195
e-mail veronique.bouny@wanadoo.fr
website www.campinglepigeonnier.com
Peaceful, shady site close to the River Dordogne amid spectacular
scenery.
➲ 400m E via D91.
Open Apr-1 Oct **Site** 1HEC ❤ ❤ ☎ ➤ **Prices** ♠ 4-4.50 pitch 4-4.50
➤ (static)170-530 **Facilities** ♠ ⊕ ⊙ ❷ ⚒ ℗ **Services** ❞ ℃ ➕ ⊠
Leisure ⚓ P **Off-site** ⊞ ℃ ⚓L

MIMIZAN LANDES

AT MIMIZAN-PLAGE (6KM E BY D626)

CM de la Plage
bd de l'Atlantique, 40200 ☎ 558090032 ▤ 558094494
e-mail contact@mimizan-camping.com
website www.mimizan-camping.com
Open 6 Apr-Sep **Site** 16HEC ❤ ⚓ ☎ ➤ **Prices** ♠ 6-8 ➤ 1.80-2 pitch 6-9
(incl 2 persons) **Facilities** ♠ ⊕ ⊙ ❷ ⚒ ⚒ ℗ **Services** ❞ ℃ ⊠
Off-site ❞ ⚓S   *See advertisement on page 89*

Marina-Landes
40202 ☎ 558091266 ▤ 558091640
e-mail contact@clubmarina.com
website www.marinalandes.com
Set in a pine wood 0.5km from the beach.
➲ D626 from Mimizan Plage.
Open 12 May-18 Sep **Site** 9HEC ❤ ⚓ ❤ ☎ ➤ A **Facilities** ♠ ⊕ ⊙ ❷ ⚒ ℗
Services ❞ ℃ ➕ ⊠ **Leisure** ⚓ P **Off-site** ⚓LRS

See advertisement on this page

MIRANDOL-BOURGNOUNAC TARN

Clots
Les Clots, 81190 ☎ 563769278 ▤ 563769278
e-mail campclots@wanadoo.fr
website www.campinglesclots.info
A wooded area within the Viaur valley with good facilities.
➲ 5.5km N via D905, rte de Rieupeyroux.
Open May-Sep **Site** 7HEC ❤ ❤ ☎ ➤ A **Prices** ♠ 3.70-4.60 ➤ 1-1.50
pitch 3.60-6.70 ➤ (static)240-300 **Facilities** ♠ ⊞ ⊙ ❷ ⚒ ℗ **Services** ❞ ⊠
Leisure ⚓ PR

MOLIÈRES DORDOGNE

Grande Veyière
24480 ☎ 553632584 ▤ 553631825
e-mail la_grande_veyiere@wanadoo.fr
Wooded site with good sports facilities in the heart of Périgord's
bastides country.
➲ 2.4km SE.
Open Apr-5 Nov **Site** 4HEC ❤ ⚓ ❤ ☎ ➤ **Facilities** ♠ ⊞ ⊙ ❷ ⚒ ℗
Services ❞ ℃ ⊠ **Leisure** ⚓ P

MOLIÈRES TARN-ET-GARONNE

Lac du Malivert
Centre de Loisirs du Malivert, 82220 ☎ 563677637 ▤ 563676216
e-mail molieres.82@wanadoo.fr
website www.cdg82.fr/molieres
A pleasant lakeside setting.
➲ To Molières from S, towards Centre de Loisirs & Lac Malivert.
Open Jun-Sep **Site** 0.7HEC ❤ ❤ ☎ ➤ **Prices** ♠ 2.20 pitch 2.50
Facilities ♠ ⊞ ⊙ ❷ ℗ **Services** ❞ ⊠ **Leisure** ⚓ L **Off-site** ⊞ ℃ ℃ ➕

MOLIETS-PLAGE LANDES

Airotel St-Martin
av de l'Océan, 40660 ☎ 558485230 ▤ 558485073
e-mail contact@camping-saint-martin.fr
website www.camping-saint-martin.fr
Large site on the Atlantic coast with direct access to the largest sandy
beach in the region.
➲ Between village & beach.
Open Etr-Oct **Site** 18.5HEC ❤ ⚓ ❤ ☎ **Prices** pitch 17.50-46 (incl 2
persons) **Facilities** ♠ ⊞ ⊙ ❷ ⚒ ℗ **Services** ❞ ℃ ⊠ **Leisure** ⚓ P
Off-site ⚒ ⚓S ➕

Cigales
av de l'Océan, 40660 ☎ 558485118 ▤ 558483527
e-mail camping-les-cigales@wanadoo.fr
website www.camping-les-cigales.fr
On undulating ground in pine trees.
➲ 300m from beach.
Open Apr-Sep **Site** 23HEC ❤ ⚓ ❤ ☎ **Facilities** ♠ ⊞ ⊙ ❷ ⚒ ⚒ ℗
Services ❞ ℃ ➕ ⊠ **Off-site** ⚓LRS

MONCRABEAU LOT-ET-GARONNE

Mouliat
'Le Nouliat', 47600 ☎ 553654328 ▤ 553654328
A small site in a wooded location on the banks of the River La Baïse.
➲ On D219, 200m from D930.
Open Jun-15 Sep **Site** 1.3HEC ❤ ⚓ ☎ ➤ **Facilities** ♠ ⊞ ⊙ ❷ ℗
Services ❞ ℃ ⊠ **Off-site** ⚓PR

Site 6HEC (site size) ❤ grass ⚓ sand ⚓ stone ⚓ little shade ❤ partly shaded ❤ mainly shaded ☎ bungalows for hire
➤ caravans for hire A tents for hire ⊗ no dogs **Prices** ♠ adult per night ➤ car per night pp per person per night ➤ caravan per night
A tent per night ➤ (static)-caravan hire per week

MONTESQUIOU GERS

Château le Haget
32320 ☎ 562709580 📠 562709483
e-mail info@lehaget.com
website www.lehaget.com
Set in the grounds of a château.
Open Apr-Oct **Site** 12HEC 🚙 🚐 ⛺ 🏠 **Facilities** 🚿 🛍 🔌 ⚡ 🔥 🛢 [P] **Services** 🍷 🍴 ➕ 🧺 **Leisure** 🏊 P **Off-site** 🏊LR

MONTIGNAC DORDOGNE

Moulin du Bleufond
av Aristide Briand, 24290 ☎ 553518395 📠 553511992
e-mail le.moulin.du.bleufond@wanadoo.fr
website www.bleufond.com
Situated beside a river in the grounds of a 17th-century mill.
➡ *0.5km off D65 Montignac to Sergeac road.*
Open Apr-15 Oct **Site** 1.3HEC 🚙 🚐 ⛺ **Prices** 🚶 3.82-5.10 pitch 4.57-6.10 **Facilities** 🚿 🛍 🔌 ⚡ [P] **Services** 🍷 🍴 ➕ 🧺 **Leisure** 🏊 P **Off-site** 🏊R

MUSSIDAN DORDOGNE

CM Le Port
24400 ☎ 553812009
Open 15 Jun-15 Sep **Site** 0.5HEC 🚙 🚐 **Facilities** 🚿 🔌 ⚡ [P] **Services** ➕ 🧺 **Off-site** 🛍 🍷 🍴 🏊PR

NAGES TARN

Rieu Montagné
Lac du Laouzas, 81320 ☎ 563372471 📠 563371542
e-mail rieumontagne@camping-indigo.com
website www.camping-indigo.com
Wooded location beside the Laouzas lake with good recreational facilities.
➡ *4.5km S via D62.*
Open 10 Jun-17 Sep **Site** 9HEC 🚙 🚐 ⛺ 🏠 🏕 **Prices** 🚶 4.80-5.50 pitch 4.20-17.50 🏠 (static)200-640 **Facilities** 🚿 🛍 🔌 ⚡ 🔥 🛢 [P] **Services** 🍷 🍴 ➕ 🧺 **Leisure** 🏊 LP

OLORON-STE-MARIE PYRÉNÉES-ATLANTIQUES

Val du Gave-d'Aspe
rte du Somport, Gurmençon, 64400 ☎ 559360507
e-mail chalet.aspe@wanadoo.fr
website www.chalet-aspe.com
A pleasant site in the Aspe valley with picturesque Pyrenean scenery.
Open 8 Jan-4 Nov **Site** 0.5HEC 🚙 🚐 ⛺ **Prices** 🚶 3 pitch 13-16 **Facilities** 🚿 🔌 ⚡ 🅿 **Services** 🍷 ➕ 🧺 **Leisure** 🏊 P **Off-site** 🍴 🛢 🏊R

ONESSE-ET-LAHARIE LANDES

CM Bienvenu
259 route de Mimizan, 40110 ☎ 558073049 📠 558073078
A family site situated in a forest.
➡ *0.5km from village centre on D38.*
Open 15 Jun-15 Sep **Site** 1.2HEC 🚙 🚐 **Facilities** 🚿 🔌 ⚡ [P] **Services** 🍷 🍴 ➕ 🧺 **Off-site** 🛍 🍴 🏊R

OUSSE PYRÉNÉES-ATLANTIQUES

Sapins
64320 ☎ 559817421
➡ *N117 exit Pau. Or A64 exit Soumoulou.*
Open All year **Site** 1HEC 🚙 🚐 ⛺ 🏠 **Prices** 🚶 3 pitch 3.50 🏠 (static)110 **Facilities** 🚿 🔌 ⚡ [P] **Services** 🍷 🍴 ➕ 🧺 **Off-site** 🛍 🍴

PADIRAC LOT

Chênes
rte du Gouffre, 46500 ☎ 565336554 📠 565337155
e-mail les_chenes@hotmail.com
website www.campingleschenes.com
A fine position in the centre of the Haute-Quercy with good facilities.
➡ *1.5km NE on D90 towards Gouffre.*
Open May-14 Sep **Site** 5HEC 🚙 🚐 ⛺ 🏕 **Facilities** 🚿 🛍 🔌 ⚡ 🔥 🛢 [P] **Services** 🍷 🍴 ➕ 🧺 **Leisure** 🏊 P

PAMIERS ARIÈGE

Ombrages
rte d'Escosse, 9100 ☎ 561671224 📠 561601823
A pleasant site in wooded surroundings beside the River Ariège, 1.5km from the town centre.
➡ *NW on D119 beside river.*
Open All year **Site** 2.5HEC 🚙 🚐 🏠 **Facilities** 🚿 🛍 🔌 ⚡ 🔥 🛢 [P] **Services** 🍷 🍴 ➕ 🧺 **Off-site** 🏊PR

PAUILLAC GIRONDE

CM Les Gabarreys
rte de la Rivière, 33250 ☎ 556591003 📠 556733068
e-mail camping.les.gabarreys@wanadoo.fr
website www.pauillac-medoc.com
A municipal site with good sports facilities.
➡ *RN 215/D2*
Open 3 Apr-6 Oct **Site** 2HEC 🚙 🚐 ⛺ **Prices** pitch 13.60 (incl 2 persons) pp8 **Facilities** 🚿 🔌 ⚡ [P] **Services** ➕ 🧺 **Off-site** 🛍 🍷 🍴 🔥 🛢 🏊PR

PAYRAC LOT

Panoramic
rte de Loupiac, 46350 ☎ 565379845 📠 565379165
e-mail camping.panoramic@wanadoo.fr
website www.campingpanoramic.com
A peaceful family site 5km from the River Dordogne with good recreational facilities.
➡ *Off N20 N of Payrac.*
Open All year **Site** 1.8HEC 🚙 🚐 ⛺ 🏠 🏕 **Prices** 🚶 2.50-2.80 pitch 3-4 🏠 (static)100-210 **Facilities** 🚿 🔌 ⚡ 🛢 [P] **Services** 🍷 🍴 ➕ 🧺 **Off-site** 🛍 🔥 🏊P

Pins
46350 ☎ 565379632 📠 565379108
e-mail info@les-pins-camping.com
website www.les-pins-camping.com
A well-managed site, partly in forest, partly on meadowland. Sheltered from traffic noise.
➡ *S of village off N20.*
Open Apr-Sep **Site** 3.5HEC 🚙 🚐 ⛺ 🏠 🏕 **Prices** 🚶 3.75-6.30 pitch 5.50-9 🏠 (static)140-410 **Facilities** 🚿 🔌 ⚡ [P] **Services** 🍷 🍴 ➕ 🧺 **Leisure** 🏊 P **Off-site** 🛍 🔥 ➕

Facilities 🛍 shop 🚿 shower 🔌 electric points for razors ⚡ electric points for caravans [P] parking by tents permitted 🅿 compulsory separate car park
Services 🍴 café/restaurant 🍷 bar 🔥 Camping Gaz International 🛢 gas other than Camping Gaz ➕ first aid facilities 🧺 laundry
Leisure 🏊 swimming L-Lake P-Pool R-River S-Sea **Off-site** All facilities within 2km

France

PÉRIGUEUX DORDOGNE

Barnabé
80 r des Bains, Boulazac, 24750 ☎ 553534145 📠 553541662
e-mail contact@barnabe-perigord.com
website www.barnabe-perigord.com
A well-appointed site in a wooded park-like location beside the river.
➲ *Signed from N89, 2km E of town centre.*
Open Mar-Oct **Site** 1.5HEC 🌱 🌳 **Prices** 🚶 3.80 🚗 2.30 🚐 3.60 ⛺ 3.20
Facilities 🚿 🔌 🚐 Ⓟ **Services** 🍷 🍴 ✚ 🧺 **Off-site** 🛍 🍴 🍃 🏊P

PETIT-PALAIS GIRONDE

Pressoir
Queyrai Petit-Palais, 33570 ☎ 557697325 📠 557697736
e-mail camping.le.pressoir@wanadoo.fr
website www.campinglepressoir.com
An old farm in the rolling countryside around St-Emilion.
➲ *N89 Bordeaux-Périgeux, exit St-Médard de Guizières & signed.*
Open Apr-Sep **Site** 2HEC 🌱 🌳 ⛺ **Prices** pitch 7-10 pp6-6.25 🚐 (static)295-395 **Facilities** 🚿 🔌 🚐 Ⓟ **Services** 🍷 🍴 ✚ 🧺
Leisure 🏊 P

PEZULS DORDOGNE

Forêt
24510 ☎ 553227169 📠 553237779
e-mail camping.laforet@wanadoo.fr
website www.camping-dordogne.com/la-foret
Set in extensive grounds on the edge of the forest with modern facilities.
➲ *3km from village centre, site 0.6km off D703.*
Open Apr-Oct **Site** 9HEC 🌱 🌳 🏠 🚐 **Prices** 🚶 4.10-5.10 pitch 3.80-4.80
Facilities 🚿 🛍 🔌 🚐 🍃 🍖 Ⓟ **Services** 🍷 ✚ 🧺 **Leisure** 🏊 P

PONT-ST-MAMET DORDOGNE

Lestaubière
Pont-St-Mamet, 24140 ☎ 553829815 📠 553829017
e-mail lestaubiere@cs.com
website www.lestaubiere.com
Secluded site in an attractive part of the Dordogne, occupying the former outbuildings and wooded grounds of the adjacent château. Fine views of the surrounding countryside.
➲ *Off N21. 0.5km N of Pont-St-Mamet.*
Open 26 Apr-1 Oct **Site** 22HEC 🌱 🌳 🚐 ⛺ **Prices** 🚶 4.70-5.90 pitch 6.90-9.90 🚐 (static)360-420 **Facilities** 🚿 🛍 🔌 🚐 🍃 Ⓟ **Services** 🍷 🍴 ✚ 🧺
Leisure 🏊 LP

PUYBRUN LOT

Sole
46130 ☎ 565385237 📠 565109109
e-mail la-sole@wanadoo.fr
website www.la-sole.com
A well-run site in pleasant wooded surroundings with good facilities.
➲ *D703 from village towards Bretenoux, 1st turning after garage.*
Open Apr-Sep **Site** 2.1HEC 🌱 🌳 🏠 🚐 **Facilities** 🚿 🔌 🚐 🍖 Ⓟ
Services 🍷 🍴 ✚ 🧺 **Leisure** 🏊 P **Off-site** 🛍 🏊LR

PUY-L'ÉVÊQUE LOT

AT MONTCABRIER (7 KM NW)

Moulin de Laborde
46700 ☎ 565246206 📠 565365133
e-mail moulindelaborde@wanadoo.fr
website www.moulindelaborde.com
Well-equipped site surrounded by woods and hills, in a picturesque valley on the River Thèze.
➲ *NW off D673.*
Open 29 Apr-8 Sep **Site** 12HEC 🌱 🌳 🚫 **Prices** 🚶 4.64-5.80 pitch 6.40-8
Facilities 🚿 🛍 🔌 🚐 🍃 Ⓟ **Services** 🍷 🍴 ✚ 🧺 **Leisure** 🏊 LPR
Off-site 🍖

PYLA-SUR-MER GIRONDE

Dune
rte de Biscarrosse, 33260 ☎ 556227217 📠 556227401
e-mail reception@campingdeladune.fr
website www.campingdeladune.fr
A beautifully situated and quiet site partly on terraced sandy fields. A dune over 100m in height separates the site from the sea.
➲ *On road between Pyla-sur-Mer & Pilat-Plage.*
Open May-Sep **Site** 6HEC 🏖 🌳 🏠 **Prices** pitch 15-28 (incl 2 persons)
Facilities 🚿 🛍 🔌 🚐 🍃 🍖 Ⓟ **Services** 🍷 🍴 ✚ 🧺 **Leisure** 🏊 P
Off-site 🏊S

Forêt
rte de Biscarrosse, 33115 ☎ 556227328 📠 556227050
e-mail camping.foret@wanadoo.fr
website www.campinglaforet.fr
A well-equipped, mainly sandy site surrounded by pine trees. A dune over 100m high separates the site from the fine beaches at the mouth of the Arcachon Basin. There are good sports facilities and evening entertainment is provided regularly.
➲ *Follow the road between Pilat and Plage.*
Open Apr-Oct **Site** 12HEC 🌱 🌳 🏠 **Facilities** 🚿 🛍 🔌 🚐 🍃 🍖 Ⓟ
Services 🍷 🍴 ✚ 🧺 **Leisure** 🏊 PS

Pyla
rte de Biscarrosse, 33115 ☎ 556227456 📠 556221031
e-mail pylacamping@free.fr
website www.pyla-camping.com
A well-equipped family site with good recreational facilities and direct access to the sea.
Open Apr-Sep **Site** 8HEC 🌱 🏖 🌳 🏠 **Prices** pitch 14.80-32.80 (incl 2 persons) **Facilities** 🚿 🛍 🔌 🚐 🍃 🍖 Ⓟ **Services** 🍷 🍴 ✚ 🧺
Leisure 🏊 PS

Sunêlia Petit Nice
rte de Biscarrosse, 33115 ☎ 556227403 📠 556221431
e-mail info@petitnice.com
website www.petitnice.com
Sandy terraced site, partly steep slopes in pine woodland, mainly suitable for tents. Paths and standings are strengthened with timber, and there are 220 steps down to the beach.
➲ *6km S on D218.*
Open 12 Apr-Sep **Site** 5.5HEC 🌱 🏖 🌳 🏠 ⛺ **Prices** pitch 14-28 (incl 2 persons) pp4-7 **Facilities** 🚿 🛍 🔌 🚐 🍃 Ⓟ **Services** 🍷 🍴 ✚ 🧺
Leisure 🏊 PS

Site 6HEC (site size) 🌱 grass 🏖 sand 🪨 stone 🌴 little shade 🌳 partly shaded 🌲 mainly shaded 🏠 bungalows for hire 🚐 caravans for hire ⛺ tents for hire 🚫 no dogs **Prices** 🚶 adult per night 🚗 car per night pp per person per night 🚐 caravan per night ⛺ tent per night 🚐 (static)-caravan hire per week

France

Yelloh Village Panorama du Pyla
rte de Biscarrosse, 33115 ☎ 556221044 🖨 556221012
e-mail mail@camping-panorama.com
website www.camping-panorama.com
Partially terraced site among dunes, on the edge of the 100m high Dune de Pyla. Views of the sea from some pitches.
➲ *Signed on D218.*
Open 20 Apr-1 Oct **Site** 15HEC ➸ ❄ ✿ ⇆ ⅄ **Prices** ✦ 4-5.50 pitch 8-17 **Facilities** 🚿 🏠 ⊙ ⚡ ⌀ ⚊ 🏢 **Services** 🍴 🍽 🚑 ⊠ **Leisure** ⚓ PS

RAUZAN GIRONDE

Vieux Château
Route Départementale 123, 33420 ☎ 557841538 🖨 557841834
e-mail hoekstra.camping@wanadoo.fr
website www.vieux-chateau.com
A family site in a peaceful valley surrounded by vineyards and overlooked by the ruined 12th-century Rauzan castle.
➲ *1.5km from D670.*
Open Apr-Oct **Site** 2.5HEC ➸ ❄ ✿ **Prices** pitch 10-17 **Facilities** 🚿 🏠 ⊙ ⚡ ⚊ 🏢 **Services** 🍽 ⊠ **Leisure** ⚓ P **Off-site** ⊞

REYREVIGNES LOT

Papillon
46320 ☎ 565401240 🖨 565401718
e-mail info@domaine-papillon.com
website www.domaine-papillon.com
A wooded park in the heart of the Haut-Quercy region with modern facilities.
➲ *Via N653.*
Open May-Sep **Site** 3HEC ➸ ❄ ✿ **Prices** ✦ 3.50-5 pitch 4.20-6 **Facilities** 🚿 ⊙ ⚡ 🏢 **Services** 🍴 🍽 ⊠ **Leisure** ⚓ P **Off-site** ⚓LR

ROCAMADOUR LOT

Cigales
46500 ☎ 565336444 🖨 565336960
e-mail camping.cigales@wanadoo.fr
website www.camping-cigales.com
A peaceful, well-equipped site with shaded pitches and modern facilities. Fine views of Rocamadour.
Open 21 Jun-Aug **Site** 3HEC ➸ ❄ ✿ ⇆ **Facilities** 🚿 🏠 ⊙ ⚡ ⊘ 🏢 **Services** 🍴 🍽 ⊞ ⊠ **Leisure** ⚓ P

Relais du Campeur l'Hospitalet
46500 ☎ 565336328 🖨 565106821
e-mail contact@relais-du-campeur.com
website www.relais-du-campeur.com
Shady, level site with well-marked pitches and good facilities. Fine views of Rocamadour.
➲ *On D36.*
Open Apr-Sep **Site** 1.7HEC ➸ ❄ **Prices** pitch 11.40-13.90 (incl 2 persons) **Facilities** 🚿 🏠 ⊙ ⚡ ⌀ 🏢 **Services** 🍴 ⊞ ⊠ **Leisure** ⚓ P **Off-site** 🍽 ⚊

ROCHE-CHALAIS, LA DORDOGNE

Gerbes
r de la Dronne, 24490 ☎ 553914065 🖨 553903201
e-mail camping.la.roche.chalais@wanadoo.fr
Well-appointed family site on banks of River Dronne.
➲ *Off D674 in village centre, signed.*
Open 15 Apr-Sep **Site** 3.5HEC ➸ ❄ ✿ **Prices** ✦ 2.20 pitch 2.70 ⇆ (static)170 **Facilities** 🚿 🏠 ⊙ ⚡ 🏢 **Services** ⊞ ⊠ **Leisure** ⚓ R **Off-site** 🏠 🍴 🍽 ⌀ ⚊ ⚓P

ROMIEU, LA GERS

Camp de Florence
32480 ☎ 562281558 🖨 562282004
e-mail info@lecampdeflorence.com
website www.lecampdeflorence.com
Well-equipped site in rural surroundings.
➲ *D931 towards Agen-Condom, 3km before Condom left to La Romieu.*
Open Apr-6 Oct **Site** 15HEC ❄ ✿ ✿ ⇆ ⅄ **Prices** pitch 13.90-30.90 (incl 2 persons) pp3.50-6.90 ⇆ (static)230-775 **Facilities** 🚿 ⊙ ⚡ 🏢 **Services** 🍴 🍽 ⊞ ⊠ **Leisure** ⚓ P **Off-site** 🏠

ROQUEFORT LANDES

CM de Nauton
Cité Nauton, 40120 ☎ 558455046 🖨 558455363
A small municipal site with good facilities.
➲ *1.6km N on D932 towards Bordeaux.*
Open Jun-Aug **Site** 1.4HEC ➸ ❄ **Facilities** 🚿 ⊙ ⚡ 🏢 **Services** ⊞ **Off-site** 🏠 🍴 🍽 ⚓PR

ROQUELAURE GERS

Talouch
32810 ☎ 562655243 🖨 562655368
e-mail info@camping-talouch.com
website www.camping-talouch.com
A family site in picturesque wooded surroundings in the heart of Gascony. There are good sports and entertainment facilities.
➲ *N21 onto D148.*
Open Apr-Sep **Site** 9HEC ➸ ❄ ✿ ⅄ **Prices** pitch 14.70-23.15 (incl 2 persons) **Facilities** 🚿 🏠 ⊙ ⚡ ⌀ 🏢 **Services** 🍴 🍽 ⊞ ⊠ **Leisure** ⚓ P

ROUFFIGNAC DORDOGNE

Cantegrel
24580 ☎ 553054830 🖨 553052787
e-mail infos@camping-bleusoleil.com
website www.camping-bleusoleil.com
A peaceful location in the heart of the Périgord Noir, with good recreational facilities.
➲ *1.5km N via D31, rte de Thenon.*
Open Apr-1 Oct **Site** 60HEC ➸ ❄ ✿ ⇆ **Facilities** 🚿 ⊙ ⚡ ⚊ 🏢 **Services** 🍴 🍽 ⊞ ⊠ **Leisure** ⚓ P **Off-site** 🏠

ST-ANTOINE-D'AUBEROCHE DORDOGNE

Pélonie
La Bourgie ☎ 553075578 🖨 553037427
e-mail lapelonie@aol.com **website** www.lapelonie.com
In a picturesque rural location in the heart of the Périgord.
➲ *Off N89 between St Pierre de Chignac and Fossmagne.*
Open Apr-30 Oct **Site** 3HEC ➸ ❄ ✿ ✿ ⇆ ⅄ **Prices** ✦ 3.50-4.80 pitch 4.90-6.50 ⇆ (static)160-340 **Facilities** 🚿 🏠 ⊙ ⚡ ⌀ ⚊ 🏢 **Services** 🍴 🍽 ⊞ ⊠ **Leisure** ⚓ P

ST-ANTOINE-DE-BREUILH DORDOGNE

Riviere Fleurie
St Aulaye, 24230 ☎ 553248280 🖨 553248280
e-mail info@la-riviere-fleurie.com
website www.la-riviere-fleurie.com
➲ *Off D936 W of St-Antoine & 3km towards River Dordogne.*
Open Apr-Sep **Site** 2.4HEC ➸ ❄ ✿ ⇆ **Prices** ✦ 4-5 pitch 13.60-17 (incl 2 persons) ⇆ (static)140-330 **Facilities** 🚿 🏠 ⊙ ⚡ ⚊ 🏢 **Services** 🍴 🍽 ⊞ ⊠ **Leisure** ⚓ PR

Facilities 🏠 shop 🚿 shower ⊙ electric points for razors ⚡ electric points for caravans 🏢 parking by tents permitted 🅿 compulsory separate car park
Services 🍽 café/restaurant 🍴 bar ⌀ Camping Gaz International ⚊ gas other than Camping Gaz ⊞ first aid facilities ⊠ laundry
Leisure ⚓ swimming L-Lake P-Pool R-River S-Sea **Off-site** All facilities within 2km

France

ST-ANTONIN-NOBLE-VAL TARN-ET-GARONNE

Trois Cantons
82140 ☎ 563319857 🖹 563312593
e-mail info@3cantons.fr
website www.3cantons.fr
Divided into pitches, partly on sloping ground in an oak forest. Separate section for teenagers.

⮕ 8.5km NW near D926, signed.

Open 15 Apr-Sep **Site** 15HEC ⬤ ⬤ ⬤ ⬤ **Facilities** 🌣 🛁 ⊙ 🚽 ⬛ ⬤ **Services** ⬛ ⭘ 🗑 **Leisure** ⬤ P

ST-BERTRAND-DE-COMMINGES HAUTE-GARONNE

Es Pibous
chemin de St-Just, 31510 ☎ 561883142 🖹 561956383
e-mail es.pibous@wanadoo.fr
website www.espibous.fr
A quiet, shaded site in an elevated position with good facilities.

Open All year **Site** 1.8HEC ⬤ ⬤ **Prices** ⭢ 3.86 pitch 3.50 **Facilities** 🌣 🛁 ⊙ 🚽 ⬛ ⬤ **Services** 🗑 **Leisure** ⬤ P **Off-site** 🛁 ⬛ ⭘ 🏊 ⬤ LR

ST-CÉRÉ LOT

CM de Soulhol
quai A-Salesse ☎ 565381237 🖹 565381237
e-mail info@campinglesoulhol.com
website www.campinglesoulhol.com
A family site bordered by two rivers with good recreational facilities.

⮕ Via A20

Open May-Sep **Site** 4HEC ⬤ ⬤ **Prices** ⭢ 4-4.20 pitch 4.40-4.90 **Facilities** 🌣 ⊙ 🚽 ⬤ ⬤ **Services** ⬛ 🗑 **Leisure** ⬤ R **Off-site** 🛁 ⬛ ⭘ 🏊 ⬤ P

ST-CIRQ-LAPOPIE LOT

Plage
46330 ☎ 565302951 🖹 565302333
e-mail camping-laplage@wanadoo.fr
website www.campingplage.com
Site beside the River Lot with well-defined pitches and modern facilities. Boat and bicycle hire available.

⮕ Via D41 from N. Or D42 from S.

Open All year **Site** 3HEC ⬤ ⬤ ⬤ ⬤ **Facilities** 🌣 ⊙ 🚽 🏊 ⬤ **Services** ⬛ ⭘ 🗑 **Leisure** ⬤ R **Off-site** 🛁

ST-CRICQ GERS

Lac de Thoux
32440 ☎ 562657129 🖹 562657481
e-mail lacdethoux@cacg.fr
A family site with good facilities on the edge of the lake, 50m from the beach.

⮕ On D654 between Cologne & l'Isle Jourdain.

Open Apr-15 Oct **Site** 3HEC ⬤ ⬤ ⬤ 🏕 Ⓐ **Facilities** 🌣 🛁 ⊙ 🚽 ⬤ 🏊 ⬤ **Services** ⬛ ⭘ ⬛ 🗑 **Leisure** ⬤ LP

ST-CYBRANET DORDOGNE

Bel Ombrage
24250 ☎ 553283414 🖹 553596464
e-mail belombrage@wanadoo.fr
website www.belombrage.com
Quiet holiday site in wooded valley.

Open Jun-5 Sep **Site** 6HEC ⬤ ⬤ **Facilities** 🌣 ⊙ 🚽 ⬤ **Services** ⬛ 🗑 **Leisure** ⬤ PR **Off-site** 🛁 ⬛ ⭘ 🏊

ST-CYPRIEN DORDOGNE

Ferme de Campagnac
Castels, 24220 ☎ 553292603 🖹 553292603
e-mail maboureau@tiscali.fr
website www.campagnac.fr.tc
A quiet site in a sheltered position 200m from the farm.

⮕ D25 from town, signed.

Open Apr-Oct **Site** 0.8HEC ⬤ ⬤ ⬤ 🏕 **Facilities** 🌣 ⊙ 🚽 ⬤ **Services** 🗑 **Off-site** 🛁 ⬛ ⭘ ⬤ 🏊 ⬛

CM Garrit
24220 ☎ 553292056 🖹 553292056
e-mail pbecheau@aol.com
website www.campingdugarritendordogneperigord.com
A peaceful location beside the River Dordogne with safe bathing.

⮕ 1.5km S on D48.

Open Apr-Oct **Site** 2HEC ⬤ ⬤ 🏕 🏕 **Prices** pitch 12-15 (incl 2 persons) 🏕 (static)240-500 **Facilities** 🌣 🛁 ⊙ 🚽 ⬤ **Services** ⬛ ⬛ 🗑 **Leisure** ⬤ PR **Off-site** 🛁 ⭘ ⬤ 🏊 ⬤ R

ST-ÉMILION GIRONDE

Barbanne
route de Montagne, 33330 ☎ 57247580 🖹 57246968
e-mail barbanne@wanadoo.fr
website www.camping-saint-emilion.com
A peaceful country setting among vineyards, close to a 5-hectare lake.

⮕ 3km N via D122.

Open Apr-23 Sep **Site** 10HEC ⬤ ⬤ 🏕 **Facilities** 🌣 🛁 ⊙ 🚽 ⬤ ⬤ **Services** ⭘ ⬛ 🗑 **Leisure** ⬤ LPR

ST-GENIES DORDOGNE

Bouquerie
24590 ☎ 553289822 🖹 553291975
e-mail labouquerie@wanadoo.fr
website www.labouquerie.com
A family site in wooded surroundings with a variety of facilities.

⮕ N of village on D704.

Open 7 Apr-22 Sep **Site** 8HEC ⬤ ⬤ 🏕 **Prices** ⭢ 4.60-6.50 pitch 9.80-12.50 **Facilities** 🌣 🛁 ⊙ 🚽 ⬤ 🏊 ⬤ **Services** ⬛ ⭘ ⬛ 🗑 **Leisure** ⬤ LP

ST-GIRONS ARIÈGE

Pont du Nert
rte de Lacourt (D33), 09200 ☎ 561665848
e-mail dmmadre@aol.com
Grassy site between road and woodland.

⮕ 3km SE at junct D33 & D3.

Open Jun-15 Sep **Site** 1.5HEC ⬤ ⬤ **Prices** ⭢ 3.50 🏕 2 Ⓐ 2 **Facilities** 🌣 ⊙ 🚽 ⬤ **Off-site** ⬤ ⬤ R

ST-JEAN-DE-LUZ PYRÉNÉES-ATLANTIQUES

Atlantica
Quartier Acotz, 64500 ☎ 559477244 🖹 559547227
e-mail info@campingatlantica.com
website www.campingatlantica.com
A family site with good facilities at the foot of the Pyrénées close to the Spanish border, and 0.5km from the beach.

⮕ N10 exit St-Jean-de-Luz Nord for Biarritz, 1km on left.

Open Apr-Sep **Site** 3.5HEC ⬤ ⬤ 🏕 **Prices** pitch 14.30-25 (incl 2 persons) **Facilities** 🌣 🛁 ⊙ 🚽 ⬤ 🏊 ⬤ **Services** ⬛ ⭘ 🗑 **Leisure** ⬤ P
Off-site ⬤ S

See advertisement on page 95

Site 6HEC (site size) ⬤ grass ⬤ sand ⬤ stone ⬤ little shade ⬤ partly shaded ⬤ mainly shaded 🏠 bungalows for hire 🚐 caravans for hire Ⓐ tents for hire Ⓧ no dogs **Prices** ⭢ adult per night 🚗 car per night pp per person per night 🚐 caravan per night Ⓐ tent per night 🏕 (static)-caravan hire per week

Ferme d'Erromardie

64500 ☎ 59263426 ▤ 559512602

e-mail contact@camping-erromardie.com

website www.camping-erromardie.com

Site by the sea with several sections divided by roads and low hedges.

➪ *N to N10, over railway bridge & sharp right, signed.*

Open 15 Mar-15 Oct **Site** 2HEC ♨ ♣ ♠ **Prices** pitch 12.50-20 (incl 2 persons) **Facilities** ⋔ 🖺 ⊙ ⊡ ♨ ⑫ **Services** ⊉ ⓧ ➕ 🖾 **Leisure** ⚲ RS **Off-site** ∅

Tamaris Plage

quartier d'Acotz, 64500 ☎ 559265590 ▤ 559477015

e-mail tamaris1@wanadoo.fr

website www.tamaris-plage.com

Level family site with good facilities divided into sections by drives and hedges.

➪ *Signed from N10 towards sea.*

Open Apr-Sep **Site** 1.3HEC ♨ ♣ ♠ ♠ **Facilities** ⋔ 🖺 ⊡ ⑫ **Services** 🖾 **Off-site** 🖺 ⊉ ⓧ ∅ ♨ ⚲S ➕

AT SOCOA (3KM SW)

Juantcho

rte de la Corniche, 64122 ☎ 559471197 ▤ 559471197

e-mail camping@juantcho.com

website www.juantcho.com

➪ *2km W on D912.*

Open 10 Apr-Sep Oct-Mar **Site** 6HEC ♨ ♣ ♠ **Facilities** ⋔ ⊙ ⊡ ⑫ ⓟ **Services** 🖾 **Off-site** 🖺 ⊉ ⓧ ♨ ⚲RS ➕

ST-JEAN-PIED-DE-PORT PYRÉNÉES-ATLANTIQUES

Narbaïtz

rte de Bayonne, Ascarat, 64220 ☎ 559371013 ▤ 559372142

e-mail camping-narbaitz@wanadoo.fr

website www.camping-narbaitz.com

A quiet, comfortable site beside the River Berroua.

➪ *2km NW towards Bayonne.*

Open 15 Mar-Sep **Site** 2.5HEC ♨ ♣ ♠ **Facilities** ⋔ 🖺 ⊙ ⊡ ∅ ⑫ **Services** ⓧ 🖾 **Leisure** ⚲ PR **Off-site** 🖺 ⊉ ♨

ST-JULIEN-EN-BORN LANDES

Lette Fleurie

40170 ☎ 558427409 ▤ 558424151

e-mail camping-la-lette-fleurie@saint-julien-en-born.fr

On undulating ground in a pine wood with good facilities, 5 minutes from the beach.

Open Apr-Sep **Site** 18HEC ♨ ♣ ♠ ♠ **Prices** ♠ 3.80 ♠ 1.50 ♠ 3.50 Å 3.50 **Facilities** ⋔ 🖺 ⊙ ∅ ♨ ⑫ **Services** ⊉ ⓧ ➕ 🖾 **Leisure** ⚲ P **Off-site** ⚲RS

ST-JUSTIN LANDES

Pin

rte de Roquefort, 40240 ☎ 558448891 ▤ 558448891

e-mail camping.lepin@wanadoo.fr

website www.campinglepin.com

A quiet family site beside the lake. Bar and café only open May to 15 September.

➪ *2.3km N on D626.*

Open Apr-Sep **Site** 3HEC ♨ ♣ ♠ ♠ **Facilities** ⋔ ⊙ ⊡ ⑫ **Services** ⊉ ⓧ ➕ 🖾 **Leisure** ⚲ P **Off-site** 🖺

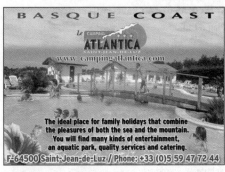

ST-LÉON-SUR-VÉZÈRE DORDOGNE

Paradis

24290 ☎ 553507264 ▤ 553507590

e-mail le-paradis@perigord.com

website www.le-paradis.com

Situated on the river bank in the picturesque Vézère valley.

➪ *S of village off D706 Les Éyzies road.*

Open Apr-25 Oct **Site** 7HEC ♨ ♣ ♠ **Prices** ♠ 5-7 pitch 7.50-11.50 ♠ (static)299-799 **Facilities** ⋔ 🖺 ⊙ ⊡ ∅ ♨ ⑫ **Services** ⊉ ⓧ ➕ 🖾 **Leisure** ⚲ PR

AT TURSAC (7KM SW)

Pigeonnier

24620 ☎ 553069690 ▤ 553069690

e-mail campinglepigeonnier@wanadoo.fr

website www.campinglepigeonnier.fr

A small, peaceful site in the heart of the Dordogne countryside.

➪ *Via D706 between Le Moustier & Les Éyzies.*

Open Jun-Sep **Site** 1.1HEC ♨ ♣ ♠ **Prices** ♠ 4 pitch 5.50 ♠ (static)270 **Facilities** ⋔ 🖺 ⊙ ∅ ⑫ **Services** ⊉ ⓧ ➕ 🖾 **Leisure** ⚲ P **Off-site** ⓧ ⚲R

Vézère Périgord

route de Montignac, 24620 ☎ 553069631 ▤ 553067966

website www.le-vezere-perigord.com

A well-equipped site in wooded surroundings close to the river.

➪ *0.8km NE on D706.*

Open Etr-Oct **Site** 6HEC ♨ ♣ ♠ **Facilities** ⋔ 🖺 ⊙ ⊡ ⑫ **Services** ⊉ ⓧ ➕ 🖾 **Leisure** ⚲ P **Off-site** ∅ ⚲R

ST-MARTIN-DE-SEIGNANX LANDES

Lou P'tit Poun

40390 ☎ 559565579 ▤ 559565371

e-mail ptitpoun@club-internet.fr

website www.les-campings.com/lou-ptit-poun

A quiet site with well-defined pitches on terraces.

➪ *A63 exit Bayonne Nord for Pau.*

Open Jun-15 Sep **Site** 7HEC ♨ ♣ ♠ ♠ Å **Facilities** ⋔ ⊙ ⊡ ∅ ♨ ⑫ ⓟ **Services** ⊉ ⓧ 🖾 **Leisure** ⚲ P

ST-MARTORY HAUTE-GARONNE

CM

rte de St-Girons, 31360 ☎ 561981465

e-mail cccsm@wanadoo.fr

Open 15 Jun-15 Sep **Site** ♨ ♣ **Facilities** ⋔ 🖺 ⊙ ⊡ ⑫ **Services** ➕ 🖾 **Off-site** 🖺 ⊉ ⓧ ∅ ♨ ⚲R

Facilities 🖺 shop ⋔ shower ⊙ electric points for razors ⊡ electric points for caravans ⑫ parking by tents permitted ⓟ compulsory separate car park **Services** ⓧ café/restaurant ⊉ bar ∅ Camping Gaz International ♨ gas other than Camping Gaz ➕ first aid facilities 🖾 laundry **Leisure** ⚲ swimming L-Lake P-Pool R-River S-Sea **Off-site** All facilities within 2km

France

ST-NICOLAS-DE-LA-GRAVE TARN-ET-GARONNE

Plan d'Eau
Base de Plein Air, et de Loisirs, 82210
☎ 563955002 ▤ 563955001
e-mail basedeloisirs.stnicolas@cg82.fr
➥ *2.5km N via D15.*
Open 15 Jun-15 Sep **Site** 1.5HEC ☙ ✿ **Prices** pitch 9.50-20.15
Facilities ↑⊙🅰℗ **Services** ➕▤ **Off-site** ➽🎹 ⛵LPR

ST-PARDOUX-LA-RIVIÈRE DORDOGNE

Château le Verdoyer
24470 ☎ 553569464 ▤ 553563870
e-mail chateau@verdoyer.fr
website www.verdoyer.fr
A small, well-equipped site in the grounds of a restored castle.
➥ *3km N via D96.*
Open 23 Apr-15 Oct **Site** 25HEC ☙ ✿ 🛏 🚐 🅧 **Facilities** ↑⊙🅰🅰⊘
℗ **Services** ➽🍴 ➕▤ **Leisure** ⛵ LP

ST-PAUL-LES-DAX LANDES

Pins du Soleil
RD459, 40990 ☎ 558913791 ▤ 558910024
e-mail pinsoleil@aol.com
website www.pinsoleil.com
On a hotel complex with modern facilities.
➥ *SW via D954.*
Open 10 Mar-10 Nov **Site** 6HEC ☙ ✿ 🛏 **Prices** 🅧 3.50 pitch 15-23 (incl 2 persons) 🚐 (static)265-671 **Facilities** ↑🚾⊙🅰⊘🚿℗ **Services** ➽🍴
▤ **Leisure** ⛵ P **Off-site** 🍴⊘🚿⛵LRS

ST-PÉE-SUR-NIVELLE PYRÉNÉES-ATLANTIQUES

Goyetchea
64310 ☎ 559541959
e-mail info@camping-goyetchea.com
website www.camping-goyetchea.com
Quiet, peaceful site in a wooded location at the foot of the Pyrénées.
➥ *2km from St Pée via D918*
Open 3 Jun-16 Sep **Site** 3HEC ☙ ✿ **Prices** pitch 13-18.50 (incl 2 persons) pp3-4.10 **Facilities** ↑🚾⊙🅰🅰℗ **Services** 🍴➕▤
Leisure ⛵ P **Off-site** ➽🍴🚿⛵R

Ibarron
64310 ☎ 559541043
e-mail camping.dibarron@wanadoo.fr
website www.camping-ibarron.com
A pleasant wooded location with level pitches and modern facilities.
➥ *2km W on D918.*
Open May-Sep **Site** 2.9HEC ☙ ✿ 🛏 🚐 **Facilities** ↑🚾⊙🅰🚿℗
Services 🍴➕▤ **Leisure** ⛵ PR **Off-site** ➽➽🍴🚿⛵LPR

ST-PIERRE-LAFEUILLE LOT

Graves
46090 ☎ 565368312 ▤ 565368312
e-mail infos@camping-lesgraves.com
website www.camping-lesgraves.com
On a small hill on the northern outskirts of the village providing fine views over the surrounding countryside.
➥ *10km N of Cahors.*
Open Apr-1 Nov **Site** 1.5HEC ☙ ✿ 🛏 🚐 **Prices** 🅧 3.20-4 pitch 4.40-5.50
Facilities ↑⊙🅰℗ **Services** 🍴▤ **Leisure** ⛵ P **Off-site** 🚾➽🍴

Quercy-Vacances
Le Mas de Lacombe, 46090 ☎ 565368715
e-mail quercyvacances@wanadoo.fr
website www.quercy-vacances.com
A well-equipped site in pleasant wooded surroundings.
➥ *On N20. 12km N of Cahors.*
Open Apr-Oct **Site** 3HEC ☙ ✿ 🛏 🚐 🅧 **Prices** 🅧 3.80-5 🚗 5-6 pitch 6.60-8.80 **Facilities** ↑🚾⊙🅰⊘℗ **Services** 🍴🍴 ➕▤ **Leisure** ⛵ P
Off-site ⛵LR

ST-RÉMY-SUR-LIDOIRE DORDOGNE

Tuilière
24700 ☎ 553824729 ▤ 553824729
e-mail la-tuiliere@wanadoo.fr
website www.campinglatuiliere.com
Pleasant wooded surroundings beside a lake. Separate car park for arrivals after 22.00 hrs.
➥ *D708 from Montpon towards Ste-Foy-la-Grande for 6km.*
Open May-15 Sep **Site** 8HEC ☙ ✿ 🛏 🚐 **Facilities** ↑🚾⊙🅰⊘🚿℗
Services 🍴🍴 ➕▤ **Leisure** ⛵ LP

ST-SERNIN-DE-DURAS LOT-ET-GARONNE

Moulin de Borie Neuve
47120 ☎ 553207073
e-mail info@borieneuve.com
website www.borieneuve.com
A pleasant site in the Dourdèze valley close to an old mill.
➥ *D244 towards St-Astier-de-Duras.*
Open 15 May-15 Oct **Site** 1HEC ☙ ✿ **Facilities** ↑⊙🅰℗
Services 🍴➕▤ **Leisure** ⛵ PR **Off-site** 🚾🍴⊘🚿⛵L

ST-SEURIN-DE-PRATS DORDOGNE

Plage
24230 ☎ 553586107 ▤ 553586107
A peaceful wooded setting beside the Dordogne with a variety of recreational facilities.
➥ *0.7km on D11.*
Open May-Sep **Site** 4.5HEC ☙ ✿ 🛏 **Facilities** ↑⊙🅰℗🅿 **Services** 🍴
🍴▤ **Leisure** ⛵ PR **Off-site** 🚾⊘🚿

STE-EULALIE-EN-BORN LANDES

Bruyères
chemin Laffont, 40200 ☎ 558097336 ▤ 558097558
e-mail bonjour@camping-les-bruyeres.com
website www.camping-les-bruyeres.com
Set in the middle of the Landes forest close to the lakes and the sea.
➥ *2.5km N via D652*
Open 14 May-29 Sep **Site** 3HEC ☙ ✿ 🛏 🚐 **Prices** 🅧 3.30-5.20 pitch 13.50-21.70 (incl 2 persons) 🚐 (static)110-470 **Facilities** ↑🚾⊙🅰⊘🚿
℗ **Services** 🍴🍴 ➕▤ **Leisure** ⛵ P **Off-site** ⛵LR

SALIGNAC DORDOGNE

'Les Peneyrals'
Le Poujol, St-Crépin Carlucet, 24590 ☎ 553288571 ▤ 553288099
e-mail camping.peneyrals@wanadoo.fr
website www.peneyrals.com
Quiet site among trees between the Vézère and Dordogne rivers.
➥ *10km N of Sarlat on D60.*
Open 15 May-15 Sep **Site** 12HEC ☙ ✿ 🛏 🚐 **Prices** 🅧 4.60-7.60 pitch 6.70-10.70 🚐 (static)260-760 **Facilities** ↑🚾⊙🅰⊘🚿℗ **Services** 🍴
🍴▤ **Leisure** ⛵ P

Site 6HEC (site size) ☙ grass ⬤ sand ⬤ stone ⬤ light shade ✿ partly shaded ⬤ mainly shaded 🛏 bungalows for hire
🚐 caravans for hire 🅧 tents for hire 🅧 no dogs **Prices** 🅧 adult per night 🚗 car per night pp per person per night 🚐 caravan per night
🅰 tent per night 🚐 (static)-caravan hire per week

SALLES GIRONDE

Val de l'Eyre

8 rte de Minoy, 33770 ☎ 556884703 ▤ 556884727
e-mail levaldeleyre2@wanadoo.fr
website www.valdeleyre.com

A well-equipped family site in a pleasant wooded location between the Landes forests and Bordeaux vineyards.

➲ *SW on D108 rte de Lugos.*

Open Apr-15 Oct **Site** 13HEC 🌊 ♨ 🚌 **Prices** ⚑ 11-17 **Facilities** ⋔ ⊙ 🚐 ♨ ℗ ℗ **Services** ⬛ 🍽 ➕ 🔓 **Leisure** ⚓ PR **Off-site** 🏪 ⊘ ⚓P

SALLES LOT-ET-GARONNE

Bastides

47150 ☎ 553408309 ▤ 553408176
e-mail info@campingdesbastides.com
website www.campingdesbastides.com

Peaceful wooded surroundings overlooking the Lède valley with good sports and entertainment facilities.

➲ *1km N via D150.*

Open Etr-Sep **Site** 6HEC 🌊 ♨ 🚌 ⚐ **Facilities** ⋔ 🏪 ⊙ 🚐 ⊘ ♨ ℗ **Services** ⬛ 🍽 🔓 **Leisure** ⚓ P

SARLAT-LA-CANÉDA DORDOGNE

Maillac

Ste-Nathalène, 24200 ☎ 553592212 ▤ 553296017
e-mail campingmaillac@wanadoo.fr
website www.campingmaillac.fr

Wooded surroundings in the heart of the Périgord Noir region with good facilities for a family holiday. Separate car park for arrivals after 23.00 hrs.

➲ *7km NE on D47.*

Open 15 May-Oct **Site** 6HEC 🌊 ♨ 🚌 **Prices** ⚑ 4.60 pitch 6 **Facilities** ⋔ 🏪 ⊙ 🚐 ⊘ ♨ ℗ **Services** ⬛ 🍽 🔓 **Leisure** ⚓ P **Off-site** ⚓LR

Moulin du Roch

rte des Éyzies, Le Roch, 24200 ☎ 553592027 ▤ 553592095
e-mail moulin.du.roch@wanadoo.fr
website www.moulin-du-roch.com

A picturesque location between the Dordogne and Vézère valleys.

➲ *10km NW via D704, D6 & D47.*

Open 28 Apr-15 Sep **Site** 8HEC 🌊 ♨ 🚌 ⊗ **Prices** ⚑ 4-7.80 pitch 15-27 (incl 2 persons) **Facilities** ⋔ 🏪 ⊙ 🚐 ⊘ ℗ **Services** ⬛ 🍽 ➕ 🔓 **Leisure** ⚓ P

See advertisement on this page

Périères

r Jean Gabin, BP98, 24203 ☎ 553590584 ▤ 553285751
e-mail les-perieres@wanadoo.fr
website www.lesperieres.com

Very well-kept terraced site in parkland and woods in the heart of the Périgord Noir, with fine views over the Sarlat valley. There are good recreational facilities and modern, well-equipped bungalows are available for hire.

➲ *1km N of town on D47.*

Open Etr-Sep **Site** 11HEC 🌊 ♨ 🚌 **Prices** pitch 18.20 (incl 2 persons) pp6.25 **Facilities** ⋔ 🏪 ⊙ 🚐 ⊘ ℗ **Services** ⬛ 🍽 ➕ 🔓 **Leisure** ⚓ P **Off-site** 🍽

Val d'Ussel

La Fond d'Ussel, 24200 ☎ 553592873 ▤ 553293825
e-mail valdussel@online.fr
website www.valdussel.com

A well-equipped site in woodland in the heart of the Périgord Noir region. Separate car park for late arrivals.

➲ *Off D704 or D56.*

Open 8 May-25 Sep **Site** 7HEC 🌊 ♨ 🚌 ⚐ **Facilities** ⋔ 🏪 ⊙ 🚐 ℗ **Services** ⬛ 🍽 🔓 **Leisure** ⚓ P

AT CARSAC-AILLAC (7KM SE VIA D704A)

Aqua Viva

24200 ☎ 553314600 ▤ 553293637
e-mail aqua-viva@perigord.com
website www.aquaviva.fr

Site with numerous terraces in beautiful wooded surroundings in the heart of the Dordogne.

➲ *On D704A Sarlat-Souillac.*

Open 16 Apr-24 Sep **Site** 11HEC 🌊 ♨ ♨ 🚌 **Facilities** ⋔ 🏪 ⊙ 🚐 ⊘ ℗ **Services** ⬛ 🍽 ➕ 🔓 **Leisure** ⚓ LP **Off-site** ⚓R

Rocher de la Cave

24200 ☎ 553281426 ▤ 553282710
e-mail rocher.de.la-cave@wanadoo.fr
website www.rocherdelacave.com

Pleasant family site on a level meadow beside the Dordogne, set in beautiful countryside.

➲ *Via D703 & D704.*

Open 15May-15 Sep **Site** 4HEC 🌊 ♨ 🚌 🚐 ⚐ **Prices** ⚑ 3.84-4.80 pitch 4.96-6.20 🚐 (static)155-278 **Facilities** ⋔ 🏪 ⊙ 🚐 ⊘ ℗ **Services** ⬛ 🍽 ➕ 🔓 **Leisure** ⚓ PR

SEIGNOSSE LANDES

Chevreuils

rte de Hossegor, 40510 ☎ 558433280 ▤ 558433280
e-mail contact@chevreuils.cegeteldsl.com
website www.chevreuils.com

Set in a pine forest close to the sea with good recreational facilities.

➲ *On CD79 rte de Hossegor.*

Open Jun-15 Sep **Site** 8HEC 🌊 ♨ 🚌 🚐 **Prices** ⚑ 5.90 pitch 21.10 🚐 (static)270-820 **Facilities** ⋔ 🏪 ⊙ 🚐 ⊘ ♨ ℗ **Services** ⬛ 🍽 ➕ 🔓 **Leisure** ⚓ P **Off-site** ⚓S

Facilities 🏪 shop ⋔ shower ⊙ electric points for razors 🚐 electric points for caravans ℗ parking by tents permitted ℗ compulsory separate car park **Services** 🍽 café/restaurant ⬛ bar ⊘ Camping Gaz International ♨ gas other than Camping Gaz ➕ first aid facilities 🔓 laundry **Leisure** ⚓ swimming L-Lake P-Pool R-River S-Sea **Off-site** All facilities within 2km

France

France

Océliances
av des Tucs, 40510 ☎ 558433030 ▤ 558416421
e-mail oceliances@wanadoo.fr
website www.oceliances.com
Very clean and tidy site in a pine forest 0.6km from the sea.
➾ *200m from Seignosse town centre.*
Open 28 Apr-Sep **Site** 13HEC ⛱ ♣ ⛺ **Prices** pitch 12.50-23.50 (incl 2 persons) ⛽ (static)279-869 **Facilities** ↿ 盦 ⊙ ⊞ ⑳ ℗ **Services** ⌁ ℺ ➕ ▤ **Leisure** ⇆ P **Off-site** 涎 涎 涎LS

Oyats
rte de la Plage des Casenres, 40510 ☎ 558433794 ▤ 558432329
e-mail cployats@atciat.com
website www.campeoles.fr
Level site, subdivided into fields and surrounded by woodland. Separate section for young people. Children's play area.
➾ *Off D79 in N outskirts towards Plage des Casernes.*
Open 15 May-15 Sep **Site** 17HEC ⛱ ♣ ⛺ Å **Prices** pitch 13.50-23.10 (incl 2 persons) **Facilities** ↿ 盦 ⊙ ⊞ ⊘ ⑳ **Services** ⌁ ℺ ➕ ▤ **Leisure** ⇆ P **Off-site** 涎S

AT SEIGNOSSE-LE-PENON (5KM W)

Forêt
40510 ☎ 558416850 ▤ 558432326
A pleasant, quiet site 300m from the sea.
Open 29 Jun-2 Sep **Site** 11HEC ⛱ ♣ ⛺ ⊗ **Facilities** ↿ ⊙ ⊞ ℗ **Services** ⌁ ℺ ➕ ▤ **Leisure** ⇆ P **Off-site** 盦 ⊘ 涎 涎LS

SEIX ARIÈGE

Haut Salat
09140 ☎ 561668178 ▤ 561669417
e-mail camping.le-haut-salat@wanadoo.fr
website www.ariege.com/campinglehautsalat
Very clean, well-kept site beside stream. Big gravel pitches for caravans. Common room with TV.
➾ *0.8km NE on D3.*
Open All year **Site** 2.5HEC ⛱ ♣ ⛺ **Facilities** ↿ 盦 ⊙ ⊞ ⊘ ⑳ **Services** ⌁ ℺ ➕ ▤ **Leisure** ⇆ PR **Off-site** ℺

SÉRIGNAC-PÉBOUDOU LOT-ET-GARONNE

Vallée de Gardeleau
47410 ☎ 553369696 ▤ 553369696
e-mail valleegardeleau@wanadoo.fr
website perso.wanadoo.fr/camping.valleegardeleau.fr
A shaded wooded position, offering peace and comfort in relaxing surroundings.
➾ *On RN21 between Lauzun & Castilonnès.*
Open 26 May-15 Sep **Site** 2HEC ⛱ ♣ ⛺ Å **Prices** ↑ 2.50-3.90 pitch 3.80-6 ⛽ (static)220-530 **Facilities** ↿ ⊙ ⊞ ⑳ **Services** ⌁ ℺ ➕ ▤ **Leisure** ⇆ P

SOUILLAC LOT

Domaine de la Paille Basse
46200 ☎ 565378548 ▤ 565370958
e-mail paille.basse@wanadoo.fr
website www.lapaillebasse.com
A family site in a picturesque wooded location in the grounds of a former château.
➾ *6.5km NW off D15 Salignac-Eyvignes road.*
Open 12 May-15 Sep **Site** 12HEC ⛱ ♣ ⛺ **Prices** ↑ 5.40-7 pitch 7.80-13 **Facilities** ↿ 盦 ⊙ ⊞ ⊘ ⑳ **Services** ⌁ ℺ ➕ ▤ **Leisure** ⇆ P

SOULAC-SUR-MER GIRONDE

Lilhan
8 allée Michel Montaigne ☎ 556097763 ▤ 556099482
e-mail contact@lelilhan.com
website www.lelilhan.com
Located in an oak tree and pine forest, a short distance from the beach
➾ *CD 101 rte des Lacs from Soulac, left at l'Amelie x-rds.*
Open Apr-Sep **Site** 4HEC ♣ ⛺ **Prices** pitch 14.95-18.95 (incl 2 persons) **Facilities** ↿ 盦 ⊙ ⊞ ⊘ 涎 ⑳ **Services** ⌁ ℺ ➕ ▤ **Leisure** ⇆ P **Off-site** 涎S

Océan
L'Améliè, 33780 ☎ 556097610 ▤ 556097475
A level site in a pine forest, 300m from the beach.
➾ *3.5km S.*
Open Jun-15 Sep **Site** 6HEC ⛱ ♣ ♣ ⛺ **Facilities** ↿ 盦 ⊙ ⊞ ⊘ ⑳ **Services** ⌁ ℺ ➕ ▤ **Off-site** 涎S

Sables d'Argent
33BD de l'Amélie, 33780 ☎ 556098287 ▤ 556099482
e-mail sables@lelilhan.com
website www.sables-d-argent.com
Set in a pine forest bordered by dunes, with direct access to the beach.
➾ *1.5km SW of village.*
Open Apr-Sep **Site** 2.6HEC ⛱ ♣ ♣ ⛺ **Facilities** ↿ 盦 ⊙ ⊞ ⊘ 涎 ⑳ **Services** ⌁ ℺ ➕ ▤ **Leisure** ⇆ S **Off-site** 涎P

AT AMÉLIE-SUR-MER, L' (4.5KM S)

Amélie-Plage
33780 ☎ 556098727 ▤ 556736426
e-mail camping.amelie.plage@wanadoo.fr
website www.camping-amelie-plage.com
Hilly wooded terrain. Lovely sandy beach.
➾ *3km S on Soulac road.*
Open Mar-Dec **Site** 8.5HEC ⛱ ♣ ♣ ⛺ **Prices** pitch 16-20 (incl 2 persons) **Facilities** ↿ 盦 ⊙ ⊞ ⊘ 涎 ⑳ **Services** ⌁ ℺ ➕ ▤ **Leisure** ⇆ S

AT LILIAN (4.5KM S)

Pins
33780 ☎ 556098252 ▤ 5577365558
e-mail contact@campingdispins.fr
website www.campingdespins.fr
Situated in a beautiful pine forest close to the beach with plenty of sports facilities.
➾ *S on D101.*
Open May-Oct **Site** 3.2HEC ⛱ ♣ ♣ ⛺ ⛽ Å **Facilities** ↿ 盦 ⊙ ⊞ ⊘ ℗ **Services** ⌁ ℺ ➕ ▤ **Off-site** 涎RS

SOUSTONS LANDES

CM Airial
61 av Port d'Albret, 40140 ☎ 558411248 ▤ 558415383
e-mail contact@camping-airial.com
website www.camping-airial.com
Situated in a shady park with plenty of recreational facilities and modern installations.
➾ *2km W on D652.*
Open Apr-15Oct **Site** 17HEC ⛱ ♣ ♣ ⛺ **Prices** ↑ 3.60-4.80 pitch 7.10-13.30 **Facilities** ↿ 盦 ⊙ ⊞ ⊘ ⑳ **Services** ⌁ ℺ ➕ ▤ **Leisure** ⇆ P

Site 6HEC (site size) ⛱ grass ⊖ sand ♣ stone ♣ little shade ⛱ partly shaded ⛱ mainly shaded ⛺ bungalows for hire ⛽ caravans for hire Å tents for hire ⊗ no dogs **Prices** ↑ adult per night ⇆ car per night pp per person per night ⛽ caravan per night Å tent per night ⛽ (static)-caravan hire per week

TARASCON-SUR-ARIÈGE ARIÈGE

Pré Lombard

BP 48, 9400 ☎ 561056194 ▤ 561057893
e-mail leprelombard@wanadoo.fr
website www.prelombard.com
Beautiful wooded surroundings beside the River Ariège with modern facilities.

➲ 1.5km SE on D23.

Open 27 Jan-11 Nov **Site** 3.5HEC ♨ ♨ ♨ ⚊ Å **Prices** pitch 15-30 (incl 2 persons) pp5-9 ♠ (static)240-790 **Facilities** ⚓ ⊙ ♠ ⊘ ⚊ ⚒ **Services** ⚑ ⚑ ⎈ ⚓ **Leisure** ⚍ PR **Off-site** ⚓

TEILLET TARN

Relais de l'Entre Deux Lacs

81120 ☎ 563557445 ▤ 563557565
e-mail contact@campingdutarn.com
website www.campingdutarn.com
Shady terraced site. Various activities arranged. Beautiful views.

➲ Off D81 towards Lacaune.

Open Apr-Oct **Site** 4HEC ♨ ♨ ♨ **Prices** ⚑ 4 pitch 11 (incl 2 persons) **Facilities** ⚓ ⊙ ♠ ⚒ **Services** ⚑ ⚑ ⎈ **Leisure** ⚍ P **Off-site** ⚓ ⊘ ⚊ ⚍ LR

THIVIERS DORDOGNE

CM Le Repaire

24800 ☎ 553526975 ▤ 553526975
e-mail campingthiviers@wanadoo.fr
A well-appointed family site in a wooded valley in the Périgord Vert region of the Dordogne, a short walk from the ancient village of Thiviers.

➲ On D707 1.5km towards Lanouaille.

Open May-Sep **Site** 11HEC ♨ ♨ ♨ ♨ **Prices** ⚑ 3.40-4.20 pitch 4-6 ♠ (static)180-250 **Facilities** ⚓ ⊙ ♠ ⚒ **Services** ⚑ ⚑ ⎈ ⚓ **Leisure** ⚍ P **Off-site** ⚓ ⚑ ⊘ ⚊ ⚍ LR

TONNEINS LOT-ET-GARONNE

CM Robinson

47400 ☎ 553790228
➲ 0.5km from town centre on N113 Agen road.
Open Jun-Sep **Site** 0.7HEC ♨ ♨ ♨ **Facilities** ⚓ ⊙ ♠ ⚒ **Services** ⚓ **Leisure** ⚍ R **Off-site** ⚍P ⎈

TOUZAC LOT

Ch'Timi

46700 ☎ 565365236 ▤ 565365323
e-mail info@campinglechtimi.com
website www.campinglechtimi.com
A well-equipped site overlooking the River Lot. Entertainment available in summer.

➲ 0.8km from Touzac on D8.

Open Apr-Sep **Site** 3.5HEC ♨ ♨ ♨ **Prices** ⚑ 3.70-4.95 pitch 5.15-6.90 **Facilities** ⚓ ⚓ ⊙ ♠ ⊘ ⚒ **Services** ⚑ ⚑ ⎈ ⚓ **Leisure** ⚍ PR

Clos Bouyssac

46700 ☎ 565365221 ▤ 565246851
e-mail camping.leclosbouyssac@wanadoo.fr
website monsite.wanadoo.fr/leclosbouyssac
On the fringe of a wooded hillside by the sandy shore of the River Lot. Good for walking.

➲ S of Touzac on D65.

Open Apr-Oct **Site** 1.5HEC ♨ ♨ ♨ ♨ Å **Prices** ⚑ 4.20 pitch 5.40 ♠ (static)309 **Facilities** ⚓ ⚓ ⊙ ♠ ⊘ ⚒ **Services** ⚑ ⚑ ⎈ ⚓ **Leisure** ⚍ PR

URRUGNE PYRÉNÉES-ATLANTIQUES

Larrouleta

210 route de socoa, 64122 ☎ 559473784 ▤ 559474254
e-mail info@larrouleta.com
website www.larrouleta.com
Hilly meadow with young trees.

➲ Via RN10 or A63

Open All year **Site** 10HEC ♨ ♨ **Prices** ⚑ 4.50-5.50 pitch 4-5 **Facilities** ⚓ ⚓ ⊙ ♠ ⚒ **Services** ⚑ ⚑ ⎈ ⚓ **Leisure** ⚍ LP **Off-site** ⊘ ⚍S

URT PYRÉNÉES-ATLANTIQUES

Etche Zahar

allée de Mesplès, 64240 ☎ 559562736
e-mail info@etche-zahar.fr
website www.etche-zahar.fr
A small, privately owned site in a wooded location and within easy reach of local tourist areas. Separate car parking for arrivals 22.00-7.00 hrs.

➲ A63 exit 8. Or A64 exit 4.

Open 24 Mar-5 Nov **Site** 2.5HEC ♨ ♨ Å **Facilities** ⚓ ⚓ ⊙ ♠ ⚊ ⚒ **Services** ⚑ ⎈ ⚓ **Leisure** ⚍ P **Off-site** ⚑ ⚑ ⊘ ⚍R

VALEUIL DORDOGNE

Bas Meygnaud

D393 Brantome, 24310 ☎ 553055844
e-mail camping-du-bas-meygnaud@wanadoo.fr
website www.basmeygnaud.com
A quiet, shady site in the Dronne valley.

➲ Off D939 at Lasserre.

Open Apr-Sep **Site** 1.7HEC ♨ ♨ ♨ Å **Prices** ⚑ 2.50 ♠ 2 ♠ 5 Å 5 **Facilities** ⚓ ⚓ ⊙ ♠ ⚒ **Services** ⚑ ⚑ ⎈ ⚓ **Leisure** ⚍ P **Off-site** ⚍R

VARILHES ARIÈGE

CM Parc du Château

av du 8 Mai 45, 9120 ☎ 561674284 ▤ 561605554
On the banks of the river and close to the town.

➲ N on N20.

Open All year **Site** 1HEC ♨ ♨ **Facilities** ⚓ ⊙ ♠ ⚒ **Services** ⎈ ⚓ **Off-site** ⚓ ⚑ ⊘ ⚊ ⚍PR

VAYRAC LOT

Bourzolles

Condat, 46110 ☎ 565321632 ▤ 565321632
e-mail leschenesclairs@laposte.net

➲ Off D20 between Condat & Vayrac.

Open May-Oct **Site** 4HEC ♨ ♨ **Prices** ⚑ 3 pitch 3 ♠ (static)200 **Facilities** ⚓ ⊙ ♠ ⚒ **Services** ⎈ ⚓ **Leisure** ⚍ P **Off-site** ⚑ ⚑ ⊘ ⚊

Facilities ⚑ shop ⚓ shower ⊙ electric points for razors ♠ electric points for caravans ⚒ parking by tents permitted ♠ compulsory separate car park
Services ⎈ café/restaurant ⚑ bar ⊘ Camping Gaz International ⚊ gas other than Camping Gaz ⎈ first aid facilities ⚓ laundry
Leisure ⚍ swimming L-Lake P-Pool R-River S-Sea **Off-site** All facilities within 2km

France

France

VENDAYS-MONTALIVET GIRONDE

Mayan

3 route de Mayan, 33930 ☎ 556417651

A small site in a pine wood.

➲ *Via N215 & D102.*

Open Jul-Aug **Site** 1HEC 😌 ♣ 🛏 **Prices** 🏕 2 pitch 4.20-6.30 🚗 (static)225 **Facilities** 🏪 ⊙ ⊖ 🅿 **Services** 🖪 🗟 **Off-site** ♨

VERDON-SUR-MER, LE GIRONDE

Royannais

88 rte de Soulac, 33123 ☎ 556096112 📠 556737067

e-mail camping.le.royannais@wanadoo.fr

website www.royannais.com

Level, sandy terrain under high pine and deciduous trees.

➲ *S of Le Verdon-sur-Mer in Le Royannais district on D1.*

Open Apr-15 Oct **Site** 3HEC 😌 ⊜ 🛏 🚗 **Facilities** 🏪 🏕 ⊙ ⊖ 🅿 ♨ ⊛ **Services** 🖪 🗟 **Off-site** ⊛RS

VERGT-DE-BIRON DORDOGNE

Patrasses

24540 ☎ 553630587 📠 553248895

Situated in the heart of the Périgord Noir region with good facilities.

➲ *3.6km S via D2E.*

Open Jun-Sep **Site** 4.7HEC 😌 ♣ 🛏 🚗 Å **Facilities** 🏪 🏕 ⊙ ⊖ 🅿 ♨ **Services** 🖪 🗟 **Leisure** ⊛ P

VÉZAC DORDOGNE

Deux Vallées

24220 ☎ 553295355 📠 553310981

e-mail les2v@perigord.com

website www.les-2-vallees.com

A level site in a picturesque location in the Dordogne valley. Good facilities for families.

➲ *Via D57 from Sarlat. Or D703 from Bergerac.*

Open All year **Site** 3.2HEC 😌 ⊜ 🚗 **Facilities** 🏪 🏕 ⊙ ⊖ 🅿 ⊘ ♨ **Services** 🖪 🗟 **Leisure** ⊛ P **Off-site** ⊛R

Plage

La Roque Gageac, 24220 ☎ 553295083 📠 553303163

Modest but attractive site in a pleasant riverside setting.

➲ *Via D703 beyond La Roque Gageac.*

Open Apr-Sep **Site** 3.5HEC 😌 ⊜ 🛏 🚗 **Prices** 🏕 3.50-4.40 🚗 1.70-2 pitch 2.15-2.80 **Facilities** 🏪 🏕 ⊙ ⊖ 🅿 ⊘ ♨ **Services** 🖪 🗟 **Leisure** ⊛ PR **Off-site** 🗟

VIELLE-ST-GIRONS LANDES

Eurosol

rte de la Plage, 40560 ☎ 558479014 📠 558477674

e-mail contact@camping-eurosol.com

website www.camping-eurosol.com

Well-maintained family site in a pine forest, 0.7km from one of the finest beaches in the country.

➲ *A63 exit Castets.*

Open 12 May-15 Sep **Site** 18HEC 😌 ⊜ ⊜ 🛏 **Prices** 🏕 4 pitch 4-25 🚗 (static)266-749 **Facilities** 🏪 🏕 ⊙ ⊖ 🅿 ⊘ ♨ **Services** 🖪 🗟 **Leisure** ⊛ P **Off-site** ⊛S

Sunelia Col Vert

Lac de Léon, 40560 ☎ 558429406 📠 558429188

e-mail contact@colvert.com

website www.colvert.com

Quiet site on lakeside in sparse pine woodland. Small natural harbour in the mouth of a stream.

➲ *Off D652 on N side of village, continue towards lake.*

Open Apr-Sep **Site** 30HEC 😌 ♣ 🛏 🚗 Å **Prices** pitch 6-17.10 (incl 2 persons) pp2-6.30 **Facilities** 🏪 🏕 ⊙ ⊖ 🅿 ⊘ ♨ ♨ ♨ **Services** 🖪 🗟 **Leisure** ⊛ LP

VIEUX-BOUCAU-LES-BAINS LANDES

CM des Sablères

bd du Marensin, 40480 ☎ 558481229 📠 558482070

e-mail camping-lessableres@wanadoo.fr

website www.lessableres.com

A family site with modern facilities and direct access to the beach.

➲ *Via N10 & D652.*

Open Apr-15 Oct **Site** 11HEC 😌 ♣ 🛏 **Prices** pitch 10.80-15.70 (incl 2 persons) **Facilities** 🏪 ⊙ ⊖ 🅿 ♨ **Services** 🖪 🗟 **Off-site** 🏕 🖪 🗟 ⊘ ♨ ⊛LS

VIGAN, LE LOT

Rêve

Revers, 46300 ☎ 565412520

e-mail info@campinglereve.com

website www.campinglereve.com

A modern family site in wooded surroundings.

➲ *D673 from Payrac towards Le Vigan & signed.*

Open 26 Apr-15 Sep **Site** 10HEC 😌 ♣ 🛏 **Prices** 🏕 2.95-4.20 pitch 4.38-6.25 **Facilities** 🏪 🏕 ⊙ ⊖ 🅿 ⊘ ♨ **Services** 🖪 🗟 **Leisure** ⊛ P

VILLEFRANCHE-DU-QUEYRAN LOT-ET-GARONNE

Moulin de Campech

47160 ☎ 553887243 📠 553880652

e-mail campech@wanadoo.fr

website www.moulindecampech.co.uk

A beautiful site in a peaceful location beside a small lake stocked with trout.

➲ *D11 towards Casteljaloux.*

Open Apr-22 Oct **Site** 4HEC 😌 ⊜ **Prices** 🏕 3.70-5.45 pitch 18.50-24.70 (incl 2 persons) **Facilities** 🏪 🏕 ⊙ ⊖ 🅿 ♨ **Services** 🖪 🗟 **Leisure** ⊛ LPR

VILLENAVE-D'ORNON GIRONDE

Gravières

35 ave Mirieu de Labarre, 33140 ☎ 556870036

➲ *2km NE.*

Open All year **Site** 3.5HEC 😌 ⊜ ⊛ ⊜ 🛏 🚗 Å **Facilities** 🏪 🏕 ⊙ ⊖ 🅿 ⊘ ♨ ♨ **Services** 🖪 🗟 **Leisure** ⊛ L **Off-site** ⊘

Site 6HEC (site size) 😌 grass ⊜ sand ⊛ stone ♣ little shade ⊜ partly shaded ⊜ mainly shaded 🛏 bungalows for hire 🚗 caravans for hire Å tents for hire ⊗ no dogs **Prices** 🏕 adult per night 🚗 car per night pp per person per night 🚗 caravan per night Å tent per night 🚗 (static)-caravan hire per week

VILLERÉAL LOT-ET-GARONNE

Château de Fonrives

Rives, 47210 ☎ 553366338 🖷 553360998

e-mail chateau.de.fontives@wanadoo.fr

website www.campingchateaufonrives.com

A beautiful natural park in the grounds of a château with good facilities for all ages.

➲ 2.2km NW via D207

Open Apr-Oct **Site** 20HEC ❤ ❤ ⛺ ⛆ ⅄ **Prices** pitch 16-24.50 (incl 2 persons) ⛆ (static)180-729 **Facilities** ⋔ 🖽 ⊙ ⊡ ⌀ ⌸ ⅌ **Services** ⅏ ⅓〇⅟ ➕ 🖫 **Leisure** ⌇ LP

VITRAC DORDOGNE

Bouysse

Caudon, 24200 ☎ 553283305 🖷 553303852

e-mail la-bouysse.24@wanadoo.fr

website www.labouysse.com

Well-appointed site in a wooded valley beside the Dordogne.

➲ 2km E, near the River Dordogne.

Open Apr-Sep **Site** 3HEC ❤ ❤ ⛺ **Prices** ⅄ 4.50-5.50 pitch 5.50-7.20 **Facilities** ⋔ 🖽 ⊙ ⊡ ⌀ ⅌ **Services** ⅏ ⅓〇 🖫 **Leisure** ⌇ PR **Off-site** 〇⅟ ⌸ ➕

Soleil Plage

Caudon par Montfort, 24200 ☎ 553283333 🖷 553283024

e-mail info@soleilplage.com

website www.soleilplage.com

Set out around an old farmhouse bordering the Dordogne with excellent facilities.

➲ 4km E on D703, turn by Camping Clos Bernard.

Open Sep **Site** 8HEC ❤ ❤ ⛺ **Prices** ⅄ 4.50-7.50 pitch 6-12 ⛆ (static)250-690 **Facilities** ⋔ 🖽 ⊙ ⊡ ⌀ ⅌ **Services** ⅏ ⅓〇 ➕ 🖫 **Leisure** ⌇ PR

See advertisement on this page

LOIRE/CENTRAL

AIGUILLON-SUR-MER, L' VENDÉE

Bel Air

85460 ☎ 251564405 🖷 251971558

e-mail camping.belair@wanadoo.fr

website www.camping-belair.com

A long, level stretch of meadowland in rural surroundings.

➲ 1.5km NW on D44 then turn left.

Open Apr-Sep **Site** 7HEC ❤ ❤ ⛺ ⛆ ⅄ **Facilities** ⋔ 🖽 ⊙ ⊡ ⌀ ⅌ **Services** ⅏ ⅓〇 ➕ 🖫 **Leisure** ⌇ P **Off-site** ⌇LRS

AIRVAULT DEUX-SÈVRES

Courte Vallée

Courte Vallée, 79600 ☎ 549647065

e-mail camping@caravanningfrance.com

website www.caravanningfrance.com

A modern site with large pitches and good facilities, situated in a river valley.

➲ On NW outskirts of town, 0.5km towards Availles.

Open All year **Site** 12HEC ❤ ❤ ⛺ **Prices** ⅄ 6-7 pitch 9-11 **Facilities** ⋔ 🖽 ⊙ ⊡ ⅌ **Services** ⅏ ⅓〇 ➕ 🖫 **Leisure** ⌇ P **Off-site** 🖽 ⅏〇⅟ ⌸ ⌇PR

Take advantage of our prices in low season to enjoy our heated pool & the beautiful scenery from your chalet or your pitch along the river

Right on the Dordogne riverside (Sand beach, swimming, fishing, canoeing)

An exceptional site, 6km from Sarlat medieval town, In the heart of Périgord beautiful landscapes & castles

Many quality facilities for couples, families or groups:
Mini-mart (fresh bread & croissants), restaurant périgourdin, pizzeria, take-away, bar, meeting room.

Numerous activities: heated **pool complex with slides, fitness, tennis, mini-golf, multi-sport pitch, hiking, cycling, golf** (1km), riding (5km), numerous visits (caves, castles, vines, farms...)

English fluently spoken

Domaine de Soleil Plage****Caudon par Montfort, Vitrac, 24200 SARLAT.
Tel: 33 5 53 28 33 33 - Fax: 33 5 53 28 30 24 - www.soleilplage.fr

ALLONNES MAINE-ET-LOIRE

Pô Doré

Le Pô Doré, 49650 ☎ 241387880 🖷 241387881

A family site in a pleasant rural setting in the heart of the Anjou region with good recreational facilities. Separate car park for arrivals after 22.00 hrs.

➲ D35 from Tours. Or N147 from Angers.

Open Apr-Oct **Site** 2HEC ❤ ❤ ⛺ ⛆ **Facilities** ⋔ 🖽 ⊙ ⊡ ⅌ **Services** ⅏ ⅓〇 🖫 **Leisure** ⌇ P

ANCENIS LOIRE-ATLANTIQUE

Ile Mouchet

La Charbonnière, 44150 ☎ 240830843 🖷 240831619

e-mail efberthelot@wanadoo.fr

website www.camping-estivance.com

Peaceful, wooded site located on the banks of the Loire.

➲ Off N23 Nantes-Ancenis.

Open Apr-8 Oct **Site** 3HEC ❤ ❤ ⛺ ⛆ **Prices** ⅄ 2.20-2.50 pitch 6-7 ⛆ (static)300-450 **Facilities** ⋔ 🖽 ⊙ ⊡ ⅌ **Services** ⅏ ⅓〇 🖫 **Leisure** ⌇ P **Off-site** ⌀ ⌸ ⌇RS

ANDONVILLE LOIRET

Domaine de la Joullière

rte de Richerelles, 45480 ☎ 238395846 🖷 238396194

e-mail domaine.joulliere@wanadoo.fr

website www.domaine.joulliere.com

Spread over a series of small, wooded valleys with good sports and leisure facilities.

➲ 1km E on Richerelles road.

Open 15 Feb-15 Dec **Site** 10HEC ❤ ❤ **Facilities** ⋔ 🖽 ⊙ ⊡ ⅌ **Services** ⅏ ⅓〇 ➕ 🖫 **Leisure** ⌇ P

Facilities 🖽 shop ⋔ shower ⊙ electric points for razors ⊡ electric points for caravans ⅌ parking by tents permitted ⓟ compulsory separate car park
Services ⅓〇 café/restaurant ⅏ bar ⌀ Camping Gaz International ⌸ gas other than Camping Gaz ➕ first aid facilities 🖫 laundry
Leisure ⌇ swimming L-Lake P-Pool R-River S-Sea **Off-site** All facilities within 2km

France (side tab)

ANGERS MAINE-ET-LOIRE

Lac de Maine
av du Lac de Maine, 49000 ☎ 241730503 🖹 241730220
e-mail camping@lacdemaine.fr
website www.lacdemaine.fr
Pleasant rural surroundings on the 100-hectare Lac de Maine. There are fine sports and entertainment facilities and the historic town of Angers is within easy reach.
➲ A11 exit Lac de Maine.
Open 25 Mar-10 Oct **Site** 4HEC 👑 🌊 🐚 ♣ 🚐 **Prices** pitch 11.50-16.50 (incl 2 persons) 🚐 (static)299-572 **Facilities** 🌳 ⊙ 🚿 ⌀ 🛒 ⓟ **Services** ✚ 🍴 🖼 **Leisure** ☀ P **Off-site** 🏠 ✚LR ➕

ANGLES VENDÉE

Atlantique
5 bis Rue de Chemin de Fer ☎ 251270319 🖹 251276972
Open 21 Apr-25 Sep **Site** 6.9HEC 👑 🌊 🐚 🚐 🚐 **Facilities** 🌳 🏠 ⊙ ⌀ ⓟ **Services** ✚ 🍴 **Leisure** ☀ P

See advertisement on this page

Moncalm et Atlantique
85750 ☎ 251975580 🖹 251289109
e-mail camping-apv@wanadoo.fr
website www.camping-apv.com
Two distinct sites, but sharing the same recreational facilities in a wooded setting close to the beach.
Open 31 Mar-22 Sep **Site** 3HEC 👑 🌊 🐚 🏠 🚐 ⛺ **Prices** ♦ 5-6.50 🚗 2.50 pitch 15.50-24 🚐 (static)125-590 **Facilities** 🌳 ⊙ 🚿 ⌀ ⌗ ⓟ **Services** 🖼 **Leisure** ☀ P **Off-site** ☀R ➕

ANGOULINS-SUR-MER CHARENTE-MARITIME

Chirats
rte de la Platère, 17690 ☎ 546569416 🖹 546566595
website www.campingleschirats.fr.
Modern site with good facilities 100m from a small sandy beach and providing panoramic views over the Bay of Fouras. The more popular, larger beaches of the area are some 3km away. Reservations are strongly recommended.
➲ 7km S of La Rochelle.
Open Apr-Sep **Site** 4.5HEC 👑 🌊 🐚 🏠 🚐 **Prices** pitch 13.50-19.50 (incl 2 persons) pp3.60-4.30 **Facilities** 🌳 🏠 ⊙ 🚿 ⌀ ⓟ 🅿 **Services** ✚ 🍴 ➕ 🖼 **Leisure** ☀ PS

APREMONT VENDÉE

Prairies du Lac
rte de Maché RD40, 85220 ☎ 251557058 🖹 251557604
e-mail infos@les-prairies-du-lac.com
website www.camping-les-prairies-du-lac.com
Site located in a country setting but near the Vendée beaches and the lake of Apremont with its water slide.
➲ D58 from Challans.
Open May-September **Site** 6HEC 👑 🌊 ♣ **Facilities** 🌳 ⊙ 🚿 ⓟ **Services** ✚ 🖼 **Leisure** ☀ P **Off-site** 🏠 ☀LR ➕

ARCES CHARENTE-MARITIME

Chez Filleux
17120 ☎ 546908433 🖹 546908433
e-mail laferme.chezfilleux@wanadoo.fr
website www.camping-chezfilleux.com
A level meadow partly shaded by trees and bushes, with modern facilities, 10 minutes from the beaches.
Open Apr-Sep **Site** 3HEC 👑 🌊 🐚 ♣ 🚐 **Prices** pitch 13 **Facilities** 🌳 🏠 ⊙ 🚿 ⓟ **Services** ✚ 🍴 ➕ 🖼 **Leisure** ☀ P

ARGENTAT CORRÈZE

Gibanel
Le Gibanel, 19400 ☎ 555281011 🖹 555288162
e-mail contact@camping-gibanel.com
website www.camping-gibanel.com
Pleasant site in the grounds of a château next to a lake.
➲ S from Tulle on N120.
Open Jun-8 Sep **Site** 6.5HEC 👑 🌊 🐚 🚐 **Prices** ♦ 3.88-4.85 🚗 4-5 🚐 4-5 🚐 (static)220-250 **Facilities** 🌳 🏠 ⊙ 🚿 ⌀ ⓟ **Services** ✚ 🍴 ➕ 🖼 **Leisure** ☀ LP

Saulou
Vergnolles, 19400 ☎ 555281233 🖹 555288067
e-mail le.saulou@wanadoo.fr **website** www.saulou.net
A peaceful site in a wooded location beside the River Dordogne. Ideal for families.
➲ 6km S on D116.
Open Apr-Sep **Site** 7.5HEC 👑 🌊 🐚 🚐 **Prices** pitch 11.80-17 (incl 2 persons) 🚐 (static)170-564 **Facilities** 🌳 🏠 ⊙ 🚿 ⌀ ⌗ ⓟ **Services** ✚ 🍴 ➕ 🖼 **Leisure** ☀ PR

AT MONCEAUX-SUR-DORDOGNE (3KM SW)

Vaurette
19400 ☎ 555280967 🖹 555288114
e-mail info@vaurette.com **website** www.vaurette.com
On the banks of the River Dordogne with a beach, swimming pool & tennis court.
➲ On D12 between Argentat & Beaulieu.
Open May-21 Sep **Site** 4HEC 👑 🌊 🐚 🏠 🚐 **Prices** pitch 14-20 (incl 2 persons) pp3-4.50 **Facilities** 🌳 🏠 ⊙ 🚿 ⌀ ⌗ ⓟ **Services** ✚ 🍴 ➕ 🖼 **Leisure** ☀ PR

ARGENTON-CHÂTEAU DEUX-SÈVRES

CM du Lac d'Hautibus
79150 ☎ 549659508 🖹 549657084
e-mail marie-argenton-chateau@cegetel.net
➲ 0.4km S on D748.
Open Apr-Oct **Site** 16.2HEC 👑 🌊 🐚 🏠 **Facilities** 🌳 ⊙ 🚿 ⓟ **Services** 🖼 **Off-site** 🏠 ✚ 🍴 ⌀ ⌗ ☀LPR ➕

Site 6HEC (site size) 👑 grass 🌊 sand 🐚 stone ♣ little shade ♣ partly shaded 🌑 mainly shaded 🏠 bungalows for hire 🚐 caravans for hire ⛺ tents for hire ⊗ no dogs **Prices** ♦ adult per night 🚗 car per night pp per person per night 🚐 caravan per night ⛺ tent per night 🚐 (static)-caravan hire per week

AVRILLÉ VENDÉE

Forges
Domaine Les Forges, 85440 ☎ 251223885 🖷 251223885
e-mail contact@domaine-des-forges.net
website www.domaine-des-forges.net
A pleasant position beside a lake, 300m from the town centre. Close to the beach, the site has a variety of leisure facilities.
Open Etr-end Sep **Site** 8HEC 🌿 ♣ 🏠 ♨ **Facilities** ⋔ 🏪 ☉ ♨ 🛒 ⛺
Services 🍴 ⍩ 🏧 ⛱ ⍥ **Leisure** ♨ LP **Off-site** ⌀

Mancelières
rte de Longeville-sur-Mer, 85440 ☎ 251903597 🖷 251903931
e-mail camping.mancellieres@wanadoo.fr
website www.lesmancellieres.com
A pleasant site in a wooded park 5km from the fine beaches of south Vendée. Separate car park for arrivals after 23.00 hrs.
➲ *1.7km S on D105 towards Longeville.*
Open May-15 Sep **Site** 2.6HEC 🌿 ♣ 🏠 ♨ 🅰 **Prices** pitch 11.20-16 (incl 2 persons) pp3.90 ♨ (static)450 **Facilities** ⋔ 🏪 ☉ ♨ ⌀ ⛺ **Services** ⍥ 🏧 ⍩ **Leisure** ♨ P **Off-site** 🍴

AZAY-LE-RIDEAU INDRE-ET-LOIRE

Parc du Sabot
r du Stade, 37190 ☎ 247454272 🖷 247454911
e-mail mairie.azaylerideau@free.fr
Site lies in a large meadow on the River Indre.
➲ *Near château in town centre.*
Open Apr-Oct **Site** 9HEC 🌿 ♣ **Facilities** ⋔ ☉ ♨ ⛺ **Services** 🏧 ⍩ **Leisure** ♨ R **Off-site** 🏪 🍴 ⍥ ⌀ 🛒 ♨P

BARRE-DE-MONTS, LA VENDÉE

Grande Côte
85550 ☎ 251685189 🖷 251492557
website www.campeoles.fr
Set in a pine forest behind dunes with direct access to the beach. Plenty of recreational facilities.
➲ *3km from village beside Noirmoutier toll bridge.*
Open 7Apr-23Sep **Site** 22HEC ♨ ♣ 🏠 🅰 **Facilities** ⋔ 🏪 ☉ ♨ ⛺ **Services** 🍴 ⍩ **Leisure** ♨ P **Off-site** ⍥ ⌀ 🛒 ♨S

BATZ-SUR-MER LOIRE-ATLANTIQUE

Govelle
rte de la Côte Sauvage, 44740 ☎ 240239163 🖷 240239163
Direct access to the sea. Supervised beach and sea-fishing nearby.
➲ *On D45 between Le Pouliguen & Batz.*
Open 20 Apr-Sep **Site** 6.8HEC 🌿 ♣ 🏠 **Prices** ⍨ 4.42 ♨ 4.57
Facilities ⋔ ☉ ♨ ⛺ 🅿 **Services** 🏧 ⍩ **Leisure** ♨ S

BAULE, LA LOIRE-ATLANTIQUE

Ajoncs d'Or
chemin du Rocher, 44500 ☎ 240603329 🖷 240244437
e-mail contact@ajoncs.com
website www.ajoncs.com
A large wooded park with well-defined pitches, close to the beach.
➲ *Signed from entrance to town.*
Open Apr-Sep **Site** 6HEC 🌿 ♣ 🏠 **Prices** ⍨ 6 pitch 19-24 ♨ (static)288-618 **Facilities** ⋔ 🏪 ☉ ♨ ⌀ 🛒 ⛺ **Services** 🍴 ⍩ 🏧 ⍩ **Leisure** ♨ P **Off-site** ♨S

Facilities 🏪 shop ⋔ shower ☉ electric points for razors ♨ electric points for caravans ⛺ parking by tents permitted 🅿 compulsory separate car park
Services 🍴 café/restaurant ⍩ bar ⌀ Camping Gaz International 🛒 gas other than Camping Gaz 🏧 first aid facilities ⍩ laundry
Leisure ♨ swimming L-Lake P-Pool R-River S-Sea **Off-site** All facilities within 2km

France

France

CM

av de Diane, 44505 ☎ 240601740 🖹 240601148
e-mail labaule@lesbalconsverts.com
website www.lesbalconsverts.com
Site consists of two sections, one for caravans, one for tents, each with separate entrance.

➲ *On NE outskirts near railway.*

Open Feb-Oct **Site** 4HEC 👪 ⬤ ⬤ 🏠 ⊗ **Prices** pitch 10-22 (incl 2 persons) pp3-5 🚐 (static)280-600 **Facilities** ↳ 🖎 ☺ 🚰 🗷 🛒 �🛱 **Services** 🍴 🍽 🚻 🗑 **Leisure** ⬤ P **Off-site** 🍽 🚠 ⬤RS

See advertisement on page 103

Eden

1315 Route De Ker Rivaud, 44500 ☎ 240600323 🖹 240119425
e-mail eden-caravaning@wanadoo.fr
website www.campingeden.com
Pleasant rural surroundings with good sports and sanitary facilities.

➲ *1km NW via N171 exit La Baule-Escoublac.*

Open Apr-5 Nov **Site** 4.7HEC 👪 ♣ 🏠 **Prices** pitch 15-21 (incl 2 persons) pp4.50-6.50 **Facilities** ↳ 🖎 ☺ 🚰 🚠 🛒 **Services** 🍴 🍽 🚻 🗑 **Leisure** ⬤ LP **Off-site** 🗷 ⬤S

Roseraie

20 av J-Sohier, 44500 ☎ 240604666 🖹 240601184
e-mail camping@laroserie.com
website www.laroseraie.com
A well-planned site in wooded surroundings with good recreational facilities.

➲ *E of N171 towards bay.*

Open Apr-Sep **Site** 5HEC 👪 ♣ 🏠 **Prices** ↟ 4.50-7.50 pitch 8-13 **Facilities** ↳ 🖎 ☺ 🚰 🗷 🚠 🛒 **Services** 🍴 🍽 🚻 🗑 **Leisure** ⬤ P **Off-site** ⬤S

BAZOUGES-SUR-LE-LOIR SARTHE

CM

rte de Cré-sur-Loir, 72200 ☎ 243459580 🖹 243453826
On the bank of the River Loir with well-defined pitches.

➲ *Off A11 towards La Flèche.*

Open 15 May-Oct **Site** 0.8HEC 👪 ♣ 🏠 **Facilities** ↳ ☺ 🚰 🛒 **Services** 🚻 🗑 **Off-site** 🖎 🍴 🍽 🗷 🚠 ⬤RS

BEAULIEU-SUR-DORDOGNE CORRÈZE

Îles

19120 ☎ 555910265 🖹 555910519
e-mail jycastanet@aol.com
website www.camping-des-iles.net
On an island in the River Dordogne, within easy reach of all facilities.

Open 15 Apr-15 Oct **Site** 4.5HEC 👪 ⬤ 🏠 🏠 🅰 **Facilities** ↳ ☺ 🚰 🚠 🛒 **Services** 🍴 🍽 🚻 🗑 **Leisure** ⬤ PR **Off-site** 🖎 🗷

BESSINES-SUR-GARTEMPE HAUTE-VIENNE

AT MORTEROLLES-SUR-SEMME (4.5KM N ON N20)

CM

87250 ☎ 555766018 🖹 555766845
e-mail ot.bessines@wanadoo.fr

➲ *A20 exit 24*

Open All year **Site** 8HEC 👪 ☺ ♣ **Prices** ↟ 2.10 pitch 6.80 (incl 2 persons) **Facilities** ↳ ☺ 🚰 🛒 **Services** 🗑 **Off-site** 🖎 🍴 🍽 🗷 ⬤R 🚻

BEYNAT CORRÈZE

Étang de Miel

19190 ☎ 555855066 🖹 555855796
e-mail camping.lac.de.miel@wanadoo.fr
A family site in a picturesque wooded setting close to the lake.

➲ *4km E on N121 Argentat road.*

Open 15 Jun-15 Sep **Site** 9HEC 👪 ♣ 🏠 **Facilities** ↳ 🖎 ☺ 🚰 🗷 🛒 **Services** 🍴 🍽 🚻 🗑 **Leisure** ⬤ LR

BIGNAC CHARENTE

Marco de Bignac

Lieudit "Les Sablons", 16170 ☎ 545217841 🖹 545215237
e-mail camping.marcodebignac@wanadoo.fr
website www.camping-marco-bignac.com
A beautiful wooded location around a large lake with fine entertainment and sports facilities.

➲ *N10 exit La Touche, W onto D11, through Vars to Basse, right onto D117 to Bignac, signed near River Charente.*

Open 15 May-15 Sep **Site** 8HEC 👪 ♣ 🏠 **Prices** pitch 15-21 (incl 2 persons) pp3-5 🚐 (static)200-450 **Facilities** ↳ 🖎 ☺ 🚰 🛒 **Services** 🍴 🍽 🚻 **Leisure** ⬤ LP **Off-site** ⬤R

BLÉRÉ INDRE-ET-LOIRE

CM

r de la Gatine, 37150 ☎ 247579260 🖹 247579260
e-mail marie@blere-touraine.com
website www.blere-touraine.com
Well-kept site beside River Cher. Two entrances.

Open 7 Apr-15 Oct **Site** 4HEC 👪 ♣ **Facilities** ↳ ☺ 🚰 🛒 🛱 **Services** 🗑 **Off-site** 🖎 🍴 🍽 ⬤P 🚻

BONNAC-LA-CÔTE HAUTE-VIENNE

Château de Leychoisier

87270 ☎ 555399343 🖹 555399343
e-mail contact@leychoisier.com **website** www.leychoisier.com
A well-managed site of roomy pitches sloping gently towards woods.

➲ *1km S off N20.*

Open 15 Apr-20 Sep **Site** 4HEC 👪 ⬤ ♣ 🏠 🏠 **Facilities** ↳ 🖎 ☺ 🚰 🛒 **Services** 🍴 🍽 🚻 🗑 **Leisure** ⬤ LP

BONNES VIENNE

CM

r de la Varenne, 86300 ☎ 549564434 🖹 549564851
e-mail camping_bonnes@hotmail.com
website camping.bonnes86.free.fr
A quiet site with plenty of recreational facilities.

➲ *S beside River Vienne.*

Open May-15 Sep **Site** 1HEC 👪 ♣ 🏠 **Prices** ↟ 2.80 🚗 1.10 pitch 2.20 **Facilities** ↳ ☺ 🚰 🛒 **Services** 🚻 🗑 **Leisure** ⬤ PR **Off-site** 🖎 🍴 🍽 🚠 ⬤L

BONNY-SUR-LOIRE LOIRET

Val

45420 ☎ 238315771 🖹 238315771
e-mail maisonpays-bonny@wanadoo.fr
Woodland site beside the Loire, near the town centre.

➲ *At junct N7 & D965.*

Open mid May-30 Oct **Site** 0.8HEC 👪 ♣ **Facilities** ↳ ☺ 🚰 🛒 **Services** 🗑 **Leisure** ⬤ R **Off-site** 🖎 🍴 🍽 🗷 🚠

Site 6HEC (site size) 👪 grass ⬤ sand ⬤ stone ♣ little shade ♣ partly shaded 🏠 mainly shaded 🏠 bungalows for hire 🚐 caravans for hire 🅰 tents for hire ⊗ no dogs **Prices** ↟ adult per night 🚗 car per night pp per person per night 🚐 caravan per night 🅰 tent per night 🚐 (static)-caravan hire per week

France

BOURGES CHER

CM Robinson

26 bd de l'Industrie, 18000 ☎ 248201685 📠 248503239
e-mail tourisme@wellbourges.fr **website** www.wellbourges.fr
In the town near Lake Auron.

➲ *Via A71, N144 or N76.*

Open 15 Mar-15 Nov **Site** 2.2HEC ♨ ♣ ♠ **Prices** ⚹ 3.70 ⛺ 3.70-4.80
Facilities ⋔ ⊙ ⊑ ⑫ **Services** ➕ ⑤ **Off-site** 🏠 ⚑ ⍾ ⌀ ⚏ ⚞LPR

BOUSSAC-BOURG CREUSE

Château de Poinsouze

rte de La Châtre - BP 12, 23600 ☎ 555650221 📠 555658649
e-mail info.camping-de-poinsouze@wanadoo.fr
website www.camping-de-poinsouze.com
A picturesque location in the grounds of a château with modern
facilities.

➲ *2km N via D917.*

Open 12 May-15 Sep **Site** 22HEC ♨ ♣ ♠ ⚟ **Prices** pitch 19-28 (incl 2
persons) pp3-6 ⛺ (static)160-820 **Facilities** ⋔ 🏠 ⊙ ⊑ ⌀ ⚏ ⑫
Services ⚑ ⍾ ➕ ⑤ **Leisure** ⚞ P

BRACIEUX LOIR-ET-CHER

CM des Châteaux

11 rue Roger Brun, 41250 ☎ 254464184 📠 254464121
e-mail campingdebracieux@wanadoo.fr
website www.campingdeschateaux.com
A pleasant shady park close to the town centre and convenient for
visiting the châteaux of Chambord, Cheverny and Villesavin.

Open 31 Mar-12 Nov **Site** 8HEC ♨ ♣ ♠ **Prices** ⚹ 4.20-4.45 pitch 5.40-
5.90 ⛺ (static)250-450 **Facilities** ⋔ ⊙ ⊑ ⑫ **Services** ➕ ⑤ **Leisure** ⚞ PR
Off-site 🏠 ⚑ ⍾ ⌀ ⚏

BRAIN-SUR-L'AUTHION MAINE-ET-LOIRE

CM Caroline

49800 ☎ 241804218
website www.campingterreoceane.com
A modern site in a pleasant wooded setting close to the river.

Open 15 Mar-16 Sep **Site** 3.5HEC ♨ ♣ ♠ ⚟ **Prices** ⚹ 2.10-3 pitch 5-9
⛺ (static)290-610 **Facilities** ⋔ ⊙ ⊑ ⑫ **Services** ⚑ ⍾ ➕ ⑤ **Leisure** ⚞ P
Off-site 🏠 ⚑ ⍾ ⌀ ⚏ ⚞R

BRÉTIGNOLLES-SUR-MER VENDÉE

Dunes

Plage des Dunes, 85470 ☎ 251905532 📠 251905485
e-mail campinglesdunes@freesurf.fr
website www.campinglesdunes.com
Direct access to the beach. All plots surrounded by hedges.

➲ *2km S turn right off D38, 1km across dunes, 150m from
beach.*

Open Apr-11 Nov **Site** 12HEC ♨ ♣ ♠ **Facilities** ⋔ 🏠 ⊙ ⊑ ⌀ ⚏ ⑫
Services ⚑ ⍾ ➕ ⑤ **Leisure** ⚞ P **Off-site** ⚞LS

Motine

4 r des Morinières, 85470 ☎ 251900442 📠 251338052
e-mail campinglamotine@wanadoo.fr
website www.lamotine.fr
Pleasant site 350m from the town centre and 400m from the beach,
with good facilities.

Open Apr-Sep **Site** 1.8HEC ♨ ♣ ♠ **Prices** ⚹ 5.50 pitch 17.50-26 (incl 2
persons) **Facilities** ⋔ ⊙ ⊑ ⚏ ⑫ **Services** ⚑ ⍾ ➕ ⑤ **Leisure** ⚞ P
Off-site 🏠 ⌀ ⚞LRS

Trevilliere

rte de Bellevue, 85470 ☎ 251900965 📠 251339404
e-mail chadotel@wanadoo.fr
website www.chadotel.com

➲ *0.9km from town centre. 2km from beach.*

Open 7 Apr-23 Sep **Site** 3.5HEC ♨ ♣ ♠ ⚟ **Prices** ⚹ 5.80 pitch 12-23.20
(incl 2 persons) ⛺ (static)220-745 **Facilities** ⋔ 🏠 ⊙ ⊑ ⌀ ⚏ ⑫
Services ⚑ ⍾ ➕ ⑤ **Leisure** ⚞ P **Off-site** ⍾ ⚞S

Vagues

20 bd du Centre, 85470 ☎ 251901948 📠 240024988
e-mail lesvagues@free.fr **website** www.campinglesvagues.fr
A family site in a delightful rural setting on the Côte de Lumière.

➲ *N on D38 towards St-Gilles-Croix-de-Vie.*

Open Apr-Sep **Site** 5HEC ♨ ♣ ♠ ⚟ **Prices** ⚹ 3.29-5 pitch 14-22
⛺ (static)244-335 **Facilities** ⋔ ⊙ ⊑ ⑫ **Services** ⚑ ⍾ ➕ ⑤
Leisure ⚞ P **Off-site** 🏠 ⍾ ⌀ ⚞LS

BRISSAC-QUINCÉ MAINE-ET-LOIRE

L'Étang

rte de St Mathurin, 49320 ☎ 241917061 📠 241917265
e-mail info@campingetang.com
website www.campingetang.com
A lakeside site in the heart of the Anjou countryside with good
recreational facilities.

➲ *D748 towards Poitiers.*

Open 15 May-15 Sept **Site** 6HEC ♨ ♣ ♠ **Prices** pitch 18-31 (incl 2
persons) ⛺ (static)350-650 **Facilities** ⋔ 🏠 ⊙ ⊑ ⌀ ⚏ ⑫ **Services** ⚑ ⍾ ➕
⑤ **Leisure** ⚞ PR **Off-site** ⍾

CANDÉ-SUR-BEUVRON LOIR-ET-CHER

Grande Tortue

3 rte de Pontlevoy, 41120 ☎ 254441520 📠 254441945
e-mail lagrandetortue@wanadoo.fr
website www.la-grand-tortue.com
A family site in a peaceful wooded setting.

➲ *D751 between Blois & Amboise, on river.*

Open 7 Apr-22 Sep **Site** 5.8HEC ♨ ♣ ♠ **Prices** pitch 19.50-30 (incl 2
persons) pp5 ⛺ (static)266-651 **Facilities** ⋔ 🏠 ⊙ ⊑ ⌀ ⚏ ⑫ **Services** ⚑
⍾ ➕ ⑤ **Leisure** ⚞ P

CHALARD, LE HAUTE-VIENNE

Vigères

Les Vigères, 87500 ☎ 555093722 📠 555099339
e-mail lesvigeres@aol.com
website www.lesvigeres.com
Generally level site in peaceful surroundings in an elevated position
with fine views. English management.

➲ *On D901 between Châlus & Le Chalard.*

Open All year **Site** 20HEC ♨ ♣ ♠ **Prices** ⚹ 3-4 pitch 3-4.50 **Facilities** ⋔
⊙ ⚏ ⑫ **Services** ➕ ⑤ **Leisure** ⚞ LP **Off-site** 🏠 ⚑ ⍾ ⚞R

CHALONNES-SUR-LOIRE MAINE-ET-LOIRE

CM Candais

rte de Rochefort, 49290 ☎ 241780227 📠 241780227
e-mail info@campingteueoceane.com
website www.campingteueoceane.com
On the banks of the River Loire at its confluence with the River Louet.

➲ *NE off D751 towards Rochefort.*

Open 15 May-Sep **Site** 3HEC ♨ ♣ ⚟ **Facilities** ⋔ ⊙ ⊑ ⑫
Services ⚑ ⍾ ➕ ⑤ **Off-site** 🏠 ⚑ ⍾ ⌀ ⚏ ⚞P

Facilities 🏠 shop ⋔ shower ⊙ electric points for razors ⊑ electric points for caravans ⑫ parking by tents permitted ❶ compulsory separate car park
Services ⍾ café/restaurant ⚑ bar ⌀ Camping Gaz International ⚏ gas other than Camping Gaz ➕ first aid facilities ⑤ laundry
Leisure ⚞ swimming L-Lake P-Pool R-River S-Sea **Off-site** All facilities within 2km

France

CHAPELLE HERMIER, LA VENDÉE

Pin Parasol

Lac du Jaunay, Chateaulong, 85220 ☎ 251346472 ▤ 251346462

e-mail campingpinparasol@free.fr

website campingpinparasol.free.fr

Set in the heart of the Vendée on the shore of Lac du Jaunay with modern facilities.

➭ *Between D6 & D12.*

Open 27 Apr-25 Sep **Site** 12HEC ❤ ♣ ☎ **Prices** pitch 11.50-24.50 (incl 2 persons) pp4.50-6 **Facilities** ♠ ⬛ ☺ ⊕ ❻ ⊘ ♨ ℗ **Services** ☎ ℣ ❶ ☒ **Leisure** ⬤ PS

CHARTRES EURE-ET-LOIR

CM des Bords de l'Eure

9 r de Launay, 28000 ☎ 237287943 ▤ 237282943

e-mail camping-roussel-chartres@wanadoo.fr

website www.auxbordsdeleure.com

Wooded surroundings beside the river.

➭ *Signed towards Orléans.*

Open 10 Apr-10 Nov **Site** 3.9HEC ❤ ♣ ☎ ❿ **Prices** pitch 11-15 (incl 2 persons) ❿ (static)250 **Facilities** ♠ ⬛ ☺ ⊕ ❻ ⊘ ♨ ℗ **Services** ☎ ℣ ❶ ☒ **Off-site** ℣ ⊘ ♨ ⬤PR

CHARTRE-SUR-LE-LOIR, LA SARTHE

Vieux Moulin

chemin des Bergivaux, 72340 ☎ 243444118 ▤ 243442406

e-mail camping@lachartre.com

website www.lachartre.com

Open Apr-Sep **Site** 2.4HEC ❤ ♣ ☎ ❿ ⋏ **Prices** pitch 9-10 (incl 2 persons) ❿ (static)180-230 **Facilities** ♠ ⬛ ☺ ⊕ ❻ ⊘ ♨ ℗ **Services** ☎ ℣ ❶ ☒ **Leisure** ⬤ PR **Off-site** ⬤LP

CHARTRIER-FERRIÈRE CORRÈZE

Magaudie

La Magaudie Ouest, 19600 ☎ 555852606

e-mail camping@lamagaudie.com

website www.lamagaudie.com

A peaceful site covering 8 hectares, half consisting of forest, 3km from Lac du Causse with beaches and water sports. The 18th-century buildings on the site have been converted to hygenic sanitary facilities.

➭ *A20 exit 53, N20 for Cahors, at rdbt onto D19 for Chasteaux, D154 left for Chartrier & Nadaillac, 3rd right for La Magaudie, 1st right, site on left.*

Open All year **Site** 8HEC ❤ ♣ ⬤ ❿ **Prices** ⋏ 3.70 pitch 3.75-5.25 ❿ (static)200-275 **Facilities** ♠ ⊕ ❻ ℗ **Services** ☎ ℣ ❶ ☒ **Leisure** ⬤ P

CHASSENEUIL-SUR-BONNIEURE CHARENTE

CM Les Charmilles

r des Écoles, 16260 ☎ 545395536 ▤ 545225245

e-mail mairie.chasseneuil@wanadoo.fr

website membres.lycos.fr/ville16260/

➭ *W of town via D27, beside River Bonnieure.*

Open 15 Apr-Oct **Site** 1.5HEC ❤ ❤ ☎ ⋏ **Prices** ⋏ 1.55 ❻ 0.88 ❿ 0.88 ⋏ 0.98 ❿ (static)122 **Facilities** ♠ ⊕ ❻ ℗ **Services** ☒ **Off-site** ⬛ ☎ ℣ ⊘ ⬤P ❶

CHÂTEAU D'OLONNE, LE VENDÉE

Pirons

r des Marchais, La Pironnière, 85180 ☎ 251952675 ▤ 251239317

e-mail contact@camping-les-pirons.com

website www.camping-les-pirons.com

Site 300m from the beach, with three swimming pools and an aquatic chute.

➭ *Off D949.*

Open Apr-Oct **Site** 7HEC ♣ ☎ ❿ ⋏ ℗ **Facilities** ♠ ⬛ ☺ ⊕ ❻ ⊘ ♨ ℗ **Services** ☎ ℣ ☒ **Leisure** ⬤ P **Off-site** ⬤S

CHÂTEAU-DU-LOIR SARTHE

CM de Coemont

72500 ☎ 243794463

Shady site on the bank of the Loir.

Open Jun-Sep **Site** 0.6HEC ❤ ♣ **Facilities** ♠ ⊕ ❻ ℗ **Services** ☒ **Leisure** ⬤ R **Off-site** ⬛ ☎ ℣ ℣ ⊘ ⬤LP ❶

CHÂTELAILLON-PLAGE CHARENTE-MARITIME

Clos des Rivages

av des Boucholeurs, 17340 ☎ 546562609

Level, well-kept site with pitches divided by trees and bushes, 0.5km from the sea.

➭ *0.5km from the village, signed.*

Open 15 Jun-5 Sep **Site** 2.5HEC ❤ **Facilities** ♠ ⬛ ☺ ⊕ ❻ ⊘ ℗ **Services** ☎ ❶ ☒ **Leisure** ⬤ P **Off-site** ℣ ⬤S

Deux Plages

17340 ☎ 546562753 ▤ 546435118

e-mail reception@2plages.com **website** www.2plages.com

Pleasant wooded surroundings 200m from the beach.

Open May-Sep **Site** 4.5HEC ❤ ♣ ⬤ ☎ **Prices** ⋏ 4.80 ❻ 2.35 **Facilities** ♠ ⬛ ☺ ⊕ ❻ ℗ **Services** ☎ ℣ ❶ ☒ **Leisure** ⬤ P **Off-site** ⊘ ♨ ⬤S

CHÂTELLERAULT VIENNE

Relais du Miel

rte d'Antran, 86100 ☎ 549020627

e-mail camping@lerelaisdumiel.com

website www.lerelaisdumiel.com

Set in the grounds of Château de Valette, beside the River Vienne.

➭ *A10 exit 26 Châtellerault Nord.*

Open 15 May-Aug **Site** 7HEC ❤ ♣ ☎ ❿ **Facilities** ♠ ⊕ ❻ ℗ **Services** ☎ ℣ ❶ ☒ **Leisure** ⬤ PR **Off-site** ⬛ ☎ ℣ ⊘ ♨

CHÂTRES-SUR-CHER LOIR-ET-CHER

CM des Saules

41320 ☎ 254980455

➭ *On N76 near bridge.*

Open May-Aug **Site** 2HEC ❤ ♣ **Facilities** ♠ ⊕ ❻ ℗ **Services** ☒ **Off-site** ⬛ ☎ ℣ ⊘ ♨ ⬤R ❶

CHAUFFOUR-SUR-VELL CORRÈZE

Feneyrolles

19500 ☎ 555253143

e-mail feneyrolles@aol.com

A quiet wooded location with good facilities. Ideal for exploring the Dordogne valley and surrounding area.

➭ *2.2km E.*

Open 15 Apr-15 Sep **Site** 4HEC ❤ ❤ ☎ ❿ **Facilities** ♠ ⬛ ☺ ⊕ ❻ ℗ **Services** ☎ ℣ ❶ ☒ **Leisure** ⬤ P

Site 6HEC (site size) ❤ grass ⬤ sand ❤ stone ♣ little shade ❤ partly shaded ❤ mainly shaded ☎ bungalows for hire ❿ caravans for hire ⋏ tents for hire ⊗ no dogs **Prices** ⋏ adult per night ❻ car per night pp per person per night ❿ caravan per night ⋏ tent per night ❿ (static)-caravan hire per week

CHEF-BOUTONNE DEUX-SÈVRES

Moulin

Treneuillet, rte de Brioux, 79110 ☎ 549297346 🖺 549297346
e-mail campinglemoulin.chef@tiscali.fr
website www.campingchef.com
Small, secluded family site in a rural setting.
➲ *1km NE via D740.*

Open All year **Site** 2.5HEC ⛺ ⛺ ⛺ **Prices** ♣ 2.50-2.70 ▲ 2.50 pitch 5.70-8 **Facilities** ⋔ ⊙ ⊕ ⚤ ⚑ ⑫ **Services** ⚑ ⍩ 🞥 🖭 ⑤ **Leisure** ♨ PR **Off-site** ⊘

CHENONCEAUX INDRE-ET-LOIRE

Moulin Fort

37150 ☎ 247238622 🖺 247238093
e-mail lemoulinfort@wanadoo.fr
website www.lemoulinfort.com
➲ *2km SE.*

Open Apr-Sep **Site** 3HEC ⛺ ⛺ **Prices** pitch 13-20 (incl 2 persons) pp3-5
Facilities ⋔ ⓘ ⊙ ⚤ ⊘ ⑫ **Services** ⚑ ⍩ 🞥 ⑤ **Leisure** ♨ PR

CHÉVERNY LOIR-ET-CHER

Les Saules

rte de Contres, 41700 ☎ 254799001 🖺 254792834
e-mail contact@camping-cheverny.com
website www.camping-cheverny.com
Set in the heart of the Val de Loire, bordered by a golf course and the Cheverny forest.
➲ *1.5km from town on D102 towards Contres.*

Open 30 Mar-Sep **Site** 8HEC ⛺ ⛺ ⛺ ▲ **Prices** pitch 15.50-25.50 (incl 2 persons) pp4.50 **Facilities** ⋔ ⓘ ⊙ ⚤ ⊘ ⚑ ⑫ **Services** ⚑ ⍩ 🞥 ⑤ **Leisure** ♨ P

CHOLET MAINE-ET-LOIRE

Lac de Ribou

av L-Mandin, 49300 ☎ 241497430 🖺 241582122
e-mail village-vacances-cholet@wanadoo.fr
website www.cholet-shorts-loisirs.fr
Well set-out site bordering a lake, with fishing, boating, tennis and volleyball.
➲ *3km from town centre.*

Open Apr-Sep **Site** 5HEC ⛺ ⛺ ⛺ ⚤ ⚑ **Facilities** ⋔ ⊙ ⚤ ⑫ **Services** ⚑ ⍩ 🞥 ⑤ **Leisure** ♨ P **Off-site** ⓘ ⊘ ♨ L

CLOYES-SUR-LE-LOIR EURE-ET-LOIR

Val Fleuri

rte de Montigny, 28220 ☎ 237985053 🖺 237983384
e-mail info@parc-de-loisirs.com
website www.parc-de-loisirs.com
On the bank of the River Loir. Extensive leisure facilities. Separate section for teenagers. Shop only open in July and August, bar and restaurant only May to September.
➲ *N10 S from Châteaudun towards Cloyes, right onto Montigny-le-Gamelon road.*

Open 15 Mar-15 Nov **Site** 5HEC ⛺ ⛺ ⛺ **Prices** ♣ 4.50-5.65 pitch 6.85-8.80 ⚑ (static)295-540 **Facilities** ⋔ ⓘ ⊙ ⚤ ⊘ ⚑ ⑫ **Services** ⚑ ⍩ 🞥 🖭 ⑤ **Leisure** ♨ P **Off-site** ⓘ ⚑ ⍩

COGNAC CHARENTE

Cognac

rte de Ste-Sévère, bd de Chatenay, 16100 ☎ 545321332 🖺 545321582
e-mail infos@campingdecognac.com
website www.campingdecognac.com
Wooded surroundings beside the River Charente with modern facilities.
➲ *2km N on D24.*

Open May-15 Oct **Site** 1.6HEC ⛺ ⛺ ⛺ **Prices** pitch 11-14.30 (incl 2 persons) **Facilities** ⋔ ⓘ ⊙ ⚤ ⑫ **Services** ⚑ ⍩ ⑤ **Leisure** ♨ PR **Off-site** ⚑ ⍩ ♨ P 🞥

CONDAT SUR GANAVEIX CORRÈZE

Moulin de la Geneste

Moulin de la Geneste ☎ 555989008 🖺 555989008
e-mail la.geneste@lineone.net **website** www.lageneste.net
Undulating land with three small lakes and a small trout river. Part of the land and small wood have been left as a nature reserve with an abundance of wildlife.
➲ *from Limoges take A20 exit 44 Uzerche travelling S. Follow signs for Condat sur Ganaveix.*

Open May-15 Sep **Site** 4HEC ⛺ ⛺ ⛺ **Prices** ♣ 3.20 pitch 2.70
Facilities ⋔ ⊙ ⚤ ⑫ **Services** 🞥 ⑤

CONTRES LOIR-ET-CHER

Charmoise

Sassay, 41700 ☎ 254795515 🖺 254795515
On a level meadow with good facilities.
➲ *N956.*

Open Apr-Oct Nov-Mar **Site** 1HEC ⛺ ⛺ **Prices** ♣ 2.30 ⚑ 1 ⚑ (static)80 **Facilities** ⋔ ⊙ ⚤ ⑫ **Services** ⑤ **Off-site** ⓘ ⚑ ⍩ ⚑

France

Facilities ⓘ shop ⋔ shower ⊙ electric points for razors ⚤ electric points for caravans ⑫ parking by tents permitted ⓟ compulsory separate car park
Services ⍩ café/restaurant ⚑ bar ⊘ Camping Gaz International ⚑ gas other than Camping Gaz 🞥 first aid facilities ⑤ laundry
Leisure ♨ swimming L-Lake P-Pool R-River S-Sea **Off-site** All facilities within 2km

France

COUHÉ-VERAC VIENNE

Peupliers
86700 ☎ 549592116 📠 549379209
e-mail info@lespeupliers.fr **website** www.lespeupliers.fr
A family site in a forest beside the river.
➔ *N of village on N10 Poitiers road.*
Open 2 May-Sep **Site** 16HEC 🌢 🌢 🏠 �caravan **Prices** 🕯 4.55-7 pitch 5.85-9
Facilities 🌲 🏠 ☺ 🔊 🅿 🗑 ☎ **Services** 🚰 🍴 🔌 🗑 **Leisure** 🏊 PR
Off-site 🔩

See advertisement on page 107

COURÁON-D'AUNIS CHARENTE-MARITIME

Garenne
21 r du Stade, 17170 ☎ 546016050 📠 546016359
Open Jul-Aug **Site** 🌢 🌢 **Facilities** 🌲 ☺ 🔊 ☎ **Services** 🗑 **Off-site** 🏠 🚰
🍴 🔩 🏊 🅿 🔌

COUTURES MAINE-ET-LOIRE

Parc de Montsabert
Montsabert, 49320 ☎ 241579163 📠 241579002
e-mail camping@parcdemontsabert.com
website www.parcdemontsabert.com
➔ *Off D751 along River Loire between Angers & Saumur.*
Open 14 Apr-16 Sep **Site** 10HEC 🌢 🌢 🏠 🕯 **Prices** pitch 15.30-23.80 (incl 2 persons) pp4.60 **Facilities** 🌲 🏠 ☺ 🔊 ☎ **Services** 🚰 🍴 🔌 🗑
Leisure 🏊 🅿 **Off-site** 🏠 🍴 🔩 🔩

See advertisement on this page

CROISIC, LE LOIRE-ATLANTIQUE

Océan
44490 ☎ 240230769 📠 240157063
e-mail camping-ocean@wanadoo.fr
website www.camping-ocean.fr
A quiet, well-appointed site 150m from the sea.
➔ *1.5km NW via D45*
Open Apr-Sep **Site** 7.5HEC 🌢 🌢 🏠 �caravan **Facilities** 🌲 🏠 ☺ 🔊 🅿 🗑 🔩 🔩 ☎
Services 🚰 🍴 🔌 🗑 **Leisure** 🏊 🅿 **Off-site** 🏊 S

See advertisement on page 119

DISSAY VIENNE

CM du Parc
r du Parc, 86130 ☎ 549628429 📠 549625872
Quiet, shady site at the foot of a 15th-century château, close to Futuroscope, the lake of St-Cyr and the forest of Mouliere.
Open Jun-15 Sep **Site** 1HEC 🌢 🌢 **Prices** 🕯 1.50 pitch 6.50 **Facilities** 🌲
☺ 🔊 ☎ **Services** 🗑 **Off-site** 🏠 🚰 🍴 🔩 R

DURTAL MAINE-ET-LOIRE

International
9 r du Camping, 49430 ☎ 241763180
e-mail contact@camping-durtal.com
website www.camping-durtal.com
A pleasant site beside the River Loire.
➔ *Near town centre, via N23 or A11.*
Open Etr-Sep **Site** 3HEC 🌢 🌢 🏠 **Prices** 🕯 3.20 pitch 10.65 (incl 2 persons) **Facilities** 🌲 ☺ 🔊 ☎ **Services** 🚰 🍴 🔌 🗑 **Off-site** 🏠 🍴 🏊 P

EYMOUTHIERS CHARENTE

Gorges du Chambon
16220 ☎ 545707170 📠 545708002
e-mail gorges.chambon@wanadoo.fr
website www.gorgesduchambon.fr
A beautiful location on a wooded hilltop.
➔ *3km N via D163.*
Open 21 Apr-22 Sep **Site** 7HEC 🌢 🌢 🏠 🅰 🚫 **Prices** pitch 12.75-22.60 (incl 2 persons) pp3.75-8.30 �caravan (static)252-570 **Facilities** 🌲 🏠 ☺ 🔊 🔩
☎ **Services** 🚰 🍴 🔌 🗑 **Leisure** 🏊 PR

FAUTE-SUR-MER, LA VENDÉE

Fautais
18 rte de la Tranche, 85460 ☎ 251564196
Situated in the village centre, with numbered pitches.
➔ *On D46.*
Open Apr-Sep **Site** 1HEC 🌢 🌢 🏠 **Facilities** 🌲 ☎ **Services** 🗑 **Off-site** 🏠
🚰 🍴 🔩 🏊 LPRS 🔌

Flots Bleus
av des Chardons, 85460 ☎ 251271111 📠 251294076
Family site only 100m from the sea.
➔ *From La Faute cross Pont de l'Aiguillons-sur-Mer, onto Route de la Pointe d'Arçay to site.*
Open 8 May-8 Sep **Site** 1.5HEC 🌢 🌢 🏠 �caravan **Facilities** 🌲 ☺ 🔊 🔩 ☎
Services 🚰 🍴 🔌 🗑 **Off-site** 🏠 🍴 LRS

FENOUILLER, LE VENDÉE

SAS SHH Le Pas Opton
rte de Nantes, 85800 ☎ 251551198 📠 251554494
website www.springharvestholidays.com
Well-equipped family site near the beach and close to the Des Vallées sailing centre.
➲ 2km N beside the River Vie on D754.
Open May-Nov **Site** ♨ ♣ ♠ Å ⊗ **Facilities** ♠ 🛋 ⊙ 🔌 ⊘ ⓟ **Services** 🍴 🍽 🚑 🔲 **Leisure** ≈ PR

FOURAS CHARENTE-MARITIME

Charmilles
St Laurent de la Pree, 17450 ☎ 546840005 📠 546840284
e-mail charmilles17@wanadoo.fr
website www.domainedescharmilles.com
Open 2 Apr-Sep **Site** 5HEC ♨ ♣ ♠ **Facilities** ♠ 🛋 ⊙ 🔌 ⓟ **Services** 🍴 🍽 🚑 **Leisure** ≈ P **Off-site** 🍽 ≈S

FRESNAY-SUR-SARTHE SARTHE

CM Sans Souci
r de Haut Ary, 72130 ☎ 243973287
e-mail camping-fresnay@wanadoo.fr
A family site with good facilities and direct access to the river.
➲ 1km SE on D310.
Open Apr-Sep **Site** 2HEC ♨ ♣ ♠ **Facilities** ♠ 🛋 ⊙ 🔌 ⊘ ⓟ **Services** 🚑 **Leisure** ≈ PR **Off-site** 🍴 🍽 🔄

FRIAUDOUR HAUTE-VIENNE

Freaudour
87250 ☎ 555765722 📠 555712393
e-mail lacsaintpardoux@wanadoo.fr
website www.lac-saint-pardoux.com
A well-equipped site beside Lac de St-Pardoux.
➲ A20 exit 25.
Open 4 Jun-10 Sep **Site** 3.5HEC ♨ ♣ ♠ **Prices** pitch 11.20-17.30 (incl 2 persons) 🔌 (static)235-570 **Facilities** ♠ 🛋 ⊙ 🔌 ⓟ **Services** 🍴 🍽 🔲 **Leisure** ≈ LP **Off-site** ⊘ 🔄

FROSSAY LOIRE-ATLANTIQUE

Migron
Le Square de la Chaussée, 44320 ☎ 240397272
A pleasant location beside the canal.
Open Jul-Sep **Site** 2.5HEC ♨ ♣ **Prices** ♟ 2.05 🔌 1.05 pitch 2.55 **Facilities** ♠ ⊙ 🔌 ⊘ ⓟ **Services** 🚑 **Leisure** ≈ R **Off-site** 🛋 🍴 🍽

GENNES MAINE-ET-LOIRE

Au Bord de Loire
av des Cadets de Saumur, 49350 ☎ 241380467 📠 241380712
e-mail auborddeloire@free.fr
website www.camping-auborddeloire.com
Peaceful location on the river.
➲ Via D952-D751
Open May-Sep **Site** 3HEC ♨ ♣ ♠ Å **Prices** pitch 8 (incl 2 persons) 🔌 (static)155-300 **Facilities** ♠ ⊙ 🔌 ⓟ **Services** 🍽 🚑 **Leisure** ≈ R **Off-site** 🛋 🍴 🍽 ⊘ 🔄 ≈P 🔲

GIEN LOIRET

Bois du Bardelet
rte de Bourges, Poilly, 45500 ☎ 238674739 📠 238382716
e-mail contact@bardelet.com **website** www.bardelet.com
A family site with a variety of sports facilities.
➲ D940 SW of Gien.
Open Apr-Sep **Site** 12HEC ♨ ♣ ♠ **Prices** pitch 18.50-30.30 (incl 2 persons) pp3.70-6.20 🔌 (static)309-903 **Facilities** ♠ 🛋 ⊙ 🔌 ⊘ ⓟ **Services** 🍴 🍽 🔲 **Leisure** ≈ P

GUÉMENÉ-PENFAO LOIRE-ATLANTIQUE

Hermitage
36 av du Paradis, 44290 ☎ 240792348 📠 240515 1187
e-mail contact@campinglhermitage.com
website www.campinglhermitage.com
A beautiful setting overlooking the Don valley with modern facilities.
➲ 1.5km E on rte de Châteaubriant.
Open Apr-Sep **Site** 2.5HEC ♨ ♣ ♠ Å **Prices** pitch 11.50-9.60 (incl 2 persons) pp3 🔌 (static) **Facilities** ♠ 🛋 ⊙ 🔌 ⊘ ⓟ **Services** 🍴 🚑 **Leisure** ≈ P **Off-site** 🍴 🍽 🔄 ≈R 🔲

GUÉRANDE LOIRE-ATLANTIQUE

Bréhadour
44350 ☎ 240249312 📠 240249277
e-mail info@homair-vacances.fr **website** www.homair-vacances.fr
A well-equipped family site with good facilities, a few kilometres from the sea.
➲ 2km NE on D51, rte de St-Lyphard.
Open 15 Apr-Sep **Site** 7HEC ♨ ♣ ♠ ♠ Å **Facilities** ♠ 🛋 ⊙ 🔌 ⓟ **Services** 🍴 🍽 🚑 **Leisure** ≈ P **Off-site** ⊘ 🔄 🔲

Domaine de Lévéno
rte de l'Étang de Sandun, 44350 ☎ 240247930 📠 240620123
e-mail domaine.leveno@wanadoo.fr
website www.camping-leveno.com
A pleasant location with good facilities.
➲ 3km E via rte de Sandun.
Open 9 Apr-2 Oct **Site** 12HEC ♨ ♣ ♠ **Facilities** ♠ 🛋 ⊙ 🔌 ⊘ 🔄 ⓟ **Services** 🍴 🍽 🔲 **Leisure** ≈ P **Off-site** ≈S

See advertisement on page 119

Pré du Château de Careil
Careil, 44350 ☎ 240602299 📠 240602299
e-mail chateau.careil@free.fr
website www.pays-blanc.com/camping-careil
Divided into pitches for caravans only. Booking advised for July and August.
➲ 2km N of La Baule on D92.
Open 22 May-12 Sep **Site** 2HEC ♨ ♣ **Facilities** ♠ ⊙ 🔌 ⓟ **Services** 🔲 🚑 **Leisure** ≈ P **Off-site** 🛋 🍴 🍽 ⊘ 🔄

HÉRIC LOIRE-ATLANTIQUE

Pindière
44810 ☎ 240576541 📠 228022543
e-mail camping.pindiere@free.fr
website www.camping-la-pindiere.com
A family site on a level meadow with good facilities.
➲ 1km from town on D16.
Open All year **Site** 3HEC ♨ ♣ ♠ **Prices** ♟ 3.20-3.60 pitch 4.50-5 **Facilities** ♠ ⊙ 🔌 🔄 ⓟ **Services** 🍴 🍽 🔲 🚑 **Leisure** ≈ P **Off-site** 🛋

Facilities 🛋 shop ♠ shower ⊙ electric points for razors 🔌 electric points for caravans ⓟ parking by tents permitted 🅿 compulsory separate car park
Services 🍽 café/restaurant 🍴 bar ⊘ Camping Gaz International 🔄 gas other than Camping Gaz 🔲 first aid facilities 🚑 laundry
Leisure ≈ swimming L-Lake P-Pool R-River S-Sea **Off-site** All facilities within 2km

France

HOUMEAU, L' CHARENTE-MARITIME

Trépied au Plomb

17137 ☎ 546509082 📠 546500133
e-mail camping@aupetitport.com **website** www.aupetitport.com
➲ NE via D106

Open Apr-Sep **Site** 2HEC 🏕 🏖 🏨 🚐 **Facilities** 🅡 ☺ 🅡 🅟 ⑳ **Services** 🍴
➕ 🅢 **Off-site** 🛒 🍴 🅾️ 🅐 ⛱S

INGRANDES VIENNE

AT ST-USTRE (2KM NE)

Petit Trianon de St-Ustre

86200 ☎ 549026147 📠 549026881
e-mail chateau@petit-trianon.fr **website** www.petit-trianon.fr
Set in a beautiful park surrounding a small 18th-century château, the site has good entertainment and recreational facilities.
➲ Off N10 at sign N of Ingrandes, site 1km.

Open 20 May-20 Sep **Site** 7HEC 🏕 🏖 🏨 🚐 **Prices** ★ 6.50-7 🚗 3.80-4 pitch 3.90-4.20 🚐 (static)260-360 **Facilities** 🅡 🛒 ☺ 🅡 🅐 **Services** ➕ 🅢 **Leisure** ⛱ P **Off-site** 🍴 🍴 ⚓

JARD-SUR-MER VENDÉE

Écureuils

rte des Goffineaux, 85520 ☎ 251334274 📠 251339114
e-mail camping-ecureuils@wanadoo.fr
website www.camping-ecureuils.com
Quiet woodland terrain 450m from the sea, with large pitches surrounded by hedges.
➲ Signed.

Open Apr-Sep **Site** 4.3HEC 🏕 🏖 🏨 🚐 ⊗ **Prices** pitch 13.95-15.50 pp1.80-4.50 🚐 (static)260-670 **Facilities** 🅡 🛒 ☺ 🅡 🅐 🅟 **Services** 🍴 🍴 ➕ 🅢 **Leisure** ⛱ P **Off-site** 🍴 ⛱S

La Mouette Cendrée

Les Malecots, St-Vincent-sur-Jard, 85520
☎ 251335904 📠 251203139
e-mail camping.mc@free.fr
website www.mouettecendree.com
Open Etr-Sep **Site** 1.2HEC 🏕 🏖 🏨 🚐 **Facilities** 🅡 ☺ 🅡 🅟 ⑳ **Services** ➕ 🅢 **Leisure** ⛱ P **Off-site** 🛒 🍴 🍴 🅐 ⛱S

Océano d'Or

r G-Clemenceau, 85520 ☎ 251336508 📠 251339404
e-mail chadotel@wanadoo.fr
website www.chadotel.com
A well-maintained site 1km from the beach and 0.5km from the town centre.
➲ Via D19.

Open 7 Apr-23 Sep **Site** 7.8HEC 🏕 🏖 🏨 **Prices** ★ 5.80 pitch 14.50-24.20 (incl 2 persons) 🚐 (static)200-730 **Facilities** 🅡 🛒 ☺ 🅡 🅐 🅟 **Services** 🍴 🍴 ➕ 🅢 **Leisure** ⛱ P **Off-site** 🍴 ⛱S

See advertisement on this page

Pomme de Pin

r Vincent Auriol, 85520 ☎ 251334385 📠 251339404
e-mail info@pommedepin.net
website www.pommedepin.net
Situated in a pine forest.
➲ 300m from town centre. 150m from beach.

Open 6 Apr-20 Sep **Site** 3HEC 🏕 🏖 🏨 **Facilities** 🅡 🛒 ☺ 🅡 🅐 🅟 **Services** 🍴 🍴 ➕ 🅢 **Leisure** ⛱ PS **Off-site** 🍴

JARGEAU LOIRET

Isle aux Moulins

r du 44ème RI, 45150 ☎ 238597004 📠 238591223
e-mail kas@wanadoo.fr
Wooded location beside the Loire.
Open Mar-15 Nov **Site** 7HEC 🏕 🏖 🏨 🚐 **Facilities** 🅡 🛒 ☺ 🅡 🅐 🅟 **Services** ➕ 🅢 **Leisure** ⛱ R **Off-site** 🍴 🍴 🅐

JAUNAY CLAN VIENNE

Croix du Sud

rte de Neuville, 86130 ☎ 549625814
e-mail camping@la-croix-du-sud.fr
website www.la-croix-du-sud.fr
Within easy reach of Futuroscope, the European Park of the Moving Image.
➲ Via A10 & D62.

Open 29 Mar-13 Sep **Site** 4HEC 🏕 🏖 🏨 **Facilities** 🅡 🛒 ☺ 🅡 🅐 🅟 **Services** 🍴 🍴 🅢 **Leisure** ⛱ P

LAGORD CHARENTE-MARITIME

CM Parc

r du Parc, 17140 ☎ 546676154 📠 546006201
e-mail mairie.lagord@wanadoo.fr
Pleasant municipal site within easy reach of the coast.
➲ Via N137/D735.

Open Jun-Sep **Site** 🏕 🏖 🚐 **Facilities** 🅡 ☺ 🅡 🅟 **Services** ➕ 🅢 **Off-site** 🛒 🍴 🍴 🅐 🅐 ⛱P

LESSAC CHARENTE

Roufferies
16500 ☎ 545302126 🖪 545302126
Rural grassland site surrounded by trees and hidden from the road.
Large lake for swimming.
➮ *From Potiers towards Confolens, through Preesac & left for Leesac, 5km signed on right.*
Open Apr-Sep **Site** 20HEC � ♣ ♣ **Facilities** ⋒ ℗ **Leisure** ⇆ L
Off-site 🗐 🕯 ❍ ⚓

LIMERAY INDRE-ET-LOIRE

Jardin Botanique
9 r de la Rivière ☎ 247301682 🖪 247301732
e-mail info@camping-jardinbotanique.com
website www.camping-jardinbotanique.com
Set in wooded shady parkland.
➮ *6km NE of Amboise on N152.*
Open Apr-Sep **Site** 1.5HEC 🌤 ♣ 🚃 **Prices** pitch 12-13.50 (incl 2 persons) pp2.60-3.40 🚃 (static)200-450 **Facilities** ⋒ 🗐 ⊙ ♣ ℗ **Services** 🕯 ❍
Leisure ⇆ P

See advertisement on this page

Marked and shady pitches.
Free: swimming-pool - play ground
- tennis - table tennis - TV.
RN 152 - 6 Kms from Amboise
towards Blois - 37530 Limeray

☎ +033(0)2.47.30.13.50 Fax:+033(0)2.47.30.17.32
www.camping-jardinbotanique.com

LINDOIS, LE CHARENTE

Étang
16130 ☎ 545650267 🖪 545650896
website www.campingdeletang.com
Well-shaded site with a natural lake, ideal for swimming and fishing with a small beach.
➮ *From Rochefoucauld D13 towards Montemboeuf.*
Open Apr-Nov **Site** 10HEC 🌤 ♣ ♣ **Prices** ♠ 3.50-4.50 pitch 5.50-7
Facilities ⋒ 🗐 ⊙ ♣ ℗ **Services** 🕯 ❍ ➕ 🖫 **Leisure** ⇆ L
Off-site 🗐 ⌀ ⚓

LION D'ANGERS, LE MAINE-ET-LOIRE

CM Frénes
49220 ☎ 241953156
A municipal site on the banks of the River Oudon, 300m from the town centre.
➮ *NE on N162.*
Open May-Sep **Site** 2HEC 🌤 ♣ **Prices** ♠ 1.79-11 🚃 4 pitch 1.90-11
Facilities ⋒ ⊙ ♣ ℗ **Leisure** ⇆ R **Off-site** 🗐 🕯 ❍ ⌀ ⚓ ⇆P ➕

LONGEVILLE VENDÉE

Brunelles
Le Bouil, 85560 ☎ 251335075 🖪 251339821
e-mail camping@les-brunelles.com
website ww.camp-atlantique.com
A well-appointed site in a wooded location 0.7km from the beach.
➮ *On coast between Longeville & Jard-sur-Mer.*
Open 3 Mar-9 Sep **Site** 3HEC 🌤 ♣ ♣ 🚃 **Prices** pitch 15-21 (incl 2 persons) 🚃 (static)110-590 **Facilities** ⋒ 🗐 ⊙ ♣ ⌀ ⚓ ℗ **Services** 🕯 ❍
➕ 🖫 **Leisure** ⇆ P **Off-site** ⇆S

Clos des Pins
Les Conches, 85560 ☎ 251903169 🖪 251903068
e-mail philip.jones@freesbee.fr **website** campinginfrance.com
A family run site with good facilities, 250m from a sandy beach.
➮ *Between Longeville & La Tranche.*
Open Apr-Sep **Site** 1.6HEC 🌤 ♣ 🌤 ♣ 🚃 Å **Facilities** ⋒ 🗐 ⊙ ♣ ⚓ ℗
Services 🕯 ❍ ➕ 🖫 **Leisure** ⇆ P **Off-site** ⌀ ⇆S

Jarny Océan
Le Bouil, 85560 ☎ 251334221 🖪 251339537
e-mail jarny-ocean@wanadoo.fr
Subdivided well-tended meadow, with a holiday complex of the same name and shopping facilities. A forest path leads 0.8km to the sea.
➮ *Off D105 3km S of Longeville.*
Open May-Sep **Site** 7.6HEC 🌤 ♣ 🚃 🚃 **Facilities** ⋒ 🗐 ⊙ ♣ ℗
Services 🕯 ❍ ➕ 🖫 **Leisure** ⇆ P **Off-site** ❍ ⌀ ⇆S

AT CONCHES, LES (4KM S)

Dunes
av de la Plage, 85560 ☎ 251333293 🖪 251903861
e-mail contact@camping-lesdunes.com
website www.camping-lesdunes.com
Well-kept site among dunes in a pine forest.
➮ *6km S of Longeville on D105.*
Open May-Sep **Site** 5HEC ⚓ ♣ 🚃 **Facilities** ⋒ 🗐 ⊙ ♣ ⌀ ℗
Services 🕯 ❍ ➕ 🖫 **Leisure** ⇆ P **Off-site** ❍ ⇆PRS

See advertisement on page 112

LUCHÉ-PRINGÉ SARTHE

CM de la Chabotière
Place des Tilleuls, 72800 ☎ 243451000 🖪 243451000
e-mail lachabotiere@ville-luche-prange.fr
website www.ville-luche-prange.fr
Site by a river just 100m from the village and a short drive from several Loire chateaux. Large marked sites on terraces above the river, and most cars are kept in a car park to ensure safe play areas for children.
Open Apr-15 Oct **Site** 2HEC 🌤 ♣ 🚃 Å **Prices** ♠ 2.05-3.05
🚃 1.55 pitch 2.05 **Facilities** ⋒ ⊙ ♣ ℗ **Services** ➕ 🖫 **Leisure** ⇆ PR
Off-site 🗐 🕯 ❍ ⌀ ⚓

Facilities 🗐 shop ⋒ shower ⊙ electric points for razors ♣ electric points for caravans ℗ parking by tents permitted ❻ compulsory separate car park
Services ❍ café/restaurant 🕯 bar ⌀ Camping Gaz International ⚓ gas other than Camping Gaz ➕ first aid facilities 🖫 laundry
Leisure ⇆ swimming L-Lake P-Pool R-River S-Sea **Off-site** All facilities within 2km

LUSIGNAN VIENNE

CM Vauchiron

Vauchiron, 86600 ☎ 549433008 ▤ 549436119

e-mail lusignan@cg86.fr

A quiet wooded location beside the River Vonne with good facilities.

➲ *0.5km NE on N11.*

Open 15 Apr-14 Oct **Site** 4HEC ♨ ♣ ⚘ **Facilities** ⋔ ⊙ ⊑ ⊛ **Services** ⊠
Leisure ⚲ R **Off-site** ⚑ ⌗ 🍴 ∅ ⚱ ⊞

LUYNES INDRE-ET-LOIRE

CM Granges

Les Granges, 37230 ☎ 247557905

e-mail campinglesgrangesluynes@yahoo.fr

Quiet site close to the village. Ideal for visiting historical sites, fishing, and wine tasting

➲ *S via D49.*

Open Jun-1 Oct **Site** 0.8HEC ♨ ♣ ⚘ **Prices** ⚹ 3.50 pitch 3.50
Facilities ⋔ ⊙ ⊑ ∅ ⊛ **Services** ⊞ ⊠ **Off-site** ⚑ ⌗ 🍴 ⚲PR

MACHÉ VENDÉE

Val de Vie

r du Stade, 85190 ☎ 251602102 ▤ 251602102

e-mail campingvaldevie@aol.com

Open May-Sep **Site** 2.2HEC ♨ ♣ ⚘ **Prices** pitch 14.40-18 (incl 2 persons) **Facilities** ⋔ ⊙ ⊑ ⊛ **Services** ⊞ ⊠ **Leisure** ⚲ P
Off-site ⚑ ⌗ 🍴

MAGNAC-BOURG HAUTE-VIENNE

Écureuils

rte de Limoges, 87380 ☎ 555008028 ▤ 555004909

e-mail mairie.magnac-bourg@wanadoo.fr

A grassy site close to the historic village

➲ *25km S on N20.*

Open Apr-Sep **Site** 1.3HEC ♨ ♣ **Prices** ⚹ 3.50 pitch 3.50 **Facilities** ⋔ ⊙ ⊑ ⊛ **Services** ⊠ **Off-site** ⚑ ⌗ 🍴 ∅ ⚱ ⊞

MANSIGNÉ SARTHE

CM de la Plage

rte du Plessis, 72510 ☎ 243461417 ▤ 243461665

e-mail campingmansigne@wanadoo.fr

A holiday complex set in extensive parkland around a 24-hectare lake with good recreational facilities.

➲ *On D13, 4km from D307.*

Open Etr-Oct **Site** 3.4HEC ♨ ♣ ⚘ **Facilities** ⋔ ⊙ ⊑ ⊛ **Services** ⌗ 🍴
⊞ ⊠ **Leisure** ⚲ LP **Off-site** ⚑ ∅ ⚱

MARANS CHARENTE-MARITIME

CM Le Bois Dinot

rte de Nantes, 17230 ☎ 546011051 ▤ 546011051

e-mail campingboisdinot.marans@wanadoo.fr

website www.ville-marans.fr

Separate car park for arrivals after 22.00 hrs.

➲ *Via N137.*

Open May-Sep **Site** 6HEC ♨ ♣ ⚘ **Prices** ⚹ 3.10 ⚗ 1.90 ⊟ 1.90
Facilities ⋔ ⊙ ⊑ ⊛ **Services** ⊞ ⊠ **Off-site** ⚑ ⌗ 🍴 ∅ ⚱ ⚲PR

MARÇON SARTHE

Lac des Varennes

72340 ☎ 4243441372 ▤ 4243445431

e-mail camping.des.varennes.marcon@wanadoo.fr

website www.ville-marcon.fr

An attractive site bordering the lake in the heart of the Loire valley, with spacious pitches and well-maintained installations.

Open 25 Mar-10 Oct **Site** 7HEC ♨ ♣ ⚘ ⊟ **Facilities** ⋔ ⚑ ⊙ ⊑ ⊛
Services ⌗ 🍴 ⊞ ⊠ **Leisure** ⚲ LR **Off-site** ∅

MATHES, LES CHARENTE-MARITIME

Charmettes

av de la Palmyre, 17570 ☎ 546225096 ▤ 546236970

website www.camping-lescharmettes.com

Large site with plenty of organised activities. 5km from the beach.

➲ *1km SW via D141.*

Open 15 Apr-Sep **Site** 34HEC ♨ ♣ ♨ ⚘ ⊛ **Facilities** ⋔ ⚑ ⊙ ⊑ ⊛
⊕ **Services** ⌗ 🍴 ⊞ ⊠ **Leisure** ⚲ PS

Estanquet

17570 ☎ 546224732 ▤ 546225146

website www.campingestanquet.com

See advertisement on page 113

Orée du Bois

225 rte de la Bouverie, La Fouasse, 17570 ☎ 546224243 🖷 546225476

e-mail info@camping-oree-du-bois.fr

website www.oree-du-bois.fr/camping

A family site in a pine and oak forest, 5 minutes from the beach.

➲ *3.5km NW.*

Open 28 Apr-167 Sep Site 6HEC ♨ ♨ 🏕 Prices pitch 16-34 (incl 2 persons) pp7 Facilities 🌳 🍴 ⊙ 🚿 ⊘ 🚮 ⑫ 🅿 Services 🕯 🍽 🛟 ⚕ 🛋 Leisure ⚓ P Off-site ⚓S

Pinède

2103 rte de la Fouasse, 17570 ☎ 546224513 🖷 546225021

e-mail contact@campinglapinede.com

website www.campinglapinede.com

A modern family site in a wooded area around the large Aquatic Park. Excellent sports facilities. Entertainment available in July and August.

➲ *3km NW.*

Open Apr-Sep Site 7HEC ♨ ♨ ⚘ 🏕 Prices pitch 19-36.80 (incl 2 persons) Facilities 🌳 🍴 ⊙ 🚿 ⑫ Services 🕯 🍽 🛟 ⚕ 🛋 Leisure ⚓ P

MAYENNE MAYENNE

CM du Gue St Leonard

r St-Léonard, 53100 ☎ 243045714 🖷 243302110

e-mail webmestre@mairie-mayenne.fr

website www.mairie-mayenne.fr

Wooded location on the River Mayenne.

➲ *0.8km from town centre near N12.*

Open 15 Mar-Sep Site 1.8HEC ♨ ♨ 🏕 Facilities 🌳 🍴 ⊙ 🚿 ⑫ Services 🍽 🛟 🛋 Leisure ⚓ P Off-site 🍴 🕯 🍽 ⊘ 🚮 🛟

See advertisement on this page

MEMBROLLE-SUR-CHOISILLE, LA INDRE-ET-LOIRE

CM

rte de Foudettes, 37390 ☎ 247412040

On level meadow in sports ground beside River Choisille.

➲ *N on N138 Le Mans road.*

Open May-Sep Site 1.5HEC ♨ ♨ Prices pitch 10 (incl 2 persons) pp2.80 Facilities 🌳 ⊙ 🚿 ⑫ Services 🛟 🛋 Leisure ⚓ R Off-site 🍴 🕯 🍽 ⚓L

MERVENT VENDÉE

Chêne Tord

34 chemin du Chêne Tord, 85200 ☎ 251002063 🖷 251002794

e-mail mervent.aventures@tele2.fr

website www.vacances-en-vendee.com/lechenetord

A well-appointed site 200m from a large artificial lake in the heart of the Mervent forest.

➲ *Via D99.*

Open Apr-Nov Site 4HEC ♨ ♨ 🏕 🚐 Prices ⚡ 2.20-2.70 🚐 1.35-1.75 pitch 4.50-6 🚐 (static)243-252 Facilities 🌳 ⊙ 🚿 ⑫ Services 🛋 Off-site 🍴 🕯 🍽 ⚓LR

MESLAND LOIR-ET-CHER

Parc du Val de Loire

rte de Fleuray, 41150 ☎ 254702718 🖷 254702171

e-mail parcduvaldeloire@wanadoo.fr

website www.parcduvaldeloire.com

A sheltered position among Touraine vineyards with good recreational facilities.

➲ *1.5km W between A10 & N152.*

Open 30 Mar-29 Sep Site 13.6HEC ♨ ♨ 🏕 Prices pitch 14-24.50 (incl 2 persons) Facilities 🌳 🍴 ⊙ 🚿 ⊘ 🚮 ⑫ 🅿 Services 🕯 🍽 🛟 🛋 Leisure ⚓ P

France

Facilities 🏠 shop 🌳 shower ⊙ electric points for razors 🚘 electric points for caravans ⑫ parking by tents permitted 🅿 compulsory separate car park
Services 🍽 café/restaurant 🕯 bar ⊘ Camping Gaz International 🚮 gas other than Camping Gaz 🛟 first aid facilities 🛋 laundry
Leisure ⚓ swimming L-Lake P-Pool R-River S-Sea Off-site All facilities within 2km

MESQUER LOIRE-ATLANTIQUE

Au Soir d'Été

44420 ☎ 240425726 🖷 251739776
e-mail nadine-houssais@wanadoo.fr
website www.camping-soirdete.com
Open 26 Mar-Oct **Site** 1.5HEC 😃 😃 🏚 **Facilities** ↾ ⊙ ⌨ ♨ ⊕
Services ☎ 🍴 ⊞ 🖸 **Leisure** ⚓ P **Off-site** 🏖 🖉 ⚓ S

Beaupré

rte de Kervarin, Kercabellec, 44420 ☎ 240426748 🖷 2440426672
e-mail camping.beaupre@wanadoo.fr
A well-equipped site 0.5km from the beach.
➲ Signed on road between Mesquer & Quimiac.
Open 15 Jun-15 Aug **Site** 0.6HEC 😃 😃 🏚 🚐 **Facilities** ↾ ⊙ ⌨ ⊕
Services ⊞ 🖸 **Off-site** 🏖 🍴 🍴 🖉 ⚓ S

Château de Petit Bois

44420 ☎ 240426877 🖷 240426558
e-mail camping_du_petit_bois@wanadoo.fr
website www.campingdupetitbois.com
Set in the extensive grounds of an 18th-century château with shaded,
well-defined pitches.
Open Apr-Sep **Site** 10HEC 😃 😃 🏚 **Facilities** ↾ ⊙ ⊙ ⌨ ♨ ⊕
Services 🍴 🍴 🖸 **Leisure** ⚓ P **Off-site** 🖉 ⚓ S ⊞

Praderoi

alleé des Barges, Quimiac, 44420 ☎ 240426672 🖷 240426672
e-mail camping.praderoi@wanadoo.fr
website perso.wanadoo.fr/mtger.debonne
On level ground 70m from Lanseria beach.
➲ 300m from Quimiac.
Open 15 Jun-15 Sep **Site** 0.5HEC 😃 **Prices** pitch 13-16 (incl 2
persons) pp4 🚐 (static)230-340 **Facilities** ↾ ⊙ ⌨ ⊕ **Services** ⊞ 🖸
Off-site 🏖 🍴 🍴 🖉 ⚓ S

Welcome

r de Bel-Air, 44420 ☎ 240425085 🖷 240425085
e-mail lewelcom@club-internet.fr
website www.lewelcome.com
Pleasant wooded surroundings, 0.6km from the coast. Separate car
park for arrivals after 22.30 hrs.
➲ 1.8km NW via D352.
Open Apr-Oct **Site** 2HEC 😃 😃 🏚 🚐 **Prices** pitch 12-15 (incl 2 persons)
pp4-5 🚐 (static)180-400 **Facilities** ↾ ⊙ ⊙ ⌨ ⊕ **Services** 🖸
Leisure ⚓ P **Off-site** 🍴 🍴 🖉 ⚓ S ⊞

MESSE DEUX-SÈVRES

Grande Vigne

79120 ☎ 549293943
e-mail admin@grande-vigne.com
website www.grande-vigne.com
Flat orchard site bordered by fruit trees and set in rural countryside.
No boundaries or marked pitches as only 5 pitches are let at any one
time.
➲ Off RN10 between Poitiers & Anguleme.
Open All year **Site** 0.5HEC 😃 😃 🏚 **Prices** pitch 14-18.50 **Facilities** ↾ ⊙
⌨ ⊕ **Services** 🖸 **Leisure** ⚓ P

MISSILLAC LOIRE-ATLANTIQUE

CM des Platanes

10 r du Château, 44780 ☎ 240883888
➲ 1km W via D2, 50m from the lake.
Open Jul-Aug **Site** 2HEC 😃 😃 **Prices** pitch 7.55 (incl 2 persons)
Facilities ↾ ⊙ ⌨ ⊕ **Services** 🖸 **Off-site** 🏖 🍴 🍴 ⊞

MONTARGIS LOIRET

Forêt

rte de Paucourt, 45200 ☎ 238980020
Set in the forest of Montargis.
➲ 1.5km NE near station & stadium.
Open Feb-Nov **Site** 5.5HEC 😃 😃 **Facilities** ↾ ⊙ ⌨ ⊕ **Services** ⊞ ⊞
Off-site 🏖 🍴 🍴 🖉 🍴 ⚓ LPR

MONTGIVRAY INDRE

CM Solange Sand

2 r du Pont, 36400 ☎ 254061036 🖷 254061039
e-mail mairie.montgivray@wanadoo.fr
A pleasant riverside site in the grounds of a château.
Open 15 Mar-15 Oct **Site** 1HEC 😃 😃 **Prices** ⚘ 1.95 pitch 2.77
Facilities ↾ ⊙ ⌨ 🖉 ⊕ **Services** 🖸 **Leisure** ⚓ R **Off-site** 🏖 🍴 🍴 🖉 🍴

MONTLOUIS-SUR-LOIRE INDRE-ET-LOIRE

Peupliers

37270 ☎ 247508190 🖷 380379583
e-mail aquadis1@wanadoo.fr
website www.aquadis-loisirs.com
On level meadow.
➲ 1.5km W on N751, next to swimming pool near railway
bridge.
Open Apr-Oct **Site** 6HEC 😃 😃 🏚 **Prices** pitch 14.70 (incl 2 persons)
pp4.20 **Facilities** ↾ 🏖 ⊙ ⌨ 🖉 ♨ ⊕ **Services** 🍴 🍴 ⊞ 🖸 **Leisure** ⚓ R
Off-site ⚓ R

MONTMORILLON VIENNE

CM Allochon

av F-Tribot, 86500 ☎ 549910233 🖷 549915826
e-mail montmorillon@cg86.fr
A well-equipped municipal site close to the river and 1.5km from the
town centre.
➲ SE via D54.
Open Mar-Oct **Site** 2HEC 😃 😃 **Prices** ⚘ 1.20 🚗 0.71 pitch 0.71
Facilities ↾ ⊙ ⌨ ⊕ **Services** 🖸 **Off-site** 🏖 🍴 🍴 🖉 🍴 ⚓ PR ⊞

MONTSOREAU MAINE-ET-LOIRE

Isle Verte

av de la Loire, 49730 ☎ 241517660 🖷 241510883
e-mail isleverte@cvtloisirs.co.uk
website www.campingisleverte.com
Wooded surroundings beside the River Loire.
➲ On D947 between road & river.
Open Apr-Sep **Site** 2HEC 😃 😃 🏚 ⚑ **Prices** ⚘ 3-3.20 pitch 12.90-16.80
Facilities ↾ ⊙ ⌨ 🍴 ⊕ **Services** 🍴 🍴 ⊞ 🖸 **Leisure** ⚓ P
Off-site 🏖 🖉 ⚓ R

Site 6HEC (site size) 😃 grass ⚌ sand 😃 stone ♣ little shade ♣ partly shaded ♣ mainly shaded 🏚 bungalows for hire
🚐 caravans for hire Ⓐ tents for hire ⊗ no dogs **Prices** ⚘ adult per night 🚗 car per night pp per person per night 🚐 caravan per night
Ⓐ tent per night 🚐 (static)-caravan hire per week

MOUTIERS-EN-RETZ, LES LOIRE-ATLANTIQUE

Domaine du Collet
44760 ☎ 240214092 ⓘ 240214512
e-mail info@domaine-du-collet.com
website www.domaine-du-collet.com
Open 30 Mar-Sep **Site** 5HEC 😊 ✿ 🏠 Å **Prices** pitch 25 **Facilities** 🍴 🛆
😊 🔌 🔌 🚿 ⑨ **Services** 🍴 🍽 ➕ 🅸 **Leisure** 🏊 PR

Village de la Mer
18 r de Prigny, 44760 ☎ 240646590 ⓘ 251746317
e-mail info@village-mer.fr
website www.village-mer.fr
Quiet site close to a village and the beach
➲ *9km S of Pornic on D97.*
Open 15 Jun-15 Sep **Site** 7HEC 😊 ✿ 🏠 Å **Prices** pitch 16-27 (incl 2
persons) **Facilities** 🍴 😊 🔌 🔌 🚿 ⑨ **Services** 🍴 🍽 🅸 **Leisure** 🏊 P
Off-site 🛆 🍽 🔌 🏊S

MUIDES-SUR-LOIRE LOIR-ET-CHER

Château des Marais
27 r de Chambord ☎ 254870542 ⓘ 254870543
website www.chateau-des-marais.com
A wooded campsite set in the spacious grounds of an old stone
manor house. The campsite retains the atmosphere of a country
estate and the waterpark features waterslides and spacious sun
terraces.
➲ *Autoroute A10 Orleans-Blois, exit 16*
Open 12 May-14 Sep **Site** 12HEC 😊 🏠 🔌 **Prices** pitch 23-31 (incl 2
persons) pp6 🔌 (static)212 **Facilities** 🍴 🛆 😊 🔌 **Services** 🍴 🍽
Leisure 🏊 P

See advertisement on this page

NANTES LOIRE-ATLANTIQUE

Petit Port
bd du Petit Port 21, 44300 ☎ 240744794 ⓘ 240742306
e-mail camping-petit-port@nge-nantes.fr
website www.nge-nantes.fr
A modern, well-kept park by a river.
➲ *In N of town near Parc du Petit Port. N137 Rennes road from
town centre & signed.*
Open All year **Site** 8.5HEC 😊 ✿ 🏠 **Prices** 🏕 2.65-3.25 Å 3.30-4.10 pitch
6.80-8.60 **Facilities** 🍴 🛆 😊 🔌 ⑨ **Services** ➕ 🅸 **Off-site** 🍴 🍽 🚿 🏊PR

NEUVILLE-SUR-SARTHE SARTHE

Vieux Moulin
72190 ☎ 243253182 ⓘ 243253811
e-mail info@lemanscamping.net
website www.lemanscamping.net
A pleasant site with good recreational facilities, close to the village.
➲ *Via N138 & D197.*
Open Jul-Aug **Site** 4.8HEC 😊 ✿ 🏠 **Prices** pitch 13 (incl 2 persons)
Facilities 🍴 🛆 😊 🔌 🔌 🚿 ⑨ **Services** ➕ 🅸 **Leisure** 🏊 P
Off-site 🍴 🍽 🏊R

Château des Marais
41500 Muides sur Loire
Tel. : +33 2 54 87 05 42
Fax : +33 2 54 87 05 43
www.chateau-des-marais.com
chateau.des.marais@wanadoo.fr

NIBELLE LOIRET

Nibelle
rte de Boiscommun, 45340 ☎ 238322355 ⓘ 238320387
website www.parc-nibelle.com
Level site in the clearing of an oak woodland.
➲ *Off D921 E to Nibelle, signed.*
Open Mar-Nov **Site** 12HEC 😊 ✿ 🏠 🔌 **Prices** 🏕 12 🚗 2-3 🔌 4 Å 2-4
🔌 (static)206-258 **Facilities** 🍴 😊 🔌 🚿 ⑨ **Services** 🍴 🍽 🅸 **Leisure** 🏊
P **Off-site** 🛆 🍽 🔌

NOIRMOUTIER, ILE DE VENDÉE

BARBÂTRE

Onchères
85630 ☎ 251398131 ⓘ 251397365
Quiet setting on dunes, south of village on D95.
Open Apr-Sep **Site** 10HEC 😊 ✿ **Facilities** 🍴 🛆 😊 🔌 🔌 🚿 ⑨
Services 🍴 🍽 ➕ 🅸 **Leisure** 🏊 PS

GUERINIERE, LA

Caravan'Ile
BP N4, 85680 ☎ 251395029 ⓘ 251358685
e-mail contact@caravanile.com
website www.caravanile.com
Located near fine sand beaches. Swimming pool with aquatic
toboggan.
Open Mar-15 Nov **Site** 9HEC 😊 ✿ 🏠 **Prices** 🏕 2.90-4.50 pitch 13.50-
21.50 **Facilities** 🍴 🛆 😊 🔌 ⑨ **Services** 🍴 🍽 🅸 **Leisure** 🏊 PS

France

NOTRE-DAME-DE-MONTS VENDÉE

Beauséjour
85690 ☎ 251588388
➲ *2km NW on D38.*
Open Etr-Sep **Site** 1.3HEC ❤ ♣ ❤ ⛺ **Facilities** ⛬ ⊙ ❤ ∅ ❷ **Services** ➕ 🖥 **Off-site** 🏠 🍴 ⚓S

Grand Jardin
Le Grand Jardin, 50 r de la Barre, 85690 ☎ 228112175
e-mail contact@legrandjardin.net
website www.legrandjardin.net
A family site in a picturesque location facing the Ile d'Yeu. Modern sanitary installations and plenty of sports facilities. 1km from the beach.
➲ *0.6km N.*
Open All year **Site** 4HEC ❤ ♣ ❤ ⛺ **Prices** ♙ 3.10-4.50 ⛂ 2 pitch 17-24 (incl 2 persons) ⛂ (static)260-590 **Facilities** ⛬ ⊙ ❤ ⚒ ❷ 🅿 **Services** 🖥 🍴 ➕ 🖥 **Leisure** ⚓ PR **Off-site** 🏠 ∅ ⚓S

OLÉRON, ILE D' CHARENTE-MARITIME
BOYARDVILLE

Signol
17190 ☎ 546470122 🖨 546472346
e-mail contact@signol.com
website www.signol.com
Attractive surroundings in a pine forest, close to the village centre and 0.8km from the beach.
➲ *D126 W from town by AVIA fuel station, signed for 0.6km.*
Open Apr-Sep **Site** 8HEC ⚪ ❤ ⛺ ⛂ **Facilities** ⛬ ⊙ ❤ ❷ **Services** 🖥 ➕ 🖥 **Leisure** ⚓ P **Off-site** 🏠 ⚓S

CHÂTEAU-D'OLÉRON, LE

Airotel d'Oléron
Domaine de Montreavail, 17480 ☎ 546476182 🖨 546477967
e-mail info@camping-airotel-oleron.com
website www.camping-airotel-oleron.com
A peaceful, parklike setting 1km from the beach and the town centre.
➲ *Signed from town centre.*
Open Mar-1 Nov **Site** 4HEC ❤ ♣ ⛺ **Prices** pitch 13-21 (incl 2 persons) ⛂ (static)250-580 **Facilities** ⛬ 🏠 ⊙ ❤ ∅ ❷ ❷ **Services** 🖥 🍴 ➕ 🖥 **Leisure** ⚓ LPS

Brande
rte des Hu116tres, 17480 ☎ 546476237 🖨 546477170
e-mail info@camping-labrande.com
website www.camping-labrande.com
A family site with good facilities in beautiful surroundings.
➲ *2.5km NW, 250m from the sea.*
Open 15 Mar-15 Nov **Site** 5.5HEC ❤ ♣ ⚪ ❤ ⛺ **Prices** pitch 16-35 (incl 2 persons) **Facilities** ⛬ 🏠 ⊙ ❤ ∅ ❷ ❷ **Services** 🖥 🍴 ➕ 🖥 **Leisure** ⚓ P **Off-site** ⚓S

COTINIÈRE, LA

Tamaris
72 av des Pins, 17310 ☎ 546471051 🖨 546472796
Level site in a pleasant olive grove 150m from the sea.
➲ *W side of island. N of town.*
Open 15 Mar-15 Nov **Site** 5HEC ❤ ♣ ⛺ ⚠ **Facilities** ⛬ ⊙ ❤ ❷ ❷ **Services** 🖥 🍴 ➕ 🖥 **Leisure** ⚓ P **Off-site** 🏠 ∅ ⚓S

DOLUS-D'OLÉRON

Ostréa
rte des Huîtres, 17550 ☎ 546476236 🖨 546752001
e-mail camping.ostrea@wanadoo.fr
website www.camping-ostrea.com
A well-equipped site in wooded surroundings close to the beach.
➲ *3.5km NE.*
Open Apr-Sep **Site** 2HEC ❤ ⚪ ♣ ⛺ ⛂ **Prices** pp3.50-5 ⛂ (static)190-390 **Facilities** ⛬ 🏠 ⊙ ❤ ∅ ❷ ❷ **Services** 🖥 🍴 ➕ 🖥 **Leisure** ⚓ PS

DOMINO

International Rex
Domino, 17190 ☎ 546765597 🖨 546766788
Pleasant seaside site with good recreational facilities and access to the beach.
Open May-14 Sep **Site** 0.8HEC ⚪ ❤ ♣ ⛺ **Facilities** ⛬ 🏠 ⊙ ❤ ∅ ❷ **Services** 🖥 🍴 ➕ 🖥 **Leisure** ⚓ PS **Off-site** 🍴

ST-DENIS-D'OLÉRON

Phare Ouest
7 Impasse des Beaupins, 17650 ☎ 251975550 🖨 251289109
e-mail camping-apv@wanadoo.fr
website www.camping-apv.com
On level ground with direct access to the beach.
➲ *1km NW towards lighthouse.*
Open Apr-Sep **Site** 3.5HEC ❤ ♣ ⚪ ⛺ **Facilities** ⛬ 🏠 ⊙ ❤ ∅ ❷ ❷ **Services** 🖥 🍴 🖥 **Leisure** ⚓ S **Off-site** ➕

Site 6HEC (site size) ❤ grass ⚪ sand ♣ stone ♣ little shade ❤ partly shaded ⛺ mainly shaded ⛺ bungalows for hire ⛂ caravans for hire Ⓐ tents for hire ⊗ no dogs **Prices** ♙ adult per night ⛂ car per night pp per person per night ⛂ caravan per night Ⓐ tent per night ⛂ (static)-caravan hire per week

St-Georges-d'Oléron

Gros Joncs

17190 ☎ 546765229 🖷 546766774
e-mail camping.gros.joncs@wanadoo.fr
website www.camping-les-gros-joncs.com
Quiet location on undulating land in lovely pine woodland.
➲ *5km NW from La Cotinière towards Domino, 1km SW of St-Georges-d'Oléron.*
Open All year **Site** 5.2HEC 🐘 ➱ ♣ 🏠 **Prices** ♣ 5.60-11.20 pitch 14.70-40.10 (incl 2 persons) **Facilities** 🌣 🖻 ⊙ 🖴 🅿 ⑳ **Services** 🍴 🍽 🛨 🖭
Leisure ⚲ PS **Off-site** ⌀

Quatre Vents

La Jousselinière, 17190 ☎ 546756547 🖷 546361566
e-mail 4vents.oleron@wanado.fr
A peaceful site with good facilities.
➲ *3km E via N739.*
Open Mar-Nov **Site** 7.2HEC 🐘 ♣ 🏠 **Facilities** 🌣 🖻 ⊙ 🖴 🚿 ⑳
Services 🍴 🍽 🛨 🖭 **Leisure** ⚲ P **Off-site** ⚲S

Signol

av de Albatros, Boyardville, 17190 ☎ 546470122 🖷 546472346
e-mail contact@signol.com
website www.signol.com
Situated among pine and oak trees, 0.8km from a sandy beach.
Open Apr-Sep **Site** 8HEC 🐘 ➱ ♣ 🏠 🖴 ⊗ **Facilities** 🌣 ⊙ 🖴 🚿 🅿
Services 🍴 🍽 **Leisure** ⚲ PS **Off-site** ⌀

See advertisement on page 116

Suroît

rte Touristique Côte Ouest, l'Ileau, 17190 ☎ 546470725
e-mail info@camping-lesuroit.com
website www.camping-lesuroit.com
Level ground sheltered by dunes with fine modern facilities.
➲ *5km SW of town.*
Open Apr-Sep **Site** 5HEC 🐘 ➱ ♣ ♣ 🏠 **Prices** 🖴 2-3 pitch 15-22 (incl 2 persons) 🖴 (static)260-650 **Facilities** 🌣 🖻 ⊙ 🖴 ⌀ ⑳ **Services** 🍴 🍽 🛨
🖭 **Leisure** ⚲ PS **Off-site** 🚿

Verébleu

La Jousselinière, 17190 ☎ 546765770
website www.verebleu.tm.fr
➲ *1.7km SE via D273*
Open 28 May-11 Sep **Site** 7.5HEC 🐘 ♣ 🏠 ⊗ **Facilities** 🌣 🖻 ⊙ 🖴 ⌀ ⑳
🅿 **Services** 🍴 🍽 🛨 🖭 **Leisure** ⚲ P **Off-site** 🍽 🚿

St-Pierre-d'Oléron

Aqua Trois Masses

Le Marais Doux, 17310 ☎ 546472396 🖷 546751554
e-mail accueil@campingaqua3masses.com
website www.campingaqua3masses.com
A well-equipped site in a picturesque location 2.5km from the beach.
Open Apr-Sep **Site** 3HEC 🐘 ♣ 🏠 **Prices** pitch 14-22 (incl 2 persons) pp5
🖴 (static)230-720 **Facilities** 🌣 🖻 ⊙ 🖴 ⑳ **Services** 🍴 🍽 🛨 🖭
Leisure ⚲ LP **Off-site** ⚲S

Open from
the 1st of April till
the 30th of September

· Aquatic Park
· Heated swimming pools
· Paddling pool-Slide
· Playing-room
· Animation-Mini club

RENTAL OF COTTAGES MOBILE HOMES

· Direct access to the beach by a forest-path.
· Lots of cycling-tracks.
· At 5 minutes from the centre of Sables d'Olonne.

RD 80 - 85340 LES SABLES D'OLONNE
Phone: 02 51 33 10 59 · Fax: 02 51 33 15 16
www.l-oree.com · E-mail: loree@free.fr

Pierrière

18 rte de St-Georges, 17310 ☎ 546470829 🖷 546751282
e-mail camping-la-pierriere@wanadoo.fr
website www.camping-la-pierriere.com
A pleasant site in wooded surroundings with well-defined pitches.
➲ *NW towards St-Georges-d'Oléron.*
Open 9 Apr-18 Sep **Site** 4HEC 🐘 ➱ ♣ 🏠 **Facilities** 🌣 ⊙ 🖴 ⑳ **Services** 🍴
🍽 🖭 **Leisure** ⚲ P **Off-site** 🖻 🍽 ⌀ 🚿 ⚲S 🛨

OLIVET LOIRET

CM Olivet

r du Pont Bouchet, 45160 ☎ 238635394 🖷 238635896
Site lies partly on shaded peninsula, partly on open lawns beside river.
➲ *2km E, signed from village.*
Open Apr-Oct **Site** 1HEC 🐘 ➱ **Facilities** 🌣 🖻 ⊙ 🖴 ⌀ ⑳ **Services** 🛨 🖭

OLONNE-SUR-MER VENDÉE

Domain de l'Oree

rte des Amis de la Nature, 85340 ☎ 251331059 🖷 251331516
e-mail loree@free.fr
website www.l-oree.com
➲ *3km N.*
Open Apr-Sep **Site** 7HEC 🐘 ♣ 🏠 **Facilities** 🌣 🖻 ⊙ 🖴 ⌀ 🚿 ⑳
Services 🍴 🍽 🛨 🖭 **Leisure** ⚲ P **Off-site** ⚲LRS

See advertisement on this page

Facilities 🖻 shop 🌣 shower ⊙ electric points for razors 🖴 electric points for caravans ⑳ parking by tents permitted 🅿 compulsory separate car park
Services 🍽 café/restaurant 🍴 bar ⌀ Camping Gaz International 🚿 gas other than Camping Gaz 🛨 first aid facilities 🖭 laundry
Leisure ⚲ swimming L-Lake P-Pool R-River S-Sea **Off-site** All facilities within 2km

France

Loubine

1 rte de la Mer, 85340 ☎ 251331292 🗎 251331271

e-mail camping.la.loubine@wanadoo.fr

Situated on the edge of a forest bordering the beach.

➲ N via D87/D80.

Open 2 Apr-24 Sep **Site** 8HEC 🌣 🍃 🌣 ⊗ **Facilities** 🏲 🖻 ⊙ 🖻 🖉 ⊛ **Services** 🗒 🍽 🔄 🖾 **Leisure** ⊛ P **Off-site** ⊛S

Moulin de la Salle

r.des Moulin de la salle, 85340 ☎ 251959910 🗎 251969613

Pleasant surroundings close to the beach with good facilities.

➲ 2.7km W.

Open Apr-Oct **Site** 3.1HEC 🌣 🍃 🌣 **Facilities** 🏲 ⊙ 🖻 🛎 ⊛ **Services** 🗒 🍽 🔄 🖾 **Leisure** ⊛ P **Off-site** 🖻

ONZAIN LOIR-ET-CHER

Dugny

rte de Chambon-sur-Cisse, 41150 ☎ 254207066 🗎 254337169

e-mail info@dugny.fr

website www.dugny.fr

On a small lake, surrounded by farmland with well-marked pitches shaded by poplars.

➲ CD45 from Onzain for Chambon-sur-Cisse.

Open All year **Site** 10HEC 🌣 🍃 🌣 🌣 Å **Prices** 🕇 7-14 pitch 5.50-9 **Facilities** 🏲 🖻 ⊙ 🖻 🖉 🛎 ⊛ **Services** 🗒 🍽 🔄 🖾 **Leisure** ⊛ P

PALMYRE, LA CHARENTE-MARITIME

Bonne Anse Plage

17570 ☎ 546224090 🗎 546224230

e-mail bonne.anse@wanadoo.fr

website www.campingbonneanseplage.com

An extensive, gently undulating site in a pine wood, 400m from the beach.

➲ 1km from La Palmyre rdbt, signs for Ronce-les-Bains.

Open 17 May-3 Sep **Site** 17HEC 🌣 🍃 🌣 🌣 ⊗ **Prices** pitch 32.50 (incl 2 persons) **Facilities** 🏲 🖻 ⊙ 🖻 🖉 ⊛ **Services** 🗒 🍽 🔄 🖾 **Leisure** ⊛ P **Off-site** 🖉 🛎 ⊛S

Palmyr Océana

26 av des Mathes, 17570 ☎ 546224035 🗎 546236476

e-mail contact@palmyr-oceana.fr

website www.palmyr-oceana.fr

A well-equipped family site in a delightful wooded setting close to the beach. A variety of recreational facilities is available.

Open 26 Jun-4 Sep **Site** 17HEC 🌣 🍃 🌣 🌣 **Prices** 🕇 5 pitch 15-25 (incl 2 persons) 🚐 (static)310-430 **Facilities** 🏲 🖻 ⊙ 🖻 🛎 ⊛ **Services** 🗒 🍽 🔄 🖾 **Leisure** ⊛ P **Off-site** 🖉 ⊛RS

PERRIER, LE VENDÉE

CM de la Maison Blanche

85300 ☎ 251493923 🗎 251681430

A family site on level ground, with pitches divided by trees. 6km from the coast.

Open Jun-15 Sep **Site** 3.2HEC 🌣 🍃 🌣 **Prices** pitch 10-11.45 (incl 2 persons) pp3.50 **Facilities** 🏲 ⊙ 🖻 ⊛ **Services** 🖾 **Leisure** ⊛ PR **Off-site** 🖻 🗒 🍽 🖉 🛎 🔄

PIRIAC-SUR-MER LOIRE-ATLANTIQUE

Parc du Guibel

44420 ☎ 240235267 🗎 240155024

e-mail camping@parcduguibel.com

website www.parcduguibel.com

On level ground in a delightful wooded setting with good recreational facilities.

➲ 3.5km E via D52.

Open 5 Apr-27Sep **Site** 14HEC 🌣 🍃 🌣 🌣 **Facilities** 🏲 🖻 ⊙ 🖻 🛎 ⊛ **Services** 🗒 🍽 🔄 🖾 **Leisure** ⊛ P **Off-site** ⊛PS

PLAINE-SUR-MER, LA LOIRE-ATLANTIQUE

Tabardière

44770 ☎ 240215817 🗎 240210268

e-mail info@camping-la-tabardiere

website www.camping-la-tabardiere.com

A wooded, terraced site 3km from the sea.

➲ Off D13 between Pornic & La Plaine-sur-Mer.

Open Apr-Sep **Site** 6HEC 🌣 🍃 🌣 **Prices** 🕇 3.30-5.50 🚗 3.20 pitch 2.70-6.80 🚐 (static)170-600 **Facilities** 🏲 🖻 ⊙ 🖻 🖉 🛎 ⊛ **Services** 🗒 🍽 🔄 🖾 **Leisure** ⊛ P **Off-site** 🍽

PONS CHARENTE-MARITIME

Chardon

Chardon, 17800 ☎ 546950125

e-mail chardon2@wanadoo.fr

Quiet location on the edge of a small village, next to a farm.

➲ D732 W from Pons towards Royan, site 2.5km on left. Or A10 exit 36, towards Pons, site 0.8km on right.

Open Apr-Oct **Site** 1.6HEC 🌣 🍃 🌣 🌣 **Facilities** 🏲 🖻 ⊙ 🖻 ⊛ **Services** 🗒 🍽 🖾 **Off-site** ⊛R 🔄

PONT-L'ABBÉ-D'ARNOULT CHARENTE-MARITIME

Parc de la Garenne

24 av Bernard Chambenoit, 17250 ☎ 546970146

e-mail info@lagarenne.net

website www.lagarenne.net/gb

Peaceful site in a parkland setting. Shady individual pitches.

➲ Via A10, N137 & D18.

Open 15 May-25 Sep **Site** 2.8HEC 🌣 🍃 🌣 **Facilities** 🏲 ⊙ 🖻 ⊛ **Services** 🗒 🍽 🖾 **Leisure** ⊛ P **Off-site** 🖻 🗒 🍽 🖉 🛎 ⊛R 🔄

PONTS-DE-CÉ, LES MAINE-ET-LOIRE

Ile du Château

rte de Cholet, av de la Boire Salée, 49130

☎ 241446205 🗎 241446205

e-mail ile-du-chateau@wanadoo.fr

website www.camping-ileduchateau.com

Situated on a small island in the Loire close to the Château des Ponts-de-Cé. Separate car park for arrivals after 21.00 hrs.

➲ SW of Angers towards Cholet.

Open Apr-Sep **Site** 2.3HEC 🌣 🍃 🌣 🌣 Å **Prices** 🕇 2.40-2.80 pitch 10.10-12.60 (incl 2 persons) 🚐 (static)130-340 **Facilities** 🏲 🖻 ⊙ 🖻 🛎 ⊛ **Services** 🗒 🍽 🔄 🖾 **Leisure** ⊛ PR **Off-site** 🖉

Site 6HEC (site size) 🌣 grass 🍃 sand 🌣 stone 🍃 little shade 🌣 partly shaded 🌣 mainly shaded 🌣 bungalows for hire 🚐 caravans for hire Å tents for hire ⊗ no dogs **Prices** 🕇 adult per night 🚗 car per night pp per person per night 🚐 caravan per night Å tent per night 🚐 (static)-caravan hire per week

PORNIC LOIRE-ATLANTIQUE

Boutinardière

r de la Plage de la, Boutinardière, 44210
☎ 240820568 📠 240824901
e-mail info@boutinardiere.com
website www.camping-boutinardiere.com
The site has three outdoor pools with water slides. Also a heated indoor pool.
Open Apr-Sep **Site** 7.5HEC 🐃 ♣ 🏠 **Prices** pitch 13-29 (incl 2 persons) **Facilities** ↑ 🖾 ⊕ 🖼 ⌀ 🛒 ℗ **Services** 🍴 🍽 ➕ 🗄 **Leisure** ⚓ P
Off-site ⚓ S

See advertisement on this page

Sunelia le Patisseau

29 rue de Patisseau, 44210 ☎ 240821039 📠 240822281
e-mail contact@lepatisseau.com **website** www.lepatisseau.com
Wooded surroundings close to the beach with good recreational facilities.

➲ *3km E via D751.*

Open 8 Apr-6 Nov **Site** 4.3HEC 🐃 ♣ 🏠 🅰 **Prices** 🚲 4 pitch 24-39 (incl 2 persons) **Facilities** ↑ 🖾 ⊕ 🖼 ⌀ 🛒 ℗ **Services** 🍴 🍽 ➕ 🗄 **Leisure** ⚓
P **Off-site** ⚓ S *See advertisement on this page*

PORNICHET LOIRE-ATLANTIQUE

Bel Air

150 av de Bonne Source, 44380 ☎ 240611078
website www.belairpornichet.com
A pleasant wooded location 50m from the beach.
Open 24 Mar-1 Oct **Site** 6HEC 🐃 ♣ 🏠 **Prices** pitch 19-30 (incl 2 persons) **Facilities** ↑ 🖾 ⊕ 🖼 ⌀ 🛒 ℗ **Services** 🍴 🍽 🗄 **Leisure** ⚓ P
Off-site ⚓ S ➕

France

Facilities 🖾 shop ↑ shower ⊕ electric points for razors 🖼 electric points for caravans ℗ parking by tents permitted 🅿 compulsory separate car park
Services 🍽 café/restaurant 🍴 bar ⌀ Camping Gaz International 🛒 gas other than Camping Gaz ➕ first aid facilities 🗄 laundry
Leisure ⚓ swimming L-Lake P-Pool R-River S-Sea **Off-site** All facilities within 2km

France

Forges

98 rte de Villes Blais, 44380 ☎ 240611884 🖹 240601184
e-mail camping@campinglesforges.com
website www.campinglesforges.com
Wooded surroundings with well-defined pitches and good recreational facilities.
➲ *Via N171.*
Open Jul-Aug **Site** 2HEC ⚑ ♣ 🏠 **Prices** ↟ 6 pitch 8-0.50 **Facilities** ⋔ 🏠 ⊙ 🖪 ∅ ♨ ℗ **Services** ➕ 🗟 **Leisure** ≈ P **Off-site** ≈L

PRAILLES DEUX-SÈVRES

Lambon

Plan d'eau du Lambon, 78370 ☎ 549799041 🖹 549797862
e-mail comcanton.celles@wanadoo.fr
A peaceful rural site by a stretch of water, with a beach for bathing.
➲ *D948 from Niort towards Limoges, signs for Celle-sur-Belle, site 6km N.*
Open Jun-Sep **Site** 1HEC ⚑ ♣ 🏠 **Facilities** ⋔ ⊙ 🖪 ∅ ℗ **Services** ➕ 🗟 **Leisure** ≈ L **Off-site** ≈R

RÉ, ILE DE CHARENTE-MARITIME

ARS-EN-RÉ

Cormoran

rte de Radia, 17590 ☎ 546294604 🖹 546292936
e-mail info@cormoran.com
Situated on the edge of a forest 0.5km from village of Ars.
Facilities ⋔ ⊙ 🖪 **Services** ➕ 🍽 **Leisure** ≈ P

BOIS-PLAGE-EN-RÉ, LE

Antioche

17580 ☎ 546092386 🖹 546094334
A quiet, wooded area among dunes with direct access to the beach.
➲ *3.5km SE of village towards beach.*
Open 27 Mar-Sep **Site** 2.7HEC ⚑ ♣ 🏠 **Facilities** ⋔ 🏠 ⊙ 🖪 ℗ **Services** ➕ 🍽 ➕ 🗟 **Leisure** ≈ S **Off-site** ∅

Camping Interlude-Gros-Jonc

rte de Gros Jonc, 17580 ☎ 546091822 🖹 546092338
e-mail infos@interlude.fr
website www.interlude.fr
A pleasant wooded location 50m from the beach. The site has a fitness centre and can arrange guided tours of the area.
Open 31 Mar-11 Nov **Site** 7.5HEC ⚑ ♣ 🏠 **Prices** pitch 23-46 (incl 2 persons) **Facilities** ⋔ 🏠 ⊙ 🖪 ∅ ℗ **Services** ➕ 🍽 🗟 **Leisure** ≈ P **Off-site** ➕

COUARDE-SUR-MER, LA

Océan

50 Route d'Ars, 17670 ☎ 546298770 🖹 546299213
e-mail campingdelocean@wanadoo.fr
website www.campingocean.com
A fine position facing the sea with modern facilities.
➲ *3km NW on N735.*
Open Apr-Sep **Site** 8HEC ⚑ ♣ 🏠 **Prices** pitch 14.95-38.20 **Facilities** ⋔ 🏠 ⊙ 🖪 ♨ ℗ **Services** ➕ 🍽 ➕ 🗟 **Leisure** ≈ P **Off-site** ≈S

See advertisement on this page

Tour des Prises

rte d'Ars, B.P. 27 ☎ 546298482
e-mail camping@lesprises.com
website www.camping-la-tour-des-prises.com
Located in the heart of the island, next to a wood, in a peaceful and quiet location. The trees dotted throughout the site offer many shady areas.
Open 23 Mar-Sep **Site** 2.5HEC ⚑ ♣ 🏠 **Prices** pitch 14-32 **Facilities** ⋔ 🏠 ⊙ 🖪 ℗ ℗ **Services** 🍽 🗟 **Leisure** ≈ P **Off-site** 🍽 ∅ ≈S ➕

FLOTTE, LA

Blanche

Deviation de la Flotte, 17630 ☎ 546095243 🖹 546093694
website www.ileblanche.com
A popular family site in a wooded location.
➲ *N on D735 towards St-Martin.*
Open Apr-Sept **Site** 4HEC ♣ 🏠 **Facilities** ⋔ ⊙ 🖪 ∅ ℗ **Services** 🍽 🍽 ➕ 🗟 **Leisure** ≈ P **Off-site** 🏠 ≈S

Peupliers

17630 ☎ 546096235 🖹 546095976
e-mail contact@les-peupliers.com
website www.camp-atlantique.com
Siutated in a large, wooded park 0.8km from the sea with good sports facilities.
➲ *1.3km SE.*
Open 31 Mar-Sep **Site** 4.4HEC ♣ 🏠 **Prices** pitch 15-28 (incl 2 persons) **Facilities** ⋔ 🏠 ⊙ 🖪 ∅ ♨ ℗ **Services** 🍽 🍽 ➕ 🗟 **Leisure** ≈ P **Off-site** ≈S

Site 6HEC (site size) ⚑ grass ⚍ sand ⚑ stone ♣ little shade ♣ partly shaded 🏠 mainly shaded 🏠 bungalows for hire 🖪 caravans for hire Å tents for hire ⊗ no dogs **Prices** ↟ adult per night 🚗 car per night pp per person per night 🚐 caravan per night Å tent per night 🚐 (static)-caravan hire per week

Loix

Ilates

Le Petit Boucheau, rte du Grouin, 17111
☎ 546290543 ◎ 546290679
e-mail ilates@wanadoo.fr
➾ *E towards Pointe du Grouin, 0.5km from sea.*
Open Apr- 12 Nov **Site** 4.5HEC ⚊ ♣ ⚍ **Facilities** ⚘ ☉ ⊞ ℗
Services ⚑ ⑩ ⊞ ⚊ **Leisure** ⚈ P **Off-site** ⚐ ⚑ ⑩ ⊘ ⚌ ⚈S

Ste Marie-de-Re

Camping les Grenettes

rte du Boise Plage, 17740 ☎ 546302247 ◎ 546302464
Open All year **Site** 7HEC ⚊ ♣ ⚍ **Facilities** ⚘ ⚐ ☉ ⊞ ⊘ **Services** ⚑
⑩ ⊞ **Leisure** ⚈ PS

See advertisement on this page

St-Martin-de-Ré

CM

r du Rempart, 17410 ☎ 546092196 ◎ 546099418
Pleasant wooded surroundings at the foot of the 17th-century ramparts.
➾ *N, beyond La Flotte.*
Open 15 Feb-15 Nov **Site** 4HEC ⚊ ♣ ⚍ ⚍ **Prices** pitch 19 (incl 3 persons) pp4.20 **Facilities** ⚘ ⚐ ☉ ⚐ ℗ **Services** ⚑ ⑩ ⊞
Off-site ⚈S ⊞

Rille INDRE-ET-LOIRE

Huttopia Rille

lac de Pincemaille ☎ 247246297 ◎ 247246361
e-mail rille@huttopia.com
website www.huttopia.com
Site located at the edge of a lake surrounded by forest in the chateaux area of the Loire. Home to some 190 species of birds. Spacious shady piches.
Open Apr-Oct **Site** 7HEC ⚊ ⚊ ♣ ⚍ ⚍ ⚊ **Prices** ♦ 4.50-5.20 ⚍ 3.80-14
⚍ (static)350-690 **Facilities** ⚘ ⚐ ☉ ⚐ ⊘ ℗ **Services** ⚑ ⑩ ⊞
Leisure ⚈ LP

Rosiers, Les MAINE-ET-LOIRE

Val de Loire

6 r Ste-Baudruche, 49350 ☎ 241519433 ◎ 241518913
e-mail contact@camping-valdeloire.com
website www.camping-valdeloire.com
A comfortable site partly on the banks of the River Loire with good recreational facilities.
➾ *N via D59*
Open Apr-15 Oct **Site** 3HEC ⚊ ♣ ⚍ ⚍ ⚊ **Prices** pitch 13-1613 (incl 2 persons) pp3.90 ⚍ (static)230-520 **Facilities** ⚘ ⚐ ☉ ⚐ ⚌ ℗
Services ⚑ ⑩ ⊞ ⊞ **Leisure** ⚈ P **Off-site** ⑩ ⊘ ⚈R

Royan CHARENTE-MARITIME

AT MÉDIS (4KM NE)

Chênes

La Verdonneric, 17600 ☎ 546067138
Wooded location with good facilities. Separate car park for late arrivals after 22.00 hrs.
➾ *2km from Royan on Saintes-Royan road.*
Open All year **Site** 6.5HEC ⚊ ♣ ⚍ **Facilities** ⚘ ⚐ ☉ ⚐ ⊘ ⚌ ℗
Services ⚑ ⑩ ⊞ **Leisure** ⚈ P

AT PONTAILLAC (2KM NE ON D25)

Clairfontaine

allée des Peupliers, 17200 ☎ 546390811 ◎ 546381379
e-mail camping.clairfontaine@wanadoo.fr
website www.camping-clairfontaine.com
A well-equipped site in wooded surroundings 300m from the beach with a variety of recreational facilities.
Open 20 May-15 Sep **Site** 5HEC ⚊ ♣ **Facilities** ⚘ ⚐ ☉ ⚐ ⊘ ℗ ℗
Services ⚑ ⑩ ⊞ ⊞ **Leisure** ⚈ PS

Sables-D'Olonne, Les VENDÉE

Dune des Sables

La Paracou, 85100 ☎ 251323121 ◎ 251339404
e-mail chadotel@wanadoo.fr
website www.chadotel.com
A fine location facing the sea and close to the beach.
Open 7 Apr-23 Sep **Site** 6HEC ⚊ ♣ ⚍ **Prices** ♦ 5.80 pitch 14.50-24.20 (incl 2 persons) **Facilities** ⚘ ⚐ ☉ ⚐ ⊘ ⚌ ℗ **Services** ⚑ ⑩ ⊞ ⊞
Leisure ⚈ PS **Off-site** ⑩ ⚈S

Roses

1 r des Roses, 85100 ☎ 251951042 ◎ 251339404
e-mail chadotel@wanadoo.fr
website www.chadotel.com
A level site shaded by trees and bushes, 0.5km from the Remblai beach.
➾ *Close to town centre off D949.*
Open 7 Apr-3 Nov **Site** 3.5HEC ⚊ ♣ ⚍ **Prices** ♦ 5.80 pitch 14.50-24.20 (incl 2 persons) **Facilities** ⚘ ⚐ ☉ ⚐ ⊘ ⚌ ℗ **Services** ⚑ ⑩ ⊞
Leisure ⚈ P **Off-site** ⑩ ⚈S

Facilities ⚐ shop ⚘ shower ☉ electric points for razors ⚐ electric points for caravans ℗ parking by tents permitted ℗ compulsory separate car park
Services ⑩ café/restaurant ⚑ bar ⊘ Camping Gaz International ⚌ gas other than Camping Gaz ⊞ first aid facilities ⊞ laundry
Leisure ⚈ swimming L-Lake P-Pool R-River S-Sea **Off-site** All facilities within 2km

France

SABLÉ-SUR-SARTHE SARTHE

Hippodrome

allée du Quebec ☎ 243954261 🗎 24927482
e-mail camping-sable@wanadoo.fr
website www.sable-sur-sarthe.com
A peaceful wooded setting with a great variety of recreational facilities.
➲ *450m from town.*
Open Apr-Oct **Site** 3HEC 🌣 🌣 🛖 🚐 **Prices** 🛆 1.70-2.16 pitch 3.13-4.17
Facilities 🌰 🏬 ⊙ 🚐 ⌀ 🏵 **Services** 🖪 🖹 **Leisure** ⚓ P **Off-site** 🍴 🍽 🛆

ST-AIGNAN-SUR-CHER LOIR-ET-CHER

CM Cochards

41110 ☎ 254751559 🗎 254754472
e-mail camping@lescochards.com
website www.lescochards.com
On beautiful meadowland, completely surrounded by hedges.
➲ *1km from bridge on D17 towards Selles.*
Open Apr-15 Oct **Site** 4HEC 🌣 🌣 🛖 🚐 pitch 14.50-17.50 (incl 3 persons) pp3.70-4.20 🚐 (static)190-530 **Facilities** 🌰 🏬 ⊙ 🚐 🛆 🏵
Services 🍴 🍽 🖪 🖹 **Leisure** ⚓ P **Off-site** ⚓R

ST-AMAND-MONTROND CHER

CM Roche

chemin de la Roche, 18200 ☎ 248960936 🗎 248960936
e-mail camping-la-roche@wanadoo.fr
website www.ville-saint-armond-montrond.fr
A lovely wooded location between the River Cher and the Berry Canal with modern facilities.
➲ *1.5km SW near river & canal.*
Open Apr-Sep **Site** 4HEC 🌣 🌣 **Prices** 🛆 2.60 pitch 3.70 **Facilities** 🌰 ⊙
🚐 🏵 **Services** 🖪 🖹 **Leisure** ⚓ R **Off-site** 🏬 🍴 🍽 ⚓P

ST-ANDRÉ-DES-EAUX LOIRE-ATLANTIQUE

CM Les Chalands Fleuris

r du Stade, 44117 ☎ 240012040 🗎 240915424
e-mail chalfleu@club-internet.fr
website www.chalandsfleuris.com
A peaceful site with good facilities in the middle of a natural park.
➲ *1km NE.*
Open 15 Apr-15 Oct **Site** 4HEC 🌣 🌣 🛆 **Prices** 🛆 3.80 pitch 20
Facilities 🌰 🏬 ⊙ 🚐 🛆 🏵 **Services** 🖪 🖹 **Leisure** ⚓ P **Off-site** 🍴 🍽 ⌀

ST-AVERTIN INDRE-ET-LOIRE

CM Rives du Cher

61 r de Rochepinard, 37550 ☎ 247272760 🗎 247258289
e-mail contact@camping-lesrivesducher.com
website www.camping-lesrivesducher.com
Municipal site on the banks of the River Cher. Only caravans weighing less than 1000kg accepted.
➲ *400m N of town centre. 4km from Tours.*
Open Apr-15 Oct **Site** 3HEC 🌣 🌣 🛖 🚐 **Prices** 🛆 3.60 🚗 2.40 🚐 4.10
🛆 3.60 🚐 (static)160-295.40 **Facilities** 🌰 🏬 ⊙ 🚐 ⌀ 🛆 🏵 **Services** 🖪 🖹
Off-site 🍴 🍽 ⚓LPR

ST-BRÉVIN-LES-PINS LOIRE-ATLANTIQUE

CM Courance

100/110 av Ml-Foch, 44250 ☎ 240272291 🗎 240272291
e-mail info@campinglacourance.fr
website www.campinglacourance.fr
Set in a pine forest with direct access to the beach.
➲ *S off D305.*
Open All year **Site** 4HEC 🌣 🌣 🌣 🛖 🚐 🛆 **Prices** pitch 10.20-11.90 (incl 2 persons) 🚐 (static)185-595 **Facilities** 🌰 🏬 ⊙ 🚐 ⌀ 🏵 **Services** 🍴 🍽 🖪
🖹 **Leisure** ⚓ S **Off-site** 🛆 ⚓P

Site 6HEC (site size) 🌣 grass 🌣 sand 🌣 stone 🌣 little shade 🌣 partly shaded 🌣 mainly shaded 🛖 bungalows for hire
🚐 caravans for hire 🛆 tents for hire 🚫 no dogs **Prices** 🛆 adult per night 🚗 car per night pp per person per night 🚐 caravan per night
🛆 tent per night 🚐 (static)-caravan hire per week

Fief
57 chemin du Fief, 44250 ☎ 240272386 240644619
website www.lefief.com
A family site adjacent to a long sandy beach. The pitches are surrounded by trees and bushes and there are modern facilities.
➲ *From town centre onto Route Bleue to Centre Leclerc & 2nd right to site.*
Open Apr-15 Oct **Site** 7HEC **Prices** 4-8 pitch 14-32
Facilities **Services** **Leisure** P
Off-site S

See advertisement on page 122

ST-BRÉVIN-L'OCÉAN LOIRE-ATLANTIQUE

Pierres Couchées
L'Ermitage, 44250 ☎ 240278564 240849703
e-mail contact@pierres-couchees.com
website www.pierres-couchees.com
Extensive, well-screened terrain made up of three sites.
➲ *300m from sea. 2km on D213 toward Pornic.*
Open Apr-8 Oct **Site** 14HEC **Prices** pitch 16-26 (incl 2 persons) pp4-6.50 **Facilities** **Services**
Leisure P **Off-site** S

See advertisement on this page

ST-CYR VIENNE

Flower du Lac
86130 ☎ 549625722 549522858
e-mail contact@lacdesaintcyr.com
website www.lacdesaintcyr.com
A delightful setting in a spacious park beside a lake. The Futuroscope is within easy reach via the A10.
➲ *1.5km NE via D4/D82.*
Open Apr-Sep **Site** 5HEC **Prices** pitch 10-21 (incl 2 persons) pp2.60-5.50 **Facilities** **Services**
Leisure L

SAINTES CHARENTE-MARITIME

Au Fill de l'Eau
6 r de Courbiac, 17100 ☎ 546930800 546936188
Site lies beside the River Charente, 0.9km from the town centre.
➲ *1km on D128.*
Open May-Oct **Site** 7HEC **Prices** 3.35-4.55 pitch 4.30-4.30 (static)300-500 **Facilities** **Services**
Leisure PR **Off-site**

ST-FLORENT-LE-VIEIL MAINE-ET-LOIRE

Ile Batailleuse
44370 ☎ 240834501
e-mail serge.rabec@tiscali.fr
➲ *6km SE. N of Lac du Boudon.*
Open Apr-16 Nov **Site** 2.7HEC **Prices** 7-8.50 pitch 7 (static)250 **Facilities** **Services** **Leisure** R
Off-site P

France

Facilities shop shower electric points for razors electric points for caravans parking by tents permitted compulsory separate car park
Services café/restaurant bar Camping Gaz International gas other than Camping Gaz first aid facilities laundry
Leisure swimming L-Lake P-Pool R-River S-Sea **Off-site** All facilities within 2km

France

ST-GAULTIER INDRE

Oasis du Berry

r de la Pierre Plate, 36800 ☎ 254471704
e-mail campoasisduberry@aol.com
website www.campoasisduberry.com
Open All year **Site** 2.5HEC ꠥ ♨ ☎ ♣ ▲ **Facilities** ⋔ ⊙ ⊕ ⌀ ⍟
Services ☂ ⍟⍥ ⊞ ⍟ **Leisure** ♣ P **Off-site** ⍨ ♣R

ST-GEORGES-DE-DIDONNE CHARENTE-MARITIME

Bois Soleil

2 av de Suzac, 17110 ☎ 546050594 ▤ 546062743
e-mail camping.bois.soleil@wanadoo.fr
website www.bois-soleil.com
Pitches lie on different levels. Direct access to the beach.
⮩ *2.5km S of town on D25 Meschers road.*
Open 31 Mar-4 Nov **Site** 9HEC ꠥ ♨ ☎ **Prices** pitch 14-34 (incl 2 persons) pp3.50-7 ♨ (static)200-940 **Facilities** ⋔ ⍟⊙⊕⌀⌀⍟ **Services** ☂ ⍟⍥ ⊞ ⍟ **Leisure** ♣ PS

Ideal Camping No 1

Av de Suzac, 17110 ☎ 546052904 ▤ 546063236
e-mail info@ideal-camping.com
website www.ideal-camping.com
A well-equipped, peaceful site in a pine forest 200m from Suzac beach.
⮩ *W of St-Georges-de-Didonne via D25.*
Open 28 Apr-9 Sep **Site** 8HEC ꠥ ♨ ☎ ♨ ⊗ **Prices** pitch 14.50-23 (incl 3 persons) ♨ (static)274-630 **Facilities** ⋔ ⍟⊙⊕⌀⌀⍟⍟ **Services** ☂ ⍟⍥ ⊞ ⍟ **Leisure** ♣ P **Off-site** ⍨S

ST-GEORGES-LÈS-BAILLARGEAUX VIENNE

Futuriste

86130 ☎ 549524752 ▤ 549372333
e-mail camping-le-futuriste@wanadoo.fr
website www.camping-le-futuriste.fr
An elevated position having fine views over the Parc du Furturoscope and the Clain valley. Booking advised for June to August.
Open All year **Site** 4HEC ꠥ ♨ ☎ **Prices** ♦ 1.80-2.50 pitch 13.50-18.50 (incl 3 persons) **Facilities** ⋔ ⍟⊙⊕⌀ ⍟ **Services** ☂ ⍟⍥ ⍟ **Leisure** ♣ LP **Off-site** ⊞

ST-GILLES-CROIX-DE-VIE VENDÉE

Bahamas Beach

168 rte des Sables, 85800 ☎ 251546916 ▤ 251339404
e-mail chadotel@wanadoo.fr
website www.chadotel.com
Site lies 0.6km from the beach.
⮩ *2km from town centre*
Open 7 Apr-23 Sep **Site** 5HEC ꠥ ♨ ☎ ♨ **Prices** pitch 14.50-24.20 (incl 2 persons) pp5.50 **Facilities** ⋔ ⍟⊙⊕⌀ ⍟ **Services** ☂ ⊞ ⍟ **Leisure** ♣ PS **Off-site** ⍨S

Domaine de Beaulieu

Givrand, 85800 ☎ 251555946 ▤ 251339404
e-mail chadotel@wanadoo.fr
website www.chadotel.com
⮩ *4km from town. 1km from beach.*
Open 7 Apr-23 Sep **Site** 7HEC ꠥ ♨ ☎ ♨ **Prices** pitch 12-23.20 (incl 2 persons) pp5.80 **Facilities** ⋔ ⍟⊙⊕⌀⌀ ⍟ **Services** ☂ ⍟⍥ ⊞ ⍟ **Leisure** ♣ PS **Off-site** ♣R

ST-HILAIRE-DE-RIEZ VENDÉE

Biches

rte de Notre-Dame-de-Riez, 85270 ☎ 251543882 ▤ 251543074
e-mail campingdesbiches@wanadoo.fr
website www.campingdesbiches.com
A well-equipped site in a pine forest and close to the sea.
⮩ *2km N.*
Open 15 May-15 Sep **Site** 10HEC ꠥ ♨ ☎ **Facilities** ⋔ ⍟⊙⊕⌀⌀⍟ **Services** ☂ ⍟⍥ ⊞ ⍟ **Leisure** ♣ P

Bois Tordu

84 av de la Pège, 85270 ☎ 251543378 ▤ 251540829
e-mail leboistordu@wanadoo.fr
website www.leboistordu.com
Wooded location with good facilities.
⮩ *5.3km NW.*
Open 15 May-15 Sep **Site** 2HEC ꠥ ♨ ☎ **Prices** pitch 26-32.50 (incl 3 persons) pp5.20-6.50 ♨ (static)300-690 **Facilities** ⋔ ⍟⊙⊕⌀⌀⍟ **Services** ☂ ⍟⍥ ⊞ ⍟ **Leisure** ♣ P **Off-site** ⍟⍥ ♣S

Chouans

108 av de la Faye, 85270 ☎ 251543490 ▤ 251540592
e-mail info@sunmarina.com
website www.sunmarina.com
Wooded location on the edge of a national forest.
⮩ *2.5km NW.*
Open 15 May-15 Sep **Site** 5HEC ꠥ ♨ ☎ **Prices** pitch 24-30 (incl 3 persons) ♨ (static)400-800 **Facilities** ⋔ ⍟⊙⊕⌀⌀⍟ **Services** ☂ ⍥ ⍟ **Leisure** ♣ P **Off-site** ♣S

Ecureuils

100 av de la Pège, 85270 ☎ 251543371 ▤ 251556908
e-mail info@camping-aux-ecureuils.com
Pleasant surroundings 250m from a fine sandy beach, with good recreational facilities.
⮩ *D178 & D753 from Nantes to St-Hilaire-de-Riez.*
Open May-15 Sep **Site** 4HEC ꠥ ♨ ♣ **Prices** pitch 24.50-32.70 (incl 2 persons) pp4.60-5.65 **Facilities** ⋔ ⍟⊙⊕⍟ **Services** ☂ ⍟⍥ ⊞ ⍟ **Leisure** ♣ P **Off-site** ⌀ ♣S

Padrelle

1 r Prévot, La Corniche de Sion/l'Océan, 85270 ☎ 251553203
A rural setting 50m from the beach and 5 minutes from the town.
Open May-Sep **Site** 1.5HEC ꠥ ♨ ♨ **Prices** ♠ 2 pitch 10 (incl 2 persons) pp3 ♨ (static)200-270 **Facilities** ⋔ ⊙⊕⍟ **Services** ⍟ **Off-site** ⍟⊞ ☂ ⍟⍥ ⌀⌀ ♣S ⊞

Plage

106 av de la Pège, 85270 ☎ 251543393 ▤ 251559702
e-mail campinglaplage@campingscollinet.com
website www.campingscollinet.com
On a meadow with trees. Access to beach via dunes.
⮩ *5.7km NW.*
Open 15 Apr-10 Sep **Site** 5.5HEC ꠥ ♨ ☎ ♨ ▲ **Facilities** ⋔ ⊙⊕⌀⌀⍟ ⍟ **Services** ☂ ⍟⍥ ⊞ ⍟ **Leisure** ♣ PS **Off-site** ⍟

Site 6HEC (site size) ꠥ grass ⊜ sand ꠥ stone ♣ little shade ♣ partly shaded ꠥ mainly shaded ☎ bungalows for hire ♨ caravans for hire ▲ tents for hire ⊗ no dogs Prices ♦ adult per night ♠ car per night pp per person per night ♨ caravan per night ▲ tent per night ♨ (static)-caravan hire per week

Prairie

chemin des Roselières, 85270 ☎ 251540856 ▤ 251559702

e-mail campinglaprairie@campingscollinet.com
website www.campingscollinet.com

A family site with pitches shaded by trees. Booking advised in summer.

➲ 5.5km NW, 0.5km from beach.

Open 15 May-10 Sep **Site** 4.7HEC ⛺ ❀ ⌂ ⇔ **Prices** pitch 22.50-25 (incl 2 persons) pp4.50-5 ⇔ (static)380-470 **Facilities** ⋔ ⊙ ⌂ ⌀ ⚌ ⓟ **Services** ⛚ ᵢⓄᵢ ◙ **Leisure** ⚓ P **Off-site** 圄 S

Puerta del Sol

Les Borderies - D59, 85270 ☎ 251491010 ▤ 251498484

e-mail info@campinglapuertadelsol.com
website campinglapuertadelsol.com

A peaceful site with well-defined pitches in a wooded location. Good facilities for family recreation.

➲ 4.5km N.

Open Apr-Sep **Site** 4HEC ⛺ ❀ ⌂ ⇔ ⚎ **Prices** pitch 19-29 (incl 2 persons) pp5-6.50 ⇔ (static)285-780 **Facilities** ⋔ 圄 ⊙ ⇔ ⓟ **Services** ⛚ ᵢⓄᵢ ✚ ◙ **Leisure** ⚓ P **Off-site** ✚   *See advertisement on this page*

Sol-à-Gogo

61 av de la Pège, 85270 ☎ 251542900 ▤ 251548874

e-mail solagogo@wanadoo.fr **website** www.solagogo.com

A family site with good recreational facilities, including an aquaslide, with direct access to the beach.

➲ 4.8km NW of St-Hilaire, 6km S of St-Jean-de-Monts.

Open 15 May-15 Sep **Site** 4HEC ⛺ ❀ ⌂ ⇔ **Prices** pitch 26-32.50 (incl 3 persons) ⇔ (static)330-690 **Facilities** ⋔ 圄 ⊙ ⇔ ⓟ **Services** ⛚ ᵢⓄᵢ ✚ ◙ **Leisure** ⚓ PS **Off-site** ᵢⓄᵢ ⌀ ⚌

ST-HILAIRE-LA-FORÊT VENDÉE

Batardières

85440 ☎ 251333385

A pleasant site surrounded by mature trees and shrubs, with large pitches separated by hedges.

➲ W on D70.

Open Jul-Aug **Site** 1.6HEC ⛺ ❀ **Prices** pitch 20 (incl 2 persons) **Facilities** ⋔ ⊙ ⚓ ⓟ **Services** ◙ **Off-site** 圄 ⛚ ᵢⓄᵢ ⌀ ⚌

Grand' Métairie

8 r de la Vineuse en Plaine, 85440 ☎ 251333238 ▤ 251332569

e-mail grand-metairie@wanadoo.fr
website www.la-grand-metairie.com

Site with flowers and trees with clearly marked sites. Entertainment for children and teenagers. Free shuttle available to nearby sandy beach.

Open Apr-Sep **Site** 3.8HEC ⛺ ❀ ⌂ ⚎ **A** **Facilities** ⋔ ⊙ ⇔ ⌀ ⚌ ⓟ ⓟ **Services** ⛚ ᵢⓄᵢ ✚ ◙ **Leisure** ⚓ P **Off-site** 圄 ⚓ LS

ST-HILAIRE-PEYROUX CORRÈZE

Le Chazal

19560 ☎ 555257296

e-mail camping.lechazal@wanadoo.fr
website perso.wanadoo.fr/camping.lechazal/

A peaceful site on the edge of the Massif Central with fine views over the Couze valley.

➲ Off N89 at Malemort onto D141 at rdbt to Venarsal & 1.5m for St-Hilaire-Peyroux, left onto C13 for site.

Open Apr-1 Nov **Site** 1.5HEC ⛺ ❀ ⌂ **Prices** ⚑ 3.50 ⇔ 4 **Facilities** ⋔ ⊙ ⇔ ⓟ **Services** ᵢⓄᵢ ✚ ◙ **Off-site** 圄 ⛚ ᵢⓄᵢ

A cosy campsite with magnificent pine and oak trees, ideal for family holidays in a calm and peaceful area with 216 marked-off pitches. ENTERTAINMENT PROGRAMME for adults and children during the day and every evening during the peak season (karaoke, disco, concerts, tabletop football,...). Heated pool with water slide, paddling pool, children's club, petanque, tennis, volleyball, newly renovated hall, basketball, bike-rental,... RENTAL OF MOBILE HOMES, CHALETS AND PITCHES. Reservation advisable

85270 ST-HILAIRE-DE-RIEZ Tel 02 51 49 10 10 Fax 02 51 49 84 84
info@campinglapuertadelsol.com www.campinglapuertadelsol.com

ST JEAN-D'ANGELY CHARENTE-MARITIME

Val de Boutonne

☎ 546322616
e-mail info@valba.net
website www.valbanet.com

Wooded location near the river.

➲ NE of town.

Open 16 May-Sep **Site** 1.8HEC ⛺ ❀ ⌂ **Facilities** ⋔ ⊙ ⇔ ⓟ **Services** ◙ **Leisure** ⚓ PR **Off-site** 圄 ⛚ ᵢⓄᵢ ⌀ ⚌ ✚

ST-JEAN-DE-MONTS VENDÉE

Abri des Pins

rte de Notre-Dame-de-Monts, 85160 ☎ 251588386 ▤ 251593047

e-mail abridespins@aol.com
website www.abridespins.com

A family site on level grassland with pitches subdivided by hedges, bushes and trees. Short walk from the beach.

➲ 4km N on D38 Notre-Dame-de-Monts road.

Open 3 May-12 Sep **Site** 3HEC ⛺ ❀ ❀ ⌂ **Facilities** ⋔ 圄 ⊙ ⇔ ⓟ **Services** ⛚ ᵢⓄᵢ ✚ ◙ **Leisure** ⚓ P **Off-site** ⌀ ⚌ ⚓ S

Facilities 圄 shop ⋔ shower ⊙ electric points for razors ⇔ electric points for caravans ⓟ parking by tents permitted ⓟ compulsory separate car park   **Services** ᵢⓄᵢ café/restaurant ⛚ bar ⌀ Camping Gaz International ⚌ gas other than Camping Gaz ✚ first aid facilities ◙ laundry   **Leisure** ⚓ swimming L-Lake P-Pool R-River S-Sea **Off-site** All facilities within 2km

Bordering a pine forest
1/2 mile from the beach

les Amiaux
★★★★

223 route de Notre Dame
85169 Saint Jean de Monts
www.amiaux.fr
e-mail : accueil@amiaux.fr

Waterslides, indoor pool
Grocery, bar, restaurant
Playgrounds, tennis courts

TEL +33 2 51 58 22 22   FAX +33 2 51 58 26 09

Amiaux
223 rte de Notre-Dame de Monts, 85160
☎ 251582222 🖹 251582609
e-mail accueil@amiaux.fr
website www.amiaux.fr
A well-equipped site on the edge of a forest, 0.7km from the beach.
➲ *3.5km NW of D38.*
Open Etr-Sep **Site** 16HEC ⚬ ⚬ ⚬ 🏠 **Prices** ⚬ 3.80 pitch 10.40-23.40
Facilities 🏠 ⚬ ⊙ ⚬ ⊘ ℗ **Services** ⚬ 🎱 ⚬ 🗑 **Leisure** ⚬ P
Off-site ⚬S

See advertisement on this page

Avenhiriers de la Calypso
rte de Notre-Dame-de-Monts, Les Tonnelles, 85160
☎ 251597966 🖹 251597967
e-mail camping_apv@wanadoo.fr
website www.lesaventuriersdelacalypso.com
A holiday village with modern facilities, 0.7km from Tonnelles beach.
Open Apr-Sep **Site** 5HEC ⚬ ⚬ ⚬ 🏠 △ **Facilities** 🏠 ⚬ ⊙ ⚬ ⊘ ℗
Services ⚬ 🎱 ⚬ 🗑 **Leisure** ⚬ P **Off-site** ⚬S 🗑

Bois Dormant
168 r des Sables, 85160 ☎ 251586262 🖹 251582997
e-mail boisdormant@siblu.fr
Open 8 Apr-9 Sep **Site** 11.5HEC ⚬ ⚬ ⚬ ⚬ 🏠 △ ⊗ **Facilities** 🏠 ⚬ ⊙ ⚬
⊘ ⚬ ℗ **Services** ⚬ 🎱 🗑 🗑

Bois Joly
46 r de Notre-Dame-de-Monts, BP 507, 85165
☎ 251591163 🖹 251591106
e-mail boisjoly@compuserve.com
website www.camping-leboisjoly.com
A pleasantly landscaped, terraced site set among pine trees. Good facilities. Close to the beach and the town centre.
Open Apr-24 Sep **Site** 7.5HEC ⚬ ⚬ 🏠 **Prices** ⚬ 2-4.50 pitch 15-26 (incl 2 persons) **Facilities** 🏠 ⚬ ⊙ ⚬ ⊘ ⚬ ℗ **Services** ⚬ 🎱 ⚬ 🗑
Leisure ⚬ PR **Off-site** ⚬S

Bois Masson
149 r des Sables, 85160 ☎ 251586262 🖹 251582997
e-mail boismasson@siblu.fr
website www.siblu.com
A family site with a variety of facilities in a wooded setting near the beach. Aquatic complex includes covered and outdoor pools, water chutes, jacuzzi and sauna.
➲ *2km SE.*
Open 8 Apr-16 Sep **Site** 7.5HEC ⚬ ⚬ ⚬ ⚬ 🏠 ⚬ ⊗ **Facilities** 🏠 ⚬ ⊙ ⚬ ⊘ ⊘
℗ **Services** ⚬ 🎱 ⚬ 🗑 🗑 **Leisure** ⚬ P **Off-site** ⚬S

Clarys Plage
av des Epines, 85160 ☎ 251581024 🖹 251595196
e-mail leclarys@wanadoo.fr
website www.leclarys.com
A family site with good facilities including an indoor swimming pool and an outdoor pool with a water slide.
➲ *S of town 300m from beach.*
Open 15 May-15 Sep **Site** 8HEC ⚬ ⚬ ⚬ 🏠 **Prices** pitch 26-32.50 (incl 3 persons) 🏠 (static)305-690 **Facilities** 🏠 ⚬ ⊙ ⚬ ℗ **Services** ⚬ 🎱 ⚬ 🗑 🗑
Leisure ⚬ P **Off-site** 🎱 ⊘ ⚬ ⚬S

Forêt
190 chemin de la Rive, 85160 ☎ 251588463 🖹 251588463
e-mail camping-la-foret@wanadoo.fr
website www.hpa-laforet.com
A well-equipped family site in a pleasant rural setting.
➲ *Off D38*
Open 15 Apr-20 Sep **Site** 1HEC ⚬ ⚬ ⚬ 🏠 **Prices** ⚬ 3-5 pitch 16-23.50
(incl 2 persons) **Facilities** 🏠 ⚬ ⊙ ⚬ ⊘ ℗ **Services** 🗑 🗑 **Leisure** ⚬ P
Off-site ⚬ 🎱 ⚬ ⚬S

Zagarella
rte des Sables, 85160 ☎ 251581982 🖹 251593528
e-mail zagarella@wanadoo.fr
website www.zagarella.fr
Open 15 May-15 Sep **Site** 4.2HEC ⚬ ⚬ 🏠 **Facilities** 🏠 ⚬ ⊙ ⚬ ⚬ ℗
Services ⚬ 🎱 🗑 **Leisure** ⚬ P **Off-site** ⚬S

AT OROUET (6KM SE)

Yole
chemin des Bosses, 85160 ☎ 251586717 🖹 251590535
e-mail contact@la-yole.com
website www.la-yole.com
Set in rural surroundings 1km from a fine sandy beach.
➲ *Signed from D38 in Orouet.*
Open 2 Apr-28 Sep **Site** 7.5HEC ⚬ ⚬ ⚬ 🏠 **Prices** pitch 16-29 (incl 2 persons) 🏠 (static)305-650 **Facilities** 🏠 ⚬ ⊙ ⚬ ⊘ ℗ **Services** ⚬ 🎱
🗑 **Leisure** ⚬ P **Off-site** ⚬ ⚬S

Site 6HEC (site size) ⚬ grass ⚬ sand ⚬ stone ⚬ little shade ⚬ partly shaded ⚬ mainly shaded 🏠 bungalows for hire
🏠 caravans for hire △ tents for hire ⊗ no dogs **Prices** ⚬ adult per night ⚬ car per night pp per person per night 🏠 caravan per night
△ tent per night 🏠 (static)-caravan hire per week

ST-JULIEN-DES-LANDES VENDÉE

Fôret
85150 ☎ 251466211 ▤ 251466087
e-mail camping@domainelaforet.com
website www.domainelaforet.com
A picturesque setting in the grounds of a château with well-defined pitches and modern facilities.
⮑ *NE on D55, rte de Martinet.*
Open 15 May-15 Sep **Site** 50HEC 👪 ♨ ♠ **Facilities** 🗽 🏠 ⊙ 🔌 ⌀ ℗
Services ⊡ 🍽 ➕ 🅂 **Leisure** ⇆ P

Garangeoire
85150 ☎ 251466539 ▤ 251466985
e-mail info@garangeoire.com
website www.camping-la-garangeoire.com
Family site set in 200-hectare estate with a variety of recreational facilities. Pitches separated by hedges.
⮑ *2km N of village.*
Open 2 Apr-23 Sep **Site** 18HEC 👪 ♨ ♠ **Prices** 🏕 4.50-7.50 pitch 17-37 (incl 2 persons) **Facilities** 🗽 🏠 ⊙ 🔌 ⌀ ℗ **Services** ⊡ 🍽 ➕ 🅂
Leisure ⇆ LP

Guyonnière
La Guyonnière, 85150 ☎ 251466259 ▤ 251466289
e-mail info@laguyonniere.com
website www.laguyonniere.com
A pleasant site with pitches divided by hedges with good sanitary and recreational facilities.
⮑ *2km from town centre towards St-Gilles-Croix-de-Vie.*
Open 28 Apr-29 Sep **Site** 30HEC 👪 ♨ ♠ **Prices** pitch 11-29.40 (incl 2 persons) **Facilities** 🗽 🏠 ⊙ 🔌 ⌀ ⤵ ℗ **Services** ⊡ 🍽 ➕ 🅂
Leisure ⇆ LP

ST-JUST-LUZAC CHARENTE-MARITIME

Castel Camping Séquoia Parc
La Josephtrie, 17320 ☎ 546855555 ▤ 546855556
e-mail sequoia.parc@wanadoo.fr
website www.sequoiaparc.com
Situated in a spacious park on the La Josephtrie estate, which contains an attractive château, 5km from the coast.
⮑ *A10 exit Saintes, D728 for Ile d'Oléron & signed from St-Just.*
Open 12 May-16 Sep **Site** 45HEC 👪 ♨ ♠ **Prices** pitch 17-41 (incl 2 persons) pp4 **Facilities** 🗽 🏠 ⊙ 🔌 ℗ **Services** ⊡ 🍽 ➕ 🅂
Leisure ⇆ P

ST-LAURENT-NOUAN LOIR-ET-CHER

Amitié
r du Camping, 41220 ☎ 254870152 ▤ 254870993
On the shore of the River Loire between Blois and Orléans.
⮑ *On D951.*
Open All year **Site** 2HEC 👪 ♨ 🔌 **Prices** pitch 10-14 (incl 2 persons) pp4 🔌 (static)210-380 **Facilities** 🗽 ⊙ 🔌 ℗ **Services** 🅂 **Leisure** ⇆ R
Off-site 🏠 ⊡ 🍽 ⌀ ⤵

ST-LÉONARD-DE-NOBLAT HAUTE-VIENNE

CM Beaufort
87400 ☎ 555560279 ▤ 555560279
e-mail campingdebeaufort@cegetel.net
Set in pleasant wooded surroundings with good facilities.
⮑ *Off D39.*
Open 14 Apr-Sep **Site** 2HEC 👪 ♨ ♠ **Prices** pitch 10-12 🔌 (static)200-500 **Facilities** 🗽 🏠 ⊙ 🔌 ⌀ ℗ **Services** ⊡ 🍽 ➕ 🅂 **Leisure** ⇆ R
Off-site 🍽 ⤵

ST-MALÔ-DU-BOIS VENDÉE

La Vallee de Poupet
85590 ☎ 251923145 ▤ 251923865
e-mail camping@valleedepoupet.com
website www.valleedepoupet.com
A picturesque location beside the River Sèvre Nantaise, surrounded by woodland.
⮑ *D72 from village, 1km left fork & signed.*
Open 15 May-15 Sep **Site** 3HEC 👪 ♨ ♠ **Prices** 🏕 2.80-3.10 pitch 11.70-14 (incl 2 persons) **Facilities** 🗽 ⊙ 🔌 ⤵ ℗ **Services** ➕ 🅂 **Leisure** ⇆ PR
Off-site 🏠 ⊡ 🍽 ⌀

ST-PALAIS-SUR-MER CHARENTE-MARITIME

Ormeaux
44 av de Bernezac, 17420 ☎ 546390207 ▤ 546385666
e-mail campingormeaux@tiscali.fr
website www.camping-ormeaux.com
Well-equipped site in wooded surroundings, 0.5km from the beach.
⮑ *1km N.*
Open Apr-Oct Nov-Mar **Site** 3.5HEC 👪 ♨ ♠ 🔌 🅰 **Facilities** 🗽 🏠 ⊙ 🔌 ⌀ ⤵ ℗ **Services** ⊡ 🍽 ➕ 🅂 **Leisure** ⇆ P **Off-site** ⇆ LS

Puits de l'Auture
La Grande Côte, 17420 ☎ 546232031 ▤ 546232638
e-mail camping-lauture@wanadoo.fr
website www.camping-puitsdelauture.com
A family site in a picturesque location at the edge of a forest facing the sea.
⮑ *2km NW on D25 La Palmyre road.*
Open May-Sep **Site** 5HEC 👪 ♨ ♠ ⊗ **Prices** pitch 15-31 (incl 2 persons) pp5-7 🔌 (static)330-1420 **Facilities** 🗽 🏠 ⊙ 🔌 ⌀ ℗ **Services** ⊡ 🍽 ➕ 🅂
Leisure ⇆ P **Off-site** ⇆ S

See advertisement on this page

France

ST-REVÉRÉND VENDÉE

Pont Rouge

av Georges Clémenceau, 85220 ☎ 251546850 📱 251546850
e-mail camping.pontrouge@wanadoo.fr
website www.camping-lepontrouge.com
Quiet site in the Vendée countryside within easy reach of the sea.
➲ *D6 E from St Gilles, turning to St-Revérénd.*
Open Apr-Oct **Site** 2.1HEC ⛺ ⛺ 🏠 🚽 🅰 **Facilities** 🚿 🏪 ☺ 🚰 ⌀ 🚿 ⓟ
Services 🔌 🅱 **Leisure** ⚓ PR **Off-site** 🔌 🍽

ST-VINCENT-SUR-JARD VENDÉE

'Bolée d'Air'

rte du Bouil, 85520 ☎ 251903605 📱 251339404
e-mail chadotel@wanadoo.fr
website www.chadotel.com
A family site on level ground with pitches divided by hedges. Good recreational facilities, including a water slide, and 0.9km from Bouil beach.
➲ *2km E via D21.*
Open Apr-Sep **Site** 6.5HEC ⛺ ⛺ ⚓ 🏠 🅰 **Prices** 🧍 5.80 pitch 12-23.20 (incl 2 persons) **Facilities** 🚿 🏪 ☺ 🚰 ⌀ 🚿 ⓟ **Services** 🔌 🍽 🔌 🅱 **Leisure** ⚓ P **Off-site** 🍽 ⚓ S

STE-CATHERINE-DE-FIERBOIS INDRE-ET-LOIRE

Parc de Fierbois

37800 ☎ 247654335 📱 247655375
e-mail parc.fierbois@wanadoo.fr
website www.fierbois.com
Beside artificial lake, good bathing area.
➲ *Off N10 onto D101, 1.5km SE.*
Open 14 May-14 Sep **Site** 20HEC ⛺ ⛺ 🏠 **Prices** pitch 16-39 (incl 2 persons) 🚐 (static)224-910 **Facilities** 🚿 🏪 ☺ 🚰 ⓟ **Services** 🔌 🍽 🔌 🅱 **Leisure** ⚓ LP

See advertisement on this page

STE-REINE-DE-BRETAGNE LOIRE-ATLANTIQUE

Château du Deffay

BP 18, 44160 ☎ 240880057 📱 240016655
e-mail campingdudeffay@wanadoo.fr
website camping-le-deffay.com
Set in the beautiful Parc de Brière providing fishing, walking and horse riding. Games and TV rooms.
➲ *4.5km W on D33 rte de Pontchâteau.*
Open May-Sep **Site** 13HEC ⛺ ⛺ 🏠 **Prices** 🧍 3.10-5 pitch 10.70-15.20 **Facilities** 🚿 🏪 ☺ 🚰 ⓟ **Services** 🔌 🍽 🔌 🅱 **Leisure** ⚓ LP

Site 6HEC (site size) ⛺ grass ⛺ sand ⚓ stone ⚓ little shade ⛺ partly shaded ⛺ mainly shaded 🏠 bungalows for hire
🚐 caravans for hire 🅰 tents for hire ⊗ no dogs **Prices** 🧍 adult per night 🚗 car per night pp per person per night 🚐 caravan per night
🅰 tent per night 🚐 (static)-caravan hire per week

SANTROP HAUTE-VIENNE

Santrop

87640 ☎ 555710808 ▤ 555712393
e-mail lacsaintpardoux@wanadoo.fr
website www.lac-saint-pardoux.com
A well-equipped family site on the shore of Lac de St-Pardoux with good facilities for water sports.

➥ *A20 exit 25.*

Open 8 May-20 Sep **Site** 4.5HEC ♨ ♣ ♠ **Prices** ♠ 3.10-4.10 pitch 9.70-15.80 (incl 2 persons) **Facilities** ♠ ⓘ ⊙ ♠ ⊘ ♨ ℗ **Services** ⚑ ⛾ **Leisure** ♨ L

SAUMUR MAINE-ET-LOIRE

Chantepie

49400 ☎ 241679534 ▤ 241679585
e-mail info@campingchantepie.com
website www.campingchantepie.com
A pleasant site with a fine view over the River Loire.

➥ *D751 towards Gennes.*

Open 15 May-15 Sep **Site** 10HEC ♨ ♣ ♠ ⚊ **Prices** ♠ 4.50-7 pitch 15-28 **Facilities** ♠ ⓘ ⊙ ♠ ⊘ ℗ **Services** ⚑ ⛾ **Leisure** ♨ P **Off-site** ⛾

Ile d'Offard

av de Verden, 49400 ☎ 241403000 ▤ 241673781
e-mail iledoffard@cvtloisirs.fr
website www.cvtloisirs.com
On island in the middle of the Loire near municipal stadium. Some facilities are only available during summer.

Open Mar-Oct **Site** 4.5HEC ♨ ♣ ♠ ⚊ **Prices** pitch 15.50-24 (incl 2 persons) **Facilities** ♠ ⓘ ⊙ ♠ ♨ ℗ **Services** ⚑ ⛾ **Leisure** ♨ P **Off-site** ⊘ ♨R

SELLE CRAONNAISE, LA MAYENNE

Rincerie

Base de Loisirs la Rincerie, 53800 ☎ 243061752 ▤ 243075020
e-mail larincerie@wanadoo.fr
website www.la-rincerie.com
A modern site offering a good selection of sports facilities. Separate car park for arrivals after 22.00 hrs.

➥ *N of La Selle-Craonnaise towards Ballots.*

Open Mar-Nov **Site** 5HEC ♨ ♣ ♠ **Prices** ♠ 5.95-9.70 **Facilities** ♠ ⊙ ♠ ℗ **Services** ⛾ **Off-site** ⚑

SILLÉ-LE-GUILLAUME SARTHE

Privé du Landereau

72140 ☎ 243201269

➥ *1.5km NW via D304*

Open Etr-15 Oct **Site** 2.5HEC ♠ ♣ ♠ ♠ **Facilities** ♠ ⊙ ♠ ⊘ ℗ **Services** ⚑ ⛾ **Off-site** ⛾ ♨ ♨LR

SILLÉ-LE-PHILIPPE SARTHE

Château de Chanteloup

72460 ☎ 243275107 ▤ 243890505
e-mail chanteloup.souffront@wanadoo.fr
website www.chateau-de-chanteloup.com
Set partly in wooded clearings and open ground within the park surrounding an old mansion. Good sanitary installations.

➥ *17km NE of Le Mans on D301.*

Open Jun-Sep **Site** 20HEC ♨ ♣ **Prices** ♠ 5.50-7 pitch 9-12 **Facilities** ♠ ⓘ ⊙ ♠ ℗ **Services** ⚑ ⛾ **Leisure** ♨ LP

SOUTERRAINE, LA CREUSE

Suisse Océan

Le Cheix, 23300 ☎ 555633332

➥ *1.8km E via D912 near the lake.*

Open All year **Site** 2HEC ♨ ♣ ♠ ♠ **Facilities** ♠ ⊙ ♠ ℗ **Services** ⚑ ⛾ **Off-site** ⛾ ♨L

SUÈVRES LOIR-ET-CHER

Château de la Grenouillère

41500 ☎ 254878037 ▤ 254878421
e-mail la.grenouillere@wanadoo.fr
website www.camping-loire.fr
Site divided into pitches, and the castle is now a hotel with common room for campers. Each pitch 150 sq m. Separate area for overnight campers.

➥ *A10 exit 16 Mer/Chambord, RN152 in direction Blois. Site 2km after Mer on right.*

Open May-5 Sep **Site** 11HEC ♨ ♣ ♠ **Prices** ♠ 5-7 ♠ 19-31 **Facilities** ♠ ⓘ ⊙ ♠ ⊘ ℗ **Services** ⚑ ⛾ **Leisure** ♨ P

SULLY-SUR-LOIRE LOIRET

Hortus Jardin de Sully

rte de St Benoit - D60 ☎ 238363594 ▤ 238363594
e-mail info@camping-hortus.com
website www.camping-hortus.com
On a level meadow beside the River Loire.

➥ *W on D60 towards St-Benoît-sur-Loire.*

Open All year **Site** 5HEC ♨ ♣ ♠ ♠ **Prices** ♠ 2-5 ♠ 1-1.50 pitch 3-3.50 **Facilities** ♠ ⓘ ⊙ ♠ ℗ **Services** ⚑ ⛾ **Leisure** ♨ PR **Off-site** ♨L

TALMONT-ST-HILAIRE VENDÉE

Littoral

Le Porteau, 85440 ☎ 251220464 ▤ 251220537
e-mail info@campinglelittoral.fr
website www.campinglelittoral.fr
Situated near Port Bourgenay, 80m from the sea. Good facilities and entertainment available during the season.

Open Apr-Sep **Site** 8.5HEC ♨ ♣ ♠ **Prices** pitch 17-34 (incl 2 persons) **Facilities** ♠ ⓘ ⊙ ♠ ♨ ℗ **Services** ⚑ ⛾ **Leisure** ♨ P **Off-site** ♨S

TOURS INDRE-ET-LOIRE

AT BALLAN-MIRÉ (8.5KM W D751)

Mignardière

22 av des Aubepines, 37510 ☎ 247733100 ▤ 247733101
e-mail info@mignardiere.com
website www.mignardiere.com
A well-maintained site with a variety of sports facilities.

➥ *2.5km NE.*

Open 10 Apr-Sep **Site** 3.5HEC ♨ ♣ ♠ ♠ **Facilities** ♠ ⓘ ⊙ ♠ ⊘ ♨ ℗ **Services** ⛾ **Leisure** ♨ P **Off-site** ⚑ ⛾

France

Facilities ⓘ shop ♠ shower ⊙ electric points for razors ♠ electric points for caravans ℗ parking by tents permitted ℗ compulsory separate car park
Services ⛾ café/restaurant ⚑ bar ⊘ Camping Gaz International ♨ gas other than Camping Gaz ✚ first aid facilities ⬚ laundry
Leisure ♨ swimming L-Lake P-Pool R-River S-Sea **Off-site** All facilities within 2km

37220 TROGUES

Phone: 00 33 (0)2 47 58 60 60
Fax: 00 33 (0)2 47 95 24 04

4 stars residential estate in an impressive natural environment of a shady 16 hectares park with a magnificent lake and nicely situated along the banks of the Vienne. Rental of pitches for mobile homes, camping. With lots of outdoor activities : Covered heated swimming pool, water slide, tennis and ping pong, mountain bike circuit, multi sports terrain, fishing in the lake and in the river, playing area for kids, fitness room and animation in July and August

www.parc-des-allais.com • contact@parc-des-allais.com

TRANCHE-SUR-MER, LA VENDÉE

Almadies
rte de la Roche-sur-Yon, 85360 ☎ 251303694 ▤ 251303704
e-mail info@lesalmadies.com
website www.lesalmadies.com
Situated on the banks of a canal 3km from the sea.
➲ *300m E on D46.*
Open Apr-Oct **Site** 11HEC 💥 ♣ ♨ ⌂ ▲ **Facilities** 🏪 🛁 ⊙ ♨ ⊘ ℗
Services ⬚ 🍴 🛒 📺 **Leisure** ⚓ PR

Bale d'Aunis
10 r du Pertuis, 85360 ☎ 251274736 ▤ 251274454
e-mail info@camping-baiedaunis.com
website www.camping-baiedaunis.com
On level land by the sea, 50m from the beach and 400m from the town centre with a variety of leisure activities.
➲ *300m E on D46.*
Open 27 Apr-16 Sep **Site** 2.4HEC ♨ 💥 ♣ ⌂ ⊗ **Prices** pitch 24.70-28.70 (incl 2 persons) ⊞ (static)290-660 **Facilities** 🏪 ⊙ ♨ ⊘ ℗ **Services** ⬚ 🍴 📺 **Leisure** ⚓ PS **Off-site** 🛁 🍴 ⚒ 🛒

Bel
r du Bottereau, 85360 ☎ 251304739 ▤ 251277281
e-mail campbel@wanadoo.fr
A quiet, family-run site 450m from a magnificent beach and a marine lake. Plenty of sports and entertainment facilities.
➲ *400m from town centre.*
Open 26 May-2 Sep **Site** 3.5HEC 💥 ♨ ♣ ⊗ **Prices** pitch 26 (incl 2 persons) **Facilities** 🏪 🛁 ⊙ ♨ ℗ **Services** ⬚ 🍴 🛒 📺 **Leisure** ⚓ PS **Off-site** 🍴 ⊘ ⚒ 🛒

Cottage Fleuri
La Grière-Plage, 85360 ☎ 251303457 ▤ 251277477
A level site with modern facilities.
➲ *2.5km E, 0.5km from beach.*
Open Apr-15 Oct **Site** 7.5HEC 💥 ♣ ⌂ ⌂ **Facilities** 🏪 ⊙ ♨ ⚒ ℗
Services ⬚ 🍴 🛒 📺 **Leisure** ⚓ P **Off-site** ⚒ S

Escale du Perthuis
120 bd Tassigny ☎ 251303896 ▤ 251277148
Meadowland site by the sea and a lovely sandy beach. Site only offers mobile homes to let.
➲ *On D46 4.5km towards l'Aiguillon.*
Open 15 Apr-15 Sep **Site** 6HEC ♨ ♣ ♨ ⌂ ⌂ **Facilities** 🏪 🛁 ⊙ ♨ ℗
Services ⬚ 🍴 🛒 📺 **Leisure** ⚒ PS

Jard
123 bd de Lattre-de-Tassigny, 85360 ☎ 251274379 ▤ 251274292
e-mail info@campingdujard.fr
website www.campingdujard.fr
A family site on level ground with clearly defined pitches, 0.7km from the beach, with plenty of recreational facilities.
➲ *Via D747.*
Open 19 May-15 Sep **Site** 6HEC 💥 ♣ ⌂ ⊗ **Prices** pitch 21.50-27.60
Facilities 🏪 🛁 ⊙ ♨ ℗ **Services** ⬚ 🍴 🛒 📺 **Leisure** ⚒ P **Off-site** ⊘ ⚒

Savinière
85360 ☎ 251274270 ▤ 251274048
Set in a beautiful natural park with modern facilities.
➲ *1.5km NW via D105.*
Open Apr-Sep **Site** 2.5HEC 💥 ♨ ♣ ⌂ **Facilities** 🏪 🛁 ⊙ ♨ ℗
Services ⬚ 🍴 🛒 📺 **Leisure** ⚒ P **Off-site** ⊘ ⚒ S

TROCHE CORRÈZE

Domaine Vert
Les Magnes ☎ 555735989 ▤ 555735989
website www.ledomainevert.nl
Peaceful farm site surrounded by grass and woodland where campers can select their own pitch. Simple facilities and the opportunity to try the organic produce from the farm.
➲ *A20 exit 45, to Vigeois, after Vigeois right onto D50 for Lubersac, site 5km.*
Open Apr-1 Oct **Site** 3HEC 💥 ♣ ⌂ **Prices** 🚶 4.50 pitch 7-9.50
Facilities 🏪 ⊙ ♨ ℗ **Services** ⬚ 🍴 🛒

TROGUES INDRE-ET-LOIRE

Château de la Rolandière
37220 ☎ 247585371 ▤ 247585371
e-mail contact@larolandiere.com
website www.larolandiere.com
Situated in parkland surrounding a fine château. A good base for visiting the châteaux of the Loire.
➲ *A10 exit 25, road for Chinon for 6km.*
Open May-Sep **Site** 4HEC 💥 ♣ ⌂ **Prices** 🚶 5-6 pitch 7-8.50 **Facilities** 🏪 🛁 ⊙ ♨ ℗ **Services** ⬚ 🍴 🛒 📺 **Leisure** ⚒ P **Off-site** ⚒ R

Parc des Allais

☎ 247586060 🖹 247952404
e-mail contact@parc-des-allais.com
website www.chloro-parc.com

A natural environment site at the heart of the Loire châteaux. On the banks of the Vienne river and beside a fine lake.

⮑ *A10 autoroute from Tours exit 25 Ste Maure de Touraine. Follow directions for Pouzay.*

Open Aug-Sep **Site** 16HEC 😃 **⚘ Prices** pitch 21.95-26.35 (incl 2 persons) pp3.95-4.75 **Facilities** ⚑ 🏚 **Services** ☎ 🍽 🗑 **Leisure** ⚓ LPR

See advertisement on page 130

TURBALLE, LA LOIRE-ATLANTIQUE

Parc Ste-Brigitte

Domaine de Bréhet, 44420 ☎ 240248891 🖹 240156572
e-mail saintebrigitte@wanadoo.fr
website www.campingsaintebrigitte.com

Parkland site in the grounds of a château, divided into pitches and surrounded by hedges.

⮑ *E of village on D99 Guérande road.*

Open Apr-Sep **Site** 6HEC 😃 😃 😃 ⚘ **Prices** ⚑ 5.90 ⚘ 3.10 pitch 6.70-13.40 ⚘ (static)350-685 **Facilities** ⚑ 🏚 ⊙ ⚡ ⌀ ⚑ **Services** ☎ 🍽 🗑 **Leisure** ⚓ P **Off-site** ⚓S

VALENÁAY INDRE

CM Chènes

rte de Loches, 36600 ☎ 254000392 🖹 254000392

A quiet site on level ground with well-defined pitches.

⮑ *1km W on D960.*

Open 27 Apr-29 Sep **Site** 5HEC 😃 😃 **Facilities** ⚑ ⊙ ⚡ ⚑ **Services** ☎ 🗑 **Leisure** ⚓ LP **Off-site** 🏚 ☎ 🍽 ⌀ ⚘ ⚓R

VARENNES-SUR-LOIRE MAINE-ET-LOIRE

Étang de la Brèche

5 Impasse de la Brèche, 49730 ☎ 241512292 🖹 241512724
e-mail etang.breche@wanadoo.fr
website www.etang-breche.com

Relaxing site in the heart of the Loire valley, ideal base for visiting sites of historical interest.

⮑ *4.5km NW via N152.*

Open 12 May-15 Sep **Site** 24HEC 😃 😃 ⚘ **Prices** ⚑ 5-7 pitch 18.50-31 (incl 2 persons) ⚘ (static)230-810 **Facilities** ⚑ 🏚 ⊙ ⚡ ⌀ ⚘ ⚑ **Services** ☎ 🍽 🗑 **Leisure** ⚓ P

VELLES INDRE

Grands Pins

Les Maisons Neuves, 36330 ☎ 254366193 🖹 254361009
e-mail contact@les-grands-pins.fr
website www.les-grands-pins.fr

The site has individual pitches and easy access to the countryside. Swimming pool only available July and August.

⮑ *7km S of Châteauroux on N20.*

Open All year **Site** 5HEC 😃 😃 😃 **Prices** ⚑ 4.50 pitch 4.50 **Facilities** ⚑ ⊙ ⚡ ⚑ **Services** ☎ 🍽 🗑 **Leisure** ⚓ P

VENDÔME LOIR-ET-CHER

Grand Prés

r G-Martel, 41100 ☎ 254770027 🖹 254894101
e-mail campings@cpvendome.com

Site lies on a meadow, next to a sports ground.

⮑ *E of town on right bank of Loire.*

Open 10 Jun-Aug **Site** 3HEC 😃 😃 ⚘ **Facilities** ⚑ ⊙ ⚡ ⚑ **Services** ⊞ 🗑 **Leisure** ⚓ PR **Off-site** 🏚 ☎ 🍽 ⚓

VILLIERS-LE-MORHIER EURE-ET-LOIR

Ilots de St Val

☎ 237827130 🖹 237827767
e-mail lesilots@campinglesilotsdestval.com
website www.campinglesilotsdestval.com

A peaceful rural setting between Maintenon and Nogent-le-Roi, nestling above the Eure river. A haven for wildlife.

⮑ *On D983*

Open All year **Site** 😃 😃 ⚘ ⚘ **Prices** ⚑ 5.90 pitch 5 ⚘ (static)140-205 **Facilities** ⚑ ⊙ ⚡ ⌀ ⚘ ⚑ **Services** 🗑 **Off-site** ⚓R

VINEUIL LOIR-ET-CHER

Rives de Loire

Lac de Loire, 41350 ☎ 254788205 🖹 254786203

Level site on the River Loire with modern buildings. Boating. Bathing not recommended.

⮑ *From Blois towards St-Dye, after modern bridge towards Lac de Loire for 1.5km.*

Open June-15 Sept **Site** 30HEC 😃 😃 **Facilities** ⚑ ⊙ ⚡ ⚑ **Services** ⊞ 🗑 **Leisure** ⚓ PR

BRITTANY/NORMANDY

ALENÇON ORNE

CM de Guéramé

65 r de Guéramé, 61000 ☎ 233263495 🖹 233263495

Set in open country near a stream, 0.5km from town centre.

⮑ *Via boulevard Périphérique in SW part of town.*

Open Apr-Oct **Site** 1.5HEC 😃 😃 **Prices** ⚑ 2.30 ⚘ 4.90 ⚑ 4.90 **Facilities** ⚑ ⊙ ⚡ ⚑ **Services** ⊞ 🗑 **Leisure** ⚓ R **Off-site** 🏚 ☎ 🍽 ⌀ ⚘ ⚓P

ALLINEUC CÔTES-D'ARMOR

Lac de Bosméléac

Bosméléac, 22460 ☎ 296288788 🖹 296288097

Wooded site beside a lake with a beach.

⮑ *RN12 Brest-Paris exit Loudéac.*

Open 14 Jun-15 Sep **Site** 1.2HEC 😃 😃 😃 ⚘ **Prices** ⚑ 2.30 ⚘ 2.80 ⚑ 2.80 **Facilities** ⚑ ⊙ ⚡ ⚑ **Services** ☎ 🍽 ⊞ 🗑 **Leisure** ⚓ L **Off-site** ⚓R

Facilities 🏚 shop ⚑ shower ⊙ electric points for razors ⚡ electric points for caravans ⚑ parking by tents permitted ⦿ compulsory separate car park
Services 🍽 café/restaurant ☎ bar ⌀ Camping Gaz International ⚘ gas other than Camping Gaz ⊞ first aid facilities 🗑 laundry
Leisure ⚓ swimming L-Lake P-Pool R-River S-Sea **Off-site** All facilities within 2km

France

Camping "Le Ty Nadan"

from the 31st of march for unforgettable holidays!

www.tynadan-vacances.fr

ARRADON MORBIHAN

Penboch
9 chemin de Penboch, 56610 ☎ 297447129 🖨 297447910
e-mail camping.penboch@wanadoo.fr
website www.camping-penboch.fr
An well-appointed site in a pleasant wooded location 200m from the beaches of the Gulf of Morbihan. The swimming pool has a large chute with 4 waterslides.
➔ *Signed from N165.*
Open 5 Apr-22 Sep **Site** 4HEC 👑 🏖 🏠 ⊞ **Prices** ⚑ 3-5.90 pitch 3.95-18 (incl 2 persons) ⊞ (static)215-810 **Facilities** ⚘ 🔟 ⊖ ⊕ 🅿 ⚗ 🖳 ⚘ **Services** ⛵ 🍽 ➕ 🔲 **Leisure** ⚓ PS **Off-site** 🔟 ⚓S

ARZANO FINISTÈRE

Ty Nadan
rte d'Arzano, 29310 ☎ 298717547 🖨 298717731
e-mail infos@camping-ty-nadan.fr
website www.camping-ty-nadan.fr
A quiet riverside site in attractive parkland in the Ellé valley.
➔ *3km W. N165 exit Quimperlé for Arzano.*
Open 30 Mar-6 Sep **Site** 12HEC 👑 🏖 🏠 ⚑ **Prices** ⚑ 4.30-8.70 pitch 8.70-22 ⊞ (static)322-1127 **Facilities** ⚘ 🔟 ⊖ ⊕ 🅿 ⚗ **Services** ⛵ 🍽 ➕ 🔲 **Leisure** ⚓ PR

See advertisement on this page

AUDIERNE FINISTÈRE

Loquéran
BP 55, 29770 ☎ 298749506 🖨 298749114
e-mail campgite.loqueran@free.fr
A terraced woodland site in calm and peaceful surroundings, a short distance from the sea.
Open 01 May-30 Sep **Site** 1HEC 👑 🏖 🏠 ⚑ **Prices** ⚑ 3 🚗 1.50 pitch 3
Facilities ⚘ ⊖ ⊕ ⚗ **Services** ➕ 🔲 **Off-site** 🔟 ⛵ 🍽 ⚓S

BADEN MORBIHAN

Mané Guernehué
r Mane er Groez, 56870 ☎ 297570206 🖨 297571543
e-mail mane-guernehue@wanadoo.fr
website www.mane-guernehue.com
A pleasant location at the head of the Gulf of Morbihan with good recreational facilities.
➔ *1km SW via Mériadec road.*
Open Apr-Sep **Site** 10HEC 👑 🏖 🏠 ⚑ **Prices** ⚑ 3.10-6.80 pitch 10.50-19.20
Facilities ⚘ 🔟 ⊖ ⊕ 🅿 ⚗ **Services** ⛵ 🍽 ➕ 🔲 **Leisure** ⚓ P
Off-site ⌀ ⚓ ⚓S

BARNEVILLE-CARTERET MANCHE

Vikings
St-Jean-de-la-Rivière ☎ 233538413 🖨 233530819
website www.campingviking.com
A family site with level terrain, 400m from the sea and a fine sandy beach.
➔ *SE of Barneville-Carteret off D904*
Open 15 Mar-15 Nov **Site** 6HEC 👑 🏖 🏠 **Facilities** 🔟 **Services** ⛵ 🍽 🔲
Leisure ⚓ P

BAYEUX CALVADOS

CM Calvados
bd d'Eindhoven, 14400 ☎ 231920843 🖨 231920843
website www.mairie-bayeux.fr
Very clean and tidy site with tarmac drive and hardstanding for caravans. Adjoins football field.
➔ *N side of town on Boulevard Circulaire.*
Open 28 Apr-Sep **Site** 2.9HEC 👑 🏖 **Prices** ⚑ 3.10 🚗 3.83 ⚑ 3.83
Facilities ⚘ ⊖ ⊕ 🅿 ⚗ **Services** ➕ 🔲 **Off-site** 🔟 ⛵ 🍽 ⌀ ⚓ ⚓P

BEG-MEIL FINISTÈRE

Kervastard
chemin de Kervastard, 29170 ☎ 298949152 🖨 298949983
e-mail camping.le.kervastard@wanadoo.fr
A pleasant wooded site 250m from a fine sandy beach with plenty of leisure facilities.
➔ *In village.*
Open May-Sep **Site** 2HEC 👑 🏖 🏠 🏕 **Prices** ⚑ 3.30-5.50 pitch 7.40-10.20
⚑ (static)228.67-548.81 **Facilities** ⚘ ⊖ ⊕ 🅿 ⚗ **Services** ➕ 🔲
Leisure ⚓ P **Off-site** 🔟 ⛵ 🍽 ⌀ ⚓S

Site 6HEC (site size) 👑 grass 🏖 sand ⚘ stone ⚘ little shade 🏖 partly shaded 🌳 mainly shaded 🏠 bungalows for hire
⚑ caravans for hire 🏕 tents for hire ⊗ no dogs **Prices** ⚑ adult per night 🚗 car per night pp per person per night ⚑ caravan per night
🏕 tent per night ⚑ (static)-caravan hire per week

Roche Percée

29170 ☎ 298949415 ▤ 298944805
e-mail contact@camping-larochepercée.com
website www.camping-larochepercée.com
Wooded family site 400m from the Roche Percée beach.

⮑ *1km from Beg Meil towards Fouesnant.*

Open 8 Apr-26 Sep **Site** 2HEC ❀ ❤ ⊞ **Prices** ★ 3-4.50 pitch 8.50-11.50
⊞ (static)250-730 **Facilities** ↟ 🗎 ⊙ ⊞ ↡ ⑰ **Services** ﹢ ⛱ ➕ ⓢ
Leisure ⛱ P **Off-site** ⓘ ⌀ ⛱S

BÉNODET FINISTÈRE

Letty

29950 ☎ 298570469 ▤ 298662256
e-mail reception@campingduletty.com
website www.campingduletty.com
Site bordering beach, divided into sectors. Good sanitary installations,
ironing rooms and games room. Good beach for children. Use of car
park compulsory after 23.00 hrs.

⮑ *1km SE beside sea.*

Open 15 Jun-6 Sep **Site** 10HEC ❀ ❤ ⊞ **Prices** ★ 5.40 pitch 9
⊞ (static)350-520 **Facilities** ↟ 🗎 ⊙ ⊞ ↡ ⑰ **Services** ﹢ ⛱ ➕ ⓢ
Leisure ⛱ S

Pointe St-Gilles

Corniche de la Mer, 29950 ☎ 298570537 ▤ 298572752
e-mail sunelia@stgilles.fr
website www.stgilles.fr
Holiday site south of village, on fields by beach. Divided into sectors
with individual pitches. Well-equipped sanitary blocks.

⮑ *D34 Quimper-Bénodet, signposted in town. From N165 take
exit for Concarneau, turn right following signs for Bénodet, site
signed.*

Open 27 Apr-9 Sep **Site** 7HEC ❀ ❤ ⊞ ⊗ **Prices** pitch 18-38 (incl 2
persons) **Facilities** ↟ 🗎 ⊙ ⊞ ⌀ ↡ ⑰ **Services** ﹢ ➕ ⓢ **Leisure** ⛱ PS
Off-site ⓘ

Yelloh Village Port de Plaisance

7 rte de Quimper, Prad Poullou, 29950
☎ 298570238 ▤ 298572525
e-mail info@campingbenodet.fr
website www.campingbenodet.fr
A well-equipped family site on the outskirts of the town, 0.5km from
the harbour.

⮑ *NE off D34 at entrance to town.*

Open 15 May-Sep **Site** 12HEC ❀ ❤ ⊞ **Prices** ★ 4-7 pitch 6-20
⊞ (static)210-980 **Facilities** ↟ 🗎 ⊙ ⊞ ↡ ⑰ **Services** ﹢ ⛱ ➕ ⓢ
Leisure ⛱ P **Off-site** ⌀ ⛱RS

BÉNOUVILLE CALVADOS

Hautes Coutures

rte de Ouistréham, 14970 ☎ 231447308 ▤ 231953080
e-mail camping-hautes-coutures@wanadoo.fr
website www.leshautescoutures.free.fr
Pleasant site with good facilities near the Canal Maritime and within
easy reach of the Caen-Portsmouth ferry.

⮑ *From Caen towards Ouistréham on dual carriageway, site
after Pegasus Bridge exit.*

Open Apr-Sep **Site** 8HEC ❀ ❤ ⊞ **Prices** ★ 6.50 pitch 7.50 **Facilities** ↟ 🗎
⊙ ⊞ ↡ ⑰ **Services** ﹢ ⛱ ➕ ⓢ **Leisure** ⛱ PR **Off-site** ⛱S

BINIC CÔTES-D'ARMOR

Palmiers

Kerviarc'h, 22520 ☎ 296737259 ▤ 296737259
e-mail campingpalmiers.chantal@laposte.net
website www.campingpalmiers.com
A well-equipped site within the Parc Tropical de Bretagne, just over
1km from the town centre.

⮑ *Via N12/D786.*

Open 15 Jul-Sep **Site** 2HEC ❤ ⊞ **Prices** pitch 14-26 (incl 3 persons)
Facilities ↟ 🗎 ⊙ ⊞ ↡ ⑰ **Services** ﹢ ⛱ ➕ ⓢ **Leisure** ⛱ P **Off-site** ⓘ
⛱RS

BLANGY-LE-CHÂTEAU CALVADOS

Brévedent

14130 ☎ 231647288 ▤ 231643341
e-mail contact@campinglebrevedent.com
website www.campinglebrevedent.com
Situated in the grounds of an 18th-century manor house with good
facilities.

⮑ *3km SE on D51 beside lake.*

Open May-25 Sep **Site** 5.5HEC ❀ ❤ ⊞ ⊗ **Facilities** ↟ 🗎 ⊙ ⊞ ⌀ ⑰
Services ﹢ ⓘ ➕ ⓢ **Leisure** ⛱ P **Off-site** ⓘ

Domaine du Lac

14130 ☎ 231646200 ▤ 231641591
Open Apr-Oct **Site** 4HEC ❀ ❤ **Facilities** ↟ 🗎 ⊙ ⊞ ⌀ ↡ ⑰
Services ﹢ ⓘ ➕ ⓢ **Leisure** ⛱ LR

BLANGY-SUR-BRESLE SEINE-MARITIME

CM

r des Étangs, 76340 ☎ 235945565 ▤ 235940614
In the middle of the local leisure park comprising 80 hectares of
woodland, lakes and streams.

⮑ *300m on N28.*

Open 15 Mar-15 Oct **Site** 8HEC ❀ ❤ **Facilities** ↟ ⊙ ⊞ ⑰ ⓟ
Services ➕ ⓢ **Off-site** ⌀ ↡ ⛱R

BLONVILLE-SUR-MER CALVADOS

Village Club le Lieu Bill

Le Lieu Bill, 14910 ☎ 231879727 ▤ 231814715
e-mail info@villageclub.fr
website www.villageclub.fr
A family site convenient for Le Havre and other ferry ports.

⮑ *Off D118 Villers-sur-Mer to Pont-l'Évêque.*

Open Apr-Sep **Site** 7HEC ❀ ❤ ⊞ **Facilities** ↟ ⊙ ⊞ ↡ ⑰
Services ﹢ ⓘ ➕ ⓢ **Leisure** ⛱ P **Off-site** 🗎 ⛱S

BOURG-ACHARD EURE

Clos Normand

235 rte de Pont-Audemer, 27310 ☎ 232563484
A peaceful location within an apple orchard.

⮑ *A13 exit Bourg-Achard, site 1km.*

Open Apr-Sep **Site** 1.5HEC ❀ ❤ ⊞ **Facilities** ↟ ⊙ ⊞ ⑰ **Services** ﹢ ⓘ
➕ ⓢ **Leisure** ⛱ P **Off-site** 🗎 ⌀ ↡

Facilities 🗎 shop ↟ shower ⊙ electric points for razors ⊞ electric points for caravans ⑰ parking by tents permitted ⓟ compulsory separate car park
Services ⓘ café/restaurant ﹢ bar ⌀ Camping Gaz International ↡ gas other than Camping Gaz ➕ first aid facilities ⓢ laundry
Leisure ⛱ swimming L-Lake P-Pool R-River S-Sea **Off-site** All facilities within 2km

France

CALLAC CÔTES-D'ARMOR

CM Verte Vallée

22160 ☎ 296455850

➔ *W on D28 towards Morlaix.*

Open 15 Jun-15 Sep **Site** 1HEC 👑 ♣ 🏠 🚘 **Prices** ♠ 2.32 🚙 1.16 pitch 1.79
Facilities 🏪 ⊙ 🚰 ⊘ **Services** 🗄 **Off-site** 🛒 🛏 🍴 ⊘ 🛒

CAMARET-SUR-MER FINISTÈRE

Grand Large

Lambezen, 29570 ☎ 298279141 📠 298279372

Situated at the tip of the Armorique regional park, facing the sea.

➔ *Entering Camaret, at rdbt right onto D355, 2km turn right.*

Open 29 Mar-Sep **Site** 2.8HEC 👑 ♣ 🏠 🚘 **Facilities** 🏪 🛏 ⊙ 🚰 ⊘ 🛏 ⊛
Services 🛒 🍴 🛒 🗄 **Leisure** 🛶 P **Off-site** 🛒 S

Lambézen

29570 ☎ 298277733 📠 298273838

e-mail contact@campingarmorique.com

website www.campingarmorique.com

Situated beside the sea on the edge of the Armorique regional park
with a variety of recreational facilities.

➔ *3km NE on D355 rte de Roscanvel.*

Open 29 Mar-Sep **Site** 2.5HEC 👑 ♣ 🏠 🚘 **Facilities** 🏪 🛏 ⊙ 🚰 ⊘ 🛏 ⊛
Services 🛒 🍴 🗄 🛒 **Leisure** 🛶 P **Off-site** 🛒 S

Plage de Trez Rouz

29570 ☎ 298279396

e-mail camping-plage-de-trez-rouz@wanadoo.fr

website www.trezrouz.com

On level ground 50m from the beach.

➔ *3km from Camaret-sur-Mer on D355 towards Pointe-des-
Espagnols.*

Open 15 Mar-15 Oct **Site** 3.1HEC 👑 ♣ 🏠 🚘 **Prices** ♠ 3.80-4.60 🚙 1.50-
2 pitch 3.20-4.20 🚘 (static)156-360 **Facilities** 🏪 ⊙ 🚰 ⊘ ⊛ **Services** 🛒
🍴 🗄 🛒 **Off-site** 🍴 🛒 S

CANCALE ILLE-ET-VILAINE

Notre Dame du Verger

35260 ☎ 299897284 📠 299896011

Terraced site overlooking the sea with direct access to the beach.

➔ *2km from Pointe-du-Grouin on D201.*

Open 29 Mar-28 Sep **Site** 2.2HEC 👑 ♣ **Facilities** 🏪 🛏 ⊙ 🚰 ⊘ ⊛
Services 🛒 🍴 🗄 🛒 **Off-site** 🛒 S

CARANTEC FINISTÈRE

Mouettes

Grande Grève, 29660 ☎ 298670246 📠 298783146

e-mail camping@lesmouettes.com

website www.les-mouettes.com

Level site divided by low shrubs and trees.

➔ *1.5km SW on rte de St-Pol-de-Léon towards sea.*

Open May-9 Sep **Site** 12HEC 👑 ♣ 🏠 **Prices** ♠ 5-8 pitch 17-43 (incl 2
persons) **Facilities** 🏪 🛏 ⊙ 🚰 ⊘ ⊛ 🅿 **Services** 🛒 🗄 🛒 **Leisure** 🛶 P
Off-site 🍴 🛒 S

CARENTAN MANCHE

CM le Haut Dyck

30 chemin du Grand-Bas Pays, 50500

☎ 233421689 📠 233421689

e-mail lehautdick@aol.com

website www.camping-municipal.com

A level site in wooded surroundings with well-defined pitches.

➔ *Village road off N13 towards Le Port.*

Open 15 Jan-1 Nov **Site** 2.5HEC 👑 ♣ 🏠 🚘 **Prices** ♠ 2.50 🚙 1.20
🚘 3.80 Å 3.80 **Facilities** 🏪 ⊙ 🚰 ⊛ **Services** 🛒 🗄 **Off-site** 🛒 🍴 🍴 ⊘
🛏 🛒 PR   *See advertisement on this page*

CARNAC MORBIHAN

Bruyères

Kerogile, 56340 ☎ 297523057 📠 297523057

e-mail camping.les.bruyeres@wanadoo.fr

Partly wooded site with modern facilities close to the local beaches.

➔ *N of Carnac on C4, 2km from Plouharnel.*

Open Apr-14 Oct **Site** 2HEC 👑 ♣ 🏠 **Prices** ♠ 3.05-4 pitch 5.90-7.40
🚘 (static)150-535 **Facilities** 🏪 🛏 ⊙ 🚰 ⊘ 🛏 ⊛ **Services** 🛒 🗄
Off-site 🛒 🍴

Étang

67 rte de Kerlann, 56340 ☎ 297521406 📠 297522319

A rural setting with pitches divided by hedges, 2.5km from the coast.

➔ *2km N at Kerlann on D119.*

Open Apr-15 Oct **Site** 2.5HEC 👑 ♣ 🏠 🚘 **Prices** ♠ 3.10-5 pitch 4.80-6.50
🚘 (static)320 **Facilities** 🏪 🛏 ⊙ 🚰 ⊘ ⊛ **Services** 🛒 🍴 🗄 🛒
Leisure 🛶 P

Grande Métairie

rte des Alignements, de Kermario, 56342

☎ 297522401 📠 297528358

e-mail info@lagrandemetairie.com

website www.lagrandemetairie.com

Holiday site with modern amenities, completely divided into pitches.

➔ *2.5km NE on D196.*

Open 31 Mar-8 Sep **Site** 15HEC 👑 ♣ 🏠 🚘 **Facilities** 🏪 🛏 ⊙ 🚰 ⊘ ⊛
Services 🛒 🍴 🗄 🛒 **Leisure** 🛶 PS **Off-site** 🛒 L

See advertisement on page 135

Moulin de Kermaux

56340 ☎ 297521590 🗎 297528385
e-mail moulin-de-kermaux@wanadoo.fr
website www.camping-moulinkermaux.com
A quiet location surrounded by trees and bushes, with good facilities.
Within easy reach of the coast and the local megaliths.
➲ *2.5km NE.*
Open 3 Apr-15 Sep **Site** 3HEC 🌢 ♣ ⛺ **Prices** ♠ 4.50 pitch 14
Facilities 🏕 🖾 ⊙ ⊡ ℗ **Services** ⊑ ◉ ➕ 🗟 **Leisure** ♒ P
Off-site ◉ ⊘ ♒RS

Moustoir

rte du Moustoir, 56340 ☎ 297521618 🗎 297528837
e-mail info@lemoustoir.com **website** www.lemoustoir.com
Well-equipped site in a rural setting close to the sea.
➲ *3km NE of Carnac.*
Open 7 Apr-23 Sep **Site** 5HEC 🌢 ♣ ⛺ ⛁ **Prices** ♠ 4.40 pitch 5-16
Facilities 🏕 🖾 ⊙ ⊡ ℗ **Services** ⊑ ◉ ➕ 🗟 **Leisure** ♒ P
Off-site ⊘ ♒S

Ombrages

56430 ☎ 297521652
Wooded location with shaded pitches divided by hedges.
➲ *Rte Carnac to Auray, left at Shell fuel station.*
Open Jun-10 Sep **Site** 1HEC 🌢 ♣ ⛺ ⛁ **Facilities** 🏕 🖾 ⊙ ⊡ ⊘ ℗
Services ➕ 🗟 **Off-site** ⊑ ◉ ♒LS

Saules

rte de Rosnual, 56340 ☎ 297521498 🗎 297526584
Grassland family site with good facilities site between road and
deciduous woodland, subdivided by hedges and shrubs.
➲ *2.5km N on D119.*
Open Apr-Sep **Site** 2.5HEC 🌢 ♣ ⛺ ⛁ ⛁ **Facilities** 🏕 🖾 ⊙ ⊡ ⊘ ℗
Services ➕ 🗟 **Leisure** ♒ P **Off-site** ⊑ ◉

AT CARNAC-PLAGE (1KM S)

Druides

55 chemin de Beaumer, 56340 ☎ 297520818 🗎 297529613
e-mail camping-les-druides@wanadoo.fr
website www.camping-le-druides.com
Family site with well-defined pitches, 400m from a fine sandy beach.
➲ *SE of town centre. Approach via D781 or D119.*
Open 27 Apr-10 Sep **Site** 2.5HEC 🌢 ♣ ⛺ **Prices** ♠ 3.50-5.60 pitch 18-29
(incl 2 persons) **Facilities** 🏕 ⊙ ⊡ ℗ **Services** ➕ 🗟 **Leisure** ♒ P
Off-site 🖾 ⊑ ◉ ⊘ ⛩ ♒S

Men Dû

22 bis Chemin de Beaumer, 56340 ☎ 297520423
e-mail mendu@wanadoo.fr **website** www.camping-mendu.com
Peaceful site in a wooded setting close to the beach.
➲ *1km from Carnac Plage via D781 & D186.*
Open 2 Apr-2 Oct **Site** 1.5HEC 🌢 ♣ ⛺ **Prices** ♠ 3-4.50 pitch 15-22 (incl 2
persons) ⛁ (static)200-580 **Facilities** 🏕 ⊙ ⊡ ⛩ ℗ **Services** ⊑ ◉ 🗟
Off-site 🖾 ⊘ ♒PRS ➕

Menhirs

allée St-Michel, 56343 ☎ 297529467 🗎 297522538
e-mail contact@lesmenhirs.com **website** www.lesmenhirs.com
A family site near the beach and shops with good recreational facilities
and modern sanitary blocks, including toilets suitable for the disabled.
Open 29 Apr-Sep **Site** 6HEC 🌢 ♣ ⛺ **Facilities** 🏕 🖾 ⊙ ⊡ ℗
Services ⊑ ◉ ➕ 🗟 **Leisure** ♒ P **Off-site** ⊑ ◉ ⊘ ⛩ ♒S

See advertisement on this page

France

Facilities 🖾 shop 🏕 shower ⊙ electric points for razors ⊡ electric points for caravans ℗ parking by tents permitted 🅿 compulsory separate car park
Services ◉ café/restaurant ⊑ bar ⊘ Camping Gaz International ⛩ gas other than Camping Gaz ➕ first aid facilities 🗟 laundry
Leisure ♒ swimming L-Lake P-Pool R-River S-Sea **Off-site** All facilities within 2km

France

CAUREL CÔTES-D'ARMOR

Nautic International
rte de Beau Rivage, 22530 ☎ 296285794 🖹 296260200
e-mail contact@campingnautic.fr **website** www.campingnautic.fr
A terraced site in woodland on the edge of Lake Guerlédan with a variety of recreational facilities.
➲ *N164 towards Beau Rivage.*
Open 15 May-25 Sep **Site** 3.6HEC 👾 ♨ 🏠 **Prices** ♠ 3.30-6 pitch 5.40-8 **Facilities** 🚿 🖻 ⊙ ⊖ ⑫ **Services** 🖪 🖺 **Leisure** ⚓ LP **Off-site** 🍴 🍽

CHAPELLE-AUX-FILZMÉENS, LA ILLE-ET-VILAINE

Domaine du Logis
35190 ☎ 299452545 🖹 299453040
e-mail domainedulogis@wanadoo.fr
website www.domainedulogis.com
A quiet, pleasant site in the wooded grounds of an 18th-century château.
➲ *NE of town towards Combourg.*
Open Apr-27 Oct **Site** 6HEC 👾 ♨ 🏠 **Prices** ♠ 4-5 pitch 6-17 🚐 (static)250-650 **Facilities** 🚿 🖻 ⊙ ⊖ 🖳 🖉 ♨ ⑫ **Services** 🍴 🍽 🖪 🖺 **Leisure** ⚓ P **Off-site** ⚓R

CHÂTEAULIN FINISTÈRE

La Pointe Superbe
rte St-Coulitz, 29150 ☎ 298865153 🖹 298865153
e-mail lapointecamping@aol.com
website www.lapointesuperbecamping.com
Set in a wooded valley close to the town with modern facilities. Pitches divided by hedges. British owners.
➲ *D770 S from Châteaulin centre for Quimper, 1km left to St-Coulitz, site 100m on right.*
Open 15 Mar-Oct **Site** 2.5HEC 👾 ♨ **Prices** pitch 7-14 (incl 2 persons) pp3 **Facilities** 🚿 ⊙ ⊖ 🖳 ⑫ **Leisure** ⚓ R **Off-site** 🖻 🍴 🍽 🖉 ♨ ⚓PS 🖪

CLOÎTRE-ST-THEGONNEC, LE FINISTÈRE

Bruyères
29410 ☎ 298797176
A small, secluded site in a picturesque setting within the Amorique regional park.
➲ *12km S of Morlaix via D769.*
Open Jul-15 Sep **Site** 2.5HEC 👾 ♨ **Prices** ♠ 4 🚗 3 pitch 4 **Facilities** 🚿 🖉 ⑫ **Services** 🖪 🖺 **Off-site** 🖻 🍴 🍽 ♨

COMBOURG ILLE-ET-VILAINE

Bois Coudrais
Cuguen, 35270 ☎ 299732745 🖹 299731308
e-mail info@vacancebretagne.com
website www.vacancebretagne.com
A small, level site with fine views.
➲ *Off D83.*
Open May-Sep **Site** 2.2HEC 👾 ♨ 🏠 **Prices** ♠ 2.50 pitch 8.50 **Facilities** 🚿 ⊙ 🖳 ⑫ **Services** 🍴 🍽 🖪 🖺 **Leisure** ⚓ P **Off-site** 🖻

CONCARNEAU FINISTÈRE

Prés Verts
Kernous Plage, BP612, 29900 ☎ 298970974 🖹 298973206
e-mail info@presverts.com
website www.presverts.com
A landscaped site with good facilities overlooking Concarneau Bay.
➲ *1.2km NW.*
Open Apr-Sep **Site** 2.5HEC 👾 ♨ 🏠 **Prices** pitch 16-22 (incl 2 persons) pp4.70-6.50 **Facilities** 🚿 🖻 ⊙ ⊖ ⑫ ⑫ **Services** 🖺 **Leisure** ⚓ P **Off-site** 🍴 🖉 ♨ ⚓S

COUTERNE ORNE

Clos Normand
rte de Bagnoles-Lac, 61410 ☎ 233379243
e-mail contact@camping-clos-normand.fr
website www.camping-clos-normand.fr
A pleasant site in rural surroundings in a sheltered position close to the thermal spa of Bagnoles-de-l'Orne.
➲ *Approach D916.*
Open May-Sep **Site** 1.3HEC 👾 ♨ 🏠 **Prices** ♠ 2.87 pitch 4.70 (incl 1 persons) 🚐 (static)181-341 **Facilities** 🚿 ⊙ 🖳 ⑫ **Services** 🍴 🍽 🖺 **Off-site** 🖻 🖉 ♨ ⚓PR

CRACH MORBIHAN

Fort Espagnol
rte de Fort Espagnol, 56950 ☎ 297551488 🖹 297300104
e-mail fort-espagnol@wanadoo.fr
website www.fort-espagnol.com
A family site in a secluded, wooded location, with a variety of recreational facilities.
➲ *E of Crach towards coast.*
Open 29 Apr-10 Sep **Site** 4.5HEC 👾 ♨ 🏠 🅰 **Facilities** 🚿 🖻 ⊙ 🖳 🖉 ♨ ⑫ **Services** 🍴 🍽 🖪 🖺 **Leisure** ⚓ P **Off-site** ⚓RS

CRIEL-SUR-MER SEINE-MARITIME

Mouettes
r de la Plage, 76910 ☎ 235867073 🖹 235506494
website www.camping-lesmouettes.fr
Small grassy site overlooking the sea.
Open Apr-2 Nov **Site** 2HEC 👾 ♨ 🏠 **Prices** ♠ 8-9 pitch 7.90-8.90 **Facilities** 🚿 🖻 ⊙ 🖳 🖉 ⑫ **Services** 🍴 🖺 **Off-site** 🍽 ⚓RS 🖪

CROZON FINISTÈRE

Pen ar Menez
bd de Pralognan, 29160 ☎ 298271236
On fringe of a pine wood. Water sports 5km away. Cycles for hire.
Open All year **Site** 2.6HEC 👾 ♨ 🏠 🚐 **Facilities** 🚿 ⊙ 🖳 ⑫ **Services** 🍴 🍽 🖺 **Off-site** 🖻 🍽 🖉 ♨ ⚓S 🖪

Plage de Goulien
Kernaveèno, 29160 ☎ 298271710 🖹 298272195
e-mail campingdelaplagedegoulien@presquile-crozon.com
website www.presquile-crozon.com
Grassy site in wooded surroundings 150m from the sea.
➲ *5km W on D308.*
Open 10 Jun-15 Sep **Site** 2.5HEC 👾 ♨ 🏠 🚐 **Facilities** 🚿 🖻 ⊙ ⊖ 🖉 ⑫ **Services** 🖪 🖺 **Off-site** 🍴 🍽 ⚓S

Site 6HEC (site size) 👾 grass ⊖ sand 👾 stone ♨ little shade ♨ partly shaded 🏠 mainly shaded 🏠 bungalows for hire 🚐 caravans for hire 🅰 tents for hire ⊗ no dogs **Prices** ♠ adult per night 🚗 car per night pp per person per night 🚐 caravan per night 🅰 tent per night 🚐 (static)-caravan hire per week

DEAUVILLE CALVADOS

AT ST-ARNOULT (3KM S)

Vallée
route de Beaumont, 14800 ☎ 231885817 📄 231881157
e-mail loreca@free.fr
A pleasant wooded setting with plenty of recreational facilities.
➲ *1km S via D27 & D275.*
Open Apr-3 Nov **Site** 19HEC 🏕 🛁 🏠 **Facilities** 🌲 ⊙ 🗪 ⬛ ⑳
Services 🍴 🍽 🗄 **Leisure** ⬗ LPR **Off-site** 🏠 ⬗S ➕

AT TOUQUES (3KM SE)

Haras
chemin du Calvaire, 14800 ☎ 231884484 📄 231889708
e-mail les.haras@wanadoo.fr
A partially residential site in pleasant surroundings. Ideal for overnight
stops, but booking advised for July and August.
➲ *N on D62, to Honfleur.*
Open Feb-Nov **Site** 4HEC 🏕 🛁 🏠 🗪 **Facilities** 🌲 ⊙ 🗪 ⬗ 🔥 ⑳
Services 🍴 🍽 ➕ 🗄 **Off-site** 🏠 ⬗P

DÉVILLE-LÈS-ROUEN SEINE-MARITIME

CM
12 rue Jules-Ferry, 76250 ☎ 235740759 📄 235763521
Open All year **Site** 1.5HEC 🏕 🛁 🛁 **Prices** ⚡4.10 🗪 2.90 ⛺1.60
Facilities 🌲 ⊙ 🗪 ⑳ **Services** ➕ 🗄 **Off-site** 🏠 🍴 🍽 ⬗PR

DIEPPE SEINE-MARITIME

AT HAUTOT-SUR-MER (6KM SW)

Source
Petit Appeville, 76550 ☎ 235842704 📄 235822502
e-mail reception@camping-la-source.fr
website www.camping-la-source.fr
Open 15 Mar-15 Oct **Site** 2.5HEC 🏕 🛁 🏠 **Prices** ⚡3.60-5.20 🗪 1 🗪 7 ⛺5
🗪 (static)100-260 **Facilities** 🌲 ⊙ 🗪 ⬗ ⑳ **Services** 🍴 🍽 ➕ 🗄
Leisure ⬗ PR **Off-site** 🏠 ⬗S

DOL-DE-BRETAGNE ILLE-ET-VILAINE

Château des Ormes
35120 ☎ 299735300 📄 299735355
e-mail info@lesormes.com
website www.lesormes.com
Site in grounds of château, within a large leisure complex with
excellent facilities.
➲ *7km S on N795 Rennes road.*
Open 19 May-9 Sep **Site** 50HEC 🏕 🛁 🏠 **Prices** ⚡4.70-7 pitch 15-22
🗪 (static)306-1010 **Facilities** 🌲 🏠 ⊙ 🗪 ⬗ ⑳ **Services** 🍴 🍽 ➕ 🗄
Leisure ⬗ LP

CM Les Tendieres
r des Tendieres, 35120 ☎ 299481468
On level meadow.
➲ *SW from town centre on rte de Dinan 400m.*
Open 15 May-15 Sep **Site** 1.7HEC 🏕 🛁 **Facilities** 🌲 ⊙ 🗪 ⑳ **Services** 🗄
Leisure ⬗ R **Off-site** 🏠 🍴 🍽 ⬗P

AT BAGUER-PICAN (4KM E ON N176)

Camping du Vieux Chêne
35120 ☎ 299480955 📄 299481337
e-mail vieux.chene@wanadoo.fr
website www.camping-vieuxchene.fr
Spacious site in a pleasant lakeside location. Farm produce available.
➲ *5km E of Dol-de-Bretagne on D576.*
Open 31 Mar-22 Sep **Site** 12HEC 🏕 🛁 🏠 **Prices** ⚡4.75-6 pitch 6-17.50
Facilities 🌲 🏠 ⊙ 🗪 ⬗ ⑳ **Services** 🍴 🍽 ➕ 🗄 **Leisure** ⬗ P

DOUARNENEZ FINISTÈRE

Kerleyou
Tréboul, 29100 ☎ 298741303 📄 298740961
e-mail campingdekerleyou@wanadoo.fr
website www.camping-kerleyou.com
Family site in wooded surroundings near the beach. Separate car park
for arrivals after 23.00 hrs.
➲ *1km W on r de Préfet-Collignon towards sea.*
Open May-24 Sep **Site** 3HEC 🏕 🛁 🏠 **Prices** ⚡3.20-3.80 🗪 1.10-1.80
pitch 3.40-6.30 **Facilities** 🌲 🏠 ⊙ 🗪 ⑳ **Services** 🍴 🍽 ➕ 🗄 **Leisure** ⬗ P
Off-site 🍽 ⬗ 🔥 ⬗S

AT POULLAN-SUR-MER (5KM W ON D765)

Pil Koad
29100 ☎ 298742639 📄 298745597
e-mail info@pil-koad.com **website** www.pil-koad.com
A natural wooded setting with a variety of recreational facilities.
➲ *E on D7 towards Douarnenez.*
Open Apr-Sep **Site** 5.5HEC 🏕 🛁 🏠 ⛺ **Prices** ⚡3-4.50 pitch 6.50-15
Facilities 🌲 🏠 ⊙ 🗪 ⬗ 🔥 ⑳ **Services** 🍴 🍽 ➕ 🗄 **Leisure** ⬗ P **Off-site** ⬗S

See advertisement on this page

ERDEVEN MORBIHAN

Ideal
Route de la plage ☎ 297556766
e-mail info@camping-l-ideal.com
website www.camping-l-ideal.com
Open Apr-1 Nov **Site** 0.5HEC 🌱 🏖 🏠 **Prices** ♦ 4-5 pitch 8.80-11
🚐 (static)260-670 **Facilities** 🛒 🚻 ⊙ 🚰 🅿 **Services** 🍴 🛒 **Leisure** 🏊 P
Off-site 🏪 🏄RS

See advertisement on this page

Sept Saints
56410 ☎ 297555265 🖹 297552267
e-mail info@septsaints.com
website www.septsaints.com
Wooded surroundings with good recreational facilities.
➲ *2km NW via D781 rte de Plouhinec.*
Open 15 May-15 Sep **Site** 5HEC 🌱 🏖 🏠 **Prices** ♦ 4-6 pitch 10-17
Facilities 🛒 🚻 ⊙ 🚰 🖉 🚿 ⚲ **Services** 🍴 🛒 **Leisure** 🏊 P **Off-site** 🍴
🏄LRS

ERQUY CÔTES-D'ARMOR

Hautes Greés
123 r St-Michel, 22430 ☎ 296723478 🖹 296723015
e-mail hautesgrees@wanadoo.fr
website www.camping-hautes-grees.com
Good family site, 2km from the town centre and 400m from the
beach.
➲ *0.5km from sea.*
Open Apr-Sep **Site** 3HEC 🌱 🏖 🏠 **Prices** ♦ 3.10-4.90 pitch 5.60-8.50
🚐 (static)260-580 **Facilities** 🛒 🚻 ⊙ 🚰 🖉 ⚲ **Services** 🍴 🛒
Leisure 🏊 P **Off-site** 🍴 🛒 🖉 ⚲ 🏄S

Roches
Caroual Village, 22430 ☎ 296723290 🖹 296635784
e-mail info@camping-les-roches.com
website www.camping-les-roches.com
A rural setting with well-marked pitches, 0.8km from the beach.
➲ *3km SW off D786.*
Open Apr-15 Sep **Site** 3.1HEC 🌱 🏖 🏠 **Prices** ♦ 3.80 🚗 2.80 pitch 3.80
Facilities 🛒 🚻 ⊙ 🚰 ⚲ **Services** 🛒 **Off-site** 🏄S

St-Pabu
22430 ☎ 296722465 🖹 296728717
e-mail camping@saintpabu.com
website www.saintpabu.com
On big open meadow with several terraces in beautiful, isolated
location by sea. Divided into pitches.
➲ *W on D786, signed from la Coutre.*
Open Apr-10 Oct **Site** 5.5HEC 🌱 🏖 🏠 **Prices** pitch 7.50-8.90 pp4-4.80
🚐 (static)270-630 **Facilities** 🛒 🚻 ⊙ 🚰 🖉 ⚲ **Services** 🍴 🛒 🚽 🛒
Leisure 🏊 S

Vieux Moulin
r des Moulins, 22430 ☎ 296723423 🖹 296723663
e-mail camp.vieux.moulin@wanadoo.fr
website www.camping-vieux-moulin.com
Clean tidy site divided into pitches and surrounded by a pine forest.
Suitable for children.
➲ *On D783.*
Open 28 Apr-8 Sep **Site** 6.5HEC 🌱 🏖 🏠 ⚑ **Prices** ♦ 4.50-5.70 pitch 14-19
Facilities 🛒 🚻 ⊙ 🚰 🖉 ⚲ **Services** 🍴 🛒 🚽 🛒 **Leisure** 🏊 P **Off-site** ⚲ 🏄S

ÉTABLES-SUR-MER CÔTES-D'ARMOR

Abri Côtier
22680 ☎ 296706157 🖹 296706523
e-mail camping.abricotier@wanadoo.fr
website www.camping-abricotier.fr
A pleasant family site in a wooded location close to the sea.
➲ *1km N of town centre on D786.*
Open 5 May-9 Sep **Site** 2HEC 🌱 🏖 🏠 **Facilities** 🛒 🚻 ⊙ 🚰 🖉 ⚲
Services 🍴 🛒 **Leisure** 🏊 P **Off-site** 🛒 🏄S

ETRÉHAM CALVADOS

Reine Mathilde
14400 ☎ 231217655 🖹 231221833
e-mail camping.reine_mathilde@wanadoo.fr
website campingreinemathilde.com
A quiet rural setting 4km from the sea.
➲ *1km W via D123*
Open Apr-Sep **Site** 6.5HEC 🌱 🏖 🏠 **Prices** ♦ 5.35-6 pitch 5-5.60
🚐 (static)389.55-555.45 **Facilities** 🛒 🚻 ⊙ 🚰 ⚲ **Services** 🍴 🛒 🚽 🛒
Leisure 🏊 P

FAOUËT, LE MORBIHAN

Beg Er Roch
rte de Lorient, 56320 ☎ 297231511 🖹 297231166
e-mail camping.lefaouët@wanadoo.fr
Pleasant surroundings on the banks of a river. A popular site with
modern sanitary facilities and opportunities for many sports.
Open 10 Mar-Sep **Site** 3.5HEC 🌱 🏖 🏠 🅰 **Prices** ♦ 2.65-3.60 🚗 1-2.10
pitch 2.15-3.20 🚐 (static)195-440 **Facilities** 🛒 ⊙ 🚰 ⚲ **Services** 🛒
Leisure 🏊 R **Off-site** 🏪 🍴 🛒 🖉 ⚲ 🚽

FORÊT-FOUESNANT, LA FINISTÈRE

Européen de la Plage
5 r de Port la Forêt, 29940 ☎ 298569625 🖹 298369625
e-mail laplage.camp@wanadoo.fr
website www.campingdelaplage-kerleven.com
➲ *2.5km SE on D783.*
Open 15 Mar-15 Oct **Site** 1HEC 🌱 🏖 🏠 **Prices** ♦ 4.50 🚗 1.50 pitch 4.90
Facilities 🛒 ⊙ 🚰 ⚲ **Services** 🛒 **Off-site** 🏪 🍴 🛒 🖉 ⚲ 🏄S 🚽

Kérantérec

29940 ☎ 298569811 🖹 298568173
e-mail info@camping-keranterec.com
website www.camping-keranterec.com
Well-kept terraced site, divided into sections by hedges and extending to the sea.
➲ 3km SE.
Open 10 Apr-19 Sep **Site** 6.5HEC 🌺 ♣ 🏠 **Facilities** 🝙 ☺ 🚱 ♨ ℗ ℗
Services 🗜 🍽 🚼 🗟 **Leisure** ⬤ PS **Off-site** 🚿 🍽

Manoir de Pen Ar Steir

29940 ☎ 298569775 🖹 298568049
e-mail info@camping-penarsteir.com
website www.camping-penarsteir.com
Well-tended site close to Port La Forêt, a major yachting arena.
➲ NE off D44.
Open Feb-15 Nov **Site** 3HEC 🌺 ♣ 🏠 **Facilities** 🝙 ☺ 🚱 ♨ ℗ ℗
Services 🚼 🗟 **Off-site** 🚿 🗜 🍽 ⬤PS

Pontérec

Pontérec, 29940 ☎ 298569833 🖹 298569347
A modern site with well-defined pitches separated by hedges, 2.5km from the beach.
➲ On D44 0.5km towards Bénodet.
Open Apr-Sep **Site** 3HEC 🌺 ♣ 🏠 🚐 **Facilities** 🝙 ☺ 🚱 ℗ **Services** 🚼 🗟
Off-site 🚿 🗜 🍽

St-Laurent

Kerleven, 29940 ☎ 298569765 🖹 298569251
e-mail info@camping-du-saint-laurent.fr
website www.camping-du-saint-laurent.fr
On rocky coast. Divided into pitches.
➲ 3.5km SE of village.
Open 2 May-8 Sep **Site** 5.2HEC 🌺 ♣ 🏠 **Prices** pitch 16-37 (incl 2 persons) 🚐 (static)182-1085 **Facilities** 🝙 🚿 ☺ 🚱 ℗ **Services** 🗜 🍽 🗟
Leisure ⬤ PS **Off-site** 🚿 ♨ 🚼

FOUESNANT FINISTÈRE

Atlantique

rte de Mousterlin, 29170 ☎ 298561444 🖹 298561867
e-mail sunelia@latlantique.fr
website www.latlantique.fr
Modern site with plenty of amenities 400m from the beach.
➲ 4.5km S on road to Mousterlin.
Open May-15 Sep **Site** 9HEC 🌺 ♣ 🏠 ⊗ **Prices** pitch 22-39 (incl 2 persons) **Facilities** 🝙 🚿 ☺ 🚱 ♨ ℗ **Services** 🗜 🍽 🚼 **Leisure** ⬤ P
Off-site 🍽 ♨ ⬤S

Piscine

51 Hent Kerleya, 29170 ☎ 298565606 🖹 298565764
e-mail contact@campingdelapiscine.com
website www.campingdelapiscine.com
A beautiful location 1.5km from the beach.
➲ 4km NW towards Kerleya.
Open 15 May-15 Sep **Site** 5HEC 🌺 ♣ 🏠 **Prices** 🕇 3.90-5.75 pitch 7.80-11.50 **Facilities** 🝙 🚿 ☺ 🚱 ♨ ℗ **Services** 🚼 🗟 **Leisure** ⬤ PS

Yelloh Village Le Grand Large

Pointe de Mousterlin, 29170 ☎ 298560406 🖹 298565826
e-mail info@yellohvillage-grand-large.com
website www.villagelegrandlarge.com
A family site in a wooded setting with direct access to the beach. Plenty of modern facilities.
➲ S of Fouesnant via D145.
Open 31 Mar-16 Sep **Site** 6HEC 🌺 ♣ 🏠 ⚠ **Prices** 🕇 5-7 pitch 17-37 (incl 2 persons) **Facilities** 🝙 🚿 ☺ 🚱 ♨ ℗ **Services** 🗜 🍽 🚼 **Leisure** ⬤ PR
Off-site ⬤S   *See advertisement on page 140*

FOUGÈRES ILLE-ET-VILAINE

CM Paron

rte de la Chapelle Janson, 35300 ☎ 299994081 🖹 299942794
A well-managed site suitable for overnight stays.
➲ 1.5km E via D17
Open Apr-Oct **Site** 2.5HEC 🌺 ♣ **Prices** 🕇 2.20 🚐 1.55 pitch 2-2.45
Facilities 🝙 ☺ 🚱 ℗ **Services** 🗟 **Off-site** 🚿 🗜 🍽 ♨ ⬤PR 🚼

GUILLIGOMARC'H FINISTÈRE

Bois des Ecureuils

29300 ☎ 298717098 🖹 298717098
e-mail bois-des-ecureuils@tiscali.fr
website bois-des-ecureuils.com
Tranquil 1.6-hectare wooded site set among oak, chestnut and beech trees. An ideal base for walking, cycling, horse riding and fishing.
➲ D769 N of Plouay, turn W to Guilligomarc'h for 2km.
Open Jun-1 Sep **Site** 2.5HEC 🌺 ♣ ⚠ **Prices** 🕇 3 pitch 5 **Facilities** 🝙 🚿
☺ 🚱 ♨ ℗ **Services** 🚼 🗟

GUILVINEC FINISTÈRE

Yelloh Village La Plage

rte de Penmarc'h, 29730 ☎ 298586190 🖹 298588906
e-mail info@yellohvillage-la-plage.com
website www.villagelaplage.com
On level meadow. Divided into pitches. Flat beach suitable for children.
➲ 2km W of village on Corniche towards Penmarc'h.
Open Apr-16 Sep **Site** 14HEC ⬤ ♣ 🏠 ⚠ **Prices** 🕇 5-7 pitch 17-38
Facilities 🝙 🚿 ☺ 🚱 ♨ ℗ **Services** 🗜 🍽 🚼 🗟 **Leisure** ⬤ PS

See advertisement on page 140

HAYE-DU-PUITS, LA MANCHE

Étang des Haizes

50250 ☎ 233460116 🖹 233472380
e-mail etang.des.haizes@wanadoo.fr
website www.etang-des-haizes.com
A well-equipped family site bordering a lake, shaded by apple trees.
➲ D903 from Carentan.
Open 10 Apr-15 Oct **Site** 5HEC 🌺 ♣ 🏠 🚐 **Prices** 🕇 4-6 pitch 6-17 (incl 2 persons) **Facilities** 🝙 ☺ 🚱 ℗ **Services** 🗜 🍽 🚼 🗟 **Leisure** ⬤ LP
Off-site 🚿 🍽

France (side tab)

Facilities 🚿 shop 🝙 shower ☺ electric points for razors 🚱 electric points for caravans ℗ parking by tents permitted ℗ compulsory separate car park
Services 🍽 café/restaurant 🗜 bar ♨ Camping Gaz International ♨ gas other than Camping Gaz 🚼 first aid facilities 🗟 laundry
Leisure ⬤ swimming L-Lake P-Pool R-River S-Sea **Off-site** All facilities within 2km

France

HOULGATE CALVADOS

Vallée

88 r de la Vallée, 14510 ☎ 231244069 🖷 231244242
e-mail camping.lavallee@wanadoo.fr
website campinglavallee.com
Site with good recreational facilities, 0.9km from the beach.
➲ *1km S.*

Open Apr-Sep **Site** 11HEC 👙 ♣ 🏠 **Facilities** 🌂 🗓️ ⊙ 🐶 🖉 ⏁ ℗ Ⓟ
Services 🍴 🍽 ➕ 🖸 **Leisure** ● P **Off-site** ● S

See advertisement on this page

IFFENDIC ILLE-ET-VILAINE

Domaine de Trémelin

35750 ☎ 299097379 🖷 299097069
A lakeside site in beautiful wooded surroundings with good sports and
entertainment facilities.
➲ *S of town towards Plélan-le-Grand.*

Open Apr-Sep **Site** 2HEC 👙 ♣ 🏠 **Facilities** 🌂 ⊙ 🐶 ℗ **Services** 🍴 🍽
➕ **Leisure** ● L

JULLOUVILLE MANCHE

Chaussée

1 av de la Libération, 50610 ☎ 233618018 🖷 233614526
e-mail jmb@camping-lachaussee.com
website www.campinglachaussee.com
On large meadow, completely divided into pitches. Separated from
the beach and coast road by a row of houses.

Open 8 Apr-17 Sep **Site** 6HEC 👙 ♣ 🏠 **Facilities** 🌂 🗓️ ⊙ 🐶 🖉 ℗
Services 🍴 ➕ 🖸 **Leisure** ● P **Off-site** 🗓️ 🍴 🍽 ● S ➕

Site 6HEC (site size) 👙 grass 🌊 sand 🌊 stone ♣ little shade ♣ partly shaded 👙 mainly shaded 🏠 bungalows for hire
🚐 caravans for hire 🅰 tents for hire ⊗ no dogs **Prices** 🔺 adult per night 🚗 car per night pp per person per night 🚐 caravan per night
🅰 tent per night 🚐 (static)-caravan hire per week

AT ST-MICHEL-DES-LOUPS (4KM SE)

JUMIÈGES SEINE-MARITIME

Forêt
rue Mainberthe, 76480 ☎ 235379343 📄 235377648
e-mail info@campinglaforet.com
website www.campinglaforet.com
Located in the heart of the Brotonne regional park beside the Seine.
➲ *A13 exit Bourg-Achard, site 10km.*
Open 7 Apr-28 Oct **Site** 2.5HEC 🌡 ♣ ⛺ **Prices** ♠ 4-4.50 pitch 15.50-18 (incl 2 persons) 🚐 (static)280-480 **Facilities** 🅵 🚿 ⊙ 🔌 ⌀ ℗ **Services** ➕ 🚿 **Leisure** ⚓ P **Off-site** 🍴 🍺 ⚓R

KERLIN FINISTÈRE

Étangs de Trévignon
Pointe de Trévignon, Kerlin, 29910 ☎ 298500041
e-mail camp.etangsdetrevignon@wanadoo.fr
website www.camping-etangs.com
A family site with modern facilities. A path leads to the beach, 0.8km away.
Open Jun-15 Sep **Site** 3.5HEC 🌡 ♣ ⛺ 🏕 **Prices** ♠ 5.80 pitch 6.60
Facilities 🅵 🚿 ⊙ 🔌 ℗ **Services** 🍺 ➕ 🚿 **Leisure** ⚓ P **Off-site** 🍴 ⚓S

LANDAUL MORBIHAN

Le Pied-à-Terre
Branzého, 56690 ☎ 297245270
e-mail jimrolland@wanadoo.fr **website** www.lepiedaterre.net
A pleasant, quiet location, 15 minutes from the sea.
➲ *1km from N165, signed from Landaul.*
Open 15 May-15 Sep **Site** 2.6HEC 🌡 ♣ ⛺ **Prices** ♠5 🚐 2 🚐 4 🏕 4
Facilities 🅵 ⊙ 🔌 ℗ **Services** 🍺 ➕ 🚿 **Off-site** 🚿 🍴

LANDÉDA FINISTÈRE

Abers
Dunes de Ste-Marguerite, 29870 ☎ 298049335 📄 298048435
e-mail camping-des-abers@wanadoo.fr
website www.camping-des-abers.com
Very quiet beautiful site among dunes. Ideal for children.
➲ *2.5km NW on peninsula between bays Aber-Wrac'h & Aber Benoît.*
Open May-26 Sep **Site** 4.5HEC 🌡 ♣ ⛺ **Facilities** 🅵 🚿 ⊙ 🔌 ⌀ ℗ **Services** ➕ 🚿 **Leisure** ⚓ S **Off-site** 🍺 🍴 ⚓R

LESCONIL FINISTÈRE

Dunes
7 r P-Langevin, 29740 ☎ 298878178 📄 298822705
A family site on slightly sloping landscaped ground, 0.8km from the town centre and the harbour.
➲ *Via D53, turn S in Plobannalac & signed.*
Open end May-15 Sep **Site** 2.8HEC 🌡 ♣ **Prices** ♠ 4.60 pitch 10.95
Facilities 🅵 ⊙ 🔌 ℗ **Services** ➕ 🚿 **Leisure** ⚓ S **Off-site** 🚿 🍺 🍴 ⚓R

Grande Plage
71 r P-Langevin, 29740 ☎ 298878827 📄 298878827
e-mail campinggrandeplage@hotmail.com
Well-equipped site on level ground, surrounded by woodland, 300m from the sea.
Open 2 May-Sep **Site** 2.5HEC 🌡 ♣ ⛺ 🚐 **Prices** ♠ 3.40-4.25 pitch 5.05-6.30 🚐 (static)180-345 **Facilities** 🅵 ⊙ 🔌 ⌀ ℗ **Services** ➕ 🚿 **Off-site** 🚿 🍺 🍴 ⚓S

LITTEAU CALVADOS

Orée du Bois
14490 ☎ 231222208 📄 662544722
e-mail camping.loreedubois@wanadoo.fr
website www.camping-loree-du-bois.com
See advertisement on this page

LOUVIERS EURE

Bel Air
Hameau de St-Lubin, rte de la Haye Malherbe, 27400
☎ 232401077 📄 232401077
e-mail le.belain@wanadoo.fr
website www.lebelair.fr.st
Small site on the edge of a forest with landscaped pitches and good facilities.
➲ *3km from town centre via D81.*
Open 15 Mar-15 Oct **Site** 2.5HEC 🌡 ♣ ⛺ **Prices** ♠ 3.70-4.20 pitch 4.40-5 **Facilities** 🅵 🚿 ⊙ 🔌 ⛽ ℗ **Services** ➕ 🚿 **Leisure** ⚓ P

LUC-SUR-MER CALVADOS

Capricieuse
2 r Brummel, 14530 ☎ 231973443 📄 231968278
e-mail info@campinglacaprieuse.com
A large family site 100m from the beach.
➲ *On W outskirts. A13 exit Douvres.*
Open Apr-Sep **Site** 4.5HEC 🌡 ♣ ⛺ 🚐 **Prices** ♠ 3.04-3.80 🚐 3.68-4.60 pitch 3.04-3.80 🚐 (static)221-420 **Facilities** 🅵 ⊙ 🔌 ℗ **Services** ➕ 🚿 **Off-site** 🚿 🍺 🍴 ⌀ 🚿 ⚓PS

Facilities 🖼 shop 🅵 shower ⊙ electric points for razors 🔌 electric points for caravans ℗ parking by tents permitted ℗ compulsory separate car park
Services 🍴 café/restaurant 🍺 bar ⌀ Camping Gaz International 🚿 gas other than Camping Gaz ➕ first aid facilities 🚿 laundry
Leisure ⚓ swimming L-Lake P-Pool R-River S-Sea **Off-site** All facilities within 2km

France

MARTIGNY SEINE-MARITIME

2 Rivières
76880 ☎ 235856082 🖹 235859516
e-mail martigny.76@wanadoo.fr
website www.camping-2-rivieres.com
On the shore of a lake in pleasant surroundings 8km from Dieppe.
➲ *Via D154.*
Open 30 Mar-11 Oct **Site** 6.8HEC ⬠ ♣ ⬠ **Prices** pitch 15.50 (incl 3 persons) **Facilities** ⬠ ⬠ ⊙ ⬠ ⬠ ⬠ **Services** ⬠ ⬠ **Off-site** ⬠PS

MARTRAGNY CALVADOS

Château de Martragny
14740 ☎ 231802140 🖹 231081491
e-mail chateau.martragny@wanadoo.fr
website www.chateau-martragny.com
Family site in grounds of a château, which also offers accommodation.
➲ *N13 exit Martragny, through St-Léger, site on right.*
Open May-15 Sep **Site** 15HEC ⬠ ♣ **Prices** ⬠ 4.50-5.50 pitch 10.50-110
Facilities ⬠ ⬠ ⊙ ⬠ ⬠ ⬠ ⬠ **Services** ⬠ ⬠ ⬠ **Leisure** ⬠ P **Off-site** ⬠R

MAUPERTUS-SUR-MER MANCHE

Anse du Brick
50330 ☎ 233543357 🖹 233544966
e-mail welcome@anse-du-brick.com
website www.anse-du-brick.com
Terraced site in a landscaped park between the sea and a forest.
➲ *200m from beach.*
Open Apr-Sep **Site** 17HEC ⬠ ♣ ⬠ ⬠ **Prices** ⬠ 4-7 pitch 18.50-33
⬠ (static)329-735 **Facilities** ⬠ ⬠ ⊙ ⬠ ⬠ ⬠ ⬠ **Services** ⬠ ⬠ ⬠ ⬠
Leisure ⬠ P **Off-site** ⬠S

MERVILLE-FRANCEVILLE CALVADOS

Peupliers
Allée des Pins, 14810 ☎ 231240507 🖹 231240507
e-mail asl-mondeville@wanadoo.fr
website www.asl-mondeville.com
A rural setting 300m from the beach. The sanitary facilities include a bathroom for babies. Shop, bar and café available in summer.
➲ *2km E from sign on D514.*
Open Apr-Oct **Site** 3.6HEC ⬠ ⬠ ⬠ ⬠ **Prices** ⬠ 6.50 pitch 7.20
⬠ (static)180-370 **Facilities** ⬠ ⬠ ⊙ ⬠ ⬠ ⬠ ⬠ **Services** ⬠ **Leisure** ⬠ P
Off-site ⬠ ⬠RS ⬠

MONTERBLANC MORBIHAN

Haras
Aérodrome Vannes-Meucon, 56250
☎ 297446606 🖹 297444941
e-mail campingvannes@free.fr
website campingvannes.free.fr
➲ *4km from Vannes towards Aerodrome Vannes-Meucon.*
Open All year **Site** 14HEC ⬠ ♣ ⬠ ⬠ ⬠ **Prices** ⬠ 3-4 ⬠ 1-2 ⬠ 3-4 ⬠ 2-3 ⬠ (static)170-550 **Facilities** ⬠ ⬠ ⊙ ⬠ ⬠ ⬠ **Services** ⬠ ⬠ ⬠ ⬠
Leisure ⬠ P

MONT-ST-MICHEL, LE MANCHE

Gué de Beauvoir
5 rte du Mont-St-Michel, Beauvoir, 50170 ☎ 233600923
A level site in an orchard close to the River Couesnon.
➲ *4km S of Abbey on D776 Pontorson road.*
Open Etr-Sep **Site** 0.6HEC ⬠ ♣ **Prices** ⬠ 2.50 ⬠ 1.50 ⬠ 2.50 ⬠ 2.50
Facilities ⬠ ⊙ ⬠ ⬠ ⬠ **Services** ⬠ ⬠ ⬠ ⬠ **Off-site** ⬠ ⬠

MORGAT FINISTÈRE

Bruyeres
Le Bouis, 29160 ☎ 298261487
e-mail camping.les.bruyeres@presquile-crozon.com
website www.presquile-crozon.com
On a meadow surrounded by woodland with pitches divided by hedges on the edge of the Parc Naturel Régional d'Armorique.
➲ *From Morgat D255 towards Cap de la Chèvre, 1.5km right towards Bouis.*
Open May-Sept **Site** 3HEC ⬠ ♣ ⬠ **Prices** ⬠ 3.70 ⬠ 1.90 pitch 3.70
Facilities ⬠ ⬠ ⊙ ⬠ ⬠ **Services** ⬠ ⬠ **Off-site** ⬠ ⬠ ⬠ ⬠ ⬠

MOYAUX CALVADOS

Colombier
14590 ☎ 231636308 🖹 231631597
e-mail chateau@camping-lecolombier.com
website www.camping-lecolombier.com
Well-kept site in grounds of manor house.
➲ *3km NE on D143.*
Open May-15 Sep **Site** 10HEC ⬠ ♣ **Facilities** ⬠ ⬠ ⊙ ⬠ ⬠ ⬠
Services ⬠ ⬠ ⬠ ⬠ **Leisure** ⬠ P

NÉVEZ FINISTÈRE

Deux Fontaine
Feuntelin Vehan, 29920 ☎ 298068191 🖹 2980697180
e-mail info@les2fontaines.fr
website www.les2fontaines.fr
Mainly level site, subdivided into several fields surrounded by woodland with good recreational facilities including an aquaslide.
➲ *0.7km from Ragunès beach.*
Open 5 May-8 Sep **Site** 7HEC ⬠ ♣ ⬠ **Prices** ⬠ 3.70-5.60 ⬠ 2.10-3.20
pitch 8-14.40 **Facilities** ⬠ ⬠ ⊙ ⬠ ⬠ ⬠ **Services** ⬠ ⬠ ⬠ ⬠ **Leisure** ⬠
P **Off-site** ⬠RS

NOYAL-MUZILLAC MORBIHAN

Moulin de Cadillac
Moulin de Cadillac, 56190 ☎ 297670347 🖹 297670002
e-mail infos@moulin-cadillac.com
website www.camping-moulin-cadillac.com
A well-equipped family site in a pleasant wooded location with good facilities.
➲ *Via N165, N through Muzillac.*
Open May-Sep **Site** 3HEC ⬠ ♣ ⬠ ⬠ ⬠ **Prices** ⬠ 3-4 pitch 4.12-5.50
Facilities ⬠ ⬠ ⊙ ⬠ ⬠ ⬠ **Services** ⬠ ⬠ ⬠ ⬠ **Leisure** ⬠ P

Site 6HEC (site size) ⬠ grass ⬠ sand ⬠ stone ⬠ little shade ⬠ partly shaded ⬠ mainly shaded ⬠ bungalows for hire
⬠ caravans for hire ⬠ tents for hire ⊗ no dogs **Prices** ⬠ adult per night ⬠ car per night pp per person per night ⬠ caravan per night
⬠ tent per night ⬠ (static)-caravan hire per week

PÉNESTIN-SUR-MER MORBIHAN

Cénic
56760 ☎ 299904565 🖷 299904505
e-mail info@lecenic.com
website www.lecenic.com
A forested area 2km from the sea. The spacious grassy pitches are ideal for families.
➩ *D34 from La Roche-Bernard.*
Open Apr-Sep **Site** 7HEC 🐛 ♣ 🏠 **Prices** 🏕 4.50-6 pitch 5-10 🚐 (static)185-460 **Facilities** 🍴 🖺 ⊙ 🖎 🖉 🅿 ⊛ **Services** 🍴 🍽 🖳 **Leisure** ⇌ P **Off-site** 🍽 ⇌S

Iles
La Pointe du Bile, 56760 ☎ 299903024 🖷 299904455
e-mail contact@camping-des-iles.fr
website www.camping-des-iles.fr
A family site with direct access to the beach and a separate residential section.
➩ *3km S on D201.*
Open Apr- 15 Oct **Site** 4HEC 🐛 ♣ 🏠 🛆 **Prices** 🏕 2.30-5 pitch 16-35 (incl 2 persons) 🚐 (static)231-854 **Facilities** 🍴 🖺 ⊙ 🖎 🖉 **Services** 🍴 🍽 🖳 🖺 **Leisure** ⇌ PS

Inly
56760 ☎ 299903509 🖷 299904093
e-mail inly-info@wanadoo.fr
website www.camping-inly.com
Set in the centre of a nature reserve close to the coast, with good recreational facilities.
➩ *2km SE via D201.*
Open 7 Apr-23 Sep **Site** 30HEC 🐛 ♣ 🏠 🛆 **Prices** 🏕 4.50-6.70 🚐 2.20-2.60 pitch 8-11.50 🚐 (static)217-651 **Facilities** 🍴 🖺 ⊙ 🖎 🖉 ⊛ **Services** 🍴 🍽 🖳 **Leisure** ⇌ LP **Off-site** 🖉 ⇌ ⇌RS 🖳

PENTREZ-PLAGE FINISTÈRE

Tamaris
29550 ☎ 298265395 🖷 298265248
e-mail camping-kerys@wanadoo.fr
website www.ker-ys.com
Level site divided into pitches 20m from the beach.
➩ *Via D887.*
Open May-14 Sep **Site** 3HEC 🐛 ♣ 🏠 **Prices** 🏕 3.60-5.30 **Facilities** 🍴 🖺 ⊙ 🖎 ⇲ ⊛ 🅿 **Services** 🖳 🖺 **Leisure** ⇌ PS **Off-site** 🍴 🍽

PERROS-GUIREC CÔTES-D'ARMOR

Claire Fontaine
Toul ar Lann, 22700 ☎ 296230355 🖷 296490619
website www.camping-claire-fontaine.com
Spacious, level site in a rural setting.
➩ *1.2km SW of town centre, 0.8km from Trestraou beach.*
Open Etr-Sep **Site** 3HEC 🐛 ♣ 🏠 🚐 **Facilities** 🍴 ⊙ 🖎 🖉 ⊛ **Services** 🍴 🖳 🖺 **Off-site** 🖺 ⇌S

AT LOUANNEC (3KM SE)

CM Ernest Renan
rte de Perros-Guirec, 22700 ☎ 296231178 🖷 293490447
e-mail mairie-lovannec@wanadoo.com
Site next to the sea. Takeaway food, games room.
➩ *1km W.*
Open May-Sep **Site** 4.5HEC 🐛 ♣ 🏠 🚐 **Facilities** 🍴 🖺 ⊙ 🖎 🖉 ⊛ **Services** 🖳 🍽 🖺 **Leisure** ⇌ LRS **Off-site** 🍽

AT PLOUMANACH(2KM NW)

Ranolien
22700 ☎ 296916565 🖷 296914190
e-mail leranolien@yellovillage.com
website www.leranolien.fr
The site is divided into pitches by hedges, with separate sections for caravans.
➩ *0.5km from village.*
Open 31 Mar-16 Sep **Site** 16HEC 🐛 ♣ 🏠 **Prices** pitch 17-39 (incl 2 persons) **Facilities** 🍴 🖺 ⊙ 🖎 🖉 ⊛ **Services** 🍴 🍽 🖳 🖺 **Leisure** ⇌ P **Off-site** ⇌S

PIEUX, LES MANCHE

Grand Large
50340 ☎ 233524075 🖷 233525820
e-mail le-grand-large@wanadoo.fr
website legrandlarge.com
An unspoiled location with direct access to the beach.
➩ *3km from town centre on D117.*
Open 7 Apr-16 Sep **Site** 4HEC 🐛 ♣ 🏠 🚐 **Prices** 🏕 4-6 pitch 17-29 (incl 2 persons) pp4-5.20 🚐 (static)250-830 **Facilities** 🍴 🖺 ⊙ 🖎 🖉 ⊛ **Services** 🍴 🍽 🖳 🖺 **Leisure** ⇌ PS

PLÉRIN CÔTES-D'ARMOR

Mouettes
Les Rosaires les Mouettes, 22190 ☎ 296745148
Open Jul-Sep **Site** 1HEC 🐛 ♣ 🚐 **Facilities** 🍴 ⊙ 🖎 ⊛ **Services** 🖳 🖺 **Off-site** 🖺 🍴 🍽 🖉 ⇌PRS

PLEUBIAN CÔTES-D'ARMOR

Port la Chaîne
22610 ☎ 296229238 🖷 296228792
e-mail info@portlachaine.com
website www.portlachaine.com
A peaceful, terraced site on the Wild Peninsula, with direct access to the sea, with good facilities.
➩ *2km N via D20.*
Open May-Sep **Site** 5HEC 🐛 ♣ 🏠 🛆 **Facilities** 🍴 🖺 ⊙ 🖎 🖉 ⇲ ⊛ **Services** 🖳 🍽 🖳 🖺 **Leisure** ⇌ PS

PLOBANNALEC-LESCONIL FINISTÈRE

Yelloh Manoir de Kerlut
29740 ☎ 298822389 🖷 298822649
e-mail info@yellohvillage-manoir-de-kerlut.com.
website www.domainemanoirdekerlut.com
A peaceful site located in the grounds of a manor house some 2km from the beach.
➩ *1.6km S via D102.*
Open 5 May-16 Sep **Site** 12HEC 🐛 ♣ 🏠 🛆 **Prices** 🚐 2 pitch 17-37 (incl 2 persons) pp5-7 **Facilities** 🍴 🖺 ⊙ 🖎 🖉 ⊛ **Services** 🍴 🍽 🖳 🖺 **Leisure** ⇌ PS **Off-site** 🍽

France

Facilities 🖺 shop 🍴 shower ⊙ electric points for razors 🖎 electric points for caravans ⊛ parking by tents permitted 🅿 compulsory separate car park **Services** 🍽 café/restaurant 🖳 bar 🖉 Camping Gaz International ⇲ gas other than Camping Gaz 🖳 first aid facilities 🖺 laundry **Leisure** ⇌ swimming L-Lake P-Pool R-River S-Sea **Off-site** All facilities within 2km

PLOËMEL MORBIHAN

Kergo
56400 ☎ 297568066 ▤ 297568066
e-mail camping.kergo@wanadoo.fr
Pleasant wooded surroundings close to the beaches.
➲ *2km SE via D186*
Open 15 Apr-Sep **Site** 2.5HEC ❦ ♣ ⌂ ♠ **Prices** ⚹ 3.50 ♠ 1.80
pitch 4.10 ♠ (static)260-290 **Facilities** ⋔ 🗄 ⊙ ⊕ ♨ **Services** ⊞ ▨
Off-site ⬆ ⚬I

PLOEMEUR MORBIHAN

Ajoncs
Beg Minio, 56270 ☎ 297863011 ▤ 297863011
e-mail secretariat@campingclub.asso.fr
website www.campingclub.asso.fr
A rural site set in an orchard.
➲ *From town centre towards Fort-Bloqué.*
Open 18 Mar-Sep **Site** 2HEC ❦ ♣ **Prices** ⚹ 2.53 ♠ 2.53 ♠ 2.53
Facilities ⋔ ⊙ ⊕ ♨ **Services** ▨ **Off-site** ⬆ ⚬I ⬆LPS

PLOËRMEL MORBIHAN

Lac
Les Belles Rives, Taupont, 56800 ☎ 297740122
e-mail camping.du-lac@wanadoo.fr
website www.camping-du-lac-ploermel.com
A lakeside family site with plenty of facilities for water sports.
➲ *2km from village centre beside lake.*
Open Apr-Oct **Site** 3HEC ❦ ♣ ⌂ **Facilities** ⋔ 🗄 ⊙ ⊕ ♨ ♨ ⓟ
Services ⬆ ⚬I ⊞ ▨ **Leisure** ⬆ L **Off-site** ⬆P

Vallée du Ninian
Le Rocher, 56800 ☎ 297935301 ▤ 297935727
e-mail infos@camping-ninian.com
website www.camping-ninian.com
Peaceful family site beside the River Ninian in the heart of Brittany.
The owners specialise in homemade cider.
➲ *W of Taupont towards river.*
Open 15 May-Sep **Site** 2.7HEC ❦ ♣ ⌂ ♠ **Prices** ⚹ 2.70-3.40 ♠ 4.20-5.30
♠ (static)200-430 **Facilities** ⋔ 🗄 ⊙ ⊕ ♨ ⓟ **Services** ⬆ ⊞ ▨
Leisure ⬆ PR **Off-site** ⚬I

PLOMEUR FINISTÈRE

Torche
Pointe de la Torche, Roz an Tremen, 29120
☎ 298586282 ▤ 298588969
e-mail info@campingdelatorche.fr
website www.campingdelatorche.fr
A family site with pitches surrounded by trees and bushes, 1.5km from
the beach.
➲ *3.5km W.*
Open 3 Apr-25 Sep **Site** 4HEC ❦ ⬤ ♣ ⌂ ♠ **Facilities** ⋔ 🗄 ⊙ ⊕ ♨ ⌀ ♨
ⓟ **Services** ⬆ ⚬I ⊞ ▨ **Leisure** ⬆ P **Off-site** ⚬I ⬆S

PLOMODIERN FINISTÈRE

Iroise
Plage de Pors-ar-Vag, 29550 ☎ 298815272 ▤ 298812610
e-mail campingiroise@aol.com
website www.camping-iroise.com
A family site with fine recreational facilities, providing magnificent
views over the Bay of Douarnenez.
➲ *5km SW, 150m from the beach.*
Open 10 Apr-20 Sep **Site** 2.5HEC ❦ ⬤ ♣ ⌂ **Prices** ⚹ 4.60-6.10 pitch 9.10-
12.10 **Facilities** ⋔ 🗄 ⊙ ⊕ ♨ ⌀ ♨ ⓟ **Services** ⬆ ⚬I ⊞ ▨ **Leisure** ⬆ P
Off-site ⚬I ⬆S

PLONÉVEZ-PORZAY FINISTÈRE

International de Kervel
29550 ☎ 298925154 ▤ 298925496
e-mail camping.kervel@wanadoo.fr
website www.kervel.com
One of the best sites in the region and 0.8km from the sea. Ideal for
families.
➲ *SW of village on D107 Douarnenez road for 3km, turn at x-
rds towards coast.*
Open 30 Apr-10 Sep **Site** 7HEC ❦ ⬤ ♣ ⌂ ♠ Å **Facilities** ⋔ 🗄 ⊙ ⊕ ♨ ⌀
♨ ⓟ **Services** ⬆ ⚬I ⊞ ▨ **Leisure** ⬆ P **Off-site** ⬆S

See advertisement on this page

Tréguer-Plage
Ste-Anne-la-Palud, 29550 ☎ 298925352 ▤ 298925489
e-mail camping-treguer-plage@wanadoo.fr
website www.camping-treguer-plage.com
A level site with direct access to the beach.
➲ *1.3km N.*
Open 15 Jun-15 Sep **Site** 6HEC ❦ ⬤ ♣ ⌂ ♠ **Prices** ⚹ 3.80 ♠ 2.60 pitch
3.80 ♠ (static)155-360 **Facilities** ⋔ 🗄 ⊙ ⊕ ♨ ⌀ ♨ ⓟ **Services** ⬆ ⚬I ▨
Leisure ⬆ S **Off-site** ⬆S ⊞

PLOUÉZEC CÔTES-D'ARMOR

Cap Horn
Port Lazo, 22470 ☎ 296206428 ▤ 296206388
e-mail lecaphorn@hotmail.com
website www.lecaphorn.com
An elevated position overlooking the Ile de Bréhat with direct access
to the beach.
➲ *2.3km NE via D77 at Port-Lazo.*
Open Apr-Sep **Site** 5HEC ❦ ♣ ⌂ ♠ **Prices** ⚹ 4.50 ♠ 7.50 pitch 7.50
Facilities ⋔ 🗄 ⊙ ⊕ ♨ ⌀ ⓟ **Services** ⬆ ⚬I ▨ **Leisure** ⬆ PS **Off-site** ♨

Site 6HEC (site size) ❦ grass ⬤ sand ♣ stone ♣ little shade ♣ partly shaded ❦ mainly shaded ⌂ bungalows for hire
♠ caravans for hire Å tents for hire ⊗ no dogs **Prices** ⚹ adult per night ♠ car per night pp per person per night ♠ caravan per night
Å tent per night ♠ (static)-caravan hire per week

PLOUEZOCH FINISTÈRE

Baie de Térénez

Moulin de Caneret, 29252 ☎ 298672680 ▤ 298672680
e-mail campingbaiedeterenez@wanadoo.fr
website www.campingbaiedeterenez.com
A well-equipped site in a pleasant rural setting.
➲ 3.5km NW via D76.
Open Apr-Sep **Site** 3HEC ⛺ ♣ 🏕 **Prices** ⚹ 3.50-5 ▲ 5.80
pitch 4.50-6.20 🚐 (static)180-610 **Facilities** 🅝 ⊙ 🚰 ⌀ ⬜ ⓟ **Services** ⛽
⚑ ⬚ 🅖 **Leisure** ⛱ P **Off-site** ⚓RS

PLOUGASNOU FINISTÈRE

Etangs de Mesqueau

26930 ☎ 298673745 ▤ 0298678279
e-mail commune.de.plougasnou@wanadoo.fr
Large municipal site with good recreational facilities.
➲ 3.5km S via D46.
Open Jul-Aug **Site** 7HEC ⛺ ♣ **Facilities** 🅝 ⊙ 🚰 ⓟ ⓟ **Services** ⚑ ⬚
Leisure ⛱ R **Off-site** ⚑ ⚑ ⚓S

Trégor

Kerjean, 29630 ☎ 298673764
e-mail bookings@campingdutregor.com
website www.campingdutregor.com
A sheltered site with numbered, grassy pitches. Surrounded by
hedges.
➲ Off D46 towards Morlaix.
Open Etr-Oct **Site** 1HEC ⛺ ♣ 🚐 **Prices** ⚹ 2.40-2.90 ⚹ 1-1.20 ▲ 1.80-
2.10 ▲ 1.80-2.10 🚐 (static)200-360 **Facilities** 🅝 ⊙ 🚰 ⬜ ⬜ **Services** 🅖
Off-site ⓘ ⚑ ⚑ ⚓S ⬚

PLOUHA CÔTES-D'ARMOR

AT TRINITÉ, LA (2KM NE)

Domaine de Keraval

rte de Port Moguer, 22580 ☎ 296224913
e-mail keraval@wanadoo.fr
website www.keraval.com
Forested site built around an elegant country mansion, 1km from the
sea.
Open 15 May-Sep **Site** 5HEC ⛺ ♣ 🏕 **Prices** ⚹ 5.20-6.50 pitch 8.64-10.80
Facilities 🅝 ⓘ ⊙ 🚰 ⌀ ⬜ **Services** ⬚ 🅖 **Leisure** ⛱ P **Off-site** ⚓S

PLOUHARNEL MORBIHAN

Étang de Loperhet

56340 ☎ 297523468 ▤ 297523468
e-mail info@camping-loperhet.com
website www.camping-loperhet.com
➲ 1km NW via D781
Open Apr-Sep **Site** 6HEC ⛺ ♣ ♣ 🏕 🚐 **Prices** ⚹ 3.10-4.80 pitch 5-7.90
🚐 (static)165-590 **Facilities** 🅝 ⓘ ⊙ 🚰 ⌀ ⬜ **Services** ⚑ 🍽 🅖
Leisure ⛱ P **Off-site** 🍽 ⚑ ⚓S ⬚

Kersily

Ste-Barbe, 56340 ☎ 297523965 & ▤ 297524476
e-mail camping.kersily@wanadoo.fr
website www.camping-kersily.com
Open Apr-Oct **Site** 4HEC ⛺ ♣ 🏕 🚐 **Prices** ⚹ 2.80-4.40 ⚹ 1.50-1.80
pitch 3.80-5.40 **Facilities** 🅝 ⓘ ⊙ 🚰 ⬜ **Services** ⚑ 🍽 ⬚ 🅖
Leisure ⛱ P **Off-site** ⚓S

Lande

Kerzivienne, 56340 ☎ 297523148 ▤ 297523148
e-mail campdelalande@aol.com
On partially shaded terrain, 0.6km from the beach.
Open Jun-27 Sep **Site** 1HEC ⛺ ♣ 🏕 🚐 **Prices** pitch 12.50 (incl 2
persons) 🚐 (static)250-300 **Facilities** 🅝 ⊙ 🚰 ⌀ ⬜ **Services** ⬚ 🅖
Off-site ⓘ ⚑ 🍽 ⌀ ⚓S

PLOUHINEC MORBIHAN

Moténo

rte du Magouer, 56680 ☎ 297367663 ▤ 297858184
e-mail camping-moteno@wanadoo.fr
website www.camping-le-moteno.com
On slightly sloping ground, subdivided into several fields in a wooded
area 0.6km from the beach.
➲ S beside Mer d'Etel.
Site 4HEC ⛺ ♣ 🏕 🚐 **Prices** ⚹ 2.60-4.20 pitch 4.50-9.50 🚐 (static)170-
585 **Facilities** 🅝 ⓘ ⊙ 🚰 ⌀ ⬜ **Services** ⚑ 🍽 ⬚ 🅖 **Off-site** ⚓PS

PLOZÉVET FINISTÈRE

Corniche

rte de la Corniche, 29710 ☎ 298913394 ▤ 298914153
e-mail info@campinglacorniche.com
website www.campinglacorniche.com
Peaceful rural site 1.5km from the sea.
Open Apr-Sep **Site** 2HEC ⛺ ♣ 🏕 **Prices** ⚹ 4.50 pitch 6 **Facilities** 🅝 ⓘ ⊙
🚰 ⌀ ⬜ **Services** ⚑ 🍽 ⬚ 🅖 **Leisure** ⛱ P **Off-site** ⚑ 🍽 ⚑ ⚓LRS

PONTAUBAULT MANCHE

Vallée de la Sélune

7 rue Mal Leclerc, 50220 ☎ 233603900 ▤ 233603900
e-mail campselune@wanadoo.fr
website www.camping-normandy.com
This site is in a quiet village near the River Sélune. Ideal base for
exploring the Normandy/Brittany area.
➲ Off N175.
Open Apr-20 Oct **Site** 1.6HEC ⛺ ♣ 🏕 🚐 **Prices** ⚹ 3 🚐 3 🚐 3 ▲ 2-3
🚐 (static)150-190 **Facilities** 🅝 ⓘ ⊙ 🚰 ⌀ ⬜ **Services** ⚑ 🍽 ⚓R
Off-site 🍽 ⚑ ⚓R

PONT-AVEN FINISTÈRE

Domaine de Kerlann

29930 ☎ 298060177 ▤ 0870 242 9999
e-mail kerlann@haven.fr
website www.haveneurope.com
A wooded park with shady pitches featuring an indoor pool complex
with waterslide and spa bath.
➲ 3m E of Pont Aven.
Open 19 Mar-21 Oct **Site** 26HEC ⛺ ♣ ▲ ⬚ **Facilities** 🅝 ⓘ ⊙ 🚰 🚐 ⬜
Services ⚑ 🍽 ⬚ 🅖 **Leisure** ⛱ P **Off-site** ⓘ ⚑

PONT-L'ABBÉ FINISTÈRE

Bois Soleil

29120 ☎ 298870339 ▤ 298870339
website www.camping-finistere.com
Shady site set in a wooded park with good recreational facilities.
➲ 3.5km NE on D44.
Open May-Sep **Site** 3HEC ⛺ ♣ 🏕 🚐 **Prices** ⚹ 2.80-3.50 ⚹ 1.50-1.80
pitch 3.50-4.40 🚐 (static)220-340 **Facilities** 🅝 ⓘ ⊙ 🚰 ⌀ ⬜ ⬜
Services ⚑ 🍽 ⬚ 🅖 **Leisure** ⛱ P **Off-site** ⚓P

France

Facilities ⓘ shop 🅝 shower ⊙ electric points for razors 🚰 electric points for caravans ⬜ parking by tents permitted ⓟ compulsory separate car park
Services 🍽 café/restaurant ⚑ bar ⌀ Camping Gaz International ⬜ gas other than Camping Gaz ⬚ first aid facilities 🅖 laundry
Leisure ⛱ swimming L-Lake P-Pool R-River S-Sea **Off-site** All facilities within 2km

France

PONTORSON MANCHE

Haliotis

chemin des Soupirs ☎ 233681159 ▤ 233589536
e-mail info@camping-haliotis-mont-saint-michel.com
website www.camping-haliotis-mont-saint-michel.com
On the banks of a river, a short distance from Mont St Michel.

⊃ *Off D976 in direction Avranches*

Open Apr-5 Nov **Site** 6HEC ❤ ❤ ⚐ **Prices** ♦ 4.50-6 pitch 5-7
Facilities ♠ ⊙ ⊡ ℗ **Services** ☎ ⦿ ➕ ▣ **Leisure** ⚓ P
Off-site ⚐ ⦿ ⌀ ⚒

PORDIC CÔTES-D'ARMOR

Madières

rte de Vau Madec, 22590 ☎ 296790248 ▤ 296794667
e-mail lesmadieres@wanadoo.fr
website www.campinglesmadieres.com
A quiet coastal site in a well-shaded position.

⊃ *1.5km from village on D786 towards St-Brieuc.*

Open Apr-Oct **Site** 2HEC ⊜ ❤ ⚐ ⚐ **Facilities** ♠ ⚐ ⊙ ⊡ ⌀ ⚒ ℗
Services ☎ ⦿ ➕ ▣ **Leisure** ⚓ P **Off-site** ⚓S

PORT-EN-BESSIN CALVADOS

Port'land

14520 ☎ 231510706 ▤ 231517649
e-mail campingportland@wanadoo.fr
website www.camping-portland.com
Situated in rural surroundings near Omaha Beach, with an indoor
heated swimming pool on site.

Open 31 Mar-8 Nov **Site** 8.6HEC ⊜ ❤ ❤ ⚐ **Prices** pitch 15.50-27.30
pp4.80-7.30 **Facilities** ♠ ⚐ ⊙ ⊡ ℗ **Services** ☎ ⦿ ➕ ▣ **Leisure** ⚓ LP
Off-site ⚐ ☎ ⦿ ⌀ ⚒ ⚓S

PORT-MANECH FINISTÈRE

St-Nicolas

29920 ☎ 298068975 ▤ 298067461
e-mail info@campinglesaintnicolas.com
website www.campinglesaintnicolas.com
Divided into hedge-lined pitches in beautiful surroundings close to the
beach.

Open May-Sep **Site** 3.5HEC ⊜ ❤ ⚐ **Prices** ♦ 4.90 pitch 8.90 **Facilities** ♠
⊙ ⊡ ℗ **Services** ➕ ▣ **Leisure** ⚓ P **Off-site** ⚐ ☎ ⦿ ⌀ ⚒ ⚓S

POSES EURE

Ile Adeline

27740 ☎ 232593581 ▤ 232598895
A well-equipped site close to the Lery-Poses leisure centre.

⊃ *A13 exit 19 for Val-de-Reuil.*

Open Apr-Sep **Site** 2.5HEC ⊜ ❤ ⚐ **Facilities** ♠ ⚐ ⊙ ⊡ ℗ **Services** ☎
⦿ ➕ ▣ **Off-site** ⚓LR

POULDU, LE FINISTÈRE

Embruns

r du Philosophe Alain, 29360 ☎ 298399107 ▤ 298399787
e-mail camping-les-embruns@wanadoo.fr
website www.camping-les-embruns.com
A pleasant site with good facilities and easy access to the beach.
Separate car park for arrivals after 22.00 hrs.

Open 7 Apr-15 Sep **Site** 5HEC ⊜ ❤ ⚐ **Prices** pitch 10.50-28.20 pp3.90-
5.30 **Facilities** ♠ ⚐ ⊙ ⊡ ⌀ ⚒ ℗ **Services** ☎ ⦿ ➕ ▣ **Leisure** ⚓ P
Off-site ⦿ ⚓RS

QUETTEHOU MANCHE

Rivage

rte de Morsalines, 50630 ☎ 233541376
e-mail camping.lerivage@wanadoo.fr
website www.camping-lerivage.fr
Quiet, sheltered site, 400m from the sea.

⊃ *Via D14.*

Open Apr-Sept **Site** 2HEC ⊜ ❤ ⚐ **Facilities** ♠ ⊙ ⊡ ⌀ ⚒ ℗
Services ☎ ⦿ ➕ ▣ **Leisure** ⚓ P **Off-site** ⚐ ☎ ⦿ ⌀ ⚓S ➕

QUIBERON MORBIHAN

Bois d'Amour

rue St-Clement, 56170 ☎ 297501352 ▤ 297504267
e-mail info@homair-vacances.fr
website www.homair-vacances.fr
A family site with plenty of recreational facilities close to the area's fine
beaches.

⊃ *1.5km SE at La Pointe de la Presqu'île, 100m from beach.*

Open Apr-Oct **Site** 5.5HEC ⊜ ❤ ⚐ ⚐ ⚐ **Facilities** ♠ ⚐ ⊙ ⊡ ℗
Services ☎ ⦿ ▣ **Leisure** ⚓ P **Off-site** ⚐ ☎ ⦿ ⌀ ⚒ ⚓S ➕

Conguel

bd Teignouse, 56170 ☎ 297501911
Directly on the beach, with fine recreational facilities.

⊃ *Near aerodrome towards Pointe de Conguel.*

Open Apr-Oct **Site** 5HEC ⊜ ❤ ⚐ **Facilities** ♠ ⚐ ⊙ ⊡ ℗ **Services** ☎
⦿ ➕ ▣ **Leisure** ⚓ P **Off-site** ⚓S

QUIMPER FINISTÈRE

Orangerie de Lanniron

Chateau de Lanniron, 29336 ☎ 298906202 ▤ 298521556
e-mail camping@lanniron.com
website www.lanniron.com
Set in the grounds of the former residence of the bishops of Quimper
beside the River Odet and surrounded by tropical vegetation.

⊃ *2.5km from town centre via D34.*

Open 15 May-15 Sep **Site** 27HEC ⊜ ❤ ⚐ ⚐ **Prices** ♦ 4.25-6.80 ♣ 7.50-
12.20 pitch 15.50-24.40 **Facilities** ♠ ⚐ ⊙ ⊡ ⌀ ⚒ ℗ **Services** ☎ ⦿ ➕
▣ **Leisure** ⚓ PR

RAGUENÈS-PLAGE FINISTÈRE

Airotel International Raguenès-Plage

19 r des Iles, Raguenez, 29920 ☎ 298068069 ▤ 298068905
e-mail info@camping-le-raguenes-plage.com
website www.camping-le-raguenes-plage.com
Site with asphalt drives, 400m from beaches.

⊃ *From Pont-Aven to Nevez, signs to Raguenès.*

Open Apr-Sep **Site** 7HEC ⊜ ❤ ⚐ ⚐ **Prices** ♦ 4.40-5.60 pitch 7.70-15.80
⚐ (static)247.50-820 **Facilities** ♠ ⚐ ⊙ ⊡ ⌀ ⚒ ℗ ℗ **Services** ☎ ⦿ ➕ ▣
Leisure ⚓ PS

Site 6HEC (site size) ⊜ grass ⊜ sand ❤ stone ♣ little shade ❤ partly shaded ❤ mainly shaded ⚐ bungalows for hire
⚐ caravans for hire ♣ tents for hire ⊗ no dogs **Prices** ♦ adult per night ♣ car per night pp per person per night ⚐ caravan per night
♣ tent per night ⚐ (static)-caravan hire per week

RAVENOVILLE-PLAGE MANCHE

Cormoran

50480 ☎ 233413394 🖷 233951608
e-mail lecormoran@wanadoo.fr
website www.lecormoran.com
A pleasant family site with well-defined pitches, 20m from the sea.
⮑ *300m from town towards Utah Beach.*
Open Apr-24 Sept **Site** 8.5HEC ☸ ☸ 🐾 **Prices** pitch 16.50-34 (incl 2 persons) pp4-7 🚐 (static)280-780 **Facilities** 🌳 🛍️ ⊙ 🔌 ⌀ 🚿 ® **Services** 🗜 🍽 🛟 🗄 **Leisure** ⚓ P **Off-site** 🍽 ⚓S

ROCHE-BERNARD, LA MORBIHAN

CM Patis

3 chemin du Patis, 56130 ☎ 299906013 🖷 299908828
On banks of River Vilaine.
⮑ *100m from village centre.*
Open Apr-Sep **Site** 1HEC ☸ ☸ 🐾 **Facilities** 🌳 ⊙ 🔌 ® **Services** 🛟 🗄 **Leisure** ⚓ R **Off-site** 🛍️ 🗜 🍽 ⌀ 🚿 ⚓P

ROCHEFORT-EN-TERRE MORBIHAN

Moulin Neuf

56220 ☎ 297433752 🖷 297433545
A well-equipped site in wooded surroundings. The shop contains only basic items but there is a supermarket nearby.
⮑ *Signed from D744 in village.*
Open May-Sep **Site** 2.5HEC ☸ ☸ 🐾 **Facilities** 🌳 ⊙ 🔌 ® 🅿 **Services** 🛟 🗄 **Leisure** ⚓ P **Off-site** 🗜 🍽 ⚓LR 🛟

ROSTRENEN CÔTES-D'ARMOR

Fleur de Bretagne

Kerandouaron, 22110 ☎ 296291545 🖷 296291645
e-mail info@fleurdebretagne.com
website www.fleurdebretagne.com
A spacious site in a picturesque, sheltered valley with modern facilities.
⮑ *D764 from Rostrenen 1.5km towards Pontivy.*
Open All year **Site** 6HEC ☸ ☸ 🐾 **Prices** ♠ 3-5 ▲ 3-4 pitch 5-7 🚐 (static)200-300 **Facilities** 🌳 ⊙ 🔌 ® **Services** 🗜 🍽 🗄 **Leisure** ⚓ LP **Off-site** 🛍️ ⌀ 🚿 🛟

ST-ALBAN CÔTES-D'ARMOR

St-Vrêguet

St-Vréguet, 22400 ☎ 296329021
e-mail vreguet@wanadoo.fr
A peaceful site in a pleasant park with good sanitary and recreational facilities.
Open Jun-Sep **Site** 1HEC ☸ ☸ 🐾 **Prices** ♠ 2.90 🚗 1.40 pitch 1.80 🚐 (static)290 **Facilities** 🌳 🛍️ ⊙ 🔌 ⌀ ® **Services** 🗜 🛟 🗄 **Off-site** ⚓R

ST-AUBIN-SUR-MER SEINE-MARITIME

CM Mesnil

76740 ☎ 235830283
A family site attached to a typical Norman farm.
⮑ *2km W on D68.*
Open Apr-Oct **Site** 2.3HEC ☸ ☸ **Prices** ♠ 5.47 🚗 2.12 pitch 3.02 **Facilities** 🌳 ⊙ 🔌 ® **Services** 🍽 🛟 🗄 **Off-site** 🛍️ ⚓S

ST-AUBIN-SUR-MER CALVADOS

Yelloh Village Côte de Nacre

17 r du General Moulton, 14750 ☎ 231971445 🖷 231972211
e-mail camping-cote-de-nacre@wanadoo.fr
website www.camping-cote-de-nacre.com
A pleasant site with good recreational facilities. Reservations recommended in high season. Separate car park for late arrivals.
Open 31 Mar-16 Sep **Site** 10HEC ☸ ☸ **Prices** pitch 17-41 (incl 2 persons) **Facilities** 🌳 🛍️ ⊙ 🔌 ® **Services** 🗜 🍽 🛟 🗄 **Leisure** ⚓ P **Off-site** ⚓S

See advertisement on this page

ST-BRIAC ILLE-ET-VILAINE

Emeraude

7 chemin de la Souris, 35800 ☎ 299883455
e-mail camping.emeraude@wanadoo.fr
website www.camping-emeraude.com
Well-kept site in pleasant quiet location and divided into pitches.
⮑ *Left off D786 for 0.8km.*
Open Apr-Sep **Site** 2HEC ☸ ☸ 🐾 🐾 **Facilities** 🌳 🛍️ ⊙ 🔌 ⌀ 🚿 ® **Services** 🗜 🛟 🗄 **Off-site** 🍽 ⚓S

ST-BRIEUC CÔTES-D'ARMOR

Vallées

Parc de Brézillet, 22000 ☎ 296940505
e-mail campingdesvallees@wanadoo.fr
Situated on the edge of the town. Restaurant only open July and August.
Open Etr-15 Oct **Site** 4.8HEC ☸ ☸ 🐾 🐾 **Prices** ♠ 3.70-4.60 pitch 12-9.60 🚐 (static)330-670 **Facilities** 🌳 🛍️ ⊙ 🔌 ® **Services** 🗜 🍽 🛟 🗄 **Leisure** ⚓ R **Off-site** ⌀ ⚓PS

Camping
★★★★

Le P'tit Bois
Saint Malo
City of the sea

Saint Malo
35430 St Jouan des Guérêts

Booking:
Tel. 33 (0)2 99 21 14 30
Fax 33 (0)2 99 81 74 14
E-mail: camping.ptitbois@wanadoo.fr
www.ptitbois.com

ST-CAST-LE-GUILDO CÔTES-D'ARMOR

Château de Galinée
22380 ☎ 296411056 🖹 296410372
e-mail contact@chateaudegalinee.com
website www.chateaudegalinee.com
A family site in a 2-hectare wood incorporating the buildings of an old farm, 3km from the beaches.
➲ *1km from CD786. Signed.*
Open 12 May-9 Sep **Site** 14HEC 🌳 ♨ ☘ 🏠 ⚠ **Prices** ♦ 4-6 pitch 8.50-15 **Facilities** 🍴 🕍 ⊙ 🚰 ⚑ ⊕ **Services** 🛒 ⛱ **Leisure** ⚓ P **Off-site** ⌀ ⚓LS

Châtelet
r des Nouettes, 22380 ☎ 296419633 🖹 296419799
e-mail chateletcp@aol.com
website www.lachatelet.com
Superb landscaped surroundings overlooking the sea with good sports facilities.
➲ *1km W, 250m from beach.*
Open May-10 Sep **Site** 8HEC 🌳 ♨ ☘ 🏠 **Prices** ♦ 4-6 pitch 12.50-20 ⚑ (static)310-790 **Facilities** 🍴 🕍 ⊙ 🚰 ⌀ ⊕ **Services** 🛒 ⛱ 🚻 ⛁ **Leisure** ⚓ LPS **Off-site** 🚿

Crique
r de la Mare, 22380 ☎ 296418919
A tiered site with exceptional views across Fort Lalette and the sea. Direct access to the beach.
Open 15 Mar-2 Jan **Site** 2.8HEC 🌳 ♨ ☘ 🏠 **Facilities** 🍴 ⊙ 🚰 ⌀ ⊕ **Services** 🛒 ⛱ 🚻 ⛁ **Off-site** ⚓S

Mielles
22380 ☎ 296418760 🖹 296810477
Ideally positioned at the heart of the resort and within walking distance of the beach. Spacious defined pitches.
➲ *0.5km NE on coast.*
Open 15 Mar-2 Jan **Site** 3.5HEC 🌳 ♨ ☘ 🏠 **Facilities** 🍴 ⊙ 🚰 ⌀ ⊕ **Services** ⛱ 🚻 ⛁ **Leisure** ⚓ P

ST-EFFLAM CÔTES-D'ARMOR

CM
r de Ian-Carré, 22310 ☎ 296356215 🖹 296350975
e-mail campingmunicipalplestin@wanadoo.fr
website www.camping-bretagne.com/camping
On a level meadow with well-defined pitches 100m from a magnificent beach.
Open Apr-Sep **Site** 4HEC 🌳 ☘ 🏠 **Prices** ♦ 2.21-2.60 ⚑ 1.30-1.60 pitch 2.86-3.40 **Facilities** 🍴 ⊙ 🚰 ⊕ **Services** 🛒 ⛱ ⛁ **Off-site** ⛱ ⌀ ⚓S

ST-GERMAIN-SUR-AY MANCHE

Aux Grands Espaces
50430 ☎ 233071014 🖹 233072259
website www.aux-grand-espaces.com
On slightly sloping ground among dunes, 0.5km from the sea. Children's play area.
➲ *Off D650 W of town onto D306 signed Plage.*
Open May-15 Sep **Site** 15HEC 🌳 ♨ ☘ 🏠 ⚠ **Prices** ♦ 5.20 pitch 6.50 ⚑ (static)560 **Facilities** 🍴 🕍 ⊙ 🚰 🚿 ⊕ **Services** 🛒 ⛱ 🚻 ⛁ **Leisure** ⚓ P **Off-site** ⚓S

ST-GILDAS-DE-RHUYS MORBIHAN

Menhir
rte de Port Crouesty, 56730 ☎ 297452288 🖹 297453718
e-mail campingmenhir@aol.com
website www.campingdumenhir.com
A family site with good facilities, 1km from the beach.
➲ *3.5km N.*
Open 26 May-5 Sep **Site** 3HEC 🌳 ♨ ☘ 🏠 **Facilities** 🍴 🕍 ⊙ 🚰 ⊕ **Services** 🛒 ⛱ 🚻 ⛁ **Leisure** ⚓ PS **Off-site** ⌀ ⚓S

ST-JOUAN-DES-GUÉRÊTS ILLE-ET-VILAINE

P'tit Bois
35430 ☎ 299211430 🖹 299817414
e-mail camping.ptitbois@wanadoo.fr
website www.ptitbois.com
A pleasant family site in quiet wooded surroundings.
➲ *Via N137 exit St-Jouan-des-Guerets (D4).*
Open 7 Apr-8 Sep **Site** 6HEC 🌳 ♨ ☘ 🏠 **Prices** ♦ 5-8 pitch 8-19 **Facilities** 🍴 🕍 ⊙ 🚰 ⌀ ⊕ **Services** 🛒 ⛱ 🚻 ⛁ **Leisure** ⚓ P **Off-site** 🚿 ⚓R

See advertisement on this page

ST-LÉGER-DU-BOURG-DENIS SEINE-MARITIME

Aubette
23 r Vert Buisson, 76160 ☎ 235084769 🖹 235084769
Set in a wooded valley 3km E of Rouen.
Open All year **Site** 0.8HEC 🌳 ☘ 🏠 **Prices** ♦ 3 pitch 3.10 **Facilities** 🍴 ⊙ 🚰 🚿 ⊕ 🅿 **Services** 🚻 ⛁ **Off-site** 🕍 🛒 ⛱ ⌀ ⚓R

Site 6HEC (site size) 🌳 grass ♨ sand 🌳 stone ☘ little shade ☘ partly shaded 🏠 mainly shaded 🏠 bungalows for hire ⚑ caravans for hire ⚠ tents for hire ⊗ no dogs **Prices** ♦ adult per night ⚓ car per night pp per person per night ⚑ caravan per night ⚠ tent per night ⚑ (static)-caravan hire per week

ST-LUNAIRE ILLE-ET-VILAINE

Longchamp
od de St-Cast, 35800 ☎ 299463398 ◫ 299460271
website www.camping-longchamp.com
A beautiful wooded setting 100m from the sea on the Emerald coast
with a good range of facilities.
⊃ *Off D786 towards St-Briac at end of village, site on left.*
Open 17 May-10 Sep **Site** 5HEC ❄ ♣ **Prices** ♠ 5.20 ♠ 3.60 ♠ 5.80
▲ 5.80 **Facilities** ⋔ 🏕 ⊙ ⊕ ⌀ ℗ **Services** 🍴 ⍩ ⊞ ◙ **Off-site** ⊶S

Touesse
35800 ☎ 299466113 ◫ 299160258
e-mail camping.la.touesse@wanadoo.fr
website www.campinglatouesse.com
A well-equipped family site, 300m from the beach.
⊃ *2km E via D786.*
Open Apr-Sep **Site** 2.8HEC ❄ ♣ 🏠 ♠ **Prices** ♠ 4-5.10 ♠ 2.60-3.10
♠ 5-6.20 ▲ 5-6.20 (static)175-370 **Facilities** ⋔ 🏕 ⊙ ⊕ ⌀ ℗
Services 🍴 ⍩ ⊞ ◙ **Off-site** ⊶PS

ST-MALO ILLE-ET-VILAINE

CM le Nicet
av de la Varde Rotheneuf, 35400 ☎ 299402632 ◫ 299219262
e-mail camping@ville-saint-malo.fr
website www.ville-saint-malo.fr/campings
Site 100m from the beach, access via stairs. Water sports and other
activities available.
Open Jul-1 Sep **Site** 2.9HEC ❄ ♣ **Prices** ♠ 5.50 pitch 12 **Facilities** ⋔ ⊙
⊕ ℗ **Services** ⊞ ◙ **Leisure** ⊶ S **Off-site** 🏕 ⍩ ⌀ ⊸ ⊶S

Domaine de la Ville Huchet
rte de la Passagère, 35400 ☎ 299811183 ◫ 299815189
e-mail info@lavillehuchet.com
website www.lavillehuchet.com
⊃ *5km S via N137.*
Open 28 Apr-22 Sep **Site** 6HEC ❄ ♣ 🏠 ♠ **Prices** ♠ 3.45-5.20 pitch 9-12.40
♠ (static)295-575 **Facilities** ⋔ 🏕 ⊙ ⊕ ⌀ ℗ **Services** 🍴 ⍩ ⊞ ◙
Leisure ⊶ P **Off-site** ⊶R

ST-MARCAN ILLE-ET-VILAINE

Balcon de la Baie
35120 ☎ 299802295 ◫ 299802295
A beautiful location overlooking the bay of Mont-St-Michel.
⊃ *10km NW of Pontorson on D797.*
Open Apr-Oct **Site** 2.7HEC ❄ ♣ 🏠 ♠ **Prices** ♠ 4.50 pitch 5 ♠ (static)460
Facilities ⋔ ⊙ ⊕ ⊸ ℗ **Services** ◙ **Leisure** ⊶ P **Off-site** 🍴 ⍩

ST-MARTIN-DES-BESACES CALVADOS

Puits
14350 ☎ 231678002 ◫ 231678002
e-mail camping.le.puits@wanadoo.fr
website www.lepuits.com
A small family run site surrounded by a pleasant garden and lush
fields.
⊃ *Off N175.*
Open Mar-Oct **Site** 3.6HEC ❄ ♣ **Prices** ♠ 3 pitch 8 **Facilities** ⋔ ⊙ ⊕ ℗
Services 🍴 ⍩ ⊞ ◙ **Off-site** ⍩ ⌀ ⊸

ST-MARTIN-EN-CAMPAGNE SEINE-MARITIME

Goélands
r des Grèbes, Saint Martin Plage, 76370
☎ 235838290 ◫ 235832179
e-mail g4sdomaine@wanadoo.com
website www.lesdomaines.org
Site with good recreational facilities in an area of woodland, 100m
from a small lake. Shop and bar only open in summer.
⊃ *NE of Dieppe, 2km from D925.*
Open Apr-Oct **Site** 4.5HEC ❄ ♣ ♣ 🏠 **Prices** ♠ 3 ♠ 21-24 ▲ 10.50-15.50
Facilities ⋔ 🏕 ⊙ ⊕ ⌀ ⊸ ℗ **Services** ⊞ ◙ **Off-site** 🍴 ⍩ ⊶PS

ST-MICHEL-EN-GRÈVE CÔTES-D'ARMOR

Capucines
Kervourdon, 22300 ☎ 296357228 ◫ 296357898
e-mail les.capucines@wanadoo.fr
website lescapucines.fr
A peaceful setting near the beach with a large variety of facilities.
⊃ *On D786 Lannion-Morlaix road.*
Open 15 Mar-5 Nov **Site** 4HEC ❄ ♣ 🏠 **Prices** ▲ 13-18 pitch 7 14-26.60
(incl 2 persons) pp3.90-5.40 **Facilities** ⋔ 🏕 ⊙ ⊕ ⊸ ℗ **Services** 🍴 ⍩
⊞ ◙ **Leisure** ⊶ P **Off-site** ⍩ ⌀ ⊶S

ST-PAIR-SUR-MER MANCHE

Ecutot
50380 ☎ 233502629 ◫ 233506494
e-mail camping.ecutot@wanadoo.fr
website www.ecutot.com
Set in an orchard 1km from the sea.
⊃ *On main road between Granville & Avranches.*
Open Jun-15 Sep **Site** 5HEC ❄ ♣ 🏠 **Prices** ♠ 8 pitch 7 **Facilities** ⋔ ⊙
⊕ ℗ **Services** 🍴 ◙ **Leisure** ⊶ P **Off-site** 🏕 ⍩ ⌀ ⊸ ⊶S ⊞

Lez-Eaux
St-Aubin-des-Preaux, 50380 ☎ 233516609 ◫ 233519202
e-mail bonjour@lez-eaux.com
website www.lez-eaux.com
Situated in grounds of a château. Bank, TV and reading room. Fishing
available.
⊃ *7km SE via D973 rte d'Avranches.*
Open Apr-Dec **Site** 12HEC ❄ ♣ 🏠 **Prices** ♠ 5 pitch 14-40 (incl 2
persons) pp8.50 **Facilities** ⋔ 🏕 ⊙ ⊕ ℗ **Services** 🍴 ⍩ ⊞ ◙
Leisure ⊶ P **Off-site** ⌀ ⊸

Mariénée
50380 ☎ 233906005 ◫ 233906005
Set in the grounds of an old farm 2km from the sea.
⊃ *2km S of town on D21.*
Open Apr-Sep **Site** 1.2HEC ❄ ♣ 🏠 ♠ **Facilities** ⋔ ⊙ ⊕ ⊸ ℗
Services ⊞ ◙ **Off-site** 🏕 🍴 ⍩ ⌀ ⊶PS

France

Facilities 🏕 shop ⋔ shower ⊙ electric points for razors ⊕ electric points for caravans ℗ parking by tents permitted ℗ compulsory separate car park
Services ⍩ café/restaurant 🍴 bar ⌀ Camping Gaz International ⊸ gas other than Camping Gaz ⊞ first aid facilities ◙ laundry
Leisure ⊶ swimming L-Lake P-Pool R-River S-Sea **Off-site** All facilities within 2km

ST-PHILIBERT-SUR-MER MORBIHAN

Palmiers

Kernivilit, 56470 ☎ 297550117 📠 297300391
e-mail contact@campinglespalmiers.com
website www.campinglespalmiers.com
Beautiful, well-kept site divided by hedges.

➲ 2km W via D781.

Open All year **Site** 2.7HEC ❤ ❤ 🏠 **Prices** ♠ 4-5.10 🚗 2.60-3 pitch 6.90-9
🚐 (static)480-570 **Facilities** 🏪 🔦 ⊙ 🚻 ⌀ 🏦 **Services** 🍴 🍽 🛒 🖨
Leisure ⊛ P **Off-site** 🏠 ⊛RS

ST-PIERRE-DU-VAUVRAY EURE

St-Pierre

1 r du Château, 27430 ☎ 232610155 📠 232610155
e-mail eliane-dareissac@wanadoo.fr
website www.lecampingdesaintpierre.com
Wooded surroundings with pitches divided by hedges, 50m from the
River Seine.

➲ Via A13/N15.

Open 7 Jan-25 Dec **Site** 3HEC ❤ ❤ **Prices** ♠ 3.50 pitch 5 **Facilities** 🏪 ⊙
🚻 🏦 **Services** 🖨 **Leisure** ⊛ P **Off-site** 🏠 🍴 🍽 ⊛R

ST-PIERRE-QUIBERON MORBIHAN

Park-er-Lann

56170 ☎ 297502493 📠 297502493

➲ 1.5km S on D768.

Open Etr-Sep **Site** 2.5HEC ❤ ❤ 🏠 **Facilities** 🏪 ⊙ 🚻 🚰 🏦
Services 🍴 🍽 🛒 🖨 **Off-site** 🏠 ⌀ ⊛S

ST-QUAY-PORTRIEUX CÔTES-D'ARMOR

Bellevue

68 bd du Littoral, 22410 ☎ 296704184 📠 269705546
e-mail campingbellevue@free.fr
website www.campingbellevue.net
A terraced site adjacent to the sea with numbered pitches.

➲ 0.8km from town centre off D786.

Open May-16 Sep **Site** 4HEC ❤ ❤ 🏠 **Prices** ♠ 3.80-4.80 pitch 5.60-7.50
Facilities 🏪 🔦 ⊙ 🚻 ⌀ 🏦 **Services** 🛒 🖨 **Leisure** ⊛ PS **Off-site** 🏠 🍴
🍽 🚰

ST-VAAST-LA-HOUGUE MANCHE

Gallouette

r de la Gallouette, 50550 ☎ 233542057 📠 233541671
e-mail contact@camping-lagallouette.fr
website www.camping-lagallouette.fr
A well-equipped site, 300m from the town centre and with direct
access to the beach.

Open Apr-Sep **Site** 3.5HEC ❤ ❤ ♣ 🏠 **Prices** ♠ 4.50-5.50 pitch 6.20-9.80
🚐 (static)265-687 **Facilities** 🏪 🔦 ⊙ 🚻 ⌀ 🚰 🏦 **Services** 🍴 🍽 🖨
Leisure ⊛ PS **Off-site** 🍽

STE-MARIE-DU-MONT MANCHE

Utah Beach

La Madeleine, 50480 ☎ 233715369 📠 233710711
e-mail utah.beach@wanadoo.fr
website www.camping-utahbeach.com
On a level meadow 100m from the beach.

➲ 6km NE via D913 & D421.

Open Apr-Sep **Site** 3.5HEC ❤ ❤ ♣ 🏠 **Facilities** 🏪 🔦 ⊙ 🚻 🚰 🏦
Services 🍴 🍽 🖨 **Leisure** ⊛ P **Off-site** ⊛S

STE-MARINE FINISTÈRE

Hellès

29120 ☎ 298563146 📠 298563146
e-mail contact@le-helles.com
website www.le-helles.com

➲ 400m from beach.

Open May-15 Sep **Site** 3HEC ❤ ❤ 🏠 🚐 **Facilities** 🏪 🔦 ⊙ 🚻 ⌀ 🏦
Services 🛒 🖨 **Leisure** ⊛ P **Off-site** 🏠 🍴 🍽 ⊛S

SARZEAU MORBIHAN

Ferme de Lann Hoedic

rte du Roaliguen, 56370 ☎ 297480173 📠 297417287
e-mail contact@camping-lannhoedic.fr
website www.camping-lannhoedic.fr
Quiet site 0.8km from a sheltered beach, accessible by foot or bike by
a forest path. Pitches in sunny or shady locations, some surrounded
by landscaped hedges.

➲ From Vannes exit for Sarzeau, continue for Arzon, left at 1st
rdbt by Super U, 2km left for Lann Hoedic.

Open Apr-Oct **Site** 3.6HEC ❤ ❤ 🏠 🚐 **Prices** ♠ 3.30-4.20 pitch 6-7.50
🚐 (static)230-590 **Facilities** 🏪 🔦 ⊙ 🚻 🚰 🏦 **Services** 🛒 🖨 **Off-site** 🏠 🍴
🍽 ⌀ ⊛S

Treste

rte de la Plage du Roaliguen, 56370 ☎ 297417960 📠 297413621
e-mail letreste@campingletreste.com
website www.campingletreste.com
A family site with good facilities, 0.8km from Roaliguen beach.

➲ 2.5km S.

Open 16 Jun-9 Sep **Site** 5HEC ❤ ❤ 🏠 **Prices** ♠ 4.48-5.60 pitch 7.88-9.85
🚐 (static)180-520 **Facilities** 🏪 🔦 🏠 ⊙ 🚻 ⌀ 🏦 **Services** 🍴 🖨 **Leisure** ⊛ P
Off-site 🍽 🚰 ⊛S 🛒

AT POINTE-ST-JACQUES (5.5KM S)

CM St-Jacques

56370 ☎ 297417929 📠 297480445
e-mail camping-stjacques.com
website www.camping-stjacques.com
On beach protected by dunes. Well-kept site with asphalt drives in a
pleasant wooded location.

Open Apr-Sep **Site** 7.6HEC ❤ ❤ 🏠 🚐 🅰 **Facilities** 🏪 🔦 ⊙ 🚻 ⌀ 🚰 🏦
Services 🍴 🍽 🛒 🖨 **Leisure** ⊛ S **Off-site** 🏠 🍽

SUBLIGNY MANCHE

Grand Chemin

50870 ☎ 233513096
Small site in a rural setting with well-defined pitches within easy reach
of the village.

➲ N175 towards Avranches, onto D39 & signed.

Open All year **Site** 2HEC ❤ ❤ 🚐 **Prices** ♠ 2.28 🚐 3.75 🅰 1.52
Facilities 🏪 🔦 ⊙ 🚻 🏦 **Services** 🖨

Site 6HEC (site size) ❤ grass ⊖ sand ❤ stone ♣ little shade ♣ partly shaded ❤ mainly shaded 🏠 bungalows for hire
🚐 caravans for hire 🅰 tents for hire ⊗ no dogs **Prices** ♠ adult per night 🚗 car per night pp per person per night 🚐 caravan per night
🅰 tent per night 🚐 (static)-caravan hire per week

France

TELGRUC-SUR-MER FINISTÈRE

Panoramic
rte de la Plage, 29560 ☎ 298277841 ▤ 298273610
e-mail info@camping-panoramic.com
website www.camping-panoramic.com
Quiet terraced site with views across a wide sandy beach. Secluded pitches.
➲ W on D887, S onto D208.
Open Jun-15 Sept **Site** 4HEC ♨ ♣ 🏠 **Prices** ⚑ 5 pitch 10 **Facilities** ⚑ 🏠
⊙ ⌂ ⌀ ⍉ **Services** ▦ 🍴 ➕ 🅂 **Leisure** ⚓ P **Off-site** ⚓S

THEIX MORBIHAN

Rhuys
Le Poteau Rouge, Atlantheix, 56450 ☎ 297541477
e-mail campingderhuys@wanadoo.fr
Site directly on the sea with modern facilities.
➲ 3.5km NW via N165.
Open Apr-15 Oct **Site** 2HEC ♨ ♨ ♣ 🏠 **Prices** ⚑ 4-5.10 pitch 4.50
Facilities ⚑ ⊙ ⌂ ⌕ ⍉ ⍉ **Services** ➕ 🅂 **Leisure** ⚓ P **Off-site** 🏠 ▦ 🍴

THURY-HARCOURT CALVADOS

Vallée du Traspy
rue du Pont Benôit, 14220 ☎ 231796180 ▤ 231796180
Level meadow site near a small reservoir, 250m from Centre Aquatique de la Suisse Normande.
Open 15 Apr-Sep **Site** 1.5HEC ♨ ♣ ♣ 🏠 **Prices** ⚑ 4.50 pitch 4.50
🏠 (static)380-480 **Facilities** ⚑ 🏠 ⊙ ⌂ ⍉ **Services** ▦ 🍴 ➕ 🅂
Leisure ⚓ LPR **Off-site** ⌀ ⍅

TINTÉNIAC ILLE-ET-VILAINE

Peupliers
La Besnelais, 35190 ☎ 299454975
e-mail camping.les.peupliers@wanadoo.fr
A peaceful site in a wooded location with good facilities.
➲ 2km SE via N137.
Open Apr-Sep **Site** 4.5HEC ♨ ♣ 🏠 **Prices** ⚑ 4.80 pitch 6.50 **Facilities** ⚑
🏠 ⊙ ⌂ ⍅ ⍉ **Services** ▦ 🍴 ➕ 🅂 **Leisure** ⚓ P **Off-site** 🍴 ⌀

TOLLEVAST MANCHE

Village Vert
50470 ☎ 233430078
e-mail le.village.vert@wanadoo.fr
website www.le-village-vert.com
A peaceful site in a pine grove within an extensive park.
➲ From Cherbourg ferry terminal N13 to Auchan Hypermarket, site 200m on left.
Open All year **Site** 5.5HEC ♨ ♣ ♣ ⚑ **Facilities** ⚑ 🏠 ⊙ ⌂ ⍅ ⍉
Services ➕ 🅂 **Off-site** ⌀ ⍅

TOURLAVILLE MANCHE

Espace Loisirs de Collignon
50110 ☎ 233201688 ▤ 233448171
e-mail camping-collignon@wanadoo.fr
A pleasant site with good facilities, 1km from town centre.
➲ Site in Collignon Leisure Park
Open May-Sep **Site** 2HEC ♨ ♣ 🏠 **Prices** ⚑ 4.40 pitch 6.25
⚑ (static)302-520 **Facilities** ⚑ 🏠 ⊙ ⌂ ⍉ **Services** 🅂 **Leisure** ⚓ S
Off-site ▦ 🍴 ⚓PS ➕

TOURNIÈRES CALVADOS

Picard Holidays
14330 ☎ 231228244 ▤ 231517028
e-mail paul.palmer@wanadoo.fr
website www.camp-france.com
A quiet site between Cherbourg and Caen, with pleasant sheltered pitches.
➲ Via N13 & D15/D5.
Open All year **Site** 2HEC ♨ ♣ ⍉ 🏠 **Prices** ⚑ 5 pitch 5 ⚑ (static)415-560
Facilities ⚑ 🏠 ⊙ ⌂ ⍉ ⍉ ⍉ **Services** ▦ 🍴 ➕ 🅂 **Leisure** ⚓ LP **Off-site** ⚓R

TRÉBEURDEN CÔTES-D'ARMOR

Armor-Loisirs
rue de Kernevez-Lors-Mabo, 22560 ☎ 296235231 ▤ 296154036
e-mail info@armorloisirs.com
website www.armorloisirs.com
Modern site with individual pitches surrounded by hedges. Hardstandings for caravans.
➲ 0.5km S of Kernévez road.
Open Apr-Sep **Site** 2.2HEC ♨ ♣ 🏠 **Prices** ⚑ 3.50-6 ⚑ 2-2.50
pitch 5.50-8 **Facilities** ⚑ 🏠 ⊙ ⌂ ⍉ ⌀ ⍅ ⍉ **Services** ▦ 🍴 ➕ 🅂
Leisure ⚓ P **Off-site** ⚓RS

TRÉGUNC FINISTÈRE

Pommeraie
St-Philibert, 29910 ☎ 298500273 ▤ 298500791
e-mail pommeraie@club-internet.fr
website www.campingdelapommeraie.com
A well-equipped site with good facilities for children, 1.2km from the beach.
➲ S via D1.
Open May-Sep **Site** 7HEC ♨ ♣ 🏠 **Prices** ⚑ 4-5.60 pitch 8.50-12.10
Facilities ⚑ 🏠 ⊙ ⌂ ⍅ ⍉ **Services** ▦ 🍴 ➕ 🅂 **Leisure** ⚓ P
Off-site ⌀ ⚓S

TRÉLÉVERN CÔTES-D'ARMOR

Port l'Epine
Pors-Garo, 22660 ☎ 296237194 ▤ 296237783
e-mail camping-de-port-lepine@wanadoo.fr
website www.camping-port-lepine.com
Well-shaded site directly on the sea.
Open 30 Mar-21 Sep **Site** 3HEC ♨ ♣ 🏠 ⚑ **Prices** ⚑ 5 ⚑ 2.50 pitch
14.50-27 (incl 2 persons) **Facilities** ⚑ 🏠 ⊙ ⌂ ⌀ ⍅ ⍉ **Services** ▦ 🍴 ➕
🅂 **Leisure** ⚓ PS

TRÉPORT, LE SEINE-MARITIME

CM les Boucaniers
r Mendes-France, 76470 ☎ 235863547 ▤ 235865582
e-mail camping@ville-le-treport.fr
website www.ville-le-treport.fr
Well-kept site on flat meadow on eastern edge of village. Sports and games nearby.
Open Apr-Sep **Site** 5.5HEC ♨ ♣ 🏠 **Prices** ⚑ 3.15 ⚑ 2.65 ⚑ 2.75-6.65
⚑ 2.75-6.65 **Facilities** ⚑ ⊙ ⌂ ⍉ ⍉ **Services** ▦ ➕ 🅂 **Off-site** 🏠 ▦ 🍴
⍅ ⚓PRS

Facilities 🏠 shop ⚑ shower ⊙ electric points for razors ⌂ electric points for caravans ⍉ parking by tents permitted ⍉ compulsory separate car park
Services 🍴 café/restaurant ▦ bar ⌀ Camping Gaz International ⍅ gas other than Camping Gaz ➕ first aid facilities 🅂 laundry
Leisure ⚓ swimming L-Lake P-Pool R-River S-Sea **Off-site** All facilities within 2km

Parc International du Golf

102 rte de Dieppe, 76470 ☎ 227280150 🖹 227280151
Set in a park on the cliffs.
⤳ *1km W on D940.*
Open Apr-20 Sep 5HEC ♨ ♣ **Prices** 🛉 6-7.50 **Facilities** 🌳 ☺ 🖾 ⑫
Services ➕ 🖸 **Off-site** 🖾 📞 🅾 🥾 ⛱PS

AT MESNIL-VAL

Parc Val d'Albion

1 r de la Mer, 76910 ☎ 235862142 🖹 235867851
Terraced site in wooded parkland next to the sea.
⤳ *3km S from Le Tréport on D126.*
Open Jun-15 Sep 3HEC ♨ ♣ **Prices** 🛉 7.50 **Facilities** 🌳 ☺ 🖾 ⑫
Services ➕ 🖸 **Off-site** 🖾 📞 🅾 ⛱S

TRÉVOU-TRÉGUIGNEC CÔTES-D'ARMOR

Mât

38 r de Trestel, 22660 ☎ 296237152
e-mail camping-le-mat@wanadoo.fr
A family site on level ground, 50m from the beach.
⤳ *Via D38.*
Open 15 Apr-15 Sep **Site** 1.6HEC ♨ ♣ 🏠 🚐 **Prices** 🛉 4.20 pitch 5.30
🚐 (static)320 **Facilities** 🌳 🖾 ☺ 🖾 🅾 ⑫ **Services** 📞 📍 ➕ 🖸
Leisure ⛱ P **Off-site** ⛱LS

TRINITÉ-SUR-MER, LA MORBIHAN

Baie

Plage de Kervilen, 56470 ☎ 297557342 🖹 297558881
e-mail contact@campingdelabaie.fr
website www.campingdelabaie.fr
Several strips of land divided by tall trees on the edge of a fine sandy beach.
⤳ *Signed towards Kerbihan.*
Open 15 May-15 Sep **Site** 2.4HEC ♨ ♣ 🚐 **Facilities** 🌳 🖾 ☺ 🖾 🅾 ⑫
Services 📞 📍 ➕ 🖸 **Leisure** ⛱ P **Off-site** ⛱S

Kervilor

56470 ☎ 297557675 🖹 297558726
e-mail ebideau@camping-kervilor.com
website www.camping-kervilor.com
A pleasant wooded location 1.5km from the port. Plenty of recreational facilities.
⤳ *1.6km N.*
Open May-9 Sep 5HEC ♨ ♣ 🚐 **Prices** 🛉 3.68-4.90 pitch 9.75-13
Facilities 🌳 🖾 ☺ 🖾 🅾 ⑫ **Services** 📞 📍 ➕ 🖸 **Leisure** ⛱ P **Off-site** 📍
🥾 ⛱S

See advertisement on this page

Plage

Plage de Kervilen, 56470 ☎ 297557328 🖹 297558831
e-mail camping@camping-plage.com
website www.camping-plage.com
A family site divided into pitches behind dunes, with direct access to the beach.
⤳ *1km S towards Carnac-Plage.*
Open 12 May-16 Sep **Site** 3HEC ♨ ♣ 🚐 **Prices** 🛉 5 pitch 6.90-23.50
🚐 (static)276-757 **Facilities** 🌳 ☺ 🖾 ⑫ **Services** ➕ 🖸 **Leisure** ⛱ P
Off-site 🖾 📞 📍 🅾 ⛱S

VEULES-LES-ROSES SEINE-MARITIME

Paradis

chemin de Manneville, 76980 ☎ 235976142
A municipal site on the southern outskirts of the town.
Open mid May-mid Sep 0.9HEC ♨ ♣ **Facilities** 🌳 ☺ 🖾 ⑫
Services ➕ 🖸 **Off-site** 🖾 📞 📍 🅾 🥾 ⛱PRS ➕

VILLERS-SUR-MER CALVADOS

Ammonites

rte de la Corniche, 14640 ☎ 231870606 🖹 231871800
e-mail camping-lesammonites@wanadoo.fr
website www.camping-les-ammonites.com
⤳ *4km SW via rte de Cabourg & D163 towards Auberville.*
Open Apr-Oct **Site** 3HEC ♨ ♣ 🏠 **Facilities** 🌳 🖾 ☺ 🖾 🅾 🥾 ⑫
Services 📍 📞 ➕ 🖸 **Leisure** ⛱ P

France

PARIS/NORTH

ACY-EN-MULTIEN OISE

Ancien Moulin
60620 ☎ 344872128 ▤ 344872128.
website www.campingclub.asso.fr
Situated beside a river and a small lake with good sports facilities.
Open All year **Site** 5HEC ♨ ♣ **Prices** ⌂ 17.61-20 **Facilities** ⋔ ⊙ ⊟ ⑫
Services ▣ **Leisure** ⇜ LR **Off-site** ⬜ ⬤ ⭐ ⌀ ⚌ ➕

AMIENS SOMME

Parc des Cynes
111 r de Montières ☎ 322432928 ▤ 322435942
e-mail camping.amiens@wanadoo.fr
website www.parcdescygnes.com
A well maintained site on the outskirts of Amiens. Pitches are grassy and flat in varying sizes and some specially designed for motor homes. Pitches are marked but there is little shade.
➲ Off N1
Open Apr-14 Oct **Site** 3.2HEC ♨ ♣ ⬛ **Prices** pitch 14-19.50 (incl 2 persons) pp5.70 **Facilities** ⋔ ⊙ ⊟ ⌀ ⑫ **Services** ⭐ ➕ **Off-site** ⇜R

ARDRES PAS-DE-CALAIS

AT AUTINGUES (2KM S)

St-Louis
223 r Leulène, 62610 ☎ 321354683 ▤ 321001978
e-mail domirine@aol.com
website www.campingstlouis.com
A well-equipped site in pleasant wooded surroundings.
➲ Off N43 1km SE of Ardres onto D224 & signed.
Open Apr-Oct **Site** 1.7HEC ♨ ♣ ⬛ **Prices** ⌂ 3 pitch 9 ⬛ (static)200-220
Facilities ⋔ ⊙ ⊟ ⚌ ⑫ **Services** ⭐ ⭐ ➕ ▣ **Off-site** ⬜ ⇜L

AUDRUICQ PAS-DE-CALAIS

CM Les Pyramides
62370 ☎ 321355917
A site with good sanitary and sports facilities beside the canal.
Open Apr-Sep **Site** ♨ ♣ **Facilities** ⋔ ⊙ ⊟ ⑫ ⑫ **Services** ➕ ▣
Off-site ⬜ ⭐ ⭐ ⌀ ⇜P

BEAUVAIS OISE

Clos Normand
1 r de l'Abbaye, St-Paul, 60650 ☎ 344822730
A small site on a lake with facilities for fishing.
➲ 6km W via N31 towards Rouen.
Open Apr-Sep **Site** 1.3HEC ♨ ♣ **Facilities** ⋔ ⊙ ⊟ ⚌ ⑫
Services ▣ **Off-site** ⭐ ⭐ ⇜R

BERCK-SUR-MER PAS-DE-CALAIS

Orée du Bois
chemin Blanc 251, Rang-du-Fliers, 62180
☎ 321842851 ▤ 321842856
e-mail oree.du.bois@wanadoo.fr
website www.loreedubois.com
A modern site in wooded surroundings with good sports facilities.
➲ 2km NE.
Open Apr-Oct **Site** 18.5HEC ♨ ♣ ♣ ⬛ **Prices** ⌂ 5-6 ⚠ 12-17
pitch 18-24 (incl 2 persons) **Facilities** ⋔ ⊙ ⊟ ⚌ ⑫ **Services** ⭐ ⭐ ➕ ▣
Off-site ⬜ ⌀

BERNY-RIVIÈRE AISNE

Croix du Vieux Pont
2290 ☎ 323555002 ▤ 323550513
e-mail lacroixduvieuxpont@wanadoo.fr
website www.la-croix-du-vieux-pont.com
Wooded surroundings beside the River Aisne with good facilities.
➲ N of N31. Over River Aisne, site 0.5km E of Vic-sur-Aisne on D91.
Open All year **Site** 19HEC ♨ ♣ ⬛ **Facilities** ⋔ ⬜ ⊙ ⊟ ⌀ ⑫
Services ⭐ ⭐ ➕ ▣ **Leisure** ⇜ P **Off-site** ⚌

BERTANGLES SOMME

Château
r du Château, 80260 ☎ 360656836 ▤ 322936836
e-mail camping@chateaubertangles.com
website www.chateaubertangles.com
Site in an old orchard of a château.
➲ Signed off Amiens-Doullens road.
Open 20 Apr-10 Sep **Site** 0.8HEC ♨ ♣ **Prices** ⚠ 3.35 ⬛ 2.30 ⬛ 3.40
⚠ 3.40 **Facilities** ⋔ ⊙ ⊟ ⌀ ⑫ **Services** ▣ **Off-site** ⬜ ⭐ ⭐

BEUVRY PAS-DE-CALAIS

CM
r Victor-Dutériez, 62660 ☎ 321650800
Open 15 Jun-15 Sep **Site** 1HEC ♨ ♣ **Prices** ⚠ 2 ⬛ 3 ⚠ 3
Facilities ⋔ ⊙ ⊟ ⑫ **Services** ▣ **Off-site** ⬜ ⭐ ⭐ ⌀ ⚌ ⇜P

BLANDY-LES-TOURS SEINE-ET-MARNE

Pre de L'Etang
34 r St Martin, 77115 ☎ 160669634 ▤ 160669634
On the outskirts of the village, surrounded by fields in a calm and peaceful location and containing a large pond.
➲ A5 exit 16 for Chatillon La Borde & Blandy-Les-Tours, then towards St Méry.
Open 15 Feb-15 Dec **Site** 2HEC ♨ ♣ ⬛ **Prices** pitch 14.80 (incl 2 persons) ⬛ (static)195 **Facilities** ⋔ ⊙ ⊟ ⌀ ⑫ **Services** ▣ **Off-site** ⬜ ⭐ ⭐ ⚌ ⇜R ➕

BOIRY-NOTRE-DAME PAS-DE-CALAIS

Paille Haute
1 r Verte, 62156 ☎ 321481540 ▤ 321220724
e-mail lapaillehaute@wanadoo.fr
website www.la-paille-haute.com
On a level meadow with a variety of recreational facilities.
➲ A1 exit 15 towards Cambrai, site on D34. Or A26 exit 8 towards Arras.
Open Apr-Oct **Site** 4.9HEC ♨ ♣ ⬛ **Prices** pitch 20 ⬛ (static)300-450
Facilities ⋔ ⊙ ⊟ ⑫ **Services** ⭐ ⭐ ▣ **Leisure** ⇜ P **Off-site** ⬜ ⌀ ⚌

BOISSY-LE-CUTTE ESSONNE

Boulinière
La Boulinière, 91590 ☎ 164576523 ▤ 145448516
e-mail secretariat@campingclub.asso.fr
website www.campingclub.asso.fr
Situated in a wood 0.8km from the village.
➲ Via N20 & D148.
Open All year **Site** 4HEC ♨ ♣ ♣ ⬛ **Facilities** ⋔ ⊙ ⊟ ⑫ **Services** ▣
Off-site ⬜ ⭐ ⭐ ⌀ ⚌ ⇜R ➕

France

Facilities ⬜ shop ⋔ shower ⊙ electric points for razors ⊟ electric points for caravans ⑫ parking by tents permitted ⑫ compulsory separate car park
Services ⭐ café/restaurant ⭐ bar ⌀ Camping Gaz International ⚌ gas other than Camping Gaz ➕ first aid facilities ▣ laundry
Leisure ⇜ swimming L-Lake P-Pool R-River S-Sea **Off-site** All facilities within 2km

BOUBERS-SUR-CANCHE PAS-DE-CALAIS

Petit St Jean
27 rue de Frevent, 62270 ☎ 321048520 📠 321048520
e-mail arielle.triart@wanadoo.fr
website www.camping-loisir-boubers.com
A peaceful rural setting within easy reach of the village.
➲ E via D340 towards Frévent.
Open Apr-15 Oct **Site** 1HEC 👪 ♣ 🚐 **Facilities** 🏪 ⊙ 🖲 ♨ ⑫
Services 🍴 🛒 🗑 **Off-site** 🏢 ⛊PR

BOULANCOURT SEINE-ET-MARNE

Ile de Boulancourt
6 allée des Marronniers, 77760 ☎ 164241338 📠 164241043
e-mail camping-ile-de-boulancourt@wanadoo.fr
A peaceful site shaded by mature trees in a convenient location in the Essonne valley.
➲ Via D410.
Open All year **Site** 5HEC 👪 ♣ 🚐 **Prices** 🖈 4 pitch 4.80 🚐 (static)120
Facilities 🏪 ⊙ 🖲 ⑫ **Services** 🛒 🗑 **Leisure** ⛊ R **Off-site** 🏢 🍴 🌐 🥢 ♨

BRAY-DUNES NORD

Perroquet-Plage
59123 ☎ 328583737 📠 328583701
e-mail camping-perroquet@wanadoo.fr
website www.campingduperroquet.com
Situated among dunes with direct access to the beach.
➲ 3km NE towards La Panne.
Open Apr-Sep **Site** 28HEC 👪 🍴 ♣ 🚐 🚐 **Prices** 🖈 5 🚗 2 🚐 2.80 🅰 2
🚐 (static)250 **Facilities** 🏪 🏢 ⊙ 🖲 🥢 ♨ ⑫ **Services** 🍴 🍽 🛒 🗑
Leisure ⛊ S

CAMIERS PAS-DE-CALAIS

Sables d'Or
62176 ☎ 321849515
Wooded location with good recreational facilities.
Open All year **Site** 10HEC 👪 🍴 ♣ 🚐 **Facilities** 🏪 ⊙ 🖲 ⑫ **Services** 🛒 🗑
Leisure ⛊ P

CAYEUX-SUR-MER SOMME

Voyeul
rte des Canadiens, 80410 ☎ 322266084 📠 322266084
Pleasant surroundings 400m from the sea, with pitches enclosed by hedges and flowerbeds.
➲ 1.5km S on D140.
Open Apr-15 Oct **Site** 1.7HEC 👪 ♣ **Facilities** 🏪 ⊙ 🖲 ♨ ⑫
Services 🍴 🍽 🛒 🗑 **Off-site** ⛊S

CONDETTE PAS-DE-CALAIS

Château
21 r Nouvelle, 62360 ☎ 321875959 📠 321875959
e-mail campingduchateau@libertysurf.fr
website camping-caravaning-du-chateau.com
Pleasant parkland bordered by a forest, 0.5km from the town centre. Separate car park for arrivals after 23.00 hrs.
➲ D940 towards Hardelot.
Open Apr-Oct **Site** 1.2HEC 👪 ♣ 🚐 🚐 **Prices** 🖈 4.80-5.60 pitch 15.30-
18.70 🚐 (static)270-330 **Facilities** 🏪 ⊙ 🖲 ⑫ **Services** 🛒 🗑 **Off-site** 🏢
🍴 🍽 🥢 ♨ ⛊L

COUDEKERQUE NORD

Bois des Forts
59280 ☎ 328610441
➲ 0.7km NW on D72.
Open All year **Site** 4HEC 👪 ♣ 🚐 🚐 **Facilities** 🏪 ⊙ 🖲 ♨ ⑫ **Services** 🍴
🍽 🗑 **Off-site** 🏢 🥢 ⛊R

CROTOY, LE SOMME

Aubépines
r de la Maye, Saint Firmin, 80550 ☎ 322270134 📠 322271366
e-mail contact@camping-lesaubepines.com
website www.camping-lesaubepines.com
A peaceful verdant location surrounded by hawthorn trees on the Picardy coast and Somme estuary. The nearest beach, 1km away, is part of a nature reserve.
➲ D940 from Abbeville.
Open 30 Mar-3 Nov **Site** 4HEC 👪 ♣ 🚐 **Prices** 🖈 4.30-4.70 pitch 16-21
Facilities 🏪 ⊙ 🖲 ♨ ⑫ **Services** 🛒 🗑 **Leisure** ⛊ P
Off-site 🍴 🍽 🥢 ⛊S

Ridin
lieu dit Mayocq ☎ 322270322 📠 322277076
e-mail contact'@campingleridin.com
website www.campingleridin.com
Situated in the heart of the Somme bay, conveniently located for Paris and Lille.
➲ From Calais take A16 exit 24 towards Rue then Le Crotoy. At roundabout turn right and then 2nd right.
Open 30 Mar-3 Nov **Site** 4HEC 👪 ♣ 🚐 **Prices** pitch 16.20-18
Facilities 🏪 ⊙ 🖲 ♨ ⑫ **Services** 🍴 🍽 🛒 **Leisure** ⛊ P
Off-site 🥢 ⛊S

DUNKERQUE (DUNKIRK) NORD

Licome
1005 bd de l'Europe, 59240 ☎ 328692668 📠 328695621
e-mail campinglalicorne@ville-dunkerque.fr
Open Apr-Nov **Site** 10HEC 👪 ♣ **Prices** 🖈 5.95 🚗 2.80 🚐 5.60 🅰 5.60
Facilities 🏪 ⊙ 🖲 ⑫ 🅿 **Services** 🍴 🍽 🛒 🗑 **Off-site** 🏢 🍴 🍽 🥢 ♨
⛊PS 🛒

ÉPERLECQUES PAS-DE-CALAIS

Château de Gandspette
62910 ☎ 321934393 📠 321957498
e-mail contact@chateau-gandspette.com
website www.chateau-gandspette.com
A peaceful site, surrounded by woodland.
➲ 11.5km NW on N43 & D207.
Open Apr-Sep **Site** 11HEC 👪 ♣ 🚐 **Prices** 🖈 5-6 pitch 6-10 🚐 (static)350-
580 **Facilities** 🏪 ⊙ 🖲 ⑫ **Services** 🍴 🍽 🛒 🗑 **Leisure** ⛊ P
Off-site 🏢

EQUIHEN-PLAGE PAS-DE-CALAIS

CM la Falaise
r C-Cazin, 62224 ☎ 321312261 📠 321805401
e-mail camping.equinhen.plage@orange.fr
website www.ville-equinhen-plage.fr
Between Boulogne and le Touquet.
Open Apr-Oct **Site** 8HEC 👪 ♣ 🚐 **Prices** 🖈 4.50 🚗 3 pitch 4.50
Facilities 🏪 ⊙ 🖲 ⑫ **Services** 🗑 **Off-site** 🏢 🍴 🍽 🥢 ♨ ⛊S

Site 6HEC (site size) , 👪 grass ⛱ sand 👪 stone ♣ little shade 🍴 partly shaded 🚐 mainly shaded 🏠 bungalows for hire
🚐 caravans for hire 🅰 tents for hire ⊗ no dogs **Prices** 🖈 adult per night 🚗 car per night pp per person per night 🚐 caravan per night
🅰 tent per night 🚐 (static)-caravan hire per week

ÉTAMPES ESSONNE

Vauvert
Ormoy La Rivière, 91150 ☎ 164942139 🖹 169927259
A pleasant woodland location beside the river.
➲ 2km S via D49.
Open 15 Jan-15 Dec **Site** 11HEC 🌢 🌢 **Facilities** 🌣 ☺ ⊘ �# ℗
Services 🍴 🍽 🚼 **Leisure** ⇌ R **Off-site** ⇌LP

ÉTAPLES PAS-DE-CALAIS

Pinède
62630 ☎ 321943451
A well-equipped site among dunes and surrounded by pine trees,
close to the marina and shopping facilities.
Open 15 Feb-15 Dec **Site** 3HEC 🌢 🌢 🌢 **Facilities** 🌣 ☺ ☺ 🚼 ℗
Services 🍴 🍽 🗄 **Off-site** ⊘ �# ⇌R 🚼

FELLERIES NORD

CM La Boissellerie
~ de la Place, 59740 ☎ 327590650 🖹 327590288
➲ take RN2 southbound
Open 15 Apr-Sep **Site** 1HEC 🌢 🌢 **Prices** ⚹ 3 🚘 2 🚐 2 🅰 2
Facilities 🌣 ☺ 🚐 ℗ 🅿 **Off-site** 🗄 🍴 🍽 ⊘ �# 🚼

FERTÉ-SOUS-JOUARRE, LA SEINE-ET-MARNE

Bondons
47/49 r des Bondons, 77260 ☎ 160220098 🖹 160229701
e-mail castel@chateaudesbondons.com
Set in a beautiful wooded park. Reserved for caravans.
➲ 2km NE via D402 & D70.
Open All year **Site** 28HEC 🌢 🌢 **Prices** ⚹ 7 pitch 10 **Facilities** 🌣 ☺ 🚐
Services 🍴 🍽 🚼 🗄 **Off-site** 🗄 🍴 🍽 �# ⇌PR

FORT-MAHON-PLAGE SOMME

Royon
rte de Quend ☎ 322234030 🖹 322236515
e-mail info@campingleroyon.com
website www.campingleroyon.com
A family site with good facilities and well-marked pitches, 2.5km from
the beach.
Open 10 Mar-1 Nov **Site** 5.5HEC 🌢 🌢 🌢 **Prices** ⚹ 7 pitch 17-30 (incl 3
persons) **Facilities** 🌣 🗄 ☺ 🚐 ⊘ �# ℗ **Services** 🍴 🍽 🚼 🗄 **Leisure** ⇌ P
Off-site ⇌S

GOUVIEUX OISE

César
rte de Toutevoie 10, 60270 ☎ 344570205 🖹 344570205
e-mail lemontcesar@wanadoo.fr
website www.lemontcesar.com
On a hill overlooking the River Oise.
➲ A1 to Gouvieux town centre, then towards Creil.
Open Apr-Oct **Site** 6HEC 🌢 🌢 🌢 **Prices** ⚹ 4 pitch 5 🚐 (static)200
Facilities 🌣 ☺ 🚐 ℗ **Services** 🚼 🗄 **Off-site** 🗄 🍴 🍽 ⊘ �# ⇌P

GRAND-FORT-PHILIPPE NORD

Camping de la Plage
r Ml-Foch, 59153 ☎ 328653195
e-mail vpa@club-internet.fr
website www.camping-de-la-plage.info
On a level meadow separated from the beach (0.5km)
➲ Via A16
Open Apr-Oct **Site** 1.5HEC 🌢 🌢 🌢 **Prices** ⚹ 2.29-4.18 🚘 0.97-1.63
🚐 1.73-3.26 🅰 1.73-3.25 **Facilities** 🌣 ☺ 🚐 🚼 ℗ **Services** 🗄 **Off-site** 🗄
🍴 🍽 ⊘ ⇌S 🚼

GREZ-SUR-LOING SEINE-ET-MARNE

CM Près
chemin des Près, 77880 ☎ 164457275 🖹 164457275
website camping-grez@wanadoo.fr
➲ NE towards Loing.
Open end Mar-11 Nov **Site** 6HEC 🌢 🌢 🌢 🚐 **Prices** ⚹ 2.60 🚘 1.90 🚐 2.60
🅰 2.10-2.60 🚐 (static)140-190 **Facilities** 🌣 🗄 ☺ 🚐 �# 🚼 **Services** 🗄
Off-site 🍴 🍽 ⊘ ⇌R 🚼

GUINES PAS-DE-CALAIS

Bien Assise
62340 ☎ 321352077 🖹 321367920
e-mail castel@bien-assise.com
website www.bien-assise.com
Rural site near to a large forest and a charming little town.
➲ D231 towards Marquise.
Open 19 Apr-21 Sep **Site** 12HEC 🌢 🌢 🌢 🚐 **Prices** ⚹ 5.40 pitch 14
Facilities 🌣 🗄 ☺ 🚐 ⊘ ℗ **Services** 🍴 🍽 🚼 🗄 **Leisure** ⇌ P

HIRSON AISNE

Cascade
Site de Blangy, 2500 ☎ 323581897 🖹 323587451
e-mail tourisme.info.hirson@wanadoo.fr
A picturesque woodland setting with modern facilities.
➲ 1.8km N on N43 towards La Capelle.
Open 15 Apr-15 Sep **Site** 1.6HEC 🌢 🌢 🌢 **Facilities** 🌣 🗄 ☺ 🚐 ⊘ ℗
Services 🍴 🚼 🗄 **Leisure** ⇌ P **Off-site** �#

ISQUES PAS-DE-CALAIS

Cytises
r de l'Église, 62360 ☎ 321311110 🖹 321311110
A pleasant rural setting beside the River Liane.
➲ A16 exit 28
Open Apr-15 Oct **Site** 2.5HEC 🌢 🌢 🌢 🚐 **Prices** pitch 3.10-3.40
🚐 (static)210-280 **Facilities** 🌣 ☺ 🚐 ℗ **Services** 🍴 🍽 🚼 🗄 **Off-site** 🗄
⊘ �# ⇌R

JABLINES SEINE-ET-MARNE

International
77450 ☎ 160260937 🖹 160264333
e-mail welcome@camping-jablines.com
website www.camping-jablines.com
Only 9km from Disneyland Paris.
➲ A1 or A3 towards Marne-la-Vallée, onto N3.
Open 31 Mar-28 Oct **Site** 3.5HEC 🌢 🌢 🌢 🌢 **Prices** ⚹ 5-6 pitch 20-23
(incl 2 persons) 🚐 (static)385-590 **Facilities** 🌣 🗄 ☺ 🚐 ℗ **Services** 🍴
🍽 🗄 **Off-site** ⇌L

Facilities 🗄 shop 🌣 shower ☺ electric points for razors 🚐 electric points for caravans ℗ parking by tents permitted 🅿 compulsory separate car park
Services 🍽 café/restaurant 🍴 bar ⊘ Camping Gaz International �# gas other than Camping Gaz 🚼 first aid facilities 🗄 laundry
Leisure ⇌ swimming L-Lake P-Pool R-River S-Sea **Off-site** All facilities within 2km

France

France

Camping ★★★ Loisirs des Groux

78270 Mousseaux sur Seine
Phone : 00 33 (0)1 34 79 33 86

45 minutes from Paris by A13 :
visit of the capital and the
Palace of Versailles.

45 minutes from Rouen by A13 :
visit of "the town of 100 bell-towers".

15 minutes from Giverny : the road of the impressionists
Monet museum.

At 500 meters : leisure park close to pool and golf 18 holes.

www.loisirsdesgroux.com • infos@loisirsdesgroux.com

LAON AISNE

CM La Chênaie

allée de la Chênaie, 02000 ☎ 323202556 ▤ 323202556
A peaceful family site with good facilities close to the city centre.
➲ W of city centre towards N44.
Open May-Sep **Site** 3.3HEC ⛺ ♣ **Facilities** ⚘ ☉ ⊕ ⊕ ℗ **Services** ➕ ⊠
Off-site 🏧 ⌀ ≛ ⇔LPR

LICQUES PAS-DE-CALAIS

Canchy

r de Canchy, 62850 ☎ 321826341 ▤ 321826341
e-mail camping.lecanchy@wanadoo.fr
website www.camping-lecanchy.com
A quiet site on an open, level meadow. Well situated for the ferries
and the Channel Tunnel.
Open 15 Mar-Oct **Site** 1HEC ⛺ ♣ ⊞ ⊞ **Prices** ⚹ 3.50 pitch 4.50
⊞ (static)150-200 **Facilities** ⚘ 🏧 ☉ ⊕ ⊕ ⌀ ≛ ℗ **Services** ⌨ ℩ ➕ ⊠
Leisure ⇔ R

MAISONS-LAFFITTE YVELINES

International

1 r Johnson, 78600 ☎ 139122191 ▤ 139127050
e-mail ci.mlaffitte@wanadoo.fr
website ww.campint.com
A well-kept site in a residential area on the banks of the Seine.
Modern installations, heated in cold weather.
➲ 8km N of St-Germain-en-Laye. Or A86 exit Colombos-Ouest.
Open 30 Mar-Oct **Site** 6.5HEC ⛺ ♣ ⊞ **Prices** pitch 20-23 (incl 2 persons)
pp5.30-5.80 **Facilities** ⚘ 🏧 ☉ ⊕ ⊕ ⌀ ℗ **Services** ⌨ ℩ ➕ ⊠
Off-site ≛ ⇔PR

MAUBEUGE NORD

Camping Municipal de Clair de Lune

rte de Mons, 59600 ☎ 327622548 ▤ 327622548
➲ 1.5km N via N2 Bruxelles road.
Open All year **Site** 2.1HEC ⛺ ♣ ⊞ **Facilities** ⚘ ☉ ⊕ ⊕ ℗ **Services** ➕ ⊠
Off-site 🏧 ⌨ ℩ ⌀ ≛

MELUN SEINE-ET-MARNE

Belle Étoile

Quai Joffre, 77000 ☎ 164394812 ▤ 164372555
e-mail info@campinglabelleetoile.com
website www.campinglabelleetoile.com
Pleasant grassy site with two central blocks.
➲ At La Rochette on River Seine, 1km from town.
Open Apr-22 Oct **Site** 3.5HEC ⛺ ♣ ⊞ ⊞ ⛺ **Prices** ⚹ 4.90-5.40
pitch 5-5.40 ⊞ (static)225 **Facilities** ⚘ 🏧 ☉ ⊕ ⊕ ⌀ ℗ **Services** ⌨ ℩ ⊠
⊠ **Leisure** ⇔ P **Off-site** ℩ ⌀ ⇔LPR

MERLIMONT PAS-DE-CALAIS

St-Hubert

RD 940, 62155 ☎ 321891010 ▤ 321891012
e-mail sthubert62@wanadoo.fr
website www.sthubert62.com
Pleasant wooded surroundings with good recreational facilities.
➲ 3km S via D940, near Parc de Bagatelle.
Open Apr-Oct **Site** 16HEC ⛺ ♣ **Facilities** ⚘ 🏧 ☉ ⊕ ⌀ ≛ ℗ **Services**
⌨ ℩ ➕ ⊠ **Leisure** ⇔ P

MILLY-LA-FORÊT ESSONNE

Musardière

rte des Grandes Vallées, 91490 ☎ 164989191 ▤ 164989191
e-mail lamusardiere@infonie.fr
Pleasant wooded surroundings.
➲ 4km SE via D948.
Open 16 Feb-1 Dec **Site** 12HEC ⛺ ⊜ ♣ ⊞ ⛺ **Prices** ⚹ 6 ⇐ 3.20
⊞ 5.50 ⚠ 3.20 ⊞ (static)189-217 **Facilities** ⚘ ☉ ⊕ ⊕ ℗ **Services** ➕
Leisure ⇔ P

MONNERVILLE ESSONNE

Bois de la Justice

91930 ☎ 164950534 ▤ 164951731
website www.camping-boislajustice.com
Pitches separated by trees and hedges in beautiful natural woodland
with good facilities.
➲ N20 Orléans to Étampes.
Open Feb-Nov **Site** 5.5HEC ⛺ ♣ ⊞ **Prices** ⚹ 6 ⇐ 2.50 ⊞ 5 ⚠ 5
Facilities ⚘ ☉ ⊕ ⊕ ≛ ℗ **Services** ⌨ ℩ ➕ ⊠ **Leisure** ⇔ P

MONTIGNY-LE-BRETONNEUX YVELINES

Parc Étang

Base de Loisirs-de-St Quentin, 78180 ☎ 130585620 ▤ 134600714
Beautiful rural surroundings beside a leisure centre with easy access to
Paris and Versailles.
➲ SE of town centre towards Centre de Volle.
Open Mar-Oct **Site** 12HEC ⛺ ♣ ⊞ **Facilities** ⚘ 🏧 ☉ ⊕ ⊕ ⌀ ≛ ℗
Services ⌨ ℩ ➕ ⊠ **Off-site** ℩ ⇔LP

Site 6HEC (site size) ⛺ grass ⊜ sand ⛺ stone ♣ little shade ♣ partly shaded ⛺ mainly shaded ⊞ bungalows for hire
⊞ caravans for hire ⚠ tents for hire ⊗ no dogs **Prices** ⚹ adult per night ⇐ car per night pp per person per night ⊞ caravan per night
⚠ tent per night ⊞ (static)-caravan hire per week

MONTREUIL-SUR-MER PAS-DE-CALAIS

CM Fontaine des Clercs

1, Rue de L'eglise, 62170 ☎ 321060728
e-mail freddy.monchaux@wanadoo.fr
➲ N of town on N1.
Open All year **Site** 2HEC 🌳🌲🅰 **Facilities** 🚿☺🅿⑲ **Services** ➕🔲
Leisure ⚓ R **Off-site** 🏠🍺🍴🛢🔥⚓P

MOUSSEAUX SUR SEINE YVELINES

Loisirs des Groux

chemin de Vetheuil, 78270 ☎ 134793382
e-mail infos@loisirsdesgroux.com
website www.loisirsdesgroux.com
Convenient location for visiting Paris, Giverny and Versailles.
Open Mar-Nov **Site** 3.5HEC 🌳🌲🏠🚃 **Facilities** 🚿☺🅿⑲
Services 🔲 **Leisure** ⚓ LR **Off-site** 🏠🍺🍴⚓L ➕

See advertisement on page 156

MOYENNEVILLE SOMME

Val de Trie

Bouillancourt-sous-Miannay, 80870 ☎ 322314888 🖷 322313533
e-mail raphael@camping-lavaldetrie.fr
website www.camping-levaldetrie.fr
A small site in a picturesque wooded location with good facilities including a lake for fishing.
➲ 1km from D925.
Open Apr-1 Nov **Site** 3HEC 🌳🌲🏠 **Prices** 🧍3.10-4.80 🚐1.60 pitch 5.80-6.50 **Facilities** 🚿🏠☺🅿🛢🔥⑲ **Services** 🍺🍴➕🔲 **Leisure** ⚓ P **Off-site** 🔥

See advertisement on this page

NESLES-LA-VALLÉE VAL-D'OISE

Parc de Séjour de l'Étang

10 Chemin des Belles Vues, 95690 ☎ 134706289 🖷 134706289
e-mail brehinier1@hotmail.com
website www.campingparcset.com
Level site near a small lake.
➲ A15 exit 10, D927 & D79. Or N1 exit l'Isle Adam.
Open Mar-Oct **Site** 6HEC 🌳🌲 **Prices** 🧍4 pitch 4 **Facilities** 🚿☺🅿⑲
Services ➕🔲 **Off-site** 🏠🍺🍴🛢🔥

NEUVILLE, LA NORD

Leu Pindu

2 r du Gle-de-Gaulle, 59239 ☎ 320865087 🖷 320865177
➲ N on D8.
Open All year **Site** 1.2HEC 🌳🌲🏠 **Facilities** 🚿☺🅿🛢🔥⑲
Services 🍺🍴➕🔲 **Off-site** 🏠🍺⚓L

ORVILLERS-SOREL OISE

Sorel

60490 ☎ 344850274 🖷 355521165
Divided into pitches. Local tradesmen supply provisions.
➲ A1 onto N17, turn right for 400m.
Open Feb-15 Dec **Site** 3HEC 🌳🌲🏠🚃 **Facilities** 🚿🏠☺🅿🛢⑲
Services 🍺🍴➕🔲

Camping le Val de Trie ★★★

Situated at only 1 hour from Calais (A16)
Ideal spot for first or last night or longer stay
12 km from the coast

www.camping-levaldetrie.fr
raphael@camping-levaldetrie.fr

80870 MOYENNEVILLE
Tel : +33 3 22 31 48 88
Fax : +33 3 22 31 35 33

OYE-PLAGE PAS-DE-CALAIS

Oyats

272 Digue Vert, 62215 ☎ 321851540 & 🖷 328603833
e-mail bnilliet.nicolas@wanadoo.fr
➲ 4.5km NW on beach.
Open May-Sep **Site** 5HEC 🌳🌲 **Prices** 🧍6 pitch 7 **Facilities** 🚿🏠☺🅿
⑲ **Services** 🍴➕🔲 **Leisure** ⚓ PS

PARIS

Bois de Boulogne

2 allée du Bord de l'Eau, 75016 ☎ 145243000 🖷 142244295
e-mail camping_boulogne@stereau.fr
website www.campingparis.fr
This popular site is close to the city centre and it can be crowded during the summer, as it is the only site in central Paris.
Open All year **Site** 7HEC 🌳🌲🌲🏠 **Facilities** 🚿🏠☺🅿🛢⑲
Services 🍺🍴➕🔲

PLESSIS-FEU-AUSSOUX SEINE-ET-MARNE

Château-de-Chambonnières

77540 ☎ 164041585 🖷 0164041336
➲ On D231 towards Provins.
Open All year **Site** 5HEC 🌳🌲🏠🚃 **Facilities** 🚿🏠☺🅿🛢⑲
Services ➕🔲

France

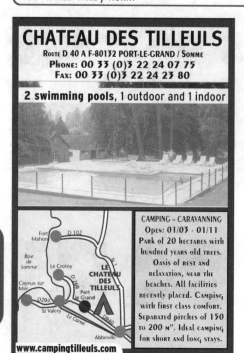

POIX-DE-PICARDIE SOMME

Bois des Pêcheurs
rte de Forges-les-Eaux, 80290 ☎ 322901171 📠 322903291
e-mail camping@ville-poix-de-picardie.fr
website www.ville-poix-de-picardie.fr
A quiet riverside location with a high standard of sanitary facilities.
➲ Exit 13 on A29
Open Apr-Sep **Site** 2.4HEC 🌱 🏕 **Prices** 🔺 8 pitch 11 (incl 2 persons) pp2 **Facilities** 🅿 ⊙ 🚰 ⓟ **Services** 🚻 🔲 **Off-site** 🏧 🚿 🍴 ⌀ 🚿 ⚓PR

POMMEUSE SEINE-ET-MARNE

Chêne Gris
24 pl de la gare de, Faremoutiers-Pommeuse, 77515
☎ 164042180 📠 164200589
e-mail info@lechene.gris.com
website www.lechenegris.com
Woodland site within easy travelling distance of Disneyland Resort Paris and the capital itself.
➲ N34 towards Coulommiers-Crécy, onto D25 to Pommeuse, signed on right after station.
Open 23 Apr-Oct **Site** 5HEC 🌱 🏕 🏠 🔺 **Prices** pitch 29-35 pp2-3.50 🚐 (static)308-623 **Facilities** 🅿 🏧 🚰 ⓟ **Services** 🚻 🍴 🔲 **Leisure** ⚓ P **Off-site** ⚓R

PORT-LE-GRAND SOMME

Chateau des Tilleuls
rte D40 A, 80132 ☎ 322240775 📠 322242380
e-mail contact@campingtilleuls.com
website www.campingtilleuls.com
On gently sloping meadow surrounding a farm.
➲ 1 km SE on D940A.
Open Mar-Oct **Site** 5HEC 🌱 🏖 🏠 🏕 **Facilities** 🅿 🏧 ⊙ 🚰 ⌀ 🚿 ⓟ **Services** 🚻 🔲 **Leisure** ⚓ P **Off-site** ⚓R

See advertisement on this page

PROYART SOMME

Loisir la Violette
rte de Mericourt, 80340 ☎ 322858136 📠 322851737
Open Mar-Oct **Site** 1.8HEC 🌱 🏖 🏕 **Prices** 🔺 2.10 🚐 1 pitch 1.30 **Facilities** 🅿 ⊙ 🚰 ⓟ **Services** 🔲 **Off-site** 🏧 🚻 🍴 🚿 ⚓P 🔲

QUEND-PLAGE-LES-PINS SOMME

Roses
80120 ☎ 322277617 📠 322239306
e-mail info@campingdesroses.com
website www.campingdesroses.com
Well-kept site with trees and hedges surrounding individual pitches.
➲ Off D940 at Quend onto D102, site 0.5km on left.
Open 15 Mar-23 Oct **Site** 9HEC 🌱 🏖 🏕 **Facilities** 🅿 ⊙ 🚰 🚿 ⓟ **Services** 🚻 🍴 🔲 **Leisure** ⚓ LP **Off-site** 🏧 ⌀ ⚓S

Vertes Feuilles
25 rte de la Plage, Monchaux ☎ 322235512 📠 322190752
e-mail contact@lesvertesfeuilles.com
website www.lesvertesfeuilles.com
Situated 3km from the sea between the Somme Bay and Authe Bay.
➲ A16 exit 24, follow D32 direction Quend Plage
Open Apr-Nov **Site** 1.4HEC 🌱 🏖 🏕 🔺 **Prices** pitch 14-23 (incl 2 persons) pp3.50-4 **Facilities** 🏧 ⊙ 🚰 🚿 ⓟ **Services** 🔲 **Leisure** ⚓ P **Off-site** 🚻 🍴 ⌀

ST-AMAND-LES-EAUX NORD

Mont des Bruyères
806 r Basly, 59230 ☎ 327485687 📠 327485687
➲ 3.5km SE in forest of St-Amand.
Open Mar-Nov **Site** 3.5HEC 🌱 🏖 **Facilities** 🅿 🏧 ⊙ 🚰 🚿 ⓟ **Services** 🚻 🔲 **Off-site** 🍴 ⌀ ⚓LPR

ST-CHÉRON ESSONNE

Parc des Roches
La Petite Beauce, 91530 ☎ 164566550 📠 164565450
e-mail info@parcdesroches.com
website www.parcdesroches.com
Set in a wooded park.
Open 10 Apr-15 Oct **Site** 23HEC 🌱 🏖 🏠 **Prices** 🔺 6.60 🚐 2.60 🚐 5 🔺 5 🚐 (static)420 **Facilities** 🅿 ⊙ 🚰 🚿 ⓟ **Services** 🚻 🍴 🔲 **Leisure** ⚓ P **Off-site** ⌀

Site 6HEC (site size) 🌱 grass 🏖 sand 🏔 stone ♣ little shade 🏕 partly shaded 🌳 mainly shaded 🏠 bungalows for hire 🚐 caravans for hire 🔺 tents for hire ⊗ no dogs **Prices** 🔺 adult per night 🚗 car per night pp per person per night 🚐 caravan per night 🔺 tent per night 🚐 (static)-caravan hire per week

ST-CYR-SUR-MORIN SEINE-ET-MARNE

Choisel

Courcelles la Roue, 77750 ☎ 160238493 🖹 160248174
e-mail campingduchoisel@wanadoo.fr
A pleasant location. Separate car park for arrivals after 22.00 hrs.

➲ *2km W via D31.*

Open Mar-Nov **Site** 3.5HEC 👽 ⛺ 🏠 🚐 **Prices** 🛆 4.50 🚐 6.90 ⛺ 3
🚐 (static)182.94 **Facilities** 🏕 ⊙ 🚱 ⚒ ® **Services** 🛒 🍽 ➕ 🔲
Off-site ⊘ ⇆LPR

ST-JANS-CAPPEL NORD

Domaine de la Sablière

Le Mont Noir, 59270 ☎ 328494634 🖹 328426290
A pleasant family site in a wooded location with large, well-defined
pitches.

➲ *3.5km NE via D10 & D318.*

Open 15 Apr-15 Oct **Site** 3.6HEC ⛺ **Facilities** 🏕 ⊙ 🚱 🚐 ®
Services ➕ 🔲 **Off-site** 🛖 🍽 ⊘ ⇆LP

ST-LEU-D'ESSERENT OISE

Campix

☎ 44560848 🖹 44562875
e-mail campixfr@aol.com
website www.campingcampix.com
Set in wooded surroundings within easy reach of Chantilly.

➲ *3.5km NE via D12.*

Open 7 Mar-1 Dec **Site** 6HEC 👽 ⛺ **Prices** 🛆 3-5.50 pitch 3.50-5.50
Facilities 🏕 ⊙ 🚱 ® **Services** ➕ 🔲 **Off-site** 🛖 🍽 ⇆LP

ST-QUENTIN AISNE

CM

bd J-Bouin, 02100 ☎ 323626866
A good site in pleasant wooded surroundings near the canal.

Open Mar-Nov **Site** 1.9HEC 👽 ⛺ **Facilities** 🏕 🚱 ® **Off-site** ⊘
⇆PR ➕

ST-VALÉRY-SUR-SOMME SOMME

Domaine du Château de Drancourt

80230 ☎ 322269345 🖹 322268587
e-mail chateau.drancourt@wanadoo.fr
website www.chateau-drancourt.com
Set within the grounds of a former hunting lodge surrounded by
woods, fields and lakes.

➲ *3.5km S via D48.*

Open 30 Mar-5 Nov **Site** 15HEC 👽 ⛺ 🏠 **Prices** pitch 12-33 (incl 2
persons) **Facilities** 🏕 🛖 ⊙ 🚱 ⊘ ⚒ ® **Services** 🛒 🍽 ➕ 🔲 **Leisure** ⇆ P
Off-site 🍽 ⇆L

SALENCY OISE

Étang du Moulin

54 r du Moulin, 60400 ☎ 344099981
A small site opposite a trout fishing lake and recreational area under
the ownership of the site proprietors.

➲ *3km from Noyon on N32 towards Chauny.*

Open All year **Site** 0.4HEC 👽 ⛺ **Prices** 🛆 2 🚐 2.50 🚐 4 ⛺ 4
Facilities 🏕 ⊙ 🚱 ® **Services** 🛒 🍽 **Off-site** ⇆PR ➕

SERAUCOURT-LE-GRAND AISNE

Pêche du Vivier aux Carpes

10 r Ch-Voyeux, 02790 ☎ 323605010 🖹 323605169
e-mail camping.du.vivier@wanadoo.fr
website www.camping-picardie.com
A peaceful site bordered by lakes. Separate car park for arrivals after
22.00 hrs.

➲ *A26 exit 11, left onto D1, onto D72 Essigny.*

Open Mar-Oct **Site** 3HEC 👽 ⛺ **Prices** pitch 17.50 (incl 2 persons)
pp3.50 **Facilities** 🏕 ⊙ 🚱 ⊘ ⚒ ® **Services** ➕ 🔲 **Leisure** ⇆ L
Off-site 🛖 🛒 🍽 ⇆R

SOISSONS AISNE

CM

av du Mail, 02200 ☎ 323745269 🖹 323596772
e-mail officedetourisme@ville-soissons.fr
website www.ville-soissons.fr
Pleasant surroundings with modern facilities.

Open All year **Site** 1.8HEC 👽 ⛺ **Facilities** 🏕 ⊙ 🚱 ® ℗ **Services** ➕ 🔲
Off-site 🛖 🛒 🍽 ⊘ ⚒ ⇆P ➕

THIEMBRONNE PAS-DE-CALAIS

Pommiers

rte de Desvres, 62560 ☎ 321395019 🖹 321957920
A family site in pleasant wooded surroundings

➲ *NW on D132.*

Open 15 Mar-15 Oct **Site** 1.8HEC 👽 ⛺ 🏠 **Prices** 🛆 3.50-4.20 🚐 1.80-
2.80 pitch 3.50-4.20 🚐 (static)190-280 **Facilities** 🏕 ⊙ 🚱 ⊘ ⚒ ®
Services ➕ 🔲 **Leisure** ⇆ P **Off-site** ⇆R

TOLLENT PAS-DE-CALAIS

Val d'Authie

CD 119 Rt de Berck, 62390 ☎ 321471427 🖹 321471427
A pleasant wooded location with wide, well-marked pitches.

➲ *SE via D119.*

Open Apr-Sep **Site** 5.7HEC 👽 ⛺ 🏠 **Prices** pitch 15 🚐 (static)370
Facilities 🏕 🛖 ⊙ 🚱 ® **Services** 🛒 🍽 ➕ 🔲 **Leisure** ⇆ LP **Off-site** ⇆R

TORCY SEINE-ET-MARNE

Parc de la Colline

rte de Lagny, 77200 ☎ 160054232 🖹 164800517
e-mail camping.parc.de.la.colline@wanadoo.fr
website www.camping-de-la-colline.com
An ideal base for visiting Paris (30 minutes from the centre by Metro).
Separate car park for arrivals after 22.00 hrs.

➲ *A104 exit 10, onto D10E.*

Open All year **Site** 10HEC 👽 ⛺ 🏠 ⛺ **Prices** 🛆 6.90 pitch 11 **Facilities** 🏕
🛖 ⊙ 🚱 ⊘ ® **Services** 🛒 🍽 ➕ 🔲 **Off-site** 🍽 ⇆LP

TOUQUIN SEINE-ET-MARNE

Étangs Fleuris

rte de la Couture, 77131 ☎ 164041636 🖹 164041228
e-mail contact@etangs-fleuris.com
website www.etangsfleuris.com
Wooded surroundings with well-defined pitches and modern facilities.

➲ *E of town towards Provins.*

Open 15 Apr-15 Sep **Site** 5.5HEC 👽 ⛺ **Prices** 🛆 9 **Facilities** 🏕 ⊙ 🚱 ®
Services 🛒 🍽 **Leisure** ⇆ P **Off-site** 🛖 🍽

France

Facilities 🛖 shop 🏕 shower ⊙ electric points for razors 🚱 electric points for caravans ® parking by tents permitted ℗ compulsory separate car park
Services 🍽 café/restaurant 🛒 bar ⊘ Camping Gaz International ⚒ gas other than Camping Gaz ➕ first aid facilities 🔲 laundry
Leisure ⇆ swimming L-Lake P-Pool R-River S-Sea **Off-site** All facilities within 2km

France

TOURNEHEM PAS-DE-CALAIS

Bal Parc
500 r du Vieux Château, 62890 ☎ 321356590 🗎 321351857
e-mail balparc@wanadoo.fr
A peaceful site in rural surroundings with modern facilities.
➲ *D218 from village centre.*
Open All year **Site** 1.6HEC 🌿 🌿 🏠 �caravan **Facilities** ☍ 🗑 ⊙ 🚿 ⌀ 🛒 ☂
Services 🍴 ⍟ 🔀 🛒 **Off-site** ⇔R

VAILLY-SUR-AISNE AISNE

Domaine de la Nature
chemin de Boufaud, Pont de Vailly, 02370
☎ 323547455 🗎 323547829
e-mail roger.paris@club-internet.fr
website www.camping-vailly-02.com
A pleasant rural setting alongside the canal with well-defined pitches and modern sanitary facilities.
➲ *4km W via D144 near canal & lake.*
Open All year **Site** 3HEC 🌿 🌿 🏠 �caravan 🛖 **Prices** pitch 12.50 (incl 2 persons) �caravan (static)380-530 **Facilities** ☍ ⊙ 🚿 ⌀ 🛒 ☂ **Services** 🍴 ⍟ 🔀 🛒
Off-site 🗑 ⍟ ⇔R

VERNEUIL-SUR-SEINE YVELINES

Lac de Seine
chemin du Rouillard, 78480 ☎ 139281620 🗎 139711860
e-mail scc-client@valdeseine78.com
website www.valdeseine78.com
Set on the outskirts of Paris in a pine forest.
Open Apr-Sep **Site** 3.5HEC 🌿 **Prices** ♦ 3.25-3.75 �car 1.60 pitch 3.20-5.30 **Facilities** ☍ 🗑 ⊙ 🚿 ☂ **Services** ⍟ 🔀 🛒 **Leisure** ⇔ L

VERSAILLES YVELINES

Huttopia Versailles
31 av Berthelot ☎ 139512361 🗎 139536829
e-mail versailles@huttopia.com
website www.huttopia.com
Site in forest location 2.5km from the palace of Versailles. Very convenient for Paris.
➲ *400m from RER C station at Porchefontaine.*
Open All year **Site** 4.5HEC 🌿 🌿 🛖 **Prices** ♦ 6-7 pitch 10-20
Facilities ☍ ⊙ 🚿 ⌀ 🏥 **Services** 🍴 ⍟ 🔀 **Leisure** ⇔ P **Off-site** 🗑 🔀

VILLENNES-SUR-SEINE YVELINES

Club des Renardières
rte de Vernouillet, 78670 ☎ 139758897
Site for caravans only, in beautiful hilly park laid out with hedges, lawns and flower beds. Fully divided into completely separated pitches.
➲ *D113 to Maison Blanche, turn right for 3km.*
Open All year **Site** 7HEC 🌿 🌿 🏠 **Prices** ♦ 2.02 pitch 9.41 **Facilities** ☍ ⊙ 🚿 **Services** 🛒 **Off-site** 🗑 🍴 ⍟ ⇔LPR

VILLERS-HÉLON AISNE

Castel des Biches
Chateau Alexandre Dumas, 2600 ☎ 323729393 🗎 323729333
e-mail pacal.ginailhac@wanadoo.fr
website www.castel-des-biches.com
Attractive site in grounds of an old castle.
➲ *N2 onto D2 for 7km via Longport.*
Open All year **Site** 10HEC 🌿 🌿 🏠 �caravan 🛖 **Facilities** ☍ ⊙ 🚿 ☂
Services 🔀 🛒 **Off-site** 🗑 ⌀ 🏥 ⇔LR

VILLERS-SUR-AUTHIE SOMME

Val d'Authie
20 rte de Vercourt, 80120 ☎ 322299247 🗎 322299330
e-mail camping@valdauthie.fr
website www.valdauthie.fr
A well-designed site between the forest of Crécy and the sea. Bar and café only open in summer.
➲ *Via N1.*
Open Apr-15 Oct **Site** 7HEC 🌿 🌿 🏠 **Prices** ♦ 6 �car 2.50 �caravan 3.50 🛖 3.50 **Facilities** ☍ 🗑 ⊙ 🚿 ⌀ 🛒 ☂ **Services** 🍴 ⍟ 🔀 **Leisure** ⇔ P **Off-site** ⇔R

VIRONCHAUX SOMME

Peupliers
221 r du Cornet, 80150 ☎ 322235427 🗎 322290519
e-mail les-peupliers2@wanadoo.fr
website www.camping-les-peupliers2.com
A peaceful site 3km from the forest of Crécy.
➲ *Via N1 & D938.*
Open Apr-Oct **Site** 2.5HEC 🌿 🌿 🏠 **Prices** ♦ 3.60 �caravan 3.10 pitch 4.20 **Facilities** ☍ 🗑 ⊙ 🚿 🏥 ☂ **Services** 🍴 ⍟ 🔀 🛒 **Off-site** 🍴

WACQUINGHEN PAS-DE-CALAIS

Éscale
62250 ☎ 321320069 🗎 321320069
e-mail camp-escale@wanadoo.fr
website www.escale-camping.com
A landscaped park with modern facilities 5 minutes from the coast.
➲ *Via A16 & D231.*
Open 15 Mar-15 Oct **Site** 11HEC 🌿 🌿 🏠 **Prices** ♦ 4.20 �caravan 2.20 🛖 4.20 🛖 3.20 **Facilities** ☍ 🗑 ⊙ 🚿 🏥 ☂ **Services** 🍴 ⍟ 🔀 🛒 **Off-site** ⌀ 🏥

AUVERGNE

ALLANCHE CANTAL

CM Pont Valat
15160 ☎ 471204587 🗎 471204181
e-mail mairie.allanche@wanadoo.fr
➲ *1km S on D679 towards St-Flour.*
Open 15 Jun-15 Sep **Site** 3HEC 🌿 🌿 **Prices** ♦ 1.40 �car 0.50 pitch 0.80 �caravan (static)200 **Facilities** ☍ ⊙ 🚿 ☂ **Services** 🛒 **Off-site** 🗑 🍴 ⍟ ⌀ 🏥 ⇔R

ALLEYRAS HAUTE-LOIRE

CM
43580 ☎ 471575686 🗎 471575686
Pleasant surroundings on level ground beside the River Allier.
➲ *2.5km NW.*
Open Apr-Oct **Site** 1HEC 🌿 🌿 🏠 **Prices** ♦ 8 pitch 8 (incl 2 persons) **Facilities** ☍ ⊙ 🚿 ⌀ ☂ **Services** 🔀 🛒 **Off-site** 🗑 🍴 ⍟ 🏥 ⇔R

Site 6HEC (site size) 🌿 grass 🏖 sand 🪨 stone ♣ little shade 🌿 partly shaded 🌿 mainly shaded 🏠 bungalows for hire �caravan caravans for hire Å tents for hire ⊗ no dogs **Prices** ♦ adult per night �car car per night pp per person per night �caravan caravan per night Å tent per night �caravan (static)-caravan hire per week

AMBERT PUY-DE-DÔME

Trois Chênes
rte du Puy, 63600 ☎ 473823468 🖷 473823468
e-mail tourisme-ambert@wanadoo.fr
Open May-Sep **Site** 😃 ♣ 🏕 **Facilities** ♠ ⊕ 🔌 ℗ **Services** 🛒 🗑
Off-site 🛒 🍴 🍽 ⊘ ⚒ ⛱LP

ANSE RHÔNE

Porte du Beaujolais
chemin des Grandes Levées, 69480 ☎ 474671287 🖷 474099097
e-mail campingbeaujolais@wanadoo.fr
A pleasant, modern site in the heart of the Beaujolais country beside
the River Saône.
⊃ *Via A6 or N6 then D39.*

Open 15 Mar-30 Oct **Site** 7HEC 😃 ♣ 🏕 ⊗ **Facilities** ♠ 🛒 ⊕ 🔌 ⊘ ℗
Services 🛒 🍴 🗑 🗑 **Leisure** ⚓ PR **Off-site** 🍴 ⚒

ARNAC CANTAL

Gineste
15150 ☎ 471629190 🖷 471629272
e-mail lagineste@mairie-arnac.fr
website www.mairie-arnac.fr
Situated on a peninsula in Lake Enchanet with modern facilities and
access to ski slopes.
⊃ *NW of Arnac towards lake.*

Open All year **Site** 3HEC 😃 ♣ 🏕 🔌 **Facilities** ♠ 🛒 ⊕ ℗ **Services** 🛒
🍴 🗑 🗑 **Leisure** ⚓ LP

ARPAJON-SUR-CÈRE CANTAL

Cère
r F-Ramond, 15130 ☎ 471645507
⊃ *S towards Rodez on D920, site beside river.*

Open Jun-Sep **Site** 2HEC 😃 ♣ 🏕 **Prices** 🔌 11 ⚠ 8.50 **Facilities** ♠ ⊕ ⚡
℗ **Services** 🗑 **Leisure** ⚓ PR **Off-site** 🛒 🍴 🍽 ⊘ 🗑

AUBIN AVEYRON

CM
12110 ☎ 565630386
⊃ *100m from the lake.*

Open 15 Apr-Sep **Site** 4HEC 😃 ♣ 🏕 ♣ **Facilities** ♠ ⊕ 🔌 ℗ **Services** 🗑
Off-site 🛒 🍴 🍽 ⊘ ⚒ ⛱PR

AT BELLERIVE-SUR-ALLIER (3KM W)

Acacias
r Claude-Decloître, 03700 ☎ 470323622 🖷 470598852
e-mail campingacacias@club-internet.fr
website www.camping-acacias.com
Well-managed site, sub-divided into numbered pitches by hedges.
Clean sanitary installations. Library, billiard room. Water sports are
available nearby on lake.
⊃ *From Vichy left after bridge beside Esso fuel station & along
river for 0.5km.*

Open 5 Apr-15 Oct **Site** 3HEC 😃 ♣ 🏕 **Prices** 🔌 3.40-4.90 pitch 3.40-4.90
Facilities ♠ 🛒 ⊕ 🔌 ⚒ ℗ 🅿 **Services** 🛒 🍴 🗑 🗑 **Leisure** ⚓ LPR
Off-site 🛒 🍴

Beau Rivage
r Claude Decloître, 03700 ☎ 470322685 🖷 470320394
e-mail camping-beaurivage@wanadoo.fr
website www.camping-beaurivage.com
Neat meadowland with marked out pitches. Well-kept sanitary
installations. TV.
⊃ *Turning over bridge onto left bank of River Allier.*

Open Apr-Sep **Site** 1.5HEC 😃 ♣ 🏕 ♣ **Prices** 🔌 3.50-4.80 ♣ 3.50-4.80
pitch 3.50-4.80 ♣ (static)161-230 **Facilities** ♠ 🛒 ⊕ 🔌 ⊘ ℗ **Services** 🛒
🍴 🗑 🗑 **Leisure** ⚓ PR

BOURBON-L'ARCHAMBAULT ALLIER

CM Parc Bignon
Parc Jean Bignon, 03160 ☎ 470670883 🖷 470673535
⊃ *1km SW on N153, rte de Montluçon, turn right.*

Open Mar-Oct **Site** 3HEC 😃 ♣ **Prices** 🔌 2.10 ♣ 0.80 ♣ 1.20 ⚠ 1.20
Facilities ♠ ⊕ 🔌 ℗ **Services** 🗑 🗑 **Off-site** 🛒 🍴 🍴 🍽 ⊘ ⚒ ⛱LP

BOURG-ARGENTAL LOIRE

Astrée
'L'Allier', 42220 ☎ 477397297 🖷 477397621
e-mail prl@bourgargental.fr
Pleasant surroundings with good recreational facilities.
⊃ *Via N82.*

Open All year **Site** 2HEC 😃 ♣ 🏕 **Prices** 🔌 2.50-3.50 ♣ 1.25-1.75 ♣ 5-7
⚠ 2.50-3.50 **Facilities** ♠ ⊕ 🔌 ℗ **Services** 🍴 🗑 **Leisure** ⚓ R **Off-site** 🛒
🛒 🍴 ⊘ ⚒ ⛱P 🗑

BRAIZE ALLIER

Champ de la Chapelle
03360 ☎ 470061545 🖷 470061545
e-mail ccdlp@aol.com
A family site in the centre of the Tronçais forest with good recreational
facilities.
⊃ *7km SE via D28 & D978.*

Open 17 Apr-19 Sep **Site** 5.6HEC 😃 ♣ 🏕 ♣ **Facilities** ♠ ⊕ 🔌 ℗
Services 🍴 🗑 🗑 **Leisure** ⚓ P

BRUSQUE AVEYRON

VAL Camping Les Pibouls
Domaine de Céras, 12360 ☎ 565495066
Open Jul-Aug **Site** 1HEC 😃 ♣ **Facilities** ♠ ⊕ 🔌 🅿 **Services** 🛒 🍴 🗑
Leisure ⚓ L **Off-site** 🛒 🗑

Facilities 🛒 shop ♠ shower ⊕ electric points for razors 🔌 electric points for caravans ℗ parking by tents permitted 🅿 compulsory separate car park
Services 🍴 café/restaurant 🍴 bar ⊘ Camping Gaz International ⚒ gas other than Camping Gaz 🗑 first aid facilities 🗑 laundry
Leisure ⚓ swimming L-Lake P-Pool R-River S-Sea **Off-site** All facilities within 2km

France

France

CANET-DE-SALARS AVEYRON

Caussanel

Lac de Pareloup, 12290 ☎ 565468519 📠 565468985

e-mail info@lecaussanel.com

website www.lecaussanel.com

Well-equipped site on the shore of Lake Pareloup.

➲ *Via D911.*

Open 12 May-15 Sep **Site** 10HEC 🌲 🌲 🏘 **Prices** pitch 13.20-26.10 (incl 2 persons) **Facilities** 🌴 🛱 ☺ ☻ ⌀ ☜ **Services** 🍴 🍽 ➕ 🔲 **Leisure** ⚓ LP

Soleil Levant

Lac de Pareloup, 12290 ☎ 565460365 📠 565460362

e-mail contact@camping-soleil-levant.com

website www.camping-soleil-levant.com

A family site set on terraces on the shores of Lac de Pareloup with good recreational facilities.

➲ *S of Canet-de-Salars on D933 towards Salles-Curan.*

Open Apr-Sep **Site** 11HEC 🌲 🌲 🏘 **Prices** pitch 12-13 (incl 2 persons) pp4-5 🚐 (static)545-595 **Facilities** 🌴 ☺ 🛱 ⌀ 🔦 ☜ **Services** 🍴 🍽 ➕ 🔲 **Leisure** ⚓ L

CAPDENAC-GARE AVEYRON

CM Rives d'Olt

bd Paul-Ramadier, 12700 ☎ 565808887

A quiet site on level ground with pitches divided by hedges on the bank of a river.

➲ *7km from Figeac via N140 towards Rodez, onto D35 to Capendac.*

Open Apr-Sep **Site** 1.3HEC 🌲 🌲 🏘 **Prices** 🧍 2.70 🚗 1.80 🚐 2.80 ⛺ 2 **Facilities** 🌴 ☺ 🛱 ☜ **Services** ➕ 🔲 **Leisure** ⚓ R **Off-site** 🛱 🍴 🍽 ⌀ 🔦 ⚓ P

CHAMPAGNAC-LE-VIEUX HAUTE-LOIRE

Chanterelle

Le Plan d'Eau, 43440 ☎ 471763400 📠 471763400

e-mail camping@champagnac.com

website www.champagnac.com

Situated in the heart of the Auvergne beside a wooded lake.

➲ *1km N via D5.*

Open Apr-Oct **Site** 4HEC 🌲 🌲 🏘 🚐 ⛺ **Prices** 🧍 2.70 🚗 1.70 pitch 5.20 **Facilities** 🌴 ☺ 🛱 ☜ **Services** ➕ 🔲 **Leisure** ⚓ L **Off-site** 🛱 🍴 🍽 ⌀ 🔦 ⚓ R ➕

CHAMPS-SUR-TARENTAINE CANTAL

Tarentaine

15270 ☎ 471787125

An attractive location surrounded by lakes and woodland.

➲ *1km SW via D679 & D22 beside River Tarentaine.*

Open 15 Jun-15 Sep **Site** 4HEC 🌲 🚐 **Prices** 🧍 2.30 🚗 8-1.45 🚐 9-1.70 ⛺ 9-1.70 🚐 (static)250 **Facilities** 🌴 ☺ 🛱 ☜ **Services** 🔲 **Leisure** ⚓ R **Off-site** 🛱 🍴 🍽 🔦 ⚓ P ➕

CHÂTEL-DE-NEUVRE ALLIER

Deneuvre

Les Graves, 03500 ☎ 470420451 📠 470420451

e-mail campingdeneuvre@wanadoo.fr

website www.deneuvre.com

Pleasant surroundings within a nature reserve beside the River Allier.

➲ *0.5km N via D9.*

Open Apr-Sep **Site** 1HEC 🌲 🌲 🏘 🚐 **Prices** 🧍 3.30-4.05 pitch 3.30-4.05 🚐 (static)225-295 **Facilities** 🌴 ☺ 🛱 ⌀ ☜ **Services** 🍴 🍽 ➕ 🔲 **Leisure** ⚓ R **Off-site** 🛱

CHÂTEL GUYON PUY-DE-DÔME

Clos de Balanède

r de la Piscine, 63140 ☎ 473860247 📠 473860564

e-mail clos-balanede.sarl-camping@wanadoo.fr

website www.balanede.com

A pleasant site set in an orchard.

➲ *Via A71 & D685.*

Open 15 Apr-2 Oct **Site** 4HEC 🌲 🌲 🏘 🚐 **Prices** 🧍 3.30-4.50 🚗 1-1.40 pitch 2-2.70 🚐 (static)135-180 **Facilities** 🌴 🛱 ☺ 🛱 ⌀ 🔦 ☜ **Services** 🍴 🍽 ➕ 🔲 **Leisure** ⚓ P **Off-site** ⚓ R

CHÂTEL-MONTAGNE ALLIER

Croix Cognat

03250 ☎ 470593138

e-mail campinglacroixcognat@wanadoo.fr

website perso.wanadoo.fr/mairie-chatel-montagne

Well-equipped site at an altitude of 540m.

➲ *0.5km NW on D25 towards Vichy.*

Open May-1Oct **Site** 1HEC 🌲 🌲 🏘 🚐 **Prices** pitch 11 🚐 (static)360 **Facilities** 🌴 🛱 ☺ 🛱 ⌀ 🔦 ☜ **Services** 🍴 🍽 ➕ 🔲 **Leisure** ⚓ P **Off-site** 🍴 ⚓ R

CHAUDES-AIGUES CANTAL

CM du Couffour

15110 ☎ 471235708 📠 471235708

website www.chaudesaigues.com

Tastefully sited around the town football pitch in the local leisure area.

➲ *2km S via D921.*

Open May-20 Oct **Site** 2.5HEC 🌲 🌲 🏘 🚐 **Prices** 🧍 2.50 🚗 1.20 pitch 1.50 **Facilities** 🌴 ☺ 🛱 ☜ **Services** ➕ 🔲 **Off-site** 🛱 🍴 🍽 ⌀ 🔦 ⚓ PR

CONDRIEU RHÔNE

Belle Rive

La Plaine, 69420 ☎ 474595108

Wooded surroundings bordering the Rhône.

➲ *11km S of Vienne on N86.*

Open Apr-Sep **Site** 5HEC 🌲 🌲 🏘 🚐 **Prices** 🧍 3.70 🚗 1.60 pitch 4 🚐 (static)150-250 **Facilities** 🌴 🛱 ☺ 🛱 ⌀ ☜ **Services** 🍴 🍽 ➕ 🔲 **Leisure** ⚓ PR

Site 6HEC (site size) 🌲 grass 🌊 sand 🪨 stone 🌳 little shade 🌲 partly shaded 🌳 mainly shaded 🏘 bungalows for hire 🚐 caravans for hire ⛺ tents for hire ⊗ no dogs **Prices** 🧍 adult per night 🚗 car per night pp per person per night 🚐 caravan per night ⛺ tent per night 🚐 (static)-caravan hire per week

CONQUES AVEYRON

Beau Rivage

12320 ☎ 565698223 ▤ 565728929
e-mail camping.conques@wanadoo.fr
website www.campingconques.com
Peaceful site beside the river with spacious, well-marked pitches.
➲ On D901.
Open Apr-Sep Site 1HEC ☸ ♨ ♠ **Prices** ♣ 3.50-4 ♠ 2.50-3 pitch 4-5
Facilities ⋔ ⬟ ⊙ ⊞ ⌀ ⅀ **Services** ꜝ⬚ ﴾◯ ⌺ **Leisure** ✦ PR
Off-site ⬚ ➕

COURNON-D'AUVERGNE PUY-DE-DÔME

CM Pré des Laveuses

r de Laveuses, 63800 ☎ 473848130 ▤ 473846590
e-mail camping@cournon-auvergne.fr
website www.cournon-auvergne.fr/camping
A rural setting beside a 7-hectare lake, close to the River Allier.
➲ 1.5km E towards Billom.
Open All year Site 5HEC ☸ ♨ ♨ ♠ ♠ **Facilities** ⋔ ⊙ ⊞ ⌀ ⅀ ➕ ⊞
Services ꜝ⬚ ﴾◯ ➕ ⌺ **Leisure** ✦ LR **Off-site** ⬚ ⌀ ⅀ ✦P

DALLET PUY-DE-DÔME

Ombrages

rte de Pont-du-Château, 63111 ☎ 473831097 ▤ 473831097
e-mail lesombrages@hotmail.com
website www.lesombrages.com
Wooded location beside the River Allier.
Open 15 May-15 Sep Site 4HEC ☸ ♨ ♠ ⚠ ⅀ **Prices** ♣ 5 pitch 7.50 (incl 2
persons) **Facilities** ⋔ ⊙ ⊞ ⅀ **Services** ꜝ⬚ ﴾◯ ➕ ⌺ **Leisure** ✦ PR
Off-site ⬚ ⌀

DARDILLY RHÔNE

International de Lyon

Porte de Lyon, 69570 ☎ 478356455 ▤ 472170426
e-mail lyon@huttopia.com
website www.camping-lyon.com
Generously arranged and equipped site divided into pitches. Ideal for
overnight stays near motorway. Concrete platforms for caravans.
➲ A6 exit Lyon La Garde, site 9km N.
Open All year Site 6.5HEC ☸ ♨ ♨ ♠ ♠ **Prices** ♣ 3.10-3.72 ♠ 8.50-10.20
⚠ 6.50-7.80 **Facilities** ⋔ ⊙ ⊞ ⅀ **Services** ➕ ⌺ **Leisure** ✦ P **Off-site** ⬚
ꜝ⬚ ﴾◯ ⌀ ⅀

EBREUIL ALLIER

Filature de la Sioule

Ile de Nieres, 3450 ☎ 470907201 ▤ 470907948
e-mail camping.filature@libertysurf.fr
website www.campingfilature.com
A peaceful, well-equipped in an orchard beside the River Sioule.
➲ A71 exit 12, site signed.
Open 30 Mar-Sep Site 3.6HEC ☸ ♨ ⊙ ⊞ ⌀ ⅀ **Prices** pitch 16 (incl 2 persons)
pp5 **Facilities** ⋔ ⬚ ⊙ ⊞ ⌀ ⅀ **Services** ꜝ⬚ ﴾◯ ➕ ⌺ **Leisure** ✦ R
Off-site ﴾◯ ⅀

FERRIÈRES-ST-MARY CANTAL

Vigeaires

15170 ☎ 471206188
A level site surrounded by woodland close to the River Allagnon with
modern facilities.
➲ A75 exit Massiac for Aurillac.
Open 15 Jun-Aug Site 0.6HEC ☸ ♨ ♠ **Facilities** ⋔ ⊙ ⊞ ⅀ **Services** ➕
⌺ **Leisure** ✦ R **Off-site** ⬚ ꜝ⬚ ﴾◯ ⌀ ⅀

FLAGNAC AVEYRON

Port de Lacombe

12300 ☎ 565601097 ▤ 565601688
e-mail info@campingportdelacombe.com
website www.campingportdelarcombe.com
A shady site in the Lot valley. Water activities including fishing and
canoeing on the river and an aquatic area incorporating a large water
chute.
➲ A75 towards Rodez, turn for Decazeville/Flagnac.
Open 15 May-15 Sep Site 4HEC ☸ ♨ ♠ ♠ **Facilities** ⋔ ⬚ ⊙ ⊞ ⌀ ⅀ ⅀
Services ꜝ⬚ ﴾◯ ➕ ⌺ **Leisure** ✦ R

FLEURIE RHÔNE

CM la Grappe Fleurie

69820 ☎ 474698007 ▤ 474698571
e-mail info@fleurie.org
website www.fleurie.org
A good quality municipal site in a picturesque setting in the heart of
the Beaujolais region.
➲ 0.6km SE on D119 E.
Open mid Mar-mid Oct Site 2.5HEC ☸ ♨ ♠ **Prices** ♣ 3.50 pitch 10 (incl
2 persons) **Facilities** ⋔ ⊙ ⊞ ⅀ **Services** ⌺ **Leisure** ✦ P **Off-site** ⬚ ꜝ⬚
﴾◯ ⌀ ⅀ ➕

See advertisement on this page

GOUDET HAUTE-LOIRE

Bord de l'Eau

Plaine du Chambon, 43150 ☎ 471571682 ▤ 471571288
e-mail auborddeleaugoudet@wanadoo.fr
Well-equipped site in wooded surroundings below the ruins of the
castle.
➲ W via D49, beside River Loire.
Open Mar-15 Oct Site 4HEC ☸ ♨ ♠ **Prices** ♣ 4.50 ♠ 4.50 ♠ 4.50
♠ (static)250-480 **Facilities** ⋔ ⬚ ⊙ ⊞ ⌀ ⅀ **Services** ꜝ⬚ ﴾◯ ➕ ⌺
Leisure ✦ PR

France

ISLE-ET-BARDAIS ALLIER

Écossais

3360 ☎ 470066257 📠 470066399

e-mail campingecossais@aol.com

A peaceful location in the heart of the forest of Tronçais, beside the Pirot lake.

➲ *Via A71/E11.*

Open Apr-Sep **Site** 25HEC 🌱 🌳 🏠 **Prices** 🚶 2.11-2.58 🚗 1.08-1.22 pitch 1.08-1.22 🚐 (static)199-419 **Facilities** 🚿 🛒 ⊙ 🚐 ∅ Ⓟ **Services** 🍷 ✚ 🧺 **Leisure** 🏊 L **Off-site** 🍴

JASSAT PUY-DE-DÔME

Ribeyre

63790 ☎ 473886429 📠 473886841

e-mail laribeyre@free.fr

website laribeyre.free.fr

A flat grassy site in the heart of the Auvergne among lakes and mountains. Access to a private beach with swimming.

➲ *A71 exit 6, D978/D996 to Murol, D5 S.*

Open May-15 Sep **Site** 10HEC 🌱 🌳 🏠 **Facilities** 🚿 🛒 ⊙ 🚐 ∅ Ⓟ **Services** 🍷 🍴 🧺 **Leisure** 🏊 LPR **Off-site** 🍴 ⛵ ✚

JENZAT ALLIER

Champ de Sioule

rte de Chantelle, 03800 ☎ 470568635 📠 470568538

e-mail mairie-jenzat@pays-allier.com

Open 14 Apr-22 Sep **Site** 1HEC 🌱 🌳 **Prices** 🚶 2.50 🚗 1.10 🚐 2.50 ⛺ 1.40 **Facilities** 🚿 ⊙ 🚐 Ⓟ **Services** ✚ 🧺 **Off-site** 🛒 🍷 🍴 ⛵ 🏊R

LACAPELLE-VIESCAMP CANTAL

Puech des Ouilhes

15150 ☎ 471464238 📠 471464738

e-mail campingpuech@infonie.fr

On a wooded peninsula on Lake St-Étienne-Cantalès.

Open 15 May-15 Sep **Site** 2HEC 🌱 🌲 🏠 🚫 **Prices** 🚗 1.80 pitch 13 (incl 2 persons) pp3.50 **Facilities** 🚿 🛒 ⊙ 🚐 ∅ Ⓟ **Services** ✚ 🧺 **Leisure** 🏊 LP **Off-site** 🍷 🍴

LANGEAC HAUTE-LOIRE

Gorges de l'Allier

Domaine du Prad'Eau, 43300 ☎ 471770501 📠 471772734

e-mail langeac@wanadoo.fr

Set in wooded surroundings within a nature reserve, 0.8km from the river. Good recreational facilities.

➲ *Off N102.*

Open Apr-Oct **Site** 14HEC 🌱 🌲 🏠 🚐 **Facilities** 🚿 ⊙ 🚐 Ⓟ **Services** 🍷 🧺 **Leisure** 🏊 PR **Off-site** 🛒 🍷 🍴 ∅ ⛵ ✚

LAPEYROUSE PUY-DE-DÔME

CM Les Marins

La Loge, 63700 ☎ 473520273 📠 473520389

e-mail marie.lapeyrouse63@wanadoo.fr

website 63lapeyrouse.free.fr

A modern, lakeside site with good facilities set among the rolling hills of the Combtaille.

➲ *2km E via D998.*

Open 15 Jun-1 Sep **Site** 2HEC 🌱 🌳 🏠 **Facilities** 🚿 ⊙ 🚐 Ⓟ **Services** 🍷 🍴 ✚ 🧺 **Leisure** 🏊 L **Off-site** 🛒 🍴 ⛵

LEMPDES HAUTE-LOIRE

Club A.Tou.Vert

43410 ☎ 471765369

Open 15 Apr-Sep **Site** 2HEC 🌱 🌳 🏠 **Prices** pitch 11-12 (incl 2 persons) pp3-3.50 **Facilities** 🚿 ⊙ 🚐 Ⓟ **Services** ✚ 🧺 **Leisure** 🏊 R **Off-site** 🛒 🍷 🍴 ∅

LOUBEYRAT PUY-DE-DÔME

Colombier

63410 ☎ 473866694

➲ *1.5km S via D16.*

Open May -14 Oct **Site** 1.3HEC 🌱 🌳 🏠 🚐 **Prices** 🚶 1.50-2.30 🚗 0.75-1.15 🚐 0.75-1.15 🚐 (static)153-351 **Facilities** 🚿 ⊙ 🚐 Ⓟ **Services** ✚ 🧺 **Leisure** 🏊 P **Off-site** 🍷 🍴

MALZIEU-VILLE, LE LOZÈRE

Piscine

48140 ☎ 66314763

Peaceful shaded site on the banks of a river near to the municipal sports complex.

➲ *A75 exit St Chély d'Apcher to Malzieu, right before bridge over river.*

Open May-Sep **Site** 1HEC 🌱 🌳 🏠 **Facilities** 🚿 🛒 ⊙ 🚐 Ⓟ **Services** 🍷 🧺 **Off-site** 🍴 🏊PR

MARTRES-DE-VEYRE, LES PUY-DE-DÔME

Camping la Font de Bleix

r des Roches, 63730 ☎ 473392649 📠 473392011

e-mail ailes_libres@tiscali.fr

website goeland03.chez.tiscali.fr/

A pleasant site beside the River Allier. A good centre for touring the surrounding area.

➲ *SE via D225 beside River Allier.*

Open All year **Site** 1.3HEC 🌱 🌴 🏠 🚐 **Facilities** 🚿 🛒 ⊙ 🚐 Ⓟ **Services** 🧺 **Leisure** 🏊 R **Off-site** 🍷 🍴 ∅ ✚

MASSIAC CANTAL

CM Allagnon

av de Courcelles, 15500 ☎ 471230393 📠 471230393

A riverside site with plenty of facilities.

➲ *0.8km W on N122.*

Open May-Sep **Site** 2.5HEC 🌱 🌲 **Prices** 🚶 1.80 🚗 1.40 🚐 1.60 ⛺ 10-1.60 **Facilities** 🚿 ⊙ 🚐 Ⓟ **Services** ✚ 🧺 **Leisure** 🏊 R **Off-site** 🛒 🍷 🍴 ∅ ⛵ 🏊P

MAURS CANTAL

AT ST-CONSTANT (4.5KM SE VIA N663)

Moulin de Chaules

rte de Calvinet, 15600 ☎ 471491102 📠 471491363

website www.eurocampings.net

Terraced site in a valley by the stream of a former watermill with modern facilities.

➲ *3km E via D28.*

Open 20 Apr-Oct **Site** 3HEC 🌱 🌳 🚐 **Facilities** 🚿 🛒 ⊙ 🚐 Ⓟ **Services** 🍷 🍴 ✚ 🧺 **Leisure** 🏊 PR

Site 6HEC (site size) 🌱 grass 🏖 sand 🪨 stone 🌴 little shade 🌳 partly shaded 🌲 mainly shaded 🏠 bungalows for hire 🚐 caravans for hire ⛺ tents for hire 🚫 no dogs **Prices** 🚶 adult per night 🚗 car per night pp per person per night 🚐 caravan per night ⛺ tent per night 🚐 (static)-caravan hire per week

MENDE LOZÈRE

Tivoli
av des Gorges-du-Tarn, 48000 ☎ 466650038 🗏 466650038
e-mail tivoli.camping@libertysurf.fr
website www.campingtivoli.com
A level site in wooded surroundings beside the river.
➲ *2km from town via A75 or N88.*
Open All year **Site** 1.8HEC 🐛 ❤ 🚐 **Prices** 🏍 4.50 🚗 2.90 🚐 2.45 🏕 2.45
Facilities 🍴 ⊙ ⊖ 🖉 🚿 ⊛ **Services** 🐶 🍴 ☺ 🗄 **Leisure** ⟳ PR **Off-site** 🖼

MEYRUEIS LOZÈRE

Ayres
rte de la Brêze, 48150 ☎ 466456051 🗏 466456051
e-mail campinglechampdayres@wanadoo.fr
website www.campinglechampdayres.com
On a wooded meadow with well-defined pitches and modern sanitary installations within easy reach of the picturesque Gorges de la Jonte. Plenty of recreational facilities.
➲ *A75 sortie S44-1*
Open 7 Apr-23 Sep **Site** 1.5HEC 🐛 ❤ 🚐 **Prices** 🏍 2.50-4 pitch 7-11 (incl 2 persons) **Facilities** 🍴 🖼 ⊙ ⊖ 🖉 🚿 ⊛ **Services** 🐶 🍴 ☺ 🗄 **Leisure** ⟳ P
Off-site 🍴 🗻 ⟳ R

Capelan
48150 ☎ 466456050 🗏 466456050
e-mail camping.le.capelan@wanadoo.fr
website www.campingcapelan.com
Set in picturesque surroundings alongside the Gorges de la Jonte with good sports facilities.
➲ *Via A75*
Open 5 May-15 Sep **Site** 4HEC 🐛 ❤ 🚐 **Prices** 🏍 3-4.10 pitch 13-19 (incl 2 persons) 🚐 (static)165-660 **Facilities** 🍴 🖼 ⊙ ⊖ 🖉 🚿 ⊛ **Services** 🐶 🍴 ☺ 🗄
🗄 **Leisure** ⟳ PR **Off-site** 🍴 🗻

MILLAU AVEYRON

Côté Sud
av de L'Aigoual, 12100 ☎ 565611883 🗏 565611883
e-mail campingcotesud@wanadoo.fr
website www.campingcotesud.com
➲ *1km E on D591 next to River Dourbe.*
Open Apr-Sep **Site** 3.5HEC 🐛 ❤ 🚐 **Prices** pitch 12.10-18.30 **Facilities** 🍴
🖼 ⊙ ⊖ 🖉 ⊛ **Services** 🐶 🍴 🗄 **Leisure** ⟳ PR

CM Millau Plage
rte de Millau Plage, 12100 ☎ 565601097 🗏 565601688
e-mail info@campingmillauplage.com
website www.campingmillauplage.com
Beside the River Tarn, flat shady parkland.
➲ *Via D187.*
Open 30 Mar-Sep **Site** 5HEC 🐛 ❤ 🚐 🏕 **Prices** pitch 25 🚐 (static)
150-630 **Facilities** 🍴 🖼 ⊙ ⊖ 🖉 🚿 ⊛ **Services** 🐶 🍴 ☺ 🗄 **Leisure** ⟳ PR

Rivages
av de l'Aigoual, 12100 ☎ 565610107 🗏 565590356
e-mail campinglesriveages@wanadoo.fr
website campinglesrivages.com
A family site with good facilities beside the River Dourbie.
➲ *1.7km E via D991.*
Open May-Sep **Site** 7HEC 🐛 ❤ 🚐 🏕 **Facilities** 🍴 🖼 ⊙ ⊖ 🖉 ⊛
Services 🐶 🍴 ☺ 🗄 **Leisure** ⟳ PR **Off-site** 🗻

Viaduc
121 av de Millau Plage ☎ 565601575 🗏 565613651
e-mail info@camping-du-viaduc.com
website www.camping-du-viaduc.com
Open 27 Apr-24 Sep **Site** 5HEC 🐛 ❤ 🚐 🚐 🏕 **Prices** pitch 13-22 (incl 2 persons) pp3-5 🚐 (static)195-620 **Facilities** 🍴 🖼 ⊙ ⊖ 🖉 ⊛ **Services** 🐶
🍴 ☺ **Leisure** ⟳ PR

MIREMONT PUY-DE-DÔME

Confolant
63380 ☎ 473799806
e-mail campingdelaplag@cegetel.net
website campingdelaplage.ifrance.com
➲ *7km NE via D19 & D19E.*
Open Jun-10 Sep **Site** 2.5HEC 🐛 ❤ 🚐 🚐 **Prices** pitch 10-13 **Facilities** 🍴
🖼 ⊙ ⊖ 🖉 ⊛ **Services** 🐶 🍴 ☺ 🗄 **Leisure** ⟳ L

MONTAIGUT-LE-BLANC PUY-DE-DÔME

CM
Le Bourg, 63320 ☎ 473967507 🗏 473957005
e-mail montaigut-le-blanc@wanadoo.fr
website www.ville-montaigut-le-blanc.fr
A quiet, level municipal site with good recreational facilities.
Open May-Sep **Site** 1.5HEC 🐛 ❤ 🚐 **Prices** 🏍 2.20-3.70 pitch 3.10
Facilities 🍴 ⊙ ⊖ ⊛ **Services** ☺ 🗄 **Leisure** ⟳ PR **Off-site** 🖼 🐶 🍴

MONT-DORE, LE PUY-DE-DÔME

CM du L'Esquiladou
rte des Cascades, 63240 ☎ 473652374 🗏 473652374
e-mail camping.esquiladou@wanadoo.fr
Mountainous location within a national park.
Open 28 Apr-16 Oct **Site** 2HEC ❤ ⟳ 🚐 **Prices** 🏍 3-3.10 pitch 2.60-2.75
Facilities 🍴 ⊙ ⊖ ⊛ **Services** ☺ 🗄 **Off-site** 🖼 🐶 🍴 🖉 ⟳ R

MORNANT RHÔNE

CM de la Trillonière
bd du Général-de-Gaulle, 69440 ☎ 478441647 🗏 478449170
e-mail mairiemornant@wanadoo.fr
website www.ville-mornant.fr
A rural setting on the southern outskirts of the town at an altitude of 333m.
➲ *Off D30 towards La Condamine.*
Open May-Sep **Site** 1.6HEC 🐛 ❤ ⊛ **Prices** 🏍 2.71-3.90 pitch 2.90
Facilities 🍴 ⊙ ⊖ 🚐 ⊛ **Services** ☺ 🗄 **Leisure** ⟳ R **Off-site** 🖼 🐶 🍴 🖉 🗻
⟳ LP

MUROL PUY-DE-DÔME

Europe
☎ 473397666 🗏 473397661
e-mail europe.camping@wanadoo.fr
website www.camping-europ.com
A family site in rural surroundings on the slopes of a forested valley close to the banks of Lake Chambon.
➲ *Via A71/75 & D996.*
Open 26 May-2 Sep **Site** 5.5HEC 🐛 ❤ 🚐 **Prices** 🏍 2.30-5.30 pitch 4.70-10.70 **Facilities** 🍴 🖼 ⊙ ⊖ 🖉 ⊛ **Services** 🐶 🍴 ☺ 🗄 **Leisure** ⟳ P
Off-site 🍴 ⟳ LR ☺

France

Facilities 🖼 shop 🍴 shower ⊙ electric points for razors 🚐 electric points for caravans ⊛ parking by tents permitted 🅿 compulsory separate car park
Services 🍴 café/restaurant 🐶 bar 🖉 Camping Gaz International 🗻 gas other than Camping Gaz ☺ first aid facilities 🗄 laundry
Leisure ⟳ swimming L-Lake P-Pool R-River S-Sea **Off-site** All facilities within 2km

Plage

Plage du Lac Chambon, 63790 ☎ 473886004 ▤ 473888008
Busy site beside lake. Caravan section divided into pitches, terraced area for tents. Asphalt drive.

➲ *1.2km from village centre. Onto allée de Plage before village & signed.*

Open May-Sep **Site** 7HEC ❤ ❤ ☎ **Facilities** ⋔ ⓘ ⊙ ⊡ ⊘ ⏺ **Services** ⊞ ⓘ◯ ⊞ ⊠ **Leisure** ⊛ LR **Off-site** ⊿

Pré-Bas

Lac Chambon, 63790 ☎ 473886304 ▤ 473886593
e-mail prebas@lac-chambon.com
website www.campingauvergne.com
On the side of Lake Chambon with direct access to the beach and windsurf beach.

➲ *SW off D996.*

Open May-Sep **Site** 3.5HEC ❤ ❤ ☎ **Prices** ⋔ 3.90-5.20 pitch 5.20-9.50 **Facilities** ⋔ ⊙ ⊡ ⏺ **Services** ⊞ ⓘ◯ ⊠ **Leisure** ⊛ LP **Off-site** ⓘ ⓘ◯ ⊘ ⊛LR

Ribeyre

Jassat, 63790 ☎ 473886429 ▤ 473886841
e-mail laribeyne@free.fr
website www.laribeyne.free.fr
A modern site in a beautiful mountain location 1km from Lac Chambon.

➲ *1.2km S on rte de Jassat.*

Open May-15 Sep **Site** 10HEC ❤ ❤ ☎ **Facilities** ⋔ ⓘ ⊙ ⊡ ⏺ **Services** ⊞ ⓘ◯ ⊠ **Leisure** ⊛ LPR **Off-site** ⊿ ⊞

NANT AVEYRON

Val de Cantobre

12230 ☎ 565584300 ▤ 565621036
e-mail info@valdecantobre.com
website www.valdecantobre.com
Beside the river in the picturesque Gorges de la Dourbie with fine views from the terraced pitches.

➲ *4km N of Nant, off D591 towards Millau.*

Open 15 May-13 Sep **Site** 6.5HEC ❤ ❤ ❤ ☎ **Facilities** ⋔ ⓘ ⊙ ⊡ ⊘ ⏺ **Services** ⊞ ⓘ◯ ⊞ ⊠ **Leisure** ⊛ PR

NAUCELLE AVEYRON

Lac de Bonnefon

L'etang de Bonnefon, 12800 ☎ 565593320 ▤ 56693209
e-mail campingdulac@hotmail.com
A peaceful site in a wooded location beside a lake with modern facilities and well-marked pitches.

➲ *NW of N88, signed.*

Open Apr-30 Oct **Site** 2.6HEC ❤ ❤ ☎ ⊗ **Facilities** ⋔ ⊙ ⊡ ⏺ **Services** ⊞ ⓘ◯ ⊞ ⊠ **Leisure** ⊛ P **Off-site** ⓘ ⓘ◯ ⊘ ⊿

NAUSSAC LOZÈRE

Terrasses du Lac

Lac de Naussac, 48300 ☎ 466692962 ▤ 466692478
e-mail naussac@club-internet.fr
website www.naussac.com
Situated beside the lake at an altitude of 1000m with fine views.

➲ *Autoroute 75 exit 88 for Langogne.*

Open 15 Apr-Sep **Site** 5.8HEC ❤ ❤ ☎ **Prices** pitch 12.50 (incl 2 persons) pp3.50 **Facilities** ⋔ ⊙ ⊡ ⏺ **Services** ⊞ ⓘ◯ ⊞ ⊠ **Leisure** ⊛ LP **Off-site** ⓘ ⊘ ⊿

NÉBOUZAT PUY-DE-DÔME

Domes

Les Quatre routes de Neébouzat, 63210
☎ 473871406 & ▤ 473871881
e-mail camping.les-domes@wanadoo.fr
website www.les-domes.com
A comfortable site with hard-standing for caravans. Advance reservations recommended.

➲ *Off RN89 Clermont-Bordeaux*

Open 6 May-16 Sep **Site** 1HEC ❤ ❤ ☎ ☎ **Prices** ⋔ 6-9.50 ☎ (static)216-360 **Facilities** ⋔ ⓘ ⊙ ⊡ ⊘ ⏺ **Services** ⊞ ⊠ **Leisure** ⊛ P **Off-site** ⊞ ⓘ◯ ⊛R

NÉRIS-LES-BAINS ALLIER

du Lac

av Marx-Dormoy, 03310 ☎ 470032470 ▤ 470037999
website www.ville-neris-les-bains.fr
Situated in a spa town, close to the centre. Some pitches are close to a road, the remainder are in a shaded valley by a stream.

Open 4 Apr-24 Oct **Site** 7HEC ❤ ❤ ☎ ☎ **Facilities** ⋔ ⊙ ⊡ ⏺ ⓟ **Services** ⊞ ⓘ◯ ⊞ ⊠ **Off-site** ⓘ ⊞ ⓘ◯ ⊛P

NEUVÉGLISE CANTAL

Belvédère du Pont de Lanau

15260 ☎ 471235050 ▤ 471235893
e-mail belvedere.cantal@wanadoo.fr
website perso.wanadoo.fr/belvedere.cantal/

➲ *5km S on D921.*

Open Apr-15 Oct **Site** 5HEC ❤ ❤ ☎ ☎ Å **Facilities** ⋔ ⓘ ⊙ ⊡ ⊘ ⊿ ⏺ **Services** ⊞ ⓘ◯ ⊞ ⊠ **Leisure** ⊛ P **Off-site** ⊛LR

OLLIERGUES PUY-DE-DÔME

Chelles

63880 ☎ 473955434
e-mail camping.les.chelles@wanadoo.fr
website www.camping-les-chelles.com
A family site in wooded surroundings with good leisure facilities.

➲ *5km from town centre.*

Open May-Sep **Site** 3.5HEC ❤ ❤ ☎ ☎ **Facilities** ⋔ ⓘ ⊙ ⊡ ⏺ **Services** ⊞ ⓘ◯ ⊞ ⊠ **Leisure** ⊛ P

ORCET PUY-DE-DÔME

Clos Auroy

r de la Narse, 63670 ☎ 473842697 ▤ 473842697
e-mail contact@campingclub.info
website www.camping-le-clos-auroy.com
Terraced site in a green valley next to a small river.

➲ *A75 exit 5 to Orcet, signed.*

Open All year **Site** 2.5HEC ❤ ❤ ☎ ☎ **Prices** ⋔ 1.90-4.20 pitch 8.40 (incl 2 persons) ☎ (static)200-475 **Facilities** ⋔ ⓘ ⊙ ⊡ ⊘ ⏺ **Services** ⊞ ⊠ **Leisure** ⊛ PR **Off-site** ⓘ◯ ⊿ ⊞

Site 6HEC (site size) ❤ grass ❤ sand ❤ stone ♣ little shade ❤ partly shaded ❤ mainly shaded ☎ bungalows for hire ☎ caravans for hire Å tents for hire ⊗ no dogs **Prices** ⋔ adult per night ☎ car per night pp per person per night ☎ caravan per night Å tent per night ☎ (static)-caravan hire per week

PEUX-ET-COUFFOULEUX AVEYRON

Bouyssiére de Blanc
☎ 65495517
e-mail vacances@labouyssiere.com
website www.labouyssiere.com
Several shaded terraces in a peaceful wooded mountainside setting.
➲ *From Brusque cross Dordou river, onto D119 signed Murat, site 6km on left.*
Open 29 Apr-Sep **Site** 2HEC 🏕 ♣ 🏠 **Prices** 🚶 3.50-4 pitch 4-5 **Facilities** 🚿 ⊙ 🚐 🔥 Ⓟ **Services** 🍷 🍴 ✚ 🧺 **Leisure** 🏊 P

OLLIONNAY RHÔNE

Col de la Luère
Col de la Luere, 69290 ☎ 478458111 📠 478458947
e-mail contact@camping-coldelaluere.com
website camping-coldelaluere.com
Situated in the Monts du Lyonnais, 20 minutes from Lyon.
Open All year **Site** 5HEC 🏕 ♣ 🏠 🚐 ⊗ **Prices** 🚶 3-3.60 🚗 2.55-3 🚐 2.55-3 ⛺ 2.55-3 🚐 (static)120-150 **Facilities** 🚿 🛍 ⊙ 🚐 ⊘ 🔥 Ⓟ **Services** 🍷 🍴 ✚ 🧺 **Leisure** 🏊 P

PONT-DE-SALARS AVEYRON

ac
12290 ☎ 565468486 📠 565743310
e-mail camping.du.lac@wanadoo.fr
website camping-du-lac.fr.st
A terraced site on the shore of a 200hect lake with good water sports.
➲ *1.5km N via D523.*
Open Jun-15 Sep **Site** 4.8HEC 🏕 ♣ 🏠 🚐 ⛺ ⊗ **Facilities** 🚿 🛍 ⊙ 🚐 ⊘ 🔥 Ⓟ **Services** 🍷 🍴 ✚ 🧺 **Leisure** 🏊 LP

Terrasses du Lac
rte du Vibal, 12290 ☎ 565468818 📠 565468538
e-mail campinglesterrasses@wanadoo.fr
website www.campinglesterrasses.com
Pleasant lake-side site with terraced pitches overlooking the Pont-de-Salars lake.
➲ *4km N via D523.*
Open Apr-Sep **Site** 6HEC 🏕 ♣ 🏠 🚐 ⛺ **Prices** pitch 10-21 (incl 2 persons) pp3.95-4.95 🚐 (static)260-620 **Facilities** 🚿 🛍 ⊙ 🚐 ⊘ 🔥 Ⓟ **Services** 🍷 🍴 🧺 **Leisure** 🏊 LP

PONTGIBAUD PUY-DE-DÔME

CM
rte de la Miouze, 63230 ☎ 473889699 📠 473887777
Set in a wooded area beside the River Sioule.
➲ *0.5km SW on D986 towards Rochefort-Montagne.*
Open 15 Apr-15 Oct **Site** 4.5HEC 🏕 ♣ 🏠 **Facilities** 🚿 ⊙ 🚐 Ⓟ **Services** 🍴 ✚ 🧺 **Leisure** 🏊 R **Off-site** 🛍 🍷 🍴 ⊘ 🔥 🏊L

PRADEAUX, LES PUY-DE-DÔME

Châteaux la Grange Fort
63500 ☎ 473710593 📠 473710769
e-mail chateau@lagrangefort.com
website www.lagrangefort.com
Set in a park surrounding a château on the River Allier.
➲ *A75 exit 13 for Parentignat, onto D999 & signed.*
Open Etr-15 Oct **Site** 22HEC 🏕 ⛰ ♣ 🏠 🚐 ⛺ **Prices** 🚶 4.20-5.50 🚗 2.25 🚐 6.20-8.30 ⛺ 6.20-8.30 🚐 (static)250-575 **Facilities** 🚿 ⊙ 🚐 ⊘ 🔥 Ⓟ **Services** 🍷 🍴 ✚ 🧺 **Leisure** 🏊 PR **Off-site** 🛍

PUY, LE HAUTE-LOIRE

Camping du Puy-en-Velay
43000 ☎ 615082359 &
On a wooded meadow with a section reserved for motor caravans.
➲ *From town centre towards Clermont-Ferrand, right at lights by church of St-Laurent, signed, site 0.5km on left.*
Open Apr-1 Oct **Site** 1HEC 🏕 ♣ **Prices** 🚶 2.95 🚗 1.70 🚐 2.90 ⛺ 2.60 **Facilities** 🚿 ⊙ 🚐 Ⓟ **Services** ✚ 🧺 **Off-site** 🛍 🍷 🍴 ⊘ 🔥 🏊P

AT BLAVOZY (9KM E)

Moulin de Barette
43700 ☎ 471030088 📠 471030051
A pleasant woodland site beside a picturesque stream.
➲ *N88 onto D156.*
Open Apr-15 Oct **Site** 2HEC 🏕 ♣ 🏠 **Facilities** 🚿 🛍 ⊙ 🚐 🔥 Ⓟ **Services** 🍷 🍴 🧺 **Leisure** 🏊 PR

AT BRIVES-CHARENSAC (4.5KM E)

Audinet
Av des Sports, 43700 ☎ 471091018 📠 471091018
e-mail camping.audinet@wanadoo.fr
website www.brives-charensac.fr
A peaceful site in a wooded setting beside the River Loire with good recreational facilities.
➲ *E on N88.*
Open 14 Apr-15 Sep **Site** 4.5HEC 🏕 ♣ 🏠 🚐 **Prices** 🚶 2.50 🚗 1.20 🚐 10.40 ⛺ 8.20 🚐 (static)124-180 **Facilities** 🚿 ⊙ 🚐 Ⓟ **Services** 🍷 🍴 🧺 **Off-site** 🛍 🏊PR

RIOM-ÈS-MONTAGNES CANTAL

Sédour
rte de Condat, 15400 ☎ 471780571
A pleasant location beside the River Véronne.
➲ *Via D678.*
Open May-Sep **Site** 1.5HEC 🏕 ♣ 🏠 **Facilities** 🚿 ⊙ 🚐 Ⓟ **Services** ✚ 🧺 **Leisure** 🏊 R **Off-site** 🛍 🍷 🍴 ⊘ 🔥 🏊LP

RIVIÈRE-SUR-TARN AVEYRON

Peyrelade
rte des Gorges-du-Tarn, 12640 ☎ 565626254 📠 565626561
e-mail campingpeyrelade@wanadoo.fr
website www.campingpeyrelade.com
Wooded surroundings close to the Gorges du Tarn.
➲ *2km E via D907, beside River Tarn.*
Open 15 May-15 Sep **Site** 4HEC 🏕 ♣ 🏠 ⛺ **Prices** 🚶 3.50-5 pitch 14-21 (incl 2 persons) 🚐 (static)210-650 **Facilities** 🚿 🛍 ⊙ 🚐 ⊘ Ⓟ **Services** 🍷 🍴 ✚ 🧺 **Leisure** 🏊 PR

RODEZ AVEYRON

CM Layoule
12000 ☎ 565670952 📠 565671143
Clean, tidy site in valley below town, completely divided into pitches.
➲ *NE of town centre, signed.*
Open Jun-Sep **Site** 3HEC 🏕 ⛰ ♣ **Prices** 🚶 2 ⛺ 4 pitch 12 (incl 3 persons) **Facilities** 🚿 ⊙ 🚐 Ⓟ **Services** ✚ 🧺 **Off-site** 🛍 🍷 🍴 ⊘ 🔥

Facilities 🛍 shop 🚿 shower ⊙ electric points for razors 🚐 electric points for caravans Ⓟ parking by tents permitted 🅿 compulsory separate car park
Services 🍴 café/restaurant 🍷 bar ⊘ Camping Gaz International 🔥 gas other than Camping Gaz ✚ first aid facilities 🧺 laundry
Leisure 🏊 swimming L-Lake P-Pool R-River S-Sea **Off-site** All facilities within 2km

France

ROYAT PUY-DE-DÔME

Indigo Royat

rte de Gravenoire, 63130 ☎ 473359705 🖹 473356769

e-mail royat@camping-indigo.com

website www.camping-indigo.com

A natural setting at the foot of the Puy de Dome and overlooking Clermont Ferrand. The pitches are laid out in terraces and are comfortably shaded.

➲ *Off D941 SW of Royat.*

Open 8 Apr-29 Oct **Site** 7HEC 👹 🌑 👹 🌑 ⛺ 🚐 Å **Prices** ♠ 4-4.70 pitch 4.70-9.80 🚐 (static)300-640 **Facilities** 🏠 🖨 ⊙ 🚻 🖉 ⑫ **Services** ⚑ 🍴 🖾 **Leisure** ⚓ P **Off-site** 🍴 ⚓LR ➕

RUYNES-EN-MARGERIDE CANTAL

A Touvert le Petit Bois

15320 ☎ 471234226 🖹 467363542

e-mail a.tou.vert@net-up.com

A pleasant, well-equipped, park-like site on the bank of the River Charente.

➲ *0.5km SW on D13 rte de Garabit, signed.*

Open Apr-15 Oct **Site** 7HEC 👹 ⛺ 🚐 **Facilities** 🏠 ⊙ 🚻 ⑫ **Services** ➕ 🖾 **Off-site** 🍴 ⚑ 🍴 🖉 ⚓P

SAIGNES CANTAL

Bellevue

15240 ☎ 471406840 🖹 471406165

e-mail saignes-mairie@wanadoo.fr

A pleasant rural site in the Sumène valley.

Open Jul-Aug **Site** 0.9HEC 👹 ⛺ **Facilities** 🏠 ⊙ 🚻 ⑫ **Services** 🍴 🖾 **Off-site** 🍴 ⚑ 🍴 🖉 ⚓P ➕

ST-ALBAN-SUR-LIMAGNOLE LOZÈRE

Galier

48120 ☎ 466315880 🖹 466314183

e-mail campinglegalier48@wanadoo.fr

Well-equipped site beside the river.

➲ *A75 exit 34.*

Open Mar-15 Nov **Site** 4HEC 👹 ⛺ ⛺ 🚐 **Prices** pitch 10.40-13.20 (incl 2 persons) pp2.80-3.40 🚐 (static)230-460 **Facilities** 🏠 ⊙ 🚻 🖉 🔺 ⑫ **Services** ⚑ 🍴 ➕ 🖾 **Leisure** ⚓ PR **Off-site** 🍴 🍴

ST-AMANT-ROCHE-SAVINE PUY-DE-DÔME

CM Saviloisirs

63890 ☎ 473957360 🖹 473957262

e-mail saviloisirs@wanadoo.fr

website www.saviloisirs.com

Run by the local tourist authority with plenty of sports facilities within easy reach.

Open May-Sep **Site** 1.5HEC 👹 ⛺ 🚐 **Prices** ♠ 2.70 🚐 1.50 Å 1.50 **Facilities** 🏠 ⊙ 🚻 ⑫ **Services** ➕ 🖾 **Off-site** 🍴 ⚑ 🍴 ⚓R

ST-BONNET-TRONÇAIS ALLIER

Champ-Fossé

3360 ☎ 470061130 🖹 470061501

e-mail champfosse@aol.com

Set in the forest of Tronçais beside a lake with plenty of recreational facilities.

➲ *Via A71-E11.*

Open Apr-Sep **Site** 35HEC 👹 ⛺ 🚐 **Prices** ♠ 3-3.90 🚐 1.10 pitch 2 🚐 (static)255-449 **Facilities** 🏠 🖨 ⊙ 🚻 🖉 ⑫ **Services** ⚑ 🍴 ➕ 🖾 **Leisure** ⚓ LP **Off-site** 🍴

ST-CLÉMENT-DE-VALORGUE PUY-DE-DÔME

Narcisses

63660 ☎ 473954576

e-mail nobilet.catherine@wanadoo.fr

website www.campinglenarcisses.com

A beautiful natural setting within the Livradois-Forez regional park.

Open May-Sep **Site** 1.3HEC 👹 ⛺ 🚐 **Facilities** 🏠 🖨 ⊙ 🚻 🔺 ⑫ **Services** ⚑ 🍴 ➕ 🖾 **Leisure** ⚓ PR **Off-site** 🖉 ⚓L

ST-GAL-SUR-SIOULE PUY-DE-DÔME

Pont de St-Gal

63440 ☎ 473974471

A pleasant site with shaded, well-defined pitches, and access to the river for boating and fishing.

➲ *E on D16 towards Ebreuil, beside River Sioule.*

Open May-Sep **Site** 1HEC 👹 ⛺ 🚐 Å **Facilities** 🏠 🖨 ⊙ 🚻 🖉 🔺 ⑫ **Services** ⚑ 🍴 ➕ 🖾 **Leisure** ⚓ R

ST-GENIEZ-D'OLT AVEYRON

Campéole La Boissière

rte de la Cascade, 12130 ☎ 565704043 🖹 565475639

website www.campeoles.fr

A comfortable site in wooded surroundings with good facilities. Entertainment provided in July and August.

➲ *A75 exit 41 for St-Geniez-d'Olt.*

Open 20 Apr-Sep **Site** 4.5HEC 👹 ⛺ 🚐 **Facilities** 🏠 🖨 ⊙ 🚻 🖉 ⑫ **Services** ⚑ 🍴 ➕ 🖾 **Leisure** ⚓ PR **Off-site** 🍴 🔺

Marmotel

12130 ☎ 565704651 🖹 565474138

website www.marmotel.com

Grassy family site on River Lot with a variety of recreational facilities.

➲ *On D19 1km NW of St Geniez-d'Olt.*

Open 12 May-12 Sep **Site** 5HEC 👹 ⛺ 🚐 **Prices** pitch 17.50-31 (incl 2 persons) 🚐 (static)220-655 **Facilities** 🏠 ⊙ 🚻 ⑫ **Services** ⚑ 🍴 ➕ 🖾 **Leisure** ⚓ PR **Off-site** 🍴 🖉

ST-GERMAIN-DE-CALBERTE LOZÈRE

Garde

48370 ☎ 466459482

e-mail camping-lagarde@wanadoo.fr

A pleasant location on the edge of the Cevennes national park.

➲ *Via A7 or A75.*

Open Jun-15 Sep **Site** 2.4HEC 👹 ⛺ ⛺ **Facilities** 🏠 ⊙ 🚻 ⑫ **Services** 🍴 🖾 **Leisure** ⚓ P **Off-site** 🍴 ⚑ 🖉 🔺 ⚓R ➕

Site 6HEC (site size) 👹 grass ⊖ sand 👹 stone ⛺ little shade ⛺ partly shaded ⛺ mainly shaded ⛺ bungalows for hire 🚐 caravans for hire Å tents for hire ⊗ no dogs **Prices** ♠ adult per night 🚗 car per night pp per person per night 🚐 caravan per night Å tent per night 🚐 (static)-caravan hire per week

France

ST-GÉRONS CANTAL

Presqu'île d'Espinet
Espinet, 15150 ☎ 471622890
e-mail camping.despinet@wanadoo.fr
website www.camping-espinet.com
On a wooded peninsula jutting into the lake with fine views of the Cantal mountains.
➲ 8.5km SE, 300m from Lake St-Étienne-Cantalès.
Open 15 Jun-Aug **Site** 3HEC 😊 ♣ 🏠 **Prices** pitch 13 (incl 2 persons) pp3.50 🚐 (static)250-450 **Facilities** 🏪 🏚 ⊙ 🚰 ⊘ ℗ **Services** 🍴 🍽 ➕ 🗄
Leisure ➽ LP **Off-site** 🚿

ST-GERVAIS-D'AUVERGNE PUY-DE-DÔME

CM de l'Étang Philippe
rte de St-Eloy-les-Mines, 63390 ☎ 473857484
e-mail campingstgervais@wanadoo.fr
website www.camping-loisir.com
A small municipal site beside a small lake.
➲ Via N987.
Open Etr-Sep **Site** 5HEC 😊 ♣ ♣ 🏠 **Facilities** 🏪 ⊙ 🚰 ℗ **Services** 🍴 ➕ 🗄
Leisure ➽ L **Off-site** 🏚 🍴 ⊘

ST-JACQUES-DES-BLATS CANTAL

CM des Blats
rte de la Gare, 15800 ☎ 471470590 🖨 471470709
e-mail i-tourisme-st-jacques@wanadoo.fr
A small site on the banks of the River Cère. A good centre for exploring the surrounding Volcanic Park area.
Open May-Sep **Site** 1HEC 😊 ♣ 🏠 **Facilities** 🏪 ⊙ 🚰 ℗ **Services** ➕ 🗄
Leisure ➽ R **Off-site** 🏚 🍴 🍽

ST-JODARD LOIRE

CM
42590 ☎ 477634242 🖨 477634001
e-mail mairie.st.jodard@wanadoo.fr
Open May-Sep **Site** 0.3HEC 😊 ♣ ♣ 🏠 **Prices** 🚶 1.38-1.90 🚐 0.69-0.95 pitch 0.69-0.95 **Facilities** 🏪 ⊙ 🚰 ℗ **Services** 🗄 **Off-site** 🏚 🍴 🍽 ⊘ 🚿 ➽P

ST-JUST CANTAL

CM
Le Bourg, 15320 ☎ 471737257 🖨 471737144
e-mail commune.stjust@wanadoo.fr
website www.saintjust.com
Set in the centre of the village beside the river.
Open Etr-Sep **Site** 2HEC 😊 ♣ 🏠 **Facilities** 🏪 ⊙ 🚰 ℗ **Services** ➕ 🗄
Leisure ➽ P **Off-site** 🏚 🍴 🍽 ⊘ 🚿 ➽R

ST-MARTIN-VALMEROUX CANTAL

Moulin du Teinturier
rte de Loupiac, 15140 ☎ 471694312 🖨 4719692452
e-mail mairie.saintmartin-valmeroux@wanadoo.fr
Wooded valley site close to medieval market town.
➲ Off D922 Aurillac-Mauriac.
Open Jun-Sep **Site** 2.8HEC 😊 🏠 ⚠ **Prices** 🚶 2.50 pitch 7.20 **Facilities** 🏪 ⊙ 🚰 ℗ **Services** 🗄 **Leisure** ➽ R **Off-site** 🏚 🍴 🍽 ⊘ 🚿 ➽P ➕

ST-NECTAIRE PUY-DE-DÔME

Vallée Verte
rte des Granges, 63710 ☎ 473885268
e-mail lavalleeverte@libertysurf.fr
website www.campinglavalleeverte.com
Wooded surroundings by a river within the Auvergne volcanic park.
➲ On R146, 400m from R996.
Open 15 Apr-Sep **Site** 2.5HEC 😊 ♣ 🏠 🚐 **Facilities** 🏪 ⊙ 🚰 ⊘ 🚿 ℗
Services 🍴 🍽 🗄 **Leisure** ➽ R **Off-site** 🚿 ➽PR ➕

ST-OURS PUY-DE-DÔME

Bel-Air
63230 ☎ 473887214
e-mail camping.belair@free.fr
website camping.belair.free.fr
➲ 1km SW on D941.
Open Apr-1 Oct **Site** 2HEC 😊 ♣ 🏠 🚐 **Prices** 🚶 4.10 🚐 1 pitch 4 🚐 (static)150-250 **Facilities** 🏪 🏚 ⊙ 🚰 ⊘ 🚿 ℗ **Services** 🍴 ➕ 🗄
Off-site 🍽

ST-PIERRE-COLAMINE PUY-DE-DÔME

Ombrage
63610 ☎ 473967787 🖨 473963040
e-mail campombrage@infonie.fr
website www.campombrage.com
A pleasant site in peaceful wooded surroundings at an altitude of 800m on the edge of the Auvergne Volcano Park. All the usual services are provided and there are good recreational facilities.
➲ 300m from D978.
Open All year **Site** 2HEC 😊 ♣ 🏠 **Prices** 🚶 4 🚐 1.10 pitch 3.30
Facilities 🏪 🏚 ⊙ 🚰 ⊘ 🚿 ℗ **Services** 🍴 ➕ 🗄 **Leisure** ➽ P
Off-site 🍽 ➽R

ST-RÉMY-SUR-DUROLLE PUY-DE-DÔME

CM Chanterelles
63550 ☎ 473943171 🖨 473943171
e-mail mairie-saint-remy-sur-durolle@wanadoo.fr
website www.saint-remy-sur-durolle.fr
Pleasant wooded surroundings close to the lake.
➲ 3km NE via D201.
Open May-Sep **Site** 6HEC 😊 ♣ **Facilities** 🏪 ⊙ 🚰 ⊘ ℗ **Services** ➕ 🗄
Off-site 🏚 🍴 🍽 🚿 ➽LP

ST-ROME-DE-TARN AVEYRON

Cascade
12490 ☎ 565625659 🖨 565625862
e-mail campingdelacascade@wanadoo.fr
website www.campingdelacascade.com
Terraced site beside the River Tarn.
➲ 0.3km N via D993.
Open All year **Site** 4HEC 😊 ♣ 🏠 🚐 ⚠ **Facilities** 🏪 🏚 ⊙ 🚰 ⊘ 🚿 ℗
Services 🍴 🍽 🗄 **Leisure** ➽ LPR **Off-site** 🍽 ➕

Facilities 🏚 shop 🏪 shower ⊙ electric points for razors 🚰 electric points for caravans ℗ parking by tents permitted 🅿 compulsory separate car park
Services 🍽 café/restaurant 🍴 bar ⊘ Camping Gaz International 🚿 gas other than Camping Gaz ➕ first aid facilities 🗄 laundry
Leisure ➽ swimming L-Lake P-Pool R-River S-Sea **Off-site** All facilities within 2km

ST-SALVADOU AVEYRON

Muret
12200 ☎ 565818069 🖨 565818069
e-mail info@lemuret.com
website www.campinglemuret.com
A modern site in peaceful, rural surroundings beside the lake.
⮥ *3km SE.*

Open Apr-Oct **Site** 3HEC 👪 ♣ ⛺ 🚐 🅰 **Prices** ♠ 2.40-3 pitch 7-8.50 🚐 (static)275-575 **Facilities** 🏪 🛁 ⊙ 🚿 ⊘ 🚮 ℗ **Services** 🍴 🍽 ➕ 🛒 **Leisure** ⚓ L **Off-site** 🛁

STE-CATHERINE RHÔNE

CM du Châtelard
69440 ☎ 478818060 🖨 478818773
e-mail mairie-ste-catherine@wanadoo.fr
A quiet, well-equipped site providing magnificent views over the surrounding countryside.
⮥ *2km S.*

Open Mar-Nov **Site** 4HEC 👪 ♣ **Prices** ♠ 2.05 🚐 2.35 **Facilities** 🏪 ⊙ 🚿 ℗ **Services** ➕ 🛒 **Off-site** 🛁 🍴 🍽 ⊘ 🚮 ⚓R

STE-SIGOLÈNE HAUTE-LOIRE

Vaubarlet
Vaubarlet, 43600 ☎ 471666495 🖨 471661198
e-mail camping@vaubarlet.com
website www.vaubarlet.com
Set in a beautiful wooded valley beside the River Dunières with a variety of supervised family activities.
⮥ *D44 exit to Ste-Sigolène, D43 towards Grazac, signed after 10km.*

Open May-Sep **Site** 3.5HEC 👪 ♣ ⛺ 🚐 🅰 **Prices** pitch 14.40-18 (incl 2 persons) pp3.20-4 🚐 (static)180-500 **Facilities** 🏪 🛁 ⊙ 🚿 ⊘ ℗ **Services** 🍴 🍽 🛒 **Leisure** ⚓ PR **Off-site** 🍽

SALLES-CURAN AVEYRON

Beau Rivage
Route des Vernhes, Lac de Pareloup, 12410 ☎ 565463332
e-mail camping-beau-rivage@wanadoo.fr
website www.beau-rivage.fr
A terraced site located on the shore of Lac de Pareloup. There are facilities for water sports and the site's popularity makes booking advisable.
⮥ *A75 exit 44.1, follow D991.*

Open Apr-Oct **Site** 2HEC 👪 ♣ ⛺ 🚐 🅰 **Prices** pitch 11.50-26 (incl 2 persons) 🚐 (static)182-395 **Facilities** 🏪 🛁 ⊙ 🚿 ⊘ 🚮 ℗ **Services** 🍴 🍽 ➕ 🛒 **Leisure** ⚓ LP

Genêts
12410 ☎ 565463534 🖨 565780072
e-mail contact@camping-les-genets.fr
website www.camping-les-genets.fr
On the edge of the Papeloup lake.
⮥ *7km W via D577.*

Open Jun-Sep **Site** 3HEC 👪 ♣ ⛺ 🅰 **Facilities** 🏪 🛁 ⊙ 🚿 ⊘ 🚮 ℗ **Services** 🍴 🍽 ➕ 🛒 **Leisure** ⚓ LP

SAZERET ALLIER

Petite Valette
03390 ☎ 470076457 🖨 470072548
e-mail la.petite.valette@wanadoo.fr
website www.valette.nl
A well-equipped site attached to a farm with well-defined pitches and organised activities for children.
⮥ *A71 exit 11 & signed.*

Site 4HEC 👪 ♣ ⛺ 🚐 🅰 **Prices** ♠ 3.95-5.15 pitch 5.95-7.50 **Facilities** 🏪 ⊙ 🚿 ℗ **Services** 🍽 ➕ 🛒 **Leisure** ⚓ LP

SEMBADEL-GARE HAUTE-LOIRE

Casses
43160 ☎ 471009472
A family site in a rural setting at an altitude of 1000m, 2km from a lake.
⮥ *1km W via D22.*

Open Jul-20 Sep **Site** 2.4HEC 👪 ♣ **Facilities** 🏪 ⊙ 🚿 ℗ **Services** 🛒 **Off-site** 🍴 🍽 🚮 ⚓LR

SÉNERGUES AVEYRON

Étang du Camp
12320 ☎ 565796225 🖨 565728158
e-mail conques@conques.com
website www.conques.com
Well-equipped site in a wooded setting beside the lake.
⮥ *6km SW via D242.*

Open 15 Jun-15 Sep **Site** 3HEC 👪 ♣ ⛺ 🚐 **Facilities** 🏪 ⊙ 🚿 ⊘ 🚮 ℗ **Services** ➕ 🛒

SÉVÉRAC-L'ÉGLISE AVEYRON

Grange de Monteillac
Monteillac, 12310 ☎ 565702100 🖨 565702101
e-mail info@la-grange-de-monteillac.com
website www.la-grange-de-monteillac.com
A family site in a quiet wooded location with good recreational facilities.
⮥ *Via A75 & N88.*

Open May-15 Sep **Site** 4.5HEC 👪 ♣ ⛺ 🚐 🅰 **Prices** pitch 15.05-23.50 (incl 2 persons) **Facilities** 🏪 🛁 ⊙ 🚿 ⊘ ℗ **Services** 🍴 🍽 **Leisure** ⚓ P **Off-site** 🚮

SINGLES PUY-DE-DÔME

Moulin de Serre
D 73 Vallee de la Burande, 63690 ☎ 473211606 🖨 473211256
e-mail moulin-de-serre@wanadoo.fr
website www.moulindeserre.com
A well-equipped site beside the River Burande.
⮥ *1.7km S of La Guinguette via D73.*

Open 13 Apr-16 Sep **Site** 7HEC 👪 ♣ ⛺ 🚐 🅰 **Prices** ♠ 2.90-3.90 pitch 9.95-16.60 🚐 (static)145-385 **Facilities** 🏪 🛁 ⊙ 🚿 ⊘ 🚮 ℗ **Services** 🍴 🍽 ➕ 🛒 **Leisure** ⚓ PR

Site 6HEC (site size) 👪 grass ⛱ sand 👪 stone ♣ little shade ♣ partly shaded 🌳 mainly shaded ⛺ bungalows for hire 🚐 caravans for hire 🅰 tents for hire ⊗ no dogs **Prices** ♠ adult per night 🚗 car per night pp per person per night 🚐 caravan per night 🅰 tent per night 🚐 (static)-caravan hire per week

THÉRONDELS AVEYRON

Source
Presqu'île de Laussac, 12600 ☎ 565660562 🖷 565662100
e-mail info@camping-la-source.com
website camping-la-source.com
A beautiful location beside Lake Sarrans.

Open 12 May-9 Sep **Site** 4.5HEC 👪 ⚬ ⚬ 🛈 **Prices** 🛉 3-4.50
pitch 15.50-24.50 (incl 2 persons) **Facilities** 🌳🛈⚬🕿⊘® **Services** 🛒
🍴🖪 **Leisure** ⚓ LP

TRIZAC CANTAL

Pioulat
15400 ☎ 471786420 🖷 471786540
e-mail mairie.trizac@wanadoo.fr
Open 16 Jun-16 Sep **Site** 4.7HEC 👪 ⚬ 🛐 **Prices** 🛉 1.60 ⚬ 1.20 🛐 1.40
🛐 1.40 **Facilities** 🌳⚬🕿® **Services** 🖪 **Leisure** ⚓ LR **Off-site** 🛈🛒🍴
⊘⚒🔁

URÇAY ALLIER

CM
r de la Gare, 3360 ☎ 470069691 🖷 470069330
Open 15 May-30 Aug **Site** 0.7HEC 👪 ⚬ 🛈 **Facilities** 🌳⚬🕿®
Services 🖪 **Leisure** ⚓ R **Off-site** 🛈🛒🍴⊘⚒🔁

VARENNES-SUR-ALLIER ALLIER

Château de Chazeuil
03150 ☎ 470450010 🖷 470450010
e-mail camping-de-chazeuil@ifrance.com
website www.camping-de-chazeuil.com
On well-kept meadow within the château park.
➲ 3km NW on N7.
Open 15 Apr-15 Oct **Site** 1.5HEC 👪 ⚬ **Facilities** 🌳⚬🕿® **Services** 🔁
🖪 **Leisure** ⚓ P **Off-site** 🛈🛒🍴⊘⚓R

VERRIÈRES-EN-FOREZ LOIRE

Ferme Le Soleillant
Le Soleillant, 42600 ☎ 477762273
e-mail camille.rival@wanadoo.fr
website www.le-soleillant.com
A small terraced site within the grounds of a farm.
➲ RD496 between Montbrison and St Anthème. Campsite signed.
Open All year **Site** 3.2HEC 👪 ⚬ 🛐 **Prices** 🛉 3 ⚬ 0.80 pitch 2.20
Facilities 🌳⚬🕿® **Services** 🍴🔁🖪 **Off-site** 🛈🛒🍴⊘⚒⚓R

VIC-SUR-CÈRE CANTAL

Pommeraie
15800 ☎ 471475418 🖷 471496330
e-mail pommeraie@wanadoo.fr
website camping-la-pommeraie.com
A well-equipped family site in a peaceful location with good recreational facilities.
➲ 2km SE.
Open Apr-15 Sep **Site** 4HEC 👪 ⚬ 🛐 🛐 **Prices** pitch 15-21 (incl 2 persons) **Facilities** 🌳🛈⚬🕿⚒® **Services** 🛒🍴🔁🖪 **Leisure** ⚓ P
Off-site ⊘⚓R

VILLEFORT LOZÈRE

Palhère
rte du Mas de la Bque, 48800 ☎ 466468063
website www.villefort.free.fr
A well-equipped, peaceful site on the edge of the Parc National des Cévennes.
➲ 4km SW via D66 beside river.
Open May-Sep **Site** 2HEC 👪 ⚬ ⚬ **Facilities** 🌳⚬🕿® **Services** 🛒🍴
🔁🖪 **Leisure** ⚓ PR **Off-site** 🛈⊘⚒⚓L

VILLEFRANCHE-DE-PANAT AVEYRON

Cantarelles
Alrance, 12430 ☎ 565464035 🖷 565464035
e-mail cantarelles@wanadoo.fr
website www.lescantarelles.com
On level grassland by Lac de Villefranche-de-Panat.
➲ On D25 3km N.
Open May-Sep **Site** 3.5HEC 👪 ⚬ 🛐 🛐 **Prices** pitch 16 (incl 2 persons) pp4.40 🛐 (static)295-529 **Facilities** 🌳⚬🕿⊘⚒® **Services** 🛒🍴🔁
🖪 **Leisure** ⚓ L

VILLEFRANCHE-DE-ROUERGUE AVEYRON

Rouergue
12200 ☎ 565451624 🖷 565451624
e-mail campingrouergue@wanadoo.fr
website www.villefranche.com/camping
A comfortable site in a pleasant, shady location beside the River Aveyron.
➲ 1.5km SW via D47 rte de Monteils.
Open Apr-Sep **Site** 2HEC 👪 ⚬ 🛐 🛐 🛈 **Prices** pitch 10.50-13.50 (incl 2 persons) 🛐 (static)150-270 **Facilities** 🌳🛈⚬🕿⊘® **Services** 🛒🍴🖪
Off-site ⚒⚓PR🔁

YSSINGEAUX HAUTE-LOIRE

CM Choumouroux
43200 ☎ 471655344
➲ 0.8km S of town off rte de Puy.
Open May-Sep **Site** 0.8HEC 👪 ⚬ 🛐 **Facilities** 🌳⚬🕿® **Services** 🔁🖪
Off-site 🛈🛒🍴⊘⚒⚓P

SOUTH COAST/RIVIERA

AGAY VAR

Agay Soleil
1152 bd de la Plage, rte de Cannes RN 98, 83530
☎ 494820079 🖷 494828870
e-mail camping-agay-soleil@wanadoo.fr
website www.agay-soleil.com
A small site in a shady position directly on a sandy beach. The facilities are good and water sports are available nearby.
➲ Between N98 & sea.
Open 25 Mar-5 Nov **Site** 0.7HEC 👪 ⚬ ⚬ 🛐 **Prices** pitch 21-26.50 (incl 3 persons) pp5.20-5.50 **Facilities** 🌳⚬🕿⊘® **Services** 🛒🍴🔁🖪
Leisure ⚓ S **Off-site** 🛈

Facilities 🛈 shop 🌳 shower ⚬ electric points for razors 🕿 electric points for caravans ® parking by tents permitted ⚬ compulsory separate car park
Services 🍴 café/restaurant 🔁 bar ⊘ Camping Gaz International ⚒ gas other than Camping Gaz 🔁 first aid facilities 🖪 laundry
Leisure ⚓ swimming L-Lake P-Pool R-River S-Sea **Off-site** All facilities within 2km

Estérel

rte de Valescure, 83530 ☎ 494820328 🖩 494828737
e-mail contact@esterel-caravaning.fr
website www.esterel-caravaning.fr
A pleasant family-site. Riding and cycling can be enjoyed in the surrounding hills and woods.

➲ *3km N from Agay-Plage towards Valescure, near golf course.*

Open Apr-Sep **Site** 15HEC 🎇 🏖 🛖 **Prices** ⋔ 8 pitch 22-42 (incl 2 persons) 🚐 (static)650-999 **Facilities** ⋒ 🖄 ⊙ 🚰 ⚍ 🛒 🛱 **Services** 🍴 🍴 ➕ 🖻 **Leisure** ⚓ P **Off-site** ⚓LR

AGDE HÉRAULT

Escale

Rte de la Tamarissière, 34300 ☎ 467212109 🖩 467211024
e-mail camping-lescale@hotmail.fr
website www.camping-lescale.com
A riverside site, 0.9km from the sea, with good recreational facilities.

Open Apr-Sep **Site** 3HEC 🎇 🏖 🛖 🛱 **Prices** pitch 15.70-27.20 (incl 2 persons) 🚐 (static)270-630 **Facilities** ⋒ 🖄 ⊙ 🚰 ⚍ 🛒 🛱 **Services** 🍴 🍴 ➕ 🖻 **Leisure** ⚓ PR **Off-site** ⊘ ⚓S

Mer et Soliel

rte de Rochelongue, 34300 ☎ 467942114 🖩 467948194
e-mail contact@camping-mer-soleil.com
website www.camping-mer-soleil.com
A modern, well-equipped family site within easy reach of the beach.

Open 31 Mar-13 Oct **Site** 7.9HEC 🎇 🏖 🛖 🛱 🅰 **Prices** 🚐 3 🅰 3 pitch 17-36 (incl 2 persons) pp3.20-7 🚐 (static)210-945 **Facilities** ⋒ 🖄 ⊙ 🚰 ⊘ ⚍ 🛒 **Services** 🍴 🍴 ➕ 🖻 **Leisure** ⚓ P **Off-site** ⚓RS

Romarins

rte du Grau ☎ 467941859 🖩 467265880
e-mail contact@romarins.com
website www.romarins.com
Located in a busy Mediterranean fishing village south of the city of Agde. On the left bank of the Herault river with fine sandy beaches.

➲ *Autoroute A9 exit 34 Agde/Bessan, proceed 12km towards Agde and exit at Grau d'Agde, first turning after bridge. Turn left at supermarket and proceed alongside river for 1.5km direction Grau d'Agde.*

Open 15 Apr-25 Sep **Site** 2.2HEC 🎇 🏖 🛖 **Prices** pitch 11.70-20.55 pp3.90-6.30 🚐 (static)177-755 **Facilities** ⊙ 🚰 ⚍ 🛒 **Services** 🍴 🍴 ➕ 🖻 **Leisure** ⚓ P **Off-site** 🖄 ⊘ ⚓RS

AT ROCHELONGUE-PLAGE (4KM S)

Champs Blancs

rte de Rochelongue, 34300 ☎ 467942342 🖩 467948781
e-mail champs.blancs@wanadoo.fr
website www.champs-blancs.fr
Quiet shady site with hedged pitches and surrounded by exotic vegetation. Good sports and entertainment facilities.

➲ *Between Agde & Cap d'Agde on route de Rochelongue.*

Open Apr-Sep **Site** 4HEC 🎇 🏖 🛖 🛱 **Prices** ⋔ 8 pitch 18-39 **Facilities** ⋒ 🖄 🚰 ⚍ 🛒 **Services** 🍴 🍴 ➕ 🖻 **Leisure** ⚓ P **Off-site** 🍴 ⊘ ⚓RS

AIGUES MORTES GARD

Camping Village La Petite Camargue

Quartier du Mole, BP21, 30220 ☎ 466539898 🖩 466539880
e-mail info@yellohvillage-petite-camargue.com
website www.yellohvillage-petite-camargue.com
A grassy site among vineyards on the D62, 3.5km from the sea.

➲ *Autoroute exit Gallargues for La Grande Motte.*

Open 28 Apr-15 Sep **Site** 10HEC 🎇 🏖 🛖 🛱 **Prices** ⋔ 3-7.50 pitch 17-43 (incl 2 persons) **Facilities** ⋒ 🖄 ⊙ 🚰 ⊘ ⚍ 🛒 **Services** 🍴 🍴 ➕ 🖻 **Leisure** ⚓ P **Off-site** ⚓S

AIX-EN-PROVENCE BOUCHES-DU-RHÔNE

Arc en Ciel

Pont de Trois Sautets, rte de Nice, 13100 ☎ 442261428
website www.campingarcenciel.fr
A pleasant terraced site on both sides of a stream.

➲ *N7 exit 3 Sautets for Toulon, 3km SE near Pont des Trois Sautets.*

Open Apr-Sep **Site** 3HEC 🎇 🏖 🛖 🛱 **Prices** ⋔ 6 pitch 5.50 **Facilities** ⋒ ⊙ 🚰 ⊘ 🛒 **Services** ➕ 🖻 **Leisure** ⚓ PR **Off-site** 🖄 🍴 🍴 ⚍

Chantecler

Val St Andre, 13100 ☎ 442261298 🖩 442273353
Extensive, uneven site on a hill. Terraced pitches.

➲ *A8 exit Aix-Est, 2.5km SE of town.*

Open All year **Site** 8HEC 🎇 🏖 🛖 🛱 **Facilities** ⋒ 🖄 ⊙ 🚰 ⊘ ⚍ 🛒 **Services** 🍴 🍴 ➕ 🖻 **Leisure** ⚓ P **Off-site** ⚓S

ALET-LES-BAINS AUDE

Val d'Aleth

chemin de la Paoulette, 11580 ☎ 468699040 🖩 468699460
e-mail camping@valdaleth.com
website www.valdaleth.com
Picturesque surroundings beneath the historic ramparts, on the banks of the River Aude.

➲ *D118 S from Carcassonne, through Limoux, site 8km S off D118.*

Open All year **Site** 0.5HEC 🎇 🏖 🛖 🛱 **Prices** ⋔ 2.75 pitch 12 (incl 2 persons) pp3.40 🚐 (static)164.50-235 **Facilities** ⋒ 🖄 ⊙ 🚰 ⊘ ⚍ 🛒 **Services** ➕ 🖻 **Leisure** ⚓ R **Off-site** 🖄 🍴 🍴 ⚓P

ALLEGRE GARD

Domaine des Fumades

☎ 466248078
On sloping meadow near the river. Extensive leisure facilities. Liable to flooding at certain times.

➲ *Turn off D7 (Bourgot-les-Allrègre) at TOTAL filling station and follow signs.*

Open 15 May-15 Sep **Site** 15HEC 🎇 🏖 🛖 **Facilities** ⋒ 🖄 🚰 ⊘ ⚍ 🛒 **Services** 🍴 🍴 ➕ 🖻 **Leisure** ⚓ PR

See advertisement on page 173

ANDUZE GARD

Arche

30140 ☎ 466617408 🖩 466618894
e-mail resa@camping-arche.fr
website www.camping-arche.fr
A beautiful location on the River Gard in the Cevennes region.

➲ *A7 exit Bollène onto D907.*

Open Apr-Sep **Site** 10HEC 🎇 🏖 🛖 🅰 **Facilities** ⋒ 🖄 ⊙ 🚰 ⊘ ⚍ 🛒 **Services** 🍴 🍴 ➕ 🖻 **Leisure** ⚓ R

Site 6HEC (site size) 🎇 grass 🏖 sand 🛖 stone ♣ little shade 🌿 partly shaded 🌳 mainly shaded 🛱 bungalows for hire 🚐 caravans for hire 🅰 tents for hire ⊗ no dogs **Prices** ⋔ adult per night 🚗 car per night pp per person per night 🚐 caravan per night 🅰 tent per night 🚐 (static)-caravan hire per week

Brise des Pins

rte de St-Félix de Pallières, 30140 ☎ 466616339

A terraced site offering fine panoramic views over the surrounding countryside.

➲ *3km from Anduze.*

Open Jun-15 Sep **Site** ♨ ♣ **Prices** ♠ 8 pitch 11 (incl 2 persons)
Facilities 🖪 ⊙ ⊕ ☻ ⑫ **Services** 🖫

Castel Rose

610 chemin de Recoulin, 30140 ☎ 466618015

e-mail castelrose@wanadoo.fr

website www.castelrose.com

A well-equipped site on the banks of the River Gardon.

➲ *1km NW on D907.*

Open 29 Mar-21 Sep **Site** 7HEC ♨ ♣ ♣ 🏠 **Facilities** 🖪 ⊙ ⊕ ☻ ∅ ⑫
Services 🖾 🍴 ⊞ 🖫 **Leisure** ⚓ R **Off-site** ☖ ♨ ➕

Cévennes Provence

30140 ☎ 466617310 📠 466616074

e-mail marais@camping-cevennes-provence.com

website www.camping-cevennes-provence.com

Situated in a valley bordered by two rivers. Choice of pitches in varying levels of shade and terrain.

➲ *From Anduze take D907 towards St Jean du Gard for 3km and turn right to Corbes on D284.*

Open 20 Mar-1Nov **Site** 30HEC ♨ ♣ ♣ 🏠 **Prices** pitch 13.20-18.90 (incl 2 persons) **Facilities** 🖪 ☖ ⊙ ☻ ∅ ♨ ⑫ **Services** 🖾 🍴 ➕ 🖫
Leisure ⚓ R

AT ATTUECH (5KM SE ON D907)

Fief

30140 ☎ 466618171 📠 466618171

On level meadow, divided by flowerbeds and shrubs.

➲ *Off D982 E of Attuech, continue 400m on partly rough track.*

Open Apr-Sep **Site** 4.5HEC ♨ ♣ 🏠 **Facilities** 🖪 ☖ ⊙ ☻ ∅ ⑫
Services 🖾 🍴 ➕ 🖫 **Leisure** ⚓ P **Off-site** ⚓LR

Azur Rivage

RN 98, 83530 ☎ 494448312 📠 494448439

website www.camping-azur-rivage.com

Well-equipped site close to a sandy beach.

Open Etr-Sep **Site** 1HEC ♨ ♣ ♣ 🏠 **Facilities** 🖪 ☖ ⊙ ☻ ∅ ♨ ⑫ 🅿
Services 🖾 🍴 ➕ 🖫 **Leisure** ⚓ P **Off-site** ⚓S

Viaduc

bd des Lucioles, 83530 ☎ 494448231 📠 494448231

website www.campingduviaduc.com

A quiet site 150m from a sandy beach, with good facilities.

➲ *Via N98.*

Open Jun-Sep **Site** 1.1HEC ♨ ♣ **Prices** ♠ 3.50-4.50 pitch 15-29 (incl 2 persons) **Facilities** 🖪 ⊙ ☻ ⑫ **Services** ➕ 🖫 **Off-site** ☖ 🖾 🍴 ∅ ♨ ⚓S

Domaine des Fumades

You found an oasis between the Ardèche and the Mediterranean Sea. Rental of chalets and mobile homes or pitches. Mini club during the season, swimming pools - one covered and heated, Jacuzzis.

Domaine des Fumades F-30500 ALLEGRE
Phone : 33 (0) 466 24 80 78 Fax : 33 (0) 466 24 82 42
www.campings-franceloc.com

Gard

ANTIBES ALPES-MARITIMES

Logis de la Brague

1221 rte de Nice, 06600 ☎ 493335472

e-mail contact@camping-logisbrague.com

website www.camping-logisbrague.com

On a level meadow beside a small river.

➲ *On N7.*

Open 2 May-Sep **Site** 1.7HEC ♨ ♣ 🏠 **Prices** pitch 17-21 (incl 2 persons) 🏠 (static)210-595 **Facilities** 🖪 ☖ ⊙ ☻ ∅ ⑫ **Services** 🖾 🍴 ➕ 🖫 **Leisure** ⚓ RS **Off-site** ♨

AT BIOT (7KM N ON N7 AND A8)

Eden

chemin du Val-de-Pome, 06410 ☎ 493656370 📠 493655422

Site on level meadowland, no tents allowed.

➲ *On D4.*

Open Apr-30 Oct **Site** 2.5HEC ♨ ♣ ♣ 🏠 🏠 ⊗ **Prices** ♠ 3.80-5.50 pitch 15.70-19.50 **Facilities** 🖪 ☖ ⊙ ☻ ⑫ **Services** 🖾 🍴 ➕ 🖫 **Leisure** ⚓ P
Off-site ⚓S

AT BRAGUE, LA (4KM N ON N7)

Pylône

av du Pylone, 06600 ☎ 493335286 📠 493333054

e-mail camping.pylone@wanadoo.fr

website www.campingdupylone.com

Situated between Cannes and Nice, the family site with good facilities.

➲ *N7 onto D4 for Biot, 1st left.*

Open All year **Site** 16HEC ♨ ♣ 🏠 ⊗ **Prices** ♠ 5 ♣ 4 pitch 18 (incl 2 persons) **Facilities** 🖪 ☖ ⊙ ☻ ∅ ♨ ⑫ **Services** 🖾 🍴 ➕ 🖫 **Leisure** ⚓ PR **Off-site** ⚓S

Facilities ☖ shop 🖪 shower ⊙ electric points for razors ☻ electric points for caravans ⑫ parking by tents permitted 🅿 compulsory separate car park
Services 🍴 café/restaurant 🖾 bar ∅ Camping Gaz International ♨ gas other than Camping Gaz ➕ first aid facilities 🖫 laundry
Leisure ⚓ swimming L-Lake P-Pool R-River S-Sea **Off-site** All facilities within 2km

ARGELÈS-SUR-MER PYRÉNÉES-ORIENTALES

Criques de Porteils

La Corniche de Collioure, 66700 ☎ 468811273 🖷 468958576

e-mail criques.costa@wanadoo.fr

website www.lescriques.com

Terraced site with beautiful view of sea.

➲ *4km S on N114, left through railway underpass & continue 0.3km.*

Open Mar-Oct/Nov **Site** 5HEC 🌱 🏖 🗻 **Facilities** ⋔ 🖻 ☺ 🖭 🖉 ⅌ **Services** ⬚ 🍽 ➕ 🗄 **Leisure** ⚓ S

Dauphin

rte de Taxo à la Mer, 66704 ☎ 468811754 🖷 468958260

e-mail info@campingledauphin.com

website www.campingledauphin.com

On a long stretch of grassland shaded by poplars, 1.5km from the sea.

➲ *3km N of town, turn right at Taxo d'Avall.*

Open 19 May-22 Sep **Site** 8.5HEC 🌱 🏖 🗻 **Prices** pitch 16-25.30 (incl 2 persons) pp4-6.20 **Facilities** ⋔ 🖻 ☺ 🖭 🖉 ⚒ ⅌ ❿ **Services** ⬚ 🍽 ➕ 🗄 **Leisure** ⚓ P **Off-site** ⚓LRS

Galets

rte de Taxo a la Mer, 66700 ☎ 468810812 🖷 468816876

e-mail lesgalets@campinglesgalets.fr

website www.campmed.com

A well-equipped family site with trees, bushes and exotic plants.

➲ *4km N.*

Open 31 Mar-Sep **Site** 5HEC 🌱 🏖 🗻 **Prices** pitch 19.50-33 (incl 2 persons) � (static)175-854 **Facilities** ⋔ 🖻 ☺ 🖭 ⅌ **Services** ⬚ 🍽 ➕ 🗄 **Leisure** ⚓ P **Off-site** 🖉 ⚓RS

Marsouins

chemin de la retirada, 66702 ☎ 468811481 🖷 468959358

e-mail marsouins@campmed.com

website www.campmed.com

A large family site with good facilities.

➲ *2km NE towards Plage Nord.*

Open 8 Apr-Sep **Site** 10HEC 🌱 🏖 🗻 **Prices** pitch 14-29 (incl 2 persons) **Facilities** ⋔ 🖻 ☺ 🖭 🖉 ⚒ ⅌ **Services** ⬚ 🍽 ➕ 🗄 **Leisure** ⚓ P **Off-site** ⚓S

Massane

66702 ☎ 468810685 🖷 468815918

e-mail camping.massane@infonie.fr

website www.camping-massane.com

Shady, well-planned site 1km from the sea.

➲ *Beside D618 near municipal sports field.*

Open 15 Mar-15 Oct **Site** 3HEC 🌱 🏖 🗻 🗻 🗻 **Prices** pitch 11.50-24 (incl 2 persons) pp2.50-5 🚐 (static)170-410 **Facilities** ⋔ 🖻 ☺ 🖭 🖉 ⚒ ⅌ **Services** ⬚ ➕ 🗄 **Leisure** ⚓ P **Off-site** 🖻 🖉 🍽 ⚓S

Neptune

Plage Nord, 66702 ☎ 468810298 🖷 468810041

e-mail neptune@parcpemin.com

Flat site with both sunny and shady pitches 350m from the northern beach. Modern sanitary facilities. Water-slide. Separate car park for arrivals after 23.00 hrs.

Open May- 15 Sep **Site** 4.5HEC 🌱 🏖 🗻 🗻 **Facilities** ⋔ 🖻 ☺ 🖭 ⚒ ⅌ ❿ **Services** ⬚ 🍽 ➕ 🗄 **Leisure** ⚓ P **Off-site** 🖉 ⚓LS

Ombrages

av du Général-de-Gaulle, 66702 ☎ 468812983 🖷 468958187

e-mail les-ombrages@freesurf.fr

website www.les-ombrages.com

A picturesque wooded setting 300m from the beach. The well-equipped site has good recreational facilities and defined pitches.

Open Jun-Sep **Site** 4HEC 🌱 🏖 🗻 **Prices** ⋔ 3.80-5.20 pitch 17.50-25 (incl 2 persons) **Facilities** ⋔ 🖻 ☺ 🖭 🖉 ⅌ **Services** 🗄 **Off-site** 🖻 🍽 🍽 ⚓LPRS ➕

Pujol

rte du Tamariguer, 66700 ☎ 468810025 🖷 468812121

A lush setting with a variety of recreational facilities.

➲ *0.5km from village, 1km from beach.*

Open Jun-Sep **Site** 6.3HEC 🌱 🏖 🗻 **Facilities** ⋔ 🖻 ☺ 🖭 🖉 ⚒ ⅌ **Services** ⬚ 🍽 ➕ 🗄 **Leisure** ⚓ P **Off-site** ⚓S

Sirène

rte de Taxo d'Avall, 66702 ☎ 468810461 🖷 468816974

e-mail contact@camping.lasirene.fr

website www.camping-lasirene.fr

A well-appointed family site with good facilities in a delightful wooded setting.

➲ *4km NE.*

Open 7 Apr-27 Sep **Site** 17HEC 🌱 🏖 🗻 **Prices** ⋔ 6-9 🚗 4-6 pitch 23-43 (incl 3 persons) 🚐 (static)248-945 **Facilities** ⋔ 🖻 ☺ 🖭 🖉 ⅌ **Services** ⬚ 🍽 ➕ 🗄 **Leisure** ⚓ P **Off-site** ⚒ ⚓S

AT ARGELÈS-PLAGE (2.5KM E VIA D618)

Pins

av du Tech, 66702 ☎ 468811046 🖷 468813506

e-mail cpglespins@frre.fr

website www.les-pins.com

A peaceful family site on a narrow stretch of grassland with some poplar trees.

Open May-Sep **Site** 4HEC 🌱 🏖 🗻 **Facilities** ⋔ ☺ 🖭 ⅌ **Services** 🍽 🗄 **Off-site** 🖻 🖉 ⚒ ⚓PS

Soleil

rte du Littoral, Plage Nord, 66702 ☎ 468811448 🖷 468814434

e-mail camping.soleil@wanadoo.fr

website campmed.com

Peaceful site in wide meadow surrounded by tall trees. Private beach, natural harbour. Popular therefore pitches must be booked in advance.

➲ *N from town on rte du Littoral & 1.5km towards beach.*

Open 12 May-23 Sep **Site** 16HEC 🌱 🏖 🗻 ⊗ **Prices** ⋔ 6.15-8.20 pitch 9.22-12.30 🚐 (static)252-602 **Facilities** ⋔ 🖻 ☺ 🖭 🖉 ⚒ ⅌ **Services** ⬚ 🍽 ➕ 🗄 **Leisure** ⚓ PRS

ARLES BOUCHES-DU-RHÔNE

Rosiers

Pont de Crau, 13200 ☎ 490960212 🖷 490933672

e-mail lesrosiers.arles@wanadoo.fr

website www.arles-camping-club.com

On level ground, shaded by bushes.

➲ *Autoroute exit Arles Sud. Or via N443.*

Open All year **Site** 3.5HEC 🌱 🏖 🗻 🚐 **Prices** pitch 13-16 (incl 2 persons) pp3-3.50 🚐 (static)340-560 **Facilities** ⋔ ☺ 🖭 ⚒ ⅌ **Services** ⬚ 🍽 ➕ 🗄 **Leisure** ⚓ P **Off-site** 🖻 🖉 ⚓LR

Site 6HEC (site size) 🌱 grass 🏖 sand 🗻 stone ♣ little shade ♣ partly shaded 🌳 mainly shaded 🏠 bungalows for hire 🚐 caravans for hire Å tents for hire ⊗ no dogs **Prices** ⋔ adult per night 🚗 car per night pp per person per night 🚐 caravan per night Å tent per night 🚐 (static)-caravan hire per week

ARLES-SUR-TECH PYRÉNÉES-ORIENTALES

Riuferrer

66150 ☎ 468391106 ▤ 468391209

e-mail campingriuferrer@libertysurf.fr

website www.campingduriuferrer.fr

Quiet holiday site on gently sloping ground in pleasant area. Clean sanitary installations. Separate area reserved for overnight stops.

➲ *Signed from N115.*

Open Feb-1 Nov **Site** 4.5HEC ⬣ ⬤ ⬤ ⬤ **Prices** ⚹ 3.20-4.50 pitch 4 ⬤ (static)170-300 **Facilities** ⬤ ⊙ ⬤ ⬤ ⬤ ⬤ **Services** ⬤ ⬤ ⬤ **Leisure** ⬤ R **Off-site** ⬤ ⬤ ⬤P

ARPAILLARGUES GARD

Mas de Rey

rte d'Anduze, 30700 ☎ 466221827 ▤ 466221827

e-mail info@campingmasderey.com

website www.campingmasderey.com

Quiet wooded surroundings with pitches divided by trees and bushes. There are good sports facilities and modern sanitary arrangements.

➲ *3km from Uzès towards Anduze.*

Open 7Apr-15 Oct **Site** 3HEC ⬤ ⬤ ⬤ ⬤ **Prices** pitch 17 (incl 2 persons) **Facilities** ⬤ ⊙ ⬤ ⬤ ⬤ ⬤ **Services** ⬤ ⬤ ⬤ ⬤ **Leisure** ⬤ P **Off-site** ⬤ ⬤

AUBIGNAN VAUCLUSE

Intercommunal du Brégoux

chemin du Vas, 84810 ☎ 490626250 ▤ 490626521

e-mail camping-lebregoux@wanadoo.fr

website www.camping-lebregoux.fr,

A level site with good views of Mt Ventoux.

➲ *On S outskirts of town. D7 onto D55 towards Caromb for 0.5km.*

Open Mar-Oct **Site** 3.5HEC ⬤ ⬤ ⬤ **Prices** ⚹ 3.05 pitch 2.95 ⬤ (static)240-460 **Facilities** ⬤ ⊙ ⬤ ⬤ **Services** ⬤ ⬤ **Off-site** ⬤ ⬤ ⬤ ⬤ ⬤R

AUPS VAR

International

rte de Fox-Amphoux, 83630 ☎ 494700680 ▤ 494701051

e-mail info@internationalcamping-aups.com

website www.internationalcamping-aups.com

Wooded surroundings with well-defined pitches and good recreational facilities. A good base for exploring the magnificent Gorges du Verdon.

➲ *0.5km W on D60 towards Fox-Amphoux.*

Open Apr-Sep **Site** 4HEC ⬤ ⬤ ⬤ **Prices** ⚹ 6 ⬤ 5.20 ⬤ (static)460 **Facilities** ⬤ ⊙ ⬤ ⬤ **Services** ⬤ ⬤ ⬤ **Leisure** ⬤ P **Off-site** ⬤ ⬤ ⬤ ⬤

See advertisement on this page

AURIBEAU ALPES-MARITIMES

Parc des Monges

635 Chemin du Gabre, 06810 ☎ 493609171 ▤ 493609171

e-mail parcdesmonges@tiscali.fr

website www.parcdesmonges.com

Wooded setting on the banks of a good fishing river, surrounded by mimosa fields.

➲ *A8 exit Mandelieu for Grasse.*

Open Apr-1 Oct **Site** 1.4HEC ⬤ ⬤ ⬤ ⬤ **Prices** pitch 14.50-21 (incl 2 persons) pp3.50-4.50 ⬤ (static)240-400 **Facilities** ⬤ ⊙ ⬤ ⬤ **Services** ⬤ ⬤ ⬤ ⬤ **Leisure** ⬤ PR **Off-site** ⬤ ⬤ ⬤

AVIGNON VAUCLUSE

Bagatelle

Ile de la Barthelasse, 84000 ☎ 490863039 ▤ 490271623

e-mail camping.bagatelle@wanadoo.fr

website www.campingbagatelle.com

Pleasant site with tall trees on the Isle of Barthelasse. All pitches are numbered, on hard standing and divided by hedges. Separate section for young people.

➲ *Along town wall & river to Rhône bridge (Nîmes road), signed on right.*

Open All year **Site** 4HEC ⬤ ⬤ ⬤ ⬤ **Prices** pitch 9.60-17.80 (incl 2 persons) **Facilities** ⬤ ⬤ ⊙ ⬤ ⬤ ⬤ **Services** ⬤ ⬤ ⬤ ⬤ **Off-site** ⬤PR

CM Pont St-Bénézet

10 chemin de la Barthelasse, 84000 ☎ 490806350 ▤ 490852212

e-mail info@camping-avignon.com

website www.camping-avignon.com

Set on an island near the bridge with fine views of town. Several tiled sanitary blocks with individual wash cabins. Individual pitches with divisions for tents and caravans.

➲ *NW of town on right bank of Rhône, 370m upstream from bridge on right. (N100 towards Nîmes.)*

Open Mar-Oct **Site** 7.5HEC ⬤ ⬤ ⬤ **Prices** pitch 10-21.50 **Facilities** ⬤ ⬤ ⊙ ⬤ ⬤ ⬤ **Services** ⬤ ⬤ ⬤ ⬤ **Leisure** ⬤ P

AXAT AUDE

Crémade

11140 ☎ 468205064

website www.lacremade.com

A shady, peaceful site, ideal for water sports.

Open Etr-end Sep **Site** 4HEC ⬤ ⬤ ⬤ **Prices** ⚹ 3.60 pitch 4 **Facilities** ⬤ ⬤ ⊙ ⬤ ⬤ ⬤ **Services** ⬤ ⬤ ⬤ **Off-site** ⬤PR

Moulin du Pont d'Alies

11140 ☎ 468205327 ▤ 468206277

e-mail contact@alies.fr

website www.alies.fr

A picturesque location at the entrance to the Gorges de la Pierre.

➲ *Junct D117 & D118, 0.8km from Axat.*

Open Apr-Oct **Site** 2HEC ⬤ ⬤ ⬤ **Prices** ⚹ 4-6 pitch 6-10 **Facilities** ⬤ ⬤ ⊙ ⬤ ⬤ **Services** ⬤ ⬤ ⬤ **Leisure** ⬤ PR

Facilities ⬤ shop ⬤ shower ⊙ electric points for razors ⬤ electric points for caravans ⬤ parking by tents permitted ⬤ compulsory separate car park
Services ⬤ café/restaurant ⬤ bar ⬤ Camping Gaz International ⬤ gas other than Camping Gaz ⬤ first aid facilities ⬤ laundry
Leisure ⬤ swimming L-Lake P-Pool R-River S-Sea **Off-site** All facilities within 2km

France

BANDOL VAR

Vallongue

83150 ☎ 494294955 ▤ 494294955
e-mail camping.vallongue@wanadoo.fr
website www.campingvar.com
Parts of the terraced site have lovely sea views.

Open Apr-Sep **Site** 1.5HEC ❀ ♣ ☎ **Prices** ♠ 4-4.50 pitch 11-14 (incl 2 persons) **Facilities** ♠ ⊙ ⊕ ℗ **Services** ⬚ ⍟ ⊞ ▤ **Leisure** ◈ P **Off-site** ☖ ⧄ ⩲

BARCARÈS, LE PYRÉNÉES-ORIENTALES

Bousigues

av des Corbières, 66420 ☎ 468861619 ▤ 468862844
e-mail lasbousigues@wanadoo.fr
website www.camping-barcares.com
Well-equipped family site 1km from the sea. Bar and café only open July and August.

⮕ *D83 exit 10.*

Open 31 Mar-Sep **Site** 3HEC ❀ ♣ ☎ Å **Prices** pitch 11-41 (incl 2 persons) ⛺ (static)143-713 **Facilities** ♠ ☖ ⊙ ⊕ ⩲ **Services** ⬚ ⍟ ⊞ ▤ **Leisure** ◈ P **Off-site** ◈RS

California

rte de St-Laurent, 66423 ☎ 468861608 ▤ 468861820
e-mail camping-california@wanadoo.fr
website www.camping-california.fr
A friendly family site with regular organised entertainment in a pleasant wooded location close to the beach.

⮕ *1.5km SW via D90.*

Open 4 Apr-10 Sep **Site** 5.5HEC ❀ ♣ ☎ **Prices** ♠ 3-5 Å 5 pitch 9-22 ⛺ (static)196-385 **Facilities** ♠ ☖ ⊙ ⊕ ℗ **Services** ⬚ ⍟ ⊞ ▤ **Leisure** ◈ P **Off-site** ⍟ ◈LRS

Europe

rte de St-Laurent, 66420 ☎ 468861536 ▤ 468864788
e-mail reception@europe-camping.com
website www.europe-camping.com
A holiday village type of site with good recreational facilities, 0.5km from the beach.

⮕ *Via D90 2km SW, 200m from Agly.*

Open All year **Site** 6HEC ❀ ♣ ☎ ⛺ **Prices** pitch 18-36.50 (incl 2 persons) **Facilities** ♠ ☖ ⊙ ⊕ ⧄ ℗ **Services** ⬚ ⍟ ⊞ ▤ **Leisure** ◈ P **Off-site** ⧄ ◈RS

Presqu'île

66420 ☎ 468861280 ▤ 468862509
e-mail contact@lapresquile.com
website www.lapresquile.com
A well-equipped family site on the edge of Lake Leucate and close to the beach.

⮕ *2km on rte de Leucate, turn right.*

Open 9 Apr-1 Nov **Site** 3.5HEC ❀ ♣ ☎ ⛺ **Facilities** ♠ ☖ ⊙ ⊕ ⧄ ℗ **Services** ⬚ ⍟ ⊞ ▤ **Leisure** ◈ LP **Off-site** ⍟ ◈RS

Sable d'Or

r des Palombes, 66420 ☎ 468861841 ▤ 466743730
A wooded site between the sea and Lac Marin.

⮕ *A9 exit 40 for Grand Plage.*

Open All year **Site** 4HEC ❀ ♣ ☎ ⛺ **Facilities** ♠ ☖ ⊙ ⊕ ℗ **Services** ⬚ ⍟ ⊞ ▤ **Leisure** ◈ PS **Off-site** ⧄ ◈L

BEYNES ALPES-DE-HAUTE-PROVENCE

Célestine

rte de Moustiers (D907), 4270 ☎ 492355254 ▤ 492355007
e-mail info@camping-lacelestine.com
website www.camping-lacelestine.com
A quiet site on flat ground in the heart of the Haute Provence country park and surrounded by mountains.

⮕ *On D907 before climb to village.*

Open May-Sep **Site** 3HEC ❀ ♣ ☎ **Facilities** ♠ ☖ ⊙ ⊕ ℗ **Services** ⬚ **Leisure** ◈ PR

BOISSET-ET-GAUJAC GARD

Domaine de Gaujac

Boisset, 30140 ☎ 466618065 ▤ 466605390
e-mail gravieres@clubinternet.fr
website www.domaine-de-gaujac.com
A family site in wooded surroundings on the banks of a river.

⮕ *Via D910.*

Open Apr-Sep **Site** 10HEC ❀ ♣ ☎ ⛺ **Prices** ♠ 3.50-4.50 pitch 15-23 ⛺ (static)135-370 **Facilities** ♠ ☖ ⊙ ⊕ ⧄ ⩲ ℗ **Services** ⬚ ⍟ ⊞ ▤ **Leisure** ◈ PR

BOISSON GARD

Château de Boisson

Boisson, 30500 ☎ 466248561 ▤ 466248014
e-mail reception@chateaudeboisson.com
website www.chateaudeboisson.com
A peaceful, well-equipped site in the beautiful Cevennes region. Painting, bridge and cookery courses are available.

⮕ *D7 towards Fumades, Boisson 10km on right, site signed.*

Open 7 Apr-29 Sep **Site** 7.8HEC ❀ ♣ ☎ ⛺ **Prices** ♠ 5.30-6.50 pitch 19-40 ⛺ (static)252-798 **Facilities** ♠ ☖ ⊙ ⊕ ℗ **Services** ⬚ ⍟ ⊞ ▤ **Leisure** ◈ P

BOLLÈNE VAUCLUSE

Barry

Lieu Dit St-Pierre, 84500 ☎ 490301320 ▤ 490404864
website www.campinglebarry.com
Well-kept site near ruins of Barry troglodite village.

⮕ *Signed from Bollène via D26.*

Open All year **Site** 3HEC ❀ ♣ ☎ **Facilities** ♠ ☖ ⊙ ⊕ ⧄ ℗ **Services** ⬚ ⍟ ⊞ ▤ **Leisure** ◈ P **Off-site** ◈LR

Simioune

Quartier Guffiage, 84500 ☎ 490304462 ▤ 490304477
e-mail la-simioune@wanadoo.fr
website www.la-simioune.fr
Pleasant wooded surroundings close to the River Rhône

⮕ *Off A7 for Carpentras, at 3rd x-rds left for Lambisque, site signed.*

Open All year **Site** 2.5HEC ❀ ♣ ☎ ⛺ **Prices** ♠ 3.50 ⛺ 3.50 Å 3 ⛺ (static)300 **Facilities** ♠ ⊙ ⊕ ℗ **Services** ⬚ ⍟ ⊞ ▤ **Leisure** ◈ P **Off-site** ◈R

Site 6HEC (site size) ❀ grass ⬤ sand ♣ stone ♣ little shade ♣ partly shaded ❀ mainly shaded ☎ bungalows for hire ⛺ caravans for hire Å tents for hire ⊗ no dogs **Prices** ♠ adult per night ⛟ car per night pp per person per night ⛺ caravan per night Å tent per night ⛺ (static)-caravan hire per week

BORMES-LES-MIMOSAS VAR

Clau Mar Jo
895 chemin de Benat, 83230 ☎ 494715339
A well-shaded site with good facilities 1.2km from the sea.
➲ *N98 onto D298.*
Open Apr-Sep **Site** 1HEC ♨ ♣ ♠ **Facilities** ↿ ⊙ ♻ ⑳ **Services** ⊞ ⌑
Off-site 🏠 ↿ ⌑ ⌑ ⌑ ⌑S

Manjastre
150 Chemin des Girolles, 83230 ☎ 494710328 ▤ 494716362
e-mail manjastre@infonie.fr
A peaceful site 6km from the Mediterraneean beaches.
➲ *5km NW via N98 on road to La Môle/Cogolin.*
Open All year **Site** 8HEC ♨ ♣ ♠ ⊗ **Facilities** ↿ 🏠 ⊙ ♻ ⌑ ⌑ ⑳
Services ⊞ ↿ ⌑ ⊞ ⌑ **Leisure** ⌑ P

AT FAVIÈRE, LA (3KM S)

Domaine
83230 ☎ 494710312 ▤ 494151867
e-mail mail@campdudomaine.com
website www.campdudomaine.com
A very attractive setting with a long sandy beach and numbered
pitches. Fine views of sea and sports facilities.
➲ *0.5km E of Bormes-Cap Bénat road.*
Open Apr-Oct **Site** 38HEC ♨ ♣ ♠ ♠ **Prices** pitch 17-30.50
♠ (static)540-750 **Facilities** ↿ 🏠 ⊙ ♻ ⌑ ⌑ ⑳ **Services** ⊞ ↿ ⌑ ⊞ ⌑
Leisure ⌑ S

BOULOU, LE PYRÉNÉES-ORIENTALES

Mas Llinas
66165 ☎ 468832546
e-mail info@camping-mas-llinas.com
website www.camping-mas-llinas.com
A family site in wooded surroundings with a variety of leisure facilities.
➲ *3km N via N9.*
Open Feb-Nov **Site** 15HEC ♨ ♣ ♠ ♠ **Prices** ↑ 4.20-5.20 pitch 4.70-6.60
Facilities ↿ ⊙ ♻ ⑳ **Services** ⊞ ↿ ⌑ ⊞ ⌑ **Leisure** ⌑ P **Off-site** 🏠 ↿ ⌑ ⌑ ⊞

BOULOURIS-SUR-MER VAR

Ile d'Or
83700 ☎ 494955213 ▤ 494955213
A quiet location with well-equipped pitches 50m from a private beach.
➲ *E off N98.*
Open Apr-Nov **Site** 10HEC ♨ ♣ ♠ ♠ **Prices** ↑ 5.60 pitch 25.90 (incl 2
persons) ♠ (static)480 **Facilities** ↿ 🏠 ⊙ ♻ ⌑ ⌑ ⑳ **Services** ⊞ ↿ ⌑ ⊞
Leisure ⌑ S

BOURDEAUX DRÔME

AT POÀT-CÉLARD, LE (3KM NW)

Couspeau
Quartier Bellevue, 26460 ☎ 475533014 ▤ 475533723
e-mail info@couspeau.com
website www.couspeau.com
A beautiful natural setting with well-maintained facilities.
➲ *1.3km SE via D328A.*
Open 15 Apr- 15 Sep **Site** 6HEC ♨ ♣ ♠ ♠ **Prices** pitch 16-26
♠ (static)220-580 **Facilities** ↿ 🏠 ⊙ ♻ ⌑ ⑳ **Services** ⊞ ↿ ⌑ ⊞ ⌑
Leisure ⌑ P

BRISSAC HÉRAULT

Val d'Hérault
St-Étienne d'Issensac, 34190 ☎ 467737229 ▤ 467733081
A terraced site in a quiet location. Bar and restaurant only open July
and August.
➲ *4km S via D4.*
Open 15 Mar-12 Nov **Site** 3.4HEC ♨ ♣ ♠ ♠ **Facilities** ↿ 🏠 ⊙ ♻ ⌑
⌑ ⑳ **Services** ⊞ ↿ ⌑ ⌑ **Leisure** ⌑ PR **Off-site** ⊞

BROUSSES-ET-VILLARET AUDE

Martinet Rouge
11390 ☎ 468265198 ▤ 468265198
e-mail martinet.bv@free.fr
website camping-lemartinetrouge.com
A pleasant, well-equipped site on gently sloping terrain. Terraced, with
well-marked pitches.
➲ *Via D48.*
Open Apr-15 Oct **Site** 2.8HEC ♨ ♣ ♠ ♠ **Prices** pitch 10.50-12.50 (incl 2
persons) ♠ (static)330 **Facilities** ↿ 🏠 ⊙ ♻ ⌑ ⌑ ⑳ **Services** ⊞ ↿ ⌑ ⊞
⌑ **Leisure** ⌑ P **Off-site** ⌑R

CADENET VAUCLUSE

Val de Durance
Les Routes, 84160 ☎ 490683775 ▤ 490681634
e-mail info@homair-vacances.fr
website www.homair-vacances.fr
A well-equipped family site on the shore of a lake and close to the
River Durance.
Open 30 Mar-Sep **Site** 11HEC ♨ ♣ ♠ Å **Prices** ↑ 3-8 pitch 6-14
Facilities ↿ 🏠 ⊙ ♻ ⑳ **Services** ⊞ ↿ ⌑ ⊞ ⌑ **Leisure** ⌑ LP **Off-site** 🏠
⊞ ↿ ⌑ ⌑ ⌑R

CAGNES-SUR-MER ALPES-MARITIMES

Colombier
35 chemin de Ste-Colombe, 06800 ☎ 493731277 ▤ 493731277
e-mail campinglecolombier06@wanadoo.fr
website www.campinglecolombier.fr
Well-equipped site in a wooded location 2km from the sea.
Open Apr-Sep **Site** 0.6HEC ♨ ♣ ♠ ♠ ⊗ **Prices** pitch 15.50-22.20
(incl 2 persons) **Facilities** ↿ ⊙ ♻ ⌑ ⑳ ⑭ **Services** ⊞ ↿ ⌑ ⊞ ⌑
Leisure ⌑ P **Off-site** 🏠 ↿ ⌑ ⌑S

Green Park
159 bis, Vallon-des-Vaux, 06800 ☎ 493070996 ▤ 493143655
e-mail info@greenpark.fr
website www.greenpark.fr
A modern site with well-defined pitches in pleasant wooded
surroundings with good recreational facilities.
➲ *A8 exit Cagnes-sur-Mer onto N7 for Nice.*
Open 26 Mar-15 Oct **Site** 5.4HEC ♨ ♣ ♠ ♠ Å **Prices** pitch 13-33.20
(incl 2 persons) pp4.50-4.80 ♠ (static)273-826 **Facilities** ↿ 🏠 ⊙ ♻ ⑳ ⑭
Services ⊞ ↿ ⌑ ⊞ ⌑ **Leisure** ⌑ P

Facilities 🏠 shop ↿ shower ⊙ electric points for razors ♻ electric points for caravans ⑳ parking by tents permitted ⑭ compulsory separate car park
Services ↿ café/restaurant ⌑ bar ⌑ Camping Gaz International ⌑ gas other than Camping Gaz ⊞ first aid facilities ⌑ laundry
Leisure ⌑ swimming L-Lake P-Pool R-River S-Sea **Off-site** All facilities within 2km

France (side tab)

France

CAMPING – CARAVANNING

"LA RIVIERE" ★ ★

06800 Cagnes sur Mer Chemin des Salles
(via Val de Cagnes, dir. Haut de Cagnes)
Tel: 04.93.20.62.27 Fax: 04.93.20.72.53
A shady, flat, quiet site.
We offer, among other things grocery
shop, restaurant, bar, free swimming pool
and rent of caravans. Reservation of a
pitch is possible. Small sanitary block.
Cabin for disabled.

La Rivière

168 chemin des Salles, 06800 ☎ 493206227 🗎 493207253
Secluded wooded surroundings with modern facilities.
➲ *4km N beside River Cagne.*
Open All year **Site** 1.2HEC �],🌱🚍 **Prices** pitch 13.30 (incl 2 persons)
pp3.50 **Facilities** 🏕 🛁 ⊙ 🚰 🅿 ⊛ **Services** 🍴 🍽 🕂 🗓 **Leisure** ⊛ P

See advertisement on this page

Todos

159 Vallon des Vaux, 06800 ☎ 493312005 🗎 492128166
e-mail info@letodos.fr
website www.letodos.fr
A beautiful Mediterranean setting, exceptionally shady with a mixture
of flat and terraced sites. Use of car park compulsory after 23.00 hrs.
➲ *N7 towards Nice.*
Open Apr-Sep **Site** 6HEC 🌱🌱🚍🚍 Ⓐ **Prices** pitch 13-33.20 (incl 2
persons) pp4.50-5.70 🚍 (static)329-693 **Facilities** 🏕 🛁 ⊙ 🚰 ⓟ Ⓟ
Services 🍴 🍽 🕂 🗓 **Leisure** ⊛ P

AT CROS-DE-CAGNES (2KM S)

Panoramer

30 chemin des Gros Buaux, 06800 ☎ 493311615 🗎 493311615
Pleasant terraced site with sea view. Separate sections for tents and
caravans.
➲ *2km N of town.*
Open Mar-Oct **Site** 1.4HEC 🌱 🌱 **Facilities** 🏕 ⊙ 🚰 ⓟ ⊛ **Services** 🍴
🍽 🕂 🗓 **Off-site** 🛁

CAMURAC AUDE

Domaine les Sapins

11340 ☎ 468203811 🗎 468314123
e-mail camping@lessapins-camurac.com
website www.lessapins-camurac.com
A picturesque wooded site on the edge of a forest with views of the
surrounding mountains.
➲ *1.5km from village.*
Open All year **Site** 3HEC 🌱🌱🌱🌱🚍 Ⓐ **Prices** pitch 12-17.50 (incl 2
persons) pp4-5 🚍 (static)250-475 **Facilities** 🏕 ⊙ 🚰 ⓟ 🛁 **Services** 🍴
🍽 🕂 🗓 **Leisure** ⊛ P **Off-site** 🛁 ⊛L

CANET-PLAGE PYRÉNÉES-ORIENTALES

Mar Estang

1 rte de St-Cyprien, 66140 ☎ 468803553 🗎 468733294
e-mail marestang@wanadoo.fr
website www.marestang.com
Open 28 Apr-23 Sep **Site** 15HEC 🌱🌱🚍 Ⓐ **Prices** pitch 15-30 (incl 2
persons) **Facilities** 🏕 🛁 ⊙ 🚰 🅿 🛁 ⊛ **Services** 🍴 🍽 🕂 🗓 **Leisure** ⊛ PS
Off-site 🍽 ⊘

See advertisement on page 179

AT CANET-VILLAGE (2KM W)

Brasilia

Voie de la Crouste, Zone Technique du Port, 66140
☎ 468802382 🗎 468733297
e-mail camping-le-brasilia@wanadoo.fr
website www.brasilia.fr
Site near the beach, with pitches divided by bushes and flowerbeds.
➲ *Off main road in village towards beach for 2km.*
Open 29 Apr-Sep **Site** 15HEC 🌱🌱🚍 **Prices** pitch 17-43 (incl 2 persons)
pp4.50-7.50 **Facilities** 🏕 🛁 ⊙ 🚰 ⊘ ⊛ **Services** 🍴 🍽 🕂 🗓
Leisure ⊛ PS **Off-site** 🛁

Peupliers

Voie de la Crouste, 66140 ☎ 468803587 🗎 468733875
e-mail contact@camping-les-peupliers.fr
Quiet, level site divided into pitches by hedges with a variety of leisure
facilities. Booking advised for July and August.
Open Jun-Sep **Site** 4HEC 🌱🌱🚍 Ⓐ **Prices** 🕴 4.80-6.20 pitch 11.70-15.60
🚍 (static)288-546 **Facilities** 🏕 🛁 ⊙ 🚰 ⊘ ⊛ Ⓟ **Services** 🍴 🍽 🕂 🗓
Leisure ⊛ PS

Ma Prairie

Av des Coteaux, 66140 ☎ 468732617 🗎 468732882
e-mail ma.prairie@wanadoo.fr
website www.maprairie.com
Grassland site in a hollow surrounded by vineyards.
➲ *N617 Perpignan-Canet-Plage onto D11 towards Elne.*
Open 5 May-25 Sep **Site** 4.5HEC 🌱🌱🚍 **Facilities** 🏕 🛁 ⊙ 🚰 ⊘ ⊛
Services 🍴 🍽 🕂 🗓 **Leisure** ⊛ P **Off-site** 🛁

CANNES ALPES-MARITIMES

Parc Bellevue

67 av M Chevalier, 6150 ☎ 493472897 🗎 493486625
e-mail contact@parcbellevue.com
website www.parcbellevue.com
➲ *A41 exit Cannes, right at 1st lights.*
Open Apr-Sep **Site** 4HEC 🌱🌱🚍🚍 **Prices** 🕴 3-4 pitch 7-10
🚍 (static)170-350 **Facilities** 🏕 🛁 ⊙ 🚰 ⊘ ⊛ **Services** 🍴 🍽 🕂 🗓
Leisure ⊛ PS **Off-site** ⊛S

AT CANNET, LE

Grand Saule

24 bd J-Moulin, 06110 ☎ 493905510 🗎 493472455
e-mail info@legrandsaule.com
website www.legrandsaule.com
Separate sections for families and groups of young people. Peaceful
surroundings and fine views with a variety of sports and leisure
activities. Beach nearby.
➲ *A8 towards Ranguin.*
Open May-Sept **Site** 1HEC 🌱🌱🚍 **Facilities** 🏕 ⊙ 🚰 ⊛ **Services** 🍴 🍽
🕂 🗓 **Leisure** ⊛ P **Off-site** 🛁 ⊘ 🛁 ⊛S

Site 6HEC (site size) 🌱 grass 🍥 sand 🌱 stone 🌱 little shade 🌱 partly shaded 🌱 mainly shaded 🚍 bungalows for hire
🚍 caravans for hire Ⓐ tents for hire ⊗ no dogs **Prices** 🕴 adult per night 🚗 car per night pp per person per night 🚍 caravan per night
Ⓐ tent per night 🚍 (static)-caravan hire per week

Ranch

chemin St-Joseph, L'Aubarède, 6110 ☎ 493460011 ⓕ 493464430
website www.leranchcamping.fr
On a wooded hillside 2km from the local beaches with good facilities.
⮑ *A8 exit 41 or 42.*

Open 2 Apr-29 Oct **Site** 2HEC ⬥⬥⬥🛒 **Prices** ⚡ 6 ⬥ 3 pitch 10-16
🛒 (static)250-510 **Facilities** ⋔ ⬟⊙⬟⬟ℓ⑫ **Services** ✚⬥ **Leisure** ⬥ P
Off-site ⛽🍴⬥S

CARCASSONNE AUDE

Breil d'Aude

Le Breil d'Aude, rte de Limoux, Preixan, 11250
☎ 468268818 ⓕ 468268507
e-mail air.hotel.grand.sud@wanadoo.fr
website www.camping-grandsud.com
Wooded location beside a private lake with free fishing.
⮑ *1.5km N via D118.*

Open Mar-1 Oct **Site** 11HEC ⬥⬥⬥⬥🛒 **Prices** pitch 19-26.50 (incl 2
persons) **Facilities** ⋔ ⬟⬟⬟⑫ **Services** ⛽🍴⬟ **Leisure** ⬥ LPR
Off-site ⬟✚

Cité

rte de St-Hilaire, 11000 ☎ 468251177
website www.campeoles.fr
Wooded surroundings beside the River Aude. A good base for
exploring the region.
⮑ *Via A61 or A9.*

Open 15 May-10 Oct **Site** 7HEC ⬥⬥⬥ **Facilities** ⋔ ⬟⊙⬟⬟ℓ⑫
Services ⛽🍴⬟ **Leisure** ⬥ P **Off-site** ⬥R

CARPENTRAS VAUCLUSE

Lou Comtadou

Route de St Didier, 881 av P-de-Coubertin, 84200
☎ 490670316 ⓕ 490460181
e-mail info@campingloucomtadou.com
website www.campingloucomtadou.com
Near the Carpentras swimming pool in pleasant surroundings with
modern facilities.
⮑ *SE of town centre towards St-Didier.*

Open Mar-Oct **Site** 2.5HEC ⬥⬥🛒 **Prices** pitch 15-18.50 (incl 2 persons)
pp8.50-10.50 🛒 (static)190-390 **Facilities** ⋔ ⬟⊙⬟ℓ⑫ **Services** ⛽
🍴⬟ **Off-site** ⬟⬥P✚

CARQUEIRANNE VAR

Beau-Vezé

rte de la Moutonne, 83320 ☎ 494576530 ⓕ 494576530
e-mail info@camping-beauveze.com
website www.camping-beauveze.com
Set in a beautiful wooded park with modern facilities.
⮑ *2.5km NW via N559 & D76 between Hyères & Toulon.*

Open 15 May-15 Sep **Site** 7HEC ⬥⬥🛒 **Prices** ⚡ 6.30 pitch 8.50
Facilities ⋔ ⬟⊙⬟⬟ℓ⑫ **Services** ⛽🍴✚⬟ **Leisure** ⬥ PS

CASTELLANE ALPES-DE-HAUTE-PROVENCE

International

rte Napoléon, 04120 ☎ 492836667
Family site at the foot of the Col des Lèques and close to the Gorges
du Verdon.
⮑ *1km from village centre, signed.*

Open Apr-Sep **Site** 6HEC ⬥⬥⬥🛒 **Facilities** ⋔ ⬟⊙⬟⬟⬟⑫
Services ⛽🍴⬟ **Leisure** ⬥ P **Off-site** ℓ

Nôtre Dame

rte des Gorges du Verdon, 04120 ☎ 492836302 ⓕ 492836302
e-mail camping-notredame@wanadoo.fr
website www.camping-notredame.com
Meadowland site with deciduous and fruit trees.
⮑ *0.5km from village centre on D952.*

Open Apr-14 Oct **Site** 0.6HEC ⬥⬥🛒 **Prices** pitch 11-15 (incl 2 persons)
🛒 (static)240-490 **Facilities** ⋔ ⬟⊙⬟ℓ⑫ **Services** ⛽✚⬟
Off-site 🍴⬟⬥PR

Verdon

Domaine du Verdon, 4120 ☎ 492836129 ⓕ 492836937
e-mail contact@camp-du-verdon.com
website www.camp-du-verdon.com
Well-maintained site on meadowland on banks of River Verdon.
Divided into pitches. Rooms in rustic style. Booking advised for July
and August.
⮑ *Below D952 towards Gorges du Verdon.*

Open 15 May-15 Sep **Site** 14HEC ⬥⬥⬥🛒 **Prices** pitch 32 (incl 3
persons) pp7-12 🛒 (static)315-616 **Facilities** ⋔ ⬟⊙⬟⬟ℓ⑫ **Services** ⛽
🍴✚⬟ **Leisure** ⬥ PR **Off-site** ⬟

Facilities ⬟ shop ⋔ shower ⊙ electric points for razors ⬟ electric points for caravans ⑫ parking by tents permitted ⬟ compulsory separate car park
Services 🍴 café/restaurant ⛽ bar ℓ Camping Gaz International ⬟ gas other than Camping Gaz ✚ first aid facilities ⬟ laundry
Leisure ⬥ swimming L-Lake P-Pool R-River S-Sea **Off-site** All facilities within 2km

France

AT CHASTEUIL (9KM W ON D952)

Gorges du Verdon

Clos d'Arémus, 04120 ☎ 492836364 🖹 492837472
e-mail aremus@camping-gorgesduverdon.com
website camping-gorgesduverdon.com
Situated beside the River Verdon at an altitude of 660m, surrounded by mountains. Site divided into pitches and split into two by road. Bathing in river is not advised due to strong current.
⮑ *0.5km S of village.*
Open May-15 Sep **Site** 7HEC 👑 👑 👑 🏠 **Prices** pitch 12-23.30 (incl 2 persons) pp3.50-4.30 **Facilities** 🏕 🛁 ⊙ 🚿 🗑 *Ø* ⊛ **Services** 🍴 🍲 🔌 🛒 **Leisure** ⚓ PR

AT GARDE-CASTELLANE (7.5KM SE)

Collines de Castellane

rte de Grasse Napoléon, 04120 ☎ 492836896 🖹 492837540
e-mail info@rcn-lescollinesdecastellane.fr
website ww.rcn-campings.fr
Terraced site on wooded grassland with mountain views and fine recreational facilities.
⮑ *On Grasse road beyond La Garde.*
Open 20 Apr-23 Sep **Site** 10HEC 👑 👑 🏠 **Prices** pitch 17-40 (incl 2 persons) 🚐 (static)230-795 **Facilities** 🏕 🛁 ⊙ 🚿 🗑 ⊛ **Services** 🍴 🍲 🔌 🛒 **Leisure** ⚓ P

CAVALAIRE-SUR-MER VAR

Cros de Mouton

83240 ☎ 494641087 🖹 494646312
e-mail campingcrosdemouton@wanadoo.fr
website www.crosdemouton.com
Terraced site with individual pitches, separated for caravans and tents. Good view of sea 1.5km away.
⮑ *Off N559 in town centre & continue inland for 1.5km.*
Open 15 Mar-Oct **Site** 5HEC 👑 👑 🏠 🚐 **Prices** 🏕 6-7.50 pitch 6-7.50 🚐 (static)380-690 **Facilities** 🏕 🛁 ⊙ 🚿 🗑 *Ø* ⊛ **Services** 🍴 🍲 🔌 🛒 **Leisure** ⚓ P **Off-site** ⚓S

Pinède

Chemin des Mannes, 83240 ☎ 494641114 🖹 494641925
website www.le-camping-la-pinede.com
A family site with well-defined pitches, 0.5km from the sea.
⮑ *300m from village centre.*
Open 15 Mar-15 Oct **Site** 2HEC 👑 👑 **Prices** 🚗 2.50 pitch 14-20 (incl 2 persons) **Facilities** 🏕 🛁 ⊙ 🚿 🗑 *Ø* ⊛ **Services** 🔌 🛒 **Off-site** 🛁 🍴 🍲 ⚓S

CENDRAS GARD

Croix Clémentine

rte de Mende, 30480 ☎ 466865269 🖹 466865484
e-mail clementine@clementine.fr
website www.clementine.fr
An extensive, partly terraced site, in wooded surroundings.
⮑ *Signed W of town on D160 towards La Baume.*
Open 28 Mar-14 Sep **Site** 12HEC 👑 👑 👑 🏠 🚐 **Prices** 🏕 2.50-8 pitch 13-23 (incl 2 persons) 🚐 (static)180-380 **Facilities** 🏕 🛁 ⊙ 🚿 🗑 *Ø* ⊛ **Services** 🍴 🍲 🔌 🛒 **Leisure** ⚓ P **Off-site** ⚓R

CHABEUIL DRÔME

Grand Lierne

26120 ☎ 475598314 🖹 475598795
e-mail contact@grandlierne.com
website www.grandlierne.com
On the edge of the Vercors Regional Park.
⮑ *A7 exit Valence Sud for Chabeuil, site signed.*
Open 24 Apr-11 Sep **Site** 4.8HEC 👑 👑 🏠 🚐 ⊛ **Facilities** 🏕 🍴 ⊙ 🚿 🗑 *Ø* 🛁 ⊛ **Services** 🍴 🍲 🔌 🛒 **Leisure** ⚓ P **Off-site** ⚓LR

CHAPELLE-EN-VERCORS, LA DRÔME

Bruyères

26420 ☎ 475482146
e-mail maine.levercos@wanadoo.fr
A well-appointed municipal site in the centre of the Parc Naturel Régional du Vercors.
Open All year **Site** 1HEC 👑 👑 🏠 **Facilities** 🏕 🛁 ⊙ 🚿 🗑 ⊛ **Services** 🔌 🛒 **Off-site** 🛁 🍴 🍲 *Ø* 🛁 ⚓P

CHARLEVAL BOUCHES-DU-RHÔNE

Orée des Bois

av du Bois, 13350 ☎ 442284175 🖹 442284748
e-mail oreedesbois@village-center.com
website www.village-center.com
Spacious, well-shaded pitches 0.5km from the village.
⮑ *A7 exit Sémas, from Charleval towards Cazan.*
Open All year **Site** 5HEC 👑 👑 👑 🏠 **Prices** pitch 13.50-22 pp3-4.50 🚐 (static)189-574 **Facilities** 🏕 ⊙ 🚿 🗑 *Ø* ⊛ **Services** 🍴 🔌 🛒 **Off-site** 🛁 🍲 🛁 ⚓P

CHÂTEAU-ARNOUX ALPES-DE-HAUTE-PROVENCE

Salettes

04160 ☎ 492640240 🖹 492640240
e-mail info@lessalettes.com
website www.lessalettes.com
Some facilities (shop, café) only available in summer.
⮑ *1km E beside river.*
Open All year **Site** 4HEC 👑 👑 🏠 **Facilities** 🏕 🛁 ⊙ 🚿 🗑 *Ø* 🛁 ⊛ **Services** 🍴 🍲 🔌 🛒 **Leisure** ⚓ P

CHAUZON ARDÈCHE

Digue

07120 ☎ 475396357 🖹 475397517
e-mail info@camping-la-digue.fr
website www.camping-la-digue.fr
A beautiful wooded location with good recreational facilities.
⮑ *1km E, 100m from River Ardèche.*
Open 20 Mar-Sep **Site** 2.5HEC 👑 👑 🏠 **Facilities** 🏕 🛁 ⊙ 🚿 🗑 *Ø* ⊛ **Services** 🍴 🍲 🔌 🛒 **Leisure** ⚓ PR

CIOTAT, LA BOUCHES-DU-RHÔNE

Oliviers

rte du Bord de Mer, 13600 ☎ 442831504 🖹 442839443
website www.camping_lesolivers.com
A terraced family site between the N559 and the railway line from Nice.
⮑ *Inland off N559 at Km34 (5km E of town centre) for 150m.*
Open Mar-Sep **Site** 10HEC 👑 👑 👑 🏠 **Facilities** 🏕 🛁 ⊙ 🚿 🗑 *Ø* 🛁 ⊛ **Services** 🍴 🍲 🔌 🛒 **Leisure** ⚓ P **Off-site** ⚓S

Site 6HEC (site size) 👑 grass 🏖 sand ⚫ stone 🌳 little shade 🌿 partly shaded 🌲 mainly shaded 🏠 bungalows for hire 🚐 caravans for hire 🅰 tents for hire ⊗ no dogs **Prices** 🏕 adult per night 🚗 car per night pp per person per night 🚐 caravan per night 🅰 tent per night 🚐 (static)-caravan hire per week

St Jean

30 av de St-Jean, 13600 ☎ 442831301 📠 442714641

e-mail stjean@easyconnect.fr

website www.asther.com/stjean

Site on the right side of the coast road in an excellent position with direct access to the beach.

➲ *Between D559 & sea behind motel in NE part of town.*

Open 2 Jun-22 Sep **Site** 9.9HEC ⛺ ☺ 🚐 **Prices** pitch 21-23 **Facilities** 🚿 ⊙ 🚿 📵 **Services** 🍴 🍽 ➕ 🖾 **Leisure** 🏊 S **Off-site** 🚿 ⊘

Soleil

751 Av Emile Bodin, rte de Cassis, 13600

☎ 442715532 📠 442839581

e-mail campingdusoleil@tiscali.fr

website www.camping-du-soleil.fr

A small site, divided into pitches, 1.5km from the beach.

➲ *A50 exit 9 la Ciotat.*

Open Apr-15 Oct **Site** 0.5HEC ⛺ ☺ 🚐 **Prices** 🏕 5 pitch 5-6 🚐 (static)235-500 **Facilities** 🚿 ⊙ 🚿 📵 **Services** 🍽 ➕ 🖾 **Off-site** 🖾 ⊘ 🏊 🏊 PS

COGOLIN VAR

Argentière

chemin de l'Argentière, 83310 ☎ 494546363 📠 494540615

e-mail camping-largentiere@wanadoo.fr

website www.camping-argentiere.com

Landscaped, partly terraced site.

➲ *1.5km NW along D48 rte de St-Maur.*

Open Apr-Sep **Site** 8HEC ⛺ ☺ 🚐 **Facilities** 🚿 🖾 ⊙ 🚿 ⊘ 🏊 ⊛ **Services** 🍴 🍽 ➕ 🖾 **Leisure** 🏊 P

COLLE-SUR-LOUP, LA ALPES-MARITIMES

Castellas

rte de Roquefort, 6480 ☎ 493329705 📠 493329705

e-mail lecastellas.camping@wanadoo.fr

website www.camping-le-castellas.com

Wooded location with direct access to the river.

Open All year **Site** 1.2HEC ⛺ ☺ 🚐 🚐 **Facilities** 🚿 ⊙ 🚿 ⊘ 🏊 ⊛ **Services** 🍴 🍽 ➕ 🖾 **Leisure** 🏊 RS **Off-site** 🏊 P

Pinèdes

rte du Pont de Pierre, Departementale No.6, 6480

☎ 493329894 📠 493325020

e-mail camplespinedes06@aol.com

website www.lespinedes.com

Well-kept terraced site on steep slope with woodland providing shade, interesting walks and beautiful views.

➲ *A8 exit Cagnes-sur-Mer, onto D6, right for La Colle-sur-Loup.*

Open 15 Mar-Sep **Site** 3.8HEC ⛺ ☺ 🚐 **Prices** 🏕 4-5 🚗 2.50-4 🚐 7-13 🏕 3.50-10.50 🚐 (static)290-650 **Facilities** 🚿 ⊙ 🚿 ⊘ ⊛ **Services** 🍴 🍽 ➕ 🖾 **Leisure** 🏊 P **Off-site** 🏊 🏊 R

Vallon Rouge

rte Greolières, 06480 ☎ 493328612 📠 493328009

e-mail auvallonrouge@aol.com

website www.auvallonrouge.com

A picturesque forest location close to the river with good facilities.

➲ *3km W of town. D6 towards Gréolières, site on right.*

Open 9 Apr-24 Sep **Site** 3HEC ⛺ ☺ 🚐 **Prices** 🏕 3-4.30 pitch 9-19 🚐 (static)240-630 **Facilities** 🚿 🖾 ⊙ 🚿 🏊 ⊛ **Services** 🍴 🍽 ➕ 🖾 **Leisure** 🏊 PR **Off-site** 🍽

COURONNE, LA BOUCHES-DU-RHÔNE

Mas

Plage de Ste-Croix, La Couronne, 13500 ☎ 442807034

e-mail camping.le-mas@wanadoo.fr

website www.camping-le-mas.com

A well-equipped family site on a plateau with a fine view of the bay, and access to a sandy beach.

➲ *A55 onto D49.*

Open 15 March-15 Oct **Site** 6HEC ⛺ ☺ 🚐 🚐 **Facilities** 🚿 🖾 ⊙ 🚿 ⊛ **Services** 🍴 🍽 ➕ 🖾 **Leisure** 🏊 PS **Off-site** ➕

CRAU, LA VAR

Bois de Mont-Redon

480 chemin du Mont-Redon, 83260 ☎ 494667408 📠 494660966

e-mail mont.redon@wanadoo.fr

website www.mont-redon.com

Set among oak and pine trees with well-defined pitches and plenty of recreational facilities.

➲ *3km NE via D29*

Open 15 Jun-15 Sep **Site** 5HEC ⛺ ☺ **Prices** pitch 23.50 (incl 2 persons) 🚐 (static)310 **Facilities** 🚿 🖾 ⊙ 🚿 ⊛ **Services** 🍴 🍽 ➕ 🖾 **Leisure** 🏊 P

CRESPIAN GARD

Mas de Reilhe

30260 ☎ 466778212 📠 466802650

e-mail info@camping-mas-de-reilhe.fr

website www.camping-mas-de-reilhe.fr

Set in the grounds of a château, surrounded by pine trees with good recreational facilities.

➲ *On N110 for Lédignan, site on right before Crespian.*

Open 6 Apr-24 Sep **Site** 3HEC ⛺ ☺ 🚐 🏕 **Prices** pitch 13-19 (incl 2 persons) pp3.40-5.20 🚐 (static)250-665 **Facilities** 🚿 🖾 ⊙ 🚿 ⊛ **Services** 🍴 🍽 ➕ 🖾 **Leisure** 🏊 P

CROIX-VALMER, LA VAR

Selection

12 Boulevard de la Mer ☎ 494551030

e-mail camping-selection@wanadoo.fr

Site in a scattered pine wood, protected from wind. Many terraces and divided into pitches.

➲ *Off N559 at rdbt at Km78.5, 300m W along bd de Mer.*

Open 15 Mar-15 Oct **Site** 3.8HEC ⛺ ☺ 🚐 🚐 **Prices** pitch 22-31.50 (incl 3 persons) **Facilities** 🚿 🖾 ⊙ 🚿 ⊛ **Services** 🍴 🍽 ➕ 🖾 **Leisure** 🏊 PS **Off-site** 🏊 S *See advertisement on page 182*

DIE DRÔME

Pinède

Quartier du Pont-Neuf, 26150 ☎ 475221777 📠 475222273

e-mail info@camping-pinede.com

website www.camping-pinede.com

A picturesque mountain setting beside the River Drôme.

➲ *W via D93, over railway line & river to site.*

Open 23 Apr-10 Sep **Site** 5HEC ⛺ ☺ 🚐 🏕 **Facilities** 🚿 🖾 ⊙ 🚿 ⊘ 🏊 ⊛ **Services** 🍴 🍽 ➕ 🖾 **Leisure** 🏊 PR

Facilities 🖾 shop 🚿 shower ⊙ electric points for razors 🚿 electric points for caravans ⊛ parking by tents permitted 🅿 compulsory separate car park
Services 🍽 café/restaurant 🍴 bar ⊘ Camping Gaz International 🏊 gas other than Camping Gaz ➕ first aid facilities 🖾 laundry
Leisure 🏊 swimming L-Lake P-Pool R-River S-Sea **Off-site** All facilities within 2km

DIEULEFIT DRÔME

Source du Jabron
Jabron, 26220 ☎ 475906130 📄 475906130
website www.campinglasource.com
A terraced site in a pleasant location beside the River Jabron.
➾ *N of town on D538.*
Open May-Sep **Site** 5HEC 😃 ♨ ♣ 🏠 🚐 **Facilities** ♠ 🏠 ⊙ 🚻 ⑳ **Services** 🔧 🍴 🛒 Leisure ♠ P

ENTRECHAUX VAUCLUSE

Bon Crouzet
rte de St-Marcelin, 84340 ☎ 490460162 📄 490460162
website du.bon.crouzet.free.fr
On level ground with modern facilities beside the river.
➾ *D938 exit Vaison-la-Romaine for St-Marcelin-les-Vaison for 6km.*
Open Apr-Oct **Site** 1.2HEC 😃 ♨ ♣ **Prices** ♠ 3.20-4 pitch 4-4.50 **Facilities** ♠ 🏠 ⊙ 🚻 ⑳ **Services** 🔧 🍴 🛒 Leisure ♠ PR **Off-site** 🍴

ESPARRON-DE-VERDON ALPES-DE-HAUTE-PROVENCE

Soleil
rte de la Tuiliene, 4800 ☎ 492771378 📄 492771045
e-mail campinglesoleil@wanadoo.fr
website membres.lycos.fr/campinglesoleil
Wooded surroundings beside Lake Esparron with well-defined pitches.
Open Etr-Sep **Site** 1.5HEC 😃 ♨ 🏠 🚐 ⊗ **Facilities** ♠ 🏠 ⊙ 🚻 ⑳ 🅿 **Services** 🔧 🍴 🛒 Leisure ♠ L

FLEURY AUDE

Aux Hamacs
Les Cabanes de Fleury, 11560 ☎ 468332222 📄 468332223
e-mail info@campingauxhamacs.com
website www.campingauxhamacs.com
A large site beside the River Aude and 1km from the coast.
➾ *A9 exit Béziers, 15km W.*
Open Apr-17 Sep **Site** 10HEC 😃 ♨ ♣ 🏠 **Prices** 🅰 3.50 pitch 15.80-27.20 (incl 2 persons) **Facilities** ♠ 🏠 ⊙ 🚻 🅿 ⑳ **Services** 🔧 🍴 🛒 🛒 Leisure ♠ PR **Off-site** ♠S

FONTES HÉRAULT

Clairettes
Route de Peret, Adissan, 34320 ☎ 467250131 📄 467253864
e-mail camping-clairettes@wanadoo.fr
website www.campinglesclairettes.com
➾ *D9 10km N of Pézenas & Adissan D128.*
Open All year **Site** 2.2HEC 😃 ♨ ♣ 🏠 🚐 **Facilities** ♠ ⊙ 🚻 ⑳ **Services** 🔧 🍴 🛒 🛒 Leisure ♠ **Off-site** 🏠 🍴

FONTVIEILLE BOUCHES-DU-RHÔNE

CM Pins
r Michelet, 13990 ☎ 490547869 📄 490548125
e-mail campingmunicipal.lespins@wanadoo.fr
Set in a pine wood close to the Moulin d'Alphonse Daudet.
➾ *1km from village via D17.*
Open Apr-Sep **Site** 3.5HEC 😃 ♨ ♣ **Prices** pitch 10 (incl 2 persons) pp7 **Facilities** ♠ ⊙ 🚻 ⑳ **Services** 🛒 🛒 **Off-site** 🏠 🔧 🍴 🚐 ♠P

FORCALQUIER ALPES-DE-HAUTE-PROVENCE

Indigo Forcalquier
rte de Sigonce, 4300 ☎ 492752794 📄 492751810
e-mail forcalquier@camping-indigo.com
website www.camping-indigo.com
Open Apr-Oct **Site** 3HEC 😃 ♣ 🏠 🚐 🅰 **Prices** 🅰 4.50-5.20 pitch 3.70-10 🚐 (static)260-640 **Facilities** ♠ ⊙ 🚻 🅿 ⑳ **Services** 🔧 🍴 🛒 Leisure ♠ P **Off-site** 🏠

FRÉJUS VAR

Domaine de Colombier
1052 r des Combattants, d'Afrique du Nord, 83600
☎ 494515601 📄 494515557
e-mail info@clubcolombier.com
website www.clubcolombier.com
Extensive site on a hill with some terraces under pine trees. Good recreational facilities.
➾ *A8 exit 38.*
Open 31 Mar-15 Oct **Site** 10HEC 😃 ♣ 🏠 **Prices** 🅰 5-8 pitch 26-50 (incl 3 persons) **Facilities** ♠ 🏠 ⊙ 🚻 ⑳ **Services** 🔧 🍴 🛒 🛒 Leisure ♠ P **Off-site** 🚻

Fréjus
rte de Bagnols, 83600 ☎ 494199460 📄 494199469
e-mail contact@lefrejus.com
website www.lefrejus.com
Well-equipped site in wooded surroundings.
➾ *Via N7 & D4.*
Open 15 Jan-15 Dec **Site** 8HEC 😃 ♣ 🏠 🅰 **Facilities** ♠ 🏠 ⊙ 🚻 🚐 🚻 🅿 **Services** 🔧 🍴 🛒 🛒 Leisure ♠ P

Site 6HEC (site size) 😃 grass 😃 sand ♨ stone ♣ little shade ♣ partly shaded 🏠 mainly shaded 🏠 bungalows for hire 🚐 caravans for hire 🅰 tents for hire ⊗ no dogs **Prices** ♠ adult per night 😃 car per night pp per person per night 🚐 caravan per night 🅰 tent per night 🚐 (static)-caravan hire per week

Holiday Green

rte de Bagnols-en-Forêt, 83600 ☎ 494198830 ▤ 494198831
e-mail info@holiday-green.com
website www.holiday-green.com
A family site in a beautiful wooded location, offering fine modern
facilities and a variety of recreational and entertainment facilities.
➲ 6km N via D4.
Open Apr-Sep **Site** 15HEC ⛺ ⛱ 🏠 🚐 **Facilities** ↳ 🛁 ⊙ 🚐 ⌀ ⚒ ⓟ ⓟ
Services ⛽ 🍴 ➕ ⓢ **Leisure** ⚓ P **Off-site** ⚓L

Montourey

Quartier Montourey, 83600 ☎ 494532641 ▤ 494532675
e-mail info@campingmontourey.com
website www.campingmontourey.com
A well-equipped site 10 minutes of the beach.
➲ 2km N.
Open Apr-Sep **Site** 5HEC ⛺ ⛱ 🏠 🚐 **Facilities** ↳ 🛁 ⊙ 🚐 ⌀ ⓟ
Services ⛽ 🍴 ➕ ⓢ **Leisure** ⚓ P

Pierre Verte

rte de Bagnols, 83.6 ☎ 494400830 ▤ 494407541
e-mail info@campinglapierreverte.com
website www.campinglapierreverte.com
A large family site in a pine forest 8km from the coast.
➲ On A8 from Puget-sur-Argens.
Open Apr-Sep **Site** 28HEC ⛺ ⛱ ⛱ 🏠 🚐 **Prices** ⚓ 5-7 pitch 17-27 (incl 2
persons) **Facilities** ↳ 🛁 ⊙ 🚐 ⌀ ⚒ ⓟ **Services** ⛽ 🍴 ➕ ⓢ **Leisure** ⚓ P

Pins Parasols

rte de Bagnols-en-Forêt, 83600 ☎ 494408843 ▤ 494408199
e-mail lespinsparasols@wanadoo.fr
website lespinsparasols.com
A modern family site shaded by oaks and pines with spacious,
well-defined pitches and good recreational facilities.
➲ 4km N via D4.
Open 8 Apr-Sep **Site** 4.5HEC ⛺ ⛱ 🏠 🚐 **Prices** pitch 17.40-25.50 (incl 2
persons) pp4.40-6 **Facilities** ↳ 🛁 ⊙ 🚐 ⓟ **Services** ⛽ 🍴 ➕ ⓢ
Leisure ⚓ P **Off-site** ⚒

FRONTIGNAN HÉRAULT

Soleil

60 av d'Ingril ☎ 467430202 ▤ 467533469
e-mail campingdusoleil@wanadoo.fr
website www.logassist.fr/soleil
Family site bordering the beach.
➲ NE via D60.
Open Apr-Sep **Site** 1.2HEC ⛺ ⛱ 🏠 🚐 **Prices** pitch 14-32 **Facilities** ↳ ⊙
🚐 ⚒ ⓟ ⓟ **Services** ⛽ 🍴 ➕ ⓢ **Leisure** ⚓ PS **Off-site** 🛁

Tamaris

av d'Ingril, 34110 ☎ 467434477 ▤ 467189790
e-mail les-tamaris@wanadoo.fr
website www.les-tamaris.fr
A family site on level ground with direct access to the beach. Good
recreational facilities.
➲ N112 onto D129 & D60/D50 for 6km.
Open Apr-Sep **Site** 4.5HEC ⛺ ⛱ 🏠 🚐 **Prices** pitch 20-32 (incl 2 persons)
🚐 (static)140-390 **Facilities** ↳ 🛁 ⊙ 🚐 ⌀ ⓟ **Services** ⛽ 🍴 ➕ ⓢ
Leisure ⚓ PS

GALLARGUES-LE-MONTUEUX GARD

Amandiers

30660 ☎ 466352802
e-mail campamandiers@wanadoo.fr
website www.camping-lesamandiers.com
A family site with good facilities in a beautiful wooded location.
➲ N113 from Lunel towards Nîmes.
Open May-10 Sep **Site** 3HEC ⛺ ⛱ 🏠 🚐 ⚓ ⊗ **Facilities** ↳ 🛁 ⊙ 🚐 ⌀ ⚒
ⓟ **Services** ⛽ 🍴 ➕ ⓢ **Leisure** ⚓ P **Off-site** 🍴 ⚓R

GALLICIAN GARD

Mourgues

30600 ☎ 466733088 ▤ 466733088
e-mail info@masdemourgues.com
website www.masdemourgues.com
Situated in an old vineyard with some vines retained to separate
pitches. Views overlooking the Camargue.
➲ On N572 between St-Gilles & Vauvert at road junct to
Gallician.
Open Apr-Sep **Site** 2HEC ⛺ ⛱ 🏠 🚐 ⚓ **Prices** pitch 11-15 (incl 2
persons) pp3-4.20 **Facilities** ↳ 🛁 ⊙ 🚐 ⚒ ⓟ **Services** ⛽ ➕ ⓢ
Leisure ⚓ P **Off-site** 🍴 ⌀

GASSIN VAR

Moulin de Verdagne

83580 ☎ 494797821 ▤ 494542265
e-mail moulindeverdagne@aol.com
Flat grassy site with a family atmosphere 4km from the beach.
➲ SE of town towards coast.
Site 5HEC ⛺ ⛱ 🏠 **Facilities** ↳ 🛁 ⊙ 🚐 ⌀ ⚒ ⓟ **Services** ⛽ 🍴 ➕ ⓢ
Leisure ⚓ P

Parc St-James Gassin

rte du Bourrian, 83580 ☎ 494552020 ▤ 4945634877
Park-like site on slopes of a hill.
➲ 2.5km E of N559, via Km84.5 & Km84.9 on D89.
Site 32HEC ⛺ ⛱ 🏠 🚐 **Facilities** ↳ 🛁 ⊙ 🚐 ⌀ ⚒ ⓟ **Services** ⛽ 🍴 ➕ ⓢ
Leisure ⚓ P

GIENS VAR

Mediterranée-Les Cigales

Quartier du Pousset, bd Alsace-Lorraine, 83400
☎ 494582106 ▤ 494589673
e-mail accueil@campinglemed.fr
website www.campinglemed.fr
A well-kept site with numbered pitches. Special places for caravans.
➲ 300m E of D97.
Open Apr-end Sep **Site** 1.5HEC ⛺ ⛱ 🏠 🚐 **Prices** pitch 7.55-23 (incl 2
persons) pp3.25-4.05 🚐 (static)169-595 **Facilities** ↳ 🛁 ⊙ 🚐 ⚒ ⓟ
Services ⛽ 🍴 ⓢ **Off-site** ⌀ ⚒ ⚓S

GRANDE-MOTTE, LA HÉRAULT

Lou Gardian

603 allée de la Petite Motte, 34280 ☎ 467561414 ▤ 467563103
A well-run site with well-defined pitches, 0.5km from the beach.
Booking advised in summer.
Open 15 Apr-Sep **Site** 2.6HEC ⛺ ⛱ 🏠 **Facilities** ↳ 🛁 ⊙ 🚐 ⓟ **Services** 🍴
➕ ⓢ **Off-site** ⌀ ⚒ ⚓LPS

France

Facilities 🛁 shop ↳ shower ⊙ electric points for razors 🚐 electric points for caravans ⓟ parking by tents permitted ⓟ compulsory separate car park
Services 🍴 café/restaurant ⛽ bar ⌀ Camping Gaz International ⚒ gas other than Camping Gaz ➕ first aid facilities ⓢ laundry
Leisure ⚓ swimming L-Lake P-Pool R-River S-Sea **Off-site** All facilities within 2km

France

Lous Pibols

34280 ☎ 467565008

Well-organised. Divided into level pitches.

➲ *W on D59, 0.4km from sea.*

Open Apr-Sep **Site** 3HEC ❤ ⬤ ❤ ⚠ A **Facilities** ♠ ⓘ ☺ ⚑ ∅ ♨ ⑫
Services ⊞ ⓢ **Leisure** ⚓ P **Off-site** ☎ ⓘ◎ ⚓S

GRASSE ALPES-MARITIMES

Paoute

160 rte de Cannes, 06130 ☎ 493091142 ⓘ 493400640
e-mail camppaoute@hotmail.com
website www.campingpaoute.com

A family site in a wooded location close to the town centre.

➲ *S of town centre, E of the Cannes road just beyond Centre Commercial.*

Open Jun-Sep **Site** 2.5HEC ❤ ⬤ ❤ **Prices** pitch 18 (incl 2 persons)
Facilities ♠ ⓘ ☺ ⚑ ∅ ♨ ⑫ **Services** ☎ ◎ ⊞ ⓢ **Leisure** ⚓ P

GRAU-DU-ROI, LE GARD

Abri de Camargue

rte du Phare de l'Espiguette, Port Camargue, 30240
☎ 466515483 ⓘ 466517642
e-mail contact@abridecarmague.fr
website www.abridecamargue.fr

A pleasant site near the beach on the edge of the Camargue with well-marked pitches and modern installations.

➲ *2.5km S on l'Espiguette road.*

Open Apr-Sep **Site** 4HEC ❤ ⬤ ❤ ❅ **Prices** pitch 27-54 (incl 2 persons)
❅ (static)350-812 **Facilities** ♠ ⓘ ☺ ⚑ ∅ ♨ ⑫ **Services** ☎ ◎ ⊞ ⓢ
Leisure ⚓ P **Off-site** ⚓S

Eden

Port-Camargue, 30240 ☎ 466514981 ⓘ 466531320
e-mail camping.eden@wanadoo.fr
website www.campingleden.fr

Quiet site on both sides of the access road, 300m from the beach.

➲ *On D626 towards Espiguette.*

Open 4 Apr-3 Oct **Site** 5.2HEC ❤ ⬤ ❤ ❅ **Facilities** ♠ ⓘ ☺ ⚑ ∅ ♨ ⑫
Services ☎ ◎ ⊞ ⓢ **Leisure** ⚓ P **Off-site** ⚓LS ⊞

Elysée Résidence

980 rte de l'Espiguette, 30240 ☎ 466535400 ⓘ 466518512
e-mail elysee.residence@elysee-residence.com
website www.elysee-residence.com

Large family site on the edge of the Camargue with a variety of sports and entertainment facilities.

➲ *Via A9.*

Open 15 May-12 Sep **Site** 18HEC ❤ ⬤ ❅ **Facilities** ♠ ⓘ ☺ ⚑ ∅ ♨ ⑫
Services ☎ ◎ ⊞ ⓢ **Leisure** ⚓ LP **Off-site** ⓘ ☎ ◎ ⚓S

Jardins de Tivoli

rte de l'Éspiguette, 30240 ☎ 466539700 ⓘ 466510981
e-mail contact@lesjardinsdetivoli.com
website www.lesjardinsdetivoli.com

A modern site with well-marked pitches in a wooded setting 0.6km from the beach. There are good recreational facilities including mountain bike hire.

➲ *A9 SE through Le Grau-du-Roi.*

Open Apr-Sep **Site** 7HEC ❤ ⬤ ❅ **Prices** pitch 23-52 pp6 **Facilities** ♠ ⓘ
☺ ⚑ ∅ ⑫ **Services** ☎ ◎ ⊞ ⓢ **Leisure** ⚓ P **Off-site** ⚓S

Petits Camarguais

rte de l'Espiguette, 30240 ☎ 466511616 ⓘ 466511617
e-mail info@yellohvillage-petits-camarguais.com
website www.yellohvillage-petits-camarguais.com

A comfortable family site in woodland with a range of recreational facilities. Close to the beach.

Open 7 Apr-15 Sep **Site** 5HEC ❤ ⬤ ❤ ❅ ⊗ **Facilities** ♠ ⓘ ☺ ⚑ ⑫
Services ☎ ◎ ⊞ ⓢ **Leisure** ⚓ P **Off-site** ⚓S

GRIGNAN DRÔME

Truffières

Lieu-dit Nachony, 26230 ☎ 475469362
e-mail info@lestruffieres.com
website www.lestruffieres.com

A family site opposite the Château Grignan with good facilities.

➲ *A7 exit Montélimar Sud & N7 E.*

Open 20 Apr-Sep **Site** 3HEC ❤ ⬤ ❤ ⊗ **Facilities** ♠ ☺ ⚑ ⑫
Services ☎ ◎ ⊞ ⓢ **Leisure** ⚓ P **Off-site** ⓘ

HYÈRES VAR

Ceinturon III

L'Ayguade, 83400 ☎ 494663265 ⓘ 494664843
e-mail ceinturon3@securmail.net
website www.provence-campings.com/azur/ceinturon3.htm

Well-kept site in wooded surroundings divided into numbered pitches. Individual washing cubicles.

➲ *4km SE of Hyères on D42.*

Open Apr-Sep **Site** 3HEC ❤ ⬤ ❅ **Facilities** ♠ ⓘ ☺ ⚑ ∅ ⑫ ℗
Services ☎ ◎ ⓢ **Leisure** ⚓ S **Off-site** ♨ ⚓S ⊞

Palmiers

Quartier Ceinturon-l'Ayguade, L'Ayguade, 83400
☎ 494663966 ⓘ 494664730
e-mail info@camping-ceinturon2.com
website www.campingclub-lespalmiers.com

A popular site on level meadowland divided into pitches. 300m from the sea.

➲ *4km SE of Hyères on D42.*

Open 15 Mar-15 Oct **Site** 4.8HEC ❤ ⬤ ❅ **Prices** ♦ 3.80 pitch 28.40 (incl
3 persons) pp6.30 ❅ (static)318-825 **Facilities** ♠ ⓘ ☺ ⚑ ⑫
Services ☎ ◎ ⊞ ⓢ **Leisure** ⚓ P **Off-site** ⚓RS

ISLE-SUR-LA-SORGUE, L' VAUCLUSE

Sorguette

rte d'Apt, 84800 ☎ 490380571 ⓘ 490208461
e-mail sorguette@wanadoo.fr
website www.camping-sorguette.com

Tranquil wooded surroundings beside the River Sorguette with good sports and entertainment facilities.

➲ *N100 towards Apt.*

Open 15 Mar-15 Oct **Site** 5HEC ❤ ⬤ ❅ ❅ **Prices** ♦ 5.20-6.60 pitch 5-6
❅ (static)280-455 **Facilities** ♠ ⓘ ☺ ⚑ ∅ ♨ ⑫ **Services** ☎ ◎ ⊞ ⓢ
Leisure ⚓ R **Off-site** ⚓P

Site 6HEC (site size) ❤ grass ⬤ sand ❤ stone ♣ little shade ❅ partly shaded ❅ mainly shaded ❅ bungalows for hire
❅ caravans for hire A tents for hire ⊗ no dogs **Prices** ♦ adult per night ⚓ car per night pp per person per night ❅ caravan per night
A tent per night ❅ (static)-caravan hire per week

LAROQUE-DES-ALBÈRES PYRÉNÉES-ORIENTALES

Planes

117 av du Vallespir, rte de Villelongue dels Monts, 66740
☎ 468892136 🖹 468890142
e-mail camping.lasplanes@libertysurf.fr
website www.lasplanes.com
A picturesque setting surrounded by trees, bushes and flowers.
⮑ *Laroque towards Villelongue-del-Monts.*
Open 15 Jun-Aug **Site** 2.5HEC � 🏕 **Prices** 🏃 3.60-4 🚗 2.50 pitch 8-8.50
Facilities 🚿 ⊙ 🖭 🖉 ⑫ **Services** 🍴 🖴 Leisure ⮕ P
Off-site 🛆 🍴 🍽 ⛱

LÉZIGNAN-CORBIÈRES AUDE

CM Pinède

av Gaston-Bonheur, 11200 ☎ 468270508 🖹 468270508
e-mail campinglapinede@wanadoo.fr
website www.campinglapinede.fr
Well-kept terraced site with numbered pitches and asphalt drives,
decorated with bushes and flower beds. Shop only open July and
August.
⮑ *Signed from N113.*
Open Mar-Oct **Site** 3.5HEC � 🏕 **Prices** 🏃 3.20-4.30 pitch 5.60-7.50
🖭 (static)290-500 **Facilities** 🚿 🛆 ⊙ 🖭 🖉 ⛱ **Services** 🍽 🖴
Leisure ⮕ P **Off-site** 🍴 🛒

LONDE-LES-MAURES, LA VAR

Moulières

83250 ☎ 494015321 🖹 494015322
e-mail camping.les.moulieres@wanadoo.fr
website www.provence-campings.com/azur/moulieres
Well-tended level meadowland in quiet location. 1km from the sea.
⮑ *On W outskirts towards coast.*
Open Jun-2 Sep **Site** 3HEC � 🏕 **Prices** pitch 24 (incl 2 persons) pp5.50
Facilities 🚿 🛆 ⊙ 🖭 ⑫ 🄿 **Services** 🍴 🍽 🛒 🖴 **Off-site** ⮕S

Pansard

83250 ☎ 494668322 🖹 494665612
e-mail pansardcamping@aol.com
website www.provence-campings.com/azur/pansard
Beautiful, wide piece of land in a pine forest beside the beach.
⮑ *Off N98.*
Open Apr-Sep **Site** 6HEC � 🏕 🚐 ⊗ **Prices** pitch 26 (incl 3
persons) pp6.60 **Facilities** 🚿 🛆 ⊙ 🖭 🖉 ⛱ 🄿 **Services** 🍴 🍽 🖴
Leisure ⮕ S

LUNEL HÉRAULT

Bon Port

rte de la Petite Camargue, 34400 ☎ 467711565 🖹 467836027
e-mail bonport@free.fr
website www.bonport.free.fr
A pleasant wooded location at the gateway to the Camargue.
⮑ *Via D24.*
Open Apr-Sep **Site** 5HEC � 🏕 🚐 **Facilities** 🚿 🛆 ⊙ 🖭 🖉 ⛱ ⑫
Services 🍴 🍽 🛒 🖴 **Leisure** ⮕ P

Mas de l'Isle

85 chemin du Clapas, 34400 ☎ 467832652 🖹 467711388
A pleasant site between the Cévennes mountains and the
Mediterranean.
⮑ *1.5km SE via D34 near D61 junct.*
Open Apr-Aug **Site** 4HEC � 🏕 **Facilities** 🚿 ⊙ 🖭 🖭 ⑫ 🄿
Services 🍴 🍽 🛒 **Leisure** ⮕ P **Off-site** 🛆 🖉 ⛱ ⮕R 🛒

MALLEMORT BOUCHES-DU-RHÔNE

Durance Luberon

Domaine du Vergon, 13370 ☎ 490591336 🖹 490574662
e-mail duranceluberon@aol.com
website www.campingduranceluberon.com
⮑ *2.5km on D23c, 200m from canal.*
Open Apr-15 Oct **Site** 4.4HEC � 🏕 **Facilities** 🚿 ⊙ 🖭 ⑫
Services 🍴 🍽 🖴 **Leisure** ⮕ P **Off-site** 🛆 🍴 🖉 ⛱ ⮕R 🛒

MANDELIEU-LA-NAPOULE ALPES-MARITIMES

Cigales

505 av de la Mer, 06210 ☎ 493492353 🖹 493493045
e-mail campingcigales@wanadoo.fr
website www.lescigales.com
A riverside site with well-defined pitches, 0.8km from the sea.
⮑ *S on N7.*
Open All year **Site** 2HEC � 🏕 🏕 **Facilities** 🚿 ⊙ 🖭 ⑫ **Services** 🍴 🍽
🛒 🖴 **Leisure** ⮕ P **Off-site** 🛆 🖉 ⛱ ⮕LRS

MANOSQUE ALPES-DE-HAUTE-PROVENCE

Ubacs

av de la Repasse, 4100 ☎ 492722808 🖹 492877529
e-mail lesubacs.manosque@ffcc.asso.fr
A well-equipped site in the Durance valley, close to the town centre.
⮑ *1.5km W off D907 rte d'Apt.*
Open Apr-Sep **Site** 4HEC � 🌹 🚐 **Facilities** 🚿 ⊙ 🖭 🖉 ⛱ ⑫
Services 🍽 🖴 **Leisure** ⮕ P **Off-site** 🛒

MARSEILLAN-PLAGE HÉRAULT

Beauregard Est

250 Chemin de l'Airette ☎ 467771545 🖹 467012178
e-mail campingbeauregardest@wanadoo.fr
website www.camping-beauregard-est.com
A family camping site bordering a sandy beach sheltered by natural
sand dunes. High standard sanitary facilities.
⮑ *Access via A9, then RN112 (exit at Sète or Cap d'Agde) or
via D51 E through Marseillan village.*
Open 8 Apr-Sep **Site** 3.3HEC � 🏕 🚐 ⊗ **Prices** pitch 15-28 (incl 2
persons) pp2-5 **Facilities** 🚿 ⊙ 🖭 ⑫ **Services** 🍴 🍽 🛒 **Leisure** ⮕ S
Off-site 🛆 🖉 ⛱ ⮕L

Charlemagne

av du Camping, 34340 ☎ 467219249 🖹 467218611
e-mail info@charlemagne-camping.com
website www.charlemagne-camping.com
Quiet wooded surroundings with good sanitary and sports facilities,
200m from the beach.
⮑ *Via N112 at Marseillan Plage.*
Open 8 Apr-23 Sep **Site** 6.6HEC � 🏕 🚐 **Facilities** 🚿 🛆 ⊙ 🖭 🖉 ⛱
⑫ **Services** 🍴 🍽 🛒 **Leisure** ⮕ PS

France

Facilities 🛆 shop 🚿 shower ⊙ electric points for razors 🖭 electric points for caravans ⑫ parking by tents permitted 🄿 compulsory separate car park
Services 🍴 café/restaurant 🍽 bar 🖉 Camping Gaz International ⛱ gas other than Camping Gaz 🛒 first aid facilities 🖴 laundry
Leisure ⮕ swimming L-Lake P-Pool R-River S-Sea **Off-site** All facilities within 2km

Créole

av des campings ☎ 467219269 🖷 467265816
e-mail campinglacreole@wanadoo.fr
website www.campinglacreole.com
Open Apr-Oct **Site** 1.5HEC 👪 🏖 ⛺ 🏘 **Prices** pitch 13-24.50 (incl 2 persons) 🚐 (static)230-550 **Facilities** 🏪 ⊙ 🚻 ⚲ **Services** 🛒 🍽 **Leisure** 🏊 S
Off-site 🏧 ⚲ 🚴 ➕

See advertisement on this page

Languedoc-Camping

117 chemin du Pairollet, 34340 ☎ 467219255 🖷 467016375
e-mail languedoc.camping.fr@wanadoo.fr
website www.languedocamping.fr
A family site in wooded surroundings with direct access to the beach.
➲ *On coast road between Mediterranean & Bassin de Thau.*
Open 15 Mar-Oct **Site** 1.5HEC 👪 🏖 ⛺ 🏘 🚐 **Facilities** 🏪 🏧 ⊙ 🚻 ⚲ 🚴 ⚲ **Services** 🍽 ➕ 🛒 **Leisure** 🏊 S **Off-site** 🛒 ⚲ 🏊LPR

Plage

69 chemin du Pairollet, 34340 ☎ 467219254 🖷 467016357
e-mail info@laplage-camping.net
website www.laplage-camping.net
A family site with direct access to a sandy beach.
Open 15 Mar-Oct **Site** 1.3HEC ⛺ 🚐 **Prices** pitch 14-28 (incl 2 persons) pp3.50-4 **Facilities** 🏪 ⊙ 🚻 ⚲ **Services** 🍽 🛒 **Leisure** 🏊 S
Off-site 🏧 ➕

MAUREILLAS PYRÉNÉES-ORIENTALES

Val Roma Park

Les Thermas du Boulou, 66480 ☎ 48877910
e-mail valromapark@wanadoo.fr
➲ *2.5km NE on N9.*
Site 3.5HEC 👪 🏖 🏘 🚐 **Prices** pitch 11.25 🚐 (static)700 **Facilities** 🏪 🏧 ⊙ 🚻 🚴 ⚲ **Services** 🍽 🛒 ➕ 🛒 **Leisure** 🏊 PR **Off-site** 🏊L

MÉOLANS-REVEL ALPES-DE-HAUTE-PROVENCE

Domaine de Loisirs de l'Ubaye

4340 ☎ 492810196 🖷 492819253
e-mail info@loisirsubaye.com
website www.loisirsubaye.com
A large terraced site in a delightful wooded valley. There is a small lake and direct access to the river and good sports and recreational facilities.
➲ *7km NW of Barcelonnette.*
Site 10HEC 👪 🏖 🏘 🚐 **Facilities** 🏪 🏧 ⊙ 🚻 ⚲ 🚴 ⚲ **Services** 🍽 🛒 ➕ 🛒
Leisure 🏊 LPR

MIRABEL-ET-BLACONS DRÔME

Gervanne Camping

26400 ☎ 475400020 🖷 475400397
e-mail info@gervanne-camping.com
website www.gervanne-camping.com
A pleasant site with scattered shade and plenty of facilities beside the River Drôme.
➲ *Via D164 Crest-Die.*
Open Apr-Sep **Site** 3.8HEC 👪 🏖 🏘 🚐 **Prices** 🧍 3.50-5.30 🚗 2.30-2.70 🚐 3.20-4.50 **Facilities** 🏪 ⊙ 🚻 ⚲ 🚴 ⚲ **Services** 🍽 🛒 ➕ 🛒
Leisure 🏊 PR

MONTBLANC HÉRAULT

Rebau

34290 ☎ 467985078 🖷 467986863
e-mail gilbert@camping-lerebau.fr
website www.camping-lerebau.fr
Divided into pitches and surrounded by vineyards.
➲ *N113 from Pézenas to La Bégude de Jordy, onto D18 towards Montblanc for 2km.*
Open Mar-Oct **Site** 3HEC 👪 🏖 🏘 🚐 **Prices** pitch 19.50-31.50 (incl 2 persons) 🚐 (static)300-690 **Facilities** 🏪 ⊙ 🚻 ⚲ 🚴 ⚲ **Services** 🍽 🛒 ➕ 🛒
Leisure 🏊 P **Off-site** 🏧

MONTCLAR AUDE

Au Pin d'Arnauteille

Domaine d'Arnauteille, 11250 ☎ 468268453 🖷 468269110
e-mail arnauteille@mnet.fr
website www.arnauteille.com
A natural wooded park surrounded by mountains.
➲ *2.2km SE via D43*
Open 31 Mar-Sep **Site** 7HEC 👪 🏖 🏘 **Prices** pitch 17-33 (incl 2 persons) pp5-7.70 🚐 (static)248-595 **Facilities** 🏪 🏧 ⊙ 🚻 ⚲ 🚴 ⚲ **Services** 🍽 🛒 ➕ 🛒 **Leisure** 🏊 P **Off-site** 🏊R

MONTÉLIMAR DRÔME

Deux Saisons

Chemin des Alexis, 26200 ☎ 475018899
A well-equipped site on the bank of River Roubion.
➲ *D540 from town centre over Pont de la Libération, 1st right onto chemin des Alexis.*
Open Mar-Nov **Site** 1.5HEC 👪 🏖 🏘 🚐 **Facilities** 🏪 ⊙ 🚻 ⚲ 🚴 ⚲ **Services** 🍽 🛒 ➕ 🛒 **Leisure** 🏊 R **Off-site** 🚴 P

MONTPELLIER HÉRAULT

Floréal

rte de Palavas, 34970 ☎ 467929305 🖷 467929305
e-mail info@camping-le-floreal
website www.camping-le-floreal.com
On level ground surrounded by vineyards.
➲ *A9 exit Montpellier-Sud, site 0.5km. From town centre D986 for Palavas.*
Open Apr-3 Nov **Site** 1.6HEC 👪 🏖 🏘 **Facilities** 🏪 🏧 ⊙ 🚻 ⚲ **Services** 🍽 ➕ 🛒 **Off-site** 🏧 🍽 🍽 ⚲ 🚴 🏊PR

MONTPEZAT ALPES-DE-HAUTE-PROVENCE

Coteau de la Marine

04500 ☎ 492775333 🖹 492775934

A pleasant wooded site, providing easy access to the Verdon Gorges. There are good facilities, especially for boating.

➲ *Via D11 & D211.*

Open May-Sep **Site** 10HEC ⛺ ♣ 🏠 ♨ **Facilities** ⋔ 🏠 ⊙ 🅿 ⊘ 🚿 ℗
Services ⊠ 🍽 ➕ 🔲 **Leisure** ⊛ PR

MONTRÉAL ARDÈCHE

Moulinage

rte des Défilés de Ruoms, 7110 ☎ 475368620 🖹 475369846

e-mail moulinage@aol.com

website www.ardeche-camping.com

Well-equipped family site with a variety of bungalows, caravans and timber chalets. Close to the famous Gorges de l'Ardèche.

Open Apr-Sep **Site** 3.5HEC ♣ ♣ 🏠 ♨ 🅰 **Facilities** ⋔ ⊙ 🅿 ℗
Services ⊠ 🍽 ➕ 🔲 **Leisure** ⊛ PR

MORNAS VAUCLUSE

Beauregard

rte d'Uchaux ☎ 490370208 🖹 490370723

e-mail beaurega@wanadoo.fr

website www.camping-beauregard.com

Site 15HEC 🏠 ♨ **Facilities** 🏠 ⊙ 🅿 **Services** ⊠ 🍽 🔲

MOURIÈS BOUCHES-DU-RHÔNE

Devenson

13890 ☎ 490475201 🖹 490476309

e-mail devenson@libertysurf.fr

website www.camping-devenson.com

Terraced site among pine and olive trees in Provençal countryside.

➲ *Off N113 at La Samatane & N towards Mouriès, site in N of village.*

Open 24 Mar -15 Sep **Site** 3.5HEC ♣ ♣ ♨ **Prices** ⋔ 4.50 pitch 5.50
♨ (static)280 **Facilities** ⋔ 🏠 ⊙ 🅿 ⊘ ℗ **Services** ➕ 🔲 **Leisure** ⊛ P
Off-site ⊠ 🍽 🚿

MOUSTIERS-STE-MARIE ALPES-DE-HAUTE-PROVENCE

St-Jean

rte de Riez, 04360 ☎ 492746685 🖹 492746685

e-mail camping-st-jean@wanadoo.fr

Quiet and relaxing site located at the gateway to the Gorges du Verdon, 5 minutes from Ste-Croix Lake.

➲ *Via D952.*

Open 24 Apr -27 Sep **Site** 1.6HEC ♣ ♣ 🏠 **Facilities** ⋔ 🏠 ⊙ 🅿 ⊘ ℗
Services ➕ 🔲 **Leisure** ⊛ R **Off-site** ⊠ 🍽 🚿

Vieux Colombier

Quartier St-Michel, 04360 ☎ 492746189 🖹 492746189

e-mail contact@lvcm.fr

website www.lvcm.fr

A family site near the entrance to the Gorges du Verdon at an altitude of 630m.

➲ *0.8km S on D952 towards Castellane.*

Open Apr-Sep **Site** 2.7HEC ♣ ♣ 🏠 **Prices** ⋔ 4.20 pitch 4.40 **Facilities** ⋔
⊙ 🅿 ⊘ ℗ **Services** ⊠ 🍽 🔲 **Off-site** 🏠 🚿 ⊛R

Cigales

721 Chemin de Jas de la Paro, 83490

☎ 494451208 🖹 494458280

e-mail contact@les-cigales.com

website www.les-cigales.com

A family site set among Mediterranean vegetation with excellent facilities. Organised entertainment in summer.

➲ *A8 exit Draguignan, onto N7, site 0.8km, signed.*

Open Apr-Oct **Site** 13.5HEC ♣ ♣ 🏠 **Prices** ⋔ 3-8 ♨ 2-3 pitch 4-9
Facilities ⋔ 🏠 ⊙ 🅿 ⊘ ℗ **Services** ⊠ 🍽 🔲 **Leisure** ⊛ P **Off-site** ⊛R

Sellig

41 chemin des Valettes, 83490 ☎ 494451171

A peaceful family site in a wooded location.

➲ *1.5km W on N7.*

Open Mar-15 Oct **Site** 1.6HEC ♣ ♣ 🏠 ♨ **Facilities** ⋔ 🏠 ⊙ 🅿 ℗
Services ⊠ 🍽 ➕ 🔲 **Leisure** ⊛ P **Off-site** ⊛LR

NAPOULE, LA ALPES-MARITIMES

Azur-Vacances

bd du Bon Puits, 06120 ☎ 493499216 🖹 493499112

Site with many long terraces, on edge of mountain slope in mixed woodland.

➲ *Turn inland 200m after fork at railway station & continue 0.6km.*

Open Apr-Sep **Site** 6HEC ♣ ♣ 🏠 **Facilities** ⋔ 🏠 ⊙ 🅿 ⊘ 🚿 ℗
Services ⊠ 🍽 ➕ 🔲 **Off-site** ⊛RS

NARBONNE AUDE

Nautique

La Nautique, 11100 ☎ 468904819 🖹 468907339

e-mail info@campinglanautique.com

website www.campinglanautique.com

Situated on the salt-water Étang de Bages. There are good recreational facilities and booking is advised.

➲ *A9 exit Narbonne Sud.*

Open 15 Feb-15 Nov **Site** 16HEC ♣ ♣ ♣ 🏠 🅰 **Prices** pitch 8.50-21 (incl
2 persons) pp4.50-6.50 **Facilities** ⋔ 🏠 ⊙ 🅿 🚿 ℗ **Services** ⊠ 🍽 ➕ 🔲
Leisure ⊛ P **Off-site** ⊘ ⊛L

See advertisement on page 188

AT NARBONNE-PLAGE (15KM E D168)

CM de la Côte des Roses

11100 ☎ 468498365 🖹 468494044

A modern site nestling at the foot of the Massif of the Calpe close to the sea.

➲ *3km SW.*

Open 25 May-Sep **Site** 16HEC ♣ ♣ **Facilities** ⋔ 🏠 ⊙ 🅿 ⊘ ℗ **Services**
⊠ 🍽 ➕ 🔲 **Off-site** 🚿 ⊛S

CM Falaise

av des Vacances, 11100 ☎ 468498077 🖹 468494044

On level ground at the foot of the Massif of the Calpe with modern facilities.

➲ *W of Narbonne Plage, 400m from beach.*

Open Apr-22 Sep **Site** 8HEC ♣ ♣ **Facilities** ⋔ 🏠 ⊙ 🅿 ⊘ ℗
Services ⊠ 🍽 ➕ 🔲 **Off-site** ⊛S

France

Facilities 🏠 shop ⋔ shower ⊙ electric points for razors 🅿 electric points for caravans ℗ parking by tents permitted 🅿 compulsory separate car park
Services 🍽 café/restaurant ⊠ bar ⊘ Camping Gaz International 🚿 gas other than Camping Gaz ➕ first aid facilities 🔲 laundry
Leisure ⊛ swimming L-Lake P-Pool R-River S-Sea **Off-site** All facilities within 2km

France

NÉBIAS AUDE

Fontaulié-Sud
11500 ☎ 468201762
e-mail lefontauliesud@free.fr
website www.fontauliesud.com
A beautiful setting in the heart of the Cathare region.
➲ *0.6km S via D117.*
Open May-15 Sep **Site** 4HEC 😃 🏕 🏨 **Prices** ♠ 4.50 pitch 6 **Facilities** 🅟 🛁 ⊙ 🅡 🅐 🚿 🅟 **Services** 🍴 🍽 🔢 🔘 **Leisure** 🏊 P **Off-site** 🍽

NÎMES GARD

Domaine de la Bastide
Rte de Generac, 30900 ☎ 466380921 📱 466380921
A rural setting with excellent facilities. Shop only open in summer.
➲ *5km S of town centre on D13. A9 exit Nîmes-Ouest.*
Open All year **Site** 5HEC 😃 🌊 🏕 🏨 **Facilities** 🅟 🛁 ⊙ 🅡 🅐 🚿 🅟 **Services** 🍴 🍽 🔢 🔘 **Off-site** 🏊 L

NIOZELLES ALPES-DE-HAUTE-PROVENCE

Moulin de Ventre
4300 ☎ 492786331 📱 492798692
e-mail moulindeventre@free.fr
website www.moulindeventre.com
A rural setting with good facilities.
➲ *2.5km E via N100.*
Open 25 Mar-Sep **Site** 2.8HEC 😃 🏕 🏨 **Facilities** 🅟 🛁 ⊙ 🅡 🅐 🚿 **Services** 🍴 🍽 🔢 🔘 **Leisure** 🏊 P

NYONS DRÔME

Domaine du Sagittaire
Vinsobres, 26110 ☎ 475270000 📱 475270039
e-mail camping.sagittaire@wanadoo.fr
website www.le-sagittaire.com
Well-kept site divided by hedges in a beautiful Alpine setting.
➲ *S of town on D538 to Vaison-la-Romaine.*
Open All year **Site** 14HEC 😃 🏕 🏨 **Facilities** 🅟 🛁 ⊙ 🅡 🅐 🚿 **Services** 🍴 🍽 🔢 🔘 **Leisure** 🏊 LP **Off-site** 🏊 R

OLLIÈRES-SUR-EYRIEUX, LES ARDÈCHE

Domaine des Plantas
07360 ☎ 475662153 📱 475662365
e-mail plantas.ardeche@wanadoo.fr
website www.domainedesplantas.com
Games room, disco and other leisure activities.
Open 8 May-18 Sep **Site** 10HEC 😃 🌊 🏕 🏨 **Facilities** 🅟 🛁 ⊙ 🅡 🅐 🚿 🅐 🚿 **Services** 🍴 🍽 🔢 🔘 **Leisure** 🏊 PR

ORANGE VAUCLUSE

Jonquier
1321 r Alexis-Carrel, 84100 ☎ 490344948 📱 490511697
e-mail info@campinglejonquier.com
website www.campinglejonquier.com
➲ *On the NW outskirts.*
Open Apr-Sep **Site** 2HEC 😃 🏕 🏨 **Prices** pitch 18.50-24 (incl 2 persons) 🚐 (static)235-770 **Facilities** 🅟 🛁 ⊙ 🅡 🅐 🚿 **Services** 🍽 🔢 🔘 **Leisure** 🏊 P **Off-site** 🍽 R

PEYREMALE-SUR-CÈZE GARD

Drouilhédes
30160 ☎ 466250480 📱 466251095
A beautiful location beside the River Cèze surrounded by pine and chestnut trees.
➲ *Via A6 & D17.*
Open Mar-Sep **Site** 2HEC 😃 🏕 🏨 **Facilities** 🅟 🛁 ⊙ 🅡 🅐 🚿 **Services** 🍴 🍽 🔢 🔘 **Leisure** 🏊 R **Off-site** ⛴

PEYRUIS ALPES-DE-HAUTE-PROVENCE

Cigales
chemin de la Digue du Bevon, 04310 ☎ 492681604 📱 492681604
website www.lescigales.ifrance.com
A modern site in the heart of the Val de Durance.
➲ *Via A51 & N96.*
Open Apr-Sep **Site** 1HEC 😃 🏕 **Facilities** 🅟 ⊙ 🅡 🚿 🚿 **Services** 🔘 **Off-site** 🛁 🍴 🍽 🏊 P 🔢

PONT-D'HÉRAULT GARD

Magnanarelles
Le Rey, 30570 ☎ 467824013 📱 467825061
e-mail info@maxfrance.com
website www.maxfrance.fr
A pleasant mountain setting with well-defined pitches.
➲ *0.3km W via D999, beside river.*
Open All year **Site** 2HEC 😃 🏕 🏨 🚐 **Prices** ♠ 3.90 🚐 5.65 🚐 (static)241 **Facilities** 🅟 🛁 ⊙ 🅡 🅐 🚿 **Services** 🍽 🔢 🔘 **Leisure** 🏊 PR

Site 6HEC (site size) 😃 grass 🌊 sand 😃 stone 🏕 little shade 🏕 partly shaded 🏨 mainly shaded 🏨 bungalows for hire 🚐 caravans for hire 🅐 tents for hire ⊗ no dogs **Prices** ♠ adult per night 🚗 car per night pp per person per night 🚐 caravan per night 🅐 tent per night 🚐 (static)-caravan hire per week

PONT-DU-GARD GARD

International des Gorges du Gardon
rte de Uzès, 30210 ☎ 466228181 🖹 466229012
e-mail camping.international@wanadoo.fr
website www.le-camping-international.com
A peaceful wooded location beside the River Gardon.
➲ *1km from aqueduct on D981 Uzès road.*
Open 15 Mar-30 Oct **Site** 4.2HEC 🐾 ⛟ ⛟ 🏕 🚐 **Prices** pitch 12-17 (incl 2 persons) **Facilities** ⚡ 🏪 ⊙ ⚡ 🅿 ⓟ **Services** 🍴 🍽 ➕ 🧺 **Leisure** ⚓ PR

AT PORT-GRIMAUD (4KM E)

Club Holiday Marina
RN 98 Le Ginestel, 83310 ☎ 494560843 🖹 494562388
e-mail info@holiday-marina.com
website www.holiday-marina.com
Located close to beaches with diving tuition available.
➲ *On N98.*
Open Mar-Dec **Site** 3.5HEC 🐾 ⛟ 🚐 **Prices** pitch 19-49 (incl 2 persons) 🚐 (static)290-890 **Facilities** ⚡ 🏪 ⊙ ⚡ 🅾 ⓟ **Services** 🍴 🍽 ➕ 🧺 **Leisure** ⚓ PRS

See advertisement on this page

Domaine des Naiades
St-Pons-les-Mûres, 83310 ☎ 494556780 🖹 494556781
e-mail info@lesnaiades.com
website www.lesnaiades.com
Site on hilly land with terraces divided into pitches and with many modern facilities.
➲ *N98 onto D244, turn right & continue uphill.*
Open 31 Mar-28 Oct **Site** 27HEC ⛟ 🚐 **Prices** pitch 28-47 (incl 3 persons) **Facilities** ⚡ 🏪 ⊙ ⚡ ⓟ **Services** 🍴 🍽 ➕ 🧺 **Leisure** ⚓ P
Off-site 🍽 ⚓S

Plage
RN 98, 83310 ☎ 494563115 🖹 494564961
e-mail campingplagegrimaud@wanadoo.fr
website www.camping-de-la-plage.net
Wide area of land on both sides of road beside sea. Partly terraced and divided into pitches.
➲ *N on N98.*
Open 31 Mar-early Oct **Site** 18HEC 🐾 ⛟ ⛟ **Prices** pitch 21-25 (incl 2 persons) pp5.50-6.50 **Facilities** ⚡ 🏪 ⊙ ⚡ 🅾 🔹 ⓟ **Services** 🍴 🍽 ➕ 🧺 **Leisure** ⚓ S

Prairies de la Mer
☎ 494790909 🖹 494790910
e-mail praries@wanadoo.fr
Site 20HEC 🐾 ⛟ **Facilities** 🏪 ⊙ ⚡ **Services** 🍽 🧺

PORTIRAGNES-PLAGE HÉRAULT

Mimosas
34420 ☎ 467909292 🖹 467908539
e-mail les.mimosas.portiragnes@wanadoo.fr
website www.mimosas.com
A well-equipped family site located in a leisure park on the banks of the Canal du Midi, 1.3km from the sea.
➲ *A9 exit Béziers Est, N112 & D37 towards coast.*
Open May-15 Sep **Site** 7HEC 🐾 ⛟ 🏕 🚐 🅰 **Facilities** ⚡ 🏪 ⊙ ⚡ 🅾 🔹 ⓟ **Services** 🍴 🍽 ➕ 🧺 **Leisure** ⚓ PR **Off-site** ⚓S

Holiday Marina is a friendly, safe site ideal for families. Situated at 800 from the centre of Port Grimaud and just 950 from the beach, we are perfectly situated for visiting this famous area of France. Our touring pitches come with their own fully equipped private bathroom, heated in low season with a water and 20 amp electrical hook up. Facilities on site include pool, Jacuzzi, bar, take-away restaurant, shop, hire shop, kids club, play area. TV & Games room, car wash, WIFI, moorings with access to the Mediterranean & more.

Opening dates: March 07 – December 07.

RN98 Le Ginestrel, 83310 Grimaud, France.
Tel. + 33 494 56 08 43 Fax + 33 494 56 23 88
Web site: www.holiday-marina.com
Email: info@holiday-marina.com

Sablons
rte de Portiragnes, 34420 ☎ 467909055 🖹 467908291
e-mail les.sablons@wanadoo.fr.
website les-sablons.com
Large site subdivided into fields by fences. Beside beach. Night club and disco.
➲ *0.5km N on D37.*
Open Apr-Sep **Site** 15HEC 🐾 ⛟ ⛟ 🏕 🅰 **Facilities** ⚡ 🏪 ⊙ ⚡ 🅾 🔹 ⓟ **Services** 🍴 🍽 ➕ 🧺 **Leisure** ⚓ PS

See advertisement on page 190

PRADET, LE VAR

Mauvallon
chemin de la Gavaresse, 83220 ☎ 494213173
A well-kept site divided into pitches among young trees.
➲ *Off N559 in Le Pradet onto D86 for 2.5km towards sea.*
Open 15 Jun-15 Sep **Site** 1.2HEC 🐾 ⛟ **Facilities** ⚡ ⊙ ⚡ 🅾 ⓟ **Services** ➕ 🧺 **Off-site** 🏪 🍴 🍽 ⚓S

PRAMOUSQUIER VAR

Pramousquier
83980 ☎ 494058395 🖹 494057504
e-mail camping-lavandou@wanadoo.fr
website www.campingpramousquier.com
A terraced site set in a wooded park 400m from a fine sandy beach. Good recreational facilities.
➲ *2km E via D559*
Open May-Sep **Site** 3HEC ⛟ 🏕 **Facilities** ⚡ 🏪 ⊙ ⚡ 🅾 ⓟ **Services** 🍴 🍽 ➕ 🧺 **Off-site** ⚓S

Facilities 🏪 shop ⚡ shower ⊙ electric points for razors 🅾 electric points for caravans ⓟ parking by tents permitted 🅿 compulsory separate car park
Services 🍽 café/restaurant 🍴 bar ⚂ Camping Gaz International 🔹 gas other than Camping Gaz ➕ first aid facilities 🧺 laundry
Leisure ⚓ swimming L-Lake P-Pool R-River S-Sea **Off-site** All facilities within 2km

PRIVAS ARDÈCHE

Ardeche

rte de Montélimar, 07000 ☎ 475640580 📠 475645968

e-mail jcray@wanadoo.fr

website www.ardechecamping.fr

A comfortable municipal site with good facilities in the heart of the Ardèche region.

Open Apr-15 Sep **Site** 5.5HEC 👺 👙 🏠 ⛺ **Prices** pitch 16.50-19 (incl 2 persons) **Facilities** 🖍 ⊙ 🕿 🖾 **Services** 🍴 🍽 🛍 **Leisure** 🏖 PR **Off-site** 🏧 🍴 🍽 🖉 🚄 🏖P ➕

PUGET-SUR-ARGENS VAR

Aubrèdes

408 chemin des Aubrédes, 83480 ☎ 494455146 📠 494452892

e-mail campingaubredes@wanadoo.fr

website campingaubredes.com

Situated on undulating meadowland surrounded by pine trees with modern facilities.

⮕ A8 exit Puget-sur-Argens, site 0.85km.

Open May-15 Sep **Site** 3.8HEC 👺 👙 🏠 **Facilities** 🖍 🛍 ⊙ 🕿 🖾 ⑫ **Services** 🍴 🍽 ➕ 🛍 **Leisure** 🏖 P

Bastiane

1056, chemin des Suvières, 83480 ☎ 494555594 📠 494555593

e-mail info@labastiane.com **website** www.labastiane.com

Hilly site divided into numbered pitches in a pine and oak wood. Separate car park for arrivals after 23.00 hrs.

⮕ Via A8.

Open 25 Mar-21 Oct **Site** 3.1HEC 👺 👙 🏠 ⛺ **Prices** 🎣 3.30-6.60 🚗 1.90-3.60 🚐 14.84-35.34 🚐 (static)115-475 **Facilities** 🖍 🛍 ⊙ 🕿 ⑫ **Services** 🍴 🍽 ➕ 🛍 **Leisure** 🏖 P **Off-site** 🚄 🏖L

QUILLAN AUDE

Sapinette

21r René Delpech, 11500 ☎ 468201352 📠 468202780

A comfortable site in a forest of fir trees with pitches separated by hedges.

⮕ W via D79 rte de Ginoles.

Open Apr-Oct **Site** 1.8HEC 👺 👙 🏠 **Facilities** 🖍 ⊙ 🕿 ⑫ **Services** ➕ 🛍 **Leisure** 🏖 P **Off-site** 🏧 🍴 🍽 🖉 🏖LPRS

RACOU, LE PYRÉNÉES-ORIENTALES

Bois de Valmarie

66 ☎ 468810992 📠 68958058

e-mail contact@camping-lasirene.fr

website www.camping-lasirene.fr

A family site with plentiful recreational facilities.

⮕ N114 exit Perpignan Sud.

Open 7 Apr-27 Sep **Site** 7HEC 👺 👙 🏠 **Prices** 🚐 (static)248-945 **Facilities** 🖍 🛍 ⊙ 🕿 🖉 ⑫ **Services** 🍴 🍽 ➕ 🛍 **Leisure** 🏖 PS **Off-site** 🚄

Site 6HEC (site size) 👺 grass 👙 sand 👺 stone 🌳 little shade 👺 partly shaded 👺 mainly shaded 🏠 bungalows for hire ⛺ caravans for hire ⛺ tents for hire ⊗ no dogs **Prices** 🎣 adult per night 🚗 car per night pp per person per night 🚐 caravan per night ⛺ tent per night 🚐 (static)-caravan hire per week

RAMATUELLE VAR

Cigale
rte de L' Escalet, 83350 ☎ 494792253 ▤ 494791205
e-mail campinglacigale@wanadoo.fr
website www.camping-lacigale.fr
The site is 0.8km from the beach.
➲ A8 exit Le Luc.
Open Apr-15 Oct **Site** 1.5HEC ♨ ♣ ♠ Å **Facilities** ⚑ ▣ ☺ ☻ ⚒ ℗
Services ⚑ ⚑ ☎ 🛒 **Leisure** ♒ P **Off-site** ♒S

Tournels
rte de Camarat, 83350 ☎ 494559090 ▤ 494559099
e-mail info@tournels.com
website www.tournels.com
Lovely views to Pampelonne Bay from part of this site. 1km to beach.
➲ Off D93 Croix-Valmer to St-Tropez, signs to Cap Camarat.
Open Mar-10 Jan **Site** 20HEC ♨ ♣ ♠ **Facilities** ⚑ ☺ ☻ ∅ ℗
Services ⚑ ⚑ ☎ 🛒 **Leisure** ♒ P **Off-site** ☻ ♒S

See advertisement on this page

REMOULINS GARD

Soubeyranne
rte de Beaucaire, 30210 ☎ 466370321 ▤ 466371465
e-mail soubeyranne@franceloc.fr
website www.soubeyranne.com
A picturesque location close to the River Gard with modern facilities.
➲ S on D986.
Open Apr23 Sep **Site** 6HEC ♨ ♣ ♠ **Prices** pitch 15.50-22 (incl 2
persons) ♣ (static)154-840 **Facilities** ⚑ ▣ ☺ ☻ ∅ ⚒ ℗ **Services** ⚑ ⚑
🛒 **Leisure** ♒ P **Off-site** ♒R

Sousta
av du Pont-du-Gard, 30210 ☎ 466371280 ▤ 466372369
e-mail info@lasousta.fr
website www.lasousta.com
Picturesque forest site a short distance from the Pont du Gard.
➲ 2km NW. A9 exit for Remoulins, right after bridge towards
Pont de Gard.
Open Mar-Oct **Site** 14HEC ♨ ♣ ♠ ♣ **Facilities** ⚑ ▣ ☺ ☻ ∅ ℗
Services ⚑ ⚑ ☎ 🛒 **Leisure** ♒ PR

REVENS GARD

Lou Triadou
Le Bourg, 30750 ☎ 467827358
e-mail lou.triadou@wanadoo.fr
website site.voila.fr/camping_lou_triadou
A well-equipped site in the heart of the Causse Noir.
➲ Via D159/D151.
Open 20 Jun-1Sep **Site** 0.8HEC ♨ ♣ ♠ ♣ Å **Prices** ♣ 3.40 pitch 4.60
♣ (static)185 **Facilities** ⚑ ☺ ☻ ∅ ⚒ ℗ **Services** ⚑ ⚑ ☎ 🛒 **Leisure** ♒ P

RIA PYRÉNÉES-ORIENTALES

Bellevue
8 r Bellevue, 66500 ☎ 468964896 ▤ 468964896 & 468961062
e-mail bellevue.camping@wanadoo.fr
website www.camping-bellevue-riasirach.com
Beautifully terraced site beside a former vineyard. Very well-kept.
➲ 2km S on N116, onto road to Sirach, turn right for 0.6km up
driveway (difficult for caravans).
Open Apr-Sep **Site** 2.2HEC ♨ ♣ ♠ ♣ **Prices** ♠ 2.80 pitch 3.38
♣ (static)175 **Facilities** ⚑ ☺ ☻ ∅ ℗ **Services** ⚑ ☎ 🛒
Off-site ▣ ⚑ ⚒ ♒LPR

ROQUEBRUNE-SUR-ARGENS VAR

Domaine de la Bergerie
Vallée du Fournel, 83520 ☎ 498114545 ▤ 498114546
e-mail info@domainelabergerie.com
website www.domainelabergerie.com
A large, well-run family site set in pleasant Provençal countryside with
fine recreational facilities.
➲ A8 exit Le Muy, onto N7 & D7.
Open 15 Feb-15 Nov **Site** 60HEC ♨ ♣ ♠ ♣ **Prices** pitch 17-30 (incl 2
persons) pp4.30-7.90 ♣ (static)371-560 **Facilities** ⚑ ▣ ☺ ☻ ∅ ⚒ ℗
Services ⚑ ⚑ ☎ 🛒 **Leisure** ♒ LP

France

Facilities ▣ shop ⚑ shower ☺ electric points for razors ☻ electric points for caravans ℗ parking by tents permitted ℗ compulsory separate car park
Services 🛒 café/restaurant ⚑ bar ∅ Camping Gaz International ⚒ gas other than Camping Gaz ☎ first aid facilities 🛒 laundry
Leisure ♒ swimming L-Lake P-Pool R-River S-Sea **Off-site** All facilities within 2km

Lei Suves

Quartier du Blavet, 83520 ☎ 494454395 ▤ 494816313
e-mail camping.lei.suves@wanadoo.fr
website www.lei-suves.com
Set in a picturesque forested area with good recreational facilities.
➲ *4km N via N7.*
Open 31 Mar-14 Oct **Site** 7.4HEC ♨ ♣ ⊞ ⊟ **Prices** pitch 19.50-34.50 (incl 2 persons) ⊟ (static)280-490 **Facilities** ⋔ 🏠 ⊙ ⊟ ⌀ ♨ ☎ **Services** ⊈ ⛧ ⊞ 🖥 **Leisure** ⊸ P

See advertisement on this page

Moulin des Iscles

Quartier La Valette, 83520 ☎ 494457074 ▤ 494454609
e-mail moulin.iscles@wanadoo.fr
A picturesque location beside the River Argens with modern facilities.
➲ *D7 towards St-Aygulf.*
Open Apr-Sep **Site** 1.3HEC ♨ ♣ ⊞ ⊟ **Prices** ♠ 3.20 pitch 19.50 (incl 3 persons) **Facilities** ⋔ 🏠 ⊙ ⊟ ⌀ ♨ ☎ **Services** ⊈ ⛧ ⊞ 🖥 **Leisure** ⊸ R **Off-site** ⊸L

Pêcheurs

83520 ☎ 494457125 ▤ 494816513
e-mail info@camping-les-pecheurs.com
website www.camping-les-pecheurs.com
A pleasant site with direct access to the river in a wooded location at the foot of the Roquebrune crag.
➲ *0.5km NW via D7, near lake.*
Open 31 Mar-Sep **Site** 5HEC ♨ ♣ ⊞ ⊟ **Prices** ♠ 4-6.30 pitch 17-32.50 (incl 2 persons) **Facilities** ⋔ 🏠 ⊙ ⊟ ⌀ ☎ **Services** ⊈ ⛧ ⊞ 🖥 **Leisure** ⊸ LPR

ROQUE-D'ANTHÉRON, LA BOUCHES-DU-RHÔNE

Domaine les Iscles

13640 ☎ 442504425 ▤ 442505629
e-mail iscles@village-center.com
website www.village-center.com
➲ *1.8km N via D67c.*
Open 31 Apr-16 Sep **Site** 10HEC ♨ ♣ ⊞ **Prices** ♠ 3-4.50 pitch 10.10-19 ⊟ (static)231-728 **Facilities** ⋔ 🏠 ⊙ ⊟ ⌀ ♨ ☎ **Services** ⊈ ⛧ ⊞ 🖥 **Leisure** ⊸ LPR

Silvacane

av de la Libération, 13640 ☎ 442504054 ▤ 442504375
e-mail silvacane@village-center.com
website www.village-center.com
Level gravelled ground with pitches of 100 sq m. Water-sports centre and stables nearby. Site in wood on slopes of hill.
Open 16 Jun-2 Sep **Site** 6HEC ♨ ♣ ⊞ **Prices** ♠ 3.60-4.50 pitch 8.80-13 **Facilities** ⋔ ⊙ ⊟ ⌀ ♨ ☎ **Services** ⊈ ⛧ ⊞ 🖥 **Leisure** ⊸ PR **Off-site** 🏠 ⊸LR

Site 6HEC (site size) ♨ grass ⊜ sand ♠ stone ♣ little shade ⊞ partly shaded ⊜ mainly shaded ⊞ bungalows for hire ⊟ caravans for hire Δ tents for hire ⊗ no dogs **Prices** ♠ adult per night ⊸ car per night pp per person per night ⊟ caravan per night Δ tent per night ⊟ (static)-caravan hire per week

ROQUETTE-SUR-SIAGNE, LA ALPES-MARITIMES

Panoramic

1630 av de la République, Quartier St-Jean, 06550
☎ 492190777 🖷 492190777
e-mail campingpanoramic@wanadoo.fr
website www.campingpanoramic.fr
A well-equipped, modern site in a wooded location affording magnificent views of the surrounding hills.

⮞ *N of village off D9.*

Open All year **Site** 1HEC 👑 😁 🏕 🛆 ⊗ **Prices** ♠ 3.50 pitch 14-15 **Facilities** 🍴 ⊙ 🔌 🗻 🅿 **Services** 🍽 🍴 ➕ 🗑 **Leisure** 🏊 P **Off-site** 🗑 🏊R

St-Louis

av de la République, 6550 ☎ 492192313 🖷 492192314
Well-equipped site in a pleasant rural setting backed by hills.

⮞ *D9 from Pégomas towards La Bocca, site 0.8km.*

Open Apr-1 Oct **Site** 5HEC 👑 😁 🏕 **Facilities** 🍴 ⊙ 🔌 🅿 🅿 **Services** ➕ 🗑 **Leisure** 🏊 P **Off-site** 🏪 🍴 🍽 🗻 🏊R ➕

RUOMS ARDÈCHE

Bastide

7120 ☎ 475396472 🖷 475397328
e-mail info@rcn-labastideardeche.fr
website www.rcn-campings.fr
Well-equipped family site in a pleasant wooded location.

⮞ *4km SW on the banks of the Ardèche.*

Open 16 Apr-8 Oct **Site** 7HEC 👑 😁 🏕 🛆 **Facilities** 🍴 🏪 ⊙ 🔌 🅿 🗻 🅿 **Services** 🍽 🍴 ➕ 🗑 **Leisure** 🏊 PR

Ternis

rte de Lagorce, 07120 ☎ 475939315 🖷 475939090
e-mail campternis@aol.com
website www.camping.leternis.com
A terraced site in a delightful setting in the southern Ardèche region, with good recreational facilities. Separate car park for arrivals from 22.00 to 08.00 hrs.

⮞ *D559 towards Lagorce.*

Open May-18 Sep **Site** 6HEC 👑 😁 🏕 🏕 **Facilities** 🍴 🏪 ⊙ 🔌 🅿 🗻 🅿 🅿 **Services** 🍽 🍴 ➕ 🗑 **Leisure** 🏊 P **Off-site** 🏊R

AT SAMPZON (6KM S)

Aloha-Plage

07120 ☎ 608988503 🖷 475891026
e-mail reception@camping-aloha-plage.fr
website www.camping-aloha-plage.fr
A fine location beside the River Ardèche, midway between Ruoms and Vallon-Pont-d'Arc. The site has two private swimming pools.

⮞ *50m from river.*

Open Apr-20 Sep **Site** 3HEC 👑 😁 🏕 🏕 **Prices** pitch 23 (incl 2 persons) pp3-4.50 🏕 (static)170-390 **Facilities** 🍴 ⊙ 🔌 🅿 🗻 🅿 **Services** 🍽 🍴 ➕ 🗑 **Leisure** 🏊 PR **Off-site** 🏪

Riviera

☎ 475396757 🖷 475939557
e-mail leriviera@wanadoo.fr
website www.campingleriviera.com
Located on the banks of the Ardèche river, just a short distance from the Pont d'Arc.

⮞ *From Valence exit autoroute at Montelimar Nord for Le Teil/Ruoms/Sampzon.*

Open Apr-Sep **Site** 6HEC 👑 😁 🏕 🛆 **Prices** pitch 15-32 **Facilities** 🍴 🏪 ⊙ 🔌 🅿 🅿 🅿 **Services** 🍽 🍴 🗑 **Leisure** 🏊 PR **Off-site** ➕

Soleil Vivarais

07120 ☎ 475396756 🖷 475396469
e-mail info@soleil-vivarais.com
website www.soleil-vivarais.com
An exceptionally well-appointed, terraced site surrounded by the imposing scenery of the Ardèche Gorge. An excellent canoeing centre with opportunities for outdoor and water activities, and regular organised entertainment.

⮞ *D579 from Vallon towards Ruoms for 5km & over River Ardèche.*

Open 31 Mar-16 Sep **Site** 12HEC 👑 😁 🏕 **Prices** pitch 17-42 (incl 2 persons) pp4.50-7.80 **Facilities** 🍴 🏪 ⊙ 🔌 🅿 🅿 🅿 **Services** 🍽 🍴 🗑 **Leisure** 🏊 PR **Off-site** 🏊S ➕

SAILLAGOUSE PYRÉNÉES-ORIENTALES

Cerdan

11 Route d'Estavar, 66800 ☎ 468047046 🖷 468040526
e-mail lecerdan@lecerdan.com
website www.lecerdan.com
Picturesque setting in meadow with some terraces. Hot meals served during peak season.

⮞ *Via N116.*

Open All year **Site** 0.8HEC 👑 😁 🏕 **Facilities** 🍴 ⊙ 🔌 🅿 🗻 🅿 🅿 **Services** 🗑 **Off-site** 🏪 🍴 🍽 🗻 🏊PR ➕

ST-ALBAN-AURIOLLES ARDÈCHE

Ranc Davaine

07120 ☎ 475396055 🖷 475393850
e-mail camping.ranc.davaine@wanadoo.fr
website www.camping-ranc-davaine.fr
Well-equipped, mainly level site with direct access to the River Chassezac and a variety of entertainment facilities.

⮞ *2.3km SW via D58.*

Open 30 Mar-16 Sep **Site** 13HEC 👑 😁 🏕 🏕 **Prices** ♠ 6.40-9.60 pitch 25.75-40.20 (incl 2 persons) 🏕 (static)287-1078 **Facilities** 🍴 🏪 ⊙ 🔌 🅿 🗻 🅿 **Services** 🍽 🍴 ➕ 🗑 **Leisure** 🏊 PR

ST-AMBROIX GARD

Beau-Rivage

Le Moulinet, 30500 ☎ 466241017 🖷 466242137
e-mail marc@camping-beau-rivage.fr
website www.camping-beau-rivage.fr
A good location between the sea and the Cevennes mountains, set beside the River Cèze.

⮞ *3.5km SE on D37.*

Open Apr-Sep **Site** 3.5HEC 👑 😁 **Prices** ♠ 6 pitch 5 **Facilities** 🍴 ⊙ 🔌 🅿 🅿 **Services** ➕ 🗑 **Leisure** 🏊 R **Off-site** 🏪 🍴 🍽

Facilities 🏪 shop 🍴 shower ⊙ electric points for razors 🔌 electric points for caravans 🅿 parking by tents permitted 🅿 compulsory separate car park
Services 🍴 café/restaurant 🍽 bar ⌀ Camping Gaz International 🗻 gas other than Camping Gaz ➕ first aid facilities 🗑 laundry
Leisure 🏊 swimming L-Lake P-Pool R-River S-Sea **Off-site** All facilities within 2km

Ideally located in the heart of the Côte d'Azur, exceptional site with friendly atmosphere on the banks of the Argens river with direct access to the fine sandy beaches (there is one for naturists). Bar, restaurant, take away food, swimming-pool which is heated in cool weather.
Entertainment: discotheque, giant barbecues, cabarets, concerts, excursions and a miniclub for children.
Mobile home and caravans available for hire.
Open from 1 April to 15 October.

Camping Caravanning Le Pont d'Argens
RN 98 Fréjus Saint Aygulf – FRANCE
Tél: 04 94 51 14 97 – Fax: 04 94 51 29 44

Clos

30500 ☎ 466241008 📄 466602562
e-mail campingleclos@wanadoo.fr
website www.camping-le-clos.com
A quiet site in a pleasant setting beside the River Cèze with modern facilities.
➲ Off church square.
Open Apr-Oct **Site** 1.8HEC 🌱 🏖 🏠 **Facilities** 🚿 ⊙ 🚰 ⊘ 🚮 ⊛ **Services** 🍴 🍽 🔋 🛒 **Leisure** ⚓ PR **Off-site** 🛁

ST-ANDIOL BOUCHES-DU-RHÔNE

St-Andiol

13670 ☎ 490950113
e-mail mendez11@viola.fr
Site on the edge of the village, divided into pitches.
➲ Via A7.
Open All year **Site** 1HEC 🌱 🏠 **Facilities** 🚿 ⊙ 🚰 ⊛ **Services** 🍴 🔋 🛒 **Leisure** ⚓ P **Off-site** 🛁 🍽

ST-AYGULF VAR

Étoile d'Argens

chemin des Étangs, 83370 ☎ 494810141 📄 494812145
e-mail info@etoiledargens.com
website www.etoiledargens.com
Pleasant wooded surroundings 2km from the beach, which can be reached by a private boat service.
➲ 5km NW, beside River Argens.
Open Apr-Sep **Site** 11HEC 🌱 🏖 🏠 🚐 **Prices** ♠ 5-8 🚗 4 pitch 20-49 (incl 2 persons)245-917 🚐 **Facilities** 🚿 🛁 ⊙ 🚰 ⊘ 🚮 ⊛ **Services** 🍴 🍽 🔋 🛒 **Leisure** ⚓ PR **Off-site** ⚓L

Paradis des Campeurs

La Gaillarde Plage, 83380 ☎ 494969355 📄 494496299
website www.paradis-des-campeurs.com
A quiet family site in a picturesque location with direct access to the beach.
➲ 2.5km towards Gaillarde-Plage between St-Aygulf & Ste-Maxime.
Open 29 Mar-16 Oct **Site** 3.7HEC 🌱 🏖 🏠 **Facilities** 🚿 🛁 ⊙ 🚰 ⊘ ⊛ **Services** 🍴 🍽 🔋 🛒 **Leisure** ⚓ S

Pont d'Argens

RN98, 83370 ☎ 494511497 📄 494512944
website www.provence-campings.com/esterel/pont-argens.htm
A pleasant site with good facilities beside the river.
Open Apr-15 Oct **Site** 7HEC 🌱 🏖 🏠 🚐 **Prices** ♠ 5-7 🚗 2 pitch 13.50-24 **Facilities** 🚿 🛁 ⊙ 🚰 ⊘ 🚮 ⊛ **Services** 🍴 🍽 🔋 🛒 **Leisure** ⚓ PRS

See advertisement on this page

St-Aygulf

270 av Salvarelli, 83370 ☎ 494176249 📄 494810316
e-mail info@camping-cote-azur.com
A well-equipped family site in wooded surroundings with direct access to the beach.
➲ Inland from N98 at Km881.3 N of town. Entrance on right of av Salvarelli.
Open Apr-Oct **Site** 22HEC 🌱 🏖 🏠 **Prices** ♠ 3-7.50 🚗 2-4.50 🚐 3.50-6 🔺 1.20-2.50 **Facilities** 🚿 🛁 ⊙ 🚰 ⊘ 🚮 ⊛ **Services** 🍴 🍽 🔋 🛒 **Leisure** ⚓ S

See advertisement on page 195

ST-CHAMAS BOUCHES-DU-RHÔNE

Canet Plage

13250 ☎ 490509689 📄 490509689 & 490508751
e-mail canet-plage@wanadoo.fr
website www.camping-lecanet.com
A well-equipped site beside the Étang de Berre with a range of recreational facilities.
➲ On D10, S of Salon-de-Provence towards La Fare les Oliviers.
Open All year **Site** 3HEC 🌱 🏖 🏠 **Facilities** 🚿 🛁 ⊙ 🚰 🚮 ⊛ **Services** 🍴 🍽 🔋 🛒 **Leisure** ⚓ LP **Off-site** ⊘

ST-CYPRIEN PYRÉNÉES-ORIENTALES

Roussillon

chemin de la Mer, 66750 ☎ 468210645 📄 251339404
e-mail chadotel@wanadoo.fr
website www.camping_le_roussilon.fr
Close to the Spanish border, flanked on one side by the Mediterrannean sea and on the other by the Pyrenees.
Open Apr-Sep **Site** 3HEC 🌱 🏖 🏠 🚐 **Facilities** 🚿 🛁 ⊙ 🚰 ⊘ 🚮 ⊛ **Services** 🍴 🍽 🔋 🛒 **Leisure** ⚓ P **Off-site** 🍽 ⚓S

ST-CYR-SUR-MER VAR

Clos Ste-Thérèse

rte de Bandol, 83270 ☎ 494321221 📄 494322962
e-mail camping@clos-therese.com
website www.clos-therese.com
Located in the heart of the Bandol vinefields overlooking the sea. A well-shaded family site with well-defined pitches on terraces.
➲ Autoroute A50
Open Apr-Sep **Site** 4HEC 🌱 🏖 🏠 **Prices** ♠ 3.20-4.80 pitch 13.30-20 (incl 2 persons) **Facilities** 🚿 🛁 ⊙ 🚰 🚮 ⊛ **Services** 🍴 🍽 🔋 🛒 **Leisure** ⚓ P **Off-site** ⊘

ST-JEAN-LE-CENTENIER ARDÈCHE

Arches
Patrick Gaschet, 07580 ☎ 475367545 ▤ 475367545
e-mail info@camping-les-arches.com
website www.camping-les-arches.com
A family site in a wooded location with direct access to the river.
➩ *A7 exit Montélimar Nord, N102 to Mirabel, onto D458 for 0.5km.*
Open May-15 Sep **Site** 4HEC ❤️ ❤️ 🏠 🚐 **Prices** ⭐ 3.60 🚐 0.80-3 🚐 1-2 ⚠ 1-2 🚐 (static)220-260 **Facilities** 🚿 ☉ 🔌 ⓟ **Services** 🍴 🍽️ 🗑 **Leisure** ⚓ R **Off-site** 🏪 🍽️ 🏊

ST-JEAN-PLA-DE-CORTS PYRÉNÉES-ORIENTALES

Casteillets
66490 ☎ 468832683 ▤ 468833967
e-mail jc@campinglescasteillets.com
website www.campinglescasteillets.com
A family site between the sea and the mountains close to the River Tech.
➩ *A9 exit le Boulu.*
Open All year **Site** 5HEC ❤️ ❤️ 🏠 ⚠ **Prices** ⭐ 2.50-4 pitch 10.30-15.50 (incl 2 persons) 🚐 (static)220-510 **Facilities** 🚿 🏪 ☉ 🔌 🏊 ⓟ **Services** 🍴 🍽️ ➕ 🗑 **Leisure** ⚓ P **Off-site** ∅ ⚓LR

Deux Rivières
rte de Maureillas, 66490 ☎ 468832320 ▤ 468830794
website www.2rivieres.com
Situated on the banks of the River Tech with large roomy pitches.
➩ *0.5km SE via D13, beside River Tech.*
Open Apr-15 Oct **Site** 11HEC ❤️ ❤️ 🏠 🚐 **Facilities** 🚿 🏪 ☉ 🔌 ∅ 🏊 ⓟ **Services** 🍴 🍽️ 🗑 **Leisure** ⚓ PR **Off-site** ⚓L ➕

ST-JULIEN-DE-LA-NEF GARD

Isis en Cevennes
Domaine de St-Julien, 30440 ☎ 467738028 ▤ 467738848
e-mail aa@isisencevennes.com
website www.isisencevennes.com
Set in wooded surroundings with direct access to the River Hérault. Plenty of sports facilities.
➩ *5km from Ganges towards Le Vigan.*
Open Mar-Oct **Site** 14HEC ❤️ ❤️ 🏠 **Prices** ⭐ 3.90 🚐 3.30 pitch 4.20 **Facilities** 🚿 🏪 ☉ 🔌 ∅ 🏊 ⓟ **Services** 🍴 🍽️ ➕ 🗑 **Leisure** ⚓ PR

ST-LAURENT-DU-VAR ALPES-MARITIMES

Magali
1814 rte de la Baronne, 06700 ☎ 493315700 ▤ 492120133
website www.camping-magali.com
A family site on level meadowland, surrounded by trees and bushes at the foot of the southern Alps.
➩ *A8 exit St-Laurent-du-Var, cross industrial zone, turn left for 100m, then right for 2km.*
Open Feb-Oct **Site** 1.2HEC ❤️ ❤️ 🏠 🚐 **Prices** pitch 15.30-22.30 (incl 3 persons) pp3.30-3.80 🚐 (static)182-320 **Facilities** 🚿 🏪 ☉ 🔌 ∅ 🏊 ⓟ **Services** 🍽️ ➕ 🗑 **Leisure** ⚓ P **Off-site** 🍴 🍽️

The sea, the sun, the fine sandy beaches near the campsite

Parc Camping de Saint Aygulf Plage

270, avenue Salvarelli
83378 Saint-Aygulf-Plage

This park of 22 hectares at the Mediterranean Sea and surrounded by the small lakes of Villepey offers you a refreshing site in a shady pine forest. Rental of pitches, mobile homes and chalets. Extensive offer of services, sports activities and animation.

Phone.: +33 04 94 17 62 49 • Mobile: 06 12 44 36 52
Fax: 04 94 81 03 16 • www.camping-cote-azur.com

ST-LAURENT-DU-VERDON ALPES-DE-HAUTE-PROVENCE

Farigoulette
Lac de St Laurent, 4500 ☎ 492744162 ▤ 492740086
website www.camping-la-farigoulette.com
➩ *1.5km NE near Verdon.*
Open 15 May-Sep **Site** 14HEC ❤️ ❤️ ❤️ 🏠 🚐 **Facilities** 🚿 🏪 ☉ 🔌 ∅ 🏊 ⓟ **Services** 🍴 🍽️ ➕ 🗑 **Leisure** ⚓ LP **Off-site** ⚓S

ST-MAXIMIN-LA-STE-BAUME VAR

Provençal
rte de Mazaugues, 83470 ☎ 494781697 ▤ 494780022
e-mail camping.provencal@wanadoo.fr
A family site in wooded surroundings with plenty of recreational facilties. Bar, café and swimming pool only open July and August.
➩ *2.5km S via D64.*
Open Apr-Sep **Site** 5HEC ❤️ ❤️ 🚐 **Facilities** 🚿 ☉ 🔌 ∅ 🏊 ⓟ **Services** 🍴 🍽️ ➕ 🗑 **Leisure** ⚓ P **Off-site** ➕

ST-PAUL-EN-FORÊT VAR

Parc
83440 ☎ 494761535 ▤ 494847184
e-mail campingleparc@wanadoo.fr
website www.campingleparc.com
Quiet, fairly isolated site surrounded by woodland.
➩ *3km N on D4.*
Open Apr-Sep **Site** 3.1HEC ❤️ ❤️ 🏠 🚐 ⚠ **Prices** pitch 10.50-19 (incl 2 persons) pp4.10-6.20 🚐 (static)180-670 **Facilities** 🚿 🏪 ☉ 🔌 ∅ 🏊 ⓟ ⓟ **Services** 🍴 🍽️ ➕ 🗑 **Leisure** ⚓ LPS

Facilities 🏪 shop 🚿 shower ☉ electric points for razors 🔌 electric points for caravans ⓟ parking by tents permitted ⓟ compulsory separate car park
Services 🍽️ café/restaurant 🍴 bar ∅ Camping Gaz International 🏊 gas other than Camping Gaz ➕ first aid facilities 🗑 laundry
Leisure ⚓ swimming L-Lake P-Pool R-River S-Sea **Off-site** All facilities within 2km

France

ST-PAUL-LES-ROMANS DRÔME

CM de Romans
Les Chasses, 26100 ☎ 475723527
Shady pitches separated by hedges.
Open Apr-15 Oct **Site** 1HEC ꜱ ꜱ ꜱ **Prices** ♠ 2.10 ꜱ 1.20 ꜱ 2.40 Å 2.40
Facilities ꜰ ⊙ ꜱ ⅌ **Services** ꜱ ꜱ **Off-site** ꜱ ꜱ ꜱ ꜱ ꜱ ꜱ P

ST-RAPHAËL VAR

Douce Quiétude
bd J-Baudino, 83700 ☎ 494443000 ꜱ 494443030
e-mail sunelia@douce-quietude.com
website www.douce-quietude.com
Meadowland site in quiet location in attractively hilly countryside with good facilities.
➾ *Via Agay Plage past Esterel Camping towards Valescure.*
Open Apr-Sep **Site** 10HEC ꜱ ꜱ ꜱ ꜱ **Facilities** ꜰ ꜱ ⊙ ꜱ ꜱ ꜱ ꜱ ⅌ ꜱ
Services ꜱ ꜱ ꜱ ꜱ **Leisure** ꜱ P

Dramont
83700 ☎ 494820768 ꜱ 494827530
Located in a pine forest with direct access to the beach and modern facilities.
➾ *Via N98 at St-Raphaël, between Boulouris & Agay.*
Open 15 Mar-15 Oct **Site** 6.5HEC ꜱ ꜱ ꜱ ꜱ **Prices** pitch 17-37 (incl 2 persons) ꜱ (static)245-812 **Facilities** ꜰ ꜱ ⊙ ꜱ ꜱ ꜱ **Services** ꜱ ꜱ ꜱ
ꜱ **Leisure** ꜱ S

Royal
Camp Long, 83530 ☎ 494820020
Level site divided by walls and hedges. Ideal bathing for children. Bar and hall next to site.
➾ *On N98 towards Cannes.*
Open 20 Jan-30 Oct **Site** 0.6HEC ꜱ ꜱ ꜱ ꜱ **Facilities** ꜰ ꜱ ⊙ ꜱ ꜱ ꜱ
⅌ **Services** ꜱ ꜱ ꜱ ꜱ **Leisure** ꜱ S **Off-site** ꜱ ꜱ

ST-REMÈZE ARDÈCHE

Domaine de Briange
rte de Gras, 07700 ☎ 475041443
e-mail briange07@aol.com
website members.aol.com/briange07
Wooded location close to the Gorges de l'Ardèche.
➾ *1.5km NE.*
Open May-Sep **Site** 4HEC ꜱ ꜱ ꜱ ꜱ Å **Facilities** ꜰ ꜱ ⊙ ꜱ ⅌
Services ꜱ ꜱ ꜱ ꜱ **Leisure** ꜱ P **Off-site** ꜱ ꜱ

ST-RÉMY-DE-PROVENCE BOUCHES-DU-RHÔNE

Monplaisir
chemin Monplaisir, 13210 ☎ 490922270 ꜱ 490921857
e-mail reception@camping-monplaisir.fr
website www.camping-monplaisir.fr
Open Mar-10 Nov **Site** 2.8HEC ꜱ ꜱ ꜱ ꜱ **Prices** pitch 12.70-17.50
Facilities ꜰ ꜱ ⊙ ꜱ ꜱ ⅌ **Services** ꜱ ꜱ ꜱ **Leisure** ꜱ P

Pégomas
Av jean Moulin, 13210 ☎ 490920121 ꜱ 490920121
e-mail contact@campingpegomas.com
website www.campingpegomas.com
Well-tended grassland with trees and bushes. Divided into several fields with high cedars providing shade.
➾ *0.5km E of village, signed.*
Open Mar-Oct **Site** 2HEC ꜱ ꜱ ꜱ ꜱ **Prices** ♠ 8.50-11.50 pitch 9-10.50
Facilities ꜰ ꜱ ⊙ ꜱ ꜱ ⅌ **Services** ꜱ ꜱ ꜱ ꜱ **Leisure** ꜱ P
Off-site ꜱ ꜱ ꜱ

ST-ROMAIN-EN-VIENNOIS VAUCLUSE

Soleil de Provence
rte de Nyons, 84110 ☎ 490464600 ꜱ 490464037
e-mail info@camping-soleil-de-provence.fr
website www.camping-soleil-de-provence.fr
Peaceful site on an uphill meadow 12km from the foot of Mt Ventoux, with superb views of the surrounding mountains. Large swimming pool with an island and palm trees.
➾ *4km from Vaison-la-Romaine*
Open 15 Mar-Oct **Site** 5HEC ꜱ ꜱ ꜱ ꜱ ꜱ **Prices** ♠ 3.50-5.50 ꜱ 3-4 pitch
3-4 **Facilities** ꜰ ꜱ ⊙ ꜱ ꜱ ꜱ **Services** ꜱ ꜱ ꜱ ꜱ **Leisure** ꜱ P

ST-SAUVEUR-DE-MONTAGUT ARDÈCHE

Ardechois
Le Chambon, Gluiras, 07190 ☎ 475666187 ꜱ 475666367
e-mail ardechois.camping@wanadoo.fr
website www.ardechois-camping.fr
Set in the grounds of a restored 18th-century farm in rolling countryside. Fine views of the surrounding hills.
➾ *8.5km W on D102, beside River Glueyre.*
Open 27 Apr-Sep **Site** 5.5HEC ꜱ ꜱ ꜱ **Prices** pitch 19-26.50 (incl 2 persons) ꜱ (static)285-665 **Facilities** ꜰ ꜱ ⊙ ꜱ ꜱ ꜱ ⅌ **Services** ꜱ ꜱ
ꜱ ꜱ **Leisure** ꜱ PR

ST-SORLIN-EN-VALLOIRE DRÔME

Château de la Pérouze
26210 ☎ 475317021 ꜱ 475316274
e-mail campingchateaudelaperouz@libertysurf.fr
A well-appointed family site with a variety of recreational facilities.
➾ *2.5km SE via D1.*
Open 15 Jun-15 Sep **Site** 14HEC ꜱ ꜱ ꜱ ꜱ ꜱ **Facilities** ꜰ ꜱ ⊙ ꜱ ꜱ ꜱ ⅌
Services ꜱ ꜱ ꜱ ꜱ **Leisure** ꜱ LP

ST-THIBÉRY HÉRAULT

Tane
Le Causse, 34630 ☎ 467778429
website www.campinglepinparasol.com
Pleasant wooded surroundings 1km from the River Hérault.
➾ *A9 exit Agde-Pézenas.*
Open Jun-Sep **Site** 2.7HEC ꜱ ꜱ ꜱ **Prices** pitch 10-13 (incl 2 persons)
Facilities ꜰ ꜱ ⊙ ꜱ ꜱ **Services** ꜱ ꜱ ꜱ **Leisure** ꜱ P **Off-site** ꜱ ꜱ ꜱ
ꜱR ꜱ

Site 6HEC (site size) ꜱ grass ꜱ sand ꜱ stone ꜱ little shade ꜱ partly shaded ꜱ mainly shaded ꜱ bungalows for hire
ꜱ caravans for hire Å tents for hire ꜱ no dogs **Prices** ♠ adult per night ꜱ car per night pp per person per night ꜱ caravan per night
Å tent per night ꜱ (static)-caravan hire per week

ST-VALLIER-DE-THIEY ALPES-MARITIMES

Parc des Arboins

755 RN85, 06460 ☎ 493426389 ▤ 493096154
e-mail reception@parc-des-arboins.com
website www.parc-des-arboins.com
Pleasantly terraced site on a hillside with some oak trees.

➲ Off N85 at KmV36.

Open All year **Site** 4HEC 😃 😃 😃 🏠 🚐 **Facilities** � ⊙ 🚘 ⌀ 🚿 ℗
Services 🍺 🍽 ➕ ▣ **Leisure** 🏊 P **Off-site** 🖾

STE-MARIE PYRÉNÉES-ORIENTALES

AT TORREILLES (4KM NW ON D11)

Dunes de Torreilles

66440 ☎ 468283829 ▤ 468283257
e-mail lesdunes@lesdunes.net
website www.lesdunes.net
A well-equipped site in wooded surroundings with direct access to the beach.

➲ E of village off D81.

Open 15 Mar-15 Oct **Site** 16HEC 😃 😃 😃 🏠 **Prices** pitch 14.50-31
Facilities 🌫 🖾 ⊙ 🚘 ⌀ ℗ **Services** 🍺 🍽 ➕ ▣ **Leisure** 🏊 PS
Off-site 🏊R

Spa Marisol

Plage de Torreilles, 66440 ☎ 468280407 ▤ 468281823
e-mail marisol@camping-marisol.com
website www.camping-marisol.com
A family site with a variety of sports and entertainment facilities in a pleasant park-like setting 350m from the beach.

➲ Off D81 towards sea.

Open Apr-Sep **Site** 9HEC 😃 😃 😃 🏠 🛡 **Prices** 🛡 5.30-8.10 pitch 15-39
(incl 2 persons) **Facilities** 🌫 🖾 ⊙ 🚘 ⌀ 🚿 ℗ **Services** 🍺 🍽 ➕ ▣
Leisure 🏊 PS **Off-site** 🏊R

Trivoly

bd des Plages, 66440 ☎ 468282028 ▤ 468281648
e-mail chadotel@wanadoo.fr
website www.chadotel.com
A modern site with excellent facilities and well-defined pitches, 0.8km from the beach.

➲ Autoroute exit Perpignan Nord for Le Barcarès.

Open Apr-Sep **Site** 4.7HEC 😃 😃 🏠 **Prices** 🛡 5.80 pitch 14.50-24.20 (incl 2 persons) 🚐 (static)220-750 **Facilities** 🌫 🖾 ⊙ 🚘 ⌀ ℗ **Services** 🍺
🍽 ➕ ▣ **Leisure** 🏊 P **Off-site** 🍽 🏊RS

STES-MARIES-DE-LA-MER BOUCHES-DU-RHÔNE

CM Brise

13460 ☎ 490978467 ▤ 490977201
e-mail labrise@saintesmaries.com
A well-equipped family site with direct access to the beach, situated in the heart of the Camargue. Modern sanitary blocks and facilities for a variety of sports.

➲ NE on D85A towards beach.

Open 15 Dec-15 Nov **Site** 22HEC 😃 😃 😃 🏠 🛡 **Prices** 🛡 4.20-6.90 pitch 11.40-18.90 (incl 2 persons) 🚐 (static)245-592 **Facilities** 🌫 🖾 ⊙ 🚘 ⌀ ℗
Services 🍺 ➕ ▣ **Leisure** 🏊 P **Off-site** 🍽 🚿 🏊RS

Clos-du-Rhône

BP 74, 13460 ☎ 490978599 ▤ 490977885
e-mail leclos@saintesmaries.com
➲ 2km W via D38, near beach.

Open Apr-15 Nov **Site** 7HEC 😃 😃 🏠 🛡 **Prices** 🛡 4.60-7.20 pitch 14.50-20
(incl 2 persons) **Facilities** 🌫 🖾 ⊙ 🚘 ⌀ ℗ **Services** 🍺 🍽 ➕ ▣
Leisure 🏊 PRS

SALAVAS ARDÈCHE

Chauvieux

07150 ☎ 475880537 ▤ 475880537
e-mail camping.chauvieux@wanadoo.fr
website www.camping-le-chauvieux.com
A popular site in a wooded location close to the River Ardèche with plenty of recreational facilities. Advance booking recommended.

➲ NE off D579.

Open 27 Apr-9 Sep **Site** 2.3HEC 😃 😃 😃 🏠 **Prices** 🛡 5 🚐 2 pitch 13-19.90 (incl 2 persons) 🚐 (static)245-615 **Facilities** 🌫 🖾 ⊙ 🚘 ⌀ ℗
Services 🍺 🍽 ➕ ▣ **Leisure** 🏊 PR

SALERNES VAR

Arnauds

Quartier des Arnauds, 83690 ☎ 494675195 ▤ 494707557
e-mail lesarnauds@ville-salernes.fr
website www.ville-salernes.fr
Level site alongside a river and a lake.

➲ Via D560 just beyond village.

Open 2 May-Sep **Site** 3HEC 😃 😃 🏠 **Prices** 🛡 4.40-6.40 pitch 8-10
Facilities 🌫 ⊙ 🚘 ℗ **Services** 🍺 🍽 ➕ ▣ **Leisure** 🏊 R **Off-site** 🖾 🍽
⌀ 🚿

SALINS-D'HYÈRES, LES VAR

Port Pothuau

101 chemin les Ourledes, 83400 ☎ 494664117 ▤ 494663309
e-mail pothuau@free.fr
website www.campingportpothuau.com
A peaceful holiday village, completely divided into pitches with good leisure facilities.

➲ 6km E of Hyères on N98 & D12.

Open 4 Apr-19 Oct **Site** 6HEC 😃 😃 🏠 🚐 **Facilities** 🌫 🖾 ⊙ 🚘 ⌀ 🚿 ℗
Services 🍺 🍽 ➕ ▣ **Leisure** 🏊 P **Off-site** 🏊RS

SALON-DE-PROVENCE BOUCHES-DU-RHÔNE

Nostradamus

rte d'Eyguières, 13300 ☎ 490560836 ▤ 490566505
e-mail gilles.nostra@wanadoo.fr
website www.camping-nostradamus.com
Pleasant wooded surroundings with good sports facilities.

➲ 5km W on D17 towards Eyguières & Arles.

Open Mar-Oct **Site** 2.2HEC 😃 😃 🏠 **Prices** 🛡 4.76-5.60 🚐 1.62-1.90 🚐 4-4.50 🛡 4-4.50 **Facilities** 🌫 🖾 ⊙ 🚘 ⌀ ℗ **Services** 🍺 🍽 ➕ ▣
Leisure 🏊 PR

France

Facilities 🖾 shop 🌫 shower ⊙ electric points for razors 🚘 electric points for caravans ℗ parking by tents permitted 🚻 compulsory separate car park
Services 🍽 café/restaurant 🍺 bar ⌀ Camping Gaz International 🚿 gas other than Camping Gaz ➕ first aid facilities ▣ laundry
Leisure 🏊 swimming L-Lake P-Pool R-River S-Sea **Off-site** All facilities within 2km

SALVETAT, LA HÉRAULT

Goudal

rte de Lacaune, 34330 ☎ 467976044 ▤ 467976268
e-mail info@goudal.com
website www.goudal.com
A natural mountain setting within the Haut Lanquedoc park.

➲ *Via D907.*

Open May-Sep **Site** 5HEC ⚌ ♣ ☙ ᐱ **Prices** ♠ 2.50-3 ⛟ 1.20-1.50 pitch
11-22.35 (incl 2 persons) **Facilities** ℾ ▣ ☺ ☕ ♨ ⓟ **Services** ⌕ ⍟ ➕ ▦
Leisure ⚲ L **Off-site** ⚲R

SANARY-SUR-MER VAR

Campasun Parc Mogador

83110 ☎ 494745316 ▤ 494741058
e-mail mogador@campasun.com
website ww.campasun.com
Situated 0.8km from the sea, the well-kept site is divided into pitches
by hedges.

➲ *2km NW, off N559 at Km15 & next left.*

Open 15 Mar-8 Nov, 15 Dec-2 Jan **Site** 2.7HEC ⚌ ♣ ☙ ⊗ **Prices** pitch
16-35 (incl 2 persons) **Facilities** ℾ ▣ ☺ ☕ ♨ ⓟ **Services** ⌕ ⍟ ➕ ▦
Leisure ⚲ P **Off-site** ⌀ ⚲S

Girelles

chemin de Beaucours, 83110 ☎ 494741318 ▤ 494746004
website www.lesgirelles.com
A modern family site with good facilities and direct access to the sea.

➲ *3km NW via D539, beside sea.*

Open Etr-24 Sep **Site** 2HEC ⚌ ♣ ☙ ☕ **Prices** ♠ 5.30-6.30 pitch 15.90-
23.90 (incl 2 persons) ⛟ (static)410-680 **Facilities** ℾ ▣ ☺ ☕ ⌀ ⓟ
Services ⌕ ⍟ ➕ ▦ **Leisure** ⚲ S

Pierredon

652 Chemin Raoul Coletta, 83110 ☎ 494742502 ▤ 494746142
e-mail pierredon@campasun.com
website www.campasun.com
A well-equipped, wooded site providing a variety of family
entertainment, 3km from the sea.

➲ *A50 exit Bandol or Sanary.*

Open Apr-Sep **Site** 4HEC ⚌ ♣ ☙ ᐱ **Prices** pitch 16-35 (incl 2 persons)
Facilities ℾ ☺ ☕ ♨ ⓟ **Services** ⌕ ⍟ ➕ ▦ **Leisure** ⚲ P
Off-site ▣ ⌀ ➕

SAUVIAN HÉRAULT

Gabinelle

34410 ☎ 467395087
website www.gabinelle.com
A modern site in pleasant wooded surroundings with good facilities.

➲ *D19 from Sauvian towards Valras Plage.*

Open 15 Apr-15 Sep **Site** 4HEC ⚌ ♣ ☙ ⛟ ᐱ **Facilities** ℾ ☺ ☕ ⓟ
Services ⌕ ⍟ ➕ ▦ **Leisure** ⚲ P **Off-site** ⌀ ♨ ⚲R

SÉRIGNAN-PLAGE HÉRAULT

Clos Virgile

34410 ☎ 467322064 ▤ 467320542
e-mail le.clos.virgile@wanadoo.fr
website leclosvirgile.com
Situated 400m from the beach, the site is on level meadowland with
large pitches and has two well-kept sanitary blocks.

Open May-15 Sep **Site** 5HEC ⚌ ♣ ☙ ☙ **Facilities** ℾ ▣ ☺ ☕ ⌀ ♨ ⓟ
Services ⌕ ⍟ ➕ ▦ **Leisure** ⚲ PS

Grand Large

34410 ☎ 467397130 ▤ 467325815
e-mail legrandlarge@wanadoo.fr
website www.camping-grandlarge.com
Situated by the sea with private access to the beach. Good facilities
and entertainment available in summer.

Open 26 Apr-14 Sep **Site** 7HEC ⚌ ♣ ☙ ☙ ᐱ **Facilities** ℾ ▣ ☺ ☕ ⌀ ♨
ⓟ **Services** ⌕ ⍟ ➕ ▦ **Leisure** ⚲ PS

Yelloh Village Le Sérignan-Plage

34410 ☎ 467323533 ▤ 467322636
e-mail info@leserignanplage.com
website www.leserignanplage.com
On a fine sandy beach, this is a family site with good recreational
facilities.

➲ *A9 exit Béziers Est.*

Open 26 Apr-23 Sep **Site** 16HEC ⚌ ♣ ☙ **Prices** pitch 17-43 (incl 2
persons) **Facilities** ℾ ▣ ☺ ☕ ⌀ ♨ ⓟ ⓟ **Services** ⌕ ⍟ ➕ ▦
Leisure ⚲ PS

SEYNE-SUR-MER, LA VAR

Mimosas

av M-Paul, 83500 ☎ 494947315 ▤ 494873613
e-mail camping-des-mimosas@wanadoo.fr
website www.camping-mimosas.com
Situated among pine trees facing the fortress of Six-Fours. Bar and
café only open in summer.

➲ *A50 exit 13 for La Seyne centre & towards Sanary-Bandol.*

Open All year **Site** 1.1HEC ⚌ ♣ ☙ ☙ ⛟ **Prices** pitch 11-14.50 (incl 3
persons) ⛟ (static)150-470 **Facilities** ℾ ☺ ☕ ♨ ⓟ **Services** ⌕ ⍟ ▦
Off-site ▣ ⌀ ⚲P ➕

SILLANS-LA-CASCADE BOUCHES-DU-RHÔNE

Relais de la Bresque

15 chemin de la Piscine, 83690 ☎ 494046489 ▤ 494771954
e-mail info@lerelaisdelabresque.com
A beautiful setting among pine trees with good sanitary and
recreational facilities.

Open Apr-Oct **Site** 3HEC ⚌ ♣ ☙ ⛟ **Facilities** ℾ ☺ ☕ ♨ ⓟ
Services ⌕ ⍟ ➕ ▦ **Off-site** ⚲PR

SIX-FOURS-LES-PLAGES VAR

Héliosports

La Font de Fillol, 83140 ☎ 494256276
Between the town centre and the beach.

➲ *1km W.*

Open 25 Mar-15 Oct **Site** 0.5HEC ⚌ ♣ ☙ **Facilities** ℾ ☺ ☕ ⓟ
Services ▦ **Off-site** ▣ ⌀ ⌕ ⍟ ♨ ⚲PS

Site 6HEC (site size) ⚌ grass ☙ sand ⚌ stone ♣ little shade ☙ partly shaded ☙ mainly shaded ☙ bungalows for hire
⛟ caravans for hire ᐱ tents for hire ⊗ no dogs **Prices** ♠ adult per night ⛟ car per night pp per person per night ⛟ caravan per night
ᐱ tent per night ⛟ (static)-caravan hire per week

International St-Jean

av de la Collégiale, 83140 ☎ 494875151 🗎 494062823

e-mail info@campingstjean.com

website www.campingstjean.com

Site with pitches, separated by hedges and reeds. Well managed, it lies just below the Fort Six-Fours.

⮑ *Via N559 & D63, via chemin de St-Jean.*

Open All year **Site** 3HEC 😸 ♨ 🏕 **Facilities** 🏠 🛁 ⊙ 🖭 🔌 🅿 ℗ **Services** 🍴 🍽 ➕ 🗐 **Leisure** ⚓ P **Off-site** 🍽

Playes

419 r Grand, 83140 ☎ 494255757 🗎 494071990

e-mail campingplayes@wanadoo.fr

website www.campingplayes.com

Terraced site on north side of town. Trees abound in this excellent location.

⮑ *Via N559 & D63, via chemin de St-Jean.*

Open All year **Site** 1.5HEC 😸 ♨ 🏕 🏕 🅰 **Facilities** 🏠 🛁 ⊙ 🖭 🔌 🚿 ℗ 🅿 **Services** 🍴 🍽 ➕ 🗐 **Off-site** 🖉 ⚓PS

SOSPEL ALPES-MARITIMES

Domaine St-Madeleine

rte de Moulinet, 06380 ☎ 493041048 🗎 493041837

e-mail camp@camping-sainte-madeleine.com

website camping-sainte-madeleine.com

A peaceful site in beautiful, unspoiled surroundings.

⮑ *4.5km NW via D2566.*

Open 26 Mar-2 Oct **Site** 3.5HEC 😸 ♨ 🏕 **Prices** pitch 19 (incl 2 persons) pp4.20 🏕 (static)210-410 **Facilities** 🏠 ⊙ 🖭 🔌 🚿 ℗ **Services** 🍴 ➕ 🗐 **Leisure** ⚓ P

SOUBÈS HÉRAULT

Les Rials

rte de Poujols, 34700 ☎ 467441553

e-mail mendez11@voila.fr

website www.campinglesrials.site.voila.fr

A terraced site in wooded surroundings on the banks of the River Lergue.

⮑ *4km from Lodève. 10km from Lac du Salagou.*

Open 25 Jun-Aug **Site** 3.5HEC 😸 ♨ **Facilities** 🏠 ⊙ 🖭 ℗ **Services** 🍴 ➕ 🗐 **Leisure** ⚓ PR **Off-site** 🛁 🍽

Sources

Soubes, 34700 ☎ 467443202 🗎 467443202

e-mail jlsources@wanadoo.fr

website www.campingdessources.cjb.net

A small, friendly site in a quiet location beside a river.

⮑ *5km NE, signed on N9.*

Open 15 May-15 Sep **Site** 1.3HEC 😸 ♨ ⊗ **Prices** pitch 14 (incl 2 persons) pp4.50 **Facilities** 🏠 ⊙ 🖭 ℗ **Services** 🍴 🍽 🗐 **Leisure** ⚓ PR **Off-site** 🛁 🍽 🖉 🚿 ⚓L ➕

TAIN-L'HERMITAGE DRÔME

CM Lucs

24 av Prés-Roosevelt, 26600 ☎ 475083282 🗎 475083206

e-mail camping.tainlhermitage@wanadoo.fr

Good overnight stopping place but some traffic noise.

⮑ *S of town near N7. Turn towards River Rhône at Esso fuel station.*

Open 15 Mar-Oct **Site** 1.5HEC 😸 ♨ **Prices** pitch 13.50-16.40 (incl 2 persons) **Facilities** 🏠 ⊙ 🖭 ℗ **Services** 🍴 🍽 ➕ 🗐 **Leisure** ⚓ P **Off-site** 🛁 🖉

THOR, LE VAUCLUSE

Jantou

Quartier le Bourdis, 84250 ☎ 490339007 🗎 490337984

e-mail accueil@lejantou.com

website www.lejantou.com

Wooded surroundings beside a river. Separate car park for arrivals after 22.00 hrs.

⮑ *Via N100.*

Open 15 Mar-Oct **Site** 6HEC 😸 ♨ 🏕 🏕 **Facilities** 🏠 🛁 ⊙ 🖭 🖉 ℗ **Services** 🍴 🍽 ➕ 🗐 **Leisure** ⚓ PR **Off-site** ➕

TOURNON-SUR-RHÔNE ARDÈCHE

Manoir

rte de Lamastre, 07300 ☎ 475080250 🗎 475085710

e-mail info@lemanoir-ardeche.com

website www.lemanoir-ardeche.com

Picturesque wooded surroundings with modern facilities.

⮑ *Off N86 onto Lamastre road for 3km.*

Open Apr-Sep **Site** 2HEC 😸 ♨ 🏕 🏕 🅰 **Prices** pitch 11-16 🏕 (static)200-380 **Facilities** 🏠 🛁 ⊙ 🖭 🔌 🚿 ℗ **Services** 🍴 🍽 🗐 **Leisure** ⚓ PR

Tournon

1 Promenade Roche de France, 07300

☎ 475080528 🗎 475080528

e-mail camping.tournon@wanadoo.fr

website www.camping-tournon.com

Well laid-out site in town centre beside River Rhône.

⮑ *NW on N86.*

Open All year **Site** 1HEC 😸 ♨ 🏕 **Facilities** 🏠 ⊙ 🖭 🖉 🚿 ℗ **Services** ➕ 🗐 **Leisure** ⚓ R **Off-site** 🛁 🍴 🍽 ⚓P

TOURRETTES-SUR-LOUP ALPES-MARITIMES

Camassade

523 rte de Pie Lombard, 06140 ☎ 493593154 🗎 493593181

e-mail courrier@camassade.com

website www.camassade.com

Quiet site under oak trees and pines with several terraces.

⮑ *From Vence turn left just after Tourette.*

Open All year **Site** 2HEC 😸 ♨ ♨ 🏕 🏕 **Prices** 🚶 4.25 🚗 2.95 pitch 9.40 🏕 (static)300 **Facilities** 🏠 🛁 ⊙ 🖭 🖉 🚿 ℗ **Services** ➕ 🗐 **Leisure** ⚓ P

France

Facilities 🛁 shop 🏠 shower ⊙ electric points for razors 🖭 electric points for caravans ℗ parking by tents permitted 🅿 compulsory separate car park
Services 🍽 café/restaurant 🍴 bar 🖉 Camping Gaz International 🚿 gas other than Camping Gaz ➕ first aid facilities 🗐 laundry
Leisure ⚓ swimming L-Lake P-Pool R-River S-Sea **Off-site** All facilities within 2km

Rives du Loup

rte de la Colle, 6140 ☎ 493241565 📄 493245370
e-mail info@rivesduloup.com
website www.rivesduloup.com
Wooded riverside setting with modern facilities adjacent to a small hotel.

⮑ *Between Vence & Grasse, 3km from Pont-du-Loup on road to La Colle-sur-Loup CD6.*

Open Apr-Sep **Site** 2.2HEC 🌱 🏖 ♣ 🌳 🏠 **Prices** ♣ 4 pitch 13.50-22.50 (incl 2 persons) 🚐 (static)195-610 **Facilities** 🚿 🛁 ⊙ 🚪 🥄 🔥 **Services** 🍴 🍽 ⊞ 🗑 **Leisure** 🏊 PR

UCEL ARDÈCHE

Domaine de Gil

rte de Vais les Bains, Quartier Chamboulas, 07200
☎ 475946363 📄 475940195
e-mail info@domaine-de-gil.com
website www.domaine-de-gil.com
Pleasant location on the River Ardèche, surrounded by beautiful countryside.

⮑ *N of Aubenas off N104.*

Open 14 Apr-16 Sep **Site** 4.5HEC 🌱 🏖 ♣ 🌳 🏠 **Prices** pitch 14-29 (incl 2 persons) **Facilities** 🚿 🛁 ⊙ 🚪 🥄 🌳 **Services** 🍴 🍽 ⊞ 🗑 **Leisure** 🏊 PR

UR PYRÉNÉES-ORIENTALES

Gare d'Ur

rte d'Espagne, UR, 66760 ☎ 468048095
website www.cerdagne-capcir.com
A pleasant mountainous setting with well-defined pitches. 0.5km from the village.

Open Nov-Sep **Site** 1HEC 🌱 ♣ 🌳 🏠 **Prices** ♣ 2.80 pitch 3.50 🚐 (static)200-350 **Facilities** 🚿 ⊙ 🚪 🥄 🔥 🌳 **Services** 🗑 **Off-site** 🍽 🏊R ⊞

UZÈS GARD

AT ST-QUENTIN-LA-POTERIE (4KM NE)

Moulin Neuf

30700 ☎ 466221721 📄 466229182
e-mail le.moulin.neuf@wanadoo.fr
website www.le-moulin-neuf.com
Quiet site on extensive meadowland within an estate.

⮑ *4km NE on D982.*

Open Etr-Sep **Site** 5HEC 🌱 🏖 ♣ 🌳 🏠 **Prices** pitch 12.50-18.50 pp3.50-4.50 **Facilities** 🚿 🛁 ⊙ 🚪 🥄 🌳 **Services** 🍴 🍽 ⊞ 🗑 **Leisure** 🏊 P

VAISON-LA-ROMAINE VAUCLUSE

International Carpe Diem

rte de St-Marcellin, 84110 ☎ 490360202 📄 490363690
e-mail contact@camping-carpe-diem.com
website www.camping-carpe-diem.com
Wooded surroundings close to Mont Ventoux with a variety of leisure facilities.

⮑ *S of town towards Malaucène.*

Open 25 Mar-1 Nov **Site** 10HEC 🌱 🏖 ♣ 🌳 🏠 🏕 **Facilities** 🚿 🛁 ⊙ 🚪 🥄 🌳 **Services** 🍴 🍽 ⊞ 🗑 **Leisure** 🏊 P **Off-site** 🥄 🏊R

Théâtre Romain

Quartier des Arts, chemin du Brusquet, 84110
☎ 490287866 📄 490287876
e-mail info@camping-theatre.com
website www.camping-theatre.com

⮑ *The site lies 0.5km from the town centre near Roman theatre.*

Open 15 Mar-15 Nov **Site** 1.5HEC 🌱 🏖 🏠 **Prices** ♣ 5-6 pitch 5-7.60 **Facilities** 🚿 ⊙ 🚪 🚪 🌳 **Services** ⊞ 🗑 **Leisure** 🏊 P **Off-site** 🛁 🍴 🍽 🥄 🥄 🏊LR

VALENCE DRÔME

CM

chemin de l'Epervière, 26000 ☎ 475423200 📄 475562067
e-mail eperviere@vacanciel.com
A well-equipped site bordering the Rhône.

⮑ *A7 exit Valence Sud.*

Open Feb-15 Dec **Site** 3.5HEC 🌱 🏖 ♣ 🌳 **Facilities** 🚿 ⊙ 🚪 🌳 **Services** 🍴 🍽 🗑 **Leisure** 🏊 P **Off-site** 🛁 🥄 🏊 ⊞

VALLABRÈGUES GARD

Lou Vincen

30300 ☎ 466592129 📄 466590741
e-mail campinglouvincen@wanadoo.fr
website www.campinglouvincen.com
A pleasant shady location in a Provençal village.

Open 24 Mar-15 Oct **Site** 1.4HEC 🌱 🏖 🏠 **Prices** pitch 11.50-14 pp3.60-4.60 🚐 (static)262-493 **Facilities** 🚿 ⊙ 🚪 🥄 🌳 **Services** ⊞ 🗑 **Leisure** 🏊 P **Off-site** 🛁 🍴 🍽 🥄 🏊LR ⊞

VALLERAUGE GARD

Corconne

Pont D'Hérault ☎ 467824682 📄 467824682
e-mail lacorconne@wanadoo.fr
website www.lacorconne.com
Unspoiled site in the Cevennes. Spacious terraced pitches blending into the wooded landscape. The river l'Herault is suitable for swimming.

⮑ *Off A75 from Millau, 3km N of Pont d'Herault.*

Open All year **Site** 7HEC 🌱 🏖 ♣ 🏠 **Prices** ♣ 4-4.20 🚐 4-4.20 🏕 4-4.20 **Facilities** 🚿 🛁 ⊙ 🚪 🥄 🥄 🌳 🅿 **Services** 🍴 🍽 ⊞ 🗑 **Leisure** 🏊 R

Site 6HEC (site size) 🌱 grass 🏖 sand 🌊 stone ♣ little shade ♣ partly shaded 🌳 mainly shaded 🏠 bungalows for hire 🚐 caravans for hire 🏕 tents for hire ⊗ no dogs **Prices** ♣ adult per night 🚗 car per night pp per person per night 🚐 caravan per night 🏕 tent per night 🚐 (static)-caravan hire per week

VALLON-PONT-D'ARC ARDÈCHE

Camping Nature Park L'Ardechois

07150 ☎ 475880663 🗎 475371497
e-mail ardecamp@bigfoot.com
website www.ardechois-camping.com
A pleasant location in the Ardèche gorge. Good access for caravans and plentiful sports facilities.

⮑ *D290 from Vallon towards St-Martin, site signed.*

Open Apr-Sep **Site** 6HEC 🌑 ⛺ 🚐 **Prices** pitch 24-40 (incl 2 persons) pp5.50-8.50 **Facilities** 🏕 🏪 ⊙ 🔌 ⌀ ⑫ **Services** 🍴 🍽 🕂 🖳 **Leisure** ⬳ PR **Off-site** ⚎

See advertisement on this page

Mondial

rte des Gorges de l'Ardèche, 7150 ☎ 475880044 🗎 475371373
e-mail reserv-info@mondial-camping.com
website www.mondial-camping.com
Modernised site on the bank of the Ardèche with good sanitary arrangements.

⮑ *D290 from Vallon-Pont-d'Arc towards Gorge d'Ardèche, site 0.8km.*

Open 24 Mar-Sep **Site** 4.2HEC 🌑 ⛺ 🚐 ⚑ ⛺ **Prices** pitch 18-32 (incl 2 persons) 🚐 (static)390-740 **Facilities** 🏕 🏪 ⊙ 🔌 ⌀ ⚎ ⑫ **Services** 🍴 🍽 🕂 🖳 **Leisure** ⬳ PR

See advertisement on this page

Plage Fleurie

Les Mazes, 7150 ☎ 475880115 🗎 475881131
e-mail info@laplagefleurie.com
website www.laplagefleurie.com
Holiday site in an unspoiled village beside river.

⮑ *D579 towards Ruoms, 2.5km left towards Les Mazes.*

Open 29 Apr-15 Sep **Site** 12HEC 🌑 ⛺ 🚐 ⚑ **Facilities** 🏕 🏪 ⊙ 🔌 ⌀ ⑫ 🅿 **Services** 🍴 🍽 🖳 **Leisure** ⬳ PR

VALRAS-PLAGE HÉRAULT

Lou Village

chemin des Montilles, 34350 ☎ 467373379 🗎 467375356
e-mail info@louvillage.com
website www.louvillage.com
Situated along a sandy beach, bordered by dunes.

⮑ *2km SW, 100m from beach.*

Open May-9 Sep **Site** 8HEC 🌑 ⛺ ⚑ 🚐 **Prices** pitch 19.50-38.50 (incl 2 persons) 🚐 (static)249-537 **Facilities** 🏕 🏪 ⊙ 🔌 ⌀ ⚎ ⑫ **Services** 🍴 🍽 🕂 🖳 **Leisure** ⬳ PS **Off-site** ⬳R

Occitanie

BP29, 34350 ☎ 467395906 🗎 467325820
e-mail campingoccitanie@wanadoo.fr
website www.campingoccitanie.com
Family site on rising ground to the north of town, 1km from the beach.

⮑ *A9 exit Béziers-Est for Valras.*

Open 26 May-8 Sep **Site** 6HEC 🌑 ⛺ 🚐 ⚑ **Prices** pitch 17-27 (incl 2 persons) pp2-4.50 🚐 (static)217-595 **Facilities** 🏕 🏪 ⊙ 🔌 �
 ⑫ **Services** 🍴 🍽 🕂 🖳 **Leisure** ⬳ P **Off-site** ⌀ ⚎ ⬳RS

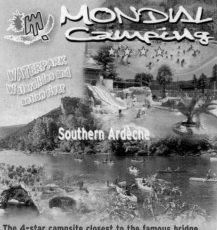

France

Facilities 🏪 shop 🏕 shower ⊙ electric points for razors 🔌 electric points for caravans ⑫ parking by tents permitted 🅿 compulsory separate car park
Services 🍴 café/restaurant 🍽 bar ⌀ Camping Gaz International ⚎ gas other than Camping Gaz 🕂 first aid facilities 🖳 laundry
Leisure ⬳ swimming L-Lake P-Pool R-River S-Sea **Off-site** All facilities within 2km

Plage & Bord du Mer
rte de Vendres ☎ 467303637 🖷 467315015
Open 25 May-6 Sep Site 10HEC 🌾 🌊 ♨ 🚐 ⊗ Facilities 🏕 🏪 ⊙ 🖫 ⌀ ⑫
Services 🛒 ⑩ 🚻 🗑

See advertisement on this page

Vagues
Vendres Plage, 34350 ☎ 467373312 🖷 467375036
website www.lesvagues.net
A well-organised family site 400m from the sea with a variety of sports
and entertainment facilities.
Open Apr-Sep Site 7HEC 🌾 🌊 ♨ 🚐 🏖 Facilities 🏕 🏪 ⊙ 🖫 ⌀ 🛒 ⑫
Services 🛒 ⑩ 🚻 🗑 Leisure ⌀ P Off-site ⌀S

New
AQUAPARK
WITH
WATERSLIDE

★★★★

**Domaine
de la Yole**

Children's paradise

BUNGALOWS AND MOBIL-HOMES FOR RENT

Until 16/06
and from 25/08 :
Children under 16
FREE

Special offer 2007 ★
All in price of 18 € ★
periods and conditions on our website
www.campinglayole.com

400 m from the beach, playground, youth-
club, Tennis, Multisport area.

Domaine de la Yole - BP 23 F - 34350 Valras Plage
Tél : 00.33.467.37.33.87 Fax : 00.33.467.37.44.89
layole34@aol.com

Yole
34350 ☎ 467373387 🖷 467374489
e-mail layole34@aol.com
website www.campinglayole.com
Very comfortable site divided into pitches. Good sanitary installations
with individual washing cubicles. Sailing boats for hire. Riding stables
in village. Booking advised for July and August.
⮡ SW of D37E towards Vendres.
Open 28 Apr-22 Sep Site 20HEC 🌾 🌊 ♨ 🚐 🏖 Prices pitch 18-37.35 (incl
2 persons) 🚐 (static)350.70-820.75 Facilities 🏕 🏪 ⊙ 🖫 ⌀ 🛒 ⑫
Services 🛒 ⑩ 🚻 🗑 Leisure ⌀ P Off-site ⌀S

See advertisement on this page

VEDÈNE VAUCLUSE

Flory
rte d'Entraigues, 84270 ☎ 490310051 🖷 490234679
e-mail campingflory@wanadoo.fr
website www.campingflory.com
Well-kept site with good facilities on a pine covered hill.
⮡ Off motorway onto D942 for 0.8km.
Open 15 Mar-Sep Site 6.5HEC 🌾 🌊 ♨ 🚐 🏖 Prices ♦ 4.50-5.50 pitch 5-6
🚐 (static)150-250 Facilities 🏕 🏪 ⊙ 🖫 ⌀ 🛒 ⑫ Services 🛒 ⑩ 🚻 🗑
Leisure ⌀ P

VENCE ALPES-MARITIMES

Domaine de la Bergerie
133 Chemin de la Sine, 06140 ☎ 493580936 🖷 493598044
e-mail info@camping-domainedelabergerie.com
website www.camping-domainedelabergerie.com
Well-kept site on hilly land. Pitches near to a wood. Some facilities are
only available in summer.
⮡ 3km W on D2210.
Open 25 Mar-15 Oct Site 13HEC 🌾 🌊 ♨ 🏖 Prices ♦ 4.90 pitch 14.50-30
Facilities 🏕 🏪 ⊙ 🖫 ⌀ 🛒 ⑫ Services 🛒 ⑩ 🚻 🗑 Leisure ⌀ P

VERCHENY DRÔME

Acacias
26340 ☎ 475217251 🖷 475217398
e-mail infos@campinglesacacias.com
website campinglesacacias.com
Pleasant site beside the River Drôme.
⮡ Via D93.
Open Apr-Sep Site 3.7HEC 🌾 🌊 🚐 🏖 Facilities 🏕 🏪 ⊙ 🖫 ⌀ 🛒 ⑫
Services 🛒 ⑩ 🚻 🗑 Leisure ⌀ R

VÉREILLES HÉRAULT

Sieste
34260 ☎ 467237296 🖷 467237538
e-mail campinglasieste@wanadoo.fr
A rural setting on the River Orb.
⮡ NE of Bédarieux, 10km from Lodève.
Open 15 Jun-Aug Site 2HEC 🌾 🌊 🚐 🏖 Prices ♦ 7-10 🚐 (static)110-200
Facilities 🏕 🏪 ⊙ 🖫 ⌀ 🛒 ⑫ Services 🛒 ⑩ 🚻 🗑 Leisure ⌀ PR

Site 6HEC (site size) 🌾 grass 🌊 sand 🌾 stone ♨ little shade 🌊 partly shaded 🌊 mainly shaded 🏖 bungalows for hire
🚐 caravans for hire 🛖 tents for hire ⊗ no dogs Prices ♦ adult per night 🚗 car per night pp per person per night 🚐 caravan per night
🛖 tent per night 🚐 (static)-caravan hire per week

VIAS HÉRAULT

Air Marin

34450 ☎ 467216490 📠 467217679
e-mail info@camping-air-marin.fr
website www.camping-air-marin.fr
A well-equipped family site in wooded surroundings, a 10-minute walk from the beach.

➔ *A6 exit Bierre-les-Semur/RN954*

Open 15 May-15 Sep **Site** 7HEC 🌳 🛖 🌳 🚐 **Prices** pitch 15.50-31 (incl 2 persons) pp3.50-7 **Facilities** 🏕 🛆 ⊙ 🚐 🚿 ℗ **Services** 🏪 🍽 🖲 **Leisure** ⚓ P **Off-site** 🛆 🖉 ⚓RS ➕

Carabasse

rte de Farinette, 34450 ☎ 467216401 📠 467217687
e-mail lacarabasse@siblu.fr
website www.siblu.com
A lively camping park with a range of activites, especially for young families and teenagers, centred around a lagoon pool complex and entertainment terrace.

➔ *1.5m NE of Vias.*

Open 15 Apr-14 Sep **Site** 🌳 🛶 🛖 🌳 🚐 Å ⊗ **Facilities** 🏕 🛆 ⊙ 🚐 🚿 ℗ **Services** 🏪 🍽 ➕ 🖲 **Leisure** ⚓ P **Off-site** ⚓S

Cap Soleil

Côte Ouest, 34450 ☎ 467216477 📠 467217066
e-mail cap.soleil@wanadoo.fr
website www.capsoleil.fr
On level land near sea. Divided into pitches.

➔ *Cross Canal du Midi, S of town, then turn W.*

Open All year **Site** 5HEC 🌳 🛖 🌳 🚐 **Facilities** 🏕 🛆 ⊙ 🚐 🖉 ℗ **Services** 🏪 🍽 ➕ 🖲 **Leisure** ⚓ P **Off-site** ⚓S

Hélios

Vias-Plage, 34450 ☎ 467216366 📠 467216366
e-mail franceschi.louis@wanadoo.fr
website www.campinghelios-viasplage.com
On level ground divided into pitches.

➔ *On D137 S of village signed Farinette.*

Open May-Sep **Site** 3HEC 🌳 🛶 🛖 🌳 🚐 **Prices** pitch 12.08-16.98 (incl 2 persons) 🚐 (static)137-306 **Facilities** 🏕 🛆 ⊙ 🚐 🚿 ℗ **Services** 🏪 🍽 ➕ 🖲 **Off-site** ⚓RS

Méditerranée Plage

☎ 467909907 📠 467909917
e-mail camping.med@wanadoo.fr
website www.mediterranee-plage.com
Direct access to a fine sandy beach.

Open Apr-24 Sep **Site** 7HEC 🌳 🛖 🌳 🚐 🚿 **Prices** pitch 20.50-35.50 (incl 2 persons) **Facilities** 🏕 🛆 ⊙ 🚐 🚿 ℗ **Services** 🏪 🍽 ➕ 🖲 **Leisure** ⚓ PS

Napoléon

1171 av de la Mediterranée, 34450 ☎ 467010780 📠 467010785
website www.camping-napoleon.fr
A well-equipped family site surrounded by tropical vegetation with direct access to the beach.

➔ *A9 exit Agde-Vias.*

Open 6 Apr-Sep **Site** 3HEC 🌳 🛖 🌳 🚐 Å **Prices** pitch 16-38 (incl 2 persons) **Facilities** 🏕 🛆 ⊙ 🚐 🚿 ℗ **Services** 🏪 🍽 ➕ 🖲 **Leisure** ⚓ PS **Off-site** ⚓R

Yelloh Village Farret

34450 ☎ 467216445 📠 467217049
e-mail farret@wanadoo.fr
website www.yellohvillage-club-farret.com
On level meadow beside flat sandy beach, ideal for children.

➔ *A9 exit Agde-Vias.*

Open 29 Apr-22 Sept **Site** 7HEC 🌳 🛖 🌳 🚐 **Prices** pitch 17-44 (incl 2 persons) 🚐 (static)245 **Facilities** 🏕 🛆 ⊙ 🚐 🖉 🚿 ℗ **Services** 🏪 🍽 ➕ 🖲 **Leisure** ⚓ PS **Off-site** ⚓R

VIC-LA-GARDIOLE HÉRAULT

Europe

31 rte de Frontignan, 34110 ☎ 467781150 📠 467784859
e-mail infos@campingleurope.com
website www.campingleurope.com
A pleasant site in peaceful surroundings.

➔ *1.5km W via D114.*

Open 11 Jun-1 Sep **Site** 5HEC 🌳 🛖 🌳 🚐 **Facilities** 🏕 🛆 ⊙ 🚐 🖉 🚿 ℗ **Services** 🏪 🍽 ➕ 🖲 **Leisure** ⚓ P **Off-site** ⚓L

VIGAN, LE GARD

Val de l'Arre

rte de Ganges, 30120 ☎ 467810277 📠 467817123
e-mail valdelarre@wanadoo.fr
website www.campingfrance.com/valdelarre
Wooded surroundings beside the River Arre. Compulsory separate car park for late arrivals.

➔ *2.5km E on D999.*

Open Apr-Sep **Site** 4HEC 🌳 🛖 🌳 **Prices** pitch 11-14.50 (incl 2 persons) pp5.18-6.71 **Facilities** 🏕 🛆 ⊙ 🚐 🖉 ℗ **Services** 🏪 🍽 ➕ 🖲 **Leisure** ⚓ PR **Off-site** 🚿

VILLARS-COLMARS ALPES-DE-HAUTE-PROVENCE

Haut-Verdon

04370 ☎ 492834009 📠 492835661
e-mail campinglehautverdon@wanadoo.fr
website www.lehautverdon.com
A comfortable site in a picturesque wooded location beside the River Verdon.

➔ *N on D908.*

Open May-Sep **Site** 3.5HEC 🌳 🛶 🛖 🌳 **Facilities** 🏕 🛆 ⊙ 🚐 🖉 ℗ **Services** 🏪 🍽 ➕ 🖲 **Leisure** ⚓ PR **Off-site** 🚿

VILLEMOUSTAUSSOU AUDE

Pinhiers

chemin du Pont Neuf, 11620 ☎ 468478190 📠 468714349
e-mail campingdaspinhiers@wanadoo.fr
website www.campingcarcassonne.net

➔ *A61 towards Mazamet.*

Open Mar-15 Nov **Site** 2HEC 🌳 🛖 🌳 🚐 **Prices** 🚶 3.50-4 pitch 3.70-4.10 🚐 (static)230-450 **Facilities** 🏕 🛆 ⊙ 🚐 ℗ **Services** 🏪 🍽 🖲 **Leisure** ⚓ P **Off-site** 🍽 🖉 🚿

VILLENEUVE-DE-BERG ARDÈCHE

Domaine de Pommier

RN 102, 07170 ☎ 475948281 📠 475948390
Holiday site in beautiful setting with terraces divided into pitches.

➔ *On winding private road off N102, 2km from village.*

Open May-Sep **Site** 30HEC 🌳 🛶 🛖 🌳 🚐 **Facilities** 🏕 🛆 ⊙ 🚐 🖉 ℗ **Services** 🏪 🍽 ➕ **Leisure** ⚓ PR

France

Facilities 🛆 shop 🏕 shower ⊙ electric points for razors 🚐 electric points for caravans ℗ parking by tents permitted ℗ compulsory separate car park
Services 🍽 café/restaurant ➕ bar 🖉 Camping Gaz International 🚿 gas other than Camping Gaz ➕ first aid facilities 🖲 laundry
Leisure ⚓ swimming L-Lake P-Pool R-River S-Sea **Off-site** All facilities within 2km

France

CAMPING ★★
"LES RIVES DU LAC"

66180 VILLENEUVE DE LA RAHO

Bordering a lake, close to Spain, between the sea and mountains

- ★ Peaceful
- ★ Family atmosphere
- ★ Fishing (carp, whitebait)
- ★ Windsurfing
- ★ Swimming
- ★ Rowing
- ★ 15km from the sea

MOBILE HOMES AND CANVAS BUNGALOWS TO LET
Open from March till November
Tel: 0468558351
Fax: 0468558637
email: campingvilleneuveraho@wanadoo.fr

VILLENEUVE-DE-LA-RAHO PYRÉNÉES-ORIENTALES

Rives-du-Lac
chemin de la Serre, 66180 ☎ 468558351 ▤ 468558637
e-mail camping.villeneuveraho@wanadoo.fr
A quiet family site beside the lake.
➲ *Via RN9*
Open Mar-Nov **Site** 2.5HEC ❀ ♣ ⛺ Å **Prices** pitch 10.50-13.60 (incl 2 persons) **Facilities** ⋔ ⛺ ⊙ ⛽ �ⓟ **Services** ⚑ ⛽ ⊠ **Off-site** ⛵L ⊞

See advertisement on this page

VILLENEUVE-LÈS-AVIGNON GARD

Ile des Papes
30400 ☎ 490151590 ▤ 490151591
e-mail ile.papes@wanadoo.fr
website www.campeoles.fr
A well-equipped site on an island between the Rhône Canal and the River Rhône.
➲ *Via N7 & D228.*
Open Apr-Oct **Site** 20HEC ❀ ♣ ⛺ ⛺ Å **Prices** ♠ 4.50-6.30 pitch 16-23 (incl 2 persons) ⛽ (static)279-659 **Facilities** ⋔ ⛺ ⊙ ⛽ ⓟ ⛵ ⓟ **Services** ⚑ ⛽ ⊠ **Leisure** ⛵ P

VILLENEUVE-LOUBET-PLAGE ALPES-MARITIMES

Hippodrôme
5 av des Rives, 06270 ☎ 493200200 ▤ 492132007
e-mail blsced@aol.com
website meublecamping-hippodrome.com
A spacious park with good facilities and pitches divided by hedges.
➲ *Turn right off N7 at ATLAS furniture store.*
Open All year **Site** 7.8HEC ❀ ♣ ⛺ **Facilities** ⋔ ⊙ ⛽ ⓟ **Services** ⊞ ⊠ **Leisure** ⛵ P **Off-site** ⛺ ⚑ ⛽ ⓟ ⛵S

Panorama
6270 ☎ 493209153
Small terraced site mainly for tents 0.8km from the sea.
➲ *0.5km from Nice-Cannes autoroute.*
Open All year **Site** 1HEC ❀ ♣ ⛺ ⛺ **Facilities** ⋔ ⊙ ⛺ ⓟ ⛽ ⓟ **Services** ⚑ ⛽ ⊞ ⊠ **Off-site** ⛺ ⛵RS

Parc des Maurettes
730 av du Dr-Lefebvre, 06270 ☎ 493209191 ▤ 493737720
e-mail info@parcdesmaurettes.com
website www.parcdesmaurettes.com
Terraced site in a pine forest with modern facilities.
➲ *A8 exit Villeneuve-Loubet-Plage, N7 towards Antibes for 1km.*
Open 10 Jan-15 Nov **Site** 2HEC ❀ ⛺ ⛺ **Prices** pitch 20.70-28.60 (incl 2 persons) **Facilities** ⋔ ⊙ ⛽ ⓟ ⓟ **Services** ⊞ ⊠ **Off-site** ⛺ ⚑ ⛵S

Parc St-James Sourire
rte de Grasse (D2085), 6270 ☎ 493209611 ▤ 493220752
website www.camping-parcsaintjames.com
Parkland dominated by an 11th-century monastery.
➲ *2km W on D2085.*
Open end Mar-end Sep **Site** 8HEC ❀ ♣ ❀ ⛺ **Facilities** ⋔ ⛺ ⊙ ⛽ ⓟ ⓟ ⓟ **Services** ⚑ ⛽ ⊠ **Leisure** ⛵ P **Off-site** ⛵R

Vieille Ferme
296 bd des Groules, 06270 ☎ 493334144 ▤ 493333728
e-mail info@vielleferme.com
website www.vielleferme.com
Wooded park close to the sea. Shop and café only open in summer.
➲ *Via A8/N7 from Antibes or Cagnes-sur-Mer.*
Open All year **Site** 2.8HEC ❀ ♣ ❀ ⛺ **Prices** pitch 17.50-28.50 (incl 2 persons) **Facilities** ⋔ ⛺ ⊙ ⛽ ⓟ ⓟ **Services** ⛽ ⊞ ⊠ **Leisure** ⛵ P **Off-site** ⛵S

VILLEROUGE-LA-CRÉMADE AUDE

Pinada
11200 ☎ 468426182 ▤ 468436861
e-mail lepinada@libertysurf.fr
website camping_le_pinada.com
Pleasant rural surroundings on edge of forest.
➲ *0.6km NW on D106.*
Open Apr-15 Oct **Site** 4.5HEC ❀ ♣ ❀ ⛺ ⛺ **Facilities** ⋔ ⊙ ⛽ ⓟ ⓟ **Services** ⚑ ⛽ ⊞ ⊠ **Leisure** ⛵ P

VILLES-SUR-AUZON VAUCLUSE

Verguettes
rte de Carpentras, 84570 ☎ 490618818 ▤ 490619787
e-mail info@provence-camping.com
website www.provence-camping.com
Lying at the foot of Mont Ventoux and Nesque Gorges in a pine forest.
➲ *W via D942.*
Open Apr-15 Oct **Site** 2HEC ❀ ♣ ⛺ **Prices** pitch 16.40-18.80 pp4.50-5.50 **Facilities** ⋔ ⊙ ⛽ ⓟ **Services** ⚑ ⛽ ⊞ ⊠ **Leisure** ⛵ P **Off-site** ⛺ ⛽ ⓟ ⓟ

Site 6HEC (site size) ❀ grass ⛱ sand ♣ stone ♣ little shade ♣ partly shaded ❀ mainly shaded ⛺ bungalows for hire ⛽ caravans for hire Å tents for hire ⓝ no dogs **Prices** ♠ adult per night ⛤ car per night pp per person per night ⛽ caravan per night Å tent per night ⛽ (static)-caravan hire per week

VITROLLES BOUCHES-DU-RHÔNE

Marina Plage

13127 ☎ 442893146 🗎 442795990

e-mail information@marina-plage.com

website www.marina-plage.com

A family site in pleasant wooded surroundings with good recreational facilities.

➲ *A7 exit Vitrolles, RN113 for Roquac, left at 2nd rdbt.*

Open All year **Site** 11HEC ♨ ♨ ♨ ♨ ⊗ **Prices** ♦ 2-4 pitch 13-17 ♣ (static)287-784 **Facilities** ♠ 🛊 ⊙ ♣ ⚏ ⓟ **Services** ▐ 🍴 ☎ 🗗 🗟 **Leisure** ❧ L

VIVIERS ARDÈCHE

Domaine d' Imbours

07220 ☎ 475543950 🗎 475543920

e-mail imbours@france.location.fr

website www.domaine-imbours.com

Wooded surroundings with a variety of recreational facilities.

➲ *Via N86 & D4.*

Open 26 Mar-Oct **Site** 45HEC ♨ ♨ ♨ **Facilities** ♠ 🛊 ⊙ ♣ ⚏ ♨ ⓟ **Services** ▐ 🍴 🗗 🗟 **Leisure** ❧ P

Rochecondrie Loisirs

07220 ☎ 475527466 🗎 475527466

e-mail campingrochecondrie@wanadoo.fr

website www.campingrochecondrie.com

A level site with good facilities beside the River l'Escoutay.

➲ *N of town on N86.*

Open Apr-15 Oct **Site** 1.8HEC ♨ ♨ ♨ **Prices** pitch 10-18 (incl 2 persons) ♣ (static)230-510 **Facilities** ♠ ⊙ ♣ ⓟ **Services** ▐ 🗗 🗟 **Leisure** ❧ PR **Off-site** 🛊 🍴 ♨

VOGÜÉ ARDÈCHE

Domaine du Cros d'Auzon

Hotellerie de Plein Air, 7200 ☎ 475377586 🗎 475370102

e-mail cros.d.auzon@wanadoo.fr

website www.guideweb.com/ardeche/camping/cros-auzon

Wooded surroundings close to the Gorges de l'Ardèche with good recreational facilities.

➲ *2.5km via D579 bordering the river.*

Open 15 Apr-15 Sep **Site** 20HEC ♨ ♨ ♨ ♨ ♨ **Prices** pitch 17.50-27.50 (incl 2 persons) pp4-6.70 **Facilities** ♠ ⊙ ♣ ♨ ⓟ **Services** ▐ 🍴 🗗 🗟 **Leisure** ❧ PR **Off-site** 🛊 ❧LS

VOLONNE ALPES-DE-HAUTE-PROVENCE

Hippocampe

rte Napoléon, 4290 ☎ 492335000 🗎 492335049

e-mail camping@l-hippocampe.com

website www.l-hippocampe.com

Several strips of land, interspersed with trees, and running down the edge of lake. Surrounded by fields and gardens.

➲ *On S edge of town, 2km E of N85.*

Open 4 Apr-Sep **Site** 8HEC ♨ ♨ ♨ Å **Prices** pitch 13-39 (incl 2 persons) ♣ (static)225-1204 **Facilities** ♠ 🛊 ⊙ ♣ ♨ ⓟ **Services** ▐ 🍴 🗗 🗟 **Leisure** ❧ P

ALÉRIA HAUTE-CORSE

Marina d'Aléria

rte de la Mer, 20270 ☎ 495570142 🗎 495570429

e-mail info@marina-aleria.com

website www.marina-aleria.com

➲ *3km E of Cateraggio via RN200*

Open 15 Apr-15 Oct **Site** 10HEC ♨ ♨ ♨ ♣ **Facilities** ♠ 🛊 ⊙ ♣ ♨ ⓟ **Services** ▐ 🍴 🗟 **Leisure** ❧ S

BONIFACIO CORSE-DU-SUD

Rondinara

Suartone, 20169 ☎ 495704315 🗎 495705679

e-mail reception@rondinara.fr   **website** www.rondinara.fr

A beautiful location 300m from the beach with modern facilities and opportunities for water sports.

➲ *On N198 midway between Porto-Vecchio & Bonifacio.*

Open 15 May-Sept **Site** 6HEC ♨ ♨ ♣ ⊗ **Facilities** ♠ 🛊 ⊙ ♣ ♨ ♨ ⓟ **Services** ▐ 🍴 🗗 🗟 **Leisure** ❧ PS

CALVI HAUTE-CORSE

Dolce Vita

Ponte Bambino, 20260 ☎ 495650599 🗎 0495653125

website www.dolce-vita-org/

Set in extensive woodland with defined pitches and modern facilities.

➲ *4km SW of Calvi, between N197 to l'Ile Rousse & sea.*

Open May-Sep **Site** 6HEC ♨ ♨ **Prices** ♦ 8.30 ♣ 2.80 ♣ 4 Å 2.80 ♣ (static)469 **Facilities** ♠ 🛊 ⊙ ♣ ♨ ⓟ **Services** ▐ 🍴 🗗 🗟 **Leisure** ❧ RS

CARGESE CORSE-DU-SUD

Torraccia

Bagghiuccia, 20130 ☎ 495264239 🗎 495264239

e-mail contact@camping-torraccia.com

website www.camping-torraccia.com

Terraced site close to the Chiuni and Pero beaches and backed by some fine mountain scenery.

➲ *4km N on N199.*

Open May-Sep **Site** 3.5HEC ♨ ♣ **Prices** ♦ 5.80-6.80 ♣ 2.20-2.80 ♣ 2.50-3.10 Å 2.20-2.80 **Facilities** ♠ 🛊 ⊙ ♣ ♨ ⓟ **Services** ▐ 🍴 🗗 🗟 **Off-site** ♨ ❧S

CENTURI HAUTE-CORSE

Isulottu

20238 ☎ 495356281

A peaceful, shady site, 200m from the beach.

➲ *1km from Centuri-Port towards Morsiglia.*

Site 3HEC ♨ **Facilities** ♠ 🛊 ⊙ ♣ ♨ ⓟ ⓟ **Services** ▐ 🍴 🗗 🗟 **Off-site** ❧S

GALÉRIA HAUTE-CORSE

Deux Torrents

20245 ☎ 495620067 🗎 495620332

e-mail 2torrents@corsica-net.com

website www.corsica-net.com/2torrents

A spacious, well-equipped site nestling between two torrents at the foot of the mountains.

➲ *5km E on D51 towards Calenzana.*

Open Jun-Sep **Site** 6.3HEC ♨ ♨ ♣ ♣ **Prices** ♦ 4.95 ♣ 2.70 ♣ 4.40 Å 2.70 ♣ (static)290 **Facilities** ♠ 🛊 ⊙ ♣ ♨ ♨ ⓟ **Services** ▐ 🍴 🗟 **Off-site** ❧R

Facilities 🛊 shop ♠ shower ⊙ electric points for razors ♣ electric points for caravans ⓟ parking by tents permitted ⓟ compulsory separate car park
Services 🍴 café/restaurant ▐ bar ♨ Camping Gaz International ♨ gas other than Camping Gaz 🗗 first aid facilities 🗟 laundry
Leisure ❧ swimming L-Lake P-Pool R-River S-Sea **Off-site** All facilities within 2km

France

France

GHISONACCIA HAUTE-CORSE

Arinella-Bianca
Arinella-Bianca, 20240 ☎ 495560478 ▤ 495561254
e-mail arinella@arinellabianca.com
website www.arinellabianca.com
Wooded surroundings beside the beach with good recreational facilities.
Open 7 Apr-13 Oct **Site** 9HEC ❀ ❀ 🏚 **Prices** pitch 21-36 (incl 2 persons) 🚐 (static)160-860 **Facilities** ⌐ 🗓 ⊙ 🖻 🖉 ⑳ **Services** ⚑ 🍽 ➕ 🖂 **Leisure** ❀ LPRS

LOZARI HAUTE-CORSE

Clos des Chênes
rte de Belgodère, 20226 ☎ 495601513 (Etr-Sep) ▤ 495602116
e-mail cdc.lozari@wanadoo.fr
website www.closdeschenes.fr
A delightful wooded setting 1km from a fine sandy beach.
⤷ 1.5km S on N197 towards Belgodère.
Open Etr-end Sep **Site** 5.5HEC ❀ ❀ 🏚 **Prices** ♦ 5.60-7.80 pitch 7-9 **Facilities** ⌐ 🗓 ⊙ 🖻 🖉 ⑳ **Services** ⚑ 🍽 ➕ 🖂 **Leisure** ❀ P **Off-site** ❀S

LUMIO HAUTE-CORSE

Panoramic
rte de Lavataggio 1, 20260 ☎ 495607313 ▤ 495607313
Very clean and tidy site divided into pitches.
⤷ From Calvi, 12km on N197, 200m from main road.
Open Jun-15 Sep **Site** 6HEC ⊜ ❀ 🏚 🚐 **Prices** ♦ 6.20 🚗 2 🚐 4.40 🅰 2.40 🚐 (static)200-300 **Facilities** ⌐ 🗓 ⊙ 🖻 🖉 ⑳ ⑫ **Services** ⚑ 🍽 ➕ 🖂 **Leisure** ❀ P **Off-site** ❀S

OLMETO-PLAGE CORSE-DU-SUD

Esplanade
20113 ☎ 495760503 ▤ 495761622
e-mail campinglesplanada@clubinternet.fr
website www.camping-esplanade.com
A pleasant natural park, 100m from the sea.
Open Apr-Oct **Site** 4.8HEC ❀ ❀ 🏚 🚐 **Prices** ♦ 5-6.90 🚗 2-3.20 🚐 3-4 🅰 2.50-3.50 🚐 (static)200-455 **Facilities** ⌐ 🗓 ⊙ 🖻 🖉 ⑳ ⑫ **Services** ⚑ 🍽 ➕ 🖂 **Leisure** ❀ PS **Off-site** ❀ ❀R

PIANOTTOLI CORSE-DU-SUD

Kevano Plage
Plage de Kevano, 20131 ☎ 495718322 ▤ 495718383
A beautiful setting in the middle of woodland with modern facilities, 400m from the beach.
Open May-Sep **Site** 6HEC ❀ ❀ 🏚 **Facilities** ⌐ 🗓 ⊙ 🖻 ⑳ **Services** ⚑ 🍽 ➕ 🖂 **Off-site** 🖉 ❀S

PISCIATELLO CORSE-DU-SUD

Benista
20166 ☎ 495251930 ▤ 495259370
e-mail benista20@club-internet.fr
website www.benista.com
A beautiful wooded setting 5 minutes from the beaches. Pitches are divided by hedges and there are good sports facilities.
Open Apr-Oct **Site** 5HEC ❀ ❀ 🏚 🚐 **Prices** pitch 19.50-24.10 (incl 2 persons) pp6.50-8.10 🚐 (static)210-390 **Facilities** ⌐ 🗓 ⊙ 🖻 🖉 🖳 ⑳ **Services** ⚑ 🍽 ➕ 🖂 **Leisure** ❀ PR **Off-site** ❀S

PORTO-VECCHIO CORSE-DU-SUD

Pirellu
rte de Palombaggia, 20137 ☎ 495702344 ▤ 495706022
e-mail u-pirellu@wanadoo.fr
website www.u-pirellu.com/camping.htm
A modern site in an oak grove 300m from the beach.
⤷ S of Porto-Vecchio towards Bonifacio, 1st left after Pont du Stabiacco.
Open Apr-Sep **Site** 2.5HEC ❀ ❀ 🏚 ⊗ **Facilities** ⌐ 🗓 ⊙ 🖻 🖉 🖳 ⑫ **Services** ⚑ 🍽 ➕ 🖂 **Leisure** ❀ P

Vetta
rte de Bastia, 20137 ☎ 495700986 ▤ 495704321
e-mail info@campinglavetta.com
website www.campinglavetta.com
Set in natural parkland with modern facilities, 3km from the sea.
⤷ 5.5km N on N198.
Open 15 May-15 Oct **Site** 8HEC ❀ ❀ 🏚 **Prices** ♦ 6-7 🚗 2-2.50 🚐 2.50-3.50 🅰 2.50-3.50 **Facilities** ⌐ 🗓 ⊙ 🖻 🖉 ⑳ ⑫ **Services** ⚑ 🍽 ➕ 🖂 **Leisure** ❀ P **Off-site** ❀S

ST-FLORENT HAUTE-CORSE

U Pezzo
chemin de la Plage, 20217 ☎ 495370165 ▤ 495370165
e-mail contact@upezzo.com
website www.upezzo.com
Pleasant site, partly level, partly terraced under eucalyptus trees. Private access to large beach.
⤷ S of town on road to beach.
Open Apr-15 Oct **Site** 2HEC ⊜ ❀ ❀ 🏚 **Facilities** ⌐ 🗓 ⊙ 🖻 🖉 ⑳ **Services** ⚑ 🍽 ➕ 🖂 **Leisure** ❀ S **Off-site** ❀R

SOTTA CORSE-DU-SUD

U Moru
20114 ☎ 495712340 ▤ 495712619
e-mail u-moru@wanadoo.fr
website www.u-moru.com
A quiet family site 5 minutes from the beach.
⤷ 4km SW via D859.
Open 15 Jun-15 Sep **Site** 6HEC ⊜ ❀ 🏚 🚐 **Prices** ♦ 6.80 🚗 2.40 🚐 3.80 🅰 2.90 🚐 (static)380 **Facilities** ⌐ 🗓 ⊙ 🖻 🖉 ⑳ **Services** ⚑ 🍽 ➕ 🖂 **Leisure** ❀ P

TIUCCIA CORSE-DU-SUD

Couchants
rte de Casaglione, 20111 ☎ 495522660 ▤ 495593177
e-mail camping.les-couchants@wanadoo.fr
A quiet location facing the vast Sagone bay and close to the Liamone river.
⤷ 3km from sea.
Open All year **Site** 5HEC ❀ ❀ 🏚 🚐 **Prices** ♦ 5.50-6 🚗 2.50-3.50 🚐 4-5 🅰 2.50-3.50 🚐 (static)228-280 **Facilities** ⌐ ⊙ 🖻 🖉 🖳 ⑳ **Services** ⚑ 🍽 ➕ 🖂 **Off-site** ❀RS

Site 6HEC (site size) ❀ grass ⊜ sand ❀ stone ♣ little shade ❀ partly shaded ❀ mainly shaded 🏚 bungalows for hire 🚐 caravans for hire 🅰 tents for hire ⊗ no dogs **Prices** ♦ adult per night 🚗 car per night pp per person per night 🚐 caravan per night 🅰 tent per night 🚐 (static)-caravan hire per week

Germany

Accidents & emergencies

fire 112   **police** 110   **ambulance** 112

Emergency numbers vary from region to region.

Driving requirements

Minimum age 18 for UK licence holders driving
temporarily imported car or motorcycle.

Lights

Dipped headlights must be used in poor daytime
visibility. Driving on sidelights only is prohibited.
Replacement set of vehicle bulbs strongly
recommended. Motorcyclists must use dipped
headlights during the day.

Passengers & children

Children under 12 and/or 1.5m in height must
not travel in the front or rear seat unless using a
suitable restraint system if fitted. Never fit a
rear-facing child restraint in a seat with a frontal
airbag.

Size restrictions

Motor vehicle or trailer
height 4m, width 2.5m, length 12m

Vehicle + trailer
length 18.35m

Speed limits

Unless signed otherwise:

Car without caravan/trailer, motorcycle

Built-up areas	50kph
Outside built-up areas	100kph
Motorways	130kph*

Car towing caravan/trailer

Built-up areas	50kph
Outside built-up areas	80kph
Motorways	80kph

*recommended maximum speed

Tourist office

German National Tourist Office
(postal/telephone enquiries only)
PO Box 2695
London W1A 3TN
Tel 020 7317 0908 (Mon-Fri 10.00-16.00 hrs)
www.germany-tourism.de
www.germany-tourism.co.uk

Additional information

It is an offence to make derogatory signs or use
abusive language to other drivers. First aid kit
and warning triangle compulsory.

SOUTH EAST

AACH BEI OBERSTAUFEN BAYERN

Aach

87534 ☎ 08386 363 📠 08386 961721
e-mail info@camping-aach.de
website www.camping-aach.de
A terraced site with beautiful views of the mountains. Sauna, solarium, games room.

⮑ B308 from Oberstaufen towards Austrian border for 7km.

Open All year **Site** 2.5HEC 👙 ♣ 🛶 **Prices** ♠ 3.60-4 �car 6-7 ▲ 3.20-7 **Facilities** 🟢 🏚 ⊙ 🅿 ⊘ ♨ ⑫ **Services** 🍴 🍽 🗑 **Off-site** ⚓R

AITRANG BAYERN

Elbsee 3

Am Elbsee 3, 87648 ☎ 08343 248 📠 08343 1406
e-mail info@elbsee.de
website www.elbsee.de
On the E shore of the lake with good bathing facilities. Section reserved for campers with dogs.

⮑ NW from Marktoberdorf centre to Ruderatshofen & W towards Aitrang, site signed S of Aitrang (narrow winding road).

Open All year **Site** 3.5HEC 👙 ♣ 🛶 **Prices** ♠ 5.30 🚗 2.70 **pitch** 7.30-9.40 **Facilities** 🟢 🏚 ⊙ 🅿 ⊘ ♨ ⑫ **Services** 🗑 🖥 **Leisure** ⚓ L **Off-site** 🍽 ⚓P

ARLACHING BAYERN

Kupferschmiede

Trostberger Str 4, 83339 ☎ 08667 446 📠 08667 16198
e-mail campingkupfer@aol.com
website campingkupferschmiede.de
On meadowland. Partially gravel.

⮑ On Seebruck-Traunstein road.

Open Apr-Oct **Site** 2.5HEC 👙 ♣ **Prices** ♠ 4.95-5.50 🚗 1.50 🚐 4.60 ▲ 3-4 **Facilities** 🟢 🏚 ⊙ 🅿 ⊘ ♨ ⑫ **Services** 🗑 🍽 🖥 🗑 **Leisure** ⚓ L **Off-site** ⚓PR

AUGSBURG BAYERN

Augusta

Mühlhauser Str 54B, 86169 ☎ 0821 707575 📠 0821 705883
e-mail info@caravaningpark.com
website www.caravaningpark.com
Hard standings for caravans. Separate section for residential caravans.

⮑ E11 exit Augsburg-Ost, N towards Neuburg & 400m right.

Open All year **Site** 6.6HEC 👙 ♣ 🛶 **Prices** **pitch** 18-20 (incl 2 persons) **Facilities** 🟢 🏚 ⊙ 🅿 ⊘ ♨ ⑫ **Services** 🍽 **Leisure** ⚓ L **Off-site** 🗑

BAMBERG BAYERN

AT BUG (5KM S)

Insel

96049 ☎ 0951 56320 📠 0951 56321
e-mail campinginsel@web.de
website www.campinginsel.de
The site lies on the bank of the River Regnitz, S of Bamberg. Park & Ride scheme into Bamberg.

⮑ A73 exit Bamberg S, B505/B4 towards Bamberg, signed on left.

Open All year **Site** 5HEC 👙 ♣ **Prices** ♠ 4.50 **pitch** 7 **Facilities** 🟢 🏚 ⊙ 🅿 ⊘ ♨ ⑫ **Services** 🗑 🍽 🖥 🗑 **Leisure** ⚓ R

BERCHTESGADEN BAYERN

Allwegiehen

83471 ☎ 08652 2396 📠 08652 63503
e-mail urlaub@allweglehen.de
website www.allweglehen.de
A terraced site at the foot of the Untersalzberg Mountain surrounded by bushy woods. There is also a steep and narrow asphalt access road with passing places.

⮑ B305 towards Schellenberg for 3.5km.

Open All year **Site** 4HEC 👙 🛶 ♣ 🛶 ♣ 🛶 **Facilities** 🟢 🏚 ⊙ 🅿 ⊘ ♨ ⑫ **Services** 🍽 🖥 🗑 **Leisure** ⚓ P **Off-site** ⚓R

BERGEN BAYERN

Wagnerhof

Campingstr 11, 83346 ☎ 08662 8557
e-mail info@camping-bergen.de
website www.camping-bergen.de
Level site.

⮑ München-Salzburg motorway exit Bergen, right at sawmill before town.

Open All year **Site** 2.8HEC 👙 ♣ 🛶 **Prices** ♠ 4.50-5.75 **pitch** 6-7.50 **Facilities** 🟢 🏚 ⊙ 🅿 ⊘ ♨ ⑫ **Off-site** 🗑 🍽 ⚓LP 🖥

BRUNNEN FORGGENSEE BAYERN

Brunnen

Seestr 81, 87645 ☎ 08362 8273 📠 08362 8630
e-mail info@camping-brunnen.de
website www.camping-brunnen.de
Situated on E shore of Lake Forggensee.

⮑ B17 from Füssen to Schwangau, then N on minor road.

Open 21 Dec-2 Nov **Site** 6HEC 👙 🛶 ♣ **Prices** ♠ 7.50-8.50 **pitch** 4.50-10 **Facilities** 🟢 🏚 ⊙ 🅿 ⊘ ♨ ⑫ **Services** 🗑 🍽 🖥 🗑 **Leisure** ⚓ L **Off-site** ⚓P

DIESSEN BAYERN

St-Alban

86911 ☎ 08807 7305 📠 08807 1057
e-mail ivan.pavic@t-online.de
website www.camping-ammersee.de
Clean site next to St-Alban, lakeside with private bathing beach and reserved section for residential campers. Good sanitary installations also used by the public.

⮑ B12 from München towards Landsberg/Lech, near Greifenberg turn left, continue via Utting to St-Alban.

Open Apr-Oct **Site** 3.8HEC 👙 ♣ **Prices** ♠ 6 **pitch** 9 **Facilities** 🟢 🏚 ⊙ 🅿 ♨ ⑫ **Services** 🍽 🗑 **Leisure** ⚓ L **Off-site** ⊘

DINKELSBÜHL BAYERN

Romantische Strasse

91550 ☎ 09851 7817 📠 09851 7848
e-mail campdinkelsbuhl@aol.de
website www.camping-dinkelsbuehl.de
Terraced site with some hedges and trees. Separate field for young people. Good sports facilities.

⮑ A7 exit 105 to Uffenheim.

Open All year **Site** 9HEC 👙 🛶 ♣ **Prices** ♠ 4 **pitch** 8.50 **Facilities** 🟢 🏚 ⊙ 🅿 ⊘ ⑫ 🅖 **Services** 🍽 🗑 🖥 **Leisure** ⚓ L **Off-site** 🗑

Site 6HEC (site size) 👙 grass 🛶 sand 🛶 stone ♣ little shade ♣ partly shaded 👙 mainly shaded 🛶 bungalows for hire 🚐 caravans for hire ▲ tents for hire ⊗ no dogs **Prices** ♠ adult per night 🚗 car per night pp per person per night 🚐 caravan per night ▲ tent per night 🚐 (static)-caravan hire per week

NDORF, BAD BAYERN

Stein

Hintersee 10, 83093 ☎ 08053 9349 ▤ 08053 798745

A family site in wooded surroundings on the shore of the Simsee.

Open 15 May-Sep **Site** 2.5HEC ⚌ ⚌ ♨ **Prices** ♦ 5 ⟐ 2 ⟐ 4 Å 4 **Facilities** ⋔ 🏠 ⊙ ⊕ ⚑ ⊗ **Services** 🖾 **Leisure** ⚓ L **Off-site** ⧮

ERLANGEN BAYERN

Rangau

Campingstr 44, 91056 ☎ 09135 8866 ▤ 09135 724743

e-mail info@camping-rangau.de

website www.camping-rangau.de

Long stretch of land behind the sports ground, next to the Dechsendorfer Weiher lake in a nature reserve.

➲ *A3 exit Erlangen W.*

Open Apr-Sep **Site** 18HEC ⚌ ⚌ **Prices** ♦ 5 pitch 3-5 **Facilities** ⋔ ⊙ ⚑ ⚏ ⊗ **Services** ⧮ ⊞ 🖾 **Off-site** 🏠 ⚓L

ESCHERNDORF BAYERN

Escherndorf-Main

97332 ☎ 09381 2889 ▤ 09381-2889

e-mail info@campingplatz-mainschleife.de

website www.camplingplatz-escherndorf.de

Site lies on meadowland by the River Main, next to the ferry station (River Ferry Northeim).

➲ *A7 exit Würzburg Estenfeld, E for Volkach.*

Open Apr-Oct **Site** 1.5HEC ⚌ ⚌ **Prices** ♦ 5.50 ⟐ 6 Å 5 **Facilities** ⋔ 🏠 ⊙ ⚑ ⚏ ⊗ **Services** ⧮ 🖾 **Leisure** ⚓ PR

ESTENFELD BAYERN

Estenfeld

Maidbronner Str 38, 97230 ☎ 09305 228 ▤ 09305 8006

e-mail cplestenfeld@freenet.de

website www.camping-estenfeld.de

On meadowland next to sportsground.

➲ *A7 exit Würzburg/Estenfeld, B19 S for 1km.*

Open 10 Mar-23 Dec **Site** 0.5HEC ⚌ ⚌ ⟐ ⟐ **Prices** ♦ 5 pitch 4-4.50 ⟐ (static)150-420 **Facilities** ⋔ 🏠 ⊙ ⚑ ⚏ ⊗ **Services** ⧮ ⧮ ⊞ 🖾 **Off-site** ⧮ ⊘

FEILNBACH, BAD BAYERN

Tenda

Reithof 2, 83075 ☎ 08066 533 ▤ 08066 8002

e-mail info@tenda-camping.de

website www.tenda-camping.de

Well-organised site on level grassland with pitches laid out in circles and hardstandings for tourers near the entrance.

➲ *A8 exit Bad Aibling, 4km S on minor road.*

Open All year **Site** 14HEC ⚌ ⚌ ⚌ ⟐ **Prices** ♦ 4.50-5.80 ⟐ 2-7.50 Å 1.50-4 pitch 1.90-7.50 **Facilities** ⋔ 🏠 ⊙ ⚑ ⚏ ⊗ **Services** ⧮ ⊞ 🖾 **Leisure** ⚓ P **Off-site** ⧮ ⚓L

FICHTELBERG BAYERN

Fichtelsee

95686 ☎ 09272 801 ▤ 09272 909045

e-mail info@camping-fichtelsee.de

website www.camping-fichtelsee.de

Gently sloping meadow amid pleasant woodland 100m from Lake Fichtelsee.

➲ *A9 exit Bad Berneck, B303 to Fichtelsee Leisure Centre turning.*

Open 15 Dec-4 Nov **Site** 2.6HEC ⚌ ⚌ **Prices** ♦ 5.50 pitch 7 **Facilities** ⋔ 🏠 ⊙ ⚑ ⚏ ⊗ **Services** ⊞ 🖾 **Off-site** ⧮ ⧮ ⧮ ⚓LP

FINSTERAU BAYERN

Nationalpark-Ost

94151 ☎ 08557 768 ▤ 08557 1062

e-mail 085571062@t-online.de

website www.camping-nationalpark-ost.de

Terraced site on edge of extensive woodland area at the entrance to a national park.

➲ *N of Freyung towards frontier.*

Open All year **Site** 3HEC ⚌ ⚌ **Prices** ♦ 4.60 pitch 5 **Facilities** ⋔ ⊙ ⚑ ⊘ ⚏ ⊗ **Services** ⧮ ⊞ 🖾 **Off-site** 🏠 ⧮

FRICKENHAUSEN BAYERN

KNAUS Camping Park Frickenhausen

Ochsenfurter Strabe 49, 97252 ☎ 09331 3171 ▤ 09331 5784

e-mail frickenhausen@knauscamp.de

website www.knauscamp.de

On level meadow in a small poplar wood beside River Main.

➲ *On N bank of Main 0.5km E of Oshsenfurt.*

Open 9 Dec-6 Nov **Site** 3.5HEC ⚌ ⚌ ⟐ Å **Prices** ♦ 6 pitch 6-9 **Facilities** ⋔ 🏠 ⊙ ⚑ ⚏ ⊗ **Services** ⧮ ⧮ ⊞ 🖾 **Leisure** ⚓ PR **Off-site** ⧮

FÜRTH IM WALD BAYERN

Einberg

Daberger Str 33, 93437 ☎ 09973 1811 ▤ 09973 803220

e-mail camping@stadtwerke-furth.de

website www.stadtwerke-furth.de

Municipal site in Dabergerstr, near swimming pool.

➲ *NE of Cham on B20.*

Open Mar-Oct **Site** 2HEC ⚌ ⚌ **Prices** ♦ 3.90 ⟐ 2.60 ⟐ 3.10 Å 2 **Facilities** ⋔ ⊙ ⚑ ⊘ ⊗ **Services** ⊞ 🖾 **Leisure** ⚓ R **Off-site** 🏠 ⧮ ⧮ ⊘ ⧮ ⚓P

FÜSSEN BAYERN

Hopfensee

87629 ☎ 08362 917710 ▤ 08362 917720

e-mail info@camping-hopfensee.com

website www.camping-hopfensee.de

A quiet location beside a lake. Private beach. Ski-ing lessons.

➲ *4km N of Füssen.*

Open 16 Dec-4 Nov **Site** 8HEC ⚌ ⚌ **Prices** ♦ 8.35-9.55 pitch 12.40-13.75 **Facilities** ⋔ 🏠 ⊙ ⚑ ⧮ ⊗ **Services** ⧮ ⧮ ⊞ 🖾 **Leisure** ⚓ LP

Facilities 🏠 shop ⋔ shower ⊙ electric points for razors ⚑ electric points for caravans ⊗ parking by tents permitted ❷ compulsory separate car park
Services ⧮ café/restaurant ⧮ bar ⊘ Camping Gaz International ⧮ gas other than Camping Gaz ⊞ first aid facilities 🖾 laundry
Leisure ⚓ swimming L-Lake P-Pool R-River S-Sea **Off-site** All facilities within 2km

FÜSSING, BAD BAYERN

Kur-und Fereincamping Fuchs

94072 ☎ 08537 356 🖹 08537 912083
e-mail info@kurcamping-fuchs.de
website www.kurcamping-fuchs.de

On meadow divided into pitches and 1km from spa baths at Bad Füssing.

⮑ *Turn at Passau end of Tutling on B12 to Kircham & signs to site on Egglfinger Strasse, 2km from Bad Füssing.*

Open All year **Site** 1.5HEC ⚊ ⚊ ⚊ ⚊ **Prices** ⚡ 4.50-5 ▲ 4-4.50 pitch 5.50-6.50 **Facilities** 🌣 🛁 ⊙ 🚽 ⚊ ⚑ **Services** ⚑ ⚑ ⚑ ⚑ **Leisure** ⚊ P **Off-site** ⚊R

Max I

Falkenstr 12, Egglfing, 94072 ☎ 08537 96170 🖹 08537 961710
e-mail info@campingmax.de
website www.campingmax.de

On a level meadow with some trees. Good modern facilities.

⮑ *S of Bad Füssing via B12.*

Open All year **Site** 3HEC ⚊ ⚊ ⚊ **Facilities** 🌣 🛁 ⊙ 🚽 ⚊ ⚑ **Services** ⚑ ⚑ ⚑ **Leisure** ⚊ P **Off-site** ⚑

GADEN BAYERN

Schwanenplatz

Schwanenpl 1, 83329 ☎ 08681 281 🖹 08681 4276
e-mail info@schwanenplatz.de
website www.schwanenplatz.de

Site lies on a meadow, divided into sections beside one of Bavaria's warmest lakes, Waginger See.

⮑ *From Traunstein to Waging, right towards Freilassing for 2km, left to lake.*

Open Apr-3 Oct **Site** 4HEC ⚊ ⚊ ⚊ **Prices** ⚡ 5.10-6.30 pitch 5.40-6.80 **Facilities** 🌣 🛁 ⊙ 🚽 ⚊ ⚑ **Services** ⚑ ⚑ ⚑ **Leisure** ⚊ LR **Off-site** ⚑

GARMISCH-PARTENKIRCHEN BAYERN

Zugspitze

Griesener Str 4, 82491 ☎ 08821 3180 🖹 08821 947594
e-mail info@zugspitzcamping.de
website www.zugspitzcamping.de

A beautiful setting at the foot of the Zugspitze between the road and the Loisach.

⮑ *On B24 towards Austrian frontier.*

Open All year **Site** 2.9HEC ⚊ ⚊ **Facilities** 🌣 🛁 ⊙ 🚽 ⚊ ⚑ **Services** ⚑ ⚑ **Leisure** ⚊ R **Off-site** ⚑ ⚊LP

GEMÜNDEN AM MAIN BAYERN

Saaleinsel

Duivenallee 7, 97737 ☎ 09351 8574

The municipal site lies a short distance off the main road bordering the River Fränkische Saale. It is in the grounds of a sports field and has a swimming pool.

⮑ *Signed off B26.*

Open Apr-15 Oct **Site** 5.1HEC ⚊ ⚊ **Prices** ⚡ 5 ⚑ 3 ⚑ 3 ▲ 3 **Facilities** 🌣 ⊙ 🚽 ⚊ ⚑ **Services** ⚑ ⚑ **Leisure** ⚊ PR **Off-site** 🛁 ⚑ ⚊

GEMÜNDEN-HOFSTETTEN BAYERN

Schönrain

97737 ☎ 09351 8645 🖹 09351 8721
e-mail info@spessart-camping.de
website www.spessart-camping.de

Slightly sloping, partly terraced meadowland E of River Main.

⮑ *From Gemünden/Main along left bank of River Main, 3km downstream. Turn left off B26 through Hofstetten to site.*

Open Apr-Sep **Site** 7HEC ⚊ ⚊ ⚊ ⚊ **Prices** ⚡ 5-6.10 pitch 6.70-7.20 ⚑ (static)232-290 **Facilities** 🌣 🛁 ⊙ 🚽 ⚊ ⚊ ⚑ **Services** ⚑ ⚑ **Leisure** ⚊ P

GOTTSDORF BAYERN

DUG-Ferienzentrum Bayerwald

Mitterweg 11, Untergriesbach, 94107
☎ 08593 880 🖹 08593 88111

Extensive terrain in quiet location.

⮑ *Off A3 Regensburg-Passau onto B388.*

Open 27 Mar-30 Oct **Site** 12HEC ⚊ ⚊ ⚊ **Facilities** 🌣 🛁 ⊙ 🚽 ⚊ ⚑ **Services** ⚑ ⚑ **Off-site** ⚑ ⚊LPR

GRIESBACH, BAD BAYERN

Kur-Und Feriencamping Dreiquellenbad

94086 ☎ 08532 96130 🖹 08532 961350
e-mail info@camping-bad-griesbach.de
website www.camping-bad-griesbach.de

Pleasant wooded surroundings with modern facilities.

⮑ *1km S of Griesbach Spa, on the Karpfham-Schwaim road.*

Open All year **Site** 3.7HEC ⚊ ⚊ ⚊ ⚊ **Prices** ⚡ 6.10 ⚑ 9.90-10.40 **Facilities** 🌣 🛁 ⊙ 🚽 ⚊ ⚑ **Services** ⚑ ⚑ ⚑ **Leisure** ⚊ P **Off-site** ⚑R

HASLACH BAYERN

Feriencenter Wertacher Hof

87466 ☎ 08361 770 🖹 08361 9344

Well-kept site on Lake Grüntensee.

⮑ *Near Wertach-Haslach railway station.*

Open All year **Site** 3.5HEC ⚊ ⚊ ⚊ **Prices** ⚡ 5.65 pitch 5 **Facilities** 🌣 🛁 ⊙ 🚽 ⚊ ⚊ ⚑ **Services** ⚑ ⚑ **Leisure** ⚊ L

HOFHEIM BAYERN

Brugger am Riegsee

82418 ☎ 08847 728 🖹 08847 228
e-mail office@camping-brugger.de
website www.camping-brugger.de

A lakeside site in a rural setting with modern facilities.

Open May-Sep **Site** 6HEC ⚊ ⚊ ⚊ **Prices** ⚡ 4.80 ▲ 4.80-7 pitch 8.50-14.50 **Facilities** 🌣 🛁 ⊙ 🚽 ⚊ ⚊ ⚑ **Services** ⚑ ⚑ ⚑ **Leisure** ⚊ L

HOHENWARTH BAYERN

Fritz-Berger-Comfort

93480 ☎ 09946 367 🖹 09946 477
e-mail cpl.hohenwarth@fritz-berger.de

Meadowland in the valley of the Weissens Regens with views of the mountain range and town above.

⮑ *From Cham on B85 S to Miltach, continue via Kotzing to Hohenwarth.*

Site 12HEC ⚊ ⚊ **Facilities** 🌣 🛁 ⊙ 🚽 ⚊ ⚊ ⚑ **Services** ⚑ **Leisure** ⚊ LP

Site 6HEC (site size) ⚊ grass ⚊ sand ⚊ stone ⚊ little shade ⚊ partly shaded ⚊ mainly shaded ⚊ bungalows for hire ⚑ caravans for hire ▲ tents for hire ⊗ no dogs **Prices** ⚡ adult per night ⚑ car per night pp per person per night ⚑ caravan per night ▲ tent per night ⚑ (static)-caravan hire per week

INGOLSTADT BAYERN

AZUR Camping Auwaldsee

85053 ☎ 0841 9611616 ▤ 0841 9611617

e-mail ingolstadt@azur-camping.de

website www.azur-camping.de/ingolstadt

Near to Auwaldsee, this site lies in a beautiful setting beside the München-Ingolstadt motorway.

➲ *A9 exit Ingolstadt-Süd.*

Open All year **Site** 10HEC ❤ ♣ **Prices** ♠ 5.50-7.50 ➡ 3.50-5 ➡ 6-9 ▲ 4.50-6 **Facilities** ↿ 🖻 ⊙ ➡ ⌀ ⚒ ℗ **Services** ⊌ ➕ ⓢ **Leisure** ⚌ L **Off-site** ⚌P

ISSIGAU BAYERN

Schloss Issigau

Altes Schloss 3, 95188 ☎ 09293 7173 ▤ 09293 7050

e-mail schloss_issigau@t.online.de

website www.schloss-issigau.de

➲ *A9 exit Berg/Bad Steben, 5km W.*

Open 15 Mar-Oct & Xmas-New Year **Site** 2HEC ❤ ♣ ➡ **Prices** ♠ 4.50 ➡ 6 ▲ 5 ➡ (static)266 **Facilities** ↿ ⊙ ➡ ⚒ ℗ **Services** ⊌ ⊎ ⓢ **Off-site** 🖻

JODITZ BAYERN

Auensee

95189 ☎ 09295 381 ▤ 09281 1706666

e-mail koeditz@landkreis-hof.de

website www.gemeinde-koeditz.de

Municipal site on partly terraced meadowland above lake.

➲ *München-Berlin motorway exit Berg-Bad Steben, site 4km E.*

Open All year **Site** 9HEC ❤ ♣ **Prices** ♠ 4 ➡ 1 ➡ 5 ▲ 2.50-4 **Facilities** ↿ ⊙ ➡ ⚒ ℗ **Services** ➕ ⓢ **Leisure** ⚌ L **Off-site** 🖻 ⊌ ⚌PR

KIPFENBERG BAYERN

AZUR-Camping Altmühltal

Campingstr, 85110 ☎ 08465 905167 ▤ 08465 3745

e-mail kipfenberg@azur-camping.de

website www.azur-camping.de/kipfenberg

Well-equipped site in an unspoiled wooded location with good canoeing facilities.

Open Apr-Oct **Site** 5.5HEC ❤ ♣ **Facilities** ↿ 🖻 ⊙ ➡ ℗ **Services** ⊌ ➕ ⓢ **Leisure** ⚌ R **Off-site** ⊌ ⚌P

KIRCHZELL BAYERN

AZUR-Camping Odenwald

Siegfriedstr, 63931 ☎ 09373 566 ▤ 09373 7375

e-mail kirchzell@azur-camping.de

website www.azur-camping.de/kirchzell

Site on natural terraced meadowland in wooded hilly country. No admission after 21.30 hrs.

➲ *From Amorbach towards Eberbach road for 5km, site 1km from town.*

Open Apr-Oct **Site** 7HEC ❤ ♣ **Prices** ♠ 5.50-7.50 ▲ 4.50-6 pitch 6-9 **Facilities** ↿ 🖻 ⊙ ➡ ⚒ ℗ **Services** ⊌ ➕ ⓢ **Leisure** ⚌ P

KISSINGEN, BAD BAYERN

Bad Kissingen

Euerdorfer Str 1, D-97688 ☎ 0971 5211 ▤ 0971 5211

e-mail info@campingpark-badkissingen.de

website www.campingpark-badkissingen.de

Set in a park beside the River Saale.

➲ *Near S bridge over the Saale.*

Open Apr-15 Oct **Site** 1.8HEC ❤ ♣ **Facilities** ↿ 🖻 ⊙ ➡ ⌀ ⚒ ℗ **Services** ⊌ ➕ ⓢ **Off-site** ⚌P

KITZINGEN BAYERN

Schiefer Turm

Marktbreiter Str 20, 97318 ☎ 09321 33125 ▤ 09321 384795

e-mail info@camping-kitzingen.de

website www.camping-kitzingen.de

➲ *A3 exit Biebelried/Kitzingen.*

Open Apr-15 Oct **Site** 2.3HEC ❤ ♣ ➡ **Prices** ♠ 5 ▲ 3.50 pitch 6 **Facilities** ↿ 🖻 ⊙ ➡ ⚒ ℗ **Services** ⊌ ⊌ ⓢ **Leisure** ⚌ R **Off-site** ⚌P

KLINGENBRUNN BAYERN

NationalPark

94518 ☎ 08553 727 ▤ 08553 6930

website www.camping-nationalpark.de

Pleasant wooded surroundings set around the restaurant.

➲ *Off B85 12km SE of Regen near Kirchdorf, 6km E towards Klingenbrunn.*

Open All year **Site** 5HEC ❤ ♣ ➡ **Prices** ♠ 4 ▲ 3.30 pitch 4.10 **Facilities** ↿ 🖻 ⊙ ➡ ⌀ ⚒ ℗ **Services** ⊌ ➕ ⓢ **Off-site** ⊌ ⚌LP

KÖNIGSDORF BAYERN

Königsdorf

Am Bibisee, 82549 ☎ 08171 81580 ▤ 08171 81165

e-mail mail@camping-koenigsdorf.de

website www.camping-koenigsdorf.de

Unspoiled site in natural setting in meadowland. A number of individual pitches for tourers.

➲ *2km N of town 0ff B11, just beyond edge of forest.*

Open All year **Site** 8.6HEC ❤ ♣ **Facilities** ↿ 🖻 ⊙ ➡ ⌀ ⚒ ℗ **Services** ⊌ ➕ ⓢ **Leisure** ⚌ L **Off-site** ⊌ ⚌PRS

KÖNIGSSEE BAYERN

Mühlleiten

83477 ☎ 08652 4584 ▤ 08652 69194

e-mail buchung@camping-muehlleiten.de

website www.camping-muehlleiten.de

A pleasant site in wooded surroundings adjacent to a small guesthouse. Beautiful views of the Berchtesgaden mountains.

➲ *N of Königsee towards Berchtesgaden.*

Open All year **Site** 1.5HEC ❤ ♣ **Facilities** ↿ 🖻 ⊙ ➡ ⌀ ⚒ ℗ **Services** ⊌ ⓢ **Leisure** ⚌ R **Off-site** ⊌ ⊌ ⚌LP

Germany

Facilities 🖻 shop ↿ shower ⊙ electric points for razors ➡ electric points for caravans ℗ parking by tents permitted ℗ compulsory separate car park
Services ⊌ café/restaurant ⊌ bar ⌀ Camping Gaz International ⚒ gas other than Camping Gaz ➕ first aid facilities ⓢ laundry
Leisure ⚌ swimming L-Lake P-Pool R-River S-Sea **Off-site** All facilities within 2km

Germany

KRUN BAYERN

Tennsee
82493 ☎ 08825 170 ▤ 08825 17236
e-mail info@camping-tennsee.de
website www.camping-tennsee.de
A partially terraced site with fine views of the Karwendel and Zugspitz mountains.

➲ *From München-Garmisch-Partenkirchen motorway B2 to Mittenwald & signed.*

Open 15 Dec-6 Nov **Site** 5HEC ♨ ♨ ♣ ♠ **Prices** ♠ 7.50-8 Å 6-7 pitch 8.50-12 (incl 2 persons) **Facilities** ♠ ▤ ⊙ ⊕ ⊘ ♨ ⑦ **Services** ♨ ⑩ ➕ ▣ **Off-site** ♨L

KÜHNHAUSEN BAYERN

Stadler
Strandbadstr 11, 83367 ☎ 08686 8037 ▤ 08685 1049
Level meadow on lake with private beach.

➲ *2m E shore of Lake Waginger.*

Open Apr-Sep **Site** 0.8HEC ♨ ♣ ♠ ♠ **Prices** ♠ 4.50 ♠ 1.50 ♠ 4-6 Å 2-5 **Facilities** ♠ ⊙ ⊕ ⑦ **Services** ▣ **Leisure** ♨ LS **Off-site** ▤ ♨⑩ ⊘ ➕

LACKENHÄUSER BAYERN

KNAUS Lackenhäuser
Lackenhäuser 127, 94089 ☎ 08583 311 ▤ 08583 91079
e-mail lackenhaeuser@knauscamp.de
website www.knauscamp.de
Extensive site with woodland parks, waterfalls. Many health resort facilities.

Open 22 Dec-5 Nov **Site** 15HEC ♨ ♣ ♠ ♠ Å **Prices** ♠ 6 pitch 4-8 **Facilities** ♠ ▤ ⊙ ⊕ ♨ ⑦ **Services** ⑩ **Leisure** ♨ P **Off-site** ♨ ♨L ➕

LANGLAU BAYERN

Langlau
Seestr 30, Kleiner Brombachsee, 91738
☎ 09834 96969 ▤ 09834 96968
e-mail mail@seecamping-langlau.de
website www.seecamping-langlau.de
On the shores of the Kleiner Brombachsee.

➲ *From Gunzevhausen towards Pleinfield for 10km.*

Open Mar-15 Nov **Site** 12.4HEC ♨ ♣ ♠ **Prices** ♠ 6.25 pitch 7 ♠ (static)180 **Facilities** ♠ ▤ ⊙ ⊕ ♨ ⑦ **Services** ♨ ⑩ ▣ **Off-site** ⑩ ♨L ➕

LECHBRUCK BAYERN

DCC Stadt Essen
Oberer Lechsee, 8923 ☎ 08862 8426 ▤ 08862 7570
Terraced site, very tidy and well-maintained on Oberen Lech lake. Separate section for dog owners.

➲ *Signed from town centre.*

Open All year **Site** 20HEC ♨ ♣ **Facilities** ♠ ▤ ⊙ ⊕ ⊘ ⑦ **Services** ⑩ ➕ ▣ **Leisure** ♨ L **Off-site** ♨P

LENGFURT BAYERN

Main-Spessart-Park
Spessartstrasse 30, 97855 ☎ 09395 1079 ▤ 09395 8295
e-mail info@camping-main-spessart.de
website www.camping-main-spessart.de
Site lies partly on terraced meadowland and partly on the E slopes of the Main valley. Some water sports and nearby private mooring on the River Main.

➲ *A3 exit Markheidenfeld, N to Altfled, 6km E to Lengfurt (NW edge of village).*

Open All year **Site** 10HEC ♨ ♣ **Prices** ♠ 5 ♠ 2 ♠ 3.50 Å 3 **Facilities** ♠ ▤ ⊙ ⊕ ⊘ ⑦ **Services** ⑩ ▣ **Off-site** ♨PR ➕

LINDAU IM BODENSEE BAYERN

Gitzenweiler Hof
88131 ☎ 838294940 ▤ 8382949415
e-mail info@gitzenweiler-hof.de
website www.gitzenweiler-hof.de
Located in hilly meadow ground near Lake Constance surrounded with trees and hedges.

➲ *A96 exit Weissenberg.*

Open All year **Site** 14HEC ♨ ♣ ♠ ♠ Å **Prices** ♠ 7 ♠ 2 Å 5-8 pitch 9 ♠ (static)600-800 **Facilities** ♠ ▤ ⊙ ⊕ ⊘ ♨ ⑦ **Services** ♨ ⑩ ➕ ▣ **Leisure** ♨ P

AT ZECH (4KM SE)

Lindau am See
Fraunhoferstr 20, 88131 ☎ 08382 72236 ▤ 08382 976106
e-mail info@park-camping.de
website www.park-camping.de
Site lies on meadowland with trees, reaching down to the lake. Very large sanitary blocks. Common room, reading room, field for ball games and a separate common room for young people.

➲ *B31 from Lindau towards Bregenz, turn right (signed) before level crossing, site 0.5km.*

Open 15 Mar-Oct **Site** 5HEC ♨ ♣ **Prices** ♠ 5-6.50 ♠ 2.40-3 Å 1.50-2.50 **Facilities** ♠ ▤ ⊙ ⊕ ♨ ⑦ **Services** ♨ ⑩ ➕ ▣ **Leisure** ♨ L **Off-site** ♨P

MEMMINGEN BAYERN

AT BUXHEIM (5KM NW)

See International
Am Weiherhaus 7, 87740 ☎ 08331 71800 ▤ 08331 63554
website www.camping-buxheim.de
Terraced site beyond public bathing area.

➲ *Leave Um-Kempten motorway at Memminger Kreuz then right to Buxheim.*

Open May-15 Sep **Site** 42HEC ♨ ♣ **Prices** ♠ 4.20 ♠ 3 ♠ 7.50-9.50 Å 2.50 **Facilities** ♠ ▤ ⊙ ⊕ ♨ ⑦ **Services** ♨ ⑩ ➕ ▣ **Leisure** ♨ L **Off-site** ⑩ ⊘ ♨P

MÖRSLINGEN BAYERN

Mörslingen
89435 ☎ 09074 4024
e-mail mail@camping-moerslingen.de
website www.camping-moerslingen.de

➲ *6km N of Dillengen.*

Open All year **Site** 1HEC ♨ ♣ ♠ ♠ **Prices** ♠ 5 ♠ 2 ♠ 8 Å 8 **Facilities** ♠ ⊙ ⊕ ♨ ⑦ **Services** ➕ ▣ **Leisure** ♨ LP **Off-site** ▤

Site 6HEC (site size) ♨ grass ♨ sand ♨ stone ♣ little shade ♣ partly shaded ♣ mainly shaded ♠ bungalows for hire ♠ caravans for hire Å tents for hire ⊗ no dogs **Prices** ♠ adult per night ♠ car per night pp per person per night ♠ caravan per night Å tent per night ♠ (static)-caravan hire per week

MÜHLHAUSEN BEI AUGSBURG BAYERN

Lech
Seeweg 6, 86444 ☎ 08207 2200 🗎 08207 2202
e-mail info@lech-camping.de
website www.lech-camping.de
Level grassland with swimming facilities beside lake.

⭕ 4km N towards Neuburg.

Open Apr-15 Sep **Site** 3HEC 😊 ♣ 🚎 **Prices** ♣ 5.20-5.70 🚐 2 🚐 7 🛇 5-7
🚐 (static)282-482 **Facilities** 🏠 ⊕ 🖭 ⌀ 🚿 ® **Services** 🍴 ⊞ 🗓
Leisure ⚓ L **Off-site** 🗓 ⚓P

Ludwigshof am See
Augsburger Str 36, 86444 ☎ 08207 96170 🗎 08207 961770
e-mail info@bauer-caravan.de
website www.bauer-caravan.de
Clean site with small lake away from motorway, near restaurant of the
same name. Separate section for residential pitches.

⭕ Motorway exit 73 Augsburg Ost, 1.5km towards Neuberg.

Open Apr-Oct **Site** 12HEC 😊 ♣ **Prices** ♣ 4.50 🚐 5-9 **Facilities** 🏠 🗓 ⊙
🚐 ⌀ 🚿 ® **Services** 🛒 🍴 ⊞ 🗓 **Leisure** ⚓ L **Off-site** 🗓 ⚓PR

MÜNCHEN (MUNICH) BAYERN

AT OBERMENZING

München-Obermenzing
Lochhausener Str 59, 81247 ☎ 089 812235 🗎 089 844807
e-mail campingplatz-obermenzing@t-online.de
website www.campingplatz-muenchen.de
Park-like site near motorway.

⭕ 1km from end of Stuttgart-München motorway.

Open 15 Mar-Oct **Site** 5.5HEC 😊 ♣ ⚓ ♣ ♣ ♣ 🚐 🚐 **Prices** ♣ 4.50 🚐 3
🚐 6 🛇 3.50 **Facilities** 🏠 🗓 ⊙ 🚐 ⌀ 🚿 ® **Services** 🛒 🍴 ⊞ 🗓
Off-site 🛒 🍴 ⚓LPR

NEUBÄU BAYERN

Seecamping
Seestr 4, 93426 ☎ 09469 331
e-mail seecamp-neubau@t-online.de
Meadowland site along lakeshore.

⭕ B85 from Schwandorf towards Cham.

Site 5HEC 😊 ♣ **Facilities** 🏠 🗓 ⊙ 🚐 ⌀ 🚿 ® **Services** 🛒 🍴 ⊞ 🗓
Leisure ⚓ L

NEUKIRCHEN VORM WALD BAYERN

Rotbrunn
Pilling 22 ☎ 08504 920260 🗎 08504 920265
e-mail camping.rotbrunn@vr-web.de
Terraced and partially shaded site on edge of small town with shops
and services.

⭕ A3 exit Aicha W, 6km to Neukirchen.

Open All year **Site** 😊 ♣ **Facilities** 🏠 ⊙ 🚐 ® **Services** 🍴 🗓 **Leisure** ⚓ L
Off-site 🗓 🛒 🍴 ⌀ ⊞

NEUSTADT BAYERN

Main-Spessart-Camping-International
97845 ☎ 09393 639 🗎 09393 1607
e-mail info@camping-neustadt-main.de
website www.camping-neustadt-main.de
Beautiful location alongside the River Main. Waters sports include
water skiing.

⭕ A3 exit Marktheidenfeld towards Lohr.

Open Apr-Sep **Site** 5.6HEC 😊 ♣ **Prices** ♣ 5-5.50 pitch 6.50 **Facilities** 🏠
🗓 ⊙ 🚐 ⌀ 🚿 ® **Services** 🍴 ⊞ 🗓 **Leisure** ⚓ PR **Off-site** 🍴

NÜRNBERG (NUREMBERG) BAYERN

Knaus Campingpark Nürnberg
Hans-Kalb-Str 56, 90471 ☎ 0911 9812717 🗎 0911 9812718
e-mail nuernberg@knauscamp.de
website www.knauscamp.de
Well-kept municipal site in beautiful location in a forest between a
stadium with a swimming pool and the Trade Fair Centre.

⭕ A9 exit Nürnberg-Fischbach towards stadium.

Open All year **Site** 2.7HEC 😊 ♣ 🚐 🛇 **Prices** ♣ 6 🚐 4 pitch 12
Facilities 🏠 🗓 ⊙ 🚐 ⌀ ® **Services** 🍴 ⊞ **Off-site** 🛒 ⚓LP

OBERAMMERGAU BAYERN

Oberammergau
Ettaler Str 56, 82847 ☎ 08822 94105 🗎 08822 94197
e-mail campingpark-oberammergau@t-online.de
website www.campingpark-oberammergau.de
A year-round site with modern facilities and fine views of the Bavarian
Alps.

⭕ Signed from town.

Open All year **Site** 2.6HEC 😊 ♣ 🚐 🚐 **Facilities** 🏠 🗓 ⊙ 🚐 ⌀ 🚿 ®
Services 🛒 🍴 ⊞ 🗓 **Leisure** ⚓ R **Off-site** ⚓P

OBERSTDORF BAYERN

Oberstdorf
87561 ☎ 08322 6525 🗎 08322 809760
e-mail camping-oberstdorf@t-online.de
website www.camping-oberstdorf.de/
Level grassland site with fine mountain views.

⭕ 0.8km N of town centre near railway line.

Open All year **Site** 16HEC 😊 ♣ **Prices** ♣ 4.60-5.10 🚐 2.60-2.60
🚐 4.60-5.10 🛇 2.60-4.60 **Facilities** 🏠 🗓 ⊙ 🚐 ⌀ 🚿 ® **Services** 🍴 ⊞ 🗓
Off-site 🗓 ⚓LPR

Facilities 🗓 shop 🏠 shower ⊙ electric points for razors 🚐 electric points for caravans ® parking by tents permitted ❷ compulsory separate car park
Services 🍴 café/restaurant 🛒 bar ⌀ Camping Gaz International 🚿 gas other than Camping Gaz ⊞ first aid facilities 🗓 laundry
Leisure ⚓ swimming L-Lake P-Pool R-River S-Sea **Off-site** All facilities within 2km

Germany

OBERWÖSSEN BAYERN

Litzelau

83246 ☎ 08640 8704 ▤ 08640 5265
e-mail camping-litzelau@t-online.de
website www.camping-litzelau.de
Almost level meadowland surrounded by forested slopes.

⮑ *A8 exit 106 Bernau, B305 S through Marquartstein & Unterwössen.*

Open All year **Site** 4.5HEC ⛺ ⛱ ⛺ 🏠 **Prices** ⋔ 4.20 🚐 6.60 🛆 3.60 **Facilities** 🏪 🏕 ⊙ 🚰 ⬮ 🚿 ℗ **Services** 🍴 🍽 ➕ 🛒 **Leisure** ⬮ R **Off-site** ⬮LP

PASSAU BAYERN

Dreiflüsse

94113 ☎ 08546 633 ▤ 08546 2686
e-mail dreifluessecamping@t-online.de
website www.dreifluessecamping.privat.t-online.de
A well-equipped site in pleasant wooded surroundings.

⮑ *A3 exit Passau-Nord, site signed.*

Open Apr-Oct **Site** 5HEC ⛺ ⛱ ⛺ 🛆 **Prices** ⋔ 4.50 🚐 4 pitch 5-9.50 **Facilities** 🏪 🏕 ⊙ ⊙ 🚰 ⬮ 🚿 ℗ **Services** 🍴 🍽 ➕ 🛒 **Leisure** ⬮ P

PFRAUNDORF BAYERN

Kratzmühle

85125 ☎ 08461 64170 ▤ 08461 641717
e-mail info@kratzmuehle.de
website www.kratzmuehle.de
Terraced site, divided into pitches, on a wooded hillside overlooking the River Altmühl.

⮑ *From village turn to Kratzmühle.*

Open All year **Site** 9.6HEC ⛺ ⛱ ⛺ 🏠 🛆 **Facilities** 🏪 🏕 ⊙ ⊙ 🚰 ⬮ 🚿 ℗ **Services** 🍽 ➕ 🛒 **Leisure** ⬮ LR

PIDING BAYERN

Staufeneck

83451 ☎ 08651 2134 ▤ 08651 710450
e-mail camping-staufeneck@t-online.de
website www.camping-berchtesgadener-land.de
Beautiful and quiet location beside the River Saalach.

⮑ *A8 exit Bad Reichenall for 2.5km & turn right.*

Open Apr-Oct **Site** 2.7HEC ⛺ ⛱ ⛺ **Facilities** 🏪 🏕 ⊙ 🚰 ⬮ 🚿 ℗ **Services** ➕ 🛒 **Leisure** ⬮ R **Off-site** 🍴 🍽 🚿

PIELENHOFEN BAYERN

Naabtal

93188 ☎ 09409 373 ▤ 09409 723
e-mail camping.pielenhofen@t-online.de
website www.camping-pielenhofen.de
The site is well-situated beside the River Nab, and has a special section for overnight visitors.

⮑ *A3 exit Nittendorf, via Etterzhausen.*

Open All year **Site** 6HEC ⛺ ⛱ ⛺ 🏠 **Prices** ⋔ 5.25 pitch 6.10 **Facilities** 🏪 🏕 ⊙ 🚰 🚿 ℗ **Services** 🍴 🍽 ➕ 🛒 **Leisure** ⬮ R

PRIEN AM CHIEMSEE BAYERN

Hofbauer

Bernauerstrasse 110, 83209 ☎ 08051 4136 ▤ 08051 62657
e-mail ferienhaus-campingpl.hofbauer@t-online.de
website www.camping-prien-chiemsee.de
A peaceful location among the Bavarian foothills of the Alps with fine views of the mountains. Site divided into separate plots.

⮑ *A8 exit 106 for Bernau, right for Prien, site 3km on left.*

Open Apr-Oct **Site** 2HEC ⛺ ⛱ ⛺ 🏠 **Prices** ⋔ 5.90-7.50 🛆 3 pitch 5.20 **Facilities** 🏪 🏕 ⊙ 🚰 🚿 ℗ **Services** 🍴 🍽 🛒 **Leisure** ⬮ P **Off-site** 🏕 🍽 ⬮L ➕

ROSSHAUPTEN BAYERN

Warsitzka

87669 ☎ 08367 406 ▤ 08367 1256
e-mail info@camping-warsitzka.de
website www.camping-warsitzka.de
A well-kept site with good installations.

⮑ *B16 from Füssen towards Rosshaupten for 10km, right 2km before village & bridge.*

Open 16 Dec-Oct **Site** 4.5HEC ⛺ ⛱ ⛺ **Facilities** 🏪 🏕 ⊙ ⊙ 🚰 ⬮ 🚿 ℗ **Services** 🍴 🍽 ➕ 🛒 **Leisure** ⬮ LR

ROTHENBURG OB DER TAUBER BAYERN

Tauber-Idyll

Detwang 28A, 91541 ☎ 09861 3177 ▤ 09861 92848
e-mail campingtauber-ldyll@t-online.de
The well-kept site lies on a meadow scattered with trees and bushes, on the outskirts of the N suburb of Detwang and next to the River Tauber.

⮑ *B25 from Nordinger Str W along River Tauber towards Bad Mergentheim. Signed from main roads.*

Open 1 wk before Etr-Oct **Site** 0.5HEC ⛺ ⛱ ⛺ **Prices** ⋔ 4.50 🚐 1.50 🚐 3.50 🛆 3 **Facilities** 🏪 🏕 ⊙ 🚰 🚿 ℗ **Services** ➕ 🛒 **Off-site** 🍴 ⬮L ⬮F

Tauber-Romantik

Detwang 39, 91541 ☎ 09861 6191 ▤ 09861 86899
e-mail info@camping-tauberromantik.de
website www.camping-tauberromantik.de
Open 15 Mar-4 Nov **Site** 1.2HEC ⛺ ⛱ ⛺ 🏠 **Prices** ⋔ 4.80-5 🚐 2 🛆 4.50-5 pitch 6-6.80 🚐 (static)190-200 **Facilities** 🏪 🏕 ⊙ 🚰 ⬮ 🚿 ℗ **Services** 🍴 🍽 🛒 **Off-site** ⬮R

ROTTENBUCH BAYERN

Terrassen-Camping am Richterbichl

82401 ☎ 08867 1500 ▤ 08867 8300
e-mail christof.echtler@t-online.de
website www.camping-rottenbuch.de
Several pleasant terraces with good views.

⮑ *On S outskirts on B23.*

Open All year **Site** 1.2HEC ⛺ ⛱ ⛺ 🏠 **Prices** ⋔ 4.50-5.10 pitch 5.40-6 🚐 (static)224-266 **Facilities** 🏪 🏕 ⊙ ⊙ 🚰 ⬮ 🚿 ℗ **Services** 🍴 🍽 🛒 **Leisure** ⬮ L **Off-site** 🍽 ⬮PR ➕

Site 6HEC (site size) ⛺ grass ⛱ sand ⛺ stone ♣ little shade ♣ partly shaded ♣ mainly shaded 🏠 bungalows for hire 🚐 caravans for hire 🛆 tents for hire ⊗ no dogs **Prices** ⋔ adult per night 🚐 car per night pp per person per night 🚐 caravan per night 🛆 tent per night 🚐 (static)-caravan hire per week

RUHPOLDING BAYERN

Ortnerhof
Ort 5, 83324 ☎ 08663 1764 📠 08663 5073
e-mail camping-ortnerhof@t-online.de
website www.ruhpolding.de/camping
Well-kept site on a meadow at the foot of the Rauschberg Mountain,
opposite the cable-car station.
➲ *Off Deutsche Alpenstr.*
Open All year **Site** 3HEC 🌳🌳🌳⛺ ⊗ **Prices** ⚑ 5 ⇄ 1.50 ⊞ 4.50
⛺ 4.50 **Facilities** ⋔ ⊙ ⊕ ⌀ ⓟ **Services** ⍟ ⊞ 🗑 **Off-site** 🛒 ⚒

SCHECHEN BAYERN

Erlensee
Rosenheimer Str 63, 83135 ☎ 08039 1695 📠 08039 9416
The site lies on the shores of an artificial lake.
➲ *From Rosenheim, 10km N onto B15 towards Wasserburg,
turn right entering Schechen.*
Open All year **Site** 6HEC 🌳⛺ **Prices** ⚑ 5.20 ⇄ 2 ⛺ 3.50-6.50 pitch 9
Facilities ⋔ ⊙ ⊕ ⚒ ⓟ **Services** ⊞ 🗑 **Leisure** � L **Off-site** 🛒 ⍟ ⍟

SCHÖNAU AM KÖNIGSSEE BAYERN

Grafenlehen
Königsseer Fussweg 71, 83471 ☎ 08652 4140 📠 08652 690768
e-mail camping-grafenlehen@t-online.de
website www.camping-grafenlehen.de
A well-drained terraced site on the edge of the Berchtesgadener
national park. A peaceful location near Königssee lake.
➲ *Motorway exit Reichenhall, B20 to Berchtesgaden, right at
railway station, B20 to Königssee, right before car park.*
Open Jan-Oct , 11-31 Dec **Site** 3HEC 🌳🌳⛺ **Facilities** ⋔ ⊡ ⊙ ⊕
Services ⍟ ⍟ 🗑 **Off-site** ⚒ P

SEEFELD BAYERN

Strandbad Pilsensee
Graf Toerringstr 11, 82229 ☎ 08152 7232 📠 08152 78473
e-mail campingplatz@toerring-seefeld.de
website www.schloss-seefeld.de
➲ *S towards Pilsensee.*
Open All year **Site** 10HEC 🌳⛺⊞ **Prices** ⚑ 5.10-6 ⇄ 1 ⊞ 5.70-6.70
⛺ 5.70-6.70 ⊞ (static)196 **Facilities** ⋔ ⊡ ⊙ ⊕ ⌀ ⚒ **Services** ⍟ ⊞ 🗑
Leisure � L

SOMMERACH AM MAIN BAYERN

Katzenkopf am See
97334 ☎ 09381 9215 📠 09381 6028
website www.camping-katzenkopf.de
On level ground beside the river Main. Pitches divided by bushes and
good recreational facilities.
➲ *A3 exit Kitzingen-Schwarzach-Volkach for Volkach for 7km.*
Open Apr-Oct **Site** 10HEC 🌳🌳⛺⊞ **Prices** ⚑ 6-6.50 pitch 6-7
Facilities ⋔ ⊡ ⊙ ⊕ ⌀ ⚒ ⓟ **Services** ⍟ ⍟ ⊞ 🗑 **Leisure** � LR
Off-site ⚒ P

See advertisement on this page

STADTSTEINACH BAYERN

Stadtsteinach
95346 ☎ 09225 800394 📠 09225 800395
e-mail info@camping-stadtsteinach.de
website www.camping-stadtsteinach.de
Terraced site on SE facing slope with a view over the town and
surrounding hills.
➲ *Via Badstr.*
Open All year **Site** 3.8HEC 🌳⛺ **Facilities** ⋔ ⊡ ⊙ ⊕ ⌀ ⚒ ⓟ
Services ⍟ ⍟ ⊞ 🗑 **Off-site** ⚒ P

TETTENHAUSEN BAYERN

Gut Horn
83329 ☎ 08681 227 📠 08681 4282
e-mail info@gut-horn.de
website www.gut-horn.de
Quiet site sheltered by forest, divided into pitches on lake shore.
➲ *SE on Wagingersee.*
Open Mar-Nov **Site** 5HEC 🌳⛺⊞ **Prices** ⚑ 5-5.50 pitch 5.50-7.50
Facilities ⋔ ⊡ ⊙ ⊕ ⚒ ⓟ **Services** ⍟ 🗑 **Leisure** � L
Off-site ⌀ ⚒ PR ⊞

TITTMONING BAYERN

Seebauer
84529 ☎ 08683 1216 📠 08683 7175
e-mail info@camping-seebauer.de
website www.camping-seebauer.de
On meadow with a few terraces. Near a farm, beside a lake.
➲ *3km NW towards Burghausen.*
Open 15 Apr-15 Oct **Site** 2.3HEC 🌳⛺ **Prices** ⚑ 5 pitch 6.50-7.80
Facilities ⋔ ⊡ ⊙ ⊕ ⌀ ⚒ ⓟ **Services** ⍟ ⊞ 🗑 **Leisure** � LP
Off-site ⍟ ⚒ L

Facilities 🏪 shop ⋔ shower ⊙ electric points for razors ⊕ electric points for caravans ⓟ parking by tents permitted ⊗ compulsory separate car park
Services ⍟ café/restaurant ⍟ bar ⌀ Camping Gaz International ⚒ gas other than Camping Gaz ⊞ first aid facilities 🗑 laundry
Leisure � swimming L-Lake P-Pool R-River S-Sea **Off-site** All facilities within 2km

Germany

TRAUSNITZ BAYERN

Trausnitz
92555 ☎ 09655 1304 ▤ 09655 1304
website www.camping-trausnitz.de
Wooded surroundings on the shores of a lake with modern facilities.
➲ A93 exit Pfreimd.
Open All year **Site** 3.5HEC ⚘ ❦ ❦ **Prices** ♣ 4 ↫ 5 Å 3.50-8
Facilities ⌂ ☖ ⊙ ➋ ⬟ ⑫ **Services** ⑩ ➕ ◙ **Leisure** ⚓ LR

TÜCHERSFELD BAYERN

Fränkische Schweiz
Tüchersfeld, 91278 ☎ 09242 1788 ▤ 09242 1040
e-mail spaetling@t-online.de
website www.campingplatz-fraenkishe-schweiz.info
➲ A9 exit Pegnitz, 12km W on B470 towards Forchheim.
Open 20 Mar-9 Oct **Site** 2HEC ⚘ ❦ **Facilities** ⌂ ☖ ⊙ ➋ ⬟ ⑫
Services ⑩ ⑩ ➕ ◙ **Leisure** ⚓ R

VELBURG BAYERN

Hauenstein
92355 ☎ 09182 454 ▤ 09182 902251
e-mail campingamhauenstein@t-ouline.de
A well-appointed site, lies on several terraces and is completely
divided into individual pitches. All with electric points.
➲ A3 exit Velburg, S through village signed Naturbad.
Open All year **Site** 5HEC ⚘ ❦ **Prices** ♣ 5.20 ↫ 3 ↫ 4 Å 3.20
Facilities ⌂ ☖ ⊙ ➋ ⬟ ⑫ **Services** ⑩ ➕ ◙ **Off-site** ⚓L

VIECHTACH BAYERN

KNAUS Viechtach
Waldfrieden 22, 94234 ☎ 09942 1095 ▤ 09942 902222
e-mail viechtach@knauscamp.de
website www.knauscamp.de
Site on slightly undulating meadow, divided by rows of trees. The site
has modern installations.
➲ Off Freibad Viechtach onto B85, signed.
Open 22 Dec-7 Jan, 30 Mar-5 Nov **Site** 5.7HEC ⚘ ❦ ❦ ↫ Å **Prices** ♣ 6
pitch 2 **Facilities** ⌂ ☖ ⊙ ➋ ⬟ ⑫ **Services** ⑩ ➕ ◙ **Leisure** ⚓ P

WAGING BAYERN

Strandcamping
Am See 1, 83329 ☎ 08681 552 ▤ 08681 45010
e-mail strandcamp@aol.com
website www.strandcamp.de
Extensive, level grassland site divided in two by access road to
neighbouring sailing club. The site lies near the Strandbad and
Kurhaus bathing area and spa, and the Casino. There is a Kneipp
(hydrotherapeutic) pool in the camp.
➲ Signed to Strandbad bathing area.
Open Apr-Oct **Site** 34HEC ⚘ ❦ ❦ ⊗ **Prices** ♣ 5.50-6.90 pitch 6.20-7.20
↫ (static)354.40-465.30 **Facilities** ⌂ ☖ ⊙ ➋ ⬟ ⑫ **Services** ⑩ ⑩ ➕
◙ **Leisure** ⚓ L

WALTENHOFEN BAYERN

Insel-Camping am See
87448 ☎ 08379 881 ▤ 08379 7308
e-mail info@insel-camping.de
website www.insel-camping.de
A well-equipped site beside the lake with access to ski slopes.
➲ Off B19, S of Memhölz.
Open All year **Site** 1.6HEC ⚘ ❦ **Prices** ♣ 4 ↫ 1.50 Å 3-5 pitch 5-7.50
Facilities ⌂ ⊙ ➋ ⬟ ⑫ **Services** ⑩ ➕ ◙ **Leisure** ⚓ L
Off-site ☖ ⑩ ⚓PR

WEISSACH BAYERN

Wallberg
Rainerweg 10, 83700 ☎ 08022 5371 ▤ 08022 670274
e-mail campingplatz-wallberg@web.de
website www.campingplatz-wallberg.de
The well-kept site lies on a level meadow with a few trees beside a
stream.
➲ B318 from Gmund to Tegernsee, Bad Wiessee to Wiessach,
continue 9km.
Open All year **Site** 3HEC ⚘ ❦ ❦ **Prices** ♣ 5.80-6.50 ↫ 2.50
↫ 5.70-6.70 Å 4.50 **Facilities** ⌂ ☖ ⊙ ➋ ⬟ ⑫ **Services** ⑩
Leisure ⚓ R **Off-site** ⑩ ⚓LP ➕

WEISSENSTADT BAYERN

Weissenstädter See
Badstr 91, 8687 ☎ 09253 288 ▤ 09253 8507
e-mail info@weissenstadt.de
website www.weissenstadt.de
This municipal site is in close proximity to a swimming pool and a
lake, so offering numerous sports facilities.
➲ 1km NW of town.
Open All year **Site** 1.7HEC ⚘ ❦ **Facilities** ⌂ ⊙ ➋ ⬟ ⑫
Services ⑩ ⑩ ➕ **Leisure** ⚓ LP **Off-site** ☖

WEMDING BAYERN

AZUR Waldsee Wemding
Wolferstadter Str 100, 86650 ☎ 09092 90101 ▤ 09092 90100
e-mail info@campingpark-waldsee.de
website www.campingpark-waldsee.de
A wooded lakeside setting with excellent recreational facilities.
Open All year **Site** 9HEC ⚘ ❦ ❦ ↫ **Prices** ♣ 4.50-6 Å 3.50-4.50 pitch
5.50-7.50 **Facilities** ⌂ ☖ ⊙ ➋ ⬟ ⑫ **Services** ⑩ ➕ ◙ **Leisure** ⚓ L
Off-site ⑩ ⬟ ⚓PR

WERTACH BAYERN

Grüntensee
Grüntenseestr 41, 87497 ☎ 08365 375 ▤ 08365 1221
e-mail info@gruentensee.de
website www.gruentensee.de
A modern site beside Lake Grünten.
➲ From Kempten, turn right entering Nesselwerg & signed.
Open All year **Site** 5HEC ⚘ ❦ ❦ **Facilities** ⌂ ⊙ ➋ ⬟ ⑫
Services ⑩ ⑩ ➕ ◙ **Leisure** ⚓ L **Off-site** ⚓P

Site 6HEC (site size) ⚘ grass ❦ sand ❦ stone ❦ little shade ❦ partly shaded ❦ mainly shaded ⌂ bungalows for hire
↫ caravans for hire Å tents for hire ⊗ no dogs **Prices** ♣ adult per night ↫ car per night pp per person per night ↫ caravan per night
Å tent per night ↫ (static)-caravan hire per week

WINKL BEI BISCHOFSWIESEN BAYERN

Winkllandthal

83483 ☎ 08652 8164 🖹 08652 979831
e-mail camping-winkl@t-online.de
website www.camping-winkl.de
Meadowland site between the B20 and the edge of woodland.
➔ *From Bad Reichenhall to Berchtesgaden for 8km.*
Open Dec-Oct **Site** 2.5HEC 👋 ⬤ 👋 �#️ **Prices** ♠ 6.50 pitch 6
�# (static)420 **Facilities** ⋔ ☎ ⊙ ⬤ ∅ ⚊ ℗ **Services** ⬛ ⭕ ➕ ⬚
Leisure ⬤ R

ZWIESEL BAYERN

AZUR-Ferienzentrum Bayerischer Wald

Waldesruhweg 34, 94227 ☎ 09922 802595 🖹 09922 802594
e-mail info@azur-camping.de
website www.azur-camping.de
A modern site. Clean sanitary installations.
Open All year **Site** 16HEC 👋 ⬤ **Prices** ♠ 5-7 🚗 3-4.50 🅰 4-5.50 pitch
5.50-8.50 **Facilities** ⋔ ⊙ ⬤ ∅ ⚊ ℗ **Services** ⭕ ➕ ⬚ **Off-site** ☎ ⬤P

SOUTH WEST

ABTSGMÜND BADEN-WÜRTTEMBERG

AT POMMERTSWEILER (6KM N)

Hammerschmiede-See

Hammerschmiede 6, 73453 ☎ 07963 369 🖹 07963 840032
e-mail camping.hammerschmiede@t-online.de
website www.camping-hammerschmiede.de
A terraced site in a wooded setting beside the lake. Partly divided into
pitches with concrete paths.
➔ *From Abtsgmünd for 3km then N to Pommertsweiler, signed.*
Open May-Sep **Site** 6HEC 👋 ⬤ **Prices** ♠ 3.10-6 🚗 2.60-5 🚗 2.60-5
🅰 2.30-4.50 **Facilities** ⋔ ☎ ⊙ ⬤ ∅ ℗ **Services** ⭕ ➕ ⬚ **Leisure** ⬤ L

ACHERN BADEN-WÜRTTEMBERG

Städtischer Campingplatz am Achernsee

Am Achernsee 8, 77855 ☎ 07841 25253 🖹 07841 508835
e-mail camping@achern.de
website www.achern.de
Open All year **Site** 6.5HEC 👋 ⬤ ⬤ **Facilities** ⋔ ☎ ⊙ ⬤ ∅ ℗
Services ⭕ ➕ ⬚ **Leisure** ⬤ L **Off-site** ⬛ ⬤P

ALTENSTEIG BADEN-WÜRTTEMBERG

Schwarzwald

72213 ☎ 07453 8415
e-mail info@schwarzwaldcamping.de
website www.schwarzwaldcamping.de
Parkland site of motor sports club Altensteig beside the River Nagold.
Separate section for dog owners.
➔ *On road to Garrweiler 1km from Altensteig.*
Open All year **Site** 3.3HEC 👋 ⬤ **Facilities** ⋔ ☎ ⊙ ⬤ ∅ ℗
Services ⭕ ➕ ⬚ **Leisure** ⬤ R **Off-site** ⬤P

ALTNEUDORF BADEN-WÜRTTEMBERG

Steinachperle

Altneudorf, 69250 ☎ 06228 467 🖹 06228 8568
e-mail campingplatz-steinachperle@t-online.de
The site lies in the narrow shady valley of the River Steinach.
➔ *Next to Gasthaus zum Pflug on outskirts of Altneudorf.*
Open Apr-Sep **Site** 3.5HEC 👋 ⬤ **Facilities** ⋔ ☎ ⊙ ⬤ ∅ ⚊ ℗
Services ⭕ ➕ ⬚ **Leisure** ⬤ R

BADENWEILER BADEN-WÜRTTEMBERG

Badenweiler

Weilertalstr 73, 79410 ☎ 07632 1550 🖹 07632 5268
e-mail info@camping-badenweiler.de
website www.camping-badenweiler.de
Level meadowland site surrounded by beautiful Black Forest scenery.
Good facilities for local walking.
➔ *A5 exit Neuenburg.*
Open 16 Jan-14 Dec **Site** 1.6HEC 👋 ⬤ **Facilities** ⋔ ☎ ⊙ ⬤ ∅ ⚊ ℗
Services ⬛ ⭕ ➕ ⬚ **Leisure** ⬤ P **Off-site** ⭕

BUCHHORN BEI ÖHRINGEN BADEN-WÜRTTEMBERG

Seewiese

Seestr 11, 74629 ☎ 07941 61568 🖹 07941 38527
e-mail campingseewiese@t-online.de
website www.camping-seewiese.de
A well-equipped site on a meadow beside a lake with fine views of the
surrounding mountains. Good recreational facilities.
➔ *7km S of Öhringen via Pfedelbach.*
Open All year **Site** 5.5HEC 👋 ⬤ **Prices** ♠ 5 🚗 3 🚗 4 🅰 2-4 **Facilities** ⋔
☎ ⊙ ⬤ ⚊ ℗ **Services** ⬛ ⭕ ➕ ⬚ **Leisure** ⬤ LP

BÜHL BADEN-WÜRTTEMBERG

Adam

Campingstr 1, 77185 ☎ 07223 23194 🖹 07223 8982
e-mail webmaster@campingplatz-adam.de
website www.campingplatz-adam.de
On level grassland, by lake.
➔ *A5 exit Bühl, 1km towards Lichtenau.*
Open All year **Site** 15HEC 👋 ⬤ 🚗 🚗 **Prices** ♠ 7-9.80 🚗 6.50-8.50
🅰 4.80-5.50 **Facilities** ⋔ ☎ ⊙ ⬤ ∅ ⚊ ℗ **Services** ⬛ ⭕ ➕ ⬚
Leisure ⬤ L **Off-site** ⬤P

CREGLINGEN BADEN-WÜRTTEMBERG

Camping Romantische Strasse

97993 ☎ 07933 20289 🖹 07933 990019
e-mail camping.hausotter@web.de
website www.camping-romantische-strasse.de
The site lies on the S outskirts of Münster and is divided into pitches.
Children's playground. Individual washing cubicles.
➔ *From Bad Mergentheim or Rothenburg/Tauber onto road to
Creglingen, turn S for 3km to Münster.*
Open 15 Mar-15 Nov **Site** 6HEC 👋 ⬤ 🚗 **Prices** ♠ 4.80-5.90 🅰 3.10-3.60
pitch 6-7 **Facilities** ⋔ ☎ ⊙ ⬤ ∅ ℗ **Services** ⭕ ⬚ **Leisure** ⬤ PR
Off-site ⬤L

Germany

Facilities ☎ shop ⋔ shower ⊙ electric points for razors ⬤ electric points for caravans ℗ parking by tents permitted ℗ compulsory separate car park
Services ⭕ café/restaurant ⬛ bar ∅ Camping Gaz International ⚊ gas other than Camping Gaz ➕ first aid facilities ⬚ laundry
Leisure ⬤ swimming L-Lake P-Pool R-River S-Sea **Off-site** All facilities within 2km

Germany

DINGELSDORF BADEN-WÜRTTEMBERG

Fliesshorn
78465 ☎ 07533 5262
At a farm, on meadowland with fine trees.
⮑ In town turn off Stadd-Dettingen road & signed NW for 1.3km.
Open Apr-Sep **Site** 5HEC ❤ ♣ ⊗ **Facilities** ⋔ 🛁 ⊙ ⊕ ⌀ **Services** 🛒 🗑 Off-site 🍴 ⮑LS

DONAUESCHINGEN BADEN-WÜRTTEMBERG

Riedsee
78166 ☎ 0771 5511 📄 0771 5511
e-mail info@riedsee-camping.de
website www.riedsee-camping.de
Level meadow on lakeside.
⮑ A81 exit Geisingen, B31 towards Pfohren, 13km left, continue 1km.
Open All year **Site** 8HEC ❤ ♣ Å **Facilities** ⋔ 🛁 ⊙ ⊕ ⌀ ⛽ ⊕ **Services** 🛒 🍴 🗑 **Leisure** ⮑ L

DÜRRHEIM, BAD BADEN-WÜRTTEMBERG

Sunthauersee
78073 ☎ 07706 712 📄 07706 922906
e-mail kurcamping@web.de
website www.kurcamping.net
Open All year **Site** 10HEC ❤ ♣ 🚐 **Facilities** ⋔ ⊙ ⊕ ⌀ ⊕ **Services** 🍴 🛒 🗑 Off-site 🛁 🍴

ELLWANGEN-JAGST BADEN-WÜRTTEMBERG

AZUR Ellwangen
Rotenbacherstr 45, 73479 ☎ 07961 7921 📄 07961 562330
e-mail ellwangen@azur-camping.de
website www.azur.camping.de/ellwangen
A modern site with good facilities in a wooded loaction on the banks of the River Jagst.
Open Apr-Oct **Site** 3.5HEC ❤ ♣ **Prices** ⚮ 5.50-7.50 Å 4.50-6 pitch 6-9 **Facilities** ⋔ 🛁 ⊙ ⊕ ⌀ ⊕ **Services** 🛒 🍴 🗑 **Leisure** ⮑ R Off-site ⮑LPR

ERPFINGEN BADEN-WÜRTTEMBERG

AZUR Schwäbische Alb (Rosencamping)
72820 ☎ 07128 466 📄 07128 30137
e-mail info@azur-camping.de
website www.azur-camping.de
Extensive site on a hill.
⮑ From Reutlingen on B312 SE to Groöngstingen, then S on Schwabische Albstr (B313) for 3.5km to Haid, right to Erpfingen, site on W outskirts.
Open All year **Site** 9HEC ❤ ♣ **Facilities** ⋔ 🛁 ⊙ ⊕ ⌀ ⛽ ⊕ **Services** 🛒 🍴 🗑 **Leisure** ⮑ P Off-site ⮑L

ETTENHEIM BADEN-WÜRTTEMBERG

Oase
77955 ☎ 07822 445918 📄 07822 445919
e-mail info@campingpark-oase.de
website www.campingpark-oase.de
Wooded location with modern facilities.
⮑ A5 exit Ettenheim.
Open Mar-Oct **Site** 5HEC ❤ ♣ ♣ **Prices** ⚮ 6.50 pitch 6 **Facilities** ⋔ 🛁 ⊙ ⊕ ⌀ ⊕ **Services** 🍴 🛒 🗑 Off-site 🍴 ⮑P

FREIBURG IM BREISGAU BADEN-WÜRTTEMBERG

Breisgau
Seestr 20, 7801 ☎ 07665 2346
Extensive level grassland site on outskirts of town. Section reserved for campers with dogs.
⮑ Autobahn exit Freiburg Nord, site 0.5km E.
Open All year **Site** 6.5HEC ❤ ♣ **Facilities** ⋔ 🛁 ⊙ ⊕ ⌀ ⛽ ⊕ **Services** 🍴 🗑 **Leisure** ⮑ L

Möslepark
Waldseestr 77, 79117 ☎ 0761 7679333 📄 0761 77578
e-mail information@camping-freiburg.com
website www.camping-freiburg.com
On outskirts of town near Busse's Waldschänke inn.
⮑ Right after town hall over railway & Waldseestr towards Littenweiler.
Open 20 Mar-28 Oct **Site** 0.7HEC ❤ ♣ 🚐 Å **Prices** ⚮ 5.50 Å 2.50 pitch 5.50 🚐 (static)280 **Facilities** ⋔ 🛁 ⊙ ⊕ ⌀ ⛽ ⊕ **Services** 🛒 🍴 🗑 Off-site 🍴 ⮑PR

FREUDENSTADT BADEN-WÜRTTEMBERG

Langenwald
Strassburgerstr 167, 72250 ☎ 07441 2862 📄 07441 2893
e-mail info@camping-langenwald.de
website www.camping-langenwald.de
The site consists of several sections and lies next to a former mill beside the River Forbach.
⮑ 4km W of Freudenstadt below the B28.
Open Apr-Nov **Site** 2HEC ❤ ♣ 🚐 **Prices** ⚮ 2.75-5.50 ⮒ 2.75-3 🚐 3.25-4 Å 3.25-4 **Facilities** ⋔ 🛁 ⊙ ⊕ ⌀ ⛽ ⊕ **Services** 🍴 🛒 🗑 **Leisure** ⮑ PR

HALLWANGEN BADEN-WÜRTTEMBERG

Königskanzel
72280 ☎ 07443 6730 📄 07443 4574
e-mail info@camping-koenigskanzel.de
website www.camping-koenigskanzel.de
Set on an elevated position in the centre of the Black Forest.
⮑ B28 from Freudenstadt towards Altensteig, past Hallwangen junct, signed on right.
Open All year **Site** 6HEC ❤ ♣ 🚐 **Prices** ⚮ 5-5.50 pitch 6.50 **Facilities** ⋔ 🛁 ⊙ ⊕ ⌀ ⛽ ⊕ **Services** 🛒 🍴 🗑 **Leisure** ⮑ P Off-site 🍴

HAUSEN BADEN-WÜRTTEMBERG

Wagenburg
88637 ☎ 07579 559
On meadowland between the railway bank and the Danube. Site has spectacular view of surrounding landscape. Entrance through subway.
Open May-Sep **Site** 1.2HEC ❤ ♣ ♣ **Facilities** ⋔ 🛁 ⊙ ⊕ ⌀ ⛽ ⊕ **Services** 🛒 🍴 🗑 **Leisure** ⮑ R Off-site 🍴

HEIDELBERG BADEN-WÜRTTEMBERG

Heidelberg-Neckartal
Schlierbacher Landstr 151, 69118
☎ 06221 802506 📄 06221 802506
e-mail mail@camping-heidelberg.de
website camping-heidelberg.de
Open 15 Mar-15 Oct **Site** 3HEC ❤ ♣ ♣ 🏠 🚐 Å **Facilities** ⋔ 🛁 ⊙ ⊕ ⌀ ⛽ ⊕ **Services** 🛒 🍴 🗑 **Leisure** ⮑ R

Site 6HEC (site size) ❤ grass ⬤ sand ♣ stone ♣ little shade ♣ partly shaded ❤ mainly shaded 🏠 bungalows for hire 🚐 caravans for hire Å tents for hire ⊗ no dogs **Prices** ⚮ adult per night ⮒ car per night pp per person per night 🚐 caravan per night Å tent per night 🚐 (static)-caravan hire per week

HERBOLZHEIM BADEN-WÜRTTEMBERG

Herbolzheim

Im Laue 1, 79336 ☎ 07643 1460 ▧ 07643 913382
e-mail s.hugoschmidt@t-online.de
website www.laue-camp.de
A pleasant rural setting with good facilities, a short distance from the
Europa-Park Rust amusement park.

⮑ *On B3 between Freiburgh & Offenburg.*

Open 10 Apr-15 Oct **Site** 8HEC ♨ ♣ **Prices** ♠ 5 ♣ 7 ▲ 6 **Facilities** ⋔ ⊙
🏠 ∅ ☂ **Services** 🍴 🍽 🕂 🛏 **Off-site** 🏠 ♨ LP

HÖFEN AN DER ENZ BADEN-WÜRTTEMBERG

Quellgrund

75339 ☎ 07081 6984 ▧ 07081 6984
Well-maintained municipal site on grassland between the B294 and
the River Enz.

⮑ *B294 SW from Pforzheim to Quelle inn/ARAL fuel station at
entrance to Höfen, turn right.*

Open All year **Site** 3.6HEC ♨ ♣ **Prices** ♠ 5.50 ♣ 2 ♣ 4-4.50 ▲ 3.50-4
Facilities ⋔ 🏠 ⊙ 🔧 ∅ ☂ **Services** 🍽 🛏 **Leisure** ♨ R **Off-site** ♨ P 🕂

HORB BADEN-WÜRTTEMBERG

Schüttehof

72160 ☎ 07451 3951 ▧ 07451 1348
Situated on a flat mountain top.

⮑ *From Horb towards Freudenstadt, 1.5km after town
boundary turn towards stables & site, continue 1km.*

Open All year **Site** 6HEC ♨ ♣ **Facilities** ⋔ 🏠 ⊙ 🔧 ∅ ☂ **Services** 🍽
🕂 🛏 **Leisure** ♨ P

ISNY BADEN-WÜRTTEMBERG

Waldbad Isny

Lohbauerstr.59-69, 88316 ☎ 07562 2389 ▧ 07562 2004
e-mail info@isny-camping.de
website www.isny-camping.de
Wooded surroundings beside a lake.

⮑ *Lindau-Kempten B12*

Open Jan-Oct **Site** 3HEC ♨ ♣ **Prices** ♠ 6.40 pitch 9 **Facilities** ⋔ 🏠 ⊙ 🔧
☂ **Services** 🍽 🕂 🛏 **Leisure** ♨ LP **Off-site** ∅ 🛏

KEHL BADEN-WÜRTTEMBERG

Kehl-Strassburg

77694 ☎ 07851 2603 ▧ 07851 73076
Park-like site divided into separate sections for young campers, transit
and holiday campers.

⮑ *Turn left at Rhine dam on outskirts of town.*

Open 15 Mar-Oct **Site** 2.3HEC ♨ ♣ **Facilities** ⋔ 🏠 ⊙ 🔧 🛏 ☂
Services 🍽 🕂 🛏 **Off-site** ♨ PR

KIRCHBERG BADEN-WÜRTTEMBERG

Christophorus

Werte 61, 88486 ☎ 07354 663 ▧ 07354 91314
e-mail info@camping-christophorus.de
website www.camping-christophorus.de
Completely enclosed, clean site.

⮑ *A7 exit Illereichen Allenstadt to town centre & towards
railway station.*

Open All year **Site** 9.2HEC ♨ ♣ **Prices** ♠ 5.60-5.70 ♣ 3.30-3.60 ♣ 3.30
▲ 3.30 **Facilities** ⋔ 🏠 ⊙ 🔧 ∅ 🛏 ☂ **Services** 🍽 🕂 🛏 **Leisure** ♨ LP

KIRCHZARTEN BADEN-WÜRTTEMBERG

Kirchzarten

Diefenbacher Str 17, 79199 ☎ 07661 9040910 ▧ 07661 61624
e-mail info@camping-kirchzarten.de
website www.camping-kirchzarten.de
Extensive site with trees providing shade.

⮑ *8km E of Freiburg im Breisgau off B31.*

Open All year **Site** 5.9HEC ♨ ♣ ♣ **Prices** ♠ 6-9.20 pitch 6-7.40
♣ (static)334-432 **Facilities** ⋔ 🏠 ⊙ 🔧 ∅ 🛏 ☂ **Services** 🍴 🍽 🕂 🛏
Leisure ♨ P

KRESSBRONN BADEN-WÜRTTEMBERG

Gohren am See

88079 ☎ 07543 60590 ▧ 07543 605929
e-mail info@campingplatz-gohren.de
website www.campingplatz-gohren.de
A large site beside the lake. It has an older section divided by many
hedges reserved for residential campers, and a newer section with
fewer bushes.

⮑ *3km from Kressbronn, signed from B31.*

Open 22 Mar-15 Oct **Site** 38HEC ♨ ♣ ♣ ▲ **Prices** ♠ 6.50 pitch 5.80
Facilities ⋔ 🏠 ⊙ 🔧 ∅ 🛏 ☂ **Services** 🍴 🍽 🕂 🛏 **Leisure** ♨ L
Off-site ♨ P

LAICHINGEN BADEN-WÜRTTEMBERG

Heidehof

Heidehofsh 50, 89150 ☎ 07333 6408 ▧ 07333 21463
e-mail heidehof.camping@t-online.de
website www.camping-heidehof.de
Well-cared for site on hillside with some high firs. Asphalt roads.
Separate section outside enclosure for overnight campers.

⮑ *A8 exit Merkingen, site 2km S via Machtolsheim.*

Open All year **Site** 25HEC ♨ ♣ ♣ **Prices** ♠ 6 ♣ 7 **Facilities** ⋔ 🏠 ⊙ 🔧
∅ 🛏 ☂ **Services** 🍽 🕂 🛏 **Leisure** ♨ P

LAUTERBURG BADEN-WÜRTTEMBERG

Hirtenteich

73457 ☎ 07365 296 ▧ 07365 251
e-mail camphirtenteich@aol.com
website www.campingplatz-hirtenteich.de
This site lies on gently sloping terrain, near the Hirtenteich recreation
area.

⮑ *Off B29 in Essingen S for 5km.*

Open All year **Site** 4HEC ♨ ♣ **Prices** ♠ 4.50 pitch 5-6 **Facilities** ⋔ 🏠 ⊙
🔧 ∅ 🛏 ☂ **Services** 🍽 🕂 🛏 **Leisure** ♨ P

LENZKIRCH BADEN-WÜRTTEMBERG

Kreuzhof

Bonndorfer Str 65, 79853 ☎ 07653 700 ▧ 07653 6623
e-mail info@brauerei-rogg.de
website www.brauerei-rogg.de
Grassland near former farm below the Rogg Brewery on the B315.

⮑ *B317 from Titisee towards Schaffhausen, onto B315 to
Lenzkirch, site 2km from centre.*

Open All year **Site** 2HEC ♨ ♣ ☂ **Prices** ♠ 4.60-8 ♣ 6 ♣ 6 ▲ 6
Facilities ⋔ 🏠 ⊙ 🔧 ∅ 🛏 ☂ **Services** 🍴 🕂 🛏 **Leisure** ♨ P

Facilities 🏠 shop ⋔ shower ⊙ electric points for razors 🔧 electric points for caravans ☂ parking by tents permitted ❶ compulsory separate car park
Services 🍽 café/restaurant 🍴 bar ∅ Camping Gaz International 🛏 gas other than Camping Gaz 🕂 first aid facilities 🛏 laundry
Leisure ♨ swimming L-Lake P-Pool R-River S-Sea **Off-site** All facilities within 2km

LIEBELSBERG BADEN-WÜRTTEMBERG

Erbenwald

75387 ☎ 07053 7382 ▤ 07053 3274
e-mail info@camping-erbenwald.de
website www.camping-erbenwald.de
Pleasant site on edge of wood.

➾ *B463 S from Calw, 6km turn right just before Neubulach,
continue N 2km.*

Open All year **Site** 7.2HEC ❤ ♣ ⚏ ⛺ **Facilities** ⚊ ⬜ ⊙ ⚑ ⊘ ♨ ⑦
Services ➍ ⍟ ⚑ ⬛ ⊠ **Leisure** ⬥ P

LIEBENZELL, BAD BADEN-WÜRTTEMBERG

Bad-Liebenzell

Pforzheimerstr.34, 75378 ☎ 07052 935680 ▤ 07052 935681
e-mail campingpark@abelundneff.de
website www.campingpark-badliebenzell.de
Municipal site with trees near tennis courts. Divided by hedges and
asphalt roads.

➾ *B463 S from Pforzheim for 19km, left 500m before Bad
Liebenzell to site beside River Nagold.*

Open All year **Site** 3HEC ❤ ♣ ⚏ ▲ ⊗ **Prices** ♦ 5.80 ▲ 4.30 pitch 6.50
⚑ (static)320-450 **Facilities** ⚊ ⬜ ⊙ ⚑ ⊘ ⑦ **Services** ➍ ⍟ ⚑ ⊠
Leisure ⬥ PR **Off-site** ⍟

LÖRRACH BADEN-WÜRTTEMBERG

Grütt

Grüttweg 8, 79539 ☎ 07621 82588 ▤ 07621 165034
Level, grassy site near frontier.

➾ *A98 exit Lörrach, onto B316 & Freiburger Str, bridge over
Wiesse, 100m left.*

Open 18 Mar-Oct **Site** 2.4HEC ❤ ♣ **Facilities** ⚊ ⬜ ⊙ ⚑ ⊘ ⑦ **Services** ⍟
⊠ **Off-site** ⬜ ⍟ ⍥ ♨ ⬥PR ⚑

LUDWIGSHAFEN AM BODENSEE BADEN-WÜRTTEMBERG

See Ende

78346 ☎ 07773 5366 ▤ 07773 7375
website www.see-ende.de
Meadowland with tall trees W of town, between railway and lake.

➾ *From Ludwigshafen towards Radolfzell.*

Open May-Sep **Site** 2.6HEC ❤ ♣ ⊗ **Facilities** ⚊ ⬜ ⊙ ⚑ ⊘ ♨ ⑦
Services ➍ ⍟ ⚑ ⊠ **Leisure** ⬥ L

MARKDORF BADEN-WÜRTTEMBERG

Wirthshof

88677 ☎ 07544 96270 ▤ 07544 962727
e-mail info@wirthshof.de
website www.wirthshof.de
Open 15 Mar-30 Oct **Site** 10HEC ❤ ♣ **Prices** ♦ 5.90-6.90 pitch 10.40-
11.40 **Facilities** ⚊ ⬜ ⊙ ⚑ ⊘ ⑦ **Services** ⍟ ⚑ ⊠ **Leisure** ⬥ P
Off-site ➍ ⍟ ⬥L

MÖRTELSTEIN BADEN-WÜRTTEMBERG

Germania

Mühlwiese 1, 6951 ☎ 06261 1795 ▤ 06261 37455
The site lies between the River Neckar and a wooded hillside.

➾ *B292 W towards Sinsheim, just after Oberigheim N onto
narrow steep road into Neckar valley.*

Open Apr-Oct **Site** 0.8HEC ❤ ♣ ⚑ **Facilities** ⚊ ⬜ ⊙ ⚑ ⊘ ♨ ⑦
Services ⍟ ⊠ **Leisure** ⬥ R **Off-site** ⍟ ⚑

MÜNSTERTAL BADEN-WÜRTTEMBERG

Münstertal

Dietzelbachstr.6, 79244 ☎ 07636 7080 ▤ 07636 7448
e-mail info@camping-muenstertal.de
website www.camping-muenstertal.de
Level, grassy site in pleasant location with fine views.

➾ *Motorway exit Bad Kroningen, SE via Stauffen to W outskirts
of Untermünstertal.*

Open All year **Site** 7HEC ❤ ⬤ ♣ ♣ ⚏ ⛺ **Prices** ♦ 6.60-7.65 pitch 10.50-
13.40 **Facilities** ⚊ ⬜ ⊙ ⚑ ⊘ ♨ ⑦ **Services** ⍟ ⚑ ⊠ **Leisure** ⬥ P

MURRHARDT BADEN-WÜRTTEMBERG

AT FORNSBACH (6KM E)

Waldsee

71540 ☎ 07192 6436 ▤ 07192 935717
e-mail waldsee@murrhardt.de
website www.murrhardt.de
The site lies near Lake Waldsee. Asphalt paths and pitches, with gravel
surface.

➾ *Murrhardt towards Fornsbach, site on E shore of lake.*

Open All year **Site** 2HEC ❤ ♣ ⚑ **Prices** ♦ 3.50-4 ⛢ 2.50-3.50 ⚑ 3-3.50
▲ 3-3.50 ⚑ (static)175-224 **Facilities** ⚊ ⬜ ⊙ ⚑ ⊘ ♨ ⑦ **Services** ⍟
⚑ ⊠ **Leisure** ⬥ L

NECKARGEMÜND BADEN-WÜRTTEMBERG

Haide

69151 ☎ 06223 2111 ▤ 06223 71959
e-mail info@camping-haide.de
website www.camping-haide.de
A well-appointed site in the picturesque Neckar valley, directly on the
river on the outskirts of Heidelberg.

➾ *Follow river towards castle & Neckarsteinach.*

Open Apr-Oct **Site** 3.6HEC ❤ ♣ ⛺ **Facilities** ⚊ ⊙ ⚑ ⑦ **Services** ➍ ⍟
⚑ ⊠ **Leisure** ⬥ R **Off-site** ⬜ ⊘ ⬥P ⚑

NECKARZIMMERN BADEN-WÜRTTEMBERG

Cimbria

74865 ☎ 06261 2562 ▤ 06261 35716
Site lies on level meadowland on the bank of the River Neckar.

➾ *Signed from B27.*

Open Apr-Oct **Site** 3HEC ❤ ♣ **Facilities** ⚊ ⊙ ⚑ ⊘ ♨ ⑦ **Services** ➍
⍟ ⊠ **Leisure** ⬥ PR **Off-site** ⬜ ⚑

NEUENBURG BADEN-WÜRTTEMBERG

Dreiländer Camping und Freizeitpark

Oberer Wald, 79395 ☎ 07631 7719 ▤ 07635 3393
e-mail info@camping-gugel.de
website www.camping-gugel.de
An excellent site, very extensive, providing many entirely separate
pitches.

➾ *A5 exit Müllheim/Neuenburg, 3km to site.*

Open All year **Site** 12.8HEC ❤ ♣ ⊙ ⛺ **Prices** ♦ 6.25 ⛢ 4.20 ▲ 3.50
5.70 **Facilities** ⚊ ⬜ ⊙ ⚑ ⊘ ♨ ⑦ **Services** ⍟ ⚑ ⊠ **Leisure** ⬥ P
Off-site ⬥LR

Site 6HEC (site size) ❤ grass ⬤ sand ⚏ stone ♣ little shade ♣ partly shaded ❤ mainly shaded ⛺ bungalows for hire
⚑ caravans for hire ▲ tents for hire ⊗ no dogs **Prices** ♦ adult per night ⛢ car per night pp per person per night ⚑ caravan per night
▲ tent per night ⚑ (static)-caravan hire per week

NUSSDORF BADEN-WÜRTTEMBERG

Nell

Bodensee, 88662 ☎ 07551 4254 🗐 07551 944458
e-mail info@campingplatz-nell.de
website www.camping-nell.de
Site within orchard between farm of same name and the lakeside
promenade. Small private beach.
➲ *Under railway bridge, then turn right.*
Open 20 Mar-20 Oct **Site** 0.6HEC 👺 ♣ ⊗ **Prices** ♠ 4.50-6 ➡ 3 ➡ 5 ▲ 5
Facilities 🌑 ⊙ 🔁 ⑫ **Services** 🖪 🖫 **Leisure** ⚊ L **Off-site** 🖹 🗓 🍴
🖉 🎬 ⚊P

ÖSTRINGEN BADEN-WÜRTTEMBERG

Kraichgau Camping Wackerhof

76684 ☎ 07259 361 🗐 07259 2431
e-mail info@wackerof.de
website www.wackerhof.de
A modern terraced site.
➲ *A5 exit Kronau/Bad Schönborn, B292 to Östringen.*
Open 25 Mar-15 Oct **Site** 3HEC 👺 ♣ **Prices** ♠ 3 pitch 3 **Facilities** 🌑 🖹
⊙ 🔁 🖉 🎬 ⑫ **Services** 🖫

PFORZHEIM BADEN-WÜRTTEMBERG

International Schwarzwald

Freibadweg 4, 75242 ☎ 07234 6517 🗐 07234 5180
e-mail fam.frech@t-online.de
website www.camping-schwarzwald.de
Site on edge of wood with southerly aspect. Separate fields for
residential, overnight and holiday campers.
➲ *S through Huchenfeld from Pforzheim to Schellbron (15km).*
Open All year **Site** 4HEC 👺 ♣ ➡ **Prices** ♠ 4.60 pitch 6.20
➡ (static)252-490 **Facilities** 🌑 🖹 ⊙ 🔁 🖉 🎬 ⑫ **Services** 🍴 🖪 🖫
Leisure ⚊ P **Off-site** ⚊R

RHEINMÜNSTER BADEN-WÜRTTEMBERG

AT STOLLHOFEN

Freizeitcenter-Oberrhein

77836 ☎ 07227 2500 🗐 07227 2400
e-mail info@freizeitcenter-oberrhein.de
website www.freizeitcenter-oberrhein.de
Modern leisure complex next to Rhine.
Open All year **Site** 36HEC 👺 ♣ ➡ **Prices** ♠ 5-8 pitch 5-8 **Facilities** 🌑 🖹
⊙ 🔁 🖉 🎬 ⑫ **Services** 🗓 🍴 🖪 🖫 **Leisure** ⚊ L

ROSENBERG BADEN-WÜRTTEMBERG

Hüttenhof

Hüttenhof 1, 73494 ☎ 07963 203 🗐 07963 8418894
e-mail huettenhof@web.de
website www.waldcamp.de
Flat meadow on incline in quiet woodland area, next to large farm.
➲ *From Ellwangen N towards Crailsheim for 3km, turn W
towards Adelmannsfelden & 8km turn N at Gaishardt.*
Open 18 Mar- 7 Nov **Site** 4HEC 👺 ♣ **Prices** ♠ 4.50 pitch 4 **Facilities** 🌑
🖹 ⊙ 🔁 🖉 🎬 ⑫ **Services** 🍴 🖪 🖫 **Leisure** ⚊ L

ST PETER BADEN-WÜRTTEMBERG

Steingrübenhof

79271 ☎ 07660 210 🗐 07660 1604
e-mail info@camping-steingrubenhof.de
website www.camping-steingrubenhof.de
On a level plateau, surrounded by delightful mountain scenery.
➲ *Via A5 & B294.*
Open All year **Site** 2HEC 👺 ♣ ➡ **Facilities** 🌑 🖹 ⊙ 🔁 🖉 🎬 ⑫
Services 🍴 🖫 **Off-site** ⚊P

SCHAPBACH BADEN-WÜRTTEMBERG

Alisehof

77776 ☎ 07839 203 🗐 07839 1263
e-mail info@camping-online.de
website www.camping-online.de
The site lies on well-kept ground with several terraces and is separated
from the road by the River Wolfach.
➲ *Off B924 in Wolfach at Kinzighbrücke for 8km N to
Schapbach, site 1km N of village.*
Open Jan-Oct & Dec **Site** 3HEC 👺 ♣ ➡ ➡ **Prices** ♠ 5.90-6.70 pitch
4.90-5.90 ➡ (static)210 **Facilities** 🌑 🖹 ⊙ 🔁 🖉 🎬 ⑫ **Services** 🗓 🍴 🖪
🖫 **Leisure** ⚊ R **Off-site** 🍴 ⚊LP

SCHILTACH BADEN-WÜRTTEMBERG

Schiltach

77761 ☎ 07836 7289 🗐 07836 7466
e-mail info@campingplatz-schiltach.de
website www.campingplatz-schiltach.de
The site lies on meadowland on the banks of the River Kinzig and is
well-placed for excursions.
Open 21 Apr-7 Oct **Site** 3.6HEC 👺 ♣ ➡ ⊗ **Prices** ♠ 4 ➡ 2.50 ➡ 3.50
▲ 3.50 **Facilities** 🌑 🖹 ⊙ 🔁 🖉 🎬 ⑫ **Services** 🍴 🖪 🖫 **Leisure** ⚊ R
Off-site ⚊P

SCHÖMBERG BADEN-WÜRTTEMBERG

Höhen-Camping-Langenbrand

75328 ☎ 07084 6131 🗐 07084 931435
e-mail eberhardt@hoehencamping.de
website www.hoehencamping.de
Open All year **Site** 1.6HEC 👺 ♣ ➡ **Prices** ♠ 4.50-5 ➡ 5-6.50 ➡ 5-6.50 ▲ 5
Facilities 🌑 ⊙ 🔁 🖉 🎬 ⑫ **Services** 🖪 🖫 **Off-site** 🖹 🗓 🍴 ⚊P

SCHUSSENRIED, BAD BADEN-WÜRTTEMBERG

Reiterhof von Steinhausen

Reiterhof, 88427 ☎ 07583 3060 🗐 07583 1004
e-mail xschmid@t.online.de
website www.campingplatz.de
A pleasant rural setting.
➲ *Via B30 Ulm-Bad Waldsee.*
Open All year **Site** 1HEC 👺 ♣ ➡ **Facilities** 🌑 ⊙ 🔁 🖉 🎬 ⑫
Services 🍴 🖪 🖫 **Off-site** 🗓 🍴 ⚊LPR

Facilities 🖹 shop 🌑 shower ⊙ electric points for razors 🔁 electric points for caravans ⑫ parking by tents permitted 🅿 compulsory separate car park
Services 🍴 café/restaurant 🗓 bar 🖉 Camping Gaz International 🎬 gas other than Camping Gaz 🖪 first aid facilities 🖫 laundry
Leisure ⚊ swimming L-Lake P-Pool R-River S-Sea **Off-site** All facilities within 2km

SCHWÄBISCH GMÜND BADEN-WÜRTTEMBERG

AT RECHBERG (6KM S)

Schurrenhof

73072 ☎ 07165 8190 📠 07165 1625

The site lies in a beautiful setting on the edge of a forest, and has a lovely view of the surrounding countryside.

➲ *B29 S from Schwäbisch Gmünd, through Strassdorf & Rechberg towards Reichenbach on B10, turn towards Schurrenhof.*

Open All year **Site** 3HEC 🏕 ♣ 🚐 **Facilities** 🏪 🖾 ⊙ 🚰 ∅ ♨ ☺ **Services** �🍴 ➕ 🖾 **Leisure** ◈ P

SCHWÄBISCH HALL BADEN-WÜRTTEMBERG

Steinbacher See

Mühlsteige 26, 74523 ☎ 0791 2984 📠 0791 9462758

e-mail camping@hohenlohe2000.de

A modern site in the beautiful Kocher valley. There are good sports facilities and many places of interest nearby in the medieval town.

➲ *Via B14/19 to Steinbach.*

Open All year **Site** 1.4HEC 🏕 ♣ **Facilities** 🏪 ⊙ 🚰 ♨ ☺ **Services** ⛽🍴 🖾 **Off-site** 🖾 🍴 ➕

STAUFEN BADEN-WÜRTTEMBERG

Belchenblick

Münstertaler Str 43, 79219 ☎ 07633 7045 📠 07633 7908

e-mail camping.belchenblick@t-online.de

website www.camping-belchenblick.de

Well-kept site on level ground.

➲ *Motorway exit Bad Krozingen/Staufen, site 4km SE.*

Open All year **Site** 2.4HEC 🏕 ♣ **Prices** 🧍 6-7.50 pitch 8-8 **Facilities** 🏪 🖾 ⊙ 🚰 ∅ ♨ ☺ **Services** ⛽🍴 ➕ 🖾 **Leisure** ◈ PR **Off-site** 🍴

STEINACH BADEN-WÜRTTEMBERG

Kinzigtal

77790 ☎ 07832 8122 📠 07832 6619

e-mail webmaster@campingplatz-kinzigtal.de

website www.campingplatz-kinzigtal.de

Site on level meadowland with tall trees, situated next to the municipal heated swimming pool.

➲ *Signed from Steinach.*

Open All year **Site** 2.6HEC 🏕 ♣ 🚐 🅰 **Prices** 🧍 5-5.50 pitch 4.50-6.50 **Facilities** 🏪 🖾 ⊙ 🚰 ∅ ♨ ☺ **Services** ⛽🍴 ➕ 🖾 **Off-site** ◈PR

STUTTGART BADEN-WÜRTTEMBERG

Canstatter Wasen

Mercedesstr 40, 70372 ☎ 0711 556696 📠 0711 557554

e-mail info@campingplatz-stuttgart

website www.campingplatz-stuttgart.de

Level site with tall poplar trees alongside the River Neckar.

➲ *Via Bad Cannstatt near sports stadium.*

Open All year **Site** 1.7HEC 🏕 ♣ 🚐 **Facilities** 🏪 🖾 ⊙ 🚰 ∅ ☺ **Services** 🍴 ➕ 🖾 **Off-site** ◈P

TITISEE-NEUSTADT BADEN-WÜRTTEMBERG

Bankenhof

Bruderhalde 31a, 79822 ☎ 07652 1351 📠 07652 5907

e-mail info@bankenhof.de

website www.bankenhof.de

A family site in a wooded location close to the lake. Access road closed 22.00-06.00 hrs.

➲ *From Titisee signed Camping Platz.*

Open All year **Site** 3.5HEC 🏕 ♣ 🚐 🅰 **Prices** 🧍 5.80 pitch 6.90 🚐 (static)364 **Facilities** 🏪 🖾 ⊙ 🚰 ∅ ♨ ☺ **Services** ⛽🍴 ➕ 🖾 **Leisure** ◈ R **Off-site** ◈L

Bühlhof

Bühlhofweg 13, 79822 ☎ 07652 1606 📠 07652 1827

e-mail hertha-jaeger@t-online.de

website www.camping-buehlhof.de

Pleasant location on a hillside above a lake.

Site 10HEC 🏕 ♣ **Prices** 🧍 5-5.50 pitch 5.20-7 **Facilities** 🏪 🖾 ⊙ 🚰 ∅ ♨ ☺ **Services** ⛽🍴 🖾 **Off-site** ◈LP ➕

Sandbank

79822 ☎ 07651 8243 & 8166 📠 07651 8286 & 88444

e-mail info@camping-sandbank.com

website www.camping-sandbank.com

Lakeside terrain landscaped with trees, upper part terraced.

➲ *From Titisee, N bank of lake, turn into old Feldbergstr, left at SW end of lake onto private road through Camping Bankenhof (closed 22.00-06.00 hrs) to site 0.7km on SE bank of lake.*

Open Apr-20 Oct **Site** 2HEC 🏕 ♣ 🚐 ♣ **Facilities** 🏪 🖾 ⊙ 🚰 ∅ ♨ ☺ **Services** 🍴 ➕ 🖾 **Leisure** ◈ L **Off-site** ◈P

Weiherhof

Bruderhalde 26, 79822 ☎ 07652 1468 📠 07652 1478

e-mail kontakt@camping-titisee.de

website www.camping-titisee.de

Mainly level site with trees, bordering on lake shore for some 400m.

➲ *Signed from Titisee.*

Open 15 May-15 Oct **Site** 2HEC 🏕 ♣ **Prices** 🧍 3.50-4.80 🚗 3.20-3.50 🚐 3.20-4 🅰 3.20-4 **Facilities** 🏪 🖾 ⊙ 🚰 ∅ ☺ **Services** 🍴 ➕ 🖾 **Leisure** ◈ L **Off-site** ◈P

TODTNAU BADEN-WÜRTTEMBERG

Hochschwarzwald

D-79674 ☎ 07671 1288 📠 07671 9999943

e-mail camping.hochschwarzwald@web.de

website www.camping-hochschwarzwald.de

Terraced site, partially grassland, by ski-lift.

➲ *6km NW of Todtnau.*

Open All year **Site** 2.5HEC 🏕 ♣ ♣ **Prices** 🧍 4.80-5.30 🅰 4.20-5.90 pitch 5.90-6.40 **Facilities** 🏪 🖾 ⊙ 🚰 ∅ ♨ ☺ **Services** 🍴 ➕ 🖾 **Leisure** ◈ R

Site 6HEC (site size) 🏕 grass 🏖 sand 🪨 stone ♣ little shade ♣ partly shaded 🌳 mainly shaded 🏠 bungalows for hire 🚐 caravans for hire 🅰 tents for hire ⊗ no dogs **Prices** 🧍 adult per night 🚗 car per night pp per person per night 🚐 caravan per night 🅰 tent per night 🚐 (static)-caravan hire per week

TÜBINGEN BADEN-WÜRTTEMBERG

Tübingen
Fremdenverkehrsgesellschaft, Rappenberghalde 61, 72070
☎ 07071 43145 ▤ 07071 793391
e-mail mail@neckarcamping.de
website www.neckarcamping.de
A quiet site on the River Neckar.
➲ *From town centre over Neckar bridge, turn right, S through Uhlandstr or Bahnhofstr to next bridge, over bridge & upstream to Rappenberghalde hill.*
Open Apr-Oct **Site** 1HEC ⛺ ♣ ♠ ▲ **Prices** ⚑ 5.50 ▲ 4.20 pitch 7.80
Facilities ⋔ ☖ ⊙ ☕ ∅ ℗ **Services** ▮ ⦿ ➕ ▨ **Leisure** ⌇ R
Off-site ⌇LP

ÜBERLINGEN BADEN-WÜRTTEMBERG

Überlingen
Bahnhofstr 57, 88662 ☎ 07551 64583 ▤ 07551 945895
e-mail info@campingpark-uberlingen.de
website www.campingpark-uberlingen.de
The site lies on the western outskirts of the town, between the railway line and the road on one side, and the concrete shore wall on the other. It is divided into several sections by low wooden barriers and has a very small beach. No individual youths under 18.
➲ *Off B31 towards lake.*
Open Apr-5 Oct **Site** 3HEC ⛺ ♣ **Prices** ⚑ 5.50-6.30 ♣ 4 pitch 9-10
Facilities ⋔ ☖ ⊙ ☕ ∅ ♨ ℗ **Services** ⦿ ➕ ▨ **Leisure** ⌇ L
Off-site ▮ ⌇P

UHLDINGEN BADEN-WÜRTTEMBERG

AT SEEFELDEN (1KM W)

Seeperle
88690 ☎ 07556 5454 ▤ 07556 966221
e-mail info@camping-seeperle.de
website www.camping-seeperle.de
This site has some large trees along the shore of the lake and a landing stage.
➲ *Off B31 at Oberuhldingen towards Seefelden, site 1km.*
Open 15 Apr-15 Sep **Site** 0.7HEC ⛺ ♣ ♠ **Facilities** ⋔ ☖ ⊙ ☕ ∅ ♨ ℗
Services ➕ **Leisure** ⌇ L **Off-site** ▮ ⦿ ⌇P

WALDKIRCH BADEN-WÜRTTEMBERG

Elztalblick
79183 ☎ 07681 4212 ▤ 07681 4213
e-mail eltztalblick@t-online.de
website www.camping-elztalblick.de
A small site with terraced pitches in the heart of the Black Forest.
➲ *Autobahn exit Waldkirch Ost, signed for 3km.*
Open 15 Mar-25 Oct **Site** 2HEC ⛺ ♣ **Facilities** ⋔ ☖ ⊙ ☕ ∅ ♨ ℗
Services ▮ ⦿ ➕ ▨ **Off-site** ⦿ ⌇P

WALDSHUT BADEN-WÜRTTEMBERG

Rhein-Camping
Jahnweg 22, 79761 ☎ 07751 3152 ▤ 07751 3252
e-mail rheincamping@t-online.de
website www.rheincamping.de
Wooded surroundings beside the River Rhein.
➲ *1km from Waldshut towards Swiss border.*
Open All year **Site** 8HEC ⛺ ♣ ♠ ♠ **Prices** ⚑ 4.90 ♠ 8.50 ▲ 4.90-8.50
Facilities ⋔ ⊙ ☕ ∅ ♨ ℗ **Services** ▮ ⦿ ➕ ▨ **Leisure** ⌇ R
Off-site ☖ ⌇P

WERTHEIM BADEN-WÜRTTEMBERG

AZUR Wertheim
An den Christwiesen 35, 97877 ☎ 09342 83111 ▤ 09342 83171
e-mail wertheim@azur-camping.de
website www.azur-camping.de/wertheim
Site lies on a level, long stretch of meadowland on the banks of the River Main next to a swimming pool.
➲ *Towards Miltenberg, 1km right at ARAL fuel station towards site.*
Open Apr-Oct **Site** 7HEC ⛺ ♣ **Facilities** ⋔ ⊙ ☕ ∅ ℗ **Services** ⦿ ➕
▨ **Leisure** ⌇ R **Off-site** ☖ ⌇P

AT BETTINGEN (5KM E)

Wertheim-Bettingen
Geiselbrunnweg 31, 97877 ☎ 09342 7077 ▤ 09342-913077
Peaceful wooded area beside a river.
➲ *A3 exit 66 Wertheim/Lengfurt, site 1km.*
Open Apr-Oct **Site** 7.5HEC ⛺ ♣ **Prices** ⚑ 4.50 ♠ 1.50 ♠ 2.50 ▲ 2.50
Facilities ⋔ ☖ ⊙ ☕ ∅ ♨ ℗ **Services** ⦿ ➕ ▨ **Leisure** ⌇ R
See advertisement on this page

WILDBAD IM SCHWARZWALD BADEN-WÜRTTEMBERG

AZUR-Camping Schwarzwald
75323 ☎ 07055 1320 ▤ 07055 929081
e-mail info@azur-camping.de
website www.azur-freizeit.de
Long narrow site with some terraces, set between the River Enz and the wooded hillside. Separate section for young campers.
➲ *From Pforzheim B294 S via Calmbach.*
Open All year **Site** 2.5HEC ⛺ ♣ **Facilities** ⋔ ☖ ⊙ ☕ ∅ ♨ ℗
Services ⦿ ➕ ▨ **Leisure** ⌇ R

Kleinenzhof
75323 ☎ 07081 3435 ▤ 07081 3770
e-mail info@kleinenzhof.de
website www.kleinenzhof.de
A family site with modern facilities.
➲ *Via B294 3km S of Calmbach.*
Open All year **Site** 8HEC ⛺ ♣ ♠ **Prices** ⚑ 6.20-6.40 pitch 8.10-8.30
Facilities ⋔ ☖ ⊙ ☕ ∅ ♨ ℗ **Services** ⦿ ➕ ▨ **Leisure** ⌇ PR

Germany

Facilities ☖ shop ⋔ shower ⊙ electric points for razors ☕ electric points for caravans ℗ parking by tents permitted ℗ compulsory separate car park
Services ⦿ café/restaurant ▮ bar ∅ Camping Gaz International ♨ gas other than Camping Gaz ➕ first aid facilities ▨ laundry
Leisure ⌇ swimming L-Lake P-Pool R-River S-Sea **Off-site** All facilities within 2km

Germany

BERLIN AND EASTERN PROVINCES

ALT SCHWERIN MEKLENBURG-VORPOMMERN

See
An der Schaftannen Nr 1, 17214
☎ 039932 42073 ▤ 039932 42072
e-mail info@camping-alt-schwerin.de
website www.camping-alt-schwerin.de
A pleasant lakeside site with modern facilities.
➲ *Via B192.*
Open Apr-Oct **Site** 3.6HEC ❤ ❤ ❤ **Prices** pitch 17.90-21.90 ❤ (static)320
Facilities ⚡ ⛺ ⊙ ❤ ⊘ ♨ ⊛ **Services** ⛽ ▣ **Leisure** ⚓ L

BERLIN

Gatow
Kladower Damm 213-217, 14089
☎ 04930 3654340 ▤ 04930 36808492
e-mail info@dccberlin.de
website www.dccberlin.de
A good stopover close to the river.
➲ *Via B5.*
Open All year **Site** 2.7HEC ❤ ❤ ❤ **Prices** ⚡ 5.80 ⚡ 5 pitch 8
Facilities ⚡ ⛺ ⊙ ❤ ♨ ⊛ **Services** ⛽ ⛽ ▣ **Off-site** ⚓LR ⊞

AT KLADOW

DCC Else-Eckert-Platz
Krampnitzer Weg 111-117, 14089 ☎ 030 3652797 ▤ 030 3651245
e-mail info@dccberlin.de
website www.dccberlin.de
Large site in woodland close to the lake. Modern facilities.
➲ *B5 & B2 exit Berlin Spandau.*
Open All year **Site** 7HEC ❤ ❤ ❤ **Prices** ⚡ 5.80 ⚡ 5 pitch 8 **Facilities** ⚡
⛺ ⊙ ❤ ♨ ⊛ **Services** ⛽ ⛽ ▣ **Off-site** ⚓LR ⊞

AT SCHMÖCKWITZ

BODSTEDT MECKLENBURG-VORPOMMERN

Bodstedt
Damm 43, 18356 ☎ 038231 4226 ▤ 038231 4820
A pleasant site on the shore of the Saaler Bodden with good boating
facilities.
➲ *B105 exit Zingst/Barth.*
Site 3.5HEC ❤ ❤ ❤ ❤ **Facilities** ⚡ ⊙ ❤ ⊛ **Off-site** ⛽ ⚓LR

CAPUTH BRANDENBURG

Himmelreich
Wentorfinsel, Geltow, 14542 ☎ 033209 70475 ▤ 033209 20100
e-mail himmelreich@campingplatz-caputh.de
website www.campingplatz-caputh.de
Open All year **Site** 7.5HEC ❤ ❤ ❤ **Prices** ⚡ 4 ⚡ 2 ❤ 6 ⚡ 3-5
Facilities ⚡ ⛺ ⊙ ❤ ⊘ ♨ ⊛ ⓟ **Services** ⛽ ⛽ ⊞ ▣ **Leisure** ⚓ LR

COLDITZ SACHSEN

Waldbad
D-04680 ☎ 034381 43122 ▤ 034381 43122
e-mail info@campingplatz.colditz.de
website www.colditz.de/camping
Wooded surroundings with some shaded pitches.
➲ *E176 exit Zschadras.*
Open Apr-Sep **Site** 2HEC ❤ ❤ ❤ **Prices** ⚡ 3 ⚡ 2 ❤ 3-6 ⚡ 7
Facilities ⚡ ⊙ ❤ ⊘ ⊛ **Services** ⛽ ⊞ ▣ **Leisure** ⚓ LPRS
Off-site ⛽ ⛽ ⛽

DRESDEN SACHSEN

Wostra
An der Wostra 7, 01259 ☎ 0351 2013254 ▤ 0351 2025448
e-mail cp-wostra@freenet.de
website www.dresden.de
Café only open May to September.
➲ *B172 towards Heidenau, site signed.*
Open Apr-Oct **Site** 1.8HEC ❤ ❤ **Prices** ⚡ 3.50 ⚡ 2.50 ❤ 5.50 ⚡ 3-6
Facilities ⚡ ⊙ ❤ ⊛ **Services** ⊞ ▣ **Off-site** ⛽ ⛽ ⚓LP

FALKENBERG BRANDENBURG

Erholungsgebiet Kiebitz
04895 ☎ 035365 2135 ▤ 035365 38533
e-mail info@kiebitz-eg-urlaub.de
website www.kiebitz-eg-urlaub.de
➲ *E55 exit Duben, B87/B101 for Herzberg.*
Open Apr-Oct **Site** 5.2HEC ❤ ❤ ❤ ❤ **Facilities** ⚡ ⊙ ❤ ⊘ ♨ ⊛
Services ⊞ ▣ **Leisure** ⚓ L **Off-site** ⛽ ⛽

FREEST MECKLENBURG-VORPOMMERN

Waldcamp
17440 ☎ 038370 20538 ▤ 038370 20525
A modern site in wooded surroundings with good facilities.
➲ *300m from Freest centre.*
Open Apr-Oct **Site** 2HEC ❤ ❤ ❤ ❤ ❤ **Facilities** ⚡ ⊙ ❤ ⓟ **Services** ▣
Off-site ⛽ ⛽ ⛽ ⊘ ♨ ⚓S

GEORGENTHAL THÜRINGEN

Georgenthal
99887 ☎ 036253 41314 ▤ 036253 25207
e-mail campingplatz70@hotmail.com
website www.campingplatz-georgenthal.de
Open Apr-Oct **Site** 1.2HEC ❤ ❤ ❤ ❤ **Facilities** ⚡ ⛺ ⊙ ❤ ⊘ ⊛ ⓟ
Services ⛽ ▣ **Leisure** ⚓ P **Off-site** ⛽ ⛽ ⚓L ⊞

GROSS-LEUTHEN BRANDENBURG

Spreewaldtor
15913 ☎ 035471 303 ▤ 035471 310
e-mail eurocamp.spreewaldtor@t-online.de
website www.eurocamp-spreewaldtor.de
On a level meadow beside the Gorss Leuthener See.
➲ *N of town off B179.*
Open All year **Site** 9HEC ❤ ❤ ❤ ❤ ❤ **Facilities** ⚡ ⛺ ⊙ ❤ ⊘ ♨ ⊛
Services ⛽ ⊞ ▣ **Off-site** ⚓L

Site 6HEC (site size) ❤ grass ❤ sand ❤ stone ❤ little shade ❤ partly shaded ❤ mainly shaded ⚡ bungalows for hire
❤ caravans for hire ⚡ tents for hire ⊗ no dogs **Prices** ⚡ adult per night ⚡ car per night pp per person per night ❤ caravan per night
⚡ tent per night ❤ (static)-caravan hire per week

GROSS-QUASSOW MECKLENBURG-VORPOMMERN

Havelberge am Wobiltzsee

17237 ☎ 03981 24790 🖷 03981 247999
e-mail info@haveltourist.de
website www.haveltourist.de
A rural setting beside the lake. Restricted facilities during March.
➲ *1.5km S of town, signed.*
Open All year **Site** 14HEC 😊 😊 😊 🚐 🖚 🛆 **Facilities** �${\sf r}$ 🖾 ⊙ 🖳 ⊘ 🚿 ℗
Services 🍴 🍺 ➕ 🖸 **Leisure** ⚓ L

See advertisement on this page

KAMENZ SACHSEN

AZUR Waldbad Deutschbaselitz

Grobteichstr 30, 01917 ☎ 03578 301489 🖷 03578 308316
e-mail deutschbaselitz@azur.freizeit.de
website www.azur-camping.de/deutschbaselitz
The shop and café are only open May to September.
Open 15 Mar-Oct **Site** 5HEC 😊 😊 😊 🚐 **Facilities** �${\sf r}$ 🖾 ⊙ 🖳 🚿 ℗
Services 🍴 **Leisure** ⚓ L

KELBRA THÜRINGEN

Südharz

Lange Str 150, 6537 ☎ 034651 45290 / 45291 🖷 034651 45292
e-mail info@seecampingharz.de
website www.seecampingharz.de
Open All year **Site** 6.5HEC 😊 ⚓ 🚐 **Facilities** �${\sf r}$ 🖾 ⊙ 🖳 ⊘ 🚿 ℗
Services 🍴 ➕ **Leisure** ⚓ LP **Off-site** 🍺

KLEINMACHNOW BRANDENBURG

Yacht-Caravan-Club

Bäkehang 9a, 14532 ☎ 033203 79684 🖷 033203 77913
e-mail spandau@city-camping-berlin.de
website www.citycamp-berlin.de
A riverside site with an hotel SW of town off A115.
Open All year **Site** 2.2HEC 😊 ⚓ **Prices** 🏃 5 🚗 2.50 🚐 3-5
🛆 3-5 **Facilities** �${\sf r}$ ⊙ 🖳 ⊘ ℗ **Services** 🍺 🍴 ➕ 🖸
Leisure ⚓ R

KLEINRÖHRSDORF SACHSEN

LuxOase

Arnsdorfer Str 1, 01900 ☎ 035952 56666 🖷 035952 56024
e-mail info@luxoase.de
website www.luxoase.de
A beautiful, peaceful location among meadows and woods, bordering a lake.
➲ *A4 exit Pulsnitz for Radeberg, 4km through Leppersdorf, 1km turn right.*
Open Mar- 9 Nov **Site** 7.2HEC 😊 ⚓ ⚓ 🚐 **Prices** 🏃 4-6 🚐 7.50 🛆 7
🚐 (static)368-508 **Facilities** �${\sf r}$ 🖾 ⊙ 🖳 ⊘ 🚿 ℗ **Services** 🍺 🍴 ➕ 🖸
Leisure ⚓ L

KLEINSAUBERNITZ SACHSEN

Olbasee

Olbaweg 16, 02694 ☎ 035932 30232 🖷 035932 30886
e-mail natur@campingplatz-olbasee.de
website www.campingplatz-olbasee.de
A rural location on the Olbasee.
➲ *Via S109*
Open 13 Apr- 21 Oct **Site** 7HEC 😊 ⚓ ⚓ 🚐 **Prices** 🏃 4.30 🚗 2.60 🚐 3.10
🛆 2.60 **Facilities** �${\sf r}$ 🖾 ⊙ 🖳 ⊘ ℗ **Services** 🍴 ➕ 🖸 **Leisure** ⚓ L
Off-site 🍴 🚿

KÖNIGSTEIN SACHSEN

Königstein

Schandauer Str 25e, 01822 ☎ 035021 68224 🖷 035021 60725
e-mail camp.koenigstein@t-online.de
website www.camping-koenigstein.de
On level ground in a wooded location with fine views of the surrounding mountains.
➲ *B172 within Königstein near Dresden.*
Open Apr-Oct **Site** 2.4HEC 😊 ⚓ 🚐 🚐 **Prices** 🏃 4.90 🚗 3 🚐 1.50-3
🛆 1.50-3 🚐 (static)245 **Facilities** �${\sf r}$ 🖾 ⊙ 🖳 ⊘ 🚿 ℗ **Services** 🍴 🖸
Off-site 🍺 🍴 ⚓PR ➕

LASSAN MECKLENBURG-VORPOMMERN

Lassan

Garthof 5-6, 17440 ☎ 038374 80373 🖷 038374 80373
e-mail naturcampingplatzlassan@gmx.de
website www.campingplatz-lassan.de
A pleasant site on the Achterwasser.
➲ *Via B110.*
Open Apr-Sep **Site** 1.4HEC 😊 ⚓ ⚓ 🚐 **Facilities** �${\sf r}$ ⊙ 🖳 ℗ **Services** 🍴 🖸
Leisure ⚓ LRS **Off-site** 🖾 🍺 ⊘ ⚓P ➕

Facilities 🖾 shop �`r` shower ⊙ electric points for razors 🖳 electric points for caravans ℗ parking by tents permitted 🅟 compulsory separate car park
Services 🍴 café/restaurant 🍺 bar ⊘ Camping Gaz International 🚿 gas other than Camping Gaz ➕ first aid facilities 🖸 laundry
Leisure ⚓ swimming L-Lake P-Pool R-River S-Sea **Off-site** All facilities within 2km

Germany (vertical text, right margin)

Germany

LEHNIN BRANDENBURG

Seeblick am Klostersee
D-14797 ☎ 03382 700274 ▤ 03382 700274
website www.campingplatz-lehnin.de
➲ On E30.
Open Apr-5 Oct **Site** 1.5HEC ⚑ ♣ **Facilities** ⚑ 🏠 ⊙ ⚑ ℗ **Services** ➕ ▤
Leisure ⚓ L **Off-site** 🏠 🍴 ⊘

MÜHLBERG THÜRINGEN

Drei Gleichen
99869 ☎ 036256 22715 ▤ 036256 86801
e-mail service@campingplatz-muehlberg.de
website www.campingplatz-muehlberg.de
Pleasant wooded surroundings.
➲ A4 exit Wandersleben, Mühlberg signed.
Open All year **Site** 2.8HEC ⚑ ♣ **Prices** ⚑ 4.70 ⚑ 1.60 ⚑ 5.20 ⚑ 3
Facilities ⚑ ⊙ ⚑ ⊘ ♨ ℗ **Services** 🍴 ▤ **Off-site** 🍴 ⚓ L ➕

NIESKY SACHSEN

Tonschächte
02902 ☎ 03588 205771 ▤ 03588 259315
e-mail camping_touschacht@gmx.de
Open 15 Apr-15 Oct **Site** 15HEC ⚑ ♣ **Prices** ⚑ 3.50 ⚑ 1.50 ⚑ 4 ⚑ 3
Facilities ⚑ ⊙ ⚑ ⊘ ♨ ℗ **Services** 🍴 ▤ **Leisure** ⚓ L **Off-site** 🍴

NIEWISCH BRANDENBURG

Schwielochsee-Camping
Uferweg Nord 16, 15848 ☎ 033676 5186 ▤ 033676 5226
e-mail fischer.camping@12move.de
website www.fischer-camping.de
A family site in pleasant wooded surroundings on the banks of the Schwielochsee.
Open All year **Site** 4.2HEC ⚑ ⚑ ♣ ⚑ **Facilities** ⚑ 🏠 ⊙ ⚑ ⊘ ♨ ℗ ℗
Services 🍴 ➕ ▤ **Leisure** ⚓ L

PLÖTZKY SACHSEN

Ferienpark Plötzky
Campingplatz Kleiner Waldsee, 39245
☎ 039200 50155 ▤ 039200 76082
e-mail info@ferienpark-ploetzky.de
website www.ferienpark-ploetzky.de
Set in a wooded location beside a small lake with well-defined pitches.
➲ Access via A2 & B246.
Open All year **Site** 12HEC ⚑ ⚑ ⚑ ⚑ **Prices** ⚑ 3-4 ⚑ 2-3 ⚑ 5-6 ⚑ 3-4
⚑ (static)210-250 **Facilities** ⚑ 🏠 ⊙ ⚑ ⊘ ♨ ℗ **Services** 🍴 ➕ ▤
Leisure ⚓ L

POTSDAM BRANDENBURG

Sanssouci-Gaisberg
An der Pirscheide, Templiner See 41, 14471 ☎ 0331 9510988
e-mail info@recra.de
website www.camping-potsdam.de
Wooded surroundings close to Templiner See.
➲ Signed from B1.
Open Apr-1 Nov **Site** 6HEC ⚑ ⚑ ♣ **Prices** ⚑ 9.30 ⚑ 1.30 ⚑ 8.90
Facilities ⚑ 🏠 ⊙ ⚑ ⊘ ♨ ℗ **Services** 🍴 🍴 ➕ **Leisure** ⚓ LR
Off-site ⚑ P

REICHENBERG SACHSEN

Sonnenland
Dresdner Str 115, 01468 ☎ 0351 8305495 ▤ 0351 8305494
e-mail bad-sonnenland@t-online.de
website www.moritzburg.de
A pleasant location beside the lake with modern facilities.
➲ A4 exit Wilder Mann. 3km S of Moritzburg.
Open Apr-Oct **Site** 18HEC ⚑ ⚑ ♣ ⚑ **Facilities** ⚑ 🏠 ⊙ ⚑ ℗ **Services** 🍴
➕ ▤ **Leisure** ⚓ L **Off-site** 🍴 ⚑ P

SUHRENDORF MECKLENBURG-VORPOMMERN

Suhrendorf
18569 ☎ 038305 82234 ▤ 038305 8165
Open All year **Site** 90HEC ⚑ ⚑ ♣ **Facilities** ⚑ 🏠 ⊙ ⚑ ⊘ ♨ ℗
Services ⚑ 🍴 ▤ **Leisure** ⚓ S

ZINNOWITZ MECKLENBURG-VORPOMMERN

Pommernland
Dr.Wachsmann-Strabe 40, 17454
☎ 038377 40348 ▤ 038377 40349
e-mail camping-pommernland@m-vp.de
website www.camping-pommernland.m-vp.de
Wooded surroundings on the coast.
➲ Via B111.
Open All year **Site** 7.7HEC ⚑ ⚑ ⚑ ♣ ⚑ **Prices** ⚑ 5.25 ⚑ 3 ⚑ 9-11
⚑ 4-6 ⚑ (static)380 **Facilities** ⚑ 🏠 ⊙ ⚑ ⊘ ♨ ℗ **Services** ⚑ 🍴 ➕ ▤
Leisure ⚓ S **Off-site** ⚑ P

CENTRAL

ASBACHERHÜTTE RHEINLAND-PFALZ

Harfenmühle
55758 ☎ 06786 7076 ▤ 06786 7570
e-mail camping-harfenmuehle@t-online.de
website www.camping-harfenmuehle.de
A quiet site, beautifully situated in the Fischbach valley. Level grassland, partly terraced.
➲ 3km NW of B327 towards Kempfeld.
Open All year **Site** 6.2HEC ⚑ ⚑ ♣ ⚑ **Facilities** ⚑ 🏠 ⊙ ⚑ ⊘ ♨ ℗
Services ⚑ 🍴 ➕ ▤ **Leisure** ⚓ L

ATTENDORN NORDRHEIN-WESTFALEN

Biggesee-Waldenburg
57439 ☎ 02722 95500 ▤ 02722 955099
e-mail info@camping-waldenburg.de
website www.biggesee.com
Generously terraced recreational site on the northern shore of the Bigge reservoir, with adjoining public bathing area. Private sunbathing area.
➲ Via A45/A4
Open Apr-Oct **Site** 6.5HEC ⚑ ⚑ ♣ **Prices** ⚑ 3.90-4 ⚑ 9-11 pitch 12-13
Facilities ⚑ 🏠 ⊙ ⚑ ⊘ ♨ ℗ **Services** ➕ ▤ **Leisure** ⚓ L **Off-site** 🍴 ⚑ P

Site 6HEC (site size) ⚑ grass ⚑ sand ⚑ stone ♣ little shade ⚑ partly shaded ⚑ mainly shaded ⚑ bungalows for hire
⚑ caravans for hire ⚑ tents for hire ⊗ no dogs **Prices** ⚑ adult per night ⚑ car per night pp per person per night ⚑ caravan per night
⚑ tent per night ⚑ (static)-caravan hire per week

Hof Biggen
Finnentroper Str 131, 57439 ☎ 02722 95530 ▤ 02722 955366
e-mail info@hof-biggen.de
website www.hof-biggen.de
Well-equipped terraced site, surrounded by woodlands.
➲ *Atterdorn road to Ahauser reservoir, entrance near Haus am See inn.*
Open All year **Site** 18HEC ❀ ❀ ♣ ♠ **Prices** ♠ 3.50-5 ♠ 1.75-2.50 ♠ 3.50-5 ♣ 3.50-5 ♠ (static)195-265 **Facilities** ♠ ☺ ☺ ♠ ⌀ ⚑ ⓟ **Services** ⚏ ◍ ➕ ⬚ **Off-site** ⇔R

BACHARACH RHEINLAND-PFALZ

Sonnenstrand
Strandbadweg 9, 55422 ☎ 06743 1752 ▤ 06743 3192
e-mail info@camping-sonnenstrand.de
website www.camping-sonnenstrand.de
On grassland beside the Rhine with some high trees. Close to a main road and two railway lines.
➲ *Turning off B9 into site can be difficult for caravans coming from N, due to one-way traffic.*
Open 15 Mar-Oct **Site** 1.4HEC ❀ ❀ ♣ ♠ **Facilities** ♠ ☺ ☺ ♠ ⌀ ⓟ **Services** ⚏ ◍ ⬚ **Leisure** ⇔ R

BALHORN HESSEN

Erzeberg
34308 ☎ 05625 5274 ▤ 05625 7116
e-mail info@campingplatz-erzeberg.de
website www.campingplatz-erzeberg.de
Site lies on meadowland on slightly sloping ground above the village.
➲ *On B450 between Istha & Fritzlar.*
Open All year **Site** 5HEC ❀ ❀ **Prices** ♠ 3.50 ♠ 7 ♣ 7 **Facilities** ♠ ☺ ♠ ⌀ ⓟ **Services** ⚏ ◍ ⬚ **Leisure** ⇔ P **Off-site** ☺ ⚑ ➕

BARNTRUP NORDRHEIN-WESTFALEN

Schwimmbad
Fischteiche 4, 32683 ☎ 05263 2221 ▤ 05263 956991
e-mail info@ferienparkteutoburgerwald.de
website www.ferienparkteutoburgerwald.de
A well-kept site next to an open-air swimming pool (available in summer).
➲ *Signed from Barntrup on B66.*
Open Apr-Oct **Site** 2.4HEC ❀ ♣ ♠ **Prices** ♠ 4 ♠ 2 **Facilities** ♠ ☺ ♠ ⓟ **Services** ➕ ⬚ **Leisure** ⇔ P **Off-site** ⚏ ◍

BERNKASTEL-KUES RHEINLAND-PFALZ

Kueser Werth
Am Hafen 2, 54470 ☎ 06531 8200 ▤ 06531 8282
website www.camping-kueser-werth.de
Grassy site near Mosel and boating marina, with view of Landshut castle.
➲ *On S outskirts of town.*
Open Apr-Oct **Site** 2.2HEC ❀ ♣ **Facilities** ♠ ☺ ☺ ♠ ⌀ ⚑ ⓟ **Services** ⚏ ◍ ➕ ⬚

BIRKENFELD RHEINLAND-PFALZ

Waldwiesen
55765 ☎ 06782 5215 ▤ 06782 5219
e-mail info@waldwiesen.de
website www.waldwiesen.de
A wooded location close to the lake.
➲ *Off B41 E of Birkenfeld, signed.*
Open Etr-Oct **Site** 9.5HEC ❀ ❀ ♠ ♠ **Prices** ♠ 5.75 ♣ 5.75 pitch 6.75-8.25 **Facilities** ♠ ☺ ♠ ⌀ ⓟ **Services** ➕ ⬚ **Leisure** ⇔ L **Off-site** ☺ ⚏ ◍ ⇔P

BÖMIGHAUSEN HESSEN

Barenberg
34508 ☎ 05632 1044 ▤ 05632 1044
e-mail berthold.trachte@t-online.de
Beautifully terraced site at Neerdar reservoir.
➲ *Via B251 between Korbach & Brilon.*
Open All year **Site** 0.5HEC ❀ ❀ ♣ **Prices** ♠ 3 ♠ 3 ♣ 3 **Facilities** ♠ ☺ ♠ ⌀ ⓟ **Services** ⬚ **Leisure** ⇔ LR

BRAUNFELS HESSEN

Braunfels
Am Weiherstieg 2, 35619 ☎ 06442 4366 ▤ 06442 6895
A terraced site surrounded by a pine forest and deciduous trees. Separate meadow for touring campers.
➲ *A45 exit Limburg, B49 towards town.*
Open All year **Site** 5.2HEC ❀ ❀ ♣ ♠ **Facilities** ♠ ☺ ♠ ⌀ ⓟ **Services** ◍ ⬚ **Off-site** ☺ ⚑ ⇔P

BREISIG, BAD RHEINLAND-PFALZ

Rheineck
53498 ☎ 02633 95645 ▤ 02633 472008
e-mail info@camping-rheineck.de
website www.camping-rheineck.de
A quiet, well-kept site on a level meadow in Vinxtbach valley.
➲ *B9 NW from Koblenz to Bad Breisig, turn left, over railway & continue 400m.*
Open All year **Site** 5HEC ❀ ❀ ♣ **Prices** ♠ 4.50 ♠ 3 ♣ 3.50 ♣ 3 **Facilities** ♠ ☺ ☺ ♠ ⌀ ⚑ ⓟ **Services** ⚏ ➕ ⬚ **Leisure** ⇔ R **Off-site** ◍ ⇔P

BRUNGERSHAUSEN HESSEN

Auenland
Zum Dammhammer 2 ☎ 06420 7172 ▤ 06420 822846
e-mail info@campingplatz-auenland.de
website www.campingplatz-auenland.de
Attractive location in a protected area at the foot of the Rimberg mountains. Variety of bird and plant life.
➲ *A2/A3 from North to A45 exit Dillenburg towards Biedenkopf on B62. Exit Brungershausen, site signed.*
Open All year **Site** 22HEC ❀ ❀ ♣ **Prices** ♠ 4 ♠ 1.50 ♣ 4 ♣ 3-4 **Facilities** ♠ ☺ ♠ ⌀ ⚑ ⓟ ⓟ **Services** ⚏ ◍ ➕ **Leisure** ⇔ PR **Off-site** ☺

Facilities ☺ shop ♠ shower ☺ electric points for razors ♠ electric points for caravans ⓟ parking by tents permitted ⓟ compulsory separate car park
Services ◍ café/restaurant ⚏ bar ⌀ Camping Gaz International ⚑ gas other than Camping Gaz ➕ first aid facilities ⬚ laundry
Leisure ⇔ swimming L-Lake P-Pool R-River S-Sea **Off-site** All facilities within 2km

Germany

BULLAY RHEINLAND-PFALZ

Bären-Camp

Am Moselüfer 1/3, 56859 ☎ 06542 900097 📄 06542 900098
e-mail info@baeren-camp.de
website www.baeren-camp.de
On a level meadow beside the Mosel, next to the football ground.
Fine view.

➲ *Via B49 Cochem-Alf, over bridge, through village, signed.*
Open Etr-1 Nov **Site** 1.8HEC 😾 ♣ **Prices** ♠ 6 🚗 3.20 🚐 3.20 ⚑ 3.20
Facilities 🌳 🚻 ⊙ 🚰 🅿 ⌀ 🚿 ☎ **Services** 🍴 🍽 🛒 **Leisure** 🏊 R
Off-site 🏊P ➕

COCHEM RHEINLAND-PFALZ

Freizeitzentrum

Stadionstr, 56812 ☎ 02671 4409 📄 02671 910719
e-mail info@campingplatz-cochem.de
website www.campingplatz-cochem.de
Level meadowland with trees beside the Mosel, downstream from the
swimming pool and sports ground.

➲ *From B49 in Cochem follow Freizeitzentrum signs, over
downstream bridge, left after swimming pool.*
Open Etr-Oct **Site** 2.8HEC 😾 ♣ **Prices** ♠ 4.50 pitch 5-8 🚐 (static)216
Facilities 🌳 🚻 ⊙ 🚰 🅿 ⌀ 🚿 ☎ 🅿 **Services** 🍴 🍽 ➕ 🛒 **Leisure** 🏊 R
Off-site 🍽 🏊P

AT LANDKERN (7KM N)

Altes Forsthaus

Haupstr 2, 56814 ☎ 02671 8701 📄 02671 8722
e-mail info@landkern.com
website www.landkern.com
The partly terraced site lies near woodland in the valley below
Landkern.

➲ *A48 exit Kaisersesch, S to Landkern, site signed.*
Open All year **Site** 10HEC 😾 ♣ **Prices** ♠ 4 🚗 2 🚐 5-7 ⚑ 5-7
Facilities 🌳 🚻 ⊙ 🚰 ⌀ 🚿 ☎ **Services** 🍴 🍽 ➕ 🛒 **Leisure** 🏊 P
Off-site 🚻 🍽

DAHN RHEINLAND-PFALZ

Büttelwoog

66994 ☎ 06391 5622 📄 06391 5326
e-mail buettelwoog@t-online.de
website www.camping-buettelwoog.de
Site lies in a magnificent pine forest, partly surrounded by steep hills
and rocks. Section reserved for young people with tents.

➲ *B10 from Pirmasens to Hinterweidenthal then B427 S to
Dahn.*
Open All year **Site** 6HEC 😾 ♣ 🍃 ♣ 🚐 **Prices** ♠ 5.50 🚐 6.50 pitch 6.50
🚐 (static)245 **Facilities** 🌳 🚻 ⊙ 🚰 🅿 ⌀ 🚿 ☎ **Services** 🍴 🍽 ➕ 🛒
Off-site 🏊P

DAUSENAU RHEINLAND-PFALZ

Lahn-Beach

Hallgarten 16, 56132 ☎ 02603 13964 📄 02603 919935
e-mail info@canutours.de
website www.campingplatz-dausenau.de
A riverside site in a wooded setting.
Open Apr-Oct **Site** 3HEC 😾 ♣ 🍃 ♣ **Facilities** 🌳 ⊙ 🚰 ☎ **Services** 🍴 🍽 🛒
Leisure 🏊 R **Off-site** 🚻

DIEMELSEE-HERINGHAUSEN NORDRHEIN-WESTFALEN

AZUR-Camping Hohes Rad

34519 ☎ 05633 99099 📄 05633 99010
website www.camping.diemelsee.de
A terraced site in the Sauerland hills overlooking Lake Diemel.

➲ *Via B251 Korbach-Beilon.*
Open All year **Site** 2.8HEC 😾 ♣ ♣ **Facilities** 🌳 🚻 ⊙ 🚰 🅿 ⌀ 🚿 ☎
Services 🍴 🍽 **Off-site** 🍽 🏊LP ➕

DIEZ RHEINLAND-PFALZ

Ochsenwiese

65582 ☎ 06432 2122 📄 06432 924193
e-mail info@camping-diez.de
website www.camping-diez.de
On a meadow beside the River Lahn, below Schloss Oranienstein.

➲ *From N A3 exit Diez (from S exit Limburg-Nord), onto B54
for 7km.*
Open Apr-Oct **Site** 7HEC 😾 ♣ ♣ **Prices** ♠ 3.60 🚗 3 🚐 4 ⚑ 2.20-3.80
🚐 (static)210 **Facilities** 🌳 🚻 ⊙ 🚰 🅿 ⌀ 🚿 ☎ **Services** 🍴 🍽 🛒
Leisure 🏊 R **Off-site** 🏊L

DORSEL AN DER AHR RHEINLAND-PFALZ

Stahlhütte

53533 ☎ 02693 438 📄 02693 511
website www.campingplatz-stahlhuette.de
Site with individual pitches, on meadowland with trees near River Ahr.

➲ *Off B258 Aachen-Koblenz road.*
Open All year **Site** 7HEC 😾 ♣ ♣ **Facilities** 🌳 🚻 ⊙ 🚰 🅿 ⌀ 🚿 ☎
Services 🍴 🍽 ➕ 🛒 **Leisure** 🏊 R

DORTMUND NORDRHEIN-WESTFALEN

Hohensyburg

Syburger Dorfstr 69, 44265 ☎ 0231 774374 📄 0231 7749554
e-mail info@camping-hohensyburg.de
website www.camping-hohensyburg.de
Terraced site on hilly grassland near Weitkamp inn.

➲ *Via B54.*
Open All year **Site** 10HEC 😾 ♣ **Facilities** 🌳 🚻 ⊙ 🚰 ⌀ ☎
Services 🍴 🍽 ➕ 🛒 **Leisure** 🏊 LR

DREIEICH-OFFENTHAL HESSEN

Offenthal

Bahnhofstr 77, 63303 ☎ 06074 5629 📄 06074 5629
e-mail schoenweitz@t-online.de
website www.campingplatz-dreieich.de
A well-equipped site in wooded surroundings.

➲ *Off B486 at Dreieich-Offenthal towards Dietzenbach.*
Open All year **Site** 3.2HEC 😾 ♣ ⊗ **Prices** ♠ 4.20 🚗 0.50 🚐 5.20
⚑ 4 **Facilities** 🌳 🚻 ⊙ 🚰 🚿 ☎ **Services** ➕ **Leisure** 🏊 P **Off-site** 🍽 ⌀

DROLSHAGEN NORDRHEIN-WESTFALEN

Gut Kalberschnacke

57489 ☎ 02763 7501 📄 02763 7879
e-mail camping-kalberschnacke@t-online.de
website www.camping-kalberschnacke.de
Terraced site above the Bigge-Lister reservoir in wooded area.

➲ *A45 exit Wegringhausen, site 4km NE.*
Open All year **Site** 13.5HEC 😾 ♣ **Facilities** 🌳 🚻 ⊙ 🚰 ⌀ 🚿 ☎
Services 🍽 🛒 **Off-site** 🏊L

Site 6HEC (site size) 😾 grass 🍃 sand 😾 stone ♣ little shade ♣ partly shaded ♣ mainly shaded 🏠 bungalows for hire
🚐 caravans for hire ⚑ tents for hire ⊗ no dogs **Prices** ♠ adult per night 🚗 car per night pp per person per night 🚐 caravan per night
⚑ tent per night 🚐 (static)-caravan hire per week

DÜLMEN NORDRHEIN-WESTFALEN

Tannenwiese

Borkenbergstr 217, 48249 ☎ 02594 991759
website www.camping-tannenwiese.de
The site lies on meadowland in a well-wooded area, near the
gliderdrome.
➲ B51 from Recklinghausen to Hausdülmen, follow sign
Segelflügplatz Borkenberge.
Open Mar-30 Oct **Site** 3.7HEC ❤ ♣ **Prices** ♦ 4.25 ♠ 1 ♣ 3.70 ▲ 2.50-
3.50 **Facilities** ℝ 🏕 ⊙ ➋ ♨ ⑳ **Services** 🖪 🗑 **Off-site** 🛒 🍴

DÜRKHEIM, BAD RHEINLAND-PFALZ

KNAUS Bad Dürkheim

In den Almen 3, 67098 ☎ 06322 61356 🗎 06322 8161
e-mail badduerkheim@knauscamp.de
website www.knauscamp.de
Lakeside site on level meadow between vineyards, adjoining a
sportsfield.
➲ Access from E outskirts of town. Turn N at railway viaduct,
near Jet fuel station.
Open Dec-Oct **Site** 16.4HEC ❤ ♣ ♣ ▲ **Prices** ♦ 6 pitch 7-12
Facilities ℝ 🏕 ⊙ ➋ ♨ ⑳ **Services** 🛒 🍴 🖪 **Leisure** ♦ L **Off-site** ♦ P

DÜSSELDORF NORDRHEIN-WESTFALEN

Unterbacher See

Kleiner Torfbruch 31, 40627 ☎ 0211 8992038 🗎 0211 8929321
e-mail service@unterbachersee.de
website www.unterbachersee.de
Site on sloping grassland.
➲ From Düsseldorf B326 to Erkrath exit, left by Unterbacher
lake.
Open Mar-Oct **Site** 6.5HEC ❤ ♣ ⑧ **Prices** ♦ 5 ▲ 6 pitch 9.50 (incl 2
persons) **Facilities** ℝ ⊙ ➋ ⌀ ⑫ **Services** 🍴 🖪 🗑 **Leisure** ♦ LP
Off-site 🏕 🛒 🍴

ESCHWEGE HESSEN

Knaus Campingpark Eschwege

37269 ☎ 05651 338883 🗎 05651 338884
e-mail eschwege@knauscamp.de
website www.knauscamp.de
Site beside the Werratalsee.
➲ A7 exit Eschwege, signed.
Open 30 Mar-5 Nov **Site** 6.8HEC ❤ ♣ ♣ ▲ **Prices** ♦ 6 pitch 4-9
Facilities ℝ 🏕 ⊙ ➋ ♨ ⑳ **Services** 🍴 **Leisure** ♦ L **Off-site** ⌀

ESSEN NORDRHEIN-WESTFALEN

AT WERDEN (10KM S)

Essen-Werden

Im Löwental 67, 45239 ☎ 0201 492978 🗎 0201 8496132
e-mail stadtcamping@gmx.de
website www.stadtcamping-essen.de
Several fields divided by bushes and surrounded by thick hedges.
➲ From Essen centre towards Werden, turn towards railway
station & signed.
Open All year **Site** 6HEC ❤ ❤ ♣ ❤ **Facilities** ℝ 🏕 ⊙ ➋ ⌀ ♨
Services 🛒 🍴 🖪 🗑 **Leisure** ♦ R **Off-site** 🏕 ♦ P

FÜRTH IM ODENWALD HESSEN

Tiefertswinkel

Am Schwimmbad, 64658 ☎ 06253 5804 🗎 06253 3717
e-mail info@camping-fuerth.de
website www.camping-fuerth.de
Pleasantly landscaped site in beautiful setting next to the municipal
open-air swimming pool.
➲ A5 Darmstadt-Heidelberg
Open Mar-Nov **Site** 4.2HEC ❤ ♣ ♣ ⑧ **Prices** ♦ 3.30-3.90 ♣ 5.50-6
▲ 4-6 **Facilities** ℝ 🏕 ⊙ ➋ ⌀ ♨ ⑳ **Services** 🛒 🖪 🗑 **Off-site** 🍴 ♦ P

GAMMELSBACH HESSEN

Freienstein

Neckartalstr 172, 64743 ☎ 06068 1306 🗎 06068 912121
The site lies just off the B45 in a landscaped preservation area. It is
terraced and divided into pitches.
Open Apr-Sep **Site** 5HEC ❤ ♣ **Facilities** ℝ ⊙ ➋ ♨ ⑳ **Services** 🗑

GEISENHEIM HESSEN

Geisenheim

Postfach 1323, 65366 ☎ 06722 75600 🗎 06722 75600
website www.rheingau-camping.de
Level grassland site.
➲ Between B42 road & River Rhine.
Open Mar-Oct **Site** 5HEC ❤ ♣ ♣ **Facilities** ℝ 🏕 ⊙ ➋ ⑳ **Services** 🍴
🗑 **Leisure** ♦ R **Off-site** ⌀ ♦ P

GERBACH RHEINLAND-PFALZ

AZUR-Camping Pfalz

67813 ☎ 06361 8287 🗎 06361 22523
e-mail gerbach@azur-camping.de
website www.azur-camping.de/gerbach
➲ A8 junct Enkenbach-Hochspeyer, N on B48 via
Rockenhausen, at Dielkirchen 4.5km E to Gerbach.
Open Apr-Oct **Site** 8.5HEC ❤ ♣ **Facilities** ℝ 🏕 ⊙ ➋ ⌀ ⑳ **Services** 🍴
🖪 🗑 **Leisure** ♦ P

GILLENFELD RHEINLAND-PFALZ

Feriedorf Pulvermaar

54558 ☎ 06573 996500 🗎 06592 982662
website www.feriendorf-pulvermaar.de
Partly terraced municipal site on a slightly sloping meadow at Pulver
Maar, surrounded by woods.
➲ A48 exit Mehren/Daun, B421 S, 1st turning to Gillenfeld, near
village turn for Pulver Maar.
Open All year **Site** 3HEC ❤ ♣ ♣ **Prices** ♦ 3-3.50 ♠ 1-2 ♣ 4.50-8
▲ 4.50-6.50 **Facilities** ℝ ⊙ ➋ ♨ ⑳ **Services** 🛒 🍴 🖪 🗑
Off-site 🏕 ⌀ ♦ LP

GRÜNBERG HESSEN

Spitzer Stein

Alsfelderstr 57, 35305 ☎ 06401 804117 🗎 06401 1804103
e-mail s.moebus@gruenberg.de
Beautiful location at a forest swimming pool.
➲ A5 exit Homberg, site 8km S.
Open Mar-Oct **Site** 4HEC ❤ ♣ **Prices** ♦ 4 pitch 2 **Facilities** ℝ 🏕 ⊙ ➋
♨ ⑳ **Services** 🍴 🖪 🗑 **Leisure** ♦ P **Off-site** 🏕 🍴

Germany

Facilities 🏕 shop ℝ shower ⊙ electric points for razors ➋ electric points for caravans ⑳ parking by tents permitted ❼ compulsory separate car park
Services 🍴 café/restaurant 🛒 bar ⌀ Camping Gaz International ♨ gas other than Camping Gaz 🖪 first aid facilities 🗑 laundry
Leisure ♦ swimming L-Lake P-Pool R-River S-Sea **Off-site** All facilities within 2km

GRUNDMÜHLE BEI QUENTEL HESSEN

Grundmühle Quentel

37235 ☎ 05602 3659 🖥 05602 915811

A sunny, forest site. Siesta 13.00-15.00 hrs.

➲ B83 from Melsungen to Röhrenfurth, right towards Furstenhagen & via Eiterhagen to Quentel.

Open All year **Site** 1.8HEC 🌢 ❅ ♣ **Facilities** 🖍 ☺ 🖭 ⊘ ♨ ☺ **Services** 🍴 🖩 **Leisure** ⊸ P **Off-site** 🖹 🍴 🍴

GULDENTAL RHEINLAND-PFALZ

Guldental

55452 ☎ 06707 633 🖥 06707 18468

Site lies in the Guldenbach valley. Some terraces are reserved for tourers and there is a lake suitable for bathing.

➲ B48 N from Bad Kreuznach to Langenlonsheim, left to Guldental.

Open All year **Site** 8HEC 🌢 ♣ **Facilities** 🖍 🖹 ☺ 🖭 ♨ ☺ **Services** 🍴 🍴 ➕

HALDERN NORDRHEIN-WESTFALEN

Strandhaus Sonsfeld

46459 ☎ 02857 2247 🖥 02857 7171

On meadowland at the Hagener-Meer next to B8 and railway line.

Open All year **Site** 15HEC 🌢 ♣ **Facilities** 🖍 ☺ 🖭 ♨ ☺ **Services** 🍴 🍴 ➕ 🖩 **Leisure** ⊸ L

HAUSBAY RHEINLAND-PFALZ

AT PFALZFELD-HAUSBAY

Schinderhannes

56291 ☎ 06746 80280 🖥 06746 802814

e-mail info@countrycamping.de

website www.countrycamping.de

Terraced site on S facing slope, broken up by trees and shrubs beside a small lake. Separate section for young people.

➲ E of B327. 29km S of Koblenz.

Open All year **Site** 30HEC 🌢 🌢 ♣ **Prices** 🏃 6 pitch 8 **Facilities** 🖍 🖹 ☺ 🖭 ⊘ ♨ ☺ **Services** 🍴 🖩 **Leisure** ⊸ L **Off-site** 🍴 🍴 ➕

HEIDENBURG RHEINLAND-PFALZ

Moselhöhe

54426 ☎ 06509 99016 🖥 06509 99017

e-mail dieter@qasem.de

website www.campingplatz-moselhoehe.de

A small, well-appointed site on an open meadow.

➲ A1 exit Mehring towards Thalfang am Erbestopf.

Open 15 Dec-14 Nov **Site** 3HEC 🌢 ♣ **Prices** 🏃 4.90 🚗 2.60 🚐 4-4.20 🅰 3-3 **Facilities** 🖍 ☺ 🖭 ⊘ ☺ **Services** 🍴 🍴 🖩 **Off-site** 🖹 ➕

HEIMBACH NORDRHEIN-WESTFALEN

Rurthal

52396 ☎ 02446 3377 🖥 02446 911126

e-mail info@campingplatz-rurthal.de

website www.campingplatz-rurthal.de

Site with individual pitches on meadowland beside the River Ruhr.

➲ From Düren S via Nideggen & Abenden to Blens, over bridge & left.

Site 7HEC 🌢 ♣ 🌢 ☺ **Prices** 🏃 3.50 🚗 2.90 🚐 3.20 🅰 2.70 🚐 (static)147 **Facilities** 🖍 🖹 ☺ 🖭 ⊘ 🖭 ♨ ☺ **Services** 🍴 🖩 **Leisure** ⊸ P **Off-site** 🍴 ⊸R

HEIMERTSHAUSEN HESSEN

Heimertshausen

Ehringshauser Str, 36320 ☎ 06635 206 🖥 06635 918359

e-mail info@campingplatz-heimertshausen.de

website www.campingplatz-heimertshausen.de

Near swimming pool in grassy, wooded valley.

➲ A5 exit Alsfeld west, continue via Romrod & Zell.

Open Apr-Sep **Site** 3.6HEC 🌢 ♣ 🚐 **Prices** 🏃 3.50 pitch 6-7 🚐 (static)140-175 **Facilities** 🖍 🖹 ☺ 🖭 ⊘ ♨ ☺ **Services** 🍴 🍴 🖩 **Off-site** ⊸P

HELLENTHAL NORDRHEIN-WESTFALEN

Hellenthal

Platiss 1, 53940 ☎ 02482 1500 🖥 02482 2171

e-mail info@camphellenthal.de

website www.camphellenthal.de

On extensive meadowland.

➲ 0.5km S of town.

Open All year **Site** 6HEC 🌢 ♣ **Prices** 🏃 4 pitch 8 **Facilities** 🖍 ☺ 🖭 ☺ **Services** 🍴 🍴 ➕ 🖩 **Leisure** ⊸ P **Off-site** 🖹 ⊘ ♨

HERINGEN HESSEN

Werra

36266 ☎ 06624 919043 🖥 06624 915597

Municipal site on slightly sloping ground at the swimming pool.

Open All year **Site** 4HEC 🌢 ♣ **Facilities** 🖍 🖹 ☺ 🖭 ⊘ ☺ **Services** 🍴 ➕ 🖩 **Off-site** ⊸PR

HIRSCHHORN AM NECKAR HESSEN

Odenwald

Langenthalerstr 80, 69430 ☎ 06272 809 🖥 06272 3658

e-mail odenwald-camping-park@t-online.de

website www.odenwald-camping-park.de

Extensive site in wooded valley. Divided by River Ülfenbach and hedges.

➲ Off B37 towards Wald-Michelbach & continue 1.5km.

Open 30 Mar-4 Oct **Site** 8HEC 🌢 ♣ 🌢 **Prices** 🏃 5.10 pitch 8.40 🚐 (static)220 **Facilities** 🖍 🖹 ☺ 🖭 ⊘ ♨ ☺ **Services** 🍴 🍴 ➕ 🖩 **Leisure** ⊸ PR

HOFGEISMAR HESSEN

Parkschwimmbad

Schöneberger Str 16, 3520 ☎ 05671 1215

Municipal site, subdivided by hedges. Next to a swimming pool. Mobile shop.

Open All year **Site** 1.5HEC 🌢 ♣ **Facilities** 🖍 ☺ 🖭 ♨ ☺ **Services** 🍴 ➕ 🖩 **Leisure** ⊸ P **Off-site** ⊘

AT LIEBENAU-ZWERGEN (9KM W)

Ponyhof Camping Club

Teichweg 1, 34396 ☎ 05676 1509 🖥 05676 8880

e-mail ponyhofcamping@t-online.de

website www.ponyhofcamping.de

A south-facing terraced site among magnificent scenery, 300m from a swimming pool.

➲ Off B83 at Hofgeismar W towards Liebenau. Or off B7 at Obemeiser N towards Liebenau.

Open 20 Mar-10 Nov **Site** 7HEC 🌢 ♣ 🌢 **Prices** 🏃 6.50-7.50 🚗 2 pitch 11.50-12.50 **Facilities** 🖍 🖹 ☺ 🖭 ♨ ☺ **Services** 🍴 🍴 ➕ **Leisure** ⊸ R **Off-site** ⊸LP ➕

Site 6HEC (site size) 🌢 grass 🌢 sand 🌢 stone ♣ little shade ♣ partly shaded 🌢 mainly shaded 🏠 bungalows for hire 🚐 caravans for hire 🅰 tents for hire ⊗ no dogs **Prices** 🏃 adult per night 🚗 car per night pp per person per night 🚐 caravan per night 🅰 tent per night 🚐 (static)-caravan hire per week

HONNEF, BAD NORDRHEIN-WESTFALEN

AT HONNEF-HIMBERG, BAD (7KM E)

Jillieshof
Ginsterbergweg 6, 53604 ☎ 02224 972066 🖹 02224 972067
e-mail hpefferoth@t-online.de
website www.camping-jillieshof.de
➲ Via A3 2km
Open All year **Site** 4HEC ⛺ ♣ **Prices** ♦ 4.50 ➡ 6 ➡ 6 Å 4 **Facilities** ⋔
🗋 ⊙ ➡ ⌀ 🚿 ⅋ **Services** ➕ 🗑 **Off-site** 🍴 🍽️

HORN-BAD MEINBERG NORDRHEIN-WESTFALEN

Eggewald
Kempener Str 33, 32805 ☎ 05255 236 🖹 05255 1375
e-mail j.glitz@traktoren-museum.de
website www.traktoren-museum.de
Site lies in well-wooded countryside.
➲ Off B1 in Horn-Bad Meinberg at Waldschlosschen onto
Altenbeken road for 8km to Kempen.
Open All year **Site** 2HEC ⛺ ♣ **Prices** ♦ 3 pitch 5 **Facilities** ⋔ ⊙ ➡ 🚿 ⅋
Services 🍴 ➕ 🗑 **Leisure** ⛱ P

INGENHEIM RHEINLAND-PFALZ

SC Klingbachtal
76831 ☎ 06349 6278
website www.klingbachtal.de
Municipal site lies on level meadowland at the edge of the village,
next to the sports ground.
➲ 8km S of Landau via B38, signed.
Open Apr-Oct **Site** 1.5HEC ⛺ ♣ **Facilities** ⋔ ⊙ ➡ 🚿 **Services** ➕
Off-site 🗋 🍽️ 🍴 ⌀ 🚿 ⛱P

IRREL RHEINLAND-PFALZ

Nimseck
54666 ☎ 06525 314 🖹 06525 1299
e-mail info@camping-nimseck.de
website www.camping-nimseck.de
Site on long grassy strip in wooded valley on the bank of River Nims.
➲ B257 SW from Bitburg, at turning from bypass to Irrel turn
left.
Open 18 Mar-2 Nov **Site** 7HEC ⛺ ♣ ♣ **Facilities** ⋔ ⊙ ➡ ⌀ 🚿 ⅋
Services 🍴 ➕ 🗑 **Leisure** ⛱ PR **Off-site** 🗋

KALLETAL-VARENHOLZ NORDRHEIN-WESTFALEN

Weser Freizeit-Zentrum
32689 ☎ 05755 444 🖹 05755 723
e-mail info@camping-wfz-kalletal.de
website www.camping-wfz-kalletal.de
Extensive site in Weser recreation area near River Weser N of Schloss
Varenholz. Separate field and common room for young campers.
➲ A2 exit Exter, via Vlotho towards Rintein.
Open Feb-Oct **Site** 12HEC ⛺ ♣ ➡ ⊗ **Facilities** ⋔ 🗋 ⊙ ➡ ⌀ 🚿 ⅋
Services 🍴 🍽️ ➕ 🗑 **Leisure** ⛱ L

KELL RHEINLAND-PFALZ

Freibad Hochwald
54427 ☎ 06589 1695
On meadow on slightly sloping wooded hillside, near a public open-
air swimming pool. Booking advised in summer.
➲ 2km from B407 towards Trier.
Open May-Sep **Site** 2HEC ⛺ ♣ **Prices** ♦ 5 ➡ 2.50 ➡ 5 Å 5
Facilities ⋔ ⊙ ➡ ⅋ **Services** 🍴 🍽️ ➕ **Leisure** ⛱ P

KIRCHHEIM HESSEN

Seepark Kirchheim
36275 ☎ 06628 1525 🖹 06628 8664
e-mail info@campseepark.de
website www.campseepark.de
This terraced site, with individual pitches, is part of an extensive and
well-equipped leisure and recreation centre.
Open All year **Site** 10HEC ⛺ ♣ ➡ ➡ **Facilities** ⋔ 🗋 ⊙ ➡ ⌀ 🚿
Services 🍴 🍽️ ➕ 🗑 **Leisure** ⛱ LPR

KIRN RHEINLAND-PFALZ

Papiermühle
Krebsweilererstr 8, 55606 ☎ 06752 2267
➲ B41 exit Meisenheim.
Open All year **Site** 6HEC ⛺ ♣ **Prices** ♦ 4 ➡ 3 ➡ 3 Å 3
Facilities ⋔ ⊙ ➡ ⌀ 🚿 ⅋ **Services** 🍴 🍽️ ➕ 🗑

KOBLENZ (COBLENCE) RHEINLAND-PFALZ

AT WINNINGEN (9KM SW)

Ziehfurt
Raiffeisen Str. 16, 56333 ☎ 02606 1800 & 357 🖹 02606 2566
website www.mosel-camping.com
Site lies on level wooded meadowland.
➲ From Koblenz B416 towards Trièr for 11km, access to site at
Schwimmbad (swimming pool).
Open Etr-Sep **Site** 7HEC ⛺ ♣ **Prices** ♦ 6 pitch 6 **Facilities** ⋔ 🗋 ⊙ ➡ ⌀
🚿 **Services** 🍴 🍽️ ➕ 🗑 **Leisure** ⛱ R **Off-site** ⛱P

KÖLN (COLOGNE) NORDRHEIN-WESTFALEN

Berger
Uferstr. 71, Rodenkirchen, 50996
☎ 0221 9355240 🖹 0221 9355246
e-mail camping.berger@t-online.de
website www.camping-berger-koeln.de
Situated on a meadow beside the River Rhine. Beautiful surrounding
area and modern facilities.
Open All year **Site** 6HEC ⛺ ♣ **Prices** ♦ 6 ➡ 3 ➡ 3 Å 3-3
Facilities ⋔ 🗋 ⊙ ➡ ⌀ 🚿 **Services** 🍴 🍽️ ➕ 🗑 **Leisure** ⛱ R

KÖNEN RHEINLAND-PFALZ

Horsch
Könenerstr 36, 54329 ☎ 06501 17571
Open Apr-14 Oct **Site** ⛺ ♣ ➡ **Prices** Å 3 pitch 14-16 (incl 2 persons)
Facilities ⋔ 🗋 ⊙ ➡ ⌀ 🚿 **Services** 🍴 🍽️ ➕ **Leisure** ⛱ LPR

Facilities 🗋 shop ⋔ shower ⊙ electric points for razors ➡ electric points for caravans 🚿 parking by tents permitted 🅿 compulsory separate car park
Services 🍴 café/restaurant 🍽️ bar ⌀ Camping Gaz International 🚿 gas other than Camping Gaz ➕ first aid facilities 🗑 laundry
Leisure ⛱ swimming L-Lake P-Pool R-River S-Sea **Off-site** All facilities within 2km

Germany (side tab)

KÖNIGSTEIN IM TAUNUS HESSEN

AT EPPSTEIN (8KM SW)

Hubertushof

Bezirksstr 2, 65817 ☎ 06198 7000 ▤ 06198 7002
e-mail info@taunuscamp.de
website www.taunuscamp.de
Site in the Taunus landscape preservation area.

⮕ *B455 from Königstein.*

Open All year **Site** 7HEC ꙮ ꙮ ꙮ ꙮ **Prices** ⋔ 6-7 pitch 6-7
ꙮ (static)196-240 **Facilities** ꙮ ▤ ⊙ ꙮ ⌀ ⚲ ⚘ **Services** ✚
Off-site ✚ ▯〇|

KREUZBERG RHEINLAND-PFALZ

Viktoria Station

☎ 02643 8338 ▤ 02643 3391
e-mail mail@viktoria-station.de
website www.viktoria-station.de
Shady site on meadows by the River Ahr, close to a forest, vineyards
and castles.

⮕ *A61 exit Meckenheim for Altenahr, site 7km.*

Open Apr-Oct **Site** 5.5HEC ꙮ ꙮ **Prices** ⋔ 4.60 ꙮ 6.90 ⚊ 6.70
Facilities ꙮ ⊙ ꙮ ⌀ ⚘ **Services** 〇| ⚲ **Leisure** ⚘ R **Off-site** ▯ ⚊ ✚

KRÖV RHEINLAND-PFALZ

Kröver-Berg

54536 ☎ 06541 70040 ▤ 06541 700444
website www.kroverberg.de
Open All year **Site** 2HEC ꙮ ꙮ ꙮ **Prices** ⋔ 3.50 ⚊ 7.50-12 pitch 5 (incl 2
persons) **Facilities** ꙮ ⊙ ꙮ ꙮ ⌀ ⚊ ⚲ ⚘ **Services** ✚| 〇| **Off-site** ⚘P

LADBERGEN NORDRHEIN-WESTFALEN

Waldsee

Waldseestr 81, 49549 ☎ 05485 1816 ▤ 05485 3560
e-mail info@waldsee-camping.de
website www.waldsee-camping.de
Site lies at the inn, near the bathing area of the lake.

⮕ *2km N. A1 exit Ladbergen for Saerbeck/Emsdetten, 100m
turn right.*

Open All year **Site** 10.5HEC ꙮ ꙮ ꙮ ꙮ **Prices** ⋔ 3.60 pitch 6.60
ꙮ (static)196 **Facilities** ꙮ ▤ ⊙ ꙮ ⌀ ⚊ ⚲ ⚘ **Services** ✚| 〇| ✚ ⚲
Leisure ⚘ LP **Off-site** ⚘R

LAHNSTEIN RHEINLAND-PFALZ

Burg Lahneck

56112 ☎ 02621 2765 ▤ 02621 18290
Level grassland site with a sunny aspect and terraces that provide
shade. Situated next to Lahneck castle with a pleasant view of the
Rhine valley.

⮕ *B42 from Koblenz to Lahnstein, follow signs Burg Lahneck,
1.5km to site.*

Open Apr-Oct **Site** 1.8HEC ꙮ ꙮ **Facilities** ꙮ ▤ ⊙ ꙮ ⌀ ⚘ **Services** ✚
⚲ **Off-site** 〇| ⚘P

LEIWEN RHEINLAND-PFALZ

AEGON-Ferienpark Sonnenberg

54340 ☎ 06507 93690 ▤ 06507 936936
e-mail sonnenberg@landal.de
website www.landal.de
Extensive terraced site in one of the largest wine growing areas of this
district. Lies above the River Mosel.

⮕ *Off B53 (Mosel valley road) over River Mosel at Thornich
then via Leiwen to site.*

Open 4 Feb-22 Jan **Site** 25HEC ꙮ ꙮ ꙮ **Facilities** ꙮ ▤ ⊙ ꙮ ⚘
Services ✚| 〇| ✚ **Leisure** ⚘ PR **Off-site** ▯ ✚| 〇| ⌀

LEMGO NORDRHEIN-WESTFALEN

Alten Hansestadt

Regenstorstr, 32657 ☎ 05261 14858 ▤ 05261-188324
e-mail info@camping-lemgo.de
website www.camping-lemgo.de
The site lies by the swimming pool directly on the river.

Open All year **Site** 15HEC ꙮ ꙮ ꙮ **Facilities** ꙮ ⊙ ꙮ ⌀ ⚘ **Services** ⚲
Leisure ⚘ R **Off-site** ▯ ✚| 〇| ⚘P ✚

LIBLAR NORDRHEIN-WESTFALEN

Liblarer See

50374 ☎ 02235 3899
This site lies at Lake Liblar, with its own bathing area.

⮕ *SW from Cologne on B265 for 15km, 1km before Liblar left
towards lake.*

Open All year **Site** 10HEC ꙮ ꙮ ꙮ **Prices** ⋔ 3.50 ⚊ 3.50-5 pitch 8
Facilities ꙮ ▤ ⊙ ꙮ ⌀ ⚊ ⚲ **Services** ✚| 〇| ✚ ⚲ **Leisure** ⚘ L

LINDENFELS HESSEN

Terrassencamping Schlierbach

Am Zentbuckel 11, 64678 ☎ 06255 630 ▤ 06255 3526
e-mail info@terrassencamping-schlierbach.de
website www.terrassencamping-schlierbach.de
Site is fenced and lies on sloping terrain.

⮕ *B47 Bensheim-Michelstadt, turn off in Lindenfels SW to
Schlierbach.*

Open Apr-Oct **Site** 3.2HEC ꙮ ꙮ ꙮ **Prices** ⋔ 3.80-4.50 ⚊ 3-6 pitch 4.40-6
Facilities ꙮ ▤ ⊙ ꙮ ⌀ ⚊ ⚲ **Services** ✚ ✚ **Off-site** ✚| 〇| ⚘P

LINGERHAHN RHEINLAND-PFALZ

Mühlenteich

56291 ☎ 06746 533 ▤ 06746 1566
e-mail info@muehlenteich.de
website www.muehlenteich.de
Site lies on slightly sloping meadowland, divided into sections by a
group of trees. Isolated location at the edge of woodland and
adjoining the forest swimming pool (free entry for campers). Trout
fishing.

⮕ *A61 exit Pfalzfeld. Easier approach for caravans A61 exit
Laudert.*

Open All year **Site** 15HEC ꙮ ꙮ **Prices** ⋔ 4 ⚊ 4 ꙮ 4 ⚊ 4
Facilities ꙮ ▤ ⊙ ꙮ ⌀ ⚊ ⚲ **Services** ✚| 〇| ✚ **Leisure** ⚘ P
Off-site ⚘R

Site 6HEC (site size) ꙮ grass ꙮ sand ꙮ stone ꙮ little shade ꙮ partly shaded ꙮ mainly shaded ꙮ bungalows for hire
ꙮ caravans for hire ⚊ tents for hire ⊗ no dogs **Prices** ⋔ adult per night ⚊ car per night pp per person per night ꙮ caravan per night
⚊ tent per night ꙮ (static)-caravan hire per week

LORCH HESSEN

Suleika
Im Bodenthal 2, 65391 ☎ 06726 9464 🖨 06726 9440
website suleika-camping.de
Well laid-out terraced site in an ideal location for exploring the Rhine valley. Separate car park for users of the smaller pitches.
➲ B42 from Assmannshausen towards Lorch for 3km, turn right to site through railway underpass. Larger caravans turn right 1km before Lorch.
Open 15 Mar-Oct **Site** 4HEC 👑 🕭 🛏 🛱 **Prices** ♠ 5 ← 2 ← 5 ▲ 3-5 🛱 (static)210 **Facilities** 🟦 🖻 ⊙ 🖾 ⌀ 🚿 🅿 **Services** 🎱 🔯 🔁 🖾
Off-site 🔯 🗢 LR

LOSHEIM SAARLAND

AZUR-Camping Reiterhof Girtenmühle
Girtenmuhle, 66679 ☎ 06872 90240 🖨 06872 902411
e-mail losheim@azur-camping.de
website www.azur-camping.de/losheim
➲ Via B268 Trier-Losheim.
Open All year **Site** 5HEC 👑 🕭 **Prices** ♠ 4-6 ▲ 3-5 pitch 4.50-7.50
Facilities 🟦 ⊙ 🖾 ⌀ 🅿 **Services** 🔯 🔁 🖾 **Off-site** 🖻 🗢 LP

MAINZ-KOSTHEIM HESSEN

Mainz-Wiesbaden Maarau
55246 ☎ 06134 4383 🖨 06134 4383
e-mail info@kakg.de
Shop closed in April.
Open 15 Mar-Oct **Site** 2HEC 👑 🕭 **Facilities** 🟦 🖻 ⊙ 🖾 🅿 **Services** 🔯
🖾 **Off-site** 🗢 PR

MARBURG AN DER LAHN HESSEN

GC Lahnaue
Tro je damm 47, 35037 ☎ 06421 21331 🖨 06421 175882
e-mail info@lahnaue.de
website www.lahnaue.de
Municipal site on level meadowland next to the Sommerbad (swimming pool) in the W part of this town on the River Lahn.
Open Apr-30 Oct **Site** 1HEC 👑 🕭 **Prices** ♠ 4 ← 2 ▲ 4 pitch 7
Facilities 🟦 ⊙ 🖾 ⌀ 🅿 **Services** 🔯 🖾 **Leisure** 🗢 R **Off-site** 🗢 P

MEERBUSCH NORDRHEIN-WESTFALEN

AZUR-Camping Meerbusch
Zur Rheinfähre 21, 40668 ☎ 02150 911817 🖨 02150 912289
e-mail info@azur-camping.de
website www.azur-camping.de
A peaceful location on the Rhine within easy reach of Dusseldorf.
➲ Via A57 Neuss-Krefeld.
Open 01Apr-13Oct **Site** 3.8HEC 👑 🕭 **Facilities** 🟦 🖻 ⊙ 🖾 🚿 ⊛
Services 🔯 🔁 **Leisure** 🗢 R

MEHLEM NORDRHEIN-WESTFALEN

Genienau
53179 ☎ 0228 344949 🖨 0228 3294989
e-mail genienau@freenet.de
The site lies opposite the Drachenfels.
Open All year **Site** 1.8HEC 👑 🕭 **Prices** ♠ 6 ← 3-4 ← 4-10 ▲ 3-8
Facilities 🟦 ⊙ 🖾 ⌀ ⊛ **Services** 🔯 🔁 **Leisure** 🗢 R **Off-site** 🖻 🔯 ⌀
🚿 🗢 P

MESCHEDE NORDRHEIN-WESTFALEN

Knaus Campingpark Hennesee
Mielinghausen 7 ☎ 0291 952720 🖨 0291 9527229
e-mail hennesee@knauscamp.de
website www.knauscamp.de
Terraced site on the eastern side of a lake in an attractive location of mountains and forests.
Open 15 Dec-5 Nov **Site** 17HEC 👑 🕭 🛱 ▲ **Prices** ♠ 6 pitch 7-12
Facilities 🟦 🖻 ⊙ 🖾 🚿 ⊛ **Services** 🔯 🔁 **Leisure** 🗢 LP **Off-site** 🔯

MESENICH RHEINLAND-PFALZ

Family Camping Club
56820 ☎ 02673 4556 🖨 02673 9629829
e-mail info@familycamping.de
website www.familycamping.de
A family site with plenty of recreational facilities beside the River Moselle. Pitches are divided by trees and hedges.
Open May-Sep **Site** 3HEC 👑 🕭 ▲ **Facilities** 🟦 🖻 ⊙ 🖾 ⌀ 🚿
Services 🔯 🔯 🔁 🖾 **Leisure** 🗢 PR

MITTELHOF RHEINLAND-PFALZ

Eichenwald
57537 ☎ 02742 910643 🖨 02742 910645
e-mail camping@hatzfeldt.de
website www.camping-im-eichenwald.de
Set in an oak wood, mainly divided into pitches.
➲ B62 from Siegen towards Wissen, turn to site 4km NE of Wissen.
Open All year **Site** 10HEC 👑 🕭 🛏 ▲ **Facilities** 🟦 ⊙ 🖾 🚿 ⊛
Services 🔯 🔯 🔁 🖾 **Off-site** 🖻 🗢 P

MONSCHAU NORDRHEIN-WESTFALEN

Perlenau
Eifel, 52156 ☎ 02472 4136 🖨 02472 4493
e-mail familie.rasch@monschau-perlenau.de
website www.monschau-perlenau.de
Open Apr-Oct **Site** 2HEC 👑 🕭 **Prices** ♠ 5 ← 3 ← 5 ▲ 5 **Facilities** 🟦 🖻
⊙ 🖾 ⌀ 🚿 ⊛ **Services** 🔯 🔯 🖾 **Leisure** 🗢 PR **Off-site** 🔁

MONTABAUR RHEINLAND-PFALZ

AT GIROD (4KM E)

Eisenbachtal
56412 ☎ 06485 766 🖨 06485 4938
Situated in the Nassau nature reserve.
➲ A3 exit 40 for Montabaur, before town left towards Limburg for 5km.
Open All year **Site** 3HEC 👑 🕭 🕭 **Prices** ♠ 4 pitch 7 **Facilities** 🟦 🖻 ⊙ 🖾
⌀ 🚿 ⊛ **Services** 🔯 🔯 🔁 🖾 **Off-site** 🗢 P

MÖRFELDEN-WALLDORF HESSEN

Arndt Mörfelden
Am Zeltplatz 5, 64546 ☎ 06105 22289 🖨 06105 277459
e-mail campingplatz.moerfelden@t-online.de
website www.campingplatz-moerfelden.de
Well laid-out site in two sections near the motorway.
➲ A5 exit Langen/Mörfelden, site 0.3km, signed.
Open All year **Site** 6HEC 👑 🕭 🕭 **Prices** ♠ 5 pitch 7-10 **Facilities** 🟦 ⊙ 🖾
🚿 ⊛ **Services** 🔯 🖾 **Off-site** 🖻 🔯 🔯 ⌀ 🗢 LP 🔁

Germany

Facilities 🖻 shop 🟦 shower ⊙ electric points for razors 🖾 electric points for caravans ⊛ parking by tents permitted 🅿 compulsory separate car park
Services 🔯 café/restaurant 🔯 bar ⌀ Camping Gaz International 🚿 gas other than Camping Gaz 🔁 first aid facilities 🖾 laundry
Leisure 🗢 swimming L-Lake P-Pool R-River S-Sea **Off-site** All facilities within 2km

MÜLHEIM RHEINLAND-PFALZ

Mülheim
54486 ☎ 06534 940157 📠 06534 940157
e-mail info@campingmuelheim.nl
website www.campingmuelheim.nl
Near Mülheim-Lieser bridge over the Mosel.
➲ *B53 from Bernkastel towards Trier for 5.5km.*
Open Etr-Oct **Site** 1.5HEC 😃 ♨ 🚐 **Prices** ⚡ 4-5.50 🚗 5-7 ▲ 3.50-4
Facilities 🌳 ⊙ 🚿 ⚑ ⑦ **Services** ⊞ 🍴 🛒 **Leisure** ✦ R **Off-site** 🏧 ⊘ 🛒 ⊞

MÜLHEIM AN DER RUHR NORDRHEIN-WESTFALEN

Entenfangsee
45481 ☎ 0203 760111 📠 0203 765162
Extensive site near a lake. Touring pitches near railway line. Adventure playground.
➲ *Motorway exit Duisburg-Wedau for Bissingheim & lake.*
Open All year **Site** 12.5HEC 😃 ♨ **Facilities** 🌳 🏧 ⊙ 🚿 ⚑ ⊘ ⑦
Services 🍴 ⊞ 🛒 **Leisure** ✦ L **Off-site** ✦P ⊞

MÜLLENBACH RHEINLAND-PFALZ

Nürburgring
53520 ☎ 02692 224 📠 02692 1020
e-mail rezeption@camping-am-nuerburgring.de
website www.camping-am-nuerburgring.de
A large, well-equipped site in a wooded location with direct access to the Nürburgring Grand-Prix circuit.
➲ *Via A61/A48 & B412.*
Open All year **Site** 30HEC 😃 ♨ ♨ 🚐 **Prices** ⚡ 11-12 **Facilities** 🌳 🏧 ⊙
🚿 ⊘ 🛒 ⑦ **Services** 🍴 ⊞ 🛒

NEHREN RHEINLAND-PFALZ

Nehren
56820 ☎ 02673 4612 📠 02671 910754
e-mail campingnehren@aol.com
website www.campingplatz-nehren.de
On level terrain beside the River Moselle. Separate section for teenagers. Liable to flood at certain times of the year.
➲ *Off B49 in Nehren.*
Open Apr-15 Oct **Site** 5HEC 😃 ♨ **Prices** ⚡ 4.50 🚐 8 ▲ 6
Facilities 🌳 🏧 ⊙ 🚿 ⚑ 🛒 ⑦ **Services** ⊞ 🍴 ⊞ 🛒 **Leisure** ✦ R **Off-site** ⊞

NIEDEREISENHAUSEN HESSEN

Hinterland
Ouotshauser Weg 32, Steffenberg, 35329 ☎ 06464 7564
e-mail camphinterland01@aol.com
➲ *Follow signs to Schwimmbad.*
Open All year **Site** 2HEC 😃 ♨ 🚐 **Facilities** 🌳 ⊙ 🚿 🛒 ⑦ **Services** ⊞
🍴 ⊞ 🛒 **Off-site** 🏧 ⊘ ✦PR

NIEDERKRÜCHTEN NORDRHEIN-WESTFALEN

Lelefeld
Lelefeld 4, 41372 ☎ 02163 81203 📠 2163 81203
e-mail gblut@aol.com
website www.camping-lelefeld.com
A quiet wooded location on the outskirts of the village.
➲ *Signed from Elmpt.*
Open All year **Site** 1.5HEC 😃 ♨ 🚐 **Prices** ⚡ 3.10 🚗 1.50 🚐 3.10 ▲ 3.10
🚐 (static)175 **Facilities** 🌳 🏧 ⊙ 🚿 ⊘ 🛒 ⑦ **Services** ⊞ ⊞ 🛒
Off-site 🍴 ✦LPR

OBERSGEGEN RHEINLAND-PFALZ

Reles-Mühle
Kapellenstr 3, 54675 ☎ 06566 8741 📠 06566 31064
e-mail info@eifelcamping.com
website www.eifelcamping.com
Set in rural surroundings next to a farmhouse, on a level meadow by a brook with trees and bushes.
➲ *B50 from Bitburg towards Vianden, site near Luxembourg frontier.*
Open All year **Site** 2HEC 😃 ♨ ♨ 🚐 **Prices** ⚡ 2.50 🚗 2.10 🚐 2.10
▲ 1.50-2.10 🚐 (static)133-168 **Facilities** 🌳 🏧 ⊙ 🚿 ⑦ **Services** ⊞ 🛒
Leisure ✦ R **Off-site** 🏧 ⊞ 🍴 ⊘ 🛒 ✦P

OBERWEIS RHEINLAND-PFALZ

Prümtal-Camping
In der Klaus 5, 54636 ☎ 06527 92920 📠 06527 929232
e-mail info@pruemtal.de
website www.pruemtal.de
A family site in pleasant wooded surroundings with good sports facilities.
➲ *B50 from Bitburg towards Luxembourg border.*
Open All year **Site** 3HEC 😃 ♨ ♨ 🚐 **Prices** ⚡ 4.35-5.80 pitch 5.21-9.30
Facilities 🌳 🏧 ⊙ 🚿 ⊘ 🛒 ⑦ **Services** ⊞ 🍴 🛒 **Leisure** ✦ PR
Off-site ⊞

OLPE NORDRHEIN-WESTFALEN

AT KESSENHAMMER

Biggesee-Kessenhammer
Kessenhammer 3, 57462 ☎ 02761 94420 📠 02761 944299
e-mail info@camping-kessenhammer.de
website www.biggesee.com
Long, narrow partly terraced site in quiet woodland setting on eastern shore of the Bigge reservoir.
➲ *A45 exit Olpe, B54 to Olpe, E on B55, exit Rhode.*
Open Apr-Oct **Site** 5.7HEC 😃 ♨ ♨ **Prices** ⚡ 3.90-4 ▲ 9-11 pitch 12-13
Facilities 🌳 🏧 ⊙ 🚿 ⊘ 🛒 ⑦ **Services** ⊞ 🛒 **Leisure** ✦ L **Off-site** 🍴

AT SONDERN

Biggesee-Vier Jahreszeiten
Sonderner Kopf 3, 57462 ☎ 02761 944111 📠 02761 944141
e-mail info@camping-sonderner.de
website www.biggesee.com
A popular site in wooded surroundings on the shore of the Biggesee.
➲ *A45 exit Olpe for Attendorn, 6km turn for Erholungsanlage Biggesee-Sondern.*
Open All year **Site** 6HEC 😃 ♨ ♨ **Prices** ⚡ 3.90-4.50 pitch 12-14
Facilities 🌳 🏧 ⊙ 🚿 ⊘ 🛒 ⑦ **Services** 🍴 ⊞ 🛒 **Leisure** ✦ L **Off-site** 🍴

Site 6HEC (site size) 😃 grass ⊜ sand 😃 stone ♨ little shade ♨ partly shaded 😃 mainly shaded 🏠 bungalows for hire
🚐 caravans for hire ▲ tents for hire ⊗ no dogs **Prices** ⚡ adult per night 🚗 car per night pp per person per night 🚐 caravan per night
▲ tent per night 🚐 (static)-caravan hire per week

PORTA WESTFALICA NORDRHEIN-WESTFALEN

Grosser Weserbogen

32457 ☎ 05731 6188 ▤ 05731 6601
e-mail info@grosserweserbogen.de
website www.grosserweserbogen.de
⮑ A2 towards Dortmund, exit Porta Westfalica-Minden.
Open All year **Site** 7HEC ⛺ ♣ ⊗ **Facilities** ⋔ ▣ ⊙ ➋ ⊘ ⊛ **Services** ⫮
➕ ▣ **Leisure** ⚲ L **Off-site** ⚲P

PRÜM RHEINLAND-PFALZ

Waldcampingplatz

54591 ☎ 06551 2481 ▤ 06551 6555
e-mail info@waldcamping-pruem.de
website www.waldcamping-pruem.de
Site lies on both side of the River Prüm and is surrounded by woods.
Divided into three sections of level meadowland.
⮑ On NW edge of Prüm.
Open All year **Site** 3.5HEC ⛺ ♣ **Facilities** ⋔ ▣ ⊙ ➋ ⊘ ⚞ ⊛
Services ⫮ ➕ ▣ **Leisure** ⚲ R **Off-site** ▣ ⫮ ⫮ ⚲P

REINSFELD RHEINLAND-PFALZ

AZUR Camping Hunsrück

54421 ☎ 06503 95123 ▤ 06503 95124
e-mail reinsfeld@azur-camping.de
website www.azur-camping.de/reinsfeld
A peaceful location close to Trier on the Luxembourg border,
surrounded by hills.
⮑ Via B52 or B407.
Open All year **Site** 20HEC ⛺ ♣ ➊ **Prices** ⋔ 5.50-7.50 ▲ 4.50-6 pitch 6-9
Facilities ⋔ ▣ ⊙ ➋ ⊘ ⚞ ⊛ **Services** ⫮ ⫮ ➕ ▣ **Leisure** ⚲ P

ROTHEMANN HESSEN

Rothemann

Maulkuppenstr 17, 36124 ☎ 06659 2285
A small, well-kept site surrounded by a hedge, next to the main Fulda
road.
⮑ A7 onto A66 exit Fulda Süd, 3km S on B27 towards Bad
Brükenau.
Open Apr-Oct **Site** 5.4HEC ⛺ ♣ **Prices** ⋔ 4.30 ➊ 2.20 ➊ 2.20 ▲ 2
Facilities ⋔ ▣ ⊙ ➋ ⊘ ⚞ ⊛ **Services** ➕ **Off-site** ⫮

RÜDESHEIM HESSEN

Rhein

65385 ☎ 06722 2528 & 2582 ▤ 06722 941046 & 406783
website www.campingplatz-ruedesheim.de
Near the open-air swimming pool and the River Rhine.
Open May-3 Oct **Site** 3HEC ⛺ ♣ **Prices** ⋔ 4.70 ➊ 3.70 ➊ 4.70 ▲ 4.30-
4.70 **Facilities** ⋔ ▣ ⊙ ➋ ⊘ ⚞ ⊛ **Services** ⫮ ⫮ ▣ **Off-site** ⫮ ⚲P ➕

SAARBURG RHEINLAND-PFALZ

Landal Greenpark Warsberg

54439 ☎ 06581 91460 ▤ 06581 914646
e-mail warsberg@landal.de
website www.landal.de
Open site in a quiet hilltop location. A chairlift (700m) goes down to
the town.
⮑ Signed at N end of town off B51 Trier road, 3km uphill.
Open 31 Mar-Oct **Site** 11HEC ⛺ ♣ ➊ ➊ **Facilities** ⋔ ▣ ⊙ ➋ ⊘ ⚞ ⊛
Services ⫮ ⫮ ➕ ▣ **Leisure** ⚲ P

Leukbachtal

54439 ☎ 06581 2228 ▤ 06581 2228
e-mail camping.leukbachtal@web.de
Municipal site on level meadows on both sides of the Leuk-Bach
(brook).
⮑ B51 from Saarburg towards Trassen, turn left after x-rds.
Open Apr-Oct **Site** 3HEC ⛺ ♣ ➊ **Facilities** ⋔ ⊙ ➋ ⊘ ⚞ ⊛
Services ⫮ ⫮ ➕ ▣ **Off-site** ▣ ⚲P

Waldfrieden

Im Fichtenhain 4, 54439 ☎ 06581 2255 ▤ 06581 5809
e-mail info@campingwaldfrieden.de
website www.campingwaldfrieden.de
Site lies next to the Café Waldfrieden on unspoiled, slightly rising
meadowland in woods.
⮑ S of town off B51 or B407 towards Nennig (Luxembourg),
200m to site.
Open Mar-3 Nov **Site** 2.3HEC ⛺ ♣ ➊ **Prices** ⋔ 2.70-4.20 ▲ 3.38-5 pitch
8 **Facilities** ⋔ ⊙ ➋ ⊘ ⚞ ⊛ **Services** ⫮ ⫮ ➕ ▣ **Leisure** ⚲ P
Off-site ▣ ⚲R ➕

SAARLOUIS SAARLAND

AZUR-Camping Saarlouis

Marschall-Ney-Weg 2, 66740 ☎ 06831 3691 ▤ 06831 122970
e-mail campsls@aol.com
website www.camping-saarlouis.de
Divided into pitches, and set on level meadowland with tall trees.
⮑ Off B51 in suburb of Roden, over new bridge over River Saar
to site beyond sports hall.
Open 15 Mar-Oct **Site** 2HEC ⛺ ♣ ➊ **Prices** ⋔ 4.80 ➊ 5.50 ▲ 3.50
Facilities ⋔ ⊙ ➋ ⚞ ⊛ **Services** ⫮ ➕ ▣ **Off-site** ▣ ⫮ ⫮ ⚲P

ST GOAR RHEINLAND-PFALZ

Friedenau

Gruendelbach 103, 35629 ☎ 06741 368 ▤ 06741 368
e-mail info@camping-friedenau.de
website www.camping-friedenau.de
On level, narrow stretch of meadowland at Gasthaus Friedenau.
⮑ Off B9 in St-Goar, through railway underpass towards
Emmelshausen for 1km.
Open Mar-1 Dec **Site** 2HEC ⛺ ♣ ➊ **Prices** ⋔ 4.20-4.50 ➊ 2.50 ➊ 2.50-
3 ▲ 2-2.50 ➊ (static)140 **Facilities** ⋔ ▣ ⊙ ➋ ⊘ ⚞ ⊛ **Services** ⫮ ⫮
➕ ▣ **Leisure** ⚲ R **Off-site** ⚲P

Germany

Facilities ▣ shop ⋔ shower ⊙ electric points for razors ➋ electric points for caravans ⊛ parking by tents permitted ➌ compulsory separate car park
Services ⫮ café/restaurant ⫮ bar ⊘ Camping Gaz International ⚞ gas other than Camping Gaz ➕ first aid facilities ▣ laundry
Leisure ⚲ swimming L-Lake P-Pool R-River S-Sea **Off-site** All facilities within 2km

ST GOARSHAUSEN RHEINLAND-PFALZ

Loreleystadt

56346 ☎ 06771 2592 📄 02137 929641

Municipal site on level meadow beside the Rhine. Near a sports field and opposite Rheinfels castle.

⮕ *Via B42.*

Open 15 Mar-Oct **Site** 1.5HEC 😃 🍃 **Facilities** 🌳 🏪 ⊙ 🚿 🅿 ⊘ ⊗ **Services** 🍴 🚌 🖻 **Leisure** ⚓ R **Off-site** 🍴

SCHACHEN HESSEN

Hochrhön

36129 ☎ 06654 7836 📄 06654 7836

e-mail campinghochrhoen@aol.com

Site lies 1.5km from the Kneipp (hydrotherapeutic) Spa area of Gersfeld.

⮕ *2km N of Gersfeld.*

Open All year **Site** 3HEC 😃 🍃 **Prices** 🧍 3.50 pitch 4.50 **Facilities** 🌳 ⊙ 🚿 ⊘ ᾱ ⊗ **Services** 🍴 🖻 **Off-site** 🏪 🍴 ⚓P 🚌

SCHALKENMEHREN RHEINLAND-PFALZ

Camp am Maar

Maarstr 22, 54552 ☎ 06592 95510 📄 06592 955140

e-mail hotelschneider@t-online.de

website www.hotelschneider.de

Terraced lakeside site on meadowland at the Schalkenmehrener Maar (water-filled crater).

⮕ *A48 exit Mehren/Daun, B42 to Mehren, turn SW.*

Open All year **Site** 1HEC 😃 🍃 **Facilities** 🌳 🏪 ⊙ 🚿 ⊘ ᾱ 🅿 **Services** 🍴 🍴 🖻 **Leisure** ⚓ LP **Off-site** 🚌

SCHLEIDEN NORDRHEIN-WESTFALEN

Schleiden

Im Wiesengrund 39, 53937 ☎ 02445 7030 📄 02445 5980

Site lies on hilly, well-wooded country.

⮕ *On B258 to Monschau, 1km to site.*

Open All year **Site** 5HEC 😃 🍃 **Prices** 🧍 4 🚗 1.80 🚐 4.80 🏕 4.60-6.20 **Facilities** 🌳 🏪 ⊙ 🚿 ⊘ ᾱ ⊗ **Services** 🍴 🚌 🖻 **Off-site** 🏪 🍴 🍴 ⚓P 🚌

SCHLÜCHTERN HESSEN

AT HUTTEN (8KM E)

Hutten Heiligenborn

Helga Herzog-Gericke, 36381 ☎ 06661 2424 📄 06661 917581

e-mail helga.herzog-gericke@online.de

Site lies at Heiligenborn and has a pleasant southerly aspect.

⮕ *B40 from Fulda towards Frankfurt to Flieden for 19km, turn left via Rückers to Hutten (8km).*

Open All year **Site** 3.5HEC 😃 🍃 **Facilities** 🌳 🏪 ⊙ 🚿 ⊘ ᾱ ⊗ **Services** 🍴 🚌 🖻 **Off-site** ⚓P

SCHÖNENBERG SAARLAND

Ohmbachsee

66901 ☎ 06373 4001 📄 06373 4002

e-mail ohmbachsee@profimail.de

website www.campingpark-ohmbachsee.de

Terraced site on sloping ground above eastern bank of the Ohmbachsee. Separate field for young people.

⮕ *Signed.*

Open All year **Site** 7.8HEC 😃 🍃 🏠 **Facilities** 🌳 🏪 ⊙ 🚿 ⊘ ᾱ ⊗ **Services** 🍴 🍴 🚌 🖻 **Leisure** ⚓ P **Off-site** ⚓L

SCHOTTEN HESSEN

Nidda-Stausee

Vogelsbergstr 184, 63679 ☎ 06044 1418 📄 06044 987995

e-mail campingplatz@schotten.de

website www.schotten.de

A pleasant family site on the shore of a lake.

⮕ *Via B455.*

Open All year **Site** 3.2HEC 😃 🍃 **Prices** 🧍 4 🚐 4.50 🏕 3.50-4.50 **Facilities** 🌳 ⊙ 🚿 ⊘ ⊗ **Services** 🍴 🚌 🖻 **Off-site** 🍴 ⚓LP

SECK RHEINLAND-PFALZ

Weiherhof

56479 ☎ 02664 8555 📄 02664 6388

e-mail info@camping-park-weiherhof.de

website www.camping-park-weiherhof.de

Site lies on level meadowland next to a small lake in a wooded nature reserve. Special section reserved for young people. Many bathers at weekends.

⮕ *B255 from Rennerod to Hellenbahn-Schellenberg, turn S for 2km.*

Open 15 Mar-15 Oct **Site** 10HEC 😃 🍃 🏠 **Prices** 🧍 4.50 🏕 4 pitch 6 🚐 (static)280 **Facilities** 🌳 🏪 ⊙ 🚿 ᾱ ⊗ **Services** 🍴 🍴 🚌 🖻 **Leisure** ⚓ L

SENHEIM RHEINLAND-PFALZ

Internationaler Holländischer Hof

56820 ☎ 02673 4660 📄 02673 4100

e-mail holl.hof@t-online.de

website www.moselcamping.com

On level meadowland, divided into pitches beside the River Mosel (mooring facilities).

⮕ *B49 from Cochem towards Zell, at Senhals over bridge & left.*

Open 15 Apr-1 Nov **Site** 4HEC 😃 🍃 🏠 🚐 ⊗ **Facilities** 🌳 🏪 ⊙ 🚿 ⊘ ᾱ 🅿 **Services** 🍴 🍴 🚌 🖻 **Leisure** ⚓ R

SENSWEILER MÜHLE RHEINLAND-PFALZ

Oberes Idartal

55758 ☎ 06786 2114 📄 06786 2222

e-mail cpoberesidartal@aol.com

website www.oberes-idartal.de

Site lies on a farm by the Idar, set on several small meadows and partly on terraced terrain next to Camping Sensweiler Mühel.

⮕ *B422 from Idar-Oberstein for 10km NW, site between Katzenloch & Allenbach.*

Open All year **Site** 2HEC 😃 🍃 🏠 🚐 **Facilities** 🌳 🏪 ⊙ 🚿 ⊘ ᾱ ⊗ **Services** 🚌 🖻 **Leisure** ⚓ R **Off-site** 🍴 🍴 ⚓P

Site 6HEC (site size) 😃 grass ⊖ sand 😃 stone 🍃 little shade 🍃 partly shaded 😃 mainly shaded 🏠 bungalows for hire 🚐 caravans for hire 🏕 tents for hire ⊗ no dogs **Prices** 🧍 adult per night 🚗 car per night pp per person per night 🚐 caravan per night 🏕 tent per night 🚐 (static)-caravan hire per week

Sensweiler-Mühle

Bundestat 422, 55758 ☎ 06786 2395 🗎 06781 35147

e-mail info@sensweiler-muehle.de

website www.sensweiler-muehle.de

On extensive grassland beside the Idar, partially terraced, in rural area near a farm. Views of wooded range of hills. Next to Camping Oberes Idartal. Separate section for young groups.

⊃ *B422 from Idar-Oberstein for 10km NW, site between Katzenloch & Allenbach.*

Open 3 Oct- 11-Feb **Site** 4HEC 👐 🏕 **Facilities** 🏪 ⊙ 🔛 🅿 ⑰ **Services** 🍽 ➕ 🗑 **Leisure** 🏊 R **Off-site** 🗐 🍴 🍽 L

SOLINGEN NORDRHEIN-WESTFALEN

AT GLÜDER

Waldcamping Glüder

42659 ☎ 0212 242120 🗎 0212 2421234

e-mail info@camping-solingen.de

website www.camping-solingen.de

Site on level terrain surrounded by woodland on banks of the River Wupper.

⊃ *B299/B224 from Solingen towards Witzhelden via Burg Hohenscheid.*

Open All year **Site** 2HEC 👐 🏕 **Facilities** 🏪 🗐 ⊙ 🔛 🅿 🚿 ⑰ **Services** 🍴 🍽 ➕ 🗑 **Off-site** 🍽 P

STADTKYLL RHEINLAND-PFALZ

Landal Wirftt

54589 ☎ 06597 92920 🗎 06597 929250

e-mail wirfttal@landal.de

website www.landal.de

Extensive, level grassland beside the upper of two small reservoirs, 1km outside the town.

⊃ *A1 S from Euskirchen, through Blankenheim towards Stadtkyll.*

Open All year **Site** 6.4HEC 👐 👐 🏕 🏕 **Prices** pitch 13-28 (incl 2 persons) **Facilities** 🏪 🗐 ⊙ 🔛 🅿 🚿 ⑰ **Services** 🍴 🍽 ➕ 🗑 **Leisure** 🏊 P

STEINEN RHEINLAND-PFALZ

Hofgut Schönerlen

56244 ☎ 02666 207 🗎 02666 8429

e-mail camping-kopper@t-online.de

website www.camping-westerwald.de

Beautiful and quiet site at Lake Hausweiher. Young campers under 18 years old not accepted unless with adults.

⊃ *B8 to Steinen & left to site.*

Open Dec-Oct **Site** 15HEC 👐 👐 🏕 🔛 ⑰ **Prices** 🏕 4.10-4.60 pitch 5.20-5.70 **Facilities** 🏪 🗐 ⊙ 🔛 🅿 🚿 ⑰ **Services** ➕ 🗑 **Leisure** 🏊 L **Off-site** 🍴 🍽

STUKENBROCK NORDRHEIN-WESTFALEN

Furlbach

Am Furlbach 33, 33758 ☎ 05257 3373 🗎 05257 940373

e-mail info@campingplatzamfurlbach.de

website www.campingplatzamfurlbach.de

Extensive site, partly on level, open meadow and partly in woodland. Separate section for dog owners. Old barn is used as a common room for young campers.

⊃ *A2 exit Bielefeld/Sennenstadt, onto B68 for 12km towards Paderborn, turn at Km44.2 to site 400m.*

Open Apr-1 Nov **Site** 9HEC 👐 🏕 **Prices** 🏕 4 🚐 3 🚗 4 ⛺ 3.50-4 pitch 7 **Facilities** 🏪 🗐 ⊙ 🔛 🚿 ⑰ **Services** 🍽 ➕ 🗑 **Off-site** 🍴 🍽

TANN HESSEN

Ulstertal

Dippach 4, 36142 ☎ 06682 8292 🗎 06682 10086

Terraced site on slightly sloping meadowland.

⊃ *Off B278 Bischofsheim-Tann in Wendershausen SE to Dippach.*

Open All year **Site** 2.4HEC 👐 🏕 🏕 **Facilities** 🏪 🗐 ⊙ 🔛 🅿 🚿 🚿 ⑰ **Services** 🍽 ➕ 🗑

TREIS-KARDEN RHEINLAND-PFALZ

Mosel-Islands

56253 ☎ 02672 2613 🗎 02672 912102

e-mail mosel-boating-center@t-online.de

An extensive, level site on a grassy island in the Mosel next to a yacht marina.

⊃ *Off B49 in Treis onto S coast road.*

Open Apr-Oct **Site** 4.5HEC 👐 🏕 🏕 **Facilities** 🏪 ⊙ 🔛 🚿 ⑰ **Services** 🗑 **Leisure** 🏊 R **Off-site** 🗐 🍴 🍽 🍽 P ➕

TRENDELBURG HESSEN

Trendelburg

34388 ☎ 05675 301 🗎 05675 5888

e-mail conradi-camping@t-online.de

website campingplatz-trendelburg.de

Site located at the foot of the castle, subdivided on the banks of the River Diemel. Covered tennis court.

⊃ *B83 N from Kessel via Hofgeismar to Trendelburg, over bridge & sharp left to site.*

Open All year **Site** 2.7HEC 👐 🏕 🏕 **Prices** 🏕 3.10 pitch 4.60 **Facilities** 🏪 🗐 ⊙ 🔛 🚿 🚿 ⑰ **Services** 🍽 🍴 🍽 🗑 **Leisure** 🏊 R **Off-site** 🍽 P

TRIER RHEINLAND-PFALZ

Treviris

Luxemburger Str 81, 54294 ☎ 0651 8200911 🗎 0651 8200567

Level site owned by the Rowing Club Treviris, beside the Mosel 1.6km from the city centre.

⊃ *On Luxembourg road between Romer bridge & Adenauer bridge.*

Open Apr-Oct **Site** 1.5HEC 👐 🏕 ⛺ **Prices** 🏕 6 ⛺ 4-5 pitch 6.50 **Facilities** 🏪 🗐 ⊙ 🔛 🚿 ⑰ **Services** 🍴 🗑 **Leisure** 🏊 R **Off-site** 🍽 🍽 P

TRIPPSTADT RHEINLAND-PFALZ

Sägmühle

Sägmühle 1, 67705 ☎ 06306 92190 🗎 06306 2000

e-mail info@saegmuehle.de

website www.saegmuehle.de

The site lies in a wooded valley beside Sägmühle (Saw Mill) lake. It consists of several unconnected sections, some of them terraced.

⊃ *14km S of Kaiserslautern.*

Open 14 Dec-Oct **Site** 10HEC 👐 🏕 🏕 **Prices** 🏕 6.70-7.70 pitch 7.30-9.30 **Facilities** 🏪 🗐 ⊙ 🔛 🚿 ⑰ **Services** 🍽 🍴 ➕ 🗑 **Leisure** 🏊 L **Off-site** 🍽 P

Facilities 🗐 shop 🏪 shower ⊙ electric points for razors 🔛 electric points for caravans ⑰ parking by tents permitted 🅿 compulsory separate car park
Services 🍴 café/restaurant 🍽 bar 🚿 Camping Gaz International 🚿 gas other than Camping Gaz ➕ first aid facilities 🗑 laundry
Leisure 🏊 swimming L-Lake P-Pool R-River S-Sea **Off-site** All facilities within 2km

VINKRATH BEI GREFRATH NORDRHEIN-WESTFALEN
SC Waldfrieden
An der Paas 13, 47929 ☎ 02158 3855 🖷 02158 3685
e-mail ferienpark-waldfrieden@t-online.de
website www.ferienpark-waldfrieden.de
Site within a nature reserve.
➔ *Off B509 at Grefrath N towards Wankum, 3km turn right.*
Open All year **Site** 4.5HEC ⚅ ♣ 🏠 🚐 **Prices** ⋏ 4.50 pitch 6-10
🚐 (static)180 **Facilities** 🏠 ⊙ 🚻 ⌀ ⚒ ⑳ ⑫ **Services** 🔆 🖨 **Off-site** 🖿 🛒
🍴 ⚓LPR

VLOTHO NORDRHEIN-WESTFALEN
Borlefzen
Borlefzen 2, 32602 ☎ 05733 80008 🖷 05733 89728
e-mail info@borlefzen.de
website www.borlefzen.de
Open Apr-Oct **Site** 40HEC ⚅ ♣ 🚐 **Prices** ⋏ 4.50 pitch 6 **Facilities** 🏠 🖿
⊙ 🚻 ⌀ ⑳ **Services** 🛒 🍴 🔆 🖨 **Leisure** ⚓ LR

WARBURG NORDRHEIN-WESTFALEN
Eversburg
34414 ☎ 05641 8668
Site lies next to restaurant of the same name on the SE outskirts of the town.
Open All year **Site** 4.5HEC ⚅ ♣ 🚐 **Prices** ⋏ 4 🚗 1.50 🚐 8 🅰 4-6
Facilities 🏠 🖿 ⊙ 🚻 ⌀ ⑳ **Services** 🔆 🍴 🖨 **Leisure** ⚓ R
Off-site ⚓P

WASSERFALL NORDRHEIN-WESTFALEN
Wasserfall
Aurorastr 9, 59909 ☎ 02905 332
Terraced site surrounded by woodland, next to Fort Fun leisure centre.
Little room for touring campers during the winter.
➔ *Turn S off B7 10km E of Meschedes, pass Gevelinghausen to Wasserfall.*
Open All year **Site** 0.7HEC ⚅ ♣ 🚐 🅰 **Facilities** 🏠 ⊙ 🚻 ⚒ ⑫
Services 🔆 🍴 🖨 **Off-site** ⚓PR

WAXWEILER RHEINLAND-PFALZ
AEGON-Ferienpark Im Prümtal
Schwimmbadstrasse 7, 54649 ☎ 06554 92000 🖷 06554 920029
e-mail info@ferienpark-waxweiler.de
website www.ferienpark-waxweiler.de
Site lies on level terrain and is divided into pitches, with a separate field on the opposite side of the River Prüm. Near swimming pool.
➔ *From N end of Waxweiler turn towards River Prüm.*
Open Apr-Oct **Site** 3HEC ⚅ ♣ 🏠 🚐 **Prices** pitch 13.50-18.50 **Facilities** 🏠 🖿
⊙ 🚻 ⑳ **Services** 🍴 🖨 **Leisure** ⚓ PR **Off-site** 🔆 🍴 ⚓P

WEILBURG HESSEN
AT ODERSBACH
Odersbach
Runkler Str 5A, 35781 ☎ 06471 7620 🖷 06471 379603
e-mail camping-odersbach@t-online.de
website www.camping-odersbach.de
An attractive setting beside the River Lahn, next to a public swimming pool.
➔ *On S outskirts of town.*
Open Apr-Oct **Site** 6HEC ⚅ ♣ 🚐 🅰 **Prices** ⋏ 3.60 🚗 2.70 🚐 3.50
🅰 2.10-13.40 **Facilities** 🏠 ⊙ 🚻 ⌀ ⑳ **Services** 🍴 🖨 🖨 **Leisure** ⚓ PR
Off-site 🖿 🛒 🍴

WINTERBERG NORDRHEIN-WESTFALEN
AT NIEDERSFELD (8.5KM N)
Vossmecke
59955 ☎ 02985 8418 🖷 02985 553
e-mail info@camping-vossmecke.de
website www.camping-vossmecke.de
A pleasant wooded location with facilities for winter camping.
➔ *Off B480 towards Winterberg.*
Open All year **Site** 4HEC ⚅ ♣ ♣ **Prices** 🅰 10.95-11.95 pitch 19.40-22.40
(incl 2 persons) **Facilities** 🏠 🖿 ⊙ 🚻 ⌀ ⑳ **Services** 🍴 🖨 **Off-site** 🖿
🍴 ⚓P

WISSEL NORDRHEIN-WESTFALEN
Wisseler See
Zum Wisseler See 15, 47546 ☎ 02824 96310 🖷 02824 963131
e-mail wisseler-see@t-online.de
website www.wisseler-see.de
Well-kept municipal site with modern equipment beside Lake Wissel.
There is a separate car park next to the open-air swimming pool. The pool belongs to the camp.
➔ *B57 from Kieve towards Xanten, 9km turn left, continue 3km towards Wissel.*
Open All year **Site** 35HEC ⚅ ♣ ♣ ♣ **Prices** ⋏ 5.50 🚗 3.25 🚐 8.50
🅰 6.50 **Facilities** 🏠 🖿 ⊙ 🚻 ⌀ ⚒ ⑳ ⑫ **Services** 🔆 🍴 🖨
Leisure ⚓ L **Off-site** ⚓P

WITZENHAUSEN HESSEN
Werratal
Am Sande 11, 37213 ☎ 05542 1465 🖷 05542 72418
website www.campingplatz-werratal.de
The site lies on meadow between the outskirts of Witzenhausen and the banks of the Werra.
➔ *Hannover-Kassel motorway exit Werratal, onto B80 to Witzenhausen, signed from market place.*
Open All year **Site** 3HEC ⚅ ♣ 🏠 🚐 **Prices** ⋏ 3.15-4.50 pitch 3.80-7
🚐 (static)245 **Facilities** 🏠 🖿 ⊙ 🚻 ⌀ ⑳ **Services** 🔆 🖨
Leisure ⚓ R **Off-site** 🍴 ⚓P

Site 6HEC (site size) ⚅ grass ⚊ sand ⚇ stone ♣ little shade ♣ partly shaded ⚅ mainly shaded 🏠 bungalows for hire
🚐 caravans for hire 🅰 tents for hire ⊗ no dogs **Prices** ⋏ adult per night 🚗 car per night pp per person per night 🚐 caravan per night
🅰 tent per night 🚐 (static)-caravan hire per week

WOLFSTEIN RHEINLAND-PFALZ

AZUR Campingpark am Königsberg

Am Schwimmbad 1, 67752 ☎ 06304 4143 ▤ 06304 7543
e-mail benspruijt@gmx.de
website www.camping-wolfstein.com
Beside small River Lauter next to an open-air swimming pool.

➲ *Site at S end of Wolfstein on right of B270 from Kaiserslautern.*

Open All year **Site** 1.5HEC ⛺ ♣ ♠ � **Prices** ♦ 4.50-6 ▲ 3.70-4.50 pitch
5.50-7.50 🚲 (static)400 **Facilities** 🛉 ⊕ ⌨ ♨ ⅋ ℗ **Services** 🍴 🍽 🗑
Off-site 🛒 ⌀ ⇆LPR ➕

ZERF RHEINLAND-PFALZ

Rübezahl

54314 ☎ 06587 814 ▤ 06587 814
e-mail seyffardt-zerf@t-online.de
Meadowland site in natural grounds on wooded hillside.

➲ *B268 from Zerf S towards Saarbrücken & turn towards Oberzerf, site 2.5km. Or B407 from Saarburg, turn right after Vierherrenhorn onto track for 60m.*

Open Apr-Oct **Site** 2.5HEC ⛺ ♣ **Prices** ♦ 4 pitch 5 **Facilities** 🛉 ⊕ ⌨ ⌀
℗ **Services** ➕ **Leisure** ⇆ P

ZWESTEN HESSEN

Waldcamping

Hinter dem Wasser, 34596 ☎ 05626 379 ▤ 06695 1320
e-mail info@doering-jesberg.de
website www.waldcamping.de
Site in bend of River Schwalm. For touring campers there is an overflow site.

➲ *Access from Kassel in SW direction via Fritzlar to Zwesten.*

Open All year **Site** 5HEC ⛺ ♣ **Prices** ♦ 4.50 pitch 5.50 **Facilities** 🛉 ⊕ ⌨
♨ ℗ **Services** 🍴 🍽 ➕ 🗑 **Leisure** ⇆ PR **Off-site** 🛒 🍽

NORTH

ALTENAU NIEDERSACHSEN

Okertalsperre

Kornhardtweg 1, 38707 ☎ 05328 702 ▤ 05328 911708
e-mail camping-okertal@t-online.de
website www.camping-okertal.de
On a long stretch of grassland at the south end of the Oker reservoir.

➲ *Signed from B498 Oker-Altenau.*

Open All year **Site** 4HEC ⛺ ♠ ♣ 🚲 **Prices** ♦ 3.15-3.50 pitch 6 🚲 (static)210-
280 **Facilities** 🛉 🛒 ⊕ ⌨ ⌀ ♨ ℗ **Services** 🍽 ➕ 🗑 **Leisure** ⇆ L

BLECKEDE NIEDERSACHSEN

Alt-Garge (ADAC)

Am Waldbad 23, 21354 ☎ 05854 311 ▤ 05854 1640
e-mail adac-camping-altgarge@t-online.de
website www.camping-urlaub.de
A modern site at the south-east end of Alt-Garge, next to a heated swimming pool in the woods. The camp has archery butts and its own gas-filling station.

➲ *5km SE of Bleckede.*

Open All year **Site** 6.6HEC ⛺ ♠ ♣ **Facilities** 🛉 🛒 ⊕ ⌨ ♨ ℗
Services ➕ **Off-site** 🍽 ⌀ ⇆LPR

BODENWERDER NIEDERSACHSEN

Himmelspforte

Ziegeleiweg 1, 37619 ☎ 05533 4938 ▤ 05533 4432
e-mail himmelspforte@yahoo.de
website www.camping-weserbergland.de
Site on grassland, with a fruit orchard, next to River Weser. Good possibilites for water sports. Separate section and common room for young campers.

➲ *Cross River Weser & right towards Rühle, site 2km.*

Open All year **Site** 11HEC ⛺ ♠ **Prices** ♦ 3.50 pitch 4.50 **Facilities** 🛉 🛒
⊕ ⌨ ♨ ℗ **Services** 🍴 🍽 ➕ **Leisure** ⇆ R **Off-site** ⇆P

Rühler Schweiz

Grosses Tal 1, 37619 ☎ 05533 2486 ▤ 05533 5882
e-mail info@brader-ruehler-schweiz.de
website www.brader-ruehler-schweiz.de
This site lies on well-kept meadowland by the River Weser.

➲ *4km from Weser bridge in Bodenwerder towards Rühle.*

Open Mar-Oct **Site** 7HEC ⛺ ♠ ♠ ♣ 🚲 **Prices** ♦ 4 ▲ 3 pitch 5.50
Facilities 🛉 🛒 ⊕ ⌨ ♨ ℗ **Services** 🍴 🍽 ➕ 🗑 **Leisure** ⇆ PR
Off-site 🍽

BOTHEL NIEDERSACHSEN

Hanseat

27384 ☎ 04266 355 ▤ 04266 355
Open All year **Site** 4.5HEC ⛺ ♣ **Facilities** 🛉 ⊕ ⌨ ⌀ ℗ **Services** ➕ 🗑
Off-site 🛒 🍴 🍽 ⇆P

BRAUNLAGE NIEDERSACHSEN

AT ZORGE (14KM S)

Harz Camping Im Waldwinkel

37449 ☎ 05586 1048 ▤ 05586 8113
A site on different levels, surrounded by high trees, 200m from an open-air woodland pool in Kunzen valley.

Open All year **Site** 1.5HEC ⛺ ♠ ♠ ♣ 🚲 **Prices** pitch 9.70-14 (incl 2
persons) **Facilities** 🛉 🛒 ⊕ ⌨ ⌀ ♨ ℗ **Services** ➕ 🗑 **Off-site** 🍴 🍽 ⇆P

BREMEN BREMEN

Stadtwaldsee

Hochschulring 1, 28359 ☎ 0421 8410748 ▤ 0421 8410749
e-mail contact@camping-stadtwaldsee.de
website www.camping-stadtwaldsee.de
Situated near a lake in forest close to the city.

➲ *A27 exit 18.*

Open All year **Site** 5.8HEC ⛺ ♠ ♠ ♣ 🚲 **Prices** ♦ 6-7 🚲 1-1.50 🚲 9-10
▲ 3-4 🚲 (static)175 **Facilities** 🛉 🛒 ⊕ ⌨ ⌀ ℗ **Services** 🍴 🗑
Off-site 🍽 ⇆LP ➕

BRIETLINGEN-REIHERSEE NIEDERSACHSEN

Reihersee 1

Alte Salzstr 8, 21382 ☎ 04133 3671 & 3577 ▤ 04133 4391
Divided into pitches by hedges and pine trees. Private bathing area.

➲ *Turn E at car park 2km beyond Brietlingen towards Reihersee for 0.8km.*

Open All year **Site** 6.2HEC ⛺ ♠ ♣ 🚲 **Facilities** 🛉 ⊕ ⌨ ♨ ℗ **Services** 🍽
➕ 🗑 **Leisure** ⇆ LR **Off-site** 🛒

Facilities 🛒 shop 🛉 shower ⊕ electric points for razors ⌨ electric points for caravans ℗ parking by tents permitted ⅋ compulsory separate car park
Services 🍽 café/restaurant 🍴 bar ⌀ Camping Gaz International ♨ gas other than Camping Gaz ➕ first aid facilities 🗑 laundry
Leisure ⇆ swimming L-Lake P-Pool R-River S-Sea **Off-site** All facilities within 2km

Germany

BÜCHEN SCHLESWIG-HOLSTEIN

Waldschwimmbad

21514 ☎ 04155 5360 ▤ 04155 499140
e-mail camping-hintz@t-online.de
website www.camping-buechen.de
On gently sloping grassland. Siesta 13.00-15.00 hrs.

➲ *From Lauenburg or Mölln to Büchen then signed.*

Open All year **Site** 1.6HEC ♨ ♣ ♨ Å **Facilities** ♠ 🏠 ⊙ ♨ ∅ ♨ ⑫
Services ☎ 🍴 ➕ 🗗 **Off-site** ♨PR

BURG (ISLAND OF FEHMARN) SCHLESWIG-HOLSTEIN

AT KLAUSDORF (5KM NW)

Klausdorfer Strand

23769 ☎ 04371 2549 ▤ 04371 2481
e-mail info@camping-klausdorferstrand.de
website www.camping-klausdorferstrand.de
A grassy site with sea views. Divided into pitches. Sandy beach.

➲ *From Burg turn off main road 2.5km before Klausdorf onto narrow asphalt road.*

Open Apr-15 Oct **Site** 12HEC ♨ ♣ ♨ **Facilities** ♠ 🏠 ⊙ ♨ ∅ ♨ ⑫
Services 🍴 ➕ 🗗 **Leisure** ♨ PS **Off-site** ♨L

BURGWEDEL NIEDERSACHSEN

Erholungsgebiet Springhorstsee

30938 ☎ 05139 3232 ▤ 05139 27070
e-mail springhorstsee@aol.com
website www.springhorstsee.de
On level ground beside a lake with well-defined pitches and modern facilities.

➲ *A7 exit 54, site 2km.*

Open All year **Site** 29HEC ♨ ♣ ♨ ⚏ ♨ **Prices** ♠ 3.50 ♨ 6 Å 3.50
♨ (static)126 **Facilities** ♠ ⊙ ♨ ♨ ⑫ **Services** ☎ 🍴 ➕ 🗗 **Leisure** ♨ LP
Off-site 🏠 ∅

BUTJADINGEN NIEDERSACHSEN

Burhave

Burhave Strand ☎ 04733 1683 ▤ 04733 173206
e-mail burhave@knauscamp.de
website www.knauscamp.de
Situated next to a national park with access to fine beaches.

Open 4 Apr-15 Oct **Site** 10HEC ♨ ♣ ♨ **Prices** ♠ 6 pitch 5-8 **Facilities** ♠
🏠 ⊙ ♨ ♨ ⑫ **Services** ➕ **Leisure** ♨ S

CLAUSTHAL-ZELLERFELD NIEDERSACHSEN

Prahljust

38678 ☎ 05323 1300 ▤ 05323 78393
e-mail camping@prahljust.de
website www.prahljust.de
The site lies on slightly sloping grassland in an area of woodland and lakes.

➲ *B242 SE from outskirts towards Braunlage, 2km turn right, site 1.5km.*

Open All year **Site** 13HEC ♨ ♣ **Prices** ♠ 4.60 Å 2.50 pitch 4.70
Facilities ♠ 🏠 ⊙ ♨ ∅ ⑫ **Services** ☎ 🍴 🗗 **Leisure** ♨ LP
Off-site ♨ ➕

Waldweben

Spiegelthalerstr 31, 38678 ☎ 05323 81712 ▤ 05323 962134
website www.campingplatz-waldweben.de
Holiday village with individual pitches in open meadow and coniferous woodland by three small lakes.

➲ *Signed from B241 towards Goslar.*

Open All year **Site** 4.5HEC ♨ ♣ ♨ ⚏ **Prices** ♠ 4-5 ♨ 2.50 ♨ 3 Å 2.50
Facilities ♠ 🏠 ⊙ ♨ ♨ ⑫ **Services** 🍴 🗗 **Off-site** 🍴 ♨LP ➕

DAHRENHORST NIEDERSACHSEN

Irenensee

Dahrenhorst, 31311 ☎ 05173 98120 ▤ 05173 981213
e-mail info@irenensee.de
website irenensee.de
A lakeside site on meadowland, partly surrounded by woods, with separate section for tourers, statics and residentials.

➲ *B188 from Burgdorf towards Uetze for 15km.*

Open Apr-Oct **Site** 120HEC ♨ ♣ ♨ ⚏ Å **Prices** ♠ 6.10-9 ♨ 2.70-3
♨ 2.70-6.20 ♨ (static)199-2.99 **Facilities** ♠ 🏠 ⊙ ♨ ∅ ♨ ⑫ **Services** 🍴
➕ 🗗 **Leisure** ♨ L

DETERN NIEDERSACHSEN

Jümmesee

26847 ☎ 04957 1808 ▤ 04957 8112
e-mail info@detern.de
website www.detern.de

➲ *Via B72 Aurich-Cloppenburg.*

Open All year **Site** 11.5HEC ♨ ♣ ♨ **Prices** ♠ 5 Å 4 pitch 5.50
Facilities ♠ ⊙ ♨ ♨ ⑫ **Services** 🍴 ➕ 🗗 **Leisure** ♨ LR **Off-site** ♨PS

DORUM NIEDERSACHSEN

AZUR Nordseecamp Dorumer Tief

Am Kutterhafen, 27632 ☎ 04741 5020 ▤ 04741 914061
e-mail dorum@azur-camping.de
website www.azur-camping.deldorum
Next to a small harbour. Separated from the beach by a dyke.

➲ *Via A27 Bremerhaven-Cuxhaven.*

Open Apr-Sep **Site** 7HEC ♨ ♣ ⑧ **Prices** ♠ 4-6 ♨ 3.50 Å 3-5 pitch 4.50-
7.50 **Facilities** ♠ 🏠 ⊙ ♨ ♨ ⑫ **Services** 🍴 ➕ 🗗 **Leisure** ♨ PS

ECKWARDERHÖRNE NIEDERSACHSEN

Eckwarderhörne

Butjadinger Str.116 ☎ 04736 1300 ▤ 04736 102593
e-mail eckwarderhoerne@knauscamp.de
website www.knauscamp.de
Parkland site adjoining the North Sea.

Open 30 Mar-5 Nov **Site** 7.7HEC ♨ ♣ ♨ Å **Prices** ♠ 6 pitch 5-8
Facilities ♠ 🏠 ⊙ ♨ ♨ ⑫ **Services** 🍴 **Leisure** ♨ S

Site 6HEC (site size) ♨ grass ♨ sand ♨ stone ♣ little shade ♨ partly shaded ♨ mainly shaded ⚏ bungalows for hire
♨ caravans for hire Å tents for hire ⑧ no dogs **Prices** ♠ adult per night ♨ car per night pp per person per night ♨ caravan per night
Å tent per night ♨ (static)-caravan hire per week

EGESTORF NIEDERSACHSEN

AZUR-Camping Lüneburger Heide

21272 ☎ 04175 661 📠 04175 8383

e-mail egestorf@azur-camping.de

website www.azurcamping.de/egestorf

Modern site on wooded heathland on the edge of the Lüneburg heath nature reserve, 2km S of town on slightly sloping terrain with asphalt internal roads.

➲ A7 exit Egestorf or Evendorf.

Open All year **Site** 22HEC 👪 ♣ ♨ ♣ **Prices** ♠ 5-7 ▲ 4-5.50 pitch 5.50-8.50 **Facilities** ♠ 🛍 ⊙ ♀ ⌀ ♨ ℗ **Services** 🍴 🍽 🖫 **Leisure** ⇌ P **Off-site** 🍴

EIMKE NIEDERSACHSEN

Eimke Im Extertal

32699 ☎ 05262 3307 📠 05262-992404

e-mail info@campingpark-eimke.de

website www.campingpark-eimke.de

Extensive, partly terraced site on slightly sloping meadowland with two ponds.

➲ A2 exit 35, B238 past Rinteln, left onto External-Barntrup road for 18km.

Open All year **Site** 20HEC 👪 ♣ 🚐 **Prices** ♠ 5 pitch 5 🚐 (static)280 **Facilities** ♠ 🛍 ⊙ ♀ ⌀ ♨ ℗ **Services** 🍴 🍽 🖫 **Leisure** ⇌ L **Off-site** 🍽 ⇌P

ELISABETH SOPHIENKOOG (ISLAND OF NORDSTRAND) SCHLESWIG-HOLSTEIN

Elisabeth-Sophienkoog

Nordstrand, 25845 ☎ 04842 8534 📠 04842 8306

e-mail camping-nordstrand@t-online.de

On meadowland behind the sea dyke.

➲ Via Husum to Island of Nordstrand.

Open Apr-Oct **Site** 1.7HEC 👪 ♣ 🚐 **Prices** ♠ 3.90 🚗 2.40 🚐 4.50 ▲ 3.90 🚐 (static)280 **Facilities** ♠ 🛍 ⊙ ♀ ⌀ ℗ **Services** 🍽 🖫 **Leisure** ⇌ S

ESENS-BENSERSIEL NIEDERSACHSEN

Bensersiel

Am Strand, 26427 ☎ 04971 917121 📠 04971 917190

e-mail camping@bensersiel.de

website www.bensersiel.de

Well-managed, extensive leisure centre with harbour, good fish restaurant and reading room. Swimming pools have sea water and artificial waves.

➲ B210 NE from Aurich to Ogenbargenn then via Esens.

Open Etr-15 Oct **Site** 10HEC 👪 ♣ ♣ 🚐 ℗ **Prices** ♠ 3.40 🚗 1.60 🚐 7 ▲ 7 **Facilities** ♠ 🛍 ⊙ ♀ ℗ **Services** 🍴 🍽 🖫 **Leisure** ⇌ PS **Off-site** ⌀ ♨ ⇌P

EUTIN-FISSAU SCHLESWIG-HOLSTEIN

Prinzenholz

Prinzenholzweg 20, 23701 ☎ 04521 5281 📠 04521 3601

e-mail info@nc-prinzenholz.de

website www.nc-prinzenholz.de

Terraced lakeside site divided by trees and bushes. Mobile shop.

➲ N of town onto Malente road, 2km turn right.

Open Apr-Oct **Site** 2HEC 👪 ♣ 🚐 **Facilities** ♠ 🛍 ⊙ ♀ ⌀ ♨ ℗ **Services** 🍽 🖫 **Leisure** ⇌ L **Off-site** 🍴 🍽 ⇌P 🖫

FALLINGBOSTEL NIEDERSACHSEN

Böhmeschlucht

Vierde 22, 29683 ☎ 05162 5604 📠 05162 5160

e-mail campingplatz-boehmeschlucht@t-online.de

website www.bohmeschlucht.de

Site located in a nature reserve beside the river Böhme.

➲ A7 exit 46/47, site signed 3km N.

Open All year **Site** 4HEC 👪 ♣ 🚐 **Prices** ♠ 2.80 pitch 11.50 **Facilities** ♠ ⊙ ♀ ℗ ℗ **Services** 🍴 🍽 🖫 **Leisure** ⇌ R **Off-site** 🛍

FEHMARNSUND SCHLESWIG-HOLSTEIN

Miramar

23769 ☎ 04371 3220 📠 04371 868044

e-mail campingmiramar@t-online.de

website www.camping-miramar.de

A family site on meadowland at the southern end of the island.

➲ Off B207 at 1st turning after Sundbrücke (bridge) towards Svendorf.

Open All year **Site** 13HEC 👪 ♣ 🚐 **Prices** ♠ 4-7 pitch 8.50-12 🚐 (static)245-490 **Facilities** ♠ 🛍 ⊙ ♀ ⌀ ♨ ℗ **Services** 🍴 🍽 🖫 **Leisure** ⇌ LS

GANDERSHEIM, BAD NIEDERSACHSEN

DCC Kur-Campingpark

Braunschweiger Str 12, 37581 ☎ 05382 1595 📠 05382 599

website www.camping-bad-gandersheim.de

On a level meadow, divided in two by a brook beside a public park. Good sports facilities. Separate section for young people.

➲ A7 exit 67 Soesen onto B64 W.

Open All year **Site** 9HEC 👪 ♣ **Prices** ♠ 3.60-4 🚐 8.50 ▲ 6 **Facilities** ♠ 🛍 ⊙ ♀ ℗ **Services** 🍽 🖫 **Off-site** ⇌P

GARTOW NIEDERSACHSEN

Gartow am See

Am Helk, 29471 ☎ 05846 8250 📠 05846 2151

e-mail campingpark@gartow.de

website ww.campingpark-gartow.de

Situated in woodland with an adjoining meadow.

➲ NE on A493 from Lüchow.

Open All year **Site** 14HEC 👪 ♣ ♣ 🚐 **Facilities** ♠ 🛍 ⊙ ♀ ♨ ℗ **Services** 🖫 **Leisure** ⇌ P **Off-site** 🛍 🍽 ⇌LR 🖫

GIFHORN NIEDERSACHSEN

AT RÖTGESBÜTTEL (8KM S)

Glockenheide

38531 ☎ 05304 1581 📠 05304 1581

e-mail camping-glockenheide@T-online.de

website www.glockenheide.de

Tranquil site in heathland.

➲ In Rötgesbüttel turn left & left again after level crossing.

Open All year **Site** 5HEC 👪 ♣ ♣ 🚐 **Prices** ♠ 3.40 🚗 2.60 🚐 2.60 ▲ 2.60 **Facilities** ♠ ⊙ ♀ ♨ ℗ **Services** 🖫 **Off-site** 🛍 🍽

GLÜCKSBURG-HOLNIS SCHLESWIG-HOLSTEIN

Ostseecamp Glücksburg-Holnis

Am Kurstrand 3, 24960 ☎ 04631 622071 📠 04631 622072

e-mail info@ostseecamp-holnis.de

website www.ostseecamp-holnis.de

Open Apr-Oct **Site** 6HEC 👪 ♣ 🚐 **Prices** ♠ 3.90-4.90 🚗 2-2.50 🚐 5-7.50 ▲ 4-6 **Facilities** ♠ ⊙ ♀ ♨ ℗ **Services** 🍽 🖫 **Off-site** 🛍 🍽 ⇌S

Facilities 🛍 shop ♠ shower ⊙ electric points for razors ♀ electric points for caravans ℗ parking by tents permitted ℗ compulsory separate car park
Services 🍽 café/restaurant 🍴 bar ⌀ Camping Gaz International ♨ gas other than Camping Gaz 🖫 first aid facilities 🖫 laundry
Leisure ⇌ swimming L-Lake P-Pool R-River S-Sea **Off-site** All facilities within 2km

Germany

GRUBE SCHLESWIG-HOLSTEIN

Rosenfelder Strand Ostsee

23749 ☎ 04365 979722 🖹 04365 979594
e-mail info@rosenfelder-strand.de
website www.rosenfelder-strand.de
Excellently managed family site beside the sea with a 1km-long beach. Divided into separate fields by rows of bushes. Children's playground in woodland between site and sea.

➲ *E47 exit Oldenburg, north of Lübeck*

Open 23 Mar-14 Oct **Site** 24HEC ❤ ♣ 🖙 ⊗ **Prices** ♦ 5.20 pitch 10.40-12.20 🖙 (static)210-490 **Facilities** 🖙 🖻 ⊙ 🖼 ⊘ ⊸ ⊛ **Services** 🔧 ⍾ 🖸 🖸 **Leisure** ⊛ S **Off-site** ⊛S

HADDEBY SCHLESWIG-HOLSTEIN

Haithabu

24866 ☎ 04621 32450 🖹 04621 33122
e-mail info@campingplatz-haithabu.de
website www.campingplatz-haithabu.de
Clean, tidy site beside the River Schlei.

➲ *B76 from Schleswig towards Eckernförde.*

Open Apr-Oct **Site** 5HEC ❤ ♣ 🖙 **Prices** ♦ 3.50 🖙 2 🖙 9 Å 6 **Facilities** 🖙 🖻 ⊙ 🖼 ⊸ ⊛ **Services** ⍾ 🖸 🖸 **Leisure** ⊛ R

HADEMSTORF NIEDERSACHSEN

Waldhaus Allertal

29693 ☎ 05071 1872 🖹 05071 1912516
A picturesque wooded setting with pitches separated by hedges and bushes.

➲ *Via A27/A7.*

Open Apr-Sep **Site** 4HEC ❤ ♣ **Facilities** 🖙 🖻 ⊙ 🖼 ⊘ ⊸ ⊛ **Services** 🔧 ⍾ 🖸 **Off-site** ⊛R 🖸

HAHNENKLEE NIEDERSACHSEN

Kreuzeck

38644 ☎ 05325 2570 🖹 05325 3392
e-mail kreuzeck@aol.com
website www.campingground.de
Terraced site in a forest beside a lake. Separate section for dog owners.

➲ *Beside Café am Kreuzeck at junct B241 & road to Hahnenklee.*

Open All year **Site** 5HEC ❤ ⊜ ♣ ♣ 🖙 Å **Prices** ♦ 4.05 🖙 1.80 🖙 4.45 Å 4.45 🖙 (static)227.50 **Facilities** 🖙 🖻 ⊙ 🖼 ⊸ ⊛ ⊕ **Services** ⍾ 🖸 🖸 **Leisure** ⊛ LP **Off-site** ⊘

HAMELN NIEDERSACHSEN

Waldbad

Pfedeweg 2, 31787 ☎ 05158 2774 🖹 05158 2774
A grassy terraced site on the edge of woodland beside a public swimming pool.

➲ *Follow swimming pool signs from Havelstorf.*

Open Apr-Oct **Site** 2.8HEC ❤ ♣ 🖙 **Facilities** 🖙 ⊙ 🖼 ⊸ ⊛ **Services** ⍾ 🖸 **Off-site** 🖻 ⊛P

HANNOVER NIEDERSACHSEN

AT GARBSEN (10KM W)

Blauer See

30823 ☎ 05137 89960 🖹 05137 899677
e-mail info@camping-blauer-see.de
website www.camping-blauer-see.de
On a small lake beside the Garbsen service area on the A2 motorway.

Open All year **Site** 22HEC ❤ ♣ 🖙 **Prices** ♦ 6.80-7.90 🖙 2 Å 2.60-4.20 pitch 4.20-6.20 **Facilities** 🖙 🖻 ⊙ 🖼 ⊘ ⊛ **Services** ⍾ 🖸 🖸 **Leisure** ⊛ L

AT ISERNHAGEN (16KM NE)

Parksee Lohne

Alter Postweg 12, 30916 ☎ 05139 88260 🖹 05139 891665
e-mail parksee-lohne@t-online.de
website www.parksee-lohne.de
Recreation area by a lake. On the flight approach path for Hannover Langenhagen airport. Separate section for tourers.

➲ *Motorway exit Kirchorst, Altwarmbüchen road to Isernhagen.*

Open All year **Site** 16HEC ❤ ♣ **Facilities** 🖙 ⊙ 🖼 ⊸ ⊛ **Services** 🔧 ⍾ 🖸 🖸 **Leisure** ⊛ L

HARDEGSEN NIEDERSACHSEN

Ferienpark Solling

37181 ☎ 05505 5585 🖹 05505 5585
Terraced site in forested area. Separate field for touring pitches.

➲ *In town onto Waldgebiet Gladeberg road.*

Open All year **Site** 2.4HEC ❤ ♣ 🖙 **Facilities** 🖙 ⊙ 🖼 ⊸ ⊛ **Services** 🔧 ⍾ 🖸 🖸 **Off-site** 🖻 ⍾ ⊘ ⊛P

HASSENDORF NIEDERSACHSEN

Stürberg

27367 ☎ 04264 9124 🖹 04264 821440
e-mail campingpark-stuerberg@gmx.de
website www.stuerberg.de
Pleasant wooded surroundings beside a lake.

➲ *A1 exit 50 Stuckenborstel, B75 for Rotenburg for 5km.*

Open 15 Mar-Oct **Site** 2HEC ❤ ♣ **Prices** ♦ 3.50 🖙 8 Å 6 **Facilities** 🖙 ⊙ 🖼 ⊘ ⊸ ⊛ **Services** 🔧 ⍾ 🖸 **Leisure** ⊛ L **Off-site** ⍾

HATTEN NIEDERSACHSEN

Freizeitzentrum Hatten

Kreyenweg 8, 26209 ☎ 04482 677 🖹 04482 928027
e-mail info@fzz.hatten.de
Open All year **Site** 2HEC ❤ ♣ Å **Prices** ♦ 5 Å 2.60 pitch 6 **Facilities** 🖙 🖻 ⊙ 🖼 ⊘ ⊛ **Services** ⍾ 🖸 **Leisure** ⊛ P

HATTORF NIEDERSACHSEN

Oderbrücke

37197 ☎ 05521 4359 🖹 05521 4360
e-mail oderbruecke@t-online.de
website www.oderbruecke.top.ms
A pleasant wooded location with good recreational and sanitary facilities.

➲ *On B27 towards Herzberg.*

Open All year **Site** 2.5HEC ❤ ♣ **Prices** ♦ 3.15-3.50 pitch 5.20 **Facilities** 🖙 🖻 ⊙ 🖼 ⊘ ⊸ ⊛ **Services** 🔧 ⍾ 🖸 **Leisure** ⊛ R **Off-site** 🖸

Site 6HEC (site size) ❤ grass ⊜ sand ❤ stone ♣ little shade ♣ partly shaded ♣ mainly shaded 🏠 bungalows for hire 🖙 caravans for hire Å tents for hire ⊗ no dogs **Prices** ♦ adult per night 🖙 car per night pp per person per night 🖙 caravan per night Å tent per night 🖙 (static)-caravan hire per week

HEIKENDORF SCHLESWIG-HOLSTEIN

Möltenort

24226 ☎ 0431 241316 ▤ 0431 2379920
e-mail gronau.heikendorf@freenet.de
website www.camping-ostsee-online.de
Terraced site by the Kieler Förde.
➲ *15km NE of Kiel to W of road B502. Access via narrow, winding road.*
Open Apr-1 Oct **Site** 2HEC ♨ ♣ **Prices** ♦ 4 ♣ 8-10 ▲ 7-8
Facilities ♠ ☎ ☉ ☻ ☻ ⑳ **Services** ➕ ▣ **Leisure** ♨ S **Off-site** ☝ ☚ ⌀ ⚬ ♨

HELMSTEDT NIEDERSACHSEN

Waldwinkel

Maschweg 46, 38350 ☎ 05351 37161
Set in an orchard next to the Gasthaus Waldwinkel.
➲ *Autobahn exit Helmstedt, site signed.*
Open All year **Site** 10HEC ♨ ♣ **Facilities** ♠ ☎ ☉ ☻ ⌀ ♨ ⑳
Services ☚ ➕ ▣ **Off-site** ☚P

HEMELN NIEDERSACHSEN

Hemeln

34346 ☎ 05544 1414 ▤ 05544 1414
e-mail camping-hemeln@gmx.de
website www.wesercamping.de
Well-kept site on N outskirts of village, beside the River Weser.
➲ *A7 exit Gothenburg, B3 to Dransfeld & signed.*
Open All year **Site** 24HEC ♨ ♣ ♣ ♠ ♣ **Prices** ♦ 4 ♣ 2.10 ♣ 3.50
▲ 2.50 ♣ (static)28.50 **Facilities** ♠ ☎ ☉ ☻ ⌀ ♨ ⑳ **Services** ☚ ➕ ▣
Leisure ♨ R **Off-site** ☚P

HERMANNSBURG NIEDERSACHSEN

Örtzetal

29320 ☎ 05052 3072 & 1555
website www.campingplatz-oldendorf.de
Site lies on meadows on the east bank of the River Örtze, set in unspoiled woodlands on Lüneburg heath. Boat landing stage.
➲ *Off B3 in Bergen NE towards Hermannsburg & Eschwege.*
Open 15 Mar-Oct **Site** 6HEC ♨ ♣ ♣ ♠ ♣ **Prices** ♦ 4-4.50 ♣ 1 ♣ 4.50
▲ 2.50-3 **Facilities** ♠ ☉ ☻ ⑳ **Services** ☚ ☚ ➕ ▣ **Leisure** ♨ R
Off-site ☎ ☚ ☚P

HOHEGEISS NIEDERSACHSEN

Bärenbache

Bärenbachweg 10, 38700 ☎ 05583 1306 ▤ 05583 1300
e-mail info@campingplatz-hohegeiss.de
website www.campingplatz-hohegeiss.de
Terraced site. Well-organised.
Open All year **Site** 2.8HEC ♨ ♣ ♣ **Prices** ♦ 4.80 pitch 4.90 ♣ (static)175-245 **Facilities** ♠ ☉ ☻ ⌀ ♨ ⑳ **Services** ☚ **Off-site** ☎ ☚P

HOLLE NIEDERSACHSEN

AT DERNEBURG (2KM NW ON UNCLASS ROAD)

Seecamp-Derneburg

An der B6, Derneburg, 31188 ☎ 05062 565 ▤ 05062 8785
e-mail info@campingplatz-derneburg.de
website www.campingplatz-derneburg.de
A terraced lakeside site on a hill slope with a southerly aspect. Separate towing field. Useful stopover site near autobahn.
➲ *Motorway exit Derneburg onto B6.*
Open Apr-15 Sep **Site** 7.8HEC ♨ ♣ ♠ ♣ **Prices** ♦ 4.50 ♣ 2.50 ♣ 5
▲ 4.50 **Facilities** ♠ ☎ ☉ ☻ ⌀ ⑳ **Services** ☚ ➕ ▣ **Leisure** ♨ L
Off-site ☚R

KLEINWAABS SCHLESWIG-HOLSTEIN

Ostsee Heide

24369 ☎ 04352 2530 ▤ 04352 1398
e-mail info@waabs.de
website www.waabs.de
Divided into pitches and pleasantly landscaped. Large games room for teenagers.
Open Mar-Oct **Site** 22HEC ♨ ♣ ♠ ♣ **Prices** ♦ 3-5 pitch 8-13.50
Facilities ♠ ☎ ☉ ☻ ⌀ ♨ ⑳ **Services** ☚ ☚ ▣ **Leisure** ♨ PS

KLINT-BEI-HECHTHAUSEN NIEDERSACHSEN

Geesthof

Am Ferienpark 1, 21755 ☎ 04774 512 ▤ 04774 9178
e-mail ferienpark.geesthof@t-online.de
website www.ferienpark-geesthof.de
On dry meadowland next to the River Oste, in quiet setting with trees.
➲ *Off B73 in Hechthausen W towards Lamstedt for 3km.*
Open All year **Site** 15HEC ♨ ♣ ♠ ♣ **Prices** ♦ 4-5 ♣ 4-9 ▲ 3-5
Facilities ♠ ☎ ☉ ☻ ♨ ⑳ **Services** ☚ ➕ ▣ **Leisure** ♨ P

LAUTERBERG, BAD NIEDERSACHSEN

Wiesenbeker Teich

37431 ☎ 05524 2510 ▤ 05524 932089
e-mail info@campingwiesenbek.de
website www.campingwiesenbek.de
Wooded surroundings on the Wiesenbeker Teich.
➲ *Approach via B243 SE of Bad Lauterberg.*
Open All year **Site** 10HEC ♨ ♣ ♣ ♠ **Facilities** ♠ ☉ ☻ ⌀ ♨ ☻
Services ☚ ☚ ➕ ▣ **Leisure** ♨ L **Off-site** ☎ ♨ ☚P

LOOSE SCHLESWIG-HOLSTEIN

Gut Ludwigsburg

24369 ☎ 04358 370 ▤ 04358 460
e-mail info@ostseecamping-ludwigsburg.de
website www.ostseecamping-ludwigsburg.de
This partly wooded holiday site lies between an inland lake and the sea, with a 100m-long private beach. Divided into pitches.
➲ *From Eckernförde towards Klein-Wabbs, at Gut Ludwigsburg onto track for 2km.*
Open Apr-Sep **Site** 10HEC ♨ ♣ ♠ ♣ **Prices** ♦ 4 pitch 6-11
♣ (static)224-301 **Facilities** ♠ ☎ ☉ ☻ ⌀ ♨ ⑳ **Services** ☚ ➕ ▣
Leisure ♨ LS **Off-site** ♨S

Germany

Facilities ☎ shop ♠ shower ☉ electric points for razors ☻ electric points for caravans ⑳ parking by tents permitted ☻ compulsory separate car park
Services ☚ café/restaurant ☚ bar ⌀ Camping Gaz International ♨ gas other than Camping Gaz ➕ first aid facilities ▣ laundry
Leisure ♨ swimming L-Lake P-Pool R-River S-Sea **Off-site** All facilities within 2km

Germany

MALENTE-GREMSMÜHLEN SCHLESWIG-HOLSTEIN

Schwentine
Wiesenweg 14, 23714 ☎ 04523 4327 ▨ 04523 202799
e-mail info@camping-bad-malente.de
website www.camping-bad-malente.de
A park-like setting with trees and bushes, at a river within the village of Malente.

➲ *A17 18km NW of Eutin.*

Open Apr-4 Oct **Site** 2.5HEC ✿ ♣ **Prices** ⋔ 3.60-4.50 ⇔ 1.60-2 ⇔ 4.80-6 Ⓐ 4.80-6 **Facilities** ⋔ 🛁 ⊙ 🞲 🖉 🚿 ⑳ **Services** 🍽 🞧 🗟 **Leisure** ⚓ R **Off-site** ⚓LP

NEUSTADT SCHLESWIG-HOLSTEIN

Strande
Sandberger Weg 94, 23730 ☎ 04561 4188 ▨ 04361 7125
e-mail info@amstrande.de
website www.amstrande.de
The site is divided into small sections and slopes down to the sea. Narrow sandy beach.

➲ *From Neustadt towards Pelzerhaken, 1st site on right.*

Open Apr-Sep **Site** 4.7HEC ✿ ♣ ⇔ **Prices** ⋔ 4 pitch 6-9 **Facilities** ⋔ ⊙ 🞲 🚿 ⑳ **Services** 🞧 🗟 **Leisure** ⚓ S **Off-site** 🛁 🞲 🍽 🖉

NORTHEIM NIEDERSACHSEN

Sultmer Berg
Sultmerberg 3, 37154 ☎ 05551 51559 ▨ 05551 5656
e-mail campingplatzmajora@web.de
website www.campingplatzsultmerberg.de
Grassland site with views of surrounding hills.

➲ *B3 from town centre.*

Open All year **Site** 2.7HEC ✿ ♣ ⇔ **Facilities** ⋔ 🛁 ⊙ 🞲 🖉 🚿 ⑳ **Services** 🍽 🞧 🗟 **Leisure** ⚓ P **Off-site** 🞲 🍽 ⚓LR

OEHE-DRAECHT SCHLESWIG-HOLSTEIN

Oehe-Draecht
24376 ☎ 04642 6124 & 6029 ▨ 04642 69159
e-mail Gut-oehe@T-online.de
website www.oehe-draecht.de
Grassy site, divided into pitches, on sandy ground behind a sea dyke.

➲ *B199 from Kappeln, turn towards Hasselberg & signed Strand.*

Open 23 Mar-22 Sep **Site** 6HEC ✿ ⚊ ♣ ⇔ ⇔ **Facilities** ⋔ 🛁 ⊙ 🞲 🖉 🚿 ⑳ **Services** 🞲 🍽 🞧 🗟 **Leisure** ⚓ LS

ORTSTEIL GÖTTINGERODE NIEDERSACHSEN

Harz-Camp Göttingerode
Kreisstr 66, 38667 ☎ 05322 81215 ▨ 05322 877533
e-mail harz-camp@t-online.de
website www.harz-camp.de
On outskirts of village next to main road. Terraced site with separate touring field.

➲ *On B6 between Bad Harzburg & Goslar.*

Open All year **Site** 6.5HEC ✿ ♣ ⇔ **Facilities** ⋔ 🛁 ⊙ 🞲 🖉 🚿 ⑳ **Services** 🍽 🞧 🗟 **Leisure** ⚓ P

OSNABRÜCK NIEDERSACHSEN

Niedersachsenhof
Nordstr 109, 49084 ☎ 0541 77226 ▨ 0541 70627
e-mail osnacamp@aol.com
website www.osnacamp.de
The site lies on a gently sloping meadow bordering a forest, near a converted farmhouse with an inn.

➲ *5km NW from town centre on B51/65 towards Bremen, turn right, site 300m.*

Open All year **Site** 3HEC ✿ ♣ ⇔ **Prices** ⋔ 4 pitch 7.50 **Facilities** ⋔ ⊙ 🞲 🚿 ⑳ **Services** 🍽 🞧 🗟 **Off-site** 🛁 🞲 🍽 🖉 ⚓PRS 🞧

OSTERODE NIEDERSACHSEN

Sösestausee
37520 ☎ 05522 3319 ▨ 05522 72378
e-mail harzcamp@t-online.de
website www.harzcamp.de
Terraced site on edge of woodland and by reservoir.

➲ *B498 from Osterode towards Altenau, 3km right to site.*

Open All year **Site** 4HEC ✿ ♣ ⇔ **Facilities** ⋔ 🛁 ⊙ 🞲 🖉 🚿 ⑳ **Services** 🍽 🞧 🗟 **Leisure** ⚓ LR **Off-site** 🞲 🍽

OSTRHAUDERFEHN NIEDERSACHSEN

Frieizeitanlage Idasee
Idafehn-Nord 77 B, 26842 ☎ 04952 994297 ▨ 04952 808628
e-mail nlappe2611@aol.com
website www.camping-idasee.de
A lakeside site between Oldenburg and the Dutch border with good water sports.

➲ *Via B27 Cloppenburg-Aurich.*

Open All year **Site** 11HEC ✿ ♣ ⇔ Ⓐ **Prices** ⋔ 4.30 Ⓐ 5.50 pitch 7.80 **Facilities** ⋔ 🛁 ⊙ 🞲 🖉 ⑳ **Services** 🍽 🞧 🗟 **Leisure** ⚓ L

OTTERNDORF NIEDERSACHSEN

See Achtern Diek
Deichstr 14, 21762 ☎ 04751 2933 ▨ 04751 3016
e-mail campingplatz@otterndorf.de
website www.otterndorf.de
A family site with good facilities close to the coast.

➲ *Via B73 Cuxhaven-Hamburg.*

Open Apr-Oct **Site** 13HEC ✿ ♣ **Facilities** ⋔ ⊙ 🞲 ⑳ **Services** 🗟 **Leisure** ⚓ L **Off-site** 🛁 🞲 🍽 🖉 🚿 ⚓LPRS 🞧

OYTEN NIEDERSACHSEN

Oyten
Erholungsgebiet Oyter See ☎ 04207 2878 ▨ 04207 909005
e-mail oyten@knauscamp.de
website www.knauscamp.de
Parkland site next to a lake on the outskirts of Bremen

Open Apr-5 Nov **Site** 15.6HEC ✿ ♣ **Prices** ⋔ 6 pitch 2 **Facilities** ⋔ ⊙ 🞲 🚿 ⑳ **Services** 🍽 🞧 **Leisure** ⚓ L

PLÖN SCHLESWIG-HOLSTEIN

Spitzenort
Ascheberger Str 76, 24306 ☎ 04522 2769 ▨ 04522 4574
A pleasant site with hedges surrounded by Plön lake on three sides. Ideal for water sports.

➲ *B430 from Plön towards Neumünster.*

Open Apr-15 Oct **Site** 4.5HEC ✿ ♣ **Facilities** ⋔ 🛁 ⊙ 🞲 🖉 ⑳ **Services** 🍽 🞧 🗟 **Leisure** ⚓ L **Off-site** 🍽 ⚓P

Site 6HEC (site size) ✿ grass ⚊ sand ♦ stone ♣ little shade ♣ partly shaded ✿ mainly shaded ⊞ bungalows for hire ⇔ caravans for hire Ⓐ tents for hire ⊗ no dogs **Prices** ⋔ adult per night ⇔ car per night pp per person per night ⇔ caravan per night Ⓐ tent per night ⇔ (static)-caravan hire per week

PYRMONT, BAD NIEDERSACHSEN

AT LÜGDE-ELBRINXEN (3KM S)

Eichwald
Obere Dorfstr 80, 32676 ☎ 05283 335 🖷 05283 640
e-mail campingeichwald@t-online.de
website www.camping-eichwald.de
Pleasant grassy site near woodland and a pool.
➲ *S of Lüdge towards Rischenau to Elbrinxen.*
Open All year **Site** 10HEC 😃 ♣ ♨ **Prices** ♠ 4.60 pitch 5.20 **Facilities** ⋒
⊙ ♨ ∅ ⚲ ⑦ **Services** ⊞ ⑩ 🖆 **Off-site** 🖄 ⚫P ➕

RIESTE NIEDERSACHSEN

Alfsee
Am Campingpark 10, 49597 ☎ 05464 92120 🖷 05464 5837
e-mail info@alfsee.de
website www.alfsee.com
Open All year **Site** 15.5HEC 😃 ♣ ♨ ⚘ **Prices** ♠ 3.20-5.20 pitch 7.60-10.70
Facilities ⋒ 🖄 ⊙ ♨ ∅ ⚲ ⑦ **Services** ⊞ ⑩ ➕ 🖆 **Leisure** ⚫ L

RINTELN NIEDERSACHSEN

Doktor-See
Am Doktor-See, 31722 ☎ 05751 964860 🖷 05751 964888
e-mail info@doktorsee.de
website doktorsee.de
A beautiful location beside a recreation area and the Doktor See
bathing beach. Section for touring campers.
➲ *In town turn downstream at River Weser bridge along left
bank for 1.5km.*
Open All year **Site** 152HEC 😃 ♣ ♨ **Prices** ♠ 4.40-6.30 pitch 3.70-5.25
Facilities ⋒ 🖄 ⊙ ♨ ∅ ⚲ ⑦ **Services** ⊞ ⑩ ➕ 🖆 **Leisure** ⚫ L
Off-site ⚫PR

ST ANDREASBERG NIEDERSACHSEN

Erikabrücke
37444 ☎ 05582 923056 🖷 05582 1431
e-mail camping@erikabruecke.de
website www.erikabruecke.de
➲ *Off B27 from Bad Lauterberg towards Braunlage.*
Open All year **Site** 5.5HEC 😃 ♣ ♨ ♣ **Facilities** ⋒ 🖄 ⊙ ♨ ∅ ⚲ ⑦
Services ⊞ ⑩ ➕ 🖆 **Leisure** ⚫ LR

SCHOBÜLL SCHLESWIG-HOLSTEIN

Seeblick
25875 ☎ 04841 3321 🖷 04841 5773
e-mail info@camping-seeblick.de
website www.camping-seeblick.de
Beautiful location beside the sea. Site divided into two sections.
➲ *Off B5 on N outskirts of Husum towards Insel Nordstrand for
4km to Schobüll.*
Open Apr-15 Oct **Site** 3.4HEC 😃 ♣ ♣ **Prices** ♠ 3.20-3.60 ♣ 6.50-8.50
▲ 5-6.50 ♣ (static) 98-175 **Facilities** ⋒ 🖄 ⊙ ♨ ⚲ ⑦ **Services** ⑩ ➕ 🖆
Leisure ⚫ S **Off-site** ⑩ ⚫P

STELLE NIEDERSACHSEN

Steller See
Zum Steller See 15, 28816 ☎ 04206 6490 🖷 04206 6668
e-mail steller.see@t-online
website www.steller-see.de
➲ *Delmenhorst-Ost exit off motorway. Site 300m.*
Open Apr-Sep **Site** 16HEC 😃 ♣ **Prices** ♠ 4-4.50 ♣ 2 ♣ 5-5.50 ▲ 4-4.50
Facilities ⋒ 🖄 ⊙ ♨ ∅ ⑦ ⚲ **Services** ⊞ ⑩ ➕ 🖆
Leisure ⚫ L

SUDERBURG NIEDERSACHSEN

AT HÖSSERINGEN (5KM SW)

Hardausee
29556 ☎ 05826 7676 🖷 05826 8303
e-mail info@camping-hardausse.de
website www.camping-hardausse.de
Grassland site without firm internal roads. Statics have individual
pitches and outbuildings. Separate fields for tourers.
➲ *From Uelzen S on B4, 9km turn right, continue via Suderburg
to site on right before Hösseringen.*
Open All year **Site** 12HEC 😃 ♣ ♣ **Prices** ♠ 4.50-5 ♣ 3 ♣ 3 ▲ 3
Facilities ⋒ 🖄 ⊙ ♨ ∅ ⚲ ⑦ **Services** ⑩ 🖆 **Off-site** ⚫L

TARMSTEDT NIEDERSACHSEN

Rethbergsee
27412 ☎ 04283 422 🖷 04283 980139
e-mail camping-rethbergsee@t-online.de
website www.rethbersee-wochenendpark.de
Level site on a grand scale.
➲ *Halfway between Bremen-Lilienthal & Zeven.*
Open All year **Site** 10HEC 😃 ♣ ♨ ♣ **Prices** ♠ 4.50 pitch 5 **Facilities** ⋒
🖄 ⊙ ♨ ∅ ⚲ ⑦ **Services** ⊞ ⑩ 🖆 **Leisure** ⚫ L **Off-site** ➕

TELLINGSTEDT SCHLESWIG-HOLSTEIN

Tellingstedt
Teichstr, 25789 ☎ 04838 657 🖷 04838 786969
Divided by a row of high shrubs.
➲ *Off B203 towards swimming pool.*
Open May-15 Sep **Site** 1.2HEC 😃 ♣ **Prices** ♠ 3 ♣ 1.50 ♣ 3.50 ▲ 2.50
Facilities ⋒ ⊙ ♨ ⑦ **Services** ⑩ ➕ 🖆 **Leisure** ⚫ P **Off-site** 🖄 ⊞ ⑩ ∅

TINNUM (ISLAND OF SYLT) SCHLESWIG-HOLSTEIN

Südhörn
25980 ☎ 04651 3607 🖷 04651 3619
Well-kept site divided into pitches.
➲ *Signed from railway. No road connection between island &
mainland railway from Niebüll to Westerland.*
Open All year **Site** 2HEC 😃 ♣ ♨ ♣ **Facilities** ⋒ 🖄 ⊙ ♨ ∅ ⑦
Services ⑩ **Off-site** ⊞ ⑩ ⚫PS ➕

Germany

Facilities 🖄 shop ⋒ shower ⊙ electric points for razors ♨ electric points for caravans ⑦ parking by tents permitted ⚲ compulsory separate car park
Services ⑩ café/restaurant ⊞ bar ∅ Camping Gaz International ⚲ gas other than Camping Gaz ➕ first aid facilities 🖆 laundry
Leisure ⚫ swimming L-Lake P-Pool R-River S-Sea **Off-site** All facilities within 2km

TÖNNING SCHLESWIG-HOLSTEIN

Lilienhof

Katinger Landstr 5, 25832 ☎ 04861 439 ▤ 04861 610 159
e-mail info@camping-lilienhof.de
website www.camping-lilienhof.de
Well-maintained site in the woodland grounds of an old manor house next to a quiet country road.
➲ *Off B202 at end of Tönning & 2km W towards Welt.*
Open All year **Site** 2HEC ❤ ♣ ♨ 🚐 **Prices** ♠ 4.50 pitch 7 **Facilities** ♠ ☺ 🚐 ♨ ⑳ **Services** ⚑ 🍴 ➕ 🛒 **Off-site** 🛒🍴 ⊘ ⛱PR

TOSSENS NIEDERSACHSEN

Tossens

Tossener Deich ☎ 04736 219 ▤ 04736 102168
e-mail tossens@knauscamp.de
website www.knauscamp.de
Situated next to the beach facing the North Sea.
Open 4 Apr-15 Oct **Site** 8HEC ❤ ♣ **Prices** ♠ 6 pitch 5-8 **Facilities** ♠ 🛒 ☺ 🚐 ♨ ⑳ **Services** 🍴 ➕ **Leisure** ⛱ S **Off-site** ⛱P

WALKENRIED NIEDERSACHSEN

KNAUS Walkenried

Ellricher Str 7, 37445 ☎ 05525 778 ▤ 05525 2332
e-mail walkenreid@knauscamp.de
website www.knauscamp.de
An attractive location in the southern Harz area.
➲ *A7 exit Seesen, B243 via Herzberg & Bad Sachsa.*
Open 22 Dec-16 Jan, 30 Mar-6 Nov **Site** 5.5HEC ❤ ♣ ♨ 🚐 ⚠ **Prices** ♠ 6 pitch 4-8 **Facilities** ♠🛒 ☺ 🚐 ♨ ⑳ **Services** 🍴 ➕ **Off-site** ⚑⎯

WALLENSEN NIEDERSACHSEN

Ferienpark Humboldt See

☎ 05186 957140 ▤ 05186 957139
website www.ferienpark.de
Fine location in a protected area for nature and wildlife close to the Humboldt lake and convenient for the mountain country surrounding the river Weser and the town of Hamlin.
Open All year **Site** 6.5HEC ❤ ♣ ♨ 🚐 **Facilities** ♠ ☺ 🚐 **Services** 🍴 🛒 **Off-site** ⛱L

WEENER NIEDERSACHSEN

Weener

Am Erholungsgebiet 4, 26826 ☎ 04951 1740 ▤ 04951 8613
e-mail weener@t-online.de
website www.weener.de
A municpal site, pleasantly landscaped and set inside a leisure centre with swimming pool and harbour.
➲ *Off B75 in centre of Weener & signed.*
Open 26 Mar-Oct **Site** 3.2HEC ❤ ♣ ♨ 🚐 **Facilities** ♠ ☺ 🚐 ♨ ⑳ **Services** ➕ 🛒 **Leisure** ⛱ P **Off-site** 🛒🍴 ⊘ ⛱R

WIETZENDORF NIEDERSACHSEN

Südsee

Soltau-Süd, 29649 ☎ 05196 980116/7 ▤ 05196 980299
e-mail AA@sudseecamp.de
website www.5-sterne-camping.de
Beautiful location in a forest beside a lake.
➲ *A7 exit 45 Soltau-Süd, B3 S towards Bergen for 2km, at underpass in Bokel left for Wietzendorf for 4km.*
Open All year **Site** 80HEC ❤ ♣ ♨ 🚐 **Prices** pitch 17-39 (incl 2 persons) 🚐 (static)315-560 **Facilities** ♠ 🛒 ☺ 🚐 ⊘ ♨ ⑳ **Services** ⚑ 🍴 ➕ 🛒 **Leisure** ⛱ LP

WILSUM NIEDERSACHSEN

AZUR-Ferienpark Wilsumer Berge

49849 ☎ 05945 1029 ▤ 05945 511
e-mail info@wilsumerberge.nl
website www.wilsumerberge.nl
Parts of the site adjoin a large lake. The separate section for touring campers has its own sanitary building.
➲ *B403 from Nordhorn via Uelsen to Wilsum, turn right near Wilsum.*
Open All year **Site** 88HEC ❤ ♣ ♨ 🚐 **Facilities** ♠ 🛒 ☺ 🚐 ♨ ⑳ **Services** ⚑ 🍴 ➕ 🛒 **Leisure** ⛱ L

WINGST NIEDERSACHSEN

Knaus Wingst

Schwimmbadallee 13, 21789 ☎ 04778 7604 ▤ 04778 7608
e-mail wingst@knauscamp.de
website www.knauscamp.de
This modern comfortable site extends over several terraces, above a small artificial lake on the northern edge of an extensive forest. Municipal recreation centre across the road.
➲ *Off B73 between Stade & Cuxhaven, 3km S of Cadenberge.*
Open 30 Mar-5 Nov **Site** 11.6HEC ❤ ♣ 🚐 🚐 ⚠ **Facilities** ♠ 🛒 ☺ 🚐 ⑳ **Services** 🍴 **Off-site** ⛱P

WINSEN NIEDERSACHSEN

Hüttensee

☎ 05056 941880 ▤ 05056 941881
e-mail info@campingpark-huettensee.de
website www.campingpark-huettensee.de
Site beside a large stretch of water on Lüneburg heath, suitable for swimming and water sports. Fine sandy beach. The area is rich in wildlife.
Open All year **Site** 17HEC ❤ ♣ ♨ 🚐 **Prices** ♠ 4.50-6 🚗 2 ⚠ 3.50-13 pitch 6-9 **Facilities** ♠ 🛒 ☺ 🚐 ♨ ⑳ **Services** 🍴 ➕ 🛒 **Leisure** ⛱ LP

WINSEN-ALLER NIEDERSACHSEN

Winsen

29308 ☎ 05143 93199 ▤ 05143 93144
e-mail info@camping-winsen.de
website www.camping-winsen.de
Site lies on meadowland at the River Aller. Water sports available.
➲ *NW from Celle to Winsen.*
Open All year **Site** 12HEC ❤ ♣ **Prices** ♠ 4-6 🚗 2.10-3.30 🚐 3-4 ⚠ 3-4 pitch 5-7 **Facilities** ♠ 🛒 ☺ 🚐 ⊘ ♨ ⑳ **Services** 🍴 ➕ 🛒 **Leisure** ⛱ R **Off-site** ♨ ⛱P

Site 6HEC (site size) ❤ grass ⬤ sand ♨ stone ♣ little shade ♣ partly shaded ❤ mainly shaded 🏠 bungalows for hire 🚐 caravans for hire ⚠ tents for hire ⊗ no dogs **Prices** ♠ adult per night 🚗 car per night pp per person per night 🚐 caravan per night ⚠ tent per night 🚐 (static)-caravan hire per week

WITTENBORN SCHLESWIG-HOLSTEIN

Weisser Brunnen

23829 ☎ 04554 1757 & 1413 ▣ 04554 4833

e-mail gert.petzold@t-online.de

website www.naturcamping-weisser-brunnen.de

A lakeside site consisting of several sections, hilly in parts, next to Lake Mözen. A public road, leading to the lake, passes through part of the site.

➲ *Off B206 at Km23.6 towards lake.*

Open Apr-Oct **Site** 7HEC ⊛ ♣ ⊞ **Prices** ♠ 5 ▲ 4.50-6 pitch 7 ⊞ (static)245-330 **Facilities** ⋔ ⓐ ☉ ⊕ ∅ ⊼ ⑫ **Services** ⊮ Ⓞ ⊞ ▤ **Leisure** ⇜ L

WULFEN (ISLAND OF FEHMARN) SCHLESWIG-HOLSTEIN

Wulfener Hals

23769 ☎ 04371 86280 ▣ 04371 3723

e-mail camping@wulfenerhals.de

website www.wulfenerhals.de

A meadowland site beside the Baltic Sea and an inland lake (Burger Binnensee), with a 1.7km-long private beach.

➲ *Off B20 (Vogelfluglinie) after Sundbrücke towards Avendorf, then Wulfen & Wulfener Hals.*

Open All year **Site** 34HEC ⊛ ♣ ⊞ ⊞ **Prices** ♠ 3.70-7.90 pitch 7.40-21 ⊞ (static)182-819 **Facilities** ⋔ ⓐ ☉ ⊕ ⑫ **Services** ⊮ Ⓞ ⊞ ▤ **Leisure** ⇜ PS

See advertisement on this page

Luneberg Heide

Germany

Italy

Accidents & emergencies
fire 115　**police** 113 (carabinieri 112)
ambulance 118

Driving requirements
Minimum age 18 for UK licence holders driving temporarily imported cars (or motorcycles over 125cc or with passenger). All valid UK driving licences should be accepted in Italy. This includes the older, all-green style UK licences, although the European Commission appreciates that these may be more difficult to understand and that drivers may wish to voluntarily update them before travelling abroad, if time permits. Application form D750 is available from most Post Offices. Alternatively, older licences may be accompanied by an International Driving Permit (IDP) see page 10.

Lights
Use of dipped headlights during the day is compulsory outside built-up areas and during snow and rain / poor visibility. Rear fog lights may only be used when visibility is less than 50 metres or in case of strong rain or intense snow.

Passengers & children
Children under 3 must not travel in the front or rear seats unless using a suitable restraint system. Children between 4 and 12 may only travel in front seat if using such equipment. Never fit a rear-facing child restraint in a seat with a frontal airbag.

Size restrictions
Motor vehicle or trailer
height 4m, width 2.55m, length 6.5m one axle, 12m two or more axles

Vehicle + trailer
length 18.75m

Speed limits
Unless signed otherwise:

Private car without caravan/trailer**
motorcycle***

Built-up areas	50kph
Outside built-up areas	90kph
	110kph*
Motorways	130kph

Car towing caravan/trailer

Built-up areas	50kph
Outside built-up areas	70kph
Motorways	80kph

*according to type/quality of road as indicated by signs.

**these limits also apply to cars towing one axle (two wheeled) luggage trailers. On some three-lane (plus emergency lane) motorways 150kph. In wet weather upper limits reduced to 90kph.

***motorcycles under 150cc cannot exceed 90kph and are not allowed on motorways.

Tourist office
Italian Government Tourist Board (ENIT)
1 Princes Street
London W1B 2AY
Tel 020 7408 1254 (Mon-Fri 09.00-17.00 hrs)
www.enit.it

Additional information
Vehicles travelling in opposite directions and wishing to turn left must pass in front of each other, and not behind as in the UK. Warning triangle compulsory. The wearing of a reflective jacket/waistcoat is compulsory if driver and/or passengers exit vehicle which is immobilised on the carriageway at night or in poor visibility.

Motorways
www.autostrade.it
To join a motorway follow the green signs. Vehicles that cannot exceed 40kph and motorcycles under 150cc are prohibited.

Services
It is usually possible to obtain services for a car and/or occupants every 30-50km. Emergency telephones are sited every 2km on most motorways. Some are marked SOS and have automatic push-button controls to summon medical and/or mechanical help.

Breakdown
Use of warning triangle compulsory.

Toll payments, *pedaggio*

On the majority of the toll motorways a travel ticket is issued on entry and a toll is paid on leaving the motorway. The travel ticket gives all relevant information about the toll charges, including the toll category of the vehicle. At the exit the ticket is handed in. If you cannot produce a travel ticket, a charge will be calculated from the furthest entry point. On some motorways — notably A8, A9, A11, A14 (Pescara - Lanciano) and A12 (Roma - Civitavécchia) — the toll is paid at intermediate toll booths for each section of the motorway used. On a few motorways the destination must be declared and the toll paid on entering the motorway. No refund on break of journey. Toll booths will not exchange traveller's cheques — ensure you have sufficient currency to meet the high toll charges. Tolls are charged according to the distance travelled. Most cars pay the toll quoted if the entire section of motorway is used. The charges in the following tables are a guide only and may change.

Tolls

Tolls		car	car & caravan	Tolls		car	car & caravan
A1	Milano - Bologna	€10.90	€13.30	A14	Bologna - Ancona	€10.40	€12.60
A1	Bologna - Firenze	€6.00	€7.20	A14	Ancona - Pescara	€7.00	€8.50
A1	Firenze - Roma	€13.30	€16.10	A14	Pescara - Bari	€15.50	€18.79
A1	Roma - Napoli	€10.60	€12.80	A14	Bari - Taranto	€3.50	€4.19
A1	Milano - Napoli	€41.20	€50.10	A14	Pescara - Taranto	€19.70	€23.90
A3	Napoli - Salerno	€4.00	€4.90	A14	Bologna - Taranto	€38.70	€47.10
A4	Torino - Milano	€7.00	€8.50	A15	Parma - La Spezia	€10.40	€13.80
A4	Milano - Brescia	€7.20	€8.70	A16	Napoli - Bari	€15.20	€18.50
A4	Brescia - Verona	€2.60	€3.20	A20	Furiano - Cefalu	€0.50	€0.60
A4	Verona - Padova	€3.40	€4.20	A20	Cefalu - Buonfornello	€0.80	€0.90
A4	Padova - Venezia	€1.70	€2.09	A21	Torino - Alessandria	€4.80	€6.10
A4	Milano - Venezia	€14.70	€18.00	A21	Alessandria - Piacenza	€4.20	€5.20
A4	Venezia - Trieste	€5.50	€6.90	A21	Torino - Piacenza	€9.50	€11.80
A5	Santhia - Aosta	€12.90	€17.20	A21	Piacenza - Brescia	€3.50	€4.30
A5	Torino - Aosta	€14.30	€19.10	A22	Brenner Pass - Trento	€8.30	€10.10
A6	Torino - Savona	€9.89	€13.30	A22	Trento - Verona	€5.10	€6.20
A7	Milano - Tortona	€3.40	€4.10	A22	Verona - Modena	€4.90	€5.90
A7	Milano - Génova	€7.00	€8.50	A22	Brenner Pass - Modena	€18.29	€22.20
A8	Milano - Varese	€2.20	€2.60	A23	Udine - Tarvisio	€5.50	€6.60
A8/A9	Milano - Chiasso	€2.70	€3.20	A24	Roma - L'Aquila	€7.40	€8.89
A10	Genova - Savona	€2.20	€2.60	A24	L'Aquila - Teramo	€3.20	€3.90
A10	Savona - Ventimiglia - Border	€12.70	€20.20	A24	Roma - Teramo	€10.90	€13.10
A11	Firenze - Pisa	€5.40	€6.80	A25	Roma - Pescara	€12.80	€15.60
A12	Genova - La Spezia	€8.60	€11.10	A26	Genova - Alessandria	€4.00	€4.80
A12	La Spezia - Rosignano Marittimo	€10.30	€13.80	A26	Road,Genova - Arona	€9.50	€11.50
A12	Genova - Viareggio	€10.60	€13.90	A27	Mestre - Belluno	€5.00	€6.00
A12	Genova - Rosignano Marittimo	€16.60	€21.80	A30	Caserta - Salerno	€5.10	€6.20
A12	Civitavecchia - Roma	€1.50	€1.90	A31	Vicenza - Piovene Rocchette	€1.40	€1.70
A13	Bologna - Pádova	€5.10	€6.20	A32	Road,Torino - Bardonecchia	€10.20	€15.50
A13	Bologna - Ferrara	€1.70	€2.09				
A13	Ferrara - Padova	€4.10	€4.90	**Bridges & tunnels**			
A14/A14	Bologna - Ravenna	€3.70	€4.60	E70 Tunnel del Frejus		€31.20	€41.30
				E25 Tunnel Monte Bianco		€31.90	€42.10
				Sankt Bernhard Tunnel		€22.40	€34.80
				Munt La Schera Tunnel		€10.00	€13.50

NORTH WEST/ALPS & LAKES

ANFO BRESCIA

Palafitte
via Calcaterra, 25070 ☎ 0365 809051 🖹 0365 809051
Pleasant site divided into plots, sloping to a lake and trees.
➲ Signed on S outskirts to Pilù campsite, then turn right.
Open 22 Apr-17 Sep **Site** 20HEC ⚊ ⚌ ⚍ **Facilities** 🍴 ⛺ ⊙ 🚿 ⍉ ⑫
Services ⚑ 🍽 🛒 **Leisure** ⚐ LP **Off-site** ⛺ 🍽

Pilù
via Venturi 4, 25070 ☎ 0365 809037 🖹 0365 809207
e-mail info@pilu.it
website www.pilu.it
A well-maintained, slightly sloping site subdivided by trees and rows of
shrubs. Separated from the pebble beach by a public footpath.
➲ Signed on S outskirts.
Open Apr-Sep **Site** 2HEC ⚊ ⚌ ⚍ **Prices** ⚑ 5-6.50 pitch 8.50-12.50
Facilities 🍴 ⛺ ⊙ 🚿 ⍉ ≛ ⑫ **Services** ⚑ 🍽 🛒 **Leisure** ⚐ LPR
Off-site 🍽

ANGERA VARESE

Città di Angera
via Bruschera 99, 21021 ☎ 0331 930736 🖹 0331 960367
e-mail info@campingcittadiangera.it
website www.campingcittadiangera.it
Large family site with plenty of recreational facilities.
➲ Signed.
Open All year **Site** 6.7HEC ⚊ ⚌ **Facilities** 🍴 ⛺ ⊙ 🚿 ⍉ ≛ ⑫
Services ⚑ 🍽 🛒 **Leisure** ⚐ LP

ARONA NOVARA

AT DORMELLETTO (5KM S)

Lago Azzurro
via E-Fermi 2, 28040 ☎ 0322 497197 🖹 0322 497197
e-mail info@campinglagoazzuro.it
website www.campinglagoazzuro.it
A lakeside site in beautiful surroundings with fine sports facilities.
➲ S of Arona off SS Sempione 33.
Open All year **Site** 2.5HEC ⚊ ⚌ ⚍ **Prices** ⚑ 6-7 pitch 7.50-10
⚍ (static)65-70 **Facilities** 🍴 ⛺ ⊙ 🚿 ⍉ ⑫ **Services** ⚑ 🍽 🛒
Leisure ⚐ LP

Lago Maggiore
via L-da-Vinci 7, 28040 ☎ 0322 497193 🖹 0322 497193
e-mail info@lagomag.com
website www.lagomag.com
Well-maintained site divided into plots, pleasantly landscaped by the
lakeside.
➲ Off SS33, signed.
Open Apr-Sep **Site** 5HEC ⚊ ⚌ ⚍ **Prices** ⚑ 4.50-7 pitch 7-14
⚍ (static)350-700 **Facilities** 🍴 ⛺ ⊙ 🚿 ≛ ⑫ **Services** ⚑ 🍽 🛒
Leisure ⚐ LP

Lido Holiday Inn
via M-Polo 1, 28040 ☎ 0322 497047 🖹 0322 497047
e-mail info@lidoholidayinn.com
website www.lidoholidayinn.com
Site on bank of the lake, with some trees.
➲ Off SS33 at Km60/VII & IP fuel station.
Open Apr-29 Sep **Site** 3.5HEC ⚊ ⚌ ⛺ **Facilities** 🍴 ⛺ ⊙ 🚿 ⍉ ⑫ ⑫
Services ⚑ 🍽 🛒 **Leisure** ⚐ LP **Off-site** ⍉

Smeraldo
via Cavour 131, 28040 ☎ 0322 497031 🖹 0322 497031
e-mail info@camping-smeraldo.com
website www.camping-smeraldo.com
Well-landscaped site in woodland deside a lake. Divided into plots.
➲ Off SS33.
Open Mar-Oct **Site** 24HEC ⚊ ⚌ ⛺ **Prices** ⚑ 5.50-8 ⚍ 6-7 ⚍ 12-16.50
⚑ 12-16.50 **Facilities** 🍴 ⊙ 🚿 ⍉ ≛ ⑫ **Services** ⚑ 🍽 🛒 🛒
Leisure ⚐ LP **Off-site** 🛒 ⚑ 🍽

ARVIER AOSTA

Arvier
via Chaussa 17, 11011 ☎ 0165 99088 🖹 0165 99045
e-mail campingarvier@yahoo.it
website www.campingarvier.com
Quiet wooded site close to mountains and a peaceful village.
Open Jun- Aug **Site** 1HEC ⚊ ⚌ ⚍ **Prices** ⚑ 5.40-6 ⚍ 3.60-4
⚍ 5.20-5.80 ⚑ 5.20-5.80 **Facilities** 🍴 ⛺ ⊙ 🚿 ⑫ **Services** 🛒
Leisure ⚐ P **Off-site** 🛒 ⚑ 🍽 ⍉ ⚐ ⚐R

BASTIA MONDOVI CUNEO

Cascina
Loc. Pieve 23, 12060 ☎ 0174 60181 🖹 0174 60181
e-mail info@campinglacascina.it
website www.campinglacascina.it
A peaceful site on level land surrounded by mountains.
➲ Towards Bastia.
Open Jan-30 Aug, Oct-Dec **Site** 4HEC ⚊ ⚌ ⚍ **Prices** ⚑ 5.50 pitch 5
Facilities 🍴 ⛺ ⊙ 🚿 ≛ ⑫ **Services** ⚑ 🍽 🛒 **Leisure** ⚐ PR
Off-site 🛒 🍽

BAVENO NOVARA

Tranquilla
via Cave 2, 28831 ☎ 0323 923452 🖹 0323 923452
e-mail info@tranquilla.com
website www.tranquilla.com
A peaceful location with panoramic views of the surrounding
mountains and Lake Maggiore. Modern facilities.
➲ 4km from Stresa.
Open 20 Mar-10 Oct **Site** 1.8HEC ⚊ ⚌ ⚍ **Prices** ⚑ 4.90-5.80 pitch 6.70-
9.50 **Facilities** 🍴 ⊙ 🚿 ⑫ **Services** ⚑ 🍽 🛒 **Leisure** ⚐ P **Off-site** 🛒 ⍉
≛ ⚐LR ⚑

BELLAGIO COMO

Azienda Agricola Clarke
via Valassina 170/c, 22021 ☎ 031 951325
e-mail elizabethclarke@tin.it
website www.bellagio-camping.com
A small, secluded site on a horsebreeding farm close to Lake Bellagio,
up towards the mountains with fine views.
Open Jun-Sep **Site** 0.5HEC ⚊ ⚌ **Prices** ⚑ 7 pitch 10 **Facilities** 🍴 ⊙ 🚿
⑫ **Services** ⚑ **Off-site** 🛒 ⚑ 🍽 ⚐LP

Site 6HEC (site size) ⚊ grass ⚌ sand ⚍ stone ⚌ little shade ⚌ partly shaded ⚌ mainly shaded ⛺ bungalows for hire
⚍ caravans for hire Ⓐ tents for hire ⊗ no dogs **Prices** ⚑ adult per night ⚍ car per night pp per person per night ⚍ caravan per night
Ⓐ tent per night ⚍ (static)-caravan hire per week

BOLZANO-BOZEN BOLZANO

Moosbauer

Moritzingerweg 83, 39100 ☎ 0471 918492 🖺 0471 204894
e-mail info@moosbauer.com
website www.moosbauer.com
Small site in attractive valley at the Gateway to the Dolomites.
Open All year **Site** 1.2HEC 🌱 🌢 🏖 **Facilities** 🌲 🛆 ⊙ 🚱 ⌀ 🅿
Services 🍴 🍽 🖫 **Leisure** 🏊 P **Off-site** ➕

BRÉCCIA COMO

International

via Cecilio, 22100 ☎ 031 521435 🖺 031 521435
e-mail campingint@hotmail.com
website www.internazionale.it
On a level meadow near the motorway.
➲ *Off A9 Como-Milan.*
Open 28 Mar-30 Oct **Site** 1.3HEC 🌱 🌢 🏖 🏕 **Prices** 🧍 5.50 🚗 3.50
🚐 4.50 ⛺ 4 **Facilities** 🌲 🛆 ⊙ 🚱 ⌀ 🏳 ⅏ ℗ **Services** 🍴 🍽 ➕ 🖫
Leisure 🏊 P

BRESSANONE-BRIXEN BOLZANO

Löwenhof

via Brennero 60 ☎ 0472 836216 🖺 0472 801337
e-mail info@loewenhof.it
website www.loewenhof.it
Site offers rafting and canoeing school as well as a sauna and pool,
which are avaliable in the Dolomiti resort 8km away.
➲ *Bolzano-Brennero motorway exit Varna, site just before
Brixen.*
Open Apr-30 Oct **Site** 0.5HEC 🌱 🏖 **Prices** 🧍 7-8 🚗 3-5 🚐 10-15 ⛺ 5-8
Facilities 🌲 🛆 ⊙ 🚱 ⌀ ⅏ ℗ 🅿 **Services** 🍴 🍽 🖫 **Leisure** 🏊 PR
Off-site 🏊 L ➕

CALCERANICA TRENTO

Al Pescatore

via dei Pescatori 1, 38050 ☎ 0461 723062 🖺 0461 724212
e-mail trentino@campingpescatore.it
website www.campingpescatore.it
The site consists of several sections of meadowland, inland from the
lake shore road to Lago di Caldonazzo. Well maintained with private
beach.
Open 22 May-15 Sep **Site** 3.8HEC 🌱 🏖 **Prices** 🧍 7.50 pitch 10
Facilities 🌲 🛆 ⊙ 🚱 ⌀ ℗ **Services** 🍴 🍽 🖫 **Leisure** 🏊 LP **Off-site** ➕

Fleiola

via Trento 42, 38050 ☎ 0461 723153 🖺 0461 724386
e-mail info@campingfleiola.it
website www.campingfleiola.it
Site is divided into sectors beside lake.
➲ *Verona-Brennero motorway exit Trento, signs for Pergine &
Caldonazzo.*
Open Apr-5 Oct **Site** 1.2HEC 🌱 🌢 🏖 **Prices** 🧍 5.50-8 pitch 6.50-13.50
Facilities 🌲 🛆 ⊙ 🚱 ⌀ ℗ **Services** 🍴 🍽 🖫 **Leisure** 🏊 L
Off-site 🍽 ⅏ ➕

Riviera

viale Venezia 10, 38050 ☎ 0461 724464 🖺 0461 718689
e-mail riviera@dnet.it
website www.campingriviera.net
Open Etr-15 Sep **Site** 1.5HEC 🌱 🏖 **Prices** 🧍 5.50-8 pitch 6-10
Facilities 🌲 ⊙ 🚱 ℗ **Services** 🍴 🍽 🖫 **Leisure** 🏊 L **Off-site** 🛆 ⅏ ➕

CAMPITELLO DI FASSA TRENTO

Miravalle

vicolo camping 15, 38031 ☎ 0462 750502 🖺 04621 751563
e-mail info@campingmiravalle.it
website www.campingmiravalle.it
Wooded mountain setting beside the River Avisio and close to the
town centre.
➲ *Signed.*
Open Jun-Sep & Dec-Apr **Site** 3HEC 🌱 🏖 🏕 **Prices** 🧍 7.50-9.50
🚐 7.50-9.50 ⛺ 7.50 (static)280-420 **Facilities** 🌲 ⊙ 🚱 ⌀ ⅏ ℗ 🅿
Services ➕ 🖫 **Leisure** 🏊 R **Off-site** 🛆 🍴 🍽 ⌀ ⅏ 🏊P

CANAZEI TRENTO

Marmolada

via Pareda 60, 38032 ☎ 0462 601660 🖺 0462 601722
Grassland site extending to the river, part of it in spruce woodland.
➲ *On S outskirts on right of road to Alba Penia.*
Open All year **Site** 3HEC 🌱 🏖 **Facilities** 🌲 ⊙ 🚱 ⌀ ⅏ ℗ **Services** 🍴
🍽 🖫 **Leisure** 🏊 R **Off-site** 🛆 🍽 🏊P ➕

CANNOBIO NOVARA

International Paradis

via Casali Darbedo 12, 28052 ☎ 0323 71227 🖺 0323 72591
e-mail info@campingglagomaggiore.it
website www.campingglagomaggiore.it
A level site on the bank of a lake.
➲ *Off SS34 at Km35/V.*
Open 20 Mar-15 Oct **Site** 1.2HEC 🌱 🌢 🏖 🏕 ⊗ **Prices** 🧍 5.50-7 pitch 9-12
🚐 (static)290.50-385 **Facilities** 🌲 🛆 ⊙ 🚱 ⌀ ⅏ ℗ **Services** 🍴 🍽 ➕ 🖫
Leisure 🏊 L **Off-site** 🍽 🏊R

Residence Campagna

via Casali Darbedo 20/22, 28822 ☎ 0323 70100 🖺 0323 71190
e-mail info@campingcampagna.it
website www.campingcampagna.it
A well-equipped site in a pleasant lakeside location.
➲ *Off SS34 to Locarno at Km35/V on N outskirts of village. W
of lake on road 21.*
Open 20 Mar-Nov **Site** 1.2HEC 🌱 🌢 🏖 🏕 **Prices** 🧍 5.50-7 pitch 9-12
🚐 (static)322-434 **Facilities** 🌲 🛆 ⊙ 🚱 ⌀ ⅏ ℗ **Services** 🍴 🍽 🖫
Leisure 🏊 L **Off-site** 🏊R ➕

Valle Romantica

via Valle Cannobina, 28822 ☎ 0323 71249 🖺 0323 71249
e-mail valleromantico@riviera-valleromantica.com
website www.riviera-valleromantica.com
A pleasant site with trees, shrubs and flowers. Internal roads are
asphalted and a mountain stream provides bathing facilities.
➲ *1.5km w off road to Malesco.*
Open 23 Mar-Sep **Site** 25HEC 🌱 🌢 🏖 🏕 ⛺ **Prices** 🧍 6.50-7.50 pitch 9-12
🚐 (static)370-545 **Facilities** 🌲 🛆 ⊙ 🚱 ⌀ ℗ **Services** 🍴 🍽 🖫
Leisure 🏊 PR **Off-site** 🏊L ➕

Italy

Facilities 🛆 shop 🌲 shower ⊙ electric points for razors 🚱 electric points for caravans ℗ parking by tents permitted 🅿 compulsory separate car park
Services 🍽 café/restaurant 🍴 bar ⌀ Camping Gaz International ⅏ gas other than Camping Gaz ➕ first aid facilities 🖫 laundry
Leisure 🏊 swimming L-Lake P-Pool R-River S-Sea **Off-site** All facilities within 2km

CASTELLETTO TICINO NOVARA

Italia Lido

via Cicognola 104, 28053 ☎ 0331 923032 ▤ 0331 923032
e-mail campingitalialido.campin@tin.it
website www.campingitalialido.it
A large family site with its own private beach on Lake Maggiore. The site is popular with families and there are good recreational facilities.

➔ *A8 onto A26 & signed.*

Open Mar-30 Oct **Site** 3HEC ⛺ ⛱ 🏕 🚐 **Prices** ⅄ 4-5.10 🚗 4 pitch 7.20-11.70 **Facilities** 🍴 🛁 ☺ 🚿 🖉 🛒 ⊕ **Services** 🎪 🍽 🛍 **Leisure** ⚊ L
Off-site 🛁 ➕

CHIUSA-KLAUSEN BOLZANO

Gamp

Griesbruck 10, 39043 ☎ 0472 847425 ▤ 0472 845067
e-mail info@camping-gamp.com
website www.camping-gamp.com
The site lies next to the Gasthof Gamp, between the Brenner railway line and the motorway bridge, which passes high above the site.

➔ *Motorway exit onto SS12, signed.*

Open All year **Site** 0.6HEC ⛺ ⛱ **Facilities** 🍴 🛁 ☺ 🚿 ⊕ **Services** 🎪 🍽 🛍 **Leisure** ⚊ P **Off-site** 🖉 🛒 ⚊P ➕

CHIUSI DELLA VERNA TRENTO

La Verna

Vezzano ☎ 0575 532121 ▤ 0575 532041
e-mail info@campinglaverna.it
website www.campinglaverna.it
On the borders of the Casentino Forest Park in attractive Tuscan scenery. Pitches are of varying sizes and levels of shade.

Open Etr-Oct **Site** 2.2HEC 🏕 🚐 **Prices** ⅄ 4.50-6 pitch 6-8 **Facilities** 🍴 ☺ 🚿 🛒 **Services** 🎪 🍽 🛍 **Leisure** ⚊ PR **Off-site** 🛁

COLFOSCO BOLZANO

Colfosco

via Sorega 15, 39030 ☎ 0471 836515 ▤ 0471 830801
e-mail info@campingcolfosco.org
website www.campingcolfosco.org
A beautiful setting at the foot of the Sella mountains.

Open Dec-Etr & 15 May-5 Oct **Site** 2.5HEC ⛺ ⛱ ⚊ ⛲ 🏕 **Prices** ⅄ 5-6.50 🚗 3-5.50 🚐 8-13.50 ⅄ 4-10.50 **Facilities** 🍴 🛁 ☺ 🚿 🖉 🛒 🚿 **Services** 🎪 🍽 🛍 **Leisure** ⚊ PR **Off-site** 🍽 ⚊L ➕

COLOMBARE BRESCIA

Sirmione

via Sirmioncino 9, 25019 ☎ 030 919045 ▤ 030 919045
e-mail www.camping-sirmione.com
website info@camping-sirmione.com
A well-equipped site in a beautiful location on the Sirmione peninsula, with direct access to Lake Garda.

➔ *SS11 towards Sirmione, 0.4km turn right.*

Open 25 Mar-5 Oct **Site** 3.5HEC ⛺ ⚊ ⛱ 🏕 **Prices** ⅄ 6-9 ⅄ 6-9 pitch 9-15 **Facilities** 🍴 🛁 ☺ 🚿 🚿 **Services** 🎪 🍽 ➕ 🛍 **Leisure** ⚊ LP **Off-site** 🛁 🖉 🛒

DESENZANO DEL GARDA BRESCIA

Vò

via Vò 9, 25015 ☎ 030 9121325 ▤ 030 9120773
e-mail vo@voit.it
website www.voit.it
Situated on Lake Garda, 1.5km from Desenzano, surrounded by meadows and woods.

➔ *Between Padenghe & Sirmione on Lake Garda, 2km from Desenzano.*

Open Apr-Sep **Site** 5HEC ⛺ ⛱ 🏕 **Prices** ⅄ 6-8 pitch 9-12 **Facilities** 🍴 🛁 ☺ 🚿 🚿 **Services** 🎪 🍽 🛍 **Leisure** ⚊ LP **Off-site** 🖉 ➕

DIMARO TRENTO

Dolomiti di Brenta

via Gole 105, 38025 ☎ 0463 974332 ▤ 0463 973200
e-mail info@campingdolomiti.com
website www.campingdolomiti.com
The site has large flat plots surrounded by tall pines. Good sports facilities and tuition for canoeing and white-water rafting.

➔ *Off SS42 at Km173.5.*

Open Jun-Sep, 6 Dec-15 Apr **Site** 4HEC ⛺ ⛱ 🏕 **Facilities** 🍴 🛁 ☺ 🚿 🖉 🛒 🚿 **Services** 🎪 🍽 ➕ 🛍 **Leisure** ⚊ P **Off-site** ⚊R

DOMASO COMO

Gardenia

via Case Sparse 164, 22013 ☎ 0344 96262 ▤ 0344 83381
e-mail campingardenia@interfree.it
website www.campingardenia.it

➔ *N at Case Sparse.*

Open Apr-Sep **Site** 20HEC ⛺ ⛱ 🏕 ⊗ **Facilities** 🍴 🛁 ☺ 🚿 🖉 🛒 🚿 **Services** 🎪 🍽 🛍 **Leisure** ⚊ L **Off-site** ⚊R ➕

EDOLO BRESCIA

Adamello

via Campeggio 10, 25048 ☎ 0364 71694 ▤ 0364 71694
e-mail enrico.adamello@libero.it
A terraced site in wooded surroundings, 1km from the lake.

➔ *1.5km W of SS39.*

Open All year **Site** 1.2HEC ⛺ ⛱ 🏕 **Prices** ⅄ 5 🚗 2.50 🚐 7 ⅄ 5-7 🚐 (static)30-50 **Facilities** 🍴 🛁 ☺ 🚿 🖉 🛒 🚿 **Services** 🎪 🍽 ➕ 🛍 **Off-site** 🍽 ⚊LPR

FERIOLO NOVARA

Orchidea

via Repubblica dell'Ossola, 28835 ☎ 0323 28257 ▤ 0323 28573
e-mail info@campingorchidea.it
website www.campingorchidea.it
A modern site on Lake Maggiore with good sports and entertainment facilities.

➔ *Via SS33.*

Open 18 Mar-9 Oct **Site** 4HEC ⛺ ⛱ 🏕 🚐 **Facilities** 🍴 🛁 ☺ 🚿 🖉 🛒 🚿 **Services** 🎪 🍽 ➕ 🛍 **Leisure** ⚊ L

Site 6HEC (site size) ⛺ grass ⛱ sand ⚊ stone ⛲ little shade ⛱ partly shaded ⛱ mainly shaded 🏕 bungalows for hire
🚐 caravans for hire ⅄ tents for hire ⊗ no dogs **Prices** ⅄ adult per night 🚗 car per night pp per person per night 🚐 caravan per night
⅄ tent per night 🚐 (static)-caravan hire per week

FONDOTOCE NOVARA

Continental Lido

via 42 Martiri 156, 28924 ☎ 0323 496300 🖹 0323 496218
e-mail info@campingcontinental.com
website www.campingcontinental.com
By Lake Mergozzo and 1km from Lake Maggiore.

⮕ *On right of road Verbania Fondotoce-Gravellona.*

Open 6 Apr-18 Sep **Site** 8HEC 😃 😄 😄 **Facilities** ⋔ 🏢 ⊙ 🚃 ⌀ ☻
Services 🍴 🍽 🗑 **Leisure** ⇔ L **Off-site** 🚿 ⇔R

Lido Toce

via per Feriolo 41, 28924 ☎ 0323 496298 🖹 0323 496220
e-mail perucchinigiovanna@tiscalli.it
website web.tiscali.it.lidotoce
A beautiful location with spectacular views on the eastern shore of the lake. Good recreational facilities.

Open 20 Apr-Sep **Site** 2HEC 😃 😄 😄 **Prices** ⋔ 4.20-5.40 pitch 8.10-10.90
Facilities ⋔ 🏢 ⊙ 🚃 ☻ **Services** 🍴 🍽 🚑 🗑 **Leisure** ⇔ LR **Off-site** ⌀ 🚿 ⇔P

Village Isolino

via Per Feriolo 25, 28924 ☎ 0323 496080 🖹 0323 496414
e-mail info@isolino.com
website www.isolino.it
Open 30 Mar-24 Sep **Site** 12HEC 😃 😄 😄 **Prices** ⋔ 4.30-7.30 pitch 18.25-32.85 (incl 2 persons) 🚃 (static)246.50-875 **Facilities** ⋔ 🏢 ⊙ 🚃 ⌀ ☻
Services 🍴 🍽 🚑 🗑 **Leisure** ⇔ LP **Off-site** ⇔R

FUCINE DI OSSANA TRENTO

Cevedale

Via di Sottopila 4, 38026 ☎ 0463 751630 🖹 0463 751630
e-mail info@campingcevedale.it
website www.campingcevedale.it
A well-equipped site in a peaceful location at an altitude of 900m, close to the local ski resorts.

⮕ *4km W of Savona.*

Open All year **Site** 3.7HEC 😃 😄 😄 ⊗ **Prices** ⋔ 7-8 pitch 5-12
Facilities ⋔ 🏢 ⊙ 🚃 ⌀ ☻ **Services** 🍴 🍽 🚑 🗑 **Leisure** ⇔ R
Off-site 🍽 ⇔L

GERMIGNAGA VARESE

Il Boschetto

via Mameli, 21010 ☎ 0332 534740 🖹 0332 500791
e-mail boshol@tin.it
website www.boschettoholiday.it
A pleasant location beside Lake Maggiore with a variety of facilities and opportunities for water sports.

Open Apr-29Sep **Site** 1HEC 😃 😄 🚃 **Facilities** ⋔ ⊙ 🚃 ☻ **Services** 🍴
🍽 🗑 **Leisure** ⇔ LPR **Off-site** 🏢 🍽 ⌀ 🚑 🚑

IDRO BRESCIA

AZUR Vantone

25074 ☎ 0365 83125 🖹 0365 823663
e-mail idro@azur-freizeit.de
website www.azur-camping.de/idro
The site lies at the mouth of the river of same name beside Lake Idro. Subdivided into pitches (separate pitches for youths) on grass and woodland at the foot of strange rock formations.

⮕ *Approach from Idro direction of Vantone & signed.*

Open Apr-Oct **Site** 4.5HEC 😃 😄 😄 🚃 🏕 **Prices** ⋔ 5-8 pitch 7-10.50
Facilities ⋔ 🏢 ⊙ 🚃 ⌀ 🚑 ☻ **Services** 🍴 🍽 🚑 🗑 **Leisure** ⇔ LPR

Vantone Pineta

via Capovalle 11, 25074 ☎ 0365 823385
e-mail campingpineta@libero.it
website www.vantonepineta.it
On eastern shore of lake. Grassland enclosed by rush and willow fencing. Part of site in a small wood on the bank of a stream.

⮕ *Approach from Idro & signs for Camping Idro Rio Vantone.*

Open 31 Mar-Oct **Site** 2HEC 😃 😄 🚃 **Facilities** ⋔ 🏢 ⊙ 🚃 ⌀ ☻
Services 🍴 🍽 🗑 **Leisure** ⇔ LP **Off-site** ⌀ 🚑 🚑

ISEO BRESCIA

Punta d'Oro

via Antonioli 51/53, 25049 ☎ 030 980084 🖹 030 980084
e-mail info@camping-puntadoro.com
website www.camping-puntadoro.com
A well-set out site with roads and paths to every pitch.

⮕ *A4 exit Rovato, signs for Iseo.*

Open Apr-Oct **Site** 0.6HEC 😃 😄 😄 🚃 **Prices** ⋔ 4.50-6.90 pitch 9-14.50
🚃 (static)303.10-483 **Facilities** ⋔ ⊙ 🚃 ☻ **Services** 🍴 🍽 🗑
Leisure ⇔ L **Off-site** 🍽 ⌀ 🚑 ⇔P 🚑

Quai

via Antonioli 73, 25049 ☎ 0309 821610 🖹 0309 981161
e-mail info@campingquai.it
website www.campingquai.it
Shady site close to the edge of Lake d'Iseo.

⮕ *W of town, signed.*

Open 8 Apr-26 Sept **Site** 1.3HEC 😃 😄 😄 ⊗ **Facilities** ⋔ ⊙ 🚃 ☻ 🅿
Services 🍴 🍽 🗑 **Leisure** ⇔ L **Off-site** 🏢 🍽 ⌀ ⇔P 🚑

Sassabanek

via Colombera 2, 25049 ☎ 030 980300 🖹 030 9821360
e-mail sassabanek@sassabanek.it
website www.sassabanek.it
A pleasant wooded location on the shore of Lake Iseo with good recreational facilities.

Open Apr-Sep **Site** 3.5HEC 😃 😄 ⊗ **Prices** ⋔ 4.30-7.90 🏕 2.30-5.10 pitch
8.50-15.50 **Facilities** ⋔ 🏢 ⊙ 🚃 ⌀ 🅿 **Services** 🍴 🍽 🗑 **Leisure** ⇔ LP
Off-site 🚑

KALTERN BOLZANO

St Josef am Kalterer See

Welnstr 75, 39052 ☎ 0471 960170
e-mail camping.st.josef@dnet.it
website www.kalterersee.com/camping
On level ground surrounded by trees close to the lake.

⮕ *Signed from Kalten-Tramin road.*

Open 15 Mar-10 Nov **Site** 1.4HEC 😃 😄 😄 **Facilities** ⋔ 🏢 ⊙ 🚃 ⌀ ☻
Services 🍴 🍽 🗑 **Leisure** ⇔ L

LAIVES-LEIFERS BOLZANO

Steiner

Kennedystr 34, 39055 ☎ 0471 950105 🖹 0471 951572
e-mail info@campingsteiner.com
website www.campingsteiner.com
The site lies behind the Gasthof Steiner, the AGIP fuel station and a bungalow estate.

⮕ *Off SS12 on N outskirts of village.*

Open 18 Mar-4 Nov **Site** 2.5HEC 😃 😄 😄 ⊗ **Prices** ⋔ 5-7 pitch 11-14
Facilities ⋔ 🏢 ⊙ 🚃 ☻ **Services** 🍴 🍽 🗑 **Leisure** ⇔ P

Italy

LATSCH BOLZANO

Latsch an der Etsch
Reichstr 4, 39021 ☎ 0473 623217 ▤ 0473 622333
e-mail info@camping-latsch.com
website www.camping-latsch.com
A terraced site beside the river.
➲ *Signed on SS38.*
Open 11 Dec-10 Nov **Site** 2.2HEC ❣ ❤ ✿ **Prices** ♠ 6.20-7.20 Å 8.70-9.70 pitch 11.90-13.40 **Facilities** ⋒ 🛈 ⊙ ☮ ⌀ 🌢 ☼ **Services** ⚑ 🍴 ➕ 🖫 **Leisure** ❤ PR

LECCO COMO

Rivabella
via Alla Spiaggia 35, 23900 ☎ 0341 421143 ▤ 0341 421143
e-mail rivabellalecco@libero.it
On a private, guarded beach on the shore of Lake Como.
➲ *3km S towards Bergamo.*
Open 25 Apr-Sep **Site** 2HEC ❣ ❤ ✿ **Prices** ♠ 5.50 pitch 10 **Facilities** ⋒ 🛈 ⊙ ☮ ⌀ ☼ **Services** ⚑ 🍴 ➕ 🖫 **Leisure** ❤ L **Off-site** 🍴

LEVICO TERME TRENTO

Due Laghi
Loc Costa 3, 38056 ☎ 0461 706290 ▤ 0461 707381
e-mail info@campingclub.it
website www.campingclub.it
Mainly family site with 400 large flat grass pitches.
➲ *From Trento signs for Pergine & Lake Caldonazza.*
Open 25 May-10 Sep **Site** 12HEC ❣ ❤ ✿ **Prices** ♠ 6-9 pitch 11-14 **Facilities** ⋒ 🛈 ⊙ ☮ ⌀ 🌢 ☼ **Services** ⚑ 🍴 ➕ 🖫 **Leisure** ❤ LP

Jolly
Loc Pleina, 38056
☎ 0461 706934 & 701933 ▤ 0461 700227 & 701933
e-mail mail@campingjolly.com
website www.campingjolly.com
The site is divided into plots and lies 200m from the lake. Three inside swimming pools.
Open Apr-1 Oct **Site** 2HEC ❣ ❤ ✿ **Prices** ♠ 5.50-9.50 pitch 8-12.50 **Facilities** ⋒ 🛈 ⊙ ☮ ⌀ ☼ **Services** ⚑ 🍴 ➕ 🖫 **Leisure** ❤ P **Off-site** 🍴 ❤LR

Levico
38056 ☎ 0461 706491 ▤ 0461 707735
e-mail mail@campinglevico.com
website www.campinglevico.com
Site is by a lake with a private beach.
➲ *SS47 exit Levico/Caldonazzo, site signed.*
Open Apr-10 Oct **Site** 5HEC ❣ ❤ ✿ ✿ **Facilities** ⋒ 🛈 ⊙ ☮ ⌀ 🌢 ☼ **Services** ⚑ 🍴 ➕ 🖫 **Leisure** ❤ LR **Off-site** ❤P

LIMONE PIEMONTE CUNEO

Luis Matlas
12015 ☎ 0171 927565 ▤ 0171 927565
This tidy site offers winter facilities and skiing lessons are provided by the owner. Fishing is also available.
➲ *N of town off Limone-Nice road.*
Open 18 May-6 Oct, 28 Oct-6 May **Site** 1.5HEC ❣ ❤ ✿ **Prices** ♠ 5.50 Å 4 pitch 6 **Facilities** ⋒ ⊙ ☮ ⌀ ☼ **Services** ⚑ 🍴 🖫 **Leisure** ❤ R **Off-site** 🛈 🍴 ➕

LIMONE SUL GARDA BRESCIA

Nanzel
via 4 Novembre 3, 25010 ☎ 0365 954155 ▤ 0365 954468
e-mail campingnanzel@cibero.it
Well-managed site, with low terraces in olive grove.
➲ *Access from Km101.2 (Hotel Giorgiol).*
Open Apr-15 Oct **Site** 0.7HEC ❤ ✿ **Prices** ♠ 4.90-6.20 pitch 9.50-12.70 **Facilities** ⋒ 🛈 ⊙ ☮ ⌀ ☼ **Services** ⚑ 🍴 🖫 **Leisure** ❤ L **Off-site** 🍴 🌢 ➕

MACCAGNO VARESE

AZUR-Lago Maggiore
21010 ☎ 0332 560203 ▤ 0332 561263
e-mail maccagno@azur-camping.de
website www.azur-camping.de/maccagno
A popular site on the shore of the lake.
➲ *Off SS394 in village at Km43/III towards lake, 0.5km turn right.*
Open 15 Mar-15 Nov **Site** 1.5HEC ⊖ ❤ ✿ **Facilities** ⋒ 🛈 ⊙ ☮ ⌀ ☼ **Services** 🍴 ➕ 🖫 **Leisure** ❤ LR **Off-site** 🍴

Brancheito
via Pietraperzia 13, 21010 ☎ 045 6784029
Open All year **Site** 1.6HEC ❤ ✿ ✿ **Facilities** ⋒ 🛈 ⊙ ☮ ⌀ 🌢 ☼ **Services** ⚑ 🍴 ➕ 🖫 **Off-site** 🍴

Lido
via Pietraperzia 13, 21010 ☎ 0332 560250 ▤ 0332 560250
e-mail campinglido@boschettoholiday.it
website www.boschettoholiday.it
Lakeside site with good facilities, 200m from the river.
Open Apr-Sep **Site** 0.8HEC ❤ ✿ **Facilities** ⋒ ⊙ ☮ ☼ ☼ **Services** ⚑ 🍴 🖫 **Leisure** ❤ LR **Off-site** 🍴 ⌀ 🌢 ❤R

MANERBA DEL GARDA BRESCIA

Belvedere
via Cavalle 5, 25080 ☎ 0365 551175 ▤ 0365 552350
e-mail info@camping-belvedere.it
website www.camping.belvedere.it
Terraced site by Lake Garda.
➲ *Signed from SS572.*
Open Apr-7 Oct **Site** 2.1HEC ❣ ❤ ❤ ✿ ✿ ✿ **Prices** ♠ 3-6.80 ✿ 2.60-4 ✿ 8-15 ✿ (static)210-364 **Facilities** ⋒ 🛈 ⊙ ☮ ⌀ 🌢 ☼ **Services** ⚑ 🍴 🖫 **Leisure** ❤ LP **Off-site** 🍴 ➕

Rio Ferienglück
via del Rio 37, 25080 ☎ 0365 551075 ▤ 0365 551044
➲ *Off SS572 Desenzano-Salo between Km8 & Km9, site 4km N.*
Open Apr-Sep **Site** 5HEC ❣ ❤ ✿ ✿ **Prices** ♠ 4.50-6.50 ✿ 4-6 ✿ 5-6.50 Å 4.50-6 **Facilities** ⋒ 🛈 ⊙ ☮ ⌀ 🌢 ☼ **Services** ⚑ 🍴 ➕ 🖫 **Leisure** ❤ LPR

Rocca
via Cavalle 22, 25080 ☎ 0365 551738 ▤ 0365 552045
e-mail info@laroccacamp.it
website www.laroccacamp.it
A picturesque location with fine views over the gulf of Manerba.
Open 31 Mar-Sep **Site** 5HEC ❣ ❤ ✿ ✿ **Prices** ♠ 3.80-7 pitch 8.80-14 ✿ (static)210-714 **Facilities** ⋒ 🛈 ⊙ ☮ 🌢 ☼ **Services** ⚑ 🍴 🖫 **Leisure** ❤ LP

Site 6HEC (site size) ❣ grass ⊖ sand ❤ stone ✿ little shade ✿ partly shaded ❤ mainly shaded ✿ bungalows for hire ✿ caravans for hire Å tents for hire ⊗ no dogs **Prices** ♠ adult per night ✿ car per night pp per person per night ✿ caravan per night Å tent per night ✿ (static)-caravan hire per week

Zocco

via del Zocco 43, 25080 ☎ 0365 551605 🖹 0365 552053
e-mail info@campingzocco.it **website** www.campingzocco.it
The site consists of several, terraced sections. The section below the
maintenance/supply building lies on a sloping olive grove and is
somewhat obstructed by bungalows.

➲ *0.5km S of Gardonicino di Manerba.*

Open 8 Apr-24 Sep **Site** 5HEC 🏕 🏕 🏕 🏕 🛦 **Prices** ↟ 4.50-7 pitch 9-14
Facilities 🖍 🖻 ⊙ 🕳 ⌀ ℗ **Services** 🍴 🍷 🛅 🛠 **Leisure** 🏊 LP

MARONE BRESCIA

Riva di San Pietro

via Cristini 9, 25054 ☎ 030 9827129 🖹 030 9827129
e-mail rivasanpietro@hotmail.com
A modern site on the eastern side of Lake Iseo. Plenty of recreational
facilities.

➲ *Milano-Venezia road exit Rovato or Palazzolo for Iseo,
Marone 10km N.*

Open May-Sep **Site** 2HEC 🏕 🏕 🏕 **Prices** ↟ 5-6 �car 10-12 🛦 7.50-10
Facilities 🖍 ⊙ 🕳 ⌀ ℗ **Services** 🍴 🍷 🛅 **Leisure** 🏊 LP **Off-site** 🛒 🛠 🛠

MOLINA DI LEDRO TRENTO

International Camping Al Sole

via Maffei, 38060 ☎ 0464 508496 🖹 0464 508496
e-mail info@campingalsole.it
website www.campingalsole.it
A family site with modern facilities on Lake Ledro at an altitude of
655m.

➲ *W of Molina beside the lake.*

Open 20 Apr-Sep **Site** 3HEC 🏕 🏕 🏕 🏕 **Facilities** 🖍 🛒 ⊙ 🕳 ⌀ ℗
Services 🍴 🍷 🛠 🛅 **Leisure** 🏊 LP **Off-site** 🛠

MOLVENO TRENTO

Spiaggia-Lago di Molveno

via Lungolago 27, 38018 ☎ 0461 586978 🖹 0461 586330
e-mail camping@molveno.it **website** www.molveno.it/camping
A picturesque setting by the lake, at the foot of the Brenta Dolomites.

➲ *Signed from SS421.*

Open All year **Site** 4HEC 🏕 🏕 🏕 **Prices** ↟ 5-9 pitch 8.50-15.50 **Facilities** 🖍
🛒 ⊙ 🕳 ℗ **Services** 🍴 🍷 🛠 🛅 **Leisure** 🏊 LP **Off-site** 🛠 🏊P 🛠

MONIGA DEL GARDA BRESCIA

Fontanelle

via Magone 13, 25080 ☎ 0365 502079 🖹 0365 503324
e-mail info@campingfontanelle.it
website www.campingfontanelle.it
Peaceful site on the shores of Lake Garda shaded by olive trees.

Open 28 Apr-23 Sep **Site** 45HEC 🏕 🏕 🏕 🏕 ⌀ ℗ **Services** 🍴 🍷 🛠 🛅 **Leisure** 🏊 LP **Off-site** 🛠

San Michele

via San Michele 8, 25080 ☎ 0365 502026 🖹 0365 503443
e-mail info@campingsanmichele.it
website www.campingsanmichele.it
A family site with good facilities and direct access to the lake via a
private beach.

➲ *A4 exit Desenzano, site 8km towards Salo.*

Open 10 Mar-2 Nov **Site** 3HEC 🏕 🏕 🏕 **Prices** ↟ 4.50-6.50 pitch 8.50-
15.50 **Facilities** 🖍 🛒 ⊙ 🕳 ℗ **Services** 🍴 🍷 🛠 🛅 **Leisure** 🏊 LP
Off-site ⌀ 🛠

NATURNO-NATURNS BOLZANO

Wald

Dornsbergweg 8, 39025 ☎ 0473 667298 🖹 0473 668072
e-mail info@waldcamping.com
website www.waldcamping.com
The site lies on gently rising ground, in a forest of pine and deciduous
trees.

➲ *Off SS38 near Gasthof Alderwirt in village, 0.8km S over
railway line.*

Open 15 Mar-5 Nov **Site** 2.3HEC 🏕 🏕 🏕 **Facilities** 🖍 🛒 ⊙ 🕳 🛠 ℗
Services 🛠 🛅 **Leisure** 🏊 P **Off-site** 🍴 🍷 ⌀ 🏊R

NOVATE MEZZOLA SONDRIO

El Ranchero

via Nazionale 3, 23025 ☎ 0343 44169 🖹 0343 44169
Located on the edge of the Mezzola lake in front of a spectacular view
of the mountains.

Open May-15 Oct **Site** 1HEC 🏕 🏕 🏕 🏕 🏕 ⊗ **Prices** ↟ 5 �car 5 �car 5-7 🛦 5-7
Facilities 🖍 ⊙ 🕳 ℗ **Services** 🍴 🍷 🛅 **Leisure** 🏊 L **Off-site** 🛒 🍴 ⌀ 🛠
🏊PR 🛠

ORTA SAN GIULIO NOVARA

Cusio

Lago d'Orta, 28016 ☎ 0322 90290 🖹 0322 90290
e-mail cusio@tin.it
website www.orta.net/cusio
Site surrounded by woodland on Lake Orta in a picturesque alpine
valley. Good facilities.

➲ *S of Omegna towards Borgomanero.*

Open Apr-Nov **Site** 2HEC 🏕 🏕 🏕 **Prices** ↟ 4.50-6.20 🛦 3.50-4.90
pitch 7.50-10.90 **Facilities** 🖍 ⊙ 🕳 ℗ **Services** 🍴 🍷 🛅 **Leisure** 🏊 P
Off-site 🛒 🏊L 🛠

PADENGHE BRESCIA

Cá

via S.Cassiano 12, 25080 ☎ 030 9907006 🖹 030 9907693
e-mail lacafab@tiscalinet.it
website www.laca.it
A park-like setting on terraced ground.

➲ *Off the road along Lake Garda, 1.5km N turn for Padenghe
& down steep road towards lake.*

Open Mar-30 Oct **Site** 2HEC 🏕 🏕 🏕 🏕 **Prices** ↟ 3.60-6.60 pitch 5-13.50
�car (static)196-339.50 **Facilities** 🖍 🛒 ⊙ 🕳 ⌀ ℗ **Services** 🍴 🍷 🛅
Leisure 🏊 LP

Villa Garuti

via del Porto 5, 25080 ☎ 030 9907134 🖹 030 9907817
e-mail villagaruti@gardaleke.it
A campsite and holiday village in the garden of the old Villa Garuti,
beside the lake with its own beach.

➲ *A4 exit Desenzano, SS572 to Padenghe.*

Open Mar-20 Oct **Site** 1.5HEC 🏕 🏕 🏕 🏕 **Prices** ↟ 5-8 🚗 3-5 🚐 8-12.50
🛦 6.50-12.50 🚐 (static)120-280 **Facilities** 🖍 ⊙ 🕳 ⌀ 🛠 ℗ **Services** 🍴
🍷 🛠 🛅 **Leisure** 🏊 LP **Off-site** 🛒

Italy

Facilities 🛒 shop 🖍 shower ⊙ electric points for razors 🕳 electric points for caravans ℗ parking by tents permitted ℗ compulsory separate car park
Services 🍴 café/restaurant 🍷 bar ⌀ Camping Gaz International 🛠 gas other than Camping Gaz 🛠 first aid facilities 🛅 laundry
Leisure 🏊 swimming L-Lake P-Pool R-River S-Sea **Off-site** All facilities within 2km

PEIO TRENTO

Val di Sole
Loc Dossi di Cavia, 38020 ☎ 0463 753177 ▤ 0463 753176
e-mail valdisole@camping.it
website www.camping.it/trentino/valdisole
The site lies on terraced slopes at the foot of the Ortier mountain range.

⮕ *400m off SP87.*

Open Jun-5 Nov & Dec-5 May **Site** 2.3HEC ❤ ♣ ⚏ **Facilities** ↑ 🗎 ⊙ ⌷
⌀ ≞ ℗ **Services** ⌁ 🍴 🗑 **Off-site** 🍴 ⌁P

PERA DI FASSA TRENTO

Soal
via Dolomiti 32, 38030 ☎ 0462 764519 ▤ 0462 764609
e-mail info@campingsoal.com
website www.campingsoal.com
Breath-taking location among the Dolomites, ideal for skiing and walking.

Open All year **Site** 30HEC ❤ ♣ **Facilities** ↑ 🗎 ⊙ ⌷ ⌀ ≞ ℗
Services ⌁ 🍴 🗑 **Leisure** ⌁ R

PÉRGINE TRENTO

Punta Indiani
Lago di Caldonazzo, 38058 ☎ 0461 548062 ▤ 0461 548607
e-mail info@campingpuntaindiani.it
website www.campingpuntaindiani.it
On level ground surrounded by trees with direct access to 400m of private beach on the banks of the lake.

⮕ *A22 exit Trento, signs for Pergine, S Cristoforo & Caldonazzo.*
Open May-Sep **Site** 1.5HEC ❤ ♣ ⊗ **Prices** ♠ 8 pitch 7-12
Facilities ↑ ⊙ ⌷ ℗ **Services** 🗑 **Leisure** ⌁ L **Off-site** 🗎 ⌁ 🍴 ⌀ ≞ 🞧

San Cristoforo
via dei Pescatori, 38057 ☎ 0461 512707 ▤ 0461 707381
e-mail info@campingclub.it
website www.campingclub.it
A family-run site in a prime position on the sunniest side of lake.

⮕ *Road 47 from Trento towards Venice for 14km, site in centre of S Cristoforo.*
Open 26 May-2 Sep **Site** 2.5HEC ❤ ♣ **Prices** ♠ 6-9 pitch 10-14
Facilities ↑ ⊙ ⌷ ℗ **Services** ⌁ 🍴 🞧 🗑 **Leisure** ⌁ LP
Off-site 🗎 ⌀ ≞

PIEVE DI MANERBA BRESCIA

Faro
via Repubblica 52, 25080 ☎ 0365 651704 ▤ 0365 651704
e-mail campeggioilfaro@virgilio.it
Set in a peaceful rural area close to the sea.

⮕ *Off A4 at Desenzano onto N572 to Manerba del Garda.*
Open 15 Apr-15 Sep **Site** 1HEC ❤ ❤ ⌷ **Facilities** ↑ ⊙ ⌷ ℗
Leisure ⌁ P **Off-site** 🗎 ⌁ 🍴 ⌀ ≞ ⌁L 🞧

PISOGNE BRESCIA

Eden
via Piangrande 3, 25055 ☎ 0364 880500 ▤ 0364 880500
e-mail info@campeggioeden.com
website www.campeggioeden.com
The site lies on eastern lake shore with tall trees and a level beach.

⮕ *Off SS510 at Km37/VII, over railway towards lake.*
Open 2 Apr-28 Sep **Site** 2.5HEC ❤ ♣ ⌷ **Prices** ♠ 4-5.80 ♠ 3.60-5.20
pitch 7.50-11.50 **Facilities** ↑ ⊙ ⌷ ℗ **Services** ⌁ 🍴 ℗ **Leisure** ⌁ L
Off-site 🍴 ⌀ ≞ ⌁PR 🞧

PONTE TRESA VARESE

Trelago
via Trelago 20, 21030 ☎ 0332 716583 ▤ 0332 719650
e-mail info@3lagocamping.com
website www.3lagocamping.com
Lakeside site with grassy pitches shaded by tall trees.

⮕ *Signs from Milan to Varese & Ghirla, site 15km from Varese.*
Open Apr-15 Sep **Site** 3.3HEC ❤ ♣ ⌷ ⌷ **Prices** ♠ 5.50 pitch 7
⌷ (static)189 **Facilities** ↑ 🗎 ⊙ ⌷ ⌀ ≞ ℗ **Services** ⌁ 🍴 🞧 🗑
Leisure ⌁ LP **Off-site** 🍴

PORLEZZA COMO

Paradiso
Via Calbiga 30, 22018 ☎ 0344 70393 ▤ 0344 70715
e-mail info@campingoklarivetta.com
website www.campingoklarivetta.com
The site lies in meadowland on the north eastern lake shore.

⮕ *S from SS340.*
Open 15 Mar-15 Nov **Site** 5HEC ❤ ♣ ⌷ ℗ **Prices** ♠ 4.50-5.50 pitch 9-11.50
Facilities ↑ 🗎 ⊙ ⌷ ℗ **Services** ⌁ 🍴 🗑 **Leisure** ⌁ LP **Off-site** 🍴 ⌀
≞ ⌁R

POZZA DI FASSA TRENTO

Caravan Garden Vidor
Loc.Vidor 5, 38036 ☎ 0462 763247 ▤ 0462 764780
e-mail info@campingvidor.it
website www.campingvidor.it
A traditional family-run site in a pine forest. Ideal for skiers, nature lovers and families.

⮕ *Signed from SS48.*
Open Jan-Apr, June-Dec **Site** 2.5HEC ❤ ♣ ⌷ **Prices** ♠ 5.50-7.50
pitch 7.50-10 **Facilities** ↑ 🗎 ⊙ ⌷ ⌀ ≞ ℗ **Services** ⌁ 🍴 🞧 🗑
Off-site 🍴 ⌁R

Rosengarten
via Avisio 15, Loc Puccia, 38036 ☎ 0462 763305 ▤ 0462 763501
e-mail campingcatinacciorosen@tin.it
website www.catinacciorosengarten.com
A well-tended site in the heart of the Dolomites. A good base for a skiing or walking holiday.

⮕ *Signed from SS48.*
Open 10 Jun-Sep, 13 Nov-Apr **Site** 3HEC ❤ ❤ ♣ ⌷ ⌷ **Prices** ♠ 6.70-8.50
♠ 6-7.10 pitch 7.20-8.50 ⌷ (static)280 **Facilities** ↑ ⊙ ⌷ ⌀ ≞ ℗
Services ⌁ 🍴 🞧 🗑 **Leisure** ⌁ R **Off-site** 🗎 🍴 ⌁P

Italy

RASUN BOLZANO

Corones

39030 ☎ 0474 496490 ▤ 0474 498250
e-mail info@corones.com
website www.corones.com
A modern site in an ideal mountain location with good sports facilities.
⊃ *Milan-Brenner motorway exit Val Pusteria, through Brunico &*
Valdaora to Rasun.
Open All year **Site** 2.7HEC 👑 👑 👑 🏕 **Prices** � 18-25.50 ⬥ 15-20
Facilities 🍴 🛁 ⊙ 🖻 🖉 🛒 ⓟ **Services** 📞 🍽 ➕ 🖾 **Leisure** 🏊 P

RIVA DEL GARDA TRENTO

Bavaria

viale Rovereto 100, 38066 ☎ 0464 552524 ▤ 0464 559126
e-mail camping@bavarianet.it
website www.bavarianet.it
⊃ *On SS240 towards Rovereto.*
Open Apr-Oct **Site** 6HEC 👑 👑 ⊙ 👑 **Facilities** 🍴 ⊙ 🖻 ⓟ **Services** 📞 🍽
➕ **Leisure** 🏊 L **Off-site** 🛁 🖉 🛒

Monte Brione

via Brione 32, 38066 ☎ 0464 520885 ▤ 0464 520890
e-mail campingbrione@rivadelgarda.com
website www.campingbrione.com
This site is at the foot of a hill covered with olive trees with good
sports facilities.
⊃ *250m from San Nicolo' tourist centre.*
Open Etr-Sep **Site** 3.3HEC 👑 👑 **Facilities** 🍴 🛁 ⊙ 👑 ⓟ **Services** 📞 🍽
🖾 **Leisure** 🏊 P **Off-site** 🍽 🏊L

RIVOLTELLA BRESCIA

San Francesco

strada Vicinale San Francesco, 25010 ☎ 030 9110245 ▤ 030 9119464
e-mail moreinfo@campingsanfrancesco.com
website www.campingsanfrancesco.com
This well-kept site is divided into many sections by drives, vineyards
and orchards and has a private gravel beach.
⊃ *At Km268 on SSN11.*
Open Apr-Sep **Site** 10.4HEC 👑 👑 🏕 � **Prices** ⬥ 5.70-10 pitch 12-30
Facilities 🍴 🛁 ⊙ 🖻 🖉 🛒 ⓟ **Services** 📞 🍽 ➕ 🖾 **Leisure** 🏊 LP

SAN ANTONIO DI MAVIGNOLA TRENTO

Faé

38084 ☎ 0465 507178 ▤ 0465 507178
e-mail campingfae@campiglio.it
website www.campiglio.it/campingfae
Situated in the winter skiing region of Madonna di Campiglio. Good
base for climbing in the Brenta range. Set on on four gravel terraces,
and an alpine meadow in a hollow.
⊃ *Off SS239.*
Open Jun-Sep & 1 Dec-30 Apr **Site** 2.1HEC 👑 👑 🚐 **Prices** ⬥ 7-8 pitch
8-11 **Facilities** 🍴 🛁 ⊙ 🖻 🖉 🛒 ⓟ **Services** 📞 🍽 🖾 **Off-site** 🍽 ➕

SAN FELICE DEL BENACO BRESCIA

Camping Europa-Silvella

via Silvella ☎ 0365 651095 ▤ 0365 654395
e-mail info@europasilvella.it **website** www.europasilvella.it
Site separated in two by the approach road. The beach is 80m below.
⊃ *Signed.*
Open Apr-Sep **Site** 7.5HEC 👑 👑 🏕 **Prices** ⬥ 4-8 pitch 9.50-21
Facilities 🍴 🛁 ⊙ 🖻 ⓟ **Services** 📞 🍽 ➕ 🖾 **Leisure** 🏊 LP

See advertisement on this page

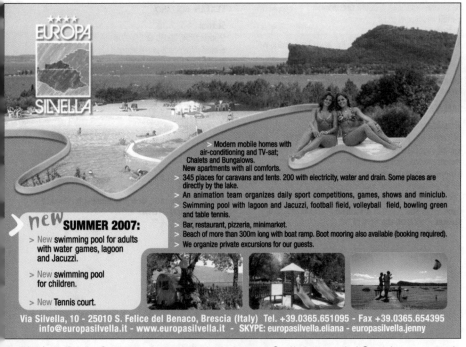

Italy

Facilities 🛁 shop 🍴 shower ⊙ electric points for razors 🖻 electric points for caravans ⓟ parking by tents permitted ⓟ compulsory separate car park
Services 🍽 café/restaurant 📞 bar 🖉 Camping Gaz International 🛒 gas other than Camping Gaz ➕ first aid facilities 🖾 laundry
Leisure 🏊 swimming L-Lake P-Pool R-River S-Sea **Off-site** All facilities within 2km

Fornella

via Fornella 1, 25010 ☎ 0365 62294 📄 0365 559418
e-mail fornella@fornella.it
website www.fornella.it
A quiet site in an ideal location on the shore of Lake Garda.
➲ Signed from SS572 Salo-Desenzano.
Open 28 Apr-3 Sep **Site** 9.2HEC ❤ ❤ ❀ ❀ ▲ **Prices** ♠ 4.60-8.80 pitch
9.30-16.50 ❖ (static)392-696 **Facilities** ❀ ⚲ ⊙ ❀ ⌀ ⑦ **Services** ❄ ⑩
⑤ **Leisure** ❤ LP

Gardiola

via Gardiola 36, 25010 ☎ 0365 559240 📄 0365 557625
e-mail info@lagardiola.com
website www.baiaholiday.com
A terraced site with a variety of good facilities on the shore of Lake
Garda.
➲ S of San Felice del Benaco off SS572.
Open Apr-22 Oct **Site** 0.4HEC ❤ ❀ ❀ ❖ **Prices** ♠ 3.30-7.80 pitch 15.60-
34.90 (incl 2 persons) ❖ (static)210-524.30 **Facilities** ❀ ⚲ ⊙ ❀ ⑦ **Services**
❄ ⑩ ⑤ **Leisure** ❤ L **Off-site** ⚲ ⑩ ⌀ ➷ ❤PR ➕

Ideal Molino

25010 ☎ 0365 62023 📄 0365 559395
e-mail info@campingmolino.it
website www.campingmolino.it
Charming and quiet site beside Lake Garda, set among beautiful
scenery 1km from S Felice. On the beach there is a pier and boat
moorings. Pedal boats can be hired for lake trips.
Open 23 Mar-Sep **Site** 1.7HEC ❤ ❀ ❀ ❀ ❖ ⑧ **Prices** ♠ 3.60-7.90 pitch
9.90-16.40 **Facilities** ❀ ⚲ ⊙ ❀ ⑦ **Services** ❄ ⑩ ⑤ **Leisure** ❤ L
Off-site ⌀ ➷

Weekend

via Vallone della Selva 2, 25010 ☎ 0365 43712 📄 0365 42196
e-mail info@weekend.it
website www.weekend.it
A quiet family site with modern facilities, situated in a olive grove
overlooking Lake Garda.
➲ A4 exit Desenzano, to Cisano, signed S Felice D-B.
Open 23 Apr-25 Sept **Site** 9HEC ❤ ❀ ❀ **Facilities** ❀ ⚲ ⊙ ❀ ❀
Services ❄ ⑩ ➕ ⑤ **Leisure** ❤ P **Off-site** ❤L

SAN MARTINO DI CASTROZZA TRENTO

Sass Maor

via Laghetto 48, 38058 ☎ 0439 68347 📄 0439 68347
e-mail info@campingsassmaor.it
website www.campingsassmaor.it
A winter sports site in a beautiful mountain setting.
➲ From Trento travel to Ora, Cavalese and S Martino di
Castrozza.
Open All year **Site** 0.2HEC ❤ ❀ **Facilities** ❀ ⚲ ⊙ ❀ ⌀ ➷ ⑦ ⑫
Services ❄ ⑩ ⑤ **Off-site** ❤LPR ➕

SAN PIETRO DI CORTENO GOLGI BRESCIA

Villaggio Aprica

via Nazionale 507, 25040 ☎ 0342 710001
e-mail info@campingaprica.it
website www.campingaprica.it
A small natural park ideal for winter skiing and summer walking.
➲ On SS39 Aprica-Edolo.
Open All year **Site** 2.1HEC ❤ ❀ ❀ ❀ **Prices** ♠ 4.55-6.80 pitch 4.90-11.60
❖ (static)200-500 **Facilities** ❀ ⚲ ⊙ ❀ ⌀ ➷ ⑦ **Services** ❄ ⑩ ⑤
Leisure ❤ R **Off-site** ❤LPS ➕

SAN VIGILIO DI MAREBBE BOLZANO

Al Plan

39030 ☎ 0474 501694 📄 0474 506550
e-mail camping.alplan@rolmail.net
website www.campingalplan.com
Wooded Alpine setting at an altitude of 1200m.
➲ Off A22.
Open Dec-15 Apr Jun-Oct **Site** 2HEC ❤ ❀ ❀ ❀ **Prices** ♠ 5-7.50 ❖ 10-12
▲ 5-7 **Facilities** ❀ ⚲ ⊙ ❀ ⌀ ➷ **Services** ❄ ⑩ ⑤ **Off-site** ❤PR ➕

SARRE AOSTA

Monte Bianco

Fraz St Maurice 15, 11010 ☎ 0165 257523 📄 0165 257275
e-mail info@campingmontebianco.it
website www.campingmontebianco.it
Wooded surroundings close to the town centre.
➲ SS26 towards Aosta & Courmayer.
Open Apr-Sep **Site** 7.5HEC ❤ ❀ **Prices** ♠ 4.50-4.80 ❖ 2.50-2.70 ❖ 3.90-
4.20 ▲ 3.90-4.20 **Facilities** ❀ ⊙ ❀ ⑦ **Services** ➕ ⑤ **Leisure** ❤ R
Off-site ⚲ ❄ ⑩ ⌀ ➷ ❤P

SEXTEN BOLZANO

Sexten

St-Josefstr 54, 39030 ☎ 0474 710444 📄 0474 710053
e-mail info@caravanparksexten.it
website www.caravanparksexten.it
Open 4 Dec-5 Nov **Site** 6HEC ❤ ❀ ❀ ❖ **Prices** ♠ 7-11.50 pitch 4-19.50
❖ (static)301-518 **Facilities** ❀ ⚲ ⊙ ❀ ⌀ ➷ ⑦
Services ❄ ⑩ ⑤ **Leisure** ❤ PR

SORICO COMO

Au Lac De Como

via C-Battisti 18, 22010 ☎ 0344 84035 📄 0344 84802
The well-kept site lies on the right of the River Mera as it flows into
Lake Como.
➲ Off SS340d at Km25 near Total fuel station, 200m towards
lake.
Open All year **Site** 17HEC ❤ ❀ ❀ ❖ **Facilities** ❀ ⚲ ⊙ ❀ ⌀ ➷
Services ❄ ⑩ ➕ ⑤ **Leisure** ❤ LR

Site 6HEC (site size) ❤ grass ❤ sand ❤ stone ❤ little shade ❀ partly shaded ❀ mainly shaded ❀ bungalows for hire
❖ caravans for hire ▲ tents for hire ⑧ no dogs **Prices** ♠ adult per night ❖ car per night pp per person per night ❖ caravan per night
▲ tent per night ❖ (static)-caravan hire per week

TORBOLE TRENTO

Porto

38069 ☎ 0464 505891 🖹 0464 505891

e-mail info@campingalporto.it

website www.campingalporto.it

A site with modern facilities, situated in a quiet position near the lake. Ideal for sports and families.

⮑ *From Torbole onto SS240, signed.*

Open Apr-Oct **Site** 1.1HEC 😾 � **Prices** ♠ 6.50-6.90 pitch 7.80-10 **Facilities** ⋔ ⊙ ☒ ⓟ **Services** ⍾ ⍾ 🖺 **Off-site** 🖾 ⍾ ⍾ ⍾ ⮕LR

TORRE DANIELE TORINO

Mombarone

via Nazionale 54, 10010 ☎ 0125 757907 🖹 0125 757396

website www.campingmombarone.com

⮑ *13km N of Ivrea on SS26. Close to river.*

Open All year **Site** 1.2HEC 😾 😾 🚃 🚐 **Prices** ♠ 5 🚗 2 🚐 4 ⛺ 3 **Facilities** ⋔ ⊙ ☒ ⓟ **Services** ⍾ ⍾ 🖺 **Leisure** ⮕ PR **Off-site** 🖾 ⍾ ⍾ 🎝

TOSCOLANO MADERNO BRESCIA

Chiaro di Luna

via Statale 218, 25088 ☎ 0365 641179 🖹 0365 641179

website www.chiarodiluna.org

Open Apr-29 Sep **Site** 9HEC 😾 😾 🚐 **Facilities** ⋔ 🖾 ⊙ ☒ 🚃 ⓟ **Services** ⍾ ⍾ 🖺 **Leisure** ⮕ L **Off-site** ⍾

VALNONTEY AOSTA

Lo Stambecco

11012 ☎ 0165 74152 🖹 0165 749213

e-mail campingstambecco@tiscali.it

website www.campinglostambecco.com

Open 15 May-25 Sep **Site** 1.6HEC 😾 😾 🚐 **Facilities** ⋔ ⊙ ☒ ⍾ 🚃 ⓟ **Services** ⍾ ⍾ 🖺 **Leisure** ⮕ R **Off-site** 🖾 ⍾ ⍾

VIVERONE VERCELLI

Rocca

via Lungo Lago 35, 13886 ☎ 0161 98416 🖹 0161 98416

e-mail Felicitaa@libero.it

website www.la-rocca.org

Open 15 Mar-15 Oct **Site** 1HEC 😾 😾 🚐 **Facilities** ⋔ 🖾 ⊙ ☒ ⓟ **Services** ⍾ ⍾ 🖺 **Leisure** ⮕ P **Off-site** ⍾ 🚃 ⮕L

VENICE/NORTH

ARSIE BELLUNO

Gajole

Loc Soravigo, 32030 ☎ 0439 58505 🖹 0439 58505

e-mail campinggajole@libero.it

website www.campinggajole.it

A delightful, peaceful setting on the shore of Lake Corlo.

⮑ *Off SS50.*

Open Apr-Sep **Site** 1.5HEC 😾 😾 **Prices** ♠ 5-7 pitch 5-8 **Facilities** ⋔ 🖾 ⊙ ☒ ⓟ **Services** ⍾ ⍾ 🖺 **Leisure** ⮕ L

ASIAGO VICENZA

Ekar

Loc.Ta' Ekar, 36012 ☎ 0424 455157 🖹 0424 455161

e-mail campingasiago@keycomm.itg-ekar

On a level meadow in a striking setting among wooded hills in a popular ski-ing region.

Open 18 May-Sep & 15 Nov-27 Apr **Site** 3.5HEC 😾 😾 **Facilities** ⋔ 🖾 ⊙ ☒ 🚃 ⓟ **Services** ⍾ ⍾ 🖺

AURISINA TRIESTE

Imperial

Aurisina Cave 55, 34011 ☎ 040 200459 🖹 040 200459

e-mail campimperial@libero.it

website www.campingimperialcarso.it

A well-maintained site in a secluded, wooded location.

⮑ *Via SS14 Sistiana-Aurisina.*

Open Jun-Sep **Site** 1.5HEC 😾 😾 🚐 **Prices** ♠ 3.80-6.50 🚗 4.50-7.50 ⛺ 4-5 pitch 9.50-14.50 🚐 (static)189-266 **Facilities** ⋔ 🖾 ⊙ ☒ ⓟ **Services** 🖺 **Leisure** ⮕ P

BARDOLINO VERONA

Continental

Localita Reboin, 37011 ☎ 045 7210192 🖹 045 7211756

e-mail continental@campingarda.it

website www.campingarda.it

A pleasant site directly on the lake with modern facilities.

Open Apr-10 Oct **Site** 3.5HEC 😾 😾 🚃 **Prices** ♠ 4.70-7 pitch 9.50-15.50 **Facilities** ⋔ 🖾 ⊙ ☒ ⍾ ⓟ **Services** ⍾ ⍾ 🖺 **Leisure** ⮕ L **Off-site** ⮕L

Rocca

S Pietro, 37011 ☎ 045 7211111 🖹 045 7211300

e-mail info@campinglarocca.com

website www.campinglarocca.com

Slightly sloping grassland broken by rows of trees, separated from the lake by a public path (no cars). Part of site is on the other side of the main road, terraced among vines and olives with lovely view of lake.

⮑ *Below SS249 at Km40/IV.*

Open 30 Mar-7 Oct **Site** 8HEC 😾 😾 🚃 🚐 **Prices** ♠ 4.50-6.80 pitch 9-17 🚐 (static)189-273 **Facilities** ⋔ 🖾 ⊙ ☒ 🚃 ⓟ **Services** ⍾ ⍾ 🖺 **Leisure** ⮕ LP **Off-site** ⍾

BIBIONE VENEZIA

Villagio Turistico Internazionale

via Colonie 2, 30020 ☎ 0431 442611 🖹 0431 442699

e-mail info@vti.it

website www.vti.it

Mostly sandy terrain under pine trees. Some meadowland with a few deciduous trees. Wide sandy beach. Tennis court.

⮑ *Signed along approach.*

Open 21 Apr-23 Sep **Site** 13HEC 😾 😾 🚃 🚐 **Prices** ♠ 3.50-9.50 🚗 4-5 pitch 9-22.50 🚐 (static)245-1029 **Facilities** ⋔ 🖾 ⊙ ☒ ⍾ 🚃 ⓟ **Services** ⍾ ⍾ 🖺 **Leisure** ⮕ PS

Italy

Facilities 🖾 shop ⋔ shower ⊙ electric points for razors ☒ electric points for caravans ⓟ parking by tents permitted ⓟ compulsory separate car park
Services ⍾ café/restaurant ⍾ bar ⍾ Camping Gaz International 🚃 gas other than Camping Gaz ⍾ first aid facilities 🖺 laundry
Leisure ⮕ swimming L-Lake P-Pool R-River S-Sea **Off-site** All facilities within 2km

BRENZONE VERONA

Primavera

via Benaco 5, 37010 ☎ 045 7420421 ⬚ 045 7420421
e-mail info@camping-primavera.com
website www.camping-primavera.com
Small site on the shore of Lake Garda.

Open Apr-Oct **Site** 0.8HEC ⚌ ⬥ ⊞ **Facilities** ⬥ ⬚ ⊙ ⬚ ⬚ ⬚ ⬚ ⬚
Services ⬚ ⬚ ⬚ **Leisure** ⬚ L **Off-site** ⬚ ⬚

CA'NOGHERA VENEZIA

Alba d'Oro

via Triestina 214/B, 30030 ☎ 041 5415102 ⬚ 041 5475971
e-mail albadoro@tin.it
website www.ecvacanze.it
On level ground directly on the lagoon with modern facilities including moorings for small boats. Regular bus service to Venice.

⮕ Off SS14.

Open Feb-Oct **Site** 7HEC ⚌ ⬥ ⬥ ⬚ Å **Facilities** ⬥ ⬚ ⊙ ⬚ ⬚ ⬚ ⬚ ⬚
Services ⬚ ⬚ ⬚ **Leisure** ⬚ PR **Off-site** ⬚ LS ⬚

CAORLE VENEZIA

San Francesco

via Selva Rosata, 25080 ☎ 0421 2982 ⬚ 0421 299284
e-mail info@villaggiosfrancesco.com
website www.villaggiosfrancesco.com
A generously laid-out site, on level lawns with shady poplars, in a holiday village.

⮕ Signed from Caorle.

Open 12 Apr-29 Sep **Site** 32HEC ⚌ ⬥ ⬥ ⬥ ⬥ ⬚ **Facilities** ⬥ ⬚ ⊙ ⬚ ⬚ ⬚ ⬚ ⬚ ⬚ **Services** ⬚ ⬚ ⬚ ⬚ **Leisure** ⬚ PS

CASSONE VERONA

Bellavista

37010 ☎ 045 7420244
e-mail info@campingbellavistamalcesine.com
website www.campingbellavistamalcesine.com
A fine position in an olive grove overlooking Lake Garda with modern sanitary installations. Access to the lake is by an underpass and water sports are available.

Open All year **Site** 27HEC ⚌ ⬥ ⬥ ⬥ ⬚ **Facilities** ⬥ ⬚ ⊙ ⬚ ⬚ ⬚ ⬚
Services ⬚ ⬚ ⬚ ⬚ **Leisure** ⬚ L **Off-site** ⬚ PR

CASTELLETTO DI BRENZONE VERONA

Maior

VIA Croce N.10, 37010 ☎ 045 7430333 ⬚ 045 7430333
e-mail camp_lemaior@libero.it
website www.campinglemaior.it
A comfortable, modern site in a pleasant, quiet location.

Open Etr-29 Sep **Site** 8HEC ⚌ ⬥ ⬥ ⬚ **Prices** ⬧ 7-8.50 pitch 10-12
Facilities ⬥ ⬚ ⊙ ⬚ ⬚ ⬚ ⬚ **Services** ⬚ ⬚ ⬚ **Off-site** ⬚ ⬚ L ⬚

San Zeno

via A.Vespucci 97, 37010 ☎ 045 7430231 ⬚ 045 4430171
e-mail info@campingsanzeno.it
website www.campingsanzeno.it
Situated close to the lake and surrounded by hundred-year old olive groves.

⮕ Motorway exit Rovereto/Trento, continue S, site 10km S of Malcesine.

Open May-Sep **Site** 1.4HEC ⚌ ⬥ ⬥ ⬚ **Prices** ⬧ 4.70-6.50 pitch 7.50-10
Facilities ⬥ ⬚ ⊙ ⬚ ⬚ ⬚ ⬚ **Services** ⬚ ⬚ ⬚ **Off-site** ⬚ ⬚ L

CAVALLINO VENEZIA

Cavallino

via delle Batterie 164, 30013 ☎ 041 966133 ⬚ 041 5300827
e-mail info@campingcavallino.com
website www.baiaholiday.com
Set in a pine wood close to the sea with plenty of recreational facilities.

Open Apr-21 Oct **Site** 11.4HEC ⚌ ⬥ ⬥ ⬥ ⬥ ⬚ **Facilities** ⬥ ⬚ ⊙ ⬚ ⬚ ⬚ ⬚
Services ⬚ ⬚ ⬚ ⬚ **Leisure** ⬚ PS

Europa

via Fausta 332, 30013 ☎ 041 968069 ⬚ 041 5370150
e-mail info@campingeuropa.com
website www.campingeuropa.com
On grassland reaching to the sea, with some poplars.

⮕ Signed on Punta Sabbioni road.

Open 2 Apr-Sep **Site** 11HEC ⚌ ⬥ ⬥ ⬥ ⬚ **Prices** ⬧ 4.30-7.60 pitch 8.40-19.80 **Facilities** ⬥ ⬚ ⊙ ⬚ ⬚ ⬚ ⬚ **Services** ⬚ ⬚ ⬚ **Leisure** ⬚ S **Off-site** ⬚

Italy

via Fausta 272, 30013 ☎ 041 968090 ⬚ 041 5370076
e-mail info@campingitaly.it
website www.campingitaly.it
Small family site on a peninsula 6km from Lido di Jesolo. Venice can be reached by public ferry.

⮕ Brennero-Venezia motorway exit signs for Jesolo-Cavallino.

Open 20 Apr-18 Sep **Site** 3.9HEC ⚌ ⬥ ⬥ ⬥ ⬚ **Prices** ⬧ 4.60-7.40 pitch 7.80-19.20 ⬚ (static)329-574 **Facilities** ⬥ ⬚ ⊙ ⬚ ⬚ ⬚ **Services** ⬚ ⬚ ⬚ **Leisure** ⬚ PS **Off-site** ⬚

Joker

via Fausta 318, 30013 ☎ 041 5370766 ⬚ 041 968216
e-mail jokercamping@iol.it
website www.jokercamping.it
Between coastal road and the sandy beach with tall poplars. Partially subdivided.

Open May-Sep **Site** 4.4HEC ⚌ ⬥ ⬥ ⬥ Å ⬚ **Facilities** ⬥ ⬚ ⊙ ⬚ ⬚ ⬚ ⬚ **Services** ⬚ ⬚ ⬚ ⬚ **Leisure** ⬚ PS

Residence

via F. Baracca 47, 30013 ☎ 041 968027 ⬚ 041 5370164
e-mail info@residencevillage.com
website www.residencevillage.com
Well-laid out site on level, wooded grassland, by a sandy beach, between Jesolo and Cavallino.

⮕ Signed.

Open 5 May-22 Sep **Site** 8HEC ⚌ ⬥ ⬥ ⬥ ⬥ ⬚ **Prices** ⬧ 4.30-8.60 pitch 8.50-20.90 **Facilities** ⬥ ⬚ ⊙ ⬚ ⬚ ⬚ ⬚ **Services** ⬚ ⬚ ⬚ **Leisure** ⬚ PS **Off-site** ⬚ R

Sant' Angelo

via F-Baracca 63, 30013 ☎ 041 968882 ⬚ 041 5370242
e-mail info@santangelo.it
website www.santangelo.it
A large beach site decorated by trees and flower beds. Good entertainment, sports and eating facilities.

⮕ Outside Venice signs for Caposile & Jesolo, cross bridge just after Lido di Jesolo & right to coast.

Open 6 May-24 Sep **Site** 20HEC ⚌ ⬥ ⬥ ⬥ ⬥ ⬚ **Facilities** ⬥ ⬚ ⊙ ⬚ ⬚ **Services** ⬚ ⬚ ⬚ ⬚ **Leisure** ⬚ PS

Site 6HEC (site size) ⚌ grass ⬤ sand ⬥ stone ⬧ little shade ⬥ partly shaded ⬥ mainly shaded ⊞ bungalows for hire ⬥ caravans for hire Å tents for hire ⬚ no dogs **Prices** ⬧ adult per night ⬥ car per night pp per person per night ⬥ caravan per night Å tent per night ⬥ (static)-caravan hire per week

Scarpiland
via A-Poerio 14, 30010 ☎ 041 966488 📠 041 966488
e-mail info@scarpiland.com
website www.scarpiland.com
A beautiful location surrounded by a pine wood with sea views and direct access to the beach.
Open 25 Apr-22 Sep **Site** 4.5HEC 😃 ♨ ♨ ☎ ♤ **Facilities** 🚿 🛍 ⊙ 🖸 🖉 ⚏ ⑭ **Services** 🍴 🍽 🖪 🖸 **Leisure** ⚓ S

Silva
via F-Baracca 53, 30013 ☎ 041 968087 📠 041 968087
The site lies on sand and grassland and is located between road and beach, divided by a vineyard. The section of site near the beach is quiet.
Open 11 May-16 Sep **Site** 3.3HEC 😃 ♨ ♤ **Prices** ⚹ 3.50-6.50 ♨ 7-16 ⚑ 6-16 **Facilities** 🚿 🛍 ⊙ 🖸 🖉 ⑭ **Services** 🍴 🍽 🖸 **Leisure** ⚓ S
Off-site ⚓R 🖸

Union-Lido
via Fausta 258, 30013 ☎ 041 2575111 📠 041 5370355
e-mail info@unionlido.com
website www.unionlido.com
This large site lies on a long stretch of land next to a 1km-long beach. Separate section for tents and caravans. Minimum stay during peak period is one week. Ideal for families.
⤵ *Motorway from Tarvisio via Udine, San Dona di Piave then signed to Jesolo & Cavallino.*
Open May-Sep **Site** 60HEC 😃 ♨ ♤ ⊗ **Prices** ⚹ 6.20-9.30 pitch 11.40-24 **Facilities** 🚿 🛍 ⊙ 🖸 🖉 ⚏ ⑭ **Services** 🍴 🍽 🖸 🖸 **Leisure** ⚓ PS

Villa al Mare
via del Faro 12, 30013 ☎ 041 968066 📠 041 5370576
e-mail info@villaalmare.it
website www.villaalmare.com
Level site divided into plots on a peninsula behind the lighthouse. Direct access to a long, sandy beach.
Open May-Sep **Site** 2HEC 😃 ♨ ♨ ☎ ♤ ⊗ **Prices** ⚹ 3.90-7.50 pitch 7.90-17.70 ♨ (static)311.60-796 **Facilities** 🚿 🛍 ⊙ 🖸 🖉 ⚏ ⑭ **Services** 🍴 🍽 🖸 🖸 **Leisure** ⚓ RS

CHIOGGIA VENEZIA

Miramare
via A-Barbarigo 103, 30019 ☎ 041 490610 📠 041 490610
e-mail campmir@tin.it
website www.miramarecamping.com
Longish site reaching as far as the beach, clean and well-maintained.
⤵ *SS309 Strada Romeo towards Chioggia Sottomarina, turn right at beach, site 0.5km.*
Open 5 Apr-20 Sep **Site** 5HEC 😃 ♨ ☎ ♤ ⊗ **Prices** ⚹ 4.50-7.20 ⚑ 7.50-10.60 pitch 8.50-16 **Facilities** 🚿 🛍 ⊙ 🖸 🖉 ⚏ ⑭ **Services** 🍴 🍽 🖸 **Leisure** ⚓ PS **Off-site** 🖸

Villaggio Turistico Isamar
via Isamar 9, Isolaverde, 30015 ☎ 041 5535811 📠 041 490440
e-mail info@villaggioisamar.com
website www.villaggioisamar.com
The site lies on level grassland at the mouth of the River Etsch. Shade is provided by high poplars. Good beach.
⤵ *Off SS309. Caravans are advised to approach via Km84/VII near Brenta.*
Open 29 Apr-29 Sep **Site** 33HEC 😃 ♨ ☎ ♤ ⊗ **Facilities** 🚿 🛍 ⊙ 🖸 🖉 ⑭ **Services** 🍴 🍽 🖸 🖸 **Leisure** ⚓ PRS

CHIOGGIA SOTTOMARINA VENEZIA

Oasi
via A-Barbarigo 147, 30019 ☎ 041 5541145 📠 041 490801
e-mail info@campingoasi.com **website** www.campingoasi.com
A well-equipped site on a wooded peninsula near the mouth of the Brenta River with a wide private beach.
⤵ *W of town centre towards river & beach.*
Open 30 Mar-Sep **Site** 3HEC 😃 ♨ ♨ ☎ ♤ **Prices** ⚹ 4.50-7.20 pitch 8-16.30 **Facilities** 🚿 🛍 ⊙ 🖸 🖉 ⚏ ⑭ **Services** 🍴 🍽 🖸 **Leisure** ⚓ PRS
Off-site 🖸

CISANO VERONA

Cisano
via Peschiera, 37011 ☎ 045 6229098 📠 045 6229059
e-mail cisano@camping-cisano.it
website www.camping-cisano.it
Quiet, partly terraced site beside Lake Garda with good water sports and entertainment.
⤵ *Brenner-Verona motorway exit AFFI, site 4km.*
Open 29 Mar-3 Oct **Site** 14HEC 😃 ♨ ♨ ☎ ♤ **Facilities** 🚿 🛍 ⊙ 🖸 🖉 ⚏ ⑭ **Services** 🍴 🍽 🖸 🖸 **Leisure** ⚓ LP

San Vito
via Pralesi 3, 37010 ☎ 045 6229026 📠 045 6229059
e-mail cisano@camping-cisano.it **website** www.camping-cisano.it
A tranquil and shady site with many modern facilities.
⤵ *Off Brennero motorway, signed to S of Cisano.*
Open 29 Mar-4 Oct **Site** 5HEC 😃 ♨ ☎ ♤ ⊗ **Facilities** 🚿 🛍 ⊙ 🖸 🖉 ⚏ ⑭ **Services** 🍴 🍽 🖸 🖸 **Leisure** ⚓ LP

CORTINA D'AMPEZZO BELLUNO

Cortina
via Campo 2, 32043 ☎ 0436 867575 📠 0436 867917
e-mail campcortina@tin.it
This site lies among pine trees several hundred metres from the edge of town.
⤵ *Off Dolomite road towards Belluno, site 1km by small river.*
Open All year **Site** 4.6HEC 😃 ♨ ♨ **Prices** ⚹ 4.50-7.50 pitch 7-9 **Facilities** 🚿 🛍 ⊙ 🖸 🖉 ⚏ ⑭ **Services** 🍴 🍽 🖸 **Leisure** ⚓ PR

Dolomiti
via Campo di Sotto, 32043 ☎ 0436 2485 📠 0436 5403
e-mail campeggiodolomiti@tin.it
website www.campeggiodolomiti.it
The site is beautifully situated on grassland with pine trees in a hollow, not far from the Olympic ski jump.
⤵ *2.7km S of Cortina. Off Dolomite road towards Belluno, site 1.5km.*
Open Jun- 19 Sep **Site** 5.4HEC 😃 ♨ **Prices** ⚹ 4.50-7.50 pitch 7-9 **Facilities** 🚿 🛍 ⊙ 🖸 🖉 ⚏ ⑭ **Services** 🍴 🖸 **Leisure** ⚓ PR **Off-site** 🍽 ⚓L

Olympia
Fiames 1, 32043 ☎ 0436 5057 📠 0436 5057
e-mail info@campingolympiacortina.it
website www.campingolympiacortina.it
A very beautiful site set in the centre of the centre of the magnificent Dolomite landscape.
⤵ *N of town off SS51.*
Open 5 Dec-5 Nov **Site** 4HEC 😃 ♨ **Prices** ⚹ 4.50-7.50 pitch 7-9 **Facilities** 🚿 🛍 ⊙ 🖸 🖉 ⚏ ⑭ **Services** 🍴 🍽 🖸 🖸 **Leisure** ⚓ R
Off-site ⚓LP 🖸

Italy

Facilities 🛍 shop 🚿 shower ⊙ electric points for razors 🖸 electric points for caravans ⑭ parking by tents permitted 🅿 compulsory separate car park
Services 🍽 café/restaurant 🍴 bar 🖉 Camping Gaz International ⚏ gas other than Camping Gaz 🖸 first aid facilities 🖸 laundry
Leisure ⚓ swimming L-Lake P-Pool R-River S-Sea **Off-site** All facilities within 2km

LAGO DI GARDA è...
Consorzio di Promozione e Commercializzazione Turistica

www.lagodigarda-e.it • info@lagodigarda-e.it

CAMPING in LAZISE

Camping DU PARC Lazise - Lago di Garda

I-37017 LAZISE (VERONA)
Tel. 0039 045 7580127
Fax 0039 045 6470150
duparc@camping.it
www.campingduparc.com

Camping ★★★ Spiaggia D'Oro

I-37017 LAZISE (VERONA)
Tel. 0039 045 7580007
Fax 0039 045 7580611
info@campingspiaggiadoro.com
www.campingspiaggiadoro.com

Camping La Quercia ... mehr als ein Camping!

Loc. Bottona • I-37017 LAZISE (VERONA)
Tel. 0039 045 6470577
Fax 0039 045 6470243
laquercia@laquercia.it
www.laquercia.it

Camping Park Delle Rose ★★★

Loc. Vanon • I-37017 LAZISE (VERONA)
Tel. 0039 045 6471181
Fax 0039 045 7581356
info@campingparkdellerose.it
www.campingparkdellerose.it

Piani di Clodia ★★★★

Loc. Bagatta • I-37017 LAZISE (VERONA)
Tel. 0039 045 7590456
Fax 0039 045 7590939
info@pianidiclodia.it
www.pianidiclodia.it

CAMPING in PACENGO near LAZISE

Camping Lido ★★★ Pacengo Lago di Garda

I-37010 PACENGO DI LAZISE (VERONA)
Tel. 0039 045 7590030 - 045 7590611
Tel. and Fax in winter 0039 045 7580334
Fax 0039 045 7590611
info@campinglido.it
www.campinglido.it

Regione Veneto

★★★ Eurocamping Pacengo Lago di Garda

I-37010 PACENGO DI LAZISE (VERONA)
Via del Porto 13
Tel. and Fax 0039 045 7590012
info@eurocampingpacengo.it
www.eurocampingpacengo.it

Italy

LAZISE
LAKE GARDA

PACENGO - LAKE GARDA

Italy

Facilities 🏠 shop 🚿 shower ⊙ electric points for razors 🔌 electric points for caravans ⊛ parking by tents permitted Ⓟ compulsory separate car park
Services 🍽 café/restaurant 🍷 bar ⊘ Camping Gaz International ⛽ gas other than Camping Gaz ✚ first aid facilities 🧺 laundry
Leisure 🏊 swimming L-Lake P-Pool R-River S-Sea **Off-site** All facilities within 2km

Rocchetta

via Campo 1, 32043 ☎ 0436 5063 🖹 0436 5063
e-mail camping@sunrise.it
website www.campingrocchetta.it
Set in beautiful wooded surroundings.

➲ *S from Cortina via SS51.*

Open Jun-20 Sep & Dec-10 Apr **Site** 2.5HEC 🌺 🌿 **Prices** ♠ 4.50-8 pitch
7-9 **Facilities** ⋔ ⬚ ⊙ ⬛ ∅ ⬚ ℗ **Services** ⛽ 🍽 ⬛ **Leisure** ⬿ R
Off-site 🍽 ⬿L

DUINO-AURISINA TRIESTE

AT SISTIANA

Marepinetá

34019 ☎ 040 299264 🖹 040 299265
e-mail info@marepineta.com
website www.baiaholiday.com
A modern site in a pleasant wooded location near the harbour and
beach with a range of recreational facilities. Free bus service to the
beach.

➲ *A4 exit Duino, 1km on SS14.*

Open Apr-Oct **Site** 10.8HEC 🌺 🌿 🐝 🐟 **Prices** pitch 15.60-34.40 (incl 2
persons) 🚐 (static)210-531 **Facilities** ⋔ ⬚ ⊙ ⬛ ∅ ⬚ ℗ **Services** ⛽ 🍽
⬛ 🖨 **Leisure** ⬿ P **Off-site** ⬿S

ERACLEA MARE VENEZIA

Portofelice

viale dei Fiori 15, I-30010 ☎ 0421 66411 🖹 0421 66021
e-mail info@portofelice.it
website www.portofelice.it
A well-equipped family village site separated from the beach by a pine
wood. A variety of recreational facilities is available.

➲ *A4 exit Venice/Mestre, signs for Carole & Eraclea Mare.*

Open 5 May-16 Sep **Site** 17.5HEC 🌺 🌿 🐝 🐟 **Prices** ♠ 3.40-9.40 pitch
7.40-20.70 **Facilities** ⋔ ⬚ ⊙ ⬛ ∅ ⬚ ℗ ℗ **Services** ⛽ 🍽 ⬛ 🖨
Leisure ⬿ PS **Off-site** ⬿R

FUSINA VENEZIA VENEZIA

Fusina

via Moranzani 79, 30030 ☎ 041 5470055 🖹 041 5470050
e-mail info@camping-fusina.com
website www.camping-fusina.com
This well-equipped site is ideal for those visiting Venice and the
Lagoon.

Open All year **Site** 5.5HEC 🌺 🌿 🐝 🚐 🏕 **Prices** ♠ 8-9 🚗 5 🚐 9 🏕 9
Facilities ⋔ ⬚ ⊙ ⬛ ∅ ⬚ ℗ **Services** ⛽ 🍽 ⬛ 🖨 **Leisure** ⬿ S

GEMONA DEL FRIÚLI UDINE

Ai Pioppi

via del Bersaglio 118, 33013 ☎ 0432 980358 🖹 0432 980358
e-mail bar-camping-taxi@aipioppi.it
website www.aipioppi.it
Quiet, well-equipped site in a pleasant mountain setting.

➲ *1km from town centre via N13.*

Open 15 Mar-30 Oct **Site** 11HEC 🌺 🌿 🐝 🚐 **Prices** ♠ 4.50-5 **Facilities** ⋔
⊙ ⬛ ∅ ⬚ ℗ **Services** ⛽ 🍽 🖨 **Off-site** ⬚ ⬿PR ⬛

GRADO GORIZIA

Europa

34073 ☎ 0431 80877 🖹 0431 82284
e-mail info@villaggioeuropa.com
website www.villaggioeuropa.com
Level terrain under half-grown poplars, and partly in pine forest.

➲ *On road to Monfalcone, 20km from Palmanova via Aquileia.*

Open 28 Apr-22 Sep **Site** 22HEC 🌺 🌿 🐝 🐟 **Prices** ♠ 5.50-9.50 pitch 8-
18.50 🚐 (static)385-490 **Facilities** ⋔ ⬚ ⊙ ⬛ ∅ ⬚ **Services** ⛽ 🍽 ⬛ 🖨
Leisure ⬿ PS

Tenuta Primero

via Monfalcone 14, 34073 ☎ 0431 896900 🖹 0431 896901
e-mail info@tenutaprimero.com
website www.tenutaprimero.com
The site lies in extensive level grassland between the road and the
dam, which is 2m high along the narrow and level beach. Tennis
court.

➲ *Signed off Monfalcone road.*

Open May-18 Sep **Site** 20HEC 🌺 🌿 🐝 🐟 **Prices** ♠ 7-11 pitch 12-18
Facilities ⋔ ⬚ ⊙ ⬛ ∅ ⬚ ℗ **Services** ⛽ 🍽 ⬛ 🖨 **Leisure** ⬿ PS

JÉSOLO, LIDO DI VENEZIA

AT JÉSOLO PINETA (6KM E)

Malibu Beach

viale Oriente 78, 30017 ☎ 0421 362212 🖹 0421 961338
e-mail info@campingmalibubeach.com
website www.campingmalibubeach.com
Set in a pine wood facing the sea and a fine sandy beach.

➲ *From Venezia via Cavallino on coast road to Cortellazzo.*

Open 12 May-15 Sep **Site** 10HEC 🌺 🌿 🐝 🐟 **Prices** ♠ 4.55-7.45 🚗 2.70-
5.35 🏕 8-16 pitch 12.80-20.40 **Facilities** ⋔ ⬚ ⊙ ⬛ ∅ ⬚ **Services** ⛽ 🍽
⬛ 🖨 **Leisure** ⬿ PS

Waikiki

viale Oriente 144, 30017 ☎ 0421 980186 🖹 0421 378040
e-mail info@campingwaikiki.com
website www.campingwaikiki.com
A family site in a pine wood with direct access to the beach. Regular
bus service to Venice passes the site.

Open 12 May-15 Sep **Site** 5.2HEC 🌺 🌿 🐝 🐟 **Prices** ♠ 3.65-6.80 🏕 6.90-
14.55 pitch 10-18.40 **Facilities** ⋔ ⬚ ⊙ ⬛ ∅ ⬚ **Services** ⛽ 🍽 ⬛ 🖨
Leisure ⬿ PS **Off-site** ∅ ⬚ ⬿R

LAZISE VERONA

Parc

Loc Sentieri, 37017 ☎ 045 7580127 🖹 045 6470150
e-mail duparc@camping.it
website www.campingduparc.com
Well-kept, lakeside site off main road.

➲ *From Garda, site on S side of Lazise just after turning for
Verona.*

Open 15 Mar-30 Oct **Site** 6HEC 🌺 🌿 🐝 🚐 **Prices** ♠ 5.50-7.90 pitch
10.90-18 **Facilities** ⋔ ⬚ ⊙ ⬛ ⬚ **Services** ⛽ 🍽 ⬛ 🖨 **Leisure** ⬿ LP
Off-site ∅ ⬚

See advertisements on pages 262-263

Site 6HEC (site size) 🌺 grass 🌿 sand 🌺 stone 🌿 little shade 🌿 partly shaded 🌺 mainly shaded 🐝 bungalows for hire
🚐 caravans for hire 🏕 tents for hire 🐟 no dogs **Prices** ♠ adult per night 🚗 car per night pp per person per night 🚐 caravan per night
🏕 tent per night 🚐 (static)-caravan hire per week

Camping La Quercia

☎ 045 6470577 ▤ 045 6470243

e-mail laquercia@laquercia.it

website www.laquercia.it

The site is divided into many large sections by tarred drives and lies on terraced ground that slopes gently down to the lake. There is a large private beach.

➲ Off SS49 at Km31/8 & site 400m.

Open Apr-3 Oct **Site** 20HEC ⛺ ⛺ ⛟ **Facilities** ⋔ ⓐ ⊙ ⊕ ⊘ ⑦ **Services** ⛽ 🍽 ➕ �� **Leisure** ⚓ LP **Off-site** ⚒

See advertisement on page 266

LIGNANO SABBIADORO UDINE

Sabbiadoro

via Sabbiadoro 8, 33054 ☎ 0431 71455 ▤ 0431 721355

e-mail campsab@lignano.it

website www.campingsabbiadoro.it

A peaceful site in a pine grove close to the beach.

➲ Via A4 Venice-Trieste (exit Latisana) onto S354.

Open 31 Mar-Sep **Site** 13HEC ⛺ ⛺ ⛟ ⛭ Å **Prices** ⋔ 4.50-8.60 pitch 6.80-13.80 ⛭ (static)280-728 **Facilities** ⋔ ⓐ ⊙ ⊕ ⊘ ⚒ ⑦ **Services** ⛽ 🍽 ➕ 🔳 **Leisure** ⚓ P **Off-site** ⚓S

MALCESINE VERONA

Claudia

Gardesana 394, 37018 ☎ 045 7400786 ▤ 045 7400786

e-mail info@campingclaudia.it

website www.campingclaudia.it

Flat grassy site only 30m from the lake. Excellent facilities, especially for water sports.

➲ From Rome/Brennero motorway, continue via Trento, Arco & Torbole, site on outskirts of Malcesine.

Open Apr-20 Oct **Site** 1HEC ⛺ ⛺ **Prices** ⋔ 5-6.50 pitch 10-12 **Facilities** ⋔ ⓐ ⊙ ⊕ ⑦ **Services** ⛽ 🍽 🔳 **Off-site** 🍽 ⊘ ⚒ ⚓L

MALGA CIAPELA BELLUNO

Malga Ciapela Marmolada

32020 ☎ 0437 722064 ▤ 0437 722064

e-mail camping.mc.marmolada@dolomiti.com

A terraced site in tranquil wooded surroundings at the foot of Mt Marmolada.

➲ Brenner-Verona motorway exit Bozen, signs for Canazei, Malga Ciapela & site at Marmolada.

Open Jun-23 Sep, Dec-25 Apr **Site** 3HEC ⛺ ⛺ ⛟ **Prices** ⋔ 5.50-6.50 Å 5-5.50 pitch 6-7 **Facilities** ⋔ ⓐ ⊙ ⊕ ⊘ ⚒ ⑦ **Services** ⛽ 🔳 **Leisure** ⚓ R **Off-site** 🍽

MARGHERA VENEZIA

Jolly delle Querce

via A-de-Marchi 7, 30175 ☎ 041 920312 ▤ 041 920312

The site lies on meadowland scattered with poplars.

➲ Autostrada exit Venezia, SS309 for 200m towards Chioggia.

Open Apr-Oct **Site** 1.2HEC ⛺ ⛺ ⛟ ⛭ **Facilities** ⋔ ⓐ ⊙ ⊕ ⊘ ⚒ ⑦ **Services** ⛽ 🍽 ➕ 🔳 **Off-site** ⚓PRS

MASARÈ BELLUNO

Alleghe

32022 ☎ 0437 723737 ▤ 0437 723874

e-mail alleghecamp@dolomites.it

website www.camping.dolomites.com/alleghe

Several terraces on a wooded incline below a road.

Open 14 Jun-29 Sep, 6 Dec-Apr **Site** 2HEC ⛺ ⛺ ⛟ ⑦ **Prices** ⋔ 6.50-7 Å 4.50-5.50 pitch 7-8 **Facilities** ⋔ ⊙ ⊕ ⊘ ⚒ ⑦ **Services** ⛽ 🍽 🔳 **Off-site** ⓐ 🍽 ⚓LP

MONTEGROTTO TERME PADOVA

Sporting Center

35036 ☎ 049 793400 ▤ 049 8911551

e-mail sporting@sportingcenter.it

website www.sportingcenter.it

A peaceful site in a pleasant setting in the Euganean hills with good facilities including a thermal treatment centre.

Open Mar-12 Nov **Site** 6.5HEC ⛺ ⛺ ⛟ **Prices** ⋔ 5.50-7.50 ⛭ 11-15 Å 7.50-10.20 **Facilities** ⋔ ⊙ ⊕ ⑦ **Services** ⛽ 🍽 🔳 **Leisure** ⚓ P **Off-site** ⓐ ⊘

ORIAGO VENEZIA

Serenissima

via Padana 334, 30030 ☎ 041 920286 ▤ 041 920286

e-mail campingserenissima@shineline.it

website www.campingserenissima.com

A well-looked after site with shade provided by the local woodland. Local bus service every 20 minutes to Venice.

➲ A4 to Venice, SS11 at Oriago.

Open Etr-10 Nov **Site** 2HEC ⛺ ⛺ ⛟ ⛭ **Prices** ⋔ 6-7.50 Å 5 pitch 8-12 **Facilities** ⋔ ⓐ ⊙ ⊕ ⊘ ⑦ **Services** ⛽ 🍽 🔳 **Leisure** ⚓ R **Off-site** ➕

PACENGO VERONA

Camping Lido

via Peschiera 2, 37010 ☎ 045 7590611 ▤ 045 7590030

e-mail info@campinglido.it

website www.campinglido.it

Open Apr-Oct **Site** 10HEC ⛺ ⛺ ⛟ **Facilities** ⋔ ⓐ ⊙ ⊕ ⊘ ⑦ **Services** ⛽ 🍽 ➕ 🔳 **Leisure** ⚓ LP

PALAFAVERA BELLUNO

Palafavera

32010 ☎ 0437 788506 ▤ 0437 788857

e-mail palafavera@sunrise.it

website www.camping.dolomiti.com/palafavera

A beautiful location in the heart of the Dolomites at an altitude of 1514m. Modern sanitary installations and plenty of recreational facilities.

Open Jun-Sep **Site** 5HEC ⛺ ⛺ ⑦ **Facilities** ⋔ ⓐ ⊙ ⊕ ⊘ ⚒ ⑦ **Services** ⛽ 🍽 ➕ 🔳 **Leisure** ⚓ LPR **Off-site** ⚓P

PESCHIERA DEL GARDA VERONA

Bella Italia

via Bella Italia 2, 37019 ☎ 045 6400688 ▤ 045 6401410

e-mail bellaitalia@camping-bellaitalia.it

website www.camping-bellaitalia.it

Extensive lakeside site. No animals or motorcycles allowed.

➲ Off Brescia road between Km276.2 & Km275.8 towards lake.

Open 24 Mar-7 Oct **Site** 20HEC ⛺ ⛺ ⛟ ⛭ Å ⑦ **Prices** ⋔ 6-11.50 pitch 12-21 **Facilities** ⋔ ⓐ ⊙ ⊕ ⊘ ⑦ **Services** ⛽ 🍽 🔳 **Leisure** ⚓ P **Off-site** ⊘ ⚒ ⚓LR ➕

Facilities ⓐ shop ⋔ shower ⊙ electric points for razors ⊕ electric points for caravans ⑦ parking by tents permitted ⊕ compulsory separate car park
Services 🍽 café/restaurant ⛽ bar ⊘ Camping Gaz International ⚒ gas other than Camping Gaz ➕ first aid facilities 🔳 laundry
Leisure ⚓ swimming L-Lake P-Pool R-River S-Sea **Off-site** All facilities within 2km

The Camping **No. 1** of Lake Garda!

Sought-after relaxation in the nature

Enjoy a unique relax in the **Camping La Quercia**, in a clean and safe environment with an exceptional comfort. In the spirit of the true camping, we make people happy since 49 years.

If you wish a place where everything smiles on you, discover our hospitality in the midst of Nature.

Shadow for everybody, in a place of extraordinary beauty.

A very clean beach where one can play in all safety.

A lot of services for a vacation of true relax.

Try AquaFun, an exciting amusement.

Shady parking places – Warmed toilet services for both grownups and children – Warm water 24 hours out of 24 – Restaurant – Pizzeria – Cocktail Bar – Funny Bar on the beach – Swimming-pools and 'Maxicaravan'-slides with sight on the lake – Professional animateurs – Animation for both children and boys – Warmed underwater massage bath – Full-comfort bungalows for 4 and 5 people – The widest beach in the lake – Theatre – Supermarket – Butcher's shop – Pastry-shop and bakery – Typical products of the lake – Fresh fruits and vegetables all days – Tobacconist's shop – International news-stall – Rent-a-car service – Fax service Tennis – Canoes – Archery – Surfing – Judo – Football – Fitness hall – Fencing – Spinning – Horse-riding.

Reserve at once your relax vacation!
Call now!
++39.045.6470577

CAMPING ★★★★
LAQUERCIA
...more than a camping!

LAZISE SUL GARDA
VERONA - **ITALY**

Anniversario
1958-2008

Information
www.laquercia.it
laquercia@laquercia.it

Bergamini

via Bergamini 51, Porto Bergamini, 37010
☎ 045 7550283 ▤ 045 7550283
website www.campingbergamini.it
Ideal for young families as site has two children's pools and extensive play areas.

➲ Signs for Porto Bergamini.

Open May-20 Sep **Site** 1.4HEC ♨ ♣ ♠ ♣ **Prices** ⚑ 7-8.50 pitch 12-16 **Facilities** ⋔ ☖ ⊙ ♿ ⑫ **Services** ᵀ ⎮⚬⎮ ⊞ ☑ **Leisure** ⚲ LP **Off-site** ⌀ ♒

San Benedetto

via Bergamini 14, 37010 ☎ 045 7550544 ▤ 045 7551512
e-mail info@campingsanbenedetto.it
website www.campingsanbenedetto.it
A family site in a fine position overlooking the lake.

Open 24 Mar-Sep **Site** 22HEC ♨ ♠ ♣ **Prices** ⚑ 4-7.50 pitch 8-14 **Facilities** ⋔ ☖ ⊙ ♿ ⑫ **Services** ᵀ ⎮⚬⎮ ☑ **Leisure** ⚲ LP **Off-site** ⌀ ♒ ⚲R ⊞

PORTO SANTA MARGHERITA VENEZIA

Pra'delle Torri

Viale Altanea 201, 30021 ☎ 0421 299063 ▤ 0421 299035
e-mail torri@vacanze-natura.it
website www.pradelletorri.it
Extensive site on flat ground.

➲ 3km W by beach.

Open 8 Apr-Mar **Site** 120HEC ♨ ♣ ♠ ♣ Å ⚑ **Prices** ⚑ 3.76-8.60 pitch 4.90-22 **Facilities** ⋔ ☖ ⊙ ♿ ⌀ ♒ ⑫ **Services** ᵀ ⎮⚬⎮ ⊞ ☑ **Leisure** ⚲ PS

PUNTA SABBIONI VENEZIA

Marina di Venezia

via Montello 6, 30010 ☎ 041 5302511 ▤ 041 966036
e-mail camping@marinadivenezia.it
website www.marinadivenezia.it
Extensive, well-organised and well-maintained holiday centre, extremely well-appointed, with ample shade by trees. A section of the site is designated for dog owners, caravans and tents.

➲ Along coast road, 0.5km before end turn onto narrow asphalt road towards sea, signed.

Open 21 Apr-Sep **Site** 70HEC ♨ ♣ ♠ ♣ **Prices** ⚑ 4.05-8 pitch 10.20-19.50 **Facilities** ⋔ ☖ ⊙ ♿ ⑫ **Services** ᵀ ⎮⚬⎮ ⊞ ☑ **Leisure** ⚲ PS

Miramare

Lungomare D-Alighieri 29, 30010 ☎ 041 966150 ▤ 041 5301150
e-mail info@camping-miramare.it
website www.camping-miramare.it
A magnificent location overlooking the lagoon.

Open Apr-Nov **Site** 1.8HEC ♨ ♣ ♠ ⑫ **Facilities** ⋔ ☖ ⊙ ♿ ⌀ ⑫ **Services** ᵀ ⎮⚬⎮ ⊞ ☑ **Off-site** ⚲S

ROSOLINA MARE ROVIGO

Margherita

via Foci Adige 10, 45010 ☎ 0426 68212 ▤ 0426 329016
e-mail lamargherita@lamargherita.it
website www.lamargherita.it
A well-equipped family site situated between the sea and a pine wood in the Po Delta Park.

Open May-25 Sep **Site** 6.4HEC ♨ ♣ ♠ ♣ **Facilities** ⋔ ☖ ⊙ ♿ ⌀ ⑫ **Services** ᵀ ⎮⚬⎮ ⊞ ☑ **Leisure** ⚲ PRS

Rosapineta

Strada Nord 24, 45010 ☎ 0426 68033 ▤ 0426 68105
e-mail info@rosapineta.it
website www.rosapineta.com
The site lies in the grounds of an extensive holiday camp. Pitches for caravans and tents are separate.

➲ Strada Romea towards Ravenna & over River Adige, 0.8km turn off, over bridge towards Rosolina Mare & Rosapineta (8km).

Open 11 May-15 Sep **Site** 47HEC ♨ ♣ ♠ ♣ **Prices** ⚑ 4-6.30 ♣ 7.40-10.70 Å 4.90-7.30 ♣ (static)143.50-385 **Facilities** ⋔ ☖ ⊙ ♿ ⌀ ♒ ⑫ **Services** ᵀ ⎮⚬⎮ ☑ **Leisure** ⚲ PS **Off-site** ⚲R

TREPORTI VENEZIA

Ca' Pasquali Village

via Poerio 33, 30010 ☎ 041 966110 ▤ 041 5300797
e-mail info@capasquali.it
website www.capasquali.it
Sandy, meadowland site with poplar and pine trees.

➲ Off Cavallino-Punta Sabbioni coast road onto asphalt road for 400m.

Open 28 Apr-22 Sep **Site** 9HEC ⚇ ♣ ♠ ⑫ **Prices** ⚑ 4.20-8.50 Å 3-8 pitch 7.20-22.50 **Facilities** ⋔ ☖ ⊙ ♿ ⑫ **Services** ᵀ ⎮⚬⎮ ⊞ ☑ **Leisure** ⚲ PS **Off-site** ⌀ ♒

Cá Savio

via di Ca'Savio 77, 30010 ☎ 041 966017 ▤ 041 5300707
e-mail info@casavio.it
website casavio.it
A level site along the edge of the sea with private, sandy beach. Separate pitches for caravans and tents.

➲ From Cá Savio turn at lights towards sea, 0.5km to beach.

Open May-Sep **Site** 26.8HEC ⚇ ♣ ♠ ♣ ⑫ **Prices** ⚑ 4.50-8.50 pitch 9-19 **Facilities** ⋔ ☖ ⊙ ♿ ⑫ **Services** ᵀ ⎮⚬⎮ ⊞ **Leisure** ⚲ PS **Off-site** ⌀

Fiori

via Vettor Pisani 52, Località Cà vio, 30010
☎ 041 966448 ▤ 041 966724
e-mail fiori@vacanze-natura.it
website www.deifiori.it
The site stretches over a wide area of dunes and pine trees with separate sections for caravans and tents.

➲ A4 from Venice onto coast road via Jesolo to Lido del Cavallino.

Open 21 Apr-3 Sep **Site** 11HEC ⚇ ♣ ♠ ♣ ⑫ **Prices** ⚑ 4.40-8.80 Å 6.80-17.50 pitch 8.30-21.70 **Facilities** ⋔ ☖ ⊙ ♿ ⑫ **Services** ᵀ ⎮⚬⎮ ⊞ ☑ **Leisure** ⚲ PS **Off-site** ⌀

Mediterráneo

via delle Batterie 38, Ca'Vio, 30010 ☎ 041 966721 ▤ 041 966944
e-mail mediterraneo@vacanze-natura.it
website campingmediterraneo.it
Slightly hilly grassland site with trees and sunshade roofs.

➲ Signed from Jesolo.

Open May-22 Sep **Site** 17HEC ♨ ♣ ♠ ♣ ⑫ **Prices** ⚑ 4-8.50 pitch 6.80-21.30 **Facilities** ⋔ ☖ ⊙ ♿ ⑫ **Services** ᵀ ⎮⚬⎮ ⊞ ☑ **Leisure** ⚲ PS **Off-site** ⌀ ♒ ⚲R

Italy

Facilities ☖ shop ⋔ shower ⊙ electric points for razors ♿ electric points for caravans ⑫ parking by tents permitted ⑫ compulsory separate car park
Services ⎮⚬⎮ café/restaurant ᵀ bar ⌀ Camping Gaz International ♒ gas other than Camping Gaz ⊞ first aid facilities ☑ laundry
Leisure ⚲ swimming L-Lake P-Pool R-River S-Sea **Off-site** All facilities within 2km

VICENZA VICENZA

Vicenza
Strada Pelosa 239, 36100 ☎ 0444 582311 ▤ 0444 582434
e-mail camping@viest.it
A modern, well-equipped site.
➲ *A4 exit Vicenza-Est.*
Open Apr-Sep **Site** 3HEC 🌿 🏖 🏕 🚐 **Prices** ⚬ 5.60-7.40 🚗 5.50-7.20
🚐 11.30-14.70 ⚬ 5.70-7.40 **Facilities** ⬦ ⊙ 🚻 ⑫ **Services** 🍴 🍽 🗑
Off-site 🚿 🍽 ⌀ 🚿R

ZOLDO ALTO BELLUNO

Pala Favera
32010 ☎ 0437 788506 ▤ 0437 788857
e-mail palafavera@sunrise.it
website www.campingpalafavera.com
Site with some woodland, at the foot of Monte Pelmo.
Open Dec-Apr, Jun-Sep **Site** 5HEC 🌿 🏖 🏕 **Prices** ⚬ 4.80-6.70 ⚬ 4-5
pitch 5.80-8.20 **Facilities** ⬦ 🚿 ⊙ 🚻 ⌀ 🛁 ⑫ **Services** 🍴 🍽 🗑
Leisure 🚿 R **Off-site** 🚿P ➕

NORTH WEST/MED COAST

ALBENGA SAVONA

Bella Vista
Campochiesa, Reg Campore 23, 17031
☎ 0182 540213 ▤ 0182 554925
e-mail info@campingbellavista.it
website www.campingbellavista.it
A friendly, family orientated site with good facilities. Pitches are divided by bushes and flowerbeds.
➲ *1km from Km613.5 on SS1.*
Open All year **Site** 1.4HEC 🌿 🏖 🏕 🚐 **Facilities** ⬦ 🚿 ⊙ 🚻 **Services** 🍴
➕ 🗑 **Leisure** 🚿 P **Off-site** 🍽 🚿S

Roma
Regione Foce, 17031 ☎ 0182 52317 ▤ 0182 555075
e-mail info@campingroma.com
website www.campingroma.com
The site is divided into pitches and laid out with many flower beds.
➲ *N of bridge over Centa, turn left.*
Open Apr-29 Sep **Site** 1HEC 🌿 🏖 🏕 🏕 🚐 **Facilities** ⬦ 🚿 ⊙ 🚻 ⑫
Services 🍴 🍽 🗑 **Leisure** 🚿 RS **Off-site** ⌀ 🛁 🚿P ➕

ALBINIA GROSSETO

Acapulco
via Aurelia Km155, 58010 ☎ 0564 870165 ▤ 0564 870165
e-mail campeggioacapulco@virgilio.it
website campeggioacapulco.interfree.it
Set on hilly terrain in pine woodland.
➲ *Off via Aurelia at Km155 onto coast road.*
Open May-14 Sep **Site** 2HEC 🏖 🏕 🚐 ⊗ **Prices** ⚬ 5-9.50 pitch 6.50-
12.50 🚐 (static)175-525 **Facilities** ⬦ 🚿 ⊙ 🚻 ⌀ 🛁 🅿 **Services** 🍴 🍽 ➕
🗑 **Leisure** 🚿 S

Hawaii
58010 ☎ 0564 870164 ▤ 0564 872952
e-mail hawaiigr@libero.it
website www.campinghawaii.it
The site lies in a pine forest on rather hilly ground.
➲ *Off via Aurelia at Km154/V towards sea.*
Open 16 Apr-27 Sep **Site** 4HEC 🌿 🏖 🏕 🚐 ⊗ **Facilities** ⬦ 🚿 ⊙ 🚻 ⌀ 🅿
Services 🍴 🍽 ➕ 🗑 **Leisure** 🚿 S

BARBERINO VAL D'ELSA FIRENZE

Semifonte
50021 ☎ 055 8075454 ▤ 055 8075454
e-mail semifonte@semifonte.it
website www.semifonte.it
Terraced site with pitches of various sizes.
Open 15 Mar-30 Oct **Site** 1.7HEC 🌿 🏕 🚐 **Facilities** ⬦ 🚻 **Services** 🗑
Leisure 🚿 P **Off-site** 🚿 🍽

BIBBONA, MARINA DI LIVORNO

Capanne
via Aurelia KM.273, 57020 ☎ 0586 600064 ▤ 0586 600198
e-mail info@campinglecapanne.it
website www.campinglecapanne.it
A pleasant family site set in a spacious wooded park in magnificent Tuscan scenery. Defined pitches and a variety of recreational facilities.
➲ *Access from Km273 via Aurelia travelling inland.*
Open 14 Apr-Sep **Site** 6HEC 🌿 🏖 🏕 🚐 **Facilities** ⬦ 🚿 ⊙ 🚻 ⌀ 🛁 ⑫
Services 🍴 🍽 ➕ 🗑 **Leisure** 🚿 P **Off-site** 🚿S

Capannino
via Cavalleggeri Sud 26, 57020 ☎ 0586 600252 ▤ 0586 600720
e-mail capannino@capannino.it
website www.capannino.it
Well-tended park site in pine woodland with private beach.
➲ *Off via Aurelia at Km272/VII towards sea.*
Open Apr-Sep **Site** 3HEC 🌿 🏖 🏕 🚐 ⊗ **Facilities** ⬦ 🚿 ⊙ 🚻 ⌀ 🛁 ⑫
Services 🍴 🍽 ➕ 🗑 **Leisure** 🚿 S

Casa di Caccia
via del Mare 40, Marina di Bibbona, 57020
☎ 0586 600000 ▤ 0586 600000
e-mail info@campingcasadicaccia.com
website www.campingcasadicaccia.com
A tranquil site by the sea direct access to a private beach.
➲ *A12 exit Rosignano for Cecina, 6km exit La California, site 3km S.*
Open 15 Mar-30 Oct **Site** 3.5HEC 🏖 🏕 🚐 ⊗ **Prices** ⚬ 4.20-9.50
🚗 3.20-5 🚐 6.90-11.50 ⚬ 6.90-11.50 🚐 (static)217-525 **Facilities** ⬦ 🚿 ⊙
🚻 ⌀ 🛁 ⑫ **Services** 🍴 🍽 ➕ 🗑 **Leisure** 🚿 S

Forte
via dei Platani 58, 57020 ☎ 0586 600155 ▤ 0586 600123
e-mail campeggiodelforte@campeggiodelforte.it
website www.campeggiodelforte.it
Level site, grassy, sandy terrain.
Open 15 Apr-17 Sep **Site** 8HEC 🌿 🏖 🏕 ⊗ **Facilities** ⬦ 🚿 ⊙ 🚻 ⌀ 🛁 ⑫
Services 🍴 🍽 ➕ 🗑 **Leisure** 🚿 P **Off-site** 🚿S

Site 6HEC (site size) 🌿 grass 🏖 sand 🏕 stone 🌳 little shade 🌲 partly shaded 🌴 mainly shaded 🏠 bungalows for hire
🚐 caravans for hire ⚬ tents for hire ⊗ no dogs **Prices** ⚬ adult per night 🚗 car per night pp per person per night 🚐 caravan per night
⚬ tent per night 🚐 (static)-caravan hire per week

Free Beach

via Cavalleggeri Nord 88, 57020 ☎ 0586 600388 ▤ 0586 602984
e-mail info@campingfreebeach.it
website www.campingfreebeach.it
Situated 300m from the sea through pine woods.

➲ *From SS206 at Cecina signs to S Guido.*

Open 5 Apr-Sep **Site** 9HEC ❤ ➳ ⚘ ⇔ **Prices** ♠ 10 ▲ 9 pitch 13
Facilities ⋔ 🖻 ⊙ ⊕ ⊘ ⇔ **Services** ☝ ⟆ **Leisure** ⬳ P
Off-site ⬳S

Il Gineprino

via dei Platani 56a, 57020 ☎ 0586 600550 ▤ 0586 636866
e-mail ilgineprino@tiscalinet.it
website www.ilgineprino.it
A modern site situated on the Tuscany coast and shaded by a pine
wood. There are good recreational facilities and the beach is within
300m.

➲ *Motorway exit La California for Marina di Bibbona.*

Open Apr-Sep **Site** 1.5HEC ❤ ➳ ⚘ ⇔ **Facilities** ⋔ 🖻 ⊙ ⊕ ⇔ ⊘ ⊕
Services ☝ ⟆ ⟆ **Leisure** ⬳ P **Off-site** ⊘ ⬳S ⊞

BOGLIASCO GENOVA

Genova Est

via Marconi, Cassa, 16031 ☎ 010 3472053 ▤ 010 3472053
e-mail info@camping-genova-est.it
website www.camping-genova-est.it
Quiet and shady site 1km from the sea. A free bus service operates
from the site to the railway station for links to Genoa and Portofino.

➲ *A12 exit Nervi, 8km E.*

Open 10 Mar-30 Oct **Site** 1.2HEC ❤ ➳ ⚘ ⇔ **Prices** ♠ 5.30-5.60 ⇔ 3
⇔ 5.70-6 ▲ 4.80-7.40 ⇔ (static)210 **Facilities** ⋔ 🖻 ⊙ ⊕ ⇔ ⊘ **Services** ☝
⟆ ⟆ **Off-site** ⬱ ⬳PS ⊞

BOTTAI FIRENZE

Internationale Firenze

via S Cristoforo 2, 50029 ☎ 055 2374704 ▤ 055 2373412
e-mail internazionale@florencecamping.it
website www.florencecamping.com
Situated on the Florentine hills, the site offers a restful atmosphere
close to many historic places.

Open Apr-29 Oct **Site** 6HEC ❤ ⬳ ➳ ⚘ ⇔ **Prices** ♠ 9.50 pitch 15-16
⇔ (static)50 **Facilities** ⋔ 🖻 ⊙ ⊕ ⇔ ⊘ ⊕ **Services** ☝ ⟆ **Leisure** ⬳ P
Off-site ⬱ ⬳LR ⊞

CALENZANO FIRENZE

Autosole

via V-Emanuele 11, 50041 ☎ 055 8827819 ▤ 055 8827819

➲ *A1 exit Calenzano-Sesto Fiorentino, left at lights, 200m on left.*

Open All year **Site** 2.2HEC ❤ ⬳ ⚘ **Facilities** ⋔ ⊙ ⇔ ⊕ **Services** ⟆
Leisure ⬳ P **Off-site** 🖻 ☝ ⟆ ⬱

CAPALBIO GROSSETO

Costa d'Argento

Monte Alzato, 58010 ☎ 0564 893007 ▤ 0564 893107
e-mail info@costadargento.it
website www.costadargento.it
A camping village in the middle of a nature reserve, 1km from the
Maremma coast.

➲ *12km from Orbetello via SS Aurelia.*

Open Apr-Sep **Site** 6HEC ❤ ➳ ⚘ ⇔ **Facilities** ⋔ 🖻 ⊙ ⊕ ⊘ ⊕
Services ☝ ⟆ ⟆ **Leisure** ⬳ P **Off-site** ⬳S

CAPANNOLE AREZZO

Chiocciola

via G-Cesare 14, 52020 ☎ 055 995776 ▤ 055 995776
e-mail tourcountry@virgilio.it
website www.campinglachiocciola.com
A modern site in a rural setting among chestnut trees at an altitude of
250m.

Open Mar-1 Nov **Site** 3HEC ⬳ ➳ ⚘ ▲ **Prices** ♠ 8-10 ⇔ 3-4 ⇔ 10-12
▲ 9-11 ⇔ (static)400-560 **Facilities** ⋔ 🖻 ⊙ ⊕ ⊘ ⇔ **Services** ☝ ⟆
⊞ ⟆ **Leisure** ⬳ P **Off-site** ⬳LR

CASALE MARITTIMO PISA

Valle Gaia

56040 ☎ 0586 681236 ▤ 0586 683551
e-mail info@vallegaia.it
website www.vallegaia.it
Site among pines and olive trees in a quiet rural location.

➲ *Autostrada/superstrada exit Casale Marittimo for Cecina, site
signed.*

Open 31 Mar-14 Oct **Site** 4HEC ⬳ ➳ ⚘ **Prices** ♠ 4.40-7.60 pitch
8.10-13.70 **Facilities** ⋔ 🖻 ⊙ ⊕ ⊘ ⊕ **Services** ☝ ⟆ ⊞ ⟆ **Leisure** ⬳ P

CASTAGNETO CARDUCCI LIVORNO

Climatico Le Pianacce

via Bolgherese, 57022 ☎ 0565 763667 ▤ 0565 766085
e-mail info@campinglepiancce.it
website www.campinglepianacce.it
Terraced site on slopes of mountain in typical Tuscany landscape,
enhanced by site landscaping. Pleasant climate due to height.

➲ *Off via Aurelia at Km344/VIII towards Castagneto
Carducci/Sassetta, 3.2km left for Bolgheri, 0.5km right towards
mountains.*

Open 20 Apr-23 Sep **Site** 9HEC ⬳ ➳ ⚘ ⊗ **Prices** ♠ 4.80-8.60 pitch
8.20-14 **Facilities** ⋔ 🖻 ⊙ ⊕ ⊘ ⬱ ⊕ **Services** ☝ ⟆ ⊞ ⟆ **Leisure** ⬳ PS

CASTEL DEL PIANO GROSSETO

Amiata

via Roma 15, 58033 ☎ 0564 955107 ▤ 0564 955107
e-mail info@amiata.org
website www.amiata.org
A grassland site with a separate section for dog owners.

➲ *On outskirts of Castel del Piano, on SS323 towards Arcidosso.*

Open All year **Site** 4.2HEC ⬳ ➳ ⚘ **Prices** ♠ 5.10-6.40 pitch 5.10-6.40
Facilities ⋔ 🖻 ⊙ ⊕ ⊕ **Services** ☝ ⟆ ⊞ ⟆ **Off-site** ⊘ ⬱ ⬳P ⊞

CASTIGLIONE DELLA PESCAIA GROSSETO

Santa Pomata

Strada della Rocchette, 58043 ☎ 0564 941037 ▤ 0564 941221
e-mail info@campingsantapomata.it
website www.campingsantapomata.it
Site in hilly woodland terrain with some pitches among bushes. Flat
clean sandy beach.

➲ *Off SS322 at Km20 towards Le Rocchette 4.5km NW,
continue to sea, site 1km on left.*

Open Apr-20 Oct **Site** 6HEC ❤ ➳ ⚘ ⇔ **Facilities** ⋔ 🖻 ⊙ ⊕ ⊘ ⬱ ⊕
Services ☝ ⟆ ⊞ ⟆ **Leisure** ⬳ S

Italy

Facilities 🖻 shop ⋔ shower ⊙ electric points for razors ⇔ electric points for caravans ⊕ parking by tents permitted ⊕ compulsory separate car park
Services ⟆ café/restaurant ☝ bar ⊘ Camping Gaz International ⬱ gas other than Camping Gaz ⊞ first aid facilities ⟆ laundry
Leisure ⬳ swimming L-Lake P-Pool R-River S-Sea **Off-site** All facilities within 2km

CERIALE SAVONA

Baciccia

via Torino 19, 17023 ☎ 0182 990743 ▤ 0182 993839
e-mail info@campingbaciccia.it
website www.campingbaciccia.it
An orderly site, lying inland off the via Aurelia, 0.5km from the sea.

➲ *Entrance 100m W of Km612/V.*

Open All year **Site** 1.2HEC ⚌ ⚌ ⚌ ㊉ Å **Prices** ♠ 5-9 pitch 9-19
⚌ (static)245-686 **Facilities** ℿ ▣ ⊙ ㊉ ⊘ ⊛ **Services** ☎ ☏ ▣
Leisure ⚘ P **Off-site** ≛ ⚘S ➕

CERVO IMPERIA

Lino

via N Sauro 4, 18010 ☎ 0183 400087 ▤ 0183 400089
e-mail info@campinglino.it
website www.campinglino.it
A clean, well-managed seaside site shaded by grape vines. There is a knee-deep lagoon suitable for children.

➲ *Off via Aurelia at Km637/V near railway underpass onto via Nazionale Sauro towards sea.*

Open Apr-21 Oct **Site** 1.1HEC ⚌ ⚌ ㊉ **Prices** pitch 20-43 (incl 2 persons)
Facilities ℿ ▣ ⊙ ㊉ ⊛ **Services** ☎ ☏ ➕ ▣ **Off-site** ⊘ ≛ ⚘PS

CUTIGLIANO PISTOIA

Betulle

via Cantamaggio 6, 51024 ☎ 0573 68004
e-mail info@campeggiolebetulle.it
website www.campeggiolebetulle.it
A pleasant year-round site with good facilities in a central location with access to three popular ski stations.

Open All year **Site** 4HEC ⚌ ⚌ ㊉ **Prices** ♠ 5.50 ⚌ 1.50 ⚌ 6.50 Å 5.50
Facilities ℿ ▣ ⊙ ㊉ ⊛ **Services** ☎ ☏ ▣ **Leisure** ⚘ LR

DEIVA MARINA LA SPEZIA

La Sfinge

Gea 5, 19013 ☎ 0187 825464 ▤ 0187 825464
e-mail lasfinge@camping.it
website www.campinglasfinge.com
Partly terraced site in pleasant wooded surroundings. Ideal for both nature lovers and families.

➲ *Via A12 Genova-La Spezia.*

Open All year **Site** 1.8HEC ⚌ ⚌ ㊉ Å **Prices** ♠ 6-7 ⚌ 3-3.50 ⚌ 9-14
Å 6-14 **Facilities** ℿ ▣ ⊙ ㊉ ⊘ ≛ ⊛ **Services** ☎ ☏ ➕ ▣
Leisure ⚘ RS **Off-site** ☏

Villaggio Turistico Arenella

Arenella, 19013 ☎ 0187 825259 ▤ 0187 815861 / 826884
e-mail info@campingarenella.it
website www.campingarenella.it
Set in a beautiful quiet valley 1.5km from the sea with good facilities.

➲ *Via A12 Genoa-La Spezia.*

Open Dec-Oct **Site** 16.2HEC ⚌ ⚌ ⚌ ㊉ **Prices** ♠ 7-8.50 ⚌ 2 ⚌ 7-8.50
Å 6-7.50 **Facilities** ℿ ▣ ⊙ ㊉ ☻ **Services** ☎ ☏ ▣ **Off-site** ☎ ☏ ☻
≛ ⚘S ➕

See advertisement on this page

DONORATICO LIVORNO

Continental

Casella postale n.5, Marina di Castagneto
☎ 0565 744014 ▤ 0565 744014
e-mail info@campingcontinental.it
website www.campingcontinental.it
Situated directly on a blue flag beach within an ancient pine forest.

Open Apr-Sep **Site** 6.5HEC ⚌ ⚌ **Prices** ♠ 5-8.50 pitch 7.50-14
Facilities ▣ ⊙ ㊉ ≛ ⊛ **Services** ☎ ☏ ➕ **Leisure** ⚘ S

LACONA

Lacona Pineta

Lacona CP 186, 57037 ☎ 0565 964322 ▤ 0565 964087
e-mail info@campinglaconapineta.com
website www.campinglaconapineta.com
A picturesque location on a thickly wooded hillside sloping gently towards a sandy beach, with plenty of recreational facilities.

Open Apr-Oct **Site** 4HEC ⚌ ⚌ ㊉ **Facilities** ℿ ▣ ⊙ ㊉ ⊘ ⊛ **Services** ☎
☏ ➕ ▣ **Leisure** ⚘ S **Off-site** ⊘

NISPORTO

Sole e Mare

57039 ☎ 0565 934907 ▤ 0565 961180
e-mail info@soleemare.it
website www.soleemare.it
A well-equipped, modern site in pleasant wooded surroundings close to the beach. A variety of recreational facilities is available.

➲ *From Portoferraio towards Porto Azzurro, turn towards Rio nell'Elba-Nisporto.*

Open Apr-15 Oct **Site** 2HEC ⚌ ⚌ ㊉ ⚌ **Prices** ♠ 5-13 ⚌ 7-23 Å 5-23
⚌ (static)170-720 **Facilities** ℿ ▣ ⊙ ㊉ ⊘ ≛ ⊛ **Services** ☎ ☏ ➕ ▣
Leisure ⚘ S

Site 6HEC (site size) ⚌ grass ⚌ sand ⚌ stone ⚌ little shade ⚌ partly shaded ⚌ mainly shaded ㊉ bungalows for hire
⚌ caravans for hire Å tents for hire ⊗ no dogs **Prices** ♠ adult per night ⚌ car per night pp per person per night ⚌ caravan per night
Å tent per night ⚌ (static)-caravan hire per week

ORTANO

Canapai
Loc Ortano, 57038 ☎ 0565 939165
Camping Card Compulsory.

Open Apr-Sep **Site** 4HEC ♨ ♠ ● ♠ **Facilities** ↑ 🖾 ⊙ ♀ ⌀ ♨ **Services** 🍴 🍽 🚻 **Leisure** ♠ P **Off-site** ♠ S

OTTONE

Rosselba le Palme
Ottone 3, 57037 ☎ 0565 933101 🖹 0565 933041
e-mail info@rosselbalepalme.it
website www.rosselbalepalme.it

Pitches are on varying heights up from the beach. Shade is provided by large palm trees.

➲ *8km from Portferraio around bay via Bivo Bagnaia.*

Open 25 Apr-Sep **Site** 30HEC ♨ ♠ ● ♠ **Prices** ↟ 6-13 ♠ 2-4.70 ♠ 9-17.50 ▲ 5-12.60 **Facilities** ↑ 🖾 ⊙ ♀ ⌀ **Services** 🍴 🍽 🚻 🗲 **Leisure** ♠ PS

PORTO AZZURRO

Reale
57036 ☎ 0565 95678 🖹 0565 920127
e-mail campingreale@tin.it
website www.isolaelbacampingreale.com

A well-equipped site in a wooded location with direct access to the beach.

➲ *From Portoferraio towards Porto Azzurro for 13km, towards Rio Marina for 2km & signed.*

Open Apr-5 Oct **Site** 2.5HEC ♨ ♠ ● ♠ **Facilities** ↑ 🖾 ⊙ ♀ ♨ **Services** 🍴 🍽 🚻 **Leisure** ♠ S **Off-site** ♠ P 🗲

PORTOFERRAIO

Acquaviva
Acquaviva, 57037 ☎ 0565 919103 🖹 0565 915592
e-mail campingacquaviva@elbalink.it
website www.campingacquaviva.it

This seafront site is surrounded by trees and has excellent facilities for scuba diving and water sports.

➲ *3km W of town.*

Open Etr-Oct **Site** 1.7HEC ♨ ♠ ● ♠ ♠ **Facilities** ↑ 🖾 ⊙ ♀ ⌀ ♨ ℗ ℗ **Services** 🍴 🍽 🚻 **Leisure** ♠ S

Enfola
Enfola, Casella Postale 147, 57037 ☎ 0565 939001 🖹 0565 918613
e-mail info@campingenfola.it
website www.campingenfola.it

Located on the Isle of Elba, ideal for scuba-diving, sailing and sunshine.

Open Etr-Oct **Site** 0.8HEC ♨ ♠ ● ♠ ♠ **Facilities** ↑ 🖾 ⊙ ♀ ♨ ℗ **Services** 🍴 🍽 🚻 **Off-site** ♠ S

Scaglieri
via Biodola 1, 57037 ☎ 0565 969940 🖹 0565 969834
e-mail info@campingscaglieri.it
website www.campingscaglieri.it

Sloping terraces 10m from the sea make up this site. Facilities such as tennis and golf are avaliable at the nearby Hotel Hermitage.

➲ *Island accessible by plane & ferry. Site on N coast 7km from Portoferraio.*

Open 12 Apr-17Oct **Site** 1.7HEC ♨ ♠ ● ♠ **Prices** ↟ 7-13.50 ♠ 2.50-4.50 ♠ 11-18.50 ▲ 10-18 **Facilities** ↑ 🖾 ⊙ ♀ ⌀ ♨ **Services** 🍴 🍽 🚻 **Leisure** ♠ P **Off-site** ♠ S

FIÉSOLE FIRENZE

Panoramico
via Peramonda 1, 50014 ☎ 055 599069 🖹 055 59186
e-mail panoramico@florencecamping.com
website www.florencecamping.com

Site stretches over wide terraces on the Fiesole hillside surrounded by tall evergreens.

➲ *A1 exit Firenze Sud, signs through city to Fiesole, site on SS Bolognese.*

Open All year **Site** 5HEC ♨ ♠ ● ♠ ♠ **Prices** ↟ 10-10.50 pitch 15-15.75 **Facilities** ↑ 🖾 ⊙ ♀ ⌀ ℗ **Services** 🍴 🍽 🚻 **Leisure** ♠ P **Off-site** ♨

FIGLINE VALDARNO FIRENZE

Norcenni Girasole
via Norcenni 7, 50063 ☎ 055 915141 🖹 055 9151402
e-mail girasole@ecvacanze.it
website www.ecvacanze.it

Terraced site on partial slope. Separate section for young people.

➲ *A1 exit onto road 69 for Figline, right for Greve & signed.*

Open 24 Mar-29 Oct **Site** 15HEC ♨ ♠ ● ♠ ▲ **Prices** ↟ 7-11 ♠ 4-6.10 ▲ 5.90-8.80 pitch 10.30-15.20 **Facilities** ↑ 🖾 ⊙ ♀ ⌀ ♨ ℗ **Services** 🍴 🍽 🚻 🗲 **Leisure** ♠ PR

FIRENZE (FLORENCE) FIRENZESEE ALSO TROGHI

Semifonte
via Ugo Foscolo 4, Barberino Val d'Elsa, 50021
☎ 055 8075454 🖹 055 8075454
e-mail semifonte@semifonte.it
website www.semifonte.it

A peaceful, terraced site offering panoramic views over the Chianti Hills. Regular bus services to Firenze and Siena.

➲ *25km S of Firenze & N of Barberino Val d'Elsa.*

Open 15 Mar-20 Oct **Site** 1.6HEC ♨ ♠ **Facilities** ↑ 🖾 ⊙ ♀ ⌀ ♨ ℗ **Services** 🚻 **Leisure** ♠ P **Off-site** 🍴 🍽 🗲

AT MARCIALLA

Toscana Colliverdi
via Marcialla 349, Certaldo, 50020
☎ 0571 669334 🖹 0571 669334
e-mail toscolverdi@virgilio.it

A sloping, terraced site with good facilities, surrounded by vineyards and olive groves.

➲ *Autostrada del Sole exit Firenze-Certosa. Or Autostrada del Palio exit Tavarnelle Valpesa.*

Open Apr-Sep **Site** 2.2HEC ♨ ♠ **Facilities** ↑ 🖾 ⊙ ♀ ⌀ ℗ **Services** 🍴 🍽 🚻 🗲 **Leisure** ♠ P **Off-site** 🖾 🍴 🍽

Facilities 🖾 shop ↑ shower ⊙ electric points for razors ♀ electric points for caravans ℗ parking by tents permitted ℗ compulsory separate car park
Services 🍽 café/restaurant 🗲 bar ⌀ Camping Gaz International ♨ gas other than Camping Gaz 🚻 first aid facilities 🍴 laundry
Leisure ♠ swimming L-Lake P-Pool R-River S-Sea **Off-site** All facilities within 2km

GROSSETO, MARINA DI GROSSETO

La Marze

St Statale della Collacchie ☎ 0564 35501 🗎 0564 35534
e-mail lemarze@ecvanze.it
website www.ecvacanze.it

➲ *Via SS322.*

Open 15 Apr-14 Oct **Site** 20HEC 🌿 ⬤ ⬤ ♨ **Ⓐ Facilities** ⌂ 🏪 ⊙ ⊕ ∅ ⊘
⬤ **Ⓟ Services** ⏏ 🍴 ⊞ ⬚ **Leisure** ⬤ PS

Rosmarina

via delle Colonie 37, 58046 ☎ 0564 36319 🗎 0564 34758
e-mail info@campingrosmarina.it
website www.campingrosmarina.it

A modern site in a pine wood close to the sea. Beautiful views, and various sports and entertainments for everyone.

Open May-Sep **Site** 1.4HEC ⬤ ⬤ **Ⓐ Prices** ⚥ 6-11 **Ⓐ** 5-10 pitch 7-14
Facilities ⌂ 🏪 ⊙ ⊕ ∅ ⬤ **Services** ⏏ 🍴 ⊞ ⬚ **Off-site** ⬤S

LERICI LA SPEZIA

Maralunga

via Carpanini 61, Maralunga, 19032
☎ 0187 966589 🗎 0187 966589

This terraced site is directly on the seafront and surrounded by olive groves.

➲ *Access from Sarzana-La Spezia motorway.*

Open Jun-Sep **Site** 1HEC ⬤ ⬤ **Prices** ⚥ 7.60-10.10 ⬤ 6.80-8.60 ⬤ 13-15.10 **Ⓐ** 9.40-14.40 **Facilities** ⌂ 🏪 ⊙ ⊕ ∅ **Ⓟ Services** ⏏ 🍴 ⊞
Leisure ⬤ S **Off-site** 🍴

LIMITE FIRENZE

San Giusto

via Castra 71, 50050 ☎ 055 8712304 🗎 055 8711856

A useful site on slightly sloping ground within easy reach of Florence by car or public transport.

Open Etr-Oct **Site** 2.5HEC ⬤ ⬤ ♨ ⬤ **Facilities** ⌂ ⊙ ⊕ ∅ **Services** ⏏
🍴 **Off-site** ⬤P

MASSA, MARINA DI MASSA CARRARA

Giardino

viale delle Pinete 382, 54037 ☎ 0585 869291 🗎 0585 240781
e-mail cgiardono@tin.it
website www.campinggiardino.com

Site in pine woodland and on two meadows, shade provided by roof matting.

➲ *On island side of SS328 to Pisa.*

Open Apr-Sep **Site** 3.2HEC ⬤ ⬤ ♨ ⬤ **Facilities** ⌂ 🏪 ⊙ ⊕ ⬤ ⬤ ⬤
Services ⏏ 🍴 ⬚ **Leisure** ⬤ P **Off-site** ⬤S ⊞

MONÉGLIA GENOVA

Villaggio Smeraldo

Preata, 16030 ☎ 0185 49375 🗎 0185 490484
e-mail info@villaggiosmeraldo.it
website www.villaggiosmeraldo.it

A pleasant site in a pine wood overlooking the sea with modern facilities and direct access to the beach.

➲ *Via A12/SS1.*

Open All year **Site** 1.5HEC ⬤ ⬤ ♨ ⬤ **Facilities** ⌂ 🏪 ⊙ ⊕ ⬤ ⬤
Services ⏏ 🍴 ⬚ **Leisure** ⬤ S **Off-site** ∅

MONTECATINI TERME PISTOIA

Belsito

via delle Vigne 1/A, Vico, 51016 ☎ 0572 67373 🗎 0572 67373
e-mail cbelsito@tin.it
website www.campingbelsito.it

A quiet site at an altitude of 250m with good sized pitches.

Open Apr-Sep **Site** 3.5HEC ⬤ ⬤ ♨ **Prices** ⚥ 5-7 ⬤ 3-4 ⬤ 7-8.50
Ⓐ 5.50-8.50 **Facilities** ⌂ 🏪 ⊙ ⊕ ∅ ⬤ **Services** ⏏ 🍴 ⊞ ⬚
Leisure ⬤ P

MONTE DI FO FIRENZE

Sergente

50030 ☎ 055 8423018 🗎 055 8423907
e-mail info@campingilsergente.it
website www.campingilsergente.it

The site is at 780m above sea level on a hill. The pitches are flat. Ideal for walkers.

➲ *SS65 exit Barberino Mugello & signs for Monte di Fo.*

Open All year **Site** 3HEC ⬤ ⬤ ♨ ⬤ **Facilities** ⌂ 🏪 ⊙ ⊕ ∅ ⬤ ⬤
Services ⏏ 🍴 ⊞ ⬚

MONTERIGGIONI SIENA

Piscina Luxor Quies

Loc. Trasqua, 53032 ☎ 0577 743047 🗎 0577 743047
e-mail info@luxorcamping.com
website www.luxorcamping.com

Lies on a flat-topped hill, partly in an oak wood, partly in meadowland.

➲ *Off SS2 at Km239/II or Km238/IX, site 2.5km over railway line. Very steep & winding road to site.*

Open 20 May-10 Sep **Site** 1.5HEC ⬤ ⬤ ♨ **Prices** ⚥ 7.70 ⬤ 3.30 ⬤ 4.40
Ⓐ 4.10 **Facilities** ⌂ 🏪 ⊙ ⊕ ∅ ⬤ **Services** ⏏ 🍴 ⊞ ⬚ **Leisure** ⬤ P

MONTESCUDÁIO LIVORNO

Montescudáio

via del Poggetto, 56040 ☎ 0586 683477 🗎 0586 630932
e-mail info@camping-montescudaio.it
website www.camping-montescudaio.it

This modern site on a hill is divided into individual pitches, some of which are naturally screened.

➲ *From SS1 via Aurelia at Cecinia towards Guardistallo for 2.5km.*

Open 11 May-16 Sep **Site** 25HEC ⬤ ⬤ ♨ ⬤ ⬤ **Prices** ⚥ 5.50-7.50 pitch 11.50-22.50 ⬤ (static)238-941 **Facilities** ⌂ 🏪 ⊙ ⊕ ∅ ⬤ ⬤ **Services** ⏏
🍴 ⬚ **Leisure** ⬤ PS **Off-site** ⊞

MONTICELLO AMIATA GROSSETO

Lucherino

Lucherino, 58047 ☎ 0564 992975 🗎 0564 992975
e-mail meichu@tiscalinet.it
website www.campinglucherino.com

A peaceful site 735m above sea level on the slopes of Mt Amiata. The shady but sloping site is ideal for walkers.

➲ *SS223 to Paganico then signs to Monte Amiata.*

Open May-15 Oct **Site** 2HEC ⬤ ⬤ ♨ ⬤ **Prices** ⚥ 4.50-7.50 pitch 6.50-9.50 ⬤ (static)210-315 **Facilities** ⌂ ⊙ ⊕ ∅ ⬤ **Ⓟ Services** ⏏ 🍴 ⊞ ⬚
Leisure ⬤ P **Off-site** 🏪 ⬤R

Site 6HEC (site size) 🌿 grass ⬤ sand ⬤ stone ♨ little shade ⬤ partly shaded ⬤ mainly shaded ⬤ bungalows for hire
⬤ caravans for hire **Ⓐ** tents for hire ⬤ no dogs **Prices** ⚥ adult per night ⬤ car per night pp per person per night ⬤ caravan per night
Ⓐ tent per night ⬤ (static)-caravan hire per week

PEGLI GENOVA

Villa Doria

via al Campeggio 15n, 16156 ☎ 010 6969600 ▤ 010 6969600
e-mail villadoria@camping.it
website www.camping.it/liguria/villadoria
Quiet site in pleasant wooded surroundings.

➲ *Signed via SS1.*

Open All year **Site** 0.4HEC ⛺ ⛺ ⛺ ⊞ **Prices** ⋔ 8 pitch 11 **Facilities** ⋔ 🏠 ⊙ 🔌 😊 **Services** ⛽ 🍽 🛒 **Off-site** 🍽 ∅ ⇆S

PISA PISA

Torre Pendente

viale della Cascine 86, 56122 ☎ 050 561704 ▤ 050 561734
e-mail info@campingtorrependente.it
website www.campingtorrependente.it
Pleasant, modern site on level ground in a rural setting. 1km walk to the Leaning Tower.

➲ *SS12 from Lucca to Pisa, continue N with town on left for 1km, site on right.*

Open Apr-15 Oct **Site** 2.5HEC ⛺ ⛺ ⊞ **Prices** ⋔ 8-8.50 🚗 4.50-5 🚐 7-8 ⛺ 7-7.50 **Facilities** ⋔ 🏠 ⊙ 🔌 ∅ 😊 **Services** ⛽ 🍽 🛒 **Leisure** ⇆ P **Off-site** ⇆ ⇆PR 🛒

POPULÓNIA LIVORNO

Sant'Albínia

via della Principessa, 57025 ☎ 0565 29389 ▤ 0565 221310
e-mail arci.piobino@etruscan.li.it
A good overnight stopping place with plenty of facilities. Ideally placed for the ferry ports.

➲ *10km N of Piombino on San Vincenzo road.*

Open May-15 Sep **Site** 3HEC ⛺ ⛺ ⛺ ⛺ ⊗ **Facilities** ⋔ 🏠 ⊙ 🔌 ⇆ **Services** ⛽ 🍽 **Leisure** ⇆ S

RIOTORTO LIVORNO

Orizzonte

Perelli, 57020 ☎ 0565 28007 ▤ 0565 28033
A fine coastal position overlooking the island of Elba.

Open All year **Site** 10HEC ⛺ ⛺ ⊞ ⛺ **Facilities** ⋔ 🏠 ⊙ 🔌 ∅ **Services** ⛽ 🍽 🛒 **Leisure** ⇆ P **Off-site** ⇆S

SAN BARONTO FIRENZE

Barco Reale

via Nardini 11, 51030 ☎ 0573 88332 ▤ 0573 856003
e-mail info@barcoreale.com
website www.barcoreale.com
A well-equipped site in a hilly, wooded location.

➲ *Signed from Lamporecchio.*

Open Apr-Sep **Site** 10HEC ⛺ ⛺ ⊞ **Prices** ⋔ 6.70-9.10 🚗 3.40-5.10 🚐 5.80-13.40 ⛺ 4.20-7.40 **Facilities** ⋔ 🏠 ⊙ 🔌 ∅ 😊 **Services** ⛽ 🍽 🛒 **Leisure** ⇆ P

SAN GIMIGNANO SIENA

Boschetto di Piemma

Santa Lucia, 53037 ☎ 0577 940352 ▤ 0577 907453
e-mail info@boschettodipiemma.it
website www.boschettodipiemma.it
This small grassy site is well-equipped and has many facilities for both families and idividuals.

Open Apr-Oct **Site** 6HEC ⛺ ⛺ ⊞ **Prices** ⋔ 6-7.80 🚗 2-3 🚐 6.30-7.50 ⛺ 5-6.80 **Facilities** ⋔ 🏠 ⊙ 🔌 ∅ ⇆ 😊 **Services** ⛽ 🍽 🛒 🛒 **Leisure** ⇆ P

SAN PIERO A SIEVE FIRENZE

Village Mugello Verde

via Massorondinaio 39, 50037 ☎ 055 848511 ▤ 055 8486910
e-mail mugelloverde@florencecamping.com
website www.florencecamping.com
Terraced site in wooded surroundings.

➲ *Motorway exit 18 & signed.*

Open All year **Site** 12HEC ⛺ ⛺ ⊞ **Facilities** ⋔ 🏠 ⊙ 🔌 😊 **Services** ⛽ 🍽 🛒 🛒 **Leisure** ⇆ P **Off-site** ⇆ ⇆R

SAN VINCENZO LIVORNO

Park Albatros

Pineta di Torre Nuova, 57027 ☎ 0565 701018 ▤ 0565 703589
e-mail info@parkalbatros.it
website www.ecvacanze.it
The site lies among beautiful tall pine trees, 1km from the sea.

➲ *Off SP23 beyond San Vincenzo at Km7/III & continue 0.6km inland.*

Open Apr-12 Oct **Site** 11.4HEC ⛺ ⛺ ⊞ **Prices** ⋔ 5.60-11 pitch 7.20-16.80 **Facilities** ⋔ 🏠 ⊙ 🔌 ∅ 😊 **Services** ⛽ 🍽 🛒 🛒 **Leisure** ⇆ P **Off-site** ⇆S

SARTEANO SIENA

Bagno Santo

via del Bagno Santo 29, 53047 ☎ 0578 26971 ▤ 0578 265889
e-mail info@parcodellepiscine.it
website www.parcodellepiscine.it
A well shaded location on a plateau surrounded by hills. The pools on the site are fed by mineral rich spring water.

➲ *A1 exit 29 Chiusi-Chianciano terme. Follow signs to Sarteano for 5km. Cross main square and follow main road, site on left.*

Open Apr-Sep **Site** 15HEC ⛺ ⛺ ⊞ ⊗ **Prices** ⋔ 10-14 🚗 4-6.50 🚐 10-14 ⛺ 10-14 **Facilities** ⋔ 🏠 ⊙ 🔌 😊 **Services** ⛽ 🍽 🛒 🛒 **Leisure** ⇆ P **Off-site** 🏠

SARZANA LA SPEZIA

Iron Gate

via XXV Aprile 54, 19038 ☎ 0187 676370 ▤ 0187 675014
A modern site with good facilities attached to the Iron Gate Marina.

Open All year **Site** 2HEC ⛺ ⛺ ⊞ **Facilities** ⋔ 🏠 ⊙ 🔌 😊 **Services** ⛽ 🍽 🛒 **Leisure** ⇆ PR **Off-site** ∅ ⇆

SESTRI LEVANTE GENOVA

Fossa Lupara

via Costa 31, 16039 ☎ 0185 43992 ▤ 0185 43992
Open All year **Site** 1.5HEC ⛺ ⛺ ⛺ **Facilities** ⋔ 🏠 ⊙ 🔌 ∅ ⇆ 😊 **Services** ⛽ 🍽 🛒 **Off-site** ⇆S

SIENA SIENA

Montagnola

Soviille, 53018 ☎ 0577 314473 ▤ 0577 314473
e-mail montagnolacamping@libero.it
website www.campingtoscana.it/montagnola
Quiet site in an oak wood with individual plots separated by hedges. Facilities are modern and extensive.

➲ *A1 W exit Siena, site signed towards Soviille.*

Open Etr-29 Sep **Site** 2.5HEC ⛺ ⛺ ⛺ ⊞ **Prices** ⋔ 6 pitch 8 **Facilities** ⋔ 🏠 ⊙ 🔌 ⇆ 😊 **Services** ⛽ 🛒 **Leisure** ⇆ R **Off-site** 🍽 🛒

Italy

Facilities 🏠 shop ⋔ shower ⊙ electric points for razors 🔌 electric points for caravans 😊 parking by tents permitted 😊 compulsory separate car park
Services 🍽 café/restaurant ⛽ bar ∅ Camping Gaz International ⇆ gas other than Camping Gaz 🛒 first aid facilities 🛒 laundry
Leisure ⇆ swimming L-Lake P-Pool R-River S-Sea **Off-site** All facilities within 2km

Siena Colleverde

Strada di Scacciapensieri 47, 53100
☎ 0577 280044 🖹 0577 333298
e-mail campingsiena@terresiena.it
website www.terresiena.it

The site offers both large areas for caravans and mobile homes and a large grassy area for tents. There is a local bus service to the centre of Siena.

➲ *Only site in Siena, situated just to N.*

Open Etr-10 Nov **Site** 4.5HEC ♨ ♨ **Facilities** ⋔ ⊙ ⌨ ≞ ⑫ **Services** ⛟ ⛝ 🖸 **Leisure** ⇜ P **Off-site** 🖾 ⊕

Soline

Casciano di Murlo, 53010 ☎ 0577 817410 🖹 0577 817415
e-mail camping@lesoline.it
website www.lesoline.it

Terraced hilly site surrounded by woodland with a variety of sports facilities and family entertainment.

➲ *Via SS223*

Open All year **Site** 6HEC ♨ ♨ ♨ ⌂ **Prices** ⋔ 7 ⇜ 1.50 ⌨ 6.50 ⛰ 5-6 **Facilities** ⋔ 🖾 ⊙ ⌨ ⌀ ≞ ⑫ **Services** ⛟ ⛝ ⊕ 🖸 **Leisure** ⇜ P

STELLA SAN GIOVANNI SAVONA

Stella

via Rio Basco 62, 17040 ☎ 019 703269 🖹 019 703269
e-mail campingdolcevita@libero.it
website www.campingdolcevita.it

Wooded surroundings with well-defined pitches, 5.5km from the coast.

➲ *Via SS334.*

Open Apr-Sep **Site** 10HEC ♨ ♨ **Prices** ⋔ 5-6 pitch 10-17 (incl 2 persons) **Facilities** ⋔ 🖾 ⊙ ⌨ ⌀ ≞ ⑫ **Services** ⛟ ⛝ ⊕ 🖸 **Leisure** ⇜ PR **Off-site** ⊕

TORRE DEL LAGO PUCCINI LUCCA

Burlamacco

viale G-Marconi Int, 55048 ☎ 0584 359544 🖹 0584 359387
e-mail info@campingburlamacco.com
website www.campingburlamacco.com

A beautiful wooded location 1km from the sea on the Versilia Riviera, close to the former home of Puccini. A variety of facilities are available.

Open Apr-29 Sep **Site** 4.5HEC ♨ ♨ ♨ ⌂ ⌨ ⊗ **Prices** pitch 18-29 (incl 2 persons) ⌨ (static)210-280 **Facilities** ⋔ 🖾 ⊙ ⌨ ⌀ ≞ ⊕ **Services** ⛟ ⛝ 🖸 **Leisure** ⇜ P **Off-site** ⇜LS ⊕

Europa

Viale dei Tigli, 55048 ☎ 0584 350707 🖹 0584 342592
e-mail info@europacamp.it
website www.europacamp.it

Site in pine and poplar woodland.

➲ *From Viareggio, on land side of Viale dei Tigli.*

Open 31 Mar-13 Oct **Site** 60HEC ♨ ♨ ♨ ⌂ ⌨ **Prices** ⋔ 4-8.50 ⌨ 8.50-12 ⛰ 6-10 **Facilities** ⋔ 🖾 ⊙ ⌨ ⌀ ≞ ⑫ **Services** ⛟ ⛝ 🖸 **Leisure** ⇜ P **Off-site** ⇜S

Italia

52 viale dei Tigli, 55048 ☎ 0584 359828 🖹 0584 341504
e-mail info@campingitalia.net **website** www.campingitalia.net

This site is divided into pitches and lies in meadowland planted with poplar trees.

➲ *Inland off Viareggio road (viale dei Tigli).*

Open 19 Apr-23 Sep **Site** 9HEC ♨ ♨ ♨ ⌂ ⊗ **Prices** ⋔ 4.50-8.50 ⌨ 8.50-11.50 ⛰ 6.50-11.50 **Facilities** ⋔ 🖾 ⊙ ⌨ ⌀ ≞ ⑫ ⊕ **Services** ⛟ ⛝ ⊕ 🖸 **Off-site** 🖾 ⛟ ⛝ ⌀ ≞ ⇜LS

Tigli

Viale dei Tigli, 54, 55048 ☎ 0584 341278 🖹 0584 341278
e-mail info@campingdeitigli.com
website www.campingdeitigli.com

Shady site close to a Regional Park, Lake Massaciuccoli, and the villa where Puccini wrote much of his music.

Open Apr-Sep **Site** 9HEC ♨ ♨ ♨ ⌂ **Prices** ⋔ 5-9 ⌨ 9-15 ⛰ 9-15 **Facilities** ⋔ 🖾 ⊙ ⌨ ⌀ ≞ ⑫ **Services** ⛟ ⛝ ⊕ 🖸 **Leisure** ⇜ P **Off-site** ⇜LS

TROGHI FIRENZE

Il Poggetto

via il Poggetto 143, 50010 ☎ 055 8307323 🖹 055 8307323
e-mail info@campingilpoggetto.com
website www.campingilpoggetto.com

A modern site with good facilities. Large, level, grassy pitches.

➲ *A1 exit Incisa Valdarno, site 5km.*

Open Apr-15 Oct **Site** 4.5HEC ♨ ⌂ ⌨ ⌨ **Prices** ⋔ 7.50-7.80 pitch 13-13.50 ⌨ (static)420-665 **Facilities** ⋔ 🖾 ⊙ ⌨ ⌀ ≞ ⑫ **Services** ⛟ ⛝ ⊕ 🖸 **Leisure** ⇜ P **Off-site** ⇜L

VADA LIVORNO

Flori

Località Campo ai Fiori 4, 57018 ☎ 0586 770096 🖹 0586 770323
e-mail campofiori@multinet.it
website www.campingcampodeifiori.it

Level grassland surrounded by fields. Shade provided by roof matting

➲ *A12 to Rosignano.*

Open 7 Apr-23 Sep **Site** 15HEC ♨ ⌂ ⌨ **Prices** ⋔ 6-11 ⌨ 6-10 ⛰ 6-10 **Facilities** ⋔ 🖾 ⊙ ⌨ ⌀ ≞ ⑫ **Services** ⛟ ⛝ ⊕ 🖸 **Leisure** ⇜ P **Off-site** ⇜S

VIAREGGIO LUCCA

Pineta

via dei Lecci, 55049 ☎ 0584 383397
e-mail campinglapineta@interfree.it
website www.campinglapineta.com

A well-organised site in a wooded location, 1km from a private beach

➲ *Via SSN1 between Km354 & Km355.*

Open 5 Apr-22 Sep **Site** 3.2HEC ♨ ♨ ⌂ ⌨ **Prices** ⋔ 5-9 ⛰ 6.50-11 pitch 10.50-16.50 **Facilities** ⋔ 🖾 ⊙ ⌨ ⌀ ≞ ⊕ **Services** ⛟ ⛝ ⊕ 🖸 **Leisure** ⇜ P **Off-site** ⇜S

Site 6HEC (site size) ♨ grass ♨ sand ♨ stone ♣ little shade ♣ partly shaded ♣ mainly shaded ⌂ bungalows for hire ⌨ caravans for hire ⛰ tents for hire ⊗ no dogs **Prices** ⋔ adult per night ⇜ car per night pp per person per night ⌨ caravan per night ⛰ tent per night ⌨ (static)-caravan hire per week

Viareggio

via Comparini 1, 55049 ☎ 0584 391012 ▤ 0584 391012
e-mail campingviareggio@tin.it
website www.campingviareggio.it
The site lies in a poplar wood 0.7km from the beach.
➲ *1.5km S of town. From Km354/V towards coast.*
Open Apr-29 Sep **Site** 2HEC ⛺ ⚌ ⚏ **Prices** ♦ 6-9 ⊕ 8-12 ▲ 8-12
Facilities ♠ ⌂ ⊙ ➡ ⧄ ⚒ ⚖ **Services** ⊫ ⓧ ✚ ▣ **Leisure** ◆ P
Off-site ◆PS

ZINOLA SAVONA

Buggi International

via N S del Monte 15, 17049 ☎ 019 860120 ▤ 019 804573
A well-equipped site with plenty of space for tents, 0.9km from the
sea.
Open All year **Site** 2HEC ⛺ ⚌ ⚏ ⊕ **Prices** ♦ 5 ⊕ 5 ⊕ 7 ▲ 5
⊕ (static)400 **Facilities** ♠ ⌂ ⊙ ➡ ⚖ **Services** ⊫ ⓧ **Off-site** ⧄ ▵ ◆S
✚

NORTH EAST/ADRIATIC

ALBA ADRIATICA TERAMO

AT TORTORETO, LIDO (4KM S)

Salinello

c da Piane a Mare, 64019 ☎ 0861 786306 ▤ 0861 786451
e-mail salinello@camping.it
website www.camping.it/salinello
Well-tended meadowland site with numerous rows of poplars. Private
beach.
➲ *On S outskirts, signed from Km405 of SS16.*
Open May-Sep **Site** 15HEC ⛺ ⚌ ⚏ ⊗ **Facilities** ♠ ⌂ ⊙ ➡ ⧄ ▵ ⚒
Services ⊫ ⓧ ✚ ▣ **Leisure** ◆ PS **Off-site** ◆R

ASSISI PERUGIA

Village Assisi

Campiglione No. 110, 06081 ☎ 075 813710 ▤ 075 812335
e-mail info@campingassisi.it
website www.campingassisi.it
Set at the foot of the hill on which Assisi stands, this modern, well-
equipped site is a good touring base.
➲ *W via SS147.*
Open Apr-Oct **Site** 3HEC ⛺ ⚌ ⚏ ⊕ ▲ **Prices** ♦ 7-8 ⊕ 2-3 ⊕ 7-8 ▲ 6-
7 **Facilities** ♠ ⌂ ⊙ ➡ ⧄ ▵ **Services** ⊫ ⓧ ▣ **Leisure** ◆ P **Off-site** ◆R

BARREA L'AQUILA

Genziana

Parco Nazionale d'Abruzzo, Tre Croci, 67030
☎ 0864 88101 ▤ 0864 88101
e-mail pasettanet@tiscali.it
website www.campinglagenzianapasetta.it
Picturesque wooded surroundings on the shore of a lake.
Open All year **Site** 2HEC ⛺ ⚌ ⚏ ⊕ ▲ **Prices** ♦ 7.20 ⊕ 3 ⊕ 8 ▲ 7.20-8
Facilities ♠ ⌂ ⊙ ➡ ⚒ **Services** ⊫ ⓧ **Off-site** ⌂ ⧄ ▵ ◆L ✚

BELLARIA FORLI

Happy

via Panzini 228, 47814 ☎ 0541 346102 ▤ 0541 346408
e-mail info@happycamping.it
website www.happycamping.it
The site is in a quiet position on the sea shore close to the centre of
town.
➲ *A14/SS16 exit Bellaria Cagnona S Mauro Mare, signs for
Acquabell, over level crossing, site on right.*
Open All year **Site** 4HEC ⚌ ⚏ ⊕ **Prices** ♦ 5-9 pitch 10.50-17.80
Facilities ♠ ⌂ ⊙ ➡ ⧄ ▵ ⚒ **Services** ⊫ ⓧ ✚ ▣ **Leisure** ◆ PS
Off-site ◆R

BEVAGNA PERUGIA

Pian di Boccio

Pian di Boccio 10, 06031 ☎ 0742 360164 ▤ 0742 360391
e-mail piandiboccio@tiscalinet.it
website www.piandiboccio.com
In wooded surroundings in the centre of the Umbria region with
modern facilities. Popular with families.
Open Apr-Sep **Site** 8.5HEC ⛺ ⚌ ⚏ ⊕ **Prices** ♦ 5.50-6.50 ⊕ 2-2.50
⊕ 6-7 ▲ 3.50-6.50 **Facilities** ♠ ⌂ ⊙ ➡ ⧄ ▵ ⚒ **Services** ⊫ ⓧ ▣
Leisure ◆ LP

BOLOGNA BOLOGNA

Citta di Bologna

via Romita 12/IVA, 40127 ☎ 051 325016 ▤ 051 325318
e-mail info@hotelcamping.com
website www.hotelcamping.com
Located in the northern part of this ancient town this site offers a
cheap and convenient alternative to hotels.
Open All year **Site** 6.3HEC ⛺ ⚌ ⚏ **Prices** ♦ 5-7 pitch 8-13 **Facilities** ♠
⌂ ⊙ ➡ ⚒ **Services** ⊫ ⓧ ✚ ▣ **Leisure** ◆ P **Off-site** ⓧ ⧄ ▵

BORGHETTO PERUGIA

Badiaccia

via Trasimenoi, no.91, 6061 ☎ 075 9659097 ▤ 075 9659019
e-mail info@badiaccia.com
website www.badiaccia.com
A well-equipped site with large grassy pitches and direct access to the
lake.
➲ *A1 exit Valdichiana for Perugia & signs for Lake Trasimeno.*
Open Apr-Sep **Site** 5.5HEC ⛺ ⚌ ⚏ ⊕ **Facilities** ♠ ⌂ ⊙ ➡ ⧄
Services ⊫ ⓧ ▣ **Leisure** ◆ LP **Off-site** ▵

CASAL BORSETTI RAVENNA

Adria

via Spallazzi N30, 48010 ☎ 0544 445217
The site lies in a field behind the Ristorante Lugo.
➲ *Motorway exit Ravenna. Or SS309 (Romea) Km13 N of
Ravenna.*
Open May-20 Sep **Site** 5.5HEC ⛺ ⚌ ⚏ **Facilities** ♠ ⌂ ⊙ ➡ ⧄ ▵ ⚒
Services ⊫ ⓧ ✚ ▣ **Leisure** ◆ PS

Italy

Facilities ⌂ shop ♠ shower ⊙ electric points for razors ➡ electric points for caravans ⚒ parking by tents permitted ⓟ compulsory separate car park
Services ⓧ café/restaurant ⊫ bar ⧄ Camping Gaz International ▵ gas other than Camping Gaz ✚ first aid facilities ▣ laundry
Leisure ◆ swimming L-Lake P-Pool R-River S-Sea **Off-site** All facilities within 2km

Reno

via Spallazzi 11, 48010 ☎ 0544 445020 ▤ 0544 442056
e-mail info@campingreno.it
website www.camping.it/emiliaromagna/reno
Meadowland in sparse pine woodland and separated from the sea by dunes.

➦ *Off SS309 at Km8 or Km14.*

Open Apr-Oct **Site** 3HEC ❤❤ 🛏 🚐 **Prices** ♠ 4.60-6.80 pitch 8-11 (incl 4 persons) 🚐 (static)200-396 **Facilities** ⚲ ▥ ⊙ 🚿 ⌀ ♨ ⑳ **Services** ⬧ ⬧ ➕ ⬧ **Off-site** ⬧S

CASTIGLIONE DEL LAGO PERUGIA

Listro

via Lungolago, 6061 ☎ 075 951193 ▤ 075 951193
e-mail listro@listro.it
website www.listro.it
Attractive site on a peninsula in Lake Trasimeno.

Open Apr-Sep **Site** 1HEC ❤❤ **Prices** ♠ 3.80-4.50 🚗 1.30-1.80 🚐 3.80-4.50 Δ 3.80-4.50 **Facilities** ⚲ ▥ ⊙ 🚿 ♨ ⑳ **Services** ⬧ ⬧ ⬧ **Leisure** ⬧ L **Off-site** ⬧ ⌀ ⬧P➕

CERVIA RAVENNA

Adriatico

via Pinarella 90, 48015 ☎ 0544 71537 ▤ 0544 72346
e-mail info@campingadriatico.net
website www.campingadriatico.net
Level meadowland site with plenty of shade, pleasantly landscaped with olives, willows, elms and maples.

➦ *Site before Pinarella di Cervia off SS16 Caduti per le Liberta, 0.6km from sea.*

Open 21 Apr-9 Sep **Site** 3.4HEC ❤❤ 🛏 **Prices** ♠ 5-7.80 🚐 10.10-14 Δ 7.90-12.30 **Facilities** ⚲ ▥ ⊙ 🚿 ⌀ ♨ ⑳ **Services** ⬧ ⬧ ➕ ⬧ **Leisure** ⬧ P **Off-site** ▥ ⬧ ⬧ ♨ ⬧L ➕

CESENATICO FORLI

Cesenatico

via Mazzini 182, 47042 ☎ 0547 81344 ▤ 0547 672452
e-mail info@campingcesenatico.com
website www.campingcesenatico.com
The site stretches over an area of land belonging to the Azienda di Soggiomo e Turismo.

➦ *1.5km N, off the SS16 at Km178 towards sea.*

Open All year **Site** 18HEC ❤❤ 🛏 🚐 **Facilities** ⚲ ▥ ⊙ 🚿 ♨ ⑳ **Services** ⬧ ⬧ ⬧ **Leisure** ⬧ PS **Off-site** ➕

Zadina

via Mazzini 184, 47042 ☎ 0547 82310 ▤ 0547 672802
e-mail info@campingzadina.it
Very pleasant terrain in dunes on two sides of a canal.

Open 23 Apr-16 Sep **Site** 6HEC ❤❤ 🛏 **Facilities** ⚲ ▥ ⊙ 🚿 ⌀ ♨ ⑳ **Services** ⬧ ⬧ ➕ ⬧ **Leisure** ⬧ S

CITTA DI CASTELLO PERUGIA

La Montesca

06012 ☎ 075 8558566 ▤ 075 8520180
e-mail info@lamontesca.it **website** www.lamontesca.it
Set in a large wooded park with excellent facilities. A good base for exploring the area.

➦ *3km from town beside River Tiber.*

Open 15 May-15 Sep **Site** 5HEC ❤❤ 🛏 **Facilities** ⚲ ⊙ 🚿 ♨ ⑳ **Services** ⬧ ⬧ ➕ ⬧ **Leisure** ⬧ P **Off-site** ⬧R

CUPRA MARITTIMA ASCOLI PICENO

Calypso

via Boccabianca 8, 63012 ☎ 0735 778686 ▤ 0735 778106
e-mail calypso@camping.it
website www.campingcalypso.it
Open Apr-29 Sep **Site** 26HEC ❤❤ 🛏 🚐 **Facilities** ⚲ ▥ ⊙ 🚿 ⌀ ♨ ⑳ **Services** ⬧ ⬧ ➕ ⬧ **Leisure** ⬧ PS

DANTE, LIDO DI RAVENNA

Classe

viale Catone, 48100 ☎ 0544 492005 ▤ 0544 492058
e-mail info@campingclasse.it
website www.campingclasse.it
Level meadowland in grounds of former farm.

➦ *Off SS16 at Km154/V towards sea, 9km to site.*

Open 28 Mar-10 Oct **Site** 7HEC ❤❤ 🛏 🚐 **Prices** ♠ 6-10 pitch 10-15 🚐 (static)280-770 **Facilities** ⚲ ▥ ⊙ 🚿 ♨ ⑳ **Services** ⬧ ⬧ ⬧ **Leisure** ⬧ PS **Off-site** ⌀ ⬧LR

ESTENSI, LIDO DEGLI FERRARA

International Mare Pineta

via delle Acacie 67, 44024 ☎ 0533 330110 ▤ 0533 330052
e-mail info@campingmarepineta.com
website www.campingmarepineta.com
Extensive site on slightly hilly ground under pines and deciduous trees, providing shade. Near the beach and has numerous mobile homes.

➦ *2km SE of Port Garibaldi.*

Open 19 Apr-23 Sep **Site** 16HEC ❤❤ 🛏 🚐 **Prices** ♠ 3.90-8.50 🚗 2.60-4.30 pitch 7.25-14.20 **Facilities** ⚲ ▥ ⊙ 🚿 ⌀ ♨ ⑳ **Services** ⬧ ⬧ ⬧ **Leisure** ⬧ PS

FANO PESARO & URBINO

Mare Blu

61032 ☎ 0721 884201 ▤ 0721 884389
e-mail mareblu@camping.it
website www.camping.it/mareblu
The site is surrounded by tall poplars with direct access to a sandy beach. Facilities for most water sports, and entertainment for children and families.

➦ *A14 exit Fano, site 3km S.*

Open Apr-Sep **Site** 2.5HEC ❤❤ 🚐 **Prices** ♠ 5.50-8 pitch 11-14 🚐 (static)359-459 **Facilities** ⚲ ▥ ⊙ 🚿 ⌀ ♨ ⑳ Ⓟ **Services** ⬧ ⬧ ➕ ⬧ **Leisure** ⬧ S **Off-site** ⬧PR

FERRARA FERRARA

Estense

via Gramicia 76, 44100 ☎ 0532 752396 ▤ 0532 752396
e-mail camping.estense@libero.it
A good overnight stop on the way south.

➦ *NE outskirts of Ferrara.*

Open 25 Feb-15 Jan **Site** 3.3HEC ❤❤ 🚐 **Prices** ♠ 5 pitch 6.50-7.50 **Facilities** ⚲ ⊙ 🚿 ⑳ **Off-site** ▥ ⬧ ⬧ ⬧P

Site 6HEC (site size) ❤ grass ⬤ sand ❤ stone ♣ little shade ♣ partly shaded ❤ mainly shaded 🛏 bungalows for hire 🚐 caravans for hire Δ tents for hire ⊗ no dogs **Prices** ♠ adult per night 🚗 car per night pp per person per night 🚐 caravan per night Δ tent per night 🚐 (static)-caravan hire per week

FIORENZUOLA DI FOCARA PESARO & URBINO

Panorama
Strada Panoramica, 61010 ☎ 0721 208145 ▤ 0721 209860
e-mail info@campingpanorama.it
website www.campingpanorama.it
Located in a park 100m above sea level this site welcomes families, animals and cyclists.
⊃ *Signed off SS16. 10km from Gabicce, 7km from Pesaro.*
Open May-Sep **Site** 2.2HEC ⛺ ⚌ ♠ ♠ **Prices** ♦ 5.50-8.50 ♠ 2.50 ♠ 7-10.50 ▲ 7-10.50 ♠ (static)336-490 **Facilities** ♠ ⚐ ⊕ ♠ ⊘ ⚒ ⑨ **Services** ⚑ ⑩ ⊞ ⓢ **Leisure** ⚘ PS

GATTEO MARE FORLI

Delle Rose
via Adriatica 29, 47043 ☎ 0547 86213 ▤ 0547 87583
e-mail info@villaggiorose.com
website www.villaggiorose.com
A peaceful setting close to the sea and the town centre.
⊃ *Off SS16 at Km186.*
Open 22 Apr-25 Sep **Site** 4HEC ⛺ ⚌ ⚌ ♠ ♠ **Prices** ♦ 4.20-8.20 pitch 9-16.60 ♠ (static)200-525 **Facilities** ♠ ⚐ ⊕ ♠ ⊘ ⚒ ⑨ **Services** ⚑ ⑩ ⊞ ⓢ **Leisure** ⚘ PS **Off-site** ⚘R

GIULIANOVA LIDO TERAMO

Baviera
Lungomare Zara, 64022 ☎ 085 8000053 ▤ 085 8004420
A family site in a wooded location with direct access to a private beach. A variety of sports and entertainment facilities are available, particularly in July and August, when all cars must use the designated car park.
⊃ *Access via A14 & SS80.*
Open 31 May-15 Sep **Site** 1.8HEC ⛺ ⚌ ⚌ ♠ **Facilities** ♠ ⚐ ⊕ ♠ ⊘ ⚒ ⑨ **Services** ⚑ ⑩ ⓢ **Leisure** ⚘ PS

GUBBIO PERUGIA

Villa Ortoguidone
Ortoguidone 214, 06024 ☎ 075 9272037 ▤ 075 9276620
e-mail info@gubbiocamping.com
website www.gubbiocamping.com
One of two well-equipped sites in the same location. Plenty of space for tents.
⊃ *Via SS298 Gubbio-Perugia.*
Open 4 Apr-16 Sep **Site** 0.5HEC ⛺ ⚌ ⚌ ♠ ♠ **Prices** ♦ 6.50-9 ♠ 2.50 ♠ 9-10.50 ▲ 7-9 ♠ (static)210-280 **Facilities** ♠ ⚐ ⊕ ♠ ⊘ ⑨ **Services** ⚑ ⑩ **Leisure** ⚘ P **Off-site** ⚐ ⚑ ⑩ ⊘ ⚒

MARCELLI DI NUMANA ANCONA

Conero Azzurro
via Litoranea, 60026 ☎ 071 7390507 ▤ 071 7390986
e-mail coneroazzurro@camping.it
Well-equipped site between the Adriatic and Mt Canero.
Open Jun-15 Sep **Site** 5HEC ⛺ ⚌ ♠ ⑨ **Prices** ♦ 8-11 ♠ 4-6 ♠ 10-14 ▲ 10-14 **Facilities** ♠ ⚐ ⊕ ♠ ⊘ **Services** ⚑ ⑩ ⊞ ⓢ **Leisure** ⚘ PS **Off-site** ⚒

MAROTTA PESARO & URBINO

Gabbiano
via Faa' di Bruno 95, 61035 ☎ 0721 96691 ▤ 0721 96691
e-mail info@campingdelgabbiano.it
website www.campingdelgabbiano.it
Quiet location surrounded by trees overlooking the sea.
⊃ *A14 exit Marotta, SS16 for Fano for 2.5km.*
Open May-Sep **Site** 1.9HEC ⛺ ⚌ ♠ ⑨ **Facilities** ♠ ⚐ ⊕ ♠ ⊘ ⚒ ⑨ **Services** ⚑ ⑩ ⊞ ⓢ **Leisure** ⚘ PS

MARTINSICURO TERAMO

Duca Amedeo
Lungomare Europa 158, 64014 ☎ 0861 797376 ▤ 0861 797264
e-mail ducaamedeo@camping.it
website www.ducaamedeo.it
A pleasant location close to the sea, surrounded by trees and lush vegetation.
⊃ *A14 exit Martinsicuro.*
Open May-28 Sep **Site** 1.5HEC ⛺ ♠ ♠ **Prices** ♦ 2.50-9 ▲ 4-9 pitch 7-16 **Facilities** ♠ ⊕ ♠ ⊘ ⑨ **Services** ⚑ ⑩ ⊞ ⓢ **Leisure** ⚘ PS **Off-site** ⚐ ⑩

MILANO MARITTIMA RAVENNA

Romagna
viale Matteotti 190, 48016 ☎ 0544 949326 ▤ 0544 949345
e-mail info@campeggioromagna.it
website www.campeggioromagna.it
Level and flat site with young trees.
⊃ *SS16 Strada Adriatica, turn off after Milano Marittima & signed.*
Open 12 Apr-15 Sep **Site** 40HEC ⛺ ⚌ ⚌ ♠ ⑨ **Prices** ♦ 4.50-8.50 ▲ 6-12 pitch 7-14 **Facilities** ♠ ⚐ ⊕ ♠ ⊘ ⑨ **Services** ⚑ ⑩ ⓢ **Leisure** ⚘ S **Off-site** ⚘P ⊞

MONTECRETO MODENA

Parcodei Castagni SRL
via del Parco 5 ☎ 0536 63595 ▤ 0536 63630
e-mail camping@parcodeicastagni.it
website www.parcodeicastagni.it
Site set among mature chestnut trees in an environmentally friendly location. A chair lift provides access to the surrounding high mountains.
Open All year **Site** ⛺ ⚌ ⚌ ♠ ▲ **Prices** ♦ 5-8 ▲ 4-6 pitch 8-10 **Facilities** ♠ ⊕ ♠ ⊘ ⑨ **Services** ⚑ ⑩ ⓢ **Leisure** ⚘ P **Off-site** ⚐ ⚒

MONTENERO, MARINA DI CAMPOBASSO

Costa Verde
86036 ☎ 0873 803144 ▤ 0873 803144
e-mail info@costaverde.it
website www.costaverde.it
A level site with good facilities and direct access to the beach east of San Salvo Marino.
⊃ *Off SS16 coast road at Km525/VII onto farm road for 300m.*
Open 15 May-15 Sep **Site** 1HEC ⛺ ⚌ ♠ ♠ ▲ ⑨ **Prices** ♦ 4.50-7.50 pitch 5-11 **Facilities** ♠ ⚐ ⊕ ♠ ⊘ ⚒ ⑨ **Services** ⚑ ⑩ ⊞ ⓢ **Leisure** ⚘ PRS **Off-site** ⊞

Italy

Facilities ⚐ shop ♠ shower ⊕ electric points for razors ♠ electric points for caravans ⑨ parking by tents permitted ⑨ compulsory separate car park
Services ⑩ café/restaurant ⚑ bar ⊘ Camping Gaz International ⚒ gas other than Camping Gaz ⊞ first aid facilities ⓢ laundry
Leisure ⚘ swimming L-Lake P-Pool R-River S-Sea **Off-site** All facilities within 2km

NARNI TERNI

Monti del Sole
strada di Borgheria 22 ☎ 0744 796336 ▤ 0744 796336
e-mail info@campingmontidelsole.it
website www.campingmontidelsole.it
A spacious wooded site, shaded and flat. All plots are grassed and easily reached by firm lanes.

➲ *A1 exit Magliano Sabina for Terni, signs for Narni.*

Open Apr-Sep **Site** ❤ ❤ ❤ **Prices** ⋔ 5.50-6.50 ⇔ 1.50 ⇔ 5.50-6.50 ▲ 4.50-5.50 **Facilities** ⋔ ⊙ ⊖ ⊕ ⊗ **Services** ⊉ ⍩ **Leisure** ❤ P

NAZIONI, LIDO DELLE FERRARA

Tahiti
viale Libia 133, 44020 ☎ 0533 379500 ▤ 0533 379700
e-mail info@campingtahiti.com
website www.campingtahiti.com
Attractively planned site, 0.65km from the sea. The site's private beach is accessible via a miniature railway.

➲ *Off SS309 near Km32.5 & 2km to site, signed.*

Open 12 Apr-24 Sep **Site** 12HEC ❤ ❤ ❤ ❤ ⊞ ⊞ ⊗ **Prices** ⋔ 4.50-8.90 pitch 8.90-18.90 **Facilities** ⋔ ☎ ⊙ ⊖ ⊘ ⊘ ⊕ ⊗ **Services** ⊉ ⍩ ⊞ ⊠ **Leisure** ❤ P **Off-site** ❤ S

PERUGIA PERUGIA

Rocolo
strada Fontana la Trinita, 06074 ☎ 075 5178550 ▤ 075 5178550
e-mail daimon@ilrocolo.it
website www.ilrocolo.it
Open 15 Apr-15 Oct **Site** 2.4HEC ❤ ❤ ▲ **Prices** ⋔ 5.50-6.50 ⇔ 2-2.50 ⇔ 5.50-6.50 ▲ 4-5 **Facilities** ⋔ ☎ ⊙ ⊖ ⊘ ⊗ **Services** ⊉ ⍩ ⊞ ⊠ **Off-site** ⊾ ❤P

PARMA PARMA

Cittadella
parco Cittadella, 43100 ☎ 0521 961434
Camping Card Compulsory.
Open Apr-Oct **Site** 4HEC ❤ ❤ ❤ **Facilities** ⋔ ⊙ ⊖ ⊕ ⊗ **Off-site** ☎ ⊉ ⍩ ⊘ ⊾ ⊞

PASSIGNANO PERUGIA

Europa
Loc San Donato, 06065 ☎ 075 827405 ▤ 075 827405
e-mail info@camping-europa.it
website www.camping-europa.it
Situated by Lake Trasimeno with a private beach.

➲ *Motorway exit Passignano Est, site signed.*

Open Etr-Oct **Site** 3HEC ❤ ❤ ⊞ ❤ ⊞ **Prices** ⋔ 5.50-6.50 ⇔ 2.50-3 ⇔ 6-7 ▲ 5.30-6.30 ⊞ (static)290-434 **Facilities** ⋔ ☎ ⊙ ⊖ ⊘ ⊗ **Services** ⊉ ⍩ ⊞ ⊠ **Leisure** ❤ LP

Kursaal
viale Europa 24, 06065 ☎ 075 828085 ▤ 075 827182
e-mail info@campingkursaal.it
website www.campingkursaal.it
The site lies between the road and the lake, near the villa of the same name.

➲ *Off SS75 at Km35.2.*

Open Apr-29 Oct **Site** 1HEC ❤ ❤ ❤ ❤ **Prices** ⋔ 6-7.50 pitch 12-14 **Facilities** ⋔ ☎ ⊙ ⊖ ⊗ **Services** ⊉ ⍩ ⊠ **Leisure** ❤ LP **Off-site** ⊞

Spaggia
Viale Europa 22 ☎ 075 827246 ▤ 075 827246
e-mail info@campinglaspiaggia.it
website www.campinglaspiaggia.it
On the northern shore of Lake Trasimeno in a tranquil wooded location. Large grassy pitches.

Open Apr-Sep **Site** 1.6HEC ❤ ❤ ⊞ **Prices** ⋔ 5.50-7 ⇔ 2.50 ⇔ 6-7.50 ▲ 5-7 **Facilities** ⋔ ⊙ ⊖ ⊘ ⊾ ⊗ **Services** ⊉ ⍩ ⊠ **Leisure** ❤ L **Off-site** ☎ ⍩ ⊘ ❤P ⊞

PIEVEPELAGO MODENA

Fra Dolcino
41027 ☎ 0536 71229
Open All year **Site** 3.6HEC ❤ ❤ ❤ ❤ **Facilities** ⋔ ☎ ⊙ ⊖ ⊕ ⊾ ⊗ **Services** ⊉ ⍩ ⊠ **Off-site** ⍩ ❤PR ⊞

Rio Verde
via M.di Canossa 34, 41027 ☎ 0536 72204 ▤ 0536 72204
e-mail campingrioverde@libero.it
website www.abetour.it
Wooded mountain setting close to the river with modern facilities.

➲ *SS12 from Modena*

Open All year **Site** 1.8HEC ❤ ❤ ⊞ ❤ **Prices** ⋔ 5-6 ⇔ 6-7 ▲ 4-6 **Facilities** ⋔ ⊙ ⊖ ⊕ ⊘ **Services** ⊉ ⍩ ⊠ **Leisure** ❤ R **Off-site** ☎ ⊘ ⊾ ❤LP ⊞

PINARELLA RAVENNA

Safari
viale Titano 130, 48015 ☎ 0544 987356 ▤ 0544 987356
e-mail csafari@cervia.com
website www.cervia.com
The site is divided into several sections. Only families are accepted.
Open May-15 Sep **Site** 3.1HEC ❤ ❤ ⊗ **Facilities** ⋔ ☎ ⊙ ⊖ ⊘ ⊾ ⊗ **Services** ⊉ ⍩ ⊞ ⊠ **Off-site** ⍩ ❤S

PINETO TERAMO

Heliopolis
Contrada Villa Fumosa, 64025 ☎ 085 9492720 ▤ 085 9492171
e-mail info@heliopolis.it
website www.heliopolis.it
Situated near a golden sandy beach. Various activies for all, and idyllic scenery for relaxing walks.

Open Apr-Sep **Site** 12HEC ❤ ❤ ❤ ❤ **Facilities** ⋔ ☎ ⊙ ⊖ ⊕ ⊘ ⊾ ⊕ **Services** ⊉ ⍩ ⊞ ⊠ **Leisure** ❤ PS

International
Loc Torre Cerrano, 64025 ☎ 085 930639 ▤ 085 930639
e-mail info@internationalcamping.it
website www.internationalcamping.it
Site on level terrain with young poplars. Sunshade roofing on the beach.

➲ *Off SS16 at Km431.2 & under railway underpass, site next to railway line.*

Open May-Sep **Site** 1.5HEC ❤ ❤ ⊞ ⊗ **Prices** ⋔ 4.50-9 ▲ 3-6 pitch 8.50-16 **Facilities** ⋔ ☎ ⊙ ⊖ ⊘ ⊾ ⊕ ⊕ **Services** ⊉ ⍩ ⊞ ⊠ **Leisure** ❤ S

Site 6HEC (site size) ❤ grass ❤ sand ❤ stone ❤ little shade ❤ partly shaded ❤ mainly shaded ⊞ bungalows for hire ⊞ caravans for hire ▲ tents for hire ⊗ no dogs **Prices** ⋔ adult per night ⇔ car per night pp per person per night ⇔ caravan per night ▲ tent per night ⊞ (static)-caravan hire per week

Pineto Beach

S.s 16 km425, 64025 ☎ 085 9492724 ▤ 085 9492796
e-mail pinetobeach@camping.it
website www.pinetobeach.it
A well-equipped site in wooded surroundings with direct access to the beach.
➲ *On SS16 Adriatica at Km425.*
Open 15 May-29 Sep **Site** 3HEC ❤ ❤ ❤ ➤ **Facilities** ↑ 🅰 ⊙ 🔌 🅰 ⏀ 🅿
Services 🍴 🍽 ➕ 🖸 **Leisure** ❤ PS

POMPOSA FERRARA

International Tre Moschettieri

via Capanno Garibaldi 22, 44020 ☎ 0533 380376 ▤ 0533 380377
e-mail info@tremoschettieri.com
website www.tremoschettieri.com
Site set beneath pine trees next to sea.
➲ *Signed from SS309.*
Open 23 Apr-23 Sep **Site** 11HEC ❤ ❤ ❤ ❤ ➤ **Prices** ⋔ 4-8 pitch 9-15
➤ (static)210-420 **Facilities** ↑ 🅰 ⊙ 🔌 🅰 ⏀ **Services** 🍴 🍽 🖸
Leisure ❤ PS **Off-site** ⏀ ❤L

PORTO SANT'ELPÍDIO ASCOLI PICENO

Risacca

via Gabbie 6, 63018 ☎ 0734 991423 ▤ 0734 997276
e-mail info@larisacca.it
website www.larisacca.it
Clean, well-kept site on level meadowland, with some trees surrounded by fields.
➲ *Off SS16 N of village, towards sea under railway (narrow underpass maximum height 3m) & 1.2km along field paths to site. Caravan access 400m further S along SS16, under railway & along field paths to site.*
Open 19 May-14 Sep **Site** 8HEC ❤ ❤ ❤ ▲ Ⓧ **Prices** ⋔ 3-8 pitch 7-16
➤ (static)150-364 **Facilities** ↑ 🅰 ⊙ 🔌 🅰 ⏀ 🅿 **Services** 🍴 🍽 ➕ 🖸
Leisure ❤ PS **Off-site** ❤R

PRECI PERUGIA

Il Collaccio

Castelvecchio di Preci, 6047 ☎ 0743 939005 ▤ 0743 939094
e-mail info@ilcollaccio.com
website www.ilcollaccio.com
Beautiful natural surroundings with plenty of roomy pitches and good recreational facilities.
➲ *Via SS 209.*
Open Apr-Sep **Site** 10HEC ❤ ❤ ➤ **Prices** ⋔ 5.50-7.50 ➤ 2-3.50 ➤ 6.50-
9 ▲ 5.50-7.50 **Facilities** ↑ 🅰 ⊙ 🔌 🅰 ⏀ **Services** 🍴 🍽 **Leisure** ❤ P
Off-site ❤R

AT PUNTA MARINA TERME (4.5KM S)

Adriano

via dei Campeggi 7, 48020 ☎ 0544 437230 ▤ 0544 438510
e-mail info@campingadriano.com
website www.campingadriano.com
A landscaped site among the dunes of the Punta Marina, 300m from the sea.
➲ *On SS309 via Lido Adriano to Punta Marina.*
Open 17 Apr-21 Sep **Site** 14HEC ❤ ❤ ❤ ❤ ➤ **Facilities** ↑ 🅰 ⊙ 🔌 🅰 ⏀
🅰 ⏀ **Services** 🍴 🍽 ➕ 🖸 **Leisure** ❤ PS

Coop 3

via dei Campeggi 8, 48020 ☎ 0544 437353 ▤ 0544 438144
e-mail info@campingcoop3.it
Level site with some high pines and poplars. Beach 300m away across flat dunes.
➲ *Signed.*
Open 21 Apr-10 Sep **Site** 7HEC ❤ ❤ ➤ **Prices** ⋔ 4.20-7.30 ▲ 2.90-5.60
pitch 8.40-13.10 ➤ (static)283.50-497 **Facilities** ↑ 🅰 ⊙ 🔌 🅰 ⏀
Services 🍴 🍽 **Off-site** ⏀ ❤PS ➕

RAVENNA, MARINA DI RAVENNA

International Piomboni

Viale Della Pace 421, 48023 ☎ 0544 530230 ▤ 0544 538618
e-mail info@campingpiomboni.it
website www.campingpiomboni.it
Site on slightly undulating mainly grassy terrain with pines and poplars. Separate section for tents.
➲ *Access from SS309 or A14.*
Open 20 Apr-16 Sep **Site** 5HEC ❤ ❤ ❤ ❤ ➤ **Prices** ⋔ 4.10-7.20 pitch 7.50-
11.20 ➤ (static)189-336 **Facilities** ↑ 🅰 ⊙ 🔌 🅰 ⏀ **Services** 🍴 🍽 ➕
🖸 **Leisure** ❤ S

RICCIONE FORLI

Alberello

via Torino 80, 47036 ☎ 0541 615402 ▤ 0541 615248
e-mail direzione@alberello.it
website www.alberello.it
On the seafront connected to the beach by a private subway. Popular with families, with a range of recreational facilities.
➲ *Via A14 & SS16.*
Open 5 Apr-24 Sep **Site** 4HEC ❤ ❤ ❤ Ⓧ **Prices** ⋔ 3.80-7.95 pitch 8.50-
13.75 **Facilities** ↑ 🅰 ⊙ 🔌 🅰 ⏀ **Services** 🍴 🍽 🖸 **Off-site** ❤LPRS ➕

Fontanelle

via Torino 56, 47838 ☎ 0541 615449 ▤ 0541 610193
e-mail info@campingfontanelle.com
website www.campingfontanelle.com
On southern outskirts, separated from the beach by the coast road (underpass to public beach).
➲ *Off SS16 between Km216 & Km217.*
Open 21 Apr-22 Sep **Site** 6HEC ❤ ❤ ➤ **Prices** ⋔ 3.80-7.95
➤ 6 pitch 8.50-13.75 **Facilities** ↑ 🅰 ⊙ 🔌 🅰 ⏀ **Services** 🍴 🍽 ➕ 🖸
Leisure ❤ S

Riccione

via Marsala N10, 47838 ☎ 0541 690160 ▤ 0541 690044
e-mail info@campingriccione.it
website www.campingriccione.it
Extensive flat meadowland with poplars, 300m from the sea.
➲ *Off SS16 on S outskirts of town towards sea for 200m.*
Open 6 Apr-16 Sep **Site** 6.5HEC ❤ ❤ ➤ **Prices** ⋔ 3.70-7.70 pitch 8.60-
22.70 **Facilities** ↑ 🅰 ⊙ 🔌 🅰 ⏀ **Services** 🍴 🍽 ➕ 🖸 **Leisure** ❤ PS
Off-site ❤S

Italy

Facilities 🅰 shop ↑ shower ⊙ electric points for razors 🔌 electric points for caravans ⏀ parking by tents permitted 🅿 compulsory separate car park
Services 🍽 café/restaurant 🍴 bar ⏀ Camping Gaz International 🅰 gas other than Camping Gaz ➕ first aid facilities 🖸 laundry
Leisure ❤ swimming L-Lake P-Pool R-River S-Sea **Off-site** All facilities within 2km

ROSETO DEGLI ABRUZZI TERAMO

Eurcamping-Roseto
Lungomare Trieste Sud 90, 64026
☎ 085 8993179 ▤ 085 8930552
e-mail eurcamping@camping.it
website www.eurcamping.it
A meadow site at the S end of the beach road.
➔ *Off SS16 in town, site 0.5km.*
Open Apr-Oct **Site** 5HEC ⚘ ⚘ ⌂ **Prices** ⚹ 4-9 pitch 8-16 **Facilities** ⋒ ⓘ
⊙ ⊕ ⌀ ⅏ ⓟ **Services** ⓩ ⓘ ⅀ **Leisure** ⚘ PS **Off-site** ⚘R

Gilda
viale Makarska, 64026 ☎ 085 8941023 ▤ 085 8941023
e-mail gilda@camping.it
A picturesque wooded setting with modern facilities and direct access
to the beach.
Open Jun-12 Sep **Site** 1.5HEC ⚘ ⚘ ⌂ ⌀ **Facilities** ⋒ ⓘ ⊙ ⊕ ⅏ ⓟ
Services ⓩ ⓘ ⅀ **Leisure** ⚘ S **Off-site** ⌀ ⚘P

SALSOMAGGIORE TERME PARMA

Arizona
via Tabiano 42 A, 43030 ☎ 0524 565648 ▤ 0524 567589
e-mail info@camping-arizona.it
website www.camping-arizona.it
Family site with plenty of activities, and close to two thermal cure
establishments.
➔ *Off A1 to Tabiano.*
Open Apr-15 Oct **Site** 13HEC ⚘ ⚘ ⌂ ⌀ **Prices** ⚹ 6-7.75 ⌂ 8-12.50 ⚹ 6-
12.50 ⌂ (static)399-644 **Facilities** ⋒ ⓘ ⊙ ⊕ ⌀ ⓟ **Services** ⓩ ⓘ ⅀
Leisure ⚘ P **Off-site** ⅏ ⊞

S ARCANGELO SUL TRASIMENO PERUGIA

Polvese
via Montivalle, 6060 ☎ 075 848078 ▤ 075 848050
e-mail cpolvese@interfree.iti
website www.polvese.com
A peaceful location beside Lake Trasimeno with plenty of recreational
facilities.
Open Apr-Sep **Site** 5HEC ⚘ ⚘ ⌂ **Facilities** ⋒ ⓘ ⊙ ⊕ ⌀ ⓟ
Services ⓩ ⓘ ⅀ **Leisure** ⚘ LP

Villaggio Italgest
via Martiri di Cefalonia, 06060 ☎ 075 848238 ▤ 075 848085
e-mail camping@italgest.com
website www.italgest.com
Situated by a lake and surrounded by woodland. There are modern
facilities and various recreations are available.
Open Apr-Sep **Site** 5.5HEC ⚘ ⚘ ⌂ ⚹ **Prices** ⚹ 6-8.40 ⚘ 2-2.50 ⌂ 6-8.50
⚹ 6-8.50 **Facilities** ⋒ ⓘ ⊙ ⊕ ⌀ ⅏ ⓟ **Services** ⓩ ⓘ ⊞ ⅀ **Leisure** ⚘ LP

SAN MARINO

Centro Turistico San Marino
Strada San Michele 50, 47893 ☎ 0549 903964 ▤ 0549 907120
e-mail info@centrovacanzesanmarino.com
website www.centrovacanzesanmarino.com
A quiet wooded location close to the centre of the Republic of San
Marino.
➔ *A14 exit Rimini Sud.*
Open All year **Site** 10HEC ⚘ ⚘ ⌂ ⚹ **Prices** ⚹ 6-9 ⚘ 2-4 ⌂ 4-12 ⚹ 3-8
Facilities ⋒ ⓘ ⊙ ⊕ ⌀ ⅏ ⓟ **Services** ⓩ ⓘ ⅀ **Leisure** ⚘ P
Off-site ⚘S ⊞

SAN PIERO IN BAGNO FORLI

Altosavio
strada per Alfero 37c, 47026
☎ 0543 903409 ▤ 0543 903409/917397
e-mail i4std@libero.it
website www.bagnodiromagnaturismo.it
On level ground at an altitude of 600m with good facilities.
➔ *E45 exit Bagno di Romagna for San Piero in Bagno.*
Open 24 Apr-Sep **Site** 1.3HEC ⚘ ⚘ **Prices** ⚹ 4.60-5.30 pitch 8
Facilities ⋒ ⊙ ⊕ ⓟ **Services** ⓩ ⓘ ⅀ **Off-site** ⓘ ⅏ ⚘LR ⊞

SASSO MARCONI BOLOGNA

Piccolo Paradiso
via Sirano, Marzabotto, 40037 ☎ 051 842680 ▤ 051 6756581
e-mail piccoloparadiso@aruba.it
website www.campingpiccoloparadiso.com
Pleasant site with plenty of trees. A sports centre less than 100m from
the site provides excellent facilities for sports and recreation.
➔ *A1 exit for town, towards Vado for 2km, signed.*
Open All year **Site** 6.5HEC ⚘ ⚘ ⌂ ⌀ **Facilities** ⋒ ⓘ ⊙ ⊕ ⌀ ⅏ ⓟ
Services ⓩ ⓘ ⅀ **Off-site** ⚘LPR

AT SAVIGNANO SUL RUBICONE

Rubicone
via Matrice Destra 1, 47039 ☎ 0541 346377 ▤ 0541 346999
e-mail info@campingrubicone.com
website www.campingrubicone.com
An extensive, level site divided into two sections by a narrow canal.
Site extends to the beach.
➔ *0.8km from fork at Km187/0 off SS16 Strada Adriatica.*
Open May-Sep **Site** 13HEC ⚘ ⚘ ⌂ ⊗ **Prices** ⚹ 5-9.10 pitch 10.90-15.50
Facilities ⋒ ⓘ ⊙ ⊕ ⌀ ⓟ **Services** ⓩ ⓘ ⊞ ⅀ **Leisure** ⚘ PS

SCACCHI, LIDO DEGLI FERRARA

Florenz
via alpi Centrali 199, 44020 ☎ 0533 380193 ▤ 0533 381456
e-mail info@campingflorenz.com
website www.campingflorenz.com
Site with dunes extending to the sea.
➔ *Off Strada Romea for Lido Degli Scacchi, continue on
asphalt road to beach.*
Open Apr-22 Sep **Site** 8HEC ⚘ ⚘ ⌂ **Prices** ⚹ 4-8.30 pitch 9.50-15.70
Facilities ⋒ ⓘ ⊙ ⊕ ⌀ ⅏ ⓟ **Services** ⓩ ⓘ ⅀ **Leisure** ⚘ PS

SENIGALLIA ANCONA

Summerland
via Podesti 236, 60019 ☎ 071 7926816 ▤ 071 7927758
website www.camping.it/marche/summerland
A pleasant site with good facilities, 150m from the sea.
➔ *SS16 exit Senigallia, site 3km.*
Open Jun-15 Sep **Site** 4.5HEC ⚘ ⚘ ⌂ ⊗ **Facilities** ⋒ ⓘ ⊙ ⊕ ⌀ ⓟ
Services ⓩ ⓘ ⊞ ⅀ **Off-site** ⚘PS

Site 6HEC (site size) ⚘ grass ⚘ sand ⚘ stone ⚘ little shade ⚘ partly shaded ⚘ mainly shaded ⌂ bungalows for hire
⌂ caravans for hire ⚹ tents for hire ⊗ no dogs **Prices** ⚹ adult per night ⚘ car per night pp per person per night ⌂ caravan per night
⚹ tent per night ⌂ (static)-caravan hire per week

SPINA, LIDO DI FERRARA

Spina

via del Campeggio 99, 44024 ☎ 0533 330179 ▤ 0533 333566
e-mail spina@clubdesole.com
website www.clubdesole.com
Extensive site on level meadowland and slightly hilly dune terrain. Separate section for dog owners.
➲ *Signed off SS309.*
Open Mar-Oct **Site** 24HEC ✹ ✿ ▥ **Facilities** ⬕ ⛺ ⊙ ⊡ ⌀ ⓟ **Services** ⬚ ⦿ ⬛ **Leisure** ⚘ PS **Off-site** ⬛

SPOLETO PERUGIA

Monteluco

S.Pietro, 06049 ☎ 0743 220358 ▤ 0743 220358
e-mail campeggiomonteluco@libero.it
website www.campingspoleto.com
A modern site on the slopes of Monteluco.
➲ *SS75 exit Foligno, onto SS3 for Spoleto, Monteluco road to site.*
Open Apr-Sep **Site** 6HEC ✹ ✦ ✿ ▥ ▲ **Prices** ⚹ 5-6 ⟐ 2-3 ▥ 4-6 ▲ 4-6 ▥ (static)140-200 **Facilities** ⬕ ⊙ ⊡ ⊡ ⓟ ⓟ **Services** ⬚ ⦿ ⬛ **Leisure** ⚘ P **Off-site** ⛺ ⌀ ⚘P ⬛

TORINO DI SANGRO MARINA CHIETI

Belvedere

66020 ☎ 0873 911381
Open Jun-6 Sep **Site** 1.5HEC ✹ ✿ ▥ **Facilities** ⬕ ⛺ ⊙ ⊡ ⊡ ⌀ ▤ ⓟ **Services** ⬚ ⦿ ⬛ **Leisure** ⚘ S **Off-site** ⦿ ⚘P ⬛

VALLICELLA DI MONZUNO BOLOGNA

Le Querce

Rioveggio, 40036 ☎ 051 6770248 ▤ 051 6770394
A well-equipped site in a wooded mountain setting.
➲ *Access via Autostrada del Sole.*
Open May-Sep **Site** 12HEC ✹ ✿ ▥ ▲ **Prices** ⚹ 6 ▥ 8 ▲ 7 ▥ (static)120 **Facilities** ⬕ ⛺ ⊙ ⊡ ⌀ ▤ ⓟ ⓟ **Services** ⬚ ⦿ ⬛ **Leisure** ⚘ LPR

VASTO CHIETI

Europa

66055 ☎ 0873 801988 ▤ 0873 802553
e-mail info@campingeuropasrl.it
website www.campingeuropasrl.it
Site on level terrain by the road with poplars.
➲ *On SS16 at Km522.*
Open Apr-Sep **Site** 2.3HEC ✹ ✿ ▥ **Facilities** ⬕ ⛺ ⊙ ⊡ **Services** ⬚ ⦿ ⬛ **Leisure** ⚘ S **Off-site** ⬛

Grotta del Saraceno

via Osca 6, loc Vignola, 66054 ☎ 0873 310213 ▤ 0873 310295
e-mail info@grottadelsaraceno.it
website www.grottadelsaraceno.it
Site in olive grove on steep coastal cliffs with lovely views. Steep path to beach.
➲ *Off SS16 at Km512.2.*
Open 15 Jun-15 Sep **Site** 12HEC ✹ ✿ ▥ **Facilities** ⬕ ⛺ ⊙ ⊡ ▤ **Services** ⬚ ⦿ ⬛ **Leisure** ⚘ S **Off-site** ⌀ ▤

Pioppeto

66055 ☎ 0873 801466 ▤ 0873 801466
website www.ilpioppeto.it
Camping Card Compulsory.
Open 15 May-14Sep **Site** 1.7HEC ✹ ✿ **Prices** ⚹ 6-7.50 pitch 11-15
Facilities ⬕ ⛺ ⊙ ⊡ ⌀ ⓟ **Services** ⬚ ⦿ ⬛ **Leisure** ⚘ S **Off-site** ⬛

ZOCCA MODENA

Montequestiolo

via Montequestiolo 184, 41059 ☎ 059 985045 ▤ 059 985045
e-mail jagatzz@libero.it
Open All year **Site** 1.8HEC ✹ ✦ ✿ ▥ ▲ **Prices** ⚹ 6-8 ⟐ 5-8 ▲ 6-8 pitch 10-12 ▥ (static)90-120 **Facilities** ⬕ ⛺ ⊙ ⊡ ⓟ **Services** ⬚ ⦿ ⬛ ⬛ **Off-site** ⌀ ⚘P

ROME

BOLSENA VITERBO

Blu International

via Cassia km 111,650, 01023 ☎ 0761 798855 ▤ 0761 798855
e-mail info@blucamping.it
website www.blucamping.it
A modern site with good facilities in a wooded location on the shore of Lake Bolsena. Compulsory separate car parking in July and August.
➲ *A1 exit Orvieto, then via Cassia at Km111.65.*
Open 4 Apr-Sep **Site** 3HEC ✹ ✿ ▥ **Prices** pitch 17-22.50 (incl 2 persons) **Facilities** ⬕ ⛺ ⊙ ⊡ ⌀ ⓟ **Services** ⬚ ⦿ ⬛ **Leisure** ⚘ LP **Off-site** ⌀ ▤ ⬛

Lido

via Cassia km111, 01023 ☎ 0761 799258 ▤ 0761 796105
e-mail info@bolsenacamping.it
website www.bolsenacamping.it
A lakeside family site with modern facilities.
➲ *Motorway exit Orvieto.*
Open Apr-Sep **Site** 10HEC ✹ ✿ ▥ ⊗ **Prices** ⚹ 4.80-6.90 pitch 8.90-10.90 ▥ (static)269.50-458.50 **Facilities** ⬕ ⛺ ⊙ ⊡ ⌀ ▤ ⓟ **Services** ⬚ ⦿ ⬛ **Leisure** ⚘ LP

BRACCIANO ROMA

Porticciolo

via Porticciolo, 00062 ☎ 06 99803060 ▤ 06 998803030
e-mail info@porticciolo.it
website www.porticciolo.it
A family site in a pleasant location on the shore of a lake.
➲ *SS493 to Bracciano.*
Open Apr-Sep **Site** 3.2HEC ✹ ✿ ▥ **Prices** ⚹ 4.20-6 pitch 11 (incl 2 persons) ▥ (static)147-250 **Facilities** ⬕ ⛺ ⊙ ⊡ ⌀ ⓟ **Services** ⬚ ⦿ ⬛ **Leisure** ⚘ L **Off-site** ⬛

FIANO ROMANO ROMA

Bungalow Park I Pini

via delle Sassete 1A, 00065 ☎ 0765 453349 ▤ 0765 453057
e-mail ipini@camping.it
website www.ecvacanze.it
A modern, well-equipped site within easy reach of the centre of Rome. A good base for excursions.
➲ *A1 exit Fiano Romana.*
Open 24 Mar-4 Nov **Site** 5HEC ✹ ✿ ✿ **Prices** ⚹ 8.50-10 pitch 8-11.50 **Facilities** ⬕ ⛺ ⊙ ⊡ ⌀ ▤ ⓟ **Services** ⬚ ⦿ ⬛ ⬛ **Leisure** ⚘ P

Facilities ⛺ shop ⬕ shower ⊙ electric points for razors ⊡ electric points for caravans ⓟ parking by tents permitted ⓟ compulsory separate car park
Services ⦿ café/restaurant ⬚ bar ⌀ Camping Gaz International ▤ gas other than Camping Gaz ⬛ first aid facilities ⬛ laundry
Leisure ⚘ swimming L-Lake P-Pool R-River S-Sea **Off-site** All facilities within 2km

Italy

FORMIA LATINA

Gianola
via delle Vigne, 04023 ☎ 0771 720223 ▤ 0771 720223
e-mail gianolacamping@tiscalinet.it
website www.gianolacamping.it
A narrow grassland area near a stream and trees amid agricultural land. Pleasant sandy beach edged by rocks.
➲ *Off Roma-Napoli road, 0.8km from S Croce.*
Open Apr-Sep **Site** 4HEC ❤ ⬭ 🏠 **Prices** ♠ 3.10-8 ⬛ 6-15 **Facilities** � 🛁 ⊙ ⬛ **Services** ▥ 🍽 🖻 **Leisure** ⬧ RS **Off-site** ⬧ ᐟᐟ 🚻 ➕

MINTURNO, MARINA DI LATINA

Golden Garden
via Dunale 74, 04020 ☎ 0771 681425 ▤ 0771 614059
e-mail servizio.clienti@goldengarden.it
website www.goldengarden.it
Secluded quiet site within agricultural area by the sea.
➲ *SS7 over river bridge (Garigliano), continue 4.6km (last 1km sandy track).*
Open Apr-20 Sep **Site** 2.3HEC ❤ ⬭ 🏠 🏠 ⊗ **Prices** pitch 24-45 (incl 2 persons) pp8-13 **Facilities** � 🛁 ⊙ ⬛ ᐟᐟ ⬛ ⊕ **Services** ▥ 🍽 🖻 **Leisure** ⬧ S **Off-site** 🍽 ⬧PR ➕

MONTALTO DI CASTRO, MARINA DI VITERBO

California
01014 ☎ 0766 802848 ▤ 0766 801210
e-mail info@californiacampingvillage.com
website www.californiacampingvillage.com
Situated on the coast below an ancient pine grove with good facilities for sports and leisure.
Open May-14 Sep **Site** 1.4HEC ❤ ⬭ 🏠 🏠 ⊗ **Facilities** � 🛁 ⊙ ⬛ ᐟᐟ ⊕ **Services** ▥ 🍽 🖻 **Leisure** ⬧ PS

Internazionale Pionier Etrusco
via Vulsinia, 01014 ☎ 0766 802199 ▤ 0766 801214
e-mail meleute@tin.it
website www.campingpionieretrusco.com
Situated in a pine forest close to the beach. Various leisure and sports activities, and a relaxing atmosphere.
Open Mar-15 Oct **Site** 6HEC ❤ ⬭ 🏠 🏠 **Prices** ⬛ 17-32 ▲ 3.60-6.50 **Facilities** � ⊙ ⬛ ᐟᐟ ⊕ **Services** ▥ 🍽 🖻 **Off-site** 🛁 ⬧RS ➕

ROMA (ROME) ROMA

Flaminio Village
via Flaminia Nuova 821, 00189 ☎ 06 3332604 ▤ 06 3330653
e-mail info@villageflaminio.com
website www.villageflaminio.com
An extensive site with good facilities, set on narrow hill terraces in a quiet valley.
➲ *Off ring road onto SS3 (via Flaminia) for 2.5km towards city centre.*
Open All year **Site** 8.4HEC ❤ 🏠 🏠 **Prices** ♠ 9.50-10.70 ⬛ 10.40-13.40 ▲ 5.30-6.90 **Facilities** � 🛁 ⊙ ⬛ ᐟᐟ ⊕ **Services** ▥ 🍽 🖻 **Leisure** ⬧ P **Off-site** ⬧R ➕

Happy
via Prato della Corte 1915, 123 ☎ 06 33626401 ▤ 06 33613800
e-mail info@happycamping.net
website www.happycamping.net
Convenient location in the north of the town. Modern installations, electricity and hot water free throughout.
➲ *Grande Raccordo Anulare (ring road) exit 5.*
Open Mar-6 Nov **Site** 3.6HEC ❤ ⬭ 🏠 🏠 **Prices** ♠ 8.50-9.80 ⬅ 2.90 ⬛ 6.20-7.50 ▲ 4.30-5.20 **Facilities** � 🛁 ⊙ ⬛ ᐟᐟ **Services** ▥ 🍽 🖻 **Leisure** ⬧ P

Roma
via Aurelia 831, 00165 ☎ 06 6623018 ▤ 06 66418147
e-mail campingroma@ecvacanze.it
website www.ecvacanze.it
The site lies on terraces on a hill near the AGIP Motel. Various excursions can be arranged.
➲ *From ring road onto SS1 (via Aurelia) for 1.5km towards town centre, turn to site at Km8/11.*
Open All year **Site** 3HEC ❤ ⬭ 🏠 🏠 ▲ **Facilities** � 🛁 ⊙ ⬛ ᐟᐟ ⊕ **Services** ▥ 🍽 🖻 **Leisure** ⬧ P **Off-site** ➕

Seven Hills
via Cassia 1216, 00189 ☎ 06 30310826 ▤ 06 30310039
e-mail info@sevenhills.it
website www.sevenhills.it
A fine, partly terraced site in beautiful rural surroundings. Well placed for access to the city by bus or underground.
➲ *Outer ring road exit 3, site 2.5km NE.*
Open Mar-1 Nov **Site** 5HEC ❤ ⬭ 🏠 🏠 ▲ **Prices** pitch 27.50-31 (incl 2 persons) pp8.50-9.50 **Facilities** � 🛁 ⊙ ⬛ ᐟᐟ ⊕ **Services** ▥ 🍽 ➕ 🖻 **Leisure** ⬧ P

Tiber
via Tiberina Km1400, 188 ☎ 06 33610733 ▤ 06 33612314
e-mail info@campingtiber.com
website www.campingtiber.com
On level grassland, shaded by poplars beside the Tiber.
➲ *Ring road exit 3, site signed N of city. From S signs for Prima Porta.*
Open Apr-Oct **Site** 5HEC ❤ ⬭ 🏠 **Prices** ♠ 9.20-10.50 ⬅ 4.30-5.10 ⬛ 6.50-8.30 ▲ 3.10-6.90 **Facilities** � 🛁 ⊙ ⬛ ᐟᐟ ⊕ **Services** ▥ 🍽 ➕ 🖻 **Leisure** ⬧ PR

SALTO DI FONDI LATINA

Fondi Holiday Camp
via Flacca Km 6800, 04020 ☎ 0771 555009 ▤ 0771 556281
e-mail info@holidayvillage.it
website www.holidayvillage.it
A well-shaded and well-equipped site beside the Mediterranean.
Open Apr-Sep **Site** 4HEC ❤ ⬭ 🏠 ⊗ **Prices** pitch 29-58 (incl 2 persons) **Facilities** � 🛁 ⊙ ⬛ ᐟᐟ ⊕ **Services** ▥ 🍽 ➕ 🖻 **Leisure** ⬧ PS

Site 6HEC (site size) ❤ grass ⬭ sand ⬮ stone ♣ little shade ❦ partly shaded ❤ mainly shaded 🏠 bungalows for hire ⬛ caravans for hire ▲ tents for hire ⊗ no dogs **Prices** ♠ adult per night ⬅ car per night pp per person per night ⬛ caravan per night ▲ tent per night ⬛ (static)-caravan hire per week

TERRACINA LATINA

Badino

Porto Badino, 04019 ☎ 0773 764430 ▤ 0773 764430

Wooded surroundings with direct access to the beach.

⊃ *Off Roma-Napoli road towards canal (Porto Canale Badino) & sea.*

Open Apr-15 Oct **Site** 1.8HEC ❤ ❤ ❤ ♠ ♣ **Prices** ♦ 4.50-7.40 pitch 7.60-13.60 ➡ (static)300-480 **Facilities** ♠ ☺ ⊕ ♠ ⊘ ᴬ ♠ **Services** ⊻ ⓘ ◙ **Leisure** ⊛ S **Off-site** ☷ ⓘ

SOUTH

BAIA DOMIZIA CASERTA

Baia Domizia

Camping Villaggio Baia Domizia, 81030
☎ 0823 930164 ▤ 0823 930375

e-mail info@baiadomizia.it

website www.baiadomizia.it

Part of this extensive seaside site is laid out with flower beds. Good sports and leisure facilities. Ideal for families. No radios allowed.

⊃ *Off SS7 (qtr) at Km6/V & 3km towards sea.*

Open 29 Apr-17 Sep **Site** 30HEC ❤ ❤ ❤ ♠ ♣ ⊗ **Facilities** ♠ ☷ ⊕ ♠ ⊘ ᴬ ⑫ **Services** ⊻ ⓘ ➕ ◙ **Leisure** ⊛ PS

BATTIPAGLIA SALERNO

Lido Mediterraneo

via Litoranea, Salerno Paestum, 84091
☎ 0828 624097 ▤ 0828 624097

e-mail mediterraneo.campania@camping.it

website www.camping.it/campania/mediterraneo

Set in a pine wood with direct access to a private beach.

Open 10 Mar-22 Sept **Site** 1.2HEC ❤ ❤ ♠ ♣ **Facilities** ♠ ☷ ⊕ ♠ ⊘ ᴬ ⑫ **Services** ⊻ ⓘ **Leisure** ⊛ S **Off-site** ⓘ ⊛P ➕

BRIATICO CATANZARO

Dolomiti

89817 ☎ 0963 391355 ▤ 0963 393009

e-mail info@dolomitisulmare.com

website www.dolomitisulmare.com

The site is in a delightful setting on two terraces planted with olive trees. It lies by the road and 150m from railway.

⊃ *Off road 522 between Km17 & Km18 towards sea.*

Open 24 Jun-24 Sep **Site** 5HEC ❤ ❤ ♠ ♣ **Facilities** ♠ ☷ ⊕ ♠ ⑫ **Services** ⊻ ⓘ ◙ **Leisure** ⊛ PS **Off-site** ⊘ ᴬ ⊛P ➕

CAMEROTA, MARINA DI SALERNO

Risacca

via delle Barche 11, Lentiscella, 84059
☎ 0974 932415 ▤ 0974 932415

e-mail larisacca@its2001.it

website www.larisacca.com

On level ground, shaded by olive trees, with direct access to a sandy beach.

⊃ *Approach via SS18.*

Open 20 May-20 Sep **Site** 2HEC ❤ ❤ ♠ **Facilities** ♠ ☷ ⊕ ♠ ⑫ **Services** ⊻ ⓘ ➕ **Leisure** ⊛ S **Off-site** ⊘ ᴬ

CAPO VATICANO CATANZARO

Gabbiano

San Nicolo di Ricadi, 89865 ☎ 0963 663159 ▤ 0963 663384

e-mail info@villaggioilgabbiano.com

website www.villaggioilgabbiano.com

Open Apr-Oct **Site** ❤ ❤ ❤ ♠ **Facilities** ♠ ☷ ⊕ ᴬ ⑫ **Services** ⊻ ⓘ ➕ ◙ **Leisure** ⊛ PS **Off-site** ➕

CAROVIGNO BRINDISI

AT SPECCHIOLLA, LIDO

Pineta al Mare

Lido Specchiolla, 72012 ☎ 0831 987024 ▤ 0831 987803

e-mail info@campingpinetamare.com

website www.campingpinetamare.com

Site in pine woodland with sandy beach and some rocks.

⊃ *E of Bari-Brindisi road at Km21.5.*

Open Apr-20 Sep **Site** 5.5HEC ❤ ❤ ♠ **Prices** ♦ 5.90-9 ➡ 1.90-3 ➡ 6.20-9 ⚠ 4.80-7 **Facilities** ♠ ☷ ⊕ ♠ ⊘ ᴬ ⑫ **Services** ⊻ ⓘ ◙ **Leisure** ⊛ PS

CIRÚ MARINA CATANZARO

Punta Alice

88811 ☎ 0962 31160 ▤ 0962 373823

e-mail info@puntalice.it

website www.puntalice.it

Meadowland among lush Mediterranean vegetation, bordering a fine gravel beach some 50m wide.

⊃ *2km from town. Off SS106 Strada Ionica at Km290 to Cira Marina, through village & beach road towards lighthouse for 1.5km.*

Open Apr-Sep **Site** 5.5HEC ❤ ❤ ♠ **Facilities** ♠ ☷ ⊕ ♠ ⊘ ᴬ ⑫ **Services** ⊻ ⓘ ➕ ◙ **Leisure** ⊛ PS

Villaggio Torrenova

via Torrenova, 88811 ☎ 0962 31482

Directly on sea, with on site facilities to suit all the family.

Open May-Sep **Site** 1.2HEC ❤ ❤ ♠ ♣ **Facilities** ♠ ☷ ⊕ ♠ ᴬ ⑫ **Services** ⊻ ⓘ ◙ **Leisure** ⊛ S

CORIGLIANO CÁLABRO COSENZA

Thurium

Contrada Ricota Grande, 87060 ☎ 0983 851101 ▤ 0983 851955

e-mail info@campingthurium.com

website www.thurium.it

The site is close to the beach and has all the facilites needed for an enjoyable camping break. It is just a walk away from the woodland and ideal for peaceful walks.

Open 24 May-Dec **Site** 16HEC ❤ ❤ ♠ **Prices** ♦ 2.50-9.80 ➡ 0.50-4.10 ➡ 2.80-12 ⚠ 2.80-12 **Facilities** ♠ ☷ ⊕ ♠ ⊘ ᴬ ⑫ ⑫ **Services** ⊻ ⓘ ➕ ◙ **Leisure** ⊛ PS

Italy

Facilities ☷ shop ♠ shower ⊕ electric points for razors ♠ electric points for caravans ⑫ parking by tents permitted ⑫ compulsory separate car park
Services ⓘ café/restaurant ⊻ bar ⊘ Camping Gaz International ᴬ gas other than Camping Gaz ➕ first aid facilities ◙ laundry
Leisure ⊛ swimming L-Lake P-Pool R-River S-Sea **Off-site** All facilities within 2km

EBOLI SALERNO

Paestum

Foce Sele, 84020 ☎ 0828 691003 ▤ 0828 691003

e-mail info@campingpaestum.it

website www.campingpaestum.it

Sandy, meadowland site in tall poplar wood by the mouth of a river. Steps and bus service to private beach, 0.6km from site.

⮑ Off Litoranea at Km20 at fork to Santa Cecilia, continue 300m, signed.

Open 15 May-15 Sep **Site** 8HEC ⛺ 🌳 🏠 🚐 **Prices** ⭢ 4-7 ⛺ 8-12 pitch 11-19 🚐 (static)420-630 **Facilities** 🏪 🗟 ⊙ 🚐 ⌀ 🚿 🅟 **Services** 🏴 🍽 ➕ 🖸 **Leisure** 🏊 P **Off-site** 🏊RS

GALLIPOLI LECCE

Baia di Gallipoli

73014 ☎ 0833 273210

e-mail info@baiadigallipoli.com

website www.baiadigallipoli.com

A holiday village set amid pine woods close to the sea with good facilities.

⮑ 5km SE of Gallipoli.

Open All year **Site** 14HEC ⛺ 🏠 🏠 **Facilities** 🏪 🗟 ⊙ 🚐 🅟 🅟 **Services** 🏴 🍽 🖸 **Leisure** 🏊 P **Off-site** 🏊S

Vecchia Torre

73014 ☎ 0833 209083

This clean, well-kept site lies among dunes in a pine wood. Small pitches.

⮑ 5km N of Gallipoli and 200m S of Hotel Rivabella at seaward side of coast road.

Open Jun-Sep **Site** 8HEC 🏖 🌳 🏠 ⊗ **Facilities** 🏪 🗟 ⊙ 🚐 ⌀ 🚿 🅟 **Services** 🏴 🍽 ➕ 🖸 **Leisure** 🏊 S

GIOVINAZZO BARI

Campofreddo

Stada Statale 16, Focalita Ponte, 70054

☎ 080 3942112 ▤ 080 3942290

e-mail torraco@libero.it

website www.campofreddo.com

Site in level terrain by the sea, mainly under sunshade roofing.

⮑ Off SS16 at Km784.3, 20km N of Bari.

Open 20 May-20 Sep **Site** 34HEC ⛺ 🌳 🌳 🏠 **Facilities** 🏪 🗟 ⊙ 🚐 🚿 🚿 **Services** 🏴 🍽 ➕ 🖸 **Off-site** 🍽 🏊S

GUARDAVALLE, MARINA DI CATANZARO

Dello Ionio

via Nazionale, 88065 ☎ 0967 86002 ▤ 0967 86271

e-mail calandrusa@yahoo.it

website www.calalandrusa.it

Site on the seafront with a 4km sandy beach. All pitches are under the shade of tall trees and have large grassy areas.

⮑ 2km from Santa Caterina dello Jonio on SS106.

Open Jun-15 Sep **Site** 7HEC ⛺ 🌳 🏠 **Facilities** 🏪 🗟 ⊙ 🚐 ⌀ 🚿 **Services** 🏴 🍽 ➕ 🖸 **Leisure** 🏊 PS

LÁURA SALERNO

Hera Argiva

84063 ☎ 0828 851193

Site in sandy terrain in eucalyptus grove by the sea.

⮑ Signed from Km88/VII SS18.

Open Apr-Sep **Site** 40HEC ⛺ 🌳 🏠 🚐 **Facilities** 🏪 🗟 ⊙ 🚐 ⌀ 🅟 **Services** 🏴 🍽 🖸 **Leisure** 🏊 S **Off-site** ➕

LEPORANO, MARINA DI TARANTO

Porto Pirrone

Litoranea Salentina, 74020 ☎ 099 5334844 ▤ 099 5334844

e-mail info@portopirrone.it

website www.portopirrone.it

Set in a pine wood offering flat large plots for both tents and caravans. Good sports and entertainment. No animals.

⮑ A14 from Massafra towards Taranto & Leporano, site near marina.

Open Jun-Sep **Site** 3.2HEC ⛺ 🌳 🌳 🏠 🚐 ⊗ **Facilities** 🏪 🗟 ⊙ 🚐 🚿 🅟 **Services** 🏴 🍽 ➕ **Leisure** 🏊 S **Off-site** 🍽 ⌀ ➕

MÁCCHIA FOGGIA

Monaco

71030 ☎ 0884 530280 ▤ 0884 530280

A pleasant location with good facilities and direct access to the beach.

Open Jun-15 Sep **Site** 5.3HEC ⛺ 🌳 🏠 🚐 **Facilities** 🏪 🗟 ⊙ 🚐 ⌀ 🅟 **Services** 🏴 🍽 ➕ 🖸 **Leisure** 🏊 PS

MANFREDONIA FOGGIA

Ippocampo

SS 159, 71043 ☎ 0884 571121

e-mail campingippocampo@email.it

website www.campingippocampo.too.it

Set in the grounds of a holiday village.

Open May -Sep **Site** 8HEC ⛺ 🌳 🌳 🏠 🚐 ⛺ **Facilities** 🏪 🗟 ⊙ 🚐 🅟 **Services** 🏴 🍽 ➕ **Leisure** 🏊 S **Off-site** 🏊P

MASSA LUBRENSE NAPOLI

Villa Lubrense

via Partenope 31, 80061 ☎ 081 5339781

website www.villalubrense.it

Open All year **Site** 2.5HEC ⛺ 🌳 🏠 🚐 **Facilities** 🏪 🗟 ⊙ 🚐 ⌀ **Services** 🏴 🍽 ➕ **Leisure** 🏊 PS

MATTINATA FOGGIA

Villaggio Turistico San Lorenzo

71030 ☎ 0884 550152 ▤ 0884 552042

e-mail info@sanlorenzo.it **website** www.sanlorenzo.it

The site lies above the coast road towards Viesta. Bungalows for hire.

Open All year **Site** 3HEC ⛺ 🌳 🏠 **Facilities** 🏪 ⊙ 🚐 🅟 🅟 **Services** 🏴 🍽 🖸 **Leisure** 🏊 PS **Off-site** 🗟 ⌀ 🚿 ➕

METAPONTO, LIDO DI MATERA

Camel Camping Club

viale Magna Grecia, 75010 ☎ 0835 741926 ▤ 0835 745585

e-mail kammel@kammel.it

website www.kammel.it

A modern, well-organised site. Sports and entertainment avaliable all season. Ideal for both relaxing and sightseeing.

Open Jun-18 Sep **Site** 3.5HEC 🏖 🌳 🏠 🚐 **Facilities** 🏪 🗟 ⊙ 🚐 🚿 **Services** 🏴 🍽 **Leisure** 🏊 P **Off-site** ⌀ 🏊RS ➕

Site 6HEC (site size) ⛺ grass 🏖 sand 🌊 stone ♣ little shade 🌳 partly shaded 🌳 mainly shaded 🏠 bungalows for hire 🚐 caravans for hire ⛺ tents for hire ⊗ no dogs **Prices** ⭢ adult per night 🚗 car per night pp per person per night 🚐 caravan per night ⛺ tent per night 🚐 (static)-caravan hire per week

OTRANTO LECCE

Mulino d'Acqua

via S Stefano, 73028 ☎ 0836 802191 🗎 0836 802196
e-mail mulino.camping@anet.it
website www.mulinodacqua.it
Shaded by olive trees, close to the beach and with plenty of organised activities.

Open 27 May-12 Sep **Site** 10HEC ❤ ❤ 🏠 **Prices** ♦ 9-14.50 ➡ 8-18 ▲ 5-15 **Facilities** ⋔ ⓐ ⊙ ⚱ ⚑ ❷ **Services** ⊈ ⓞ 🗑 **Leisure** ≋ PS
Off-site ➕

PALMI REGGIO DI CALABRIA

San Fantino

via S-Fantino, 89015 ☎ 0966 479430 🗎 0966 479430
Site on several terraces with lovely views of the bay of Lido di Palmi. 200m to the beach.

⤷ *Off SS18 towards sea N of Palmi.*
Open All year **Site** 4HEC ❤ ❤ 🏠 ▲ **Facilities** ⋔ ⓐ ⊙ ⚱ ⚑ ⚒ ❷ **Services** ⊈ ⓞ 🗑 **Off-site** ≋ PS ➕

PESCHICI FOGGIA

Centro Turistico San Nicola

Loc San Nicola, 71010 ☎ 0884 964024
Terraced site in lovely location by the sea, in a bay enclosed by rocks. Can become overcrowded.

⤷ *Off Peschici-Vieste coast road, signed along winding road to site in 1km.*
Open Apr-15 Oct **Site** 14HEC ❤ ❤ 🏠 **Prices** ♦ 7-11.50 ➡ 3.50-6 ➡ 8.50-14 ▲ 5.50-8.50 **Facilities** ⋔ ⓐ ⊙ ⚱ ⚒ ⚑ ❷ **Services** ⊈ ⓞ ➕ 🗑 **Leisure** ≋ S

Internazionale Manacore

71010 ☎ 0884 911020 🗎 0884 911049
e-mail manacore@grupposaccia.it
website www.grupposaccia.it
Meadowland with a few terraces in attractive bay, surrounded by wooded hills.

⤷ *Off Peschici-Vieste coast road towards sea on wide U bend.*
Open 15 May-Sep **Site** 22HEC ❤ ❤ 🏠 **Prices** ♦ 5.50-14 ➡ 3.50-5 ➡ 7-16 ▲ 5.50-14 **Facilities** ⋔ ⓐ ⊙ ⚱ ⚒ ⚑ **Services** ⊈ ⓞ ➕ **Leisure** ≋ S

PIZZO CATANZARO

Pinetamare

89812 ☎ 0963 534871 🗎 0963 534871
A sandy site surrounded by tall pine trees. Most water sports are avaliable along the private beach and families are welcome.

⤷ *Salerno-Reggio motorway exit Pizzo, site N of town.*
Open Jun-Sep **Site** 10HEC ❤ ❤ 🏠 ⚱ **Facilities** ⋔ ⓐ ⊙ ⚱ ⚒ ⚑ ❷ **Services** ⊈ ⓞ ➕ 🗑 **Leisure** ≋ PS **Off-site** ≋ L

POMPEI NAPOLI

Spartacus

via Plinio 127, 80045 ☎ 081 8624078 🗎 081 8624078
e-mail campingspartacus@tin.it
website www.campingspartacus.it
Site is on a level meadow with orange trees.

⤷ *Motorway exit Pompei, off Napoli road, opp Scavi di Pompei near IP fuel station.*
Open All year **Site** 9HEC ❤ ❤ 🏠 ⚱ ▲ **Prices** ♦ 5.50-6 ➡ 2-3 ➡ 5.50-6 ➡ (static)203-252 **Facilities** ⋔ ⓐ ⊙ ⚱ ⚒ ⚑ ❷ **Services** ⊈ ⓞ ➕ 🗑

POZZUOLI NAPOLI

Vulcano Solfatara

via Solfatara 161, 80078 ☎ 081 5267413 🗎 081 5263482
e-mail info@solfatara.it
website www.solfatara.it
Clean and orderly site in a deciduous forest near the crater of the extinct Solfatara volcano.

⤷ *From Nuova via Domiziana (SS7 qtr) at Km60/1 (6km before Napoli) turn inland through stone gate.*
Open Apr-Oct, 24 Dec-8 Jan **Site** 3HEC ❤ ❤ 🏠 ⚱ **Prices** ♦ 7.60-9.20 pitch 11.70-13.70 **Facilities** ⋔ ⓐ ⊙ ⚱ ⚒ ⚑ ❷ **Services** ⊈ ⓞ ➕ 🗑 **Leisure** ≋ P **Off-site** ⚑ ≋ S

AT VARCATURO, MARINA DI (12KM N)

Partenope

80014 ☎ 081 5091076 🗎 081 5096767
e-mail info@campingpartenope.it
website www.campingpartenope.it
Partially undulating terrain in woodland of medium height.

⤷ *Off SS7 (via Domiziana) at Km45/II towards sea for 300m.*
Open Jun-8 Sep **Site** 6HEC ❤ ❤ 🏠 ⚱ **Facilities** ⋔ ⓐ ⊙ ⚱ ⚒ ⚑ ❷ **Services** ⊈ ⓞ ➕ **Leisure** ≋ LPRS

PRÁIA A MARE COSENZA

International Camping Village

87028 ☎ 0985 72211 🗎 0985 72211
e-mail reception@campinginternational.it
website www.campinginternational.it
A beautiful location on the gulf of Policastro with fine recreational facilities.

⤷ *A3 to Falerna, onto SS18.*
Open May-Sep **Site** 5.5HEC ❤ ❤ 🏠 ⚱ **Facilities** ⋔ ⓐ ⊙ ⚱ ⚒ ⚑ ❷ **Services** ⊈ ⓞ ➕ 🗑 **Leisure** ≋ PS

RODI GARGANICO FOGGIA

Ripa

Contrada Ripa, 71012 ☎ 0884 965367 🗎 0884 965695
e-mail info@villaggioripa.it
website www.villaggioripa.it
Well-equipped and attractive site close to the beach.

Open 15 Jun-15 Sep **Site** 6HEC ❤ ❤ 🏠 **Prices** ♦ 5-8 ➡ 5-7 **Facilities** ⋔ ⓐ ⊙ ⚱ ⚒ ⚑ ❷ **Services** ⊈ ⓞ ➕ 🗑 **Leisure** ≋ PS **Off-site** ➕

ROSSANO SCALO COSENZA

Marina di Rossano

Contrada Leuca, 87068 ☎ 0983 516054 🗎 0983 514106
e-mail marina.club@tiscalinet.it
website www.marinadirossano.it
Wooded surroundings close to the beach with modern facilities.

⤷ *Via N106.*
Open 15 May-29 Sep **Site** 7HEC ❤ ❤ 🏠 **Prices** ♦ 3.61-6.46 pitch 15.49-23.24 **Facilities** ⋔ ⓐ ⊙ ⚱ ❷ **Services** ⊈ ⓞ ➕ 🗑 **Leisure** ≋ PS
Off-site ⚒

Italy

Facilities ⓐ shop ⋔ shower ⊙ electric points for razors ⚱ electric points for caravans ❷ parking by tents permitted ❷ compulsory separate car park
Services ⓞ café/restaurant ⊈ bar ⚒ Camping Gaz International ⚑ gas other than Camping Gaz ➕ first aid facilities 🗑 laundry
Leisure ≋ swimming L-Lake P-Pool R-River S-Sea **Off-site** All facilities within 2km

SAN MENÁIO FOGGIA

Valle d'Oro

Locacita A/A Del Cervone, 71010 ☎ 0884 991580 ▤ 0884 991580
e-mail info@campingvalledoro.it
website www.campingvalledoro.it
Site in an olive grove with some terraces and surrounded by wooded hills, 2km from the sea.

➔ *Off SS89 onto SS528 to site at Km1.800.*

Open 15 Jun-15 Sep **Site** 3HEC 🌿 🌿 🏠 **Prices** ♣ 3.50-5.50 🚐 2-4 🚍 5-7 Å 4-6.50 **Facilities** 🏪 🛈 ⊙ 🖭 🚿 **Services** 🍴 🍽 **Off-site** 🛈 🤿 🚿PS ⊞

SANTA CESÁREA TERME LECCE

Scogliera

73020 ☎ 0836 949802 ▤ 0836 949794
Attractive site close to the sea.

➔ *1km S on SS173.*

Open All year **Site** 8HEC 🌿 🌿 🏠 ⊗ **Prices** ♣ 4-10 🚐 2-3 🚍 5-10 Å 4-9 **Facilities** 🏪 🛈 ⊙ 🖭 🤿 **Services** 🍴 🍽 **Leisure** 🏊 P **Off-site** 🚿 �S ⊞

SANTA MARIA DI CASTELLABATE SALERNO

Trezene

84072 ☎ 0974 965027 ▤ 0974 965013
e-mail trezene@costacilento
website www.trezene.it
The site is partly divided into pitches and consists of two sections lying either side of the access road. Pitches between road and fine sandy beach are reserved for touring campers.

Open Apr-Oct **Site** 2.5HEC 🌿 🌿 🏠 ⊗ **Facilities** 🏪 🛈 ⊙ 🖭 ⑫ **Services** 🍴 🍽 🖥 **Leisure** 🏊 S **Off-site** 🛈 🤿 🚿 ⊞

SORRENTO NAPOLI

Santa Fortunata Campogaio

via Capo 39, 80067 ☎ 081 8073579 ▤ 081 8073590
e-mail info@santafortunata.com
website www.santafortunata.com
A well-appointed, terraced site shaded by olive trees and with direct access to the sea (50m).

➔ *2km from town centre. 400m after exit from SS145 on road towards Massa Lubrense.*

Open Apr-20 Oct **Site** 20HEC 🌿 🌿 🌿 🏠 🏠 Å **Facilities** 🏪 🛈 ⊙ 🖭 🤿 🚿 ⑫ **Services** 🍴 🍽 ⊞ 🖥 **Leisure** 🏊 PS

Giardino delle Esperidi

S.Agnello, 80065 ☎ 081 8783255 ▤ 081 8785022
e-mail info@esperidiresort.com
website www.esperidiresort.com
Set in a pleasant park surrounded by lemon and orange trees, 2km from the centre of Sorrento and 250m from La Marinella beach. There are good facilities and modern bungalows are available for hire.

Open Apr-Sep **Site** 3HEC 🌿 🌿 🏠 ⊗ **Facilities** 🏪 ⊙ 🖭 ⑫ **Services** 🍴 🍽 **Off-site** 🛈 🤿 🚿PS ⊞

International Camping Nube d'Argento

via Capo 21, 80067 ☎ 081 8781344 ▤ 081 8073450
e-mail info@nubedargento.com
website www.nubedargento.com
The site lies on narrow terraces just off a steep concrete road between the beach and the outskirts of the town.

➔ *Access difficult for caravans.*

Open Mar-Dec **Site** 1.5HEC 🌿 🌿 🏠 🏠 Å **Facilities** 🏪 🛈 ⊙ 🖭 🤿 🚿 ⑫ **Services** 🍴 🍽 ⊞ 🖥 **Leisure** 🏊 PS

TORRE RINALDA LECCE

Torre Rinalda

Litoranea Salentina, 73100 ☎ 0832 382161 ▤ 0832 382165
e-mail info@torrerinalda.it
website www.torrerinalda.it
An extensive level meadow separated from the sea by dunes. Disco.

➔ *SS613 Brindisi-Lecce exit Trepuzzi, coast road for 1.5km.*

Open Jun-Sep **Site** 15HEC 🌿 🌿 🏠 **Facilities** 🏪 🛈 ⊙ 🖭 🤿 ⑫ **Services** 🍴 🍽 ⊞ **Leisure** 🏊 PS

UGENTO LECCE

Riva di Ugento

Litoranea Gallipoli-SM diLeuca, 73059
☎ 0833 933600 ▤ 0833 933601
e-mail info@rivadiugeuto.it
website www.rivadiugeuto.it
A well-equipped site in wooded surroundings close to the beach.

Open 15 May-Sep **Site** 32HEC 🌿 🌿 🌿 🏠 🏠 Å ⊗ **Prices** pitch 18-37 🚍 (static)238-497 **Facilities** 🏪 🛈 ⊙ 🖭 🤿 ⑫ **Services** 🍴 🍽 ⊞ 🖥 **Leisure** 🏊 PS

VICO EQUENSE NAPOLI

Sant' Antonio

Marina d'Equa, 80069 ☎ 081 8028570 ▤ 081 8028570
e-mail info@campingsantantonio.it
website www.campingsantantonio.it
A modern site set among fruit trees, close to the beach with fine views over the Bay of Naples.

Open 15 Mar-30 Oct **Site** 1HEC 🌿 🌿 🏠 Å **Prices** ♣ 6.70-7.75 🚐 2.60-3.20 🚍 6.70-7.75 Å 4-6 **Facilities** 🏪 🛈 ⊙ 🖭 🤿 🚿 ⑫ **Services** 🍴 🍽 🖥 **Leisure** 🏊 S **Off-site** 🚿PS ⊞

Seiano Spiaggia

Marina Aequa, Via Murrano 15, 80069
☎ 081 8028560 ▤ 081 8028560
e-mail info@campingseiano.it
website www.campingseiano.it
Set in a plantation of evergreen and orange trees close to the sea. There are good facilities and the site is well situated for Pompeii, Naples and Vesuvius.

➔ *A3 exit Castellammare di Stabia, highway 145, after Seiano tunnel & bridge right R to Marina Aequa.*

Open Apr-Sep **Site** 1HEC 🌿 🌿 🏠 **Prices** ♣ 6.20-7 🚐 3.10-3.20 🚍 5.20-5.50 Å 4.20-4.50 **Facilities** 🏪 🛈 ⊙ 🖭 🤿 🚿 ⑫ **Services** 🍴 🍽 🖥 **Off-site** 🍽 🔾PS ⊞

Site 6HEC (site size) 🌿 grass 🌊 sand 🌿 stone 🌿 little shade 🌿 partly shaded 🌿 mainly shaded 🏠 bungalows for hire 🚍 caravans for hire Å tents for hire ⊗ no dogs **Prices** ♣ adult per night 🚐 car per night pp per person per night 🚍 caravan per night Å tent per night 🚍 (static)-caravan hire per week

Villagio Turistico Azzurro

via Murrano 9, 80066 ☎ 081 8029984 🖹 081 8029176
e-mail info@villaggioazzurro.net
website www.villaggioazzurro.net
Shaded site among ancient olive groves, by the sea and in close
proximity to the Isle of Capri.

➲ *A3 exit Castellammare, signs for Vico Equense, after 3rd tunnel & bridge right to Marina Aequa.*

Open Mar-1 Dec **Site** 11HEC 😃 ⛺ 🚐 🏕 **Prices** ⚊ 6.50-7.50 🚗 3.50-
4.50 🚐 7-7.50 🏕 6-7.50 🚐 (static)297.50-392.35 **Facilities** 🏠 🗊 ⊙ 🚰 🖉 🚿
🅿 **Services** 🍽 🍴 **Leisure** 🏊 S **Off-site** 🍴 ➕

VIESTE FOGGIA

Capo Vieste

71019 ☎ 0884 706326 🖹 0884 705993
e-mail info@capovieste.it
website www.capovieste.it
The site lies on a large area of unspoiled land, planted with a few
rows of poplar and pine trees. It is by the sea and has a large bathing
area.

➲ *Off coast road to Peschici, 7km beyond Vieste.*

Open 20 Mar-Oct **Site** 6HEC 😃 ⛺ 🌲 🚐 🏕 **Facilities** 🏠 🗊 ⊙ 🚰 🖉 🚿
🅿 **Services** 🍽 🍴 ➕ 🅖 **Leisure** 🏊 S

Umbramare

Santa Maria di Merino, 71019 ☎ 0884 706174 🖹 0884 706174
e-mail umbramare@tiscali.it
website www.umbramare.it
➲ *Off A14 at Poggio Imperiale onto route via Rodi Gargánico &
Peschici.*

Open Mar-Sep **Site** 10.5HEC 😃 ⛺ 🌲 🚐 ⊗ **Prices** ⚊ 3-8.50 pitch 6-14.50
Facilities 🏠 🗊 ⊙ 🚰 🖉 🚿 🅿 **Services** 🍽 🍴 🅖 **Leisure** 🏊 S **Off-site** 🚿

Vieste Marina

Litoranea Vieste, 71019 ☎ 0884 706471 🖹 0884 706471
e-mail viestemarina@tiscali.it
Tree-lined level site adjacent to the coast road in a quiet location with
good facilities.

➲ *5km N of Vieste, signed.*

Open Jun-Sep **Site** 5HEC 😃 ⛺ 🚐 **Facilities** 🏠 🗊 ⊙ 🚰 **Services** 🍽 🍴
➕ 🅖 **Leisure** 🏊 PS **Off-site** 🗊 🖉 🚿 🏊 LS

Village Punta Lunga

Defensola, CP 339, 71019 ☎ 0884 706031 🖹 0884 706910
e-mail puntalunga@puntalunga.com
website www.puntalunga.it
A terraced site in wooded surroundings encompassing two sandy
bathing bays and a rocky peninsula.

➲ *2km N of Vieste, signed from coast road.*

Open 28 Apr-1 Oct **Site** 6HEC 😃 ⛺ 🚐 ⊗ **Facilities** 🏠 🗊 ⊙ 🚰 🖉 🚿 🅿
Services 🍽 🍴 ➕ 🅖 **Leisure** 🏊 S

SARDEGNA (SARDINIA)

AGLIENTU SASSARI

Baia Blu la Tortuga

Pineta di Vignola Mare, 07020 ☎ 079 602200 🖹 079 602040
e-mail info@baiablu.com
website www.baiaholiday.com
Site in pine forest by the sea.

Open Apr-20 Oct **Site** 17HEC 😃 ⛺ 🌲 🚐 **Prices** ⚊ 3.30-10.30 🏕 6.50-
20.70 pitch 9-22.90 🚐 (static)210-833 **Facilities** 🏠 🗊 ⊙ 🚰 🖉 🚿 ®
Services 🍽 🍴 ➕ 🅖 **Leisure** 🏊 S

ARBATAX NUORO

Telis

Porto Frailis, 8041 ☎ 0782 667261 🖹 0782 667140
e-mail telisca@tiscalinet.it
website www.campingtelis.com
Terraced site by the sea.

➲ *SS125 between Cagliari & Olbia.*

Open All year **Site** 3HEC ⛺ 🌲 🚐 **Prices** ⚊ 6-10 🏕 6-8 pitch 7-10
Facilities 🏠 🗊 ⊙ 🚰 🖉 🚿 ® **Services** 🍽 🍴 🅖 **Leisure** 🏊 S
Off-site 🏊 P

CÁGLIARI

AT SANT'ANTIOCO

Tonnara

Loc Calasapone, 09017 ☎ 0781 809058 🖹 0781 809036
e-mail tonnaracamping@tiscali.it
website www.camping.it/italy/sardegna/cagliari
Situated in the centre of Calasapone bay with enclosed plots, good
sports facilities and access to a sandy beach.

➲ *S of Carbonia, road to island of St Antioco.*

Open Apr-Sep, Oct-Mar **Site** 7HEC ⛺ 🌲 🚐 **Prices** ⚊ 8-10.20 pitch 17.50
Facilities 🏠 🗊 ⊙ 🚰 🖉 🚿 🅖 **Services** 🍽 🍴 🅖 **Leisure** 🏊 S
Off-site 🏊 P

CALASETTA CAGLIARI

Sardi Le Saline

Le Saline, 9011 ☎ 0781 88615 🖹 0781 88615
e-mail info@campinglesaline.com
website www.campinglesaline.com
Wooded surroundings close to the beach, 0.5km from the village with
good recreational facilities.

Open May-Oct **Site** 6HEC 😃 ⛺ 🌲 🚐 **Facilities** 🏠 🗊 ⊙ 🚰
Services 🍽 🍴 ➕ 🅖 **Leisure** 🏊 S **Off-site** 🖉 🏊 ➕

CANNIGIONE DI ARZACHENA SASSARI

Isuledda

07020 ☎ 0789 86003 🖹 0789 86089
e-mail info@isuledda.it
website www.isuledda.it
Near the sea on the beautiful Costa Smeralda with modern sanitary
installations and plentiful sports and entertainment facilities.

Open Apr-15 Oct **Site** 15HEC 😃 ⛺ 🚐 ⊗ **Prices** ⚊ 5-10 🚗 2-4 🚐 13-
25 🏕 9.50-19 🚐 (static)315-955 **Facilities** 🏠 🗊 ⊙ 🚰 🖉 🅖 **Services** 🍽
🍴 ➕ 🅖 **Leisure** 🏊 S

Facilities 🗊 shop 🏠 shower ⊙ electric points for razors 🚰 electric points for caravans ® parking by tents permitted 🅿 compulsory separate car park
Services 🍴 café/restaurant 🍽 bar 🖉 Camping Gaz International 🚿 gas other than Camping Gaz ➕ first aid facilities 🅖 laundry
Leisure 🏊 swimming L-Lake P-Pool R-River S-Sea **Off-site** All facilities within 2km

LOTZORAI NUORO

Cernie

via Case Sparse 17, 08040 ☎ 0782 669472 ▤ 0782 669612
e-mail info@campinglecernie.com
website www.campinglecernie.com
Close to the beach with beautiful views on all sides. Varied sports and leisure activities.

Open All year **Site** 1.5HEC ❤ ❤ ❤ **Prices** ↟ 6-14.50 ⅄ 6 pitch 7 ❤ (static)175-420 **Facilities** ⋒ ☖ ⊙ ❷ ❷ ⊘ ❀ ❷ **Services** ❡ ⏍ ▣ **Leisure** ❧ S **Off-site** ✚

PORTO ROTONDO SASSARI

Cugnana

Loc Cugnana, 07026 ☎ 0789 33184 ▤ 0789 33398
e-mail info@campingcugnana.it
website www.campingcugnana.it
A well-appointed family site with good recreational facilities and offering free transport to the local beaches.

Open Apr-10 Oct **Site** 5HEC ❤ ❤ ❀ **Prices** ↟ 8.50-16.90 ❤ 2.50-4 **Facilities** ⋒ ☖ ⊙ ❷ ⊘ ❀ ❷ **Services** ❡ ⏍ ▣ **Leisure** ❧ P **Off-site** ❧S ✚

SANTA LUCIA NUORO

Cala-Pineta

St Statale Orientale Sarde 125, 08029
☎ 0784 819184 ▤ 0784 818128
e-mail info@calapineta.it
website www.calapineta.it
Well-equipped site 1.5km from a white sand beach.

Open 15 Jun-15 Sep **Site** 10HEC ❤ ❤ ❀ ❀ ⅄ **Facilities** ⋒ ☖ ⊙ ❷ ❷ **Services** ❡ ⏍ ▣ **Leisure** ❧ S

Selema

8029 ☎ 079 953761 ▤ 079 819068
e-mail info@selemacamping.com
website www.selemacamping.com
Wooded beach site.

Open May-Oct **Site** 7.5HEC ❤ ❤ ❤ ❀ ❀ **Facilities** ⋒ ☖ ⊙ ❷ ⊘ ❀ ❷ ❷ **Services** ❡ ⏍ ▣ **Leisure** ❧ RS **Off-site** ❀ ✚

SAN TEODORO NUORO

San Teodoro la Cinta

via del Tirren 89, 08020 ☎ 0784 865777 ▤ 0784 865777
e-mail info@campingsanteodoro.com
website www.campingsanteodoro.com
Situated in a large wooded park, the site faces the sea. Ideal for families with small children.

➲ 25km from Olbia.

Open 15 May-15 Oct **Site** 3HEC ❤ ❀ ❀ ❀ **Facilities** ⋒ ☖ ⊙ ❷ ⊘ ❀ ❷ **Services** ❡ ⏍ ✚ ▣ **Leisure** ❧ S **Off-site** ⏍ ❧R

TEULADA CAGLIARI

Porto Tramatzu

09019 ☎ 070 9283027 ▤ 070 9283028
e-mail coop.proturismo@libero.it
With extensive facilities and large individual plots. The site is less than 100m from the beautiful Port Tramatzu.

➲ SS195 from Cagliari.

Open Etr-Oct **Site** 3.5HEC ❤ ❤ ❀ **Facilities** ⋒ ☖ ⊙ ❷ ❷ **Services** ❡ ⏍ ▣ **Leisure** ❧ S

TORRE SALINAS CAGLIARI

Torre Salinas

09043 ☎ 070 999032 ▤ 070 999001
e-mail information@camping-torre-salinas.de
website www.camping-torre-salinas.de
Open Apr-14 Oct **Site** 1.5HEC ❤ ❤ ❀ ❀ ⅄ **Prices** ↟ 4.80-9.50 pitch 7-11.50 **Facilities** ⋒ ☖ ⊙ ❷ ❷ **Services** ❡ ⏍ ▣ **Leisure** ❧ S

VALLEDORIA SASSARI

Foce

via Ampurias1 C.S., 07039 ☎ 079 582109 ▤ 079 582191
e-mail info@foce.it
website www.foce.it
A delightful wooded setting separated from the beach by the River Coghinas, which can be crossed by ferry. Modern sanitary installations and plenty of recreational facilities.

Open 15 May-Sep **Site** 20HEC ❤ ❤ ❤ ❀ **Prices** ↟ 5.90-12 ❤ 1.50-3 ❤ (static)210-420 **Facilities** ⋒ ☖ ⊙ ❷ ⊘ ❀ ❷ **Services** ❡ ⏍ ▣ **Leisure** ❧ PRS

Valledoria

07039 ☎ 079 584070 ▤ 079 584058
e-mail info@campingvalledoria.com
website www.campingvalledoria.com
Located in a pine wood, this site has both white sand beaches and rocky cliffs.

Open 15 May-29 Sep **Site** 10HEC ❤ ❤ ❀ ❀ **Prices** ↟ 6.50-11 ❤ 1.80-3 ❤ (static)252-364 **Facilities** ⋒ ☖ ⊙ ❷ ⊘ ❀ ❷ **Services** ❡ ⏍ ▣ **Leisure** ❧ S **Off-site** ✚

SICILIA (SICILY)

AVOLA SIRACUSA

Pantanello

Lungomare di Avola, 96012 ☎ 0931 823275
Open All year **Site** 7.5HEC ❤ ❤ ❀ **Prices** ↟ 4-6 ❤ 2-2.50 ❤ 5.50-7 ⅄ 4-7 **Facilities** ⋒ ⊙ ❷ ❷ **Services** ❡ ⏍ **Off-site** ☖ ⏍ ⊘ ❀ ❧PS ✚

Sabbia d'Oro

96012 ☎ 0931 822415 ▤ 0931 822415 & 833233
e-mail info@campeggiosabbiadoro.com
website www.campeggiosabbiadoro.com
Situated close to the beach in a picturesque area surrounded by trees with magnificient views.

Open All year **Site** 2.2HEC ❤ ❀ **Prices** ↟ 6 ❤ 3 ❤ 9 ⅄ 10 ❤ (static)150-300 **Facilities** ⋒ ☖ ⊙ ❷ ⊘ ❀ ❷ **Services** ❡ ⏍ ▣ **Leisure** ❧ S **Off-site** ❧R ✚

Site 6HEC (site size) ❤ grass ❤ sand ❤ stone ❤ little shade ❤ partly shaded ❤ mainly shaded ❀ bungalows for hire ❤ caravans for hire ⅄ tents for hire ❀ no dogs **Prices** ↟ adult per night ❤ car per night pp per person per night ❤ caravan per night ⅄ tent per night ❤ (static)-caravan hire per week

CASTEL DI TUSA MESSINA

Scoglio

S.S. 113-Km 164, 98070 ☎ 0921 334345 📠 0921 334303
e-mail loscoglio@loscoglio.net
website www.loscoglio.net
A terraced site. No shade on the gravel beach.

⊃ *A20 from Uscita*

Open Apr-Sep **Site** 1.5HEC 🌳 🌲 ⛺ 🏠 🚐 **Prices** ⚑ 4.50-10
🚐 3-3.50 🚐 6 ▲ 6 🚐 (static)350-490 **Facilities** 🌳 🛒 ⊙ 🚿 🚐 ⌀ ⚑ ⅏
Services ⚑ 🍴 🛎 **Leisure** ⚓ PS

CATÁNIA CATANIA

Ionio

via Villini a Mare 2, 95126 ☎ 095 491139 📠 095 492277
e-mail camping@jonioeventi.it
website www.jonioeventi.it
On a clifftop plateau. Access to beach via steps.

⊃ *Off SS14 N of town towards sea.*

Open All year **Site** 1.2HEC 🌳 ⛺ 🏠 🚐 **Prices** ⚑ 7.50-10 🚐 4-6 🚐 8.50-11
▲ 7.50-10 🚐 (static)210-840 **Facilities** 🌳 🛒 ⊙ 🚿 🚐 ⌀ ⅏ ⚑ **Services** ⚑
🍴 🛎 **Leisure** ⚓ S

CEFALÚ PALERMO

Plaja degli Uccelli

90010 ☎ 0921 999068 📠 0921 999068
Wooded surroundings with modern facilities close to a fine sandy
beach.

Open Apr-10 Oct **Site** 1.8HEC 🌳 ⛺ 🏠 **Facilities** 🌳 🛒 ⊙ 🚿 🚐 ⌀ ⅏ ⚑
Services ⚑ 🍴 ➕ 🛎 **Leisure** ⚓ S

FINALE DI POLLINA PALERMO

Rais Gerbi

S.S.113KM 172,900, 90010 ☎ 0921 426570 📠 0921 426577
e-mail camping@raisgerbi.it
website www.raisgerbi.it
A well-equipped, modern site with its own private beach in
picturesque wooded surroundings.

⊃ *Off SS113 at Km172.9.*

Open All year **Site** 5HEC 🌳 ⛺ 🏠 ▲ **Prices** ⚑ 4.50-7.50 🚐 3-3.50 🚐 6-10
▲ 4.50-7.50 **Facilities** 🌳 🛒 ⊙ 🚿 🚐 ⌀ ⅏ **Services** ⚑ 🍴 🛎 **Leisure** ⚓ PS
Off-site ⅏ ➕

FÚRNARI MARINA MESSINA

Village Bazia

Contrada Bazia, 98054 ☎ 0941 800130 📠 0941 81006
e-mail info@bazia.it **website** www.bazia.it
A pleasant seaside site with plenty of recreational facilities.

Open Jun-14Sep **Site** 4HEC 🌳 🌲 ⛺ 🏠 **Prices** ⚑ 8 🚐 3 🚐 9 ▲ 9
Facilities 🌳 🛒 ⊙ 🚿 ⅏ ⚑ **Services** ⚑ 🍴 🛎 **Leisure** ⚓ PS **Off-site** ➕

ÓSOLA DELLE FÉMMINE PALERMO

La Playa

viale Marino 55, 90040 ☎ 091 8677001 📠 091 8677001
e-mail campinglaplaya@virglio.it
website www.campinglaplaya.net
A ideal site for a relaxing holiday with beautiful views and quiet
woodland walks. Direct access to the beach.

⊃ *A29 Palermo to Trapini & SS113.*

Open 15 Mar-15 Oct **Site** 2.2HEC 🌳 🌲 ⛺ 🏠 **Facilities** 🌳 🛒 ⊙ 🚐 ⌀ ⅏
⚑ **Services** ⚑ 🍴 🛎 **Leisure** ⚓ S **Off-site** 🍴 ⚓S ➕

MENFI AGRIGENTO

Palma

via delle Palme n 29, 92013 ☎ 0925 78392 📠 0925 78392
e-mail campinglapalma@li bero.it
website www.campinglapalma.com

⊃ *6km S.*

Open All year **Site** 1HEC 🌳 🌲 ⛺ 🏠 🚐 ▲ **Prices** ⚑ 6 🚐 3.50 🚐 8
▲ 6.50 🚐 (static)300 **Facilities** 🌳 🛒 ⊙ 🚿 🚐 ⌀ ⅏ ⚑ **Services** ⚑ 🍴 🛎
Leisure ⚓ S

NICOLOSI CATANIA

Etna

via Goethe, 95030 ☎ 095 914309 📠 095 914309
e-mail camping.etna@tiscalimet.it
Open All year **Site** 2.9HEC 🌲 ⛺ 🏠 🚐 ▲ **Facilities** 🌳 ⊙ 🚿 ⅏ ⚑
Services ⚑ 🍴 **Leisure** ⚓ P **Off-site** 🛒 ⚑ 🍴 ⌀

OLIVERI MESSINA

Marinello

Contrada Marinello, 98060 ☎ 0941 313000 📠 0941 313702
e-mail marinello@camping.it
website www.camping.it/sicilia/marinello
Site consists of small pitches set in a woodland area 100m from the
sea. Dogs not allowed in July and August.

⊃ *A20 exit Falcone.*

Open Apr-Oct **Site** 3.2HEC 🌳 🌲 🏠 ⊗ **Facilities** 🌳 🛒 ⊙ 🚿 🚐 ⅏ ⚑
Services ⚑ 🍴 **Leisure** ⚓ S **Off-site** 🛒 🍴 ⅏ ➕

PACHINO

AT PORTOPALO (6.6KM SE)

Capo Palssero

96010 ☎ 0931 842333
Slightly sloping site towards the sea with view of fishing harbour of
Portopalo. Disco.

⊃ *Turn S on 115 in Noto or Iolspica towards Pachino.*

Open 30 Mar-10 Oct **Site** 3.5HEC 🌳 🌲 🏠 **Facilities** 🌳 🛒 ⊙ 🚿 ⅏ ⚑
Services ⚑ 🍴 **Leisure** ⚓ PS **Off-site** ⌀ ➕

PUNTA BRACCETTO RAGUSA

Rocca dei Tramonti

97017 ☎ 0932 863208 📠 0932 918054
e-mail info@roccadeitramonti.com
website www.roccadeitramonti.com
The site lies in a quiet setting on rather barren land near a beautiful
sandy bay surrounded by cliffs.

⊃ *From Marina di Ragusa 10km W on coast road to Punta
Braccetto.*

Open May-Sep **Site** 3HEC 🌳 🌲 ⛺ 🏠 🚐 **Prices** ⚑ 2.50-5 🚐 3-4 🚐 5-7
▲ 5-6 **Facilities** 🌳 ⚑ **Leisure** ⚓ S **Off-site** 🛒 ⚑ 🍴 ⅏ ➕

RAGUSA, MARINA DI RAGUSA

Baia del Sole

Lungomare A-Doria, 97010 ☎ 0932 239844 📠 0932 230341
e-mail infobaiadelsole.it
website www.baiadelsole.it
Well-tended level site. Pitches provided with roofs of straw matting.
Open All year **Site** 3.5HEC 🌳 ⛺ 🏠 **Facilities** 🌳 🛒 ⊙ 🚐 **Services** ⚑ 🍴
Leisure ⚓ PS **Off-site** ➕

Italy

Facilities 🛒 shop 🌳 shower ⊙ electric points for razors 🚐 electric points for caravans ⅏ parking by tents permitted ⚑ compulsory separate car park
Services 🍴 café/restaurant ⚑ bar ⌀ Camping Gaz International ⅏ gas other than Camping Gaz ➕ first aid facilities 🛎 laundry
Leisure ⚓ swimming L-Lake P-Pool R-River S-Sea **Off-site** All facilities within 2km

SANT' ALESSIO SICULO MESSINA

Focetta Sicula

via Torrente Agrò, 98030 ☎ 0942 751657 ▤ 0942 756708
e-mail lafocetta@camping.it
website www.lafocetta.it

A well-equipped site with a private beach in a quiet location.

➲ *Autostrada exit Roccalumera, SS114 for Sant'Alessio & signed.*

Open All year **Site** 1.2HEC ❦ ❦ ✿ ♣ **Prices** ♠ 4-7 ♠ 3-4 ♠ 5-9 ⚠ 5-9 ♠ (static)182-315 **Facilities** ♠ ⊙ ⊕ ⊘ ♨ **Services** ⫬ ▯⏘ ☕ 🖩
Leisure ⊛ S **Off-site** ⏚

SANT' ANTONIO DI BARCELLONA MESSINA

Centro Vacanze Cantoni

98050 ☎ 090 9710165 ▤ 090 9710165
e-mail c.cantoni@hotmail.com
website www.centrovacanzecantoni.it

Open Jun-15 Sep **Site** 1HEC ❦ ❦ ✿ **Facilities** ♠ ⏚ ⊙ ⊕ ♠ ♨ ⓟ
Services ⫬ ▯⏘ ☕ 🖩 **Leisure** ⊛ PS

SECCAGRANDE AGRIGENTO

Kamemi Camping Village

92016 ☎ 0925 69212 ▤ 0925 69212
e-mail info@kamemicamping.it
website www.kamemicamping.it

Wooded surroundings close to the beach with good recreational facilities.

Open All year **Site** 5HEC ❦ ❦ ✿ **Prices** ♠ 4-7 ♠ 3-4 ♠ 8-10 ⚠ 4-10
Facilities ♠ ⏚ ⊙ ♠ ⓒ **Services** ⫬ ▯⏘ 🖩 **Leisure** ⊛ PS
Off-site ⊘ ♨ ☕

Mount Amata

Italy

Luxembourg

Accidents & emergencies
fire 112   police 113   ambulance 112

Driving requirements
Minimum age 17 for UK licence holders driving temporarily imported car or motorcycle.

Lights
When overtaking at night outside built-up areas you must flash your headlights. Parking lights are required in areas without street lighting. Motorcyclists must use dipped headlights during the day.

Passengers & children
Children under 11 and/or 1.5m in height must not travel in the front seat unless using a suitable restraint system appropriate to their size. In the rear, children under 3 must be seated in suitable restraint system and children over 3 must wear normal seat belts in absence of child seat, but permitted to wear only abdominal part of belt if under 1.5m. Never fit a rear-facing child restraint in a seat with a frontal airbag. Children under 12 not permitted as motorcycle passengers.

Size restrictions
Motor vehicle or trailer
height 4m, width 2.5m, length 12m

Vehicle + trailer
length 25m

Speed limits
Unless signed otherwise:

Car without caravan/trailer, motorcycle

Built-up areas	50kph
Outside built-up areas	90kph
Motorways	130kph

Car towing caravan/trailer

Built-up areas	50kph
Outside built-up areas	75kph
Motorways	90kph

Motorists who have held a driving licence for less than one year: 75kph outside built-up areas and 90kph on motorways.

Tourist office
Luxembourg National Trade and Tourist Office
122 Regent Street
London W1B 5SA
Tel 020 7434 2800 (Mon-Fri 10.00-17.00 hrs)
www.luxembourg.co.uk
www.ont.lu

Additional information
Warning triangle compulsory. Forbidden to carry petrol in a can in a vehicle.

BOULAIDE

Haute-Sûre

34 r J-de-Busleyden, 9639 ☎ 993061 🖹 993604
e-mail info@campinghautesure.com
website www.campinghautesure.com
Open 15 Apr-15 Sep **Site** 2HEC ♨ ♣ 🛖 **Prices** pitch 25 (incl 2 persons)
pp2.50 **Facilities** ⚘ 🖀 ⊙ 🕯 🗶 ⊛ **Services** ⚑ 🏀 🛨 🖻 **Leisure** ✦ P

CLERVAUX

Official de Clervaux

33 r Klatzewee, 9714 ☎ 920042 🖹 929728
e-mail campingclervaux@internet.lu
website www.camping-clervaux.lu
Situated next to the sports stadium, between the La Clervé stream and the railway in a forested area. Trains only run during the day and there is little noise. Separate field for tents.
➲ *0.5km SW from village.*
Open 15 Mar-30 Oct **Site** 3HEC ♨ ♣ 🛖 🚐 **Prices** ⚘ 5.30 pitch 5.50
Facilities ⚘ 🖀 ⊙ 🕯 🗶 ⊛ **Services** 🛨 🖻 **Leisure** ✦ PR
Off-site ⚑ 🏀

DIEKIRCH

Bleesbruck

9359 ☎ 803134 🖹 802718
e-mail info@camping-bleesbruck.lu
website www.camping-bleesbruck.lu
A modern site in tranquil wooded surroundings.
Open Apr-Oct **Site** 5HEC ♨ ♣ 🛖 🚐 **Facilities** ⚘ 🖀 ⊙ 🕯 🗶 ⊛
Services ⚑ 🏀 🛨 🖻 **Leisure** ✦ R **Off-site** 🏀 ✦P

Op der Sauer

rte de Gilsdorf, 9201 ☎ 808590 🖹 809470
e-mail contact@campsauer.lu
website www.campsauer.lu
➲ *0.5km from town centre on road to Gilsdorf, near stadium.*
Open All year **Site** 5HEC ♨ ♣ 🛖 **Prices** ⚘ 5 pitch 6 **Facilities** ⚘ 🖀 ⊙ 🕯
🗶 ⊛ **Services** ⚑ 🏀 🛨 🖻 **Leisure** ✦ P

DILLINGEN

Wies-Neu

12 r de la Sûre, 6350 ☎ 836110 🖹 26876438
A comfortable family site on the bank of the River Sûre.
➲ *Between Diekirch & Echternacht.*
Open Apr-30 Oct **Site** 45HEC ♨ ♣ ♣ 🛖 🚐 **Facilities** ⚘ 🖀 ⊙ 🕯 🗶 ⊛
Services 🛨 🖻 **Leisure** ✦ R **Off-site** ⚑ 🏀

ECHTERNACH

Official

5 rte de Diekirch, 6430 ☎ 720272 🖹 26720847
e-mail info@camping_echternach.lu
website www.mullerthal.lu
➲ *E42 to Echternach.*
Open 15 Mar-1 Nov **Site** 7HEC ♨ ♣ ♣ 🛖 🚐 **Facilities** ⚘ ⊙ 🕯 ⊛
Services 🛨 🖻 **Leisure** ✦ P **Off-site** 🖀 ⚑ 🏀 🗶 ✦LPR

ENSCHERANGE

Val d'Or

L-9747 ☎ 352 920691 🖹 352 929725
e-mail valdor@pt.lu
website www.valdor.lu
Quiet family site in a beautiful natural setting beside the River Clerve.
➲ *8km S of Clervaux between Drauffelt & Wilwerwiltz.*
Open All year **Site** 4HEC ♨ ♣ 🛖 🚐 **Prices** ⚘ 5 🚐 7 🅰 7
🚐 (static)175-480 **Facilities** ⚘ ⊙ 🕯 🗶 🔙 ⊛ 🅿 **Services** ⚑ 🏀 🛨
Leisure ✦ R **Off-site** 🖀 ✦LPS

ESCH-SUR-ALZETTE

Gaalgebierg

L-4001 ☎ 541069 🖹 549630
e-mail gaalcamp@pt.lu
A level park-like site with lovely trees on a hillock.
➲ *N6 SE from town centre towards Dudelange, right at motorway underpass, steep climb uphill.*
Open All year **Site** 2.5HEC ♨ ♣ 🛖 🚐 **Facilities** ⚘ 🖀 ⊙ 🕯 🗶 🔙 ⊛
Services ⚑ 🏀 🛨 🖻

HEIDERSCHEID

Fuussekaul

4 Fussekaul, 9156 ☎ 352 2688881 🖹 26888828
e-mail info@fuussekaul.lu
website www.fuussekaul.lu
A level grassland family site adjoining a woodland area. Good recreational facilities.
➲ *Off N15 Bastogne-Diekirch.*
Open All year **Site** 18HEC ♨ ♣ 🛖 🚐 **Prices** ⚘ 2.50 pitch 11.50-23 (incl 2 persons) 🚐 (static)294-679 **Facilities** ⚘ 🖀 ⊙ 🕯 🗶 🔙 ⊛ **Services** ⚑
🏀 🛨 🖻 **Leisure** ✦ P **Off-site** ✦LR

INGLEDORF

Gritt

r du Pont, 9161 ☎ 802018 🖹 802019
Set on the southern bank of the Sûre between Ettelbruck and Diekirch. A beautiful country setting ideal for fishing.
Open Apr-Oct **Site** 5HEC ♨ ♣ 🛖 🚐 **Prices** ⚘ 4.20 pitch 4.50 **Facilities** ⚘
⊙ 🕯 🗶 🔙 ⊛ **Services** ⚑ 🏀 🛨 🖻 **Leisure** ✦ R **Off-site** 🖀 ✦LP

KOCKELSCHEUER

Kockelscheuer

22 rte de Bettembourg, 1899 ☎ 471815 🖹 401243
e-mail mail@camp-kockelscheuer.lu
website www.camp-kockelscheuer.lu
A modern site on the edge of a forest.
➲ *4km from Luxembourg off N31.*
Open Etr-Oct **Site** 3.8HEC ♨ ♣ **Facilities** ⚘ 🖀 ⊙ 🕯 🗶 ⊛ **Services** 🛨 🖻
Off-site 🖀 🏀 🔙

Site 6HEC (site size) ♨ grass ♣ sand ♨ stone ♣ little shade ♣ partly shaded ♣ mainly shaded 🛖 bungalows for hire
🚐 caravans for hire 🅰 tents for hire ⊗ no dogs **Prices** ⚘ adult per night ⚗ car per night pp per person per night 🚐 caravan per night
🅰 tent per night 🚐 (static)-caravan hire per week

LAROCHETTE

Kengert

L-7633 ☎ 837186 ▤ 878323
e-mail info@kengert.lu
website www.kengert.lu
On gently sloping meadow in a pleasant rural location.
➲ *N8 towards Mersch, CR119 towards Nommern, 2km turn right.*

Open Mar-7 Nov **Site** 4HEC ⛺ ♣ 🏠 🚐 **Prices** ♠ 11-14 🚐 (static)350-500
Facilities 🚿 🛁 ⊕ 🚰 ⌀ 🚾 ⓟ **Services** 🍴 🕍 ➕ 🔒 **Leisure** 🏊 P

MAULUSMÜHLE

Woltzdal

Maison 12, 9974 ☎ 998938 ▤ 979739
e-mail info@woltzdal-camping.lu
website www.campingwoltzdal.com
Quiet family site in the deep Woltz valley.
➲ *N30 from Liege to Bastogne, N874 to Clervaux & onto N12*

Open Apr-Oct **Site** 1.5HEC ⛺ ♣ 🏠 🚐 **Prices** ♠ 5.80 🚗 2.90 🚐 2.90
🅰 2.90 🚐 (static)400 **Facilities** 🚿 🛁 ⊕ 🚰 ⌀ 🚾 ⓟ **Services** 🍴 🕍 ➕ 🔒
Leisure 🏊 R

MERSCH

Krounebierg

rue du camping, 7572 ☎ 329756 ▤ 327987
e-mail contact@campingkrounebierg.lu
website www.campingkrounebierg.lu
A clean, well-kept site on five terraces, split into sections by hedges.
➲ *0.5km W of village church.*

Open 15 Apr-Oct **Site** 5.5HEC ⛺ ♣ 🚐 🅰 **Prices** pitch 19.80-31.90
(incl 2 persons) 🚐 (static)350-490 **Facilities** 🚿 🛁 ⊕ 🚰 ⌀ ⓟ **Services** 🍴
🕍 ➕ 🔒 **Leisure** 🏊 P

NOMMERN

Europe Nommerlayen

r Nommerlayen, 7465 ☎ 878078 ▤ 879678
e-mail nommerlayen@vo.lu
website www.nommerlayen-ec.lu
A terraced site in wooded surroundings with plenty of recreational facilities.

Open Feb-Nov **Site** 15HEC ⛺ ♣ 🏠 🚐 🅰 **Prices** ♠ 5.50 🚗 3.75
pitch 18-37 🚐 (static)290-830 **Facilities** 🚿 🛁 ⊕ 🚰 ⌀ 🚾 ⓟ
Services 🍴 🕍 ➕ 🔒 **Leisure** 🏊 P

OBEREISENBACH

Kohnenhof

1 Maison, 9838 ☎ 929464 ▤ 929690
e-mail kohnenho@pt.lu
website www.campingkohnenhof.lu
Quiet site in a rural setting in the River Our valley.

Open 26 Mar-5 Nov **Site** 6HEC ⛺ ♣ 🏠 🚐 **Prices** ♠ 3.70-4.90 pitch 7.50-9.90 🚐 (static)250-695 **Facilities** 🚿 🛁 ⊕ 🚰 ⌀ 🚾 ⓟ **Services** 🍴 🕍 ➕
🔒 **Leisure** 🏊 R

ROSPORT

Barrage

rte d'Echternach, 6580 ☎ 730160 ▤ 735155
e-mail campingrosport@pt.lu
website www.campingrosport.com
Situated by Lake Süre on the German border at the entrance to Luxembourg's Little Switzerland.
➲ *Main road from Echternach to Wasserbillig.*

Open 15 Mar-Oct **Site** 3.2HEC ⛺ ♣ 🚐 **Prices** ♠ 2.80-3.50 pitch 3.20-4
Facilities 🚿 ⊕ 🚰 ⓟ **Services** ➕ 🔒 **Leisure** 🏊 LR **Off-site** 🛁 🍴 ⌀ 🚾

STEINFORT

Steinfort

72 rte de Luxembourg, 8440 ☎ 398827 ▤ 397410
e-mail campstei@pt.lu
website www.camping-steinfort.lu
A small family site with good recreational and entertainment facilities, well situated for exploring the Seven Castles area.
➲ *E25 exit Steinfort.*

Open All year **Site** 3.5HEC ⛺ ♣ ♣ 🏠 **Prices** ♠ 2.40-4 🅰 2.45-4.50 pitch
5-8.50 **Facilities** 🚿 ⊕ 🚰 ⌀ 🚾 ⓟ **Services** 🍴 🕍 ➕ 🔒 **Leisure** 🏊 P
Off-site 🛁

Facilities 🛁 shop 🚿 shower ⊕ electric points for razors 🚰 electric points for caravans 🚾 parking by tents permitted ⓟ compulsory separate car park
Services 🍴 café/restaurant 🕍 bar ⌀ Camping Gaz International 🚾 gas other than Camping Gaz ➕ first aid facilities 🔒 laundry
Leisure 🏊 swimming L-Lake P-Pool R-River S-Sea **Off-site** All facilities within 2km

Netherlands

Accidents & emergencies
fire 112   **police** 112   **ambulance** 112

Driving requirements
Minimum age 18 for UK licence holders driving temporarily imported cars or motorcycles.

Lights
Driving on sidelights only is prohibited. Undipped headlights cannot be used during the day and when their use inconveniences other traffic or pedestrians.

Passengers & children
Children under 12 and/or 1.3m in height must not travel in the front seat unless using a suitable restraint system. If the vehicle is not fitted with rear seatbelts children under 3 are not allowed to travel in the vehicle. Never fit a rear-facing child restraint in a seat with a frontal airbag.

Size restrictions
Motor vehicle or trailer
height 4m, width 2.55m,* length 12m**

* motorcycle 2m
** trailer with one axle up to 3,500kg 8m

Vehicle + trailer
length 18m

Speed Limits
Unless signed otherwise:

Car without caravan/trailer, motorcycle
Built-up areas	50kph
Outside built-up areas	80kph
	100kph*
Motorways	120kph

Car towing caravan/trailer
Built-up areas	50kph
Outside built-up areas	80kph
Motorways	80kph

*according to type/quality of road as indicated.

Tourist office
Netherlands Board of Tourism
(postal/telephone enquiries only)
PO Box 30783, London WC2B 6DH
Tel: 020 7539 7950 (Mon-Fri 09.00-17.30 hrs) or
09068 717777 (premium rate information line)
www.holland.com

Additional information
Hazard warning lights or warning triangle compulsory (recommended that warning triangle always be carried).

Tolls
Tolls Bridges & tunnels	car	car & caravan
Westerschelde Tunnel	€4.40	€6.60

NORTH

AMEN DRENTHE

Reservaat Diana Heide
53 Amen, 9446 ☎ 0592 389297 🖺 0592 389432
e-mail info@dianaheide.nl
website www.dianaheide.nl
An ideal site for relaxation, set away from traffic among forest and heathland.
➲ *E35 from Assen, through Amen towards Hooghalen.*
Open Apr-1 Oct **Site** 30HEC ♨ ♣ ♨ ♣ ♠ Å **Facilities** 📢 ⓘ ⊙ ♨ ⌀ ♨ ℗ **Services** ➡ 🍴 ➕ 🖥 **Leisure** ♨ P **Off-site** ♨R

ANNEN DRENTHE

Hondsrug
Annerweg 3, 9463 ☎ 0592 271292 🖺 0592 271440
e-mail info@hondsrug.nl
website www.hondsrug.nl
A family site in a pleasant rural setting with good recreational facilities.
➲ *On N34 SE of Annen.*
Open Apr-1 Oct **Site** 18HEC ♨ ♨ ♣ ♠ Å **Prices** ♠ 3.65 pitch 17.30-31.25 (incl 2 persons) ♠ (static)248-445 **Facilities** 📢 ⓘ ⊙ ♨ ⌀ ♨ ℗ **Services** 🍴 ➕ 🖥 **Leisure** ♨ P

ASSEN DRENTHE

Witterzomer
Witterzomer 7, 9405 ☎ 0592 393535 🖺 0592 393530
e-mail info@witterzomer.nl
website www.witterzomer.nl
A large site with internal asphalt roads, lying in mixed woodland near a nature reserve. Separate sections for dog owners. Individual washing facilities for the disabled.
➲ *off A28*
Open All year **Site** 75HEC ♨ ♣ ♠ ♣ Å **Prices** ♠ 3.50 pitch 20-30 (incl 4 persons) **Facilities** 📢 ⓘ ⊙ ♨ ⌀ ♨ ℗ **Services** ➡ 🍴 🖥 **Leisure** ♨ LP

BERGUM FRIESLAND

Bergumermeer
Solcamastr 30, 9262 ☎ 0511 461385 🖺 0511 463955
e-mail info@bergumermeer.nl
website www.bergumermeer.nl
Pleasant wooded surroundings with good recreational facilities, close to the marina on Bergumermeer.
➲ *N355 onto N356 S, exit E to Sumar towards Oostermeer.*
Open 27 Mar-16 Oct **Site** 29HEC ♨ ♣ ♠ ♣ Å **Facilities** 📢 ⓘ ⊙ ♨ ⌀ ♨ ℗ **Services** ➡ 🍴 ➕ 🖥 **Leisure** ♨ LP

BORGER DRENTHE

Hunzedal
De Drift 3, 9531 ☎ 0599 234698 🖺 0599 235183
e-mail info@hunzedal.nl
website www.hunzedal.nl
The site is clean, well-kept and lies north-east of the village.
➲ *Off road towards Buinen, over Buinen-Schoondoord canal, 200m E turn S for 1km.*
Open All year **Site** 30HEC ♨ ♣ ♠ **Facilities** 📢 ⓘ ⊙ ♨ ⌀ ℗ **Services** ➡ 🍴 ➕ 🖥 **Leisure** ♨ LP

DIEVER DRENTHE

Hoeve AAn den Weg
Bosweg 12, 8439 SN ☎ 0521 387269 🖺 0521 387413
e-mail camping@hoeveAAndenweg.nl
website www.hoeveAAndenweg.nl
Pleasant wooded surroundings with good recreational facilities.
➲ *Off A32*
Open Apr-Oct **Site** 9HEC ♨ ♣ ♠ ♣ **Prices** ♠ 2.10-2.75 pitch 6-8 ♠ (static)250 **Facilities** 📢 ⓘ ⊙ ♨ ⌀ ♨ ℗ ℗ **Services** ➡ 🍴 ➕ 🖥 **Leisure** ♨ P

DWINGELOO DRENTHE

Noordster
Noordster 105, 7991 ☎ 0521 597238 🖺 0521 597589
e-mail noordster@rcn-centra.nl
website www.rcn-centra.nl
A large family site with static and touring pitches, surrounded by woodland.
➲ *3km S on E35.*
Open All year **Site** 42HEC ♨ ♣ ♠ ♣ **Facilities** 📢 ⓘ ⊙ ♨ ⌀ ♨ ℗ ℗ **Services** ➡ 🍴 ➕ 🖥 **Leisure** ♨ P

FRANEKER FRIESLAND

Bloemketerp
Burg J Dykstraweg 3, 8801 ☎ 0517 395099 🖺 0517 395150
e-mail info@bloemketerp.nl
website www.bloemketerp.nl
Set in a well-equipped leisure centre near the historic city centre of Franeker.
Open All year **Site** 5HEC ♨ ♣ ♠ **Prices** pitch 15-24.50 (incl 2 persons) **Facilities** 📢 ⓘ ⊙ ♨ ℗ ℗ **Services** ➡ 🍴 ➕ 🖥 **Off-site** ⌀ ♨LPRS

GRONINGEN GRONINGEN

Stadspark
Campinglaan 6, 9727 ☎ 050 5251624 🖺 050 5250099
e-mail info@campingstadspark.nl
website www.parkcampings.nl
A well-kept site on patches of grass between rows of bushes and groups of pine and deciduous trees. Some of its pitches are naturally screened.
➲ *From SW outskirts of town towards Peize & Roden.*
Open 15 Mar-15 Oct **Site** 6HEC ♨ ♣ ♠ ♣ Å **Facilities** 📢 ⓘ ⊙ ♨ ⌀ ♨ ℗ **Services** ➡ 🍴 ➕ 🖥 **Off-site** ♨LP

HARKSTEDE GRONINGEN

Grunopark
Hoofdweg 163, 9617 ☎ 050 416371 🖺 050 424521
website www.grunopark.nl
Situated within a large water park with a great variety of sports facilities available.
Open All year **Site** 23HEC ♨ ♣ Å **Facilities** 📢 ⓘ ⊙ ♨ ⌀ ♨ ℗ **Services** ➡ 🍴 ➕ 🖥 **Leisure** ♨ L

Facilities ⓘ shop 📢 shower ⊙ electric points for razors ♨ electric points for caravans ℗ parking by tents permitted ℗ compulsory separate car park
Services 🍴 café/restaurant ➡ bar ⌀ Camping Gaz International ♨ gas other than Camping Gaz ➕ first aid facilities 🖥 laundry
Leisure ♨ swimming L-Lake P-Pool R-River S-Sea **Off-site** All facilities within 2km

HARLINGEN FRIESLAND

Zeehoeve

8862 ☎ 0517 413465 🗎 0517 416971
e-mail info@zeehoeve.nl
website www.zeehoeve.nl
A well-kept meadowland site divided into large sections by rows of bushes.

➲ *1km S of Harlingen near a dyke.*

Open Apr-Sep **Site** 10HEC 👪 ♣ ☎ 🚐 **Prices** pitch 18 🚐 (static)440 **Facilities** 🍴 ⊙ 🚻 ∅ ② **Services** 🍽️ 🍴 🍽 ⊞ 🖂 **Leisure** ◆ S **Off-site** 🖂

HEE (ISLAND OF TERSCHELLING) FRIESLAND

Kooi

Hee 9, 8882 ☎ 0562 442743 🗎 0562 442835
website www.campingdekooi.nl

➲ *5km from harbour.*

Open 15 Apr-15 Sep **Site** 8.5HEC 👪 ♣ ▲ **Prices** ⚘ 4.75 🚗 2 🚐 5 ▲ 2.50-5 **Facilities** 🍴 ⊙ 🚻 🚐 **Services** 🍽️ 🍴 ⊞ 🖂 **Off-site** 🖂 ∅ ◆LS

HINDELOOPEN FRIESLAND

Hindeloopen

Westerdijk 9, 8713 ☎ 0514 521452 🗎 0514 523221
e-mail info@campinghindeloopen.nl
website www.campinghindeloopen.nl
A peaceful site on the Ysselmeer with fishing and water sports.

➲ *Via N359*

Open Apr-Oct **Site** 16HEC 👪 ♣ ⊗ **Prices** pitch 16.50-19.50 (incl 2 persons) **Facilities** 🍴 🖂 ⊙ 🚻 ∅ ② ② **Services** 🍽️ 🍴 ⊞ 🖂 **Leisure** ◆ L

KOUDUM FRIESLAND

De Kuilart

Kuilart 1, 8723 ☎ 0514 522221 🗎 0514 523010
e-mail info@kuilart.nl
website www.kuilart.nl
A camping and water-sports centre on the shores of De Fluessen lake.

➲ *Via N359.*

Open All year **Site** 37HEC 👪 ♣ ☎ 🚐 **Prices** ⚘ 3.80 🚗 3.20 pitch 16.50-21.30 (incl 2 persons) 🚐 (static)255-500 **Facilities** 🍴 🖂 ⊙ 🚻 ∅ ☎ ② **Services** 🍽️ 🍴 ⊞ 🖂 **Leisure** ◆ LP **Off-site** ◆S

LAUWERSOOG GRONINGEN

Lauwersoog

Strandweg 5, 9976 ☎ 0159 349133 🗎 0519 349195
e-mail info@lauwersoog.nl
website www.lauwersoog.nl
A pleasant location on the shores of Lauwersmeer. A good excursion centre with water sports.

Open All year **Site** 15HEC 👪 ♣ ⊜ ☎ 🚐 **Facilities** 🍴 🖂 ⊙ 🚻 ∅ ② **Services** 🍽️ 🍴 ⊞ 🖂 **Leisure** ◆ L **Off-site** ◆S

MAKKUM FRIESLAND

Holle Poarte

Holle Poarte 2, 8754 ☎ 0515 231344 🗎 0515 231339
e-mail info@hollepoarte.nl
website www.hollepoarte.nl
A modern site with water sports on the Ijsselmeer.

Open All year **Site** 32HEC 👪 ♣ ⊜ ☎ 🚐 **Prices** pitch 14.35-16.30 (incl 2 persons) **Facilities** 🍴 🖂 ⊙ 🚻 ∅ ② ② **Services** 🍽️ 🍴 ⊞ 🖂 **Leisure** ◆ L

OPENDE FRIESLAND

Strandheem

Parkweg 2, 9865 ☎ 0594 659555 🗎 0594 658592
e-mail info@strandheem.nl
website www.strandheem.nl
A family site with modern sanitary blocks and a variety of recreational facilities.

➲ *A7 exit 31.*

Open Apr-1 Oct **Site** 15HEC 👪 ♣ ☎ 🚐 **Prices** pitch 17-22.50 (incl 2 persons) 🚐 (static)225-450 **Facilities** 🍴 🖂 ⊙ 🚻 ∅ ▲ ② ② **Services** 🍽️ 🍴 ⊞ 🖂 **Leisure** ◆ LP

RUINEN DRENTHE

Wiltzangh

Witteveen 2, 7963 ☎ 0522 471227 🗎 0522 472178
e-mail info@dewiltzangh.com
website www.dewiltzangh.com
Set in the middle of a coniferous and deciduous forest, and within the grounds of a big holiday village. Advance booking for summer.

➲ *From Ruinen towards Ansen, 3km turn N.*

Open Apr-Oct **Site** 13HEC 👪 ♣ ☎ ⊙ 🚻 ∅ ▲ ② **Services** 🍴 ⊞ 🖂 **Leisure** ◆ P

SONDEL FRIESLAND

Sondel

Beuckenswijkstr 26, 8565 ☎ 0514 602300 🗎 0514 605026
e-mail e.landman@zonnet.nl
website www.campingsondel.nl
Set in a dense wood.

➲ *Just off Sondel-Rijs road.*

Open Apr-Oct **Site** 3HEC 👪 ♣ ☎ ⊗ **Prices** pitch 13 (incl 2 persons) pp4.50 **Facilities** 🍴 ⊙ 🚻 ② ② **Services** 🍽️ 🍴 ⊞ 🖂 **Leisure** ◆ LPRS **Off-site** 🖂 ∅ ▲

TERMUNTERZIJL GRONINGEN

Zeestrand Eems-Dollard

Schepperbuurt 4a ☎ 0596 601443 🗎 0596 601209
e-mail campingzeestrand@wanadoo.nl
website www.campingzeestrand.nl
Situated on a tongue of land in the Wadden See with views of Germany. Close to a beach.

➲ *A7 exit 45 for Delfzijl, site signed.*

Open 25 Mar-1 Nov **Site** 6.5HEC 👪 ♣ ☎ 🚐 **Prices** ⚘ 3.15-3.60 🚗 1.45-1.60 🚐 3.30-3.80 ▲ 3.30-3.80 🚐 (static)180 **Facilities** 🍴 ⊙ 🚻 ∅ ▲ ② ② **Services** 🍽️ 🍴 ⊞ 🖂 **Leisure** ◆ LPRS **Off-site** 🖂

WEDDE GRONINGEN

Wedderbergen

Molenweg 2, 9698 ☎ 0597 561673 🗎 0597 562595
e-mail info@wedderbergen.nl
website www.wedderbergen.nl
Meadowland site divided by deciduous trees and hedges.

➲ *From E outskirts of village onto narrow asphalt road N, 3.2km onto Spanjaardsweg & Molenweg to site.*

Open Apr-1Nov **Site** 40HEC 👪 ♣ ☎ ▲ **Facilities** 🍴 🖂 ⊙ 🚻 ∅ ▲ ② ② **Services** 🍽️ 🍴 ⊞ 🖂 **Leisure** ◆ LR **Off-site** ◆P

Site 6HEC (site size) 👪 grass ⊜ sand 👪 stone ♣ little shade ♣ partly shaded ⊜ mainly shaded ☎ bungalows for hire 🚐 caravans for hire ▲ tents for hire ⊗ no dogs **Prices** ⚘ adult per night 🚗 car per night pp per person per night 🚐 caravan per night ▲ tent per night 🚐 (static)-caravan hire per week

CENTRAL

ALKMAAR NOORD-HOLLAND

Alkmaar
Bergerweg 201, 1817 ☎ 072 5116924
e-mail info@campingalkmaar.nl
website www.campingalkmaar.nl
The site is well-kept and divided into many sections by rows of trees and bushes.
➲ *On NW outskirts of town, off Bergen road.*
Open Mar-Oct **Site** 3HEC ⚊ ⚊ ⚏ **Prices** pitch 17.50-23.50 (incl 2 persons) **Facilities** ⚈ ⚏ ⊙ ⚊ ⚏ **Services** ⚏ ⚏ **Off-site** ⚊P

AMSTELVEEN NOORD-HOLLAND

Amsterdamse Bos
Kleine Noorddijk 1, 1432 ☎ 020 6416868 ▤ 020 6402378
e-mail info@campingamsterdamsebos.com
website www.campingamsterdamsebos.com
The site is in a park-like setting in the Amsterdam wood. The camp is near the airport flight path and is subject to noise depending on the wind direction.
➲ *From The Hague along motorway, turn at N edge of airport towards Amstelveen, signs for Aalsmeer. From Utrecht, motorway exit Amstelveen for Aalsmeer, through Bovenkerk.*
Open All year **Site** 6.8HEC ⚊ ⚊ ⚏ **Facilities** ⚈ ⚏ ⊙ ⚏ ⚏
Services ⚏ ⚏ ⚌ ⚏ **Off-site** ⚊ ⚊ ⚊LRS

AMSTERDAM NOORD-HOLLAND

Gaasper
Loosdrechtdreef 7, 1108 ☎ 020 6967326 ▤ 020 6969369
website www.gaaspercamping.nl
Situated on the edge of the beautiful Gaasperpark within easy reach of Amsterdam.
➲ *A9 exit Gaasperplas/Weesp (S113), campsite signed.*
Open 15 Mar-1 Nov **Site** 5.5HEC ⚊ ⚊ **Prices** ⚊ 4.75 ⚊ 4.25 ⚏ 6.25
⚊ 5.50-6.50 **Facilities** ⚈ ⚏ ⊙ ⚏ ⚊ ⚌ ⚏ **Services** ⚏ ⚏ ⚌ ⚏
Off-site ⚏ ⚊L

See advertisement on this page

Zeeburg
Zuider Ijdijk 20, 1095 ☎ 020 6944430 ▤ 020 6946238
e-mail info@campingzeeburg.nl
website www.campingzeeburg.nl
On an island in the Ijmeer, 15 minutes from the city centre, with good facilities. Popular with backpackers and holidaymakers alike.
➲ *A10 exit S114 for Zeeberg*
Open All year **Site** 3.8HEC ⚊ ⚊ ⚏ **Prices** ⚊ 3-5 pitch 13.50-26
Facilities ⚈ ⚏ ⊙ ⚊ ⚏ ⚌ ⚏ **Services** ⚏ ⚏ ⚏ ⚏ **Off-site** ⚊P

ANDIJK NOORD-HOLLAND

Vakantiedorp Het Grootslag
Proefpolder 4, 1619 ☎ 0228 592944 ▤ 0228 592457
e-mail info@andijkvakanties.nl
website www.andijkvakanties.nl
A well-equipped site situated on the IJsselmeer. Individual bathrooms are allocated to each pitch and a range of recreational facilities are available.
➲ *A7 exit Hoorn-Noord/Enkhuizen/Lelystad, left for Andijk, signs for Het Grootslag & Dijkweg.*
Open Apr-30 Oct **Site** 40HEC ⚊ ⚊ ⚏ **Prices** ⚊ 3 pitch 18-29
(incl 4 persons) **Facilities** ⚈ ⚏ ⊙ ⚏ ⚊ ⚌ ⚏ ⚏ **Services** ⚏ ⚏ ⚏ ⚏
Leisure ⚊ LP

APPELTERN GELDERLAND

Het Groene Eiland
Lutenkampstr 2, 6629 ☎ 0487 562130 ▤ 0487 561540
e-mail info@hetgroeneeiland.nl
website www.hetgroeneeiland.nl
Set in a water recreation park with plenty of sports facilities.
➲ *A15 exit Leeuwen & signed.*
Open 15 Mar-Oct **Site** 16HEC ⚊ ⚊ ⚏ **Prices** ⚊ 2.50 ⚊ 2.90 ⚏ 11.30
⚊ 11.30 ⚏ (static)460 **Facilities** ⚈ ⚏ ⊙ ⚏ ⚊ ⚌ ⚏ **Services** ⚏ ⚏ ⚏ ⚏
Leisure ⚊ LR **Off-site** ⚏

ARNHEM GELDERLAND

Arnhem
Kemperbergerweg 771, 6816 ☎ 026 4431600 ▤ 026 4457705
e-mail arnhem@holiday.nl
website www.campingarnhem.nl
The site lies on grassland and is surrounded by trees.
➲ *NW of town & S of E36.*
Open Apr-Oct **Site** 36HEC ⚊ ⚊ **Facilities** ⚈ ⚏ ⊙ ⚏ ⚊ ⚌ ⚏
Services ⚏ ⚏ ⚏ ⚏ **Leisure** ⚊ P

Netherlands

Facilities ⚏ shop ⚈ shower ⊙ electric points for razors ⚏ electric points for caravans ⚏ parking by tents permitted ⚏ compulsory separate car park
Services ⚏ café/restaurant ⚏ bar ⚏ Camping Gaz International ⚌ gas other than Camping Gaz ⚏ first aid facilities ⚏ laundry
Leisure ⚊ swimming L-Lake P-Pool R-River S-Sea **Off-site** All facilities within 2km

Buitengoed Hooge Veluwe
Koningsweg 14, 6816 ☎ 026 4432272 026 4436809
e-mail info@hoogeveluwe.nl
website www.hoogeveluwe.nl
Situated in a pleasant natural park with good facilities.
➲ *E36 exit Apeldoorn, NW towards Hooge Veluwe.*
Open 31 Mar-28 Oct **Site** 18HEC **Prices** pitch 18-27 (incl 2 persons) (static)220-640 **Facilities** **Services** **Leisure** P

Warnsborn
Bakenbergseweg 257, 6816 ☎ 026 4423469 026 4421095
e-mail info@campingwarnsborn.nl
website www.campingwarnsborn.nl
The site is surrounded by woodland and lies on slightly sloping meadowland. Near zoo and open-air museum.
➲ *Near E36 NW of town towards Utrecht. 200m S of Shell fuel station, continue W for 0.7km.*
Open Apr-Oct **Site** 3.5HEC **Prices** 3.75 3 4.50 2.50-4.50 (static)250-350 **Facilities** **Services** **Off-site** P

BABBERICH GELDERLAND

Rivo Torto
Beekseweg 8, 6909 ☎ 0316 247332 0316 246628
e-mail rivotorto@rivotorto.nl
website www.rivotorto.nl
A riverside site with good recreational facilities.
➲ *3km W on E36.*
Open 15 Mar-Oct **Site** 8.5HEC **Prices** 1.85 2.45 6.25 3.80 **Facilities** **Services** **Off-site**

BERKHOUT NOORD-HOLLAND

Westerkogge
Kerkebuurt 202, 1647 ☎ 0229 551208 0229 551390
e-mail info@westerkogge.nl
A fine location with sheltered pitches and a good range of recreational facilities.
➲ *A7 exit Hoorn-Berkhout or Berkhout-Avenhorn.*
Open Apr-Oct **Site** 11HEC **Facilities** **Services** **Leisure** P

BILTHOVEN UTRECHT

Bospark Bilthoven
Burg v.d Borchlaan 7, 3722 ☎ 030 2286777 030 2293888
e-mail info@bosparkbilthoven.nl
website www.bosparkbilthoven.nl
Family site in wooded surroundings with asphalt drives.
➲ *Signed from town centre.*
Open Apr-Oct **Site** 20HEC **Facilities** **Services** **Leisure** P **Off-site**

BLOKZIJL OVERIJSSEL

Tussen de Diepen
Duinigermeerweg 1A, 8356 ☎ 0527 291565 0527 292203
e-mail camping@tussendediepen.nl
website www.tussendediepen.nl
Secluded site surrounded by water. Fishing, water sports and sailing.
Open Apr-Oct **Site** 5.2HEC **Facilities** **Services** **Leisure** LR **Off-site** P

BUURSE OVERIJSSEL

't Hazenbos
Oude Buurserdijk 1, 7481 ☎ 0535 696338
e-mail info@hazenbos.nl
website www.hazenbos.nl
On several meadows, partially surrounded by trees.
➲ *7km from German border.*
Open Mar-Oct **Site** 6HEC **Prices** 2.70 1.75 2.75 2.15-2.70 **Facilities** **Services** **Off-site** L

CALLANTSOOG NOORD-HOLLAND

Recreatiecentrum de Nollen
Westerweg 8, 1759 ☎ 0224 581281 0224 582098
e-mail info@denollen.nl
website www.denollen.nl
A modern family site with plenty of facilities, less than 1.6km from the beach.
➲ *E of town towards N9.*
Open Apr-1 Nov **Site** 9HEC **Prices** pitch 14-28.50 **Facilities** **Services** **Off-site** PS

Tempelhof
Westerweg 2, 1759 ☎ 0224 581522 0224 582133
e-mail info@tempelhof.nl
website www.tempelhof.nl
Well-equipped site on level meadowland.
➲ *N9 5km*
Open All year **Site** 12.7HEC **Prices** 3.80 pitch 17-33 (incl 2 persons) **Facilities** **Services** **Leisure** P **Off-site** S

DALFSEN OVERIJSSEL

Buitenplaats Gerner
Haersolteweg 9-17, 7722 ☎ 0529 439191 0529 439199
e-mail info@gerner.nl
website www.gerner.nl
➲ *Off at Dalfsen & 2nd left.*
Open All year **Site** 12HEC **Facilities** **Services** **Leisure** P

DENEKAMP OVERIJSSEL

Papillon
Kanaalweg 30, 7591 ☎ 05413 51670 05413 55217
e-mail info@depapillon.nl
website www.depapillon.nl
Mostly a chalet site on meadowland in a coniferous and deciduous forest, 2km north of Denekamp. There are a few naturally screened pitches.
➲ *Off E72 towards Nordhorn (Germany) 300m N of sign for Almelo-Nordhorn canal, continue NE 1.5km.*
Open Apr-1 Oct **Site** 11HEC **Prices** pitch 25 pp4 **Facilities** **Services** **Leisure** LP

Netherlands

Site 6HEC (site size) grass sand stone little shade partly shaded mainly shaded bungalows for hire caravans for hire tents for hire no dogs **Prices** adult per night car per night pp per person per night caravan per night tent per night (static)-caravan hire per week

DIEPENHEIM OVERIJSSEL

Molnhofte

Nyhofweg 5, 7478 ☎ 0547 351514 📠 0547 351641
e-mail info@molnhofte.nl
website www.molnhofte.nl
A family site in a rural setting with modern bungalows for hire.

➲ *E of town.*

Open All year **Site** 6HEC ❤ ♣ 🏠 🚻 **Prices** ♠ 3.25 🚗 2.75 🚐 3.25
🅰 3.25 **Facilities** 🏪 🖪 ⊙ 🚿 🐠 🚉 ⓟ ❹ **Services** 🛒 🍴 ➕ 🗄
Leisure ⇆ P

DOESBURG GELDERLAND

Ijsselstrand

Eekstr 18, 6984 ☎ 0313 472797 📠 0313 473376
e-mail ijsselstrand@planet.nl
website www.ijsselstrand.nl
On level meadow with trees and hedges beside the River Ijssel.
Separate field for young people. Water sports available.

➲ *NE across river, signed.*

Open All year **Site** 45HEC ❤ ♣ 🏠 🚻 **Facilities** 🏪 🖪 ⊙ 🚿 🐠 🚉 ⓟ
Services 🛒 🍴 ➕ 🗄 **Leisure** ⇆ LR

DOETINCHEM GELDERLAND

Wrange

Rekhemseweg 144, 7004 ☎ 0314 324852
e-mail info@dewrange.nl
website www.dewrange.nl
On the eastern outskirts of the town, set in meadowland and
surrounded by bushes and deciduous trees.

➲ *200m E of link road between roads to Varsseveld & Terborg.*

Open All year **Site** 12HEC ❤ ♣ 🏠 🚻 **Prices** pitch 12-16.50 **Facilities** 🏪
🖪 ⊙ 🚿 🐠 🚉 ⓟ **Services** 🛒 🍴 ➕ 🗄 **Leisure** ⇆ P

DOORN UTRECHT

Bonte Vlucht

Leersumsestraatweg 23, 3941 ☎ 0343 473232 📠 0343 414517
e-mail info@bontevlucht.nl
website www.bontevlucht.nl

➲ *3km E.*

Open Apr-Oct **Site** 17HEC ❤ ♣ ♣ 🏠 ⊗ **Facilities** 🏪 ⊙ 🚿 🐠 ⓟ
Services 🛒 🍴 ➕ **Off-site** ⇆P

Het Grote Bos

Hydeparklaan 24, 3941 ☎ 0343 513644 📠 0343 512324
e-mail het-grote-bos@rcn.nl
website www.rcn.nl
Well laid-out site on wooded grassland. Varied leisure activities for
children and adults.

➲ *1km NW of Doorn.*

Open All year **Site** 80HEC ❤ ♣ ♣ 🏠 **Facilities** 🏪 🖪 ⊙ 🚿 🐠 🚉
Services 🛒 🍴 ➕ 🗄 **Leisure** ⇆ P

DRONTEN GELDERLAND

AT BIDDINGHUIZEN (9KM S)

Riviera Park

Spijkweg 15, 8256 ☎ 0321 331344 📠 0321 331402
e-mail info@riviera.nl
website www.riviera.nl
Grassland site surrounded by shrubs near a deciduous forest.

➲ *On Polder beside Veluwemeer, 5km S of Biddinghuizen turn
left.*

Open Apr-30 Oct **Site** 60HEC ❤ ♣ ♣ 🏠 🚻 🅰 **Prices** pitch 23.50-40
🚐 (static)210-590 **Facilities** 🏪 🖪 ⊙ 🚿 🐠 🚉 ⓟ **Services** 🛒 🍴 ➕ 🗄
Leisure ⇆ LP

EDAM NOORD-HOLLAND

Strandbad

Zeevangszeedijk 7a, 1135 ☎ 0299 371994 📠 0299 371510
e-mail info@campingstrandbad.nl
website www.campingstrandbad.nl
A friendly family site on the Ijssel lake with plenty of facilities and close
to the historical town of Edam.

Open Apr-Sep **Site** 5HEC ❤ ♣ 🏠 ⊗ **Facilities** 🏪 🖪 ⊙ 🚿 🐠 🚉 ⓟ
Services 🛒 🍴 ➕ 🗄 **Leisure** ⇆ L **Off-site** ⇆P

EERBEEK GELDERLAND

Landal Greenparks Coldenhove

Boshoffweg 6, 6961 ☎ 0313 659101 📠 0313 654776
e-mail coldenhove@landal.nl
website www.landal.co.uk
Set in woodland.

➲ *From Apeldoorn-Dieren road, drive 2km SW, then NW for
1km.*

Open 18 Mar-1 Nov **Site** 74HEC ❤ ♣ ♣ 🏠 ⊗ **Prices** pitch 14-31 (incl 2
persons) pp3 **Facilities** 🏪 🖪 ⊙ 🚿 🐠 🚉 ⓟ ⓟ **Services** 🛒 🍴 ➕ 🗄
Leisure ⇆ P

Robertsoord

Doonweg 4, 6961 ☎ 0313 651346 📠 0313 655751
e-mail info@robertsoord.nl
website www.robertsoord.nl
Wooded location with good recreational facilities.

➲ *1km SE.*

Open Apr-Oct **Site** 2.5HEC ❤ ♣ 🏠 **Facilities** 🏪 ⊙ 🚿 🐠 🚉 ⓟ
Services 🍴 ➕ 🗄 **Off-site** 🖪 ⇆P

EGMOND AAN ZEE NOORD-HOLLAND

Camping Egmond ann Zee

Nollenweg 1, 1931 AV ☎ 072 5061702 📠 072 5067147
website www.euroase.com
A wooded location 1.5km from the beach. One of a chain of family
sites with excellent facilities.

Open Apr-Oct **Site** 11HEC ❤ ♣ 🏠 ⊗ **Facilities** 🏪 🖪 ⊙ 🚿 🐠 🚉 ⓟ
Services 🛒 🍴 ➕ 🗄 **Leisure** ⇆ PS **Off-site** 🍴 ⇆P

Netherlands

ENSCHEDE OVERIJSSEL

De Twentse Es
Keppelerdijk 200, 7534 ☎ 053 4611372 🖹 053 4618558
e-mail info@twentse-es.nl
website www.twentse-es.nl
Wooded location with good recreational facilities.

➲ Signed on A35

Open All year **Site** 10HEC 🌱 ♨ **Prices** pitch 20.40-23 **Facilities** ⋔ 🏠 ⊙ 🚻 ⊘ ♨ ⅏ ⑦ **Services** ⊞ Ⅰ◎Ⅰ 🛒 🛢 **Leisure** ≈ P

ERMELO GELDERLAND

Haeghehorst
Fazantlaan 4, 3852 ☎ 0341 553185 🖹 0341 562751
e-mail info@haeghehorst.nl
website www.haeghehorst.nl
Well-equipped site in pleasant wooded surroundings.

➲ A28 towards Amersfoort, onto N303.

Open All year **Site** 10HEC 🌱 ♨ 🏕 🛏 ⊗ **Prices** pitch 15.80-31
Facilities ⋔ 🏠 ⊙ 🚻 ⊘ ♨ ⅏ ⑦ **Services** ⊞ Ⅰ◎Ⅰ 🛒 🛢 **Leisure** ≈ LP

GROOTE KEETEN NOORD-HOLLAND

Callassande
Voorweg 5A, 1759 ☎ 0224 581663 🖹 0224 582588
e-mail info@callassande.nl
website www.callassande.nl
A large site with fine facilities close to the sea.

Open Apr-Oct **Site** 12HEC 🌱 ♨ 🏕 🛏 **Prices** ♠ 4 ⊕ 2.50 🚐 12.50
🛆 9-12.50 **Facilities** ⋔ 🏠 ⊙ 🚻 ⊘ ⑦ 🅿 **Services** ⊞ Ⅰ◎Ⅰ 🛒 🛢 **Leisure** ≈ P
Off-site ⊘ ⅏ ≈S

HAAKSBERGEN OVERIJSSEL

't Stien'nboer
Scholtenhagenweg 42, 7481 ☎ 0535 722610 🖹 0535 729394
e-mail info@stien-nboer.nl
website www.stien-nboer.nl
A family site with good recreational facilities lying S of the town.

Open 15 Mar-1 Nov **Site** 10.5HEC 🌱 ♨ ♨ 🏕 🛆 **Facilities** ⋔ 🏠 ⊙ 🚻 ⊘ ⑦ 🅿 **Services** ⊞ Ⅰ◎Ⅰ 🛒 🛢 **Leisure** ≈ P **Off-site** 🏠 ⊞ Ⅰ◎Ⅰ

HALFWEG NOORD-HOLLAND

Houtrak
Zuiderweg 2, 1165 NA ☎ 020 4972796 🖹 020 4975887
e-mail info@campinghoutrak.nl
website www.campinghoutrak.nl
Grassy site on several levels subdivided by trees, hedges and shrubs.
Separate section for young campers.

➲ A5 exit Spaarwonde, site signed.

Open Apr-Sep **Site** 13HEC 🌱 ♨ 🏕 **Facilities** ⋔ 🏠 ⊙ 🚻 ⊘ ♨ ⑦ **Services** Ⅰ◎Ⅰ 🛒 🛢 **Leisure** ≈ L **Off-site** ≈P

HATTEM GELDERLAND

Leemkule
Leemkuilen 6, 8051 PN ☎ 038 4441945 🖹 038 4446280
e-mail info@leemkule.nl
website www.leemkule.nl
The holiday centre is in one of the largest nature reserves in the country.

➲ 2.5km SW.

Open Apr-Oct **Site** 16HEC 🌱 ♨ 🏕 ⊗ **Prices** pitch 19-26 (incl 2 persons)
Facilities ⋔ 🏠 ⊙ 🚻 ⊘ 🅿 **Services** ⊞ Ⅰ◎Ⅰ 🛒 🛢 **Leisure** ≈ P **Off-site** ⅏

HEILOO NOORD-HOLLAND

Heiloo
De Omloop 24, 1852 ☎ 072 5355555 🖹 072 5355551
e-mail info@campingheiloo.nl
website www.campingheiloo.nl
One of the best sites in the area. It is divided into many large squares by hedges.

Open Apr-Oct **Site** 4HEC 🌱 ♨ 🏕 🛏 ⊗ **Facilities** ⋔ ⊙ 🚻 ⊘ ♨ ⅏ 🅿 **Services** ⊞ Ⅰ◎Ⅰ 🛒 🛢 **Off-site** 🏠 ≈LP

Klein Varnebroek
De Omloop 22, 1852 ☎ 072 5331627 🖹 072 5331620
e-mail info@kleinvarnebroek.nl
website www.kleinvarnebroek.nl
A grassy, family site surrounded by trees.

➲ Off Alkmaar road towards swimming pool.

Open 31 Mar-25 Sep **Site** 4.9HEC 🌱 ♨ 🏕 **Prices** pitch 17-28 (incl 2 persons) **Facilities** ⋔ ⊙ 🚻 ⊘ 🅿 **Services** ⊞ Ⅰ◎Ⅰ 🛒 🛢 **Off-site** 🏠 ≈LPS

HELDER, DEN NOORD-HOLLAND

Donkere Duinen
Jan Verfailleweg 616, 1783 ☎ 0223 614731
e-mail info@donkereduinen.nl
website www.donkereduinen.nl
A quiet, pleasant site with good facilities.

➲ Signs for Nieuw-Den Helder Strand, 0.8km towards beach.

Open 28 Apr-3 Sep **Site** 7HEC 🌱 ♨ **Prices** ♠ 4.10 pitch 20.70-23.20 (incl 2 persons) **Facilities** ⋔ ⊙ 🚻 ⊘ ⑦ **Services** 🛒 🛢 **Leisure** ≈ S **Off-site** 🏠 ⊞ Ⅰ◎Ⅰ ⊘ ⅏ ≈PS

Noorder Sandt
Noorder Sandt 2, Julianadorp aan Zee, 1787
☎ 0223 641266 🖹 0233 645600
e-mail info@noordersandt.com
website www.noordersandt.com
A flat, well-maintained site on meadowland, with good sanitary blocks.

➲ Access from Den Helder to Callantsoog coast road.

Open Etr-29 Oct **Site** 10HEC 🌱 ♨ 🏕 **Prices** ♠ 4-4.80 pitch 24.50-31.10 (incl 2 persons) **Facilities** ⋔ 🏠 ⊙ 🚻 ⊘ ⅏ ⑦ **Services** ⊞ Ⅰ◎Ⅰ 🛒 🛢 **Leisure** ≈ P **Off-site** ≈S

HENGELO GELDERLAND

Kom-Es-An
Handwijzersdijk 4, 7255 ☎ 0575 467242
A family site in wooded surroundings on the outskirts of the village.

➲ NE of village towards Ruurlo.

Open Apr-Oct **Site** 10.5HEC 🌱 ♨ 🏕 **Facilities** ⋔ 🏠 ⊙ 🚻 ⊘ ♨ ⅏ ⑦ 🅿 **Services** ⊞ Ⅰ◎Ⅰ 🛒 🛢 **Leisure** ≈ P

HENGELO OVERIJSSEL

Zwaaikom
Kettingbrugweg 60, 7552 ☎ 074 2916560 🖹 074 2916785
e-mail smink_zwaaikom@planet.nl
website www.dezwaaikom.tk
A family site on the Twente canal, with good facilities.

➲ SE towards Enschede between canal & road.

Open 15 Apr-15 Sep **Site** 4HEC 🌱 ♨ ⊗ **Facilities** ⋔ 🏠 ⊙ 🚻 ⊘ ⅏ ⑦ **Services** ⊞ Ⅰ◎Ⅰ 🛒 🛢 **Leisure** ≈ P

Site 6HEC (site size) 🌱 grass ♨ sand ♨ stone 🛏 little shade 🏕 partly shaded 🏕 mainly shaded 🏠 bungalows for hire 🚐 caravans for hire 🛆 tents for hire ⊗ no dogs **Prices** ♠ adult per night 🚗 car per night pp per person per night 🚐 caravan per night 🛆 tent per night 🚐 (static)-caravan hire per week

HEUMEN GELDERLAND

Heumens Bos

Vosseneindseweg 46, 6582 ☎ 024 3581481 ▤ 024 3583862
e-mail info@heumensbos.nl
website www.heumensbos.nl

One of the best sites in the area with modern facilities and spacious pitches.

➲ *NW of village, 100m N of Wijchen road.*

Open All year **Site** 16HEC ♨ ♣ ♠ ♠ **⚑** 🏕 **Prices** ♦ 4 pitch 16-25 (incl 2 persons) **Facilities** ➊ 🚾 ⊙ ⊕ **⚑** ⊘ ⊕ **Services** ⬛ 🍴 ➕ ▤ **Leisure** ⬗ P

HOENDERLOO GELDERLAND

Pampel

Woeste Hoefweg 35, 7351 TN ☎ 055 3781760 ▤ 055 3781992
e-mail info@pampel.nl
website www.pampel.nl

A most attractive site in pleasant wooded surroundings with good facilities for families.

Open All year **Site** 14.5HEC ♨ ♣ ♠ ♣ **Facilities** ➊ 🚾 ⊙ ⊕ **⚑** ⊘ ⊕ **Services** 🍴 ➕ ▤ **Leisure** ⬗ P **Off-site** ⬛ 🍴

HOORN, DEN (ISLAND OF TEXEL) NOORD-HOLLAND

Kogerstrand

Badweg 33 ☎ 0222 317208 ▤ 0222 317018
e-mail info@rsttexel.nl
website www.rsttexel.nl

Part of the Duinen van Texel national park, close to the dunes and the sea. A separate part of the site is reserved for the 16-25 age group, and there is a restricted traffic policy. Cars may only enter the site on arrival and departure, at other times the car park must be used.

➲ *From ferry proceed to De Koog and continue along road (Nikadel). Pass Catholic church and continue along Badweg. Drive to end of road.*

Open 31 Mar-28 Oct **Site** 52HEC ♨ ♣ ♠ 🏕 **Facilities** ➊ ⊙ **⚑** ⊕ **Services** 🍴 🍴 ➕ ▤ **Leisure** ⬗ S **Off-site** 🚾 ⊘ ⬗P

Loodsmansduin

Rommelpot 19, 1797 ☎ 0222 317208 ▤ 0222 317018
e-mail info@rsttexel.nl
website www.rsttexel.nl

Extensive site, numerous large and small hollows between dunes, connected by paved paths. Several sanitary blocks. At the highest part there is a bungalow village within a shopping and administrative complex. A section is reserved for naturists and there is a naturist beach 2km away.

➲ *From ferry N towards Den Burg, left at x-rds towards Den Hoorn.*

Open 31 Mar-28 Oct **Site** 38HEC ♨ ♣ ♠ ♣ **Facilities** ➊ ⊙ **⚑** ⊘ ⊕ **Services** 🍴 🍴 ➕ ▤ **Leisure** ⬗ PS **Off-site** 🚾 ⬗S

KESTEREN GELDERLAND

Lede en Oudewaard

Hogedijkseweg 40, 4041 ☎ 0488 481477 ▤ 0488 482599
e-mail lede_oudewaard@zonnet.nl
website www.camping-ledeoudewaard.nl

On level meadowland surrounded by bushy hedges and divided into individual pitches. 100m from private beach and pool.

➲ *2km N of village, turn W off main Rhenen-Kesteren road, and continue for 2.7km.*

Open All year **Site** 30HEC ♨ ♣ ♠ **Facilities** ➊ 🚾 ⊙ ⊕ **⚑** ⊘ ⊕ ⊕ **Services** 🍴 🍴 ➕ ▤ **Leisure** ⬗ L

KOOG, DE (ISLAND OF TEXEL) NOORD-HOLLAND

Om de Noord

Boodtlaan 80 ☎ 0222 317208 ▤ 0222 317018
e-mail info@rsttexel.nl
website www.rsttexel.nl

Site with spacious pitches located close to woodlands, dunes and the beach.

➲ *From ferry to De Koog, continue along road (Nikadel), pass Catholic church on right, turn right at junct with Boodtlaan, continue to football pitch, driveway on left.*

Open 31 Mar-28 Oct **Site** 3.3HEC ♨ ♣ **Facilities** ➊ ⊙ **⚑** ⊕ **Services** ➕ ▤ **Off-site** 🚾 🍴 🍴 ⊘ ▲ ⬗PS

Shelter

Boodtlaan 43, 1796 ☎ 0222 317208 ▤ 0222 317018
e-mail info@rsttexel.nl
website www.rsttexel.nl

Small family site a short distance from the sea.

Open All year **Site** 1.1HEC ♨ ♣ 🏕 **Prices** ♦ 1.60-3 **⚑** 16-29 🏕 16-29 **Facilities** ➊ ⊙ **⚑** ⊕ **Services** ➕ ▤ **Off-site** 🚾 🍴 🍴 ⊘ ▲ ⬗S

KOOTWIJK GELDERLAND

Kerkendel

Kerkendelweg 49, 3775 ☎ 0577 456224 ▤ 0577 456545
e-mail kerkendel@kerkendel.nl
website www.kerkendel.nl

A family site with good facilities in the heart of the Veluwe national park.

Open 27 Mar-Oct **Site** 7.5HEC ♨ ♣ ♠ 🏕 **Facilities** ➊ 🚾 ⊙ ⊕ **⚑** ⊘ ⊕ **Services** 🍴 🍴 ➕ ▤ **Leisure** ⬗ P **Off-site** ⬗LR

LATHUM GELDERLAND

Mars

Marsweg 6, 6988 ☎ 0313 631131 ▤ 0313 631435
e-mail info@campingdemars.nl
website www.campingdemars.nl

Divided into pitches on level meadowland beside a dammed tributary of River Ijssel.

➲ *Off Arnhem-Doesberg road N of village & W for 1.7km.*

Open Apr-Oct **Site** 10HEC ♨ ♣ ♠ ⊕ **Prices** ♦ 3.60 **⚑** 1.75 🏕 3.25 🏕 3.25 **Facilities** ➊ 🚾 ⊙ **⚑** ▲ ⊕ ⊕ **Services** 🍴 🍴 ➕ ▤ **Leisure** ⬗ L

LUTTENBERG OVERIJSSEL

Luttenberg

Heuvelweg 9, 8105 ☎ 0572 301405 ▤ 0572 301757
e-mail info@luttenberg.nl
website www.luttenberg.nl

A large holiday park with spacious, well-defined pitches separated by bushes. Variety of recreational facilities.

Open Apr-Sep **Site** 12HEC ♨ ♣ ♠ ♠ 🏕 **Prices** pitch 17-24.50 (incl 2 persons) **Facilities** ➊ 🚾 ⊙ **⚑** ⊘ ▲ ⊕ ⊕ **Services** 🍴 🍴 ➕ ▤ **Leisure** ⬗ P

Facilities 🚾 shop ➊ shower ⊙ electric points for razors **⚑** electric points for caravans ⊕ parking by tents permitted ⊕ compulsory separate car park
Services 🍴 café/restaurant 🍴 bar ⊘ Camping Gaz International ▲ gas other than Camping Gaz ➕ first aid facilities ▤ laundry
Leisure ⬗ swimming L-Lake P-Pool R-River S-Sea **Off-site** All facilities within 2km

Netherlands

MAARN UTRECHT

Laag-Kanje
Laan van Laag-Kanje 1, 3951 ☎ 0343 441348 ▤ 0343 443295
e-mail info@laagkanje.nl
website www.laagkanje.nl
Situated 0.5km from the lake.
➲ *2km NE.*
Open Apr-Sep **Site** 28HEC ♨ ♣ ⊗ **Prices** ♠ 2.95 ♠ 2.40 ♣ 2 ▲ 3.20
Facilities ⋔ ☖ ⊕ ⊖ ⌿ ⦿ **Services** ➤☐ ↻☉ ⊞ ⊠ **Off-site** ⇔L

MIJNDEN UTRECHT

Mijnden
Bloklaan 22a, 1231 AZ ☎ 0294 233165 ▤ 0294 233402
e-mail info@mijnden.nl
website www.mijnden.nl
Situated on Loosdrechtse Plassen lake with good sports facilities.
➲ *A2 exit Hilversum, after bridge turn right, through Loenen & left.*
Open 31 Mar-1 Oct **Site** 25HEC ♨ ♣ **Prices** ♠4 ♠3 ♣7 ▲7
Facilities ⋔ ☖ ⊕ ⊖ ⌿ ⊕ ⦿ **Services** ➤☐ ↻☉ ⊞ ⊠ **Leisure** ⇔ LP
Off-site ⇔L

NEEDE GELDERLAND

Eversman
Bliksteeg 1, 7161 ☎ 0545 291906
A quiet position surrounded by trees.
➲ *W of town.*
Open Apr-Sep **Site** 3.8HEC ♨ ♣ ⚏ ♠ **Facilities** ⋔ ⊖ ⊖ ⌿ ⊕
Services ↻☉ ⊞ ⊠ **Leisure** ⇔ P

NOORD SCHARWOUDE NOORD-HOLLAND

Molengroet
Molengroet 1, 1723 ☎ 0226 393444 ▤ 0226 391426
e-mail info@molengroet.nl
website www.molengroet.nl
Site with modern facilities within easy reach of the beach and the Geestmerambacht water park.
➲ *Signed on N245.*
Open Apr-Oct **Site** 11HEC ♨ ♣ ⚏ **Facilities** ⋔ ☖ ⊕ ⊖ ⌿ ⊕ ⦿
Services ➤☐ ↻☉ ⊞ ⊠ **Leisure** ⇔ L **Off-site** ⇔PS

NUNSPEET GELDERLAND

Vossenberg
Groenlaantje 25, 8071 ☎ 0341 252458 ▤ 0341 279500
Open Apr-1 Nov **Site** 3.6HEC ♨ ♣ ⚏ ♠ ⊗ **Facilities** ⋔ ⊖ ⊖ ⌿ ⊕
Services ➤☐ ↻☉ ⊞ ⊠ **Off-site** ☖↻☉ ⇔LP

PUTTEN GELDERLAND

Strandpark Putten
Strandboulevard 27, 3882 ☎ 0341 361304 ▤ 0341 361210
e-mail info@strandparkputten.nl
website www.strandparkputten.nl
Campsite is by a lake and has a private beach. Excellent facilities for windsurfing and yachting.
➲ *off A28*
Open Apr-Oct **Site** 8HEC ♨ ♣ ▲ ⊗ **Prices** pitch 57-74 **Facilities** ⋔ ⊖
⊖ ⦿ **Services** ➤☐ ↻☉ ⊞ ⊠ **Leisure** ⇔ L **Off-site** ☖⌿⥾ ⇔P

REUTUM OVERIJSSEL

De Molenhof
Kleijsenweg 7, 7667 ☎ 0541 661165 ▤ 0541 662032
e-mail info@demolenhof.nl
website www.demolenhof.nl
A large family site in wooded surroundings with plenty of modern facilities.
➲ *Via A1*
Open 31 Mar-Sep **Site** 16HEC ♨ ♣ ⚏ ▲ **Prices** ♠5 pitch 8.50-23 (incl 2 persons) **Facilities** ⋔ ☖ ⊕ ⊖ ⌿ ⥾ ⦿ **Services** ➤☐ ↻☉ ⊞ ⊠
Leisure ⇔ P

RHENEN UTRECHT

Thymse Berg
Nieuwe Veenendaalseweg 229, 3911
☎ 0317 612384 ▤ 0317 618119
e-mail thymseberg@planet.nl
website www.thymseberg.nl
➲ *N of town.*
Open Apr-Oct **Site** 10HEC ♨ ♣ ⚏ ♠ ⊗ **Prices** ♠4 ♠ 1.20 ♣ 5.50-9.50
▲ 3.50 **Facilities** ⋔ ☖ ⊕ ⊖ ⌿ ⦿ **Services** ➤☐ ↻☉ ⊞ ⊠ **Leisure** ⇔ P
Off-site ⥾ ⇔LR

RUURLO GELDERLAND

't Sikkeler
Sikkelerweg 8, 7261 ☎ 0573 461221 ▤ 0573 461586
e-mail info@sikkeler.nl
website www.sikkeler.nl
A beautiful wooded location with modern facilities. Popular with walkers.
➲ *4km SW.*
Open All year **Site** 7HEC ♨ ♣ ⚏ **Facilities** ⋔ ☖ ⊕ ⊖ ⌿ ⊕ ⦿
Services ↻☉ ⊞ ⊠ **Off-site** ⥾ ⇔LP

ST MAARTENSZEE NOORD-HOLLAND

St Maartenszee
Westerduinweg 30, 1753 ☎ 0224 561401 ▤ 0224 561901
e-mail info@campingsintmaartenszee.nl
website www.campingsintmaartenszee.nl
Completely surrounded and divided into pitches by hedges, lying on meadowland beside a wide belt of dunes.
➲ *Via N9 in direction of Den Helder, signed in village St Maartensvlotbrug*
Open 30 Mar-Sep **Site** 5HEC ♨ ♣ ⚏ ⊗ **Prices** ♠ 3.81-4.81 pitch 9.25-17
Facilities ⋔ ☖ ⊕ ⊖ ⌿ ⥾ ⊕ **Services** ➤☐ ↻☉ ⊞ ⊠ **Off-site** ⇔LPS

SOEST UTRECHT

King's Home
Birkstr 136, 3768 ☎ 033 4619118 ▤ 033 4610808
e-mail camping@kingshome.nl
website www.kingshome.nl
Well-maintained site with modern facilities in a natural setting on the edge of woodland.
➲ *On N221 between Amersfoort & Soest.*
Open All year **Site** 5HEC ♨ ♣ ⚏ ♠ **Facilities** ⋔ ⊖ ⊖ ⌿ ⥾ ⦿
Services ➤☐ ↻☉ ⊞ ⊠ **Off-site** ☖↻☉ ⇔P

Site 6HEC (site size) ♨ grass ⊖ sand ♨ stone ♣ little shade ♣ partly shaded ♨ mainly shaded ⚏ bungalows for hire
♠ caravans for hire ▲ tents for hire ⊗ no dogs **Prices** ♠ adult per night ♠ car per night pp per person per night ♣ caravan per night
▲ tent per night ♠ (static)-caravan hire per week

Netherlands

STEENWIJK OVERIJSSEL

Kom

Bultweg 25, 8346 ☎ 0521 513736 ▤ 0521 518736
e-mail info@campingdekom.nl
website www.campingdekom.nl
Split into two sections, lying near a country house, and surrounded by a beautiful oak forest.

➲ *Off Steenwijk-Frederiksoord road.*

Open All year **Site** 12.5HEC ❄ ♣ ♣ ☎ ➤ **Prices** pitch 17.20-20.50 (incl 2 persons) **Facilities** ℾ 🏠 ⊙ ⊕ ⍉ ∅ ⑳ ⓟ **Services** ⚑ ⍓ ✚ ⑤ **Leisure** ◈ P

TEXEL (ISLAND OF) See HOORN, DEN

UITDAM NOORD-HOLLAND

Uitdam

Zeedijk 2, 1154 ☎ 020 4031433 ▤ 020 4033692
e-mail info@campinguitdam.nl
website www.campinguitdam.nl
A well-maintained site on the Markermeer adjoining the marina.

➲ *Via N247 Amsterdam-Monnickendam.*

Open Mar-Oct **Site** 21HEC ❄ ♣ ☎ ➤ **Prices** ♦ 3 pitch 19-22.50 **Facilities** ℾ 🏠 ⊙ ⊕ ⍉ ∅ ⑳ **Services** ⚑ ⍓ ✚ ⑤ **Leisure** ◈ L

URK FLEVOLAND

Hazevreugd

Vormtweg 9, 8321 ☎ 0527 681785 ▤ 0527 686298
e-mail info@hazevreugd.nl
website www.hazevreugd.nl
A modern family site in wooded surroundings with a variety of recreational facilities.

➲ *Via A6.*

Open Apr-Oct **Site** 12HEC ❄ ♣ **Facilities** ℾ 🏠 ⊙ ⊕ ⍉ ∅ ⍾ ⑳ **Services** ⚑ ⍓ ✚ ⑤ **Leisure** ◈ P **Off-site** ◈S

VOGELENZANG NOORD-HOLLAND

Vogelenzang

Doodweg Tweede 17, 2114 AP ☎ 023 5847014 ▤ 023 5849249
e-mail camping@vogelenzang.nl
website www.vogelenzang.nl
➲ *1km W.*

Open Etr-15 Sep **Site** 22HEC ❄ ♣ ◈ ⊗ **Facilities** ℾ 🏠 ⊙ ⊕ ⍉ ∅ ⍾ ⑳ **Services** ⚑ ⍓ ✚ ⑤ **Leisure** ◈ P

WEZEP GELDERLAND

Heidehoek

Heidehoeksweg 7, 8091 ☎ 038 3761382 ▤ 038 3765571
e-mail heidehoek@info.nl
website www.heidehoek.nl
➲ *0.5km W of railway station.*

Open Apr-Oct **Site** 16HEC ❄ ♣ ➤ **Facilities** ℾ 🏠 ⊙ ⊕ ⍉ ∅ ⍾ ⑳ **Services** ⚑ ⍓ ✚ ⑤ **Leisure** ◈ LP

WIJDENES NOORD-HOLLAND

Het Hof

Zuideruitweg 64, 1608 ☎ 0229 501435 ▤ 0229 503244
e-mail info@campinghethof.nl
website www.campinghethof.nl
A series of fields in a sheltered position on the shore of the Ijsselmeer.

➲ *A7 exit 8 Hoorn, onto N506 for Enkhuizen, right to Wijdenes & signed.*

Open 30 Mar-Sep **Site** 3.9HEC ❄ ♣ **Prices** ♦ 3.75 ➤ 8.50 ▲ 8.50 **Facilities** ℾ 🏠 ⊙ ⊕ ⍉ ∅ ⓟ **Services** ⚑ ⍓ ✚ ⑤ **Leisure** ◈ LP

WINTERSWIJK GELDERLAND

Twee Bruggen

Meenkmolenweg 11, 7109 ☎ 0543 565366 ▤ 0543 565222
e-mail info@detweebruggen.nl
website www.detweebruggen.nl
A family site in pleasant wooded surroundings with modern facilities.

Open All year **Site** 34HEC ❄ ♣ ☎ ➤ **Facilities** ℾ 🏠 ⊙ ⊕ ⍉ ∅ ⍾ ⑳ ⓟ **Services** ⚑ ⍓ ✚ ⑤ **Leisure** ◈ LP

SOUTH

AFFERDEN LIMBURG

Klein Canada

Dorpsstr 1, 5851 ☎ 0485 531223 ▤ 0485 532218
e-mail info@kleincanada.nl
website www.kleincanada.nl
Situated among heath and woodland close to the River Meuse.

Open All year **Site** 12.5HEC ❄ ♣ ☎ ➤ **Facilities** ℾ 🏠 ⊙ ⊕ ⍉ ∅ ⍾ ⓟ **Services** ⚑ ⍓ ✚ ⑤ **Leisure** ◈ P

BAARLAND ZEELAND

Comfort Camping Scheldeoord

Landingsweg 1, 4435 ☎ 0113 639900 ▤ 0113 639500
e-mail info@scheldeoord.nl
website www.scheldeoord.nl
A popular family site in a beautiful location by the River Scheldt.

➲ *S of town on coast.*

Open Apr-Oct **Site** 16HEC ❄ ♣ ☎ ➤ **Prices** pitch 14-39.50 **Facilities** ℾ 🏠 ⊙ ⊕ ⍉ ∅ ⍾ ⑳ **Services** ⚑ ⍓ ✚ ⑤ **Leisure** ◈ PS

BAARLE NASSAU NOORD-BRABANT

Heimolen

Heimolen 6, 5111 EH ☎ 0507 9425 ▤ 0507 7885
e-mail info@deheimolen.nl
website www.deheimolen.nl
Wooded location with modern facilities.

➲ *1.5km SW.*

Open All year **Site** 15HEC ❄ ♣ ☎ ➤ **Facilities** ℾ ⊙ ⊕ ⍉ ∅ ⍾ ⓟ **Services** ⚑ ⍓ ✚ ⑤ **Off-site** ◈P

BERG EN TERBLIJT LIMBURG

Oriëntal

Rijksweg 6, 6325 ☎ 043 6040075 ▤ 043 6042912
e-mail info@campingoriental.nl
website www.campingoriental.nl
➲ *On Maastricht-Valkenburg road 3km from Maastricht.*

Open 13 Apr-29 Oct **Site** 5.5HEC ❄ ♣ ➤ **Facilities** ℾ 🏠 ⊙ ⊕ ⍉ ∅ ⍾ ⑳ **Services** ⚑ ⍓ ✚ ⑤ **Leisure** ◈ P **Off-site** ⍓

Facilities 🏠 shop ℾ shower ⊙ electric points for razors ⊕ electric points for caravans ⑳ parking by tents permitted ⓟ compulsory separate car park
Services ⍓ café/restaurant ⚑ bar ∅ Camping Gaz International ⍾ gas other than Camping Gaz ✚ first aid facilities ⑤ laundry
Leisure ◈ swimming L-Lake P-Pool R-River S-Sea **Off-site** All facilities within 2km

Netherlands

BERGEYK NOORD-BRABANT

Paal

De Paaldreef 14, 5571 ☎ 0497 571977 ▤ 0497 577164
e-mail info@depaal.nl
website www.depaal.nl
Site catering especially for families.

➲ *Signed.*

Open Mar-Oct **Site** 41HEC ❤ ♣ **Prices** pitch 27-39 (incl 2 persons)
Facilities ↖ ▥ ⊙ ◘ ∅ ♨ ❾ **Services** ⚑ ⍭ ➕ ⬚ **Leisure** ❦ P
Off-site ❦L

BOSSCHENHOOFD NOORD-BRABANT

Langoed de Wildert

Pagnevaartdreef 3 ☎ 0165 312582 ▤ 0165 310941
website www.landgoeddewildert.nl
Peaceful location in woodland.

➲ *A58 exit 21 to Bosschenhoofd, pass church on right, site
0.5km on left.*

Open Apr-Sep **Site** 15HEC ❤ ● ♣ ⊗ **Prices** pitch 20 (incl 2 persons)
pp4 **Facilities** ↖ ⊙ ◘ ♨ **Services** ⍭ ➕ ⬚ **Off-site** ▥ ⚑ ⍭ ∅

BOXTEL NOORD-BRABANT

Dennenoord

Dennendreef 5, 5282 ☎ 0411 601280 ▤ 0411 601393
e-mail info@campingdennenoord.nl
website www.campingdennenoord.nl
Level, grassy site with hedging and groups of trees. Leisure activities
organised for adults and young people. Soundproof disco.

➲ *Off N2 at Esch towards Osterwijk, signed.*

Open Apr-1 Oct **Site** 7HEC ❤ ♣ **Facilities** ↖ ⊙ ◘ ∅ ♨ ❾
Services ⚑ ⍭ ➕ ⬚ **Leisure** ❦ P **Off-site** ▥ ❦L

BRESKENS ZEELAND

Napoleon Hoeve

Zandertje 30, 4511 ☎ 0117 383838 ▤ 0117 383550
e-mail info@napoleonhoeve.nl
website www.napoleonhoeve.nl
A family site with access to the beach.

Open All year **Site** 13HEC ❤ ♣ ☎ ❤ **Facilities** ↖ ▥ ⊙ ◘ ∅ ♨ ⊛ ❾
Services ⚑ ⍭ ➕ ⬚ **Leisure** ❦ PS

Schoneveld

Schoneveld 1, 4511 HR ☎ 0117 383220 ▤ 0117 383650
e-mail schoneveld@zeelandnet.nl
website www.zeelandnet.nl/schoneveld

➲ *3km S at beach.*

Open All year **Site** 14HEC ❤ ♣ ⚑ **Facilities** ↖ ▥ ⊙ ◘ ∅ ♨ ❾
Services ⚑ ⍭ ➕ ⬚ **Leisure** ❦ PS

BRIELLE ZUID-HOLLAND

Krabbeplaat

Oude Veerdam 4, 3231 ☎ 0181 412363 ▤ 0181 412093
e-mail info@krabbeplaat.nl
website www.krabbeplaat.com
On level ground scattered with trees and groups of bushes. It has
asphalt drives. Nearest site to the coast and ferries.

➲ *Signed.*

Open Apr-Oct **Site** 18HEC ❤ ♣ ⊗ **Facilities** ↖ ▥ ⊙ ◘ ∅ ♨ ⊛
Services ⚑ ⍭ ➕ ⬚ **Leisure** ❦ L

BROEKHUIZENVORST LIMBURG

Kasteel Ooyen

Blitterswijkseweg 2, 5871 ☎ 077 4631307 ▤ 077 4632765
e-mail info@kasteelooijen.nl
website www.kasteelooijen.nl

➲ *off A73*

Open Apr-Oct **Site** 16HEC ❤ ♣ ☎ ❤ **Prices** pitch 15.80-22.45 (incl 2
persons) pp2.90-4.15 **Facilities** ↖ ⊙ ◘ ∅ ❾ **Services** ⚑ ⍭ ➕ ⬚
Leisure ❦ P **Off-site** ▥

BROUWERSHAVEN ZEELAND

Osse

Blankersweg 4, 4318 ☎ 0111 691513 ▤ 0111 691058
e-mail denosse@zeelandnet.nl
website www.campingdenosse.nl
An attractive site with good water sports.

Open Apr-Oct **Site** 8.3HEC ❤ ♣ ☎ ❤ **Prices** pitch 22-24 (incl 2 persons)
❤ (static)292-495 **Facilities** ↖ ⊙ ◘ ♨ ⊛ ❾ **Services** ⚑ ⍭ ➕ ⬚
Leisure ❦ P **Off-site** ▥ ❦LR

BURGH-HAAMSTEDE ZEELAND

Zeeland Camping Ginsterveld

J J Boeijesweg 45, 4328 HA ☎ 0111 651590 ▤ 0111 653040
e-mail info@ginsterveld.nl
website www.ginsterveld.nl
A family holiday centre with well-defined pitches on level ground and
plenty of recreational facilities.

➲ *NW of town, signed from R107.*

Open Apr-Sep **Site** 14HEC ❤ ♣ ⊗ **Prices** pitch 18.50-30.50 (incl 2
persons) **Facilities** ↖ ▥ ⊙ ◘ ∅ ♨ ⊛ **Services** ⚑ ⍭ ➕ ⬚ **Leisure** ❦ P
Off-site ❦S

DELFT ZUID-HOLLAND

Delftse Hout

Korftlaan 5, 2616 ☎ 015 2130040 ▤ 015 2131293
e-mail info@delftsehout.nl
website www.delftsehout.nl
On a level meadow surrounded by woodland close to the lake.

➲ *1.6km E of A13, signed.*

Open All year **Site** 5.5HEC ❤ ♣ ☎ ❤ **Prices** ⚑ 2 pitch 21-25.50
(incl 2 persons) ❤ (static)280-520 **Facilities** ↖ ▥ ⊙ ◘ ∅ ♨ ❾
Services ⚑ ⍭ ➕ ⬚ **Leisure** ❦ PS **Off-site** ❦L

ECHT LIMBURG

Marisheem

Brugweg 89, 6102 ☎ 0475 481458 ▤ 0475 488018
e-mail info@marisheem.nl
website www.marisheem.nl
The site is well-kept and lies east of the village.

➲ *From town towards Echterbosch & border, 2.2km turn left.*

Open Apr-Oct **Site** 12HEC ❤ ♣ ⊗ **Facilities** ↖ ▥ ⊙ ◘ ∅ ♨ ❾
Services ⚑ ⍭ ➕ ⬚ **Leisure** ❦ P

EERSEL NOORD-BRABANT

Ter Spegelt

Postelseweg 88, 5521 ☎ 0497 512016 ▤ 0497 514162
e-mail info@terspegelt.nl
website www.terspegelt.nl
A large family-orientated site with good recreational facilities.

Open Apr-30 Oct **Site** 63HEC ❤ ♣ ☎ ❤ ▲ ⊗ **Facilities** ↖ ▥ ⊙ ◘ ∅
♨ ❾ **Services** ⚑ ⍭ ➕ ⬚ **Leisure** ❦ LP

Site 6HEC (site size) ❤ grass ● sand ❦ stone ♣ little shade ♣ partly shaded ❤ mainly shaded ☎ bungalows for hire
❤ caravans for hire ▲ tents for hire ⊗ no dogs **Prices** ♠ adult per night ❤ car per night pp per person per night ❤ caravan per night
▲ tent per night ❤ (static)-caravan hire per week

'S-GRAVENZANDE ZUID-HOLLAND

Jagtveld
Nieuwlandsedijk 41, 2691 ☎ 0174 413479 🖹 0174 422127
e-mail info@jagtveld.nl
website www.jagtveld.nl
A quiet family site on level meadowland with good facilities.
➲ *Via N220.*
Open Apr-Sep **Site** 3.3HEC 😃 ♣ ⊗ **Prices** ⚭ 3.75 ⊞ 3.75 ⊞ 8 Å 8
Facilities ⋔ ⊙ ⊝ ⊿ ⓟ ❷ **Services** ⚑ 🍴 ⊞ 🖾 **Off-site** ⊜S

GROEDE ZEELAND

Groede
Zeeweg 1, 4503 ☎ 0117 371384 🖹 0117 372277
e-mail info@campinggroede.nl
website www.campinggroede.nl
A large family site with a variety of leisure facilities and close to the beach.
Open Apr-Oct **Site** 20HEC 😃 ♣ ♨ **Facilities** ⋔ 🏠 ⊙ ❷ ⊿ ⊿ ⓟ
Services ⚑ 🍴 ⊞ 🖾 **Leisure** ⊜ S

HAAG, DEN (THE HAGUE) ZUID-HOLLAND

Kijkduinpark
Machiel Vrijenhoeklaan 450, 2555 NW
☎ 070 4482100 🖹 070 3232457
e-mail info@kijkduinpark.nl
website www.kijkduinpark.nl
A modern chalet and camping site in an extensive leisure park close to the beach with excellent recreational facilities.
Open All year **Site** 40HEC 😃 ♣ 🏠 **Facilities** ⋔ 🏠 ⊙ ❷ ⊿ ⓟ
Services ⚑ 🍴 🖾 **Leisure** ⊜ P **Off-site** ⊜S

HELLEVOETSLUIS ZUID-HOLLAND

'T Weergors
Zuiddyk 2, 3221 ☎ 0181 312430 🖹 0181 311010
e-mail weergors@publishnet.nl
website www.weergors.nl
A pleasant, peaceful site on a level meadow close to the beach. A good overnight stopping place or holiday site.
Open Apr-Oct **Site** 9.7HEC 😃 ♣ 🏠 ♨ **Prices** ⚭ 3.50 ⊞ 2.50 ⊞ 6.50
⊿ 6.50 ♨ (static)225-405 **Facilities** ⋔ 🏠 ⊙ ❷ ⊿ ⊿ ⓟ ❷ **Services** ⚑
🍴 ⊞ 🖾 **Leisure** ⊜ S

HENGSTDIJK ZEELAND

Vogel
Vogelweg 4, 4585 ☎ 0114 681625 🖹 0114 682527
e-mail info@de-vogel.nl
website www.de-vogel.nl
Open All year **Site** 33HEC 😃 ♣ 🏠 ♨ **Facilities** ⋔ 🏠 ⊙ ❷ ⊿ ⊿ ⓟ ❷
Services ⚑ 🍴 ⊞ 🖾 **Leisure** ⊜ LP

HERPEN NOORD-BRABANT

Herperduin
Schaykseweg 12, NL-5373 ☎ 0486 411383 🖹 0486 416171
e-mail info@herperduin.nl
website www.herperduin.nl
Situated in extensive woodland.
➲ *Motorway 's Hertogenbosch-Nijmegen exit Ravenstein, towards Herpen & Bergheim/Oss.*
Open Apr-20 Oct **Site** 7HEC 😃 ♣ 🏠 ⊗ **Facilities** ⋔ 🏠 ⊙ ❷ ⊿ ⓟ
Services ⚑ 🍴 ⊞ 🖾 **Leisure** ⊜ P

HILVARENBEEK NOORD-BRABANT

Beekse Bergen
Beekse Bergen 1, 5081 NJ ☎ 031 5360032 🖹 031 5366716
e-mail beeksebergen@libema.nl
website www.beeksebergen.com
Situated in a holiday centre in the Brabant afforestation on the edge of a safari park. Various facilities and the lake is suitable for swimming.
➲ *10km S of Tilburg.*
Open 30 Mar-4 Nov **Site** 400HEC 😃 ♣ 🏠 ♨ Å **Facilities** ⋔ 🏠 ⊙ ❷ ⊿
⊿ ⓟ ❷ **Services** ⚑ 🍴 ⊞ 🖾 **Leisure** ⊜ LP

HOEK ZEELAND

Braakman Holiday Park
Middenweg 1, 4542 PN ☎ 0115 481730 🖹 0115 482077
e-mail info@braakman.co.uk **website** www.braakman.co.uk
A large family site on the edge of extensive nature reserves. The pitches are shaded by woodland and there is direct access to Braakman lake. Plenty of recreational facilities.
➲ *4km W of town, signed from N61.*
Open All year **Site** 80HEC 😃 ♣ 🏠 ♨ **Facilities** ⋔ 🏠 ⊙ ❷ ⊿ ⊿ ⓟ ❷
Services ⚑ 🍴 ⊞ 🖾 **Leisure** ⊜ LP

HOEK VAN HOLLAND ZUID-HOLLAND

Hoek van Holland
Wierstraat 100, 3151 ☎ 0174 382550 🖹 0174 310210
e-mail camping.hvh@hetnet.nl
website www.campinghoekvanholland.nl
On grass, surrounded by bushes and paved drives.
➲ *From N, off E36 to beach.*
Open 15 Mar-12 Oct **Site** 5.5HEC 😃 ♣ ⊗ **Prices** pitch 25.95 (incl 4 persons) **Facilities** ⋔ 🏠 ⊙ ❷ ⊿ ⊿ ⓟ ❷ **Services** ⚑ 🍴 ⊞ 🖾 **Off-site** ⊜S

HOEVEN NOORD-BRABANT

Bosbad Hoeven
Oude Antwerpse Postbaan 81b, 4741
☎ 0165 502570 🖹 0165 504254
e-mail info@bosbadhoeven.nl **website** www.bosbadhoeven.nl
Extensive site with modern facilities.
➲ *A58 exit 20 St Willebrord, follow directions for Hoeven.*
Open Apr-30 Oct **Site** 35HEC 😃 ♣ 🏠 ♨ ⊗ **Prices** pitch 16.75-26.75 (incl 2 persons) **Facilities** ⋔ 🏠 ⊙ ❷ ⊿ ⊿ ⓟ ❷ **Services** ⚑ 🍴 ⊞ 🖾
Leisure ⊜ P

KAMPERLAND ZEELAND

Roompot
Mariapolderseweg 1, 4493 ☎ 0113 374000 🖹 0113 374170
e-mail info@roompot.nl **website** www.roompot.nl
A level, well-maintained site with a private beach.
➲ *Off Kamperland-Wissenkerke road & N for 0.5km.*
Open All year **Site** 33HEC 😃 ♣ 🏠 ♨ Å **Prices** pitch 22-35
(incl 5 persons) ♨ (static)99-720 **Facilities** ⋔ 🏠 ⊙ ❷ ⊿ ⊿ ⓟ
Services ⚑ 🍴 ⊞ 🖾 **Leisure** ⊜ PS

KATWIJK AAN ZEE ZUID-HOLLAND

Noordduinen
Campingweg 1, 2221 ☎ 071 4025295 🖹 071 4033977
Family site among dunes close to the sea.
➲ *Via Hoorneslaan.*
Open mid Mar-Oct **Site** 11HEC 😃 ♣ 🏠 ⊗ **Facilities** ⋔ 🏠 ⊙ ❷ ⊿ ⊿ ⓟ
Services ⚑ 🍴 ⊞ 🖾 **Leisure** ⊜ S

Facilities 🏠 shop ⋔ shower ⊙ electric points for razors ❷ electric points for caravans ⓟ parking by tents permitted ❷ compulsory separate car park
Services 🍴 café/restaurant ⚑ bar ⊘ Camping Gaz International ⊿ gas other than Camping Gaz ⊞ first aid facilities 🖾 laundry
Leisure ⊜ swimming L-Lake P-Pool R-River S-Sea **Off-site** All facilities within 2km

Netherlands

KORTGENE ZEELAND

De Paardekreek

Havenweg 1, 4484 ☎ 0113 302051 🗎 0113 302280
e-mail paardekreek@ardoer.com
website www.ardoer.com/paardekreek
A municipal site next to the Veerse Meer canal.
➲ *Off Zierikzee-Goes road at Chevron fuel station towards Kortgene, through village & continue SW.*
Open Apr-Oct **Site** 10HEC ❤ ♣ ♠ ▲ **Prices** pitch 16.80-30.90
🚐 (static)231-581 **Facilities** 🟢 🚻 ⊙ 🚮 🚿 ⌀ 🚼 ⊛ **Services** 🛒 🍴 🔁 🛍 **Leisure** 🏊 LP

KOUDEKERKE ZEELAND

Dishoek

Dishoek 2, 4371 ☎ 0118 551348 🗎 0118 552990
e-mail info@campingdishoek.nl
website www.roompot.nl
➲ *W on Vlissingen-Dibhoek road.*
Open 18 Mar-23 Oct **Site** 6HEC ❤ ♣ **Prices** pitch 22-37 **Facilities** 🟢 🚻 ⊙ 🚮 🚿 ⌀ 🚼 ⊛ 🅿 **Services** 🛒 🍴 🔁 🛍 **Off-site** 🏊S

Duinzicht

Strandweg 7, 4371 PK ☎ 0118 551397 🗎 0118 553222
e-mail info@campingduinzicht.nl
website www.campingduinzicht.nl
A small family site with good facilities.
➲ *1.5km SW of Koudekerke.*
Open Apr-Oct **Site** 6.5HEC ❤ ♣ 🚐 **Prices** pitch 12.50-22.50 (incl 2 persons) **Facilities** 🟢 🚻 ⊙ 🚮 🚼 ⌀ 🅿 **Services** 🍴 🔁 🛍 **Off-site** 🛒 🍴 🏊S

LAGE MIERDE NOORD-BRABANT

Vakantlecentrum de Hertenwei

Wellenseind 7-9, 5094 ☎ 013 5091295
website www.hertenwei.nl
Pleasant wooded site with modern facilities.
➲ *2km N on N269 (Tilburg-Reusel).*
Open All year **Site** 20HEC ❤ ♣ ♠ 🚐 **Prices** pitch 20-34.25 (incl 2 persons) 🚐 (static)235-470 **Facilities** 🟢 🚻 ⊙ 🚮 🚿 ⌀ 🚼 ⊛ **Services** 🛒 🍴 🔁 🛍 **Leisure** 🏊 P

LANDGRAAF LIMBURG

Bousberg

Boomweg 10, 6370 ☎ 045 5311213 🗎 045 5323143
➲ *NW towards Kakert.*
Open Apr-Oct **Site** 7.5HEC ❤ ♣ ♠ 🚐 **Facilities** 🟢 🚻 ⊙ 🚮 🚿 ⌀ 🚼 ⊛ **Services** 🛒 🍴 🔁 🛍 **Leisure** 🏊 P

LUYKSGESTEL NOORD-BRABANT

Zwarte Bergen

Zwarte Bergen Dreef 1, 5575 ☎ 0497 541373 🗎 0497 542673
e-mail info@zwartebergen.nl
website www.zwartebergen.nl
Isolated and very quiet site in a pine forest.
➲ *From Eindhoven through Valkenswaard & Bergiejkl, signed.*
Open All year **Site** 25.5HEC ❤ ♣ ♠ **Facilities** 🟢 🚻 ⊙ 🚮 🚿 ⌀ 🚼 🅿 **Services** 🛒 🍴 🔁 🛍 **Leisure** 🏊 P **Off-site** 🏊L

MAASBREE LIMBURG

BreeBronne

Lange Heide 9, 5993PB ☎ 077 4652360 🗎 077 4652095
e-mail info@breebronne.nl
website www.breebronne.nl
A family site in quiet surroundings with good facilities.
➲ *On E3 just before Venlo, on German border.*
Open All year **Site** 23HEC ❤ ♣ ♠ **Prices** pitch 19-44.30 **Facilities** 🟢 🚻 ⊙ 🚮 🚿 ⌀ 🚼 ⊛ **Services** 🛒 🍴 🔁 🛍 **Leisure** 🏊 LP

MAASTRICHT LIMBURG

Dousberg

Dousbergweg 102, 6216 ☎ 043 3432171 🗎 043 3430556
e-mail dousbergcamping@dousberg.nl
website www.dousberg.nl
A modern site with good facilities.
➲ *Eindhoven-Liège motorway exit for Hasselt, then signs to site.*
Open Apr-Oct **Site** 10HEC ❤ ♣ **Facilities** 🟢 🚻 ⊙ 🚮 🚿 ⌀ 🚼 ⊛ **Services** 🛒 🍴 🔁 🛍 **Off-site** 🏊P

MIDDELBURG ZEELAND

Middelburg

Koninginnelaan 55, 4335 ☎ 0118 625395 🗎 0118 625395
e-mail campingmiddelburg@komnaarons.nl
website www.campingmiddelburg.nl
On meadowlands surrounded by trees and bushes.
➲ *On W outskirts of town.*
Open Etr-15 Oct **Site** 3.4HEC ❤ ♣ ♠ 🚐 **Facilities** 🟢 🚻 ⊙ 🚮 🚼 ⌀ 🚼 ⊛ **Services** 🛒 🍴 🔁 🛍 **Off-site** 🚻 🏊PS

MIERLO NOORD-BRABANT

Wolfsven

Patrijslaan 4, 5731 ☎ 0492 661661 🗎 0492 663895
e-mail info@bosparkhetwolfsven.nl
website www.euroase.nl
Large site with wooded areas and several lakes. Asphalt drives.
Open 30 Mar-Oct **Site** 70HEC ❤ 🌊 ♣ ♠ 🚐 **Prices** 🚐 16-31 **Facilities** 🟢 🚻 ⊙ 🚮 🚿 ⌀ 🚼 ⊛ **Services** 🛒 🍴 🔁 🛍 **Leisure** 🏊 LP **Off-site** 🚿

NIEUWVLIET ZEELAND

Pannenschuur

Zeedijk 19, 4504 ☎ 0117 372300 🗎 0117 371415
e-mail info@pannenschuur.nl
website www.pannenschuur.nl
A modern site with good facilities. Close to the beach.
➲ *NW of town, signed.*
Open All year **Site** 14HEC ❤ ♣ ♠ 🚐 **Facilities** 🟢 🚻 ⊙ 🚮 🚿 ⌀ 🚼 🅿 **Services** 🛒 🍴 🔁 🛍 **Leisure** 🏊 PS

NOORDWIJK AAN ZEE ZUID-HOLLAND

Club Soleil

Kraaierslaan 7, 2204 ☎ 0252 374225 🗎 0252 376450
e-mail info@clubsoleil.nl
website www.clubsoleil.nl
A pleasant location near the bulb fields and the sea.
➲ *Signed.*
Open Apr-Nov **Site** 5.5HEC ❤ ♣ ♠ 🚐 **Facilities** 🟢 🚻 ⊙ 🚮 🚿 ⌀ 🅿 **Services** 🛒 🍴 🔁 🛍 **Leisure** 🏊 P **Off-site** 🏊LS

Site 6HEC (site size) ❤ grass 🌊 sand 🌿 stone ♣ little shade ♠ partly shaded 🌳 mainly shaded 🏠 bungalows for hire 🚐 caravans for hire ▲ tents for hire ⊗ no dogs **Prices** 🚶 adult per night 🚗 car per night pp per person per night 🚐 caravan per night ▲ tent per night 🚐 (static)-caravan hire per week

Noordwijkse Duinen
Kapelleboslaan 10, 2204 ☎ 0252 372485 🖹 0252 340140
e-mail info@noordwijkseduinen.nl
website www.noordwijkseduinen.nl
A well-equipped family site in a wooded location 2km from the beach.
Open 15 Mar-Sep **Site** 6HEC 😃 ♣ 🏠 ♠ **Prices** ♠ 6 pitch 20-25
(incl 4 persons) ♠ (static)300-575 **Facilities** ⌐ ⊙ ⊖ ♠ ♨ 🏖 ⊛
Services ⊞ ⊓⊙⊩ 🖸 ⊠ **Leisure** ⊛ P **Off-site** ⊛LS

OISTERWIJK NOORD-BRABANT

Reebok
Duinenweg 4, 5062 ☎ 013 5282309 🖹 013 5217592
e-mail info@dereebok.nl
website www.dereebok.nl
Situated in a large pine forest within attractive surroundings with
numerous small lakes.
➲ *SE of town.*
Open 15 Mar-Oct **Site** 8HEC ♣ 🏠 ♠ **Prices** pitch 18.50-23.50
Facilities ⌐ 🖻 ⊙ ⊖ ♠ ♨ 🏖 ⊛ **Services** ⊞ ⊓⊙⊩ 🖸 ⊠ **Off-site** ⊛LP

OOSTERHOUT NOORD-BRABANT

Katjeskelder
Katjeskelder 1, 4904 ☎ 0162 453539 🖹 0162 454090
e-mail kkinfo@katjeskelder.nl
website www.katjeskelder.nl
A large, modern family site with good sanitary and recreational
facilities.
➲ *A27 exit 17 & signed.*
Open All year **Site** 25HEC 😃 ♣ 🏠 ♠ **Facilities** ⌐ 🖻 ⊙ ⊖ ♠ ♨ ⊛ ⊕
Services ⊞ ⊓⊙⊩ 🖸 ⊠ **Leisure** ⊛ P **Off-site** ♨

OOSTKAPELLE ZEELAND

Dennenbos
Duinweg 64, 4356 ☎ 0118 581310 🖹 0118 583773
e-mail dennenbos@zeelandnet.nl
website www.dennenbos.nl
A well-maintained family site in a wooded location, 0.5km from the
beach.
Open Mar-Nov **Site** 3HEC 😃 ♣ 🏠 ♠ ⊛ **Facilities** ⌐ 🖻 ⊙ ⊖ ♠ ♨ 🏖 ⊛
Services ⊞ ⊓⊙⊩ 🖸 ⊠ **Leisure** ⊛ PS **Off-site** ⊓⊙⊩

In de Bongerd
Brouwerijstr 13, 4356 ☎ 0118 581510 🖹 0118 581510
e-mail info@campingindebongerd.nl
website www.campingindebongerd.nl
A well-kept family site, set in a meadow with hedges and apple trees.
There are fine recreational facilities and the beach is within easy reach.
➲ *0.5km S.*
Open 30 Mar-28 Oct **Site** 7.4HEC 😃 ♣ 🏠 ♠ 🅰 **Prices** ♠ 4.50 pitch
14.50-35 (incl 2 persons) ♠ (static)140-360 **Facilities** ⌐ 🖻 ⊙ ⊖ ♠ ♨ ⊛
Services ⊞ ⊓⊙⊩ 🖸 ⊠ **Leisure** ⊛ PS

Ons Buiten
Aagtekerkseweg 2a, 4356 ☎ 0118 581813 🖹 0118 583771
e-mail onsbuiten@zeelandcamping.nl
website www.zeelandcamping.nl/onsbuiten
A beautiful location with a choice of recreational activities.
➲ *From church S towards Grijpskerke, turn W for 400m.*
Open 31 Mar-Oct **Site** 11.5HEC 😃 ♣ ⊛ **Prices** ♠ 4-4.50 pitch 17-36
(incl 2 persons) **Facilities** ⌐ 🖻 ⊙ ⊖ ♠ ♨ 🏖 ⊕ **Services** ⊞
⊓⊙⊩ 🖸 ⊠ **Leisure** ⊛ PS

Pekelinge
Landmetersweg 1, 4356 ☎ 0118 582820 🖹 0118 583782
e-mail pekelinge@ardoer.com
website www.ardoer.com/pekelinge
The site facilities are only open in summer.
Open Apr-Oct **Site** 18HEC 😃 ♣ 🏠 ♠ ⊛ **Prices** ♠ 3.40 pitch 15.40-36.80
(incl 2 persons) ♠ (static)238-616 **Facilities** ⌐ 🖻 ⊙ ⊖ ♠ ♨ ⊕
Services ⊞ ⊓⊙⊩ 🖸 ⊠ **Leisure** ⊛ P **Off-site** ♨ ⊛S

OOSTVOORNE ZUID-HOLLAND

Kruininger Gors
Gorspl 2, 3233 ☎ 0181 482711 🖹 0181 485957
e-mail info@kruiningergors.nl
website www.kruiningergors.nl
A small site, divided by hedges, close to the lake.
➲ *Via A15/N218*
Open Apr-Sep **Site** 108HEC 😃 ♣ 😃 ⊛ **Prices** ♠ 2 pitch 15.70-17.70
Facilities ⌐ 🖻 ⊙ ⊖ ♠ ♨ ⊛ ⊕ **Services** ⊞ ⊓⊙⊩ 🖸 ⊠ **Leisure** ⊛ LS

OUDDORP ZUID-HOLLAND

Klepperstee
Vrijheidsweg 1, 3253 ☎ 0187 681511 🖹 0187 683060
e-mail info@klepperstee.com
website www.klepperstee.com
On level meadow divided by hedges and trees.
➲ *N57 exit Ouddorp.*
Open Apr-Oct **Site** 40HEC 😃 ♣ 🏠 ⊛ **Prices** pitch 28-33 (incl 4 persons)
Facilities ⌐ 🖻 ⊙ ⊖ ♠ ♨ ⊛ **Services** ⊞ ⊓⊙⊩ 🖸 ⊠ **Leisure** ⊛ P
Off-site ⊛LPS

PLASMOLEN LIMBURG

Eldorado
Witteweg 18, 6586 ☎ 024 6961914 🖹 024 6963017
e-mail info@eldorado-mook.nl
Well-equipped site in wooded surroundings on the Mooker See.
➲ *S of N271.*
Open Apr-1 Oct **Site** 6HEC 😃 ♣ **Facilities** ⌐ 🖻 ⊙ ⊖ ♠ ♨ ⊛
Services ⊞ ⊓⊙⊩ 🖸 ⊠ **Leisure** ⊛ L

RENESSE ZEELAND

International
Scharendijkseweg 8, 4325 ☎ 0111 461391 🖹 0111 462571
e-mail info@camping-international.net
website www.camping-international.net
On grassland, between rows of tall shrubs and trees. Between dyke
road and main road to Scharendijk on eastern outskirts of village.
Open Mar-Nov **Site** 3HEC 😃 ♣ 🏠 **Prices** ♠ 4.50 ♠ 2.50 ♠ 5 🅰 4
Facilities ⌐ 🖻 ⊙ ⊖ ♠ ♨ ⊛ ⊕ **Services** ⊞ 🖸 ⊠ **Leisure** ⊛ PS
Off-site ⊓⊙⊩

Wyde Blick
Hogezoom 23, 4325 ☎ 0111 468888 🖹 0111 468889
e-mail dewijdeblick@zeelandcamping.nl
website www.zeelandcamping.nl/dewijdeblick
A family site with good facilities.
➲ *Signed.*
Open All year **Site** 10HEC 😃 ♣ 🏠 ⊛ **Prices** pitch 15-31.50 ♠ (static)295-
695 **Facilities** ⌐ 🖻 ⊙ ⊖ ♠ ♨ ⊕ **Services** ⊞ ⊓⊙⊩ 🖸 ⊠ **Leisure** ⊛ P
Off-site ⊛S

Facilities 🖻 shop ⌐ shower ⊙ electric points for razors ⊖ electric points for caravans ⊛ parking by tents permitted ⊕ compulsory separate car park
Services ⊓⊙⊩ café/restaurant ⊞ bar ♨ Camping Gaz International ♨ gas other than Camping Gaz 🖸 first aid facilities ⊠ laundry
Leisure ⊛ swimming L-Lake P-Pool R-River S-Sea **Off-site** All facilities within 2km

Netherlands

RETRANCHEMENT ZEELAND

De Zwinhoeve
Duinweg 1, 4525 ☎ 0117 392120 ▤ 0117 392248
e-mail info@zwinhoeve.nl
website www.zwinhoeve.nl
A beautiful position backed by dunes with easy access to the fine beaches of the Zeeuws-Vlaanderen coast.

Open 23 Mar-Oct **Site** 9HEC 👐 ♣ 🚐 ▲ **Prices** ♠ 5 pitch 10 **Facilities** 🍴 🏠 ⊙ ⊙ ⌀ ♨ ⓟ ⓟ **Services** ⚑ ◉ 🔁 🖫 **Leisure** 🏊 S **Off-site** 🏊P

RIJNSBURG ZUID-HOLLAND

Koningshof
Elsgeesterweg 8, 2231 ☎ 071 4026051 ▤ 071 4021336
e-mail info@koningshofholland.nl
website www.koningshofholland.nl
Modern site on level meadow near the flower fields.

➲ A44 exit 7 to Rijnsburg, site 1km N, signed.

Open All year **Site** 7.5HEC 👐 ♣ 🚐 🚐 **Prices** ♠ 4 pitch 21.50-27.50 **Facilities** 🍴 🏠 ⊙ ⊙ ⌀ ♨ ⓟ **Services** ⚑ ◉ 🔁 🖫 **Leisure** 🏊 P **Off-site** 🏊S

ROCKANJE ZUID-HOLLAND

Waterboscamping
Duinrand 11, 3235 ☎ 0181 401900 ▤ 0181 404233
e-mail info@waterboscamping.nl
website www.waterboscamping.nl
A small, pleasant site near the beach.

➲ Via N15.

Open Apr-Sep **Site** 7HEC 👐 ♣ ⊗ **Prices** ♠ 2.40 pitch 18-23 (incl 2 persons) **Facilities** 🍴 🏠 ⊙ ⊙ ♨ ⓟ ⓟ **Services** ⚑ ◉ 🖫 **Off-site** ◉ 🏊S

ROERMOND LIMBURG

Hatenboer
Hatenboer 51, 6041 ☎ 0475 336727 ▤ 0475 310113
Situated in a water park with access to water sports.

➲ A68 exit Hatenboer.

Open Apr-1 Nov **Site** 15HEC 👐 ♣ **Facilities** 🍴 ⊙ ♨ ⓟ ⓟ **Services** ⚑ ◉ 🔁 🖫 **Leisure** 🏊 LR **Off-site** 🏠 ⌀ ♨ 🏊P

Marina Oolderhuuske
Oolderhuuske 1, 6041 ☎ 0475 588686 ▤ 0475 582652
e-mail info@oolderhuuske.nl
website www.oolderhuuske.nl
A well-equipped site within the marina area on the Maasplassen.

Open 28 Mar-1 Nov **Site** 6HEC 👐 ♣ 🚐 🚐 **Facilities** 🍴 🏠 ⊙ ⊙ ♨ ⌀ ♨ ⓟ ⓟ **Services** ⚑ ◉ 🔁 🖫 **Leisure** 🏊 LPR

ROOSENDAAL NOORD-BRABANT

Zonneland
Tufvaartsestr 6, 4709 ☎ 0165 36529
e-mail info@zonneland.nl
website www.zonneland.nl

➲ S of town towards Belgian border.

Open Mar-15 Oct **Site** 14HEC 👐 🚐 🚐 **Prices** ♠ 3.50 🚗 2 🚐 5 ▲ 5 **Facilities** 🍴 🏠 ⊙ ♨ ⓟ **Services** 🔁 🖫 **Leisure** 🏊 P

ST ANTHONIS NOORD-BRABANT

Ullingse Bergen
Bosweg 36, 5845 ☎ 0485 388566 ▤ 0485 388569
e-mail info@ullingsebergen.nl
website www.ullingsebergen.nl
A family site in natural wooded surroundings with good facilities for children.

➲ W of town.

Open Apr-Oct **Site** 11HEC 👐 ♣ 🚐 ⊗ **Facilities** 🍴 🏠 ⊙ ⊙ ♨ ⌀ ♨ ⓟ ⓟ **Services** ◉ 🔁 🖫 **Leisure** 🏊 P

ST OEDENRODE NOORD-BRABANT

Kienehoef
Zwembadweg 35-37, 5491 ☎ 0413 472877 ▤ 0413 477033
e-mail info@kienehoef.nl
website www.kienehoef.nl
An exceptionally well-appointed site in a peaceful rural setting.

➲ NW towards Boxtel.

Open All year **Site** 4HEC 👐 ♣ 🚐 ▲ ⊗ **Facilities** 🍴 🏠 ⊙ ⊙ ⌀ ♨ ⓟ **Services** ⚑ ◉ 🔁 🖫 **Leisure** 🏊 P **Off-site** ◉

SEVENUM LIMBURG

Schatberg
Midden Peelweg 5, 5975 ☎ 077 4677777 ▤ 077 4677799
e-mail receptie@schatberg.nl
website www.schatberg.nl
A well-appointed family site in wooded surroundings with plenty of leisure facilities.

➲ A67 exit 38 for Schatberg & SW towards Eindhoven.

Open All year **Site** 86HEC 👐 ♣ 🚐 🚐 ▲ **Prices** 🚐 17.50-33.95 **Facilities** 🍴 🏠 ⊙ ⊙ ⌀ ♨ ⓟ ⓟ **Services** ⚑ ◉ 🔁 🖫 **Leisure** 🏊 LP

SLUIS ZEELAND

Meldoorn
Hoogstr 68, 4524 ☎ 0117 461662 ▤ 0117 461662
e-mail meidoorn@zeelandnet.nl
website www.campingdemeidoorn.nl
A meadowland site surrounded by rows of deciduous trees.

➲ N on road to Zuidzande.

Open Apr-22 Oct **Site** 6.5HEC 👐 ♣ 🚐 **Prices** ♠ 3.80 🚗 2.30 🚐 4.45 ▲ 3.35-4.45 **Facilities** 🍴 ⊙ ♨ ⌀ ♨ ⓟ ⓟ **Services** ⚑ ◉ 🔁 🖫 **Off-site** 🏠

VALKENBURG LIMBURG

Europa
Couberg 29, 6301 ☎ 043 6013097 ▤ 043 6013525
A quiet family site within easy reach of the town.

➲ SW of town.

Open Apr-Oct **Site** 10HEC 👐 ♣ **Facilities** 🍴 🏠 ⊙ ♨ ⌀ ♨ ⓟ **Services** ⚑ ◉ 🔁 🖫 **Leisure** 🏊 P

VENRAY LIMBURG

de Oude Barrier
Maasheseweg 93, 5802 ☎ 0478 582305
e-mail info@deoudebarrier.nl **website** www.deoudebarrier.nl
A quiet site recommended for those with young children.

➲ NE of town.

Open Apr-Sep **Site** 14HEC 👐 ♣ **Prices** ♠ 3.60 🚗 2.10 🚐 1.90 ▲ 1.90 **Facilities** 🍴 ⊙ ♨ ⌀ ♨ **Services** 🔁 🖫 **Leisure** 🏊 P **Off-site** ◉ ♨

Site 6HEC (site size) 👐 grass 🌊 sand 🌑 stone ♣ little shade 🌳 partly shaded 🌲 mainly shaded 🏠 bungalows for hire 🚐 caravans for hire ▲ tents for hire ⊗ no dogs **Prices** ♠ adult per night 🚗 car per night pp per person per night 🚐 caravan per night ▲ tent per night 🚐 (static)-caravan hire per week

VROUWENPOLDER ZEELAND

Oranjezon
Koningin Emmaweg 16a, 4354 ☎ 0118 591549 ▤ 0118 591920
e-mail oranjezon@oranjezon.nl
website www.oranjezon.nl
Well-kept between tall, thick hedges and bushes. south west of the village.

⊃ *Towards Oostkapelle, 2.5km turn N for 300m.*

Open Apr-Oct **Site** 9.8HEC ♚ ♣ ⚑ **A Prices** pitch 31 (incl 4 persons) **Facilities** ⋒ ⓘ ⊙ ⓠ ⌀ ≞ ⓟ ⓟ **Services** ⚑ ⓞ ⊞ ▤ **Leisure** ⚌ PS

Sandput
Roondijk 9, 4354 ☎ 0118 597210 ▤ 0118 591954
e-mail info@roompot.nl
website www.roompot.nl
On level ground behind dunes and close to the beach.

⊃ *2km N.*

Open 18 Mar-23 Oct **Site** 12HEC ♚ ♣ ⚑ **A Facilities** ⋒ ⓘ ⊙ ⓠ ⓟ ⓟ **Services** ⚑ ⓞ ⊞ ▤ **Off-site** ⌀ ≞ ⚌LS

WASSENAAR ZUID-HOLLAND

Duinhorst
Buurtweg 135, 2244 ☎ 070 3242270 ▤ 070 3246053
e-mail info@duinhorst.nl
website www.duinhorst.nl
A peaceful site in wooded surroundings with modern facilities and fine opportunities for sports and entertainment.

Open Apr-1 Oct **Site** 11HEC ♚ ♣ ♣ ⚑ ⊛ **Prices** ♠ 4.60 ⚑ 2.60 ⚑ 4.20 A 3-3.50 **Facilities** ⋒ ⓘ ⊙ ⓠ ⌀ ⓟ **Services** ⚑ ⓞ ⊞ ▤ **Leisure** ⚌ P

Duinrell
Duinrell 1, 2242 ☎ 070 5155255 ▤ 070 5155371
e-mail info@duinrell.nl
website www.duinrell.nl
A very well-maintained site with a recreation centre nearby, which is free for campers. Some aircraft noise. Toilets have facilities for the disabled. Restricted area for cars. Naturist beach nearby.

⊃ *Off A44 at lights in Wassenaar dorp' & signed.*

Open All year **Site** 110HEC ♚ ♣ ⚑ **A Prices** ♠ 9.50 pitch 8.50-15 **Facilities** ⋒ ⓘ ⊙ ⓠ ⌀ ≞ ⓟ ⓟ **Services** ⚑ ⓞ ⊞ ▤ **Leisure** ⚌ P **Off-site** ⚌LS

See advertisement on this page

WEERT LIMBURG

Yzeren Man
Herenvennenweg 60, 6006 ☎ 0495 533202 ▤ 0495 546812
e-mail info@deyzerenman.nl
website www.deyzerenman.nl
Well-kept site with asphalt drives, set in a big nature reserve with zoo, heath and forest.

⊃ *A2 Eindhoven-Maastricht.*

Open Apr-1 Nov **Site** 8.5HEC ♚ ♣ ⚑ **Prices** ♠ 4.47 pitch 23.94 (incl 2 persons) **Facilities** ⋒ ⊙ ⓠ ≞ ⓟ ⓟ **Services** ⚑ ⓞ ⊞ ▤ **Leisure** ⚌ P **Off-site** ⓞ ⚌L

WELL LIMBURG

Leukermeer
De Kamp 5, 5855 EG ☎ 0478 502444 ▤ 0478 501260
e-mail vakantie@leukermeer.nl
website www.leukermeer.nl
Beautiful surroundings on Leukermeer with modern installations and plenty of leisure facilities.

⊃ *Signed from N271.*

Open 27 Mar-1 Nov **Site** 14HEC ♚ ♣ ⚑ ⚑ **Prices** ⚑ 19.50-34.50 **A** 19.50-34.50 **Facilities** ⋒ ⓘ ⊙ ⓠ ⌀ ≞ ⓟ ⓟ **Services** ⚑ ⓞ ⊞ ▤ **Leisure** ⚌ LP

WEMELDINGE ZEELAND

Linda
Oostkanaalweg 4, 4424 ☎ 0113 621259 ▤ 0113 622638
e-mail info@campinglinda.nl **website** www.campinglinda.nl
On meadowland surrounded by rows of tall shrubs.

⊃ *Turn opp bridge in town for 100m, over bridge to site.*

Open Apr-Nov **Site** 8HEC ♚ ♣ ⚑ **Prices** ♠ 6 ⚑ 3 ⚑ 7 **A** 3.50 ⚑ (static)235-485 **Facilities** ⋒ ⓘ ⊙ ⓠ ⌀ ≞ ⓟ **Services** ⚑ ⓞ ⊞ ▤ **Leisure** ⚌ S

WESTKAPELLE ZEELAND

Boomgaard
Domineeshofweg 1, 4361 ☎ 0118 571377 ▤ 0118 572383
A flat grassy site.

⊃ *Signed off Middleburg road on S outskirts of town.*

Open 27 Mar-24 Oct **Site** 8HEC ♚ ♣ ⚑ **Facilities** ⋒ ⓘ ⊙ ⓠ ⌀ ≞ ⓟ **Services** ⚑ ⓞ ⊞ ▤ **Leisure** ⚌ P **Off-site** ⚌S

Facilities ⓘ shop ⋒ shower ⊙ electric points for razors ⓠ electric points for caravans ⓟ parking by tents permitted ⓟ compulsory separate car park
Services ⓞ café/restaurant ⚑ bar ⌀ Camping Gaz International ≞ gas other than Camping Gaz ⊞ first aid facilities ▤ laundry
Leisure ⚌ swimming L-Lake P-Pool R-River S-Sea **Off-site** All facilities within 2km

Netherlands

Portugal

Accidents & emergency
fire 112   police 112   ambulance 112

Driving Requirements
Minimum age 18 for UK licence holders driving temporarily imported car or motorcycle (over 50cc).

Lights
Full headlights are prohibited in built-up areas. Dipped headlights in poor daytime visibility, in tunnels and on the main road linking Aveiro-Vilar Formoso at the Spanish frontier (IP5). Motorcyclists must use dipped headlights during the day.

Motorways
See page 317.

Passengers & children
Children under 12 and less than 1.5m in height cannot travel as front seat passengers. They must travel in the rear in a special restraint system adapted to their size, unless the car is a two seater, or is not fitted with seatbelts. Never fit a rear facing child in a seat with a frontal airbag. Children under 7 are not permitted as motorcycle passengers.

Size restrictions
Motor vehicle or trailer
height 4m, width 2.5m, length 12m

Vehicle + trailer
length 18m

Speed limits
Car without caravan/trailer,
motorcycle without sidecar

Built-up areas	50kph
Outside built-up areas	90kph
	100kph*
Motorways	120kph

Car towing caravan/trailer,
motorcycle with sidecar

Built-up areas	50kph
Outside built-up areas	70kph
	80kph*
Motorways	100kph

*according to type/quality of road as indicated by signs. Motorists who have held a driving licence for less than one year must not drive over 90kph.

Tourist office
Portuguese National Tourist Office
11 Belgrave Sq
London SW1X 8PP
Tel 0845 3551212
www.visitportugal.com

Additional information
By law, Photographic proof of identity must be carried at all times. The use of hazard warning lights or a warning triangle is compulsory in an accident/breakdown situation. Wearing a reflective jacket/waistcoat is compulsory if anyone exits a vehicle which is immobilised on the carriageway of motorways or main roads. The jacket must be carried in the passenger compartment of the car, not in the boot. It is illegal to carry bicycles on the back of a passenger car.

Tolls, *portagem*

Portugal Tolls		car	car & caravan
A1	Lisboa - Porto	€18.50	€18.50
A2	Lisboa - VLA (Algarve)	€17.75	€17.75
A3	Porto - Valença do Minho	€8.45	€8.45
A4	Porto - Amarante	€3.45	€3.45
A5	Lisboa - Cascais	€1.15	€1.15
A6/A2	A2/Marateca - Elvas (Spanish border)	€11.20	€11.20
A7	Vila Nova de Famalicao - Guimaraes	€7.85	€7.85
A8	Lisboa - Leiria	€8.00	€8.00
A9	A1 (Alverca) - A5 (Estadio)	€2.75	€2.75
A10	A9 - Arruda dos Vinhos - A13	€0.80	€0.80
A11	A28/Braga (A3) - Guimaraes (A7) - A4	€4.75	€4.75
A12	Setubal - Montijo	€1.75	€1.75
A13	Santo Estevao - Marateca (A2/A6)	€6.30	€6.30
A14	Figueira da Foz - Coimbra Nord	€2.15	€2.15
A15	Caldas da Rainha - Santarem	€3.25	€3.25
A21	Malveria (A8) - Mafra	€0.55	€0.55
Bridges & tunnels			
A12	Vasco da Gama Bridge (Ponte Vasco da Gama), (tolls are payable only when travelling north)	€2.10	€2.10
A2	Lisbon Tagus Bridge (Ponte 25 de Abril), (tolls are payable only when travelling north into Lisbon)	€1.20	€1.20

Please see page 317 for more toll information

Portugal

SOUTH

ALBUFEIRA ALGARVE

Albufeira
8200-55 ☎ 289587629 ▤ 289587633
e-mail campingalbufeira@mail.telepac.pt
A modern, purpose-built site with excellent sanitary blocks and a variety of sports and entertainment facilities.
➲ 1.5km from Albufeira, signed from N125.
Open All year **Site** 19HEC ⬙ ⬤ ⬤ ⬛ **Facilities** ⬤ ⬤ ⬤ ⬤ ⬤ ⬤ **Services** ⬤ ⬤ ⬤ ⬤ **Leisure** ⬤ P **Off-site** ⬤ ⬤ ⬤ S ⬤

ALVITO BAIXO ALENTEJO

Markádia
Barragem de Odivelas, Apartado 17, 7920-999
☎ 284763141 ▤ 284763102
Open savannah terrain beside a lake with modern facilities.
➲ Via N257
Open All year **Site** 10HEC ⬙ ⬤ ⬤ ⬛ **Prices** ⬤ 2.40-4.80 ⬤ 2.40-4.80 ⬤ 2.40-4.80 ⬤ 2.40-4.80 **Facilities** ⬤ ⬤ ⬤ ⬤ ⬤ ⬤ **Services** ⬤ ⬤ ⬤ ⬤ **Leisure** ⬤ L **Off-site** ⬤ P

BEJA BAIXO ALENTEJO

CM de Beja
Vasco da Gama, 7800-397 ☎ 284311911 ▤ 284311911
website www.cmbeja.pt/culturadesporto/parque.htm
Open All year **Site** 1HEC ⬤ ⬤ **Prices** ⬤ 1.11-2.22 ⬤ 0.82-1.64 ⬤ 1.14-3.28 ⬤ 0.82-1.64 **Facilities** ⬤ ⬤ ⬤ **Services** ⬤ ⬤ ⬤ ⬤ **Off-site** ⬤ ⬤ ⬤ ⬤ ⬤LPRS ⬤

OLHÂO ARGARVE

Olhâo
Pinheiros de Marim, 8703 ☎ 289700300 ▤ 289700390
e-mail parque.campismo@sbsi.pt
website www.sbsi.pt
Open All year **Site** 10HEC ⬤ ⬤ ⬛ **Facilities** ⬤ ⬤ ⬤ ⬤ ⬤ ⬤ **Services** ⬤ ⬤ ⬤ **Leisure** ⬤ P **Off-site** ⬤ S

See advertisement on this page

PORTIMÂO ALGARVE

Ria Dourada
Alvor, 8500 ☎ 282459178 ▤ 282459178
Set in a park-like area close to the beach with good facilities.
➲ N off Portimâo-Lagos road.
Open All year **Site** 4HEC ⬙ ⬤ ⬤ ⬛ ⬤ ⬤ **Facilities** ⬤ ⬤ ⬤ ⬤ ⬤ ⬤ **Services** ⬤ ⬤ ⬤ ⬤ **Leisure** ⬤ LPRS

PRAIA DA LUZ ALGARVE

AT VALVERDE

Orbitur
Estrada da Praia da Luz, 8600 ☎ 282789211 ▤ 282789213
e-mail info@orbitur.pt
website www.orbitur.pt
Well-equipped site with children's playground and tennis courts.
➲ Off N125 Lagos-Cape St Vincent road. 4km from Lagos.
Open All year **Site** 9.1HEC ⬤ ⬤ ⬛ ⬤ **Prices** ⬤ 2.90-4.90 ⬤ 2.40-4.90 ⬤ 4.30-8.20 ⬤ 3.50-7.30 **Facilities** ⬤ ⬤ ⬤ ⬤ ⬤ ⬤ **Services** ⬤ ⬤ ⬤ ⬤ **Leisure** ⬤ P **Off-site** ⬤ ⬤ ⬤ S

★★★ Open All Year

Camping Olhão
www.sbsi.pt/camping

Tennis
Football
Bar
Swimming Pool
Restaurant
Bungalows
Mobile Homes

parque.campismo@sbsi.pt
Algarve - Portugal
© 351 289 700 300

QUARTEIRA ALGARVE

Orbitur
Estrada da Forte Santa, Avenida Sá Carneiro, 8125
☎ 289302826 ▤ 289302822
e-mail info@orbitur.pt
website www.orbitur.pt
A terraced site at the top of a hill.
➲ Off M125 in Almoncil, signs to Quarteira, left 0.5km before sea.
Open All year **Site** 9.7HEC ⬤ ⬤ ⬛ ⬤ ⬤ **Prices** ⬤ 2.90-4.90 ⬤ 2.40-4.90 ⬤ 4.30-8.20 ⬤ 3.50-7.30 **Facilities** ⬤ ⬤ ⬤ ⬤ ⬤ ⬤ **Services** ⬤ ⬤ ⬤ ⬤ **Leisure** ⬤ P **Off-site** ⬤ ⬤ S

SAGRES ALGARVE

Orbitur
Cerro Das Moitas, 8650 ☎ 282624371 ▤ 282624445
e-mail info@orbitur.pt
website www.orbitur.pt
Situated in a dune and forest area.
➲ 1.5km W of N268.
Open All year **Site** 6.7HEC ⬤ ⬤ ⬛ ⬤ **Prices** ⬤ 2.40-4.40 ⬤ 2.10-4 ⬤ 3.30-6.60 ⬤ 2.90-6.10 **Facilities** ⬤ ⬤ ⬤ ⬤ ⬤ ⬤ **Services** ⬤ ⬤ ⬤ ⬤ **Off-site** ⬤ S

Facilities ⬤ shop ⬤ shower ⬤ electric points for razors ⬤ electric points for caravans ⬤ parking by tents permitted ⬤ compulsory separate car park
Services ⬤ café/restaurant ⬤ bar ⬤ Camping Gaz International ⬤ gas other than Camping Gaz ⬤ first aid facilities ⬤ laundry
Leisure ⬤ swimming L-Lake P-Pool R-River S-Sea **Off-site** All facilities within 2km

SANTO ANDRE BAIXO ALENTEJO

Lagoa de Santo Andre
7500 ☎ 269708550 ▤ 269708559
e-mail info@fpcampismo.pt
website www.fpcampismo.pt
Wooded surroundings with good facilities.
➲ *Signed.*
Open 18 Jan- 30 Oct **Site** 15HEC ⛺ ♨ ♨ ⊗ **Facilities** ⋒ ⊙ ☺ ⛱ ∅ �℗
Services ⛽ ⍩ ➕ ▣ **Off-site** ⛽ ⍩ ⊛LS

SINES BAIXO ALENTEJO

S. Tonnes
S. Tonnes, 7520 ☎ 269632105 ▤ 269862430
Set in a pine wood on the Cabo de Sines peninsula, to the N of the
town.
➲ *Signs for Algarve/S Tonnes.*
Open All year **Site** 7.5HEC ⛺ ♨ ⛺ **Facilities** ⋒ ⊙ ☺ ⛱ ⚒ ℗
Services ⛽ ⍩ ➕ ▣ **Off-site** ⊛S

VILA DO BISPO ALGARVE

AT PRAIA DE SALEMA (7.5KM SE)

Quinta dos Carriços
8650 ☎ 282695201 ▤ 28265122
e-mail quintacarrico@oninet.pt
website www.quintadoscarricos.com
A well-equipped site with good facilities. There is a naturist section in a
separate valley with its own facilities.
Open All year **Site** 20HEC ⛺ ♨ ⛺ ⛱ **Prices** ⚹ 4.60 ⛟ 4.60 ⛟ 6.50
Facilities ⋒ ⊙ ☺ ⛱ ∅ ⚒ ℗ **Services** ⛽ ⍩ ➕ ▣ **Off-site** ⊛S

VILA NOVA DE MILFONTES BAIXO ALENTEJO

Parque de Campismo de Milfontes
7645 ☎ 283996104 ▤ 283996104
e-mail parquemilfontes@netc.pt
website www.roteiro-campista.pt
Open All year **Site** 6.5HEC ♨ ⛱ ⛟ **Prices** ⚹ 2.45-3.80 ⛟ 2.30-4.20
⛟ 3.80-4.90 ⚡ 1.95-3.20 ⛟ (static)245-490 **Facilities** ⋒ ⊙ ☺ ⛱ ∅ ⚒ ℗
Services ⛽ ⍩ ▣ **Off-site** ⊛RS ➕

NORTH

CAMINHA MINHO

Orbitur
Mata do Camarido, 4910 ☎ 258921295 ▤ 258921473
e-mail info@orbitur.pt
website www.orbitur.pt
On undulating sandy ground with trees.
➲ *Off N13 at Km 89.7, W along Rio Minho for 0.8km & left.*
Open Jan-Nov **Site** 2.1HEC ⛺ ♨ ⛱ ⛟ **Prices** ⚹ 2.40-4.40 ⛟ 2.10-4 ⛟ 3.30-
6.60 ⚡ 2.90-6.10 **Facilities** ⋒ ⊙ ☺ ⛱ ∅ ℗ **Services** ⛽ ⍩ ➕ ▣
Off-site ⍩ ⊛S

CAMPO DO GERES MINHO

Cerdeira
4840 ☎ 253351005 ▤ 253353315
e-mail info@parquecerdeira.com
website www.parquecerdeira.com
A picturesque wooded location with mature oak trees surrounding the
pitches.
Open All year **Site** 7HEC ⛺ ♨ ⛺ ⛱ ⊗ **Prices** ⚹ 3.20-4.50 ⛟ 3-4.10
⛟ 3.85-6.50 ⚡ 2.75-5 **Facilities** ⋒ ⊙ ☺ ⛱ ∅ ℗ **Services** ⛽ ⍩ ➕ ▣
Leisure ⊛ P **Off-site** ⛱ ⊛LR

MATOSINHOS DOURO LITORAL

AT ANGEIRAS (12KM N)

Orbitur
Angeiras, 4455-039 ☎ 229270571 ▤ 229271178
e-mail info@orbitur.pt
website www.orbitur.pt
A modern, well-kept site in a pine wood on a hill overlooking the sea.
➲ *W of N13 x-rds at Km12.1. E of Vila do Pinheiro towards sea
for 5km.*
Open All year **Site** 7HEC ⛺ ♨ ⛺ ⛟ **Prices** ⚹ 2.60-4.60 ⛟ 2.20-4.20
⛟ 3.60-7 ⚡ 3.10-6.50 **Facilities** ⋒ ⊙ ☺ ⛱ ∅ ℗ **Services** ⛽ ⍩ ➕ ▣
Leisure ⊛ P **Off-site** ⊛S

MONDIM DE BASTO MINHO

Mondim de Basto
4880-187 ☎ 255381650 ▤ 255381650
e-mail ccporto@sapo.pt
website www.ccporto.pt
Wooded surroundings beside the River Olo.
➲ *Signed.*
Open Feb-Nov **Site** 3HEC ♨ ⛺ ⊗ **Facilities** ⋒ ⊙ ☺ ∅ ℗
Services ⛽ ⍩ ➕ ▣ **Leisure** ⊛ R **Off-site** ⛱ ⍩

PÓVOA DE VARZIM DOURO LITORAL

Rio Alto
E.N.13 - Km 13, Estela-Rio Alto, 4570-275
☎ 252615699 ▤ 252615599
e-mail info@orbitur.pt
website www.orbitur.pt
Situated near dunes, 150m from the sea.
➲ *Off NX111 towards Viana.*
Open All year **Site** 7.9HEC ⛺ ♨ ♨ ⛟ **Prices** ⚹ 2.70-4.80 ⛟ 2.40-4.7
⛟ 4.30-7.80 ⚡ 3.50-6.90 **Facilities** ⋒ ⊙ ☺ ⛱ ∅ ℗ **Services** ⛽ ⍩ ➕ ▣
Leisure ⊛ PS **Off-site** ⊛S

VIANA DO CASTELO MINHO

Orbitur
Rua Diogo Álvares, Cabedelo, 4900-161
☎ 258322167 ▤ 258321946
e-mail info@orbitur.pt
website www.orbitur.pt
A well-equipped site with direct access to a sandy beach.
➲ *Approach via N13 Porto-Viana do Castelo.*
Open All year **Site** 3HEC ♨ ⛺ ⛟ **Prices** ⚹ 2.60-4.60 ⛟ 2.20-4.20
⛟ 3.60-7 ⚡ 3.10-6.50 **Facilities** ⋒ ⊙ ☺ ⛱ ∅ ℗ **Services** ⛽ ⍩ ➕ ▣
Leisure ⊛ PS

Site 6HEC (site size) ⛺ grass ⛺ sand ♨ stone ♣ little shade ⛺ partly shaded ⛺ mainly shaded ⛱ bungalows for hire
⛟ caravans for hire ⚡ tents for hire ⊗ no dogs **Prices** ⚹ adult per night ⛟ car per night pp per person per night ⛟ caravan per night
⚡ tent per night ⛟ (static)-caravan hire per week

Portugal

VILA NOVA DE GAIA DOURO LITORAL

Orbitur
Rua do Cerro, 608, Praia da Madalena, 4405-736
☎ 227122520 🗎 227122534
e-mail info@orbitur.pt
website www.orbitur.pt
Well-equipped site in a pine wood 0.5km from Madalena beach.
Open All year **Site** 2.4HEC ⬤ ♣ ⊕ Å **Prices** ♠ 2.60-4.60 ⇄ 2.20-4.20
⇄ 3.60-7 Å 3.10-6.50 **Facilities** 🏠 🛈 ⊙ 🔌 ⊘ ℗ **Services** 🛒 🍴 🛒 ⬦
Leisure ⬦ P **Off-site** 🍴 ⬦RS

VILA REAL TRAS-OS-MONTES ALTO DOURO

Parque Campismo de Vila Real
⬦ Dr-Manuel Cardona, 5000 ☎ 259324724
⮑ In E part of town off N2 by Galp fuel station.
Open Mar-Nov **Site** 4HEC ⬤ ♣ ⊕ **Prices** ♠ 3.06-3.40 ⇄ 2.16-2.40
⇄ 4.41-4.90 Å 2.70-3 **Facilities** 🏠 🛈 ⊙ 🔌 ⊘ ℗ **Services** 🛒 🍴 🛒 ⬦
Off-site ⬦PR

CENTRAL

ABRANTES RIBATEJO

Castelo do Bode
Martinchel, 2200 ☎ 241849262 🗎 241849244
e-mail castelo.bode@fcmportugal.com
website www.fcmportugal.com
Set in natural wooded surroundings.
⮑ Signed.
Open 15 Jan-Oct **Site** 2.5HEC ⬦ ♣ ⬤ **Facilities** 🏠 ⊙ 🔌 ⊘ ℗
Services 🛒 🍴 🛒 ⬦ **Leisure** ⬦ R **Off-site** 🛈 🍴

ALENQUER ESTREMADURA

Alenquer
Estrada Nacional No.9-KM94, 2580-330
☎ 263710375 🗎 263710375
e-mail camping@dosdin.pt
website www.dosdin.pt/agirdin
A modern well-equipped terraced site surrounded by walnut trees.
Reductions available to campers presenting this publication.
⮑ Via A1
Open All year **Site** 1.5HEC ⬤ ♣ ⬤ ⊕ Å **Prices** ♠ 3.50-4 ⇄ 3.50-4
⇄ 4.50-6 Å 3.50-5 ⇄ (static)245-285 **Facilities** 🏠 🛈 ⊙ 🔌 ℗
Services 🛒 🍴 🛒 ⬦ **Leisure** ⬦ P **Off-site** ⊘ ⬦ ⬦R 🛒

ARGANIL BEIRA LITORAL

Arganil
Sarzedo, 3300 ☎ 235200133 🗎 235200134
e-mail camping@mail.telepac.pt
website www.cm-arganil.pt
A pleasant location among pine trees, close to the River Alva.
⮑ On N342-4.
Open All year **Site** 2.5HEC ⬦ ♣ ⬤ **Prices** ♠ 1.60-1.80 ⇄ 1.60-1.80
⇄ 2.20-5.20 Å 1.50-3 **Facilities** 🏠 🔌 ⊘ ℗ **Services** 🛒 🍴 🛒 ⬦
Leisure ⬦ R **Off-site** 🛈 🍴

WWW.ORBITUR.PT

ORBITUR PORTUGAL
ORBITUR · INTERCÂMBIO DE TURISMO, SA
INFORMATION AND RESERVATIONS: Rua Diogo do Couto, 1-8° F
1149-042 Lisboa · PORTUGAL Tel. +351.218117000/70
Fax +351.218117034 e-mail: info@orbitur.pt

CALDAS DA RAINHA ESTREMADURA

Orbitur Foz do Arelho
Foz Do Arelho, 2500 ☎ 262978683 🗎 262978685
e-mail info@orbitur.pt
website www.orbitur.pt
Situated in a fine lagoon on the Arelho estuary.
⮑ 3km SE of Foz do Arelho.
Open All year **Site** 6HEC ⬤ ♣ ⬤ **Facilities** 🏠 🛈 ⊙ 🔌 ℗
Services 🛒 🍴 🛒 ⬦ **Leisure** ⬦ P **Off-site** 🍴 ⬦S

See advertisement on this page

CASFREIRES BEIRA LITORAL

Quinta Chava Grande
3560-043 ☎ 232665552 🗎 232665552
e-mail chave-grande@sapo.pt
website www.chave-grande.com
A terraced site overlooking a beautiful valley. There are modern
installations and leisure facilities.
Open 15 Mar-Oct **Site** 10HEC ⬦ ♣ ⬤ **Prices** ♠ 4.50 ⇄ 4 ⬤ 4 Å 4
Facilities 🏠 ⊙ 🔌 ⊘ ℗ **Services** 🛒 🛒 ⬦ **Leisure** ⬦ P **Off-site** 🛈 🍴

COJA BEIRA LITORAL

Coja
3305 ☎ 235729666 🗎 235728945
e-mail coja@fpcampismo.pt
website www.coja.no.sapo.pt
Wooded location beside the River Alva.
⮑ Signed.
Open 15 Mar-30 Oct **Site** 3HEC ⬦ ♣ ⬤ ⊗ **Facilities** 🏠 🛈 ⊙ 🔌 ⊘ ℗
Services 🛒 🍴 🛒 ⬦ **Leisure** ⬦ R **Off-site** 🛈 ⬦R

Facilities 🛈 shop 🏠 shower ⊙ electric points for razors 🔌 electric points for caravans ℗ parking by tents permitted ⊕ compulsory separate car park
Services 🍴 café/restaurant 🛒 bar ⊘ Camping Gaz International ⬦ gas other than Camping Gaz 🛒 first aid facilities ⬦ laundry
Leisure ⬦ swimming L-Lake P-Pool R-River S-Sea **Off-site** All facilities within 2km

Portugal

COSTA DA CAPARICA ESTREMADURA

Orbitur
Av. Afonso de Albuquerque, Quinta de St.º António, 2825
☎ 212901366 🖷 212900661
e-mail info@orbitur.pt **website** www.orbitur.pt
This site has a small touring section and is 200m from a fine sandy beach.

➲ *After crossing Ponte Sul on road to Caparica, turn right at lights, site 1km on left.*

Open All year **Site** 5.7HEC 🌱 ⛱ 🏠 �caravans 🅰 **Prices** 🏃 2.70-4.80 🚗 2.40-4.70 �караван 4.30-7.80 🅰 3.50-6.90 **Facilities** 🌳 🚿 ⊙ 🚰 🅿 ⊛ **Services** 🍴 🍽 ➕ 🖾 **Off-site** 🚾 🍽 🅿 ⊛S

ÉVORA ALTO ALENTEJO

Orbitur
Estrada de Alcacovas, 7000-703 ☎ 266705190 🖷 266709830
e-mail info@orbitur.pt
website www.orbitur.pt
Wooded surroundings with modern facilities.

➲ *2km S near Km94.5.*

Open All year **Site** 3.3HEC 🌱 ⛱ 🏠 **Prices** 🏃 2.60-4.60 🚗 2.20-4.20 �караван 3.60-7 🅰 3.10-6.50 **Facilities** 🌳 🚿 ⊙ 🚰 🅿 ⊛ **Services** 🍴 🍽 ➕ 🖾 **Leisure** ⊛ P **Off-site** 🚾 🍽

ÉVORA DE ALCOBAÁA ESTREMADURA

Rural de Silveira
Capuchos, 2460-479 ☎ 262509573
e-mail silveira.capuchos@clix.pt
Set in a rural wooded location.

➲ *3km from Alcobaça on N86.*

Open May-Sep **Site** 0.5HEC 🌱 ⛱ **Prices** 🏃 3 🚗 2 �караван 3.50-4.50 🅰 2.50-3.50 **Facilities** 🌳 ⊙ 🚰 ⊛ **Services** ➕ 🖾 **Off-site** 🚾 🍴 🍽 🅿 ⊛ ⊛R

FIGUEIRA DA FOZ BEIRA LITORAL

Foz do Mondego
Cabedelo, Gala, 3080 ☎ 233402740 🖷 233402749
e-mail info@fpcampismo.pt
website www.fpcampismo.pt
Open 19 Jan- 30 Oct **Site** 4HEC 🌱 ⛱ ⊗ **Facilities** 🌳 ⊙ 🚰 🅿 ⊛ **Services** 🍴 🍽 ➕ 🖾 **Leisure** ⊛ RS **Off-site** 🚾

Orbitur
Gala, 3080 ☎ 233431492 🖷 233431231
e-mail info@orbitur.pt **website** www.orbitur.pt
An enclosed area set within a municipal park on top of Guarda hill

➲ *On NW outskirts of town. Turn left off N16 Porto road at Km177, uphill for 0.5km.*

Open All year **Site** 6HEC 🌱 ⛱ 🏠 **Facilities** 🌳 🚿 ⊙ 🚰 🅿 ⊛ **Services** 🍴 🍽 ➕ 🖾 **Leisure** ⊛ S **Off-site** ⊛S

GOUVEIA BEIRA LITORAL

Curral do Negro
6290 ☎ 238491008
e-mail info@fpcampismo.pt
website www.fpcampismo.pt
A mountain setting surrounded by woodland.

➲ *Signed.*

Open 18 Jan- 30 Oct **Site** 2HEC 🌱 ⛱ **Facilities** 🌳 ⊙ 🚰 🅿 ⊛ **Services** 🍴 🍽 ➕ 🖾 **Leisure** ⊛ P

GUINCHO ESTREMADURA

Orbitur
Areia-Guincho, 2750-053 ☎ 214870450 🖷 214872167
e-mail info@orbitur.pt
website www.orbitur.pt
On hilly ground in a pine wood in the Parque du Guincho, near the Boca do Inferno.

➲ *5km NW of Cascais, off road 247-7.*

Open All year **Site** 7.7HEC 🌱 ⛱ 🏠 �caravans 🅰 **Prices** 🏃 2.70-4.80 🚗 2.40-4.70 �караван 4.30-7.80 🅰 3.50-6.90 **Facilities** 🌳 🚿 ⊙ 🚰 🅿 ⊛ **Services** 🍴 🍽 ➕ 🖾 **Off-site** 🚾 🍽 ⊛S

LOURIÇAL BEIRA LITORAL

Tamanco
11 Casas Brancas, 3100-231 ☎ 236952551 🖷 236952551
e-mail campismo.o.tamanco@mail.telepac.pt
website www.campismo-o-tamanco.com
Pleasant wooded surroundings.

➲ *Via N109 or A1.*

Open Feb-Oct **Site** 1.5HEC 🌱 ⛱ 🏠 **Prices** 🏃 3.30 🚗 2.45 �caravan 3.55 🅰 2.45-3.20 **Facilities** 🌳 🚿 ⊙ 🚰 ⊛ **Services** 🍴 🍽 🖾 **Leisure** ⊛ P **Off-site** 🅿 ➕

LUSO BEIRA LITORAL

Orbitur
E.N 336, Pampilhosa, Quinta Do Vale Do Jorge, 3050-246
☎ 231930916 🖷 231930917
e-mail info@orbitur.pt
website www.orbitur.pt
Open All year **Site** 3HEC 🌱 ⛱ 🏠 **Prices** 🏃 2.20-4 🚗 1.90-3.70 �caravan 2.75-6.20 🅰 2.40-5.70 **Facilities** 🌳 🚿 ⊙ 🚰 🅿 ⊛ **Services** 🍴 🍽 ➕ 🖾 **Off-site** 🚾 🍽

MONTARGIL ALTO ALENTEJO

Orbitur
E.N.2, Montargil, 7425-017 ☎ 242901207 🖷 242901220
e-mail info@orbitur.pt
website www.orbitur.pt
A beautiful wooded location with good recreational facilities close to the River Alva.

➲ *N off N2.*

Open All year **Site** 6HEC 🌱 ⛱ 🏠 �caravans 🅰 **Prices** 🏃 2.40-4.40 🚗 2.10-4 �caravan 3.30-6.60 🅰 2.90-6.10 **Facilities** 🌳 🚿 ⊙ 🚰 🅿 ⊛ **Services** 🍴 🍽 ➕ 🖾 **Off-site** 🍽 ⊛L

NAZARÉ ESTREMADURA

Orbitur Valado
Valado, 2450-148 ☎ 262561609 🖷 262561137
e-mail info@orbitur.pt
website www.orbitur.pt
Set in a pine wood 2km from the village with good facilities.

➲ *300m E of village, S of road 8-4 Nazaré-Alcobaça.*

Open Feb-Oct **Site** 6.3HEC 🌱 ⛱ 🏠 �caravans 🅰 **Prices** 🏃 2.20-4 🚗 1.90-3.70 �caravan 2.75-6.20 🅰 2.40-5.70 **Facilities** 🌳 🚿 ⊙ 🚰 🅿 ⊛ **Services** 🍴 🍽 ➕ 🖾 **Off-site** 🚾 🍽 ⊛S

Site 6HEC (site size) 🌱 grass ⊜ sand 🪨 stone ♣ little shade ⛱ partly shaded ⛱ mainly shaded 🏠 bungalows for hire 🚐 caravans for hire 🅰 tents for hire ⊗ no dogs **Prices** 🏃 adult per night 🚗 car per night pp per person per night 🚐 caravan per night 🅰 tent per night 🚐 (static)-caravan hire per week

Portugal

Vale Paraiso

Estrada Nacional 242, 2450-138 ☎ 262561800 🖷 262561900
e-mail info@valeparaiso.com website www.valeparaiso.com
Situated in a beautiful natural park among tall pines. The site is well appointed with high standards of hygiene and varied recreational facilities.

Open Jan-9 Dec, 27-31 Dec Site 8.3HEC ⚌ ⚌ ⚌ 🛖 � Prices ⚊ 3.10-4.20
🚋 2.90-3.50 🚐 3.70-4.50 ▲ 2.70-5.30 🚐 (static)120-380 Facilities 🏪 🖾
🖰 🚿 ⊘ ℗ Services ⛢ 🍴 🕀 🖾 Leisure ⚌ P Off-site 🖴 ⚌S

ALHEIROS DE MIRA BEIRA LITORAL

Orbitur

Estrada Florestal N.º 1 - km 2, Dunas de Mira, 3070-792
☎ 231471234 🖷 231472047
e-mail info@orbitur.pt website www.orbitur.pt
Site lies in a dense forest.
➲ N off N334 at Km2 towards Videira, opp road fork.
Open Jan-Nov Site 3HEC ⚌ ⚌ 🛖 Prices ⚊ 2.40-4.40 🚐 2.10-4 🚐 3.30-
60 ▲ 2.90-6.10 Facilities 🏪 🖾 🖰 🚿 ⊘ ℗ Services ⛢ 🍴 🕀 🖾
Leisure ⚌ S Off-site 🖾 🍴 ⚌LS

PENACOVA BEIRA LITORAL

Penacova

Est da Carvoeira, 3360 ☎ 239477464 🖷 239477464
e-mail info@fpcampismo.pt website www.fpcampismo.pt
A pleasant riverside site in wooded surroundings.
➲ Signed.
Open 18 Jan- 30 Dec Site 1HEC ⚌ ⚌ ℗ Facilities 🏪 ⊘ 🚿 ⊘ ℗
Services ⛢ 🍴 🕀 🖾 Leisure ⚌ R Off-site 🖾

PENICHE ESTREMADURA

CM

Av. Monsenhor Bastos, 2520 ☎ 262789529 🖷 262789529
website www.cm-peniche.pt
On a sandy hillock, partly wooded, 0.5km from sea.
➲ 2km E.
Open All year Site 12.6HEC ⚌ ⚌ ⚌ 🛖 ▲ Prices ⚊ 1.13-2.25 🚐 0.93-
85 🚐 1.35-4.85 ▲ 0.93-4.55 Facilities 🏪 🖾 🖰 🚿 ⊘ ℗ Services ⛢ 🍴
🕀 🖾 Off-site 🖾 ⛢ 🍴 ⊘ 🖴 ⚌PS

Peniche Praia

2520 ☎ 262783460 🖷 262789447
e-mail penichepraia@hotmail.com website www.penichepraia.pt
On level ground 0.5km from the sea.
➲ N towards Cabo Carudeiro.
Open All year Site 1.5HEC ⚌ ⚌ ⚌ 🛖 Prices ⚊ 1.65-3.20 🚐 1.40-2.90
2.25-4 ▲ 1.65-3.20 Facilities 🏪 🖾 🖰 🚿 ⊘ Services ⛢ 🍴 🕀 🖾
Off-site ⊘ 🖴 ⚌PS 🕀

See advertisement on this page

PORTALEGRE ALTO ALENTEJO

Orbitur

Quinta da Saude, 7300-435 ☎ 245308384 🖷 245308385
e-mail info@orbitur.pt
website www.orbitur.pt
A hilltop site commanding magnificent views.
➲ Via N18 Estremoz-Castelo Branco.
Open Apr-Sep Site 2HEC ⚌ ⚌ ⚌ Facilities 🏪 🖰 🚿 ⊘ ℗ Services ⛢
🍴 🖾 Off-site 🖾 🍴

SALVATERRA DE MAGOS RIBATEJO

Parque de Campismo de Escaroupim

Mata Florestal de Escaroupim, 2120 ☎ 263595484 🖷 263595484
e-mail info@fpcampismo.pt
Open 18 Jan- 30 Oct Site 3HEC ⚌ ⚌ ℗ Facilities 🏪 🖾 🖰 🚿 ⊘ ℗
Services ⛢ 🍴 🕀 🖾 Leisure ⚌ P Off-site 🖴 ⚌R

SÃO JACINTO BEIRA LITORAL

Orbitur

E.N.327 - Km 20, 3800-901 ☎ 234838284 🖷 234838122
e-mail info@orbitur.pt
website www.orbitur.pt
Set in a dense pine wood, towards the sea from the uneven paved road from Ovar that runs alongside the lagoon.
➲ 1.5km from sea.
Open Feb-Oct Site 2.2HEC ⚌ ⚌ 🛖 Prices ⚊ 2.20-4 🚐 1.90-3.70 🚐 2.75-
6.20 ▲ 2.40-5.70 Facilities 🏪 🖾 🖰 🚿 ⊘ ℗ Services ⛢ 🍴 🖾
Leisure ⚌ R Off-site ⚌RS

SÃO PEDRO DE MOEL ESTREMADURA

Orbitur

2430 ☎ 244599168 🖷 244599148
e-mail info@orbitur.pt
website www.orbitur.pt
On a hill among pine trees.
➲ Off road 242-2 from Marinha Grande at rdbt near Shell fuel station on E outskirts of village, N for 100m.
Open All year Site 7HEC ⚌ ⚌ ⚌ 🛖 ▲ Prices ⚊ 2.70-4.80 🚐 2.40-4.70
🚐 4.30-7.80 ▲ 3.50-6.90 Facilities 🏪 🖾 🖰 🚿 ⊘ ℗ Services ⛢ 🍴 🕀 🖾
Leisure ⚌ P Off-site 🖾 🍴 ⚌PS

VISEU BEIRA ALTA

Orbitur

Fontelo, 3500 ☎ 232436146 🖷 232432076
e-mail info@orbitur.pt
website www.orbitur.pt
A pleasant, quiet site in a rural location.
➲ Via N2.
Open 15 Mar-15 Oct Site 3HEC ⚌ ⚌ ⚌ Facilities 🏪 🖾 🖰 🚿 ⊘ ℗
Services ⛢ 🍴 🕀 🖾 Off-site 🖾

Facilities 🖾 shop 🏪 shower ⊙ electric points for razors 🖰 electric points for caravans ℗ parking by tents permitted ℗ compulsory separate car park
Services 🍴 café/restaurant ⛢ bar ⊘ Camping Gaz International 🖴 gas other than Camping Gaz 🕀 first aid facilities 🖾 laundry
Leisure ⚌ swimming L-Lake P-Pool R-River S-Sea Off-site All facilities within 2km

Spain

Accidents & emergencies
fire 112   **police** 112   **ambulance** 112

Driving requirements
Minimum age 18 for UK licence holders driving temporarily imported cars (or motorcycles over 75cc). All valid UK driving licences should be accepted in Spain This includes the older, all-green style UK licences, although the European Commission appreciates that these may be more difficult to understand and that drivers may wish to voluntarily update them before travelling abroad. Alternatively, older licences may be accompanied by an International Driving Permit (IDP).

Lights
The use of full headlights in built up areas is prohibited. Dipped headlights are compulsory when passing through tunnels (even if they are well lit). Motorcyclists must use dipped headlights during the day. Replacement set of vehicle bulbs compulsory. The requirement to carry a spare set of vehicle bulbs does not apply to high intensity discharge (HID) lamp units.

Passengers & children
Children under 12 must not travel in the front seat unless using a suitable restraint system. Never fit a rear-facing child restraint in a seat with a frontal airbag.

Size restrictions
Motor vehicle or trailer
height 4m, width 2.55m, length 12m

Vehicle + trailer
length 18.75m

Speed limits
Unless signed otherwise:

Car without caravan/trailer, motorcycle
Built-up areas	50kph
Outside built-up areas	90kph
	100kph*
Motorways and dual carriageways	120kph

Car towing caravan/trailer
Built-up areas	50kph
Outside built-up areas	70kph
	80kph*
Motorways	80kph
Minimum speed on motorway	60kph

*according to type/quality of road as indicated by signs.

Tourist office
Spanish National Tourist Office
PO Box 4009, London W1A 6NB
Tel 020 7486 8077 (Mon-Fri 09.15-13.30 hrs)
www.tourspain.co.uk

Tolls, *peaje*

Spain Tolls

A1	Burgos - A68 (near Miranda de Ebro)	€8.80	€8.80
A2	Zaragoza - Tarragona	€20.75	€20.75
A4	Cadiz - Dos Hermanas (Sevilla)	€5.30	€5.30
A6	Villalba - Adanero	€8.30	€8.30
A7	La Jonquera - Barcelona	€11.28	€11.28
A7	Barcelona - Salou	€12.30	€12.30
A7	Salou - Valencia	€16.65	€16.65
A7	Valencia - Alicante (Alacant)	€11.35	€11.35
A7	Malaga - Estepona	€7.65	€7.65
A7	Estepona - Guadiaro	€2.65	€2.65
A8	Bilbao (Bilbo) - Irun	€7.90	€7.90
A9	La Coruna - Santiago de Compostela	€4.65	€4.65
A9	Santiago de Compostela - Vigo	€6.65	€6.65
A12	Leon - Astorga	€3.35	€3.35
A15/A68	Pamplona (Irunea) - Tudela	€9.00	€9.00
A16	Tunel de Garraf	€3.75	€3.75
A17	Barcelona - Montmelo	€1.15	€1.15
A19	Barcelona - Tordera	€3.25	€3.25
A37	Alicante (Alacant) - Cartagena	€5.50	€5.50
A55	La Coruna - Carballo	€2.90	€2.90
A66	Leon - Campomanes	€9.60	€9.60
A68	Zaragoza - Miranda de Ebro	€15.90	€15.90
A68	Miranda de Ebro - Bilbao (Bilbo)	€7.90	€7.90

Bridges & tunnels

Tunel del Cadi	€9.68	€9.68

Pedestrians and bicycles with auxiliary motors of less than 50cc are prohibited. Drivers must maintain a speed of 30-50kph on the bridges. Speed is checked by radar. Heavy vehicles must keep at least 20 metres (66ft) behind the preceding vehicle.

If you run out of petrol on the bridges you will be fined and will have to buy 10 litres of petrol from the bridge authorities at the official price. Motorcycles under 50cc not permitted.

Additional information

Warning triangle compulsory. The wearing of reflective jacket/waistcoat is compulsory if driver and/or passengers exit a vehicle which is immobilised on the carriageways of motorways and main or busy roads.

Motorways

To join a motorway follow signs with the international motorway symbol. Motorcycles under 50cc and motor vehicles for invalids are prohibited. The minimum speed limit is 60kph(Spain), 50kph (Portugal) except where otherwise signposted.

Services

It is usually possible to obtain services for a car and/or occupants every 30-50km. Emergency telephones are sited every 2km on most motorways.

Breakdown

Two warning triangles are compulsory for all vehicles in Spain.

Toll payments, *peaje, portagem*

On the majority of toll motorways a travel ticket is issued on entry and toll is paid on leaving the motorway. The travel ticket gives all relevant information about toll charges, including the toll category of the vehicle. At the exit point the ticket is handed in. On some motorways the toll collection is automatic; have the correct amount ready to throw in the collecting basket. If change is required use marked separate lane. Toll booths will not exchange traveller's cheques — ensure you have sufficient currency to meet the high toll charges. Alternatively, credit cards are now accepted at toll booths in Spain, but not in Portugal. Tolls are charged on most motorways according to distance travelled. Most cars pay the toll quoted if the entire section of motorway is used. On some motorways a lower toll category is used for vehicles under 900cc and a higher category for vehicles over 2000cc. Twin-axled caravans are charged at double the standard rate.

Andorra

Accidents & emergencies

fire 118 **police** 110 **ambulance** 118

mountain rescue 112

Driving requirements

Minimum age 18 for UK licence holders driving temporarily imported cars and/or motorcycles.

Lights

Dipped headlights should be used in poor daytime visibility. Motorcycles must use dipped headlights during the day.

Motor insurance

Green Card compulsory.

Passengers & children

Child under 10 cannot travel as a front seat passenger. Compulsory for front seat occupants to wear seat belts, if fitted.

Size restrictions

Motor vehicle or trailer
height 3.5m

Speed limits

Unless signed otherwise:

Vehicle with or without trailers	
Built-up areas	40kph
Outside built-up areas	70kph

Tourist office

Andorra Tourist Delegation
63 Westover Road
London SW18 2RF
Tel 020 8874 4806
www.turisme.ad
www.andorra.com

Additional information

Compulsory for visitors to equip their vehicle with a set of replacement bulbs and a warning triangle. It is wise to carry snow chains when severe winter weather has been notified.

Lost on the continent?

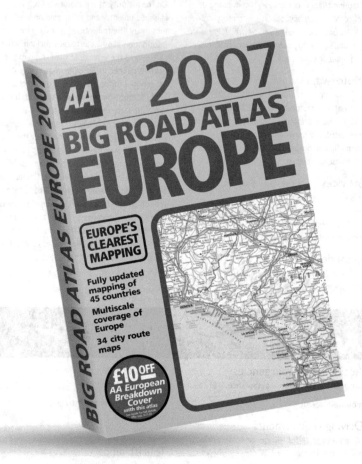

NORTH EAST COAST

BEGUR GIRONA

Begur
Ctra. D'Esclanya km2, 17255 ☎ 972 623201 ▤ 972 624566
e-mail info@campingbegur.com
website www.campingbegur.com
A terraced site in a wooded valley.
➲ 1.4km SE of town. Right of road to Palafrugell, 400m after turning for Fornells & Aiguablava.
Open Apr-Sep **Site** 8HEC ⛺ ⛺ ⛺ **Prices** ⚊ 3.21-3.10 ⛊ 3.53-7.39 ⚊ 2.25-6.10 **Facilities** ⛄ ⓘ ⊙ ⊟ ⚐ ⑬ **Services** ⛽ ⓡ ⊞ ⓢ **Leisure** ⚓ P
Off-site ⓘ ⛽ ⌀ ⚓S

Maset
Playa de sa Riera, 17255 ☎ 972 623023 ▤ 972 623901
e-mail info@campingelmaset.com
website www.campingelmaset.com
A well-kept terraced site, divided into pitches in a beautiful valley, 300m from the sea.
➲ 2km N of Begur. If entering from W, turn left just before town.
Open 2 Apr-24 Sep **Site** 1.2HEC ⛺ ⛺ ⛺ ⛊ ⑬ **Prices** ⚊ 5.03-7.17 ⛊ 4.28-6.10 ⛊ 6.21-8.88 ⚊ 5.46-8.24 **Facilities** ⛄ ⓘ ⊙ ⊟ ⚐ ⌀ ⓟ **Services** ⛽ ⓡ ⊞ ⓢ **Leisure** ⚓ P **Off-site** ⚓S

BLANES GIRONA

Bella Terra
av Villa de Madrid, 17300 ☎ 972 348017 ▤ 972 348275
e-mail info@campingbellaterra.com
website www.campingbellaterra.com
A large family site in a luxuriant pine wood beside the beach with modern facilities.
➲ Via N11.
Open Apr-Sep **Site** 10.5HEC ⛺ ⛺ ⛺ ⛺ **Facilities** ⛄ ⓘ ⊙ ⊟ ⚐ ⑬ **Services** ⛽ ⓡ ⊞ ⓢ **Leisure** ⚓ PS

Blanes
Avenida Villa de Madrid 33, 17300 ☎ 972 331591 ▤ 972 337063
e-mail info@campingblanes.com
website www.campingblanes.com
Set in a pine forest bordering the beach, 1km from the town centre.
➲ On left of Paseo Villa de Madrid coast road towards town.
Open All year **Site** 2HEC ⛺ ⛺ **Prices** ⚊ 4.70-6.52 pitch 13.85-18.83 **Facilities** ⛄ ⓘ ⊙ ⊟ ⚐ ⌀ ⑬ **Services** ⛽ ⓡ ⊞ ⓢ **Leisure** ⚓ PS
Off-site ⚓R

Masia
c Colon 44, Los Pinos, 17300 ☎ 972 331013 ▤ 972 333128
e-mail info@campinglamasia.com
website www.campinglamasia.com
A pleasant family site on level ground with shady pitches, 150m from the sea.
➲ 50m inland from Paseo Villa de Madrid coast road.
Open May-Sep **Site** 9HEC ⛺ ⛺ ⛺ **Prices** ⚊ 4.75-6.50 pitch 13.80-23.20 **Facilities** ⛄ ⓘ ⊙ ⊟ ⚐ ⌀ ⑬ **Services** ⛽ ⓡ ⊞ ⓢ **Leisure** ⚓ PRS
Off-site ⓘ ⛽ ⓡ ⌀ ⚓P

Pinar
av Villa de Madrid, 17300 ☎ 972 331083 ▤ 972 331100
e-mail camping@elpinarbeach.com
website www.elpinarbeach.com
Divided into two by the coastal road. Partially meadow under poplars.
➲ 1km on Paseo Villa de Madrid coast road.
Open Apr-Sep **Site** 5HEC ⛺ ⛺ ⛺ ⛺ **Prices** ⚊ 5.80 pitch 18 **Facilities** ⛄ ⓘ ⊙ ⊟ ⌀ ⑬ **Services** ⛽ ⓡ ⊞ ⓢ **Leisure** ⚓ PS

S'Abanell
av Villa Madrid 7-9, 17300 ☎ 972 331809 ▤ 972 350506
e-mail info@sabanell.com
website www.sabanell.com
Set within a pine wood, part of which is inland and open to the public.
➲ On either side of Avenida Villa de Madrid road. Off coast road S of Blanes.
Open 8 Jan-23 Dec **Site** 3.3HEC ⛺ ⛺ ⛺ ⛊ **Prices** ⚊ 2.83-6.52 ⛊ 2.41-6.21 pitch 9.33-18.83 ⛊ (static)168-368 **Facilities** ⛄ ⓘ ⊙ ⊟ ⌀ ⑬ **Services** ⛽ ⓡ ⊞ ⓢ **Leisure** ⚓ S

CALELLA DE LA COSTA BARCELONA

Botanic Bona Vista
Ctra. N2 KM 665, 08370 ☎ 93 7692488 ▤ 93 7695804
e-mail info@botanic-bonavista.net
website www.botanic-bonavista.net
Subdivided and well-tended terraced site on a hillside, beautifully landscaped. Steep internal roads. Access to the beach via a pedestrian underpass.
➲ Off N11 at Km665, site round blind corner.
Open All year **Site** 2.8HEC ⛺ ⛺ ⛺ **Facilities** ⛄ ⓘ ⊙ ⊟ ⚐ ⌀ ⑬ **Services** ⛽ ⓡ ⊞ ⓢ **Leisure** ⚓ PS **Off-site** ⚓P

Far
08370 ☎ 93 7690967 ▤ 93 7690967
e-mail elfar@reset.es
Terraced site on a hillock under deciduous trees with lovely view of Calella and out to sea. Steep internal roads.
➲ Travelling S on N11, site before left bend at Km666.
Open Apr-Sep **Site** 2.5HEC ⛺ ⛺ ⛺ **Facilities** ⛄ ⓘ ⊙ ⊟ ⚐ ⌀ ⑬ **Services** ⛽ ⓡ ⊞ ⓢ **Off-site** ⚏ ⚓PS

CASTELL D'ARO GIRONA

Castell d'Aro
crta S'Agaro, 17249 ☎ 972 819699 ▤ 972 819699
e-mail campingcastelldaro@yahoo.es
website www.campingsonline.com/campingcastelldaro
A quiet family site, 2km from the beach, with good recreational facilities.
➲ Off Km1 on S'Agaró road.
Open Apr-Sep **Site** 8HEC ⛺ ⛺ ⛺ **Prices** ⚊ 4.25-6 pitch 24-35 **Facilities** ⛄ ⓘ ⊙ ⊟ ⚐ ⑬ **Services** ⛽ ⓡ ⊞ ⓢ **Leisure** ⚓ P **Off-site** ⚓S

Spain

Facilities ⓘ shop ⛄ shower ⊙ electric points for razors ⚐ electric points for caravans ⑬ parking by tents permitted ⓟ compulsory separate car park
Services ⓡ café/restaurant ⛽ bar ⌀ Camping Gaz International ⚏ gas other than Camping Gaz ⊞ first aid facilities ⓢ laundry
Leisure ⚓ swimming L-Lake P-Pool R-River S-Sea **Off-site** All facilities within 2km

Catalonien Tourism Merits Medal

On the Costa Daurada, between BARCELONA and TARRAGONA, near tourist sites and PORT AVENTURA. Situated on the C-31, km 146,2, between Cubelles and Cunit at only 100 m from the beach. Hot water and swimming pool free. Horseback riding, tennis etc. close by. Consult our low-season fees. **20 % P/N red. with carnet CCI.** Communication w. Barcelona and airport per train and bus.

INFORMATION and RESERVATION:

www.la-rueda.com
(in English)

Email: **larueda@la-rueda.com**
Aptdo. Correos 261 E-08880 Cubelles.
Tel. (0034) 938 950 207
Fax (0034) 938 950 347

CASTELLÓ D'EMPURIES GIRONA

Castell-Mar
Platja de la Rubina, 17486 ☎ 972 450822 📄 972 452330
e-mail cmar@campingparks.com
website www.campingparks.com
A modern family site close to the beach on the edge of a national park.
➲ *A7 exit 3 or 4 Figueres, C260 through Castello d'Empuries for Roses.*
Open 19 May-23 Sep **Site** 4HEC 😃 😃 🏕 🏠 **Prices** ♠ 4 pitch 8-34 **Facilities** ⟑ 🏛 ⊙ ⊕ ⊛ **Services** 🍴 🍽 ➕ 🖲 **Leisure** ⋆ PS

Mas-Nou
Crta. Figueres a Roses, km38, 17486
☎ 972 454175 📄 972 454358
e-mail info@campingmasnou.com
website www.campingmasnou.com
A family site with good recreational facilities, 2.5km from the coast.
➲ *Off A7 onto Figueres-Roses road.*
Open Mar-Sep **Site** 9.8HEC 😃 🏕 🏠 **Prices** ♠ 2.46-4.70 pitch 14.44-27.28 **Facilities** ⟑ ⊙ ⊕ ⊛ **Services** 🍴 🍽 ➕ 🖲 **Leisure** ⋆ P **Off-site** 🏛 ⊘ ⋆RS

Nautic Almanta
17486 ☎ 972 454477 📄 972 454686
e-mail info@almata.com
website www.almata.com
A level meadowland site reaching as far as the sea and bordering the River Fluvia, which has been made into a canal. No shade, good facilities. Boating is possible in the canal, which flows into the sea.
➲ *Turn S off C260 at Km11, E onto track for 2.2km.*
Open 12 May-23 Sep **Site** 22HEC 😃 😃 🏠 🅰 **Prices** pitch 19.40-38.80 (incl 6 persons) pp1.82-3.65 **Facilities** ⟑ 🏛 ⊙ ⊕ ⊛ ⊘ ⊛ **Services** 🍴 🍽 🖲 **Leisure** ⋆ PRS

CUBELLES BARCELONA

La Rueda
Ctra.C-31 KM146,2, 8880 ☎ 938950207 📄 938950347
e-mail larueda@la-rueda.com
website www.la-rueda.com
Level terrain between road and railway. Access to beach by means of an underpass.
➲ *1km N of Cunit near C31 Km146.2.*
Open 31 Mar-10 Sep **Site** 6HEC 😃 😃 🏠 **Prices** ♠ 3.68-6.14 pitch 11.05-18.44 **Facilities** ⟑ 🏛 ⊙ ⊕ ⊘ ⊛ **Services** 🍴 🍽 ➕ 🖲 **Leisure** ⋆ PS

See advertisement on this page

ESCALA, L' GIRONA

Maite
Playa Riells, 17310 ☎ 972 770544 📄 972 770599
e-mail maite@campings.net
website www.campings.net/maite
An extensive site, lying inland, but near the sea, at a small lake. Partly on a hillock under pine trees.
➲ *Signed from outskirts of l'Escala towards Cala Montgo.*
Site 6HEC 😃 😃 **Facilities** ⟑ 🏛 ⊙ ⊕ ⊘ ⊛ **Services** 🍴 🍽 ➕ **Leisure** ⋆ LS

Neus
Cala Montgó, 17130 ☎ 972 770403 📄 972 222409
e-mail info@campingneus.com
website www.campingneus.com
Peaceful location among pine trees, 0.8km from the beach.
Open Jun-16 Sep **Site** 4HEC 😃 😃 🅰 **Facilities** ⟑ 🏛 ⊙ ⊕ ⊘ ⊛ **Services** 🍴 🍽 ➕ **Leisure** ⋆ P **Off-site** 🍽 ⋆S

ESTARTIT, L' GIRONA

Castell Montgri
17258 ☎ 972 751630 📄 972 750906
e-mail c.montgri@campingparks.com
website www.campingparks.com
On a large terraced meadow in pine woodlands.
➲ *100m N of GE road from Torroella de Montgri, 0.5km before l'Estartit on small hill.*
Open 12 May-Sep **Site** 25HEC 😃 😃 🏠 🅰 **Prices** ♠ 4 pitch 9-36 **Facilities** ⟑ 🏛 ⊙ ⊕ ⊘ ⊛ **Services** 🍴 🍽 ➕ 🖲 **Leisure** ⋆ P **Off-site** ⋆S

See advertisement on page 321

Site 6HEC (site size) 😃 grass 😃 sand 😃 stone 🌳 little shade 🌳 partly shaded 🌳 mainly shaded 🏠 bungalows for hire 🅰 caravans for hire 🅰 tents for hire ⊗ no dogs **Prices** ♠ adult per night 🚗 car per night pp per person per night 🚐 caravan per night 🅰 tent per night 🚐 (static)-caravan hire per week

Cámping
Caravaning **CASTELL MONTGRI**

Ctra. de Torroella a L'Estartit, Km. 4,7
17258 - L'ESTARTIT (Costa Brava) ESPAÑA
Tel. +34 972 75 16 30   Fax. +34 972 75 09 06
E-mail: cmontgri@campingparks.com

Ofertas 2007 €

12-5 → 23-6 25-8 → 30-9	14 🌙	21 🌙	28 🌙
+2 👤	164	226	290
N.H.L. 5 p	474	666	869
M.H. 6p	632	850	1048
LUXE M.H. 6p	758	1020	1255
2 👤 > 60 = 10% Dto.			

www.campingparks.com

www.campingparks.com

19-5 → 23-6 25-8 → 23-9	14 🌙	21 🌙	28 🌙
+2 👤	164	226	290
Bungalow 4 p.	390	546	712
M.H. 4p	445	622	811
M.H. 6p	603	808	990
2 👤 > 60 = 10% Dto.			

Cámping
Caravaning **CASTELL MAR**

Platja de La Rubina
17486 - CASTELLÓ D'EMPURIES (Costa Brava) ESPAÑA
Tel. +34 972 45 08 22   Fax. +34 972 45 23 30
E-mail: cmar@campingparks.com

Facilities 🏠 shop 🚿 shower ⊙ electric points for razors 🔌 electric points for caravans ⓟ parking by tents permitted 🅿 compulsory separate car park
Services 🍴 café/restaurant 🍺 bar ⌀ Camping Gaz International ⛽ gas other than Camping Gaz ➕ first aid facilities 🌀 laundry
Leisure 🏊 swimming L-Lake P-Pool R-River S-Sea **Off-site** All facilities within 2km

Estartit

Cap Villa Primavera 12, 17258 ☎ 972 751909 ▤ 972 750991
website www.campingestartit.com

Set in a valley on sloping ground, which can be steep in places. Some terraces, shaded by pines.

⮑ *200m from church & road from Torroella de Montgri.*

Open Apr-Sep **Site** 2.5HEC ⛺ ⛱ ♣ 🏠 ▲ ⊗ **Prices** ⚊ 4.77 🚗 4.77 ⛺ 5.33 ▲ 4.11 ⛺ (static)385 **Facilities** 🛁 🛒 ⊙ 🚰 ⛽ **Services** 🍴 🍴 🔁 🛒 **Leisure** ⚓ LPRS **Off-site** ⌀

Medes

17258 ☎ 972 751805 ▤ 972 750413
e-mail info@campinglesmedes.com
website www.campinglesmedes.com

Quiet holiday site in rural surroundings with clearly marked pitches and modern facilities.

⮑ *GE641 from Torroella di Montgri, turn right at Km5 & continue 1.5km .*

Open Dec-Oct **Site** 2.6HEC ⛺ ⛱ ♣ 🏠 ⊗ **Prices** ⚊ 3.74-7.16 pitch 8.23-16.05 **Facilities** 🛁 🛒 ⊙ 🚰 ⌀ ⊗ **Services** 🍴 🍴 🔁 🛒 **Leisure** ⚓ P **Off-site** ♨ ⚓S

Molino

17258 ☎ 972 750629 ▤ 972 750629
e-mail branders@teleline.es

Divided into several sections of open meadowland near the beach on grassland with young poplars. The reconstructed mill is a landmark.

⮑ *From Torroella de Montgri turn right entering l'Estartit & signed.*

Open Apr-Sep **Site** 10HEC ⛺ ♣ 🏠 **Facilities** 🛁 🛒 ⊙ 🚰 ⌀ ⊗ ⊕ **Services** 🍴 🍴 🔁 🛒 **Leisure** ⚓ S **Off-site** ⚓R

GUARDIOLA DE BERGUEDA BARCELONA

El Berguedá

08694 ☎ 93 8227432 ▤ 93 8227432
e-mail campingbergueda@gmail.com
website www.campingbergueda.com

A peaceful site in the middle of a forest at an altitude of 900m with a variety of sports facilities.

⮑ *On B400.*

Open 24 Jun-1 Sep **Site** 3HEC ⛺ ⛱ ♣ 🏠 **Prices** ⚊ 4.65 🚗 4.65 ⛺ 4.65 ▲ 4.65 **Facilities** 🛁 🛒 ⊙ 🚰 ⌀ ♨ ⊗ **Leisure** ⚓ P **Off-site** ⚓R

GUILS DE CERDANYA GIRONA

Pirineus

ctra Guils de Cerdanya, 17528 ☎ 972 881062 ▤ 972 882471
e-mail guils@stel.es
website www.stel.es

A fine level location at an altitude of 1200m with fine views over the Cerdanya valley.

⮑ *On Puigcerda-Guils de Cerdanya road.*

Open 16 Jun-11 Sep **Site** 5HEC ⛺ ⛱ ♣ 🏠 ⊗ **Facilities** 🛁 🛒 ⊙ 🚰 ⌀ ⊗ **Services** 🍴 🍴 🔁 🛒 **Leisure** ⚓ P

LLORET DE MAR GIRONA

Tucan

Ctra. de Lloret a Blanes,S/N, 17310 ☎ 972 369965 ▤ 972 360079
e-mail info@campingtucan.com
website www.campingtucan.com

A modern family site, close to the sea, with plenty of recreational facilities.

⮑ *A7 exit 9 to Lloret de Mar.*

Open 31 Mar-Sep **Site** 4HEC ⛺ ⛱ ♣ 🏠 ▲ **Prices** ⚊ 4.62-7.57 🚗 4.62-7.57 ⛺ 4.62-7.57 ▲ 4.62-7.57 **Facilities** 🛁 🛒 ⊙ 🚰 ⌀ ⊗ **Services** 🍴 🍴 🔁 🛒 **Leisure** ⚓ P **Off-site** ♨ ⚓S

MASNOU, EL BARCELONA

Masnou

ctra Nac 2, 8320 ☎ 93 5551503 ▤ 93 5551503
e-mail campingmasnou@hotmail.com

A well-equipped site in wooded surroundings, 150m from the beach on the Costa del Maresme.

⮑ *Inland from N11 at Km633.*

Open Jun- Sep **Site** 2HEC ⛺ ♣ 🏠 ▲ **Facilities** 🛁 🛒 ⊙ 🚰 ⌀ ♨ ⊗ **Services** 🍴 🍴 🔁 🛒 **Leisure** ⚓ PS

PALAFRUGELL GIRONA

AT LLAFRANC

Kim's

Font d'En Xeco 1, 17211 ☎ 972 301156 ▤ 972 610894
e-mail info@campingkims.com
website www.campingkims.com/

Terraced site with winding drives, lying on the wooded slopes of a narrow valley leading to the sea.

⮑ *Turn right off Palafrugell-Tamariu road for 1km, pass El Paranso Hotel towards Llafranc, 400m from sea.*

Open Etr-Sep **Site** 5.8HEC ⛺ ⛱ ♣ 🏠 **Prices** ⚊ 2.50-6.50 pitch 12-26 **Facilities** 🛁 🛒 ⊙ 🚰 ⌀ ⊗ **Services** 🍴 🍴 🔁 🛒 **Leisure** ⚓ P **Off-site** ⚓S   *See advertisement on this pag*

AT MONTRÁS (3KM SW)

Relax-Ge

17253 ☎ 972 301549 ▤ 972 601100
e-mail info@campingrelaxge.com
website www.campingrelaxge.com

Level meadow under poplars and olive trees.

⮑ *Off C255 at Km38.7 & 4km towards sea.*

Open Jun-Aug **Site** 3HEC ⛺ ♣ 🏠 **Prices** ⚊ 5.50 pitch 10-17 **Facilities** 🛁 🛒 ⊙ 🚰 ⌀ ⊗ **Services** 🍴 🍴 🔁 🛒 **Leisure** ⚓ P **Off-site** ⚓S

Site 6HEC (site size) ⛺ grass ⛱ sand ⛰ stone ♣ little shade ♣ partly shaded 🏠 mainly shaded 🏠 bungalows for hire
⛺ caravans for hire ▲ tents for hire ⊗ no dogs **Prices** ⚊ adult per night 🚗 car per night pp per person per night ⛺ caravan per night
▲ tent per night ⛺ (static)-caravan hire per week

TAMARIU

Tamariu
17212 ☎ 972 620422 📠 972 620592
e-mail info@campingtamariu.com
website www.campingtamariu.com
Terraced site with mixture of high young pines. Direct access to the beach.
⮕ *Turning to site at beach parking area, continue 300m.*
Open May-Sep **Site** 2HEC 🌳 ♨ ♿ 🚐 **Prices** 👤 3.50-5 🚗 3-4.30
🚐 3.50-5 ⛺ 3-4.30 **Facilities** 🍴 🛏 ⊙ 🔌 ⊘ ℗ **Services** 🍴 🍽 ➕ 🖥
Leisure 🏊 PS **Off-site** 🛏 🍴 🍽 ⊘ ➕

PALAMÓS GIRONA

Castell Park
17230 ☎ 972 315263 📠 972 315263
e-mail info@campingcastellpark.com
website www.campingcastellpark.com
Level and gently sloping meadow with poplars and pine woodland on a hill.
⮕ *At Km40 100m to right of C255 to Palamós, 3km S of Montras.*
Open 31 Mar-16 Sep **Site** 4.5HEC 🌳 ♨ ♿ 🚐 **Prices** 👤 3-5.03 pitch
10.70-21.08 **Facilities** 🍴 🛏 ⊙ 🔌 ℗ **Services** 🍴 🍽 ➕ 🖥 **Leisure** 🏊 P
Off-site 🏊 S

Coma
Ronda Est, 17230 ☎ 972314638 📠 972315470
e-mail lacoma@campinglacoma.com
website www.campinglacoma.com
Terraced terrain with young deciduous trees and some pines, 0.8km from the sea.
⮕ *Off C255 in N outskirts near Renault garage towards sea.*
Open Apr-Sep **Site** 5.2HEC 🌳 ♨ ♿ ⛺ **Facilities** 🍴 🛏 ⊙ 🔌 ⊘ ℗
Services 🍴 🍽 ➕ 🖥 **Leisure** 🏊 P **Off-site** 🏊 S

Internacional Palamós
Cami cap de Planes s/n, 17230 ☎ 972 314736 📠 972 317626
e-mail info@internacionalpalamos.com
website www.internacionalpalamos.com
A family site in a picturesque wooded location close to the beach.
⮕ *Signed.*
Open Apr-Sep **Site** 5.2HEC 🌳 ♨ ♿ 🚐 ⛺ **Prices** 👤 3.21-3.53 pitch
17.92-41.30 🚐 (static)352.03-808.92 **Facilities** 🍴 🛏 ⊙ 🔌 ℗ **Services** 🍴
🍽 ➕ 🖥 **Leisure** 🏊 PS **Off-site** ⊘ *See advertisement on this page*

Palamós
ctra la Fosca 12, 17230 ☎ 972 314296 📠 972 601100
e-mail campingpal@grn.es
website www.campingpalamos.com
A picturesque location on a wooded headland overlooking the sea.
Open 31 Mar-Sep **Site** 5.5HEC 🌳 ♨ ♨ ♿ 🚐 ⛺ **Prices** 👤 5.20-6.10 pitch
10-19.70 🚐 (static)327.60-683.90 **Facilities** 🍴 🛏 ⊙ 🔌 ℗ **Services** 🍴
🍽 ➕ 🖥 **Leisure** 🏊 PS **Off-site** 🛢

Vilarromá
calle del Mar-Avda catalunya, 17230 ☎ 972 314375 📠 972 314375
e-mail camping@vilarroma.com
website www.campingvilarroma.com
Clean and tidy site, almost completely divided into pitches.
⮕ *Off E outskirts of Palamós near big fuel station.*
Open Apr-25 Sep **Site** 1.8HEC 🌳 ♨ ♿ 🚐 ⛺ **Facilities** 🍴 🛏 ⊙ 🔌 ⊘ ℗
Services 🍴 🍽 ➕ 🖥 **Off-site** 🍽 🛢 🏊 LPS

camping · caravaning · bungalow
INTERNACIONAL PALAMÓS
ADAC 2005
costa BRAVA

Camí Cap de Planes, s/n · E-17230 Palamós ·
Costa Brava (Girona ·España)
Apartado correos 100
E-17230 Palamós
Costa Brava (Girona ·España)
Tel.: (+34) 972 314 736
Fax: (+34) 972 317 626
info@internacionalpalamos.com ·
www.internacionalpalamos.com

Modern, quiet family site, very near to the beautiful **PLAYA DE FOSCA (La Fosca Beach) and in the centre of the COSTA BRAVA.** Lots of shade from trees and many flowers give you the impression of being in a garden. 3.000 sqm. of green area with swimming pools, solarium and all install. of a good holiday site, incl free hot water 24 hours a day. Bungalows tents 'Trigano' (4 pers.), mobile homes (6 pers.) and wooden bungalows 'Campitel' for rent. **There are more sites nearby, with mainly national campers. Be sure to visit our site. Exemplary sanitary blocks.**

Acces: Take exit towards Palamós-Norte and continue towards Playa de la Fosca.   **Open: Easter - Sept.**

AT CALONGE (5KM W)

Cala Gogo
17251 ☎ 972 651564 📠 972 650553
e-mail calagogo@calagogo.es
website www.calagogo.es
Terraced site in tall pine woodland and poplars with some good views of the sea. Underpass across to section of site with private beach. Some internal dusty roads
⮕ *From Palamós 4km S on C253 coast road, site on right after Km47.*
Open 28 Apr-23 Sep **Site** 20HEC ♨ ♿ 🚐 ⛺ ⊗ **Prices** 👤 3.30-6.25
🚐 12.20-27.15 ⛺ 10.20-22.90 **Facilities** 🍴 🛏 ⊙ 🔌 ⊘ **Services** 🍴 🍽 ➕
🖥 **Leisure** 🏊 PS

Internacional de Calonge
17250 ☎ 972 651233 📠 972 652507
e-mail info@intercalonge.com
website www.intercalonge.com
Set on a pine covered hill overlooking the sea within easy reach of a sandy beach.
⮕ *On coast road between Platja d'Aro & Palamós.*
Open All year **Site** 13HEC 🌳 ♨ ♿ ⛺ **Prices** 👤 3.64-7.28 🚐 13.05-26.75
⛺ 12.57-23.91 **Facilities** 🍴 🛏 ⊙ 🔌 ⊘ ℗ **Services** 🍴 🍽 ➕ 🖥
Leisure 🏊 PS

Spain

Facilities 🛏 shop 🍴 shower ⊙ electric points for razors 🔌 electric points for caravans ℗ parking by tents permitted ℗ compulsory separate car park
Services 🍽 café/restaurant 🍴 bar ⊘ Camping Gaz International 🛢 gas other than Camping Gaz ➕ first aid facilities 🖥 laundry
Leisure 🏊 swimming L-Lake P-Pool R-River S-Sea **Off-site** All facilities within 2km

PALS GIRONA

Cypsela
17256 ☎ 972 667696 📠 972 667300
e-mail info@cypsela.com **website** www.cypsela.com
Well-kept grassy site in a pine wood.
➲ *Turn towards sea N of Pals towards Playa de Pals, turn left after Km3.*
Open 12 May-23 Sep **Site** 20HEC ⛱ ⛺ ⛺ 🚐 ⊗ **Prices** ⚊ 5.78 🚗 6.42-12.84 pitch 18.51-33.70 🚐 (static)494.34-1018.64 **Facilities** 🚿 🛁 ⊙ 🚰 🖉 🛎 **Services** 🍴 🍽 ➕ 🛒 **Leisure** ⛱ P **Off-site** ⛱S

Mas Patoxas
17256 ☎ 972 636928 📠 972 667349
e-mail info@campingmaspatoxas.com
website www.campingmaspatoxas.com
A family site in a quiet location close to the sea. Modern sanitary blocks and plenty of recreational facilities.
➲ *At Km5 on Palafrugell to Torroella.*
Open 14 Apr-Sep **Site** 5.5HEC ⛱ ⛺ ⛺ 🚐 🅰 **Facilities** 🚿 🛁 ⊙ 🚰 🖉 ⛲ 🛎 **Services** 🍴 🍽 ➕ 🛒 **Leisure** ⛱ P

AT PLAYA DE PALS

Playa Brava
17256 ☎ 972 636894 📠 972 636952
e-mail info@playabrava.com **website** www.playabrava.com
On level terrain adjoining pine woodlands, golf course, rivers and sea.
➲ *From N end of Pals turn towards sea & Playa de Pals.*
Open 13 May-17 Sep **Site** 11HEC ⛱ ⛺ ⛺ ⊗ **Facilities** 🚿 🛁 ⊙ 🚰 **Services** 🍴 🍽 ➕ 🛒 **Leisure** ⛱ LPRS **Off-site** 🛁 🍴 🍽 🖉

PINEDA DE MAR BARCELONA

Camell
Ada de los Naranjos 12, 08397 ☎ 93 7671520 📠 93 7670270
e-mail campingcamell@teleline.es
Surrounded by deciduous trees next to a small wood owned by the Taurus Hotel.
➲ *Off N11 at Km 670 onto av de los Naranjos towards sea.*
Open May-Sep **Site** 2.2HEC ⛱ ⛺ **Prices** ⚊ 4.60 pitch 13.50 **Facilities** 🚿 🛁 ⊙ 🚰 🖉 🛎 **Services** 🍴 🍽 ➕ 🛒 **Leisure** ⛱ PS **Off-site** 🍽

PLATJA D'ARO, LA GIRONA

Valldaro
Avda Castell d'Aro 63, 17250 ☎ 972 817515 📠 972 816662
e-mail info@valldaro.com **website** www.valldaro.com
Extensive level meadowland under poplars, pines and eucalyptus trees. Some large pitches without shade.
➲ *On left of GE662 towards Castell & Santa Cristinia d'Aro at Km4.*
Open 23 Mar-Sep **Site** 18HEC ⛱ ⛺ ⛺ 🚐 **Prices** ⚊ 3.74-6.15 pitch 11.02-29.10 **Facilities** 🚿 🛁 ⊙ 🚰 🖉 🛎 **Services** 🍴 🍽 ➕ 🛒 **Leisure** ⛱ P **Off-site** ⛱S

PUIGCERDÀ GIRONA

Stel
ctra Llívia, 17520 ☎ 972 882361 📠 972 140419
e-mail puigcerda@stel.es **website** www.stel.es
Modern site in the Pyrenees on level land. Has wonderful views of the mountains and surrounding area. Good sanitary installations.
➲ *Via N340 between Comarruga & Tarragona.*
Open 2 Jun-24 Sep **Site** 7HEC ⛱ ⛺ ⛺ 🚐 **Facilities** 🚿 🛁 ⊙ 🚰 🖉 🛎 **Services** 🍴 🍽 ➕ 🛒 **Leisure** ⛱ P

RIPOLL GIRONA

Solana del Ter
17500 ☎ 972 701062 📠 972 714343
e-mail hotel@solanadelter.com **website** www.solanadelter.com
A peaceful location close to ski resorts at the foot of the Pyrénées. Part of a small hotel-restaurant complex.
Open May-Oct **Site** 8.5HEC ⛱ ⛺ **Facilities** 🚿 🛁 ⊙ 🚰 🛎 **Services** 🍴 🍽 ➕ 🛒 **Leisure** ⛱ P **Off-site** 🛁

SALDES BARCELONA

Repos del Pedraforca
08697 ☎ 93 8258044 📠 93 8258061
e-mail pedra@campingpedraforca.com
website www.campingpedraforca.com
A well-equipped site situated in an area of natural beauty.
Open All year **Site** 4HEC ⛱ ⛺ ⛺ 🚐 🅰 **Facilities** 🚿 🛁 ⊙ 🚰 🖉 🛎 **Services** 🍴 🍽 ➕ 🛒 **Leisure** ⛱ P **Off-site** ⛱LR

SANTA CRISTINA D'ARO GIRONA

Mas St Josep
Ctra Sta Cristina, a Playa de Aro, 17246
☎ 972 835108 📠 972 837018
e-mail info@campingmassantjosep.com
website www.campingmassantjosep.com
A family site with plenty of recreational facilities.
➲ *At Km2 on Sta Cristina d'Aro road.*
Open 14 Mar-Dec **Site** 35HEC ⛱ ⛺ 🚐 **Prices** ⚊ 5.50-7 pitch 14.40-19 **Facilities** 🚿 🛁 ⊙ 🚰 🖉 🛎 **Services** 🍴 🍽 ➕ 🛒 **Leisure** ⛱ P

Site 6HEC (site size) ⛱ grass ⛱ sand ⛱ stone 🌱 little shade ⛺ partly shaded ⛺ mainly shaded 🏠 bungalows for hire 🚐 caravans for hire 🅰 tents for hire ⊗ no dogs **Prices** ⚊ adult per night 🚗 car per night pp per person per night 🚐 caravan per night 🅰 tent per night 🚐 (static)-caravan hire per week

Spain

SANT ANTONI DE CALONGE GIRONA

Eurocamping
Avinguda Catalunya 15, 17252 ☎ 972 650879 ▤ 972 661987
e-mail info@euro-camping.com **website** www.euro-camping.com
A family site in a peaceful location close to the sea with fine recreational facilities.

➲ *A7 exit 6.*

Open 31 Mar-23 Sep **Site** 13HEC ♨ ♨ ♨ **Prices** ♦ 2.51-6.26 pitch 17.60-29.26 **Facilities** ⌐ 🏠 ⊙ ⊕ ℗ **Services** 🍴 ⌐ 🍴 ➕ 🗑 **Leisure** ♨ P **Off-site** ⌀ ♨ ♨S

Treumal
San Feliu Quixols a Palamos, 17251 ☎ 972 651095 ▤ 972 651671
e-mail info@campingtreumal.com
website www.campingtreumal.com
A peaceful family site in a beautiful location between a pine wood and the beach.

➲ *On Sant Feliú-Platja d'Aro-Palamós road.*

Open Apr-Sep **Site** 7HEC ♨ ♨ ♨ ♨ ⊗ **Prices** ♦ 3.96-7.17 ⊕ 14.77-27.29 ▲ 14.23-26.22 **Facilities** ⌐ 🏠 ⊙ ⊕ ⌀ ℗ **Services** 🍴 ⌐ 🍴 ➕ 🗑
Leisure ♨ PS *See advertisement on page 324*

SANTA SUSANA BARCELONA

Bon Répos
08398 ☎ 93 7678475 ▤ 93 7678526
e-mail info@campingbonrepos.com
website www.campingbonrepos.com
Set in pine woodland between the railway and the beach with some sun-shade roofing.

➲ *Off N11 at Km681, via underpass (max height 2.5m) before beach.*

Open All year **Site** 6HEC ♨ ♨ ♨ ♨ **Facilities** ⌐ 🏠 ⊙ ⊕ ⌀ ℗ **Services** 🍴 ⌐ 🍴 ➕ 🗑 **Leisure** ♨ PS **Off-site** 🏠 ⌐ ♨S

SANT CEBRIÁ DE VALLALTA BARCELONA

Verneda
av Maresme, 08396 ☎ 93 7631185 ▤ 93 7631185
e-mail verneda@teleline.es
Set inland among tall trees.

➲ *Off N11 Girona-Barcelona at end of Sant Pol de Mar, turn inland at Km670, 2km to edge of village & right before bridge over River Vallala.*

Open Apr-Sep **Site** 1.6HEC ♨ ♨ ♨ **Prices** ♦ 4.80 ♠ 4.80 ⊕ 4.80 ▲ 4.80 **Facilities** ⌐ 🏠 ⊙ ⊕ ⌀ ℗ **Services** 🍴 ⌐ 🍴 ➕ 🗑 **Leisure** ♨ P

SANT FELIU DE GUIXOLS GIRONA

Sant Pol
Doctor Fleming, 17220 ☎ 972 327269 ▤ 972 222409
e-mail info@campingsantpol.com
website www.campingsantpol.com
Wooded surroundings near the beach with good facilities.

➲ *0.8km from town centre towards Palamos.*

Open 30 Mar-4 Nov **Site** 1.2HEC ♨ ♨ ♨ **Prices** ♦ 3.50-7 pitch 14-31 **Facilities** ⌐ 🏠 ⊙ ⊕ ℗ **Services** 🍴 ⌐ 🍴 ➕ 🗑 **Leisure** ♨ P **Off-site** ⌀ ♨S

Facilities 🏠 shop ⌐ shower ⊙ electric points for razors ⊕ electric points for caravans ℗ parking by tents permitted ℗ compulsory separate car park
Services 🍴 café/restaurant ⌐ bar ⌀ Camping Gaz International ♨ gas other than Camping Gaz ➕ first aid facilities 🗑 laundry
Leisure ♨ swimming L-Lake P-Pool R-River S-Sea **Off-site** All facilities within 2km

A first class site. **Fabulous situation** in the most beautiful part of the Costa Brava. Isolated and quiet. 4 beaches. Swimming pool, children's playground, bar, restaurant, supermarket, laundry, hairdressing, medical service. Exceptional sanitary facilities with free hot water. Numbered pitches. Open from 1st. of Mai until 30th. of September.
Sports and animation:
Swimmingpool, tennis, basket ball, windsurfing and diving school, compressed air for divers, table tennis, minigolf, mountain bike. Special activities for the children in July and August.
Reservation service. Bungalows and apartments for hire.

Write to:
Camping **Cala Llevadó**
Postbus 34, E-17320 **Tossa de Mar**
COSTA BRAVA - Spain
Tel. 00 34 972 34 03 14
Fax 00 34 972 34 11 87
E-mail: info@calallevado.com
Web: www.calallevado.com

EMAS
ICICT
Grupo TÜV Rheinland
UNE EN ISO 14001

Cala Llevadó
camping ★★★

SANT PERE PESCADOR GIRONA

Amfora
av J-Terradellas 2, 17470 ☎ 972 520540 ▤ 972 520539
e-mail info@campingamfora.com
website www.campingamfora.com
A pleasant site, directly on the beach, with modern sanitary facilities. There are plentiful leisure facilities.
Open 31 Mar-Sep **Site** 12HEC 👹 ⬥ 🏠 **Prices** ⋔ 3.42-4.50 pitch 14.98-36.38 **Facilities** 🏠 🛁 ⊙ 🚰 ⊘ ⊛ **Services** 🗲 †◎┃ 🚻 ⓢ
Leisure ⬥ PRS **Off-site** ⬥L

Aquarius
17470 ☎ 972 520003 ▤ 972 550216
e-mail camping@aquarius.es **website** www.aquarius.es
Level meadowland. Partially in shade, quiet well-organised site by the lovely sandy beach of Bahia de Rosas.
➲ Towards l'Escala & signed towards beach.
Open 15 Mar-Oct **Site** 8HEC 👹 ⬥ 🏠 🚐 **Prices** ⋔ 3.05-3.75 pitch 11.77-32.10 **Facilities** 🏠 🛁 ⊙ 🚰 ⊘ ⊛ **Services** 🗲 †◎┃ 🚻 ⓢ
Leisure ⬥ S

Ballena Alegre 2
17470 ☎ 902 510520 ▤ 902 510521
e-mail infb2@ballena-alegre.com
website www.ballena-alegre.com
Extensive site near wide sandy beach with dunes. Large shopping complex. Modern washing and sanitary facilities.
➲ Access from l'Escala to San Martin de Ampurias, onto site in 2km.
Open 15 May-28 Sep **Site** 24HEC 👹 ⬤ ⬥ 🏠 🚐 **Prices** ⋔ 3.75-4 pitch 15.94-43.87 **Facilities** 🏠 🛁 ⊙ 🚰 ⊘ ⊛ **Services** 🗲 †◎┃ 🚻 ⓢ
Leisure ⬥ PS *See advertisement on page 325*

Dunas
17470 ☎ 972 520400
website www.campinglasdunas.com
Level extensive grassland site with young poplars, some of medium height, on the beach, totally subdivided.
➲ 5km SE of village. From l'Escala asphalt road to San Martin then track for 2.5km.
Open May-Sep **Site** 30HEC 👹 ⬥ 🏠 🚐 🗛 **Facilities** 🏠 🛁 ⊙ 🚰 ⊘ ⊛
Services 🗲 †◎┃ 🚻 ⓢ **Leisure** ⬥ PS *See advertisement on page 327*

Palmeras
ctra de la Platja, 17470 ☎ 972 520506 ▤ 972 550285
e-mail info@campinglaspalmeras.com
website www.campinglasplmeras.com
On level grassland with plenty of shade.
➲ From Sant Pere Pescador to beach, 200m from sea.
Open 31 Mar-20 Oct **Site** 5HEC 👹 ⬥ 🏠 **Prices** ⋔ 2.46-3.85 pitch 13.05-34
Facilities 🏠 🛁 ⊙ 🚰 ⊘ ⊛ **Services** 🗲 †◎┃ 🚻 ⓢ **Leisure** ⬥ PS **Off-site** ⬥R

SITGES BARCELONA

El Garrofer
Ctra C-31-Km. 3g, 8870 ☎ 93 8941780 ▤ 93 8110623
e-mail info@garroferpark.com **website** www.garroferpark.com
An area close to the beach with many pine trees, surrounded by a golf course and the Garraf nature reserve.
Open 20 Jan-18 Dec **Site** 8HEC 👹 ⬤ ⬥ 🏠 🚐 **Prices** ⋔ 2.86-5.03
🚘 4.47-6.76 🚐 15.36-19.82 🗛 1.88-3.77 **Facilities** 🏠 🛁 ⊙ 🚰 ⊘ ⊛
Services 🗲 †◎┃ 🚻 ⓢ **Leisure** ⬥ P **Off-site** ⬥S

TARADELL BARCELONA

Vall
Cami de la Vallmitjana, 08552 ☎ 93 8126336 ▤ 93 8126027
website www.campinglavall.com
Set in the mountains near the Guilleries-Montseny, with good recreational facilities.
Open 8 Jan-21 Dec **Site** 8HEC 👹 ⬥ ⬥ 🏠 🚐 **Facilities** 🏠 🛁 ⊙ 🚰 ⊘ ⚒ ⊛
Services 🗲 †◎┃ 🚻 ⓢ **Leisure** ⬥ P

TORROELLA DE MONTGRI GIRONA

Delfin Verde
17257 ☎ 972 758450 ▤ 972 760070
e-mail info@eldelfinverde.com **website** www.eldelfinverde.com
On undulating ground with some pine trees, and an open meadow beside the long sandy beach.
➲ 2km S of Torroella de Montgri towards Begur, left towards Maspinell & sea for 4.8km.
Open Apr-Sep **Site** 35HEC 👹 ⬥ 🏠 🚐 **Prices** ⋔ 4-4.50 pitch 13-39
Facilities 🏠 🛁 ⊙ 🚰 ⊘ ⊛ **Services** 🗲 †◎┃ 🚻 ⓢ **Leisure** ⬥ PRS

See advertisement on page 328

TOSSA DE MAR GIRONA

Cala Llevadó
17320 ☎ 972 340314 ▤ 972 341187
e-mail info@calallevado.com **website** www.calallevado.com
Magnificent terraced site with hairpin roads overlooking three bays, all suitable for bathing. The narrow, winding drives are quite steep in parts. Separate section for caravans.
➲ Coast road towards Lloret de Mar, 4km turn towards sea.
Open May-Sep **Site** 17HEC 👹 ⬥ 🏠 🗛 **Facilities** 🏠 🛁 ⊙ 🚰 ⊘ ⊛ Ⓟ
Services 🗲 †◎┃ 🚻 ⓢ **Leisure** ⬥ PS *See advertisement on this page*

Site 6HEC (site size) 👹 grass ⬤ sand ⬥ stone ⬥ little shade 🏠 partly shaded ⬥ mainly shaded 🏠 bungalows for hire
🚐 caravans for hire 🗛 tents for hire ⊗ no dogs **Prices** ⋔ adult per night 🚘 car per night pp per person per night 🚐 caravan per night
🗛 tent per night 🚐 (static)-caravan hire per week

Facilities 🏠 shop 🚿 shower ⊙ electric points for razors 🔌 electric points for caravans ℗ parking by tents permitted 🅿 compulsory separate car park
Services 🍴 café/restaurant 🍺 bar ⊘ Camping Gaz International ⚒ gas other than Camping Gaz ➕ first aid facilities 🧺 laundry
Leisure ⚓ swimming L-Lake P-Pool R-River S-Sea **Off-site** All facilities within 2km

Can Marti

17320 ☎ 972 340851 ▤ 972 342461
e-mail info@campingcanmarti.net
website www.campingcanmarti.net

Pleasant, unspoiled site in a partly wooded location. Good modern facilities. English spoken.

➲ 1km from sea.

Open 25 May-11 Sep **Site** 10HEC 🌊 🌳 **Prices** ♠ 5-8 🚐 3-5 🚙 5-8 ▲ 5-8 **Facilities** ⚕ 🍴 ⊙ 🚱 ∅ ② **Services** 🛒 🍴 🛂 🗒 **Leisure** ≈ PRS
Off-site ≈L

Tossa

ctra Llagostera, 17320 ☎ 972 340547 ▤ 972 341531

Meadowland and deciduous forest in a quiet, isolated valley, 3km from the sea.

➲ 3km SW near GE 681 Tossa de Mar-Llagostera, site 0.6km along unmade road.

Open Apr-Sep **Site** 9.5HEC 🌊 🌳 🏠 **Facilities** ⚕ 🍴 ⊙ 🚱 ∅ 🚿 ② **Services** 🛒 🍴 🛂 🗒 **Leisure** ≈ PS

VALLROMANES BARCELONA

El Vedado

08188 ☎ 93 5729026 ▤ 93 5729621
e-mail vedado@campingsonline.com
website www.campingelvedado.com

A valley site surrounded by wooded mountains with the beach only a short drive away. Ideal for visiting Barcelona.

➲ A17 exit 13 for Masnou, C32 exit 8 for Granollers.

Open Mar-15 Nov **Site** 100HEC 🌊 🌊 🌳 🏠 🚐 ▲ **Prices** ♠ 6.50 🚐 6 pitch 6 🚐 (static)420 **Facilities** ⚕ 🍴 ⊙ 🚱 ∅ ② **Services** 🛒 🍴 🛂 🗒 **Leisure** ≈ P **Off-site** ≈S

VILALLONGA DE TER GIRONA

Conca de Ter

ctra Camprodon-Setcases s/n, 17869
☎ 972 740629 ▤ 972 130171
e-mail concater@concater.com
website www.concater.com

A pleasant family site in wooded surroundings with a variety of recreational facilities.

➲ Between Camprodón and Setcases, 20km from French border.

Open All year **Site** 3.2HEC 🌊 🌳 🏠 ▲ **Facilities** ⚕ 🍴 ⊙ 🚱 ∅ 🚿 ② **Services** 🛒 🍴 🛂 🗒 **Leisure** ≈ PR **Off-site** 🍴 🛒 🍴 ∅ 🚿 ≈R

VILANOVA I LA GELTRÚ BARCELONA

Vilanova Park

08800 ☎ 93 8933402 ▤ 93 8935528
e-mail info@vilanovapark.es
website www.vilanovapark.es

A well-equipped family site on the edge of a densely wooded area close to the coast in the Catalonian wine-producing area. Modern sanitary block.

➲ A7 exit 29.

Open All year **Site** 51HEC 🌊 🌊 🌳 🏠 🚐 **Facilities** ⚕ 🍴 ⊙ 🚱 ∅ 🚿 ② **Services** 🛒 🍴 🛂 🗒 **Leisure** ≈ P **Off-site** ≈LS

See advertisement on this page

OPEN ALL YEAR

VILANOVA park

Situated in a very quiet area, 50 km south of Barcelona in the wine and cava region of Catalonia. Very modern installations. 2 enormous swimming pools (1.000 m2) and paddling pools. Multicolouredfountain with water jets. Excellent restaurant in old Catalan mansion. Al facilities of a first class site. Children programmes and organised leisure. Private pine trees and palm covered park (40 ha). Ideal climate. Bus service to the beach. Golf at 1 km.
Special offers for old age pensioners from September till June on sites and Bungalows (80 with air-cond.)
Autopista highway Barcelona.-Tarragona, exit 29; coming from Tarragona exit 30 and follow signs towards Vilanova-Sitges.

Ecological private park

Apartado 64
E-08800 Vilanova i la Geltrú (Barcelona)
Tel. (34) 93 893 34 02
Fax (34) 93 893 55 28
www.vilanovapark.es
info@vilanovapark.es
reservas@vilanovapark.es

NEW: COVERED SWIMMING POOL AND SPA.

WiFi ZONE

CENTRAL

ALBARRACIN TERUEL

Ciudad de Albarracin

Camino de Gea, Arrabal, 44100 ☎ 978 710197 ▤ 978 710107
website www.campingalbarracin.com

A modern site on mainly level ground with good facilities.

➲ Signed from A1512.

Open 15 Mar-Oct **Site** 1.4HEC 🌊 🌳 🏠 **Prices** ♠ 3.37 🚐 3.37 🚙 3.47 ▲ 3.37 **Facilities** ⚕ ⊙ 🚱 ∅ ② **Services** 🛒 🍴 🛂 🗒 **Off-site** 🍴 🍴 ≈LPR

ARANJUEZ MADRID

Internacional de Aranjuez

Soto Del Rebollo S/N, 28300 ☎ 91 8911395 ▤ 91 8911395
e-mail info@campingaranjuez.com
website www.campingaranjuez.com

Site divided in two parts with trees and lawns in a large castle park.

➲ Off NIV at Km 46 into village, 200m beyond Firestone fuel station turn sharp NE for 1km.

Open All year **Site** 33HEC 🌊 🌳 🏠 **Prices** ♠ 4-5.50 🚙 4-5.50 ▲ 4-5.50 **Facilities** ⚕ 🍴 ⊙ 🚱 ∅ ② **Services** 🛒 🍴 🛂 🗒 **Leisure** ≈ PR

CABRERA, LA MADRID

Pico de la Miel

28751 ☎ 91 8688082 ▤ 91 8688541
e-mail info@picodelamiel.com **website** www.picodelamiel.com
Open All year **Site** 10HEC 🌊 🌳 🏠 **Prices** ♠ 5.60 🚐 4.80-5.60 🚙 5.60 ▲ 5.40 **Facilities** ⚕ 🍴 ⊙ 🚱 ∅ ② **Services** 🛒 🍴 🛂 🗒 **Leisure** ≈ P **Off-site** 🚿

Spain

CUENCA CUENCA

Cuenca

Carretera Cuenca-Tragacete KM7, 16147
☎ 969 231656 📄 969 231656
e-mail info@campingcuenca.com
website www.campingcuenca.com
A modern site in a peaceful wooded location.
⮞ *N towards Mariana.*

Open 16 Mar-14 Oct **Site** 23HEC 🌿 🍂 🏠 **Prices** ⋔ 4.80 🚗 4.40
🚐 5.80 ⛺ 5.80 **Facilities** 🅿 🖭 ⊙ ⊕ 🔯 ∅ ⊛ **Services** 🍴 🍽 ⊞ 🖸
Leisure ⊛ P **Off-site** ⊛LR

ESCORIAL, EL MADRID

El Escorial

ctra Guadarrama, km 3500, 28280 ☎ 91 8902412 📄 91 8961062
e-mail info@campingelescorial.com
website www.campingelescorial.com
Pleasant wooded surroundings with good recreational facilities.

Open All year **Site** 40HEC 🌿 🍂 🏠 **Prices** ⋔ 5.28-5.61 🚗 5.28-5.61
🚐 5.28-5.61 ⛺ 5.28-5.61 **Facilities** 🅿 🖭 ⊙ ⊕ 🔯 ∅ ⊛ **Services** 🍴 🍽 ⊞ 🖸
Leisure ⊛ P   *See advertisement on this page*

FUENTE DE SAN ESTEBAN, LA SALAMANCA

Cruce

37200 ☎ 923 440130
e-mail campingelcruce@yahoo.es
Useful stopover site in a quiet location in the Castillian countryside.
⮞ *50m from N620 at Km291.*

Open Jul-Sep **Site** 0.5HEC 🌿 🍂 🏠 **Prices** ⋔ 3.50 🚗 3 🚐 4
⛺ 3 **Facilities** 🅿 🖭 ⊙ ⊕ 🔯 ∅ ⊛ **Services** 🍴 ⊞ 🖸 **Off-site** 🍽 ⊛R

GARGANTILLA DE LOZOYA MADRID

Monte Holiday

28739 ☎ 91 8695278 📄 91 8695278
e-mail monteholiday@monteholiday.com
website www.monteholidays.com
A terraced site with modern facilities in a beautiful mountain setting.
⮞ *Off N1 at Km69 towards Cotos for 10km.*

Open All year **Site** 30HEC 🌿 🍂 🍃 🏠 **Facilities** 🅿 🖭 ⊙ ⊕ ∅ ⊛
Services 🍴 🍽 ⊞ 🖸 **Leisure** ⊛ P **Off-site** 🖭 🍴 🍽 ⊛LR

GETAFE MADRID

Alpha

Ctra. N-4, km 12,400, 28906 ☎ 91 6958069 📄 91 6831659
e-mail info@campingalpha.com
website www.campingalpha.com
Surrounded by pine woods at roughly the geographical centre of
Spain with well-defined pitches and modern facilities. Direct bus
service to Madrid.
⮞ *Via NIV at Km12.4.*

Open All year **Site** 4.8HEC ⊜ 🍂 🏠 ⛺ 🔯 **Prices** ⋔ 6.50 🚗 6.70 🚐 6.70
⛺ 6.70 **Facilities** 🅿 🖭 ⊙ ⊕ ∅ ⊛ ⊛ **Services** 🍴 🍽 ⊞ 🖸 **Leisure** ⊛ P

See advertisement on page 331

Site 6HEC (site size) 🌿 grass ⊜ sand 🍂 stone ♣ little shade 🌳 partly shaded 🌲 mainly shaded 🏠 bungalows for hire
🚐 caravans for hire ⛺ tents for hire ⊗ no dogs **Prices** ⋔ adult per night 🚗 car per night pp per person per night 🚐 caravan per night
⛺ tent per night 🚐 (static)-caravan hire per week

MADRID MADRID

Arco Iris

28670 ☎ 91 6160387 ▤ 91 6160059
e-mail madrid@bungalowsarcoiris.com
website www.bungalowsarcoiris.com
A family site in a peaceful location, yet with easy access to Madrid.
➲ M40 Madrid ring road exit 36 to Boadilla del Monte, continue towards Villaviciosa to Km12.
Open All year **Site** 4HEC ♨ ♨ ♨ **Prices** ⚑ 6 ⚐ 6 ⚑ 6 ⚐ 6
⚑ (static)378 **Facilities** ⚲ 🛁 ⊙ ⚡ ⊘ ⚑ ⚑ **Services** ⚑ ⚑ ⚑ ⚑
Leisure ⚭ P

Osuna

av de Logrono, 28042 ☎ 91 7410510 ▤ 91 3206365
On long stretch of land, shade being provided by pines, acacias and maple. Some noise from airfield, road and railway.
➲ N11 from town centre towards Barajas, 7.5km turn right at Km1 after railway underpass.
Open All year **Site** 2.3HEC ♨ ♨ **Prices** ⚑ 6.31 ⚐ 6.31 ⚑ 6.31 ⚑ 6.31
Facilities ⚲ 🛁 ⊙ ⚡ ⚑ **Services** ⚑ ⚑ ⚑ ⚑ **Off-site** ⚑ ⊘ ⚑ ⚑LPR

MALPARTIDA DE PLASENCIA CÁCERES

Parque Natural de Monfrague

Ctra Plasencia-Trujillo km-10, 10680 ☎ 927 459220 ▤ 927 459233
website www.campingmonfrague.com
A modern site with well-defined pitches and good facilities.
➲ 9km from Ex 208.
Open All year **Site** 7HEC ♨ ♨ ⚑ **Prices** ⚑ 3.70 ⚐ 3.20 ⚑ 3.70 ⚑ 3.70
Facilities ⚲ 🛁 ⊙ ⚡ ⊘ ⚑ **Services** ⚑ ⚑ ⚑ ⚑ **Leisure** ⚭ P **Off-site** ⚑

MÉRIDA BADAJOZ

Lago de Proserpina

Apdo 121, 06800 ☎ 924 123055 ▤ 924 317555
e-mail campingproserpina@estudiarte.com
website www.campingproserpina.com
Open May-Dec **Site** 5.5HEC ♨ ♨ ♨ ♨ ⚑ **Facilities** ⚲ 🛁 ⊙ ⚡ ⊘ ⚑
Services ⚑ ⚑ ⚑ ⚑ **Leisure** ⚭ LP **Off-site** ⚭P

MIRANDA DEL CASTAÑAR SALAMANCA

El Burro Blanco

37660 ☎ 923 161100 ▤ 923 161100
e-mail camping.elburroblanco@gmail.com
A well-equipped site in an area of woodland overlooking the village.
➲ 1km from village centre.
Open Apr-Sep **Site** 3.5HEC ♨ ♨ ♨ **Prices** ⚑ 5.14 pitch 8.56
Facilities ⚲ ⊙ ⚡ ⚑ **Services** ⚑ ⚑ ⚑ ⚑ **Off-site** 🛁 ⚑ ⊘ ⚭PR

NAVALAFUENTE MADRID

Camping Piscis

28729 ☎ 91 8432268 ▤ 91 8471341
e-mail campiscis@campiscis.com
website www.campiscis.com
Spacious pitches surrounded by oak trees.
➲ N1 exit 50 towards Guadalix de la Sierra.
Open All year **Site** 23HEC ♨ ♨ ♨ ⚑ **Prices** ⚑ 5.10-5.35 ⚐ 5.10-5.35
⚑ 5.10-5.35 ⚑ 4.20-5.35 **Facilities** ⚲ 🛁 ⊙ ⚡ ⊘ ⚑ ⚑ **Services** ⚑ ⚑ ⚑ ⚑
Leisure ⚭ P

SALAMANCA SALAMANCA

Don Quijote

ctra. Aldealengua km 4, Cabrerizos, 37193
☎ 923 209052 ▤ 923 209052
e-mail info@campingdonquijote.com
website www.campingdonquijote.com
➲ NE of town towards Aldealengua.
Open All year **Site** 6.5HEC ♨ ♨ ♨ ⚑ ⚑ **Facilities** ⚲ 🛁 ⊙ ⚡ ⊘ ⚑
Services ⚑ ⚑ ⚑ ⚑ **Leisure** ⚭ PR

See advertisement on this page

SANTA MARTA DE TORMES SALAMANCA

Regio

ctra Salamanca/Madrid Km4, 37900
☎ 923 138888 ▤ 923 138044
e-mail recepcion@campingregio.com
website www.campingregio.com
A pleasant site, divided into several fields.
➲ 100m from N501 Salamanca-Avila, behind Hotel Jardin-Regio.
Open All year **Site** 3HEC ♨ ♨ ♨ ⚑ **Facilities** ⚲ 🛁 ⊙ ⚡ ⊘ ⚑
Services ⚑ ⚑ ⚑ ⚑ **Leisure** ⚭ PR

SEGOVIA SEGOVIA

Acueducto

40004 ☎ 921 425000 ▤ 921 425000
e-mail information@campingacueducto.com
website www.campingacueducto.com
➲ SE next to N601 at Km112
Open Apr-Sep **Site** 3HEC ♨ ♨ ⚑ ⚑ **Prices** ⚑ 4.50-5 ⚐ 4.50-5 ⚑ 5-5.50
Facilities ⚲ 🛁 ⊙ ⚡ ⊘ ⚑ **Services** ⚑ ⚑ ⚑ ⚑ **Leisure** ⚭ P
Off-site ⚑ ⚭L

Facilities 🛁 shop ⚲ shower ⊙ electric points for razors ⚡ electric points for caravans ⚑ parking by tents permitted ⚑ compulsory separate car park
Services ⚑ café/restaurant ⚑ bar ⊘ Camping Gaz International ⚑ gas other than Camping Gaz ⚑ first aid facilities ⚑ laundry
Leisure ⚭ swimming L-Lake P-Pool R-River S-Sea **Off-site** All facilities within 2km

TOLEDO TOLEDO

Greco

45004 ☎ 925 220090 ▤ 925 220090
e-mail elgreco@retemail.es
website www.accom.nct/elgreco
Few shady terraces on slope leading down to the River Tajo. On SW outskirts of town.

➲ *From town centre C401 Carretera Comarcal SW for 2km, right at Km28, 300m towards Puebla de Montalban.*

Open All year **Site** 2.5HEC ❤ ❤ ❤ ➡ **Prices** ⋏ 5.80 ⋙ 5.60
➡ 5.60 Å 5.60 **Facilities** ↖ ⓘ ⊙ ⊖ ⊘ ☂ **Services** ☎ ⍩ ➕ ⊟
Leisure ⌷ PR **Off-site** ⚒

VALDEMAQUEDA MADRID

El Canto la Gallina

28295 ☎ 91 8984820 ▤ 91 8984823
e-mail camping@elcantolagallina.com
website www.elcantolagallina.com
Wooded location at the foot of a mountain.

Open All year **Site** 12.5HEC ❤ ❤ ❤ ➡ ⊗ **Prices** ⋏ 5.35-6.42 ⋙ 4.28
➡ 5.35-6.42 Å 4.81-5.35 **Facilities** ↖ ⓘ ⊙ ⊖ ⊘ ☂ **Services** ☎ ⍩ ➕ ⊟
Leisure ⌷ P **Off-site** ⌷R

VILLAMAYOR SALAMANCA

Ruta de la Plata

Camino Alto de Villamayor, 37184 ☎ 923 289574 ▤ 923 289574
e-mail reception@campingrutadelaplata.com
website www.campingrutadelaplata.com
Open All year **Site** 1.2HEC ❤ ❤ **Facilities** ↖ ⓘ ⊙ ⊖ ⊘ ☂ **Services** ☎
⍩ ➕ ⊟ **Leisure** ⌷ P **Off-site** ⍩

SOUTH EAST COAST

ALCOSSEBRE CASTELLÓN

Playa Tropicana

12579 ☎ 964 412463 ▤ 964 412805
e-mail info@playatropicana.com
website www.playatropicana.com
On a 0.5km-long sandy beach 3km from the village.

➲ *Motorway exit 44, onto CN340 N for 3km, turn towards sea at Km1018.*

Open May-Oct **Site** 3HEC ❤ ❤ ➡ ⊗ **Prices** pitch 17-58 (incl 2 persons)
pp3.20-6.40 **Facilities** ↖ ⓘ ⊙ ⊖ ⊘ ⚒ ☂ **Services** ☎ ⍩ ➕ ⊟
Leisure ⌷ PS

Ribamar

Partida Ribamar s/n, 12579 ☎ 964 761163 ▤ 964 761163
e-mail campingribamar@telefonica.net
website www.campingribamar.com
Quiet wooded site with individual pitches, set between the sea and mountains.

Open Jul-Dec **Site** 2.2HEC ❤ ❤ ❤ ➡ **Prices** ⋏ 2.80-4.50 pitch 7.90-26.75
Facilities ↖ ⓘ ⊙ ⊖ ⊘ ☂ **Services** ☎ ⍩ ➕ ⊟ **Leisure** ⌷ PS
Off-site ⌷S

ALFAZ DEL PI ALICANTE

Excalibur

Camino, Viejo del Albir s/n, 03580 ☎ 96 6867139 ▤ 96 6866928
e-mail c-m@camping-medieval.com
website www.camping-medieval.com
Open All year **Site** 12HEC ❤ ❤ ➡ **Facilities** ↖ ⓘ ⊙ ⊖ ⊘ ☂
Services ☎ ⍩ ➕ ⊟ **Leisure** ⌷ P **Off-site** ⌷S

ALTEA ALICANTE

Cap Blanch

Playa del Cap-Blanch, 3590 ☎ 96 5845946
A well-equipped site on Albir beach backed by imposing mountains.
Good sports and recreational facilities.

➲ *A7 exit 65.*

Open All year **Site** 4HEC ❤ ❤ ➡ **Prices** ⋏ 6 ⋙ 6 ➡ 7 Å 6
Facilities ↖ ⊙ ⊖ ⊘ ☂ **Services** ⍩ ➕ ⊟ **Leisure** ⌷ S **Off-site** ⓘ ⊘ ➕

AMETLLA DE MAR, L' TARRAGONA

L'Ametlla Village Platja

Paratge Santes Creus, 43860 ☎ 977 267784 ▤ 977 267868
e-mail info@campingametlla.com
website www.campingametlla.com
A modern site with good facilities and direct access to two beaches.
Improved access road.

➲ *2km W, S of A7.*

Open All year **Site** 8HEC ❤ ❤ ❤ ➡ Å **Prices** ⋏ 2.30-5.50 pitch 8-19.50
Facilities ↖ ⓘ ⊙ ⊖ ⊘ ⚒ ☂ **Services** ☎ ⍩ ➕ ⊟ **Leisure** ⌷ PS

BENICARLÓ CASTELLÓN

Alegria del Mar

Playa Norte, 12580 ☎ 964 470871 ▤ 964 470871

➲ *Via CN340 1046km.*

Open All year **Site** 10HEC ❤ ❤ ➡ **Prices** ⋏ 2.50-5 ⋙ 2.50-5 Å 2.50-5
Facilities ↖ ⓘ ⊙ ⊖ ⊘ ☂ **Services** ☎ ⍩ ➕ ⊟ **Leisure** ⌷ PS

BENICASIM CASTELLÓN

Bonterra Park

av Barcelona 47, 12560 ☎ 964 300007 ▤ 964 300008
e-mail info@bonterrapark.com
website www.bonterrapark.com
Between the railway line and avenida de Barcelona with a number of deciduous trees.

➲ *300m N towards Las Villas de Benicasim.*

Open All year **Site** 5HEC ❤ ❤ ➡ **Prices** ⋏ 3.27-5.35 ⋙ 3.64-5.35
Å 2.74-4.28 pitch 13.27-37.18 **Facilities** ↖ ⓘ ⊙ ⊖ ⊘ ⚒ ☂
Services ☎ ⍩ ➕ ⊟ **Leisure** ⌷ P **Off-site** ⊘ ⚒ ⌷PS

BENIDORM ALICANTE

Arena Blanca

av Dr Severo Ochoa 44, 03503 ☎ 96 5861889 ▤ 96 5861107
e-mail info@camping-arenablanca.es
website www.camping-arenablanca.es
A modern site with good facilities.

➲ *Via N332 Benidorm-Altea.*

Open All year **Site** 2.2HEC ❤ ❤ ➡ **Prices** ⋏ 2-6 ⋙ 2-6 ➡ 11 Å 5.50
Facilities ↖ ⓘ ⊙ ⊖ ⊘ ☂ **Services** ☎ ⍩ ➕ ⊟ **Leisure** ⌷ PS

Site 6HEC (site size) ❤ grass ❤ sand ❤ stone ❤ little shade ❤ partly shaded ❤ mainly shaded ➡ bungalows for hire
➡ caravans for hire Å tents for hire ⊗ no dogs **Prices** ⋏ adult per night ⋙ car per night pp per person per night ➡ caravan per night
Å tent per night ➡ (static)-caravan hire per week

Armanello

av Comunidad, 03500 ☎ 96 5853190 ▤ 96 5853100

e-mail armanello@camping-arenablanca.es

website www.camping-arenablanca.es

Divided by bushes with large pitches on terraces under olive and palm trees next to a small orange grove.

➲ *N of town off N332 at Km123.1.*

Open All year **Site** 1.6HEC ♨ ♣ ♠ ⚑ ⅄ **Prices** ♠ 5-5.50 ⇔ 2-5.50 ⚑ 12-16 ⅄ 5-5.50 **Facilities** ⋔ ⚕ ⊙ ☻ ⌀ ⚑ ⅋ **Services** ⛟ ⚑ ⌑ ⓢ **Leisure** ⚘ PS

Benisol

av Comunidad Valenciana S/N, 3503

☎ 96 5851673 ▤ 96 5860895

A modern family site with plenty of facilities. The large pitches are separated by hedges and the centre of Benidorm is within easy reach.

➲ *NE of Benidorm off N332 towards Altea.*

Open All year **Site** 7HEC ♨ ♣ ♠ ⚑ **Facilities** ⋔ ⚕ ⊙ ☻ ⌀ ⚑ ⅋

Services ⛟ ⚑ ⌑ ⓢ **Leisure** ⚘ P

BENISA ALICANTE

Fanadix

ctra Calpe-Moraira Km 5, 03720 ☎ 96 5747307 ▤ 96 5747307

e-mail campingfanadix@campingfanadix.com

website www.campingfanadix.com

Terraced site completely divided into pitches.

➲ *10km E & 400m from the sea. Access off of AV-1445.*

Site 1.6HEC ♨ ♣ ♠ **Facilities** ⋔ ⊙ ☻ ⚑ ⅋ **Services** ⛟ ⚑ ⌑ ⓢ **Leisure** ⚘ P **Off-site** ⚕ ⌀ ⚘ S

CAMBRILS TARRAGONA

Playa Cambrils-Don Camilo

Av Diputación 42, 43850 ☎ 977 361490 ▤ 977 364988

e-mail camping@playacambrils.com

website www.playacambrils.com

Divided into pitches, lying on both sides of the coast road in a wooded location.

➲ *2km N of town towards Salou & W of bridge over river.*

Open 30 Mar-14 Oct **Site** 9HEC ♨ ♣ ♠ **Facilities** ⋔ ⚕ ⊙ ☻ ⚑ ⌀ ⅋ **Services** ⛟ ⚑ ⌑ ⓢ **Leisure** ⚘ P **Off-site** ⚏ ⚘ S

See advertisement on this page

CAMPELLO ALICANTE

Costa Blanca

c Convento 143, 03560 ☎ 965 630670 ▤ 965 630670

e-mail info@campingcostablanca.com

website www.campingcostablanca.com

On most level ground scattered with old olive and eucalyptus trees. The Alicante-Denia railway line runs behind the camp.

➲ *Off N332 at Km94.2 & fuel station onto narrow gravel track towards sea for 0.5km.*

Open All year **Site** 1.1HEC ♨ ♣ ♠ ⚑ ⅄ **Prices** ♠ 3.35-4.75 ⇔ 3.35-4.75 ⚑ 5.25-7.05 ⅄ 3.35-4.75 **Facilities** ⋔ ⚕ ⊙ ☻ ⚑ ⌀ ⚏ ⅋ **Services** ⛟ ⚑ ⌑ ⓢ **Leisure** ⚘ P **Off-site** ⚘ S

CUNIT TARRAGONA

Mar de Cunit

Playa Cunit, 43881 ☎ 977 674058 ▤ 977 675006

e-mail mardecunit@seker.es **website** www.mardecunit.com

A friendly site on level ground overlooking the beach.

Open 15 May-15 Sep **Site** 1.2HEC ♨ ♣ ♠ **Facilities** ⋔ ⚕ ⊙ ☻ ⚑ ⌀ ⅋ **Services** ⛟ ⚑ ⌑ ⓢ **Leisure** ⚘ LS **Off-site** ⌑

GUARDAMAR DEL SEGURA ALICANTE

Mare Nostrum

3140 ☎ 96 5728073 ▤ 96 5728073

e-mail cmarenostrum@wanadoo.es

Partially terraced meadow with some shade from roofing.

➲ *Off N332 Alicante-Cartagena near Km38.5 towards sea.*

Open 15 Apr-15 Sep **Site** 20HEC ♨ ♣ ♠ **Facilities** ⋔ ⚕ ⊙ ☻ ⚑ ⌀ ⚏ ⅋ **Services** ⛟ ⚑ ⌑ ⓢ **Leisure** ⚘ PS **Off-site** ⚑ ⚘ LS

Marjal

Cartagena-Alicante Rd (N 332), 03140

☎ 966 725022 ▤ 966 726695

e-mail camping@marjal.com

website www.campingmarjal.com

Located in Dunas de Guardamar national park next to the Segura estuary, alongside pine and eucalyptus forests with access to fine sandy beaches.

Open All year **Site** 3.5HEC ♨ ♣ ♠ **Prices** ♠ 5-8 ⇔ 3 pitch 18-32 **Facilities** ⋔ ⚕ ⊙ ☻ ⌀ ⚏ ⅋ **Services** ⛟ ⚑ ⌑ ⓢ **Leisure** ⚘ P **Off-site** ⚕ ⛟ ⌑ ⚘ S

See advertisement on page 334

Spain

Site 6HEC (site size) ❀ grass ● sand ❀ stone ♣ little shade ♣ partly shaded ♣ mainly shaded ⛺ bungalows for hire ⛟ caravans for hire ⛺ tents for hire ⊗ no dogs **Prices** ⚲ adult per night ⛗ car per night pp per person per night ⛟ caravan per night ⛺ tent per night ⛟ (static)-caravan hire per week

Spain

Palm Mar

E -03140 ☎ 96 5728856 ▤ 96 5728856
e-mail campingpalmmar@hotmail.com
Open Jun-Sep **Site** 2HEC ⬤ ❀ **Prices** ♠ 5.50-6 ▲ 5.50-6 pitch 14-15
Facilities ⋔ ⓘ ⊙ ⊕ ⊘ ⓟ **Services** ⊞ ⦿ ✚ ⑤ **Leisure** ♨ S
Off-site ⦿ ♨P

HOSPITALET DE L'INFANT, L' TARRAGONA

El Templo del Sol

Platja del Torn, 43890 ☎ 977 810486 ▤ 977 811306
Site with modern sanitary installations and good recreational facilities
on a 1.5km-long beach. This is a naturist site. Only families or holders
of an International Naturism Carnet are allowed.
➲ A3 exit 38, 4km towards sea.
Open Apr-20 Oct **Site** ⬤ ❀ ⚓ ⊗ **Facilities** ⋔ ⓘ ⊙ ⊕ ⊘ ⓟ
Services ⊞ ⦿ ✚ ⑤ **Leisure** ♨ PS

JARACO VALENCIA

San Vincente

Playa Xeraco, 46770 ☎ 96 2888188 ▤ 96 2888147
website www.campingsanvincente.com
Level subdivided site with some trees.
➲ Off N332 Jaraco at Km332 towards Playa, off at Km304 &
site 3.5km.
Open All year **Site** 5HEC ⬤ ❀ **Prices** ♠ 3.73-4.25 ⊕ 5.11-5.95
▲ 3.73-4.25 **Facilities** ⋔ ⊙ ⊕ ⓟ **Services** ⊞ ⦿ ✚ ⑤ **Leisure** ♨ S
Off-site ⓘ ⊘ ⚓ ♨PR

MARINA, LA ALICANTE

International la Marina

Ctra. N-332 km76, 03194 ☎ 96 5419200 ▤ 96 5419110
e-mail info@campinglamarina.com
website www.campinglamarina.com
A modern site in a wooded setting, 0.5km from a sandy beach.
➲ At Km79 on Alicante-Cartagena road.
Open All year **Site** 6.3HEC ⬤ ⚓ **Facilities** ⋔ ⓘ ⊙ ⊕ ⊘ ⚓ ⓟ
Services ⊞ ⦿ ✚ ⑤ **Leisure** ♨ P **Off-site** ♨S

See advertisement on this page

MIRAMAR PLAYA VALENCIA

Coelius

av del Mar, 46711 ☎ 96 2819574 ▤ 96 2818897
e-mail camping@coelius.com
website www.coelius.com
A site with modern facilities, 0.5km from Miramar beach.
➲ Via N430.
Open All year **Site** 2HEC ⬤ ❀ ⚓ ⊕ **Prices** ♠ 3.04-4.55 ⊕ 3.05-4.55
⊕ 7.65-11.60 ▲ 4.55-6.80 ⊕ (static)187.74-297.13 **Facilities** ⋔ ⓘ ⊙ ⊕
⊘ ⚓ ⓟ **Services** ⊞ ⦿ ✚ ⑤ **Leisure** ♨ P **Off-site** ♨S

Facilities ⓘ shop ⋔ shower ⊙ electric points for razors ⚓ electric points for caravans ⓟ parking by tents permitted ⓟ compulsory separate car park
Services ⦿ café/restaurant ⊞ bar ⊘ Camping Gaz International ⚓ gas other than Camping Gaz ✚ first aid facilities ⑤ laundry
Leisure ♨ swimming L-Lake P-Pool R-River S-Sea **Off-site** All facilities within 2km

MONT-ROIG DEL CAMP TARRAGONA

Marius
43892 ☎ 977 810684 🖷 977 179658
e-mail schmid@teleline.es
website www.campingmarius.com
Pitches are planted with flowers and shrubs. Separate section for dog owners.
➲ *Off N340 Tarragona-Valencia at Km1137, through 4.9m-wide railway underpass (height 3.65m) towards beach.*
Site 4.5HEC 😃 😃 😃 😃 **Facilities** 🌴 🖻 ⊙ 🚿 ⌀ ® **Services** ⦿ 🍴 ➕ 🖥 **Leisure** 🏊 S

Playa Montroig
Ctra. N-340, km 1136, 43300 ☎ 977 810637 🖷 977 811411
e-mail info@playamontroig.com
website www.playamontroig.com
An ideal holiday centre for the whole family with sanitary installations of the highest quality. Situated on a fine sandy beach and surrounded by tropical gardens, this site offers a range of sports and recreational facilities and is noted for its helpful and friendly staff.
➲ *AP7 exit 37 or 38, onto N340, left at Km1136.*
Open 16 Mar-29 Oct **Site** 35HEC 😃 🏠 😃 ⊗ **Prices** 🚶 5-6 🚗 5-6 pitch 52-99 (incl 2 persons) **Facilities** 🌴 🖻 ⊙ 🚿 ⌀ ® **Services** ⦿ 🍴 ➕ 🖥 **Leisure** 🏊 PS

Torre Del Sol
43892 ☎ 977 810486 🖷 977 811306
e-mail info@latorredelsol.com
website www.latorredelsol.com
A level tidy grassland site on two levels, with young poplars and some of medium height between a long stretch of beach and the railway.
➲ *Off N340 at Km224.1 towards sea.*
Open 15 Mar-23 Oct **Site** 24HEC 😃 😃 🏠 🚿 🚗 Å ⊗ **Facilities** 🌴 🖻 ⊙ 🚿 ⌀ ® **Services** ⦿ 🍴 ➕ 🖥 **Leisure** 🏊 PS

See advertisement on page 337

NAVAJAS CASTELLÓN

Altomira
12470 ☎ 964 713211 🖷 964 713512
e-mail reservas@campingaltomira.com
website www.campingaltomira.com
Terraced site in the Palancia valley, with touring pitches on the higher levels.
➲ *A23 Sagunto to Teruec*
Open All year **Site** 2.5HEC 😃 😃 🏠 **Prices** 🚶 4.80 🚗 3.50 🚐 5.90 Å 4.50 **Facilities** 🌴 🖻 ⊙ 🚿 ⌀ **Services** ⦿ 🍴 ➕ 🖥 **Leisure** 🏊 P **Off-site** 🏊 LR

OLIVA VALENCIA

Azul
Apartado de Correos 96, 46780 ☎ 96 2854106 🖷 96 2854096
e-mail campingazul@ctv.es
website www.campingazul.com
A well-equipped site with direct access to the beach.
Open All year **Site** 2.5HEC 😃 😃 🏠 **Prices** 🚶 4.10 Å 3.50 pitch 12.50-14.50 **Facilities** 🌴 🖻 ⊙ 🚿 ⌀ ® **Services** ⦿ 🍴 ➕ 🖥 **Leisure** 🏊 S **Off-site** 🍴 🏊 R

Euro Camping
46780 ☎ 96 2854098 🖷 96 2851753
e-mail info@eurocamping-es.com
website www.eurocamping-es.com
On a wide sandy beach between orange groves and well-shaded with poplar and eucalyptus trees.
➲ *Off N332 at Km184.9, 0.6km from Oliva, towards sea for 3.3km, site signed. Narrow access road & blind corners.*
Open All year **Site** 4.5HEC 😃 😃 😃 🏠 **Prices** 🚶 2.28-4.55 pitch 8.77-31.40 **Facilities** 🌴 🖻 ⊙ 🚿 ⌀ 🚿 ® **Services** ⦿ 🍴 ➕ 🖥 **Leisure** 🏊 S **Off-site** 🏊 R

See advertisement on this page

Ferienplatz Olé
46780 ☎ 96 2857517 🖷 96 2857517
e-mail camping-ole@hotmail.com
website www.camping-ole.com
An extensive site with some pitches among dunes.
➲ *Off N332 at Km 209.9 5km S of Oliva, 3km onto part asphalt road through orchard.*
Open Apr-Sep **Site** 46HEC 😃 😃 🏠 **Facilities** 🌴 🖻 ⊙ 🚿 ⌀ ® **Services** ⦿ 🍴 ➕ 🖥 **Leisure** 🏊 S **Off-site** ➕

Site 6HEC (site size) 😃 grass 😃 sand 😃 stone 🌴 little shade 😃 partly shaded 😃 mainly shaded 🏠 bungalows for hire
🚐 caravans for hire Å tents for hire ⊗ no dogs **Prices** 🚶 adult per night 🚗 car per night pp per person per night 🚐 caravan per night
Å tent per night 🚐 (static)-caravan hire per week

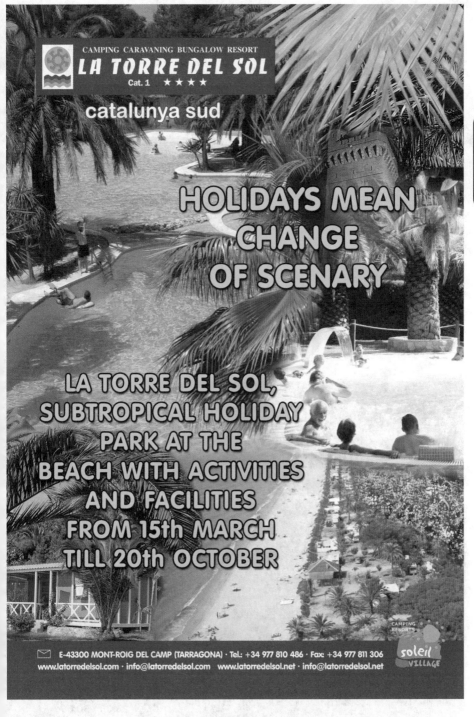

CAMPING CARAVANING BUNGALOW RESORT

LA TORRE DEL SOL
Cat. 1 ★★★★

catalunya sud

HOLIDAYS MEAN CHANGE OF SCENARY

LA TORRE DEL SOL, SUBTROPICAL HOLIDAY PARK AT THE BEACH WITH ACTIVITIES AND FACILITIES FROM 15th MARCH TILL 20th OCTOBER

E-43300 MONT-ROIG DEL CAMP (TARRAGONA) · Tel.: +34 977 810 486 · Fax: +34 977 811 306
www.latorredelsol.com · info@latorredelsol.com www.latorredelsol.net · info@latorredelsol.net

CAMPING RESORTS
soleil VILLAGE

Facilities 🏠 shop 🚿 shower ☺ electric points for razors 🔌 electric points for caravans ⛺ parking by tents permitted 🅿 compulsory separate car park
Services 🍴 café/restaurant 🍺 bar 🗭 Camping Gaz International ⛽ gas other than Camping Gaz ➕ first aid facilities 🧺 laundry
Leisure 🏊 swimming L-Lake P-Pool R-River S-Sea **Off-site** All facilities within 2km

Kiko

Playa de Oliva, 46780 ☎ 96 2850905 📠 96 2854320
e-mail kikopark@kikopark.com
website www.kikopark.com

Family holiday camp, divided into pitches, lying between marshland and vineyard. The sea can be reached by crossing a dyke and there are sunshade roofs.

➲ A7 exit 61, onto CN332 towards Oliva.

Open All year **Site** 4HEC 🌤 🌳 🏠 **Prices** ♠ 6.30 🚗 6.30 pitch 10.90-33.90 **Facilities** 🌳 🖂 ⊙ � 🕖 🏪 ⑫ **Services** 🍴 🍽 ➕ 🚿 **Leisure** ⚓ PS
Off-site ⚓ P ➕

OROPESA DEL MAR CASTELLÓN

Didota

av de la Didota, 12594 ☎ 964 319551 📠 964 319557
e-mail fenollosa@infonegocio.com

Open 16 Mar-14 Oct **Site** 1.7HEC 🌤 🌳 🏠 🏠 **Facilities** 🌳 🖂 ⊙ � 🕖 ⑫
Services 🍴 🍽 ➕ 🚿 **Leisure** ⚓ P **Off-site** ⚓ S

PEÑISCOLA CASTELLÓN

Camping Eden

Avda. Papa Luna, KM.6, 12598 ☎ 964 480562 📠 964 489828
e-mail camping@camping-eden.com
website www.camping-eden.com

A modern, well-appointed site on level ground close to the seafront.

➲ Off A7 for Peñiscola, turn towards Benicarlo.

Open All year **Site** 4HEC 🌳 🏠 **Prices** ♠ 0.80-8.07 pitch 6.83-47.90 **Facilities** 🌳 🖂 ⊙ � 🕖 🚿 ⑫ **Services** 🍴 🍽 ➕ 🚿 **Leisure** ⚓ P
Off-site 🖂 🍴 🍽 ⚓ S

PUEBLA DE FARNALS VALENCIA

Brasa

46137 ☎ 96 1460388

Level meadowland site with poplars near village centre.

➲ Motorway Barcelona-Valencia exit 3, towards Playa Puebla de Farnals.

Open All year **Site** 3.9HEC 🌤 🌳 **Facilities** 🌳 ⊙ � ⑫ **Services** 🍴 🍽 ➕ 🚿 **Leisure** ⚓ P **Off-site** 🖂 ⚓ S

RODA DE BARÀ TARRAGONA

Playa Barà

43883 ☎ 977 802701 📠 977 800456
e-mail info@barapark.es **website** barapark.es

A well maintained lively site with a Mediterranean flavour. The central avenue is lined with palm trees and colourful flowers and leads to a sandy beach.

➲ For access turn off the N340 near the Arco de Barà (triumphant arch) and drive towards the sea for 1.5 km.

Open 23 Mar-Sep **Site** 14.5HEC 🌤 🌳 🏠 **Prices** ♠ 3-9.40 🚗 4.50-9.40 � 🚗 9.40 ⚑ 3.50-9.40 **Facilities** 🌳 🖂 ⊙ � ⑫ **Services** 🍴 🍽 ➕ 🚿 **Leisure** ⚓ P **Off-site** ⚓ S *See advertisement on this page*

SALOU TARRAGONA

Pineda de Salou

Playa de la Pineda, 43840 ☎ 977 373080 📠 977 373081
e-mail info@campingglapineda.com
website www.campingglapineda.com

A well-equipped site close to the sea.

➲ At Km 5 on the Tarragona-Salou road.

Open All year **Site** 4HEC 🌤 🌳 🏠 🏠 **Facilities** 🌳 🖂 ⊙ � 🕖 🚿 ⑫ **Services** 🍴 🍽 ➕ 🚿 **Leisure** ⚓ P **Off-site** 🖂 🍴 🍽 🚿 ⚓ S

Site 6HEC (site size) 🌤 grass 🌊 sand 🌳 stone ♣ little shade 🏠 partly shaded 🌤 mainly shaded 🏠 bungalows for hire 🚗 caravans for hire ⚑ tents for hire ⊗ no dogs **Prices** ♠ adult per night 🚗 car per night pp per person per night � caravan per night ⚑ tent per night � (static)-caravan hire per week

Sanguli-Salou

43840 ☎ 977 381641 ▤ 977 384616

e-mail mail@sanguli.es

website www.sanguli.es

A large, family site in pleasant wooded surroundings, 50m from the beach, with extensive sports and entertainment facilities.

➲ *3km SW from Port Aventura, 50m inland from coast road to Cambrils.*

Open 23 Mar-28 Oct **Site** 23HEC 🌊 ☺ 🏕 **Prices** ✿ 6.42 pitch 13.91-43.87 **Facilities** ℕ 🛁 ⊕ ➡ ⌀ ⓟ **Services** ▥ ⑪ 🗙 ▤ **Leisure** ⚓ PS

See advertisement on page 340

Union

c Pompeu Fabra 37, 43840 ☎ 977 384816 ▤ 977 351444

e-mail reservas@campinglaunion.com

website www.campinglaunion.com

A well-equipped site in wooded surroundings, 350m from the sea.

➲ *On S outskirts, 1km from Port Aventura theme park.*

Open Apr-Sep **Site** 3.8HEC 🌊 ☺ 🏕 **Facilities** ℕ 🛁 ⊕ ➡ ⌀ ⓟ **Services** ▥ ⑪ 🗙 ▤ **Leisure** ⚓ PS

SANTA OLIVA TARRAGONA

Santa Oliva

Jaume Balmes 122, 43710 ☎ 977 679546 ▤ 977 679228

➲ *At Km3 on Vendrell-Santa Oliva road.*

Open All year **Site** 2HEC 🌊 🏕 **Facilities** ℕ ⊕ ➡ ⌀ ⌙ ⓟ **Services** ▥ ⑪ 🗙 ▤ **Leisure** ⚓ P **Off-site** 🛁 ⑪ ⚓S

TAMARIT TARRAGONA

Caledonia

43008 ☎ 977 650098 ▤ 977 652867

e-mail caledonia@camping-caledoia.com

website www.camping-caledonia.com

A well-appointed site in wooded surroundings, 0.8km from the sea.

➲ *On N340 at Km1172.*

Open 18 Jun-20 Sept **Site** 3.5HEC 🌊 ☺ 🏕 🏕 **Facilities** ℕ 🛁 ⊕ ➡ ⌀ ⓟ **Services** ▥ ⑪ 🗙 ▤ **Leisure** ⚓ P **Off-site** ⚓S

Trillas Platja Tamarit

43008 ☎ 977 650249 ▤ 977 650926

e-mail info@campingtrillas.com

website www.campingtrillas.com

On several terraces planted with olive trees next to a farm, 50m from the sea.

➲ *Off N340 at Km1.172 8km N of Tarragona, over narrow rail-way bridge (beware oncoming traffic).*

Open 31 Mar-8 Oct **Site** 4HEC 🏕 **Facilities** ℕ 🛁 ⊕ ➡ ⌀ ⌙ ⓟ **Services** ▥ ⑪ 🗙 ▤ **Leisure** ⚓ PRS

TARRAGONA TARRAGONA

Tamarit-Park

Platja Tamarit, 43008 ☎ 977 650128 ▤ 977 650451

e-mail tamaritpark@tamarit.com

website www.tamarit.com

Well-kept site at the sea beneath Tamarit castle. One section lies under tall shady trees, and a new section lies in a meadow with some trees.

➲ *Off N340 at Km1171.5 towards beach, left at end of road.*

Open 7 April-Oct **Site** 17HEC 🌊 ☺ 🏕 🏕 ⛺ **Facilities** ℕ 🛁 ⊕ ➡ ⌀ ⓟ **Services** ▥ ⑪ 🗙 ▤ **Leisure** ⚓ PRS

See advertisement on this page

TAMARIT PARK CAMPING, BUNGALOWS

Exceptionally beautiful situation, peaceful but well connected. 3kms.long sandy beach from Tamarit Castle to Altafulla. Perfect for families with young children. Near Tarragona (World Heritage City) and only 20kms. away from Universal Port Aventura amusement park.
• Restaurant and snack-bar by the beach and also by the swimming-pools • Sports area open until midnight. Tennis courts, football, basketball, pingpong, paddle courts, Fitness centre, snack bar, Cable TV, etc. Water sports. Activities for all ages. Disco at the Amphitheatre • Social club with two TV areas, internet, billiard tables, snack bar with terrace , live music at night • Fee reductions up to 45% outside high season • 30/03/2007 – 14/10/2007.
Platja Tamarit - Ctra. N - 340 km. 1172
43008 Tarragona
Tel. (34) 977 65 01 28 - Fax. (34) 977 65 04 51
www.tamarit.com   tamaritpark@tamarit.com

VENDRELL, EL TARRAGONA

San Salvador

av Palfuriana 68, 43880 ☎ 977 680804 ▤ 977 680804

e-mail campingsantsalvador@trx.com

website www.campingsantsalvador.com

On two large grassy terraces and has some sunshade roofs. Near the sea in the centre of the town.

➲ *A7 exit 31, in centre of Comarruga-Sant Salvador.*

Open 6 Apr-Sep **Site** 2.9HEC 🌊 ☺ 🏕 **Facilities** ℕ 🛁 ⊕ ➡ ⌀ ⓟ **Services** ▥ ⑪ 🗙 ▤ **Off-site** ⚓PS

Vendrell Platja

43820 ☎ 977 694009 ▤ 977 694106

e-mail vendrell@camping-vendrellplatja.com

website www.camping-vendrellplatja.com

A large family site in a pleasant wooded location close to the beach.

Open 7 Apr-Oct **Site** 7.3HEC 🌊 ☺ 🏕 **Facilities** ℕ 🛁 ⊕ ➡ ⌀ ⓟ **Services** ▥ ⑪ 🗙 ▤ **Leisure** ⚓ P **Off-site** ⚓S 🗙

VILANOVA DE PRADES TARRAGONA

Serra de Prades

Sant Antoni, 43439 ☎ 977 869050 ▤ 977 869050

e-mail info@serradeprades.com

website www.serradeprades.com

A fine site close to the beach and within easy reach of Barcelona and the Port Aventura theme park.

➲ *Via N-240*

Open All year **Site** 5HEC 🌊 ☺ 🏕 🏕 **Prices** ✿ 5.45 ➡ 5.45 ⛺ 5.45 **Facilities** ℕ 🛁 ⊕ ➡ ⌀ ⌙ ⓟ **Services** ▥ ⑪ 🗙 ▤ **Leisure** ⚓ P **Off-site** 🛁 ▥ ⑪ ⌀ ⌙ ⚓LR

Facilities 🛁 shop ℕ shower ⊕ electric points for razors ➡ electric points for caravans ⓟ parking by tents permitted ⓟ compulsory separate car park
Services ⑪ café/restaurant ▥ bar ⌀ Camping Gaz International ⌙ gas other than Camping Gaz 🗙 first aid facilities ▤ laundry
Leisure ⚓ swimming L-Lake P-Pool R-River S-Sea **Off-site** All facilities within 2km

Spain

PARC DE VACANCES
Sanguli Salou
CAMPING & BUNGALOW PARK
●●●● 1ª CAT.

✉ **Apartat de Correus 123**
43840 SALOU • Tarragona • España
☎ Camping   +34 977 38 16 41
☎ Bungalow +34 977 38 90 05
    Fax   +34 977 38 46 16
@ mail@sanguli.es
    www.sanguli.es

Online reservations: www.sanguli.es

Luxurious holidays at the Costa Daurada

Salou • Costa Daurada • España

VINAROZ CASTELLÓN

Garoa-Sol de Riu Playa
12500 ☎ 964 496356 ▤ 964 496368
Wooded surroundings close to the sea with modern facilities.
Open All year **Site** 5.5HEC ♛ ♨ ♨ **Facilities** ↾ ⚲ ⊕ ☯ ⌀ ⓟ
Services ⊨ ⑽ ➕ ⓢ **Leisure** ♒ PRS **Off-site** ♒R

NORTH COAST

AJO-BAREYO CANTABRIA

Cabo de Ajo
ctra al Faro, 39170 ☎ 942 670624 ▤ 942 630725
e-mail losmolinos@ceoecant.es
On level ground 2km from the coast.
➲ *A8 exit Beranga Km185.*
Open Jun-Sep **Site** ♛ ♨ **Prices** ♠ 3.50 ☯ 7.50 ▲ 3.80 **Facilities** ↾ ⊕ ☯
⌀ ⓟ **Services** ⊨ ⑽ ⓢ **Leisure** ♒ P **Off-site** ⚲ ⊨ ⑽ ♒S

BAREYO CANTABRIA

Los Molinos de Bareyo
ctra Bareyo-Güemes, 39190 ☎ 942 670569 ▤ 942 670569
e-mail losmolinosdebareyo@ceoecant.es
website www.campinglosmolinosdebareyo.com
A quiet location with fine views.
Open Jun-Sep **Site** 12HEC ♛ ♨ ♨ **Prices** ♠ 4.50-6 ☯ 8.50-12
▲ 5.50-7.50 **Facilities** ↾ ⚲ ⊕ ☯ ⌀ ⓟ **Services** ⊨ ⑽ ➕ ⓢ **Leisure** ♒ P
Off-site ♒S

BARREIROS LUGO

Gaivota
Playa de Barreiros, 27793 ☎ 982 124451 ▤ 982 124451
website www.campingpobladogaivota.com
Site leads down to a sandy beach with windsurfing. The main
buildings have been designed and built by the owner, who is a
painter.
Open 5 Jun-Sep **Site** 1HEC ♛ ♨ ♨ ▲ **Prices** ♠ 4 ☯ 4 ☯ 4.50
▲ 4 **Facilities** ↾ ⚲ ⊕ ☯ ⌀ ⓟ **Services** ⊨ ⑽ ➕ ⓢ **Leisure** ♒ S
Off-site ♒PR

BERGONDO LA CORUÑA

Santa Marta-Coruña
15166 ☎ 981 795826
e-mail info@campingsantamarta.com
website www.campingsantamarta.com
Open 15 May- 15 Sept **Site** 2.8HEC ♛ ♨ ♨ ▲ **Facilities** ↾ ⚲ ⊕ ☯ ⌀ ⚒
ⓟ **Services** ⊨ ⑽ ➕ ⓢ **Leisure** ♒ PS

CADAVEDO ASTURIAS

Regalina
ctra de la Playa, 33788 ☎ 98 5645056 ▤ 98 5645014
e-mail laregalina@la-regalina.com
website www.laregalina.com
A modern site with good facilities noted for its mountain and sea
views.
➲ *On N632 between Luarca and Avilés.*
Open All year **Site** 1HEC ♛ ♨ ♨ ▲ **Facilities** ↾ ⚲ ⊕ ☯ ⌀ ⓟ
Services ⊨ ⑽ ➕ ⓢ **Leisure** ♒ P **Off-site** ⚲ ⊨ ⑽ ⚒ ♒S ➕

CASTRO-URDIALES CANTABRIA

Castro
Barrio Campijo s/n, 39700 ☎ 942 867423 ▤ 942 630725
e-mail losmolinos@ceoecant.es
A quiet location with terraces.
➲ *A8 exit Castro-Urdiales Km151.*
Open Jun-Sep **Site** 3HEC ♛ ♨ ♨ **Facilities** ↾ ⚲ ⊕ ☯ ⌀ ⓟ
Services ⊨ ⑽ ➕ ⓢ **Leisure** ♒ P **Off-site** ♒S

COMILLAS CANTABRIA

Comillas
ctra M-Noriga, 39520 ☎ 942 720074 ▤ 942 720074
e-mail info@campingcomillas.com
website www.campingcomillas.com
Level grassland site to the right of the road to the beach.
➲ *E on C6316 at Km23.*
Open Jun-Sep **Site** 3HEC ♛ ♨ **Prices** ♠ 4.68 pitch 11.21 **Facilities** ↾ ⚲
⊕ ☯ ⌀ ⓟ **Services** ⊨ ⑽ ➕ ⓢ **Leisure** ♒ S **Off-site** ⑽ ♒P

CUDILLERO ASTURIAS

Amuravela
El Pito, 33150 ☎ 985 590995 ▤ 985 590995
e-mail www.camping@lamuravela.com
website www.lamuravela.com
Open Jun-15 Sep **Site** 2.5HEC ♛ ♨ ♨ ♨ **Facilities** ↾ ⚲ ⊕ ☯ ⌀ ⓟ
Services ⊨ ⑽ ➕ ⓢ **Leisure** ♒ P **Off-site** ♒RS

FOZ LUGO

San Rafael
Playa de Peizas, 27789 ☎ 982 132218 ▤ 982 132218
e-mail info@campingsanrafael.com
website www.campingsanrafael.com
A small site on open, level ground 50m from the beach.
➲ *2km from town centre.*
Open May-Sep **Site** 1.2HEC ♛ ♨ ♨ ▲ **Facilities** ↾ ⚲ ⊕ ☯ ⌀ ⓟ
Services ⊨ ⑽ ➕ ⓢ **Off-site** ⚒ ♒LPRS

FRANCA, LA ASTURIAS

Las Hortensias
Playa de la Franca, 33590 ☎ 98 5412442 ▤ 98 5412153
e-mail lashortensias@campinglashortensias.com
website www.campinglashortensias.com
A well-maintained site with good facilities beside the La Franca beach.
Open Jun-Sep **Site** 2.8HEC ♛ ♨ **Prices** ♠ 5.78 ☯ 4.81 ☯ 7.38 ▲ 5.94
Facilities ↾ ⚲ ⊕ ☯ ⌀ ⓟ **Services** ⊨ ⑽ ➕ ⓢ **Leisure** ♒ RS
Off-site ⚒

ISLARES CANTABRIA

Playa Arenillas
39798 ☎ 942 863152 ▤ 942 863152
e-mail cueva@mundivia.es
website www.campingplayaarenillas.com
Well-equipped site in meadowland with some pine trees, 100m from
the beach.
➲ *N off N634 at Km155.8 for 100m. Steep entrance.*
Open Apr-Sep **Site** 2HEC ♛ ♨ ▲ ⓧ **Prices** ☯ 4.66 ▲ 4.81 **Facilities** ↾
⚲ ⊕ ☯ ⌀ ⓟ **Services** ⊨ ⑽ ➕ ⓢ **Leisure** ♒ S

Facilities ⚲ shop ↾ shower ⊕ electric points for razors ☯ electric points for caravans ⓟ parking by tents permitted ⓠ compulsory separate car park
Services ⑽ café/restaurant ⊨ bar ⌀ Camping Gaz International ⚒ gas other than Camping Gaz ➕ first aid facilities ⓢ laundry
Leisure ♒ swimming L-Lake P-Pool R-River S-Sea **Off-site** All facilities within 2km

LAREDO CANTABRIA

Carlos V

pl de Carlos V, 39770 ☎ 942 605593

Camp surrounded by walls and buildings on western outskirts of Laredo.

➲ *Off N634 at Km171.6 onto avenue towards sea, left before beach, round rdbt on plaza de Carlos V.*

Open Apr-Oct **Site** 10HEC ❤ ♣ ⚏ ⚍ 🛆 **Facilities** ⋔ ⓘ ⊙ 🚰 ⌀ ⓟ **Services** ♨ 🍴 ✚ 🗑 **Off-site** 🍴 ⚍ 🏖LPRS

LLANES ASTURIAS

Barcenas

Antigua CN 634, 33500 ☎ 98 5402887 📠 98 5400175

Site beside the River Carrocedo, 100m from town centre and beaches.

➲ *SW of town beyond hospital.*

Open Jun-Sep / Easter **Site** 2.2HEC ❤ ♣ ⚏ 🛆 **Facilities** ⋔ ⓘ ⊙ 🚰 ⌀ ⓟ **Services** ♨ 🍴 ✚ 🗑 **Off-site** 🍴 ⚍ 🏖S

Palacio de Garaña

33591 ☎ 98 5410075 📠 98 5410298

e-mail info@campingpalacio.com

website www.campingpalacio.com

Situated in the grounds of the former Palace of the Marquis of Argüelles, the site is enclosed by stone walls and has good facilities.

Open May-15 Sept **Site** 2.8HEC ❤ ♣ ⚏ ⚍ **Facilities** ⋔ ⓘ ⊙ 🚰 ⌀ ⚍ ⓟ **Services** ♨ 🍴 ✚ 🗑 **Leisure** 🏖 PRS **Off-site** 🏖L

LUARCA ASTURIAS

Cantiles

33700 ☎ 98 5640938 📠 98 5640938

e-mail cantiles@campingloscantiles.com

website www.campingloscantiles.com

Meadowland site beautifully situated high above the cliffs. Limited shade from bushes. Footpath to the bay 70m below.

➲ *N634 from Oviedo, turn at Km308.5 towards Faro de Luarca after Firestone fuel station, in Villar de Luarca turn R & 1km to site.*

Open All year **Site** 2.3HEC ❤ ♣ ⚏ **Facilities** ⋔ ⓘ ⊙ 🚰 ⌀ ⓟ **Services** ♨ 🍴 ✚ 🗑 **Off-site** 🍴 ⚍ 🏖PRS ✚

MOTRICO (MUTRIKU) GUIPÚZCOA

Aitzeta

20830 ☎ 943 603356

On two sloping meadows, partially terraced. Lovely view of the sea nearby.

➲ *0.5km NE on C6212 turn at KmSS56.1.*

Open All year **Site** 1.5HEC ❤ ♣ ⚏ **Facilities** ⋔ ⓘ ⊙ 🚰 ⌀ ⓟ **Services** ♨ 🍴 ✚ 🗑 **Leisure** 🏖 S **Off-site** 🍴

NOJA CANTABRIA

Los Molinos

c,la Ria S/N, 39180 ☎ 942 630426 📠 942 630725

e-mail losmolinos@ceoecant.es

website www.campinglosmolinos.com

Pleasant surroundings close to the Emerald coast and fine beaches. Various leisure and sports activities.

Open Jun-Sep, Etr **Site** 18HEC ❤ ♣ ⚏ **Prices** ♦ 3.45-4.50 🛆 4.50-5.50 pitch 6.80-9.70 **Facilities** ⋔ ⓘ ⊙ 🚰 ⌀ ⓟ **Services** ♨ 🍴 ✚ 🗑 **Leisure** 🏖 P **Off-site** 🏖S

Playa Joyel

Playa de Ris, 39180 ☎ 942 630081 📠 942 631294

e-mail playajoyel@telefonica.net

website www.playajoyel.com

On a level meadow on a peninsula with direct access to the beach.

➲ *Between Laredo & Solares via A-8, exit 185*

Open 8 Apr-Sep **Site** 24HEC ❤ ♣ ⚏ ⚍ ⓧ **Prices** ♦ 3.96-5.89 🚗 12.84-22.47 🛆 6.42 ⚍ (static)441.91-854 **Facilities** ⋔ ⓘ ⊙ 🚰 ⌀ ⓟ **Services** ♨ 🍴 ✚ 🗑 **Leisure** 🏖 PS

ORIO GUIPÚZCOA

CM Playa de Orio

20810 ☎ 943 834801 📠 943 133433

e-mail kanpina@terra.es

On two flat terraces along cliffs and surrounded by hedges.

➲ *Off N634 near Km12.5 in Orio, before bridge over River Orio turn towards sea for 1.5km.*

Open Mar-1 Nov **Site** 3HEC ❤ ♣ ⚏ ⓧ **Facilities** ⋔ ⓘ ⊙ 🚰 ⌀ ⓟ **Services** ♨ 🍴 ✚ 🗑 **Leisure** 🏖 P **Off-site** 🏖RS

PECHÓN CANTABRIA

Arenas

39594 ☎ 942 717188 📠 942 717188

e-mail lasarenas@ctv.es

On terraces between rocks, reaching down to the sea.

➲ *Off N634 E of Unquera at Km74 towards sea & onto road S.*

Open Jun-Sep **Site** 12HEC ❤ ♣ ⚏ **Facilities** ⋔ ⓘ ⊙ 🚰 ⌀ ⓟ **Services** ♨ 🍴 ✚ 🗑 **Leisure** 🏖 PRS

PERLORA-CANDAS ASTURIAS

Perlora

33491 ☎ 98 5870048

On top of a large hill on a peninsula with a few terraced pitches.

➲ *7km W of Gijon. Off N632 towards Luanco for 5km.*

Open Jul-15 Sep **Site** 1.4HEC ❤ ♣ ♣ **Prices** ♦ 4.70 🚗 3.32 ⚍ 4.81 🛆 3.64 **Facilities** ⋔ ⓘ ⊙ 🚰 ⌀ ⓟ **Services** ♨ 🍴 ✚ 🗑 **Leisure** 🏖 S **Off-site** ⚍

REINANTE LUGO

Reinante

27279 ☎ 982 134005 📠 982 134005

Longish site beyond a range of dunes on a lovely sandy beach.

➲ *On N634 at Km391.7.*

Open All year **Site** ❤ ♣ ♣ **Prices** ♦ 3.50 🚗 3.50 ⚍ 3.50 🛆 3 **Facilities** ⋔ ⓘ ⊙ 🚰 ⌀ ⓟ **Services** ♨ 🍴 ✚ 🗑 **Leisure** 🏖 LRS

SAN SEBASTIÁN (DONOSTIA) GUIPÚZCOA

Igueldo

Aita Orkolaga Pasealekua 69, Igueldo, 20008

☎ 943 280490 📠 943 280411

e-mail info@campingigueldo.com

website www.campingigueldo.com

Terraced site on Monte Igualdo divided by hedges.

➲ *From town signs for Monte Igualdo & beach road for 4.5km.*

Open All year **Site** 5HEC ❤ ♣ ⚏ **Prices** ♦ 3.40-4.40 🚗 2.80-3.70 pitch 12.10-28.20 (incl 2 persons) **Facilities** ⋔ ⓘ ⊙ 🚰 ⌀ ⓟ **Services** ♨ 🍴 ✚ 🗑 **Off-site** 🏖S

Site 6HEC (site size) ❤ grass ⚏ sand ♣ stone ♣ little shade ♣ partly shaded ⚏ mainly shaded ⚍ bungalows for hire 🚗 caravans for hire 🛆 tents for hire ⓧ no dogs **Prices** ♦ adult per night 🚗 car per night pp per person per night ⚍ caravan per night 🛆 tent per night ⚍ (static)-caravan hire per week

Spain

SANTIAGO DE COMPOSTELA LA CORUÑA

As Cancelas

r do 25 de Xulls 35, 15704 ☎ 981 580266 ▤ 981 575553
Open All year **Site** 1.8HEC ⚌ ⚐ ⌂ ▲ **Facilities** ⋔ ⓐ ⊙ ⬛ ⊘ ⓟ
Services ⬛ ⦿ ➕ ⓢ **Leisure** ⚓ P

SANTILLANA DEL MAR CANTABRIA

Santillana

39330 ☎ 942 818250 ▤ 942 840183
e-mail complejosantillana@cantabria.com
website www.canrabria.com/complejo-santillana
Slightly sloping meadow with bushes on a hillock within the area of a
restaurant adjoining a swimming pool.
➽ *From Santander turn off after Santillana sign & continue up hill.*
Open All year **Site** 70HEC ⚌ ⚐ ⌂ ⬛ **Prices** ♣ 4.80-5.46 ⛊ 4.80-5.46
⬛ 4.80-5.46 ▲ 3.30 ⬛ (static)42.35-72.14 **Facilities** ⋔ ⓐ ⊙ ⬛ ⊘ ⓟ
Services ⬛ ⦿ ➕ ⓢ **Leisure** ⚓ P

VALDOVIÑO LA CORUÑA

Valdoviño

ctra de la Playa, 15552 ☎ 981 487076 ▤ 981 486131
Six gently sloping fields partly in shade. Located behind Cafeteria Andy
and block of flats with several villas beyond.
➽ *Off C646 towards Cedeira & sea, 0.7km to site.*
Open 10 Apr-Sep **Site** 2HEC ⚌ ⚐ ⌂ **Prices** ♣ 5.35-5.62 ⛊ 5.62-5.88
⬛ 5.88-6.21 **Facilities** ⋔ ⓐ ⊙ ⬛ ⊘ ☇ ⓟ **Services** ⬛ ⦿ ➕ ⓢ
Off-site ⚓LPRS

VIVEIRO LUGO

Vivero

27850 ☎ 982 560004
Set in tall woodland near the beach road and sea.
➽ *Off C642 Barreois-Ortueire at Km 443.1 & signed.*
Open Jun-Sep **Site** 1.2HEC ⚌ ⚐ **Facilities** ⋔ ⓐ ⊙ ⬛ ⊘ ⓟ
Services ⬛ ➕ ⓢ **Off-site** ⓐ ⬛ ⦿ ⚓RS

ZARAUZ (ZARAUTZ) GUIPÚZCOA

Talai Mendi

20800 ☎ 943 830042 ▤ 943 830042
A meadowland site on a hillside without shade, 0.5km from the sea.
Divided by internal roads.
➽ *On outskirts of town, off N634 at Km17.5 by Firestone fuel
station towards sea for 350m (narrow asphalt road).*
Open Jul-Aug **Site** 3.8HEC ⚌ ⚐ **Facilities** ⋔ ⓐ ⊙ ⬛ ⊘ ⓟ
Services ⬛ ⦿ ➕ ⓢ **Leisure** ⚓ S **Off-site** ⚓R

Zarauz

Monte Talai-Mendi, 20800 ☎ 943 831238 ▤ 943 132486
e-mail info@grancampingzarautz.com
website www.grancampingzarautz.com
Site with terraces separated by hedges.
➽ *1.8km from N634 San Sebastian-Bilbao road. Asphalt access
road from Km15.5.*
Open All year **Site** 5HEC ⚌ ⚐ ▲ **Prices** ♣ 4.70 ⛊ 4.70 ⬛ 5.20 ▲ 5.20
Facilities ⋔ ⓐ ⊙ ⬛ ⊘ ⓟ **Services** ⬛ ⦿ ➕ ⓢ **Off-site** ⚓RS

NORTH EAST

ARANDA DE DUERO BURGOS

Costajàn

9400 ☎ 947 502070
Wooded setting with good facilities.
➽ *Off N1 Burgos-Madrid at Km162.1 N of town.*
Open All year **Site** 1.8HEC ⚌ ⚐ ⌂ ⬛ **Facilities** ⋔ ⓐ ⊙ ⬛ ⊘ ⓟ
Services ⬛ ⦿ ➕ ⓢ **Leisure** ⚓ P **Off-site** ⓐ ⬛ ⦿ ☇ ⚓LR

BELLVER DE CERDANYA LLEIDA

Solana del Segre

Ctra N -260 km198, 25720 ☎ 973 510310 ▤ 973 510698
e-mail info@solanadelsegre.com
website www.solanadelsegre.com
A well-equipped site on the River Segre, known for its trout fishing.
➽ *Off N260.*
Open All year **Site** 6.5HEC ⚌ ⚐ ⌂ **Facilities** ⋔ ⓐ ⊙ ⬛ ⊘ ⓟ
Services ⬛ ⦿ ➕ ⓢ **Leisure** ⚓ PR **Off-site** ⚓L

BIESCAS HUESCA

Edelweiss

22630 ☎ 974 485084
Pleasant meadow site on a hill with deciduous trees.
➽ *Off C138 at Km97.*
Open 15 Jun-15 Sep **Site** 50HEC ⚌ ⚐ **Facilities** ⋔ ⓐ ⊙ ⬛ ⊘ ⓟ
Services ⬛ ⦿ ➕ ⓢ **Off-site** ⚓PR

BONANSA HUESCA

Baliera

N-260 km 355,5, 22486 ☎ 974 554016 ▤ 974 554099
e-mail info@baliera.com **website** www.baliera.com
A well-equipped site in a beautiful Pyrenean location on the bank of a
river.
➽ *At Km365.5 on N260.*
Open Jan-Oct & Dec **Site** 5HEC ⚌ ⚐ ⌂ **Prices** ♣ 4.23-5.29 ⬛ 4 ▲ 3.98-
4.97 **Facilities** ⋔ ⓐ ⊙ ⬛ ⊘ ☇ ⓟ **Services** ⬛ ⦿ ➕ ⓢ **Leisure** ⚓ LPR
Off-site ⦿

BORDETA, LA LLEIDA

Prado Verde

25551 ☎ 973 647172 ▤ 973 647172
e-mail foseluisperise@hotmail.com
Level meadowland on River Garona with sparse trees and sheltered by
high hedges from traffic noise.
➽ *On N230 at Km199 behind Pirelli fuel station.*
Open All year **Site** 1.7HEC ⚌ ⚐ ⌂ **Facilities** ⋔ ⓐ ⊙ ⬛ ⊘ ⓟ
Services ⬛ ⦿ ➕ ⓢ **Leisure** ⚓ LPR

BOSSOST LLEIDA

Bedurá-Park

25551 ☎ 973 648293 ▤ 973 647038
e-mail bedurapark@ibercom.com
website www.bedurapark.com
A terraced site in the Aran valley offering spectacular views over the
surrounding mountains. The site, in wooded surroundings, offers all
modern facilities and a variety of sports opportunities.
➽ *Via N230 Km174.4.*
Open Apr-15 Sep **Site** 5HEC ⚌ ⚐ ⌂ ⨯ **Facilities** ⋔ ⓐ ⊙ ⬛ ⊘ ⓟ
Services ⬛ ⦿ ➕ ⓢ **Leisure** ⚓ PR **Off-site** ⚓L

Facilities ⓐ shop ⋔ shower ⊙ electric points for razors ⬛ electric points for caravans ⓟ parking by tents permitted ⓟ compulsory separate car park
Services ⦿ café/restaurant ⬛ bar ⊘ Camping Gaz International ☇ gas other than Camping Gaz ➕ first aid facilities ⓢ laundry
Leisure ⚓ swimming L-Lake P-Pool R-River S-Sea **Off-site** All facilities within 2km

CALATAYUD ZARAGOZA

Calatayud

ctra Madrid-Barcelona KM239, 50300
☎ 976 880592 ▤ 976 880592
Open 15 March-15 Oct **Site** 1.7HEC ◕ ♣ **Facilities** ⋒ ⓘ ⊙ ⊖ ∅ ℗
Services ⊞ ⓘ⓪ ⊞ ⓢ **Leisure** ◈ P **Off-site** ⓘ⓪

ESPOT LLEIDA

Sol I Neu

ctra d'Espot, 25597 ☎ 973 624001 ▤ 973 624107
e-mail camping@solineu.com
A peaceful site in a beautiful mountain setting with modern facilities.
Organised 4WD excursions available.
Open 15 Jun-15 Sep **Site** 1.5HEC ◕ ♣ **Prices** ♠ 5 pitch 13 **Facilities** ⋒ ⓘ
⊙ ⊖ ∅ ℗ **Services** ⊞ ⓢ **Leisure** ◈ PR **Off-site** ⓘ ⊞ ⓘ⓪ ◈L

ESTELLA NAVARRA

Lizarra

Paraje de Ordoiz, 31200 ☎ 948 551733 ▤ 948 554755
Open All year **Site** 4HEC ◕ ♣ ⊕ Å **Facilities** ⋒ ⓘ ⊙ ⊖ ∅ ℗
Services ⊞ ⓘ⓪ ⊞ ⓢ **Leisure** ◈ P

GUINGUETA, LA LLEIDA

Vall d'Aneu

25597 ☎ 973 626390
Meadowland site on rising ground on both sides of the road, partially
in shade. No shade on terrace between the road and the lake.
⮕ On outskirts of town near bypass, C147.
Open May-Sep **Site** 0.5HEC ◕ ♣ **Facilities** ⋒ ⊙ ⊖ ⊿ ℗
Services ⊞ ⓘ⓪ ⊞ ⓢ **Leisure** ◈ P **Off-site** ⓘ ⊞ ⓘ⓪ ∅ ◈LR

HUESCA HUESCA

San Jorge

Ricardo del Arco, 22004 ☎ 974 227416 ▤ 974 227416
e-mail contacto@camping-san-jorge.com
website www.camping-sanjorge.com
Site with sports field surrounded by high walls. Subdivided by hedges,
sparse woodland.
⮕ M123 from town centre towards Zaragoza for 1.5km &
signed.
Open Apr-15 Oct **Site** 0.7HEC ◕ ♣ **Prices** ♠ 4.01 ◈ 4.01 ⊕ 4.28 Å 4.01
Facilities ⋒ ⊙ ⊖ ℗ **Services** ⊞ ⓘ⓪ ⊞ ⓢ **Leisure** ◈ P **Off-site** ⓘ ∅

JACA HUESCA

AT GUASA

Peña Oroel

ctra Jaca-Sabiñanigo, 22700 ☎ 974 360215
Grassland site with rows of high poplars.
⮕ On C134 Jaca-Sabiñanigo road at Km13.8.
Open 15 Jun-15 Sep **Site** 50HEC ◕ ♣ **Facilities** ⋒ ⓘ ⊙ ⊖ ∅ ℗
Services ⊞ ⓘ⓪ ⊞ ⓢ **Leisure** ◈ P

LABUERDA HUESCA

Peña Montañesa

ctra Aínsa-Francia,KM2, 22360 ☎ 974 500032 ▤ 974 500991
e-mail info@penamontanesa.com
website www.penamontanesa.com
A well-equipped family site in a wooded location near the entrance to
the Ordesa and Monte Perdido national park.
Open All year **Site** 10HEC ◕ ♣ ⊕ ⊞ **Prices** ♠ 4.40-5.90 pitch 10-18.50
Facilities ⋒ ⓘ ⊙ ⊖ ∅ ℗ **Services** ⊞ ⓘ⓪ ⊞ ⓢ **Leisure** ◈ P
Off-site ◈LR

MENDIGORRIA NAVARRA

El Molino

ctra N111, 31150 ☎ 948 340604 ▤ 948 340082
e-mail info@campingelmolino.com
website www.campingelmolino.com
Open All year **Site** 15HEC ◕ ♣ ⊕ ⊞ ⊞ Å **Prices** ♠ 3.85 ◈ 4.23 Å 4.92
Facilities ⋒ ⓘ ⊙ ⊖ ∅ ℗ **Services** ⊞ ⓘ⓪ ⊞ ⓢ **Leisure** ◈ PR
Off-site ⊿ ◈R

NÁJERA LA RIOJA

Ruedo

ps San Julian 24, 26300 ☎ 941 360102
Among poplars and the area of the bullring, almost no shade.
⮕ Off N120 Logroño-Burgos in Nájera, along river just before
stone bridge across River Majerilla & left.
Open Etr-10 Sep **Site** 0.5HEC ◕ ♣ **Prices** ♠ 5 ◈ 4.20 ⊕ 5 Å 5
Facilities ⋒ ⓘ ⊙ ⊖ ∅ ℗ **Services** ⊞ ⓘ⓪ ⊞ ⓢ **Off-site** ⊿ ◈PR

NUEVALOS ZARAGOZA

Lago Park

ctra Alhama de Aragón-Nuevalos, 50210
☎ 976 849038 ▤ 976 849038
e-mail info@campingpark.com
website www.campingpark.com
A pleasant location 100m from Laguna de la Tranquera.
⮕ NE towards Alhama de Aragon.
Open Apr-Sep **Site** 3HEC ◕ ♣ ⊕ **Prices** ♠ 5.60 ⊕ 6 Å 5.80
Facilities ⋒ ⓘ ⊙ ⊖ ∅ ℗ **Services** ⊞ ⓘ⓪ ⊞ ⓢ **Leisure** ◈ LPR

ORICAIN NAVARRA

Ezcaba

ctra Francia-Irun km7, 31194 ☎ 948 330315 ▤ 948 331316
e-mail info@campingezcaba.com
website www.campingezcaba.com
Gently sloping meadowland and a few terraces on a flat topped hill.
⮕ N of Pamplona. Off N121 at Km 7.3 towards Berriosuso, after
River Ulzama turn right & uphill.
Open All year **Site** 2HEC ◕ ♣ ⊕ ⊞ **Prices** ♠ 4.20 ◈ 6.90 ⊕ 4.90-6.90
Å 4.45 **Facilities** ⋒ ⓘ ⊙ ⊖ ∅ ⊿ ℗ **Services** ⊞ ⓘ⓪ ⊞ ⓢ **Leisure** ◈ PR
Off-site ◈PR

PANCORBO BURGOS

Desfiladero

9280 ☎ 947 354027
A well-appointed site close to the river.
⮕ Off N1 at Km305.2.
Open All year **Site** 13HEC ◕ ◕ ♣ ⊕ ⊞ **Facilities** ⋒ ⊙ ⊖ ⊞ ℗
Services ⊞ ⓘ⓪ ⊞ ⓢ **Leisure** ◈ L **Off-site** ◈PR

Site 6HEC (site size) ◕ grass ◖ sand ◕ stone ♣ little shade ♣ partly shaded ⊕ mainly shaded ⊞ bungalows for hire
⊞ caravans for hire Å tents for hire ⊗ no dogs **Prices** ♠ adult per night ◈ car per night pp per person per night ⊕ caravan per night
Å tent per night ⊞ (static)-caravan hire per week

PUEBLA DE CASTRO, LA HUESCA

Lago Barasona

crta Nacional 123 A km25, 22435 ☎ 974 545148 ▤ 974 545228
e-mail info@lagobarasona.com
website www.lagobarasona.com
A well-equipped, terraced site in a beautiful setting beside the lake and backed by mountains.
Open Apr-Sep **Site** 5HEC ❦ ♣ ♠ ➡ **Facilities** ⋔ 🖾 ⊙ 🔁 🅿 ⌀ ℗
Services 🍴⏣ 🕯 ⏣ 🖻 **Leisure** ◢ P **Off-site** ◢LR

RIBERA DE CARDÓS LLEIDA

Cardós

25570 ☎ 973 623112 ▤ 973 623183
website www.campingdelcardos.com
Long stretch of meadowland divided by four rows of poplars.
➲ Near electricity plant in Llavorsi turn NE onto Ribera road for 9km, site near hostel Soly Neu.
Open Apr-29 Sep **Site** 3HEC ❦ ♣ ♠ ➡ ⋏ **Prices** ⋏ 4.80 ➡ 4.20-4.50
➡ 4.80 ⋏ 4.80 ➡ (static)280-780 **Facilities** ⋔ 🖾 ⊙ 🔁 🅿 ⌀ ℗
Services 🍴⏣ 🕯 ⏣ 🖻 **Leisure** ◢ PR

SANTO DOMINGO DE LA CALZADA LA RIOJA

Bañares

26250 ☎ 941 342804 ▤ 941 340131
Open All year **Site** 12HEC ❦ ♣ ♠ ➡ ⋏ **Facilities** ⋔ 🖾 ⊙ 🔁 🅿 ⌀ ℗
Services 🍴⏣ 🕯 ⏣ 🖻 **Leisure** ◢ P

SOLSONA LLEIDA

Solsonès

25280 ☎ 973 482861 ▤ 973 481300
e-mail info@campingsolsones.com
website www.campingsolsones.com
A well-equipped site in a picturesque mountain setting with facilities for both summer and winter holidays.
Open All year **Site** 6.3HEC ❦ ♣ ♠ ➡ ⋏ ⊗ **Prices** ⋏ 5.20 ➡ 5.20
➡ 5.20 ⋏ 5.20 ➡ (static)210 **Facilities** ⋔ 🖾 ⊙ 🔁 🅿 ⌀ ℗
Services 🍴⏣ 🕯 ⏣ 🖻 **Leisure** ◢ P

TIERMAS ZARAGOZA

Mar del Pirineo

50682 ☎ 948 398073 ▤ 948 887177
e-mail aytosigues@hotmail.com
On broad terraces sloping down to the banks of the Embalse de Yese. Roofing provides shade for tents and cars.
➲ On N240 at Km317.7.
Open May-Sep **Site** 2.9HEC ❦ ♣ ♠ ♣ ➡ **Facilities** ⋔ 🖾 ⊙ 🔁 ⌀
Services 🍴⏣ 🕯 ⏣ 🖻 **Leisure** ◢ LP

TORLA HUESCA

Ordesa

ctra de Ordesa, 22376 ☎ 974 486146 ▤ 974 486381
e-mail hotelordesa@wanadoo.es
website www.hotelordesa.com
On three terraces between well-kept hedges.
➲ 2km N of the village at Km96 & N of C138.
Open Easter-Oct **Site** 3.5HEC ❦ ♣ ♠ ➡ **Prices** ⋏ 4.25 ➡ 4.25 ➡ 4.90
⋏ 4.25 **Facilities** ⋔ 🖾 ⊙ 🔁 ⌀ ℗ **Services** 🍴⏣ 🕯 ⏣ 🖻 **Leisure** ◢ P
Off-site ◢R

VILLOSLADA DE CAMEROS LA RIOJA

Los Cameros

ctra La Virgen, 26125 ☎ 941 747021 ▤ 941 742091
e-mail info@camping-loscameros.com
website www.camping-loscameros.com
Situated in the Sierra Cebollera national park in the Iberian mountain range.
➲ Off N111 towards Soria & onto Villoslada.
Open All year **Site** 4HEC ❦ ♣ ♠ ➡ ⋏ **Facilities** ⋔ 🖾 ⊙ 🔁 ⌀ ℗
Services 🍴⏣ 🕯 ⏣ 🖻 **Leisure** ◢ R

NORTH WEST

BAIONA PONTEVEDRA

Baiona Playa

ctra Vigo-Baiona (km 19.4), 36393 ☎ 986 350035 ▤ 986 352952
e-mail campingbayona@campingbayona.com
website www.campingbayona.com
On a long sandy peninsula on the Galicia coast with direct access to the beach. The site has modern facilities and a variety of water sports are available.
➲ Autopista AP9 Salida No 5 (Baiona Norte)
Open All year **Site** 4HEC ❦ ♣ ♠ ➡ **Prices** ⋏ 3.97-6.10 ➡ 4.25-6.53
➡ 3.97-6.10 ⋏ 3.97-6.10 **Facilities** ⋔ 🖾 ⊙ 🔁 ⌀ ℗ **Services** 🍴⏣ 🕯 ⏣ 🖻
Leisure ◢ PRS

CUBILLAS DE SANTA MARTA VALLADOLID

Cubillas

47290 ☎ 983 585002 ▤ 983 585016
e-mail info@campingcubillas.com
website www.campingcubillas.com
Meadowland with young trees, subdivided by hedges.
➲ On right of N620 from Burgos between Km100 & Km101.
Open All year **Site** 4HEC ❦ ♣ ♠ ➡ **Facilities** ⋔ 🖾 ⊙ 🔁 ⌀ ℗
Services 🍴⏣ 🕯 ⏣ 🖻 **Leisure** ◢ P **Off-site** ◢R

NIGRÁN PONTEVEDRA

Playa America

36350 ☎ 986 365404 ▤ 986 365404
e-mail oficina@campingplayaamerica.com
website www.campingplayaamerica.com
A modern site in a poplar wood, 300m from a magnificent beach.
➲ Off Vigo-Bayona road at Km 9.250.
Open 15 Jun-15 Sep **Site** 4HEC ❦ ♣ ♠ ➡ **Facilities** ⋔ 🖾 ⊙ 🔁 ⌀ ℗
Services 🍴⏣ 🕯 ⏣ 🖻 **Leisure** ◢ PS **Off-site** ◢R

PORTONOVO PONTEVEDRA

Paxariñas

36970 ☎ 986 723055
Slightly sloping site towards a bay, among dunes and tall pines and young deciduous trees. Lovely beach.
Open All year **Site** 3HEC ❦ ♣ ♠ ⋏ **Facilities** ⋔ 🖾 ⊙ 🔁 ⌀ ℗
Services 🍴⏣ 🕯 ⏣ 🖻 **Leisure** ◢ S

Facilities 🖾 shop ⋔ shower ⊙ electric points for razors 🔁 electric points for caravans ℗ parking by tents permitted 🅿 compulsory separate car park
Services 🍴 café/restaurant 🕯 bar ⌀ Camping Gaz International ⏣ gas other than Camping Gaz 🕯 first aid facilities 🖻 laundry
Leisure ◢ swimming L-Lake P-Pool R-River S-Sea **Off-site** All facilities within 2km

SANTA MARINA DE VALDEON LÉON

El Cares

24915 ☎ 987 742676 ▤ 987 742676
e-mail cares@elcares.com
website elcares.com
Wooded mountain setting with good facilities.
➔ N off N621 from Portilla de la Reina.
Open Jun-Sep **Site** 15HEC ✿ ✿ ✿ **Prices** ⚘ 3.75-4.50 ⚘ 3.75-4.50
Ⓐ 3.21-3.75 **Facilities** ⚘ 🏕 ⊙ ⚘ ⊘ ⚘ ⚘ ⚘ **Services** ⚘ ⓘ ⚘ 🖰
Leisure ⚘ R **Off-site** ⚘L

SAN VICENTE DO MAR PONTEVEDRA

Siglo XXI

36988 ☎ 986 738100 ▤ 986 738113
e-mail info@campingsiglo21.com
website www.campingsiglo21.com
A popular modern site with individual sanitary facilities attached to
each pitch.
Open Jun-Sep **Site** 1.5HEC ✿ ✿ **Prices** ⚘ 3.90-4.90 pitch 10.50-16.90
Facilities ⚘ ⊙ ⚘ ⊘ ⚘ **Services** ⚘ ⓘ ⚘ 🖰 **Leisure** ⚘ PS **Off-site** 🏕 ⚘S

TORDESILLAS VALLADOLID

Astral

Camino de Pollos 8, 47100 ☎ 983 770953 ▤ 983 770953
e-mail info@campingelastral.com
website www.campingelastral.com
A well-equipped site in a pleasant rural location close to the River
Duero.
➔ Motorway exit Tordesillas & signed.
Open Apr-Sep **Site** 3HEC ✿ ✿ ✿ ✿ **Prices** ⚘ 4.20-6 ⚘ 3.60-5 ⚘ 4.20-6
Ⓐ 4.20-6 ⚘ (static)352-672 **Facilities** ⚘ 🏕 ⊙ ⚘ ⊘ ⚘ **Services** ⚘ ⓘ ⚘
🖰 **Leisure** ⚘ P **Off-site** 🖲 ⚘R

VALENCIA DE DON JUAN LÉON

Pico Verde

Ctra C-621 Mayorga-Astorga, 24200
☎ 987 750525 ▤ 987 750525
e-mail campingpicoverd@terra.es
website www.verial.es/campingpicoverde
➔ 6km off A66
Open 23 Jun-10 Sep **Site** 2.7HEC ✿ ✿ **Prices** ⚘ 4.21 ⚘ 4.21 ⚘ 4.21
Ⓐ 4.21 **Facilities** ⚘ 🏕 ⊙ ⚘ ⊘ ⚘ **Services** ⚘ ⓘ ⚘ 🖰 **Leisure** ⚘ P
Off-site ⚘R

VILLAMEJIL LÉON

Rio Tuerto

24711 ☎ 987 605076
Open Jul-Aug **Site** 0.6HEC ✿ ✿ **Facilities** ⚘ 🏕 ⊙ ⚘ ⚘
Services ⚘ ⓘ ⚘ 🖰 **Leisure** ⚘ R **Off-site** 🏕 ⚘ ⓘ

SOUTH

ADRA ALMERIA

Habana

4770 ☎ 950 522127 ▤ 950 522274
A quiet site with good facilities and direct access to the sea.
➔ 2km W on N340 Almeria-Málaga at Km58.3 .
Open All year **Site** 1.5HEC ⚘ ✿ ⚘ Ⓐ **Facilities** ⚘ 🏕 ⊙ ⚘ ⊘ ⚘
Services ⚘ ⓘ ⚘ 🖰 **Leisure** ⚘ S

AGUILAS MURCIA

Calarreona

ctra de Aguilas a Vera, 30880 ☎ 968 413704 ▤ 968 413704
e-mail info@campingcalarreona.com
website www.campingcalarreona.com
A quiet site, 50m from the sea.
➔ Near Km4 on N332 Aguilas-Murcia.
Open All year **Site** 3.6HEC ⚘ ✿ ✿ ⚘ **Facilities** ⚘ 🏕 ⊙ ⚘ ⊘ ⚘
Services ⚘ ⓘ ⚘ 🖰 **Leisure** ⚘ S

ALCAZARES, LOS MURCIA

Cartagonova

30710 ☎ 968 575100 ▤ 968 575225
➔ On CN332 between Los Alcazares and La Union.
Open All year **Site** 30HEC ⚘ ✿ ✿ ⚘ Ⓐ **Facilities** ⚘ 🏕 ⊙ ⚘ ⊘ ⚘
Services ⚘ ⚘ 🖰 **Leisure** ⚘ PS **Off-site** ⓘ 🖰

ALMAYATE MÁLAGA

Almayate Costa

29749 ☎ 952 556289 ▤ 952 556310
e-mail almayatecosta@campings.net
website www.campings.net/almayatecosta
Open 5 May-Sep **Site** 3HEC ✿ ⚘ ✿ ⚘ ⊗ **Facilities** ⚘ 🏕 ⊙ ⚘ ⊘ ⚘
Services ⚘ ⓘ ⚘ 🖰 **Leisure** ⚘ P **Off-site** ⚘S

BAÑOS DE FORTUNA MURCIA

Fuente

30326 ☎ 968 685017 ▤ 968 685125
e-mail info@campingfuente.com
website www.campingfuente.com
A camping ground within a hotel complex with individual bathroom
facilities attached to each pitch and good recreational facilities.
➔ C3223 from Fortuna à Pinoso to Balncario de Fortuna,
signed.
Open All year **Site** 1.9HEC ⚘ ✿ ✿ **Prices** ⚘ 3.25 pitch 8-10
Facilities ⚘ 🏕 ⊙ ⚘ ⊘ ⚘ **Services** ⚘ ⓘ ⚘ 🖰 **Leisure** ⚘ P

BOLNUEVO MURCIA

Garoa Camping Playa de Mazarrón

30877 ☎ 968 150660 ▤ 968 150837
On level ground divided by a footpath and partly bordered by palm
trees.
➔ W off N332 in Puerto de Mazarrón near Km111 towards
Bolnuevo, onto MU road for 4.6km to site, 1km E of Punta Bela.
Open All year **Site** 8.5HEC ⚘ ✿ ✿ **Facilities** ⚘ 🏕 ⊙ ⚘ ⊘ ⚘
Services ⚘ ⓘ ⚘ 🖰 **Leisure** ⚘ PS

CABO DE GATA ALMERIA

Cabo de Gata

04150 ☎ 950 160443 ▤ 950 520003
e-mail info@campingcabodegata.com
website www.campingcabodegata.com
Natural parkland site with separate pitches, 1km from the beach.
➔ N340 exit 467 or 471.
Open All year **Site** 3.6HEC ⚘ ✿ ✿ **Prices** ⚘ 5.25 pitch 11.10
Facilities ⚘ 🏕 ⊙ ⚘ ⊘ 🖰 ⚘ **Services** ⚘ ⓘ ⚘ 🖰 **Leisure** ⚘ PS

See advertisement on page 347

Site 6HEC (site size) ✿ grass ✿ sand ✿ stone ✿ little shade ✿ partly shaded ✿ mainly shaded ✿ bungalows for hire
⚘ caravans for hire Ⓐ tents for hire ⊗ no dogs **Prices** ⚘ adult per night ⚘ car per night pp per person per night ⚘ caravan per night
Ⓐ tent per night ⚘ (static)-caravan hire per week

CARCHUNA GRANADA

Don Cactus

Carchuna-Motril, 18730 ☎ 958 623109 🖹 958 624294

e-mail camping@doncactus.com

website www.doncactus.com

Modern site adjoining the beach. Dogs not allowed in July and August.

⮱ *On N340 Carchuna-Motril at Km343.*

Open All year **Site** 4HEC 🏖 🏕 🛖 **Prices** ♠ 1.61-5.35 pitch 3.60-12

Facilities �showerⓘ⊙⛽🔌🚗⑳ **Services** 🔌🍴➕⬚ **Leisure** ⬤ PS

CARLOTA, LA CORDOBA

Carlos III

ctra N-4 km430, 14100 ☎ 957 300697 🖹 957 3000697

e-mail camping@campingcarlosIII.com

website www.campingcarlosIII.com

Wooded surroundings with modern facilities.

⮱ *NIV exit La Carlota.*

Open All year **Site** 7HEC 🏖 🏕 🛖 **Prices** ♠ 5 🚗 4.50 🚐 5 ⛺ 4.70

🚐 (static)590.80-698.60 **Facilities** �showerⓘ⊙⛽🔌🚗⑳ **Services** 🔌🍴➕⬚

Leisure ⬤ P **Off-site** ⬤PS

CASTILLO DE BAÑOS GRANADA

Castillo de Baños

Castillo de Baños, La Mamola, 18750

☎ 958 829528 🖹 958 829768

e-mail info@campingcastillo.com

website www.campingcastillo.com

Well-equipped site next to the beach.

⮱ *At Km 360 on N340 Castillo de Baños-La Mamola.*

Open All year **Site** 3HEC 🏖 🏕 **Facilities** �showerⓘ⊙⛽🚗⑳

Services 🔌🍴➕⬚ **Leisure** ⬤ PS

CONIL DE LA FRONTERA CÁDIZ

Fuente del Gallo

Fuente del Gallo, 11140 ☎ 956 440137 🖹 956 442036

e-mail camping@campingfuentedelgallo.com

website www.campingfuentedelgallo.com

A well-equipped site in a wooded location 300m from the beach.

⮱ *Signed from N340, Km21.6.*

Open Mar-Oct **Site** 3HEC 🏖 🏕 🛖 ⛺ **Facilities** �showerⓘ⊙⛽🚗⑳

Services 🔌🍴➕⬚ **Leisure** ⬤ P **Off-site** ⬤S

Roche

Carril de Pilahito, s/n, 11149 ☎ 956 442216 🖹 956 232319

e-mail info@campingroche.com

website www.campingroche.com

Spread among pine groves with well-defined pitches close to the beach.

⮱ *Via N-340 from Cádiz to Algeciras, 19.5km.*

Open All year **Site** 3.3HEC 🏖 🏕 🛖 **Prices** ♠ 5.50 🚗 3.70 🚐 9.50

⛺ 4.30 **Facilities** �showerⓘ⊙⛽🚗⑳ **Services** 🔌🍴➕⬚ **Leisure** ⬤ P

Off-site ⬤RS ➕

ESTEPONA MALÁGA

Parque Tropical

29680 ☎ 95 2793618 🖹 95 2793618

A modern site at the foot of the Sierra Bermeja mountains, a short walk from the sea.

⮱ *Via N340 at Km162.*

Open All year **Site** 12.4HEC 🏕 🛖 ⛺ **Prices** ♠ 3.50-5.80 🚗 4.50-6 ⛺ 4.50-6 **Facilities** �showerⓘ⊙⛽🚗⑳ **Services** 🔌🍴➕⬚ **Leisure** ⬤ PS

Off-site ⬤S

FUENTE DE PIEDRA MALÁGA

Espaciosos Rurales

Camino de la Rábita s/n ☎ 952 735294 🖹 952 735461

e-mail info@camping-rural.com

website www.camping-rural.com

Situated within a wildlife reserve on the shores of a lagoon.

Open All year **Site** 🏕 🏖 🏕 🛖 **Prices** ♠ 4.53-4.96 🚗 2.90-3.27

🚐 4.17-4.53 ⛺ 2.90-3.27 **Facilities** �showerⓘ⊙⛽⑳ **Services** 🔌🍴➕⬚

Leisure ⬤ LP **Off-site** 🚗➕

GALLARDOS, LOS ALMERIA

Gallardos

04280 ☎ 950 528324 🖹 950 469596

e-mail campinglosgallardos@hotmail.com

website www.campinglosgallardos.com

Level site with individual pitches, 11km from the sea and 10km from the old Moorish village of Mojacar.

⮱ *0.5km from Km525 on CN340.*

Open All year **Site** 3.5HEC 🏖 🏕 **Prices** ♠ 4.70 🚗 4.70 🚐 4.70 ⛺ 4.70

Facilities �showerⓘ⊙⛽🚗⑳ **Services** 🔌🍴➕⬚ **Leisure** ⬤ P

GRANADA GRANADA

Sierra Nevada

ctra de Jaen 107, 18014 ☎ 958 150062 🖹 958 150954

e-mail campingmotel@terra.es

website www.campingsierranevada.com

Almost level grassy site, in numerous sections, within motel complex.

Open Mar-1 Nov **Site** 3HEC 🏕 🏖 🛖 **Facilities** �showerⓘ⊙⛽🚗⑳

Services 🔌🍴➕⬚ **Leisure** ⬤ P **Off-site** 🚿⬤LRS

Facilities ⓘ shop 🌀 shower ⊙ electric points for razors 🔌 electric points for caravans ⑳ parking by tents permitted ⓟ compulsory separate car park

Services 🍴 café/restaurant 🔌 bar 🚗 Camping Gaz International 🚿 gas other than Camping Gaz ➕ first aid facilities ⬚ laundry

Leisure ⬤ swimming L-Lake P-Pool R-River S-Sea **Off-site** All facilities within 2km

Spain

GUIJARROSA, LA CORDOBA

Campiña

14547 ☎ 957 315303 ▤ 957 315158
e-mail info@campinglacampina.com
website www.campinglacampina.com
A quiet rural setting surrounded by olive trees and elms with modern facilities.

➲ Off N4 at Km424 or Km441 & signs to Santaella & site.
Open All year **Site** 0.7HEC ⬤ ♣ 🏠 ⚊ **Prices** ⋔ 4.25 ⇛ 4.25 ⬛ 4.35 ⚊ 4
Facilities ⬟ 🏠 ⊙ 🔒 ⊘ ⊛ **Services** ⬛ 🍴 ➕ 🔳 **Leisure** ⚍ P

ISLA CRISTINA HUELVA

Giralda

21410 ☎ 959 343318 ▤ 959 343318
e-mail campinggiralda@infonegocio.com
website www.campinggiralda.com
On level ground dotted with trees within easy reach of the beach. Modern facilities and plenty of entertainment.

➲ On Isla Cristina-La Antilla road.
Open All year **Site** 15HEC ⬤ ♣ 🏠 **Prices** ⋔ 3.89-5.19 ⇛ 3.21-4.28 ⬛ 4.21-5.62 ⚊ 3.65 **Facilities** ⬟ 🏠 ⊙ 🔒 ⊘ ⊛ **Services** ⬛ 🍴 ➕ 🔳 **Leisure** ⚍ PR **Off-site** 🍴 ⚍S

ISLA PLANA MURCIA

Madriles

ctra de la Azohia Km45, 30868 ☎ 968 152151 ▤ 968 152092
e-mail camplosmadriles@terra.es
website www.campinglosmadriles.com
A large family site with a variety of recreational facilities.

➲ Via Mazarron-Cartagena road.
Open All year **Site** 7.2HEC ⬤ ♣ 🏠 **Prices** ⋔ 4.49-5.56 pitch 13.48-16.69 **Facilities** ⬟ 🏠 ⊙ 🔒 ⊘ ⚊ ⊛ **Services** ⬛ 🍴 ➕ 🔳 **Leisure** ⚍ PS **Off-site** 🍴

MANGA DEL MAR MENOR, LA MURCIA

La Manga

30370 ☎ 968 563014 ▤ 968 63426
e-mail lamanga@caravaning.es
website caravaning.es
A large family site on the Mar Menor lagoon. Pitches separated by hedges or trees. Good recreational facilities.

➲ Off Cartagena motorway.
Open All year **Site** 32HEC ⬤ ♣ 🏠 ⬛ **Facilities** ⬟ 🏠 ⊙ 🔒 ⊘ ⚊ ⊛ **Services** ⬛ 🍴 ➕ 🔳 **Leisure** ⚍ PS

MARBELLA MÁLAGA

Buganvilla

29600 ☎ 95 2831973 ▤ 95 2831974
e-mail info@campingbuganvilla.com
website www.campingbuganvilla.com
A well-equipped site in a pine forest close to the beach.

➲ E of Marbella off N340 coast road towards Mijas.
Open All year **Site** 4HEC ⬤ ⬤ ♣ 🏠 ⬛ **Facilities** ⬟ 🏠 ⊙ 🔒 ⊘ ⚊ ⊛ **Services** ⬛ 🍴 ➕ 🔳 **Leisure** ⚍ PS

MAZAGÓN HUELVA

Mazagón

cuesta de la Barca s/n, 21130 ☎ 959 376208 ▤ 959 536256
e-mail info@campingplayamazagon.com
website www.campingplayamazagon.com
Undulating terrain among dunes in a sparse pine forest. Long sandy beach.

➲ Off N431 Sevilla-Huelva before San Juan del Puerto towards Moguer, continue S via Palso de la Frontera.
Open All year **Site** 8HEC ⬤ ♣ **Facilities** ⬟ 🏠 ⊙ 🔒 ⊘ ⊛ **Services** ⬛ 🍴 ➕ 🔳 **Leisure** ⚍ P **Off-site** ⚍S

MOJÁCAR ALMERIA

Sopalmo

Sopalmo, 04637 ☎ 950 478413
Open All year **Site** 1.7HEC ⬤ ♣ 🏠 **Facilities** ⬟ ⊙ 🔒 ⚊ ⊛ **Services** ⬛ 🍴 ➕ 🔳 **Off-site** 🍴 ⚍S

MORATALLA MURCIA

La Puerta

Caretera del Canal, Paraje La Puerta Km8
☎ 968 730008 ▤ 968 706365
e-mail lapuerta@forodigital.es
website www.campinglapuerta.com
Wooded site alongside the river Al-aharabe with big pitches and pleasant views.

➲ A30 Albacete to Murcia, onto C415 to Moratalla.
Open All year **Site** 10HEC ⬤ ♣ 🏠 **Prices** ⋔ 3.15-4 ⇛ 3.15-4 ⬛ 3.60-4.40 ⚊ 3.15-4 **Facilities** ⬟ 🏠 ⊙ 🔒 ⊘ ⚊ ⊛ **Services** ⬛ 🍴 ➕ 🔳 **Leisure** ⚍ PR **Off-site** ➕

MOTRIL GRANADA

Playa de Poniente

18613 ☎ 958 820303 ▤ 958 604191
e-mail camplapo@infogocio.com
website www.infonegocio.com/camplapo
Open All year **Site** 2.4HEC ⬤ ♣ 🏠 **Facilities** ⬟ 🏠 ⊙ 🔒 ⊘ ⚊ ⊛ **Services** ⬛ 🍴 ➕ 🔳 **Leisure** ⚍ P **Off-site** ⚍S

OTURA GRANADA

Suspiro del Moro

18630 ☎ 958 555411 ▤ 958 555411
e-mail campingsusirodelmoro@yahoo.es
website www.campingsuspirodelmoro.com
A modern site with good facilities, 5 minutes from the town centre.

➲ 10km S of Granada via N323.
Open All year **Site** 1HEC ⬤ ♣ 🏠 **Facilities** ⬟ 🏠 ⊙ 🔒 ⊘ ⊛ **Services** ⬛ 🍴 ➕ 🔳 **Leisure** ⚍ P **Off-site** ⚊ ⚍R

PELIGROS GRANADA

Granada

Cerro de la Cruz, 18210 ☎ 958 340548 ▤ 958 340548
e-mail pruizlopez1953@yahoo.es
website www.campinggranada.com
Wooded location with panoramic views.

➲ N323 exit 123 for Peligros.
Open 15 Mar-Sep **Site** 2.2HEC ⬤ ⬤ ♣ **Prices** ⋔ 5.14 pitch 11.24 **Facilities** ⬟ 🏠 ⊙ 🔒 ⊘ ⊛ **Services** ⬛ 🍴 ➕ 🔳 **Leisure** ⚍ P

Site 6HEC (site size) ⬤ grass ⬤ sand ⬤ stone ♣ little shade ♣ partly shaded 🏠 mainly shaded 🏠 bungalows for hire ⬛ caravans for hire ⚊ tents for hire ⊗ no dogs **Prices** ⋔ adult per night ⇛ car per night pp per person per night ⬛ caravan per night ⚊ tent per night ⬛ (static)-caravan hire per week

PUERTO DE SANTA MARÍA, EL CÁDIZ

Playa Las Dunas de San Anton
ps Maritimo de la Puntilla S/N, 11500
☎ 956 872210 ▤ 956 860117
e-mail info@lasdunascamping.com
website www.lasdunascamping.com
Large site with good recreational facilities close to the beach.
Open All year **Site** 13.2HEC ❤ ❤ ⛺ **Prices** ♦ 4.22-4.69 🚗 3.61-4 🚐 4.60-5.10 ▲ 4.21-4.61 **Facilities** ⚡ 🏪 ⊙ 🔌 ⊘ ⑫ **Services** 🍴 🍽 🞤 🖬 **Leisure** ⚊ PS **Off-site** 🏪 🍴 🍽 ⊘ ⛛ ⚊PRS 🞤

RONDA MÁLAGA

El Sur
ctra de Algeciras (A369 2.8km), 29400
☎ 95 2875939 ▤ 95 2877054
e-mail info@campingelsur.com
website www.elsur.com
A beautiful location in the heart of the Serrania of Ronda.
Open All year **Site** 4HEC ❤ ❤ ⛺ **Prices** ♦ 4.80 🚗 4.30 🚐 4.30-8.50 ▲ 4.30-8.50 **Facilities** ⚡ 🏪 ⊙ 🔌 ⊘ ⑫ **Services** 🍴 🍽 🞤 🖬 **Leisure** ⚊ P

ROQUETAS-DE-MAR ALMERIA

Roquetas
Los Parrales, 04740 ☎ 950 343809 ▤ 950 342525
e-mail info@campingroquetas.com
website www.campingsroquetas.com
➲ Access by road 340. 1.7km from Km428.6.
Open All year **Site** 8HEC ❤ ❤ ⛺ **Prices** ♦ 4.10 🚗 4.10 🚐 4.10 ▲ 4.10 **Facilities** ⚡ 🏪 ⊙ 🔌 ⊘ ⛛ ⑫ **Services** 🍴 🍽 🞤 🖬 **Leisure** ⚊ LPS

SANTA ELENA JAÉN

Despeñaperros
23213 ☎ 953 664192 ▤ 953 664192
e-mail campingdesp@navegalia.com
website www.campingdespenaperros.com
A clean, restful site in a nature reserve with views of the surrounding mountains.
➲ On NIV-E5 at Km257.
Open All year **Site** 5HEC ❤ ❤ **Prices** ♦ 3.60-3.80 🚗 4-3.95 🚐 3.90-4.20 ▲ 3.90-4.20 **Facilities** ⚡ 🏪 ⊙ 🔌 ⊘ ⑫ **Services** 🍴 🍽 🞤 🖬 **Leisure** ⚊ P

TARIFA CÁDIZ

Paloma
11380 ☎ 956 684203 ▤ 956 681880
e-mail info@campingpaloma.com
website www.campingpaloma.com
A modern site in a secluded location next to the prehistoric Necrolopis de los Algarbes, 400m from the beach and. Fine views of the African coast across the Straits of Gibraltar.
➲ Via N340 Cádiz-Málaga at Km74.
Open All year **Site** 4.9HEC ❤ ❤ ⛺ **Facilities** ⚡ 🏪 ⊙ 🔌 ⊘ ⑫ **Services** 🍴 🍽 🞤 🖬 **Leisure** ⚊ P **Off-site** ⚊RS

Rió Jara
11380 ☎ 956 680570 ▤ 956 680570
e-mail campingriojara@terra.es
Extensive site on meadowland with good tree cover. Long sandy beach.
➲ Off N340 at Km 79.7 towards sea.
Open All year **Site** 3HEC ❤ ❤ **Facilities** ⚡ 🏪 ⊙ 🔌 ⊘ ⑫ **Services** 🍴 🍽 🞤 🖬 **Leisure** ⚊ RS

Tarifa
11380 ☎ 956 684778 ▤ 956 684778
e-mail camping-tarifa@camping-tarifa.com
website www.camping-tarifa.com
A terraced site in wooded surroundings, 100m from the sea.
➲ At Km78 on Málaga-Cádiz road.
Open All year **Site** 3.2HEC ❤ ❤ **Facilities** ⚡ 🏪 ⊙ 🔌 ⊘ ⑫ **Services** 🍴 🍽 🞤 🖬 **Leisure** ⚊ P **Off-site** ⚊RS

AT TORRE DE LA PEÑA (7KM NW)

Torre de la Peña
11380 ☎ 956 684903 ▤ 956 681473
e-mail info@campingtp.com
website www.campingtp.com
Terraced site on both sides of through road. Upper terraces are considerably quieter. Roofing provides shade. View of the sea, Tarifa and on clear days North Africa (Tangier).
➲ Off N340 at Km76.5, turn inland by old square tower.
Open All year **Site** 3HEC ❤ ❤ ⛺ **Facilities** ⚡ 🏪 ⊙ 🔌 ⊘ ⑫ **Services** 🍴 🍽 🞤 🖬 **Leisure** ⚊ PS

VEJER DE LA FRONTERA CÁDIZ

Vejer
ctra National (N340), 11150 ☎ 956 450098 ▤ 956 450098
e-mail info@campingvejer.com
website www.campingvejer.com
A quiet family site in a pleasant shady location.
➲ On N340 Cádiz-Málaga at Km39.5.
Open Etr-end Sep **Site** 0.8HEC ❤ ❤ 🚐 ▲ **Facilities** ⚡ 🏪 ⊙ 🔌 ⑫ **Services** 🍴 🍽 🞤 🖬 **Leisure** ⚊ P

ANDORRA

SANT JULIÀ DE LÚRIA

Huguet
ctra de Fontaneda ☎ 376 843718 ▤ 376 843718
e-mail campinghuguet@hotmail.com
On level strip of meadowland with rows of fruit and deciduous trees.
➲ Off La Seu d'Urgell road N1, S of village and drive W across river.
Open All year **Site** 1.5HEC ❤ ❤ ❤ **Facilities** ⚡ ⊙ 🔌 ⑫ **Services** 🞤 🖬 **Leisure** ⚊ R **Off-site** 🏪 🍴 🍽 ⊘ ⛛ ⚊LP

Spain (vertical tab)

Facilities 🏪 shop ⚡ shower ⊙ electric points for razors 🔌 electric points for caravans ⑫ parking by tents permitted ⦿ compulsory separate car park
Services 🍽 café/restaurant 🞤 bar ⊘ Camping Gaz International ⛛ gas other than Camping Gaz 🖬 first aid facilities 🖬 laundry
Leisure ⚊ swimming L-Lake P-Pool R-River S-Sea **Off-site** All facilities within 2km

Switzerland

Accidents & emergencies
fire 118 **police** 117 **ambulance** 144

Driving requirements
Minimum age 18 for UK licence holders driving temporarily imported cars (or motorcycles over 125cc).

Lights
Use of dipped headlights during the day recommended for all motorists and motorcyclists; compulsory at all times in tunnels whether lit or not (failure to do this incurs on-the-spot fine). Driving on sidelights is prohibited.

Motorways
The Swiss authorities charge for the use of their motorway network. For vehicles up to 3.5 tonnes maximum total weight, the charge is in the form of an annual motorway tax levied on all vehicles, including motorcycles, trailers and caravans. An adhesive disc, called a *vignette*, is displayed as proof of payment. Fines are imposed for non-display. You may purchase the disc in the UK (freephone 00800 100 200 30), at the Swiss frontier, or from service stations, garages and TCS agencies throughout Switzerland. In Switzerland there is usually no warning that a tax disc is necessary.

Passengers & children
Children under 7 cannot travel as front-seat passengers unless using suitable restraint system; children between 7 and 12 must use seat belts or restraint systems appropriate to size when travelling as front or rear passengers. Never fit a rear-facing child restraint in a seat with a frontal airbag.

Size restrictions
Motor vehicle or trailer
height 4m, width 2.55m, length 12m
Vehicle and trailer
length 18.75m

Speed limits
Unless signed otherwise:

Car without caravan/trailer, motorcycle
Built-up areas	50kph
Outside built-up areas	80kph*
Semi-motoways	100kph
Motorways	120kph

Car towing caravan/trailer
Built-up areas	50kph
Outside built-up areas	80kph
Motorways	80kph
Minimum speed on motorway	60kph

*or as indicated by signs.

Tourist office
Swiss National Tourist Office
30 Bedford Street, London WC2E 9ED
Tel 00800 100 200 30 (freephone) or
020 7420 4900 (Mon, Wed & Fri 09.00-17.00,
Thu 10.00-17.00 hrs)
www.myswitzerland.com

Additional information
Warning triangle compulsory. In some areas it is compulsory to switch off your engine when waiting at traffic lights or railway crossings. It is advisable to check special regulations governing mountain roads, especially if towing a caravan/trailer.

The charges in the following table are a guide only and may change.

Tolls

Tolls Annual vignette (Swiss francs) CHF	car	car & caravan
Bridges & tunnels		
General vignette (includes use of Gotthard Tunnel and San Bernardino Tunnel)	40CHF	40CHF
Sankt Bernhard Tunnel	29CHF	46CHF
Munt La Schera Tunnel	15CHF	20CHF

NORTH

KÜNTEN AARGAU

Sulz

5444 ☎ 079 6607426 📠 056 4964879

e-mail info@camping-sulz.ch **website** www.camping-sulz.ch

Situated by a river.

⇨ *A1 exit Baden towards Bremgarten.*

Open 15 Mar-Oct **Site** 3HEC 👪 ♨ 🚐 **Prices** 👤 6 🚐 2 🚐 10-14 ⚠ 6-10
🚐 (static)250 **Facilities** 🚿 🛁 ⊙ 🚾 ⌀ 🚰 🅿 **Services** 🍴 ➕ 🗑
Leisure 🏊 PR

LÄUFELFINGEN BASEL

Läufelfingen

4448 ☎ 062 2991189

⇨ *On road from Basel to Olten.*

Open Apr-Oct **Site** 0.5HEC 👪 ♨ 🚐 **Facilities** 🚿 ⊙ 🚾 ⌀ 🅿 **Services** ➕

MÖHLIN AARGAU

Bachtalen

4313 ☎ 061 815095

e-mail info@camping-moehlin.ch

website www.camping-moehlin.ch

A pleasant site in a wooded rural setting.

⇨ *2km N towards the Rhine.*

Open Apr-Oct **Site** 1HEC 👪 ♨ 🚐 ⚠ **Prices** 👤 5-6 pitch 11-14
Facilities 🚿 ⊙ 🚾 ⌀ 🅿 **Services** ➕ 🗑 **Off-site** 🛁 🍴 🍴 🏊 PR

REINACH BASEL

Waldhort

Heideweg 16, 4153 ☎ 061 7116429 📠 061 7139835

e-mail camp.waldhort@gmx.ch

website camping-waldhort.ch

Pleasant wooded surroundings close to the Basle-Delémont road.

Open Mar-28 Oct **Site** 3.3HEC 👪 ♨ **Prices** 👤 8 🚐 18 ⚠ 11 **Facilities** 🚿
🛁 ⊙ 🚾 ⌀ 🚰 🅿 **Services** 🍴 ➕ 🗑 **Leisure** 🏊 P **Off-site** 🍴

See advertisement on this page

ZURZACH AARGAU

Oberfeld

5330 ☎ 056 2492575 📠 056 2492579

e-mail oberfield@camping-zurzach.ch

website www.camping-zurzach.ch

Open 24 Mar-27 Oct **Site** 2HEC 👪 ♨ ♨ 🚐 ⚠ **Prices** 👤 6.50 🚐 9-12
⚠ 4.50-7 🚐 (static)280-350 **Facilities** 🚿 🛁 ⊙ 🚾 ⌀ 🅿 **Services** 🍴 ➕
Leisure 🏊 PR

NORTH EAST

ALTNAU THURGAU

Ruderbaum

8595 ☎ 071 6952965 📠 071 6900632

e-mail camping@ruderbaum.ch

website www.ruderbaum.ch

A small site with ample facilities.

⇨ *Close to railway station by Lake Bodensee between Constance and Romanshorn.*

Open Apr-Oct **Site** 7.5HEC 👪 ♨ 🚐 **Facilities** 🚿 ⊙ 🚾 ⌀ 🚰 🅿 **Services** 🍴
➕ 🗑 **Leisure** 🏊 L **Off-site** 🛁 🍴

APPENZELL APPENZELL

Kau Appenzell

9050 ☎ 071 7875030

A woodland site with modern installations.

⇨ *S of Appenzell towards Wattwil.*

Open All year **Site** 2HEC 👪 ♨ ⊗ **Prices** 👤 5 🚐 3 🚐 10-12 ⚠ 9-11
Facilities 🚿 🛁 ⊙ 🚾 🚰 🅿 **Services** 🍴 ➕ 🗑

ESCHENZ THURGAU

Hüttenberg

Hüttenberg, 8264 ☎ 052 7412337 📠 052 7415671

e-mail info@huettenberg.ch

website www.huettenberg.ch

Terraced site lying above village.

⇨ *1km SW.*

Open Jan-Nov **Site** 6HEC 👪 ♨ 🚐 ⚠ **Prices** 👤 6.70-7.50 🚐 2.70-3
🚐 9.90-11 ⚠ 5.40-9 🚐 (static)385-490 **Facilities** 🚿 🛁 ⊙ 🚾 ⌀ 🚰 🅿
Services 🍴 ➕ **Leisure** 🏊 P **Off-site** 🍴 🏊 LR

GOLDINGEN ST-GALLEN

Atzmännig

8638 ☎ 055 2846434 📠 055 2846435

e-mail info@atzmaennig.ch

website www.atzmaennig.ch

Suitable for summer and winter holidays, the site is close to the main cable car and ski-lift stations and the the giant mountainside slide.

Open All year **Site** 1.5HEC 👪 ♨ **Prices** 👤 6-6 🚐 7-7 ⚠ 7-7 **Facilities** 🚿
⊙ 🚾 🚰 🅿 **Services** 🍴 ➕ 🗑

Facilities 🛁 shop 🚿 shower ⊙ electric points for razors 🚾 electric points for caravans 🅿 parking by tents permitted 🅿 compulsory separate car park
Services 🍴 café/restaurant 🍴 bar ⌀ Camping Gaz International 🚰 gas other than Camping Gaz ➕ first aid facilities 🗑 laundry
Leisure 🏊 swimming L-Lake P-Pool R-River S-Sea **Off-site** All facilities within 2km

Switzerland

KRUMMENAU ST-GALLEN

Adler
9643 ☎ 071 9941030
➲ On edge of village.
Open All year **Site** 0.8HEC 👑 ♣ **Facilities** ⋔ 🏪 ⊙ 🚰 **Services** 🍴 ➕ 🛢

MAMMERN THURGAU

Guldifuss
Guldifusstr 1, 8265 ☎ 052 7411320 🗎 052 7411342
A terraced site directly on the Untersee.
Open Apr-Oct **Site** 1.6HEC 👑 ♣ **Prices** 🛉 10 🚗 6 🚐 4 🛆 4 **Facilities** ⋔
⊙ 🚰 🗐 ⚕ 🛒 **Services** 🍴 🛢 **Leisure** 🌊 L **Off-site** 🛒 ➕

OTTENBACH ZÜRICH

Reussbrücke (TCS)
Muristr 32, 8913 ☎ 01 7612022 🗎 01 7612042
e-mail reussbruecke@tcs-ccz.ch
website www.tcs-ccz.ch
By river of same name.
➲ Access from Zürich via road 126 in SW direction, via Affoltern to Ottenbach.
Open Apr-Oct **Site** 1.5HEC 👑 ♣ 🐖 🚐 🛆 **Prices** 🛉 5.50-6.60 🚗 11-16
🚐 10-14 🛆 8-11 **Facilities** ⋔ 🏪 ⊙ 🚰 🗐 ⚕ 🛒 **Services** 🍴 ➕ 🛢
Leisure 🌊 R **Off-site** 🛒 🍴 ➷P

SCHÖNENGRUND APPENZELL

Kronenfeld
9105 ☎ 071 3611268 🗎 071 3611166
e-mail hotel.krone.schoenengrund@bluewin.ch
website www.gasthaus-krone.ch.tf
A comfortable, partly residential site with well-defined touring pitches.
Open All year **Site** 1HEC 👑 ♣ **Prices** 🛉 5.50 🚗 3 🚐 4.50-10 🛆 4.50
Facilities ⋔ ⊙ 🚰 🗐 ⚕ 🛒 **Services** 🛢 **Off-site** 🏪 ➷P ➕

WAGENHAUSEN SCHAFFHAUSEN

Wagenhausen
Hauptstr 82, 8259 ☎ 052 7414271 🗎 052 7414157
e-mail campingwagenhausen@bluewin.ch
website www.campingwagenhausen.ch
A delightful wooded location beside the River Rhein.
Open Apr-Oct **Site** 4.5HEC 👑 ♣ 🐖 **Prices** 🛉 7 🚗 4 🚐 14 🛆 7
🚐 (static)490 **Facilities** ⋔ 🏪 ⊙ 🚰 🗐 ⚕ 🛒 **Services** 🍴 🛢
Leisure 🌊 PR

WALENSTADT ST-GALLEN

See-Camping
8880 ☎ 081 7351896 🗎 081 7351841
e-mail kontakt@see-camping.ch
website www.see-camping.ch
A well-equipped family site with direct access to the Walensee.
➲ Motorway Zürich-Chur exit.
Open May-Sep **Site** 1.2HEC 👑 ♣ 🐖 **Prices** 🛉 8 🚗 4 🚐 8-15 🛆 6-15
Facilities ⋔ 🏪 ⊙ 🚰 🛒 **Services** 🍴 🛢 **Leisure** 🌊 L
Off-site 🛒 🍴 🗐 ⚕ ➕

WILDBERG ZÜRICH

Weid
☎ 052 3853388 🗎 052 3853477
e-mail campingweid@bluewin.ch
On a terraced meadow in a very peaceful location surrounded by woods.
➲ From Winterthur signs for Tösstal, right after spinning-mill in Turbenthal.
Open All year **Site** 6.1HEC 👑 ♣ 🐖 🐖 🛆 **Prices** 🛉 6 🛆 5.50 pitch 10-12
Facilities ⋔ 🏪 ⊙ 🚰 🗐 ⚕ 🛒 **Services** 🛒 🍴 ➕ 🛢 **Off-site** 🍴 ➷PR

WINTERTHUR ZÜRICH

Schützenweiher
Eichliwaldstr 4, 8400 ☎ 052 2125260 🗎 052 2125260
e-mail campingplatz@win.ch
➲ To the left of the Schaffhausen road, near Schützenhaus restaurant.
Open All year **Site** 1HEC 👑 ♣ 🐖 🛆 **Prices** 🛉 7.50 🚗 4 🚐 7.50 🛆 4.50
Facilities ⋔ ⊙ 🚰 🗐 ⚕ 🛒 **Services** ➕ 🛢 **Off-site** 🏪 🛒 🍴 ➷P

NORTH WEST/CENTRAL

AESCHI BERN

Panorama
3703 ☎ 033 2233615 🗎 033 2233656
e-mail postmaster@camping-aeschi.ch
website www.camping-aeschi.ch
➲ 400m SE of Camping Club Bern.
Open 15 May-Sep **Site** 1HEC 👑 ♣ 🐖 **Prices** 🛉 5.60 🚗 3 🚐 10-14
🛆 8-12 **Facilities** ⋔ 🏪 ⊙ 🚰 🛒 **Services** ➕ 🛢 **Off-site** 🛒 🍴 🗐

BERN (BERNE) BERN

AT WABERN

SC Eichholz
Strandweg 49, 3084 ☎ 031 9612602 🗎 031 9613526
e-mail info@campingeichholz.ch
website www.campingeichholz.ch
Set in municipal parkland with a separate section for caravans.
➲ Approach via Gossetstr & track beside river.
Open 20 Apr-Sep **Site** 2HEC 👑 ♣ 🐖 **Prices** 🛉 7.50 🚗 3.50 🚐 10
🛆 7.50-9 **Facilities** ⋔ ⊙ 🚰 🗐 🛒 **Services** 🛒 🍴 ➕ 🛢 **Leisure** 🌊 R
Off-site 🏪 🛒 🍴 ⚕ ➷P

BRENZIKOFEN BERN

Wydeli (TCS)
Wydeli 60, 3671 ☎ 031 7711141
e-mail info@camping-brenzikofen.ch
website www.camping-brenzikofen.ch
➲ 8km N of Thun.
Open May-Sep **Site** 1.3HEC 👑 ♣ 🐖 **Prices** 🛉 6.60-7.10 🚗 2-3 🚐 12-14
🚐 (static)420 **Facilities** ⋔ ⊙ 🚰 🗐 ⚕ 🛒 **Services** 🍴 🛢 **Leisure** 🌊 P
Off-site 🏪 ➕

Site 6HEC (site size) 👑 grass 🔵 sand 👑 stone ♣ little shade ♣ partly shaded 🐖 mainly shaded 🐖 bungalows for hire
🚐 caravans for hire 🛆 tents for hire ⊗ no dogs **Prices** 🛉 adult per night 🚗 car per night pp per person per night 🚐 caravan per night
🛆 tent per night 🚐 (static)-caravan hire per week

BRUNNEN SCHWYZ

Hopfreben

6440 ☎ 041 8201873 🗎 041 8201873
website www.camping-brunnen.ch
On the right bank of the Muotta stream 100m before it flows into the lake.

➲ *1km W.*

Open 20 Apr-21 Sep **Site** 1.5HEC ♨ ♣ ♠ **Prices** ♦ 5.50 ➡ 3-12 ➡ 12-16 ▲ 8-16 **Facilities** 🅟 🖾 ⊙ ➋ ⌀ ⚍ ℗ **Services** ⬛ 🍽 ➕ 🖾
Leisure ⚓ LPR **Off-site** ⚓P

COLOMBIER NEUCHÂTEL

Paradis-Plage

2013 ☎ 032 8412446 🗎 032 8414305
e-mail paradisplage@freesurf.ch
website www.paradisplage.ch
A delightful setting beside Lake Neuchâtel with modern facilities.

Open Mar-Oct **Site** 4HEC ♨ ♣ ♠ **Facilities** 🅟 🖾 ⊙ ➋ ⌀ ⚍ ℗ **Services** ⬛ 🍽 ➕ 🖾 **Leisure** ⚓ L

ERLACH BERN

Mon Plaisir

3235 ☎ 032 3381358 🗎 032 3381305
e-mail info@camping24.ch
website www.camping24.ch
Well-equipped site beside the lake.

Open All year **Site** 0.6HEC ♨ ♣ ♠ ♠ **Facilities** 🅟 🖾 ⊙ ➋ ⌀ ⚍ ℗ **Services** 🍽 ➕ 🖾 **Leisure** ⚓ L **Off-site** 🍽 ⚓PR

EUTHAL SCHWYZ

Euthal

8844 ☎ 055 4122718 🗎 055 4127673
e-mail info@hotelposteuthal.ch
website www.hotelposteuthal.ch
On the shore of the Sihlsee in a beautiful mountain setting. The site is reserved for tents only.

Open May-Oct **Site** 1HEC ♨ ♣ ⊗ **Prices** ♦ 8 ➡ 2.50 ➡ 12 ▲ 6-10 **Facilities** 🅟 ⊙ ➋ ➕ **Leisure** ⚓ L **Off-site** 🖾 ⬛ 🍽 ⌀ ⚓P ➕

FLÜELEN URI

Urnersee

6454 ☎ 041 8709222 🗎 041 8709216
e-mail info@windsurfing-urnersee.ch
website www.windsurfing-urnersee.ch
On level ground on the shore of the Vierwaldstättersee with plenty of sports facilities.

Open 15 Apr-Oct **Site** 4.5HEC ♨ ♣ **Facilities** 🅟 🖾 ⊙ ➋ ℗ **Services** ⬛ 🍽 ➕ **Leisure** ⚓ LR **Off-site** ⌀ ⚓P

FRUTIGEN BERN

Grassi

3714 ☎ 033 6711149 🗎 033 6711380
e-mail campinggrassi@bluewin.ch
website www.camping-grassi.ch
Site scattered with fruit trees beside a farm on the River Engstilgern.

➲ *From the Haupstr, turn right at Simplon Hotel.*

Open All year **Site** 1.5HEC ♨ ♣ ♠ ♠ **Prices** ♦ 6.40 pitch 8-14 **Facilities** 🅟 🖾 ⊙ ➋ ⌀ ⚍ ℗ **Services** ➕ 🖾 **Off-site** ⬛ 🍽 ⚓P

GAMPELEN BERN

Fanel (TCS)

3236 ☎ 032 3132333 🗎 032 3131407
e-mail camping.gampelen@tcs.ch
website www.campingtcs.ch
A level site on the shore of Lake Neuchâtel protected by trees and bushes.

➲ *On A5 towards Gampelen.*

Open 2 Apr-3 Oct **Site** 11.3HEC ♨ ♣ ♠ **Facilities** 🅟 🖾 ⊙ ➋ ⌀ ⚍ ℗ **Services** ⬛ 🍽 ➕ 🖾 **Leisure** ⚓ L **Off-site** ⚓R

GISWIL OBWALDEN

Giswil

6074 ☎ 041 6752355
Open Apr-20 Oct **Site** 1.9HEC ♨ ♣ ♠ **Facilities** 🅟 🖾 ⊙ ➋ ⌀ ⚍ ℗ **Services** 🍽 ➕ 🖾 **Leisure** ⚓ L

GOLDAU SCHWYZ

Bernerhöhe

6410 ☎ 041 8551887 🗎 041 8555970
On the edge of a forest with a beautiful view of Lake Lauerz. Separate field for tents.

➲ *1.5km SE & turn left.*

Open All year **Site** 2.5HEC ♨ ♣ ♠ ⊗ **Prices** ♦ 5.30 ➡ 2 ➡ 3 ▲ 3 **Facilities** 🅟 🖾 ⊙ ➋ ⌀ ℗ **Services** ➕ 🖾

GRINDELWALD BERN

Aspen

3818 ☎ 033 8531124 🗎 033 534157
Sunny hill terraces.

Open Jun-15 Oct **Site** 2.5HEC ♨ ♣ **Facilities** 🅟 ⊙ ➋ ⌀ ℗ **Services** 🖾 **Off-site** 🍽 ➕

GSTAAD BERN

Bellerive

3780 ☎ 033 7446330 🗎 033 7446345
e-mail bellerive.camping@bluewin.ch
Open All year **Site** 0.8HEC ♨ ♣ ♠ ♠ **Facilities** 🅟 ⊙ ➋ ⌀ **Services** 🍽 ➕ 🖾 **Leisure** ⚓ R **Off-site** ⚓P

INNERTKIRCHEN BERN

Aareschlucht

Hauptstr 6/11, 3862 ☎ 033 9715532 🗎 033 9715344
e-mail campaareschlucht@bluewin.ch
website www.camping-aareschlucht.ch
A beautiful Alpine location with superb mountain views.

Open May-Oct **Site** 0.5HEC ♨ ♣ ♠ **Prices** ♦ 5.70 pitch 7-14 ➡ (static)350 **Facilities** 🅟 🖾 ⊙ ➋ ⌀ ⚍ ℗ **Services** ➕ 🖾 **Off-site** ⬛ 🍽 ⚓R

Grund

3862 ☎ 033 9714409 🗎 033 9714767
e-mail info@camping-grund.ch
website www.camping-grund.ch
Next to farm on S outskirts of village.

➲ *Turn south off main road in village centre at Hotel Urweider, 0.3km turn right.*

Open All year **Site** 120HEC ♨ ♣ ♠ ▲ **Prices** ♦ 3.90-4.50 ➡ 15-19 ▲ 10-15 **Facilities** 🅟 ⊙ ➋ ℗ **Services** ➕ 🖾 **Off-site** 🖾 ⬛ 🍽 ⌀ ⚓R

Facilities 🖾 shop 🅟 shower ⊙ electric points for razors ➋ electric points for caravans ℗ parking by tents permitted 🅟 compulsory separate car park
Services 🍽 café/restaurant ⬛ bar ⌀ Camping Gaz International ⚍ gas other than Camping Gaz ➕ first aid facilities 🖾 laundry
Leisure ⚓ swimming L-Lake P-Pool R-River S-Sea **Off-site** All facilities within 2km

INTERLAKEN BERN

Hobby 3
Lehnweg 16, 3800 ☎ 033 8229652 ▤ 033 8229657
e-mail info@campinghobby.ch
website www.campinghobby.ch
Family site in a quiet location with fine views of the surrounding mountains and within easy walking distance of Interlaken.
➲ N8 exit 24 for Unterseen, follow camping sign No 3. Or N8 exit 24 (right lane in tunnel), turn right & follow camping sign No 3.
Open Apr-Sep **Site** 1.5HEC ♨ ♣ **Prices** ⚘ 6.20-7.60 pitch 22-30
Facilities ⬥ 🖾 ⊙ ➋ ⊘ ⚛ **Services** ⊞ ⬚ **Off-site** ⬚ 🍽 ⚏ ⚘LPR

See advertisements on this page

Jungfrau
Steindlerstr 50, 3800 ☎ 033 8227107 ▤ 033 8225730
e-mail info@jungfraucamp.ch
website www.jungfraucamp.ch
Beautiful views of the Eiger, the Monch and the Jungfrau.
➲ Turn right at Unterseen, through Schulhaus & Steinler Str to site.
Open May-Sep **Site** 2.5HEC ♨ ♣ ♠ **Facilities** ⬥ 🖾 ⊙ ➋ ⊘ ⚏ ⚛
Services 🍽 🍽 ⬚ **Leisure** ⚘ P **Off-site** ⚘LR ⊞

Jungfraublick
Gsteigstr 80, 3800 ☎ 033 8224414 ▤ 033 8221619
e-mail info@jungfraublick.ch
website www.jungfraublick.ch
A family site with clean, modern facilities in a fine central location.
➲ A8 exit Lauterbrunnen-Grindelwald, site 300m on left.
Open May-20 Sep **Site** 1.3HEC ♨ ♣ **Prices** ⚘ 7.60-8.60 pitch 16-30
Facilities ⬥ 🖾 ⊙ ➋ ⊘ ⚛ **Services** ⊞ ⬚ **Leisure** ⚘ P
Off-site 🍽 🍽 ⚘R

Lazy Rancho 4
Lehnweg 6, 3800 ☎ 033 8228716 ▤ 033 8231920
e-mail info@lazyrancho.ch
website www.lazyrancho.ch
A family site in a magnificent position with views of the Eiger, Mönch and Jungfrau with fine facilities.
➲ A8 exit Unterseen for Gunten, 2km turn right, left at Landhotel Golf.
Open May-15 Oct **Site** 16HEC ♨ ♣ **Prices** ⚘ 6-7.50 pitch 10-30
Facilities ⬥ 🖾 ⊙ ➋ ⊘ ⚛ **Services** ⊞ ⬚ **Leisure** ⚘ P
Off-site 🍽 🍽 ⚘LR

Manor Farm
3800 ☎ 033 8222264 ▤ 033 8222279
e-mail manorfarm@swisscamps.ch
website www.manorfarm.ch
A well-equipped site in a beautiful mountain setting.
➲ A8 exit Gunten/Beatenberg, signed.
Open All year **Site** 7.5HEC ♨ ♠ ♣ ♠ ⚏ ⚑ **Prices** ⚘ 6-10 pitch 7.80-38
⚑ (static)400-900 **Facilities** ⬥ 🖾 ⊙ ➋ ⊘ ⚛ **Services** 🍽 🍽 ⊞ ⬚
Leisure ⚘ LR

KANDERSTEG BERN

Rendez-Vous
3718 ☎ 033 6751534 🖷 033 6751737
e-mail rendez-vous.camping@bluewin.ch
website www.camping-kandersteg.ch
A delightful mountain setting with modern facilities.
➲ 0.75km E of town.
Open All year **Site** 1HEC ♨ ♣ **Prices** ⋔ 7.50 ⇝ 3 ⊞ 8-16 ▲ 8-16
Facilities ⋔ 🖹 ⊙ ⊟ ∅ ♨ ⊛ **Services** ⚑ †⊚† ⊞ 🖺 **Off-site** ⊜P

See advertisement on this page

LANDERON, LE NEUCHÂTEL

Peches
2525 ☎ 032 7512900 🖷 032 7516354
e-mail info@camping-lelanderon.ch
website www.camping-lelanderon.ch
A small site at the meeting point of the River Thielle and the Lac de Bienne.
Open Apr-15 Oct **Site** 2.1HEC ♨ ♣ ⊞ **Prices** ⋔ 8 ⇝ 4 ⊞ 12 ▲ 8.50-11
Facilities ⋔ 🖹 ⊙ ⊟ ∅ ♨ ⊛ **Services** ⚑ †⊚† ⊞ 🖺 **Leisure** ⊜ L
Off-site ⊜PR

LAUTERBRUNNEN BERN

Schützenbach
3822 ☎ 033 8551268 🖷 033 8551275
website www.schuetzenbach.ch
A fine Alpine location close to the main skiing areas and 300m from the lake.
➲ 0.8km S of village on left of road to Stechelberg opp B50.
Open All year **Site** 3HEC ♨ ♣ 🏠 ⊞ **Prices** ⋔ 6.50 ⇝ 16 ⊞ 16 ▲ 8-16
⊞ (static)350 **Facilities** ⋔ 🖹 ⊙ ⊟ ∅ ♨ ⊛ **Services** ⚑ †⊚† ⊞ 🖺
Off-site †⊚† ⊜R

LIGNIÈRES NEUCHÂTEL

Fraso-Ranch
2523 ☎ 032 7514616 🖷 032 7514614
e-mail camping.fraso-ranch@bluewin.ch
website mypage.bluewin.ch/camping_lignieres
A modern family site with good recreational facilities and a separate section for tourers.
➲ NE of Lignières on Nods road, signed.
Open All year **Site** 8.7HEC ♨ ♣ **Prices** ⋔ 6-8 pitch 5.50-15 **Facilities** ⋔ 🖹 ⊙ ⊟ ∅ ⊛ **Services** †⊚† 🖺 **Leisure** ⊜ P

LOCLE, LE NEUCHÂTEL

Communal (TCS)
2400 ☎ 032 9317493 🖷 032 9317408
e-mail camping.lelode@tcs.ch
website www.campingtcs.ch
On a level meadow surrounded by woodland. Good recreational facilities.
➲ S of town off La Sagne road.
Open 27 Apr-21 Oct **Site** 1.2HEC ♨ ♣ **Prices** ⋔ 5.40-6.40 ⊞ 10.40-14.80
▲ 7.40-8.60 **Facilities** ⋔ ⊙ ⊟ ∅ ♨ ⊛ **Services** ⚑ †⊚† ⊞ 🖺
Leisure ⊜ P **Off-site** 🖹 †⊚†

LUNGERN OBWALDEN

Obsee
6078 ☎ 041 6781463 🖷 041 6782163
e-mail camping@obsee.ch
website www.obsee.ch
A beautiful setting between the lake and the mountains with facilities for water sports.
➲ 1km W.
Open All year **Site** 1.5HEC ♨ ♣ ▲ **Prices** ⋔ 5-6 ⇝ 3 ⊞ 13 ▲ 13
Facilities ⋔ ⊙ ⊟ ∅ ♨ ⊛ **Services** ⚑ †⊚† ⊞ 🖺 **Leisure** ⊜ LPRS
Off-site 🖹

LUZERN (LUCERNE) LUZERN

Steinibachried (TCS)
Horw, 6048 ☎ 041 3403558 🖷 041 3403556
e-mail camping.horw@tcs.ch
website www.campingtcs.ch
A gently sloping meadow next to the football ground and the beach, separated from the lake by a wide belt of reeds.
➲ 3.2km S of Luzern.
Open 2 Apr-3 Oct **Site** 2HEC ♨ ♣ ⊞ **Prices** ⋔ 6-8 ⊞ 15-20 ▲ 7.50-8.50
⊞ (static)525 **Facilities** ⋔ 🖹 ⊙ ⊟ ∅ ⊘ ⊛ **Services** †⊚† ⊞ 🖺
Off-site ⚑ ⊜L

MEIRINGEN BERN

Balmweid
Balmweidstrasse 22, 3860 ☎ 033 9715115 🖷 033 9715117
e-mail camping.balmweid@popnet.ch
Mainly flat meadowland site with mountain views.
Open All year **Site** 2.2HEC ♨ ♣ **Facilities** ⋔ 🖹 ⊙ ⊟ ♨ **Services** †⊚† 🖺

MOSEN LUZERN

Seeblick
6295 ☎ 041 9171666 🖷 041 9171666
e-mail mptrunz@gmx.ch
website www.camping-seeblick.ch
Set on two strips of land on edge of lake, divided by paths into several squares.
➲ N on A26.
Open Apr-Oct **Site** 3HEC ♨ ♣ ⊞ **Prices** ⋔ 7 ⇝ 3 ⊞ 6-11 ▲ 4-5
⊞ (static)560 **Facilities** ⋔ 🖹 ⊙ ⊟ ∅ ♨ **Services** ⊞ 🖺 **Leisure** ⊜ L
Off-site †⊚†

Facilities 🖹 shop ⋔ shower ⊙ electric points for razors ⊟ electric points for caravans ⊛ parking by tents permitted ⊘ compulsory separate car park
Services †⊚† café/restaurant ⚑ bar ∅ Camping Gaz International ♨ gas other than Camping Gaz ⊞ first aid facilities 🖺 laundry
Leisure ⊜ swimming L-Lake P-Pool R-River S-Sea **Off-site** All facilities within 2km

Switzerland *(vertical side text)*

NOTTWIL LUZERN

St Margrethen
6207 ☎ 041 9371404 🖹 041 9371865
e-mail st-margrethen@swisscamps.ch
website www.swisscamps.ch
Natural meadowland with fruit trees, with own access to lake.
⮑ *Off road to Sursee 400m NW of Nottwil, towards lake for 100m.*
Open Apr-Oct **Site** 1HEC ☻ ♣ **Facilities** ↑ 🏠 ⊙ 🚿 🅿 🛒 ⑱
Services 🍴 🗓 **Leisure** ⮑ L **Off-site** 🍴 🍽 ⮑LP

PRÊLES BERN

Prêles
2515 ☎ 032 3151716 🖹 032 3155160
e-mail info@camping-jura.ch
website www.camping-jura.ch
On a wooded plateau overlooking Lake Biel.
⮑ *Off Biel-Neuchâtel road at Twann & signs for Prêles, through village, site on left.*
Open Apr-Oct **Site** 6HEC ☻ ♣ 🏠 **Prices** ⚲ 7.20-8 🚗 2.50 🚐 13 ⚠ 7-10
🚐 (static)420-470 **Facilities** ↑ 🏠 ⊙ 🚿 🅿 ⑱ **Services** 🍽 🗓 🗓
Leisure ⮑ P

SAANEN BERN

Saanen beim Kappeli
3792 ☎ 033 7446191 🖹 033 7446184
e-mail info@camping-saanen.ch
website www. camping-saanen.ch
Set in a long meadow between the railway and the River Saane.
⮑ *1km SE.*
Open Jan-Oct & Dec **Site** 0.8HEC ☻ ☺ ♣ **Prices** ⚲ 8-8.40 🚗 4.40
🚐 14-15 ⚠ 6.60-8.60 **Facilities** ↑ 🏠 ⊙ 🚿 🛒 ⑱ **Services** 🗓 🗓 **Leisure** ⮑ R
Off-site 🏠 🍴 🍽 🅿 ⮑P

SACHSELN OBWALDEN

Ewil
Brünigstrasse 258, CH-6072 ☎ 041 6663270
e-mail info@camping-ewil.ch
website www.camping-ewil.ch
On a level meadow on the SW shore of the Sarnersee.
⮑ *W of Sachseln-Ewil road towards lake.*
Open Apr-Sep **Site** 1.5HEC ☻ ♣ 🏠 **Prices** ⚲ 5.80-6.50 🚗 3 🚐 8 ⚠ 4-8
Facilities ↑ 🏠 ⊙ 🚿 🅿 ⑱ **Services** 🍴 🗓 🗓 **Leisure** ⮑ L
Off-site 🍽 ⮑R

SEMPACH LUZERN

Seeland (TCS)
6204 ☎ 041 4601466 🖹 041 4604766
e-mail camping.sempach@tcs.ch
website www.campingtcs.ch
Rectangular, level site on SW shore of lake.
⮑ *0.7km S on Luzern road by lake.*
Open Apr-Nov **Site** 5.2HEC ☻ ♣ ☺ ⚠ **Facilities** ↑ 🏠 ⊙ 🚿 🅿 🛒 ⑱
Services 🍴 🍽 🗓 🗓 **Leisure** ⮑ L

STECHELBERG BERN

Breithorn
3824 ☎ 033 8551225 🖹 033 8553561
e-mail breithorn@stechelberg.ch
A beautiful location in the Lauterbrunnen valley.
⮑ *3km S of Lauterbrunnen.*
Open All year **Site** 1HEC ☻ ♣ **Prices** ⚲ 6.70 🚐 10-12 **Facilities** ↑ 🏠 ⊙
🅿 🅿 ⑱ **Services** 🗓 🗓

SURSEE LUZERN

Sursee
Baselstrasse, Waldheim, 6216 ☎ 041 9211161 🖹 041 9211160
e-mail info@camping sursee.ch
website www.camping-sursee.ch
Next to Waldheim country estate.
⮑ *0.8km W of Sursee, 100m from Sursee-Basel road.*
Open Apr-Sep **Site** 1.7HEC ☻ ♣ **Prices** ⚲ 6.80 🚗 4 🚐 4 ⚠ 4
Facilities ↑ 🏠 ⊙ 🚿 🅿 🅿 ⑱ **Services** 🍴 🍽 🗓 🗓 **Off-site** ⮑L

VITZNAU LUZERN

Vitznau
6354 ☎ 041 3971280 🖹 041 3972457
e-mail camping-vitznau@bluewin.ch
website www.camping-vitznau.ch
Well-tended terraced site, in lovely countryside with fine views of lake.
⮑ *From N turn towards mountain at church & signed.*
Open Apr-Oct **Site** 1.8HEC ☻ ♣ 🏠 🚐 **Prices** ⚲ 8-10 pitch 15-22
Facilities ↑ 🏠 ⊙ 🚿 🅿 🛒 ⑱ **Services** 🗓 🗓 **Leisure** ⮑ P
Off-site 🍴 🍽 ⮑L

WILDERSWIL BERN

Oberei
Obereigasse 9, 3812 ☎ 033 8221335 🖹 033 8221335
e-mail oberei8@swisscamps.ch
website www.campingwilderwil.ch
A peaceful site in a picturesque village with fine views of the Jungfrau and surrounding mountains. There are good facilities and booking is advised for July and August.
Open May-Sep **Site** 0.6HEC ☻ ♣ 🏠 **Prices** ⚲ 5.60-6.20 pitch 10-20
Facilities ↑ 🏠 ⊙ 🚿 ⑱ **Services** 🗓 🗓 **Off-site** 🍴 🍽 ⮑LPR

ZUG ZUG

Innere Lorzenallmend (TCS)
Chamer Fussweg 36, 6300 ☎ 041 7418422 🖹 041 7418130
e-mail tcscamping.zug@tcs.ch
website www.campingtcs.ch
Pleasant location with beautiful view of Lake Zug and the surrounding mountains. Much traffic on the railway that passes the site.
⮑ *1km NW by lake.*
Open 2 Apr-3 Oct **Site** 1.1HEC ☻ ♣ **Facilities** ↑ 🏠 ⊙ 🚿 🅿 ⑱
Services 🍽 🗓 🗓 **Leisure** ⮑ LRS **Off-site** 🏠 🍴 🍽

Site 6HEC (site size) ☻ grass ☺ sand ☻ stone ♣ little shade ♣ partly shaded ♣ mainly shaded 🏠 bungalows for hire
🚐 caravans for hire ⚠ tents for hire ⊗ no dogs **Prices** ⚲ adult per night 🚗 car per night pp per person per night 🚐 caravan per night
⚠ tent per night 🚐 (static)-caravan hire per week

EAST

ANDEER GRAUBÜNDEN

Sut Baselgia (TCS)
7440 ☎ 081 6611453 📠 081 6611080
e-mail camping.andeer@bluewin.ch
website www.viamalaferien.ch
A pleasant, peaceful setting.
Open Dec-Oct **Site** 1.2HEC 🌳 🌲 🏠 **Prices** 🚶 6.50 🚗 3 🚐 13 ⛺ 8-13
Facilities 🚿 ⊙ 🔌 🔥 ♨ Ⓟ **Services** 🍴 ✚ 🧺 **Off-site** 🛍 🍷 🍴 🏊PR

AROSA GRAUBÜNDEN

Arosa Tourismus
7050 ☎ 081 3771745 📠 081 3773005
Open All year **Site** 0.6HEC 🌳 🌲 **Prices** 🚶 9 🚗 3 🚐 9 ⛺ 4.50
Facilities 🚿 ⊙ 🔌 🔥 Ⓟ **Off-site** 🛍 🍷 🍴 🏊LP ✚

CHUR (COIRE) GRAUBÜNDEN

Camp Au
Felsenaustr 61, 7000 ☎ 081 2842283 📠 081 2845683
e-mail info@camping-chur.ch
website www.camping-chur.ch
A summer and winter site on level ground with fine views of the surrounding mountains. Good recreational facilities.
➲ *A13 exit Chur-Süd, 2km NW of town centre on the Rhein. Access via outskirts of town.*
Open All year **Site** 2.6HEC 🌳 🌲 ⛺ **Facilities** 🚿 🛍 ⊙ 🔌 🔥 ♨ Ⓟ
Services 🍴 ✚ 🧺 **Off-site** 🏊P

CHURWALDEN GRAUBÜNDEN

Pradafenz
7075 ☎ 081 3821921 📠 081 3821921
e-mail camping@pradafenz.ch
website www.pradafenz.ch
A beautiful mountain area close to the local ski slopes.
Open Jan-22 Apr & 28 May-Oct **Site** 1.5HEC 🌳 🌲 **Facilities** 🚿 ⊙ 🔌 🔥
♨ Ⓟ **Services** 🍷 🍴 ✚ 🧺 **Off-site** 🏊PR

LENZ GRAUBÜNDEN

St Cassian
7083 ☎ 081 3842472 📠 081 3842489
e-mail camping.st.cassian@bluwin.ch
website www.st-cassian.ch
A level, shady site in a beautiful location at an altitude of 1415m above sea level. There are good facilities and the site is 1km from the town.
➲ *Motorway exit Chur-Süd, signs for Lenzerheide/St Moritz, up good mountain road.*
Open All year **Site** 25HEC 🌳 🌲 **Prices** 🚶 8 🚗 2.50 🚐 9.50 ⛺ 9.50
Facilities 🚿 ⊙ 🔌 🔥 ♨ Ⓟ **Services** 🍴 ✚ 🧺 **Off-site** 🛍 🍴

MÜSTAIR GRAUBÜNDEN

Clenga
7537 ☎ 081 8585410 📠 081 8585422
e-mail clenga@campclenga.ch
website www.campclenga.ch
Next to small river near the Italian frontier.
Open May-20 Oct **Site** 1.5HEC 🌳 🌲 🚐 **Prices** 🚶 6.50 pitch 10-12
🚐 (static)420 **Facilities** 🚿 🛍 ⊙ 🔌 🔥 ♨ Ⓟ **Services** 🍷 ✚ 🧺
Leisure 🏊 R

PONTRESINA GRAUBÜNDEN

Plauns (TCS)
7504 ☎ 081 8426285 📠 081 8345136
e-mail a.brueli@bluewin.ch
website www.pontresina.ch
Beautiful location at foot of Pit Palü.
➲ *Towards Bernina pass 4.5km beyond Pontresina. Off road 29 towards Hotel Morteratsch for 0.5km.*
Open Jun-15Oct, 15Dec-15Apr **Site** 4HEC 🌳 ⛰ 🌳 🌲 🌳 🚐
Facilities 🚿 🛍 ⊙ 🔌 🔥 ♨ Ⓟ **Services** 🍴 ✚ 🧺

POSCHIAVO GRAUBÜNDEN

Boomerang
7745 ☎ 081 8440713 📠 081 8441575
e-mail camping.boomerang@bluewin.ch
A quiet setting.
➲ *2km SE.*
Open All year **Site** 1.5HEC 🌳 🌲 🚐 **Facilities** 🚿 🛍 ⊙ 🔌 🔥 ♨ Ⓟ
Services 🍷 🍴 ✚ 🧺 **Off-site** 🍴 🏊LPR

SAMEDAN GRAUBÜNDEN

Punt Muragl
7503 ☎ 081 8428197 📠 081 8428197
e-mail camping.samedan@tcs.ch
website www.campingtcs.ch
A summer and winter site in a pleasant alpine setting.
➲ *Near Bernina railway halt, to right of fork of roads Samedan & Celerina/Schlarigna to Pontresina.*
Open Jun-3 Oct, Dec- 15 Apr **Site** 2HEC 🌳 🌲 🚐 **Prices** 🚶 8.75-9.95
🚐 15-18.40 ⛺ 7-8.20 🚐 (static)420-668 **Facilities** 🚿 🛍 ⊙ 🔌 🔥 ♨ Ⓟ
Services 🍷 🍴 ✚ 🧺 **Off-site** 🍴 🏊L

SPLÜGEN GRAUBÜNDEN

Sand
7435 ☎ 081 6641476 📠 081 6641460
e-mail camping@splugen.ch
website www.campingsplugen.ch
On the River Hinterrhein.
➲ *Off main road in village & signed.*
Open All year **Site** 0.8HEC 🌳 🌲 **Prices** ⛺ 6-16 **Facilities** 🚿 🛍 ⊙ 🔌 🔥
♨ Ⓟ **Services** 🍷 🍴 ✚ **Leisure** 🏊 R **Off-site** 🍴

SUSCH GRAUBÜNDEN

Muglinas
7542 ☎ 081 0797875689
➲ *200m W.*
Open Jun-15 Sep **Site** 1HEC 🌳 🌲 **Facilities** 🚿 ⊙ 🔌 🔥 ♨ Ⓟ
Services ✚ 🧺 **Leisure** 🏊 R **Off-site** 🛍 🍷 🍴

THUSIS GRAUBÜNDEN

Viamala
7430 ☎ 081 6512472
Pleasant wooded surroundings near the River Hinterrhein and close to the beautiful Viamala gorge.
➲ *NE towards Chur.*
Open May-Sep **Site** 4.5HEC 🌳 🌲 🚐 **Facilities** 🚿 🛍 ⊙ 🔌 🔥 Ⓟ
Services 🍷 🍴 ✚ 🧺 **Off-site** 🏊PR

Switzerland

Facilities 🛍 shop 🚿 shower ⊙ electric points for razors 🔌 electric points for caravans Ⓟ parking by tents permitted 🅟 compulsory separate car park
Services 🍴 café/restaurant 🍷 bar 🔥 Camping Gaz International ♨ gas other than Camping Gaz ✚ first aid facilities 🧺 laundry
Leisure 🏊 swimming L-Lake P-Pool R-River S-Sea **Off-site** All facilities within 2km

TSCHIERV GRAUBÜNDEN

Sternen (TCS)
Chasa Maruya, 7532 ☎ 081 8585628
e-mail maruya@gmx.net
website www.muenstertal.ch
Site in the village behind the Sternen Hotel.
⮑ *Between Ofen Pass & Santa Maria.*
Open Jun-Oct **Site** 1HEC ᴗ ♣ **Prices** ⚡ 6 Ⓐ 3 pitch 8 **Facilities** ⋔ 🖻 ☺ 🖳 ⵁ ⍟ **Services** 🍴 🍽 ➕ 🖻 **Leisure** ⛵ PR

ZERNEZ GRAUBÜNDEN

Cul
7530 ☎ 081 8561456 🖨 081 8561462
e-mail a.filli@camping-cul.ch
website www.camping-cul.ch
A delightful mountain setting close to the Swiss national park.
⮑ *Off road 27 W of Zernez.*
Open May-15 Oct **Site** 3.6HEC ᴗ ♣ **Facilities** ⋔ 🖻 ☺ 🖳 ⵁ ⵗ ⍟ **Services** 🍴 🍽 ➕ 🖻 **Leisure** ⛵ R **Off-site** 🍽 ⛵P

SOUTH

AGNO TICINO

Eurocampo
6982 ☎ 091 6052114 🖨 091 6053187
e-mail eurocampo@ticino.com
website www.eurocampo.ch
Part of site is near its own sandy beach and is divided by groups of trees.
⮑ *0.6km E on Lugano-Ponte Tresa road, opp Aeroport sign & Alfa Romeo building.*
Open Apr-Oct **Site** 6.5HEC ᴗ ♣ ⚘ **Prices** ⚡ 8-9 ⛺ 2 ⚘ 10-13 Ⓐ 8-12 **Facilities** ⋔ 🖻 ☺ 🖳 ⵁ ⵗ ⍟ **Services** 🍴 🍽 ➕ 🖻 **Leisure** ⛵ LR **Off-site** 🍽

Golfo del Sole
via Rivera 8, 6982 ☎ 091 6054802 🖨 091 6054306
e-mail info@golfodelsole.ch
website www.golfodelsole.ch
By lake. Separate play area for children.
Open 8 Apr-15 Oct **Site** 6HEC ᴗ ⚘ ♣ **Prices** ⚡ 9-10 ⛺ 2 ⚘ 10-13 Ⓐ 8-10 **Facilities** ⋔ 🖻 ☺ 🖳 ⵁ ⍟ **Services** 🍴 🍽 ➕ **Leisure** ⛵ L **Off-site** 🍽 ⛵P

CUGNASCO TICINO

Park-Camping Riarena
6516 ☎ 091 8591688 🖨 091 8592885
e-mail camping.riarena@bluewin.ch
website www.camping-riarena.ch
Beautiful park-like family site in level, natural woodland. All facilities are well-maintained and Lake Maggiore is within easy reach.
⮑ *1.5km NW. Off road 13 at BP fuel station 9km NE of Locarno & continue 0.5km.*
Open Mar-20 Oct **Site** 3.2HEC ᴗ ⛵ ⚘ ♣ Ⓐ **Prices** ⚡ 6-8 pitch 30-41 (incl 2 persons) **Facilities** ⋔ 🖻 ☺ 🖳 ⵁ ⵗ ⍟ **Services** 🍴 🍽 ➕ 🖻 **Leisure** ⛵ P **Off-site** ⛵R

GORDEVIO TICINO

Bellariva
6672 ☎ 091 7531444 🖨 091 7531764
e-mail camping.gordevio@tcs.ch
website www.campingtcs.ch
A quiet location between the road and the River Maggia.
Open Apr-Oct **Site** 2.5HEC ᴗ ⚘ ⚘ **Prices** ⚡ 7.80-9.80 Ⓐ 12-12.80 pitch 19-28.80 ⚘ (static)595-875 **Facilities** ⋔ 🖻 ☺ 🖳 ⵁ ⵗ ⍟ **Services** 🍴 🍽 ➕ 🖻 **Leisure** ⛵ PR

LOCARNO TICINO

Delta
via Respini 7, 6600 ☎ 091 7516081 🖨 091 7512243
e-mail info@campingdelta.com
website www.campingdelta.com
A beautiful, well-equipped and well-organised site at Lake Maggiore.
⮑ *2km from city.*
Open Mar-Oct **Site** 6.5HEC ᴗ ⚘ ⚘ ⊗ **Prices** ⚡ 11-18 pitch 21-57 ⚘ (static)392-700 **Facilities** ⋔ 🖻 ☺ 🖳 ⵁ ⵗ ⍟ **Services** 🍴 🍽 ➕ 🖻 **Leisure** ⛵ LR **Off-site** ⛵P

MOLINAZZO DI MONTEGGIO TICINO

Tresiana
6995 ☎ 091 6083342 🖨 091 6083142
e-mail mail@camping-tresiana
website www.camping-tresiana.ch
A family site on meadowland with trees on riverbank.
⮑ *Turn right after bridge in Ponte Tresa, site 5km.*
Open 31 Mar-21 Oct **Site** 1.5HEC ᴗ ⚘ ⚘ **Prices** ⚡ 6.50-8.50 ⚘ 3-5 ⚘ 13-25 Ⓐ 7-25 ⚘ (static)350-770 **Facilities** ⋔ 🖻 ☺ 🖳 ⵁ ⍟ **Services** 🍽 ➕ 🖻 **Leisure** ⛵ PR **Off-site** 🍴

TENERO TICINO

Campofelice
Lago Maggiore, 6598 ☎ 091 7451417 🖨 091 7451888
e-mail camping@campofelice.ch
website www.campofelice.ch
A beautifully situated and extensive site, divided into pitches and crossed by asphalt drives.
⮑ *1.9km S, signed.*
Open 23 Mar-28 Oct **Site** 15HEC ᴗ ⛵ ⚘ ⚘ ⚘ ⊗ **Prices** pitch 38-84 (incl 2 persons) **Facilities** ⋔ 🖻 ☺ 🖳 ⵁ ⵗ ⍟ **Services** 🍴 🍽 ➕ 🖻 **Leisure** ⛵ LR

Lido Mappo
Via Mappo, 6598 ☎ 091 7451437 🖨 091 7454808
e-mail camping@lidomappo.ch
website www.lidomappo.ch
A well-appointed site, beautifully situated by a lake. Teenagers must be accompanied by adults.
⮑ *0.7km SW, signed.*
Open 30 Mar-22 Oct **Site** 6.5HEC ᴗ ⚘ ⊗ **Facilities** ⋔ 🖻 ☺ 🖳 ⵁ ⵗ ⍟ **Services** 🍴 🍽 ➕ 🖻 **Leisure** ⛵ L **Off-site** ⛵PR

Site 6HEC (site size) ᴗ grass ⛵ sand ᴗ stone ♣ little shade ⚘ partly shaded ⚘ mainly shaded ⚘ bungalows for hire
⚘ caravans for hire Ⓐ tents for hire ⊗ no dogs **Prices** ⚡ adult per night ⚘ car per night pp per person per night ⚘ caravan per night
Ⓐ tent per night ⚘ (static)-caravan hire per week

Switzerland (side tab)

Tamaro

via Mappo, 6598 ☎ 091 7452161 📠 091 7456636
e-mail info@campingtamaro.ch
website www.campingtamaro.ch
Well-equipped site with direct access to the lake. Groups of young
persons must be accompanied by adults.
➥ *4km from Locano, signed from motorway.*
Open 24 Mar-22 Oct **Site** 6HEC 😃 ♣ ♣ ⊗ **Facilities** 🔥 🖫 ☺ ➡ ⌀ ♨ ⑫
Services 🍴 🍽 ➕ 🗗 **Leisure** ⚓ L **Off-site** ⚓P

SOUTH WEST

AGARN VALAIS

Gemmi

Briannenstr, 3952 ☎ 027 4731154 📠 027 4734295
e-mail info@campinggemmi.ch
website www.campinggemmi.ch
A very pleasant location on the outskirts of the town, with outstanding
views of the surrounding mountains. There are clean, modern facilities
and individual bathrooms are available for weekly hire.
➥ *A9 exit Agarn, signed.*
Open 22 Apr-14 Oct **Site** 0.9HEC 😃 ♣ **Facilities** 🔥 🖫 ☺ ➡ ⌀ ♨ ⑫
Services 🍽 ➕ 🗗 **Off-site** 🖫 🍴 🍽 ⚓P

AIGLE VAUD

Glariers (TCS)

1860 ☎ 024 4662660 📠 024 4662660
e-mail camping.aigle@tcs.ch
website www.campingtcs.ch
On level ground with trees and bushes near railway line and the
avenue des Glariers. Fine mountain views.
➥ *0.8km NE off A9 near Shell Migrol fuel station.*
Open 2 Apr-3 Oct **Site** 1HEC 😃 ♣ **Facilities** 🔥 🖫 ☺ ➡ ⌀ ⑫
Services 🍴 🍽 ➕ 🗗 **Leisure** ⚓ PR **Off-site** 🍽 ⌀

AROLLA VALAIS

Petit Praz

1986 ☎ 027 2832295
e-mail camping@arolla.com
website www.camping-arolla.com
An imposing mountain setting.
Open Jun-20 Sep **Site** 1HEC 😃 ♣ ♣ **Prices** ♦ 6.50 ➡ 3 ➡ 7-10 ⚠ 5-9
Facilities 🔥 🖫 ☺ ➡ ⌀ ♨ ⑫ **Services** 🗗

BALLENS VAUD

Bois Gentil

1144 ☎ 021 8095120 📠 021 8643840
e-mail py30@bluewin.ch
➥ *200m S of station.*
Open Apr-Oct **Site** 2.5HEC 😃 ♣ **Facilities** 🔥 🖫 ☺ ➡ ⌀ ⑫ **Services** 🍽
➕ **Leisure** ⚓ P

BOURG-ST-PIERRE VALAIS

Grand St-Bernard

1946 ☎ 027 7871411 📠 027 7871411
e-mail grand-st-bernard@swisscamps.ch
website www.campinggrand-st-bernard.ch
Set in beautiful mountain scenery with easy access to winter sports.
➥ *Between Martigny & Aosta near Italian border.*
Open May-Sep **Site** 1HEC 😃 ♣ **Facilities** 🔥 ☺ ➡ ⌀ ⑫ **Services** ➕ 🗗
Leisure ⚓ P **Off-site** 🖫 🍴 🍽 ⚓R

BOUVERET, LE VALAIS

Rive Bleue

1897 ☎ 024 4812161 📠 024 4812108
e-mail info@camping-rive-bleue.ch
website www.camping-rive-bleue.ch
Set beside a lake with a natural sandy beach and modern facilities.
➥ *Off A37 to Monthey in SW outskirts of Bouveret & continue
NE for 0.8km.*
Open Apr-Sep **Site** 3HEC 😃 ♣ ♣ ➡ **Prices** ♦ 7.90-9.70 ⚠ 6.60-10.50
pitch 10.50-13.60 ➡ (static)365 **Facilities** 🔥 🖫 ☺ ➡ ⌀ ♨ ⑫
Services ➕ 🗗 **Leisure** ⚓ LP **Off-site** 🍴 🍽 ⚓R

BULLET VAUD

Cluds

1453 ☎ 024 4541440 📠 024 4541440
e-mail vd28@campings-ccyverdon.ch
website www.campings-ccyverdon.ch
A beautiful mountain setting among pine trees.
➥ *1.5km NE.*
Open All year **Site** 1.2HEC 😃 ♣ ⚠ **Prices** ♦ 7 ➡ 3 ➡ 7-11 ⚠ 5-11
Facilities 🔥 ☺ ➡ ⌀ ♨ ⑫ **Services** 🗗 **Off-site** 🍽

CHÂTEAU-D'OEX VAUD

Berceau (TCS)

1837 ☎ 026 9246234 📠 026 9246234/ 9242526
e-mail info@chateaudoex.ch
website www.chateau-doex.ch
On level strip of grass between the mountain and the river bank.
➥ *1km SE at junct roads 77 & 76.*
Open All year **Site** 1HEC 😃 ♣ **Facilities** 🔥 ☺ ➡ ⌀ ♨ ⑫
Services 🍽 ➕ 🗗 **Leisure** ⚓ PR **Off-site** 🖫 🍽

CHÂTEL-ST-DENIS FRIBOURG

Bivouac

rte des Paccots, 1618 ☎ 021 9487849 📠 021 9487849
e-mail bivouac@swissonline.ch
website www.le-bivouac.ch
Beautiful views of the rolling Swiss countryside. Various sports and
leisure activities.
➥ *Turn E in Chatel-St Denis & continue 2km.*
Open Apr-Sep **Site** 2HEC 😃 ♣ **Prices** ♦ 5-6 pitch 10-15 **Facilities** 🔥 🖫 ☺
➡ ⌀ ♨ ⑫ **Services** 🍽 🍴 ➕ 🗗 **Leisure** ⚓ PR **Off-site** 🍽

Facilities 🖫 shop 🔥 shower ☺ electric points for razors ➡ electric points for caravans ⑫ parking by tents permitted 🅿 compulsory separate car park
Services 🍴 café/restaurant 🍽 bar ⌀ Camping Gaz International ♨ gas other than Camping Gaz ➕ first aid facilities 🗗 laundry
Leisure ⚓ swimming L-Lake P-Pool R-River S-Sea **Off-site** All facilities within 2km

CHESSEL VAUD

Grand Bois

1846 ☎ 024 4814225 🗎 024 4815113
e-mail au.grand-bois@bluewin.ch
website www.augrandbois.ch
On a level meadow close to a canal, only a few kilometres from Lake Geneva.

➲ *N of town towards lake.*

Open All year **Site** 4HEC ❤️ ♣ 🏠 **Prices** ♣ 6 ♠ 3 ♠ 9-11 Å 5-7 ♠ (static)250-380 **Facilities** ↑ 🛁 ⊙ ♀ ∅ ♨ ⊕ **Services** ▮ ◎ 🖪 **Leisure** ◔ PR

CUDREFIN VAUD

Chablais

1588 ☎ 026 6773277 🗎 026 6770767
e-mail camping@cudrefin.ch
website www.cudrefin.ch
Site by the lake, 0.5km from the town centre.

Open 15 Mar-Oct **Site** 6HEC ❤️ ♣ **Facilities** ↑ 🛁 ⊙ ♀ ⊕ **Services** 🖪 **Leisure** ◔ L **Off-site** 🛁 ▮ ◎ ∅ ◔R ➕

DÜDINGEN FRIBOURG

Schiffenensee

3186 ☎ 026 4931917 🗎 026
e-mail info@camping-schiffenensee.ch
website www.camping-schiffenen.ch

➲ *A12 exit Düdingen & N towards Murten.*

Open Apr-Oct **Site** 9HEC ❤️ ♣ **Prices** ♣ 8.50 ♠ 10 Å 8.50 **Facilities** ↑ 🛁 ⊙ ♀ **Services** ▮ ◎ ➕ 🖪 **Leisure** ◔ LP **Off-site** ∅ ♨

EVOLÈNE VALAIS

Evolène

1983 ☎ 027 2831144 🗎 027 2833255
e-mail evolene@swisscamps.ch
website www.camping-evolene.ch
On a level meadow with fine views of the surrounding mountains.

➲ *200m from town.*

Open All year **Site** 10HEC ❤️ ♣ ♠ **Prices** ♣ 7 ♠ 3 ♠ 8-10 Å 7-10 ♠ (static)300 **Facilities** ↑ ⊙ ♀ ∅ ♨ ⊕ **Services** ➕ 🖪 **Leisure** ◔ P **Off-site** 🛁 ▮ ◎ ◔R

FOULY, LA VALAIS

Glaciers

1944 ☎ 027 7831735 🗎 027 7833605
e-mail camping.glaciers@st-bernard.ch
website www.camping-glaciers.ch
At end of village in a beautiful Alpine location with fine views of the surrounding mountains.

Open 15 May-Sep **Site** 8HEC ❤️ ♣ 🏠 **Prices** ♣ 6.50 pitch 10-16 **Facilities** ↑ ⊙ ♀ ∅ ♨ ⊕ **Services** ➕ 🖪 **Off-site** 🛁 ▮ ◎

GENÈVE (GENEVA) GENÈVE

AT SATIGNY (6KM SW)

Bois-de-Bay

1242 ☎ 022 3410505 🗎 022 3410606

➲ *Off A1 at Bernex & signed.*

Open All year **Site** 2.8HEC ❤️ ♣ **Facilities** ↑ 🛁 ⊙ ♀ ∅ ♨ ⊕ **Services** ▮ ➕

AT VÉSENAZ (6KM NE)

Pointe á la Bise (TCS)

12223 ☎ 022 7521296 🗎 022 7523767
e-mail camping.geneve@tcs.ch
website www.campingtcs.ch
A pleasant wooded setting on the shore of Lake Léman.

➲ *NE between Vésenaz and Collonge-Bellerive.*

Open Etr-mid Oct **Site** 3.2HEC ❤️ ♣ 🏠 Å **Prices** ♣ 6.40-6.80 ♠ 3 Å 9.40-11.40 pitch 20.90-24.90 **Facilities** ↑ 🛁 ⊙ ♀ ∅ ♨ ⊕ **Services** ▮ ◎ ➕ 🖪 **Leisure** ◔ LP

GRANDSON VAUD

Pécos

VD24, 1422 ☎ 024 4454969 🗎 024 4462904
e-mail vd24@campings-ccyverdon.ch
website www.campings-ccyverdon.ch

➲ *400m SW of railway station between railway & lake.*

Open Apr-Sep **Site** 2HEC ❤️ ♣ ⊗ **Prices** ♣ 7.90 ♠ 3 ♠ 7-9 Å 6-12 **Facilities** ↑ 🛁 ⊙ ♀ ∅ ♨ ⊕ **Services** ◎ ➕ 🖪 **Leisure** ◔ L

GUMEFENS FRIBOURG

Lac

1643 ☎ 026 9152162 🗎 026 9152168
e-mail info@campingdulac-gruyere.ch
website www.campingdulac-gruyere.ch
On the borders of the lake.

Open Jul-Aug **Site** 1.5HEC ❤️ ♣ ⊗ **Prices** ♣ 7.20 ♠ 2.50 ♠ 8.50 Å 6.50 ♠ 8.50 **Facilities** ↑ 🛁 ⊙ ♀ ∅ ⊕ **Services** ▮ ◎ ➕ 🖪 **Leisure** ◔ L

LAUSANNE VAUD

Vidy

chemin du Camping 3, 1007 ☎ 021 6225000 🗎 021 6225001
e-mail info@clv.ch
website www.clv.ch
A delightful location among trees and flowerbeds overlooking Lac Léman. Shop and restaurant only open May to September.

Open All year **Site** 4.5HEC ❤️ ♣ 🏠 **Prices** ♣ 7 ♠ 3.50 Å 10-18 pitch 13-14 **Facilities** ↑ 🛁 ⊙ ♀ ∅ ♨ ⊕ **Services** ▮ ◎ ➕ 🖪 **Leisure** ◔ L

LEYSIN VAUD

Soleil

1854 ☎ 024 4943939 🗎 024 4942121
e-mail info@camping-leysin.ch
website www.camping-leysin.ch
A picturesque Alpine setting.

➲ *Enter village & left at Shell fuel station, site 400m.*

Open All year **Site** 1.1HEC ❤️ ♣ **Prices** ♣ 6.50 ♠ 4-5 ♠ 9 Å 4 **Facilities** ↑ 🛁 ⊙ ♀ ∅ ♨ ⊕ **Services** ▮ ◎ ➕ 🖪 **Off-site** 🛁 ▮ ◎ ◔P

MORGINS VALAIS

Morgins (TCS)

1875 ☎ 024 4772361 🗎 024 4773708
e-mail touristoffice@morgins.ch
website www.morgins.ch
Terraced site below a pine forest.

➲ *Left at end of village towards Pas de Morgins near Swiss customs.*

Open All year **Site** 1.3HEC ❤️ ❤️ ♣ **Prices** ♣ 6.70 pitch 10 **Facilities** ↑ ⊙ ♀ ⊕ **Services** ➕ 🖪 **Off-site** 🛁 ▮ ◎ ∅ ♨ ◔PR

Switzerland

RARON VALAIS

Camping Simplonblick

3942 ☎ 027 9341274 ⓘ 027 9342600
e-mail simplon-blick@bluewin.ch
website www.camping-simplonblick.ch

⮞ 300m W of Turtig.

Open All year **Site** 6HEC ❤ ❤ ♨ ⊞ Å **Facilities** ⍥ 🖀 ⊙ ⊟ ⌀ ♨ ⑫
Services ☎ ⍾ ⊞ 🗑 **Leisure** ⌲ P **Off-site** 🖀

Santa Monica

Kantonsstrasse 56, 3942 ☎ 027 9342424 ⓘ 027 9342450
e-mail info@santa-monica.ch
website www.santa-monica.ch
Open All year **Site** 4HEC ❤ ❤ ♨ **Prices** ↟ 5.50-6.50 Å 5-6 **pitch** 9.50-12
Facilities ⍥ 🖀 ⊙ ⊟ ⌀ ⑫ **Services** ⍾ ⊞ 🗑 **Leisure** ⌲ P
Off-site ☎ ⌲LR

RECKINGEN VALAIS

Ellbogen (TCS)

CH-3998 ☎ 027 9731395 ⓘ 027 9732677
e-mail info@campingaugenstern.ch
website www.campingaugenstern.ch
On an alpine meadow close to the River Rhône.

⮞ 400m S on bank of Rhône.

Open All year **Site** 3HEC ❤ ❤ ♨ **Prices** ↟ 7.50 Å 7.50 **pitch** 9.50
Facilities ⍥ 🖀 ⊙ ⊟ ⌀ ♨ ⑫ **Services** ☎ ⍾ ⊞ 🗑 **Off-site** ⌲PR

RIED-BRIG VALAIS

Tropic

3911 ☎ 027 9232537

⮞ To the left of Simplon road near entrance to village. 3km above Brig.

Open Jun-Aug **Site** 1.5HEC ❤ ❤ ♨ ⊞ **Facilities** ⍥ ⊙ ⊟ ⌀ ⑫
Services ☎ ⍾ ⊞ 🗑 **Off-site** 🖀

SAAS-GRUND VALAIS

Kapellenweg

3910 ☎ 027 9574997 ⓘ 027 9573316
e-mail camping@kapellenweg.ch
website www.kapellenweg.ch
On a level meadow in a picturesque mountain setting in the Saas valley. Modern facilities.

⮞ Over bridge & right towards Saas-Almagell.

Open May-Oct **Site** 1.5HEC ❤ ❤ ⊞ **Prices** ↟ 5.40-6 ⊕ 4-4.50 ⊞ 4-4.50
Å 4-4.50 **Facilities** ⍥ 🖀 ⊙ ⊟ ⌀ ♨ ⑫ **Services** 🗑 **Off-site** ☎ ⍾ ⊞

SALGESCH VALAIS

Swiss Plage

3970 ☎ 027 4816023 ⓘ 027 4556608
e-mail info@swissplage.ch
website swissplage.ch
Situated beside a small lake and surrounded by vineyards. Good recreational facilities.

Open Etr-1 Nov **Site** 10HEC ❤ ❤ ❤ ♨ ♨ ⊞ **Facilities** ⍥ 🖀 ⊙ ⊟
⌀ ♨ ⑫ **Services** ☎ ⍾ ⊞ 🗑 **Leisure** ⌲ LR

SEMBRANCHER VALAIS

Prairie (TCS)

1933 ☎ 027 7852206 ⓘ 027 7852131
e-mail prairie01@bluewin.ch

⮞ 0.5km from town.

Open June-Sept **Site** 50HEC ❤ ❤ **Facilities** ⍥ 🖀 ⊙ ⊟ ⌀ ⑫
Services ☎ ⍾ **Off-site** ⌲R ⊞

SIERRE (SIDERS) VALAIS

Bois de Finges (TCS)

3960 ☎ 027 4550284 ⓘ 027 4553351
e-mail camping.sierre@tcs.ch
website www.campingtcs.ch
Situated in a pine forest with well-defined pitches set on terraces.

⮞ Motorway exit Sierre-Ouest for Sierre.

Open 28 Apr-3 Oct **Site** 5HEC ❤ ❤ ❤ ♨ ⊞ **Prices** ↟ 6-7 Å 8.20-11.20
pitch 13.40-20.20 ⊕ (static)560-770 **Facilities** ⍥ 🖀 ⊙ ⊟ ⌀ ♨ ⑫
Services ☎ ⍾ ⊞ 🗑 **Leisure** ⌲ P **Off-site** ⍾ ⌲LR

SORENS FRIBOURG

Forêt

1642 ☎ 026 9151882 ⓘ 026 9150363
e-mail info@camping-la-foret.ch
website www.camping-la-foret.ch
A pleasant site on a level meadow surrounded by woodland and with plenty of vegetation.

⮞ Off A12 in Gumefens to village.

Open All year **Site** 4HEC ❤ ❤ ♨ ⊞ **Prices** ↟ 6 ⊕ 2.50 ⊞ 5 Å 5
⊞ (static)330 **Facilities** ⍥ 🖀 ⊙ ⊟ ⌀ ♨ ⑫ **Services** ⍾ ⊞ 🗑
Leisure ⌲ P

SUSTEN VALAIS

Bella Tola (TCS)

Waldstrasse 57, CH 3952 ☎ 027 4731491 ⓘ 027 4733641
e-mail info@bella-tola.ch
website www.bella-tola.ch
A peaceful, terraced site at an altitude of 750m, shielded by a belt of woodland. Good, clean modern facilities.

⮞ 2km from village.

Open 28 Apr-Oct **Site** 3.6HEC ❤ ❤ **Prices** ↟ 10 **pitch** 15-26 **Facilities** ⍥
🖀 ⊙ ⊟ ⌀ ♨ ⑫ **Services** ☎ ⍾ ⊞ 🗑 **Leisure** ⌲ P

ULRICHEN VALAIS

Nufenen

3988 ☎ 027 9731437 ⓘ 027 9731437
e-mail camping-nufenen@rhone.ch
website www.rhone.ch/camping-nufenen

⮞ 1km SE to right of road to Nufenen Pass.

Open Jun-Sep **Site** 8HEC ❤ ❤ **Facilities** ⍥ ⊙ ⊟ ⌀ ♨ ⑫ **Services** ⊞ 🗑
Leisure ⌲ R **Off-site** 🖀 ☎ ⍾

VALLORBE VAUD

Pré sous Ville (TCS)

1337 ☎ 021 8432309
A wooded riverside location. The neighbouring swimming pool is available free to campers.

⮞ On left bank of River Orbe.

Open mid Apr-mid Oct **Site** 1HEC ❤ ❤ ♨ ⊞ **Facilities** ⍥ ⊙ ⊟ ⌀ ♨ ⑫
Services ⊞ 🗑 **Leisure** ⌲ P **Off-site** 🖀 ☎ ⍾ ⌲R

Facilities 🖀 shop ⍥ shower ⊙ electric points for razors ⊟ electric points for caravans ⑫ parking by tents permitted ❷ compulsory separate car park
Services ⍾ café/restaurant ☎ bar ⌀ Camping Gaz International ♨ gas other than Camping Gaz ⊞ first aid facilities 🗑 laundry
Leisure ⌲ swimming L-Lake P-Pool R-River S-Sea **Off-site** All facilities within 2km

VERS-L'ÉGLISE VAUD

Murée (TCS)

1864 ☎ 079 4019915 ▯ 021 6345284
e-mail dagonch@bluewinch.
website www.camping-caravaningvd.com
Partially terraced site by a stream.

➲ *Signed on right at entry to village.*

Open All year **Site** 1.1HEC ⛺ ♣ 🏠 **Prices** ♦ 5-5.50 ▲ 6-11 pitch 11-13
Facilities ⛺ ⊙ ⊖ 🅟 ⦸ 🚿 ⓟ **Services** 🛒 **Leisure** ⚓ R **Off-site** 🛟

VÉTROZ VALAIS

Botza

rte du Camping 1, 1963 ☎ 027 3461940 ▯ 027 3462535
e-mail info@botza.ch
website www.botza.ch
On a level meadow with pitches divided by hedges. Fine panoramic views and good leisure facilities.

Open All year **Site** 3HEC ⛺ ♣ 🏠 ▲ **Prices** ♦ 5.40-8.60 pitch 8-22.50
Facilities ⛺ 🅑 ⊙ ⊖ ⦸ 🚿 ⓟ **Services** 🛒 🍴 🛟 🛒 **Leisure** ⚓ P

YVONAND VAUD

VD 8 Pointe D'Yvonard

1462 ☎ 024 4301655 ▯ 024 4302463
e-mail vd8@campings-ccyverdon.ch
website www.campings-ccyverdon.ch
Site borders Lake Neuchâtel with a private beach 1km away. Boat moorings, private jetty and boat hire.

➲ *3km W, signed.*

Open Apr-Sep **Site** 5HEC ⛺ ♣ 🏠 🏠 🚐 ⊗ **Prices** ♦ 7.55-9.55 🚗 3.50
🚐 7-15 ▲ 7-15 🚐 (static)750 **Facilities** ⛺ 🅑 ⊙ ⊖ 🅟 ⦸ 🚿 ⓟ **Services** 🛒
🍴 🛟 🛒 **Leisure** ⚓ L

Estaveyer-Le-Lac on the shores of Lake Neuchatel

Site 6HEC (site size) ⛺ grass ⛱ sand ⛰ stone ♣ little shade ♣ partly shaded ⛺ mainly shaded 🏠 bungalows for hire
🚐 caravans for hire ▲ tents for hire ⊗ no dogs **Prices** ♦ adult per night 🚗 car per night pp per person per night 🚐 caravan per night
▲ tent per night 🚐 (static)-caravan hire per week

COUNTRY MAP SECTION

AUSTRIA

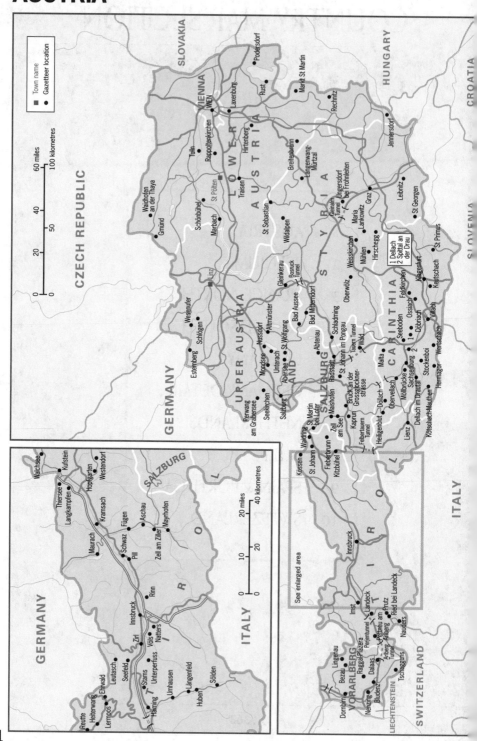

BELGIUM & LUXEMBOURG

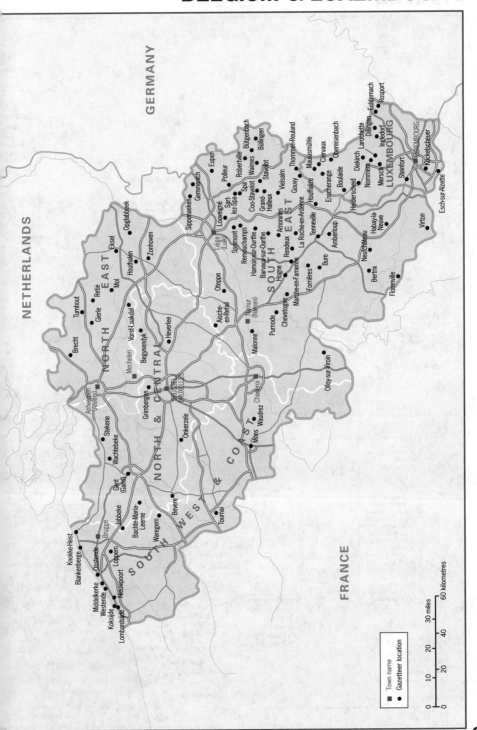

2

FRANCE

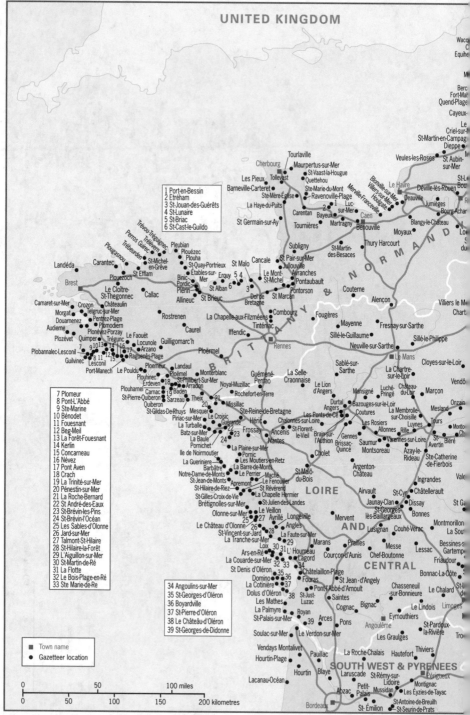

UNITED KINGDOM

1 Port-en-Bessin
2 Etréham
3 St-Jouan-des-Guérêts
4 St-Lunaire
5 St-Briac
6 St-Cast-le-Guildo

7 Plomeur
8 Pont-L'Abbé
9 Ste-Marine
10 Bénodet
11 Fouesnant
12 Beg-Meil
13 La Forêt-Fouesnant
14 Kerlin
15 Concarneau
16 Névez
17 Pont Aven
18 Crach
19 La Trinité-sur-Mer
20 Pénestin-sur-Mer
21 La Roche-Bernard
22 St André-des-Eaux
23 St-Brévin-les-Pins
24 St-Brévin-l'Océan
25 Les Sables-d'Olonne
26 Jard-sur-Mer
27 Talmont-St-Hilaire
28 St-Hilaire-la-Forêt
29 L'Aiguillon-sur-Mer
30 St-Martin-de-Ré
31 La Flotte
32 Le Bois-Plage-en-Ré
33 Ste Marie-de-Re

34 Angoulins-sur-Mer
35 St-Georges-d'Oléron
36 Boyardville
37 St-Pierre-d'Oléron
38 Le Château-d'Oléron
39 St-Georges-de-Didonne

■ Town name
● Gazetteer location

0   50   100 miles
0   50   100   150   200 kilometres

3

4

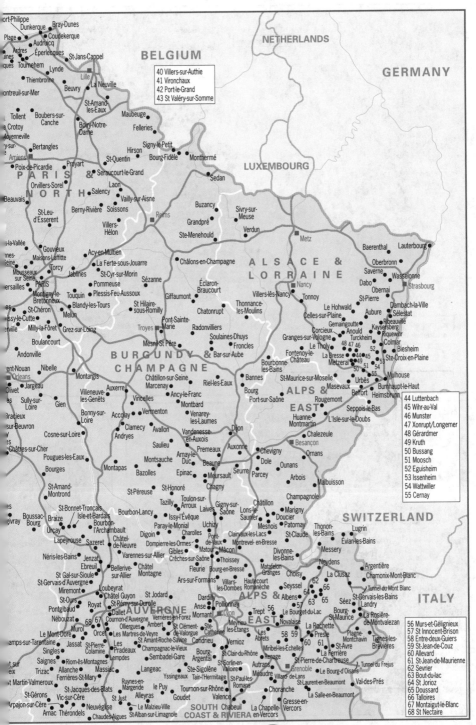

NETHERLANDS

GERMANY

BELGIUM

40 Villers-sur-Authie
41 Vironchaux
42 Port-le-Grand
43 St Valéry-sur-Somme

LUXEMBOURG

PARIS & NORTH

ALSACE & LORRAINE

BURGUNDY & CHAMPAGNE

ALPS & EAST

44 Luttenbach
45 Wihr-au-Val
46 Munster
47 Xonrupt/Longemer
48 Gérardmer
49 Kruth
50 Bussang
51 Moosch
52 Eguisheim
53 Issenheim
54 Wattwiller
55 Cernay

SWITZERLAND

ITALY

AUVERGNE

ALPS & EAST

56 Murs-et-Gélignieux
57 St Innocent-Brison
58 Entre-deux-Guiers
59 St-Jean-de-Couz
60 Allevard
61 St-Jean-de-Maurienne
62 Sevrier
63 Bout-du-lac
64 St Jorioz
65 Doussard
66 Talloires
67 Montaigut-le-Blanc
68 St Nectaire

SOUTH COAST & RIVIERA

3

FRANCE

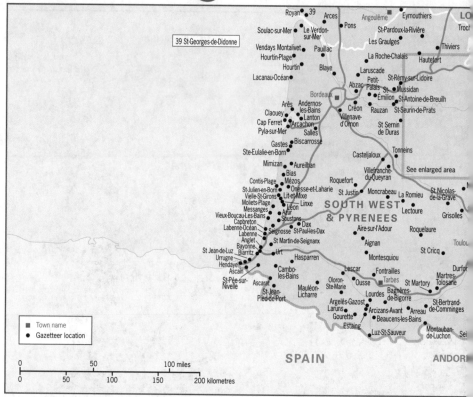

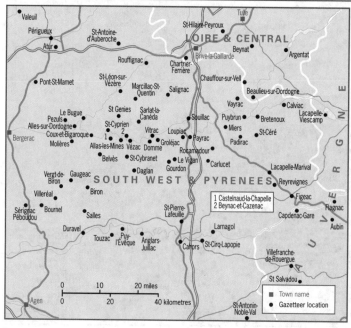

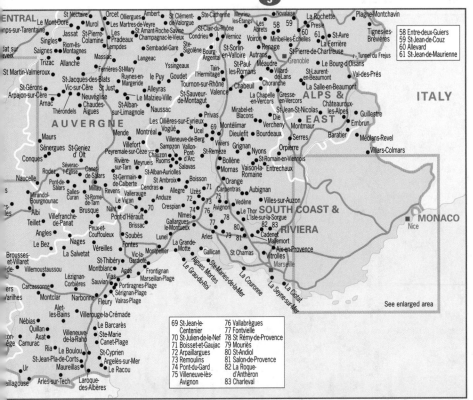

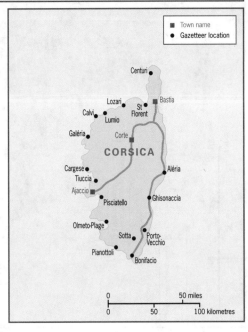

GERMANY

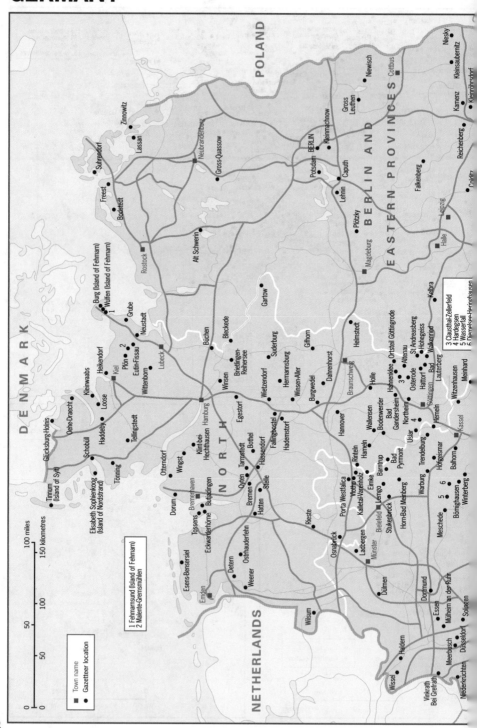

5

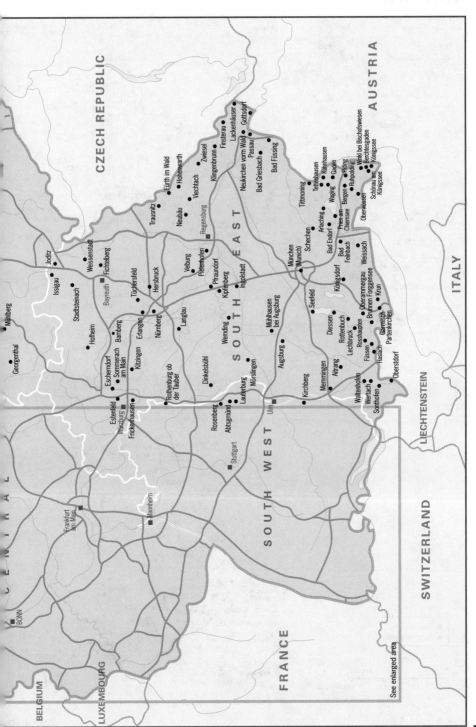

5

GERMANY

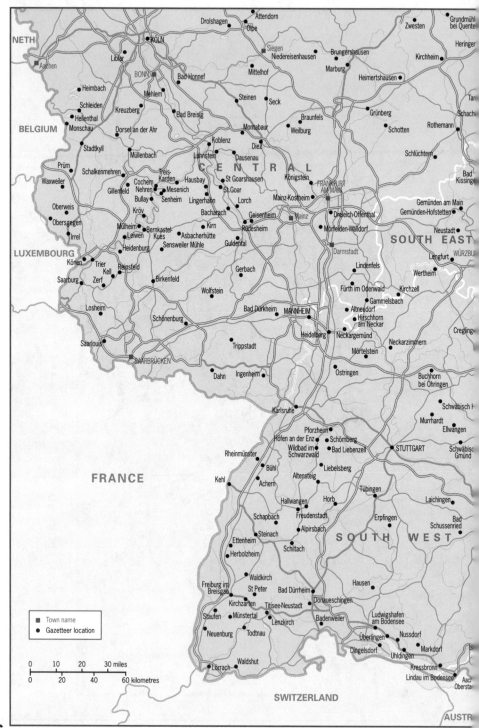

NETH

BELGIUM

LUXEMBOURG

FRANCE

SWITZERLAND

AUSTR

Attendorn
Grundmühl bei Quentel
Drolshagen
Olpe
Zwesten
Heringer
Siegen
Niedereisenhausen
Brungershausen
Kirchheim
Liblar
KÖLN
Marburg
Heimertshausen
BONN
Bad Honnef
Mittelhof
Mehlem
Steinen
Seck
Heimbach
Schleiden
Kreuzberg
Bad Breisig
Montabaur
Braunfels
Grünberg
Schotten
Rothemann
Hellenthal
Monschau
Dorsel an der Ahr
Weilburg
Stadtkyll
Koblenz
Müllenbach
Lahnstein
Diez
CENTRAL
Schlüchtern
Prüm
Schalkenmehren
Treis-Karden
Dausenau
Königstein
Bad Kissinge
Waxweiler
Cochem
Hausbay
St Goarshausen
FRANKFURT AM MAIN
Gillenfeld
Nehren
Mesenich
St.Goar
Mainz-Kostheim
Gemünden am Main
Oberweis
Bullay
Senheim
Lingerhahn
Lorch
Gemünden-Hofstetten
Obersgegen
Kröv
Bacharach
Geisenheim
Dreieich-Offenthal
Neustadt
Irrel
Mülheim
Bernkastel-Kues
Kirn
Rüdesheim
Mainz
Mörfelden-Walldorf
SOUTH EAST
Leiwen
Asbacherhütte
WÜRZBU
Heidenburg
Sensweiler Mühle
Guldental
Darmstadt
Lengfurt
Könen
Trier
Reinsfeld
Lindenfels
Wertheim
Kell
Gerbach
Fürth im Odenwald
Kirchzell
Saarburg
Zerf
Birkenfeld
Gammelsbach
Losheim
Wolfstein
Altneudorf
Cregling
Schönenburg
Bad Dürkheim
MANNHEIM
Hirschhorn am Neckar
Saarlouis
Trippstadt
Heidelberg
Neckargemünd
Neckarzimmern
SAARBRÜCKEN
Mörtelstein
Dahn
Ingenheim
Ostringen
Buchhorn bei Öhringen
Karlsruhe
Schwäbisch H
Pforzheim
Murrhardt
Ellwangen
Höfen an der Enz
Schömberg
STUTTGART
Schwäbisc Gmünd
Rheinmünster
Wildbad im Schwarzwald
Bad Liebenzell
Bühl
Liebelsberg
Kehl
Achern
Altensteig
Tübingen
Laichingen
Hallwangen
Horb
Schapbach
Freudenstadt
Erpfingen
Bad Schussenried
Steinach
Alpirsbach
SOUTH WEST
Ettenheim
Schiltach
Herbolzheim
Hausen
Waldkirch
Freiburg im Breisgau
St Peter
Bad Dürrheim
Kirchzarten
Titisee-Neustadt
Donaueschingen
Ludwigshafen am Bodensee
Staufen
Münstertal
Lenzkirch
Badenweiler
Überlingen
Nussdorf
Neuenburg
Todtnau
Dingelsdorf
Markdorf
Uhldingen
Kressbronn
Waldshut
Lindau im Bodensee
Aac
Obersta
Lörrach
Is

■ Town name
● Gazetteer location

0 10   20   30 miles
0   20   40   60 kilometres

6

NETHERLANDS

- Town name
- Gazetteer location

0   20   40   60 miles
0   50   100 kilometres

Hee
Lauwersoog
Termunterzijl
Leeuwarden
Harlingen
Franeker
Bergum
Groningen
Harkstede
Opende
NORTH
Wedde
De Koog
Makkum
Assen
Annen
Den Hoorn
Hindeloopen
Diever
Amen
Borger
Den Helder
Koudum
Dwingeloo
Groote Keeten
Sondel
Ruinen
Callantsoog
Steenwijk
St Maartenszee
Andijk
Noord Scharwoude
Urk
Blokzijl
Egmond aan Zee
Heiloo Alkmaar Berkhout
Wijdenes
Dronten
Zwolle
Dalfsen
Edam
CENTRAL
Hattem
Reutum
Uitdam
Nunspeet
Wezep
Luttenberg
Denekamp
Haarlem
Vogelenzang
Ermelo
AMSTERDAM
Halfweg
Hengelo
Noordwijk aan Zee
Amstelveen
Putten
Apeldoorn
Enschede
Rijnsburg
Aalsmeer
Mijnden
Diepenheim
Buurse
Katwijk aan Zee
Leiden
Kootwijk
Haaksbergen
Wassenaar
Bilthoven
Soest
Eerbeek
Neede
DEN HAAG
Maarn
Hoenderloo
Ruurlo
's-Gravenzande
Doorn
Lathum
Hengelo
Hoek Van Holland
Delft
Rhenen
Arnhem
Doesburg
Winterswijk
Oostvoorne
Brielle
Rotterdam
Kesteren
Babberich
Doetinchem
Rockanje
Nijmegen
Ouddorp
Hellevoetsluis
Appeltern
Renesse
Herpen
Heumen
Burgh-Haamstede
Brouwershaven
SOUTH
's-Hertogenbosch
Plasmolen
Vrouwenpolder
Hoeven
Oosterhout
St Anthonis
Oostkapelle
Kamperland
Breda
Tilburg
Boxtel
St Oedenrode
Afferden
Westkapelle
Kortgene
Roosendaal
Bosschenhoofd
Well
Zoutelande
Middelburg
Wemeldinge
Oisterwijk
Eindhoven
Venray
Broekhuizenvorst
Koudekerke
Baarle Nassau
Hilvarenbeek
Mierlo
Sevenum
Nieuwvliet
ranchement
Breskens
Baarland
Lage Mierde
Eersel
Maasbree
Groede
Hoek
Hengstdijk
Bergeyk
Sluis
Luyksgestel
Weert
Roermond
Echt

BELGIUM

GERMANY

Berg en Terblijt
Landgraaf
Maastricht
Valkenburg

FRANCE

LUX

7

ITALY

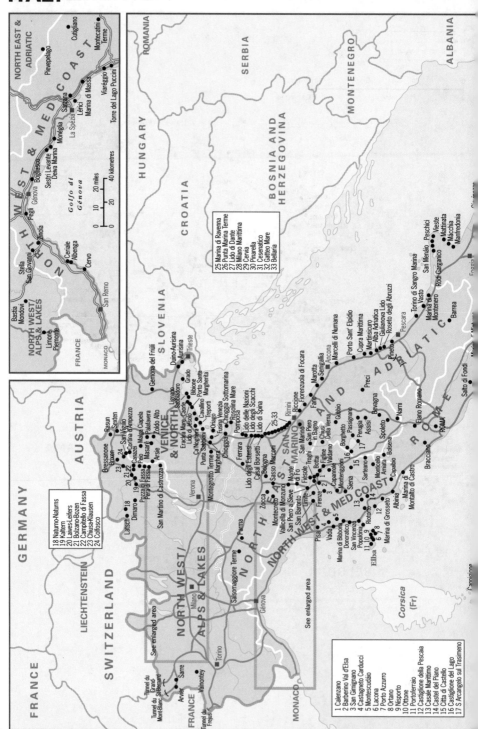

NORTH EAST & ADRIATIC

Cutigliano
Montecatini Terme
Pievepelago
Serravezza
Viareggio
Lérici
Marina di Massa
Torre del Lago Puccini
Boglasco
Pegli
Sestri Levante
Deiva Marina
Zinola
Génova

NORTH WEST / ALPS & LAKES

Stella
San Giovanni
Cerale
Albenga
Cervo
Bastia
Mondovi
Limone
Piemonte
San Remo

0   10   20 miles
0   10   20   40 kilometres
Golfo di Génova

Box (18–24):
18 Naturno-Naturns
19 Kaltern
20 Laves-Leifers
21 Bolzano-Bozen
22 Campitello di Fassa
23 Chiusa-Klausen
24 Colfosco

Box (25–33):
25 Marina di Ravenna
26 Punta Marina Terme
27 Lido di Dante
28 Milano Marittima
29 Cervia
30 Pinarella
31 Cesenatico
32 Gatteo Mare
33 Bellaria

Box (1–17):
1 Calenzano
2 Barberino Val d'Elsa
3 San Gimignano
4 Castagneto Carducci
5 Montescudaio
6 Lacona
7 Porto Azzurro
8 Ortano
9 Nisporto
10 Ottone
11 Portoferraio
12 Castiglione della Pescaia
13 Casale Marittimo
14 Castel del Piano
15 Città di Castello
16 Castiglione del Lago
17 S.Arcangelo sul Trasimeno

8

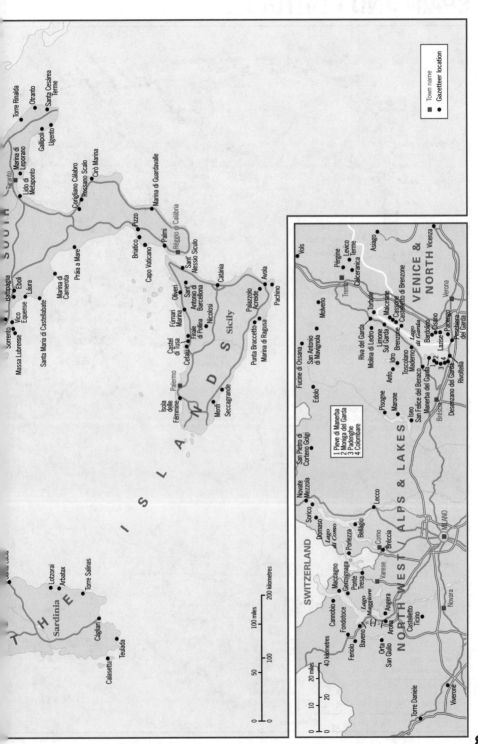

SPAIN AND PORTUGAL

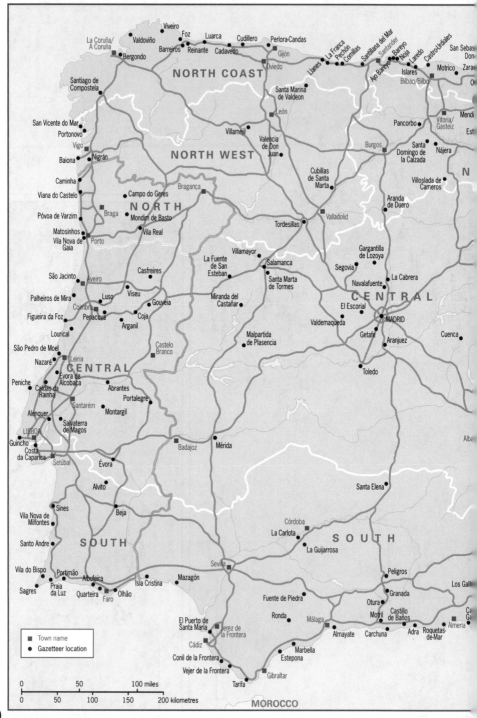

Legend:
- ■ Town name
- ● Gazetteer location

Scale:
0 — 50 — 100 miles
0 — 50 — 100 — 150 — 200 kilometres

MOROCCO

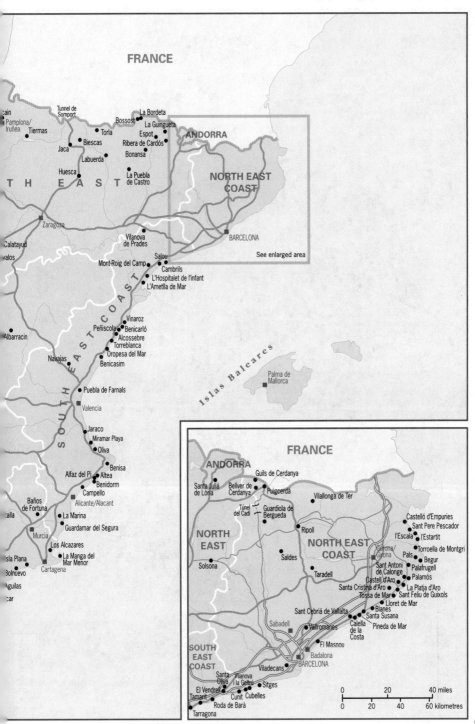

FRANCE

Tunnel de Somport
Pamplona/ Iruñea   Tiermas
Bossost   La Bordeta
Torla   La Guingueta
Biescas   Espot   ANDORRA
Jaca   Ribera de Cardós
Labuerda   Bonansa
Huesca   La Puebla de Castro   NORTH EAST COAST

THE EAST

Zaragoza
Calatayud
valos
Vilanova de Prades   BARCELONA
Salou   See enlarged area
Mont-Roig del Camp   Cambrils
L'Hospitalet de l'infant
L'Ametlla de Mar

SOUTH EAST COAST

Albarracin

Vinaroz
Peñiscola   Benicarló
Alcossebre
Torreblanca
Navajas   Oropesa del Mar
Benicasim

Islas Baleares

Puebla de Farnals

Valencia   Palma de Mallorca

Jaraco
Miramar Playa
Oliva

Benisa
Alfaz del Pi   Altea
Benidorm
Campello
Baños de Fortuna   Alicante/Alacant
talla   La Marina
Murcia   Guardamar del Segura
Los Alcazares
Isla Plana   La Manga del Mar Menor
Bolnuevo   Cartagena
Aguilas
car

FRANCE

ANDORRA
Santa Juliá de Loria   Bellver de Cerdanya   Guils de Cerdanya   Puigcerdà
Vilallonga de Ter
Túnel del Cadí   Guardiola de Bergueda
NORTH EAST   Ripoll
Solsona   Saldes   NORTH EAST COAST
Taradell   Girona/Gerona
Castelló d'Empuries
Sant Pere Pescador
l'Escala   l'Estartit
Pals   Torroella de Montgri
Begur
Sant Antoni de Calonge   Palafrugell
Castell d'Aro   Palamós
Santa Cristina d'Aro   La Platja d'Aro
Tossa de Mar   Sant Feliu de Guixols
Lloret de Mar
Sant Cebriá de Vallalta   Blanes
Santa Susana
Vallromanes   Calella de la Costa   Pineda de Mar
Sabadell
El Masnou
SOUTH EAST COAST   Badalona
Viladecans   BARCELONA
Santa Oliva   Vilanova i la Geltru
El Vendrell   Sitges
Tamarit   Cunit   Cubelles
Roda de Barà
Tarragona

0   20   40 miles
0   20   40   60 kilometres

9

SWITZERLAND

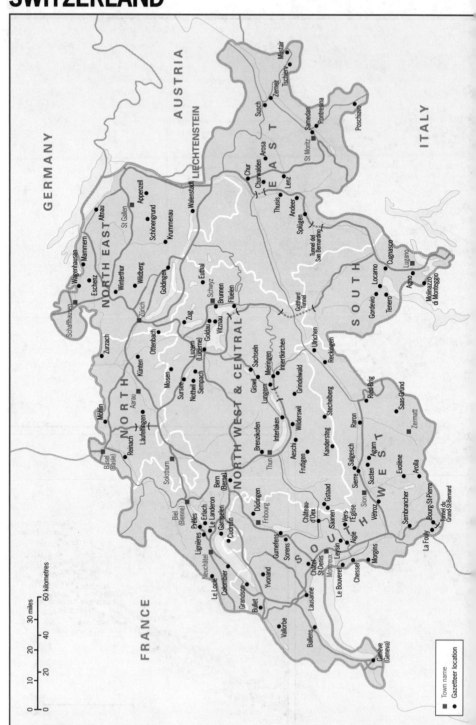

10

Index

Index

Index

Index

D

E

Index

Index

Index

N

Index

Q

R

Index

Index

Index

Index

Index

The Automobile Association would like to thank the following photographers, companies and picture libraries for their assistance in the preparation of this book.

Abbreviations for the picture credits are as follows: (t) top; (b) bottom; (l) left; (r) right; (AA) AA World Travel Library.

1 AA/A Baker; 2l AA/A Baker; 3tr AA; 3bl AA/C Sawyer; 3br AA/J Wyand; 4tl AA/M Jourdan; 6tl AA/M Jourdan; 8tl AA/M Jourdan; 9tr AA; 9r AA/A Baker; 10tl AA/M Jourdan; 11tr AA; 12tl AA/ M Jourdan; 12bl AA/T Souter; 13tr AA; 13r AA/C Sawyer; 14tl AA/M Jourdan; 15r AA/R Moore; 15tr AA; 15br AA/A Kouprianoff; 16tl AA/M Jourdan; 16b AA/W Voysey; 18tl AA/M Jourdan; 18cr AA/R Strange; 19tr AA; 20tl AA/M Jourdan; 21tr AA; 22tl AA/M Jourdan; 23tr AA; 24tl AA/M Jourdan; 25tr AA; 26tl AA/M Jourdan; 27tr AA; 28tl AA/M Jourdan; 29tr AA; 29b AA/R Strange; 30tl AA/A Baker; 45tr AA/A Kouprianoff; 45b AA/A Kouprianoff; 53tr AA/R Moss; 54tl AA/P Kenward; 207tr AA/A Baker; 207b AA/T Souter; 247b AA/P Bennett; 248tl AA/T Harris; 249tr AA/T Souter; 290b AA/K Paterson; 291tr AA/A Kouprianoff; 291b AA/A Kouprianoff; 294tl AA/A Kouprianoff; 294b AA/K Paterson; 310tl AA/M Chaplow; 316tl AA/M Chaplow; 317tr AA/A Mockford & N Bonetti; 317cr AA/S Watkins; 350tl AA/S Day; 350br AA/S Day; 362b AA/S Day.

Every effort has been made to trace the copyright holders, and we apologise in advance for any accidental errors. We would be happy to apply the corrections in the following edition of this publication.

Please send this form to:
   Editor, Caravan & Camping Europe
   AA Lifestyle Guides,
   Fanum House Floor 14,
   Basingstoke RG21 4EA

   or fax 01256 491647
   or email lifestyleguides@theAA.com

Reader's Report Form

Please use this form to recommend any caravan and camping park where you have stayed, whether it is included in the guide or not. You can also help us to improve the guide by completing the short questionnaire on the reverse.

The AA does not undertake to arbitrate between guide readers and campsites, or to obtain compensation or engage in correspondence.

Date:

Your name (block capitals)

Your address (block capitals)

....

....

....

....

email address:

Name of park:

Comments

....

....

....

....

....

....

....

(please attach a separate sheet if necessary)

Please tick here if you DO NOT wish to receive details of AA offers or products

PTO

Reader's Report Form

How often do you visit a caravan park or camp site?

Once a year ☐ Twice a year ☐ 3 times a year ☐ More than 3 times ☐

How long do you generally stay at a park or site?

1 night ☐ Up to 1 week ☐ 1 week ☐ 2 weeks ☐ Over 2 weeks ☐

Do you have a: tent ☐ caravan ☐ motorhome ☐

Which of the following is most important when choosing a site?

☐ Location ☐ Toilet/Washing facilities
☐ Personal Recommendation ☐ Leisure facilities
☐ Other

Do you prefer self-contained, cubicled washrooms with WC, shower and washhand basin to open-plan separate facilities?

Yes ☐ No ☐ Don't Mind ☐

Do you buy any other camping guides? If so, which ones?

....

Have you read the introductory pages and features in this guide? ....

Do you use the location atlas in this guide? ....

Which of the following most influences your choice of park from this guide?

Gazetteer entry information and description ☐

Photograph ☐ Advertisement ☐

Do you have any suggestions to improve the guide?

....

....

....

....

....

Thank you for completing this form

LAND ROVER BIKES

A comprehensive range of Land Rover bikes is available from your local independent bike shop. It includes fully equipped trekking bikes, off road mountain bikes, comfort bikes, childrens bikes and even a lightweight folder.

So whether your are heading for the hills for a challenging off road adventure or cruising the highways and byways in comfort, there is a Land Rover bike specific to your needs

www.landrover.co.uk
www.2x2worldwide.com

Worldwid

FUN IN THE COUNTRY